THE OXFORD HANDBOOK OF

LANGUAGE POLICY AND PLANNING

THE OXFORD HANDBOOK OF

LANGUAGE POLICY AND PLANNING

Edited by

JAMES W. TOLLEFSON

and

MIGUEL PÉREZ-MILANS

OXFORD
UNIVERSITY PRESS

Oxford University Press is a department of the University of Oxford. It furthers
the University's objective of excellence in research, scholarship, and education
by publishing worldwide. Oxford is a registered trade mark of Oxford University
Press in the UK and certain other countries.

Published in the United States of America by Oxford University Press
198 Madison Avenue, New York, NY 10016, United States of America.

The Oxford Handbook of Language Policy and Planning
Library of Congress Cataloging in Publication
Control Number: 2017045795 (print)
ISBN 978–0–19–045889–8

3 5 7 9 8 6 4

Printed by Sheridan Books, Inc., United States of America

Contents

PART II LANGUAGE POLICY AND PLANNING, NATION-STATES, AND COMMUNITIES

II.A. *Modern Nationalism, Languages, Minorities, Standardization, and Globalization*

II.B. *Language Policy and Planning in Institutions of the Modern Nation-State: Education, Citizenship, Media, and Public Signage*

II.C. Language Policy and Planning
in/through Communities

PART III LANGUAGE POLICY AND PLANNING
AND LATE MODERNITY

III.A. Language Policy and Planning, Neoliberalism, and Governmentality:
A Political Economy View of Language, Bilingualism, and Social Class

PART IV SUMMARY AND FUTURE DIRECTIONS

PREFACE

WHEN Oxford University Press first contacted us about a handbook of language policy and planning (LPP), we wondered, "Why do we need another handbook?" Later, potential authors asked the same question. Although the proliferation of handbooks in language studies in recent years has created a library of high-quality material, handbooks require enormous effort, and the authors' time required to produce these hefty manuscripts can crowd out basic research that is the foundation for any scholarly discipline. If we were to go ahead with this project, we wanted to offer a different type of handbook, one that is not primarily a retrospective summary of the history of subfields within LPP—though such retrospectives are important—but instead one that looks forward, in an effort to articulate and confront important issues underlying the transformations currently taking place in LPP and the social sciences more broadly. Accordingly, this is what we wrote to potential authors:

> Our motivation for this effort is to articulate and provide direction for the current theoretical and methodological turmoil in LPP associated with the socioeconomic, institutional, and discursive processes of change taking place under the conditions of late modernity. As an academic discipline in the social sciences, language policy is fraught with tensions between these processes of change and the still-powerful ideological framework of modern nationalism. We believe this is a thrilling time in LPP studies, and we want this project to reflect that excitement. We intend *The Oxford Handbook of Language Policy and Planning* to be a dialogue between the two major historical trends in LPP associated with processes linked to modernity and late modernity: the focus on continuity behind the institutional policies of the modern nation-state, and the attention to local processes of uncertainty, reorganization, and instability derived from the above-mentioned conditions of change. This dialogue is also aimed at overcoming the long-standing division between "top-down" and "bottom-up" analysis in LPP research, and at providing direction for theoretical and methodological innovation in LPP studies.

To our great satisfaction, the response to our call was enthusiastic across the board, and all of our contributors have responded to this challenge with great care and deep professional commitment.

As editors, we divided responsibility for the chapters according to our interests, experience, and expertise, each of us shepherding through the review process about half of the total number of chapters in the volume. Although we divided chapters in this way for administrative purposes, both of us read and fully edited every chapter, at each stage of revision. We also shared equal responsibility for writing the introductory and concluding chapters. This *Handbook*, therefore, is the result of our extensive collaboration during every phase of the project.

Many people helped us to produce this volume, above all the contributors, who responded to our multiple and repeated requests for clarification and revision as we worked to shape the volume into a coherent whole. We would also like to thank our students in our postgraduate class, *Introduction to Sociolinguistics*, which we co-taught at the University of Hong Kong in 2014. It was in this class that we began to elaborate our understanding of the tensions, paradoxes, and contradictions in LPP research and practice, in a context in which traditional institutional bodies reposition themselves as other regional and transnational actors, both governmental and nongovernmental, gain greater influence in language policymaking.

We are grateful as well for the support of our home institutions, including The University of Hong Kong, where we worked together at the time this project was initiated, and our current workplaces: the Department of English at the University of Washington, and UCL Institute of Education at University College London. We also thank Hallie Stebbens and Hannah Doyle, our editors at Oxford University Press, who patiently guided this project to its completion.

Finally, we wish to acknowledge the extraordinary formative impact of our academic mentors. For Jim, they included, at Stanford University: Gilbert Ansre, Eve V. Clark, Joseph H. Greenberg, Shirley Brice Heath, Eduardo Hernández Chávez, Beatriz Lavandera, and especially Charles A. Ferguson. For Miguel, Luisa Martín Rojo (Universidad Autónoma de Madrid), Monica Heller (University of Toronto), Ben Rampton (King's College London), and Angel Lin (The University of Hong Kong).

James W. Tollefson, Seattle
Miguel Pérez-Milans, London

CONTRIBUTORS

David Block is ICREA Research Professor in Sociolinguistics at the University of Lleida (Spain). He has published on a variety of language-related topics and currently examines issues around class, social movements, multiculturalism, and bi/multilingualism, drawing on scholarship in political economy, sociology, anthropology, and geography. His two most recent books are *Political Economy and Sociolinguistics: Redistribution and Recognition* (Bloomsbury, 2017) and (with Lídia Gallego-Balsà) *Minority Ethnic Students in Higher Education: Talking Multilingualism and Identity* (Multilingual Matters, 2017). He is a Fellow of the Academy of the Social Sciences (UK) and editor of the Routledge book series *Language, Society and Political Economy*.

Juan Eduardo Bonnin teaches Semiotics at the University of Moreno and the University of San Martín and is a researcher at the Consejo Nacional de Investigaciones Científicas y Técnicas (CONICET), Argentina. His interests include interdisciplinary research on language, inequality, and access to civil rights. His latest books are *Génesis política del discurso religioso: 'Iglesia y comunidad nacional' (1981) entre la dictadura y la democracia en Argentina* (Buenos Aires: Eudeba, 2012) and *Discurso religioso y discurso político en América Latina: Leyendo los borradores de Medellín (1968)* (Buenos Aires: Santiago Arcos, 2013).

Ildegrada da Costa Cabral was awarded a PhD at the University of Birmingham, in June 2015. She is now a Visiting Lecturer in the School of Education, University of Birmingham. Her doctoral research was a multi-scalar study of language policy processes in Timor-Leste, where Portuguese and Tetum have become co-official languages since 2002. Building on the growing tradition of linguistic ethnography, she combined ethnography of language policy with detailed analysis of multilingual classroom interaction and talk around text. Her research interests include language-in-interaction in institutional settings, linguistic ethnography and ethnography of language policy processes, multilingualism, and language and transnational migration.

Constadina Charalambous is Assistant Professor of Language Education & Literacy at the European University of Cyprus. Her research interests include language education, interactional sociolinguistics, peace education, and more specifically, language learning in contexts of conflict. She has conducted research on peace education initiatives in Cyprus and has been involved in teacher-training seminars.

She is currently conducting research on Other-language learning classes in Cyprus, investigating the role of language learning in promoting peaceful coexistence (funded by the Levehulme Trust).

Panayiota Charalambous works as a Research Associate at the European University of Cyprus, in collaboration with King's College London, in the project "Crossing Languages and Borders: Intercultural Language Education in a Conflict-Troubled Context." Her research centers around the examination of cultural practices in education in divided societies, including literature education, literacy practices, MFL teaching, and intercultural and peace education. In the past she has worked as a researcher in various Cypriot and European projects and as a teacher-trainer on related topics.

Katherine H. Y. Chen is an Assistant Professor at the University of Hong Kong. She is a sociolinguist and linguistic anthropologist, specializing in language ideologies, language and identities, multilingualism, ethnography, and sociolinguistic documentary film. She produced *Multilingual Hong Kong: A Sociolinguistic Case Study of Code-Switching*, a film that explores issues of bilingualism and prejudice. Her current research includes language and identity of multilingualism in Hong Kong; a study of the multilingual and multicultural Indonesian Chinese diaspora in Asia; and a co-authored project (with Agnes Kang) on gender stereotypes of Hong Kong women.

Eva Codó is Associate Professor of English Language and Linguistics at Universitat Autònoma de Barcelona, Spain. Her research centers on multilingual policy and practice in various social institutions, whether state or non-state, investigated using ethnographic methods. She has carried out fieldwork in a tourist information center, a state immigration office, a nongovernmental organization, and a trade union. She has also researched lifestyle migration to Barcelona, in particular discourses of cosmopolitanism and mobility, and processes of local linguistic insertion with a focus on minority languages. She adopts a critical perspective on language, inquiring into the ways in which language practice is at the heart of processes of (re)production of social inequality. Currently, she is Principal Investigator of a funded project on the intensification of English-language education in different types of secondary schools in Catalonia, and its associated linguistic and educational ideologies. She publishes regularly in scholarly journals and edited volumes, and is author of a monograph published in 2008. She has been a Visiting Professor at the University of Toronto.

Xiao Lan Curdt-Christiansen is Professor of Applied Linguistics in Education at the Department of Education, University of Bath. Her research interests encompass ideological, sociocultural-cognitive, and policy perspectives on language learning, with particular focus on children's multilingual education and biliteracy development. Her recent books include *Learning Chinese in Diasporic Communities* (with Andy Hancock, published by John Benjamins); and *Language, Ideology and*

Education: The Politics of Textbooks in Language Education (with Csilla Weninger, published by Routledge). Her publications have also appeared in *Language Policy; International Journal of Bilingualism and Bilingual Education; Journal of Multilingual and Multicultural Development; Language and Education;* and elsewhere.

Jeroen Darquennes is Professor of German and General Linguistics at the University of Namur and affiliated researcher at the Mercator European Research Centre on Multilingualism and Language Learning (Leeuwarden, The Netherlands). He is one of the general editors of *Sociolinguistica, The International Yearbook of European Sociolinguistics* (de Gruyter). In his research he mainly focuses on issues of language contact, language conflict, and language policy and planning in European indigenous language minority settings.

Alfonso Del Percio is Lecturer in Applied Linguistics at the Institute of Education, University College London. His research deals with the intersection of language and political economy and focuses on language, migration, and governmentality, and the links between language, work, and social inequality. His recent publications include "A Semiotics of Nation Branding" (Special Issue of *Signs and Society*, 2016), "Discourses of Diversity" (co-edited special issue with Zorana Sokolovska, *Language and Communication*, 2016) and "Language and Political Economy" (with Mi-Cha Flubacher and Alexandre Duchêne, *The Oxford Handbook of Language and Society*, 2017). He has also co-edited with Mi-Cha Flubacher *Language, Education and Neoliberalism: Critical Studies in Sociolinguistics* (Multilingual Matters, 2017).

Billy Fito'o, thus far one of only two PhD holders in his tribal group of Kuarafi, hails from a small rural village in the Solomon Islands. He was a schoolteacher and an education administrator for many years before taking up university studies overseas, graduating with a BA, an MA, and a PhD in education. His research focuses on citizenship education, which he argues is given only scanty coverage in most school curricula in the Pacific and needs to be given greater emphasis. He is a Lecturer in the School of Education in the Faculty of Arts, Law and Education at the University of the South Pacific in Fiji.

Kellie Frost is a PhD student and researcher at the Language Testing Research Centre in the School of Languages and Linguistics at the University of Melbourne. Her PhD research is investigating the impact of language test requirements on migrants seeking permanent residency in Australia. Her research interests include language testing and immigration policy, test impact, and the relationship between social justice and test validity.

Xuesong (Andy) Gao is an Associate Professor in the School of Education, University of New South Wales in Australia. His teaching and research interests include language education policy, reading, second language acquisition, sociolinguistics, and teacher education. His recent research includes a project on "Language

Policy and the Mass Media in Hong Kong, Guangzhou and Arizona" (with James Tollefson, 2014–2017) (RGC Ref No. HKU 17402414H).

David W. Gegeo is Research Coordinator in the Office of the Vice-Chancellor, Solomon Islands National University. Originally from the Solomon Islands, he undertook university studies in the United States, graduating with a PhD in Political Science/Political Philosophy. He has taught at the university level in the United States, New Zealand, and Fiji in the South Pacific. His research has been mostly on his own Kwara'ae culture in the Solomon Islands, where for three decades he and Karen Ann Watson-Gegeo have studied children's language acquisition, the impact of colonization on indigenous culture and languages, development, education, and Kwara'ae indigenous epistemology, among many other subjects.

Monica Heller is Professor at the Ontario Institute for Studies in Education and the Department of Anthropology at the University of Toronto. She is a Fellow of the Royal Society of Canada and a Past President of the American Anthropological Association. She has published in such journals as the *Journal of Sociolinguistics; Language in Society; Langage et Société*; and *Anthropologie et Sociétés*. With Bonnie McElhinny, she published *Language, Capitalism, Colonialism* (University of Toronto Press, 2017), and with Sari Pietikäinen and Joan Pujolar, *Critical Language Research: How to Study Language Issues That Matter* (Routledge, 2017).

Francis M. Hult is an Associate Professor at the Centre for Languages and Literature, Lund University, Sweden. His research examines multilingual language management in policy and practice, focusing on linguistic landscapes and language policy and planning through an ethnographic discourse-analytic lens. He has been a UNESCO Senior Visiting Scholar and a Visiting Researcher at the University of Calgary Language Research Centre, the National Institute of Education in Singapore, and the Center for Applied Linguistics. He is a member of the Language Policy Research Network (LPREN) advisory board and of the UNESCO International Bureau of Education network of experts. His most recent book is *Research Methods in Language Policy and Planning: A Practical Guide* (Wiley-Blackwell, 2015, with David Cassels Johnson).

Peter Ives is Professor of Political Science at the University of Winnipeg, Canada. He is author of *Gramsci's Politics of Language: Engaging the Bakhtin Circle and the Frankfurt School* (University of Toronto Press, 2004); *Language and Hegemony in Gramsci* (Pluto Press, 2004); co-editor, with Rocco Lacorte, of *Gramsci, Language and Translation* (Lexington, 2010); and with Thomas Ricento and Yael Peled, *Language Policy and Political Theory* (Springer, 2015). His articles have appeared in the journals *Language Policy; Political Studies; Educational Philosophy and Theory; Rethinking Marxism*; and the *Review of International Studies*. His writings have been translated into Spanish, German, Italian, Portuguese, and Turkish.

Jürgen Jaspers is Associate Professor of Dutch Linguistics at the Université Libre de Bruxelles (ULB), Belgium. He publishes widely on classroom interaction, linguistic standardization, and urban multilingualism. His recent work can be found in *Language in Society; Language Policy; Science Communication; Journal of Germanic Linguistics; Applied Linguistics Review; Annual Review of Anthropology*; and *International Journal of the Sociology of Language*, apart from various chapters in edited volumes.

Adam Jaworski is Chair Professor of Sociolinguistics at the School of English, The University of Hong Kong. His research interests include language and globalization, display of languages in space, media discourse, nonverbal communication, and text-based art. With Brook Bolander he co-edits the Oxford University Press book series *Oxford Studies in Sociolinguistics*.

David Cassels Johnson received his PhD in Educational Linguistics from the University of Pennsylvania. He is Associate Professor of Education at the University of Iowa. His primary area of research is educational language policy. He is the author of *Language Policy* (Palgrave Macmillan, 2013) and co-editor, with Francis M. Hult, of *Research Methods in Language Policy and Planning: A Practical Guide* (Wiley-Blackwell, 2015).

Tomasz Kamusella is a Reader in Modern History at the University of St. Andrews, specializing in language politics, ethnic cleansing, and nationalism in modern central Europe. His English-language monographs include *Creating Languages in Central Europe during the Last Millennium* (2015), *The Politics of Language and Nationalism in Modern Central Europe* (2009), and *Silesia and Central European Nationalism: The Emergence of National and Ethnic Groups in Prussian Silesia and Austrian Silesia, 1848–1918* (2006). At present, he is finishing a new monograph on the forgotten 1989 ethnic cleansing of communist Bulgaria's Turks.

Kamran Khan is currently an Associate Lecturer at the Universitat de Lleida in Catalonia, Spain, and holds a Visiting Academic position at King's College London. He was previously the ESRC (Economic and Social Research Council) Research Associate in Sociology on the project titled "The UK Citizenship Process: Exploring Immigrants' Experiences" at the University of Leicester. He completed his joint PhD at the University of Birmingham (UK) and University of Melbourne (Australia) on linguistic practices and forms of becoming within the citizenship process. His research interests include citizenship, security, multilingualism, and language testing.

Aoife Lenihan is a member of the Centre for Applied Language Studies at the University of Limerick, where she also completed her PhD research. Her primary research interests are new/digital media and sociolinguistics, including minority languages and multilingualism. Recent publications include "Virtual Ethnographic Approaches to Researching Multilingualism Online" (2017) with

Helen Kelly-Holmes in *Researching Multilingualism: Critical and Ethnographic Perspectives*, edited by Marilyn Martin-Jones and Deirdre Martin.

Marilyn Martin-Jones is an Emeritus Professor at the University of Birmingham. She is the former founding Director of the MOSAIC Centre for Research on Multilingualism. For nearly forty years, she has been involved in critical ethnographic research on multilingualism and literacy in classroom and community contexts in the United Kingdom, focusing on the ways in which language and literacy practices are bound up with local and global relations of power. Her latest publication (with Deirdre Martin) is *Researching Multilingualism: Critical and Ethnographic Perspectives*. She is also editor (with Joan Pujolar) of the Routledge book series *Critical Studies in Multilingualism*.

Luisa Martín Rojo is Professor in Linguistics at the Universidad Autónoma in Madrid, and member of the International Pragmatic Association Consultation Board (re-elected for the period 2012–2017). She has been President of the Iberian Association for Studies on Discourse and Society (EDiSo), and Distinguished Visiting Professor at the Graduate Center (City University of New York). She has conducted research in the fields of discourse analysis, sociolinguistics, and communication, mainly focused on immigration and racism. Since 2000, her research has focused on the management of cultural and linguistic diversity in schools, applying a sociolinguistic and ethnographic perspective and analyzing how inequality is constructed, naturalized, and legitimized through discourse (*Constructing Inequality in Multilingual Classrooms*, 2010), and the role of linguistic ideologies and values (*A Sociolinguistics of Diaspora: Latino Practices, Identities, and Ideologies*, 2014, co-edited with Rosina Márquez-Reiter). Currently she is exploring the interplay between urban spaces and linguistic practices in new global protest movements (*Occupy: The Spatial Dynamics of Discourse in Global Protest Movements*, 2016). She is also a member of the editorial boards of the journals *Discourse and Society; Journal of Language and Politics; Spanish in Context; Critical Discourse Studies*; and *Journal of Multicultural Discourses*.

Stephen May is Professor of Education in Te Puna Wānanga (School of Māori and Indigenous Education) in the Faculty of Education and Social Work, University of Auckland, New Zealand. He is an international authority on language rights, language policy, bilingualism and bilingual education, and critical multicultural approaches to education. He has published over 100 articles and book chapters, along with numerous books, including, most recently, *The Multilingual Turn* (2014) and *Language and Minority Rights* (2nd edition, 2012). In addition to being Editor-in-Chief of the 10-volume *Encyclopedia of Language and Education* (3rd edition, 2017), he is a Founding Editor of the interdisciplinary journal *Ethnicities*, and was from 2005 to 2015 Associate Editor of *Language Policy*. He is a Fellow of the American Educational Research Association (AERA) and the Royal Society of New Zealand (FRSNZ).

Teresa L. McCarty is the G. F. Kneller Chair in Education and Anthropology at the University of California, Los Angeles. Her research, teaching, and outreach focus on Indigenous education and critical ethnography of language planning and policy. A Fellow of the American Educational Research Association, Society for Applied Anthropology, and International Centre for Language Revitalization, her recent books include *Ethnography and Language Policy* (2011), *Language Planning and Policy in Native America: History, Theory, Praxis* (2013), and *Indigenous Language Revitalization in the Americas* (with S. Coronel-Molina, 2016). She is Principal Investigator on a 2016–2020 Spencer Foundation research grant for a national study of Indigenous-language immersion schooling.

Tim McNamara is Redmond Barry Distinguished Professor in the School of Languages and Linguistics at the University of Melbourne. His main areas of research are in language testing (particularly specific-purpose language testing, Rasch measurement, and the social context of language tests) and in poststructuralist perspectives on language and identity.

Bernadette O'Rourke is Professor of Sociolinguistics in the Department of Languages and Intercultural Studies, School of Social Sciences, at Heriot-Watt University. Her research focuses on the role of language in the construction of social difference and social inequality. Drawing on theoretical frameworks and concepts in the area of sociolinguistics and the sociology of language, she has examined these processes as they unfold in bilingual and multilingual communities. She is Deputy Director of the Intercultural Research Centre and leads a research cluster on language planning and policy, language rights, and language ideologies. She is Chair of COST Action IS1306 (2013–2017), "New Speakers in a Multilingual Europe: Opportunities and Challenges."

Yael Peled is a Postdoctoral Research Fellow in Language and Health at the Institute for Health and Social Policy and the Faculty of Law, McGill University. Her main research interests examine the complex interrelations between morality and language, ranging from the identity politics of multilingual societies to the linguistic encoding, expression, and transformation of political ethics. Alongside her work in the normative and applied ethics of language, she is also interested in the phenomenon of interdisciplinarity in the social sciences and humanities, and in the application of complexity theory (particularly complex adaptive systems) to public policy research. Her work has appeared in journals such as the *American Political Science Review; Language Policy*; the *Journal of Language and Politics*; and *Science*. Her monograph *Normative Language Policy: Ethics, Politics, Principles* (2018, with Leigh Oakes) is published by Cambridge University Press.

Miguel Pérez-Milans is Senior Lecturer in Applied Linguistics at the Centre for Applied Linguistics in the UCL Institute of Education, University College London, and is currently linked to The University of Hong Kong as Honorary

Associate Professor in the Faculty of Education. His latest research projects involve the ethnographic and sociolinguistic study of language ideology, identity, and social interaction in institutional spaces in London, Madrid, Mainland China, and Hong Kong, with specific attention to instability, social change, and interpersonal collusion under conditions of late modernity. He is author of the book *Urban Schools and English Language Education in Late Modern China: A Critical Sociolinguistic Ethnography* (Routledge Critical Series in Multilingualism, 2013). He has also edited the following monographs in the form of special issues: *Multilingual Discursive Practices and Processes of Social Change in Globalizing Institutional Spaces* (*International Journal of Multilingualism* 11[4], 2014); *Language Education Policy in Late Modernity: Insights from Situated Approaches* (*Language Policy* 14[2], 2015); and *Reflexivity in Late Modernity: Accounts from Linguistic Ethnographies of Youth* (*AILA Review* 29[1], 2016).

Joan Pujolar received his *Llicenciat* in Anglo-Germanic Philology (1987) and Catalan Philology (1988) at Universitat Autònoma de Barcelona, and his MA in Language Studies (1991) and PhD (1995) at Lancaster University. He is currently Associate Professor and Director of the Doctoral Program in Information and Knowledge Society at the Universitat Oberta de Catalunya, Director of the Research Group on Language, Culture and Identity in the Global World, President of the Catalan Society of Sociolinguistics, and Vice-Chair of the ISCH COST Action IS1306, "New Speakers in a Multilingual Europe: Opportunities and Challenges." His research focuses on how language use is mobilized in the construction of identities and its implications for access to symbolic and economic resources. He has conducted research on the use of Catalan among young people in informal contexts, in language classes for adult immigrants, and on the commodification of language in the economic sector, particularly in tourism. He has also examined the interplay between multilingualism and gender. He now leads a project on "new speakers" and the experience of people who ordinarily speak a language that is not their native one.

Ronice Müller de Quadros is a Professor and Researcher at the Federal University of Santa Catarina in Brazil and Researcher at CNPQ (*Conselho Nacional de Desenvolvimento Científico e Tecnológico*, the National Council for Scientific and Technological Development), focusing on research related to the study of sign languages. She works with longitudinal and experimental data from deaf children and bimodal bilingual hearing people in the Libras Corpus Research Group. She is also coordinating the consolidation of the National Libras Inventory, which includes several sub-projects for the composition of the Libras documentation, with funding from CNPQ and the Ministry of Culture of Brazil.

Ben Rampton is Professor of Applied and Socio Linguistics and Director of the Centre for Language Discourse and Communication at King's College London. He does interactional sociolinguistics, and his interests cover urban multilingualism, ethnicity, class, youth, and education. His publications include *Crossing: Language* *and Ethnicity among Adolescents* (Longman, 1995; St. Jerome, 2005) and *Language in Late Modernity: Interaction in an Urban School* (Cambridge University Press, 2006); he edits *Working Papers in Urban Language and Literacy*; and he was founding convener of the UK Linguistic Ethnography Forum.

Ana María Relaño-Pastor is Associate Professor of Applied Linguistics at the Department of Modern Philology (English Studies), University of Castilla-La Mancha (UCLM), Spain. She has been a Visiting Professor and Director of the program in Spanish as a Heritage Language at the Department of Spanish and Portuguese, University of Arizona, and a Postdoctoral Fellow at the Department of Ethnic Studies, University of California, San Diego. Her research interests include narrative, emotion and identity, language socialization of Latino communities in the United States, language education of immigrant communities in Spain, and bi/multilingual education in Spain. She has published in the journals *Language Policy; International Journal of Bilingual Education and Bilingualism; Spanish in Context; Narrative Inquiry; Theory into Practice*; and *Linguistics and Education*, among others. She is the author of *Shame and Pride in Narrative: Mexican Women's Experiences at the U.S.-Mexico Border* (Palgrave MacMillan, 2014).

Thomas Ricento is Professor and Research Chair, English as an Additional Language, in the Werklund School of Education, University of Calgary, Canada. His recent publications include *Language Policy and Planning: Critical Concepts in Linguistics* (Routledge, 2016); *Language Policy and Political Economy: English in a Global Context* (Oxford University Press, 2015); and *Language Policy and Political Theory: Assessing Breaches, Building Bridges* (Springer, 2015). He is founding co-editor of the *Journal of Language, Identity, and Education* (Routledge) and serves on the Editorial Advisory Boards of six international academic journals. He was a Fulbright Professor at the University of Costa Rica (2000) and at four universities in Colombia (1989), and has been a Visiting Professor/Researcher at universities in Aruba, Chile, Germany, Spain, and Switzerland.

Kristof Savski completed his PhD in linguistics at Lancaster University and is currently a Lecturer at Prince of Songkla University in Hat Yai, Thailand. His main research interests include historical and critical sociolinguistics and language policy, with a particular focus on the social impact of linguists in Slovenia since the nineteenth century, as well as on contemporary language policies in Thailand.

Qing Shao is a research student in the Faculty of Education, The University of Hong Kong. His doctoral study is based on a research project entitled "Language Policy and the Mass Media in Hong Kong, Guangzhou and Arizona," which is funded by the Research Grants Council of the Hong Kong Special Administrative Region, China (RGC Ref No. HKU 17402414H).

Sandra Silberstein is Professor of English and Director of the MATESOL Program at the University of Washington, where she also serves as Coordinator of International

Student Academic Support. Her second-language publications include the editorship of the *TESOL Quarterly*, the ELT reading textbooks *Reader's Choice* and *Choice Readings* (with Mark Clarke and Barbara Dobson), and *Techniques and Resources in Teaching Reading*. Her work in critical discourse analysis focuses on media coverage in times of national crisis and includes *War of Words: Language, Politics, and 9/11*, and a forthcoming sequel, *Languaging War and Terrorism*.

Josep Soler is Assistant Professor of Applied Linguistics at the Department of English, Stockholm University. He has degrees in English Studies and General Linguistics from the University of Barcelona, where he also obtained his PhD in Linguistics and Communication. His main research interests cover the areas of language policy and linguistic ideologies; he has recently focused on the role of English in the internationalization of higher education, and on the study of practices and ideologies in multilingual families. His research has appeared in *Current Issues in Language Planning*; *Journal of Multilingual and Multicultural Development*; *International Journal of Bilingual Education and Bilingualism*; and *Multilingua*.

James W. Tollefson is Professor Emeritus at the University of Washington and Honorary Professor in the Faculty of Education, The University of Hong Kong. His many publications include *Planning Language, Planning Inequality* (Longman, 1991); *Language Policies in Education: Critical Issues* (2nd edition, 2013); and, with Amy B. M. Tsui, *Medium of Instruction Policies: Which Agenda? Whose Agenda?* (2004) and *Language Policy, Culture and Identity in Asian Contexts* (2007). His books have also been translated into Chinese, Arabic, and Japanese. His current research focuses on language and inequality, mass media in language policy processes, and the role of language in the history of progressive and pacifist movements in the United States.

Amy B. M. Tsui is Chair Professor of Language and Education in the Faculty of Education, The University of Hong Kong (HKU), a position she has held since 1997. From 2007 to 2014, she was Pro-Vice-Chancellor and Vice-President (Teaching and Learning) at HKU, during which time she led the historical reform of undergraduate education at HKU. She has published nine books and over 100 articles on classroom discourse, conversational analysis, language policy, and teacher development. She has presented over seventy keynotes in international conferences in Asia, the United Kingdom, the United States, Europe, Australia, South Africa, and Mexico, and has served on the editorial and advisory boards of over twenty international refereed journals. She is currently co-editing with Y. C. Liu a volume on *English Language Teacher Education in Asian Contexts*, to be published by Cambridge University Press. She is a member of the International Advisory Board of the University of Helsinki and the Board of Governors of the International Baccalaureate. She was awarded an Honorary Doctoral degree in Education by the University of Edinburgh in 2015.

Virginia Unamuno holds a PhD in Philology and specializes in qualitative sociolinguistics. She works as researcher for CONICET (Consejo Nacional de Investigaciones Científicas y Técnicas) at the University of Buenos Aires. Since 2009, her research has been rooted in the CIFMA (Centro de Investigación y Formación para la Modalidad Aborigen, the Research Centre for Aboriginal Modality) of the Argentinean Chaco Province. She has been a Professor and Researcher at the Autonomous University of Barcelona for ten years, and currently teaches at the Universidad Nacional de San Martín (UNSAM) and Universidad Nacional de Tres de Febrero (UNTREF). She is the author of many scholarly articles and books. She currently coordinates a research project on the new uses and modes of transmission of indigenous languages in northern Argentina.

Karen Ann Watson-Gegeo (PhD Anthropology) is Professor of Language, Literacy, and Culture at the University of California, Davis, where she serves on multiple graduate faculties. She specializes in critical ethnography, critical discourse analysis, and social justice–oriented research in rural and urban communities of Hawai'i and the Solomon Islands; immigrant/bilingual schooling on the US mainland; and disability. She has received an AERA Research award for her work in support of ethnic minority children, and the Regents' Medal for Teaching Excellence at the University of Hawai'i. In 2004 she received the UC Davis Distinguished Graduate Mentor Award.

Li Wei is Chair of Applied Linguistics and Director of the UCL Centre for Applied Linguistics at the UCL Institute of Education, University College London. His research interests are in the broad areas of bilingualism and multilingualism. His recent publications include *Translanguaging: Language, Bilingualism and Education* (with Ofelia Garcia, 2014) which won the 2015 British Association of Applied Linguistics (BAAL) Book Prize; *The Cambridge Handbook of Linguistic Multi-Competence* (with Vivian Cook, 2016); and *Multilingualism in the Chinese Diaspora Worldwide* (2016). He is Principal Editor of the *International Journal of Bilingualism* and *Applied Linguistics Review*.

Ruth Wodak is Emerita Distinguished Professor of Discourse Studies at Lancaster University, and is affiliated with the University of Vienna. Besides various other prizes, she was awarded the Wittgenstein Prize for Elite Researchers in 1996 and an Honorary Doctorate from University of Örebro in Sweden in 2010. She is a member of the British Academy of Social Sciences and of the Academia Europaea. She has published ten monographs, twenty-seven co-authored monographs, over sixty edited volumes, and approximately 400 peer-reviewed journal papers and book chapters. Her recent book publications include *The Politics of Fear: What Right-Wing Populist Discourses Mean* (Sage, 2015; translation into the German *Politik mit der Angst. Zur Wirkung rechtspopulistischer Diskurse*, Konturen, 2016) and *The Discourse of Politics in Action: "Politics as Usual"* (Palgrave, revised edition, 2011).

THE OXFORD HANDBOOK OF

LANGUAGE POLICY AND PLANNING

CHAPTER 1

....

RESEARCH AND PRACTICE IN LANGUAGE POLICY AND PLANNING

....

JAMES W. TOLLEFSON AND MIGUEL PÉREZ-MILANS

THE idea of a *Handbook* such as the one we offer here began to take shape in February 2012. Jim had just taken a new post in the Division of English Language Education at the University of Hong Kong where Miguel was in the last year of a postdoctoral fellowship funded by the Spanish Ministry of Education. We met for the first time at a research seminar at which a postdoctoral researcher based in another university in Hong Kong presented data about Korean Chinese learning the Korean language in South Korea. Drawing heavily from Pierre Bourdieu's work (1993) on the *linguistic market* and *symbolic capital*, and relying on interview data, the speaker at that seminar provided an account of the minority participants as social actors who did not have access to the Korean linguistic market due to their lack of competence in the national language. These broad claims resonated with our own research and life experiences, and aligned well with the type of academic arguments that both of us had published in previous work. Yet, we sensed also that other issues must be considered to fully grasp language in the changing socio-institutional dynamics derived from wider patterns of sociopolitical and economic transformation that we believed to be important; we sensed also that some of these patterns complicated nationally bounded views of linguistic markets and the processes of production, distribution, and valuation of symbolic resources that operate within them.

Previous to his arrival in Hong Kong, Jim had conducted research in multiple contexts internationally while being based in the United States and Japan. Over many years, that research had illuminated the central role of language policy and planning (LPP) processes in sustaining systems of inequality under different historical conditions, including neoliberalism in the United States and East Asia (Tollefson, 2015; Tollefson & Tsui, 2007), an independent socialist alternative in Yugoslavia (Tollefson, 2002), and processes of mass migration (Tollefson, 1989, 1993). Miguel had carried out research on language education policy shifts in Madrid, mainland China, London, and Hong Kong. Committed to describing ethnographically the social patterns of global change tied to the economic conditions of late modernity, his work contributed to a body of literature preoccupied with shifting forms of inequality resulting from processes of transnational migration, late modern nationalism, institutional neoliberalization, and the commodification of diversity (see, for instance, Pérez-Milans, 2011, 2013, 2015; Pérez-Milans & Soto, 2016; Soto & Pérez-Milans, 2018).

In the context of these research trajectories, and what we believed to be interesting differences in our professional training and perspectives emerging from different periods in the development of LPP, the research seminar at the University of Hong Kong spurred a dialogue between us that led to our decision to co-teach a postgraduate class in sociolinguistics that placed theoretical and empirical developments in the field within their historical contexts. As we worked through that class, we increasingly focused on the ways in which the relationship between LPP and political-economic conditions has been understood, and how this changing relationship has shaped knowledge production in the field. It was this dialogue about the history of LPP that has led to the present volume. Equally interested in language, social critique, and inequality, our research and work experiences across different regional, national, and institutional settings—and more specifically, our latest involvement in research from and about Asian conditions—drove our attention to ongoing processes and nuances that have gradually become the focus of contemporary LPP research, in many cases forcing scholars and practitioners in the field to revisit their own assumptions, views, and methodological perspectives.

Against the background of this particular journey, we decided to embark on *The Oxford Handbook of Language Policy and Planning*—a project that aims to explore this set of issues, beyond just providing a set of summaries of specific subfields within LPP (although some will be provided as needed, or can be found elsewhere; e.g., Ricento, 2016; Spolsky, 2012). In particular, this *Handbook* addresses many of the current questions that LPP researchers face under contemporary conditions of change, with an ambition to better understand the current period in which the field operates today.

But before detailing the specific questions that have guided the organization of this volume, we first provide an overview of the foundations of the field.

Foundations of Language Policy and Planning Research

LPP activities existed long before language policy and planning emerged as a distinct field of inquiry. Tied to the rise of the bourgeoisie in the nineteenth century and to its interests in expanding economic activities both within and among unified national markets, the political and socioeconomic mode of organization of the nation-state required intensive discursive work from the start (Bauman & Briggs, 2003; see also Hobsbawm, 1990), both in the institutional arena and in everyday life, for the "imagination" (Anderson, 1983) of a monolingual citizenry (e.g., grammars, dictionaries, and other forms of regulation of speakers). However, the terms *language policy* and *language planning* emerged as such in the 1960s, in connection with what would be the early years of LPP research.

The term *language planning* referred to deliberate efforts to affect the structure (usage, corpus) or function (use, status) of languages. As evident in early scholarship (e.g., Haugen, 1966), such efforts were understood primarily as the work of planning agencies. Accordingly, in their classic book about language planning, Rubin and Jernudd (1971) defined *language planning* as follows: "language planning is *deliberate* language change; that is, changes in the system of language code or speaking or both that are planned by organizations that are established for such purposes or given a mandate to fulfill such purposes" (p. xvi). Subsequently, the most widely cited definition of *language planning* was developed by Robert Cooper, who added acquisition planning to corpus and status planning: "Language planning refers to deliberate efforts to influence the behavior of others with respect to the acquisition, structure, or functional allocation of their language codes" (Cooper, 1989, p. 45). Cooper also extended the notion of language planning to include a broad range of policy actors beyond formal state authorities (e.g., Māori community leaders who fought to extend the use of the Māori language into preschools and elementary schools in New Zealand).

Use of the term *language policy* emerged from the focus on national language planning. At times, the terms *policy* and *planning* seemed to be used interchangeably (e.g., Das Gupta, 1970; Rubin & Jernudd, 1971, p. xx). At other times, language planning was described as following from language policy, as in Fishman's discussion of corpus planning, which involves "the elaboration, codification, and implementation that go on once language-policy decisions have been reached" (1971, p. 9). This understanding accorded with Ferguson's (1968) focus on graphization, standardization, and modernization as the central processes of language planning. For other early scholars, a language policy was seen as the output of the planning process and was understood as a set of national goals (e.g., adoption of a single lingua franca) and an explicit statement about how to achieve those goals. For example, Jernudd and Das Gupta, in "Towards a Theory of Language Planning" (1971), focused on national planning processes:

> Social planning at high levels of enlargement ("macro" levels) involves the construction of an over-all design of organized action that is considered necessary for economic utilization of resources and that is directed by formally constituted authority. It consists of a structure of coordinated programs, and the latter in their turn consist of a set of coordinated projects. (p. 196)

This attention to national language policy and planning meant that the major issues investigated in early LPP research were nation building, nationalism, political and sociocultural integration, national education policies, economic development, and official languages.

In its origins, LPP was assumed to be an area of specialization in sociolinguistics. For example, written as an overview of LPP, Joshua Fishman's introduction to the foundational book *Language Problems of Developing Nations* (Fishman, Ferguson, & Das Gupta, 1968) opens with the question "what is sociolinguistics, and why?" (Fishman, 1968b, p. 3). Another early, influential volume (Fishman, 1968a) on sociolinguistics and the sociology of language included a major section on language planning, and a follow-up two-volume set included a similar section on "policy, planning and practice" (Fishman, 1972a, p. 15) as an important subfield of sociolinguistics.

Such efforts to place LPP within a disciplinary framework, as well as explicit definitions of policy and planning, were particularly evident in the remarkable formative period of LPP during the years 1964–1974. After the founding of the Center for Applied Linguistics in 1959 under its first director, Charles A. Ferguson, the need for research on LPP had become evident. Accordingly, during the early and mid-1960s, a series of meetings and conferences—often organized by Ferguson and Joshua Fishman and sponsored by the Social Science Research Council, the Ford Foundation (see Fox, 1975), and other funding agencies—produced many of the foundational early research projects and publications. These meetings took place during Joshua Fishman's year at the Center for Advanced Study in the Behavioral Sciences at Stanford University in 1963–1964; in the summer of 1964, when the Committee on Sociolinguistics of the Social Science Research Council organized an eight-week LPP seminar of linguists and social scientists (see Ferguson, 1965, for a report on this important seminar); in November 1966, at a meeting at Airlie House in Warrenton, Virginia, which focused on language and development and led directly to publication of *Language Problems of Developing Nations* (Fishman,

Ferguson, & Das Gupta, 1968); and during 1968–1969 at the East-West Center at the University of Hawaii, where Jyotirindra Das Gupta, Joshua Fishman, Björn Jernudd, and Joan Rubin spent a year that included a meeting of selected LPP scholars during April 1969.

This work at the East-West Center led to the publication of the influential *Can Language Be Planned?* (Rubin & Jernudd, 1971) and to the establishment of the International Research Project on Language Planning Processes at Stanford University (where Ferguson had founded the Committee on Linguistics [later a Department] in 1967), which eventually spawned the important book *Language Planning Processes* (Rubin et al., 1977). Other influential publications during this period included Fishman's *Advances in Language Planning* (Fishman, 1974), Fishman's reconsideration of his earlier work (Fishman, 1964) on language maintenance and shift as a field of inquiry (Fishman, 1972c), and his analysis of language and nationalism (Fishman, 1972b), as well as a growing body of case studies in contexts around the world (e.g., Das Gupta, 1970; Fishman, 1972a, volume II; Mazrui, 1968; Sibayan, 1971; Zima, 1968). In Europe, work within the Prague School was extended to LPP (Garvin, 1973; Neustupný, 1970), and case studies on LPP provided rich empirical data beyond postcolonial contexts (e.g., Lewis, 1972; Lorwin, 1972; also see Tauli, 1968). This impressive output over a period of just ten years served as the foundation for the next forty-five years of LPP scholarship.

But this scholarship has not followed a linear incremental development. Rather, LPP has been shaped by various ontological and epistemological shifts, linked to wider discussions in the social sciences and to the kind of worldwide shifting socioeconomic conditions with which we opened this introductory chapter. For the purpose of this brief discussion, and acknowledging the subsequent oversimplification of regional and interdisciplinary dynamics that it involves, we group such shifts into two major stages: namely, early work, and the contributions of the critical and ethnographic approaches. (For surveys of the field, see Jernudd & Nekvapil, 2012; Ricento, 2000; Tollefson, 1991; and Heller, Chapter 2 in this volume).

Early Work

Although social scientists frequently theorize about practice, LPP initially emerged as *essentially* pragmatic, with the aim of providing direct and explicit tools to achieve concrete social and linguistic goals. This early work—termed "classic language planning" (Ricento, 2000, p. 206) or "neoclassical language planning (Tollefson, 1991, p. 26)—viewed LPP as a practical objective science, driven by technical experts who served as the practitioners of policymaking and planning, as well as the preferred decision-makers for the complex details of policy formulation, implementation, and evaluation (see Rubin, 1971). The dominance of this positivist belief in the scientific objectivity of LPP practitioners had a direct impact on LPP methodology. In particular, the presumption of a definable underlying reality that LPP practitioners could analyze and change in predictable ways encouraged historical and quantitative methodologies, evident for example in the development of national sociolinguistic surveys, such as the influential English-language policy survey of Jordan (Harrison, Prator, & Tucker, 1975) and the language policy survey of the Philippines (Sibayan, 1971).

Although this approach generated extensive descriptive data about the language situation in many contexts, it also tended to close off process understandings of language that emerge from process methodologies (such as those that are ethnographically informed). Partly as a consequence, in LPP—and language studies generally—dominant conceptual frameworks included important ontological and epistemological assumptions such as the following: languages have reality apart from their speakers; sociolinguistic categories such as *language, dialect, diglossia,* and *national identity* have fixed meanings and clear boundaries; and there is a direct link between language and identity that places the individual speaker neatly in ethnic and national categories. Moreover, the presumption that the world is composed of identifiable chunks (languages, dialects, native speakers, communities, nations, national identities) invites causal explanation, prediction, and replication.

The work of early LPP, therefore, was aimed at finding specific, replicable techniques to achieve identifiable and quantifiable goals such as language learning and bilingualism, economic development, and political stability. Such an orientation in LPP fit well with the Chomskyan revolution in linguistic theory also taking place in the 1960s, with its assumption of universal mental structures that were essentially linguistic categories. Indeed, the universalism inherent in language research in this period meant that scholarly analysis was characterized by a sense of the potential for major breakthroughs in research and practice.

In LPP, this meant that the processes of language "modernization" and "development" (see Rostow, 1960) were understood as universally transplantable into new contexts by LPP specialists working with social scientific techniques that promised predictable outcomes. The confluence of scholars' and planners' confidence in technical analysis and expert-driven LPP, however, meant that the use of LPP to sustain systems of inequality was not sufficiently recognized. It also meant that the life trajectories of individuals living in complex social groups were subdivided into a range of discourses—linguistics, politics, economics, law, science, and more—that were impenetrable to the people whose languages and lives were being planned. It was partly in reaction to that yawning gap between analysts and their analytical objects that alternative approaches to LPP began to emerge.

Critical and Ethnographic Approaches

Although the Chomskyan revolution meant that distinctions between languages were conceptualized as surface phenomena, historical and structural analysis revealed that these distinctions can be constructed as having moral, aesthetic, and cognitive significance. Thus, along with developments in sociology, anthropology, and linguistics, the work of LPP scholarship began to examine the processes by which such constructions are developed, their social consequences, and the interests they serve. It was this understanding of LPP that led to the focus on power and ideology in LPP that was evident in critical approaches in the 1990s.

Critical approaches emerged from the wide range of alternative social scientific perspectives that undermined positivist approaches, including existentialism, deconstruction, postmodernism, and critical theory, in which notions of permanence were largely abandoned. This critical turn, which examined the processes by which language is associated with power and inequality, led to an alternative definition of LPP that became widespread in the 1990s:

> Language planning-policy means the institutionalization of language as a basis for distinctions among social groups. That is, language policy is one mechanism for locating language within social structure so that language determines who has access to political power and economic resources. Language policy is one mechanism by which dominant groups establish hegemony in language use. (Tollefson, 1991, p. 16)

Critics of earlier LPP also pointed out that corpus, status, and acquisition planning efforts in the 1960s and 1970s often failed to achieve their stated goals (see, e.g., Spolsky, 2012, p. 4). This claim that early LPP was mostly ineffective was justified in many cases, as LPP was understood primarily as the plans and policies formulated and implemented at the national level by ministries of education and similar state authorities. Critics of state LPP also pointed out that planners often ignored community concerns, and that language policies sometimes were used to sustain systems of inequality (e.g., in apartheid South Africa; see Blommaert, 1996).

The shift in LPP research to a focus on power and inequality involved the historical-structural analysis of state LPP; it did not lead to increased research on what were called the micro contexts of everyday social life, although precisely such contexts had received significant scholarly attention in linguistic anthropology, especially the ethnography of communication (e.g., Gumperz & Hymes, 1972), and interactional sociolinguistics (Gumperz, 1986). Indeed, the focus on the nation-state left little room for attention to the forms of LPP that take place in schools, individual classrooms, workplaces, nongovernmental organizations, and the private sector, where individual teachers, students, workplace supervisors, employees, and household members make critical decisions about language structure, use, and acquisition. When LPP is considered from this wider perspective, and is not limited to the plans and policies of the nation-state, then researchers begin to discover a broader range of consequences of LPP.

Analysis of such contexts required a shift toward epistemological frameworks such as those that are ethnographically informed, yet the shift to process research methods did not mean the loss of the practical focus that had characterized LPP since its founding. Indeed, ethnographic analysis is grounded fundamentally in the notion that what one learns about what it means to be human is found in examples, models, and exemplars rather than abstract principles. Whereas positivist notions of scientific objectivity assume that science is *deep* and culture is *superficial*, process methodologies seek depth of understanding through the detailed and concrete analysis of individuals-in-culture. The spread of ethnographic analysis in LPP, which followed shortly upon historical-structural analysis, revealed that understanding why individuals learn and use languages and how they adopt subject positions and identities cannot be achieved by examining structural forces and institutional social-ization alone, but rather by analyzing how these are extensions of earlier processes of socialization that take place during childhood and adolescence. If researchers want to understand language loss and language shift, the development of bi/multi-lingualism, and the complex sociolinguistic systems of daily life, then they must ex-plore the interface between individuals' life trajectories and the culture and practices of the classroom, the street, the playground, or the home, and how these are linked with national and international ideologies, discourses, and policies.

The research that is required for this undertaking is more than traditional an-thropology, however, with its focus on personal histories and group practices, and its belief that long-term immersion *in a culture* allows the researcher to develop an insider's perspective. Rather than such faith in the scholar's craft, which mirrors early faith in the technical LPP expert, what is needed is the effort to reveal the spe-cific links connecting trajectories of socially positioned actors with current social contexts, including the relationships between the use of particular linguistic forms, notions of cultural competence, and institutional forms of discursive organization (Martin-Jones & Heller, 1996), thereby shedding light "on the ways that the social order reproduces itself through everyday microlevel mechanisms" (Desmond, 2007, p. 269). The result, in LPP, was a gradual shift toward the understanding of lan-guage as social practice, and of identities as fluid and multiple, as well as research methodologies that emphasize process.

The remarkable development of LPP—from its earliest technical focus on solving concrete language-related problems of the new postcolonial nation-states using quantitative and historical analysis, to its current attention to the ways in which struc-tured communication, ideological and normative conventions, and institutional and global discourses are linked in the daily policies and practices of individuals and institutions—suggests that theoretical and conceptual issues in LPP have been, and will continue to be, transformed at a rapid pace. Indeed, the current dynamic condi-tion of LPP research, characterized by approaches and methodologies responding to the rapid global and local changes in politics, the economy, and society, reveals a discipline whose concerns are at the center of profound historical transformations. It is for this reason that this *Handbook* has a forward-looking orientation. More specifically, seeking to understand the trajectory of this current period, we ask the following set of questions: What does LPP mean today? How is our understanding of

LPP shaped by the most important issues currently confronting LPP scholars? What research methodologies are used to investigate these issues? How have changes in the conditions of the modern nation-state altered LPP policies and policymaking, and their consequences? How do the processes of late modernity, particularly neo-liberalism and various forms of globalization, impact LPP?

In the remainder of this introductory chapter, we shall try to map out some of the different threads of recent LPP research evident in this *Handbook*, highlighting the issues that scholarly analysis seeks to understand and the approaches to research used in the investigation, and to anticipate some of the generalizations that emerge.

THE CHAPTERS IN THIS *HANDBOOK*

The issues and approaches in this volume are grouped around three major points of focus. The first is concerned with the key theoretical and methodological underpinnings of past and present LPP research, which are presented as constituting a multi-angled starting point for the rest of the contributions. The second strand of discussion is focused on LPP as a window to further understand core socioeconomic, political, and institutional processes involving the modern nation-state and its role in shaping community-based relations. Finally, the third major area of focus turns our attention to shifting economic conditions in the last few decades, with a view to how they impact LPP as a field of inquiry.

Part I: Conceptual Underpinnings of Language Policy and Planning: Theories and Methods in Dialogue

Part I of the *Handbook* takes us through some of the key ontological and epistemological foundations upon which the interdisciplinary field of LPP has historically evolved, from its origins in the 1960s until contemporary developments. The review unfolds in different directions, with a focus on both theoretical and epistemological implications of such an evolving process. In Chapter 2, Monica Heller lays down the ideological underpinnings of LPP through situating its development at various historical junctures connected to political and economic interests. Far from representations of policymaking as a rational/technical activity, she aligns with the critical tradition that since the 1990s has encouraged LPP scholars to problematize their own agenda. She does so by putting forward a key argument: that if anything has changed in the field, it is in how the relationship between LPP and political economic conditions has been understood, and how this has shaped knowledge production accordingly.

In her genealogy of ideas in LPP research, Heller pays close attention to the linkages between the authoritative knowledge produced by scholars and practitioners, on the one hand, and the various forms of social, economic, and political engineering tied to the emergence and development of the modern nation-state, on the other. Drawing from literature on modern nationalism, language ideology, and late capitalism, she examines the shifts in such forms of engineering vis-à-vis the constitution of language as discursive terrain for the advancement of political economic interests, from the civilization projects of the colonial times in the nineteenth and early twentieth centuries to the decolonization movements of the 1960s—and the accompanying programs of modernization—to the extension and specialization of networks of production, circulation, and consumption driven by contemporary neoliberalism.

The subsequent chapters in Part I of the *Handbook* provide us with a road map to specific epistemological developments and innovations in LPP, against the background of the wider disciplinary shifts discussed by Heller. In his analysis of the history of LPP research methods, David Cassels Johnson in Chapter 3 considers the implications of a focus on "language problems" (Fishman, Ferguson, & Das Gupta, 1968) that derived from what Fishman (1972a, vol. II) called LPP's initial "formative half decade." This stress on practical problems, initially in postcolonial states, resulted in reliance on varied methods drawn from sociolinguistics, sociology, law, economics, and education. As a result, early LPP scholarship varied enormously in its underlying theories, epistemologies, and explanations for findings; yet without agreed-upon theoretical frameworks and methodologies, these fundamental differences could not be systematically examined. LPP-specific methods emerged only gradually and later, as empirical findings accumulated, dissatisfaction with ad hoc explanation intensified, and the need for theories and conceptual frameworks specific to LPP became clear. Thus, over time, LPP scholars began to confront deeper questions about what constituted acceptable theories and methods in LPP research. Johnson's survey of the development of such methods shows that they are associated with different epistemological foundations. As the positivist work that dominated early LPP gave way to critical approaches, researchers increasingly emphasized historical and structural analysis, with attention to power in social systems and to reflexivity, particularly the researcher's position in the research process. More recently, the shift toward critical, discursive, and ethnographic approaches to LPP focuses attention on the interplay of structure and agency and the ethics of social research.

The next three chapters offer an account of different traditions that have emerged out of the critical, discursive, and ethnographic turns which have taken place in LPP in recent decades. Marilyn Martin-Jones and Ildegrada da Costa Cabral in Chapter 4 trace the intellectual and research traditions that are the foundation of the critical ethnography of language policy. These traditions—ethnography of communication, critical sociolinguistic ethnography, linguistic anthropology (including research on language ideology), linguistic ethnography, and ethnography of language policy— developed detailed descriptions and analyses of culturally varied interactional practices and narrative styles, particularly in multilingual schools and classrooms, such as indigenous education programs in North and South America and bilingual education programs in the United States. Yet much of this work was not integrated with that of LPP scholars focusing on policy texts, policymaking processes, and wider issues of national economic development, sociocultural and politico-administrative integration of the new postcolonial nation-states, and national survey data about language in society.

As Martin-Jones and da Costa Cabral show, these two broad strands of research—historical-structural analysis within LPP and processes of the nation-state, often labeled as *macro*, and a range of types of so-called *micro* analysis of schools and other settings—have increasingly come together within the critical ethnography of language policy, a major focus of which is to overcome the macro-micro divide. The result is that LPP research has been characterized by a gradual change in focus from its early attention to the policy processes of modernity to the recent attention to the policy processes of classrooms, schools, families, and other social groups, all linked to globalization and late modern conditions such as increasing mobilities and the heteroglossia of social life. As Martin-Jones and da Costa Cabral trace these changes, they show that new issues have emerged in LPP methods, including questions of scale and the complex discursive processes of policy creation, interpretation, and appropriation.

In Chapter 5, Ruth Wodak and Kristof Savski keep our attention focused on the critical and ethnographic turns in LPP research. Yet, their approach exemplifies a very particular disciplinary tradition that stems from critical discourse studies. Aimed at demystifying ideology and power relations in language use, this tradition brings about two alternative orientations in LPP that also feature ethnographic fieldwork as a constitutive part of their discourse-based analysis: the discourse-historical approach (Reisigl & Wodak, 2015) and mediated discourse analysis (Scollon, 2008). Building on such orientations, as well as on research in the areas of sociolinguistic, linguistic, and organizational anthropology, a critical discourse-ethnographic approach such as the one presented by Wodak and Savski describes observational data and recorded practices from different sites and communicative genres in the European Parliament, all of it with reference to the historical context of such an institution and the broader sociopolitical trends that might influence the practices being observed. In so doing, they illustrate the relevance of multi-method approaches to identify, as they put it, "the repertoire of, and the facilitating factors for, different kinds of language choice, as well as the intricacies of the language regime in a transnational organizational entity such as the European Union."

Still relying on critical, ethnographic, and discourse-based perspectives, Miguel Pérez-Milans in Chapter 6 introduces yet another strand of work that comes with its own sensitivities and is potentially relevant to LPP researchers. In this case, Pérez-Milans's chapter invites us to rethink the way in which we conceptualize, investigate, and analyze texts, contexts, and meanings. Though he explicitly engages with literature in the ethnography of language policy, as discussed in Johnson's as well as in

Martin-Jones and da Costa Cabral's chapters, his claims are intended to address more generally those who, like Wodak and Savski, are interested in the ethnographic triangulation of contextual and discursive data. By drawing from contemporary work on the indexicality of language in sociolinguistics and linguistic anthropology, he advocates for a (metapragmatic) approach to LPP in which context is seen as enacted, negotiated, and made sense of in situated discursive practices across space and time.

This approach, Pérez-Milans reminds us, requires empirical commitment to the ways in which social actors connect communicative events, normative conventions, and intersubjective stances throughout their trajectories of performative identification, beyond ethnographic approaches whereby institutional events, content analysis of research interviews, and denotational descriptions of policy documents have been extensively privileged. Indeed, he states, this overemphasis on denotational analysis of texts, contexts, and meanings in LPP may have contributed to reifying a widely problematized view of policy as a cultural artifact that only shapes social life externally and whose influence in people's lives can only be (empirically) grasped through analysis of talk *about* it. In an attempt to show how performative and trajectory-based ethnographic studies of LPP may look, Pérez-Milans's chapter reports on previous fieldwork carried out in the educational space of Hong Kong.

The final chapter in Part I, Chapter 7 by Yael Peled, turns our attention toward the ethics of LPP research. Peled's chapter emerges from her extensive work examining the complex relationships between morality and language within the framework of political theory and her interest in issues related to interdisciplinarity in the social sciences and humanities. Peled argues for a role for language ethics, which she defines as "the inquiry on the moral problems, practices, and policies relating to language, on par with equivalent topics in applied ethics, such as environmental ethics or the ethics of war." Peled's normative approach to LPP, focusing on ethical theory and action, is particularly relevant to recent interest in language rights, linguistic justice, reflexivity in research, and democratic processes in language policymaking. In fact, a normative approach is particularly important for critical LPP scholars, who argue that researchers must be engaged in social change, a principle that emerges not only from the theoretical frameworks that underlie critical LPP (e.g., critical theory and Marxist approaches), but also from the early origins of the field as a practical discipline. Peled argues that this commitment to social change raises ethical questions about LPP that political theory addresses through its attention to the analysis of *what is* and *how things should be.*

Part II: Language Policy and Planning, Nation-States, and Communities

Part II includes chapters that examine the close links between LPP and nationalism and influential ideas about language and the institutions of the nation-state.

Chapters also investigate the social position of minority languages and specific communities facing profound language policy challenges.

II.A: Modern Nationalism, Languages, Minorities, Standardization, and Globalization

Since its foundational period in the 1960s, LPP research has included extensive analysis of state policies and planning processes. As critical perspectives toward LPP emerged during the 1980s and 1990s, attention to language and power meant that research focused on how LPP processes contribute to social, economic, and political inequalities and how greater opportunities for marginalized sociolinguistic groups may be opened. Thus research continued to be characterized by analysis of LPP decision-making, primarily within state planning agencies. This section of the *Handbook* examines several key areas of state LPP, in particular its role in nationalism, the treatment of linguistic minorities, and language standardization processes, as well as the expansion of the economic activities of specific social groups across different nationally constituted markets via the role that English plays in globalization.

We begin with two chapters that examine the role of the state in LPP. First, Tomasz Kamusella's Chapter 8 focuses on the use of language in nationalism within European states in the twentieth century, particularly after the collapse of the Berlin Wall in 1989. Kamusella focuses on the ethnolinguistically homogenous nation-state as the norm of legitimate statehood in Europe by tracing what he terms the "normative isomorphism" of language, nation, and state in Central Europe. As the foundation of state nationalism dating to the nineteenth century, language became a key focus of state planning, and continues to be so under the processes of globalization and the weakening of nation-state control over the economy. Kamusella examines the linkage between language and nationalism across a remarkable range of contexts, including, for example, the breakup of Yugoslavia (1990–1992), which has been accompanied by the breakup of the Serbo-Croatian language, so that the successor states of Yugoslavia (except Kosovo) have claimed their own national languages (i.e., Croatian, Serbian, Bosnian, and Montenegrin; Slovene and Macedonian were distinguished in earlier periods). Kamusella also touches on language and nationalism in other regions of the world, such as those areas where the imposition of colonial languages has prevented the normative insistence that languages should make nations. He also looks to the future and whether the European Union's push for polylingual language policies may blunt the impact of ethnolinguistic nationalism.

In the second chapter about the link between language and the nation-state, Peter Ives in Chapter 9 offers his perspective drawn from Western political theory. He examines the foundational theorists of the modern liberal tradition, John Locke and

Thomas Hobbes, as well as Rousseau's and Herder's ideas about language and the state, which have been the foundation for many versions of multiculturalism and for communitarian political theory. With regard to Locke and Hobbes, Ives delves into their differing concepts of the social contract, which, he argues, is the basis for ideas about government planning. He shows that they spelled out two competing foundational ideas about planning: Locke articulated the view that there is only a highly limited role for state LPP, whereas Hobbes provided the key philosophical argument for state language planning. Examining work by Spolsky (2004) and others, Ives shows how this difference is mirrored in contemporary LPP.

Ives also spells out the importance of this debate for contemporary discussions about global English, instrumentalism in language policy, the role of ideology in LPP, and, in particular, the rational choice theory that underlies a great deal of LPP theory and practice. As for Rousseau and Herder, Ives examines in some detail the widely held view that Herder's theories of language and the state are the foundation for ethnolinguistic nationalism. Ives's chapter suggests that the widespread attention to Herder in LPP theory deserves new analysis. Indeed, Ives argues that Herder's theories provide a more useful basis for contemporary understandings of LPP than has been previously recognized.

After the chapters by Kamusella and Ives examining the role of the state in LPP, Katherine H. Y. Chen in Chapter 10 directs our attention to language standardization as a key process whereby different social groups struggle over legitimacy within the political model of the modern nation-state. In her chapter, Chen presents us with a specific case: the analysis of LPP and modern nationalism through the lens of the ideologies of standardization of the Cantonese language in the context of contemporary Hong Kong. She uses the period leading up to the handover of Hong Kong from Britain to China, in 1997, as a point of reference to track the changing social meaning of Cantonese to the people of Hong Kong and the development of a distinct Hong Kong identity that has gained greater social and political significance in the two decades following the handover.

Chen focuses specifically on the process of standardization of Cantonese initiated by three key Cantonese language authorities; she takes this process as an index of language ideologies operating in connection with wider socioeconomic and political interests in postcolonial Hong Kong and mainland China. These interests, she claims, have never been just aesthetic or linguistic in a narrow sense; rather, they are part of a broader agenda that places language as a key discursive arena for negotiating community boundaries and identities, and thereby for furthering sociopolitical differentiation. More specifically, Chen's analysis shows how the standardization of Cantonese in Hong Kong is part of an ideological struggle over who gets to decide what counts as the *authentic* or *pure* Chinese national community.

With these chapters having established the basic logic under which the ideological framework of the modern nation-state operates, as well as the importance of language in it, Chapter 11 by Thomas Ricento expands our lens. He examines different state responses to the role of English under conditions of globalization, a process that is inherent to the consolidation and amplification of the economic activities of a transnational class across previously well-demarcated national markets. Ricento offers the perspective of political economy to analyze two competing claims about English: that it is a form of linguistic imperialism, and that it is a vehicle for social and economic mobility. Ricento's analysis looks specifically at which economic sectors and which social groups benefit from English, arguing that people in the so-called knowledge economy find English a means for economic mobility, whereas the vast majority of people in the global workforce receive no benefit or in some cases suffer economic consequences from the domination of English.

One of the important contributions of Ricento's chapter to this *Handbook* is that it introduces explicitly a political-economic approach to LPP research, in line with the arguments advanced by Heller in Chapter 2. Ricento shows that a political-economic approach avoids grand narratives about English and globalization, and instead examines English (and other languages) within the particular economic and political conditions of specific countries and regions. This approach reveals, in Ricento's words, that "the economic power of English is often assumed" rather than empirically verified, and even when there is some benefit, it is often overstated.

The focus of attention in the preceding chapters foregrounds the role of the state in LPP and the interests of the social groups who benefit the most from it, yet they say very little about minorities and their linguistic demands in the context of the ideological confines of the modern nation-state. This concern raises the issue of language rights. Although arguments for language rights are often primarily aesthetic, with diversity celebrated, honored, or appreciated rather than protected or promoted for compelling political, social, or economic reasons, Stephen May in Chapter 12 shows that language rights can make a significant contribution to social and political stability in multilingual states. In his analysis of language rights and language repression, Stephen May continues the investigation of the state and LPP by examining historical and contemporary conflicts that are often framed in ethnic terms, but that actually involve language and language policy as a central issue.

Considering cases of language rights and language repression around the world, May explores, in the final chapter of this section of the *Handbook*, three sources of the widely held belief that language diversity inevitably contributes to instability: the negative ascription of ethnicity in political and scholarly discourse; the concept drawn from European nationalism, as outlined in Kamusella's chapter, that the ideal nation-state is ethnically and linguistically homogeneous; and the implicit use of both ideas in common conceptions of citizenship and human rights. May's analysis of the historical development of these ideas reveals the underlying ideologies and official narratives that serve as the foundation for language policies of nation-states worldwide. He also presents alternative bases for minority language rights that, in his view, promote social and political stability by accommodating minority language rights and contributing to what he terms "ethnocultural and ethnolin-guistic democracy."

The ideological frameworks, processes, and struggles discussed in the previous five chapters operate in different institutions of the modern nation-state. This is the focus of the following section of Part II.

II.B: Language Policy and Planning in Institutions of the Modern Nation-State: Education, Citizenship, Media, and Public Signage

The five chapters in this section explore LPP in the institutions and daily life of the nation-state, specifically schools, citizenship and immigration, mass media, and public linguistic landscapes. Together, they provide extensive analysis of different cases, in various regional and national contexts, with which to better understand the ways in which the ideological dynamics discussed in the previous section are played out through specific institutional logics.

In Chapter 13, James W. Tollefson and Amy B. M. Tsui examine one of the most important forms of LPP in schools—medium of instruction (MOI) policies—particularly debates about the use of children's home languages in schools. Despite the success of programs that use home languages, many states have continued to promote English or other postcolonial languages. In particular, as Tollefson and Tsui show, the pressures on state educational authorities to adopt MOI policies supporting so-called global English have transformed education in many contexts, including China, European higher education, and elsewhere. As a result, parents, educators, and policymakers often must navigate contradictory personal, ped-agogical, and political agendas implicit in MOI policies. Nevertheless, despite the pressure for English in many contexts, a discourse of language rights can be a counter-force to English promotion policies. In addition, community efforts in some contexts have successfully used MOI to reduce educational inequality. This chapter suggests that LPP research adopting situated approaches can place MOI policies and practices within local and global economic, political, and social conditions, in order to make explicit the links between MOI and the social life of children, schools, families, and communities.

Focusing on a key aspect of education—language tests—Kellie Frost and Tim McNamara in Chapter 14 examine the broader linkage between language testing, immigration policy, and citizenship. Adopting the perspective of language tests as language policy (Shohamy, 2006), they show how language testing in Australia has been incorporated into immigration policy and citizenship requirements, with test scores serving as a key indicator in migrant selection processes that deter-mine individuals' eligibility to remain in Australia. However, they do not limit their analysis to state policies and institutional practices; rather, Frost and McNamara examine also the impact of testing, immigration, and citizenship requirements on individuals who are subject to policy controls. Within a poststructural analysis of the function of examinations in modern societies, they show how individuals' life chances are shaped by language-testing policies, thereby revealing the complex ways that language proficiency requirements shape the subjectivity of individuals. Their chapter has particular implications for LPP in countries where there has been a long history of policies encouraging immigration, including Australia, New Zealand, Canada, and the United States.

A growing body of research on policymaking processes has found that mass and social media can significantly constrain the language policies that are considered in a particular context and on the public understandings of those policies (Gao, 2015, 2017; Tollefson, 2015). The following two chapters in the volume speak to this issue. In their Chapter 15 on mass media and LPP, Xuesong Gao and Qing Shao focus on how the mass media discursively frame language issues and mediate the consideration of language policy alternatives. Using representation theory and the concepts of media framing (Jefferies, 2009; Scheufele & Iyengar, 2011) and legitimization (Chilton, 2004), they analyze three cases in which the media are policy actors in the policymaking process: the state print media coverage of the *dialect crisis* in mainland China, including the Protecting Cantonese Movement; high-stakes English-language examinations in mainland China; and medium of instruction in the United States and Hong Kong, including English-medium policies and the use of Putonghua as a medium of instruction for teaching Chinese in Hong Kong. Gao and Shao's chapter reveals that media may play a decisive role in determining policies, such as in Hong Kong, where media framing delegitimized Putonghua-medium instruction and thereby closed the policy window for this option. Thus Gao and Shao argue that current LPP research, in which mass media is not a central focus, deserves serious reconsideration, so that mass (and social) media can be incorporated as key policy actors in LPP processes.

Continuing Gao and Shao's focus on the role of mass media in LPP, Sandra Silberstein in Chapter 16 raises fundamental questions about media and policymaking: In media outputs with policy implications, who is allowed to speak? Whose voices count? Whose perspective is reported? Into whose identities are viewers interpellated? Silberstein is especially interested in activities of mass media during times of national crisis, when the ideological work of media framing makes crises intelligible, often without challenging the policy agendas of political elites. The questions Silberstein raises draw our attention to the intersection of media studies, discourse analysis, and LPP. She also raises questions about the boundaries of LPP scholarship.

Like Ruth Wodak's discourse-historical approach, Silberstein's work adopts critical discourse analysis in order to investigate how language is used to instantiate particular social relations of power and to show how that instantiation is a form of language policy. Silberstein's concern is how media construct "good guys" and "bad guys" through the complex discursive processes that take place in media products. In order to show how LPP scholars might trace these processes, she analyzes the case of simultaneous CNN coverage of two international crises in July 2014: the downing of Malaysian Airlines Flight 17 over Ukraine, and Israel's "Operation Protective Edge" into Gaza. Like Gao and Shao, Silberstein argues that LPP scholars should incorporate into their work a systematic analysis of the ways that media and other forms of public discourse constrain the voices and perspectives that may be heard, and thus the policy alternatives that are viewed as legitimate options.

Chapter 17 by Francis M. Hult, the last in this section, invites us to think about LPP through the lens of public signage, also known as "linguistic landscapes" (LL). Generally interested in the ways in which language is used visually in public space, LL offers a platform to examine the intersecting factors that mediate language choices such as beliefs and ideologies about languages, language policies, or communicative needs. Hult considers direct and indirect relationships between LPP and LL with reference to a wide range of contexts including Malaysia, the United States, Canada, Estonia, Spain, the Czech Republic, Ethiopia, and Cambodia, among others. In so doing, Hult's chapter brings into focus another popular and contested dichotomy in LPP research, in addition to the *micro/macro or agency/structure* referred to earlier: the *top-down/bottom-up* distinction.

The relationship between policy discourses/ideologies and LL is complex and not unidirectional. Whether explicit governmental regulations about public signage or visual language use linked to individual experiences and constructions, it may be problematic to assume any form of alignment between planning objectives related to shaping the sense of place through signage and people's beliefs about how the sense of place should be shaped. The relationship between policy and practice may include processes of resemiotization of policy discourses into LL practices. Drawing from Blommaert (2013) and Pennycook (2006), Hult shows that nongovernment forms of de facto policy can also emerge through iterative choices mediated by values about language that permeate multiple domains of society, including visual language use. Such processes, Hult points out, call for ethnographic, (critical) discourse analytic orientations and nexus analysis, or geosemiotics, to focus attention on the role of LL as a language policy mechanism in concert with other mechanisms like education and media.

These nongovernment forms of de facto policy that Hult stresses lead us to the last section of Part II.

II.C: Language Policy and Planning in/through Communities

The next five chapters investigate LPP in different communities: those whose members speak endangered languages; those that have responded critically to crises such as war and mass migration; indigenous peoples contesting and adjusting institutional views of bilingualism in public educational and healthcare systems; families, particularly those experiencing migration; and Deaf communities around the world. In the first of these five chapters, Teresa L. McCarty examines in Chapter 18 the processes and prospects for revitalizing endangered languages. Her analysis focuses on what she terms the work of "sustaining" languages (as distinct from preserving or maintaining them), in order to emphasize the complex, dynamic, heteroglossic, and often multi-sited language situation in communities working on revitalization projects. The chapter offers useful definitions of key terms and an analysis of some of the major classification systems used in language endangerment research.

McCarty then turns to discussion of three contexts for sustaining languages: the new speaker movement, involving individuals who acquire a minority language (e.g., Yiddish in Poland, Irish in Ireland, or the Manx language on the Isle of Mann) through educational programs or private study, with little or no exposure at home; indigenous-language immersion in education (including Hawaiian in the US, Māori in Aotearoa/New Zealand, and Saami in Norway, Sweden, Finland, and western Russia); and bi/multilingual education using both the endangered language and a language of the wider community (such as in Nepal, the states of Andhra Pradesh and Orissa in India, and bilingual/intercultural education in Latin America). McCarty's analysis of these widely varying language-sustaining projects reveals how the global effort for revitalization has been able to significantly disrupt what has often seemed to be the inevitable slide toward language endangerment and loss. Moreover, McCarty demonstrates that sustaining endangered languages is always political work that must challenge dominant language ideologies and entrenched systems of linguistic inequality.

From McCarty's international perspective toward LPP for revitalizing and sustaining languages, the next chapter shifts to a local lens directed toward community language policies. Virginia Unamuno and Juan Eduardo Bonnin in Chapter 19 study the formulation of national public policies linked to regional integration processes in Argentina. In their chapter, they focus on the emergence of bilinguals as an outcome of a recent phenomenon in the region: the valorization of Spanish-Wichi bilingualism as a professional qualification to apply for state positions in the field of public health care and education. Relying on ethnography, discourse analysis, and studies of interaction, they look at the practices and experiences of indigenous teachers and health workers in El Impenetrable, in Chaco Province. In their analysis, Unamuno and Bonnin reveal a conflict between institutional ideologies of "access" and indigenous ideologies of "identity," which they explain as characteristic of the struggle between modern, state-oriented language policies and grassroots activism, including language as a part of a wider repertoire of political action. Unamuno and Bonnin's chapter shows how the actual production of language policies at different levels is contested and reinterpreted from the margins by the same indigenous people who are supposed to passively implement them.

Such forms of contestation and reinterpretation can be very intensive and trans-formational, as reported by Karen Ann Watson-Gegeo, David W. Gegeo, and Billy Fito'o in Chapter 20. Based on their combined many decades of living and working in the Solomon Islands, they examine community language policies in education on the island of Malaita, where violent conflict (1998–2007) displaced thousands of speakers of Kwara'ae, the largest language in the Solomon Islands. In this new in-stallment in their ongoing research dating to the 1970s (Gegeo and Fito'o are both indigenous Kwara'ae), the chapter focuses on community responses to the forced re-turn of 20,000 Malaitans, driven from Guadalcanal back to Malaita, and the collapse of the state educational system. This crisis on Malaita was met by intense commu-nity efforts to reconstruct a new, indigenous approach to education, which Watson-Gegeo, Gegeo, and Fito'o call "critical community language policy and planning in education" (CCLPE).

CCLPE on Malaita meant that educational policymaking shifted from the nation-state to the community, with profound implications for the asymmetrical power relations that shape language-in-education policies. In this regard, CCLPE in the Solomon Islands provides further evidence of the need for epistemological and on-tological diversity, a view that is increasingly being advanced in LPP, as well as in education and development theory and related studies (see Dei, Hall & Rosenberg, 2000; Gegeo & Watson-Gegeo, 2013).

In Chapter 21, Xiao Lan Curdt-Christiansen turns to families and households by looking at explicit and implicit family language policies (FLP), particularly under conditions of transnational migration. Recent focus on FLP within LPP research emerges from the growing recognition that language policies are immanent in daily life, and that individual agency within households deserves research attention at least as much as policymaking by state agencies and institutions. As Curdt-Christiansen shows, research on FLP draws from language socialization and language acquisition research and from analysis of the language ideologies that underlie family language decisions. Why do some families retain heritage languages, whereas others undergo language shift? What are the consequences of different family language practices for the intergenerational transmission of language? How do family decisions about language interact with social, economic, and political pressures from the wider so-ciety? Curdt-Christiansen's survey of FLP research shows that such questions can be investigated with a range of research methods, including quantitative analysis, qual-itative/interpretive approaches, and sociolinguistic ethnography. Her chapter also suggests that future FLP research must extend beyond the household, to include the life trajectories of family members in a broad range of social contexts.

Ronice Müller de Quadros's Chapter 22 examines Deaf communities, which face language policy issues that are specific to sign languages, yet also overlap sig-nificantly with LPP in minority-language communities. Her overview of sign lan-guages and Deaf communities includes discussion of the sign language transmission and maintenance processes in several contexts worldwide, including those in which spoken languages are dominant. Of particular interest is her analysis of the dominant ideologies that underlie sign languages policies, which she terms a "medical view of deafness." Based on a critical analysis of the medical view, Quadros offers an agenda for Deaf LPP based on a "linguistic perspective" and a language rights discourse. She concludes by arguing that this agenda requires significant participation in policymaking processes by Deaf community members. Her advocacy for Deaf community control of Deaf LPP echoes Watson-Gegeo, Gegeo, and Fito'o's call for a critical community language policy and planning in education.

Part III: Language Policy and Planning and Late Modernity

Many chapters in Part I and Part II of the *Handbook* make reference to shifting cultural, institutional, and economic conditions in their consideration of LPP issues. Inspired by contemporary social theory (see Appadurai, 1990; Archer, 2012; Bauman, 1998; Giddens, 1991), in Part III we link these shifting conditions to the broad label of "late modernity" with reference to widespread processes of late capitalism, leading to the selective privatization of services (including education), the information revolution (associated with rapidly changing statuses and functions for languages), the repositioning of the institutions of nation-states (with major implications for language policies), and the fragmentation of overlapping and competing identities (associated with new complexities of language-identity relations and new forms of multilingual language use).

As an academic discipline in the social sciences, language policy must confront tensions between these processes of change and the powerful ideological framework of modern nationalism. The chapters in Part III place these issues at the center of our attention by approaching LPP through the lens of the following strands of research: neoliberalism and governmentality; mobility, diversity, and new social media; and new forms of engagement with language, ideology, and critique.

III.A: Language Policy and Planning, Neoliberalism, and Governmentality: A Political Economy View of Language, Bilingualism, and Social Class

As revealed in earlier chapters by Heller and Ricento, political economy has begun to be a source discipline for critical LPP research, and neoliberalism and governmentality key issues for analysis. The six chapters in this section offer conceptual and epistemological guides to the study of such issues, beginning with Eva Codó's contribution.

In Chapter 23, Codó sets up some key principles that in our view should characterize a critically oriented approach to LPP under contemporary conditions. In
alignment with Harvey (2005), she departs from accounts of globalization that only
refer to the intensification of the circulation of capital, people, and semiotic practices
around the globe, in order to argue for a view that conceptualizes globalization "as a
new mode of production predicated on the volatility of markets in rapidly evolving
technological environments and on the flexibilisation of labour." Indeed, she adds,
"flexibilisation is the buzzword of neoliberal globalisation, and the condition and
the outcome of neoliberal policy." A key research area is the changing relationship
between the state and the economic sector derived from this environment, in which
the state partially retreats from key social fields such as education, social services,
and health care, while civil society organizations and private companies increasingly
take on socially regulatory roles in lieu of or together with the state—with subsequent tensions and contradictions.

With this as a premise, Codó reviews LPP issues in three key institutional domains
transformed by neoliberalizing policies (i.e., workplace, education, and civil society
organizations). Her discussion shows that neoliberalism is not just an abstract model
of action or thought. Rather, it is a form of ethos that, while permeating institutions'
missions and discursive arrangements, shapes the production/legitimization of
moral categories about appropriate social actors and forms of knowledge (including
the linguistic) and, in turn, individual subjectivities.

These processes are further expanded and analyzed in the following chapters.
Joan Pujolar in Chapter 24 focuses on how tertiarization, neoliberalism, and globalization reconfigure the role of language in people's lives and the ways in which
individuals and organizations treat languages. He specifically looks at language as an
economic asset. Taking "linguistic commodification" (Heller, 2003) as an entry point
to ideologies and practices of governance that emerge from the changing relationship between public and non-public institutions, Pujolar reminds us that an "important point to learn from research on linguistic commodification is to appreciate
that what we are witnessing is not so much a retreat of the state, but a transformation
of its modes of intervention in public and economic life, and that language policy
makes a particularly good lens to understand this transformation." In his chapter,
he exemplifies this by exploring slightly different modes of state involvement or
non-involvement in three areas of activity: the language learning abroad industry in
Spain; the policies of Francophone economic development in Canada; and multilingual call centers from the workers' perspective.

The repositioning of the state under the economic conditions outlined by
Codó and Pujolar can be clearly identified in the institutional space of education.
Chapter 25 by Ana María Relaño-Pastor offers an analytical example of this. In her
chapter, Relaño-Pastor proposes a political economy angle to the implementation
of content and language integrated learning (CLIL), a type of bilingual education
policy aimed at enhancing English-language education while successfully meeting

the demands of the Council of Europe and the European Commission. In contrast to a dominant body of literature that has contributed to romanticizing it as a truly European approach that celebrates multilingualism, Relaño-Pastor embraces a critical sociolinguistic ethnography perspective on CLIL as policy and practice to shed light on the neoliberalization and commodification processes involved in the global spread of English in Europe. She illustrates these processes through a case study of CLIL-type English/Spanish bilingual programs in the south-central autonomous region of Castilla–La Mancha, in Spain.

Moving the focus from state institutions to multinational corporations, Alfonso Del Percio in Chapter 26 takes us through the process whereby linguistic aspects of communication get locally resignified by managers, consultants, and marketing specialists in multinational corporations as economic assets that contribute to the individualization or customization of products and services. In particular, Del Percio documents ethnographically the institutional techniques, tactics, and forms of expertise through which language and communication are governed in a Swiss multinational organization based in the major economic center of German-speaking Switzerland. He shows that corporate actors' policing is not merely linguistic. Instead, he argues, "such forms of policing are a method of enhancing multinationals' productivity and securing their competitiveness under changing market conditions." This, we believe, resonates strongly with Codó's analysis, and, as Del Percio highlights, invites LPP researchers to address language and communication "as part of a package of activities that are subjected to discipline and regimentation" and not just as "abstract entities detached from the institutional logics in which they are anchored."

Steering the discussion toward the individual subjectivities also anticipated by Codó, Luisa Martín Rojo in Chapter 27 delves into the extension of the neoliberal logic to language management and practices. By engaging with Foucault's (2009) notion of governmentality, she urges us "to understand the process by which a set of economic principles have become an ideology and a form of governance, at this moment in time when the crisis of neoliberalism as an economic and political order comes hand in hand with the rise of right- and left-leaning populism (and even neofascism) in different parts of the world." As market mechanisms begin to organize speakers' trajectories and practices, and to govern their conduct, Martín Rojo sees in linguistic governmentality an area of inquiry that allows us to understand how forms of power mutate, what key changes are currently taking place, and which languages and language policies are involved.

To us, the novelty of this perspective resides precisely in the locus of power under investigation, which, as Martín Rojo states, is "the multiple forms of activity whereby human beings, who may or may not be part of government or of an institution, seek to control the conduct of other human beings—that is, to govern them." Based on this premise, Martín Rojo discusses the ways in which the behavior of individuals, and that of the population in general, becomes regulated when one language is given prominence over others.

By this point of the narrative, it is clear that a political economy approach to LPP and the study of neoliberalism offer insightful perspectives to contemporary processes that impact our daily lives. Yet, and as David Block points out in Chapter 28, the last chapter of this section, neoliberalism continues to be ill-defined and undertheorized, particularly when it comes to analysis of social class. In his own words, "the rise of economic inequality and new forms of class struggle that have accompanied neoliberal policies and practices are effectively erased from analysis, or they are dealt with only in a cursory manner." In response, Block articulates an argument for the centrality of class as a key construct for understanding the effects of neoliberalism in LPP. Block's chapter includes concrete analysis of the ways that these are used in LPP research, as well as specific examples of how a class analysis offers insight into policymaking processes. His chapter calls for more careful definition of terms (e.g., middle class) and it includes specific suggestions for how future LPP research may better incorporate class as a central theoretical construct.

But an approach to late modernity such as we specified in the opening of Part III not only requires us to take on political economy more fully; it also invites us to adopt a self-reflective attitude toward our own assumptions as researchers.

III.B. Mobility, Diversity, and New Social Media: Revisiting Key Constructs

As the cultural, economic, and institutional conditions we inhabit change, it is part of our job as social scientists, we believe, to revisit from time to time the core concepts, notions, and analytical perspectives with which we address our objects of study. This is part of a larger paradigm shift in the study of language and society, which, according to Blommaert and Rampton (2016), has entailed, over a period of several decades, an ongoing revision of fundamental ideas about languages, about language groups and speakers, and about communication: "rather than working with homogeneity, stability, and boundedness as their starting assumptions, mobility, mixing, political dynamics, and historical embedding are now central concerns" (p. 24). In line with this spirit, the following four chapters revisit influential constructs that have continuously underpinned LPP research, either explicitly or implicitly. These are concerned with the notions of community, speaker, security, and culture.

The dominant meanings of *community* and *community language* in the language disciplines, Li Wei suggests, are today challenged by the intensification of mobility. In Chapter 29, he argues that such intensification makes it more difficult than ever to ignore that communities (1) have fuzzy and multiple boundaries, (2) are constantly intersecting and connected, and (3) constitute locations and generators of grassroots responsibilities and power. Engaging in dialogue with contemporary work on "superdiversity" (Vertovec, 2007), Li Wei provides us with a historical account of how meanings of community have shifted over time, from frames that emphasize physical closeness to those that foreground *unity of will*.

He then extends this account to the notion of *diaspora*, closely related to the phenomenon of migration, as well as to that of *multilingualism* via exploration of the ways in which the *speech community* construct has changed as a result of changing patterns of mobility and subsequent disciplinary refinements in socio- and anthropological linguistics. He also reflects on the LPP implications of a general shift of sociological attention to a practice-based notion of community, which in his view points to the importance of grassroots actions and the everyday, beyond institutionalized contexts.

In Chapter 30, Bernadette O'Rourke, Josep Soler, and Jeroen Darquennes direct our attention to the very notion of *speaker*. Relying on the discursive and ethnographic turns undertaken in contemporary LPP, they advocate for situated description of linguistic practices and trajectories of speakers outside the traditional native-speaker communities. In their account, the *new speaker* is seen as contrasting with long-standing terms such as *L2* and *non-native* in that it moves away from the notion of deficit or deficiency "and instead encapsulates the possibilities available to the speaker to expand his or her linguistic repertoire through active use of the target language." In other words, the approach described by O'Rourke, Soler, and Darquennes in their chapter compels us to foreground the lived experiences and challenges that individuals face as they become (and are recognized as) speakers of another language.

Though such an approach is not new in LPP studies, O'Rourke, Soler, and Darquennes show that it may offer new insights if expanded to different research contexts, beyond those of language revitalization in European minority-language settings. With this in mind, the authors take as a starting point examples of attempts to revitalize autochthonous minority languages, from which they turn to urban settings characterized by different forms of migration and transnational, flexible workplaces. In doing so, O'Rourke, Soler, and Darquennes argue for a reconsideration of more traditional approaches to LPP in minority-language settings in which new speakers have tended to be overshadowed by native speaker profiles, and in which "the in-between linguistic spaces and frequently more hybridized forms of language inherent in language contact situations have often been ignored."

Moving on to the construct of security, Constadina Charalambous, Panayiota Charalambous, Kamran Khan, and Ben Rampton in Chapter 31 push LPP research to look into the ways in which *security* is being reconfigured within the contemporary world, with developments in digital technology, large-scale population movements, and the privatization of public services. They welcome a shift in LPP away from a mainstream tradition that has contributed to the idealization of the sovereign nation-state through understanding security as a policy response to threats and dangers, which therefore emphasizes issues of territorial integrity and national sovereignty. They also acknowledge that this mainstream literature has devoted only superficial attention to communication.

In contrast, Charalambous, Charalambous, Khan, and Rampton align with relatively recent work in critical security studies that draws more centrally from ethnography and practice theory and that attends to context and ideology. Their chapter advocates Huysmans's conceptualization of security as "a practice of making 'enemy' and 'fear' the integrative, energetic principle of politics displacing the democratic principles of freedom and justice" (2014, p. 3); it does so through consideration of two case studies of how "enemy" and "fear" have been active principles in language policy development, in Britain and Cyprus. These two cases shed light on the processes of securitization, insecuritization, and desecuritization, which in their view "provide only a hint of the different ways in which 'security' and language policy are likely to be related in the period ahead."

The last construct to be revisited in this section is that of *culture*, particularly in relation to the impact of new media on contemporary social life. In Chapter 32, Aoife Lenihan relies on Jenkin's (2006) notion of *convergence culture*, which refers to "the technological, industrial and societal changes in contemporary culture where old and new media collide, where grassroots and corporate media intersect, where the power of the media producer and the power of the media consumer interact in unpredictable ways" (pp. 1–2). Lenihan highlights that this approach signifies a cultural shift from passive media spectatorship to a participatory culture. Her innovative approach, which emerges out of a three-year study using virtual ethnographic methods, reveals that commercial entities such as Facebook, online communities of translators, and Translation app users become both users and producers of LPP, all functioning as language policy actors capable of exerting influence over language policy and language use online.

This "convergence" of media producers and users means that contradictory processes take place in online LPP: on the one hand, the result is the commercialization of minority languages such as Irish, with the major goal being profit for the Facebook commercial entity; on the other, new forms of individual involvement in policymaking are possible, as individuals not only become translators, but they also may have direct impact on policy, for example, in terminology development and language standardization. Moreover, this individual involvement in LPP can lead to new forms of ownership of policy, as online communities take on policymaking processes (such as translation) formerly dominated by official agencies and institutions.

As the chapters in Part III show, political economy and self-reflectiveness constitute two fundamental pillars in the research agenda of LPP. As such, they point us to a possible path for a future critique in the field that does not take for granted the ideas about language, culture, power, and identity that emanated from the socioeconomic and political form of organization of the modern nation-state. This path may demand rethinking long-standing forms of critical engagement, as the chapters in the last section of Part III suggest.

III.C: Language, Ideology, and Critique: Rethinking Forms of Engagement

A form of critique that pays attention to changing forms of state involvement, as well as to alternative constructs and research perspectives such as those discussed in the preceding, requires engaging critically with certain tendencies in the field. These tendencies include the privileging of institutional domains of language planning and language engineering, and the inclusion of problematic suggestions for change in critical LPP researchers' work. Adam Jaworski addresses the former issue in Chapter 33. While acknowledging the current emphasis in the studies of language policy on political economy, diversity, social justice, and social inclusion, he claims that "turning to text-based art may offer . . . a useful lens through which to explore how hegemonic, unorthodox, non-normative, challenging, inclusive, or merely playful language ideologies may exist side by side."

In particular, Jaworski analyzes how the famous Chinese text-based artist Xu Bing reinscribes, subverts, inverts, and transcends modernist, national language ideologies through his own artwork. That is to say, Jaworki's chapter places artists as both theorists of language policy and planning and the agents implementing the very ideologies that underpin their works. The work of Xu Bing demonstrates, in Jaworski's words,

> [d]espite operating within the powerful institutional frameworks of galleries and museums, individual text-based artists . . . create their own private or personal domains of language planning and language engineering. In so doing they respond to and comment on language planning at the level of the nation-state, or they transcend the nationalist agenda by developing an internationalist dream or a democratizing stance of planning a universal language for all humanity.

The issues raised by the suggestions for change made by critical researchers are tackled by Jürgen Jaspers in Chapter 34, the last chapter of Part III. He argues that such suggestions often reproduce some of the main assumptions behind the policies that the researchers critique. Jaspers specifically examines the field of education, where teachers and other school actors tend to be positioned as those responsible for social change and increased equity. Calls for change based on this premise, Jaspers reminds us, share representations of the policy implementation process with the state authorities that they criticize; in some cases, suggestions for change complicate the emancipatory project of the school by reducing language use at school to group interests. The problem, in Jaspers's words, is "the view that education motors social change, and that to the degree that it does not, urgent (linguistic) intervention is required. In consequently insisting on teachers' responsibility, it looks as if several policy critiques share with governments a penchant for disciplining behavior."

Jaspers warns that his critique "necessitates a reconsideration of the received opposition between sociolinguistics (broadly understood) and language education policy, and requires calls for change to take a different tack." Jaspers exemplifies this line of argument in relation to research on linguistic diversity. Influenced by neo-Marxist analyses of social class reproduction, which have helped us see the school as a space of social struggle, this research tradition pushes for more inclusive policies that valorize pupils' primary languages and that pluralize the language of instruction, in line with developments in sociolinguistics (e.g., translanguaging) and educational research (e.g., critical pedagogy). Based on these concerns, Jasper highlights a need for more research that explores which opportunities and limitations emerge when employing certain types of linguistic practices in class, without reducing the struggle for social equality to an educational issue.

Part IV: Summary and Future Directions

Parts I, II, and III offer an opportunity to reflect on common issues emerging from the different strands of discussion described in the preceding. The last chapter of this *Handbook* reflects on these issues by identifying possible directions for future research. In so doing, it foregrounds those developments that, in our view, put LPP researchers in a suitable position to better grasp the transformations of the current historic juncture. The chapter also identifies unresolved problems and contradictions that we believe need further consideration.

We have intended this introduction to serve as a roadmap to the remainder of this volume, particularly the relationships among the subsequent chapters. We encourage readers to delve into the chapters in whatever order may be appropriate to their interests, yet we also hope that readers will keep in mind the importance of a historical perspective toward conceptual, theoretical, and methodological developments in LPP.

ACKNOWLEDGMENT

For reading earlier drafts of this chapter, we are grateful to Alfonso Del Percio, Monica Heller, Tom Ricento, and Sandra Silberstein.

REFERENCES

Anderson, B. (1983). *Imagined communities*. London; New York: Verso.

Appadurai, A. (1990). Disjuncture and difference in the global cultural economy. *Theory, Culture and Society* 7(2), 295–310.

Archer, M. S. (2012). *The reflexive imperative in late modernity*. Cambridge: Cambridge University Press.

Bauman, R., & C. Briggs (2003). *Voices of modernity: Language ideologies and the politics of inequality.* Cambridge: Cambridge University Press.

Bauman, Z. (1998). *Globalization: The human consequences.* New York: Columbia University Press.

Blommaert, J. (1996). Language planning as a discourse on language and society: The linguistic ideology of a scholarly tradition. *Language Problems and Language Planning* 20, 199–222.

Blommaert, J. (2013). *Ethnography, superdiversity and linguistic landscapes: Chronicles of complexity.* Bristol, UK: Multilingual Matters.

Blommaert, J., & Rampton, B. (2016). Language and superdiversity. In K. A. Arnaut, J. Blommaert, B. Rampton, & M. Spotti (Eds.), *Language and superdiversity* (pp. 21–48). New York; London: Routledge.

Bourdieu, P. (1993). *Language and symbolic power.* Cambridge, MA: Harvard University Press.

Chilton, P. (2004). *Analyzing political discourse: Theory and practice.* London: Routledge.

Cooper, R. L. (1989). *Language planning and social change.* Cambridge: Cambridge University Press.

Das Gupta, J. (1970). *Language conflict and national development: Group politics and national language policy in India.* Berkeley: University of California Press.

Dei, J. S., Hall, B. D., & Rosenberg, D. G. (Eds.). (2000). *Indigenous knowledges in global contexts: Multiple readings of our world.* Toronto: University of Toronto Press.

Desmond, M. (2007). *On the fireline: Living and dying with wildland firefighters.* Chicago: University of Chicago Press.

Ferguson, C. A. (1965). Directions in sociolinguistics: Report on an interdisciplinary seminar. *SSRC Items* 19(1), 1–4.

Ferguson, C. A. (1968). Language development. In J. A. Fishman, C. A. Ferguson, & J. Das Gupta (Eds.), *Language problems of developing nations* (pp. 27–35). New York: John Wiley & Sons.

Fishman, J. A. (1964). Language maintenance and language shift as a field of inquiry. *Linguistics* 9, 32–70.

Fishman, J. A. (Ed.). (1968a). *Readings in the sociology of language.* The Hague: Mouton.

Fishman, J. A. (1968b). Sociolinguistics and the language problems of the developing countries. In J. A. Fishman, C. A. Ferguson, & J. Das Gupta (Eds.), *Language problems of developing nations* (pp. 3–16). New York: John Wiley & Sons.

Fishman, J. A. (1971). The impact of nationalism on language planning. In J. Rubin & B. H. Jernudd (Eds.), *Can language be planned? Sociolinguistic theory and practice for developing nations* (pp. 3–20). Honolulu: University Press of Hawaii.

Fishman, J. A. (Ed.). (1972a). *Advances in the sociology of language* (Vol. I & II). The Hague: Mouton.

Fishman, J. A. (1972b). *Language and nationalism: Two integrative essays.* Rowley, MA: Newbury House.

Fishman, J. A. (1972c). Language maintenance and language shift as a field of inquiry: Revisited. In A. S. Dil (Ed.), *Language in sociocultural change: Essays by Joshua A. Fishman* (pp. 76–134). Stanford, CA: Stanford University Press.

Fishman, J. A. (Ed.). (1974). *Advances in language planning.* The Hague: Mouton.

Fishman, J. A., Ferguson, C. A., & Das Gupta, J. (Eds.) (1968). *Language problems of developing nations.* New York: John Wiley & Sons.

Foucault, M. (2009). *Security, territory, population: Lectures at the Collège de France 1977–1978*. New York: Picado.

Fox, M. (1975). *Language and development: A retrospective survey of Ford Foundation language projects 1952–1974*. 2 volumes. New York: Ford Foundation.

Gao, X. (2015). The ideological framing of "dialect": An analysis of mainland China's state media coverage of "dialect crisis" (2002–2012). *Journal of Multilingual and Multicultural Development* 36(5), 468–482.

Gao, X. (2017). Linguistic instrumentalism and national language policy in mainland China's state print media coverage of the "Protecting Cantonese Movement." *Chinese Journal of Communication* 10(2), 157–175.

Garvin, P. L. (1973). Some comments on language planning. In J. Rubin & R. Shuy (Eds.), *Language planning: Current issues and research* (pp. 24–33). Washington, DC: Georgetown University Press.

Gegeo, D. W., & Watson-Gegeo, K. A. (2013). (Re)conceptualizing language in development: Towards demystifying an epistemological paradox. *The Journal of Pacific Studies* 33(2), 137–155.

Giddens, A. (1991). *Modernity and self-identity: Self and society in the late modern age*. Cambridge: Polity Press.

Gumperz, J. (1986). Interactional sociolinguistics in the study of schooling. In J. Cook-Gumperz (Ed.), *The social construction of literacy* (pp. 45–68). Cambridge: Cambridge University Press.

Gumperz, J. J., & Hymes, D. (1972). *Directions in sociolinguistics: The ethnography of communication*. New York: Holt, Rinehart and Winston.

Harrison, W., Prator, C., & Tucker, G. R. (1975). *English-language policy survey of Jordan: A case study in language planning*. Washington, DC: Center for Applied Linguistics.

Harvey, D. (2005). *A brief history of neoliberalism*. Oxford: Oxford University Press.

Haugen, E. (1966). Linguistics and language planning. In W. Bright (Ed.), *Sociolinguistics: Proceedings of the UCLA Sociolinguistics Conference, 1964* (pp. 50–71). Janua Linguarum, Series Maior, 20. The Hague: Mouton.

Heller, M. (2003). Globalization, the new economy and the commodification of language and identity. *Journal of Sociolinguistics* 7(4), 473–492.

Hobsbawm, E. (1990). *Nations and nationalism since 1780*. Cambridge: Cambridge University Press.

Huysmans, J. (2014). *Security unbound: Enacting democratic limits*. New York: Routledge.

Jefferies, J. (2009). Do undocumented students play by the rules? Meritocracy in the media. *Critical Inquiry in Language Studies* 6, 15–38.

Jenkins, H. (2006). *Convergence culture: Where old and new media collide*. New York: New York University Press.

Jernudd, B. H., & Das Gupta, J. (1971). Towards a theory of language planning. In J. Rubin & B. H. Jernudd (Eds.), *Can language be planned? Sociolinguistic theory and practice for developing nations* (pp. 195–215). Honolulu: University Press of Hawaii.

Jernudd, B. H., & Nekvapil, J. (2012). History of the field: A sketch. In B. Spolsky (Ed.), *The Cambridge handbook of language policy* (pp. 16–36). Cambridge: Cambridge University Press.

Lewis, E. G. (1972). Migration and language in the USSR. In J. A. Fishman (Ed.), *Advances in the sociology of language* (Vol. II, pp. 310–341). The Hague: Mouton.

Lorwin, V. R. (1972). Linguistic pluralism and political tension in modern Belgium. In J. A. Fishman (Ed.), *Advances in the sociology of language* (Vol. II, pp. 396–412). The Hague: Mouton.

Martin-Jones, M., & Heller, M. (1996). Language and social reproduction in multilingual settings. *Linguistics and Education* 8(1), 3–16.

Mazrui, A. A. (1968). Some sociopolitical functions of English literature in Africa. In J. A. Fishman, C. A. Ferguson, & J. Das Gupta (Eds.), *Language problems of developing nations* (pp. 183–197). New York: John Wiley & Sons.

Neustupný, J. V. (1970). Basic types of treatment of language problems. *Linguistic Communications* 1, 77–98.

Pennycook, A. (2006). Postmodernism in language policy. In T. Ricento (Ed.), *An introduction to language policy: Theory and method* (pp. 60–76). Malden, MA: Blackwell.

Pérez-Milans, M. (2011). Being a Chinese newcomer in Madrid compulsory education: Ideological constructions in language education practice. *Journal of Pragmatics* 43(4), 1005–1022.

Pérez-Milans, M. (2013). *Urban schools and English language education in late modern China: A critical sociolinguistic ethnography*. New York; London: Routledge.

Pérez-Milans, M. (2015). Language education policy in late modernity: (Socio) linguistic ethnographies in the European Union. *Language Policy* 14(2), 99–109.

Pérez-Milans, M., & Soto, C. (2016). Reflexive language and ethnic minority activism in Hong Kong: A trajectory-based analysis. *AILA Review* 29(1), 48–82.

Reisigl, M., & Wodak, R. (2015). The discourse-historical approach. In R. Wodak & M. Meyer (Eds.), *Methods of critical discourse studies* (pp. 23–61). London: Sage.

Ricento, T. (2000). Historical and theoretical perspectives in language policy and planning. *Journal of Sociolinguistics* 4, 194–213.

Ricento, T. (Ed.). (2016). *Language policy and planning: Critical concepts in linguistics* (4 volumes). London: Routledge.

Rostow, W. W. (1960). *The stages of economic growth: A non-communist manifesto*. Cambridge: Cambridge University Press.

Rubin, J. (1971). Evaluation and language planning. In J. Rubin & B. H. Jernudd (Eds.), *Can language be planned? Sociolinguistic theory and practice for developing nations* (pp. 217–252). Honolulu: University Press of Hawaii.

Rubin, J., & Jernudd, B. H. (1971). Language planning as an element in modernization. In J. Rubin & B. H. Jernudd (Eds.), *Can language be planned? Sociolinguistic theory and practice for developing nations* (pp. xiii–xxiv). Honolulu: University Press of Hawaii.

Rubin, J., Jernudd, B. H., Das Gupta, J., Fishman, J. A., & Ferguson, C. A. (Eds.). (1977). *Language planning processes*. The Hague: Mouton.

Scheufele, D. A., & Iyengar, S. (2011). The state of framing research: A call for new directions. Retrieved from http://pcl.stanford.edu/research/2011/scheufele-framing.pdf

Scollon, R. (2008). *Analyzing public discourse: Discourse analysis in the making of public policy*. London: Routledge.

Shohamy, E. (2006). *Language policy: Hidden agendas and new approaches*. London: Routledge.

Sibayan, B. (1971). Language planning processes and the language-policy survey in the Philippines. In J. Rubin & B. H. Jernudd (Eds.), *Can language be planned? Sociolinguistic theory and practice for developing nations* (pp. 123–140). Honolulu: University Press of Hawaii.

Soto, C. & Pérez-Milans (2018). Language, neoliberalism and the discursive commodification of pedagogy. *Language and Intercultural Communication*.

Spolsky, B. (2004). *Language policy*. Cambridge: Cambridge University Press.

Spolsky, B. (Ed.). (2012). *The Cambridge handbook of language policy*. Cambridge: Cambridge University Press.

Tauli, V. (1968). *Introduction to a theory of language planning*. Acta Universitatis Upsaliensis, Studia Philologiae Scandinavicae Upsaliensia 6. Uppsala: University of Uppsala.

Tollefson, J. W. (1989). *Alien winds: The reeducation of America's Indochinese refugees*. New York: Praeger.

Tollefson, J. W. (1991). *Planning language, planning inequality: Language policy in the community*. London: Longman.

Tollefson, J. W. (1993). Language policy and power: Yugoslavia, the Philippines, and the U.S. in Southeast Asia. *International Journal of the Sociology of Language* 103, 73–95.

Tollefson, J. W. (2002). The language debates: Preparing for the war in Yugoslavia—1980–1991. *International Journal of the Sociology of Language* 154, 65–82.

Tollefson, J. W. (2015). Language policy-making in multilingual education: Mass media and the framing of medium of instruction. *Current Issues in Language Planning* 16(1–2), 132–148.

Tollefson, J. W., & Tsui, A. B. M. (2007). Issues in language policy, culture and identity. In A. B. M. Tsui and J. W. Tollefson (Eds.), *Language policy, culture, and identity in Asian contexts* (pp. 259–270). New York: Routledge.

Vertovec, S. (2007). Super-diversity and its implications. *Ethnic and Racial Studies* 30(6), 1024–1054.

Zima, P. (1968). Hausa in West Africa: Remarks on contemporary role and functions. In J. A. Fishman, C. A. Ferguson, & J. Das Gupta (Eds.), *Language problems of developing nations* (pp. 365–377). New York: John Wiley & Sons.

PART I

CONCEPTUAL UNDERPINNINGS OF LANGUAGE POLICY AND PLANNING

THEORIES AND METHODS IN DIALOGUE

CHAPTER 2

SOCIOECONOMIC JUNCTURES, THEORETICAL SHIFTS

A GENEALOGY OF LANGUAGE POLICY AND PLANNING RESEARCH

MONICA HELLER

In many ways, the premise of this *Handbook* is that language policy and planning (LPP, hereafter) and research in this field have changed recently. This chapter is meant to take account of the ways such a shift might be connected to contemporary changes in economic conditions (the *new* economy).[1] I argue here that attention to the economic value of language in a variety of forms (for example, as linked to personal income, corporate profit, or state GNP) is not, in fact, entirely new, even if it is arguably intensified and rendered more salient by contemporary shifts in relations between state and capital.

In order to separate out what is and is not new, therefore, I will begin by situating LPP in a historical frame, linking it to colonialism and capitalism, and in particular to the development of the nation-state. I will cast the institutionalized emergence of LPP as a defined field of scholarly inquiry in the 1960s in a longer history of state management of populations on the terrain of language—management necessarily connected to the interests of capital, whether in the metropole or in colonial (or, later, neocolonial) areas. I argue that LPP has always been tightly tied to political and economic conditions; if anything has changed, it is in how that relationship has been understood, and has shaped knowledge production in the field. In other words, I consider the central question to be how LPP (or whatever it was called at different moments) has been understood at various junctures to be connected to both political and economic interests, or why language has been understood as a significant, or at least useful, terrain for working out political and economic concerns. How that relationship is understood, I argue, underlies what people think LPP ought to pay attention to, ought to accomplish, and why.

Nonetheless, I take LPP to always have been centrally about what we might call anachronistically Global North states' management of diversity and inequality within their boundaries and across their spheres of influence. What is perhaps most important is the shift in legitimizing ideologies across time, first from *civilization* of subject populations, to their inscription via *emancipation* into *modern* progress, to the present moment, in which the laying bare of the relationship between LPP and profit makes LPP's goals less easily inscribed into liberal frameworks. I will begin by very briefly framing LPP in terms of the construction of state and colonial languages, and of concomitant relations among states and between metropoles and colonies, with an emphasis on liberal democracy, industrial capitalism, and colonialism in the nineteenth and early twentieth centuries.[2]

This is the period in which the engineering of language is understood as being undertaken in the interests of modern progress and liberal democracy, within a civilizing mission seeking to inscribe marginal populations into this discursive régime. This jumping-off point will allow for some discussion of tensions between state and civil society actors, and in particular of the role of intellectuals in laying the groundwork for the field, both in the Bourdieuan sense of space of social action around a set of identifiable resources, and in the narrower sense of academic discipline.

I will then turn to a consideration of the conditions of the period in which LPP was institutionalized, roughly the 1950s to the 1980s, with a peak in the 1960s and 1970s. This period was characterized by the withdrawal of imperial powers from direct political control over their colonies, the restructuring of political and economic spheres of influence (especially as influenced by the Cold War), and welfare-state industrial capitalism. We can think of these through the terms of *development* and *decolonization* within and across states, as key dimensions of the rebuilding of the postwar world order—activities that were understood to rely on various forms of social engineering.

Decolonization here refers to the movement to shake off the political control by imperial powers (often violently, as in Algeria and Indochina), to be replaced by new nation-states (a political economic form introduced by the imperial powers). *Development* refers to the process of bringing the standard of living of those states up to that enjoyed by the wealthier postwar countries, with refractions internal to welfare states in the West and to communist states devoted to a better distribution of wealth among their own citizens. Here the concern will be to understand how LPP emerged as a key element of social engineering devoted to both goals. We will see that while the nation-state was understood as the principal locus of action, LPP needs to be understood in the context of new forms of economic and political imperialism shaped by the Cold War, in which private foundations (such as the Rockefeller and Ford Foundations) and international bodies played a key role.

The conditions of the Cold War, the welfare state, and liberal democratic industrial capitalism gave way in the 1980s and 1990s to what we call variously *late capitalism, globalization*, and *neoliberalism*. The last section of the chapter will examine some key features of this shift, particularly in terms of how new conditions rendered more explicit the role of the state in supporting the expansion of capitalism, while at the same time centering language as a terrain for the advancement of political economic interests in new ways. I will argue that LPP's increasingly explicit interest in economic activity tracks a shift in locus of attention and activity, as it always has. The question for LPP has thus become the legitimacy of its mission: Whose interests does it serve, and in the name of what? As has happened in other fields, one result has been a turn to reflexivity (see Martin-Jones & da Costa Cabral, Chapter 4 in this volume). Another has been a closer examination of the role of language in economic activity, and some debate about where LPP's major interlocutors now lie (see also chapters in Part III.A. in this volume).

Language and Population Management: Nation-State, Metropole, Colony

The unification of populations on the terrain of shared and standardized language has been going on a for a long time: the developments of writing systems, of grammars, of dictionaries, and of literary canons are all arguably LPP activities with particular political and economic aims in mind. The actors have shifted, and have included religious institutions, state officials, intellectuals of a number of stripes, and other members of political, economic, and cultural élites. Here I will focus briefly on the part of the story that I think most helps us understand LPP in Western late capitalism, namely the modern understanding of how language serves as a terrain for the building of metropole-colony relations in the context of liberal democratic, industrial capitalist nation-states.

Gellner (1983) and Hobsbawm (1990) have argued that the mid- to late nineteenth century was a moment when the bourgeoisie in Europe worked at constructing national markets, international trade arrangements, and protected imperial spheres, through the mechanism of the nation-state. In contradistinction to religious or monarchical authority, understood as divine, the political legitimacy of the bourgeoisie was founded on the voice of the *people*—a people which needed to be made. As we know, one key way of making a nation was to unify it linguistically and communicatively, through the construction of a political public sphere (see Anderson, 1983; Balibar, 2007). Here, what we can consider LPP comprises the work of creating that sphere through such institutions as education, the media, and all agencies of the state with which citizens must interact. It also comprises the making of the standardized linguistic tools recognized therein as legitimate language and constituting shared modes of interaction (Grillo, 1989; Weber, 1976): the grammars, the dictionaries, the orthographies. Education in particular links the two, by socializing citizen subjects into how to use the latter to participate in the former.

But the economic basis of the power of the bourgeoisie was industrial capitalism, as tied to the imperialism that provided labor, resources, and markets. Capitalism involves competition, and the making of social difference in the interests of legitimizing the inequality which allows for maintaining cheap labor and cheap resources, fundamental to the making of profit. Thus the promise of liberal democracy to open pathways to wealth, as well as full citizenship, always meets the contradictions of the inequalities inherent in capitalism. Historically these have been managed by restricting full citizenship to those who are understood to possess reason, using social and cultural difference (gender, race) to legitimize which bodies are excluded and which are included. LPP here is a work of legitimization, arguing on the terrain of linguistic competence that certain categories of people are unable to perform the rationality understood to underlie full citizenship: their language is corrupt, or deficient, as shown by whatever specific features are constructed as deviant by the very process of standardization.

The liberal democratic nation-state as the fundamental unit of political and economic organization also constructs an additional contradiction, requiring LPP management: this is the central role of trade, both among imperial powers and between metropoles and colonies. The first required the engineering of the forms of bilingualism that would allow international cooperation without threatening the integrity of the nation-state. This is one source perhaps of the idea of élite bilingualism as a restricted good, acquirable through private means (governesses, grand tours), and limited to turning in performances of standard languages each in their whole, bounded form, with no traces of contact—or what I have called elsewhere "parallel monolingualisms" (Heller, 2007). But the period between about 1875 and 1925 also saw the emergence of a vast number of projects of construction of so-called international auxiliary languages, the most famous of which is Esperanto, which were designed to be modes of international communication that leveled the playing field, insofar as they were nobody's first language, had no attachment to specific nation-states, and were understood to be more rational than even the best of the standard national languages (Garvia, 2015; Gordin, 2015; Heller, 2017).

Between metropole and colony, LPP had a different set of concerns, depending on the specific imperial strategies involved. Certainly part of the work, some of which had already been accomplished earlier, had to do with what Hanks (2010) calls "commensuration," that is, making it possible to compare the languages of the metropole to the languages of the colony, in part for religious conversion and in part for colonial administration. Practically this usually meant constructing the main languages of interaction, whether standardized, pidgins, or creoles; and/or training an indigenous élite in the language of the metropole. It also meant using the ideologies of difference and inequality, most often racialized versions of social Darwinism, to devalue colonial languages, and to limit the legitimacy of colonial subjects as speakers of the imperial language.

In this period, then, the forms of linguistic engineering that emerged (construction of a public sphere and standardized language, legitimization of inequality through ideologies of language as reason, modes of international and intercultural communication) were centrally about the political-economic relationship between industrial capitalism, colonialism, and the nation-state. It is in that sense that I argue that LPP has always had a socioeconomic element, and indeed has long been discussed in those terms. In the next section I will jump ahead to the period in which LPP became constituted as a field; in this post–World War II context, while socieconomic concerns, I argue, remained central, it perhaps became more difficult to name them, in an effort to foreground democracy and reduce the possibilities of a critical analysis of the neocolonialism inherent in the era of the Cold War, colonial independence, and the restructuring of global spheres of influence.

DECOLONIZATION AND DEVELOPMENT: THE EMERGENCE OF LANGUAGE POLICY AND PLANNING AS A FIELD

The period after World War II, as we know, was dominated by the Cold War: the competition between communist and capitalist states to build new spheres of influence on the ruins of fascism and the collapse of empire. Former colonies were granted political independence, but were kept within both political and economic control in the interest of the expansion of wealth, whether under communism or liberal democratic capitalism. After World War II, a major concern was to ensure that the world would not again face the economic havoc associated with the Depression and the national rivalries that led to the war; this led to the restructuring of state economies and international relations (Harvey, 2005, p. 9). Reconstruction underlay a wealth boom, allowing for the rise of the welfare state in the West. Welfare-state supports also constituted an attempt to reduce the risks of insecure capitalist markets. But the nation-state as the fundamental political and economic unit remained central.

LPP had its origins in this period in two ways. One had to do with Western efforts at *development* in former colonies, as a means to bring them within the liberal democratic and capitalist-dominated political and economic order. The second had to do with achieving the promises of the welfare state to inscribe marginalized populations within states into social mobility within modernist capitalism. Both usually meant both the construction of material and institutional infrastructure, including dams, new forms of agriculture, education in engineering, medicine, and governance, as well as investment in the strategies of nation-building we are already familiar with: literacy, standard languages, and education. Decolonization and postwar reconstruction also led to labor mobility, either from former colonies or from economic peripheries into the metropoles, with concomitant concerns around language and citizenship.

Political scientists, sociologists, anthropologists, linguists, educationists, and economists were all recruited to these development efforts. While the design and goals of development were defined by states, in the United States in particular concrete efforts often took the form of projects funded by private foundations, among them those built on the wealth of the American industrialist Rockefeller and Ford families (the Rockefeller fortune was based on oil; Ford's was based on the automobile).

The linguistic dimension of development focused on two sets of concerns, both inherited from the construction of liberal democratic nation-states discussed earlier. The first had to do with the idea that nation-states ought to be monolingual, but of course, new nation-states were no more monolingual than old ones; indeed, their multilingualism itself was a product of imperial modes of control in many ways. Thus multilingualism, as always, was constructed as a problem to be solved. The Cold War heightened fears around multilingualism, to the extent that linguistic differences were understandable as flagging potential separatist or irredentist movements (especially given that colonial boundaries regularly were drawn across linguistic ones), and those movements were seen as potentially seducible by the opposite side in the Cold War. This was an acute concern not only outside the boundaries of the new world powers, but also within them.

In the United States and Europe, the emancipation movements linked to decolonization were echoed by civil rights movements. Here again, linguistic difference (whether in the form of African American English, indigenous languages, or the Spanish of what was then called the Chicano or Hispanic population) was tied to political and economic marginalization, and emancipation movements threatened the legitimacy of the state. Thus linguistic variability more broadly was understood as something to be managed.

Bringing people into the public sphere through linguistic unification was also accompanied by concerns for their preparation for entry into the modern economy. Here again, literacy and education, both at home and abroad, were considered central spheres of activity. Once again, the tools for both needed to be invented.

If anything had changed, it was perhaps the increasing focus on reason, technology, and scientific expertise. Earlier LPP struggles often involved quarrels among lay and religious intellectuals, and as the academy developed in the course of the nineteenth century, eventually between them and the scientific experts. By the 1950s, those scientific experts had won the day, establishing their authority to undertake this kind of work. Further, the Cold War was fought in important ways on the terrain of technology as the key to the better life that communism or capitalism would bring the world. Language, too, was understood as a technical problem amenable to technical solutions, in a context in which states were expected to be interventionist. LPP's context, then, is one in which state intervention in development, both domestic and international, was to be bolstered by scientific expertise.

This expertise undertook to address the questions of the management of multilingualism, the development of national standard languages, the construction of a public sphere, and inscription into global capitalism, then, as technical problems to be resolved through scientific description, construction of appropriate technical tools for amelioration, and their application through education and training interventions, especially on the terrain of literacy. Technicist approaches understood language and literacy as cognitive skills and personal achievements that, once acquired, would transform societies and individuals. If illiteracy or unfamiliarity with the standard is diagnosed as a cognitive or social deficit, linked to economic underdevelopment, then the solution to inequity is focused on individuals and on education, rather than, say, on capitalist forms of extraction that are leading to over-development in some sites and under-development in others.

Existing educational infrastructures had been installed by colonial regimes, and often continued to be staffed by them; for example, one way to do military service in France was to serve (for longer periods) in the educational institutions of former French colonies. Indigenous élites continued to be trained in the metropole, and were expected to learn to act "white" without actually being able to escape racialization (Fanon, 1967). In other cases, various forms of bilingual or multilingual education were constructed, or new standard languages were used to replace colonial ones. Some of the standard languages were constructed on the basis of existing linguistic descriptions of indigenous languages. In others, new *neutral* ones were constructed; a notable example is Bahasa Indonesia, built, in the tradition of international auxiliary languages, to be easily learned by a multilingual population (Alisjahbana, 1976).[3]

This was the context in which emerged the new field of *language planning and language policy*, in conjunction with the rise of sociolinguistics and applied linguistics. Indeed, most of the figures we associate with anglophone sociolinguistics, especially in its American form, began their careers with involvement in Ford or Rockefeller Foundation–sponsored development projects (in particular, John Gumperz, William Bright, and Charles Ferguson in 1950s India). During the same period, the Ford Foundation also set up projects in India, as well as in the Philippines, Peru, Indonesia, Tunisia, and Egypt (Fox, 1975). The same set of projects, emphasizing English as a Foreign Language (EFL) curriculum development and teacher training, included a component on the teaching of English to immigrants in California, and later to African-American children understood to not speak the standard English of schooling.

Both Foundations also undertook projects intended to lay an institutional, professional infrastructure of linguistic expertise for efforts in language standardization, literacy, management of multilingualism, and, broadly, language learning, but with an emphasis on EFL, as befits a Cold War power exploring soft power alternatives. These involved the creation of a number of research and documentation centers, which became the foundation of LPP and the contact points for government stakeholders; the first of these was the Center for Applied Linguistics in Washington, D.C., established in 1959 with Charles Ferguson as its first director, and with ties both to Georgetown University and the US State Department. Others include the Centre international de recherche sur le bilinguisme (CIRB) at Université Laval in Quebec, and the East-West Center in Honolulu. The expertise developed through the International Auxiliary Language movement also was brought to bear on LPP initiatives (as we see, for example, in the origins of the journal *Language Problems and Language Planning.*)

I now draw on some archival work I conducted in 2016 in the Rockefeller Foundation Archives, to further discuss the Foundation's involvement in the development of LPP as a field in the service of the political-economic interests of development during the Cold War. In 1963, the Rockefeller Foundation's Social Science Research Council (founded in 1923 at the initiative of a number of professional scholarly societies, such as the American Political Science Association and the American Anthropological Association, to influence social science research and its impact on public policy) set up a Committee on Sociolinguistics. This Committee, of which Ferguson was the first chair, organized what might arguably be the first scientific conference devoted to LPP (unless we count the early twentieth-century conferences of Esperantists). The Conference on "Language Problems of Developing Nations" was held in 1966 in Warrenton, Virginia. One immediate result was a 1968 volume (Fishman et al., 1968). Ford Foundation–funded work on this theme continued in 1968–1969 at the East-West Center in Hawai'i through a residency for four fellows (Fishman; Joan Rubin, then at George Washington University; Bjorn Jernudd, then at Monash; and Jyotirindra Das Gupta, then at Berkeley), and other younger scholars from India, Indonesia, and Malaysia. Ferguson organized a similar conference in Ethiopia in the same period (RF Accession 1, series 1, subseries 19, box 218, folder 1533). Together, Ferguson and Fishman were successful in obtaining a Ford Foundation grant in 1969 to continue this work, with a major comparative project in India, Indonesia, Malaysia, and Peru (see Rubin et al., 1977). Its aim was to examine all the issues of language, nationalism, and nation-building, and economic development, as it has been discussed in this section.

My point is again that at the crucible of formation of the field, LPP was intimately bound up with socioeconomic concerns. It could not have emerged as a field of scholarly inquiry without the ways in which scientific expertise was brought to bear as technical knowledge in Cold War efforts to secure capitalist forms of production and consumption, global markets, and safe imbrication of marginalized minorities in the dominant political economic forms of social organization and production and distribution of wealth. Indeed, in this period, the primary interlocutors were states, although the Rockefeller and Ford Foundations, with wealth based solidly in industrial capitalism, were, as we have seen, key players. This sets the stage for the contemporary period, in which LPP turns more explicitly to language as a form of economic resource.

Late Capitalism: The Expanding Reach of the Market and the Neoliberal State

In advanced capitalist countries, the welfare state delivered high rates of economic growth in the 1950s and 1960s, but by the end of the 1960s growth had slowed. Both liberal democratic nation-states and communist ones were unable to successfully distribute resources and regulate capitalism. These are the conditions underlying what we think of as *late capitalism,* a term I take to signal the intensification and extension of capitalism that David Harvey has described (1989, 2005), and which I understand to be manifested in the following ways (see also Duchêne & Heller, 2012):

- searches for new markets for products
- trying to sell products at a lower price than competitors, which usually means finding cheaper sources of materials and labor
- creating new kinds of customers and new kinds of desires
- specializing in specific products for specific groups (*niche* products for *niche* markets), capitalizing on preferential access to both or either

• justifying higher prices through *adding value* in some way to products.

These processes required liberation from the constraints of nation-state markets, triggering what is usually thought of as *globalization* and *neoliberalism* (Allan & McElhinny, 2017). *Globalization* marks the international flows of people, products, information, services, and capital that embody the extension and specialization of networks of production, circulation, and consumption required in order to achieve the goals set out in the preceding. *Neoliberalism* captures the legitimizing discourses connected to the dismantling of the welfare state and nation-state regulation of national markets required for such forms of globalization to be possible (see Codó, Chapter 23 in this volume).

In the Global North, governments largely dismantled or rolled back the commitments of the welfare state, including privatizing public enterprises, reducing taxes, breaking labor unions, encouraging entrepreneurial initiative, and inducing a strong inflow of foreign investment. At this time, socialism was also rolled back, ending the Cold War and reorganizing the global order. In the Global South, international bodies like the International Monetary Fund and the World Bank enforced free market fundamentalism in return for loans, or delayed loans, in a process called *structural adjustment*.

Many companies from the Global North, encouraged by deregulation and tax breaks for investment, went offshore or delocalized, meaning that they closed down workplaces, especially those involved in industrial manufacturing, in the Global North, and opened them in Asia, Africa, and Latin America. Work itself was restructured toward *flexibility*, allowing companies to respond rapidly to intensified cycles of competition and shifts in conditions of production and consumption. Thus a post-Fordist regime of flexible accumulation has emerged in place of industrial mass production, with a focus on flexible labor processes and production arrangements, and consumption focused on niche markets, all of which have transnational implications. Discussions of productivity, efficiency, and audit became pronounced at the same time that concerns about profitability rose (Urciuoli & LaDousa, 2013).

These changes have had major implications for our understandings of what language is, for whether it can or should be engineered, and if so, by and for whom, and how. Boutet (2008) pointed out that in industrial capitalism, Taylorism repressed in many ways the use of language in order to regulate manual labor. She documents the orders in French factories that forbade *unruly use* of the body and the tongue (e.g., no spitting, no talking). Communication was understood to be a distraction. Now, however, the conditions of late capitalism I outlined earlier have foregrounded language as both product and process of work (Duchêne & Heller, 2012; Heller, 2010a; see also Pujolar, Chapter 24 in this volume).

This has happened partly through tertiarization, as communication, information, and services have become increasingly necessary for the management of far-flung, diversified networks, in which intense competition produces the need for the ability to make changes rapidly (and therefore requires knowledge about what options exist). In addition, it becomes difficult to manage multilingual networks of labor, management, producers, and consumers when they are constantly changing (and so Taylorist management of language, while seductive and often practiced, is difficult to impose). Finally, niche markets and added value are often constituted through the harnessing of symbolic, often linguistic capital, which links distinction (in Bourdieu's sense) to the coupling of the symbolic and the material (Heller, 2010b; see also Del Percio, Chapter 26 and Martín Rojo, Chapter 27, both in this volume).

For LPP, then, the ground shifted radically. Rather than understanding states as the central actors, contemporary conditions shift the gaze of the field to their struggle to reposition themselves in relation to both the private sector and to the volunteer or nongovernmental organization (NGO) sector that has taken over some of the social services the state once provided (at least, where they have not been privatized). This has led to a series of new questions. These questions concern the new roles of multilingualism or linguae francae in managing extended and diversified networks of production and consumption, and the role of language in the construction of niche markets and niche products, in particular as symbolic added value. While LPP once saw language as a technical path to state economic development through the education of literate citizens, it now must confront how to understand language as a form of work, as a commodity, as a form of distinction, and as a direct contributor to gross national product (GNP). Perhaps most uncomfortably, given its liberal democratic history (at least in the West), it must confront more directly the role of capital in constraining the nature of linguistic markets and the value of linguistic capital, and it must explore their link to private profit. LPP has long been linked to emancipation; new conditions ask us to examine its darker sides.

The (socio)economic turn in LPP is both emergent and divided. In some sectors, it has meant, as has been the case for discussions of language and society more broadly, asking fewer questions about language rights and more about linguistic value (see, for example, papers in Ricento, 2015; see also Ricento, Chapter 11 in this volume). Some of this work has built on earlier analyses of how linguistic difference has been linked to both political and economic inequality to try to directly examine whether, or to what extent, claimed knowledge of named languages at an individual level correlates with income, or, at a state or multistate level, with GNP (Grin et al., 2010). This approach is meant still largely to guide states, or such multistate organizations as the European Union, regarding their policies concerning language education, and indeed it has been taken up in a traditional mode as expert knowledge for that purpose.

We see this division, or tension, also refracted in contemporary debates in the Global North about education for the multilingual global manager or flexible worker, versus the remaining interests of states in maintaining their national markets (if only as niche markets and sources of niche products that commodify national identity; Heller, 2010b). We see it refracted, too, in new iterations of old debates over multilingualism versus linguae francae for the management of a globalized economy, with proposals for loosening the Anglo-American hold on English as a lingua franca, to renewed interest in Esperanto in particular and inventing languages more generally (search "conlang" on Google, to see that we have returned to 1905 in some ways), to new forms of machine translation, or to proposals to substitute coding for language education as the ultimate in technoflexibility. Again, the interlocutor is the state or its institutions, notably education, or else the individual or his or her parents, as they try to figure out how best to succeed economically in this changing scene.

In the Global South, attention has turned to the problem of how to enter the globalized new economy in a way that fends off the negative impact of structural adjustment. Although not directly framed in these terms, I think we can treat the important body of work on so-called English fever in South Korea as a key contribution to the LPP literature, illuminating as it does how the search for English is bound up with South Korea's adjustments after its 2008 financial crisis, the end of the Cold War but persistence of North Korea as a communist state, and the risk of devaluing its own linguistic and cultural capital (Lo et al., 2015; Park & Lo, 2012). This body of work tightly ties together state policy with respect to language education, language assessment as a tool for social selection in the public and private sector, and the inequalities of both access to English and to control over what forms of English are valued; it also shows us how in destabilizing nation-states, globalization also destabilizes the ideology of the native speaker, leading to struggles over who controls the linguistic market and the value of linguistic capital. Similarly illuminating work has shown how the Philippines and Indonesia capitalize on the linguistic relics of colonialism to produce multilingual workers for export (notably as caregivers and domestic labor); to attract multinational corporations to a cheap local multilingual workforce, for such sectors as call centers or copyediting (Lorente, 2012; Tan & Rubdy, 2008); or as cheaper sites for acquiring high-value linguistic capital.

These phenomena link Asian countries among each other, as well as to the Middle East and to the Global North. They are therefore only somewhat amenable to state intervention. This is true of the globalized economy in general. Further, although communication has been Taylorized both in its repression and in scripting (Cameron, 2000), in its role as product and process of work it may be difficult to Taylorize, especially when it is key to the provision of flexible identities and subject to tension over whether to regard it as a technical skill or an authenticating inherent feature of individuals or populations (the perduring ideology of the nation, which is mobilized for purposes of saving national markets, fending off competition from global flows of labor, and adding symbolic value to niche products).

As a result, scholars increasingly examine the world of work (whether private or public sector) in order to understand what kinds of implicit or explicit language policies regulate access to jobs, job promotion, and job training (Allan, 2013; Duchêne, 2011; Duchêne et al., 2013; Garrido & Codó, 2014; Urciuoli, 2008). While LPP has tended to focus on codified, explicit policy and planning, contemporary conditions require greater attention to sectors where such codification may be undesirable or difficult, or unnecessary for legitimacy.

Finally, while LPP has not historically attended in detail to processes of resistance, contemporary conditions open up that possibility. One reason for this, alluded to earlier, has to do with the ways in which changing hegemonic regimes always open up possibilities for struggle. Some of this struggle is over whose English, English or Mandarin, multilingualism or Google translate; but some of it is over whether language can or should be commodified, that is, whether speakers are prepared to enter contemporary conditions of late capitalism as flexible speaking subjects, as communicative entrepreneurial selves.

Just as language is increasingly inscribed in the globalized new economy as work product and work process, resistance to the spread of capitalism and its increasing inequalities finds one strategy in removing it from such consideration. Ideas about the environment and indigeneity in particular put on the table alternative modes of globalization in the form of global movements of solidarity in which language is cast as inherently part of an intertwined social and physical world, one in which people are not reduced to labor and alienated from nature. This is not a world in which language can be engineered; indeed, it is not clear to what extent it is even possible to address it as a separate object. These views emerge, notably, in indigenous language revitalization movements—ironically, given that these, too, can be understood as falling within the purview of LPP, or, more properly, within the liberal democratic and scientific framework within which it has made sense as a field.

So What Is New for Language Policy and Planning?

I have argued here that LPP has always been bound up in economic interests and processes, especially insofar as it was built on ideologies of language as a system susceptible to human intervention, and of scientific expertise as the authoritative way to stake a claim to knowledge and truth, both of which are features of modernity and of the link between the nation-state and industrial capitalism. What is new is the way in which the conditions of late modernity make it difficult to maintain the nation-state as the main locus of LPP activity, and require a more direct examination of the imbrication of language and capitalism than it was perhaps possible to undertake earlier.

At the same time, this examination raises some fundamental questions about LPP as an activity; put differently, it is subject to the logic of reflexivity, which requires it to situate its own interests and to deconstruct its object (language) and its historical practice (shaping language form and practice). This no doubt helps explain the critical turn that has accompanied the socioeconomic one; if we are uncomfortable accepting language as profit and legitimization of difference and inequality, then we begin to ask what our goal is. I certainly want to argue for seeing some of the recent work on language and economic activity within the frame of LPP's intellectual history, as I have tried to summarily sketch out in this chapter. I would argue, too, for situating LPP in a broader frame of the genealogy of ideas about language and power, and of language and political economy.

Notes

1. This chapter draws heavily on sections of M. Heller & B. McElhinny (2017).
2. Let me add here a disclaimer that my focus will be too narrowly circumscribed, leaving out the many ways in which metropoles and colonies have mutually influenced each other, as well as many globally important spheres. In particular, I give short shrift to Chinese and Japanese empires, and to the work of LPP in the Soviet Union and post-1949 China, though all are important; see, e.g., Brandist (2015).
3. I am grateful to Paul Manning for pointing out this link.

References

Alisjahbana, S. T. (1976). *Language planning for modernization: The case of Indonesian and Malaysian*. Berlin: Walter de Gruyter.

Allan, K. (2013). Sites of selection. The gatekeeping of Babel: Job interviews and the linguistic penalty. In A. Duchêne, M. Moyer, & C. Roberts (Eds.), *Language, migration and social inequalities: A critical sociolinguistic perspective on institutions and work* (pp. 56–80). Bristol and Buffalo: Multilingual Matters.

Allan, K., & McElhinny, B. (2017). Neoliberalism, language and migration. In S. Canagarajah (Ed.), *The Routledge handbook on language and migration* (pp. 79–101). New York: Routledge.

Anderson, B. (1983). *Imagined communities*. London: Verso.

Balibar, R. (2007 [1974]). *Les français fictifs*. Fernelmont, BE: E.M.E.

Boutet, J. (2008). *La vie verbale au travail: Des manufactures aux centres d'appels*. Toulouse: Octares.

Brandist, C. (2015). *The dimensions of hegemony: Language, culture and politics in revolutionary Russia*. Leiden: Brill.

Cameron, D. (2000). *Good to talk? Living and working in a communication culture*. London: Sage Publications.

Duchêne, A. (2011). Néolibéralisme, inégalités sociales et plurilinguisme: L'exploitation des ressources langagières et des locuteurs. *Langage et Société* 136(2), 81–108.

Duchêne, A., & Heller, M. (Eds.) (2012). *Language in late capitalism: Pride and profit.* New York: Routledge.

Duchêne, A., Moyer, M., & Roberts, C. (Eds.) (2013). *Language, migration and social inequalities: A critical sociolinguistic perspective on institutions and work.* Bristol, UK; Buffalo, NY: Multilingual Matters.

Fanon, F. (1967). *Black skin, white masks.* New York: Grove Press.

Fishman, J., Ferguson, C., & Das Gupta, J. (Eds.) (1968). *Language problems of developing nations.* New York: John Wiley & Sons.

Fox, M. (1975). *Language and development: A retrospective survey of Ford Foundation language projects, 1952–1974.* New York: Ford Foundation.

Garrido, M. R., & Codó, E. (2014). Deskilling and delanguaging African migrants in Barcelona: Pathways of labour market incorporation and the value of 'global' English. *Globalisation, Societies and Education* 15, 22–49. doi: 10.1080/14767724.2014.944757.

Garvía, R. (2015). *Esperanto and its rivals.* Philadelphia: University of Pennsylvania Press.

Gellner, E. (1983). *Nations and nationalism.* Oxford: Blackwell.

Gordin, M. (2015). *Scientific babel: How science was done before and after global English.* Chicago: University of Chicago Press.

Grillo, R. (1989). *Dominant languages.* Cambridge: Cambridge University Press.

Grin, F., Sfreddo, C., & Vaillancourt, F. (2010). *The economics of the multilingual workplace.* New York: Routledge.

Hanks, W. (2010). *Converting words: Maya in the age of the cross.* Berkeley: University of California Press.

Harvey, D. (1989). *The condition of postmodernity: An inquiry into the origins of cultural change.* Oxford: Wiley-Blackwell.

Harvey, D. (2005). *A brief history of neoliberalism.* Oxford: Oxford University Press.

Heller, M. (2007). Bilingualism as ideology and practice. In M. Heller (Ed.), *Bilingualism: A social approach* (pp. 1–22). London: Palgrave.

Heller, M. (2010a). Language as resource in the globalized new economy. In N. Coupland (Ed.), *The handbook of language and globalization* (pp. 349–365). Oxford: Wiley Blackwell.

Heller, M. (2010b). The commodification of language. *Annual Review of Anthropology* 39, 101–114.

Heller, M. (2017). Dr. Esperanto: Or, anthropology as alternative worlds. *American Anthropologist* 118, 12–22.

Heller, M., & McElhinny, B. (2017). *Language, capitalism, colonialism: Towards a critical history.* Toronto: University of Toronto Press.

Hobsbawm, E. (1990). *Nations and nationalism since 1760.* Cambridge: Cambridge University Press.

Lo, A., Abelmann, N., Kwon, S. A., & Okazaki, S. (2015). *South Korea's education exodus: The life and times of study abroad.* Seattle: University of Washington Press.

Lorente, B. (2012). The making of "workers of the world": Language and the labor brokerage state. In A. Duchêne & M. Heller (Eds.), *Language in late capitalism: Pride and profit* (pp. 183–206). New York: Routledge.

Park, J. S. Y., & Lo, A. (Eds.). (2012). Transnational South Korea as a site for a sociolinguistics of globalization. *Journal of Sociolinguistics* 16(2), 147–307.

Ricento, T. (Ed.) (2015). *Language policy and political economy: English in a global context.* Oxford: Oxford University Press.

Rubin, J., Jernudd, B., Das Gupta, J., Fishman, J., & Ferguson, C. (1977). *Language planning processes*. The Hague; New York: Mouton.

Tan, P. K. W., & Rubdy, R. (Eds.). (2008). *Language as commodity: Global structures, local marketplaces*. London; New York: Continuum.

Urciuoli, B. (2008). Skills and selves in the new workplace. *American Ethnologist* 35(2), 211–228.

Urciuoli, B., & LaDousa, C. (2013). Language management/labour. *Annual Review of Anthropology* 42, 175–190.

Weber, E. (1976). *Peasants into Frenchmen*. Stanford, CA: Stanford University Press.

CHAPTER 3

··

RESEARCH METHODS IN LANGUAGE POLICY AND PLANNING

··

DAVID CASSELS JOHNSON

FOR much of its history, language policy and planning (LPP) has been a topic of interest, rather than a robust academic discipline with well-developed theories, research methods, and empirical findings. Early language planning research was born out of practical necessity when linguists were called upon to help primarily postcolonial nations solve what were considered to be their language problems through (what would later become known as) status- and corpus-planning efforts. It was only after these researchers began meeting to discuss this work, and publishing the results, that it became an established area of interest. Thus, for much of its history, LPP research has not relied on LPP-specific research methods. Mostly, scholars have utilized the methods developed in their disciplinary homes—(socio)linguistics, sociology, law, political theory, and economics—to study a common topic.

This interdisciplinarity (or multidisciplinarity or transdisciplinarity) is a hallmark of LPP research and reveals how the impact of language plans and policies transcends disciplinary boundaries. This also means that clear LPP-specific methods have been slow to develop, if at all. This chapter reviews the methodological history of the field, highlighting major shifts engendered by particular research approaches, and ends with some predictions about where the field might be headed as evidenced by emerging trends. First, epistemological foundations are discussed, which help clarify methodological directions and perspectives. Then, a chronological history of LPP research methods is considered, with particular attention to language planning foundations, the critical and empirical turns, and emerging trends.

EPISTEMOLOGICAL FOUNDATIONS

It is useful to begin by delineating some terminological divisions—even if such divisions will always spur debate—because they help distinguish methodological trends and clarify the discussion. We can distinguish between epistemology, theoretical framework, methodology, and method. Epistemology is the branch of philosophy focused on knowledge and, in academic research, supports, or perhaps is embedded within, the theoretical framework, methodology, and methods. What is the nature of knowledge? How do we come to know what we know? How do we ask questions about what we do not know, and how do we answer those questions? How can we be sure that what we know is accurate or real or valid? All scholars' work is grounded in some epistemology, even if they do not discuss it explicitly or even recognize their own epistemological orientation.

Crotty (1998) distinguishes between three major epistemological orientations that guide most academic research: objectivism, constructionism, and subjectivism. The objectivist believes that the things that exist in the world have meaning independent of human consciousness. That is, the tree in the forest has some objective tree meaning with or without a human observer, and it is the researcher's goal to discover the objective truth and meaning of what is being studied. The subjectivist, on the other hand, believes that trees and other objects have the meanings they have because of the human observer, who imposes a subjective meaning on the thing under consideration. Lying in the middle, so to speak, is constructionism, which posits that meaning is developed out of the interplay between the human observer and the thing being observed. Unlike in objectivism, where things have inherent meaning waiting to be discovered, for the constructionist, meaning is constructed through a partnership between the observed and the observer. Now, whether a tree in the middle of the woods, or a rock on some distant planet, *exists* without any human observation is an ontological, not an epistemological, problem. Ontology is the study of what *is*—the nature of existence—while epistemology is the study of what we *know*—the nature of knowledge. Realism, which is an ontological position stating that realities exist outside of the human mind, is not the same thing as objectivism. The belief that things exist without a human observer (realism) is perfectly compatible with the belief that things still have no meaning without a human observer (subjectivism).

Many theoretical orientations, and therefore research methods, tend to naturally fall out of particular epistemological positions. For example, positivism—the theoretical position that research should follow strict scientific guidelines, which attempts to systematically control the variables in a study, and rejects intuition and metaphysical beliefs—aligns quite clearly with objectivism. Within positivistic and postpositivistic research, experimental studies with random assignment and generalizability are the gold standard. On the other hand, postmodernism rejects modernist notions of what counts as "science" and, therefore, it is difficult to imagine an objectivist postmodern study.

Still, other research methodologies might be aligned with different epistemologies. For example, there is a strong history of objectivist ethnographic research, influenced by the biological sciences, in which the human observer attempts to unobtrusively observe the behavior of other creatures. Furthermore, while social science research has often adopted a physical science model of research, it is worth noting that the observer effect is a well-known problem in quantum mechanics (or quantum physics), which states that the mere act of observation influences the phenomenon being observed. If this is an issue when studying extremely small things, like atoms and photons, the repercussions for studying human beings would seem to be relevant. Epistemological debates have influenced LPP research as well, and the history of the field reveals a shifting epistemological landscape.

LANGUAGE PLANNING RESEARCH FOUNDATIONS

Early language planning research was dominated by objectivism. There were language *problems* to be solved—for example, what status to grant colonial languages in postcolonial nations—and solutions were proposed in the form of language planning frameworks, models, and conceptualizations. Haugen (1959, p. 8) originally defined *language planning* as "the activity of preparing a normative orthography, grammar, and dictionary for the guidance of writers and speakers in a non-homogeneous speech community." Kloss (1969) expanded on this definition, identifying what Haugen had described as *corpus planning* (i.e., planning the forms of a language), which Kloss differentiated from *status planning* (i.e., planning the functions of a language). Another focus in this early research was developing frameworks accounting for the steps in language planning. For example, Haugen (1966, 1983) delineated four steps, including (1) selection of a norm (i.e., selecting a language variety for a particular context); (2) codification (i.e., development of an explicit, usually written, form); (3) implementation (i.e., attempt to spread the language form); and (4) elaboration (i.e., continued updating of the language variety to "meet the needs of the modern world"; Haugen, 1983, p. 273).

The epistemological sway of early language planning research was influenced by an interest in excluding sociopolitical variables in the objective science of language planning. For example, Tauli (1974, p. 51) made controversial claims about the utility of languages, which "can be evaluated with objective scientific often quantitative methods. . . . Not all languages describe things equally effectively." Tauli (1974) further argued that primitive "ethnic languages" were good candidates for language planning initiatives that will improve their efficiency and descriptiveness. Such assertions were relatively extreme, and received criticism, but were indicative of an early emphasis on deliberate language planning initiatives that ignored the sociopolitical contexts in which such initiatives took place.

These early activities engendered edited volumes like *Language Problems of Developing Nations* (Fishman et al., 1968), *Can Language Be Planned?* (Rubin & Jernudd, 1971), and *Language Planning Processes* (Rubin et al., 1977). Most of the contributions were conceptual proposals, descriptive accounts of language planning projects, strategies for implementing language planning, and historical investigations of particular contexts and communities. The research was not propelled by clearly identified research methods, and the analysis of any data— government reports, policy documents, and language corpuses—was largely guided by researcher intuition. In other words, it was an exploratory time. As Fishman (1977, p. 33) said, the primary aim of the project was to demonstrate "the feasibility of studying language planning processes," rather than testing specific hypotheses or evaluating the effectiveness of particular research methods. I have called this early work *historical-textual analysis* (Johnson, 2013a), which offers potential data sources and methods of data collection, even if it does not entail particular tools of analysis (see Table 3.1).

Ricento (2000) divides the history of the field into three eras, including foundational language planning research, critical language policy (described later in the chapter), and an intermediary stage in the 1970s and 1980s. This intermediary stage was a time in which William Labov (1972) and Dell Hymes (1972) led sociolinguistic research in very different directions, with quantitative objectivism being championed in variationist studies, and qualitative anthropological methods (notably ethnography) incorporated into the ethnography of speaking, which would later become known as the ethnography of communication. Meanwhile, the aim of structuralist linguistics was questioned, and critical scholarship in the social sciences gained in popularity, foregrounding the role of the social as a determining factor in human behavior and processes. In turn, critical social theories on how power operates in society continued to influence scholars across disciplines and, within language studies, critical linguists argued that "[a]ll linguistic interaction is shaped by power differences of varying kinds, and no part of linguistic action escapes its effects" (Kress, 2001, p. 35).

Table 3.1 Research Outline for Historical–Textual Analysis

Process	Data
Policy Formulation—"deals with the decisions of formally constituted organizations with respect to either (1) the functional allocation of codes within a speech community or (2) the characteristics of one or more codes within the code matrix (linguistic repertoire) of such a community" (Fishman et al., 1971, p. 293).	Government reports and documents, organizational reports and archival materials, newspaper and journal accounts, and interviews with members of the decision-making bodies
Codification—"deals with the normalization (standardization) of regional, social, class, or other variation in usage via the preparation of recommended (or 'official') grammars, dictionaries, orthographic guides, etc." (p. 295)	Organized around the products (dictionaries, etc.) of the agencies and processes, which can be obtained via official records of their activities, and the processes, which can be obtained via interviews with participants
Elaboration—"deals with the need for intertranslatability with one or more functionally diversified languages by such means as the preparation of recommended (or 'official') word lists, in particular, the substantive, professional, or technical fields" (p. 295).	Organized around the products (word lists, etc.) of the agencies and processes, which can be obtained via official records of their activities, and the processes, which can be obtained via interviews with participants
Implementation—"refers to all efforts to gain the acceptance of the policies and 'products' of language planning, including grammars, spellers, word lists, and school curricula for the implementation of language-policy decisions" (p. 299).	Surveys among target populations to determine the impact of language planning and unstructured discussions with participants to obtain spoken and written language data

Adapted from Fishman et al. (1971).

While these influences would most notably take form in Tollefson's historical-structural approach to LPP (Tollefson, 1991), their inchoate impact began to be seen in earlier work. For example, Cobarrubias (1983, p. 41) notes that language planning processes "are not philosophically neutral [which] . . . raises ethical issues." In Ruiz's (1984, p. 2) influential article on orientations in language planning, he declares that "[o]rientations are basic to language planning in that they delimit the ways we talk about language and language issues . . . they help to delimit the range of acceptable attitudes toward language, and to make certain attitudes legitimate. In short, orientations determine what is thinkable about language in society."

This decidedly poststructuralist account of how discourses interact with power would later be reflected in many critical language policy (CLP) studies and critical language scholarship more generally. Another example is the book *Language Planning and Social Change*, in which Cooper (1989) foregrounds the sociopolitical impact of language planning, emphasizing the possibility of social change: "Language planning, concerned with the management of change, is it-self an instance of social change" (Cooper, 1989, p. 164). Both Ruiz and Cooper foreshadowed the critical turn in LPP research, which would, in turn, influence a new generation of LPP scholars and set a decidedly different epistemological and theoretical course for the field.

The Critical Turn

Early language planning research has been characterized as "technocratic" (Wiley, 1999, p. 18) and positivist (Ricento, 2000, p. 208), highlighting critiques of the assumption that the "science" of language planning—as propelled by language pla-nning scholars—can be divorced from sociopolitical forces. Tollefson was at the forefront of what Ricento (2000) describes as a third wave of LPP research (1990s through the first decade of the 2000s), which is characterized by increasing attention to how language ideologies and discourses interact with LPP processes. Tollefson (1991) refers to the earlier research as the neoclassical approach and contrasts it with the historical-structural approach, which focuses on how historical and structural forces create and sustain systems of inequality.

Tollefson (2015) portrays the historical-structural approach as part of a larger field of critical language studies, which foregrounds how relationships between language and power are created by sociocultural and sociolinguistic discourses (Fowler et al., 1979). Thus, the criticism of early language planning research—that it ignored the ideological and political nature of language planning; that it focused on individual decisions instead of social, political, and economic forces; that it was overtly and overly positivist or technocratic—reflected a more general intellectual movement toward approaches influenced by postmodernism, poststructuralism, and critical social theory.

Borrowing from Habermas (1973) and Foucault (1970), Tollefson (1991, pp. 32, 35) proposed a new conceptualization of language policy, describing it as "one mech-anism by which the interests of dominant sociopolitical groups are maintained and the seeds of transformation developed. . . . The historical-structural model presumes that plans that are successfully implemented will serve dominant class interests." Contrasted with earlier optimistic assumptions that language planning could solve language problems, Tollefson focused on how language planning leads to systemic inequality. His withering critique of early language planning research, accompanied by an innovative new vision for LPP research, was a watershed moment in the field and marked an epistemological and theoretical turning point, which would influ-ence a new generation of LPP scholars.

Like early language planning research, historical-structural analysis focuses on state policies and institutions, but emphasizes the historical events and structural mechanisms that engender social inequality. The connections between language (policy) and power are a central focus, although conceptualizations vary, and include *state power, ideological power*, and *discursive power* (Tollefson, 2015). Salient examples of each of these foci include Wiley and Wright's (2004) historical examination of how US federal educational policy has marginalized minority and indigenous language users (state power); Pan's (2011) analysis of how English language policy in China relies on ideological hegemony (ideological power); and Barakos's (2015) incorporation of governmentality (Foucault, 1991) to highlight how Welsh language policy gets recontextualized as essentialist ideologies within bilingual business practices that promote language as a neoliberal tool of consumership (discursive power). Barakos's scholarship and many others (e.g., Cincotta-Segi, 2011; Johnson, 2012) reveal how the CLP framework can be extended to focus on *micro-level interactions*, particularly when combined with discourse analytic techniques. Analyses of how policy as discourse impacts micro-level interactions in classrooms and societies have become increasingly prevalent in CLP research.

In subsequent publications, Tollefson (2002, 2006, 2012) outlines the critical in CLP research, which (1) is critical of neoclassical language planning research; (2) is influenced by critical theory; (3) emphasizes the relationships among language, power, and inequality, which are held to be central concepts for understanding language and society; and (4) entails social activism. While many researchers have taken up the first three parts of CLP, the fourth has received less attention. This is not because LPP researchers are not committed to social justice, but because research and activism are often separated in ways that reify objectivist epistemologies. Countering this, Tollefson argues that language policy researchers are not only responsible for illuminating social hierarchies and processes of power, but for changing such structures.

This demands a critical understanding of researcher subjectivity and positions the commitment to social justice as concomitant to, and reliant upon, a critical examination of interactions with participants: "[Critical language policy] researchers seek to develop a 'critical method' that includes a self-reflective examination of their relationship with the 'Others' who are the focus of research" (Tollefson, 2002, p. 4). The emphasis on research positionality as an essential component of CLP is mentioned here, but is taken up in more detail later.

Critiques of the *Critical*

The historical-structural approach has been criticized for being overly deterministic and for underestimating the role of human agency, particularly of teachers (Ricento & Hornberger, 1996), for not capturing language planning processes (Davis, 1999), and for diminishing the benevolent impact of many language planning initiatives (Fishman, 1994). Some of these criticisms are somewhat analogous to those leveled at critical discourse studies and postmodernism and poststructuralism. For example, while Foucault (1982) allows for "counter-discourses" in later writings, a consideration of human agency is largely absent, and instead humans appear trapped within powerful discourses over which they have no control. Discourse is both an effect and instrument of power, which has the ability to control human behavior and thinking: discourses are "practices that systematically form the object of which they speak" (Foucault, 1978, p. 49).

The view that we are subject to the power of language is central in many postmodernist accounts of education, which assume that discourse "worlds the world" (Lather, 1993, p. 675). However, language scholars will recognize similarities between the Foucaultian conceptualization of discourse and a similar position staked out by Benjamin Whorf (Carroll, 1956) and Edward Sapir (1921) decades earlier. According to linguistic determinism, the so-called strong version of the Sapir-Whorf hypothesis, human thinking is controlled by language, which presupposes the categories for interpreting our lived realities: "Language . . . powerfully conditions all our thinking. . . . Human beings do not live in the objective world alone . . . but are very much at the mercy of the particular language which has become the medium of expression for their society" (Sapir, 1929, p. 209). Some scholars who are influenced by postmodernism conceptualize educational discourses as mechanisms that not only shape norms of interaction and relationships of power, but also make some ideas unthinkable or less intelligible ("a problem of thinkability" according to Britzman, 1995). In other words, discourses are primary, thinking and being secondary, and the latter relies on the former. As Butler characterizes this debate: "Discourse is all there is . . . the subject is dead . . . there is no reality, only representations (1992, p. 4).

Livia and Hall (1997) make a similar argument about the connections between linguistic determinism and Foucault's discourse, but suggest one distinction: Foucault (and postmodernists) are less concerned with the lexical and morphosyntactic details within a discourse. If linguistic determinism is rejected, some of the important concepts within postmodernism lose their appeal. As it has been applied (perhaps especially in US educational research), postmodern scholars have been criticized for being nihilistic armchair radicals who do little to actually counter social problems (Schutz, 2004) besides writing in intentionally obfuscatory prose (Constas, 1998; St. Pierre, 2000). This raises a series of potential problems. Why are postmodernists uniquely positioned to transcend dominant discourses? Is arcane academic writing, which itself creates a discourse for the initiated, an effective means for social change? One might argue that a patronizing position compromises the purported commitment to an interrogation of researcher subjectivity, let alone a commitment to social justice.

A similar criticism leveled against critical discourse analysis (CDA) is that it makes unwarranted assumptions about language and (unequal) power relationships.

For example, Blommaert (2005, p. 32) argues that in CDA, "[p]ower relations are often predefined and then confirmed by features of discourse . . . politicians *always* and *intentionally* manipulate their constituencies, doctors are *by definition* and always the powerful party in doctor-patient relationships, etc." Similarly, while there is a recognition that discourse operates across many levels and that analysts should consider the connections between local and societal discourses, a multi-layered conceptualization of context is less developed in CDA. What operates as a dominant discourse in one layer may not be the case for another, and what may be viewed as subversive (by analysts) in, say, micro-level texts and discourses may be considered quite common, mainstream, or even dominant by the humans responsible for creating and interpreting those texts and discourses, at least in the context in which they were created. As Blommaert has argued, what is lacking in these critical approaches is a full analysis of how the context shapes discourse. On the other hand, it is not as if CDA practitioners are not cognizant of these limitations, and important contributions that combine CDA with ethnography, for example, are increasingly common (e.g., Kryżanowski, 2011).

The Empirical Turn

As newer generations of scholars become interested in language policy and planning, more and more researchers are examining LPP agents, processes, and discourses with empirical data collection and analysis. First, a note about the term *empirical*. Empiricism, as a philosophy of science promoted by philosophers like John Locke, describes the position that knowledge is developed through observation and experience. Innate ideas, religious and cultural traditions, metaphysical beliefs, and a priori assumptions are, therefore, not considered good evidence for answering research questions. While there is sometimes a tendency to equate *empirical* with *quantitative*, this conflicts with both historical and modern definitions. Certainly, experimental data are empirical, but so are observations and interviews, for example.

Much of the empirical turn in LPP research was propelled by longitudinal studies on language education and classroom discourse. Hornberger (1988), Davis (1994), King (2001), and McCarty (2002), for example, all utilized ethnography to study LPP processes as they related to language maintenance and education for minority and indigenous language speakers. This body of research influenced and informed the ethnography of language policy, a research methodology that focuses on the creation, interpretation, and appropriation of language policy texts and discourses across multiple levels and layers of LPP activity (Hornberger & Johnson, 2007; Johnson, 2009).

Ethnographies of language policy are nontraditional in at least two important ways. First, the object of study is not a culture or a people, as would traditionally be the case, but a policy or policies. Second, traditional ethnographies are built on long-term participant observation among a particular community or within a particular context, but ethnographies of language policy often require data collection across diverse contexts and communities of individuals. Nevertheless, multi-sited ethnographic research is useful for studying policy (Levinson & Sutton, 2001) and, even though the focus is policy, human agents who create, interpret, and appropriate policy are always at the heart of ethnographic research. Ethnography has proven useful for uncovering LPP processes across very diverse contexts, a sampling of which includes language ideology and policy in Luxembourg (Davis, 1994), bilingual education in Washington, D.C. (Freeman, 1998), indigenous language revitalization in New Zealand (Hill & May, 2011), linguistic landscapes and language ecologies in Sweden (Hult, 2007), multilingual educational policy in Mozambique (Chimbutane, 2011), and educational language policy in the Lao People's Democratic Republic (PDR) (Cincotta-Segi, 2009).

Sometimes separated from, but often combined with, ethnographic and other qualitative research approaches, different forms of discourse analysis have been leveraged to illuminate language policy creation, interpretation, and negotiation. Traditions of discourse analysis have their own methodological history, representing different foci, questions, and epistemological orientations. Grounded in the work of Sacks and Schegloff (Sacks et al., 1974), conversation analysis (CA) focuses on the organized set of practices in the structure of human interaction. While CA attends closely to the interactional moves among conversation participants, critics have argued that the context in which the interaction occurs has not historically been a focus. CDA, on the other hand, places the social context, and particularly issues of power and inequality, as central to the analysis of the text. Scholars like Fairclough (2010) and Wodak (1996) have proposed analytic frameworks for making connections between texts and contexts, often establishing complex intertextual and interdiscursive paths between multiple levels of creation, interpretation, and recontextualization.

Discourse analysts who ground their work in linguistic anthropology (e.g., Agha, 2003; Wortham, 2005) also consider the context to be of tantamount importance, but distinguish their work from CDA by an in-depth, typically ethnographically informed, understanding of the context. With a similar commitment to understanding local complexity, sociolinguistic ethnography (Pérez-Milans, 2011, 2012) combines fine-grained discourse analysis with ethnographic data collection. Echoing Blommaert's criticism of CDA, Pérez-Milans (2012, p. 63) argues that other discourse analytic approaches "have emphasized stable macro-societal processes which are taken for granted and projected on the discourse as background facts." Instead, sociolinguistic ethnography attends to the links between local practices and macro-level social processes, neither of which are monolithic or static.

Each of these discourse analytic methods has been applied to LPP studies. Bonacina's (2010) analysis of an induction classroom in France is a good example of the new wave of LPP studies that takes up Spolsky's (2004) inclusion of *language practices* as an essential part of language policy. Utilizing CA, Bonacina examines how code-switching practices emerge as a norm of interaction within the classroom, forming what she calls a "practiced language policy." Cincotta-Segi's work (2009, 2011) on language policy and education in the Lao PDR reveals how impacts of a language policy cannot necessarily be predicted based solely on the language of that policy or the perceived intentions of its authors. She combines ethnography and CDA to illuminate how the de jure intentions of the state—as expressed through governmental policy and analyzed within interviews with Ministry of Education officials—are marked by heterogeneity, and the interpretation and appropriation by teachers is equally multifarious.

Cincotta-Segi's research reveals the importance of considering the multiple intentions, ideologies, and discourses that engender policy text and discourse, as well as the multiple, unpredictable, and agentive forms of interpretation and appropriation unique to a particular context. Her analysis balances a critical focus on the power of language policy as a mechanism of hegemony (through CDA) with an understanding of the power of language policy agents (through ethnography). Mortimer (2013, p. 67) draws upon linguistic anthropology to examine language policy as "a constellation of communicative events" in which linguistic signs and social meaning emerge and change. She incorporates speech chain analysis (Agha, 2003) to trace a chain of communicative events that connect macro-level language policy with local educational practice in Paraguay. Mortimer traces two distinct meanings of what it means to speak Guaraní across diverse language policy texts, talk, and practices.

While some scholars adopt discourse analytic methodologies wholesale, others have adapted particular techniques to fit the needs of their research. Linguistic landscape analysis, for example, has emerged as a popular technique to analyze how public display of languages reflects societal language ideologies, discourses, and policies (e.g., Shohamy & Gorter, 2009). Johnson (2015) details how incorporating intertextual analysis into a discourse analytic study can highlight connections across the diverse layers of policy creation, interpretation, and appropriation.

While ethnography and different forms of discourse analysis have been widely used in empirical studies (the focus of which reflects the subjectivity of this author), LPP research is characterized by a marked multidisciplinarity as researchers leverage the methods from their disciplinary home to study LPP processes. Examples include Grin (2003), who uses economic research methods to analyze the value of language acquisition and has established the economics of language policy (Grin & Vaillancourt, 2015); May (2008) and colleagues (e.g., Sonntag, 2009), who use political theory to explore LPP processes and discourses; and Kochenov and de Varennes (2015), who consider how laws and legal systems impact LPP. This multidisciplinarity is the motivation for the annual Multidisciplinary Approaches in Language Policy and Planning Conference held at the University of Calgary and convened by Thomas Ricento (held at the University of Toronto since 2017). As well, the edited volume on research methods by Hult and Johnson (2015) represents diverse research methods and approaches in LPP, including chapters on political theory, legal theory, corpus linguistics, economics, media studies, and demography (among others).

EMERGING TRENDS IN LANGUAGE POLICY AND PLANNING RESEARCH METHODS

While most LPP scholars rely on their disciplinary expertise for methodological guidance, research methods are increasingly being adapted and sculpted for LPP-based research questions, inevitably changing them and engendering something new and LPP-specific. Ethnography of language policy (Johnson, 2013b) and economics of language policy have been proposed; perhaps in the future, we will discuss language policy discourse analysis, the language policy interview, or the demography of language policy. As more and more scholars leverage their disciplinary expertise to illuminate language policy processes, the field will undoubtedly grow. Here, two important trends, which are perhaps hallmarks of a fourth wave of LPP research, are the focus (even if there are undoubtedly more). First, the tension between approaches that focus on the power of language policies and approaches that focus on the agency of policy actors has engendered an exciting debate. Second, ethical considerations are coming to the fore in LPP research, particularly the role of the researcher in language policy processes and actions.

Structure and Agency

An essential challenge facing LPP researchers is how to balance critical analyses of the power of policy (discourses) with empirical understanding of the agency of policy actors. Menken and García's (2010) edited volume *Negotiating Language Policies in Schools: Educators as Policymakers* prioritizes this debate and, in their introduction, García and Menken (2010) argue that teachers are the final arbiters of language policy implementation (cf. Hornberger & Johnson, 2007; Menken, 2008; Ricento & Hornberger, 1996). Johnson and Johnson (2015) expand on this, conceptualizing language policy arbiters as individuals who wield a disproportionate amount of LPP power relative to other individuals in a particular context. They argue that the heterogeneity of language policy texts and the diversity of the sociolinguistic and sociocultural contexts in which policies are interpreted and appropriated create opportunities for human agency. Nevertheless, while many scholars have highlighted the possibility of agency within discursive events, they also argue that some individuals become positioned as more powerful, and this positioning tends to rely on traditional/dominant sociolinguistic and sociocultural hierarchies (Barakos, 2015; Cincotta-Segi, 2009; Johnson, 2012). As Barakos (2016) has argued, "agency and structure in both discourse and language policy dialectically shape each other" (p. 27).

Tollefson (2012) characterizes these two research approaches as the historical-structural and the creative public-sphere paradigms and argues that the distinction lies in the focus of the research, as opposed to some essential theoretical division. Indeed, much of the research epitomizing the empirical turn relies on similar theoretical foundations as CLP research (and often the theoretical foundation *is* CLP). So, while the two approaches do offer competing conceptualizations of language policy texts, discourses, and practices, they share theoretical and epistemological orientations. Whereas CLP marked a stark turning point in the field, recent research appears to expand upon earlier approaches. This is a healthy development since increasingly diverse LPP-specific research methods and approaches will better enable a new generation of scholars.

Often, structure is portrayed as a macro-level phenomenon, while agency is highlighted as something occurring at the micro-level. There is general agreement in the field that language policy should be conceptualized and studied as multiply leveled (or layered). Yet, recent research has critiqued monolithic and static depictions of the relationship between *macro* and *micro* because they do not account for the multiple constraints on social interaction, which can change over time. Furthermore, critics argue that research focusing on the micro tends to overestimate the individual's ability for novel and seminal action (Wortham & Reyes, 2015). Questioning and reconceptualizing the macro-micro dialectic is becoming an important feature within LPP research. While a multiply layered understanding of context is implicit in the macro-micro distinction (especially when other *meso* layers are added), ideologies are multiply layered as well and can change (Blommaert, 2013). As Mortimer and Wortham (2015, p. 163) argue, "[i]nstead of connecting micro-level events to macro-level structures (e.g. connecting a classroom language practice to an official policy), we must explore heterogeneous domains and scales of social organization relevant to understanding meaningful social action." Therefore, as Hult (2010) has argued, within any discursive event, there are many potential sociolinguistic scales at work, and the analyst identifies how the unique configuration of semiotic resources are made relevant within the interaction. It is tempting to equate structure with macro-level social processes/systems and agency with micro-level human interactions, yet both macro and micro discourses, and both structure and agency, can emerge in a single discursive event and shape a single policy document.

Ethics and Advocacy

Another important emerging trend is the increasing focus on researcher positionality and subjectivity. Perhaps it has become accepted as a given that most language policy scholars are *critical* since so much of the research is focused on power and/or committed to social justice; yet, traditionally, *activism* and *research* have often been separated, thus perpetuating divisions between participants and observers that reify objectivist epistemologies. De Costa (2014) argues that scholars should not only describe, critique, and transform discriminatory practices and social inequality, but also maintain critical reflexivity regarding the position of the researcher. Similarly, in Lin's (2015) interrogation of researcher epistemology in LPP, she argues that a critical perspective combines self-reflection of the researcher's position in institutional hierarchies with an interrogation of how such institutional hierarchies produce and reproduce domination and subordination. According to Lin (2015, p. 26), the goal of the researcher should be knowledge co-construction: "In the critical research paradigm, both the researcher and the researched are subjects of knowing and enter into a dialogue on equal footings." Nevertheless, Lin highlights a historical weakness in critical research, which has impacted policy less often than positivist studies. The solution might be a "dialogue with different parties in each situated context in LPP" (p. 30), which recognizes the strength in collaboration and acknowledges the limited nature of a single methodological position. Making a similar case for methodological pluralism, Fishman (1994, p. 98) argues that "neo-Marxist critics . . . of language planning . . . never seem to go beyond their critique as decisively or as productively as they state their critique." Fishman suggests, instead, that research methods should be based on "technically substantive rather than on trendy salvational grounds" (p. 97) (ostensibly portraying both ethnographic and critical approaches as trendy).

One of the areas in which researchers can openly articulate their own positions and subjectivities is in the written report. Ramanathan (2006, 2011) compellingly grapples with her own ideological conflict in researching-texting practices and criticizes LPP scholarship that presents its textual products in hermetically sealed ways—"a modus operandi that often leaves little room for addressing uncertainties and tensions in the researching-texting process" (Ramanathan, 2011, p. 256). Instead, she emphasizes that how we develop meaning in the texts we create is a process that should be rendered "porous, unstable, and changeable" (p. 247). Echoing Fishman's (1994) critique, she argues that it is crucial to interrogate the ideological aspects of research as a social practice, while also permitting a way to "complexify the researcher's voice" (p. 268). Similarly, Canagarajah and Stanley (2015, p. 41) argue that genre conventions in academic writing make it challenging to give voice to minority communities, yet it is essential that LPP scholars push back against positivistic writing genres that attempt to synthesize research findings into generalizable and monolithic truths: "Since the subjects exist in the report only through the voice of the researcher, there is a tendency for their complexity to be suppressed and their identity to be generalized (or essentialized)."

Consideration of ethics and advocacy in sociolinguistic research is nothing new. For example, Labov (1982) and Rickford (1999) have grappled with the responsibility language scholars have to the speech communities in which they collect data, and both have actively promoted social justice efforts in courts, legislatures, and public discourse. Nevertheless, Labov has consistently separated research from advocacy in ways that reify objectivist epistemologies and separate the researcher from the researched. A new wave of LPP scholars is considering how to *combine* research with application, observation with action, and critique with advocacy. There is a growing sentiment, absent in earlier language planning research, that LPP scholars should also be activists, and these two activities—research and action—can be combined in theoretically and methodologically robust ways, despite objectivist arguments to the contrary. Admittedly, this type of engagement may prove more compelling for qualitative researchers than those who specialize in surveys, economics, or demography. Nevertheless, while new LPP research has focused on empirical data collection in schools and communities, there is a burgeoning emphasis on the roles of LPP researchers, themselves, in policy processes.

CONCLUSION

In this chapter, a historical overview of LPP research methods is offered. Beginning with early language planning studies that gave birth to the field but lacked explicit methodological development, major methodological and epistemological directions and divisions are highlighted. The critical turn in the early 1990s was a watershed moment when earlier language planning models were sharply criticized, while the empirical turn, which came a little later, largely built upon critical approaches, as opposed to setting an entirely new methodological course. While LPP scholars have always leveraged discipline-specific research methods, an increasing number of LPP-specific research approaches, methods, and techniques are being proposed to study (increasingly sophisticated conceptualizations of) language policy. Because I conceptualize policy as discourse (and text and practice), discourse analytic methods are privileged in this chapter, but developments in economics, political theory, law, and demography (Hult & Johnson, 2015) are also exciting, and will benefit a new generation of LPP scholars. Two emerging trends in the field are highlighted—the tension between (1) structure and agency and (2) objectivity and advocacy—both of which will receive attention going forward and will grow the field in exciting ways.

REFERENCES

Agha, A. (2003). The social life of cultural value. *Language and Communication* 23, 231–273.

Barakos, E. (2015). Language policy and governmentality in businesses in Wales: A continuum of empowerment and regulation. *Multilingua* 35, 361–391. doi: 10.1515/multi-2015-0007.

Barakos, E. (2016). Language policy and critical discourse studies: Towards a combined approach. In E. Barakos & J. W. Unger (Eds.), *Discursive approaches to language policy* (pp. 23–49). Basingstoke, UK: Palgrave Macmillan.

Blommaert, J. (2005). *Discourse: Key topics in sociolinguistics*. Cambridge: Cambridge University Press.

Blommaert, J. (2013). Policy, policing and the ecology of social norms: Ethnographic monitoring revisited. *International Journal of the Sociology of Language* 219, 123–140.

Bonacina, F. (2010). *A conversation analytic approach to practiced language policies: The example of an induction classroom for newly-arrived immigrant children in France.* PhD thesis. University of Edinburgh.

Britzman, D. (1995). Is there a queer pedagogy? Or, stop reading straight. *Educational Theory* 45(2), 151–165.

Butler, J. (1992). Contingent foundations: Feminism and the question of "postmodernism." In J. Butler & J. W. Scott (Eds.), *Feminists theorize the political* (pp. 3–21). New York: Routledge.

Canagarajah, S., & Stanley, P. (2015). Ethical considerations in language policy research. In F. M. Hult & D. C. Johnson (Eds.), *Research methods in language policy and planning: A practical guide* (pp. 33–44). Malden, MA: Wiley-Blackwell.

Carroll, J. B. (1956) *Language, thought, and reality: Selected writings of Benjamin Lee Whorf.* Cambridge, MA: MIT Press.

Chimbutane, F. (2011). *Rethinking bilingual education in postcolonial contexts.* Clevedon, UK: Multilingual Matters.

Cincotta-Segi, A. (2009). *"The big ones swallow the small ones." Or do they? The language policy and practice of ethnic minority education in the Lao PDR: A case study from Nalae.* PhD thesis. Canberra: The Australian National University.

Cincotta-Segi, A. (2011). "The big ones swallow the small ones." Or do they? Language-in-education policy and ethnic minority education in the Lao PDR. *Journal of Multilingual and Multicultural Development* 32(1), 1–15.

Cobarrubias, J. (1983). Ethical issues in status planning. In J. Cobarrubias & J. A. Fishman (Eds.), *Progress in language planning: International perspectives* (pp. 41–86). Berlin: Walter De Gruyter.

Constas, M. A. (1998). Deciphering postmodern educational research. *Educational Researcher* 27(9), 36–42.

Cooper, R. L. (1989). *Language planning and social change.* New York: Cambridge University Press.

Crotty, S. (1998). *The foundations of social research: Meaning and perspective in the research process.* New York: SAGE Publications.

Davis, K. (1994). *Language planning in multilingual contexts: Policies, communities, and schools in Luxembourg.* Philadelphia: John Benjamins.

Davis, K. A. (1999). Dynamics of indigenous language maintenance. In T. Huebner & K. A. Davis (Eds.), *Sociopolitical perspectives on language policy and planning in the USA* (pp. 67–98). Amsterdam; Philadelphia: John Benjamins.

De Costa, P. I. (2014). Making ethical decisions in an ethnographic study. *TESOL Quarterly* 48(2), 413–422.

Fairclough, N. (2010). *Critical discourse analysis: The critical study of language.* 2nd edition. Harlow, UK: Pearson.

Fishman, J. A. (1977). Comparative study of the language planning: Introducing a survey. In J. Rubin, B. H. Jernudd, J. Das Gupta, J. A. Fishman, & C. A. Ferguson (Eds.), *Language planning processes* (pp. 31–40). The Hague: Mouton.

Fishman, J. A. (1994). Critiques of language planning: A minority languages perspective. *Journal of Multilingual and Multicultural Development* 15(2–3), 91–99.

Fishman, J. A., Das Gupta, J., Jernudd, B. H., & Rubin, J. (1971). Research outline for comparative studies of language planning. In J. Rubin & B.H. Jernudd (Eds.), *Can language be planned: Sociolinguistic theory and practice for developing nations* (pp. 293–305). Honolulu: The University Press of Hawaii.

Fishman, J., Ferguson, C. A., & Das Gupta, J. (Eds.). (1968). *Language problems of developing nations.* New York: John Wiley & Sons.

Foucault, M. (1970). *The order of things: An archeology of the human sciences.* New York: Vintage Books.

Foucault, M. (1978). *The history of sexuality.* New York: Random House.

Foucault, M. (1982). The subject and power. *Critical Inquiry* 8(Summer), 777–795.

Foucault, M. (1991). Governmentality. In G. Burchell, C. Gordon & P. Miller (Eds.), *The Foucault effect: Studies in governmentality* (pp. 87–104). Chicago: University of Chicago Press.

Fowler, R., Hodge, B., Kress, G., & Trew, T. (1979). *Language and control.* London: Routlege & Kegan Paul.

Freeman, R. D. (1998). *Bilingual education and social change.* Clevedon, UK: Multilingual Matters.

García, O., & Menken, K. (2010). Stirring the onion: Educators and the dynamics of language education policies (looking ahead). In K. Menken & O. García (Eds.), *Negotiating language policies in schools: Educators as policymakers* (pp. 249–261). London; New York: Routledge.

Grin, F. (2003). Language planning and economics. *Current Issues in Language Planning* 4(1), 1–66.

Grin, F., & Vaillancourt, F. (2015). The economics of language policy: An introduction to evaluation work. In F. M. Hult & D. C. Johnson (Eds.), *Research methods in language policy and planning: A practical guide* (pp. 21–32). Malden, MA: Wiley-Blackwell.

Habermas, J. (1973). *Theory and practice.* Boston: Beacon Press.

Haugen, E. (1959). Planning for a standard language in Norway. *Anthropological Linguistics* 1(3), 8–21.

Haugen, E. (1966). Linguistics and language planning. In W. Bright (Ed.), *Sociolinguistics* (pp. 50–71). The Hague: Mouton.

Haugen, E. (1983). The implementation of corpus planning: Theory and practice. In J. Cobarrubias & J. A. Fishman (Eds.), *Progress in language planning: International perspectives* (pp. 269–289). Berlin: Walter De Gruyter.

Hill, R., & May, S. (2011). Exploring biliteracy in Māori-medium education: An ethnographic perspective. In. T. L. McCarty (Ed.), *Ethnography and language policy* (pp. 161–183). London: Routledge.

Hornberger, N. H. (1988). *Bilingual education and language maintenance.* Dordrecht: Foris Publications.

Hornberger, N. H., & Johnson, D. C. (2007). Slicing the onion ethnographically: Layers and spaces in multilingual language education policy and practice. *TESOL Quarterly* 41(3), 509–532.

Hult, F. M. (2007). *Multilingual language policy and English language teaching in Sweden*. PhD thesis. University of Pennsylvania, Philadelphia.

Hult, F. M. (2010). Analysis of language policy discourses across the scales of space and time. *International Journal of the Sociology of Language* 202, 7–24.

Hult, F. M., & Johnson, D. C. (Eds.). (2015). *Research methods in language policy and planning: A practical guide*. Malden, MA: Wiley-Blackwell.

Hymes, D. (1972). On communicative competence. In J. B. Pride & J. Holmes (Eds.), *Sociolinguistics: Selected readings* (pp. 269–293). Harmondsworth, UK: Penguin Books.

Johnson, D. C. (2009). Ethnography of language policy. *Language Policy* 8, 139–159.

Johnson, D. C. (2012). Positioning the language policy arbiter: Governmentality and footing in the School District of Philadelphia. In J. W. Tollefson (Ed.), *Language policies in education: Critical issues* (2nd edition; pp. 116–136). London; New York: Routledge.

Johnson, D. C. (2013a). *Language policy*. Basingstoke, UK: Palgrave Macmillan.

Johnson, D. C. (Ed.). (2013b). Thematic issue, Ethnography of language policy: Theory, method, and practice. *International Journal of the Sociology of Language* 219.

Johnson, D. C. (2015). Intertextuality and language policy. In F. M. Hult & D. C. Johnson (Eds.), *Research methods in language policy and planning: A practical guide* (pp. 166–180). Malden, MA: Wiley Blackwell.

Johnson, D. C., & Johnson, E. (2015). Power and agency in language policy appropriation. *Language Policy* 14(3), 221–243.

King, K. A. (2001). *Language revitalization processes and prospects: Quichua in the Ecuadorian Andes*. Clevedon, UK: Multilingual Matters.

Kloss, H. (1969). *Research possibilities on group bilingualism: A report*. Quebec: International Center for Research on Bilingualism.

Kochenev, D., & de Varennes, F. (2015). Language and law. In F. M. Hult & D. C. Johnson (Eds.), *Research methods in language policy and planning: A practical guide* (pp. 56–66). Malden, MA: Wiley-Blackwell.

Kress, G. (2001). From Saussure to critical sociolinguistics: The turn towards a social view of language. In M. Wetherell, S. Taylor, & S. Yates (Eds.), *Discourse theory and practice* (pp. 29–38). London: Sage.

Kryżanowski, M. (2011). Ethnography and critical discourse analysis: Towards a problem-oriented research dialogue. *Critical Discourse Studies* 8(4), 231–238.

Labov, W. (1972). *Language in the inner city: Studies in the Black English Vernacular*. Philadelphia: University of Pennsylvania Press.

Labov, W. (1982). Objectivity and commitment in linguistic science: The case of the Black English trial in Ann Arbor. *Language in Society* 11(2), 165–201.

Lather, P. (1993). Fertile obsession: Validity after poststructuralism. *The Sociological Quarterly* 34(4), 673–693.

Levinson, B. A. U., & Sutton, M. (2001). Introduction: Policy as/in practice—A sociocultural approach to the study of educational policy. In B. A. U. Levinson & M. Sutton (Eds.), *Policy as practice: Toward a sociocultural analysis of educational policy* (pp. 1–22). London: Ablex.

Lin, A. M. Y. (2015). Researcher positionality. In F. M. Hult & D. C. Johnson (Eds.), *Research methods in language policy and planning: A practical guide* (pp. 21–32). Malden, MA: Wiley-Blackwell.

Livia, A., & Hall, K. (1997). It's a girl! Bringing performativity back to linguistics. In A. Livia & K. Hall (Eds.), *Queerly phrased: Language, gender, and sexuality* (pp. 3–18). New York: Oxford University Press.

May, S. (2008). *Language and minority rights: Ethnicity, nationalism, and the politics of language*. New York: Routledge.

McCarty, T. L. (2002). *A place to be Navajo: Rough Rock and the struggle for self-determination in indigenous schooling*. New York: Routledge.

Menken, K. (2008). *English learners left behind: Standardized testing as language policy*. Clevedon, UK: Multilingual Matters.

Menken, K., & García, O. (Eds.). (2010). *Negotiating language policies in schools: Educators as policymakers*. New York: Routledge.

Mortimer, K. (2013). Communicative event chains in an ethnography of Paraguayan language policy. *International Journal of the Sociology of Language* 213, 67–100.

Mortimer, K., & Wortham, S. (2015), Analyzing language policy and social identification across heterogeneous scales. *Annual Review of Applied Linguistics* 35, 160–172.

Pan, L. (2011). English language ideologies in the Chinese foreign language education policies: World-system perspective. *Language Policy* 10, 245–263.

Pérez-Milans, M. (2011). Caught in a West/China dichotomy: Doing critical sociolinguistic ethnography in Zhejiang Schools. *Journal of Language, Identity & Education* 10(3), 164–185.

Pérez-Milans, M. (2012). Beyond "safe-talk": Institutionalization and agency in China's English language education. *Linguistics and Education* 23(1), 62–76.

Ramanathan, V. (2006) Of texts AND translations AND rhizomes: Postcolonial anxieties AND deracinations AND knowledge constructions. *Critical Inquiry in Language Studies* 3(4), 223–244.

Ramanathan, V. (2011). Researching-texting tensions in qualitative research: Ethics in and around textual fidelity, selectivity, and translations. In T. McCarty (Ed.), *Ethnography and language policy* (pp. 255–270). New York; London: Routledge.

Ricento, T. (2000). Historical and theoretical perspectives in language policy and planning. *Journal of Sociolinguistics* 4(2), 196–213.

Ricento, T., & Hornberger, N. H. (1996). Unpeeling the onion: Language planning and policy and the ELT professional. *TESOL Quarterly* 30(3), 401–427.

Rickford, J. R. (1999). The Ebonics controversy in my backyard: A sociolinguist's experiences and reflections. *Journal of Sociolinguistics* 3(2), 267–275.

Rubin, J., & Jernudd, B. H. (Eds.). (1971). *Can language be planned? Sociolinguistic theory and practice for developing nations*. Honolulu: University Press of Hawaii.

Rubin, J., Jernudd, B. H., Das Gupta, J., Fishman, J. A., & Ferguson, C. A. (Eds.). (1977). *Language planning processes*. The Hague: Mouton.

Ruiz, R. (1984). Orientations in language planning. *NABE Journal* 8(2), 15–34.

Sacks, H., Schegloff, E. A., & Jefferson, G. (1974). A simplest systematics for the organization of Turn-taking for conversation. *Language* 50, 696–735.

Sapir, E. (1921). *Language: An introduction to the study of speech*. New York: Harcourt, Brace.

Sapir, E. (1929). The status of linguistics as a science. *Language* 5(4), 207–214.

Schutz, A. (2004). Rethinking domination and resistance: Challenging postmodernism. *Educational Researcher* 33(1), 15–23.

Shohamy, E., & Gorter, D. (Eds.) (2009). *Linguistic landscape: Expanding the scenery*. New York; London: Routledge.

Sonntag, S. (2009). Linguistic globalization and the call center industry: Imperialism, hegemony or cosmopolitanism? *Language Policy* 8, 5–25.

Spolsky, B. (2004). *Language policy.* Cambridge: Cambridge University Press.

St. Pierre, E. A. (2000). The call for intelligibility in postmodern educational research. *Educational Researcher* 29(5), 25–28.

Tauli, V. (1974). The theory of language planning. In J. Fishman (Ed.), *Advances in language planning* (pp. 69–78). The Hague: De Gruyter Mouton.

Tollefson, J. W. (1991). *Planning language, planning inequality: Language policy in the community.* London: Longman.

Tollefson, J. W. (2002). Introduction: Critical issues in educational language policy. In J. W. Tollefson (Ed.), *Language policies in education: Critical issues* (pp. 3–15). New York: Routledge.

Tollefson, J. W. (2006). Critical theory in language policy. In T. Ricento (Ed.), *An introduction to language policy: Theory and method* (pp. 42–59). Malden, MA: Blackwell.

Tollefson, J. W. (2012). Language policy in a time of crisis and transformation. In J. W. Tollefson (Ed.), *Language policies in education: Critical issues* (2nd edition; pp. 11–32). London; New York: Routledge.

Tollefson, J. W. (2015). Historical-structural analysis. In F. M. Hult & D. C. Johnson (Eds.), *Research methods in language policy and planning: A practical guide* (pp. 21–32). Malden, MA: Wiley-Blackwell.

Wiley, T. G. (1999). Comparative historical analysis of U.S. language policy and language planning: Extending the foundations. In T. Huebner & K. A. Davis (Eds.), *Sociopolitical perspectives on language policy and planning in the USA* (pp. 17–37). Amsterdam; Philadelphia: John Benjamins.

Wiley, T. G., & Wright, W. E. (2004). Against the undertow: Language-minority education policy and politics in the "age of accountability." *Educational Policy* 18(2), 142–168.

Wodak, R. (1996). *Disorders of discourse.* London: Longman.

Wortham, S. (2005). Socialization beyond the speech event. *Journal of Linguistic Anthropology* 5(1), 95–112.

Wortham, S., & Reyes, A. (2015). *Discourse analysis beyond the speech event.* New York: Routledge.

CHAPTER 4

THE CRITICAL ETHNOGRAPHIC TURN IN RESEARCH ON LANGUAGE POLICY AND PLANNING

MARILYN MARTIN-JONES AND ILDEGRADA DA COSTA CABRAL

THE critical ethnographic turn in language policy and planning (LPP) research is an intellectual movement that has unfolded and gathered strength over time, ever since the late 1980s and early 1990s. In this chapter, we begin by showing how different strands of ethnographic research contributed to this movement, bringing different ontological and epistemological perspectives into the frame and moving us beyond the divide between *micro* and *macro* levels of research that had characterised prior work in this field. We touch on several different strands of ethnographic research. These include ethnography of communication, critical sociolinguistic ethnography, linguistic anthropology (particularly research on language ideology), linguistic ethnography, and—the most recent development—the ethnography of language policy. Our focus will be on ethnographic research specifically related to language-in-education policymaking.

In the second section of the chapter, we consider the advantages that accrue from adopting critical ethnography as a research lens on language policy processes, arguing that it is particularly well tuned to the study of contemporary language policy processes. Following Wolcott (2008) and McCarty (2015), we weigh up the advantages of critical ethnography as a "way of seeing," as a "way of looking," and, for researchers, as a "way of being" in the field.

THE TRADITIONAL MACRO/MICRO DIVIDE IN EARLY SOCIOLINGUISTIC RESEARCH

For almost two decades, from the early 1960s onwards, there was a broad divide in sociolinguistic research that was being undertaken in multilingual contexts. On the one hand, there was macro-level research that was explicitly related to language policy and language planning; and, on the other hand, there was a distinct tradition of micro-level research of an interpretive and ethnographic nature that was being carried out in multilingual schools and classrooms where language policies were being translated into day-to-day educational practice.

The macro-level research related to language policy and language planning focused primarily on developments on a national or regional scale, and on the elite social actors involved in language status and corpus planning activities such as language selection, codification, implementation, and elaboration. Interest in this field of research was sparked by the language policy issues emerging in the new nations of the postcolonial era and in regions of existing nation-states where there were growing cultural and political movements around language rights and/or demands for particular forms of language education provision. Much of this early research was concerned with the forging of language policies, with the types of official documents and texts being produced, and with the nature and scope of the plans being developed as part of the top-down process of *implementation* of language policies. In the early years, this field of research was widely referred to (e.g., in university courses) as *language planning*, revealing, as Wiley (1999) has noted, a rather technocratic view of the role of research in relation to language policymaking. Moreover, much of the empirical work carried out in this period was based on positivist epistemology and involved the use of large-scale surveys (e.g., of language attitudes) and quantitative analysis of the data generated by such research methods. And, crucially, as several scholars have pointed out (e.g., Johnson, 2013; Ricento, 2000; Tollefson, 1991), little or no reference was made to the social and political contexts in which new language policies were being introduced.

The micro-level research taking shape at the time laid important foundations for future ethnographic research in educational settings where policy developments were having an impact. This research had its roots in the field of linguistic anthropology, notably in the work of Dell Hymes (e.g., 1972, 1974) and John Gumperz (1972, 1982). These scholars introduced significant new ontological and epistemological perspectives to the field of sociolinguistics. Gumperz and Hymes (1964, 1972) were the first to dislodge the view that local *communities* are stable, homogeneous entities and that language use is governed by community-wide norms. Instead, they argued that attention needed to be paid to the dynamic, diverse, and situated ways in which language practices contribute to the construction of social identities and relationships and to the ways in which social and cultural meanings are contextualised in and through interaction. In keeping with the social constructionist ideas that were circulating at the time (e.g., Berger & Luckman, 1966), Hymes and Gumperz approached language as a social and cultural practice rather than as a fixed entity, somehow separated from its speakers. This view of language in social life required a different approach to knowledge-building, one that focused on human interaction and meaning-making in the speech events and activities that occur in the day-to-day cycles of social life in different settings, in local life-worlds, and in institutional settings. In a landmark publication (Gumperz & Hymes, 1972), this approach came to be known as the *ethnography of communication.*

Over two decades, until the late 1980s, a considerable body of research in multilingual settings built on these foundations. This research provided detailed description and analysis of culturally distinct interactional practices and narrative styles, along with aspects of nonverbal communication (e.g., conventions around silence in conversational interaction). A good deal of this research was carried out in multilingual schools and classrooms and, in some cases, researchers worked across domains, following students from home to school. The contexts for this research included indigenous education programmes in North and South America (e.g., Hornberger, 1988; Phillips, 1983) and bilingual education programmes in the United States.

In his later work, Gumperz (1982, 1999) developed a more eclectic approach to the study of talk-in-interaction. This approach came to be known as *interactional sociolinguistics* and proved to be particularly influential in research conducted in multilingual schools and classrooms in the 1980s. It drew on ethnography but also on pragmatics, on conversation analysis, and on aspects of Erving Goffman's (1981) interaction analysis (particularly his use of the theatrical metaphor of *footing*). This later work by Gumperz provided particularly valuable analytic tools for the study of multilingual interaction, including the key notion of *contextualisation* (Gumperz, 1982). This enabled researchers to focus on the interpretive work that people do as they endeavour to assess the significance of the utterances of their interlocutors. According to Gumperz, contexualisation is made possible through the use of contextualisation cues, that is, any choice of verbal or nonverbal communicative resource that interlocutors recognise as *marked* in some way, or that depart from an expected pattern of communication. Such cues range from particular phonological, lexical, or stylistic choices or shifts between different genres of registers, within predominantly monolingual discourse, to the use and juxtapositioning of resources from different languages. Contextualisation cues also operate at the prosodic, paralinguistic, kinesic, or gestural level. They serve as the key means by which participants in a conversation (in institutional or life-world settings) negotiate their way through an interaction, making situated inferences about what is going on, signalling to interlocutors how their contributions are to be understood, and evaluating the contributions made by other participants.

In research in multilingual schools and classrooms, the study of the workings of conversational inferencing and the contextualisation of meanings, along with ethnography, generated new understandings of the ways in which teachers and students draw on the multiple verbal and nonverbal resources in their communicative repertoires in enacting the daily rituals of classroom life. For example, researchers were able to show how teachers and their students use resources from different languages to demarcate different kinds of classroom talk; to signal the transition between small talk before a lesson and the formal start of the lesson; to specify a particular addressee; to distinguish *doing the lesson* from talk about it; to change footing or make an aside; to distinguish talk about a text as opposed to reading it aloud; or to distinguish classroom management utterances from talk related to lesson content.

Although most of the research that was taking place, from the 1960s to the 1980s, in multilingual classrooms had been shaped in some way by language policy or by the introduction of new kinds of language-in-education programmes or curricula, the focus remained largely on the micro-level of teacher-student interaction (or student-student interaction). There was virtually no dialogue with researchers investigating language policy processes at the macro-level. Taking a retrospective look at this broad divide between macro-level and micro-level research in the sociolinguistics of the time, Blommaert (2007, p. 3) notes that the "connections between such levels" were often seen as "complex, difficult and unfathomable."

However, Gumperz's (1982) notion of contextualisation did offer an early glimpse into how one might capture the ways in which speakers orient to social worlds and space/times beyond the immediate moment of interaction. He saw the aim of the analysis of discourse-in-interaction as being to forge a "closer understanding of how linguistic signs interact with social knowledge in discourse" (Gumperz, 1982, p. 29). He also moved the field away from what Drew and Heritage (1992, p. 19) have called the "bucket" view of context. Context was now seen as interactively accomplished, and speakers were portrayed as having agency and the capacity to redefine or reshape the nature of an interaction, while not being entirely unfettered. In this later work, Gumperz argued that ethnographic and discourse analytic research on interaction needed to move towards "a dynamic view of social environments where history, economic forces and interactive process . . . combine to create or eliminate social distinctions" (1982, p. 29).

Moving Beyond the Macro/Micro Divide: The Development of Critical and Poststructuralist Perspectives

By the end of the 1980s, the attention of scholars concerned with different aspects of language in social life had turned to the ontological and epistemological spaces opened up by developments in social theory, notably the turn towards post-structuralist thought and critical theory (e.g., Bourdieu, 1977; Foucault, 1972; Habermas, 1979). The turn towards the incorporation of critical and poststructualist perspectives in sociolinguistics and applied linguistics took place in different ways in the two strands of research related to language policy and language practice that we have discussed so far.

In the macro-level research on language policy and planning, critical approaches were first put forward in the 1990s (e.g., Canagarajah, 1999; Phillipson, 1992; Tollefson, 1991). In a significant new move, Tollefson (1991, p. 32) proposed a historical-structural approach to language policy research, defining its aims as follows: "The major goal of policy research is to examine the historical basis of policies and to make explicit the mechanisms by which policy decisions serve or undermine particular political and economic interests." Tollefson (1991, 2002) also drew attention to the role of ideology in naturalising language practices that are linked to language policy developments, in particular, in institutional contexts such as education. Tollefson's (1991) critical approach to language policy research is widely acknowledged as constituting a major step-change in the development of the field. His choice of critical theory as a basis for theory-building shows what Pennycook (2001, p. 6) has called "a compassion grounded in a sharp critique of inequality."

At this early stage of the turn to critical, poststructuralist approaches, language policy studies retained the focus on policy processes at the level of the nation-state, foregrounding the ways in which language policymaking was bound up with asymmetries of power within specific polities. A decade later, the influence of Foucauldian thought was evident in some research related to language policy. For example, Pennycook (2002) adopted Foucault's (1991) notion of *governmentality* in a detailed historical analysis of colonial language policy in Hong Kong. Building on Foucault's view of the ways in which hegemony percolates through discourse and how particular ways of speaking and forms of action come to be construed as natural, he characterised the workings of governmentality as follows: "The notion of governmentality focuses on how power operates at the micro-level of diverse practices, rather than the macro regulation of the state. Indeed, in the notion of governmentality, these micro- and macro- relations are elided" (Pennycook, 2002, pp. 91–92).

In the early 1990s, critical approaches to ethnography were also being developed across the social sciences, as poststructuralist and critical perspectives were adopted. Commenting on these developments, May (1997, p. 197) noted that "critical ethnography adopts a perspective on social and cultural relations which highlights the role of ideology in sustaining and perpetuating inequality within particular settings." A significant number of early critical ethnographic studies in sociology and anthropology were based in educational settings and drew attention to the lived experience of schooling among working-class and minority students. Research with a focus on the role of language in the construction of social inequalities was to come later.

Critical, poststructuralist perspectives were incorporated into micro-level research in multilingual schools and classrooms in the mid-1990s, as the scope of ethnography in these research sites began to change. Starting out from classroom settings and from the interactional routines of classroom life, researchers began to seek ways of linking their detailed accounts of the interactional order of particular classrooms with an analysis of wider social and ideological processes operating at different levels of policymaking, in particular historical contexts. The goal was to provide more explanatory accounts of the day-to-day routines observed in different schools and classrooms, and to show why they were the way they were. Critical ethnographic approaches to multilingual classroom interaction were first developed by two groups of researchers: those working with teachers and learners in postcolonial contexts (e.g., Arthur, 1996; Canagarajah, 1993; Lin, 1996; Martin, 1999) and those working with linguistic minorities (e.g., Heller, 1999; Jaffe, 1999; Martin-Jones & Saxena, 1996). These researchers developed critical ethnographic approaches by drawing on different strands of social theory. Monica Heller (1999) pioneered this approach to theory-building. Drawing on ten years of ethnographic and discourse analytic research in French-language minority schools in Ontario, Canada, she developed the approach that has come to be known as critical sociolinguistic ethnography. Her main theory-building strategy was to focus on two main ways in which schools operate as institutions linked to the state: first, the ways in which schools serve as spaces within which specific language varieties (designated as national, official languages) and specific linguistic practices (ways of speaking, reading, and writing) come to be inculcated with legitimacy and authority; and second, the ways in which schools function as spaces for selecting and categorising students, for assessing performance (including linguistic performance) and providing credentials that are ultimately tied to positioning within the world of work.

The work of Bourdieu (1991) proved to be of particular relevance in pursuing these lines of theory-building, particularly his notion of *legitimate language*. Bourdieu has

provided one of the most comprehensively theorised accounts of the processes involved in the (re)production of legitimate language and of the role of schooling in
this process. Nevertheless, there are some weaknesses in Bourdieu's model of cultural reproduction. These lie in his primary focus on symbolic domination and in the
bleakness of his vision. For Bourdieu, symbolic power saturates consciousness and
remains uncontested. However, as researchers working in a critical ethnographic
vein have argued (and shown empirically), the imposition of language-in-education
policies in schools and classrooms is primarily accomplished in and through interaction. The institutional order is always indeterminate, since it is interactionally
constructed. Drawing on Giddens's theory of structuration (1984), and on Cicourel's
(1973, 1980) work on the social distribution of knowledge within institutions, Heller
(1999, 2007a) has stressed that there are always possibilities for exercising agency
and for challenging and even modifying the institutional and social order. At
the same time, it is clearly not possible to argue that the practices of teachers and
learners in schools are completely unconstrained. It is necessary to see them as being
socially positioned and, at the same time, showing agency, navigating constraints,
and actively responding to the possibilities open to them in particular school and
classroom sites.

Methodologically speaking, the core focus of this critical and ethnographic research was the interactional order of particular schools and classrooms, in particular
sociolinguistic settings. This generally involved observation and audio recording of
multilingual classroom talk, the writing of field notes, and ethnographic interviews
with participants in the research. Beyond the classroom, the ethnographic work led
these researchers to other social spaces within schools (e.g., to staff rooms, school
assemblies, and/or meetings), to other local institutional settings where language
policy and curriculum issues were addressed (e.g., in-service teacher education
sessions or meetings in local administrative offices), or even to national institutions
such as ministries of education. Visits to local and national institutions gave access
to administrators and policymakers who had been close to the process of drafting
policy and curriculum documents. The gathering of actual policy documents
and historical records took place during such visits or involved a combination of
Internet-based research and archival work.

Research of a critical sociolinguistic ethnographic nature continued into the
twenty-first century (see, e.g., Arthur Shoba & Chimbutane, 2013; Heller & Martin-
Jones, 2001; Jaffe, 2011; Lin & Martin, 2005; Martín Rojo, 2010; Pérez-Milans,
2013) and is still being consolidated and extended today. Research in the interac-
tionist tradition has also continued, with a widening of the scope of the ethnographic
work. However, as Pérez-Milans (2013, p. 31) has recently observed, what makes
critical sociolinguistic ethnography ontologically distinct from other approaches
that have been developed in socio-, applied, and educational linguistics is that it
"understands agency and social structure as mutually constitutive beyond the often-
so-called micro/macro dichotomy."

Critical ethnographic and sociolinguistic research was further strengthened in the late 1990s, with the development of significant theory-building related to language ideology in the field of linguistic anthropology (e.g., Blommaert, 1999; Schieffelin et al., 1998). This research addressed the central question of "how linguistic units came to be linked to social units" (Gal & Irvine, 1995, p. 970), how particular language resources and ways of speaking came to be associated with simplified and essentialised social categories (e.g., categories of ethnicity or gender), or how languages came to be tied to entire populations within a particular polity. This strand of work in linguistic anthropology provided a trenchant critique of grand narratives and modernist assumptions about the links between languages and particular social groups, or between entire populations and nation-states. In its critique of the language-nation-state nexus, it had a significant historical dimension and involved tracing the discursive threads involved in the construction of nationhood in primarily unitary and essentialised terms, in different historical contexts: for example, in nineteenth-century Europe (e.g., Heller, 2007b), in the language revitalisation and minority rights movements of the twentieth century (e.g., Jaffe, 1999), and in postcolonial contexts (e.g., Errington, 2008; Stroud, 2007). As Heller (2007b, p. 15) has put it, the development of this line of enquiry has foregrounded "the discourses in which processes of attribution and value to linguistic forms and practices are inscribed, along with the processes of construction of social difference and social inequality with which they are associated." She has thus proposed a reorientation of ethnographic research to a "new understanding" of multilingualism "as ideology and practice" (2007b, p. 1).

THE DEVELOPMENT OF THE CRITICAL ETHNOGRAPHY OF LANGUAGE POLICY

As we indicated earlier, from the 1960s to the 1980s, there was very little dialogue between researchers working on language planning and policy and those engaged in ethnographic and discourse-analytic research on multilingual classroom interaction. Ricento and Hornberger (1996) addressed this lack of articulation between these fields of study in a review of the state of the art in language policy research in the mid-1990s. They acknowledged the significant advances made through the development of the historical-structural and critical approaches to the study of policymaking, especially the turn towards revealing the ideological underpinning of policies. At the same time, they argued that more attention should be given to the different "agents, levels and processes" (1996, p. 408) involved in language planning and policy, and they introduced the now-familiar onion metaphor as a way of representing the multilayered nature of language policy processes.

A decade later, Hornberger and Johnson (2007) put ethnography firmly on the language policy research agenda. They argued that researchers need to go beyond studies that focus only on the global, national, and institutional dimension of policymaking and on the political and ideological processes driving language education policies. As they put it, "an (over)emphasis on the hegemonic power of policies obfuscates the potentially agentive role of local educators as they interpret and implement the policies" (2007, p. 510). They also returned to the onion metaphor and called for "multilayered" ethnographic research on language planning and policy and for "slicing the onion ethnographically" (2007, p. 509). They demonstrated, in compelling detail, why the study of language policy on paper (e.g., critical discourse analysis of policy documents) and analysis of the historical and ideological processes underpinning the creation of policies need to be combined with ethnography to avoid giving only a partial account of the ways in which policymaking unfolds. As they put it,

> An ethnography of language policy can include textual and historical analyses of policy texts but must be based in an ethnographic understanding of some local context. The texts are nothing without the human agents who act as interpretive conduits between the language policy levels (or layers of the LPP onion). (Hornberger & Johnson, 2007, p. 528)

Taking this argument further, in a later article, Johnson (2009) proposed an alternative way of conceptualising the process of policy implementation. Building on anthropological and sociological research on educational policy, he noted that

> [t]raditional divisions between policy formation and implementation implicitly ratify a top-down perspective by characterizing those in power as legislating directives that are implemented by practitioners. Instead, "policy" is a dynamic process that stretches across time, and implementation or "appropriation" is not just what happens after policy is made—it is a link in a chain of policy process in which all actors potentially have input. (Johnson, 2009, p. 142)

Instead of employing the term *implementation*, Johnson (2009) proposed that we should view language policy as "a set of processes—creation, interpretation and appropriation" (2009, p. 141). The emphasis on interpretation here is important, and appropriation is not taken to mean merely acceptance or compliance; it can also involve adaptation, recasting, or contestation of a policy. These landmark contributions by Hornberger and Johnson (2007) and Johnson (2009), and subsequent contributions by Johnson (2009, 2013), Hult and Johnson (2015), and McCarty (2011) have opened up crucial conceptual terrain at the interface with critical and ethnographic research on discourse-in-interaction in multilingual schools and classrooms.

CRITICAL ETHNOGRAPHY AS A LENS ON LANGUAGE POLICY PROCESSES

Having traced, in the preceding sections, the genealogy of critical ethnographic approaches to language policymaking, we turn now to a discussion of the particular advantages that flow from the adoption of such approaches, in different multilingual settings. We argue that critical ethnography provides a particularly appropriate research lens on contemporary processes of language-in-education policymaking. As McCarty (2015, p. 81) has recently reminded us, ethnography has its roots in anthropological ways of knowing and anthropological ways of gathering and interpreting evidence. Drawing on the work of educational anthropologist Harry Wolcott (2008), McCarty refers to ethnography as "a way of seeing" and as a "way of looking, based on long-term, first-hand fieldwork" (2015, p. 81). In addition, alluding to the work of Dell Hymes (1980) on "ethnographic monitoring" and to the ethical and political nature of the researcher/researched relationship, she adds that ethnography involves "social inquiry that is humanizing, democratizing and anti-hegemonic . . . what one might call 'a way of being' a researcher" (2015, p. 81). In this section of our chapter, we consider the benefits that accrue from adopting a critical ethnographic approach to language-in-education policy from each of these three perspectives. Extending yet further McCarty's (2015) characterisation of the three dimensions of ethnography, we take *way of seeing* as referring to its ontological basis; we take *way of looking* as referring to its epistemological and methodological basis; and we take *way of being* as referring to the ethics and politics of research and to the potential role of ethnographic researchers in contributing to social change.

Critical Ethnography as a Way of Seeing

Contemporary ethnographic research on language policymaking is rooted in a view of language as a verb (as languaging) and as a means of acting within social and institutional worlds. Adopting this ontological stance, this way of seeing means acknowledging the agentive role of speakers in contributing, in situated ways, to the construction of social life and to the building of social relationships. As we showed earlier, this way of seeing the relationship between language and social life, with its focus on human interaction and meaning-making, dates back to early work by Gumperz and Hymes (1964) on the ethnography of communication. It is ontologically quite distinct from the early structural functional research on language planning (1960s–1980s) in which language and society were seen as separate entities and in which languages were characterised as fixed and bounded objects.

In contemporary ethnographic research of a critical, poststructuralist nature, a third research lens has been developed: one that is more powerful and that allows us to see the interplay between, on the one hand, the locally situated language practices of particular social actors, in particular social spaces and at particular points in time, and, on the other hand, dominant discourses, ideologies, and conventionalised social and institutional structures. Pérez-Milans (2013, p. 31) summarises as follows the ontological assumptions underpinning research in critical sociolinguistic ethnography:

1. Social life is discursively constructed by people (including the researcher) who are considered as social agents interacting across space and time.

2. Conventional structures configure but also constrain interactions.

3. Daily interactions can also reshape conventions, often fleetingly but sometimes in more enduring ways.

4. Social agents do not interact with each other in a context of equal relations, but within economic and political forms of organisation in which symbolic and material resources are unequally (re)produced and distributed.

5. The interplay between agency, structure, constraint, and change opens up a window for analysing the operation of relations of power.

Pérez-Milans's (2013) account builds on and extends an earlier formulation, by Rampton (2006), of the assumptions underpinning analysis of social interaction. Pérez-Milans's addition is seen in the fourth point in the preceding list. This widens the ontological base of ethnography to include shedding light on the ways in which discourses, ideologies, language practices, and social interaction contribute to the (re)production of social inequalities, in keeping with the critical tradition of sociolinguistic research.

Similar assumptions have guided the development of critical approaches to research in a related field: that of the study of educational policymaking that has been developed within the anthropology of education. For instance, in an early volume entitled *Policy as Practice*, Levinson and Sutton (2001, p. 1) argued that policymaking needs to be reconceptualised as "a complex social practice, as an ongoing process of normative cultural production." In later work with a colleague, the same authors also characterised educational policymaking as "a practice of power" (Levinson et al., 2009). The specific strand of critical research on the ethnography of language policy, which we discussed earlier, echoes this broad ontological turn in policy-related research in the anthropology of education, and we see ample cross-referencing between the two fields.

Critical Ethnography as a Way of Looking

The ways of seeing, described in the preceding section, shape the epistemological decisions that ethnographers make as their research unfolds. It shapes the ways in which they develop approaches to the empirical investigation of social and institutional processes and forms of human interaction within the world of education. So, critical ethnography is also a distinctive *way of looking.* As Canagarajah (2006) has observed, ethnography is particularly well-suited to the study of the ways in which educational practitioners and students in local educational settings (schools, colleges, or universities) interpret, appropriate, negotiate, recast, or contest language-in-education policies.

First and foremost, it involves commitment to participant observation and to building an account of social and linguistic practices as they naturally occur. It involves engagement with research participants over an extended period of time and commitment to building an understanding of the beliefs and values of research participants, moving from the researcher's etic perspective to an emic perspective,[1] with a view to gaining insights into their perceptions of the significance of the language policy processes at work in their particular educational setting.

Secondly, some ethnographic work involves building an account of the life trajectories of particular research participants (e.g., teachers, students, or educational administrators), the ways in which different language and literacy resources and language ideologies have traversed these trajectories, and the ways in which the trajectories of research participants are embedded in wider historical and ideological processes. This enables researchers to place the observations they make at one point in time within a much broader picture of sociolinguistic change in particular policy contexts, taking account of the social and linguistic consequences for different social actors.

Thirdly, critical ethnographic research is typically multi-scalar in nature, so it is able to take account of policy processes at work in different social spaces, on different scales, from local to global. The notion of *scale* and a commitment to the interrogation of the links between scales are central to this epistemological orientation to the study of language policy processes.

As Blommaert (2007, p. 4) points out, "scales offer us a vertical image of [social] space, of space as stratified, and therefore power-invested, but they also suggest deep connections between spatial and temporal features." While the gaze of researchers might be directed to a particular social event occurring at one moment of time, in one particular space, they need to take into account any references that speakers make to other spaces and other times, on different scales, within a broader social order. This provides glimpses into the ways in which speakers perceive the connections between scales. This pointing to other social spaces and time periods has come to be known as indexicality (Silverstein, 2003). As Blommaert (2007, p. 4) puts it, "the connections between ... scales is indexical." Indexicality is similar to Gumperz's (1982) concept of contextualisation, mentioned earlier, though, as Rampton et al. (2015, p. 24) observe, the notion of indexicality "shifts the focus from sense-making to the utterances, things and actions that are treated as signs, and it refers to the fact that these signs are always taken as pointing beyond themselves, to something else in the past, the future or the surrounding environment." (For further discussion of multi-scalar approaches, see Hult 2010, 2015.)

Some projects start from the close study of language policy processes *on the ground* (e.g., in local schools or classrooms) and then move on to investigation of policy processes on other scales, depending on the time and resources available to the researcher. This could involve the tracking of the social, political, and ideological processes involved in policy creation, through direct observation, interviews with key social actors, or archival research. It could also involve the analysis of policy discourses and the intertextuality of different documents associated with policy creation (e.g., declarations, speeches, laws, articles in a national constitution, or a joint statement by two governments involved in bilateral cooperation). In addition, it could involve building an account of the institutional trajectories and networks through which these documents circulate, along with the discourses associated with them. Crucially, it could also involve an analysis of how actors who are positioned at different points within these trajectories and networks (e.g., in schools, in teacher education programmes, or in regional government) interpret these discourses and make institutional decisions on the basis of their interpretations. As Hult (2015, p. 222) notes, "[f]ocusing analytically on any particular scale is not about making a micro-macro distinction, but about considering a social action and the scope of its impact."

Some recent research in Global South contexts (e.g., Chimbutane, 2013; da Costa Cabral, 2015) has opened up important new perspectives in ethnography of language-in-education policy by combining detailed analysis of multilingual interaction in local classrooms, and extended engagement with educational practitioners, with the investigation of policy processes at work on scales that have not hitherto been investigated (i.e., not the usual scales of school administration or regional or national government policymaking). For example, Chimbutane (2011, 2013) has demonstrated the significant role played by nongovernmental organisations (NGOs) in the expansion of bilingual education programmes in Mozambique and even in the mobilisation of public support for these programmes. The programmes involve the use of both Portuguese (the national official language) and local African languages. Chimbutane (2013) notes that this NGO-led movement contrasts with the failure of the national government to create adequate conditions for the development of bilingual education, despite a constitutional commitment to support African languages that was made in 1990. However, he warns against extensive reliance on "donor-dependent NGOs" because of their vulnerability to changes in external sources of funding.

Ildegrada da Costa Cabral (2015) has revealed some of the key challenges facing primary school teachers in Timor-Leste, as they put into practice, on a day-to-day basis, the relatively new national language-in-education policy of employing both Portuguese and Tetum (the main lingua franca in the country) as languages of teaching and learning (LoTLs). Both languages also have the status of national official languages. The adoption of the policy of using both languages for all stages of basic education in Timor-Leste has been a bold move. One of the national curriculum objectives is "the development of the two languages at the same time in a process of mutual enrichment" (MECYS, 2004, p. 8). However, as da Costa Cabral shows through her detailed analysis of bilingual classroom talk, one impediment to the task of translating this vision into practice is that the textbooks are only in Portuguese. A significant proportion of classroom time is devoted to teacher mediation of both the language and the content of these textbooks, moving back and forth between Portuguese and Tetum. Some of the textbook content refers to life in other nations in Africa where Portuguese is an official language and is thus unfamiliar to the teachers as well as the students. On further investigation, da Costa Cabral has found that the textbooks are produced in Portugal by a team of Portuguese and East-Timorese authors for use in Timor-Leste, and the main coordinator of the team is based at a Portuguese university. Da Costa Cabral's research thus took her to a global scale as she built her account of how support for the rolling out of the national policy of reintroducing Portuguese as an LoTL is being provided. This is support that was generated as a result of a bilateral agreement between the national government of Timor-Leste and the Portuguese government.

Fourthly, as a way of looking and building knowledge, critical ethnography is embracing increasing methodological diversity. The design and conduct of critical ethnographic research often involves drawing on analytic approaches that are rooted in different research traditions in sociolinguistics or anthropology. There is already a well-established practice within ethnography of integrating different approaches to data collection and data analysis and of triangulating insights from different data sources, so drawing on different approaches to data analysis simply represents an extension of this practice. Thus far, critical ethnography has been combined with interactional sociolinguistics (as described earlier), with the New Literacy Studies (NLS) and the study of talk around texts (e.g. Martin, 1999; Martin-Jones, 2011), with critical discourse analysis (CDA) (e.g., Johnson, 2009), with both CDA and interactional sociolinguistics (e.g., Pérez-Milans, 2013), and with multimodal analysis and the study of changing schoolscapes (e.g., Laihonen & Tódor, 2015).

Last, but not least, critical ethnography is characterised by increasing researcher reflexivity. One development that has strengthened critical ethnographic approaches to language policy processes has been the turn, across the social sciences, to greater reflexivity in the design and conduct of research projects. This turn has taken place in response to the critique by scholars such as Marcus and Fischer (1986), Clifford and Marcus (1986), and Van Maanen (1988) of the long-established practices associated with ethnographic fieldwork and with the writing of research narratives. Researchers engaged in critical ethnographic research on language policy processes now have a keener awareness of the ways in which their own historically and so-cially situated subjectivity shapes different stages of the research process, especially when they are working closely with educational practitioners and students in local schools and classrooms. They are more aware of how their own subjectivity comes into play in the building of relationships in the field, in the production and use of fieldwork texts (e.g., field notes, vignettes, diaries, or transcripts) and in the writing up of the final research narrative. Heightened reflexivity about the building of field-work texts has led to considerable methodological innovation, to the design of more dialogic approaches to fieldwork, and to acknowledgement of what can be achieved through reflection on specific aspects of multilingual research practice. Such reflec-tion enables researchers to gauge the nature of the relationships they are building in the field, to make more visible the complex multilingual dynamics of fieldwork, and to create conditions for building fuller, polyphonic ethnographies. (For discussion of reflexivity in multilingual research practice, see Chimbutane, 2012; Creese et al. 2015; Martin-Jones et al., 2017).

Reflexivity and methodological innovation have been particularly evident in a rel-atively new strand of ethnographic research related to language in social life. This has come to be known as linguistic ethnography. It originated in the United Kingdom as a Special Interest Group (SiG) of the British Association for Applied Linguistics, but it has now become an extended transnational network of researchers. (For a ge-nealogy of this particular strand of ethnographic work on language in social life, and for examples of recent contributions, see Blackledge & Creese, 2010; Copland & Creese, 2015; Creese, 2010; Rampton, 2007; Rampton et al., 2004; Rampton et al., 2015; Tusting & Maybin, 2007). Partly due to its origins in applied linguistics, this strand of research has been strongly oriented to the building of close relationships with research participants, to reflexive practice, to working "from the inside out-wards," and "trying to get analytic distance on what's close to hand" (Rampton, 2007, pp. 590–591). Linguistic ethnography is thus strongly "topic-oriented," in Hymes's (1996, p. 5) original sense, and a good deal of work has been oriented to the study of language policy and practice within institutional settings that are familiar to the re-searcher (e.g., in mainstream and complementary schools, and in workplaces) and to working for social change. There is also a significant element of transdisciplinarity in this strand of ethnographic work, which has been one source for the methodolog-ical innovation.

Critical Ethnography as a Way of Being as a Researcher

Researchers engaged in critical ethnographic work related to language-in-education policy have, from the outset, expressed concern about the role that they might play in relation to educational and social change, especially when, as a result of engage-ment over time with research participants, they become aware of the ways in which particular language-in-education practices and ideologies are contributing to the construction of social inequalities. This concern about the role of the researcher was already a recurring theme in the work of Dell Hymes. In the late 1970s and early 1980s, he put forward the idea of "ethnographic monitoring" (Hymes, 1980). He did this in the context of wider interdisciplinary discussions relating to research on bilingual education in the United States. This was a time when the educational entitlements of children from linguistic minority groups were being addressed and when broader processes of change were taking place through the introduction of bilingual educa- tion programmes within the public education system. However, it was also a time when the evaluation of educational programmes was dominated by positivist models of social science and where programme outcomes were defined in primarily quanti- tative terms. Within this broader institutional and epistemological context, Hymes's proposal for ethnographic monitoring was a radical departure from the dominant tradition in educational research. Hymes argued that an ethnographic approach was essential to the investigation of a far-reaching process of change such as the intro- duction of bilingual education programmes. He pointed out that the participants in these new educational programmes were not mere "bystanders" but had "the finest possible grasp of the workings of the programs" (1980, p. 115). For these reasons, he made the case for engaging in "cooperative ethnographic monitoring" with participants, and for undertaking joint knowledge-building.

The concern about the role of the researcher with regard to social change sur- faced again in the early 1990s, with the first moves towards critical language policy research. May (1997, p. 197) characterised critical ethnography as "simultane- ously hermeneutic and emancipatory." Other researchers have confirmed and ex- tended this view (e.g., Johnson, 2013; Pennycook, 2001; Tollefson, 2002), arguing that the term *critical* signals several interconnected goals for research: first, that of shedding light on the ways in which language practices, discourses, and ideologies contribute to the reproduction of power asymmetries; secondly, that of critiquing previous technocratic approaches to language policy research that took little or no account of the social and political context of policymaking; thirdly, that of drawing on critical, poststructuralist perspectives on language in social life, including lan- guage policymaking; and last, but not least, that of challenging dominant policy discourses and the ideologies underpinning them, by raising awareness about them and working towards what Pennycook (2001, p. 8) calls "preferred futures."

There is still ongoing debate about how ethnographic research on language policy can move towards this last goal. Some researchers have exemplified the contempo- rary relevance of Hymes's notion of "ethnographic monitoring" (e.g., De Korne & Hornberger, 2017; Hornberger, 2009; Van der Aa & Blommaert, 2011, 2017). Other researchers have argued that educational practitioners should play a prominent role in language-in-education policy research on the ground (e.g., Menken & García, 2010). Extending the onion metaphor, Menken and García (2010, p. 259) have called for close engagement and collaboration between researchers and educational practitioners as "stirrers of the onion, producing the dynamism that moves the per-formance of all the actors." Yet others have called for the rethinking of the design of research on language-in-education policy so as to facilitate this kind of researcher-practitioner collaboration. Johnson (2013) envisages a type of action research that he calls Educational Language Policy Engagement and Action Research (ELPEAR). This would involve "collaboration between language policy agents from multiple levels of institutional authority doing research on educational language policies and programs, together with outside researchers" (2013, pp. 170–188). Johnson anticipates that the scope of this collaboration would include all aspects of the lan-guage policy cycle: policy creation, interpretation, and appropriation.

We expect that, in the future, there will continue to be active exploration of the ways in which collaboration between researchers and educational practitioners can be developed and consolidated, along some of the lines described in this chapter. "Cooperative ethnographic monitoring," extended researcher-practitioner engage-ment, or ELPEAR-style action research could also be incorporated into initial and in-service teacher education, as a means of fostering reflexive practice and bringing about change. Such initiatives would create significant new "epistemological circles of activity" (Van de Aa & Blommaert, 2017), away from the academy, and, as Hymes (1980) has observed, it would bring knowledge-building about language policy-making "under democratic control."

NOTE

1. A caveat is, of course, needed here since the relationships established during fieldwork are more complex than implied in the simple dichotomies between etic and emic perspectives or between outsider and insider knowledge. They also change over time. (For further discussion of this issue see, for example, McCarty, 2015, pp. 81, 84; and Martin-Jones et al., 2017).

REFERENCES

Arthur, J. (1996). Codeswitching and collusion: Classroom interaction in Botswana primary schools. *Linguistics and Education* 8(1), 17–34.

Arthur Shoba, J., & Chimbutane, F. (Eds.). (2013). *Bilingual education and language policy in the global south.* New York: Routledge.

Berger, P., & Luckman, T. (1966). *The social construction of reality.* Harmondsworth, UK: Penguin.

Blackledge, A., & Creese, A. (2010). *Multilingualism: A critical perspective.* London: Continuum.

Blommaert, J. (Ed.). (1999). *Language ideological debates.* Berlin: Mouton de Gruyter.

Blommaert, J. (2007). On scope and depth in linguistic ethnography. *Journal of Sociolinguistics* 11(5), 682–688.

Bourdieu, P. (1977). *Outline of a theory of practice.* Cambridge: Cambridge University Press.

Bourdieu, P. (1991). *Language and symbolic power.* Cambridge, MA: Harvard University Press.

Canagarajah, A. S. (1993). Critical ethnography of a Sri Lankan classroom: Ambiguities in student opposition to reproduction through ESOL. *TESOL Quarterly* 27(4), 601–626.

Canagarajah, A. S. (1999). *Resisting linguistic imperialism in English teaching.* Oxford: Oxford University Press.

Canagarajah, S. (2006). Ethnographic methods in language policy. In T. Ricento (Ed.), *An introduction to language policy: Theory and method* (pp. 153–169). Oxford: Blackwell.

Chimbutane, F. (2011). *Rethinking bilingual education in postcolonial contexts.* Bristol, UK: Multilingual Matters.

Chimbutane, F. (2012). The advantages of research in familiar locales, viewed from the perspective of the researched: Reflections on ethnographic fieldwork in Mozambique. In S. Gardner & M. Martin-Jones (Eds.), *Multilingualism, discourse and ethnography* (pp. 288–304). New York: Routledge.

Chimbutane, F. (2013). Can sociocultural gains sustain bilingual education programs in postcolonial contexts? The case of Mozambique. In J. Arthur Shoba & F. Chimbutane (Eds.), *Bilingual education and language policy in the global south* (pp. 124–145). New York: Routledge.

Cicourel, A. (1973). *Cognitive sociology: Language and meaning in social interaction.* London: Penguin.

Cicourel, A. (1980). Three models of discourse analysis: The role of social structure. *Discourse Processes* 33, 101–132.

Clifford, M., & Marcus, G. E. (1986). *Writing culture: The poetics and politics of ethnography.* Berkeley: University of California Press.

Copland, F., & Creese, A. (with F. Rock & S. Shaw). (2015). *Linguistic ethnography.* London: Sage.

Creese, A. (2010). Linguistic ethnography. In L. Litosseliti (Ed.), *Research methods in linguistics* (pp. 138–154). London: Continuum.

Creese, A., Takhi, J., & Blackledge, A. (2015). Metacommentary in linguistic ethnography. In In J. Snell, S. Shaw, & F. Copland (Eds.), *Linguistic ethnography: Interdisciplinary explorations* (pp. 266–284). Bagingstoke, UK: Palgrave Macmillan.

da Costa Cabral, I. (2015). *Multilingual talk, classroom textbooks and language values: A linguistic ethnographic study in Timor-Leste.* Unpublished PhD thesis, University of Birmingham, UK.

De Korne, H., & Hornberger, N. H. (2017). Countering unequal multilingualism through ethnographic monitoring. In M. Martin-Jones & D. Martin (Eds.), *Researching multilingualism: Critical and ethnographic perspectives* (pp. 247–258). Abingdon, UK: Routledge.

Drew, P., & Heritage, J. (1992). Analyzing talk at work: An introduction. In P. Drew & J. Heritage (Eds.), *Talk at work* (pp. 3–65). Cambridge: Cambridge University Press.

Errington, J. J. (2008). *Linguistics in a colonial world: A story of language, meaning and power.* Oxford: Blackwell.

Foucault, M. (1972). *The archaeology of knowledge.* London: Tavistock Publications.

Foucault, M. (1991). Governmentality. In G. Burchell, C. Gordon, & P. Miller (Eds.), *The Foucault effect: Studies in governmentality* (pp. 87–104). Hemel Hemstead: Harvester Wheatsheaf.

Gal, S., & Irvine, J. (1995). The boundaries of languages and disciplines: How ideologies construct difference. *Social Research* 62(4), 96–101.

Giddens, A. (1984). *The constitution of society.* Cambridge: Polity Press.

Goffman, E. (1981). *Forms of talk.* Philadelphia: University of Pennsylvania Press.

Gumperz, J. J. (1972). Introduction. In J. J. Gumperz & D. Hymes (Eds.), *Directions in sociolinguistics: The ethnography of communication* (pp. 1–25). New York: Holt, Rinehart and Winston.

Gumperz, J. J. (1982). *Discourse strategies.* Cambridge: Cambridge University Press.

Gumperz, J. J. (1999). On interactional sociolinguistic method. In C. Roberts & S. Sarangi (Eds.), *Talk, work and institutional order* (pp. 453–471). Berlin: Mouton de Gruyter.

Gumperz, J. J., & Hymes, D. (Eds.). (1964). The ethnography of communication [Special issue]. *American Anthropologist* 60(6), part 2.

Gumperz, J. J., & Hymes, D. (Eds.). (1972). *Directions in sociolinguistics: The ethnography of communication.* New York: Holt, Rinehart and Winston.

Habermas, J. (1979). *Communication and the evolution of society.* London: Heinemann.

Heller, M. (1999). *Linguistic minorities and modernity,* London: Longman.

Heller, M. (2007a). Distributed knowledge, distributed power: A sociolinguistics of structuration. *Text & Talk* 27(5–6), 633–653.

Heller, M. (Ed.). (2007b). Bilingualism as ideology and practice. In M. Heller (Ed.), *Bilingualism: A social approach* (pp. 1–24). Basingstoke, UK: Palgrave Macmillan.

Heller, M., & Martin-Jones (Eds.). (2001). *Voices of authority: Education and linguistic difference.* Westport, CT: Ablex.

Hornberger, N. H. (1988). *Bilingual education and language maintenance.* Dordrecht: Foris Publications.

Hornberger, N. H. (2009). Hymes' linguistics and ethnography in education. *Text & Talk: An Interdisciplinary Journal of Language, Discourse and Communication Studies* 29(3), 347–358.

Hornberger, N. H., & Johnson, D. C. (2007). Slicing the onion ethnographically: Layers and spaces in multilingual language education. *TESOL Quarterly* 41(3), 509–532.

Hult, F. (2010). Analysis of language policy discourses across the scales of space and time. *International Journal of the Sociology of Language* 202, 7–24.

Hult, F. (2015). Making policy connections across scales using nexus analysis. In F. Hult & D. C. Johnson (Eds.), *Research methods in language policy and planning* (pp. 217–231). Malden, MA: John Wiley & Sons.

Hult, F., & Johnson, D. C. (Eds.). (2015). *Research methods in language policy and planning.* Malden, MA: John Wiley & Sons.

Hymes, D. (1972). Models of the interaction of language and social life. In J. J. Gumperz and D. Hymes (Eds.), *Directions in sociolinguistics: The ethnography of communication* (pp. 35–71). New York: Holt, Rinehart and Winston.

Hymes, D. (1974). *Foundations of sociolinguistics: An ethnographic approach.* Philadelphia: University of Pennsylvania Press.

Hymes, D. (1980). *Language in education: Ethnolinguistic essays.* Washington, DC: Centre for Applied Linguistics.

Hymes, D. (1996). *Ethnography, linguistics, narrative inequality: Towards an understanding of voice.* London: Taylor and Francis.

Jaffe, A. (1999). *Ideologies in action: Language politics on Corsica.* Berlin and New York: Mouton de Gruyter.

Jaffe, A. (2011). Critical perspectives on language-in-education policy: The Corsican example. In T. L. McCarty (Ed.), *Ethnography of language policy* (pp. 205–229). London; New York: Routledge.

Johnson, D. C. (2009). Ethnography of language policy. *Language Policy* 8, 139–159.

Johnson, D. C. (2013). *Language policy.* Basingstoke, UK: Palgrave Macmillan.

Laihonen, P., & Tódor, E.-M. (2015). The changing schoolscape in a Szekler village in Romania: Signs of diversity in "rehungarization." *International Journal of Bilingual Education and Bilingualism* 20(3), 362–379. Retrieved from http://dx.doi.org/10.1080/13670050.2015.1051943.

Levinson, B. A. U., & Sutton, M. (2001). Introduction: Policy as/in practice—a sociocultural approach to the study of educational policy. In M. Sutton & B. A. U. Levinson (Eds.), *Policy as practice: Toward a comparative sociocultural analysis of educational policy* (pp. 1–22). Westport, CT: Ablex.

Levinson, B. A. U., Sutton, M., & Winstead, T. (2009). Education policy as a practice of power: Theoretical tools, ethnographic methods, democratic options. *Educational Policy* 23(6), 767–795.

Lin, A. M. Y. (1996). Bilingualism or linguistic segregation? Symbolic domination, resistance and codeswitching. *Linguistics and Education* 8(1), 49–84.

Lin, A. M. Y., & Martin, P. W. (Eds.). (2005). *Decolonisation, globalisation: Language-in-education policy and practice.* Clevedon, UK: Multilingual Matters.

Marcus, G. E., & Fischer, M. J. (1986). *Anthropology as cultural critique.* Chicago: Chicago University Press.

Martin, P. W. (1999). Bilingual unpacking of monolingual texts in two primary classrooms in Brunei, Darussalam. *Language and Education* 13, 38–58.

Martin-Jones, M. (2011). Languages, texts, and literacy practices: An ethnographic lens on bilingual vocational education in Wales. In T. L. McCarty (Ed.), *Ethnography of language policy* (pp. 231–253). New York: Routledge.

Martin-Jones, M., & Martin, D. (Eds.). (2017). *Researching multilingualism: Critical and ethnographic perspectives.* Abingdon, UK: Routledge.

Martin-Jones, M., & Saxena, M. (1996). Turn-taking, power asymmetries, and the positioning of bilingual participants in classroom discourse. *Linguistics and Education* 8(1), 105–123.

Martin-Jones, M., Andrews, J., & Martin, D. (2017). Reflexive ethnographic research practice in multilingual contexts. In M. Martin-Jones & D. Martin (Eds.), *Researching multilingualism: Critical and ethnographic perspectives* (pp. 189–202). Abingdon, UK: Routledge.

Martin Rojo, L. (2010). *Constructing inequality in multilingual classrooms.* Berlin: Mouton de Gruyter.

May, S. A. (1997). Critical ethnography. In N. H. Hornberger & D. Corson (Eds.), *Research methods in language and education*, Vol. 8: *Encyclopedia of language and education* (pp. 197–206). Dordrecht: Kluwer Academic.

McCarty, T. L. (Ed.). (2011). *Ethnography of language policy.* London; New York: Routledge.

McCarty, T. L. (2015). Ethnography in language planning and policy research. In F. M. Hult & D. C. Johnson (Eds.), *Research methods in language policy and planning.* (pp. 81–93). Malden, MA: John Wiley & Sons.

Menken, K., & García, O. (Eds.). (2010). *Negotiating language policy in schools: Educators as policymakers.* New York: Routledge.

Ministry of Education, Culture, Youth and Sport (MECYS). (2004). *Education policy 2004-2009.* Dili, Timor-Leste: MECYS & Republica Democrática de Timor-Leste (RDTL).

Pennycook, A. (2001). *Critical applied linguistics.* Mahwah, NJ: Lawrence Erlbaum.

Pennycook, A. (2002). Language policy and docile bodies: Hong Kong and governmentality. In J. W. Tollefson (Ed.), *Language policies in education: Critical issues* (pp. 91-110). Mahwah, NJ: Lawrence Erlbaum.

Pérez-Milans, M. (2013). *Urban schools and English language education in late modern China: A critical sociolinguistic ethnography.* New York: Routledge.

Phillips, S. (1983). *The invisible culture: Communication in classroom and community on the Warm Springs Indian reservation.* New York: Longman.

Phillipson, R. (1992). *Linguistic imperialism.* Oxford: Oxford University Press.

Rampton, B. (2006). *Language in late modernity: Interaction in an urban school.* Cambridge: Cambridge University Press.

Rampton, B. (2007). Neo-Hymesian linguistic ethnography in the United Kingdom. *Journal of Sociolinguistics* 11(5), 584-607.

Rampton, B., Tusting, K., Maybin, J. Barwell, R., Creese, A. & Lytra, V. (2004). UK linguistic ethnography: A discussion paper. Retrieved from http://www.ling-ethnog.org.uk

Rampton, B., Maybin, J., & Roberts, C. (2015). Theory and method in linguistic ethnography. In J. Snell, S. Shaw, & F. Copland (Eds.), *Linguistic ethnography: Interdisciplinary explorations* (pp. 14-50). Basingstoke, UK: Palgrave Macmillan.

Ricento, T. (2000). Historical and theoretical perspectives in language policy and planning. *Journal of Sociolinguistics* 4(2), 196-213.

Ricento, T. L., & Hornberger, N. H. (1996). Unpeeling the onion: Language planning and policy and the ELT professional. *TESOL Quarterly* 30(3), 401-428.

Schieffelin, B. B., Woolard, K. A., & Kroskrity, P. V. (Eds.). (1998). *Language ideologies: Practice and theory.* Oxford: Oxford University Press.

Silverstein, M. (2003). Indexical order and the dialectics of sociolinguistic life. *Language and Communication* 23, 193-229.

Stroud, C. (2007). Bilingualism: Colonialism and postcolonialism. In M. Heller (Ed.), *Bilingualism: A social approach* (pp. 25-49). Basingstoke, UK: Palgrave Macmillan.

Tollefson, J. W. (1991). *Planning language, planning inequality.* London: Longman.

Tollefson, J. W. (Ed.). (2002). *Language policies in education: Critical issues.* Mahwah, NJ: Lawrence Erlbaum.

Tusting, K., & Maybin, J. (2007). Linguistic ethnography and interdisciplinarity: Opening up the discussion. *Journal of Sociolinguistics* 11(5), 575-583.

Van der Aa, J. & Blommaert, J. (2011). Ethnographic monitoring: Hymes' unfinished business in education. *Anthropology and Education Quarterly* 42(4), 319-344.

Van de Aa, J. & Blommaert, J. (2017). Ethnographic monitoring and the study of complexity. In M. Martin-Jones & D. Martin (Eds.), *Researching multilingualism: Critical and ethnographic perspectives* (pp. 259-271). Abingdon, UK: Routledge.

Van Maanen, J. (1988). *Tales of the field: On ethnographic writing.* Chicago: Chicago University Press.

Wiley, T. (1999). Comparative historical analysis of U.S. language policy and language planning: Extending the foundations. In T. Heubner & K. Davis (Eds.), *Sociopolitical
perspectives on language policy and planning in the USA* (pp. 17–23). Amsterdam: John
Benjamins.

Wolcott, H. (2008). *Ethnography: A way of seeing.* 2nd edition. Lanham, MD: Altamira Press.

CHAPTER 5

CRITICAL DISCOURSE– ETHNOGRAPHIC APPROACHES TO LANGUAGE POLICY

RUTH WODAK AND KRISTOF SAVSKI

IN this chapter, we focus on the synergy that researchers in language policy have developed by integrating two other subfields of sociolinguistics: critical discourse analysis and critical ethnography. We begin by discussing the meanings of the three key concepts used in these approaches, albeit sometimes in significantly different ways: critique, ethnography, and discourse. We then examine how these concepts are relevant to contemporary analyses of language policy, focusing particularly on their potential to open new and innovative avenues of research. To demonstrate how an integrated critical discourse and ethnographic approach can be applied in concrete empirical research, we then present an analysis of language policy and practice in the European Union before providing an overview of other relevant studies in the area.

CRITIQUE, ETHNOGRAPHY, AND
DISCOURSE: KEY CONCEPTS

While concrete understandings and applications of *critique* in the social sciences vary greatly, what they all have in common is a reference to a "minimal normative standpoint" (Sayer, 2009, p. 770), by which we mean a set of grounding values that are considered indispensable to a civilized society. One such example is the concept of linguistic human rights, which are explicitly defined as "necessary to fulfil people's basic needs and for them to live a dignified life, and [. . .] therefore [. . .] so basic, so fundamental, that no state (or individual or group) is supposed to violate them" (Skutnabb-Kangas, 2006, p. 273; see also May, 2012).

In a very general sense, the aim of an ethnographic approach is "to combine close detail of local action and interaction as embedded in a wider social world" (Creese, 2008, p. 140; see also Heller, 2011, p. 40ff.). In practice, ethnography as a methodology and distinct approach involves the direct entry of the researcher into a particular context and his or her participation in or observation of local practices over an extended period (see, e.g., Agar, 1996; see also Rampton et al., 2007; Wolcott, 2008). This involves collecting several kinds of data in addition to observation, such as participants' accounts of their own practices, various types of narratives, images, documents, and so on (see Muntigl et al., 2000).

What defines a critical ethnographic approach is the overt and explicit socially normative stance of the researcher who, rather than merely observing the field and documenting practices, seeks to demystify and challenge power imbalances, from the perspective of the dominated as well as the dominant (e.g., Chilton et al., 2010; Madison, 2005; Reisigl & Wodak, 2015; Thomas, 1993). In other words, critical ethnographers seek to critique those in power, but particularly aim to engage in a dialogue with the Other, thereby voicing and advocating the needs of the disadvantaged (Madison, 2005). Following Heller, the researcher conducts such an analysis by first describing and explaining the data and findings, and then by deciding how to evaluate the emerging complex relationships and what to do about them. Thus, three stages are involved: description, evaluation, and recommendation for application (Heller, 2011, p. 11). This highlights the importance of making the position of the researcher explicit in critical research, and of constant self-reflection and self-critique (e.g., Chilton et al., 2010, pp. 491–493), characterized as follows:

> One can distinguish at least three interrelated concepts. First, critical analysis of discourse can mean to make the implicit explicit. More specifically, it means making explicit the implicit relationship between discourse, power and ideology, challenging surface meanings, and not taking anything for granted. . . . Second, for advocates of CDS [Critical Discourse Studies], being "critical" has an additional element—putting theory into action. . . . "Being critical" in CDS includes being

reflexively self-critical. In this sense, critical discourse analysis does not only mean to criticise others. It also means to criticise the "critical" itself, a point that is in line with Habermas, and was made in 1989 (Wodak, 1989: 2) and again ten years later by Chouliaraki and Fairclough (1999: 9) and by Reisigl and Wodak (2001: 32ff.). (Wodak, 2014, p. 125)

Such critical goals are also what defines many contemporary approaches to discourse. We refer particularly to the emergence of critical discourse studies (CDS, hereafter) as a field of inquiry aimed at demystifying ideology and power relations in language use (see, e.g., Chilton et al., 2010; Wodak & Meyer, 2015). While the diverse approaches that form CDS (for an overview, see Wodak & Meyer, 2015) are united by a view of discourse as a form of social practice that is constituted by and constitutive of social structure (Fairclough, Mulderrig, & Wodak, 2010), our focus in this chapter is on those that can also be categorized as *discourse–ethnographic* due to their integration of fieldwork and other ethnographic methods (cf. Krzyżanowski, 2011; see also Krzyżanowski & Oberhuber, 2007, 2008).

Two examples of the discourse–ethnographic orientation are the discourse-historical approach (DHA, hereafter) (Reisigl & Wodak, 2015; see also Wodak, 1996, 2006, 2011, 2015; Wodak et al., 2009) and mediated discourse analysis (Scollon, 2008), both of which feature ethnographic fieldwork as a constitutive part of their analysis. As explained by Heller (2011), such approaches have the potential to uncover particular discursive spaces where ideologies are "developed, contested, or reproduced in connection with the production and circulation of resources and of the regulation of access to them" (Heller, 2011, p. 41). As we discuss in the following section, this is of particular value to analyses of language policy, which need to account for both the diversity of the social spaces involved in their construction and the plurality of actors that contribute to them.

CONTRIBUTIONS OF CRITICAL DISCOURSE–ETHNOGRAPHIC APPROACHES TO LANGUAGE POLICY RESEARCH

In the last decade, critical ethnographic and discursive approaches have greatly expanded the focus of sociolinguistics as a whole, and of language policy as a distinct subfield within it. In sociolinguistics, we refer to two prominent streams. The first is Monica Heller's critical ethnographic work on minorities and postnationalism in Canada (Heller, 2011). In these studies, her work has evolved from an investigation of state policies to a multi-sited ethnography interested primarily in the trajectories of discursive change in society (for a detailed account, see Heller, 2012; see also Duchêne, 2008).

The second stream has arisen from Vertovec's (2007) assertion that the present-day effects of old and new migration patterns can no longer be analyzed as mere "diversity," but rather as a further "diversification of diversity"; the concept of "superdiversity" has become the center of a prominent stream in sociolinguistics and other paradigms in the social sciences (see, e.g., Blackledge & Creese, 2010; Blommaert, 2013; Blommaert & Rampton, 2011). Of course, the application of this concept in so many fields (from migration and policy studies to sociolinguistics) might imply that it has become an "empty signifier" onto which everybody can project their interests and meanings (Pavlenko, in press). The focus of this research is on the complexity of the linguistic practices of individuals in mobile contemporary societies, particularly in cases where these practices call into question the traditionally established boundaries between "languages" (e.g., García, 2009).

Conceptualizations of language policy have traditionally followed broader patterns in the field of sociolinguistics, particularly with the recent critical and ethnographic turns (for more detail, see Ricento, 2000). For the purposes of this chapter, we adopt Herbert Christ's very general and open-ended conceptualization of language policy as consisting of

> every public influence on the communication radius of languages, the sum of those "top-down" and "bottom-up" political initiatives through which a particular language or languages is/are supported in their public validity, their functionality and their dissemination. Like all policies it is subject to conflict and must regularly be re-ordered through constant discussion and debate. (Christ, 1991, p. 55)

Critical discursive and ethnographic approaches to language policy tend to foreground, as Christ does, its structural function as a mechanism of social control, as well as its discursive nature as the product of negotiation and co-construction (e.g., Wodak, 2000).

Various approaches (for recent overviews, see Barakos & Unger, 2016; Johnson & Ricento, 2013; McCarty, 2015) have brought attention to new research sites as well as new aspects of existing sites. In institutional settings, discursive and ethnographic approaches foreground the particular characteristics of the contexts where language policies are created, paying particular attention to the mechanisms with which they are applied and upheld, and to the range of effects they might have on the language practices of different actors. From this perspective, discourse–ethnographic studies of language policies must take into account the paradox that exists within any institution between the structural constraints that enable its existence and the agency of individuals acting within it (see, e.g., Lawrence, Suddaby, & Leca, 2009; Mahoney & Thelen, 2010).

Such mechanisms are crucial to analyses of language policies, as the relationships of power that they establish between different actors also govern the contents of policies. In other words, policies are seen as sites of struggle between different actors and different ideologies, as products of negotiations that seek to overcome such struggles, and of hegemonic and subversive efforts (Capstick, 2015; De Cillia & Wodak, 2006; Savski, 2016). As rules that have been decided upon, however, language policies are also a means of codifying a particular construction of social reality, and therefore of legitimating particular sets of actions (e.g., Levinson et al., 2009).

The inner workings of organizations also play a key role for analyses of policy implementation. Just as the genesis of a policy involves negotiation, so does its implementation in a given setting. As policy texts are recontextualized across different settings, from the transnational to the national to the local scale, for instance, the ways in which they are *read* and implemented also change (Wodak & Fairclough, 2010; Yanow, 2000). A multi-sited critical ethnographic approach gives researchers the opportunity to observe how policies are interpreted and enacted across different contexts (for more discussion, see Berthoud et al., 2013; Hult, 2015; Johnson, 2011).

The key contribution of critical ethnography in this case is that it allows insight into how the workings of a particular organization or discursive space shape policy implementation. Policy is therefore the product of a complex set of dialectic relationships that have to be observed by examining policies and how they are recontextualized in different contexts, which also necessarily influence their implementation. A particular focus is on how individual actors act to codify specific interpretations of policy (Johnson, 2013), and how their decision-making can act to both increase and decrease the agency of other actors (Hornberger, 2005).

Finally, discursive and ethnographic approaches highlight the interplay between the explicit or official level and the implicit or unofficial processes that underlie it. Therefore, these approaches not only focus on laws, regulations, declarations, and similar genres, but also involve a broader engagement with a particular context, community, or institution (McCarty, 2015). In practice, this means paying attention to how the local settings under investigation reflect broader social processes, whether this is done as part of a multi-sited ethnographic approach (see Heller, 2011) or a historical-structural analysis (see Tollefson, 1991).

In the following section, we provide an example of a recent study of language policy and practice in European Union organizations. We summarize the process of designing such a complex multilevel project, collecting context-relevant information, as well as analyzing multilingual data and interpreting findings. We show how a critical discourse–ethnographic approach can point to key events, practices, or beliefs and ideologies that underpin and influence policy in any given setting.

AN EXAMPLE: STUDYING LANGUAGE
POLICIES IN THE EUROPEAN UNION

Inspired by the recent interest in ethnographic work on language and communication, as well as building on research in the areas of sociolinguistic, linguistic, and organizational anthropology and critical discourse studies (CDS), Wodak et al. (2012) simultaneously critically analyze co-texts and contexts of multilingual practices in order to explain, understand, and evaluate how participants perform multilingualism in its manifold forms. In this research, they assumed that—depending on specific contextual cues as well as on structural constraints—different micro and macro *language ideologies* would co-determine multilingual practices.

This research, part of the multi-institutional DYLAN project (for comprehensive overviews of this project, see Berthoud et al., 2013; Unger et al., 2014), draws on a large amount of preexisting critical ethnographic field studies of EU organizations (for example, Krzyżanowski & Wodak, 2011; Muntigl et al., 2000; Wodak, 2011, 2014; Wodak & Krzyżanowski, 2011). In the course of all these investigations, over 70 members of the European Parliament (MEPs) and European Commission (CEC, hereafter) officials were interviewed; MEPs were shadowed throughout their working days, debates at the European Convention 2002–2003 were observed and documented, plenary and committee meetings at the European Parliament were audio recorded, and researchers attended small meetings (also videoconferences) in the CEC, some over the course of six months. Moreover, the legal documents and treaties were analyzed in order to trace the development of EU Language Policy since its outset in the 1960s. During a period of almost twenty years, the researchers were able to refine and develop their methodology, specifically oriented toward participant observation and critical ethnography in multilingual political institutions, as well as the discourse analysis of documented text and talk.

For example, in their fieldwork in the EP and CEC, Wodak et al. (2012) observed two distinctly different sites that condition the institutionally specific variations of the meeting-genre which impact modes of communication (Wodak, 2013). On the one hand, internal meetings in the EC are clearly conversational. Although they are also run according to minutes and/or agendas, the latter simply delineate the content, rather than determine the actual interactive and other conduct of the participants in these encounters. On the other hand, semi-plenary meetings at the EP are strictly organized and have clear rules and hierarchies. For example, the chair determines speaking times, turn-taking, and so on. Thus a detailed analysis of interaction in institutional settings needs an approach that accounts for power in/over/of discourse, always embedded in specific organizational contexts.

In broad terms, this research followed the principles of critical discursive and ethnographic approaches as outlined earlier by combining several different levels of analysis in a nonlinear, fully triangulatory approach to data collection. The major stages of the analysis, intended to explore different levels of context in a macro to micro order, included (e.g., Wodak et al., 2012) the following:

(a) *In-depth pre-fieldwork contextualization* of the object of research by exploring own and others' prior knowledge of the European Union and its multilingualism, as well as of the EU-institutional contexts in question, including their modes, patterns, practices, and "guiding" ideologies of multilingualism;

(b) *Ethnographic observations of the contexts* under study, both of their general patterns of communication and multilingualism and of the selected meetings, in order to validate the context-relevant information gathered in stage (a);

(c) *In-depth qualitative analysis of meetings* via a combination of discourse-historical and sociolinguistic analysis while focusing on issues such as power, communicative asymmetries, and so on.

By integrating findings from these different stages of research, this research program aims to adopt the *reflexive stance* that is indispensable for (critical) ethnographic endeavors in which the boundaries of interaction between "subjects" and "objects" of research are frequently difficult to delineate. This reflexivity is paramount if ethnographic research is to avoid essentializing the observations it makes and treating them as *truth* rather than merely a partial account (e.g., Clifford, 1986; Danermark et al., 2002). In the following, a brief summary of the research conducted by Wodak et al. (2012) therefore illustrates how describing observational data from different sites within an institution also necessitates studying the historical context of that institution, and the broader sociopolitical trends that might influence the practices being observed.

The Broad Context: Multilingualism in EU institutions

All major language regulations within EU institutions derive their foundations from *Regulation No. 1* of the European Council (1958), which stipulates that each member-state of the European (Economic) Community (the antecedent of the EU prior to its creation in 1993) brings its own official language with it into the organization. The official languages of the EC/EU are also the working languages of each respective country. This implies that the Union should not differentiate between the twenty-four languages and that the major institutions of the Union in particular should operate a policy of equality between all its official and working languages.

Currently, there are twenty-four official EU languages, with each EU enlargement to date resulting in new official/working languages, and in turn leading to debates about the growing linguistic repertoire in EU organizations (Krzyżanowski & Wodak, 2011 for more details). In a process that we label *hegemonic multilingualism,* a set of "traditional working languages" (mainly English, French, or German) is, indeed, replacing the set of twenty-four official languages of the European Union. Thus, a few EU working languages are given preference over the other EU working languages, constituting a set of "core languages," which are ideologically preferred (and more frequently used). This, of course, implies relevant consequences for democratic participation and representation and might provide an obstacle to the development of a public image of EU institutions as being inclusive and multilingual.

The Narrow Context: European Commission, European Parliament

Within the European Parliament (EP, hereafter) and the CEC, one can observe significant differences between the ways in which their patterns of "internal" multilingualism are regulated and practiced (Wodak, 2011). The CEC officially operates a policy whereby all official instances of communication are in fact conducted in all official languages (European Commission, 2000). Members and officials of the Commission traditionally use English, French, and (much less) German in their oral communication (particularly at a semi-official level). Among those languages, French traditionally used to be the leading one, though recently English has clearly been gaining in importance.

The EP, however, stipulates in its rules of procedure (Rule 138: Languages) that "all documents of the Parliament shall be drawn up in the official languages" (European Parliament, 2004, p. 66) and that, in plenary sessions, all members of the EP have the right to speak and be addressed in all official languages. In smaller-scale meetings (committees, delegations), this is reduced to only the "official languages used and requested by the members and substitutes of that committee or delegation" (European Parliament, 2004, p. 66, see also European Parliament, 2006).

Ethnographic Fieldwork at the CEC and the EP

The ethnographic observations in 2009 took place according to a set of predefined guidelines that were structured according to the research questions. The guidelines covered salient dimensions of linguistic interactions such as:

- *Linguistic profiles (repertoires) of the meetings*: number and variety of languages used throughout the meetings;
- *Frequency of code-switching*: convergence/divergence of code-switching with turn-taking, code-persistence over turns;
- *Topic-related versus addressee-related language choices*;
- *Language choices and CS versus degrees of formality and informality*: for example, variation between phases and stages of the meetings (before/during/after official proceedings), and between different elements of physical spaces (e.g., front rows vs. back rows);

- *Thematization of issues related to multilingualism and language use, that is, metacommunication on language*: in relation to topics under discussion, participants, the flow/efficiency of communication.

Extract 1: Example from EP: Power struggles via language choice (see transcription conventions in Appendix)

1　SP1:　(MEP, ES) Dziękuję bardzo. Thank you very much
2　　　　　　*Thank you very much*
3
4　　　　Mr (.) e-eerm kind President. aam I do agree with Mrs Harkin that there are elements
5　　　　in the Onesta and indeed in the corporate report that might enter and that we shall
6　　　　vote next week in Hungary that might set a new context for this discussion. Paso
7　　　　porque estoy hablando en ingles [unread 2.0] ((laugh)) Paso al castellano.
8
9　　　　*I'll pass because I'm speaking in English [...] ((laugh)) I'll switch over to Castilian*
10
11　　　Venga [...] [continues in Castilian for 1:40 min]
12
13　　　*OK. Let's see*
14
15　　　Bueno podría sí más que el contenido pero sí que buscaría tener esta
16　　　discusión a la próxima legislatura que en todo caso va a plantear muchas cosas.
17　　　Gracias.
18
19　　　*Well, it could be more than the content but I would like to have this discussion (around*
20　　　*the time) of the next legislature which will, in any case, raise a lot of things. Thank you.*
21
22　SP4:　(chair, MEP, PL) (1.0) Pani Sinnott
23
24　　　　　　*Mrs. Sinnott*
25
26　SP2:　(MEP, IRL) I will be very brief I have never [...] [continues in English for 0:22 min]
27　SP4:　(chair, MEP, PL) (3.0) Sir Robert
28　SP3:　Chairman eem I think I am not (unreadable 2.0) I am I am slightly deterred am by
29　　　　what Miss Harkin said because (.) as I recall when am-the Socialist group and the
30　　　　EPP group produced this report it was a working document (.) we produced it am-
31　　　　am by EVEning right and it was tabled to the committee for discussion the next day
32　　　　so it was deliberately not designed to exclude in any way shape or form
33　　　　　　　　　　　　　　　　　　　　　[
34　SP1:　　　　　　　　　　　　　　　　Oh no ((laughs))
35　　　　　　　　　　　　　　　　　　　　　　　[
36　SP3:　　　　　　　　　　　　　　　　No-no not in the slightest ((laughs in the room))
37　　　　　　　　　　　　　　　　　　　　　　　　[
38　SP2:　　　　　　　　　　　　　　　　　　(inaudible 2.0) it
39　　　　has so far been so far been the case chairman that our three colleagues (inaudible
40　　　　3.0) by September I- I would argue that of course (.) the EPP-ED and the Socialist
41　　　　group (inaudible 2.0) a majority so if it were to go to the (inaudible 2.0) that is not
42　　　　the way you want to do it no not and the whole point about this was to try and put it
43　　　　under agenda for discussion we never got to that discussion because there were ways
44　　　　whereby the discussion was prevented
45　SP1:　　　　Point of order point of order point of order point of order
46　SP4:　　　　　　　　　　　　　　[Prze-Proszę Państwa Przepraszam—y za

47   *Ladies and Gentlemen, excuse me*
48
49 SP1:   [BUT Yeah. No (0.5) it is important
50 SP4:   [Hm – Proszę bardzo
51
52   *Well—Please*
53
54 SP1:   I'm SORRY but I would request that Mr Atkins aPOlogizes to the Secretariat and
55   APOlogizes TO these members, saying that the Secretariat got to know. We know
56   how to read; we have our own facts here. I really think I really think I really think that
57   you should apologize to the Secretariat and apologize to members. This is we have
58   seen enough insulting of the high (1.0) of this committee
59 SP4:   [So-hm-sorry (.) proszę państwa proszę państwa [...]
60
61   *excuse me ladies and gentlemen excuse me ladies and gentlemen*
62
63 SP3:   [Chairman I was I was speaking before that [...]
64 SP4:   [Zaraz sir Robert może być przyjęty tylko za zgodą WZYSTKICH on nie może być
65   ponieważ on nie wynika w sposób oczywisty z regulaminu [...] (unread 1.0) proszę
66   bardzo ostatni raz jeszcze bo [...]
67
68   *in a minute Sir Robert—can be accepted only upon agreement of ALL he cannot be*
69   *understood as he does not follow all the rules* (unread 1.0) *ok so for the last time please*
70   *one more time because*
71
72 SP3:   [Ch-Chairman I was
73 SP4:   [przejdziemy stąd do yy-do-do (1.0) yy David Hammerstein
74   Minz potem Sir Robert [...]
75
76   *so we move from here to to (1.0) David Hammerstein Minz and then Sir Robert*
77   [
78 SP3:   [Ch-Chairman
79 SP4:   [zaraz David
80
81   *Just a second David*
82   Hammerstein-Minz potem Sir Robert
83
84   *Hammerstein-Minz and then Sir Robert*
85 SP3:   [Sir Chairman I was speaking before I gave way to a [unread 1.0], surely I can be
86   allowed to complete my remarks please. (1.0) Chairman, I have never set out and
87   neither has the Socialist group to make this anything other than an opportunity for
88   intellectual judgement [...] we have never had the chance to debate this document
89   so to suggest that we somehow are responsible for that; it's not my responsibility
90   it's been tabled on numerous occasions and we've never got round to debating it
91   properly. That's not my fault and I do really reject any suggestion that that is the case.
92   The whole point about the way that this committee is operated is that we try and
93   work collectively. If colleagues are unhappy with what is being proposed for whatever
94   reason and I do not want to upset David or anyone by implying somehow that they
95   have had the wool pulled over their eyes I can't
96 SP1:   [It's nice that you've said that

97   SP3:   [Ah well in which case then I withdraw the accusation unreservedly
98   my comment is that I think that there has been an attempt by the Secretariat and
99   I did not resolve from that and it is quite clear that that is the case that they don't
100   that David doesn't like what is being proposed and he is perfectly entitled to that
101   point of view. I don't have to agree with him and nor does the Socialist group. In
102   the circumstances Chairman and in order to make progress I will withdraw this
103   document for further consideration. [...]
104   SP1:   [There was no quarrel [...]

All categories were carefully documented in the field notes during the meetings and were discussed and supplemented at the end of each working day. Each meeting was observed by at least two researchers, with each focusing on different aspects of the interactions. For example, while one of the researchers was focusing on aspects of the linguistic profiles of meetings and CS, the other was taking notes and (as much as possible) pictures/sketches of the situational contexts. After the meetings, the researchers discussed their notes in order to supply missing information and exchange their observations of the interactions.

Extract 1 comes from an EP Committee on Petitions meeting that the researchers were able to observe and audio record. The meeting dealt mainly with petitions on environmental issues in various European countries and apparent violations of competition rules. Four speakers are active here: Speaker 1 (SP1, male) is a Spanish MEP from the European Green Party (2004–2009), while SP2 is a female Irish MEP from the Independence/Democracy Group and vice-chair of the committee. SP3 (male) had been a British MEP since 1999 and a member of the European People's Party (Christian Democrats) (until 2009). SP4 (male) is a Polish MEP, chair of the committee (and of the meeting) from the Union for Europe of the Nations Group.

This extract illustrates one of the very rare instances in the recorded EP committee meetings where a conflict arises with spontaneous interruptions, raised voices, and manifold code switchings. The institutionalized turn-taking mechanism (see Wodak, 2000) is temporarily abolished; SP1 and SP3 get involved in a struggle over the procedures of the Petition Committee and a draft policy paper that manifests political differences in opinions and different loyalties toward the Secretariat (i.e., the CEC representative, Mrs. Harkin, who had explained her take on the proposed document in a previous statement). The chair of the Committee attempts to intervene in this conflict five times (lines 46, 50, 59, 73, 75) by interrupting SP1, who overrides the chair's list of order of speakers and takes the floor without being invited to do so. He explicitly disagrees with SP3 on the function of the Secretariat and their reported activities as well as on the functions of the draft document and the defined scope of the committee as such (lines 1–7, 54–58). SP1 thus interrupts SP3 twice by interjecting disagreement ("No," line 34), repetition of "point of order" (line 45), and again, after SP3 proposes an alternative approach to the drafting process, in agreement and support ("It's nice that you have said that" [line 96]; "There was no quarrel" [line 104]). The latter comment marks the end of this confrontational debate and implies a redefinition and reframing of this episode as rational and "no quarrel" after SP3 justifies himself by emphasizing that he is not to blame for the draft proposal, nor is the Socialist Party to blame for the procedures.

SP1 first addresses the chair in Polish, a polite participant-related way of addressing the chair (who is Polish), yet switches to English, relating to the former speaker, Mrs. Harkin, and then explicitly comments on his switch to Spanish in line 6, as this is both his preferred and expected language in this context (of-ficial language regulations) in the EP. After SP3 puts forward his standpoint and explains the nature of the draft document from his and the Socialist Party's per-spective, SP1 becomes increasingly involved, emotional, and raises his voice—switching to English again: this time, first, by loudly interjecting "No" in line 34; then, a second time, by interrupting in line 45 ("point of order"); and then, a third time, by interrupting the chair in line 54, hedging and introducing this interrup-tion first with an apology ("I'm sorry") and then continuing with a request that SP3 should apologize to the Secretariat. It might be the case that the shift to English indicates the greater symbolic capital of English; or that he wants to avoid simul-taneous interpreting. Very likely, more than one factor co-determined this shift—interpretable and understandable due to the ethnography and careful discourse analysis.

The chair succeeds in ending SP1's attack by interrupting in line 45 (and not letting SP3 cut in, in line 59). In this way, the chair regains control over the dis-cussion and starts his longer statement, thus moving the discussion on to proce-dural matters. The chair sticks to Polish throughout his attempts to control the conflict (and the turn-taking). SP3 justifies his previous actions and opinions, and then explains why he had requested that the committee enter into a debate (because "we've never got round to debating it properly," lines 90–91). Finally, he concedes that other MEPs might have different opinions ("I do not want to upset David, or anyone by implying, somehow, that they have had 'the wool pulled over their eyes,'" lines 94–95) and proposes an alternative procedure while re-emphasizing some points of disagreement ("I don't have to agree with him and nor does the Socialist group. In the circumstances, Chairman, and in order to make progress, I will withdraw this document for further consideration," lines 101–103), in order to save face. This is supported and accepted by SP1, who continues speaking in English.

This example illustrates—albeit in a summarized way—that a multi-method approach is to be recommended for such complex studies. The qualitative dis-course analysis, based on extensive critical ethnography, manifests the reper-toire of, and the facilitating factors for, different kinds of language choice, as well as the intricacies of the language regime in a transnational organizational entity such as the European Union. As the analysis clearly demonstrates, the genre of the meetings, the language regulations of the particular organizations, the interactional dynamics, and the topic all play decisive roles in determining the organization of interactions, turn-taking, and the distribution of power; obviously, analyzing such complex interactions would be almost impossible without all the contextual information gained via critical ethnography and other methodologies.

FURTHER RELEVANT RESEARCH

The DYLAN project, of which the study described in the preceding was part, is an example of the multi-sited studies outlined by Heller (2011). Aside from researching language policies and practices in core EU institutions, its various sub-teams also conducted fieldwork in private companies (e.g., Mondada, 2012) and in educational settings (e.g., Serra & Steffen, 2010). At the same time, a fourth set of sub-teams conducted investigations into transversal issues that emerged from the three principal areas of investigation, working to situate these in broader sociohistorical and economic processes, such as the use of English as a lingua franca (Seidlhofer, 2011) and to investigate the development of fair and efficient language policies (Gazzola, 2006).

While DYLAN can be considered unique due to how comprehensively it approached the European Union as a language policy context, its foci also reflect much broader interests in the field of language policy, particularly its commitment to cross-referencing particular facets of declared policies with actions and practices in the range of social contexts and domains to which the policies are applied. Johnson's analysis of the *No Child Left Behind Act*, for instance, examines how a comprehensive reform of bilingual education in the United States was implemented at the level of a school district (see Johnson, 2010, 2011). Johnson's study identified the key role that empowered individuals, acting as *arbiters*, play in the implementation of a policy by prescribing a particular interpretation and thus limiting the agencies of others (Johnson, 2013).

As implied by Johnson and Ricento (2013), educational settings were a particularly fruitful area of investigation for early critical ethnographies of language policy, and considerable attention continues to be paid to schools and classroom settings by contemporary studies. Pérez-Milans (2013), for example, investigates how schools function as instruments of social modernization in China, focusing in particular on how curricula were developed to negotiate the gap between traditional nationalist collectivist values and the individualist demands of the liberal market.

Often, classroom studies have foregrounded the power of teachers in implementing and resisting policy initiatives. Brown (2010) illustrates how Estonian teachers charged with supporting the revitalization of the Võro language were presented with a student-centered model based on "choice," but were in practice often unable to support student choices (e.g., due to a lack of practical means), or simply ended up reproducing implicit ideas about minority language education being "less important" (Brown, 2010, p. 311). Phyak (2013) analyzes how the implementation of a similar policy in Nepal was only partly successful due to active resistance by parents and students, as well as a lack of initiative on the part of the government to support the efforts of the teachers. Such studies underline Hornberger's assertion that policies may enable or inhibit the agencies of different local actors (see Hornberger, 2005; cf. Johnson, 2013; see also Martín Rojo, 2010).

Analyzing how policies affect the lives of individuals at the grassroots level often provides a useful counterbalance to the perspectives of official actors. Capstick (2015) examines the difficult trajectory of a Pakistani family migrating to the United Kingdom, focusing in particular on the different types of literacies that its members encountered when going through the strenuous and stressful visa application process. This highlights a complex interaction between the language repertoires of migrants, official policies in destination countries, and the role of go-betweens who mediate from one to the other (see also Blackledge, 2009; Khan & Blackledge, 2015).

While the implementation of policies is a time of negotiation and conflict resolution, their creation often is a site of ideological struggle. Källkvist and Hult (2016) report on an ethnography and discourse analysis of language policy creation at a Swedish university (also see Hult & Källkvist, 2016). By conducting participant observation in the meetings of a committee charged with creating a university-level language policy, Källkvist and Hult were able to reconstruct several different discourses that come into contact and conflict during the drafting of such a text, for instance, discourses of protectionism against those of internationalization (Källkvist & Hult, 2016).

In a similar vein, Savski (2016) conducted a large-scale critical discourse–historical ethnographic study to examine the drafting of a language strategy in Slovenia, tracing features of the policy against dominant ideologies in the surrounding discourse. This research highlights how complex dynamics of political change and inter-institutional conflict impact the creation and implementation of policy. It also shows that such processes may be investigated in detail even without direct access to sites of policy negotiation by relying, for instance, on the minutes of parliamentary debates, in-depth interviews, and a complete set of drafts of the relevant policy papers.

CONCLUSIONS

Our focus in this chapter has been on outlining how the synergy between critical discursive and ethnographic methods can open new avenues in the field of language policy. As discussed in the preceding sections, language policy has now come to be a predominantly interpretive and socially engaged field, one that is not only interested in policy as a prescriptive mechanism, but also is a meeting point of different social forces, which actors can reinterpret and resist, and which is embedded in the historical context of a given society or organization.

The conduct of language policy in the European Union as a site of tension between different political agendas and ideologies offers a clear example of these dynamics. The European Union nominally has twenty-four official languages, but, as outlined earlier, these do not all carry the same weight in meetings. Instead, a small set of working languages is often used at key times of decision-making, a practice that can cause antagonisms to develop, as illustrated in the previous example.

The integration of (critical) discourse studies with ethnography allows insight into the complex working of many spontaneous discursive practices in various institutional and other sites in ways that go far beyond the use of just one methodology when analyzing the impact of language policies in micro-interaction. Relying, for example, only on the interviews or surveys would cover self-assessments and beliefs but might, of course, neglect the effect of implementing such policies. Relying only on ethnography, on the other hand, could lead to essentializing only one of many relevant perspectives, as ethnography is always constrained by access to specific sites. And finally, relying on discourse analysis of specific interactions and other (also written) genres misses important contextual knowledge that might be salient for the interpretation of meanings. Hence, a critical, multilevel approach to language policy implies both complex theoretical and methodological approaches that allow for description, interpretation, and explanation of the workings of language policies, in the processes of their production and implementation over space and time.

APPENDIX

TRANSCRIPTION CONVENTIONS

(.)	short pause (1 second or less)
(6.0), (8.0), (9.0)	longer pause (six seconds, eight seconds, nine seconds duration)
(unread. 6.0)	unclear elements of speech

[	overlapping speech
Mhm. Eeeee	paraverbal elements
((leans back)),((laughs))	nonverbal behavior
THIS	stressed/accentuated element of speech
(↑)	rising intonation (if significant)
(↓)	falling intonation (if significant)
[. . .]	omitted parts of text/utterance
	dot makes long stretches of talk more comprehensible and subsequent capital letter marks new information unit
translation	translation to English of text/utterance in languages other than English.

References

Agar, M. (1996). *The professional stranger: An informal introduction to ethnography*. Orlando, FL: Academic Press.

Barakos, E., & Unger, J. W. (Eds.) (2016). *Discursive approaches to language policy*. Basingstoke, UK: Palgrave.

Berthoud, A.-C., Grin, F., & Lüdi, G. (Eds.). (2013). *Exploring the dynamics of multilingualism*. Amsterdam: John Benjamins.

Blackledge, A. (2009). "As a country we do expect": The further extension of language testing regimes in the United Kingdom. *Language Assessment Quarterly* 6(1), 6–16.

Blackledge, A., & Creese, A. (2010). *Multilingualism: A critical perspective*. New York: Continuum.

Blommaert, J. (2013). *Ethnography, superdiversity, and linguistic landscapes: Chronicles of complexity*. Bristol, UK: Multilingual Matters

Blommaert, J., & Rampton, B. (2011). Language and superdiversity. *Diversities* 13(2), 1–21.

Brown, K. (2010). Teachers as language-policy actors: Contending with the erasure of lesser-used languages in schools. *Anthropology & Education Quarterly* 41(3), 298–314.

Capstick, A. (2015). *The multilingual literacy practices of Mirpuri migrants in Pakistan and the UK: Combining new literacy studies and critical discourse analysis*. Unpublished PhD thesis. Lancaster University, Lancaster, UK.

Chilton, P., Tian, H., & Wodak, R. (2010). Reflections on discourse and critique in China and the West. *Journal of Language and Politics* 9(4), 489–507.

Chouliaraki, L., & Fairclough, N. (1999). *Discourse in late modernity*. Edinburgh: Edinburgh University Press.

Christ, H. (1991). *Fremdsprachenunterricht für das Jahr 2000: Sprachenpolitische Betrachtungen zum Lehren und Lernen fremder Sprachen*. Tübingen: Narr.

Clifford, J. (1986). Introduction: Partial truths. In J. Clifford & G. Marcus (Eds.), *Writing culture: The poetics and politics of ethnography* (pp. 1–26). Berkeley: University of California Press.

Creese, A. (2008). Linguistic ethnography. In K. A. King & N. H. Hornberger (Eds.), *Encyclopedia of language and education* (2nd edition), Vol. 10: *Research methods in language and education* (pp. 229–241). New York: Springer.

Danermark, B., Ekström, M., Jakobsen, L. & Karlsson, J. C. (2002). *Explaining society.* London: Routledge.

De Cillia, R., & Wodak, R. (2006). *Ist Osterreich ein deutsches Land? Anmerkungen zur Sprachenpolitik in der Zweiten Republik.* Innsbruck: Studienverlag.

Duchêne, A. (2008). *Ideologies across nations: The construction of linguistic minorities at the United Nations.* Berlin: Mouton de Gruyter.

European Commission. (2000). *Rules of procedure of the European Commission.* Official Journal of the European Communities L 308/26 of 08/12/2000.

European Council. (1958). *Regulation no. 1 determining the languages to be used by the European Economic Community.* Official Journal of the European Communities 17 of 06/10/1958.

European Parliament (2004). *Rules of procedure of the European Parliament,* 16th edition, July 2004. Brussels: EP.

European Parliament. (2006). *Code of conduct on multilingualism adopted by the Bureau,* 409/2006. Brussels: EP.

Fairclough, N., Mulderrig, J., & Wodak, R. (2010). What is critical discourse analysis? In T. A. Van Dijk (Ed.), *Discourse studies: A multidisciplinary introduction* (pp. 357–378). London: Sage.

García, O. (2009). *Bilingual education in the 21st century: A global perspective.* Malden, MA; Oxford: Basil/Blackwell.

Gazzola, M. (2006). Managing multilingualism in the European Union: Language policy evaluation for the European Parliament. *Language Policy* 5(4), 395–419.

Heller, M. (2011). *Paths to post-nationalism: A critical ethnography of language and identity.* New York: Oxford University Press.

Heller, M. (2012). Rethinking sociolinguistic ethnography: From community and identity to process and practice. In S. Gardner & M. Martin-Jones (Eds.), *Multilingualism, discourse and ethnography* (pp. 24–33). New York: Routledge.

Hornberger, N. H. (2005). Opening and filling up implementational and ideological spaces in heritage language education. *Modern Language Journal* 89(4), 605–609.

Hult, F. M. (2015). Making policy connections across scales using nexus analysis. In F. M. Hult & D. C. Johnson (Eds.), *Research methods in language policy and planning* (pp. 217–232). Malden, MA: Wiley Blackwell.

Hult, F., & Källkvist, M. (2016). Global flows in local language planning: Articulating parallel language use in Swedish university policies. *Current Issues in Language Planning* 17, 56–71.

Johnson, D. C. (2010). Implementational and ideological spaces in bilingual education language policy. *International Journal of Bilingual Education and Bilingualism* 13(1), 61–79.

Johnson, D. C. (2011). Critical discourse analysis and the ethnography of language policy. *Critical Discourse Studies* 8(4), 267–279.

Johnson, D. C. (2013). Positioning the language policy arbiter: Governmentality and footing in the School District of Philadelphia. In J. W. Tollefson (Ed.), *Language policies in education: Critical issues* (2nd edition; pp. 116–136). New York; London: Routledge.

Johnson, D. C., & Ricento, T. (2013). Conceptual and theoretical perspectives in language planning and policy: Situating the ethnography of language policy. *International Journal of the Sociology of Language* 219, 7–22.

Källkvist, M., & Hult, F. (2016). Discursive mechanisms and human agency in language policy formation: Negotiating bilingualism and parallel language use at a Swedish university. *International Journal of Bilingual Education and Bilingualism* 19, 1–17.

Khan, K., & Blackledge, A. (2015). "They look into our lips": Negotiation of the citizenship ceremony as authoritative discourse. *Journal of Language and Politics* 14(3), 382–405.

Krzyżanowski, M. (2011). Ethnography and critical discourse analysis: Towards a problem-oriented research dialogue. *Critical Discourse Studies* 4 (8), 231–238.

Krzyżanowski, M., & Oberhuber, F. (2007). *(Un)doing Europe: Discourses and practices of negotiating the EU constitution.* Brussels: Peter Lang.

Krzyżanowski, M., & Oberhuber, F. (2008). Discourse analysis and ethnography. In R. Wodak & M. Krzyżanowski (Eds.), *Qualitative discourse analysis in the social sciences* (pp. 197–218). Basingstoke, UK: Palgrave Macmillan.

Krzyżanowski, M., & Wodak, R. (2011). Political strategies and language policies: The "rise and fall" of the EU Lisbon Strategy and its implications for the Union's multilingualism policy. *Language Policy* 10(2), 115–136.

Lawrence, T. B., Suddaby, R., & Leca, B. (2009). *Institutional work: Actors and agency in institutional studies of organisations.* Cambridge: Cambridge University Press.

Levinson, B., Sutton, M., & Winstead, T. (2009). Educational policy as a practice of power: Theoretical tool, ethnographic methods, democratic options. *Educational Policy* 23(6), 767–795.

Madison, D. S. (2005). *Critical ethnography: Methods, ethics, and performance.* Thousand Oaks, CA: Sage.

Mahoney, J., & Thelen, K. (2010). *Explaining institutional change: Ambiguity, agency and power.* Cambridge: Cambridge University Press.

Martín Rojo, L. (2010). *Constructing inequality in multilingual classrooms.* Berlin: Mouton de Gruyter.

May, S. (2012). *Language and minority rights: Ethnicity, nationalism and the politics of language.* 2nd edition. London: Routledge.

McCarty, T. (2015). Ethnography in language planning and policy research. In F. M. Hult & D. C. Johnson (Eds.), *Research methods in language policy and planning* (pp. 81–93). Malden, MA: Wiley Blackwell.

Mondada, L. (2012). The dynamics of embodied participation and language choice in multilingual meetings. *Language in Society* 41(2), 213–235.

Muntigl, P., Weiss, G., & Wodak, R. (Eds.) (2000). *European Union discourses on un/employment: An interdisciplinary approach to employment, policy-making and organizational change.* Amsterdam: John Benjamins.

Pavlenko, A. (in press). Superdiversity and why it isn't. In S. Breidbach, L. Küster, & B. Schmenk (Eds.), *Sloganizations in language education discourse.* Bristol, UK: Multilingual Matters.

Pérez-Milans, M. (2013). *Urban schools and English language education in late modern China: A critical sociolinguistic ethnography.* London: Routledge.

Phyak, P. (2013). Language ideologies and local languages as the medium-of-instruction policy: A critical ethnography of a multilingual school in Nepal. *Current Issues in Language Planning* 14(1), 127–143.

Rampton, B., Maybin, J., & Tusting, K. (Eds.). (2007). Linguistic ethnography in the UK: Links, problems and possibilities. Special issue of *Journal of Sociolinguistics* 11(5).

Reisigl, M., & Wodak, R. (2015). The discourse-historical approach. In R. Wodak & M. Meyer (Eds.), *Methods of critical discourse studies* (pp. 23–61). London: Sage.

Ricento, T. (2000). Historical and theoretical perspectives in language policy and planning. *Journal of Sociolinguistics* 4(2), 196–213.

Savski, K. (2016). *Slovene language policy in time and space: The trajectory of a language strategy from inception to implementation.* Unpublished PhD thesis. Lancaster University, Lancaster, UK.

Sayer, A. (2009). Who's afraid of critical social science? *Current Sociology* 57(6), 767–786.

Scollon, R. (2008). *Analyzing public discourse: Discourse analysis in the making of public policy.* London: Routledge.

Seidlhofer, B. (2011). Conceptualizing 'English' for a multilingual Europe. In A. De Houwer & A. Wilton (Eds.), *English in Europe today: Sociocultural and educational perspectives* (pp. 133–146). Amsterdam: John Benjamins.

Serra, C., & Steffen, G. (2010). Acquisition des concepts et intégration des langues et des disciplines dans l'enseignement bilingue. In R. Carol (Ed), *Apprendre en classe d'immersion. Quels concepts? Quelle théorie?* (pp. 129–186). Paris: L'Harmattan.

Skutnabb-Kangas, T. (2006). Language policy and linguistic human rights. In T. Ricento (Ed.), *An introduction to language policy: Theory and method* (pp. 273–291). Oxford: Blackwell.

Thomas, J. (1993). *Doing critical ethnography.* Newbury Park, CA: Sage

Tollefson, J. (1991). *Planning language, planning inequality: Language policy in the community.* London: Longman.

Unger, J. W., Krzyżanowski, M., & Wodak, R. (Eds.). (2014). *Multilingual encounters in Europe's institutional spaces.* Basingstoke, UK: Palgrave.

Vertovec, S. (2007). Super-diversity and its implications. *Ethnic and Racial Studies* 30(6), 1024–1054.

Wodak, R. (Ed.) (1989). *Language, power and ideology.* Amsterdam: John Benjamins.

Wodak, R. (1996). *Disorders of discourse.* London: Longman.

Wodak, R. (2000). From conflict to consensus? The co-construction of a policy paper. In P. Muntigl, G. Weiss, & R. Wodak (Eds.), *European Union discourses on un/employment: An interdisciplinary approach to employment, policy-making and organizational change* (pp. 73–114.). Amsterdam: John Benjamins.

Wodak, R. (2006). Linguistic analyses in language policies. In T. Ricento (Ed.), *An introduction to language policy: Theory and method* (pp. 170–193). Oxford: Blackwell.

Wodak, R. (2011). *The discourse of politics in action: Politics as usual.* 2nd revised edition. Basingstoke, UK: Palgrave Macmillan.

Wodak, R. (2013). Analyzing meetings in political and business contexts: Different genres similar strategies. In P. Cap & O. Okulska (Eds.), *Analyzing genres in political communication* (pp. 187–221). Amsterdam: John Benjamins.

Wodak, R. (2014). The European Parliament: Multilingual experiences in the everyday life of MEPs. In J. W. Unger, M. Krzyżanowski, & R. Wodak (Eds.), *Multilingual encounters in Europe's institutional spaces* (pp. 125–146). London: Bloomsbury.

Wodak, R. (2015). *The politics of fear: What right-wing populist discourses mean.* London: Sage.

Wodak, R., Cillia, R. D., Reisigl, M., & Liebhart, K. (2009). *The discursive construction of national identity.* 2nd revised edition. Edinburgh: Edinburgh University Press.

Wodak, R., & Fairclough, N. (2010). Recontextualizing European higher education policies: The cases of Austria and Romania. *Critical Discourse Studies* 7(1), 19–40.

Wodak, R., & Krzyżanowski, M. (2011). Language in political institutions of multilingual states and the European Union. In B. Kortmann & J. van der Auwera (Eds.), *The languages and linguistics of Europe* (pp. 625–641). Berlin: Mouton de Gruyter.

Wodak, R., Krzyżanowski, M. & Forchtner, B. (2012). The interplay of language ideologies and contextual cues in multilingual interactions: Language choice and code-switching in European Union institutions. *Language in Society* 41(2), 157–186.

Wodak, R., & Meyer, M. (Eds.). (2015). *Methods of critical discourse studies.* 3rd revised edition. London: Sage.

Wolcott, H. (2008). *Ethnography: A way of seeing.* Lanham, MD: Altamira Press.

Yanow, D. (2000). *Conducting interpretive policy analysis.* Thousand Oaks, CA: Sage.

CHAPTER 6

METAPRAGMATICS IN THE ETHNOGRAPHY OF LANGUAGE POLICY

MIGUEL PÉREZ-MILANS

DISCUSSIONS of the contributions made by ethnographic and discourse-based approaches to the field of language policy and planning (hereafter, LPP) have progressively built up over the last few decades. (For a comprehensive overview of different strands of such developments, see, in this volume, Johnson, Chapter 3; Martin-Jones & da Costa Cabral, Chapter 4; Wodak & Savski, Chapter 5). With roots going back to the 1980s, and having gathered significant momentum at the turn of the twenty-first century, this strand of LPP research has rapidly evolved, leading to a plethora of work that has examined the ways in which social actors make sense of language policies across different institutional contexts worldwide.

The emergence of this epistemological approach in LPP studies follows the ethnographic turn initiated in the social sciences in the 1960s, a smooth consolidation that was facilitated by a highly cohesive body of research that has contributed to making the developments in the linguistic, anthropological, and educational traditions palatable to researchers and practitioners with no previous training in these fields (see, particularly, Canagarajah, 2006; Davis, 1994; Hornberger, 2009; Hornberger & Johnson, 2007; Johnson, 2009; McCarty, 2011). The pedagogical contribution of such a body of work is twofold. First, it has been able to articulate an appealing rationale that builds on the field's past struggles to overcome a top-down document-based analysis, which does not lead to an adequate understanding of the ways in which policies are interpreted and appropriated by social actors throughout what Canagarajah once called the "language policy cycle" (2006, p. 158):

> Since community needs and attitudes may be ambivalent, the processes of implementing policy can be multifarious, and the outcomes of policy surprising. . . . Developing knowledge of specific situations and communities is a necessary starting point for model-building. Ethnography, which is oriented towards developing hypotheses in context, can be of help in this regard. (2006, p. 154)

He adds:

> in interpersonal . . . relationships, marginalized subjects are resisting established policies, constructing alternative practices that exist parallel to the dominant policies and, sometimes, initiate changes that transform unequal relationships. . . . Such realities point to incipient and emergent cases of "language planning from the bottom". . . . It therefore behooves LPP scholars to listen to what ethnography reveals about life at the grass-roots level—the indistinct voices and acts of individuals in whose name policies are formulated. (p. 154)

The realization that policy formulation shapes (and is shaped by) interpersonal relations in localized contexts leaves ethnographic and discourse-based work as a suitable framework in the LPP agenda. In alignment with Ricento's (2000) claim that "micro-level research (the sociolinguistics of language) will need to be integrated with macro-level investigations (the sociolinguistics of society) to provide a more complete explanation for language behaviour" (pp. 208–209), Hornberger and Johnson (2011) argue that ethnography and discourse-based analysis offers a valuable lens to

> (1) illuminate and inform the development of LPP in its various types—status, corpus, and acquisition—and across the various processes of the LPP cycle—creation, interpretation, and appropriation; (2) shed light on how official top-down LPP plays out in particular contexts, including its interaction with bottom-up LPP; and (3) uncover the indistinct voices, covert motivations, embedded ideologies, invisible instances, or unintended consequences of LPP. (p. 275)

Second, the successful consolidation of this emerging tradition in LPP studies has also been reinforced by the use of powerful methodological metaphors and heuristics widely borrowed, circulated, and applied by researchers. One of the best-known metaphors is the "onion," used for the first time by Ricento and Hornberger (1996) to highlight the multilayered nature of language policy processes. In ethnographically oriented research, this metaphor gained a heightened momentum when Hornberger and Johnson (2007) re-branded it by referring to the action of "slicing the onion ethnographically" (p. 509) in order to invite LPP scholars to document the ways in which texts, discourses, and practices intersect across different settings, from production to appropriation of specific language policies.

As for heuristics, proponents of ethnographically oriented LPP have been heavily inspired by the foundational strand of the ethnography of communication in the field of linguistic anthropology, with the goal of describing the discursive and social organization of speech communities in which language policies are put into motion. In particular, they have extensively drawn from Hymes's (1974) SPEAKING acronym, which stands for eight focal components in the analysis of language use, including Setting, Participants, Ends, Act sequence, Key, Instrumentalities, Norms, and Genre. An influential example is the grid proposed by Johnson (2009), who adjusted Hymes's heuristic to guide other ethnographers of language policy during data collection, in order for them to have a point of reference with which to describe closely relevant aspects in the process of policymaking, namely (1) agents, (2) goals, (3) processes, (4) discourses that engender and perpetuate a given policy, and (5) the dynamic social and historical contexts in which the policy exists.

Although the previously mentioned body of work has put ethnography firmly on the language policy research agenda since the turn of the twenty-first century (Martin-Jones & da Costa Cabral, Chapter 4 in this volume), I argue here that it has not yet sufficiently addressed some persistent challenges. These include (a) the reproduction of dichotomies, such as that of agency/structure, that go against well-established developments in both social theory and communication studies; (b) a focus on explicit commentaries on policy documents by participants, which are taken as the primary context of interpretation; (c) an event-based entry point to data collection/analysis that is taken as the relevant platform to understand the implementation and appropriation of policies in a given context, even in multi-sited research where a compound of events is defined a priori by researchers; and (d) a tendency toward portrayals where research participants appear as mere ciphers in the matrix.

These issues are unraveled throughout the rest of the chapter. In the next section, I review contemporary shifts undertaken in the language disciplines in relation to metapragmatic analysis of texts, contexts, and meanings—an approach that may still need further attention in ethnography of language policy research. I do so with reference to some existing work in LPP. Then I examine previous ethnographic work on language education policy in Hong Kong (see Pérez-Milans & Soto, 2016) through the proposed lens, after which the final discussion section reflects on some of the implications that can be derived from this perspective more broadly, in relation to the study of LPP processes under conditions of late modernity.

TEXT, CONTEXT, AND MEANING: A METAPRAGMATIC APPROACH

In their concluding remarks to an edited volume that reports on worldwide ethnographic studies of language policies, Hornberger and Johnson (2011) state that

[e]thnography of language policy is uniquely suited to illuminate both top-down and bottom-up LPP, but a lingering problem remains: How do we make explicit connections between macro-level language policy and local language practice? What kind of data is necessary to show that there is a connection? Unless a bilingual teacher explicitly states that, in her classroom, she has interpreted and appropriated some language policy X in explicit ways, how can we be sure that educational practice is necessarily influenced by educational policy? (p. 284)

Such (lingering) questions are not only geared toward fundamental methodological aspects in the ethnography of language policy; they also force us to reveal our own ontological assumptions as to how we conceptualize the interface between text, context, and meaning. In fact, data collection driven by the assumption that participants' explicit talk about policy documents is the only legitimate path in LPP research relies on two conceptual premises. On the one hand, this approach places denotation as the sole entry point to meaning. On the other, it frames policy documents as cultural artifacts that only shape social life externally and, as such, their influence in people's lives can only be (empirically) grasped through analysis of talk *about* it. While it may have been intended to raise greater methodological awareness among LPP researchers, the statement by Hornberger and Johnson can lead to research designs that reify the widely problematized view of societal processes as operating at two independent realms, the so-called micro and macro. Accordingly, participant's accounts are likely to be considered as (micro-societal) instances of *agency* against the background of policy documents that are then taken as (macro-societal) structural properties existing out there autonomously and which can only be made sense of (or even appropriated) by individuals.

A departure from this standpoint requires an epistemological take that pays closer attention to the participants' trajectories of reflexive engagement with conventional/normative forms of social organization brought about by policy transformations. One way to investigate this is through (1) understanding meaning as tied to performative use of language in which what is talked about cannot be detached from actors' negotiation of social position and moral stance in situated encounters and institutional contexts; and (2) displacing the locus of analysis from event to trajectory. This has been the focus of long-standing research in the language disciplines, particularly in the strands that have put a metapragmatic focus into play. Each of the two aspects will be further explored in the following, in turn, with reference to two closely interrelated disciplinary shifts.

From Denotation to Performance

As mentioned in the introduction to this chapter, ethnography of language policy has drawn, from the start, on Hymes's tradition of ethnography of speaking, which introduced a major historical shift in the choice of units of analysis in the language disciplines. Away from a historical tendency to focus on decontextualized linguistic features (i.e., sentences and utterances), Hymes proposed for the first time a non-linguistic unit: the (speech) event (1964). This shift has several consequences for LPP researchers, the most important being that context is no longer defined as "background facts" (Blommaert & Bulcaen, 2000) that are needed to interpret a set of autonomous linguistic phenomena. Instead, it requires researchers to look into the daily communicative practices through which a given speech community (re)constructs shared frames of production and interpretation of meaning. Nevertheless, this key principle can be easily jeopardized if these daily communicative practices are characterized through brushstrokes in researchers' descriptions, accompanied only by running commentaries from participants in the course of research interviews. Indeed, Hymes himself did not seem to advocate this form of inquiry; his notion of *speech event* built upon Malinowski's interest in the pragmatic use of language and the notion of *context of situation* whereby the utterance itself is seen as becoming

> only intelligible when it is placed within its context of situation, if I may be allowed to coin an expression which indicates on the one hand that the conception of *context* has to be broadened and on the other that the situation in which words are uttered can never be passed over as irrelevant to the linguistic expression. (Malinowski, 1923, p. 306)

Much of the emphasis in Malinowski's work was placed on the need for a linguistic analysis supplemented by ethnographic description of situations within which speech occurs, though he also laid down the basis for a conceptualization of language as a mode of practical action (see Goodwin & Duranti, 2000, for an in-depth overview of this foundational work). Thus, he stated, any form of situated speech reveals

> the dependence of the meaning of each word upon practical experience, and of the structure of each utterance upon the momentary situation in which it is spoken. Thus the consideration of linguistic uses associated with any practical pursuit, leads us to the conclusion that language . . . ought to be regarded and studied against the background of human activities and as a mode of human behavior in practical matters. . . . Language appears to us in this function not as an instrument of reflection but as a mode of action. (1923, p. 312)

To put it this way,

> a word is used when it can produce an action and not to describe one, still less to translate thoughts. The word therefore has a power of its own, it is a means of bringing things about, it is a handle to acts and objects and not a definition of them. . . . Meaning, as we have seen, does not come . . . from contemplation of things, or analysis of occurrences, but in practical and active acquaintance with relevant situations. The real knowledge of a word comes through the practice of appropriately using it within a certain situation. (1923, pp. 321, 325)

In his SPEAKING model, Hymes furthered our understanding of the performative nature of language by defining context as emerging from situated forms of action in which social actors engage with more durable conventions. The eight components of his grid speak to this, though due to space constraints I will illustrate this point by referring only to three of them: Situation, Participants, and Genre. Situation refers to the location of speech events in space/time, though it should be noted that Hymes operationalized it through two situational subcomponents in order to capture both the actual physical circumstances of the event (setting) and the psychological, culturally bound definition of the setting (scene). This is to address an inescapable observation: that although participants in an encounter must assume some physical dimensions of an event, they do not necessarily have to agree on the cultural conceptualization of such dimensions since these have to be represented through natural language and conventional ways of defining time and space. In his account of Hymes's model, Duranti (1985) cites an emblematic example of the culture-specific complexities of spatial and temporal arrangements in social interactions:

> Unlike our own culture, in which we have special settings for many kinds of events— classroom for classes, churches for religious rites, law courts for litigation, concert halls for music—among the Yakan a single structure, the house, [can be thought as providing] a setting for a great variety of social occasions. But a house, even a one-roomed Yakan house, is not just a space. It is a structured sequence of settings where social events are differentiated not only by the position in which they occur but also by the positions the actors have moved through to get there and the manner in which they have made those moves. (Frake, 1975, p. 37, cited in Duranti, 1985, p. 206)

The degree of cultural exotism that transpires from this quote reflects the anthropological tone of the time, and indeed participants do not need to live far away from each other (or to belong to different "tribes") to have different conventional expectations about situations. However, this does not invalidate the important argument that Frake puts forward: far from general characterizations in which the spatial and temporal dimensions of social encounters are described through static and objective emplacements (e.g., at the park in the evening), the spatiotemporal dimensions of Hymes's model require a fine-grained description of social interactions whereby participants co-construct and negotiate boundaries in their attempt to achieve a common understanding of the activity at hand. Duranti sums this up when he claims that "anyone who has ever looked at actual events from the point of view of the social interaction that goes on in them knows that the internal spatial and temporal organization of an event is always relevant to speaking patterns within the event" (1985, p. 206).

With regard to Participant in the SPEAKING grid, this category represents a departure from the speaker-hearer dyad via opening the door to more nuanced descriptions in which what social actors say/do to their interlocutors (including the researcher) must be examined against the background of the different participant positions (or ways of being a speaker/listener) that are negotiated in the course of the encounter and which function as a salient context for the interpretation of meaning. Goffman (1981, pp. 124–169), who developed this further, has shown how encounters are always embedded activities in which talk has a layering effect that impacts on the ways in which participants self/hetero-identify with what is talked about.

Someone talking to a group of five other people, for example, may position her interlocutors differently depending on whether or not these are directly addressed (verbally or otherwise) while the speaker utters her words—think of the layering effect of an instance in which the speaker is reprimanding a certain behavior that she disapproves while looking straight into the eyes of one of her interlocutors. Similarly, the speaker may take a different responsibility toward her talk by taking the inter-actional role of the "author" of the words she utters, that is, "as someone who has selected the sentiments that are being expressed and the words in which they are encoded" (Goffman, 1981, p. 144), as opposed to when she positions herself as an "an-imator" who just reproduces words uttered by others.

Finally, Genre in Hymes's model brings into focus a guiding cultural point of ref-erence against which actors negotiate content and social relations (see also Bakhtin, 1986; Briggs & Bauman, 1992; Hanks, 1987). Drawing on the notion of *speech genre*, this component is concerned with models of social situations in which specific conventions (i.e., expectations) apply regarding how participants are supposed to in-teract. Hanks (1987) followed up on this and described the interface between genre and performance (one intimately connected with the interplay between social struc-ture and individual agency) in these terms:

> The conventions of genre help define the possibilities of meaning in discourse and the level of generality or specificity at which description is cast. Whether we read a text as fiction, parody, prayer, or documentary is a generic decision with important consequences for interpretation. Viewed as constituent elements in a system of signs, speech genres have value loadings, social distributions, and typical performance styles according to which they are shaped in the course of utterance. (Hanks, 1987, p. 670)

From this perspective, conventional expectations (or cultural structures) regarding appropriate ways of participating in a given context are not considered mere ex-ternal templates to which participants must conform, but instead resources available to social actors for either confirming the established norms or for disrupting them for specific communicative purposes. This is of significance for LPP research since policy documents, and the set of normative expectations and values they carry, can be artfully manipulated to yield significant effects in situated practices, such as to reveal something about the characteristics of the content that is being talked about, or of the interpersonal relations among the involved interlocutors in the encounter.

In sum, the principles underpinning Hymes's work seem to fit uneasily with accounts of participants' talk about policies whereby the stream of talk under examination is taken as a transparent window to meaning via detachment from the situational dynamics in which it occurs. In the case of ethnography of language policy, often carried out in institutional contexts, the conceptualization of research interviews as direct routes to large-scale historical, socioeconomic, and political processes via content analysis also ignores the institutional order in which such situational dynamics are placed. As shown by subsequent developments of institutionally oriented ethnography of communication (see Cicourel, 1992; Heller, 1999; Martín Rojo, 2010; Pérez-Milans, 2013), policies are not just texts shaping social life in institutions externally; they constitute normative/moral frameworks that shape the discursive arrangement of daily routines in accordance with a set of assumptions as to what constitutes legitimate knowledge and appropriate forms of participation.

Thus, participants' performative actions in the research site need to be carefully examined against the background of the social and moral categories about "good" and "bad" participants/personae/forms of knowledge that are constructed and that emerge out of such institutionalized discursive arrangements; these in fact may constitute a point of reference for participants when they position themselves and others in the fieldwork. Put differently, language policy processes can be studied as invoked performatively by actors' situated engagement with daily normative conventions and associated types of social persona in institutional settings.

It is now worth moving on to the second disciplinary shift involved in a metapragmatic approach to LPP, one that requires an examination of social actors' trajectories of identification.

From Event to Trajectory

The opening up of traditional analytic concerns with communicative events to a preoccupation with social processes that consist of interconnected multiple events has been a common denominator across different areas, from literary studies (Bakhtin, 1981) to linguistic anthropology (Agha, 2005; Silverstein, 2005; Wortham, 2006) to sociolinguistics (Blommaert, 2010; Rampton, 2006). This preoccupation is indeed part of a long-term disciplinary conversation interested in the capacity of speech to connect historical moments or, in other words, to locate traditional models for thinking about discourse within larger sociohistorical frameworks:

> Terms like "the speech event"... (Hymes, 1974) or "the interaction order" (Goffman, 1983) are names for bounded episodes of social history in which persons encounter each other through communicative behaviors amenable to recording- and transcript-based study, thus comprising an apparently concrete and easily segmentable swatch of social life. Yet the data of social life plucked from their isolable moments invariably point to lived moments that lie beyond them. We know that anyone who effectively engages in a given discursive encounter has participated in others before it and thus brings to the current encounter a biographically specific discursive history

that, in many respects, shapes the individual's socialized ability to use and construe utterances (as well as footings, stances, identities, and relationships mediated by utterances) within the current encounter; and if the current encounter has any enduring consequences for the individual, these are manifest in (and therefore identifiable only by considering) future encounters in which that individual plays a part. Similarly, the observation that the social values of particular speech forms (lexations, speech styles, registers, etc.) change over time is a way of noting that different sociohistorical encounters instantiate different ratified values of these speech forms and thus raises questions about the social logics that mark continuities and discontinuities across these encounters. (Agha, 2005, p. 1)

In ethnographically oriented LPP research, the event-based focus has been privileged since Hymes's foundational work, and has continued to be influential in the further institutionally oriented developments mentioned in the previous section. In these strands, attention to patterns in the discursive organization of social life in institutions has often led to holistic descriptions of recurrent routines in a given set of social domains that shed little light on the indeterminacies and complexities of how individual forms of alignment and identification emerge from trajectories of socialization connecting social actors, networks, and communicative encounters. In Wortham's (2005) words,

The . . . socialization and social identification of an individual is rarely accomplished, outside of ritual events, in one discursive interaction. Individuals get socially identified only across a trajectory, as subsequent events come increasingly to presuppose identities signaled in earlier ones. Socialization happens, and social identities emerge, across several events as subsequent ones come to presuppose an identity for an individual. A "poetic structure" of signs and event-segments gets established, across events, as these signs and segments become mutually presupposing. Such a structure of mutually presupposing signs and segments allows a trajectory to form, across which an individual gets socialized and emerges as a recognizable type of person. (p. 98)

I argue that, in LPP, the full implementation of this shift requires studying chains of events with an eye on those across which social actors build alignments and/or de-alignments with policy-related normative frames. In this sense, this shift is not just one concerned with displacing the attention from isolated events to interconnected events; it involves a more in-depth change of perspective that foregrounds the *process* by which certain cultural models of action are interpersonally taken up, made sense of, and socially ratified by (reflexive) actors in their attempt to display alliances and de-alliances.

Thus, the study of this process entails tracking down series of events through which communicative (i.e., semiotic, linguistic, discursive) practices get associated with identities or social personae that, within a given social group, acquire recognizable pragmatic values and come to invoke specific relationships and stances with respect to institutional (including policy-related) transformations. Agha (2007) refers to these cultural models of action emerging through communicative practices, within specific social groups, as "registers of discourse":

> A register of discourse is a reflexive model of discourse behavior. The model is performable through utterances in the sense that producing a criterial utterance indexes a stereotypic image of social personhood or interpersonal relationship. The model is formulated by semiotic practices that differentiate a register's forms from the rest of the language, evaluate these repertoires as having specific pragmatic values . . . and make these forms and values known to a population of users through processes of communicative transmission. (pp. 80–81)

There are two major implications of this. First, the description of such a process is intimately linked to the type of performative approach to meaning that was discussed in the previous section. Agha continues,

> Our focus therefore needs to be not on things alone or personae alone but on acts of performance and construal through which the two are linked, and the conditions under which these links become determinate for actors. . . . Utterances are a very special kind of emblematic sign because, in being perceivable, utterances make the things they denote present or palpable as objects of cognition; such referents can function as . . . things to which emblematic values can be attached through their treatment as encounters within the game of interaction, e.g., through the enactment of referential stances or alignments. The large majority of such emergent emblems are highly evanescent in interaction (they emerge and fade away quickly). But individuals can also formulate persistent alignments to such emblems, and such acts can polarize interactants into factional groupings. (pp. 235–236)

Second, tracing the emergence of these situated cultural models of action brings about a certain degree of anxiety on the part of the researcher who can no longer rely on a priori decisions about where to look, and when, within a given institutional setting. Thus, this alternative approach demands methodological guidelines, and Silverstein's (2005) notion of *interdiscursivity* offers some useful basis for it. In Silverstein's view, an interdiscursive connection between two communicative events can be established when one speech event points to other events via an indexical relationship, that is, when a stretch of discourse in the here and now invokes another discourse token or feature of discourse in a remote space/time, with specific communicative purposes. An example of a discourse token is an instance of reported speech to allege that some specific utterance actually occurred in another event, while a feature of discourse may be a social type of speaker, a scenario of use, or an action type that is generically associated with the usage.

Interdiscursivity, both as a construct and methodological guidance, has proved productive in sociolinguistic and linguistic anthropological research, particularly in areas concerned with language socialization in educational settings, where it provides analytical room for describing aspects of academic socialization and classroom identity development (see Wortham, 2006). In LPP, the study of communicative event chains has also allowed tracing the links between language policy texts, talk, and practices. This is exemplified in Mortimer (2013), who identifies widely circulating images of the Guaraní speaker as they appear in policy texts, in educators' talk about policy, and in practice, in the context of Paraguay's language education policy.

Mortimer focuses on a language policy that aimed at institutionalizing the Guaraní language, together with the Spanish language, in the Paraguayan school system, both as a subject of instruction and as a medium of instruction for all students. By looking at speech chains, her analysis reveals how different policy actors (i.e., teachers, teacher trainers, school principals, and supervisors) interpreted and made sense of policy texts with reference to two main types of social persona: that of the Guaraní-speaking student, which was linked to meanings about rurality, ignorance, and low-class citizens who do not speak any Spanish; and that of the urban, middle-class Spanish-speaking student. On the basis of these types of persona that emerged from making-sense practices among such actors in different domains, Mortimer shows how the policy was effectively appropriated in a way that the Guaraní language was never fully implemented as the medium of instruction, but instead just as a subject, therefore denying Guaraní-dominant children an opportunity to learn more fully through Guaraní and putting those who speak only Spanish in a privileged position.

Yet, focusing on practices and texts through which the speaker of Guaraní is *talked about* (or described) leads Mortimer to an analytical approach that lacks a performative angle. In other words, she only looks into instances of reporting speech whereby her participants refer to policy documents to make sense (through description) of different types of speakers of Guaraní, thus resulting in denotative accounts of meaning that hardly differ from those discussed in the previous section.[1] While continuing this line of research, future work in LPP requires closer attention to how interpersonal forms of alignment and identification are enacted through patterned trajectories of socialization, in response to key language policy–related events. Drawing from previous research carried out in the educational context of Hong Kong (Pérez-Milans & Soto, 2014, 2016), the following section attempts to deliver a snapshot (or flavor) of this type of approach.

Enregisterment of Ethnic Minority Activism in Hong Kong

As Hong Kong changed from a British colony to a Special Administrative Region of the People's Republic of China, medium of instruction policies have become a heated arena linked to wider socioeconomic struggles over who gets to decide what languages should be learned or taught, by whom, when, and to what degree (see Tollefson & Tsui, Chapter 13 in this volume). After a colonial period in which the British Hong Kong government's policy over medium of instruction (MOI) was based on a laissez-faire model that allowed schools to choose either

Chinese or English as the medium of instruction, the handover to China paved the way, in September 1998, to a mandatory streaming policy that introduced Chinese as the medium of instruction in all government and aided secondary schools—taken to mean Modern Standard Chinese in traditional characters as the written MOI and Cantonese as the oral MOI—unless otherwise specified under special conditions.

As a result, only 114 schools out of over 400 were allowed to remain English-medium schools, based on the test results of their fresh intakes in English and Chinese, which caused marked public opposition in a context where English remains a matter of prestige and continues to be key to access a largely English-medium higher education system. Thus, the Government Education Bureau responded to the public demands by eliminating, in 2010, the bifurcation of institutions into English medium of instruction (EMI) and Chinese medium of instruction (CMI), therefore giving secondary schools greater autonomy over choosing their MOI, in accordance with a set of criteria specified by the education authority.

Under these circumstances, the study of a government-aided secondary school that in 2010 shifted its policy (from an only Chinese-medium one to incorporating an EMI section in which Chinese was taught just as a subject) offered a relevant case to understand the local, institutional, and interpersonal complexities involved in the process.[2] In the sections that follow, I introduce the school in question and track down the emergence of ethnic minority activism as a joint cultural model of action that allowed a group of participants to build specific alignments and de-alignments that have wider policy implications in contemporary Hong Kong.

MAT School

The school, which we call MAT, is located in a working-class area in the north-western part of Hong Kong and was initially set up by a local industrial association in the 1980s, with the official aim of targeting working-class ethnically Chinese families living in the area. This focus, however, has progressively changed, as a result of both demographic and institutional transformations in the region. On the demographic side, this area of Hong Kong has seen in the last decade an increase of working-class families migrating from Nepal and Pakistan, after Hong Kong's return to China and the subsequent agreements to grant permanent residence to those citizens who were trained as soldiers for the British army during colonial times. As for institutional changes, these are concerned with local schools being more and more pushed to compete among themselves over resources, prestige, and student enrollment, in a system where schools are categorized and ranked as band 1, band 2, or band 3, according to their students' results in the Hong Kong public university entrance examinations.

At the intersection of these transformations, low-ranked band-3 schools such as MAT have struggled to meet the minimum student intake required to keep the government's funding, mainly due to a low prestige in their local areas. Thus, MAT's administrators decided in 2010 to change the linguistic profile of the school and open up an EMI division with the goal of targeting students with Pakistani and Nepali backgrounds whose working-class parents had migrated to the school's surroundings after Hong Kong's return to China in 1997.

The shift opened MAT's doors to newly hired teachers who had previous experiences with so-called ethnic minority students and were able to teach in English through unconventional approaches, in the context of the school's discursive redefinition of its pedagogical approaches for the newly established English-based division in which "tailor-made curriculum," "critical thinking," and "non-test-taking educational philosophies" featured as core values. Indeed, such values permeated the school's brochures and other forms of institutional publicity produced and displayed to attract new enrollments from the local community. Under these circumstances, in the fall of 2011, a new cohort of students aged 12–14 started their first year of secondary education at MAT with high expectations, after years of struggling in the Chinese-based mode of instruction at their previous schools.

Nevertheless, and despite the local advertisements mobilized by the new EMI division, the core pedagogical values turned out to be difficult to implement. As Hong Kong public schools are required to follow the official curriculum and standards set up by the government, their degree of adjustment to such standards determines their institutional ranking and related status, thus making difficult the implementation of pedagogical approaches other than those preparing students for the public exams that students in Hong Kong take, at the end of secondary school. As a result, the core pedagogical values became a discursive terrain for social struggle, contestation, and performance at MAT. A critical event in the orientation of all school actors to this pedagogical terrain took place in October 2014, when two teachers in the EMI section, Mr C. and Lagan, parted ways with MAT after clashes over pedagogical agendas became irreconcilable (see Soto, 2016).

Both teachers had been initially considered as key actors in getting the new English-based section at MAT running, yet eventually the school administrators judged Mr. C and Lagan's non-textbook-based educational philosophy as too lax and inadequate. Extract 1 below, which shows how some of them make sense of all of these issues, is taken from a group interview conducted by Karen, Lisa, and Steven, three university students at the Faculty of Education in the University of Hong Kong (HKU), who were working on a class research assignment and focused their study on the Chinese language-learning experiences of students with ethnic minority backgrounds in the Hong Kong education system. Guided by their course tutor at HKU, the undergraduate students approached Mr. C and some of his former students who were still enrolled at MAT (Sita, Pramiti, and Radhika), in order to conduct a group interview with all of them.

Extract 1. "So-called high class"

1	Karen:	you guys get enough teachers? / like // like // you get- the- like /
2		different teachers for subjects or is there teachers
3		[who have to teach two things]
4	Sita:	[we have many] / I think we have teachers but-
5	Radhika:	yeah / but mostly for / CMI {Chinese-as the-medium-of-instruction section}
6	Pramiti:	(yes)*
7	Karen:	what's that mean? / they- they- they get more teachers and more
8		[resources]?
9	Pramiti:	[yes]
10	Radhika:	[yes]
11	Sita:	yes
12	Karen:	and you guys get less teachers and [less resources]
13	Sita:	[because] &
14	Pramiti:	& because ah-
15	Sita:	we're looking for / teachers who can really /
16		uh / you know / support US ↑
17	Karen:	hm
18	Pramiti:	but we are not even getting that
19	Karen:	yeah
20	{laughter}	
21	Sita:	we did!
22	Pramiti:	we did get that [before]
23	Sita:	[we lost] / that
24	Karen:	oh! that is not obviously not equal /
25		because they seem to be getting more resources than you
26		[guys]
27	Sita:	[because] the- the CMI students have been already-
28		already be- [brainwashed]
29	Pramiti:	[because] most-
30	Karen:	[{laughter}]
31	Pramiti:	[most] most of the / Chinese / uh / you know / the teachers ↑
32	Karen:	hm &
33	Pramiti:	& they / they cannot speak English very well /
34	Karen:	yeah &
35	Pramiti:	& and then / you know / for the teachers who are teaching us /
36		they can speak English quite well /
37		so I think that's also / [one of]=
38	Karen:	[oh!]
39	Pramiti:	= reasons why we have less-
40	Karen:	because the requirements to teach you guys are technically higher /
41		[because]
42	Pramiti:	[hm]
43	Karen:	= they need to speak English as well
44	Steven:	how about the Chinese lessons? do you guys learn Chinese or English /
45		like / like you said you have a hard time understanding Chinese /
46		like listening to Chinese / do they explain / in /
47		Chinese or do they explain in English? // [like for a certain word?]=
48	Sita:	[uh]
49	Steven:	= [or a] =

50	Radhika:	[in]
51	Steven:	= [certain]=
52	Radhika:	[in-]
53	Steven:	= [essay?]
54	Radhika:	[for the] high class / {making the air-quotes gesture} (so-called high class)*
55	{everyone laughs}	
56	Sita:	so-called high class {laughter}
57	Radhika:	they- they- they don't teach us in English
58	Pramiti:	in [Chinese]
59	Radhika:	[they just] speak Chinese &
60	Pramiti:	& in Chinese &
61	Karen:	& all in Chinese?
62	Pramiti:	yes
63	Sita:	but for the middle group and lower gro- group they explain us in English
64	Radhika:	yeah / [but even-]
65	Steven:	[(())] &
66	Radhika:	& yeah
67	Steven:	how are their [English]?
68	Sita:	[uh] /
69		well I had different teachers this year group
70		he kind of explain really well &
71	Karen:	& hm &
72	Sita:	& but before / uh /
73		my teacher had a hard time to explain [in English]
74	Karen:	[ah!]
75	Sita:	yeah / so I think-
76	Karen:	(()) like- because- some of the times / like /
77		we- we wanna teach the language by completely speaking that language /
78		like / for my French classes at school / they just keep talking to me in French
79	{laughter}	
80	Karen:	but I get the problem / the problem is that /
81		if I don't understand something / and ask them /
82		there is no point in them explaining it to me in French /
83		because I- [I don't understand]
84	Radhika:	[yeah yeah] {laughter}
85	Pramiti:	[yeah yeah] {laughter}
86	Karen:	do you guys face this problem as well? /
87		so do you guys prefer / like teaching being able to use two &
88	Radhika:	& yes &
89	Karen:	& like both languages to help you guys?
90	Sita:	yeah &
91	Karen:	& and not just / Chinese Chinese Chinese
92	Radhika:	yes

Extract 1 not only shows how participants talk about (or describe) some of the background issues anticipated earlier; it also reveals the extent to which pedagogy becomes a salient feature upon which interview participants negotiate social relations while at the same time layering official and unofficial voices/stances that depict MAT negatively. In so doing, they detach themselves from conventional associations established at the school between, on the one hand, teaching/learning styles related to the distribution of groupings of students within the space of the school as well as the linguistic labels typifying these groupings and, on the other, the moral values and types of social persona associated with the categories of "good student" or "desirable ways of teaching and learning" upon which such teaching/learning styles and groupings are legitimated. The forms of interpersonal alignment enacted to detach themselves from such associations are also discursively connected to the departure of Mr. C and Lagan, after months in which they and the school administrators struggled over who gets to define what counts as proper ways of teaching and learning at the English-based section in MAT (line 23).

In other words, Extract 1 captures a moment in which participant's situated forms of alignment index (i.e., point to) wider institutional struggles derived from the policy shifts undergone at MAT. This emerges throughout two key segments in the extract, one regarding the distribution of resources across the two sections at MAT (lines 1–43), and the other concerned with their teachers' linguistic accommodation in the teaching of Chinese as a subject in the English-based section (lines 44–92). In the first segment, Karen, Sita, Radikha, and Pramiti coordinate their actions to achieve a common understanding regarding how the two sections in the school are related to one another. From issues concerned with unequal distribution of the number of teachers across the two sections (1–11) to imbalance in the degree of support offered by their current teachers, in contrast to other types of teachers that they had in the past and lost (in what seems to be a reference to Mr. C and Lagan's departure) (15–23), the accounts provided are collaboratively linked to inequity (24–26), leading to further contrasts that characterize students in the Chinese-based section as "brainwashed" (27–28) and students in the English-based section as requiring teachers with "higher" teaching qualifications (31–43).

The second segment of the extract brings about a crucial instance of reflexive reanalysis whereby official labels and associated types of personhood brought about by the language policy shift at MAT get collaboratively reinterpreted. In response to Steven's shift of topic toward the Chinese subject in the English-based section of the school (lines 44–53), Radhika explains that in her group the teacher of Chinese only uses Chinese in class, a claim that is reinforced by Sita and Pramiti via repetition and overlapping (lines 54–60). In her turn, Radhika refers to her group through the label of "high class" (line 54), a meta-sign that groups together a set of school-related labels upon which the social life of MAT is institutionally arranged (e.g., "advanced students" versus "low-achieving students" placed in "low groups"). That is to say, Radhika sets up a frame of interpretation in which Chinese classes in the English-based section are presented as arranged hierarchically according to the students' proficiency, a common practice in many different subjects in public schools in Hong Kong, where students are grouped according to their academic results.

However, after uttering the "high class" label, Radhika detaches personally from it by rephrasing it ("so-called high class") and accompanying it with the air-quote gesture, in what seems to signal a parodic take on the label itself, and, in turn, of the values and types of social persona associated with it (e.g., "good students"). This layering of an institutional frame with a parodic one through which the student signals shared ambivalent attitudes (i.e., official and interpersonal voices) is taken up by the rest of the interactants, who orient toward Radhika's act by laughing out loud (line 55), followed by Sita's animation of Radhika's act of rephrasing in laughter (line 56).

From that point onward, Karen offers a platform for building a joint stance together with the school students, and against their teachers of Chinese at MAT. Following up on Sita's response that her teachers in the middle and lower groups use English in the Chinese subject—which gets immediately framed (with the guide of Steven and Radhika) as one in which, even in that case, her teachers' lack of proficiency in English does not help her fully understand (lines 63–75)—Karen recounts her own previous experiences as a learner of French during her school days in the past. In so doing, she positions herself as a confused student who felt frustrated whenever her teachers attempted to explain, without rephrasing it in English, something that she did not understand well in French. This gives way to a series of exchanges with Radhika, Pramiti, and Sita in which the students align with the interviewer through laughter (line 79), affirmative responses (lines 84, 85, 88, 90, 92), or elaborations that highlight that their teachers do not support them or try to reach out to them, contrary to what the school students believe is their teachers' duty as educators.

These group-based alignments among the actors at this newly formed section of the school became persistent over time, therefore paving the way to enregistered forms of identity performance whereby "distinct forms of [communication] come to be socially recognized (or enregistered) as indexical of speaker attributes by a population of language users" (Agha, 2005, p. 38). In the case of MAT, this process of enregisterment involved the joint enactment of doing ethnic minority-based activism within a well-defined network of social actors that included the students in the EMI section and some of their teachers (e.g., Mr. C and Lagan, among others), as well as researchers such as myself and other community-based minority activists. This register of discourse allowed the students to display their disaffiliation with MAT while at the same time aligning themselves with English-based non-government-aided secondary school institutions in Hong Kong, such as Hong Kong Liberal College (HKLC), a prestigious two-year international school that offers an International Baccalaureate diploma and which, according to its website, targets students aged 16 to 18 "who are already grounded in their own cultures but impressionable enough to learn from others" and has as its core values "international and intercultural understanding," "celebration of difference," "personal responsibility and integrity," "mutual responsibility and respect," "compassion and service," "respect for the environment," "a sense of idealism," "personal challenge," and "action and personal example."

The enregisterment of doing ethnic minority activism within the previously mentioned network is well evidenced in the case of Sita, a female of Nepali heritage born in Hong Kong who in 2015 was accepted on full scholarship to HKLC, after years of socioeconomic, academic, and emotional struggles at MAT. Her case will leave us with a better grasp of the emergence of this discourse register and its wider implications in Hong Kong.

The Case of Sita

Sita's early life has been marked by movement between Hong Kong and Nepal, and their corresponding school systems and language environments. Born in Hong Kong to Nepal-born parents, Sita gained both Hong Kong permanent residence and a Nepali passport. However, a few years after her birth, her parents parted ways, and her father, a former Gurkha (a term to refer to Nepalese soldiers who worked for the British army in colonial Hong Kong), moved to England and started a new family. Struggling to raise two daughters on her own, and having difficulty securing a kindergarten for her daughters, Sita's mother sent Sita and her younger sister to Nepal to live with their maternal grandmother. After a few years, Sita returned to Hong Kong to start primary education at an EMI school, but felt bullied by other students because she was not able to speak Cantonese outside the official English-based mode of instruction.

Following her primary-three year, though, her mother became concerned with her daughters' difficulties with writing and reading Nepali, and so Sita and her sister were returned to Nepal to finish primary school. Back in Nepal, Sita studied in a Nepali-medium school, and took English as an additional school subject. Yet, her troubles did not stop there, as Sita continued to be bullied by other Nepali students due to her low Nepali reading and writing skills. In 2011, at the end of primary school, Sita and her sister were brought back to Hong Kong to live with their mother and begin their secondary education. Upon their return, Sita had to repeat a year, and at that point her mother was convinced by Lagan to enroll both daughters at the newly formed English-based section of MAT.

Though Sita felt empowered within Mr C's critical pedagogical program and through activities organized by Lagan during her first years of secondary education, she found herself otherwise struggling within an environment of instability at MAT. As a form-one student, Sita painted herself as "ordinary" and "bored" and constrained by conflicts in her life (Pérez-Milans & Soto, 2014, p. 226). Soon after, other conflicts at MAT began to be featured in her life, most of them concerned with increasing tension and polarization of the CMI and the EMI divisions. The fact that the EMI section was initially envisioned as following a different pedagogical agenda than that of the CMI reinforced the tensions between teachers across sections, since they all needed to collaborate with each other to design standardized tests for each subject and grade in the school. Mounting tensions also involved the students in the school, leading to feelings of isolation on the part of the EMI students, who believed their peers in the CMI section did not want to interact with them because they had been divided by their teachers.

By the spring of 2015, when she was seventeen years old and in form four, Sita began to recursively articulate her feelings of connection to Nepal vis-à-vis her own school experiences at MAT and her future educational aspirations in HKLC. Two years before then, Mr. C and Lagan had turned Sita's attention toward HKLC as a site for greater academic and social attainment, as Lagan had opened doors to collaborative activities with the school that he and Mr. C considered as intellectually challenging for their students at MAT. Simultaneously, Mr. C and Lagan began preparing students who showed interest in applying for admission to HKLC, which follows the International Baccalaureate curriculum (also known as "IB curriculum") and, therefore, does not have to align with the official standards set up by the Hong Kong Education Bureau.

During the process of getting ready for her application to HKLC, which involved various rounds of short-listing and a set of interviews with an admission panel seeking candidates who meet the qualities specified earlier as core values of the institution, Sita made particularly salient identity attributes around the experiences of struggling and fighting for the rights of an imagined community who share the language and the homeland of Nepal in Hong Kong. These attributes became discursively linked to the label of "student activist" that Sita publicly attributed to herself as a new emblem of identity. Figure 6.1, a photo that she took and displayed on social media such as *Facebook*, is an example of the explicit use of this label for identity positioning, and of the linkage between the label and keywords associated with Mr. C's pedagogical interests concerned with "critical pedagogy," "Hong Kong minority students," "Freire" (in reference to the Brazilian educator Paulo Freire, author of the book *Pedagogy of the Oppressed* and pioneer of critical pedagogy as a discipline), "change," or "dreams."

The image shows a tag-name that Sita filled out and notes she took at a Hong Kong international academic symposium on ethnic minority education in 2015, three days after receiving the news that she had been admitted to HKLC. Sita and other members of our research program participated in a student panel at the conference, while Mr. C delivered a paper on his research as a critical educator in the Hong Kong local education system. But the attributes related to struggle and the fight for the rights of the Nepali community in Hong Kong were not only emblematically related to explicit labels and keywords; these identity attributes were also embedded in various activities undertaken across different domains, genres, and modalities.

In the course of Sita's trajectory, from MAT to HKLC, struggle and commitment to the Nepali community were also performed through a recurrent set of communicative practices that, in Sita's network, became "functionally reanalyzed as cultural models of action, as behaviors capable of indexing stereotypic characteristics of incumbents of particular interactional roles, and of relations among them"

FIGURE 6.1. Student activist.

(Agha, 2007. p. 55). Such practices, or demeanor indexicals that concern embodied indicators of status and character (Goffman, 1956), were built upon by two main recurrent types of action in the course of her upward academic trajectory, from a low-prestige school to a highly reputed international educational institution in Hong Kong, namely, critiquing the Hong Kong public educational system, and engaging in Nepali community-based actions.

These actions were mainly displayed in public spaces, mass media, online social media, and academic forums. With regard to critiquing the Hong Kong public education system, this type of action tended to be enacted through activities concerned with joining public gatherings to protest against educational policies on Chinese as a second language; participating at school fairs in which critical messages against government school policies on ethnic minority students were displayed; sharing with the Hong Kong and international media her personal conflicts and struggles (see Figure 6.2, taken from an interview published in the *South China Morning Post*); sending complaint letters on social justice to Hong Kong–based newspapers; joining *Facebook* group discussions with researchers, community workers, teachers, and classmates about Hong Kong education policy; displaying personal artwork on *Tumblr* and *Facebook*; participating in academic conference presentations led by Mr. C and attending other lectures at universities; and lecturing to tertiary audiences,

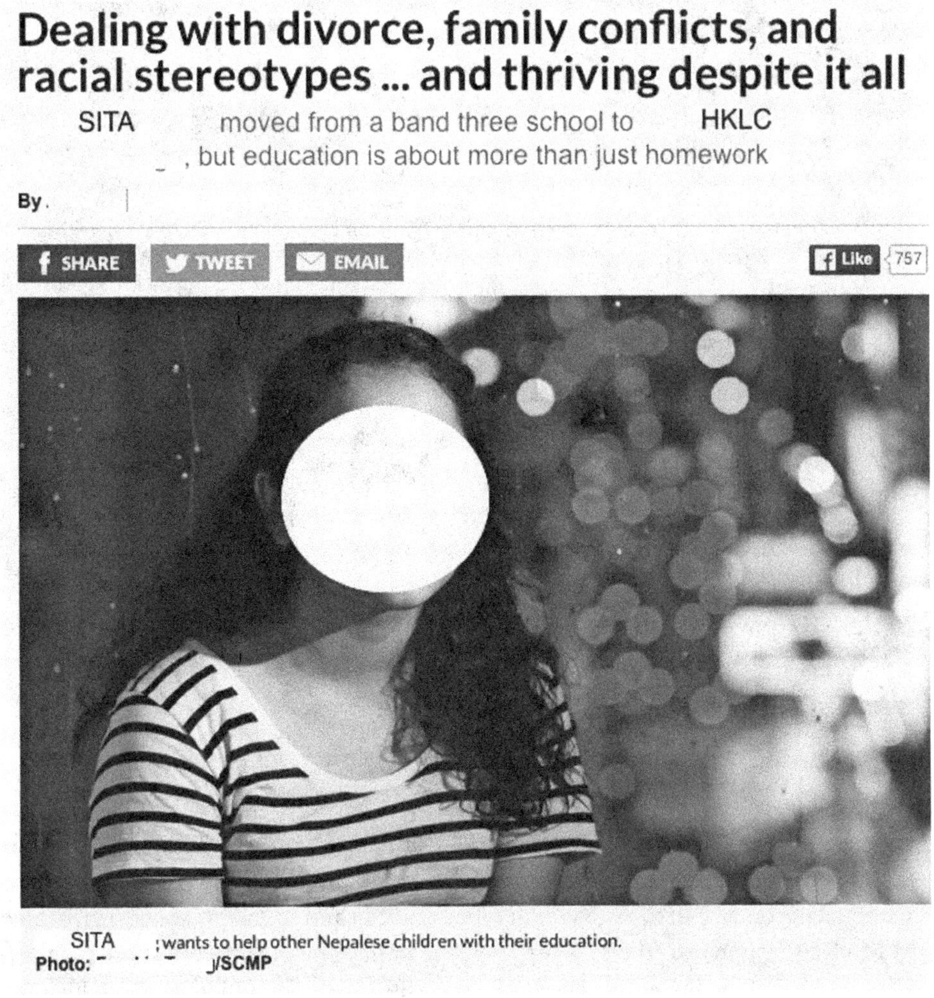
Dealing with divorce, family conflicts, and racial stereotypes ... and thriving despite it all

SITA moved from a band three school to HKLC , but education is about more than just homework

By

SHARE TWEET EMAIL Like 757

SITA ; wants to help other Nepalese children with their education.
Photo: /SCMP

FIGURE 6.2. Activism in the media.

Source: http://www.scmp.com/news/hong-kong

as part of classes on language, social class, ethnicity, and equity at the Faculty of Education in the University of Hong Kong.

As for the Nepali community-based actions, these included activities such as performing traditional Nepali dance for the Hong Kong public, in collaboration with the Nepalese Association of Hong Kong (see, for instance, Figure 6.3); arranging fundraising activities for Nepal's victims of earthquakes; participating in memorials to the Gurkha soldiers buried in Hong Kong and in monographs about their lives published in Hong Kong- and Nepali-based media; and taking part in activities online and in media connected with the Nepalese Association of Hong Kong.

FIGURE 6.3. Performing traditional Nepalese dance in Hong Kong public spaces.

In sum, Sita's trajectory of identification illustrates the process by which a specific set of communicative practices get regrouped around new identity attributes that emerged in contrast to the values and types of social and moral personae legitimated at MAT, in response to the school's language policy change and the subsequent institutional and pedagogical struggles that came with it. On the one hand, the interdiscursive performance of an ethnic minority activist social persona carries a set of alignments with critical and humanistic approaches to education in which social justice and ethnolinguistic diversity feature (and which appear incarnated in Sita's orientation to HKLC). On the other hand, this persona also enacts a dealignment with an institutional culture that is associated with MAT and is depicted as pedagogically conservative and constraining.

Beyond MAT, Sita's case has also wider implications. Although the MOI policy shift undertaken by the government in 2010 responded to public demands and gave secondary schools greater autonomy, the change does not necessarily alleviate persistent inequities publicly acknowledged in Hong Kong, where students with working-class and ethnic minority backgrounds have been reportedly failing in great numbers in secondary schools, and continue to be highly underrepresented in higher education (see Fleming, 2015). In contrast to what many assumed, changing the language of instruction does not necessarily open up the public education system to social groups other than the middle classes. Wider transformations in the institutional culture of schools are needed, as classroom activity is discursively arranged according to assumptions on what counts as proper ways of teaching and learning and/or who gets to be considered a "good" student or teacher; these moral/social labels are in turn heavily shaped by institutional normative frameworks and government-based practices and policies on curriculum and assessment. Other theoretical implications can also be extracted from this case, as I will discuss in the final section of this chapter.

CONCLUSION: LANGUAGE POLICY AND REFLEXIVITY IN LATE MODERNITY

In this chapter, I have argued that performative and trajectory-based approaches to data collection and analysis are an appropriate epistemological lens in LPP research. While ethnographic and discourse-based perspectives are well consolidated in the field, there is still a tendency toward portrayals that rely exclusively on denotational analysis of research interviews in which participants' metacommentaries on explicit questions about policy documents are taken as the only context of interpretation. This tendency, I have tried to show, may be in contradiction with the ontological underpinnings of Dell Hymes's work, often celebrated as foundational in ethnography of language policy.

In some cases, analysis of interviews is also supported by fine-grained (and ethnographically informed) descriptions of the ways in which the focal institutional settings are socially and discursively organized in daily routines, yet such descriptions tend to have the communicative event as the analytical reference and therefore leave participants backgrounded in favor of holistic characterizations of activities. In contrast to this, I have suggested a closer look at the contemporary developments in linguistic anthropology and sociolinguistics where researchers have shifted toward the study of how individual forms of alignment and identification emerge out of trajectories of socialization connecting social actors, networks, and communicative encounters. In so doing, conceptual notions such as *discourse register* and the necessary requirements for identification of interdiscursive linkages across speech chains provide a rudimentary toolkit for LPP researchers to start with.

But these suggested approaches and perspectives are not mere methodological warrants for describing or documenting processes of policy implementation/appropriation in specific (local and institutional) settings. They also offer us routes to further engage with wider ongoing sociological discussions on language, culture, and socioeconomic change. The case of Sita, for example, provides an empirical base to feedback to contemporary work in the social sciences focusing on the strengthening of reflexivity in connection with the conditions of so-called late modernity, the widespread processes of late capitalism leading to the selective privatization of services, the information revolution, the weakening of the institutions of nation-states, and the fragmentation of overlapping and competing identities (Appadurai, 1990; Bauman, 1998).

Under these conditions, reflexivity is generally defined as an emergent property of the self, an imperative form of self-governance that allows social actors to deal with social uncertainty (Beck, 1992; Bourdieu & Wacquant, 1992; Giddens, 1991). Faced with a neoliberalized and globalized labor market that pushes them to move across increasingly diversified (and trans-nationalized) contexts, social actors often find today that the customs, habits, routines, expectations, and beliefs in which they had been socialized back in their natal communities of practice are less and less reliable when making sense and acting upon the new social conditions. This is particularly salient among youth, who as a result tend now to engage in new meta-reflexive forms of action, as the dominant modes of socialization of the past, in which families and natal friends provided a key guide of action in the shaping of life toward their present and future, are no longer the main point of reference (Archer, 2007, pp. 206–248; see also Archer, 2012).

In this context, the ethnographic analysis of the discursive emergence of networked reflexive acts in Sita's trajectory pinpoints the very situated mechanisms of socialization by which individuals gain cultural capital (Bourdieu, 1986) through coordinated orientation toward strategic institutional values. Within the logic of an increasingly stratified educational system, government-aided schools in Hong Kong are pushed to compete with each other over student enrollment and to meet the curriculum and assessment requirements specified by the Education Bureau; in fact, these schools' degree of orientation toward the public university entrance examinations arranged by the government determines their institutional ranking and, in turn, their prestige and ability to attract students so as to meet the minimum intake required by the government to retain funding. Thus, MAT's initial emphasis on non-test-based educational approaches proved difficult to implement, leading to the dismissal of Mr. C and Mr. Lagan.

At the same time, private elite institutions such as HKLC operate in a parallel logic that frees them from government's pedagogical principles and allows them to creatively define their own curricula and assessment standards and classroom language use. In this regard, the enactment of an activist social persona concerned with critical pedagogy, social justice, and diversity provided Sita with a platform to become recognized by HKLC as a legitimate candidate for admission, while at the same time taking a critical stance against MAT's institutional actions, in particular, and the Hong Kong public educational system, in general.

More important, such a jointly constructed cultural model of action around ethnic minority activism constitutes empirical evidence against research approaches that separate action from structure and overemphasize individual agency when accounting for social actors' reflexive strategies in the contemporary world. At the intersection of key policy shifts, institutional events and interpersonal forms of collaboration, the tracking down of ethnic minority activism at MAT illustrates a social process by which discourse-based conventions (e.g., ways of teaching and learning) tied with normative orders operating in unequal institutional structures (e.g., moral values on what counts as "good" and "bad" models of action) get reflexively manipulated by agentive actors in their attempt to navigate their social circumstances.

Future LPP research in ethnography of language policy would benefit from closer and long-term attention to these issues. In exploring how these institutional, discursive, and cultural changes might unfold in coming years, we must continue to observe other settings and metapragmatic forms of identification and meaning-making.

ACKNOWLEDGMENT

I am grateful to Ben Rampton and Jürgen Jaspers, for reading and commenting on earlier drafts of this chapter.

NOTES

1. It should be noted that Mortimer elaborated on this approach in later work (see Mortimer & Wortham, 2015; Mortimer, 2016).
2. This section is adapted from Pérez-Milans & Soto (2016).

REFERENCES

Agha, A. (2005). Voice, footing, enregisterment. *Journal of Linguistic Anthropology* 15(1), 38–59.

Agha, A. (2007). *Language and social relations.* Cambridge: Cambridge University Press.

Appadurai, A. (1990). Disjuncture and difference in the global cultural economy. *Theory, Culture and Society* 7(2), 295–310.

Archer, M. S. (2007). *Making our way through the world: Human reflexivity and social mobility.* Cambridge: Cambridge University Press.

Archer, M. S. (2012). *The reflexive imperative in late modernity.* Cambridge: Cambridge University Press.

Bakhtin, M. (1981). *The dialogic imagination: Four essays.* Austin: University of Texas Press.

Bakhtin, M. (1986). *Speech genres and other late essays.* Austin: University of Texas Press.

Bauman, Z. (1998). *Globalization: The human consequences.* New York: Columbia University Press.

Beck, U. (1992). *Risk society: Towards a new modernity.* London: Sage.

Blommaert, J. (2010). *The sociolinguistics of globalization.* Cambridge: Cambridge University Press.

Blommaert, J., & Bulcaen, C. (2000). Critical discourse analysis. *Annual Review of Anthropology* 29, 447–466.

Bourdieu, P. (1986). The forms of capital. In J. Richardson (Ed.), *Handbook of theory and research for the sociology of education* (pp. 241–258). New York: Greenwood.

Bourdieu, P., & Wacquant, L. J. (1992). *An invitation to reflexive sociology.* Chicago: University of Chicago Press.

Briggs, C., & Bauman, R. (1992). Genre, intertextuality, and social power. *Journal of Linguistic Anthropology* 2(2), 131–172.

Canagarajah, S. (2006). Ethnographic methods in language policy. In T. Ricento (Ed.), *An introduction to language policy: Theory and method* (pp. 153–169). Oxford: Blackwell.

Cicourel, A. V. (1992). The interpenetration of communicative contexts: Examples from medical encounters. In C. Goodwin & A. Duranti (Eds.), *Rethinking context: Language as an interactive phenomenon* (pp. 291–310). Cambridge: Cambridge University Press.

Davis, K. A. (1994). *Language planning in multilingual contexts: Policies, communities, and schools in Luxembourg.* Amsterdam: John Benjamins.

Duranti, A. (1985). Sociocultural dimensions of discourse. In T. A. van Dijk (Ed.), *Handbook of discourse analysis,* Vol. 1: *Disciplines of discourse* (pp. 193–230). New York: Academic Press.

Fleming, K. (2015). *Ideology, identity and linguistic repertoires among South Asian students in Hong Kong.* PhD dissertation, University of Hong Kong. Retrieved from http://hdl.handle.net/10722/222399

Frake, C. O. (1975). How to enter a Yakan house. In M. Sanches & B. M. Blount (Eds.), *Sociocultural dimensions in language use* (pp. 205–234). New York: Academic Press.

Giddens, A. (1991). *Modernity and self-identity: Self and society in the late modern age.* Cambridge: Polity Press.

Goffman, E. (1956). The nature of deference and demeanor. *American Anthropologist* 58, 473–502.

Goffman, E. (1981). *Forms of talk.* Philadelphia: University of Pennsylvania Press.

Goffman, E. (1983). The interaction order. *American Sociological Review* 48(1), 1–17.

Goodwin, C., & Duranti, A. (2000). Rethinking context: An introduction. In C. Goodwin & A. Duranti (Eds.), *Rethinking context: Language as an interactive phenomenon* (pp. 1–42). Cambridge: Cambridge University Press.

Hanks, W. F. (1987). Discourse genres in a theory of practice. *American Ethnologist* 14(4), 668–692.

Heller, M. (1999). *Linguistic minorities and modernity. A sociolinguistic ethnography.* London; New York: Longman.

Hornberger, N. H. (2009). Hymes' linguistics and ethnography in education. *Text & Talk* 29(3), 347–358.

Hornberger, N. H., & Johnson, D. C. (2007). Slicing the onion ethnographically: Layers and spaces in multilingual language education policy and practice. *TESOL Quarterly* 14(3), 509–532.

Hornberger, N. H., & Johnson, D. C. (2011). The ethnography of language policy. In T. L. McCarty (Ed.), *Ethnography and language policy* (pp. 273–289). New York: Routledge.

Hymes, D. (1964). *Language in culture and society.* New York: Harper & Row.

Hymes, D. (1974). *Foundations in sociolinguistics: An ethnographic approach.* Philadelphia: University of Pennsylvania Press.

Johnson, D. C. (2009). Ethnography of language policy. *Language Policy* 8, 139–159.

Malinowski, B. (1923). The problem of meaning in primitive languages. In C. K. Ogden & I. A. Richards (Eds.), *The meaning of meaning* (pp. 296–336). New York: Harcourt, Brace and World.

Martín Rojo, L. (2010). *Constructing inequality in multilingual classrooms.* Berlin: Mouton.

McCarty, T. L. (Ed.). (2011). *Ethnography and language policy.* New York: Routledge.

Mortimer, K. S. (2013). Communicative event chains in an ethnography of Paraguayan language policy. *International Journal of the Sociology of Language* 291, 67–99.

Mortimer, K. S. (2016). Language policy as metapragmatic discourse: A focus on the intersection of language policy and social identification. In E. Barakos & J. W. Unger (Eds.), *Discursive approaches to language policy* (pp. 71–96). New York: Springer.

Mortimer, K. S., & Wortham S. (2015). Analyzing language policy and social identification across heterogeneous scales. *Annual Review of Applied Linguistics* 35, 160–172.

Pérez-Milans, M. (2013). *Urban schools and English language education in late modern China: A critical sociolinguistic ethnography.* New York; London: Routledge.

Pérez-Milans, M., & Soto, C. (2014). Everyday practices, everyday pedagogies: A dialogue on critical transformations in a multilingual Hong Kong school. In J. B. Clark & F. Dervin (Eds.), *Reflexivity and multimodality in language education: Rethinking multilingualism and interculturality in accelerating, complex and transnational spaces* (pp. 213–233). London; New York: Routledge.

Pérez-Milans, M., & Soto, C. (2016). Reflexive language and ethnic minority activism in Hong Kong: A trajectory-based analysis. *AILA Review* 29(1), 48–82.

Rampton, B. (2006). *Language in late modernity: Interaction in an urban school.* Cambridge: Cambridge University Press.

Ricento, T. (Ed.). (2000). *Ideology, politics and language policies: Focus on English.* Amsterdam: John Benjamins.

Ricento, T., & Hornberger, N. H. (1996). Unpeeling the onion: Language planning and policy and the ELT professional. *TESOL Quarterly* 30(3), 401–428.

Silverstein, M. (2005). Axes of evals: Token versus type interdiscursivity. *Journal of Linguistic Anthropology* 15(1), 6–22.

Soto, C. (2016). *Empowering low-income ethnic minority students in Hong Kong through critical pedagogy: Limits and possibilities in theory and practice.* PhD dissertation, University of Hong Kong. Retrieved from http://hdl.handle.net/10722/223611

Wortham, S. E. (2005). Socialization beyond the speech event. *Journal of Linguistic Anthropology* 15(1), 95–112.

Wortham, S. (2006). *Learning identity: The mediation of social identity through academic learning.* New York: Cambridge University Press.

CHAPTER 7

....

LANGUAGE ETHICS AND THE INTERDISCIPLINARY CHALLENGE

....

YAEL PELED

THE political ethics of language has attracted in recent years an increased interest and visibility from language policy researchers who seek to engage with the normative dimension of the politics of language. Examples of this engagement include the nature and scope of linguistic justice, the language rights discourse and its discontents, and the challenges of liberal neutrality and inclusive participation in multilingual democratic polities. This increased interest in complementing empirical research (*is*) with an ethical reflection (*ought*) highlights the important question of a shared interdisciplinary framework that is capable of bridging the respective fields of language policy and political philosophy in a nuanced and systematic manner.

In such a potentially rich yet largely undertheorized interface between the normative and the empirical, which theories, concepts, and methods may be potentially useful for a fuller understanding of the political ethics of language? At the heart of this attempt to identify and explore moral and political agency in language stands the question of order: namely, the process of arranging and rearranging that transpires from the fundamental reality of human difference, interdependence, and uncertainty. This chapter sets out to explore the question of order in the face of the complex relation between power, ethics, and language, which extends from the human commonalities of language and moral reasoning to the politics of language as an open-ended human activity.

In the broadest and most abstract sense, human life and experience are inextricably linked to two fundamental human capacities: the capacity for language and the capacity for moral reasoning. Extreme deviations from this basic premise, as in the case, for example, of the linguistic behavior of feral children, or the moral agency of individuals suffering from mental disorders, only reaffirm the perception of both language and moral agency as a human commonality with which all individuals are endowed, regardless of their gender, ethnicity, race, and other such particular characteristics.

Paradoxically, however, these two human commonalities are also fundamentally divisive at the same time. This is because both capacities realize themselves not in a general and abstracted form, but rather in a particular and differentiated manner. The human capacity for language manifests itself not as the capacity for some kind of a Platonic ideal of language, but rather in the form of specific (even if not discrete) systems of speech that are associated with and spoken by identifiable speech communities (e.g., German, Yiddish, Japanese). The common human capacity for language, in other words, paradoxically results in the inevitable existence of language barriers. The common human capacity for morality, likewise, manifests itself in praxis as a diverse range of moral beliefs concerning human nature, the self, and its moral relationality, expressed in a range of moral theories (e.g., consequentialism, deontology, virtue ethics, ethics of care) and likewise of political ideologies (e.g., liberalism, republicanism, Marxism, anarchism).

The challenge of the paradox of the dividing commonality, however, arises not from the mere differentiated realization of the shared capacities for language and morality, but rather, from the fact that both are, at least to an extent, mutable. Individuals may change their moral views, and likewise may elect (voluntarily or by coercion) to alter or expand their linguistic repertoires. Indeed, the possibility or even the expectation of such mutability is at the source of the politics of language. The mutability of language gives rise to the question of language regimes (e.g., to what extent is a state justified in intervening in the linguistic repertoires of its citizens), while the mutability of morality creates the sphere that allows individuals to debate their moral beliefs with fellow citizens, persuade others to reconsider their views, and be likewise persuaded themselves to do the same thing (Peled, Ricento, & Ives, 2014; Peled, forthcoming). While mutable, however, the linguistic and moral difference between individuals is irreducible or irresolvable in the sense that either form of human difference cannot be simply neutralized away, once and for all. The prospects of humanity as a whole converging on a single language is no more likely than it converging on a single moral belief.

The dividing commonalities thus raise the issue of (human) *difference*, the first of three human realities in which the political ethics of language is situated: (1) *difference*, (2) *interdependence*, and (3) *uncertainty*. As Schmidt (2006) argues, difference and interdependence are the two constitutive elements of political life, generally speaking, since

> [a]t its most basic level, all politics derive from the intersection of two realities of human existence: difference and interdependence. If we did not have "differences," if we were completely the same as all others, always in perfect harmony about everything, there would be no politics. Further, if we were totally autonomous individual beings, never needing others for anything, there would be no politics. But in combination the realities that we do have differences and yet we do need each other lead to *conflicts* that are dealt with in ways that we call political. (Schmidt, 2006, p. 98)

Politics, in other words, originates from the need to somehow reconcile irreducible human difference with unavoidable human interdependence in the form of a political *order*, namely, the power structures that result from this reconciliatory attempt. The political ethics of language, consequently, emerge from the attempt to consider the moral justifiability of these power structures, and the question of whether some power structures in language are morally better (or, of course, worse) than others. The purpose of an ethical inquiry into the politics of language, and the policies that govern it, is not simply to highlight the intricacies of power relations, structures, and disparities in language between different actors (i.e., states, communities, and citizens), but rather to reflect on existing power relations in language, to identify the moral wrongs that they may exhibit, and to develop alternative structures that are capable of righting them.

The moral evaluation of power relations in language, critically, does not generally seek to eliminate power altogether, nor perceive it as an element of social life that is intrinsically negative in any way. As the substance, or the subject matter, of politics, power is perhaps better understood as the force that holds together the irreducible tension between difference and interdependence, preventing human difference from resulting in irreversible social disintegration, on the one hand, and human interdependence from engendering a permanent convergence of social identities, on the other hand. These two extreme outcomes map, respectively, onto two ideal types that are sometimes invoked in debates over the politics of language: unfettered laissez-faire (the neutralization of human interdependence) and total assimilation (the suppression of human difference). While these approaches are often perceived as antithetical, their skepticism toward politics as a human activity nevertheless expresses a shared unease over the possibility of the existence of moral power relations (Oakes & Peled, 2018).

The irreducible tension between human difference and interdependence is further compounded by the third reality of power in language, namely *uncertainty*. Politics, in other words, is insufficiently captured as the friction generated from the interdependence of different individuals and collectives, because such a description overlooks the fact that any solutions that are found (e.g., a particular type of a language regime, a new set of language rights, etc.) are more often temporary than permanent. The significance of uncertainty is pivotal because of the underlying rationale of politics as

> the quest for finality in decisiveness in the affairs of groups, ends that are permanently frustrated by the slippery and inconclusive circumstances in which that quest occurs. One of the salient forms of human thinking is that associated with attaining ends, reaching conclusions, closing disputes, removing items from the agenda, overcoming uncertainties, or solving disagreements—all of those in conjunction with others. The finality drive is a quest rather than a realized journey because, at every stage along the projected or imagined route, the frequently displayed desire to marshal a group of people on that journey has to confront contingency, indeterminacy, and plurality, and make do with partial, temporary, and disintegrating arrangements, even when they are not immediately visible as such. (Freeden, 2013, p. 22)

Politics, therefore, emerges not only from the irresolvable tension between difference and interdependence, but also from the fact that any attempt to reconcile the two is necessarily contingent. Applied to the politics of language, this means that decisions concerning issues such as the nature of morally optimal language regimes or the scope and extent of language rights are never finite. In other words, the attempt to establish a political order in linguistic affairs is always an open-ended endeavor, highlighting the role of uncertainty as a basic reality of politics and a structural feature, rather than a dysfunction. This quest for order, as Freeden notes, is well reflected in the core conceptual vocabulary of politics in both theory and praxis, including "terms such as authority, sovereignty, rule, hegemony, order, legitimacy, electoral victory or defeat, the absoluteness and non-negotiability of rights" (Freeden, 2013, p. 23), whose purpose is to "establish a secure position, in a pecking order, for collective values and preferences" (p. 24). Such a secure position, however, is never definite and always subject to change as a result of social and political transformations that are not always or necessarily predictable.

The three human realities of difference, interdependence, and uncertainty are the basic triad at the heart of the politics of—and policy on—language. The question of their ordering and the exact nature of their complex relations is what drives empirical research on power structures in language. The moral evaluation of these power structures, with their possible alternatives, by contrast, is at the heart of a normative engagement with language politics. Such engagement includes questions such as the substance of language rights and the nature of linguistic equality, the compatibility between particular language regimes and democratic principles, or the global ethics of English as a lingua franca. Following on these and other such discussions in recent normative literature on linguistic issues, the purpose of the remainder of this chapter is to identify and explore the notion of language ethics, and its relation to the field of language policy and the politics of language more broadly.

More specifically, the remainder of the chapter progresses as follows: the next section explores the emerging debate in political philosophy on linguistic justice, particularly within contemporary liberal democratic theory. The section locates this emerging debate—and its critiques—within the broader framework of inquiry of language ethics, namely the inquiry on the moral problems, practices, and policies relating to language, on par with equivalent topics in applied ethics, such as environmental ethics or the ethics of war. The following section explores the moral inquiry on linguistic issues as a fundamentally interdisciplinary form of inquiry that aims not merely to bridge political philosophy and applied linguistics in some broad, vague, or sporadic manner, but rather to combine their distinct scientific epistemologies in a more principled and systematic way. The concluding section, finally, turns its attention to the intrinsic tension between the aim of language policy to achieve particular moral ends or outcomes (for example, to remedy historical injustices), on the one hand, and the messy, uncertain, and often unpredictable realities that shape local and global social change, on the other hand.

LANGUAGE ETHICS: THE ORDER OF THINGS

Language ethics may be defined, in comparison with topics such as environmental ethics or the ethics of war, as a topic in applied ethics (or *practical ethics*), namely, the "use of philosophical methods to treat moral problems, practices, and policies in the professions, technology, government and the like" (Beauchamp, 2003, p. 3), under the broader umbrella of normative ethics (the ethical theory concerned with the question, *how ought we to act?*) within the field of philosophy. Language ethics, in other words, applies philosophical methods to analyze the moral issues that pertain to language, such as those related, for example, to questions of linguistic freedoms, equality, autonomy, legitimacy, and dignity in multilingual and multicultural societies. It somewhat differs, however, from other more established topics in applied ethics, such as bioethics or environmental ethics, by not being used to self-identify a distinct body of literature by a distinct intellectual community. Rather, it is better understood to date as an emerging branch of (applied) ethical inquiry that is in its relatively early developmental stages. It is nevertheless possible to outline a number of common issues, approaches, and general features that characterize this emerging topic at the present moment, and which may likewise provide some clues into its future trajectories.

Normative considerations of power in language occupied, in a way, an important position in the history of the field of language policy from its early days. As Ricento (2000) notes, the seemingly technical self-perception of the field in the 1960s was followed by the development of different approaches, from critical theory-based frameworks to the linguistic human rights tradition, which called into question its "value-neutral" presupposition. However, the attribution of the label of *language ethics*, on par with other topics in applied ethics, is better understood as a result of the relatively recent interest of political philosophers in linguistic issues. The origins of this dedicated interest in the normative theorizing of language lie, as De Schutter suggests (2007; also De Schutter & Robichaud, 2015a), in two related debates within political philosophy: the individualism/communitarian debate and multiculturalism. Since the first decade of the 2000s, the normative engagement with linguistic issues has been steadily developing, focusing in particular on the question of linguistic justice and language rights from the perspective of liberal-egalitarian democratic theory (most notably, Kymlicka & Patten, 2003; Van Parijs, 2011).

What is linguistic justice, and how may it be defined? Owing to the relatively recent emergence of this debate in professional political philosophy, it is better to consider it not as a relatively unified body of literature (indeed, Van Parijs's work is the earliest published monograph to offer a systematic theorizing of linguistic justice), but rather as an emerging notion that draws on a broader philosophical interest in the nature and substance of social justice, and in connection with other specific topics in applied ethics. Broadly speaking, linguistic justice theories as developed in contemporary political philosophy are most often "statist" (i.e., state-based) theories of distributing power in language within the political boundaries of a demos. As such, they aim to

> provide an answer to the question: what is the just political management of the presence of different language groups within a political community? The question comprises sub-questions: Should we go for equality or inequality of recognition between the different languages? Should we go for sub-state territories with monolingual policies, or for states that instantiate statewide multilingualism or for some combination of both? Should linguistic minorities receive special linguistic benefits? Should we endeavour to save moribund languages? Should states have one common language that all speak and understand? (De Schutter & Robichaud, 2015b, p. 88)

Moral debates concerning the permissible scope of state intervention in response to human difference are, of course, not constrained to linguistic issues. The extent to which particular identities (e.g., gender, racial, ethnic, religious) ought to be politically accommodated is a matter of an ongoing and rich normative discussion. Where language seemingly holds a unique position in relation to other forms of human difference, however, is in the fact that it is impossible for the state to remain neutral on the language in which its laws are written, in which its public debates are held, and in which its education, health care, courts, media, and financial life operate. Due to the impossibility of linguistic neutrality, therefore, "we do not have a choice between freedom and regulation, or between neutrality and engagement. Rather we must choose between different forms of regulation and engagement, between different language policies" (De Schutter & Robichaud, 2015b, p. 89).

The two most common regulative principles put forward in the literature to date are (1) equal recognition and (2) linguistic convergence. The former advances the view that states ought to recognize equally their diverse linguistic groups, while the latter argues for a selective recognition based on a linguistic prioritization of some language(s) over others. However, "[t]he particular principle of state recognition that is favoured, as well as the particular language(s) that will be singled out for state support, will depend on an underlying account of the goal of language, of what language is thought to be good for" (De Schutter & Robichaud, 2015b, p. 90). When considering these two principles (which, in reality, operate more as ideal types), "linguistic justice theorists usually ground their theories in one or more interests in language, which language recognition can then advance. Within the possible set of interests, there are two broad types, which we can term 'identity' interests and 'non-identity' interests" (De Schutter & Robichaud, 2015b, p. 90). The former addresses the issues of individual autonomy and dignity, while the latter pertains to questions of efficiency, democracy, and equality of opportunity (De Schutter & Robichaud 2015b, pp. 91–95).

The relationships between the two principles and the identity/non-identity interests are complex, in terms of more abstracted visions of the linguistically good society, so to speak, as well as in relation to the moral evaluation of real-world cases. In reality, however, very few normative accounts of linguistic justice can be said to fully endorse only one or the other while completely neglecting or rejecting the rest of the elements along the identity/non-identity axis. A greater degree of commonality among theorists exists, however, with regard to the question of the intrinsic value of language, a view that is commonly rejected on the grounds that "language and cultures matter only insofar as they are desired by individuals" (De Schutter & Robichaud, 2015b, p. 96; see also May, 2015b), who are seen, in the eyes of liberal-egalitarian democratic theory, as the only legitimate right-holders. Essentially, "both the non-identity and the identity views . . . present distinctive accounts of what it means *for individuals* to have a language, and thereby already assume that languages are there for the benefit of their speakers" (De Schutter & Robichaud, 2015b, p. 96), rather than of the broader political community (including non-colinguals), humanity as a whole (Patten, 2014, pp. 18–21), or the languages themselves as morally autonomous entities.

The linguistic justice debate, situated in a broader liberal-egalitarian democratic framework, occupies to date the majority of present-day normative engagement with linguistic issues. At the same time, this prominent position also has attracted a number of critiques from within professional political philosophy and outside it. Within political philosophy, it has been pointed out, for example, that the nearly exclusive focus on liberal linguistic justice, while advancing liberal democratic theory (premised on ontological individualism), did not do the same for more participatory models of democratic life, where multilingual realities give rise to the challenge of *ontological multilingualism* (Schmidt, 2014). A related critique explores the influence of Locke's philosophy of language on contemporary Anglo-American political philosophy, whose underlying conception of language is often individualist and instrumental (see Ives, Chapter 9 in this volume). The perception of language as mainly a neutral vehicle for transmitting ideas among monolingual native-speaker individuals inevitably marginalizes deeper nuances of reasoning, identity, and power, thus failing to adequately capture, for example, the power and epistemic realities of English as a global lingua franca (Ives, 2014). A third type of critique questions the primacy of justice as a *hypergood*, or *the value of values*, in liberal theory, and the implications of a proceduralist normative theory of language for the broader vocabulary of political moral agency (e.g., benevolence, civility, and hope) (Peled, 2017).

Important monograph-length critiques of the liberal justice framework in theorizing language ethics also emerge from outside political philosophy. One important such critique, for example, problematizes the concept—and conceptual appeal—of language rights when considered from a situated analysis of the social life of language (Wee, 2010). Another critique considers the question of the generic and essentializing nature of international language rights advocacy as a form of global linguistic governance, and its potentially adverse effect on the freedoms of speech and expression on the other (Pupavac, 2012). More broadly, the emergent linguistic justice debate in political philosophy has been the object of repeated critiques from sociolinguistics, particularly in regard to the conception of language that underpins it, and the normative conclusions that are therefore being drawn on its basis (e.g. May, 2003, 2014, 2015a; Ricento, 2014; Wright, 2015). These and other such critiques raise a deeper question concerning the nature and substance of the linguistic justice debate, and of language ethics more broadly, not merely in terms of their theory-building efforts, but rather the disciplinary terrain in which they are situated. The question of this complex disciplinary terrain is the topic of the next section.

INTERDISCIPLINARITY: THE ORDER OF THOUGHTS

Disciplinary questions, particularly those pertaining to disciplinary boundaries, are by no means a recent phenomenon in the study of the complex social life of language, and more narrowly, in the field of language policy (Jernudd & Nekvapil, 2012; Peled, 2014; Ricento, 2000, 2006). This complexity, in turn, accounts for the current lack of an overarching theory of language policy and planning (Ricento, 2006, pp. 10–12). As Ricento notes, the field of language policy benefited historically from theories that played an important role in the evolution of LP as an interdisciplinary field, stimulating research relevant to language matters in education, economics, political science, history, sociology, geography and other fields, while insights from these same fields have contributed to the development of integrated models in LP, such as linguistic imperialism and linguistic human rights. (Ricento, 2006, p. 18)

Similarly, the field's long-standing interest in issues of power and ethics can be argued to have contributed to the evolving relationship between language policy and political philosophy, the latter itself "an interdisciplinary endeavor whose center of gravity lies at the humanities end of the happily still undisciplined discipline of political science" and an "unapologetically mongrel sub-discipline" which is situated "in relation to the academic disciplines of political science, history and philosophy" (Dryzek, Honig, & Phillips, 2012, p. ii). Broadly described, while political philosophy's

traditions, approaches and styles vary . . . [it is] united by a commitment to theorize, critique and diagnose the norms, practices and organization of political action in the past and present, in our own places and elsewhere . . . [p]olitical theorists share a concern with the demands of justice and how to fulfill them, the presuppositions and promise of democracy, the divide between secular and religious ways of life, and the nature and identity of public goods, among many other topics. (Dryzek et al., 2012, p. ii)

Political philosophy's recent interest in language, as the previous section proposes, is largely focused at present on the evolving notion of linguistic justice. However, it is important to note that interest in language among political philosophers rarely translates into an interest in *linguistics* (just as interest in politics and/or ethics among sociolinguists does not necessarily translate into interest in political science/philosophy) (Peled, 2014, p. 305). In other words, the fundamental interdisciplinary imperative of normative theorizing in language (May, 2015b; Peled, 2014) often remains more a matter of an *epistemic laissez-faire* than a systematic exploration of the political ethics of language. May in particular laments the fact that "political theorists are generally less open to such interdisciplinary engagement, although it does not stop them pronouncing on issues beyond their disciplinary expertise" (May, 2015b, p. 52), referring in particular to the weak empirical grounding of the positions articulated by Kymlicka, Pogge, Barry, and Van Parijs, all of whom are world-leading political theorists with considerable professional authority and influence over the development of the field and the models, frameworks, and conceptions it employs.

The challenge from interdisciplinarity to the normative theorizing of language comes from the fact that interdisciplinarity is, essentially, a part-whole relationship (Peled, 2015a) that has no single, clear, or definite end. In the same way that the politics of language can be described as a never-ending attempt to order human difference, interdependence, and uncertainty (see earlier discussion), the interdisciplinary nature of language ethics (and of interdisciplinarity in general) may be described as a never-ending attempt to order the disciplines that are seen as pertinent to this inquiry, and the respective theories, frameworks, concepts, and methodologies that each brings with it to the common epistemological table. The same "quest for finality and decisiveness," or "finality drive" (Freeden, 2013, p. 22), underpins the moral politics of language in the real world, as it does the complex and nuanced theoretical framework exploring it, subjected just as much to the necessity "to confront contingency, indeterminacy, and plurality, and make do with partial, temporary, and disintegrating arrangements, even when they are not immediately visible as such" (Freeden, 2013, p. 22).

One of the main challenges of language ethics as an interdisciplinary endeavor that bridges language policy and political philosophy has to do with the fact that, unlike more traditional instances of interdisciplinary fields such as economic history or social psychology, the two constitutive elements of normative theorizing of language (i.e., political philosophy and sociolinguistics) are effectively interdisciplines in their own right, each with its own internal finality quests, debates, and disagreements. As such, the emerging relationships between political philosophy and sociolinguistics certainly demonstrate the existence of deep disagreements over the most basic questions that comprise a common scientific epistemology, such as what is a good research question, which concepts and methods are important, which authors and texts are canonical, and similar issues (Peled, 2014, p. 305). This is also, presumably, one of the reasons for the prominence of the linguistic justice debate, which focuses on a relatively clearly defined framework within political philosophy (labeled by May as *Orthodox liberalism*; May, 2015b, pp. 2, 5–6), which allows philosophers to seemingly make faster progress due to the more restricted range of frameworks, theories, concepts, and methods with which they engage. Unfortunately, however, owing to the empirical weakness of parts of this normative work, the resulting literature often seems paradoxically to conflict with the interdisciplinary imperative of the normative theorizing of language, rather than promote it.

The challenge of interdisciplinarity in language ethics is, therefore, a question of *how* rather than *if*. This, however, raises the much more complex question of how *specifically* the different parts ought to be integrated into a meaningful and principled whole. The rhetoric of academic interdisciplinarity (e.g., in calls for papers and book introductions) often conceptualizes interdisciplinarity as *bridging* or *bringing together* different researchers and perspectives, without saying much on the particular forms that work across disciplines takes, or the considered reasoning that is expected to underlie such mutual engagements. As Graff (2015) notes in his historical analysis of academic interdisciplinarity in the twentieth century, there exist many paths to interdisciplinarity, some more successful and productive (e.g., genetic biology and operations research) and some less so (e.g., sociology and new literacies). Perhaps the most important insight generated from such analysis is that there is no single organisation, form, pattern of institutionalisation, or set of rules that signifies interdisciplinarity. This history warns us repeatedly of the dangers of exaggeration, successive claims of novelty, and imitation, especially of a simplified model of scientific research. It emphasises the centrality of humility, learning the basics and doing one's homework, and recognising and appreciating variety and variability. (Graff, 2015, p. 236)

The variability of normative theorizing in language is well reflected in a number of recent scholarly contributions that seek to advance the current debate on linguistic justice, its nature, substance, and limitations. These include, for example, a number of special issues produced over a relatively short period of time, primarily in linguistics (Leger & Lewis, 2017; Ricento, Peled & Ives, 2014; Tonkin, 2015) but also in political philosophy (De Schutter & Robichaud, 2015a), featuring contributions from political philosophers and sociolinguists with a common and long-standing interest in the political ethics of language. More comprehensive treatments of this complex part-whole relationship explore the intersection between linguistic diversity and social justice (Piller, 2016) and the notion of context-sensitive linguistic justice as an example of the framework of normative language policy (Oakes & Peled, 2018). None of these approaches, models, and frameworks, of course, should be regarded as capable of "winning" the epistemic quest for finality that drives this interdisciplinary endeavor, or as the ultimate recipe for the whole that correctly and conclusively integrates the different parts. What they highlight, rather, is the complex forms in which institutionalized knowledge responds to the political ethics of language, and is shaped by it.

The question of knowledge institutionalization is, of course, central to the development and consolidation processes of interdisciplines, generally speaking. As Graff (2015) demonstrates, they are greatly influenced by a complex web of perceptions, interests, and expectations within academia and outside it. The latter also holds true for the topic of language ethics, since despite the strong philosophical bias of applied ethics in general (Beauchamp, 2003, p. 3), its strong connection to language policy in theory and praxis implies that its range of stakeholders is not limited to a distinct group of academic philosophers. Debates over normative ethics in language, as in race, gender, or the environment, can make a significant contribution to the political communities in which they are situated. Among other things, they are capable of informing decision-makers and contributing conceptual depth and nuance to public debates (e.g., to critique popular language beliefs and ideologies); they can help to discuss, contextualize, and adapt ideas and concepts imported from other contexts and/or other political and linguistic cultures (e.g., introducing liberal elements to republican societies and vice versa); and they can shed light on concerns and anxieties that affect voting behavior in the face of broader social and political transformations (e.g., immigration and linguistic integration).

What they cannot offer, however, is a clear or simple answer to the question, *what should we do?* when pertaining to language policy. This is because policymaking in language, like the politics of language and the normative framework that analyzes it, is part of that unrealizable finality quest that connects human difference, interdependence, and uncertainty. This incapacity to offer finite solutions and moral prescriptions and its implications for language policy research as a field are the topic of the following and final section.

LANGUAGE POLICY: WICKED PROBLEMS
OF SOCIAL ORDER

Policymaking, in language and other domains of human life and activity, may be broadly understood as a set of actions and/or measures that aim to achieve certain stated objectives (e.g., in health, education, national security). Such an understanding, however, can be said to be simplistic, failing to capture or account, for example, for a range of covert and implicit mechanisms that underlie it (Shohamy, 2006). The nominal emphasis on "declared and conscious statements" (Shohamy, 2006, p. 3) is therefore insufficient to adequately describe real language policy as

> a device to perpetuate and impose language behaviors in accordance with the national, political, social and economic agendas. It represents the wishes of groups in authority to promote the agendas of protecting collective identities, promoting globalization, stating "who is in charge," creating "imagined communities" and maintaining social and political orders. (Shohamy, 2006, p. 3)

Understanding the relations between "overt and covert, implicit and explicit" (Shohamy, 2006, p. 3) mechanisms of language policy is, of course, an important and useful element of analyzing power in language. But the core of language policy, like the politics of language, is not simply in the competition for power and authority, but rather in the attempt of the winners to cement their victories so as to prevent future contestation to the established linguistic pecking order.

Language policy, therefore, can be seen as a set of responses (covert and overt alike) to the sought-after but equally unrealizable finality quest of power in language. The strong emphasis on the notion of language rights, for example, whether in liberal linguistic justice theories or the linguistic human rights approach, is commensurable with Freeden's observation on the appeal of rights as absolute and non-negotiable (2013, p. 23). The purpose of committing the normative debate to the language of language rights, so to speak, is precisely to shield the rights in question from the temporariness and inconclusiveness that are a structural feature of political life. This also explains the great symbolic power of language academies in being "responsible for introducing new words, imposing and promoting official policies, guarding against foreign intrusion and serving as *the final and most authoritative word* [emphasis mine] on how language should be used, both in terms of corpus and status" (Shohamy, 2006, p. 66). The fact that they exert nowadays greater influence over written norms rather than spoken norms nevertheless seems to suggest they have maintained their legitimacy as a linguistic *finality stamp* in their role as "a tool and marker of inclusion and exclusion" (Shohamy, 2006, p. 66).

This linguistic "quest for finality in decisiveness in the affairs of groups" (Freeden, 2013, p. 22) serves both as the cause and the end of language policy, whose declared aims (and covert mechanisms) are shaped in response to an existing order (e.g., a political equilibrium that threatens a minority language), and in an attempt to generate—and maintain—an alternative one (e.g., a political equilibrium that allows a minority language to thrive). The problem is, however, that often there exists no easy, clear, or straightforward process for identifying the precise mechanisms and exact causal chains that may successfully realize stated objectives (e.g., the expectation that the legal provision of minority language rights would sufficiently protect a declining minority language). Similarly, it is likewise difficult sometimes to foresee unintended outcomes and side effects (e.g., the discontent of francophone parents in Quebec over the exclusion of francophone students from English schools). Language policy, finally, is also a domain of human life that is particularly sensitive to global transformations whose dynamics are often complex and unpredictable (e.g., mass immigration).

These and other such policy challenges raise the possibility that language policy may be better understood less as a mechanistic (covertly or overtly) and linear process for realizing stated objectives, and more in terms of a linguistic set of *wicked problems*. A wicked problem is a (social) problem that is difficult or impossible to solve in any finite way due to changing circumstances, incomplete knowledge, or contradictory inputs (Australian Public Service Commissioner, 2007). Some characteristics of wicked problems include having no definitive formula (e.g., how to define poverty?) and no stopping rule, namely, no real way of knowing whether the goal, or task, has been indeed achieved; offering no ultimate test for the solution proposed; being often ill- or only partially described; and leaving little room for learning from errors due to the significance of every intervention attempt (Rittel & Webber, 1973, pp. 160–167). Applied to language policy, the vast majority of questions facing policymakers can be thought of as wicked, being "invested with symbolic and material interests for different speaker groups" (Rubin, in Lo Bianco, 2015, p. 71). Lo Bianco further argues that

> [t]his is, of course, a crucial fact about the character of language problems, which require LPP theory and policymaking, and its analysis, to be distinguished from less wicked policy problems. In democratic states the ideological preferences involve struggle about which problems, or rather "whose" problems, will be allocated resources and become the focus of policy attention. . . . It follows from this that the idea that language problems pre-exist LPP, or that they are objectively discernible and uncontentious, much less "scientific" problems, defined prior to the activity of

language planning, is an untenable basis for LPP activity, either its analysis or its practice. (Lo Bianco, 2015, pp. 71–72)

Wicked problems, Rittel and Webber argue, "rely upon elusive political judgment for resolution," stressing that such resolution is "[n]ot [a] 'solution.' Social problems are never solved. At best they are only re-solved—over and over again" (Rittel & Webber, 1973, p. 160). In other words, language policy is subjected to the same type of finality quest that underlies the politics of language and its normative analysis.

What kind of a normative response may language ethics offer to such a fluid understanding of the social and political life of language, whose most constant feature seems to be indeterminacy and unpredictability? While language ethics can be understood as a topic in applied ethics (as I have argued in the previous sections), some of the normative literature, particularly the kind labeled by May as "orthodox liberalism" (May, 2015b, pp. 2, 5–6), is not necessarily sensitive to the challenge of an unpredictable future, owing to its strong procedural reasoning. A more suitable normative framework can be found in what Shapiro (2016) calls *adaptive political theory*. In a world that is in a state of constant flux, Shapiro argues, the expectation that current democratic institutions, both existing and those proposed by theorists, are capable of ensuring justice and freedom outside history (that is, being somehow unaffected by the social and political forces of history) is misguided. Current existing democratic institutions are considerably challenged by increasing transnational threats that were formerly unimaginable, such as climate change or global security risks. Their proposed philosophical alternatives, however, are often detached from the lived experience of human reality, and implausibly advance an idealized vision of political life and arrangements (Shapiro, 2016, p. 5). Shapiro's solution is therefore to integrate into political theory an *adaptive* capacity, which will allow it to respond to the realities and demands of a changing world, rather than ground it in either utopian thinking or an ahistorical and decontextualized view of political agency (Oakes & Peled, 2018).

The notion of an adaptive approach to language policy reflects the unrealizable finality quest of the politics of language, in which power struggles over legitimacy and authority are never decided once and for all. To use Rittel and Webber's wicked problem framing, matters of power in language are never truly solved, but rather re-solved over and over again. Considering language-related political debates (and conflicts) in terms of a wicked problem acknowledges the fact that social and political transformations often take unpredictable shapes, as is evidenced, for example, by the diverse demolinguistic profile of the current European refugee crisis. It also recognizes that such problems are often resistant to precise definition and analysis, as reflected, for example, in the difficulty to define precisely the nature of *linguistic equality*—potentially referring to the identity of the equal stakeholders (equality among whom—individuals or groups?), or the currency that is being distributed (equality of what—resources, opportunities, outcomes?) (Peled, 2015b).

The wicked problems framing also recognizes that few measures, if any, may be effectively implemented across different contexts and periods in time. This may be reflected, for example, in pre- and post-statehood language policy, such as changes to the respective status, corpus, and acquisition policies of Catalan and Spanish in the event of an independent Catalonia. This is because the acquisition of political sovereignty may be followed by the need—and the desire—to redefine the power relations between the languages present within the newly sovereign territorial borders (e.g., formally designate Catalan as a national/official language, outline its scope, and consider the relative status of Castilian as well as other historical and immigrant languages in an independent Catalonia). In other words, post-statehood requires, if not necessitates, newly sovereign nations to consider and (re)define their linguistic regimes, both as a manifestation of that sovereignty and as a means of actively maintaining it.

Embracing adaptability, therefore, as a constitutive theoretical element proposes the (hypothetical) notion of adaptive language ethics; namely, an applied inquiry into the political ethics of language that is sufficiently sensitive to the effect of temporal uncertainties and limited knowledge on the extent of our present capacity to envisage—and realize—the good state of (linguistic) society (Oakes & Peled, 2018; Peled, forthcoming).

Conclusion: Normative Horizons for Language Policy Research

Language ethics as an emergent topic in applied ethics engages with the complex and undoubtedly messy reality generated by language and morality as dividing human commonalities. The normative attempt to order human difference, interdependence, and uncertainty is an open-ended endeavor, whose search for conclusiveness in a messy political and linguistic world cannot be realized outside history through seemingly finite solutions such as strict linguistic assimilation or general social disintegration. Both solutions are as impracticable as they are morally impermissible, and the attempt at either, even in a limited manner, only highlights the fact that there exists no simple solution to the challenge of the irreducible tension between these three realities of human life. A better strategy lies in acknowledging the limited capacity of language policy to achieve stated sociolinguistic objectives, and likewise the limited capacity of language ethics to provide conclusive answers to the question *what should we do?* in any kind of generic and universal sense. Any response would necessarily depend at least to some extent on local contexts, the particularities of their linguistic and political cultures, their past histories, and future social transformations. Similarly, any solution that is found would probably require a re-solution at a later stage, when the circumstances that generated previous resolutions have sufficiently changed.

The intrinsic messiness and finality quest of the politics of language are equally reflected is the disciplinary terrain in which it is situated. The interdisciplinary imperative of language ethics likewise offers no easy or simple models, frameworks, concepts, or methods that may conclusively integrate the various parts into a decisive and unified whole. The challenge of interdisciplinary inquiry in language ethics lies not in simply bringing together previously disengaged scientific epistemologies, but rather in the attempt to integrate them in a systematic and principled manner, which is capable of shedding new light on the complex relations between human difference, interdependence, and uncertainty. While such attempts are undoubtedly challenged by current realities of knowledge institutionalization in academia and outside it, they nevertheless offer a more informed and nuanced understanding of the interplay of power, language, and ethics in the lives of contemporary political communities, and in the normative debates that shape them.

More specifically, a closer engagement with normative reasoning enables language policy research to engage with the question of *what is the right thing to do?* in a manner that is systematic and principled rather than sporadic. Considering applied linguistics' increased interest in issues of legitimacy and authority, a closer engagement with existing frameworks, theories, and conceptual clusters in political philosophy can equip applied linguistics with the capable and refined normative tools required for a more complete understanding of the multifaceted interplay between language, morality, and power. Developing the normative capacities of language policy research can therefore offer better answers to ethical questions that are central to current explorations in the field, such as those concerning the scope of linguistic justice; the essence of linguistic equality; the value of linguistic diversity; the moral underpinning of linguistic inclusivity; and, more profoundly, the nature of moral and political agency in language.

Just as important, finally, is the hope that a closer engagement with political philosophy will encourage language policy research to develop a more nuanced conception—and attitude—toward power. On that view, the purpose of a normative approach to language policy is not merely to identify and critique existing power structures and dynamics, but rather to evaluate their relative legitimacy, as well as to propose and defend more permissible alternatives. In other words, a normative approach to justice in language, for example, aims not only to identify and critique current linguistic injustices, but also to offer a more complete consideration on how such injustices may be righted; on the moral justifications that underpin such righting efforts; and on their relative importance in cases of moral conflicts in the face of human difference, interdependence, and uncertainty.

REFERENCES

Australian Public Service Commissioner. (2007). Tackling wicked problems: A public policy perspective. Retrieved from http://www.apsc.gov.au/publications-and-media/archive/publications-archive/tackling-wicked-problems

Beauchamp, T. L. (2003). The nature of applied ethics. In R. G. Frey & C. H. Wellman (Eds.) *A companion to applied ethics* (pp. 1–16). Oxford: Blackwell.

De Schutter, H. (2007). Language policy and political philosophy: On the emerging linguistic justice debate. *Language Problems & Language Planning* 31(1), 1–23.

De Schutter, H., & Robichaud, D. (Eds.). (2015a). Linguistic justice—Van Parijs and his critiques: Special issue of the *Critical Review of International Social and Political Philosophy* 18(2).

De Schutter, H., & Robichaud, D. (2015b). Van Parijsian linguistic justice: Context, analysis and critiques. *Critical Review of International Social and Political Philosophy* 18(2), 87–112.

Dryzek, J. S., Honig, B., & Phillips, A. (2012). An overview of political theory. In R. E. Goodin (Ed.), *The Oxford handbook of political science* (pp. 61–88). Oxford: Oxford University Press.

Freeden, M. (2013). *The political theory of political thinking: The anatomy of a practice.* Oxford: Oxford University Press.

Graff, H. J. (2015). *Undisciplining knowledge: Interdisciplinarity in the twentieth century.* Baltimore, MD: Johns Hopkins University Press.

Ives, P. (2014). De-politicizing language: Obstacles to political theory's engagement with language policy. *Language Policy* 13(4), 335–350.

Jernudd, B., & Nekvapil, J. (2012). History of the field: A sketch. In B. Spolsky (Ed.), *The Cambridge handbook of language policy* (pp. 16–36). Cambridge: Cambridge University Press.

Kymlicka, W., & Patten, A. (Eds.). (2003). *Language rights and political theory.* Oxford: Oxford University Press.

Leger, R., & Lewis, H. (Eds.). (2017). Normative approaches to language policy and planning: Special issue of the *Journal of Multilingual and Multicultural Development* 38(7), 577–583.

Lo Bianco, J. (2015). Exploring language problems through Q-sorting. In F. M. Hult & D. C. Johnson (Eds.), *Research methods in language policy: A practical guide* (pp. 45–55). Oxford: Wiley Blackwell.

May, S. (2003). Misconceiving minority language rights. In W. Kymlicka & A. Patten (Eds.), *Language rights and political theory* (pp. 123–152). Oxford: Oxford University Press.

May, S. (2014). Contesting public multilingualism and diglossia: Rethinking political theory and language policy for a multilingual world. *Language Policy* 13(4), 371–393.

May, S. (2015a). The problem with English(es) and linguistic injustice: Addressing the limits of liberal egalitarian accounts of language. *Critical Review of International Social and Political Philosophy* 18(2), 131–148.

May, S. (2015b). Language policy and political theory. In F. M. Hult & D. C. Johnson (Eds.), *Research methods in language policy: A practical guide* (pp. 45–55). Oxford: Wiley.

Oakes, L. & Peled, Y. (2018). *Normative language policy: Ethics, politics, principles.* Cambridge: Cambridge University Press.

Patten, A. (2014). *Equal recognition.* New Haven, CT: Princeton University Press.

Peled, Y. (2014). Normative language policy: Interface and interfences. *Language Policy* 13(4), 301–315.

Peled, Y. (2015a). The domain of disciplines. *Science* 350, 168.

Peled, Y. (2015b). Parity in the plural: Language and complex equality. *Language Problems and Language Planning* 39(3), 283–297.

Peled, Y. (2017). Language and the limits of justice. *Journal of Multicultural and Multilingual Development* 38(7), 645–657.

Peled, Y. (forthcoming). Towards an adaptive approach to linguistic justice: Three paradoxes. In M. Gazzola, T. Templin, & B.-A. Wickström (Eds.), *Language policy and linguistic justice: Economic, philosophical and sociolinguistics approaches.* London: Springer.

Peled, Y., Ricento, T., & Ives, P. (2014). Introduction to the thematic volume: Language policy and political theory. *Language Policy* 13(4), 295–300.

Piller, I. (2016). *Linguistic diversity and social justice: An introduction to applied linguistics.* Oxford: Oxford University Press.

Pupavac, V. (2012). *Language rights: From free speech to linguistic governance.* London: Routledge.

Ricento, T. (2000). Historical and theoretical perspectives in language policy and planning. *Journal of Sociolinguistics* 4(2), 196–213.

Ricento, T. (2006). Language policy: Theory and practice—an introduction. In T. Ricento (Ed.), *An introduction to language policy: Theory and method* (pp. 10–23). Oxford: Blackwell.

Ricento, T. (2014). Thinking about language: What political theorists need to know about language in the real world. *Language Policy* 13(4), 351–369.

Ricento, T., Peled, Y., & Ives, P. (Eds.). (2014). Language policy and political theory: Special issue of *Language Policy* 13(4).

Rittel, H. W. J., & Webber, M. M. (1973). Dilemmas in a general theory of planning. *Policy Sciences* 4, 155–169.

Schmidt, R. (2006). Political theory and language policy. In T. Ricento (Ed.), *An introduction to language policy: Theory and method* (pp. 95–110). Oxford: Blackwell.

Schmidt, R. (2014). Democratic theory and the challenge of linguistic diversity. *Language Policy* 13(4), 395–411.

Shapiro, I. (2016). *Politics against domination.* Cambridge, MA: Harvard University Press.

Shohamy, E. (2006). *Language policy: Hidden agendas and new approaches.* London: Routledge.

Tonkin, H. (Ed.). (2015). Linguistic equality: Special issue of *Language Problems and Language Planning* 39(3).

Van Parijs, P. (2011). *Linguistic justice for Europe and for the world.* Oxford: Oxford University Press.

Wee, L. (2010). *Language without rights.* Oxford: Oxford University Press.

Wright, S. (2015). What is language? A response to Philippe Van Parijs. *Critical Review of International Social and Political Philosophy* 18(2), 113–130.

PART II

LANGUAGE POLICY AND PLANNING, NATION-STATES, AND COMMUNITIES

II.A.

Modern Nationalism, Languages, Minorities, Standardization, and Globalization

CHAPTER 8

NATIONALISM AND NATIONAL LANGUAGES

TOMASZ KAMUSELLA

In the extensive scholarly literature on nationalism, it is widely recognized that language is important for building nations and states. Discussion of the issues of language and nationalism is quite difficult, however, due to the strong and often implicit normative claims involved, and because different sets of political and social connotations may be attached to such seemingly neutral and universal terms as *nation, nation-state*, and *nationality*. These connotations may differ widely from country to country and in various languages. Another difficulty is posed by the equally unrealized Western normative dichotomy of dialect and language, in which dialects are regarded as *children* to *proper languages*. Moreover, the concept of *a language* is, simultaneously, a product of culture (including politics) and the primary instrument of generating culture (the social reality, as distinct from the material reality of bricks and mortar). Nations, nation-states, and languages are arguably invisible in the material reality, but they are the foundations of the social reality of the modern world as we know it.

In this chapter, I argue that ethnolinguistic nationalism, the foundational mechanism for creating and maintaining the social reality of nation-states in Central Europe, entails the normative isomorphism (or tight spatial and discursive overlapping) of language, nation, and state. This mechanism is presented here as a set of several procedures, which allows for operationalizing the concept of ethnolinguistic nationalism as an instrument of analysis. Apart from very few outliers elsewhere in Eurasia, most states fulfilling the requirements of this normative isomorphism are in Central Europe, where ethnolinguistic nationalism emerged as the central principle of nationalism after World War I. (Another cluster of isomorphic polities is located in Southeast and East Asia, and emerged in the wake of World War II and decolonization.) Through an examination of the case of ethnolinguistic nationalism in Central Europe, this chapter explores the historical development of the links between language and nationalism, associated conceptual and terminological complexities, and post–World War II language policies that reflect the normative isomorphism of language, nation, and state.

Nationalism Spreads across the Globe

At present we live in the global age of nationalism (as presciently predicted by Kohn, 1962). With the breakup of the Soviet Union in 1991, the last ideologically non-national polity of significance vanished from the political map of the world. The first-ever self-declared nation-states appeared in the late eighteenth century, namely the United States alongside revolutionary France and Haiti. These were followed in the first half of the following century by Spanish colonies in Latin America that rapidly won independence as national polities. During the 1820s in Europe, too, newly independent, autonomous Christian nation-states appeared in the European section of the Ottoman Empire (the so-called Balkans), that is, Montenegro, Serbia, and Greece.

In Western Europe, Belgium was created as a nation-state on a religious basis, while the Netherlands and Switzerland redefined themselves as states for one nation only. Following the founding of the Kingdom of Italy (1861) and the German Empire (1871) as nation-states par excellence, all other modern polities across Europe, with the notable exceptions of Austria-Hungary and the Russian Empire, were reinvented as national polities in order to retain or regain legitimacy as states. By World War I, the model of the nation-state had become the gold standard of statehood organization and legitimation across the Americas and in the post-Ottoman Balkans, almost entirely divided among national polities.

Outside Europe, at the turn of the twentieth century the model of the nation-state, as normatively equated with modernity and progress, was adopted by Meiji-era Japan, Republican China, and the Kingdom of Siam (Thailand), the last polity endeavoring in this way to thwart France's attempts to turn it into a French colony. The same model of national statehood spread across the British settler colonies, successively turned into a Canadian Confederation, a Commonwealth of Australia, a Dominion of New Zealand, and a Union of South Africa. Between the two World Wars, after the destruction of Austria-Hungary together with the Russian and Ottoman empires, practically all extant states in Europe (bar the Free City of Danzig or the Vatican City State) became national polities, with the marked exception of the Soviet Union, which was designed for the entire globe, as indicated by its intentionally universalist name that did not anchor the communist polity in any ethnic or geographic specificity. Many post-Ottoman territories in the Middle East and Arab North Africa gained independence and became nation-states (Egypt, Iraq, Syria, and Turkey) or were set on the road to future national independence as post-Ottoman mandates under control of the Great War Allies. The remaining independent non-Western polities urgently sought to reinvent themselves as nation-states in order to evade being made into Western colonies, especially so in the cases of Abyssinia (Ethiopia) and Persia (Iran).

After World War II, the Western maritime colonial empires were dismantled. In the wake of this massive worldwide decolonization, former colonies, upon gaining independence, invariably declared themselves to be nation-states. The process was completed in 1991 with the splitting of the non-national Soviet Union, which yielded fifteen national polities (that is, the former union republics, each complete with its own ethnolinguistically defined nation, in line with Joseph Stalin's 1930 slogan prescribing that cultures in the Soviet Union should be "national in form but socialist in content" Stalin in Vdovin, 2007, p. 145). In this way, nationalism became the first universally accepted infrastructural ideology for the legitimization of statehood organization, be it in the United States, Iran, North Korea, or Nauru, which starkly differ from one another almost in every other way but their steadfast allegiance to nationalism.

The question arises as to what is entailed in nationalism, as the late modern period's (since 1991) sole ideology of statehood organization, legitimation, and maintenance. In order to fit all the world's states, despite their vast differences, this ideology must be composed of a few, simple, widely accepted, and malleable procedures. These will be detailed in the following section.

NATIONALISM AND MIND GAMES: A KIND OF MAGIC

Briefly, nationalism proposes that in order for a polity to be legitimate it must be a nation-state, that is, a state for one nation only. In line with the post-1648 Westphalian model of the territorial polity (*Territorialstaat*), the nation-state is imagined to be a kind of spatial container that is homogeneous, either in religion, culture, language, or the status of its inhabitants construed as citizens. This homogeneous spatial container, preferably consisting of a single continuous territory, is placed under one government, which, in matters political, military, social, and sometimes economic, guards the spatially and ideologically isolated sovereign nation-state from all other polities. That is, the government guards the nation-state from unwanted influences and possible military incursions from (usually) neighboring states. Thus the nation-state appears to be an example of the human social tendency to seek safety in imagined (constructed) "morpho-immunological spheres" (Solterdijk, 2011, p. 46). In turn, the nation is proposed to be the highest imaginable taxon of human grouping, a priori precluding the possibility of any equally coherent and viable supra-national grouping. Only nations may claim to have the right to statehood (national self-determination) and simultaneously to be the font of statehood and its legitimation.

Analysis of the concept of *nation* is complicated in English or French by the fact that in these two languages this term commonly functions as a synonym for the word *state*. Hence, the academic and juridical neologism *nation-state* tends to sound like the confusing *state-state*. This difficulty does not arise, for instance, in German or Polish. In German, *state* is *Staat* and *nation* is *Volk* (or in some specialized meanings, *Nation*), while in Polish they are *państwo* and *naród*, respectively. In German and Polish the terms for *nation*, understood as a group of people (that is, *Volk* and *naród*, respectively), cannot denote *state*. The term *nation-state* is rendered in Polish as *państwo narodowe* and in German as *Nationalstaat*.

A further terminological difficulty arises in the case of the term *nationality*, for denoting either the individual's membership in a nation or (originating from the legal vocabulary of the Soviet Union) a human group that is "more than an ethnic group but less than a nation" and that may have a right to autonomy but not to national independence (some authorities prefer the neologism *proto-nation* in this meaning; see Hobsbawm, 1990, p. 72). However, in English, *nationality* most often functions as the preferred synonym for *citizenship*. *Nationality* in German is *Nationalität* and in Polish it is *narodowość*, which cannot stand for *citizenship*, or *Staatsbürgerschaft* (citizenship) in German and *obywatelstwo* in Polish. In Russian the term *nationality*, as opposed to *citizenship* (*grazhdanstvo* in Russian), comes in two different forms, namely, *narodnost'* and *natsionalnost'*, the former stemming from the word *narod* (people) and the latter from *natsiia* (nation). In the past, both terms (*narodnost'* and *natsionalnost'*) were interchangeably employed to mean "proto-nation with a right to autonomy," while only *natsionalnost'* denotes "membership in a nation." Nowadays, it is almost exclusively *narodnost'* that is employed to mean *proto-nation*. Hence, the two meanings of the term nationality are rendered with the use of two different words in today's Russian, lessening the possibility of confusion between them. Thus speakers of English, German, Polish, and Russian may mean starkly different things when they use the same English terms.

Yet human groups recognized as nations (that is, the demographic contents of nation-states) and their associated nation-states (or spatial containers) differ widely, for instance, in size. The 1.4 billion-strong Chinese nation dwarfs the fewer than 10,000 members of the Tuvaluan nation. Such differences exist without depriving any of them of the title of nation, because there are no specific material criteria that have to be met before a group can become eligible for the status of nation. The process of becoming a nation is discursive, decided by the rhetoric of power (Han, 2005), as expressed and effected through language (Bourdieu, 1992; Foucault, 2002 [1970]).

Making a nation or a nation-state is a speech act that may not immediately—if at all—alter the material reality (Austin, 1962). Entities dubbed *nations* and *nation-states* belong to the social reality generated through language that is employed in continual communication among humans and their groups (Searle, 1995). Both nations and nation-states are invisible and undetectable with instruments that natural scientists employ for probing into material reality. Either from the vantage of the observer walking on the Earth's surface or from orbit, nations and nation-states cannot be seen, whether with the naked eye or a telescope. One is unable to touch a nation or a nation-state, even though nationalists customarily propose that, if needed, one must give one's life for one's country, meaning a nation and/or a nation-state (Balch & Foster, 1898, p. 67). Thus nations and nation-states are imagined into being by people alone, that is, discursively, through language.

The Role of Language

In 1793–1794, languages other than French that were customarily employed in writing were banned from education and official use in revolutionary France, yet language was not made into the sole basis of nationhood or statehood (Certeau, Julia, & Revel, 1975). The idea of the normative equation of the demographic unit of the nation with the normative unity of a language made an appearance across the lands of the former Holy Roman Empire under the onslaught of the repeated Napoleonic attacks at the turn of the nineteenth century that led to the dissolution in 1806 of this millennium-old empire. Thus, the pre-modern polity that could have been turned into a German nation-state disappeared, barring the fledgling German national movement from following in the footsteps of the French, who had transformed the Kingdom of France into the French nation-state. The situation caused much frustration among German-speaking intellectuals (*Bildungsbürgertum*) at the beginning of the nineteenth century.

A solution to this dilemma was offered in a well-known anti-French song (Arndt, 1813), which famously proposed that the German nation-state (the German's fatherland) should extend "[a]s far as the German tongue sounds" (Arndt in Feuerzeig, 2002, p. 70). This language-related approach to the national question became a new modern norm, which postulates that speakers of a language (a speech community) naturally constitute a nation, and that a territory compactly inhabited by such a speech community should be made into a nation-state (Reiter, 1984). This norm was successfully trialed during the 1860s and 1870s when Italy and Germany were founded as ethnolinguistic nation-states. Subsequently, in the wake of World War I, the political shape of Central Europe (understood here as the vertical midsection of Europe from Scandinavia to the Balkans) was reorganized in accordance with this principle. Beginning in the second half of the nineteenth century, the question about language as the indicator of nationality (membership in a nation defined purely through language) was included in state-wide censuses held across Central Europe (Leuschner, 2004).

With the end of World War I, ethnolinguistic nation-states were erected in place of the former empires of the Habsburgs and the Ottomans, and also in the western borderlands of the erstwhile Russian Empire, alongside some eastern territories detached from the German Empire. Furthermore, during the Balkan Wars and World War I, initially ethnoreligious Balkan nation-states became increasingly ethnolinguistic. This change is best illustrated by the caesura of Albania, founded in 1912 on a purely ethnolinguistic basis. The Albanian nation was fashioned from multiconfessional Albanian-speakers who professed Islam, Orthodox Christianity, or Roman Catholicism. This novel logic of organizing the political in Central Europe was accepted by the Allies and gradually naturalized, as evidenced by the following quote from an influential 1917 tome on the subject, diligently perused by negotiators at the Paris Peace Conference: "the growing coincidence of linguistic and political boundaries must be regarded as a normal development. [. . .] For nations, like individuals, are at their best only when they are free, that is to say when the mastery of their destiny is in their own hands" (Dominian, 1917, p. 342).

As a result, during the interwar period, for instance, Estonian became the sole official and national language in Estonia, Hungarian in Hungary, Polish in Poland, and Romanian in Romania. These polities were construed to be only for their respective ethnolinguistic nations speaking the national language, that is, for the Estonian-speaking Estonians in Estonia, Hungarian-speaking Hungarians in Hungary, Polish-speaking Poles in Poland, and the Romanian-speaking Romanians in Romania. For any new polity to be recognized by the Allies as legitimate in Central Europe, it had to follow this pattern of ethnolinguistically defined national statehood. (Interestingly, the Allies had no wish to extend this principle of nation-state building to other parts of Europe, let alone to their maritime colonial empires [Mishra, 2012].)

This normative insistence on equating the nation and its nation-state with a single speech community posed a tremendous ideological and political dilemma to Czechoslovakia and the Kingdom of Serbs, Croats, and Slovenes (called Yugoslavia since 1929). The former polity was founded as a common state for the Czechs and the Slovaks, while the latter for the Serbs, the Croats, and the Slovenes. Among most politicians and inhabitants of Central Europe, the aforementioned groups were seen as (somewhat) separate nations or nationalities (proto-nations), complete with their own separate languages. Hence, neither Czechoslovakia nor the Kingdom could be a nation-state, as understood in Central Europe after 1918.

Had the two polities failed to gain legitimacy and survive, it would have been a serious blow to the Allies' diplomatic and military effort to reorganize the political shape of Central Europe in accordance with the principles of ethnolinguistic nationalism. In the case of Czechoslovakia, the solution was to proclaim the polity to be a nation-state of the Czechoslovak nation, whose sole official and national language was Czechoslovak. In everyday administrative and educational practice of interwar Czechoslovakia, Slovak was employed in Slovakia, while Czech was used in the Czech lands of Bohemia and Moravia-Silesia. In this pattern, the Czechoslovak language was interpreted as consisting of two varieties, namely, Czech and Slovak (Nekvapil, 2007, pp. 146–147). The complication of Subcarpathian Ruthenia with its own nation of Ruthenians (Rusyns) as a third constitutive ethnoterritorial part of interwar Czechoslovakia was simply disregarded. The name of the Ruthenians did not feature in the polity's name, nor was their Ruthenian (Rusyn) language added to Czechoslovak as a third variety.

The normative importance of language for constructing and legitimizing national statehood in Central Europe is evident also in the case of the Kingdom of Serbs, Croats, and Slovenes. The polity's tripartite name was changed to the unitary sobriquet of Yugoslavia in 1929, eight years after the 1921 constitutional decision to make Serbocroatoslovenian the sole official and national language of this nation-state. The tripartite name of this language was never officially changed, but after 1929 it became increasingly popular to refer to it as the *Yugoslav(ian) language*. Although the Serbs, Croats, and Slovenes became by royal fiat a single nation of Yugoslavs in 1929, in interwar Yugoslavia's everyday administrative and educational practice the Serbo-Croats and the Slovenes were de facto treated as two separate groups of the Yugoslav nation. By extension, the official Serbocroatoslovenian language came in two territorially separate varieties, that is, Slovenian employed in the Drava Region (today's Slovenia) and Serbo-Croatian used elsewhere across the nation-state and also for central administration. In addition, because the Serbo-Croatian variety of Serbocroatoslovenian was officially written both in Cyrillic and Latin, the Latin script-based Serbo-Croatian was unofficially perceived as *Croatian*, and its Cyrillic-based counterpart as *Serbian*. From the territorial perspective, the former language dominated in the Croatian Region (founded in 1939 and coterminous with today's Croatia and parts of Bosnia), while the latter dominated in the southern half of Yugoslavia (present-day Kosovo, Macedonia, Montenegro, and Serbia).

World War II dramatically altered not only the territorial arrangements in Czechoslovakia and Yugoslavia, but also the official (national) linguistic ones. In 1939 the former nation-state was broken up. Slovakia became independent, the nation-state for the Slovak-speaking Slovaks only, with Slovak as its sole official and national language. The Czech lands were incorporated into the Third Reich (wartime Germany) as a Protectorate of Bohemia and Moravia, with both German and Czech as the official languages. (Hungary annexed the Subcarpathian Ruthenia, where—unlike in interwar Czechoslovakia—Rusyn was employed in some official capacity, alongside Hungarian.) After 1945, Czechoslovakia was reconstituted as a national polity (less Subcarpathian Ruthenia, which was incorporated into the Soviet Union's Ukraine) of the Czechoslovak *people* composed, as the 1948 Constitution provided, of the two *fraternal nations* of Czechs and Slovaks. However, the Czechoslovak language was not recreated, and both Czech and Slovak were used in official and national capacity (McDermott, 2015, p. 48).

The 1941 partition of Yugoslavia among wartime Germany, Italy, Hungary, and Bulgaria also destroyed the nation-state's official and national Serbocroatoslovenian language. The Slovenian variety fell out of official use, the Slovenian ethnic territory split between Germany and Italy. In the officially named Independent State of Croatia (composed of today's Croatia and Bosnia) under joint German and Italian tutelage, bi-scriptural Serbo-Croatian was replaced with Latin Croatian, and Cyrillic was explicitly banned in official and educational use. By the same token, in rump Serbia under German military administration, Cyrillic-based Serbian superseded Serbo-Croatian. Serbian also took hold in the Italian Governorate of Montenegro, though initially Rome had planned to replace it with Montenegrin. In the part of southern Serbia (or present-day Macedonia) that was incorporated into Bulgaria, Bulgarian replaced Cyrillic-based Serbo-Croatian in official and educational use (Greenberg, 2008, p. 22; Samardžija, 2008; Scotti & Viazzi, 1987, p. 198; Vignoli, 1996).

After the war, in communist Yugoslavia, Serbocroatoslovenian was not revived, but its two interwar de facto varieties, namely, the biscriptural Serbo-Croatian and Slovenian, sprang back into life as official and national languages in their own right. In emulation of the Soviet Union, postwar Yugoslavia was re-established as a non-national federation composed of ethnolinguistically defined national republics. Slovenian became the official and national language of Slovenia in the Socialist Republic (SR) of Slovenia, with Macedonian in the SR of Macedonia. This language of Macedonian was proclaimed in 1944 when the Yugoslav communist forces had already seized most of the former southern Serbia (renamed Macedonia) from Bulgaria. As a result, by 1945 the interwar Serbocroatoslovenian language had yielded Macedonian, Serbo-Croatian, and Slovenian (Greenberg, 2008, p. 18).

Serbo-Croatian continued as the official and national language in the four Yugoslav SRs of Bosnia-Herzegovina, Croatia, Montenegro, and Serbia. This arrangement sat uncomfortably in the Central European context, which provided that every true nation, housed in its own nation-state or national republic (in the case of federations), should enjoy its own unique national language. To this end, in 1974, each of these four national SRs with Serbo-Croatian was endowed with its own national variety of this language (Greenberg, 2008, p. 23). In the SR of Croatia, its variety was officially dubbed *Croato-Serbian* or *Croatian*, and was written exclusively in Latin letters. On the other hand, the official use of Cyrillic was prescribed for the SR of Serbia, while both alphabets were permitted in the SRs of Bosnia-Herzegovina and Montenegro. Finally, the official name of Serbo-Croatian as the state language of entire Yugoslavia was altered to consensual *Serbocroatian/Croatoserbian, Croatian,* or *Serbian* (Brozović & Ivić, 1988; Tollefson, 2002).

Five years earlier, in the wake of the 1968 Soviet-led Warsaw Pact intervention in Czechoslovakia, the tentative nation-state of the bi-national Czechoslovak people was made into a non-national federation of two national republics, the Czech SR and the Slovak SR. As in federal Yugoslavia, this solution followed the Soviet model. Czech and Slovak, as previously, were official in the Czech lands and Slovakia, respectively. The significant difference was that before 1969 Czech had served as the language of the state, while afterward full and equitable official Czech-Slovak bilingualism became the norm in all spheres of public life (Nábělková, 2016).

These examples drawn from Central Europe prior to the fall of communism in 1989 clearly show that languages are entities susceptible to manipulation by humans and their groups. Humans can create and destroy languages, or merge and split them, like they do with nations and states (Kamusella, 2001). But in order to discuss the dynamics of language building and its parallels with building and destroying nations and nation-states, it is necessary to come to terms with an important conceptual and terminological problem.

Einzelsprache: The Concept of *a Language*

The entities to which we refer in English when speaking of *languages* are not a straightforward plural form of the abstract and uncountable noun *language* that is used without an article and never occurs in plural. This eternally singular form denotes the human biological capacity for speech. In turn, *a language* and its plural form mean specific actualizations of this biological capacity. Availing of this capacity, separate groups of humans have created their own specific languages, thus becoming *speech communities*. Hence, in pre-state societies, anthropologists tend to equate speech communities with ethnic groups (Shaul, 2014, p. xvi.) Therefore, while language is part of the material reality, languages, as actualizations of the biological capacity for speech, are products of humans and their groups, that is, artifacts of culture, and thus part of the social reality. Crucially, the capacity for speech (*language*) alone cannot be used for bonding and communication among humans and their groups, just as the capacity for walking is not walking. Only *languages* can play this role.

The existing words in English and other European languages that I know of do not allow for an easy and unambiguous terminological distinction between the capacity for speech and a given actualization of this capacity. A certain solution in this respect is offered only by an old German specialist term. German-speaking linguists use the common word *Sprache* for denoting the biological capacity for speech, but prefer the neologism *Einzelsprache* when it is necessary to specify clearly and unequivocally an actualization of this capacity (*a language*). Obviously, in everyday German, as in English, people speak of *Sprachen* (languages), not of *Einzelsprachen* (cf. Dreschler, 1830, p. viii).

Moreover, the concept of the discrete and self-contained *Einzelsprache* (a language) is as much a human invention as the concept of the nation (Kamusella, 2004). Both these concepts seem to have originated in Western Europe, from where they spread elsewhere in the world as part and parcel of the politico-cultural package of Western colonialism and imperialism. Prior to the imposition of the concept of *Einzelsprache* on the social reality through political decisions and compulsory elementary education for all, languages were in essence continuous, changing gradually from clan to clan, village to village, city to city, region to region, state to state, and empire to empire (Billig, 1995, pp. 29–36). Despite the tight ideological binding of modernity in its linguistic aspect (read: language politics) with the concept of *Einzelsprache* (Kamusella, 2012; Pallas, 1786–1789; Stoll, 1982), the continuous character of languages across geography survives in many areas. Such phenomena necessitated the development of an appropriate term for its spatial or social dimension, such as "dialect continuum" (Chambers & Trudgill, 1998, pp. 5–11).

The Dichotomy of Dialect and Language

It is impossible to speak about *Einzelsprachen* without mentioning the concept of dialect, which is conceptually and ideologically conjoined with the concept of *a language*. Again, this conceptual dyad seems to be a Western development that spread elsewhere in the world and now is widely seen as a standard way of describing languages in society.

This dichotomy carries numerous normative assumptions implicitly associated with it (Kamusella, 2016): first, that a language is composed of dialects; second, that dialects are lower (worse) than languages, and hence the former must act as *umbrellas* (*Dachsprachen* in German, literally "roofing languages") for the latter (Kloss, 1967); third, that each true language enjoys an established written form, while dialects are oral, that is, not commonly employed in writing.

Leaving aside the futile attempt to scientifically distinguish between languages and dialects (e.g., with the criterion of mutual [in]comprehensibility; Bloomfield, 1926; Haugen, 1966), it is important to note that the now commonsense subjection of dialects to languages is highly anachronistic. The key point is that the *Einzelsprache* is a dialect of a power center (e.g., capital), or a dialect (more appropriately, sociolect) of an elite that happened to be committed to paper and thus became an administrative instrument of power. As a result, the dominant group's speech and writing are, by definition, a language, while the speech of a subaltern group is a dialect in which writing is discouraged or even deemed normatively impossible (cf. Tollefson, 1991).

The normative dichotomy of *Einzelsprache* versus dialect is a product of power relations among human groups, and a versatile political metonymy for such unequal relations. As such, this dichotomy legitimizes the subjection of subaltern groups to dominant elite groups; or, in today's political terminology, the subjection of ethnic groups, proto-nations, and minorities to recognized nations with their own nation-states. In Central Europe, where ethnolinguistic nationalism is the ideology of statehood creation and maintenance, this normative opposition of *Einzelsprache* to dialect and the entailed subjection of the latter to the former constitute the core of this ideology's modus operandi.

These brief histories of the concept of *Einzelsprache* and of the dichotomy of dialect and language serve two purposes. On the one hand, they conclude the general discussion of the rise of the use of languages for nation- and nation-state building in Europe, while on the other, they constitute a methodological basis for the analysis of the ethnolinguistic character of nationalism in Central Europe.

THE NORMATIVE ISOMORPHISM OF LANGUAGE, NATION, AND STATE

I propose that the main normative assumption of ethnolinguistic nationalism is that all the speakers of a language (or a speech community) constitute a nation, and that the territory compactly inhabited by them should be turned into the nation's nation-state. The desired result is a tight spatial and ideological overlapping of language, nation, and state, or the normative isomorphism of these three elements. Language appears to offer an additional protective (isolating) layer to the nation's territorial-cum-demographic "morpho-immunological sphere" (Solterdijk, 2011, p. 46) that shields the nation from the dangers of the outside world. Most of the world's extant nation-states are dual in their character, namely consisting only of the tightly overlapping nation and its state. The protective immunological sphere is based on the demographic and territorial layers, whereas the ethnolinguistic nation-state also includes a third linguistic layer.

The basic follow-up principles of the normative isomorphism of language, nation, and state require that the national language is the *only* official language of the nation-state, and that this language cannot be shared with any other polity or nation. By extension, no autonomous territories with official languages other than the national one can exist within the nation-state's borders. Likewise, no autonomous territories with the national language in question as official can exist outside the nation-state, where this language properly belongs. An additional principle is that all members of the ethnolinguistic nation should be exclusively monolingual in the national language, and that no speakers of other languages should reside permanently in the nation-state in question. By the same token, no speakers of the national language should reside permanently outside their own nation-state (Kamusella, 2006).

Dialects are not included in the principles of normative isomorphism; dialect continua and dialect leveling (that is, liquidation) (Auer, 1998; Stieber, 1956) are generally ignored by ethnolinguistic nationalism. The unique status of the national language is often constitutionally guaranteed in a typical Central European nation-state, while official documents usually omit any reference to dialects. The tacit assumption is that administration, education, and mass media necessitate the disappearance of dialects, which in due course are replaced with the idealized homogenous national language that prevails across the entire nation-state and all the nation's social strata. Perhaps that is what the Italian nationalist politician and writer Massimo d'Azeglio meant when he famously opined, "We have made Italy. Now we must make Italians" (d'Azeglio, 1867, p. 7; Killinger, 2002, p. 1).

This normative isomorphism of language, nation, and state is an analytical instrument with which it is possible to examine the ethnolinguistic character of the nation-states of Central Europe, as I will show in the following section.

WHERE IS CENTRAL EUROPE?

The heuristic value of the normative isomorphism as an instrument for identifying ethnolinguistic nationalism is, however, blighted by a certain blind spot. The doctrine of sovereignty does not permit the ethnolinguistic nation-state any easy way to prevent the adoption of its own national language in official and/or national capacity in another polity or its autonomous region. When this occurs, such contexts may be termed *near-isomorphic* nation-states. For instance, in 2010 the autonomous status of Serbia's Vojvodina was revived, complete with the co-official use of Croatian, Hungarian, Romanian, Rusyn, Serbian, and Slovak (Statut, 2014; Zakon, 2009). As a result, the previously fully isomorphic nation-states of Hungary, Romania, and Slovakia became, by this development, which was outside their sovereign control, near-isomorphic polities. In assessing the importance of ethnolinguistic nationalism in Central Europe, I ignore this relatively minor difference, and group together both isomorphic and near-isomorphic nation-states.

A scan of the region for the year 2007, that is, before the founding of Kosovo as a nation-state in 2008 and prior to the rise of the officially sexta-lingual and duo-scriptural autonomous Vojvodina, yields the categories of nation-states summarized in Table 8.1.

In 2007, fourteen out of thirty-five polities in Central Europe (40%) were isomorphic nation-states, and an additional thirteen were near-isomorphic states;

Table 8.1 Central Europe's Isomorphic and Other Polities in 2007

Isomorphic States (14)	Near-Isomorphic States (13)	Other Ethnolinguistic States (4)	Non-Ethnolinguistic States (4)	Total Number of Polities	Isomorphic States, Percent of Total	Isomorphic and Near-Isomorphic States, Percent of Total
Albania	Bosnia	Austria	Mount Athos	35	40%	77%
Bulgaria	Croatia	Belarus	Russian Federation			
Czech Republic	Cyprus	Denmark	Sovereign Base Areas			
Estonia	Finland	Liechtenstein	of Akrotiri and			
Hungary	Germany		Dhekelia			
Latvia	Greece		Transnistria			
Lithuania, Macedonia	Luxembourg					
Montenegro, Norway	Moldova					
Poland	Northern Cyprus					
Romania	Serbia					
Slovakia	Sweden					
Slovenia	Turkey					
	Ukraine					

the combined total of twenty-seven states constitutes 77% of the total of all the region's states. If we consider population, out of Central Europe's total population of 416.32 million (which includes a third of the population in Russia's European region), 357.69 million (86%) reside in isomorphic or near-isomorphic states (Index Mundi, 2015). Thus Central Europe today is characterized by nation-states that are ethnolinguistic in their organization, legitimation, and maintenance.

To my knowledge only a single fully isomorphic nation-state exists in Western Europe (Iceland) and a couple of near-isomorphic ones (Malta, The Netherlands), whereas other Western European nation-states are non-isomorphic. I emphasize not that language is of no political import there; rather, language is generally not employed in Western Europe as the basis of national statehood creation, legitimation, and maintenance. For instance, officially quadrilingual Switzerland has no Swiss language movement, while France strongly supports the spread of French as an official or national language in other countries (Poissonnier & Sournia, 2006).

Not so in Central Europe. The breakup of Yugoslavia between 1991 and 2007 was followed by the split of the Serbo-Croatian language into Bosnian, Croatian, Montenegrin, and Serbian, so that each post-Yugoslav nation-state (with the exception of Kosovo, apparently wavering on an ethnolinguistic national union with Albania) has its own national language (Greenberg, 2008). As a result, the interwar Serbocroatoslovenian language has yielded six national languages to date (Bosnian, Croatian, Macedonian, Montenegrin, Serbian, and Slovenian). When post-Soviet Moldova gained independence in 1991, its Cyrillic-based Moldovan language (written in Latin letters since 1989) was renamed *Romanian*. The polity's Slavophones feared it might be the first step to a union with Romania, and in the ensuing war the easternmost strip of Moldova seceded as unrecognized Transnistria under Russian protection. The 1994 Moldovan Constitution reintroduced the old name *Moldovan* for the language to entice Transnistria back, thus far unsuccessfully. For all practical purposes, Moldovan and Romanian are almost identical, more similar to each other than American and British English (King, 1999). The recent trend is for renaming Moldovan again as *Romanian*, though Cyrillic-based Moldovan remains a co-official language in Transnistria, alongside Russian and Ukrainian, with which it shares the same script (Hotărâre, 2013).

Bulgaria was the first country to recognize the post-Yugoslav nation-state of Macedonia when it declared independence in 1991. However, Sofia does not extend this recognition either to the Macedonian language or the Macedonian nation. In the official Bulgarian view, Macedonian is a literary variety of Bulgarian. Hence, Macedonian-speakers are officially viewed as Bulgarophones, who belong to the ethnolinguistically defined Bulgarian nation. Hence, no Macedonian nation can genuinely exist, according to Bulgarian understanding (Majewski, 2013, p. 74; Shea, 1997, p. 352).

The wartime Holocaust carried out by the Germans, the dramatic change in its borders, and the postwar population transfers (that is, expulsions of ethnolinguistic groups carried out by the Allies) made postwar Poland into an unprecedentedly homogeneous ethnolinguistic nation-state with non-Polish-speaking minorities at well under 1% of the population. But in the 2011 census, quite unexpectedly, 0.85 million (over 2%) declared themselves to be members of the ethnolinguistic nation of Silesians, and over half a million declared that they speak Silesian at home and with neighbors. The 1997 Polish Constitution defines the Polish nation as the totality of all Polish citizens, irrespective of their ethnicity, languages, or religion. However, the authorities chose to disregard these Silesians and Silesian speakers in official data, which means that the national minorities and speakers of languages other than Polish remain officially below 1% (Kamusella & Nomachi, 2014).

These examples indicate that the hold of the normative isomorphism of language, nation, and state continues across Central Europe. As many as 86% of the region's population live in nation-states where administration, political parties, schools, mass media, and businesses reinforce a specifically Central European social reality. Throughout the region, ethnolinguistic nationalism is the gold standard for understandings of social and political normalcy. Thus a Central European may be surprised that people do not speak a Canadian language in Canada or a Nigerian language in Nigeria.

Apart from a few other ethnolinguistic nation-states in Eurasia (e.g., Iceland and Turkmenistan), there is another cluster in Southeast and East Asia consisting, as of 2007, of seven fully isomorphic nation-states (Cambodia, Indonesia, Japan, Laos, Myanmar, Thailand, and Vietnam) and five near-isomorphic ones (Malaysia, Mongolia, North Korea, Philippines, and South Korea). In the future, comparative research on long-distance flows of ideas and ideological connections between ethnolinguistic nationalism as practiced in Central Europe and Southeast/East Asia may open a trove of novel insights.

ETHNOLINGUISTIC NATIONALISM IN THE FUTURE

For better or worse, ethnolinguistic nationalism remains the norm of statehood construction, legitimation, and maintenance across Central Europe. This is not going to change any time soon. A clearer understanding of this type of nationalism should help decision-makers in Western Europe better comprehend what their Central European counterparts mean when they evoke the slogans of *nation* and *national language*. On the other hand, decision-makers in Central Europe can make an effort to develop better understanding of ethnolinguistic nationalism in order to be able to transcend the constraints of this ideology when the public good may require it.

At present, most multilingual areas in Central Europe are characterized by populations that consider their own language more truly national than others, which are widely perceived as a danger to national purity. Yet exceptions exist, including multilingual Vojvodina in Serbia, Moldova (where Moldovan-Romanian and Russian coexist in everyday interaction), and Finland, with two official languages of Finnish and Swedish, although the normative power of ethnolinguistic nationalism is evident in repeated initiatives to remove mandatory Swedish from its constitutionally protected status (Mandatory Swedish, 2015). Another example is Norway, where the Norwegian language consists of two different varieties (Bokmål and Nynorsk), which are as different from each other as Czech from Slovak or Dutch from German. In the Czech Republic and Slovakia, suprastandard bilingualism continues to obtain among the generations who came of age before Czechoslovakia split in 1993, meaning that communication is successfully achieved when Slovaks speak Slovak to Czechs and in return the latter reply in Czech.

In some areas, groups not speaking the national language are large or resilient enough to successfully resist assimilation. Such resilience may be supported by minority provisions imposed from outside. Examples include areas with Sorbian speakers in eastern Germany, Silesian speakers in Poland's Upper Silesia and Kashubian speakers in the north of the country, Hungarian speakers in southern Slovakia and Romania's Transylvania, Serbian speakers in northern Kosovo, Albanian speakers in western Macedonia, and Turkish speakers in eastern and southern Bulgaria and northeastern Greece.

Interestingly, few areas remain in Central Europe where two scripts are employed side by side in an official capacity or widespread informal use, although it was the norm across the region prior to the twentieth century. In Moldova, Latin orthography is used for writing Moldovan (Romanian), while Cyrillic is used for Russian. The situation is similar in Serbia's Vojvodina, where Serbian and Rusyn are written in Cyrillic, while the other four official languages are written in the Latin script. In parts of Greece and Bulgaria, Turkish is written in the Latin script, Greek in the Greek alphabet, and Bulgarian in Cyrillic. A similar pattern is repeated in Macedonia, where Albanian is written in Latin letters and Macedonian in Cyrillic. This type of biscripturality corresponds to unequal multilingualism, when members of the subaltern group develop a mastery of both scripts, but members of the dominant group use only the official state script and are monolingual in the state language.

A kind of scriptural apartheid can be observed in Bosnia and Kosovo. In Bosnian areas designated for Bosniaks and Croats and in areas in Kosovo designated for Albanians, Latin script is employed for writing Albanian, Bosnian, and Croatian. In areas set apart for Serbs in Bosnia and Kosovo, only Cyrillic is employed. In Serbia proper, despite the constitutional designation of Cyrillic as the sole official script (Constitution, 2006, Art. 10), half of all printed matter in Serbian is produced in Cyrillic and half in Latin letters. In Montenegro, the constitution provides that the national and official Montenegrin language is written in both Cyrillic and Latin scripts (Montenegro's Constitution, 2007, Art. 13). Hence, as in Serbia, the publishing industry utilizes these two alphabets. However, biscripturalism in Montenegro and Serbia is not connected to multilingualism, but to official monolingualism in the national language—Montenegrin or Serbian. Thus both languages are heirs to the biscriptural legacy of communist Yugoslavia's language of Serbo-Croatian, which remains in use on the Internet, enjoying the largest Wikipedia (written in both alphabets) among all the post-Serbo-Croatian languages (List of Wikipedias, 2015).

The Internet and the European Union constitute a wild card that in the future may challenge the ideological hold of the normative isomorphism of language, nation, and state in Central Europe. In the European Union, consisting at present of twenty-eight member nation-states, twenty-four languages are official. In most cases, the use of these languages is confined to the territory of their respective nation-states, but all of them are employed in the EU institutions across the entire Union. In addition, EU citizens moving by the millions from one member nation-state to another, in a grassroots manner, have spread the use of their native languages, either adding to preexisting multilingualism (as in London or Paris) or creating multilingualism where there was none before (for instance, in Warsaw or Germany's Land of Mecklenburg-Vorpommern).

Moreover, deterritorialized cyberspace, not (yet) controlled by nation-states, makes it possible for members of a speech community to communicate seamlessly across Europe and the world. Internet users can read, listen to, and watch rich and varied audiovisual content in their language, irrespective of where they happen to reside. A possible result may be that the integration of migrants within the European Union may not be accompanied by the loss of their native languages. In addition, unrecognized and suppressed ethnic, national, or regional speech communities may develop culture in their own languages on the web. For example, Wikipedias use Low Saxon (Low German), Cyrillic-based Moldovan, Pontic (Greek), Rusyn, and Silesian.

No *Einzelsprache* is a destiny. People can shape and reshape the social reality in seemingly infinite ways. Accordingly, language politics is also variable and open-ended. What constrains the organization of the social reality is the naturalizing character of customs and beliefs, which act as a curb on human imagination. In the case of today's Central Europe, the most important limitation of this kind is blind faith in ethnolinguistic nationalism (that is, the normative isomorphism of language, nation, and state) as the sole possible way of organizing, legitimizing, and maintaining (national) statehood.

Acknowledgments

I thank Peter Burke for kind encouragement, and Catherine Gibson, James Tollefson, Miguel Pérez-Milans, and Dorothy Bauhoff for copious remarks and suggestions, thanks to which

I could improve the chapter substantially. Obviously, I am responsible for any remaining infelicities.

REFERENCES

Arndt, E. M. (1813). Des deutschen Vaterland. In E. M. Arndt. *Fünf Lieder für deutsche Soldaten*. Berlin: Reimer.

Auer, P. (Ed). (1998). *Dialect levelling and the standard varieties in Europe*. Berlin: Mouton de Gruyter.

Austin, J. L. (1962). *How to do things with words*. Cambridge, MA: Harvard University Press.

Balch, G. T., & Foster, W. (1898). *A patriotic primer for the little citizen: An auxiliary in teaching the youth of our country the true principles of American citizenship*. Indianapolis: Levey Brothers.

Billig, M. (1995). *Banal nationalism*. London: Sage.

Bloomfield, L. (1926). A set of postulates for the science of language. *Language* 2(3), 153–164.

Bourdieu, P. (1992). *Language and symbolic power*. J. B. Thompson, Ed., translated from the French by G. Raymond & M. Adamson. Cambridge: Polity.

Brozović, D., & Ivić, P. (1988). *Jezik, srpskohrvatski/hrvatskosrpski, hrvatski ili srpski* [Izvadak iz II izdanja Enciklopedije Jugoslavije]. Zagreb: Jugoslavenski leksikografski zavod "Miroslav Krleža."

Certeau, M. de, Julia, D., & Revel, J. (1975). *Une politique de la langue : La Révolution française et les patois. L'enquête de Grégoire*. Paris: Gallimard.

Chambers, J. K., & Trudgill, P. (1998). *Dialectology*. Cambridge: Cambridge University Press.

Constitution of the Republic of Serbia. (2006). Retrieved from www.srbija.gov.rs/cinjenice_o_srbiji/ustav_odredbe.php?id=217

D'Azeglio, M. (1867). *I miei ricordi*, Vol. 1. Florence: G. Barbèra.

Dominian, L. (1917). *The frontiers of language and nationality in Europe*. London; New York: Constable; Henry Holt.

Dreschler, M. (1830). *Grundlegung zur wissenschaftlichen Construktion des gesammten Wörter- und Formenschatzes. Zunächst der Semitischen, versuchsweise und in Grundzügen auch der Indo-Germanischen Sprachen*. Palm und Enke, Erlangen.

Feuerzeig, L. (Ed.). (2002). *Deutsche Lieder für Jung und Alt*. Middleton, WI: A-R Editions.

Foucault, M. (2002 [1970]). *The order of things: Archaeology of the human sciences*. London: Routledge.

Greenberg, R. D. (2008). *Language and identity in the Balkans: Serbo-Croat and its disintegration*. Oxford: Oxford University Press.

Han, B.-C. (2005). *Was ist Macht?* Stuttgart: Reclam.

Haugen, E. (1966). Semicommunication: The language gap in Scandinavia. *Sociological Inquiry* 36(2), 280–297.

Hobsbawm, E. J. (1990). *Nations and nationalism since 1780: Programme, myth, reality*. Cambridge: Cambridge University Press.

Hotărâre Nr. 36 din 05.12.2013 privind interpretarea articolului 13 alin. (1) din Constituție în corelație cu Preambulul Constituției și Declarația de Independență a Republicii Moldova (Sesizările nr. 8b/2013 și 41b/2013). (2013). Retrieved from http://constcourt.md/download.php?file=cHVibGljL2NjZG9jL2hvdGFyaXJpL3JvLWhfMzZfMjAxMi9yby5zWGY%3D

Index Mundi. (2015). Retrieved from www.indexmundi.com/malaysia/population.html

Kamusella, T. (2001). Language as an instrument of nationalism in Central Europe. *Nations and Nationalism* 7(2), 235–252.

Kamusella, T. (2004). On the similarity between the concepts of nation and language. *Canadian Review of Studies in Nationalism* 31, 107–112.

Kamusella, T. (2006). The isomorphism of language, nation, and state: The case of Central Europe. In W. Burszta, T. Kamusella, & S. Wojciechowski (Eds.). *Nationalisms across the globe: An overview of nationalisms of state-endowed and stateless nations* (Vol 2: The World; pp. 57–92). Poznań, Poland: Wyższa Szkoła Nauk Humanistycznych i Dziennikarstwa.

Kamusella, T. (2012). The global regime of language recognition. *International Journal of the Sociology of Language* 218, 59–86.

Kamusella, T. (2016). The history of the normative opposition of "language versus dialect": From its Greco-Latin origin to Central Europe's ethnolinguistic nation-states. *Colloquia Humanistica* 5, 164–188.

Kamusella, T., & Nomachi, M. (2014). The long shadow of borders: The cases of Kashubian and Silesian in Poland. *The Eurasia Border Review* 5(2), 35–60.

Killinger, C. L. (2002). *The history of Italy*. Westport, CT: Greenwood Press.

King, C. (1999). The ambivalence of authenticity, or how the Moldovan language was made. *Slavic Review* 58(1), 117–142.

Kloss, H. (1967). "Abstand languages" and "Ausbau languages." *Anthropological Linguistics* 9(7), 29–41.

Kohn, H. (1962). *The age of nationalism: The first era of global history*. New York: Harper.

Leuschner, T. (2004). Richard Böckh (1824–1907): Sprachenstatistik zwischen Nationalitätsprinzip und Nationalstaat. *Historiographia Linguistica* 31(2–3), 389–421.

List of Wikipedias by language group. (2015). *Wikimedia: Meta-Wiki*. Retrieved from https://meta.wikimedia.org/wiki/List_of_Wikipedias_by_language_group.

McDermott, K. (2015). *Communist Czechoslovakia, 1945–89: A political and social history*. London: Palgrave.

Majewski, P. (2013). *(Re)konstrukcje narodu: Odwieczna Macedonia powstaje w XXI wieku*. Warsaw: Wydawnictwo Naukowe Katedra.

Mandatory Swedish. (2015). *Wikipedia*. Retrieved from https://en.wikipedia.org/wiki/Mandatory_Swedish

Mishra, P. (2012). *From the ruins of empire: The revolt against the West and the remaking of Asia*. London: Allen Lane.

Montenegro's Constitution of 2007. (2007). Retrieved from https://www.constituteproject.org/constitution/Montenegro_2007.pdf

Nábělková, M. (2016). The Czech-Slovak communicative and dialect continuum: With and without a border. In T. Kamusella, M. Nomachi, & C. Gibson (Eds.), *The Palgrave handbook of Slavic languages, identities and borders* (pp. 140–184). Basingstoke, UK: Palgrave Macmillan.

Nekvapil, J. (2007). On the relationship between small and large Slavic languages. *International Journal of the Sociology of Language* 183, 141–160.

Pallas, S. P. (1786–1789). *Linguarum totius orbis vocabularia comparativa* (2 vols.). St. Petersburg: Schnoor.

Poissonnier, A., & Sournia, G. (2006). *Atlas mondial de la francophonie: Du culturel au politique*. Paris: Autrement.

Reiter, N. (1984). *Gruppe, Sprache, Nation*. Wiesbaden: Harrassowitz.

Samardžija, M. (2008). *Hrvatski jezik, pravopis i jezična politika u Nezavisnoj Državi Hrvatskoj*. Zagreb: Hrvatska sveučilišna naklada.

Scotti, G., & Viazzi, L. (1987). *Le aquile delle Montagne Nere. Storia dell'occupazione e della guerra italiana in Montenegro (1941–1943)*. Milano: Mursia.

Searle, J. R. (1995). *The construction of social reality*. London: Allen Lane.

Shaul, D. L. (2014). *A prehistory of Western North America: The impact of Uto-Aztecan languages*. Albuquerque: University of New Mexico Press.

Shea, J. (1997). *Macedonia and Greece: The struggle to define a new Balkan nation*. Jefferson, NC: McFarland.

Solterdijk, P. (2011). *Spheres*, Vol 1: *Bubbles*. Translated from the German by W. Hoban. Los Angeles: Semiotext(e).

Statut Autonomne Pokrajine Vojvodine. (2014). Retrieved from www.propisi.com/statut-autonomne-pokrajine-vojvodine.html

Stieber, Z. (1956). *Z dziejów powstawania języków narodowych i literackich*. Warsaw: Państwowe Wydawnictwo Naukowe.

Stoll, D. (1982). *Fishers of men or founders of empire? The Wycliffe Bible translators in Latin America*. London: Zed Press.

Tollefson, J. W. (1991). *Planning language, planning inequality: Language policy in the community*. London: Longman.

Tollefson, J. W. (2002). The language debates: Preparing for the war in Yugoslavia, 1980–1991. *International Journal of the Sociology of Language* 154, 65–82.

Vdovin, A. I. (2007). "Russkii vopros" i "rossiiskaia natsiia" na sovremennom etape. In S. S. Sulakshin et al. (Eds), *Natsionalna identichnost' Rossii i demograficheskii krizis* (pp. 140–152). Moscow: Nauchnyi ekspert.

Vignoli, G. (1996). Lo Statuto del ripristinato Regno del Montenegro (1941). Retrieved from www.istitutobiggini.it/relazionevignoli.pdf

Zakon o utvrđivanju nadležnosti Autonomne pokrajine Vojvodine. (2009). Retrieved from: www.paragraf.rs/propisi/zakon_o_utvrdjivanju_nadleznosti_autonomne_pokrajine_vojvodine.html

CHAPTER 9

....

LANGUAGE AND THE STATE IN WESTERN POLITICAL THEORY

IMPLICATIONS FOR LANGUAGE POLICY AND PLANNING

....

PETER IVES

SINCE the turn of the twenty-first century, there has been growing interest among political theorists in language politics and language policy (e.g., de Schutter & Robichaud, 2015; Kymlicka & Patten, 2003; Leger & Lewis, 2017; Ricento, Peled, & Ives, 2015; Van Parjis, 2011). This has led to numerous calls to bring political theory closer together with the discipline of applied linguistics generally and language policy and planning (LPP) more specifically (de Schutter, 2007; May, 2012; Peled, 2011; Ricento, 2015a; Schmidt, 2005). However, much of contemporary political theory is dominated by liberal individualist approaches that assume more than investigate fundamental conceptions of language and the implications for LPP (Ives, 2015b; May, 2012, pp. 94–131).

The general prevalence of liberal individualism—whether in the economic variant of neoliberalism (Bale, 2015; Block, Gray, & Holborow, 2012; Ricento, 2015b; Shin & Park, 2016) or the more political and cultural guise of individualism (e.g., Kymlicka & Patten, 2003; Patten, 2014; Weinstock, 2015)—is one reason why it is important that LPP takes heed of the underlying conceptions of language and their differing implications for the role of the state, broadly defined.[1] This is the context in which I consider the relationship between LPP and political theory, and specifically modern European political philosophy's major figures: Thomas Hobbes, John Locke, Jean-Jacques Rousseau, and Johann Gottfried Herder. Locke and Herder have been seen by scholars of language ideology as mainstays of modern Eurocentric language ideologies central to the armature to the modern nation-state (Bauman & Briggs, 2003, pp. 29–69, 163–196; May, 2012; Woolard, 1998, pp. 16–17). While my analysis here shares much with such scholars, I show that it is fruitful for LPP to pay greater attention to the tensions and contradictions within what has been depicted as a single ideology.

This chapter illustrates how these four figures' diverse philosophical conceptions of language have differing implications for governmental policy aimed at language usage. Thus, my purpose here is to analyze connections between specific conceptions of language and various implied or explicit understandings of the relationship(s) between language use and government activity. These relationships are important whether we adopt a narrow definition of LPP as intentional, top-down (usually) government activity, or a broader understanding of LPP as practice and ideology, including bottom-up processes (see Johnson, 2013, and Spolsky, 2005, for overviews). Indeed, I will argue that Herder, often invoked as the key theorist of the one-language-one-nation model at the center of modern Eurocentric nationalism (Bauman & Briggs, 2003; Canagarajah, 2013; May, 2012), actually provides an approach to LPP that is closer to—and more appropriate for—contemporary positions on LPP than the conception of language provided by John Locke.

This is important well beyond the adequate understanding of any given political thinker, since it is arguable that Locke's individualistic approach to language continues to be pervasive and integral to liberal and neoliberal assumptions about language. My main aim is to show how the tensions within such European ideologies can provide insight into how language is conceptualized. To begin with, if government is understood from the liberal (and neoliberal) perspective as a necessary evil that should function minimally in order to allow the efficiency of market mechanisms to dominate, then the questions posed for LPP are severely restricted; whereas if politics in general—and the role of government in particular—are understood as essentially positive aspects of being human, LPP is put in a rather different light. However, this chapter goes further than merely mapping differing political theories onto LPP; rather, it focuses on what Hobbes, Locke, Rousseau, and Herder have to say about language. By showing that their conceptions of language are central to each thinker's political theory, I provide a clearer analysis of the implications for LPP than would be possible by grafting these classic positions in political theory onto the topic of language.

The first half of this chapter focuses on the crucible of the modern liberal tradition with Hobbes and Locke. I outline how their similar conceptions of the individual lead to different versions of the social contract on which they argue government is based. The last section of this first part shows that, despite important similarities between the two, Locke sees almost no role for government or language policy even in its most informal version. In contrast, for Hobbes the sovereign (i.e., government) is tasked with making sure language functions properly. Without government playing an active role to stabilize language, Hobbes suggests, it is difficult to see how society can be civil, stable, and orderly. One major reason for this difference between Locke and Hobbes, as I will show, is that Locke argues that reason should precede language use, whereas for Hobbes language and reason are inextricably bound. The question of this relationship between language and reason remains pertinent to contemporary debates within LPP, such as whether global English or other linguae francae are neutral and can function purely instrumentally for communicative purposes, separate from their histories within colonialism or domination.

The second half of the chapter turns to Rousseau and Herder, both of whom challenge the role of individualism and the views of language and politics provided by Locke and Hobbes. I show how Rousseau and Herder's conception of language moves well beyond seeing it as primarily instrumental. Rather, both see language as expressive and connected to language communities. This is the main reason why their ideas have been so influential to so-called communitarian and multicultural political theory (e.g., thinkers such as Charles Taylor). The chapter then traces the main ideas that led Rousseau to reject the very idea of language policy. Turning to the implications of Herder's conception of language, I show how he provides much more room for governments to positively influence language practices. I conclude by questioning the widely held reductionist view of Herder as a linguistic nationalist that is often presented in LPP scholarship. As we shall see, these ideas—that language is not purely an instrument for individuals to communicate with, but also has an impact on questions of identity and community formation—remain relevant today.

HOBBES'S AND LOCKE'S SOCIAL CONTRACT THEORIES

Within the trajectory of "Western" political theory, Thomas Hobbes and John Locke are often placed as the key social contract theorists who provided a base on which modern liberalism was built.[2] They challenged the dominant position of the Greek philosopher Aristotle, for whom humans are political animals. For Aristotle (1958), to participate in government, to rule and be ruled, was an essential element of being human. In contrast, modern liberal individualism sees government as a necessary evil, required due to the negative features of humanity that are obstacles to peaceful, communal living. Hobbes and Locke both foster ideas of individual freedom and equality by articulating the notion that human beings exist ontologically as individual and free, prior to entering a society with a political structure. To make this argument, both Hobbes and Locke mobilized the concept of the *state of nature*—that is, life without a state or government—as an abstraction or ideal type, in the Weberian sense, with only rough historical examples. They both aim to delimit the role of government with recourse to this state of nature. For Locke, the state of nature was merely inconvenient, prone to instability and despotism (Locke, 1998, pp. 302, 318, 350–353), whereas for Hobbes, such a condition would be "solitary, poore, nasty, brutish and short" (Hobbes, 1996, p. 89).

This is why Hobbes argues that it is not possible to have less than an absolutely powerful government, or in his words, an "absolute sovereign." Locke provides a more moderate version of Hobbes's conclusion, arguing that a weaker government is still capable of preventing humans from falling back into the state of nature. Moreover, the danger of falling back into the state of nature, as Locke describes it, is not nearly so dire. In other words, Locke tempered Hobbes's extreme conclusions and argued that it is possible to have a more restricted and thus liberal government. Locke argued that if government overstepped its bounds, rebellion against it was both ethical and rational. This is a good starting point for understanding the differences between Hobbes and Locke, but since my goal is to consider the role of language in politics, this general picture is less adequate. LPP scholars should focus more closely on the differences between how Hobbes and Locke connect language and government.

Hobbes's Theory of Language

While Hobbes is rarely seen as a theorist of language per se, many important political theorists have noted that language is central to his theory. For example, Ian Hacking points out that Hobbes's "chief works on political theory, such as *Leviathan*, all begin with a study of human nature and man's communication . . . to understand politics, thought Hobbes, one needs a good theory of speech" (Hacking, 1975, p. 24). Philip Pettit goes further, arguing that Hobbes's approach to language is what enables him to overcome Descartes' mind/body dualism and to understand humans' ability to reason and work collectively. Pettit argues that Hobbes also sees language as accounting for humans' propensity to compare themselves with others and to become antagonistic toward one another (Pettit, 2008). Sheldon Wolin insists that one of Hobbes's under-appreciated contributions to political theory is "the recognition that a political order involved more than power, authority, law and institutions: it was a sensitive system of communication dependent upon a system of verbal signs, actions, and gestures bearing generally accepted meaning" (Wolin, 2004, p. 231). From this perspective, LPP does not begin as a field of inquiry in the twentieth century (Spolsky, 2005), but is at the heart of modern political theory beginning in the seventeenth century, if not before. Most important, Hobbes argues that the sovereign had the main role in decisions over meaning and the establishment of a public language (Hobbes, 1996, pp. 117–120; Pettit, 2008, pp. 115–140). This is a key contrast with Locke, who, as we shall see, rejects the possibility that the state or sovereign *could* or should play a role in successful language usage.

For Hobbes, language is inextricable from reason and is what makes generalization possible (Hobbes, 1996, pp. 32–33; Pettit, 2008, p. 29). He argues that the same stimulus can be signified by multiple words, which facilitates a more thorough understanding of the objects that create such stimuli. Pettit contends that this is central to Hobbes's initial equation of language and reason. It is what allows humans to view a single object from various perspectives, thereby enabling the cognitive process of generalization (Hobbes, 1996, p. 31; Pettit, 2008, pp. 30–33). Thus, from his individualistic perspective, Hobbes concludes that the state or sovereign must ensure the correct functioning of language in order to stabilize society. Pettit summarizes, "The commonwealth, then, is the great facilitator of the positive capacity that language confers on human beings" (2008, p. 115). It is because of the need for a stable language that individuals are required by our reason to act *as if* we have entered a social contract that limits or relinquishes our freedom in order to create an absolute sovereign. As Pettit writes, ". . . it is the sort of incorporation whereby society is made possible among agents who, by virtue of their linguistically disordered desires, are incapable of otherwise living at peace with one another" (2008, p. 151).

It is then no small detail that Hobbes insists that the sovereign or her agents have greater right to decide interpretations of the laws than do the authors of those laws (Hobbes, 1996, pp. 190–191). That Hobbes's sovereign is tasked with defining the meaning of words is not just an extreme argument in favor of absolute authority that can be tempered by Locke's revisions. Even if Locke is correct, and the state of nature is not as bad as Hobbes contends, Hobbes's theory of language would still require the sovereign to play an active role in language use, a position inimical, as we shall see, to Locke's conception of language. For Hobbes, the instability of language in the state of nature is also a cause of the perpetual character of human conflict, which requires a social contract to bring an absolute sovereign into existence.[3]

Despite this difference between Hobbes and Locke, they both approach language from an individualistic and empiricist framework. They share an epistemology that starts not from people imbedded in society learning languages, but from the perspective of the individual interacting with the natural and social world through his or her sense perception. For both, language is a collection of words that enable individuals to communicate with one another and thus form society (Hobbes, pp. 24–31; Locke, 1995, p. 323). We shall see both Rousseau and Herder challenge this view.

Locke's Theory of Language

Recent scholarship on Locke also highlights the centrality of language to his political theory.[4] Hannah Dawson traces out many ways in which Locke's theory of language is a crucial part of his social contract, which forms the basis of the relationship between individuals and government. As Dawson summarizes, for Locke "[w]ords only make sense insofar as they coincide with the thoughts of the [individual] language user." That is, words "must signify the ideas of *someone*, and therefore are limited to the ideas of particular speakers" (Dawson, 2007, p. 188; emphasis in original). As Bauman and Briggs argue, in Locke's writings "[l]anguage was powerfully reimagined as a question of individual words spoken by individual speakers" (Bauman & Briggs, 2003, p. 38; see also Harris & Taylor, 1989; Losonsky, 2006, pp. 1–21). Locke is skeptical about the ability of language to function correctly due to semantic plurality (that different individuals will attach differing ideas to the same words or the same words to different ideas) and the "abuse of words" (Locke, 1995, pp. 397–412). This view clearly contrasts with Hobbes's position that semantic plurality is a positive attribute in addition to a source of potential conflict.

Much of Locke's concern over language is that in practice it falls well short of this communicative function. Like Hobbes (1996, pp. 25–26), Locke worries about how speakers often either wilfully abuse language or are careless and sloppy in using it. Such practices hinder the effectiveness of language in being able to transmit an individual's ideas to others. But for Locke, this can only be corrected by individual choice. No government or social intervention can help assuage such misuses of language. As Dawson explains, for Locke the main source of miscommunication is that "... while meaning is logically prior to language, in communication language is experientially prior to meaning" (Dawson, 2007, p. 241). Locke's central argument is that language problems do not have a political solution. Instead, individuals are urged to address such issues by their own use of language.

These differences between Hobbes and Locke are important to LPP, particularly in debates about the spread of English around the globe (e.g., de Swaan, 2001; Pogge, 2003; Van Parijs, 2011; see Ives, 2015c, for a critique). I now turn to implications for LPP of the contrast between Hobbes and Locke.

Contrasting Hobbes and Locke: Implications for Language Policy and Planning

Locke's admonishments concerning language usage reveal the extent to which his assumptions about language are still present in attitudes today, from ordinary language philosophy to anti-intellectual criticisms of academic jargon. It is also especially evident in persistent criticisms of non-standard language usage and the prestige of the native speaker. Locke provides a list of normative rules that people should follow in order to avoid the "Abuse of Words," including the following: not using words without having precise and distinct ideas that they stand for; using common meanings and not deviating from them, creating new terms, or embellishing meanings;[5] repeatedly making those meanings known; and being consistent with what a given word means (Locke, 1995, pp. 414–424). This emphasis on language as primarily an instrumental tool to achieve communication is seen in much contemporary political theory concerning language (Kymlicka & Patten, 2003; Van Parjis, 2011; Weinstock, 2015).

Another important tenet of Locke's approach that reverberates in contemporary debates within LPP is that language is necessarily based on the consent of the speaker. Locke argues that language cannot by definition be regulated through any form of coercion—state coercion or coercion from other sources. Locke writes, "Words being voluntary signs, they cannot be voluntary signs imposed by him on things he knows not . . . when he represents to himself other men's ideas by some of his own, if he consent to give them the same names that other men do, it is still to his own ideas . . ." (Locke, 1995, p. 324). Locke emphasizes the role of consent: ". . . no one hath the power to make others have the same ideas in their minds that he has, when they use the same words that he does. And therefore the great Augustus himself, in the possession of that power which ruled the world, acknowledged he could not make a new Latin word . . ." (Locke, 1995, p. 326).

This notion that language usage cannot be legislated because doing so goes against the nature of language has echoes in various arguments about global English, from Abram de Swaan and Sue Wright to the postmodernist-influenced Alistair Pennycook and Suresh Canagarajah (Canagarajah, 2013; de Swaan, 2001; Pennycook, 2010; Wright, 2004). The underlying presumption against the role of government in language usage also may explain, at least partially, David Crystal's neglect of the role of government language and education policies in the spread of global English (Crystal, 2003; see Ives, 2010, p. 521). Bernard Spolsky's *Language Policy* seems to follow Crystal's general conclusion that the main explanation of the spread of English across the globe is that it happened to be in the right place at the right time. Spolsky writes, "The spread of English and its development as the first genuine global language appeared to be the result rather from its being in place to take advantage of changes in the world language system over the past century" (Spolsky, 2005, p. 90). In siding with de Swaan's analysis and castigating Phillipson's notion of linguistic imperialism, Spolsky endorses de Swaan's ontological individualism, which forms the basis of his rational choice methodology (Spolsky, 2005, pp. 76–91; de Swaan, 2001, p. 19; see Ives, 2006).

The underlying acceptance of liberal individualism is also evident in Spolsky's (2005) conclusions about the general field of language policy. He writes, "Students of language policy fall naturally into two main groups: the optimists who believe management is possible and the pessimists who assume that language is out of control" (p. 223).[6] Spolsky favors the latter, arguing (tenuously in my judgment) that history shows what he calls "language management" (his preferred term over "language planning") has been a failure (2005, p. 223).[7] While Spolsky never addresses differing conceptions of language, his conclusions about the unmanageability of languages, though less categorical, are in line with Locke's. This is one of the many ways in which the underlying dominance of liberal individualism has an impact on conclusions about the very definition of LPP.

Locke's argument that using policy to affect language is at odds with the nature of language is questionable for many reasons, especially for LPP scholars. First, the argument runs against the historical realities of the role of the state in language standardization and the creation of national languages (e.g., see Anderson, 1991; Burke, 2004). Linguistic anthropologists have shown in great detail the various ways in which, as Susan Philips summarizes, language and language ideologies play a significant role in "imagining of nations in institutions centrally involved in the production of state hegemony" (1998, p. 223; see also Blommaert & Verschueren, 1998).[8] Indeed, a key question today is the extent to which many states are agents in propagating the learning and use, not of national languages, but of English. Also, as Johnson points out (2013, e.g., pp. 47–51), intentional uses of LPP can support colonialism and the marginalization of groups and individuals, and they can also help reverse language shift (especially colonial language policies) as well as help in resisting linguistic imperialism. However, Locke's view of language not only rules out authoritarian policies affecting language; it also undermines more critical and potentially progressive uses of LPP. As we shall see, Herder's conception of language and its implications for LPP fit Johnson's point that LPP can be used potentially in progressive ways to protect or help revitalize the languages and cultures of marginalized and exploited peoples.

Locke's proposals for correcting the failings of language mirror the general approach of many contemporary normative liberal political theories. They use detailed reason to set out an ideal principle of how society should be organized. They delineate the limits within which people should behave based on these ideals, and they anticipate that reasonable people will have to agree with them (e.g., Laitin & Reich, 2003; Patten, 2014; Pogge, 2003; Weinstock, 2003). In other words, much normative political theory concerned with language rights or linguistic justice implicitly accepts Locke's view that the role of theory is to demarcate the deviation of language usage from its core function, which is transmitting ideas among individuals (see Ives, 2015c). Questions of reasoning, identity, and power may be addressed or acknowledged, but they should be rendered as secondary issues subordinated to language as a tool or vehicle of communication narrowly defined.

Epistemological individualism, however, does not necessarily lead to Locke's conception of how language and government are related, and this is evident with the example of Hobbes. The key aspects of this Lockean conception of language are the combination of epistemological individualism with the separation (at least as an ideal) of language and reason. From these propositions, the very conception of LPP—and the idea that governments can have a positive (or negative) influence on language use—is made suspect. Locke provides a laissez-faire theory of language and government rooted in his concept of individualism that remains pervasive in political theory scholarship. This is important beyond political theory and LPP scholarship in that it corresponds to the general individualist assumptions of neoliberalism (Block, Gray, & Holborow, 2012).

As shown in the preceding, Hobbes provides a much stronger role for government in language usage that is also rooted in epistemological and ontological individualism. As we shall see in the second half of this chapter, the major criticisms of Hobbes's theory of language are the same as the refutations of Locke's approach to language, but this should not obscure the different implications of Locke's and Hobbes's approaches to language. Because Locke separates language and reason, he comes to a laissez-faire theory of language and government in which there seems to be no role for language policy. Hobbes, in contrast, views language and reason as inextricable, and finds that language policy is a key role of a government, needed to create peace and order. So while both view language as fundamentally a vehicle of communication, they provide very different implications for LPP.

I shall now consider the work by Jean-Jacques Rousseau and Johann Gottfried Herder from eighteenth-century Europe, as they are often seen as key figures in the trajectory of "Western" political theory in their challenges to core aspects of the Enlightenment, including rationalism and especially the individualism and empiricism of Hobbes and Locke.

ROMANTICIST CHALLENGES TO THE INDIVIDUALISM OF SOCIAL CONTRACT THEORY

Both Rousseau and Herder understand political communities as being more than mere aggregates of individuals united to secure their persons, property, and social order, as Hobbes and Locke articulated with their social contracts. In this sense, both Rousseau and Herder harken back to an Aristotelian notion of a type of public interest—or the good life—obtainable in political community with others, thus contributing to republican traditions and some versions of nationalism. Whereas for Hobbes and Locke the legitimacy of government has nothing to do with participation, but is concerned solely with questions of infringement of individual liberties in comparison with the hypothetical state of nature, for Rousseau the legitimacy of a social contract rests on the participation of citizens (Rousseau, 2011, pp. 164–167). In relation to LPP, Rousseau does not directly translate specific ideas in his political theories to language. Nevertheless, his work paves the way for Herder's insights and much of the contemporary debate about language politics, in contrast to liberal approaches that draw from Locke to focus on individuals and their freedom to use whatever language practices they wish (e.g., Kymlicka, 1995; Patten, 2014;

Weinstock, 2015). Rousseau and Herder's line of thought leads to a greater focus on democratic aspects of the public use of language(s), including a state that fosters specific language usage, both in the workings of government and in society as a whole (May, 2012).

What is crucial for LPP scholars is that both Rousseau and Herder posit a distinction between *human* language and the more mundane conception of language found in Locke and Hobbes. This difference has deep implications for the relationship between language and the state, including approaches that emphasize informal practice, language ideology, and bottom-up language policy (Johnson, 2013, pp. 3–12; Spolsky, 2005, pp. 5–7). Both Rousseau and Herder argue that the view of language as merely an instrument for transmitting ideas does not adequately capture the unique, vital, and creative nature of *human* language (Herder, 1966, pp. 107–128; Spencer, 2012, pp. 34–41; Trabant, 2009, p. 123).

Rousseau's Passionate Approach to Language

Rousseau's challenge to Locke's and Hobbes's instrumentalist approach to language is evident in his *Essay on the Origin of Languages.* The second chapter of this work is entitled "That the First Invention of Speech Is Due Not to Need But to Passion." Here he contrasts the language that humans share with animals, a language based on communicative needs, with the fundamental aspect of human language that is concerned with expressing one's self. Rousseau argues that animals communicate, but do not possess human language, not due to any lack of "adequate structure" (Rousseau, 1966, p. 10), but because they lack the feelings, passions, and expression central to humanity.

Whereas both Locke and Hobbes warn against metaphors because they are imprecise in attaching a word to the thing signified, Rousseau describes the beginnings, vitality, and power of human languages as inherently imprecise and vague. Rousseau presents the *differentia specifica* of human language as that which exceeds literal, codified signification. Rousseau provides a possible example of the first human language. Upon seeing another group of humans unknown to them, a group of people falsely assume that these beings are a threat, because they are bigger and stronger. They call them *giants*. It is only when they have more accurate knowledge that they realize these giants are merely humans like them: "That is how the figurative word is born before the literal word" (Rousseau, 1966, pp. 12–13). The word *giant* persists after the correct, more accurate information about the strangers is gathered. This expression, *giants*, including the emotion of fear, remains the vital source of language, more vital than the factual labeling of phenomena in the world, which was the concern of Hobbes and Locke. This is also related to why Rousseau places speech over writing: "We conclude that while visible signs can render a more exact imitation, sounds more effectively arouse interest" (Rousseau, 1966, p. 9). Thus, where Locke is most concerned that imprecision leads to the failure of language to fulfill its communicative role, Rousseau finds the opposite. Emotional expression is the fundamental aspect of human language because of its lack of precision.

It is important to recognize that Rousseau's goal in this essay is to explain the origins of different languages, an issue that neither Hobbes nor Locke grapple with. Crucially, Rousseau frames the issue around a tension within languages as they develop between the expressivism of voice, accent, and speech (as introduced in the *giants* example) versus the communicative precision and cold calculation of the written word, which lacks passion.

Like Hobbes, Rousseau sees in language the roots of disunity, but for Rousseau disunity is a problem for the instrumental type of language based on needs, the language whose function is mere communication, and an activity that humans share with animals. Mirroring Rousseau's critique of Hobbes, Locke, and other social contract theorists, Rousseau re-narrates the development of rational language as occurring after, and in tension with, this originary, gestural, figurative language of passion.

Unlike Hobbes and Locke, Rousseau explicitly grounds languages in locality, as does Herder. One might think that Hobbes's and Locke's individualist empiricism could lead to an appreciation for differing sensations deriving from diverse localities, but both Hobbes and Locke emphasize the common, even universal similarities of the stimuli that humans receive. Rousseau, with no pretense to an empiricist epistemology, emphasizes (even stereotypes) climatic and geographical differences as having significant impact on languages.

It is striking how Rousseau's ideas on language, including what he fears will corrupt and trouble it, are opposed to those of both Locke and Hobbes: "Feelings are expressed in speaking, ideas in writing. In writing, one is forced to use all the words according to their conventional meaning. But in speaking, one varies the meaning by varying one's tone of voice, determining them as one pleases. Being less constrained to clarity, one can be more forceful" (Rousseau, 1966, pp. 21–22).[9] He continues, arguing that "the main source of energy for a language" comes from voice, from speaking, not the precision of accurate transference of ideas (as Locke would have it). For Rousseau, the human language of expression is threatened and corrupted by the precise (cold, calculating) use of language that Locke specifically advocates.

Rousseau's opposition between language as communication (the type of language humans share with animals) and language as the expression of passions (the origins and essence of human language) leads him to see government involvement in language use (that is, LPP) as confined solely to the former. Like Locke, Rousseau is explicitly critical of academies that codify and establish standard language (Rousseau, 1966, p. 27). While not overtly condemning all state activity concerning language usage, Rousseau's romantic vision celebrates the free and unconstrained use of language. Ironically, the implications of this vision are similar to those of Locke's emphasis on the imbedded, ontological consent and spontaneity of language use: both

Locke and Rousseau conclude that governmental attempts to influence language usage will undermine the very essence of language—even if they disagree on the content of that essence.

In his final chapter, entitled "The Relationship of Languages to Government," Rousseau sums up his sweeping and dialectical vision of history: "In ancient times, when persuasion played the role of public force, eloquence was necessary. Of what use would it be today when public force has replaced persuasion." In case this tragic point is not obvious, Rousseau adds, "And since there is nothing to say to people besides *give money*, it is said with placards on street corners or by soldiers in their homes. It is not necessary to assemble anymore for that. On the contrary, the subjects must be kept apart. That is the first maxim of modern politics" (Rousseau, 1966, p. 72). In the common readings of Rousseau, especially his writings before his *Social Contract* (1762), there is an emphasis on his critique of progress, specifically the civilizing and bureaucratic tendencies of his eighteenth-century society. Focusing on language, we can see how this is connected to Rousseau's critique of language policy per se. In his writings on language, Rousseau lives up to his reputation as a ruthless critic and cheeky provocateur more than a thinker offering a model of language that can be assessed by how useful it is for addressing current issues in LPP. Herder's much less dualistic conception of language as instrument and expression is perhaps more useful for LPP.

Herder's Challenging Conception of Language

Herder mounts a similar critique to Rousseau's of the inadequacy of approaching language as merely a vehicle of communication. Rather than contrasting communication of needs with passionate and emotional human expression, however, Herder argues that humans and animals share a language of both communication and passion, but human language is unique in being rooted in human reflection (*Besonnenheit*) and reason. He places reason on the side of expressive language, expanding it to include reflection and consciousness, and thus identity. This is what Charles Taylor influentially labeled "the importance of Herder" (Taylor, 1995). For Herder, language is what makes humans distinct from animals; it is what we might now call *consciousness* or *self-consciousness*, and it is intimately connected to the notion of freedom and free will.

Herder sees language as central to all philosophy and human life. He argues that "[l]anguage is the bond of souls, the tool of education, the instrument of our highest pleasures, indeed of all social relations" (as quoted in Eggel, Liebich, & Mancini-Griffoli, 2007, p. 59). Unlike Rousseau, he never sees instrumental language as corrupting or working against expressive language. Herder's major contribution is to provide a much wider and potentially richer psychological sense of reason rooted in self-consciousness, deliberateness, and reflection (*Besonnenheit*).

Herder's discussions of the origins of human language place creativity at the center of language. Trying to describe this mysterious essence of human language, he makes the provocative contention that every child must invent language for him- or herself. He writes, "Parents never teach their children language without the latter, by themselves, inventing language along with them: Parents merely draw their children's attention to differences between things by means of certain verbal signs, and consequently they do not replace, but only facilitate and promote for them, the use of reason through language" (Herder, 1966, p. 121).[10]

As Taylor argues, Herder anticipates some key ideas of Ludwig Wittgenstein's influential philosophy of language, specifically in arguing that human consciousness is required for even what Locke and Hobbes see as a simple act of defining something, attaching a word to a thing (as Wittgenstein analyzed with his "ostensive definition") (Taylor, 1995, pp. 82–83). We could add that Herder's insistence on the dialogical character of all language—dialogical not only with respect to other speakers, but also inwardly, as we shall see—foreshadows key ideas of Mikhail Bakhtin that have influenced contemporary theories of multiculturalism. Thus, beyond critiquing Hobbes's and Locke's approaches to language, Herder is important in understanding the inextricable link between language and human reason. Herder writes, "Without language man has no reason, and without reason no language" (1966, p. 121). Taylor sees these ideas as precursors to both Wittgenstein's and Heidegger's focus on the linguistic dimension of human "forms of life" (Taylor, 1995, p. 91).

In a key passage, Herder describes the invention of language with the example of an encounter with a lamb. The human perceives the lamb through its characteristics: it is white, soft, woolly and, importantly, it bleats. But unlike a lion, wolf, or rutting ram, for whom the lamb is merely "an object of pleasure," the human creates a "distinguishing mark," a "word within," for the lamb, to know it for itself. Herder describes this as an inner recognition within the human soul, "the strongest impression, which has broke away from all the other qualities of vision and of touch, which sprang out and penetrated most deeply, the soul retains it" (Herder, 1966, p. 117). It is this conception of reflection, or *Besonnenheit*, that Taylor, Trabant, and Spencer see as a dialogical understanding of language as inextricable from reason and consciousness. This linguistic reflection is a particularly human way of encountering the world. This inner dialogue in the soul prepares the ground for the socially dialogical character of language in relations among speakers. Unlike Rousseau, Herder sees this expressive origin of language as adding to or enabling true human communication. This is part of the context within which Herder develops his concept of the *Volk*, or people, as a language community, and his argument that different languages contain differing worldviews due to their localities, histories, and cultures.

It is particularly important to address the relationship between language and community in Herder's conception of language because LPP scholars have often fallen into a superficial, at best, rendition of Herder's ideas. To take one common, if rather extreme, example: Suresh Canagarajah labels the model of *one language, one people, one nation* as the "Herderian triad," arguing that Herder's writings are the source and initial theorization of the confluence of language with identity and citizenship (Canagarajah, 2013, pp. 19–25;[11] see also Bauman & Briggs, 2003; May, 2012, pp. 55–62). As Ingrid Piller details, this is a widespread understanding within LPP, yet it is difficult to trace where in Herder's own writings such a position originates (Piller, 2016).

Indeed, Piller's concerns align well with recent scholarship on Herder. Jürgen Trabant registers his frustration in the way Herder has been characterized as a source of linguistic nationalism, arguing that "constant repetition of that prejudice [of Herder as a linguistic nationalist] does not make it true" (Trabant, 2009, p. 122; see also Barnard, 2003; Eggel, Liebich, & Mancini-Griffoli, 2007; Spencer, 2012). Spencer argues that Herder's concept of *nation* is dissimilar from modern nationalism and is not yoked to the state, but has a much wider sense. She further argues that Herder consistently criticized imperialism and all forms of exploitation, including economic, political, and especially cultural. Trabant agrees: "It is true that Herder loved the German language . . . and that he insists on the importance of expressing himself in that language. But what is more important is that he concedes the same value and the same precious qualities to *all* other languages" (Trabant, 2009, p. 122). For Spencer, Herder's project actually delegitimizes modern or official nationalism and any aggressive or violent nationalist movement (Spencer, 2012, pp. 145–155). Spencer reinforces key elements of earlier scholars of Herder by emphasizing his respect for cultural diversity, noting that his "overriding desire is to eliminate oppression, and his particular contribution to theories of justice lies in his inclusion of the injustice of cultural oppression" (Spencer, 2012, p. 195; see also Barnard, 2003).

Such interpretations of Herder should induce LPP scholars to pay closer attention to his writings. Of course, this is not the venue to assess debates within Herderian studies concerning interpretation, and I have no interest in rescuing Herder's reputation. What is crucial is the link between Herder's challenge to Locke's individualistic approach to language as solely about communication and a much richer notion of language as intricately related to reason, including expression, creativity, reflection, and consciousness. That for Herder the linguistic community is very important and not unrelated to national identity is central here. Indeed, this is partially what accounts for why his richer conception of language speaks more directly to contemporary issues concerning language politics and LPP.

Ultimately, I would argue that if LPP scholars require more specific conceptual tools to analyze the conflicts and tensions within language communities; that is, if Herder is guilty of homogenizing language communities and struggles within them with his conception of a *people* or *Volk*, they should look to the writings of twentieth-century thinkers such as Antonio Gramsci and Valentin Vološinov (see Ives, 2004). But such considerations would take me beyond the scope of this chapter.

CONCLUSIONS

It may seem that European thinkers from the seventeenth and eighteenth centuries who thought of language as fundamentally a collection of words would have little to offer current scholarship on LPP. Yet thinkers such as Hobbes, Locke, Rousseau, and Herder are still deemed by political philosophers to be important figures in defining fundamental, and fundamentally different, conceptions of what governments are, their purposes, and thus the extent to which they should be limited. It is partly for this reason that LPP scholars often invoke such figures, especially Locke and Herder. As I have argued elsewhere (Ives, 2006, 2015a), their writings can be useful in revealing the theoretical assumptions underlying numerous contemporary debates, such as those about English as a lingua franca (Dewey & Jenkins, 2010), the spread of English as an element of linguistic justice (Van Parijs, 2011), or the need for minority language rights (May, 2012).

This chapter has shown that within the common opposition between Locke's instrumental approach to language and Herder's expressive view, there exist other configurations. Hobbes shares much with Locke in his epistemological individualism and a social contract theory justifying the state, but unlike Locke's inherent pessimism about the government project to influence language usage (that is, LPP), Hobbes concludes that government must play a key role in providing stability for languages. The key explanation for why two thinkers reach such differing conclusions from such similar philosophical beginnings is that for Hobbes language is necessary for reasoning, including classifying and understanding the stimuli that we receive from our senses as individuals; whereas Locke, on the other hand, claims that reason precedes language, and language should be understood strictly as a vehicle to transfer thoughts and ideas but not affect them. I have argued that such implicit conceptions remain influential within liberal and neoliberal visions of politics and language.

In a parallel fashion, while both Rousseau and Herder reject the ontological individualism and the general political theories of Hobbes and Locke, their analyses of language and government differ from one another. Rousseau's intriguing argument that the figurative, expressive origins of human language are at odds with, and are corrupted by, the cold, calculating, precise use of language leads him to reject language planning, at least in any overt sense. In contrast, Herder does not pit the communicative and instrumental aspects of language against its expressive essence, which leads him to consider positive possibilities for language policy and planning.

While LPP scholars obviously need to move beyond the Eurocentrism of key figures in "Western" philosophy, we should also be sure to use a nuanced understanding of those figures to reveal some of the underlying assumptions about language and the implications of these assumptions for LPP. It is not mere coincidence that liberal ideology dominates much of society while language is conceived as fundamentally an instrument of communication. If we want to understand the ways in which languages are central to being and acting in the world, we should find alternative conceptions of language. Some possibilities are to be found in the writings of Rousseau and Herder.

NOTES

1. There are of course many other reasons why LPP has engaged with theoretical questions of language. As David Cassels Johnson points out, "The field of language policy is not lacking in theoretical robustness . . ." (Johnson, 2013, p. 26), and I am not suggesting here that political theory is a privileged source of theoretical inquiry for LPP.

2. I put "Western" in quotation marks to draw attention to the constructed nature of this category and to indicate that I am not suggesting there is a hermetically sealed tradition, but rather that what is usually understood as "Western" political theory constructed itself in this way, often ignoring influences from so-called "non-Western" thinkers, societies, and cultures.

3. In this regard, there are interesting similarities with Mozi (or Mo Tzu), the fifth-century B.C.E. Chinese philosopher who argued that "in the beginning" no two people shared the same language and it was a primary function of the emperor to unify language (Pocock, 1973, p. 42).

4. This section is substantially derived from my earlier article (Ives, 2015a, pp. 49–54).

5. With this rule, Locke is admonishing linguistic creativity, which is clearly related to contemporary debates about global English, including questions of who are the norm-providers and how native and non-native speakers are distinguished.

6. I am not sure why Spolsky provides only two options. He neglects the obvious other option of those who think that language management can be and has been successful, though they are against it (e.g., Robert Phillipson, whom Spolsky criticizes extensively).

7. Spolsky's example is France and French, but most historians of language find that throughout the nineteenth century, France succeeded in promoting standardized, Parisian French as a national language, though it had been the language of a minority (Weber, 1976). One can be critical of such "success," but to use it as an example that language cannot be managed seems dubious. Other cases would also seem to falsify Spolsky's conclusion, for example, Italy, politically unified in 1861 when only about 2.5% of the population spoke anything that could be considered Italian.

8. I would be remiss if I cited Philips without questioning her lengthy discussion of Antonio Gramsci in which, among other problematic interpretations, she contends, "Nor was there a special place for language or language ideologies in the core dimension of his concept of hegemony" (Philips, 1998, p. 215). I have shown in detail how misguided this position is (see Ives, 2004).

9. This prioritizing of speech over writings is the basis of Derrida's influential reading of Rousseau as a prime example of logocentrism, with its placing of writing as the supplement of speech (Derrida, 1967).

10. While beyond the scope of this chapter, this suggestion is pertinent to current discussions of creativity and conceptions of *native languages* (e.g., Kachru, 2005).

11. In addition to Bauman and Briggs (2000), Canagarajah cites Blommaert and Verschueren (1992, reprinted as 1998) as a source for the Herderian triad, but their article does not actually mention Herder at all.

References

Anderson, B. (1991). *Imagined communities.* Revised edition. London: Verso.

Aristotle. (1958). *The politics of Aristotle.* Ernest Barker, Ed. & Trans. Oxford: Oxford University Press.

Bale, J. (2015). Language policy and global political economy. In T. Ricento (Ed.), *Language policy and political economy: English in a global context* (pp. 72–96). Oxford: Oxford University Press.

Barnard, F. M. (2003). *Herder on nationality, humanity and history.* Montreal: McGill-Queens University Press.

Bauman, R., & Briggs, C. (2000). Language philosophy as language ideology: John Locke and Johann Gottfried Herder. In P. V. Kroskrity (Ed.), *Regimes of language: Ideologies, polities, and identities* (pp. 139–204). Oxford: James Curry.

Bauman, R., & Briggs, C. (2003). *Voices of modernity: Language ideologies and the politics of inequality.* Cambridge: Cambridge University Press.

Block, D., Gray, J., & Holborow, M. (Eds.) (2012). *Neoliberalism and applied linguistics.* London: Routledge.

Blommaert, J., & Verschueren, J. (1998). The role of language in European nationalist ideologies. In B. Schieffelin, K. Woolard, & P. Kroskrity (Eds.), *Language ideologies: Practice and theory* (pp. 189–210). Oxford: Oxford University Press.

Burke, P. (2004). *Languages and communities in early modern Europe.* Cambridge: Cambridge University Press.

Canagarajah, S. (2013). *Translingual practice: Global Englishes and cosmopolitan relations.* London: Routledge.

Crystal, D. (2003). *English as a global language.* 2nd edition. Cambridge: Cambridge University Press.

Dawson, H. (2007). *Locke, language and early-modern philosophy.* Cambridge: Cambridge University Press.

Derrida, J. (1967). *Of grammatology.* G. Spivak, Ed. & Trans. Baltimore, MD: Johns Hopkins University Press.

de Schutter, H. (2007). Language policy and political philosophy. *Language Problems and Language Planning* 31(1), 1–23.

de Schutter, H. & Robichaud, D. (Eds.). (2015). Special issue on linguistic justice. *Critical Review of International Political Philosophy* 18(2).

de Swaan, A. (2001). *Words of the world.* Cambridge: Polity.

Dewey, M., & Jenkins, J. (2010). English as a lingua franca in the global context. In M. Saxena & T. Omoniyi (Eds.), *Contending with globalization in world englishes* (pp. 72–92). Bristol, UK: Multilingual Matters.

Eggel, D., Liebich, A., & Mancini-Griffoli, D. (2007). Is Herder a nationalist? *Review of Politics* 69, 48–78.

Hacking, I. (1975). *Why does language matter to philosophy?* Cambridge: Cambridge University Press.

Harris, R., & Taylor, T. (1989). *Landmarks in linguistic thought,* Vol. 1. London: Routledge.

Herder, J. G. (1966 [1772]). Essay on the origin of language. In J. H. Moran (Ed.) & A. Gode (Trans.), *On the origin of language* (pp. 85–166). Chicago: University of Chicago Press.

Hobbes, T. (1996 [1651]). *The leviathan.* R. Tuck, Ed. Cambridge: Cambridge University Press.

Ives, P. (2004). *Gramsci's politics of language: Engaging the Bakhtin circle and the Frankfurt school.* Toronto: University of Toronto Press.

Ives, P. (2006). "Global English": Linguistic imperialism or practical lingua franca? *Studies in Language and Capitalism* 1, 121–141.

Ives, P. (2010). Cosmopolitanism and global English. *Political Studies* 58(3), 516–535.

Ives, P. (2015a). De-politicizing language. In T. Ricento, Y. Peled, & P. Ives (Eds.), *Language policy and political theory: Building bridges, assessing breaches* (pp. 41–56). Cham: Springer.

Ives, P. (2015b). Global English and the limits of liberalism. In T. Ricento (Ed.), *Language policy and political economy: English in a global context* (pp. 48–71). Oxford: Oxford University Press.

Ives, P. (2015c). Language and collective identity: Theorizing complexity. In C. Späti (Ed.), *Language and identity politics* (pp. 17–37) Oxford: Berghahn Books.

Johnson, D. C. (2013). *Language policy*. London: Palgrave Macmillan.

Kachru, B. (2005). *Asian Englishes: Beyond the canon*. Hong Kong: Hong Kong University Press.

Kymlicka, W. (1995). *Multicultural citizenship: A liberal theory of minority rights*. Oxford: Oxford University Press.

Kymlicka, W., & Patten, A. (Eds.). (2003). *Language rights and political theory*. Oxford: Oxford University Press.

Laitin, D., & Reich, R. (2003). A liberal democratic approach to language justice. In W. Kymlicka & A. Patten (Eds.), *Language rights and political theory* (pp. 80–105). Oxford: Oxford University Press.

Leger, R., & Lewis, H. (Eds.) (2017). Normative political theory's contribution to language policy research: Introduction to special issue. *Journal of Multilingual and Multicultural Development* 38(7), 577–583.

Locke, J. (1995 [1693]). *An essay concerning human understanding*. Amherst, NY: Prometheus Books.

Locke, J. (1998 [1690]). *Two treatises of government*. Peter Laslett, Ed. & Trans. 3rd edition. Cambridge: Cambridge University Press.

Losonsky, M. (2006). *Linguistic turns in modern philosophy*. Cambridge: Cambridge University Press.

May, S. (2012), *Language and minority rights*. 2nd edition. London: Routledge.

Patten, A. (2014). *Equal recognition: The moral foundations of minority rights*. Princeton, NJ: Princeton University Press.

Peled, Y. (2011). Language, rights, and the language of language rights. *Journal of Language and Politics* 10(3), 436–456.

Pennycook, A. (2010). *Language as local practice*. London: Routledge.

Pettit, P. (2008). *Made with words: Hobbes on language, mind, and politics*. Princeton, NJ: Princeton University Press.

Philips, S. (1998). Language ideologies in institutions of power. In B. Schieffelin, K. Woolard, & P. Kroskrity (Eds.), *Language ideologies* (pp. 211–225). Oxford: Oxford University Press.

Piller, I. (2016). Herder: An explainer for linguists. Language on the Move website. Retrieved from http://www.languageonthemove.com/herder-an-explainer-for-linguists/

Pocock, J. G. A. (1973). *Politics, language and time*. New York: Atheneum.

Pogge, T. (2003). Accommodation rights for Hispanics in the United States. In W. Kymlicka & A. Patten (Eds.), *Language rights and political theory* (pp. 105–122). Oxford: Oxford University Press.

Ricento, T. (2015a). Thinking about language: What political theorists need to know about language in the real world. In T. Ricento, Y. Peled, & P. Ives (Eds.), *Language policy and political theory: Building bridges, assessing breaches* (pp. 57–76). Cham: Springer.

Ricento, T. (2015b). Political economy and English as a "global" language. In T. Ricento (Ed.), *Language policy and political economy: English in a global context* (pp. 27–47). Oxford: Oxford University Press.

Ricento, T., Peled, Y., & Ives, P. (Eds.). (2015). *Language policy and political theory: Building bridges, assessing breaches*. Cham: Springer.

Rousseau, J.-J. (1966 [1781]). Essay on the origin of languages. In J. H. Moran (Ed.) & A. Gode (Trans.), *On the origin of language* (pp. 5–58). Chicago: University of Chicago Press.

Rousseau, J.-J. (2011 [1762]). The social contract. In D. Cress (Ed. & Trans.), *The basic political writings* (2nd edition; pp. 155–252). Indianapolis: Hackett.

Schmidt, R., Sr. (2005). Political theory and language policy. In T. Ricento (Ed.), *An introduction to language policy: Theory and method* (pp. 95–110). Oxford: Blackwell.

Shin, H., & Park, J. S.-Y. (Eds.). (2016). Researching language and neoliberalism, Special Issue. *Journal of Multilingual and Multicultural Development* 37(5).

Spencer, V. (2012). *Herder's political thought*. Toronto: University of Toronto Press.

Spolsky, B. (2005). *Language policy*. Cambridge: Cambridge University Press.

Taylor, C. (1995), *Philosophical arguments*. Cambridge, MA: Harvard University Press.

Trabant, J. (2009). Herder and language. In H. Adler & W. Koepke (Eds.), *A companion to the works of Johann Gottfried Herder* (pp. 117–139). Rochester, NY: Camden House.

Van Parijs, P. (2011). *Linguistic justice for Europe and the world*. Oxford: Oxford University Press.

Weber, E. (1976). *Peasants into Frenchmen: The modernization of rural France, 1870–1914*. Stanford, CA: Stanford University Press.

Weinstock, D. (2015). The complex normative foundations of language policy. In T. Ricento, Y. Peled, & P. Ives (Eds.), *Language policy and political theory: Building bridges, assessing breaches* (pp. 23–40). Cham: Springer.

Weinstock, D. (2003). The antinomy of language policy. In W. Kymlicka & A. Patten (Eds.), *Language rights and political theory* (pp. 250–270). Oxford: Oxford University Press.

Wolin, S. (2004). *Politics and vision*. Expanded edition. Princeton, NJ: Princeton University Press.

Woolard, K. (1998). Introduction. In B. Schieffelin, K. Woolard, & P. Kroskrity (Eds.), *Language ideologies: Practice and theory* (pp. 3–47). Oxford: Oxford University Press.

Wright, S. (2004). *Language policy and language planning: From nationalism to globalisation*. London: Palgrave Macmillan.

CHAPTER 10

IDEOLOGIES OF LANGUAGE STANDARDIZATION

THE CASE OF CANTONESE IN HONG KONG

KATHERINE H. Y. CHEN

LANGUAGE standardization is closely connected to boundary setting, group differentiation, power, and authority. Often it is imposed for political purposes and is based on political ideologies, whether these are national unification, drawing political, social, and cultural boundaries, establishing and maintaining social hierarchies, or controlling access to education and the symbolic power that comes with use of specific linguistic forms (Bourdieu & Thompson, 1991). A part of the standardization process usually involves language authorities laying out their reasoning and justifications for prescribing language use in particular ways. In the sociolinguistic literature, Milroy and Milroy (1985) term such prescriptive discourses part of a "complaint tradition" (pp. 33–34), arguing that they serve to maintain standard language varieties.

Discourses of standardization are underpinned by language ideologies specific to a community and can reveal much about that community, including its history and its changing relationships with neighboring communities. Woolard (2016) defines language ideologies as "socially, politically, and morally loaded cultural assumptions about the way that language works in social life and about the role of particular linguistic forms in a given society" (p. 6). The study of language ideologies is, therefore, the study of human beings and their social, political, and cultural relationships. It bridges the sociolinguistic micro-macro connections, since these seemingly micro-level linguistic discourses can be traced to larger issues, from the distribution of language as a symbolic resource to cultural, ethnic, and national identities that are meaningful and significant to members of the community.

This chapter presents the standardization of the Cantonese language within Hong Kong as a case study exploring language ideologies as manifested in the discourse of major linguistic authorities (each with its own political, cultural, and moral agendas) at a critical historical moment—in this case, the period leading up to the handover of Hong Kong from Britain to China in 1997. These ideologies reveal a lot about the changing social meaning of Cantonese to the people of Hong Kong and the development of a distinct Hong Kong identity that has gained greater social and political significance in the two decades following the handover.

Language standardization often goes hand in hand with the rise of nationalism and a national identity, particularly at the end of colonial periods, as in the cases of Malaysia, Singapore, and the Philippines when colonial rule ended after World War II. In Hong Kong, however, because the whole territory was to be returned to Chinese sovereignty in 1997, "[a Hong Kong] nationalism was not feasible" (Young, 1996, p. 8). Yet the idea that Hong Kong people have a distinct identity of their own was established as early as the 1960s (Turner & Ngan, 1996), alongside the rise of Cantonese as a local identity marker. The few years leading up to the handover saw a peak in interest in Cantonese standardization among academic scholars and the media, specifically the standardization of pronunciation in contrast to colloquial pronunciation, commonly known as 懶音 ("lazy pronunciation")[1]. In this use, the adjective *lazy* has a sense of moral judgment that essentializes the speakers of such linguistic features as being *lazy* in character as well. As we will see in later sections of this chapter, such ideas about the moral imperatives of language have important cultural and political implications, connected to the defining qualities of the language and the identity of the speakers. In short, this chapter will examine the prescriptive discourses of linguistic authorities surrounding so-called lazy pronunciation during the pre-handover period and the underpinning language ideologies in the Hong Kong community.

By examining the prescriptive ideologies implicit in the discursive practices of language authorities (who also frequently promote cultural, aesthetic, and political ideologies), we can understand the controversies about language in a broader social-political context. My main argument is that these language ideologies about the aesthetics and cultural qualities of Cantonese are part of a process of social and political differentiation closely associated with the renegotiation of local Hong Kong identity in the period of political change around the handover. In the following sections, I hope to demonstrate that the standardization of Cantonese is no simple linguistic matter, but is at the very center of social, cultural, and political negotiation with regard to community boundaries and identities. I start by providing a summary of the complexity of the notion of *Chinese language* in Hong Kong as a background for the politically and culturally charged linguistic discourses used by the language authorities. Next, I examine the features that characterize lazy pronunciation. I then examine the prescriptive discourses of three key Cantonese language authorities that were dominant during the years immediately before the handover: the Hong Kong government's Education Department, the politically charged Committee for Standardizing Cantonese Pronunciation, and the influential media personality 何文匯 Man Wui Ho. These discourses shed light on the relationship between Cantonese language ideologies and the different political interests and powers at work in the renegotiation and redefinition of Hong Kong identity as Hong Kong moved toward the postcolonial period. I end with implications for the understanding of standardization processes in other contexts.

The Politics of the Chinese Language in Hong Kong

The status, function, and development of a language are never purely linguistic issues, but are closely linked to social and political conditions. This section provides a summary of the politics of the Chinese language in Hong Kong as background to understanding the complex intertwined history of language, people, and place.

Before Hong Kong was returned to China in 1997, two languages, English and Chinese, were the designated official languages of Hong Kong. Because Hong Kong was a British colony, English was the sole official language from 1842, the beginning of the colonial period, to 1974, when Chinese was recognized as another official language after decades of demands from the ethnic Chinese colonial subjects. The use of the term *Chinese language* in the colonial Hong Kong context refers to a combination of spoken Cantonese and Standard Written Chinese. Standard Written Chinese is grammatically and lexically based on Mandarin, and is a construct developed during the May 4th language movement in the 1920s in China. What was until 1949 called *Mandarin*, a dialect of northern Chinese, was then renamed *Putonghua*, literally the *common language*, and was standardized, thus becoming the national language of China. Mandarin/Putonghua is linguistically distinct from Cantonese in phonology, grammar, and lexicon. In other words, the Chinese language in Hong Kong, which is commonly conceptualized as one language, in fact contains two distinct linguistic systems—Cantonese, which is a southern variety, and Standard Written Chinese based on Putonghua, a northern variety. Such a concept of *Chinese language* is unique to Hong Kong, as the term *Chinese language* in China and the rest of the world typically refers to spoken Putonghua and Standard Written Chinese. Outside of Hong Kong, therefore, the spoken and written forms of the *Chinese language* are based on a single linguistic system.[2]

This unique conception of Chinese language in Hong Kong is culturally, socially, and politically important because it set a foundation for postcolonial language debates and also for resistance to Putonghua as a medium of instruction in Chinese language teaching and as a language in other contexts within Hong Kong. Resistance to Putonghua occurs in part because many Hong Kong people associate Putonghua with China's political system and not with the Standard Written Chinese they use in daily life. Given that only spoken Cantonese has been recognized as part of the Chinese language taught in schools, while written Cantonese has been largely ignored, it is no surprise that standardization of Cantonese pronunciation, and not its grammar and lexicon, has been the focus of scholarly and media attention. (Written Cantonese, which represents Cantonese speech, is a non-standardized written variety without official recognition that is not taught in schools and is deemed by the education system a language error when found in students' writing. Nevertheless, most schoolchildren learn it from their peers and use it for informal and personal communication. In the community, written Cantonese is commonly found in certain magazines, sections of newspapers, comic books, advertisements, and social media [for more about written Cantonese, see Bauer, 1982, 1988]).

This seemingly inconsistent conception of the *Chinese language* stems from the peculiar development of Chinese language education in colonial Hong Kong and pre-PRC (People's Republic of China) southern China that was different from its development in post-PRC China. According to C. L. Wong (1996), when Hong Kong became a British colony in 1842, the privately operated village schools on Hong Kong Island were taught by intellectuals from Canton city or nearby southern China who typically spoke Cantonese and used it as a medium of instruction. Furthermore, the written materials used at the time consisted of a combination of classical Chinese, Cantonese, and Baihua or *plain speech*, a pre-standardized modern written Chinese based on Mandarin (C. L. Wong, 1996, p. 80). As the May 4th language movement in the 1920s developed and standardized Baihua as Standard Written Chinese in China, intellectuals in Hong Kong followed, using it as the default written language for literacy and education, while the spoken medium of instruction continued to be Cantonese. However, in 1949, when the PRC selected Mandarin to be standardized as the spoken national language, Putonghua, Hong Kong's intellectuals did not follow. Young (1996) explains why Hong Kong's language development departed from that of China after 1949:

> [W]ith sweeping changes taking place in the Chinese mainland, Chinese intellectuals in Hong Kong saw themselves as vanguards of the Chinese tradition. [. . .] Whereas the Chinese on the mainland were being led by a "foreign" ideology (i.e. Marxism-Leninism), Hong Kong Chinese strenuously tried to assert their "Chineseness" in that

they believed themselves to be the more "pure" Chinese—at least they spoke the real Chinese language, Tong-Wah (Tang-hua). And if they could not preserve Chinese Confucian values, they could at least preserve the prime essence of Chinese culture which, in other words, meant Cantonese culture. (pp. 8–9)

The idea that Cantonese is more real and pure, a more authentic Chinese than Mandarin, has its origin in southern China's centuries-old Lingnan culture (literally "south of the mountain" or southern Chinese) that can be traced back to the ancient history of Middle Chinese. As we shall see, the ideology of Cantonese authenticity was prevalent among southern intellectuals, including those in colonial Hong Kong, and it recurs later in the Cantonese standardization discourse, particularly in the prescriptive ideologies of Man Wui Ho, who launched the largest media campaign in history to promote *correct* Cantonese pronunciation. Thus it was Cantonese, not Putonghua, that was the subject of the language movement in Hong Kong in the 1960s and 1970s, which eventually ended with Chinese (Cantonese and Standard Written Chinese) becoming an official language of Hong Kong alongside English. Across the border, by comparison, under China's national common language policy, Cantonese, which was once a "genuine regional standard" (Ramsey, 1987, p. 99), was reduced in status to a mere *dialect*; its use was discouraged and it had limited functionality.

The establishment of the People's Republic of China and the national language policy of Putonghua in 1949, therefore, marked the divergence of Chinese language development in China and Hong Kong, as Hong Kong did not follow mainland China's language policy and practice from this point onward. The political instability in China before 1949 generated a massive migration of population from China to Hong Kong, to the extent that the colonial government started to implement large-scale projects in housing, education, infrastructure, and social welfare never attempted before. In the decade following 1949, the sense of a local community and consciousness of a specific Hong Kong identity started to take shape. Young (1996) comments:

[I]t was around this time that the designation "Hong Kong person" first surfaced. University students, in endless debates on the question of identity, decided that their parents might have been refugees, but that their home was first and foremost Hong Kong, and therefore they must be Hong Kong persons. (p. 13)

Similarly, Turner and Ngan (1996) discuss the growth of the sense of Hong Kong identity and the notion of Hong Kong people in the 1960s:

[B]y the end of the sixties the idea of "community" was no longer an irrelevance to the majority of the population. For alongside the official discourse, a local, and largely unarticulated sense of identity had begun to emerge in Hong Kong. It was a raw identity born of the common experience of dislocation. . . . It was also marked by a subjective change in Hong Kong people's attitude towards their "own" city, in part, a consequence of an increasing focus on local issues. . . . The social changes that brought about new perceptions of identity were to some extent officially promoted, such as Cantonese-medium broadcasting and primary school education. (p. 15)

Cantonese popular culture was formed at this time. Based on Cantonese pop songs, Cantonese radio and television broadcasting, Cantonese films, and Cantonese literature in the form of comic books, newspapers, and pocket-sized entertainment books, it replaced and overtook the Mandarin-oriented popular culture that existed previously. The 1960s were also the period when the movement for local Chinese language (Cantonese and Standard Written Chinese) became active, eventually leading to the *Chinese language* gaining official status. K. P. Wong (1996) notes that the 1960s and 1970s were also the time when schools that used Cantonese as the medium of instruction were most popular in Hong Kong, and the establishment in 1963 of the Chinese University of Hong Kong was a milestone in the history of the local Chinese language movement. At this time, too, discussion about the standardization of Cantonese pronunciation began in scholarly work, as well as in the public media in newspapers and on radio, continuing later in television programs (see Rao, 1980; Yu, 1989; Zhan, 1997).

Following these language developments and the rise of a local culture, by the time it was determined that Hong Kong would be returned to China in 1997, Cantonese had already been well established as a language of the Hong Kong people, embodying their cultural, social, and political identity. As Hong Kong developed along increasingly different lines from China after 1949, potential conflicts and tensions between Hong Kong and its Chinese rulers seemed inevitable.

Given this backdrop of the politics of Chinese language development in Hong Kong, I now turn to a description of *lazy pronunciation*, before moving to the linguistic authorities' prescriptive discourses on Cantonese pronunciation.

DESCRIBING LAZY PRONUNCIATION

Virtually all Hong Kong Cantonese speakers know the term 懶音 ("lazy pronunciation"), which refers to colloquial forms that differ from prescribed dictionary pronunciation. The term indicates a moral ideology in which the linguistic form becomes an indicator of the moral character of its speakers. The use of lazy pronunciation is considered unacceptable in Hong Kong's "complaint tradition" (Milroy & Milroy, 1985), though in daily life the usage is so common it is rarely commented on, except in contexts where standard Cantonese is expected, such as in news broadcasts and public speech. Although many Cantonese speakers are able to identify and demonstrate a few specific words of the lazy category, others do not perceive the difference between lazy pronunciation and the prescribed form.

Descriptive linguists of Cantonese such as Bauer and Benedict (1997) and Matthews and Yip (2013) consider such variation to be phonologically free variation and/or sound change in progress (also see Bourgerie, 1990; Yeung, 1980). The colloquial forms have existed among Cantonese speakers for at least 130 years (Ball, 1883, reprinted 1924, p. lxiii), although many Cantonese scholars such as Ho (1990), Li (1995) and Zhan (1990) believe they are a relatively recent phenomenon that has occurred only since the 1980s. Prescriptivists claim that using the lazy variants hinders communication, because in some cases the lazy variant is a homophone of another word with a different referential meaning. In actual usage in context, however, miscommunication seldom occurs.

Lazy pronunciation is a phonemic-based variation, restricted to eight pairs of syllable-initial and syllable-final consonants, and does not involve a variation of tones or vowels. Some forms of the variation occur quite commonly, to such an extent that most users do not consider them wrong. For example, the [l-] variant in the [n-/l-] pair is common, to the extent that it is less socially stigmatized than other rarer variants such as using [ʔ-] (zero initial or glottal stop) in the [ʔ-/ ŋ-] pair. Table 10.1 provides a summary of the eight pairs of variation discussed by Ho (1991), a local prescriptivist and media celebrity widely considered to be an expert in Cantonese pronunciation. The first pair, [ŋ-] and [ʔ-] (or zero initial) occurs in complementary distribution in the traditional dictionary; [ŋ-] occurs only with words in low tones (tones 4–6) while [ʔ-] occurs in high tones (tones 1–3). It is common to see hypercorrection in which speakers

Table 10.1 Phonemic–Based Variation: "Lazy Pronunciation" (懶音)

		Chinese Characters and Glosses	Dictionary Pronunciation	Colloquial ("Lazy") Pronunciation	Colloquial Version's Homophones
Syllable-initial consonants					
1	ŋ- and ʔ-	我 I	ŋɔ 5	ʔɔ 5	
2	n- and l-	你 you	neɪ 5	leɪ 5	李 surname Lee
3	k- and h-	佢 he/she/it	kœɪ 5	hœɪ 5	
4	gʷ- and g-	國 country	gwɔk⁷ 3	gɔk⁷ 3	角 horn
5	kʷ- and k-	擴 to expand	kwɔk⁷ 3	kɔk⁷ 3	確 be certain
6	ŋ- and m-	吳 surname Ng	ŋ 4	m 4	唔 no/not
Syllable-final consonants					
7	-ŋ and -n	朋 friend	pɐŋ 4	pɐn 4	貧 poor
8	-k and -t	角 horn	gɔk⁷ 3	gɔt⁷ 3	割 to cut
Hypercorrection of syllable-initial consonant					
1a	ʔ- and ŋ-	愛 love	ʔɔɪ 3	ŋɔɪ 3 (hypercorrection)	

believe only the velar nasal variant is correct for all tones (see example 1a in Table 10.1). Other variation pairs from 2 to 8 occur in overlapping distribution and are phonetically unconditioned.

The stigmatization of lazy pronunciation goes beyond a moral judgment; it is also connected with deeper cultural and political ideologies, which are evident in the prescriptive discourses of the three major linguistic authorities active in the years immediately before the 1997 handover. Each authority has its own discourse and justifications for why a certain form of pronunciation is considered incorrect. In addition to contributing to the Cantonese standardization process, the authorities' prescriptive discourses are sites for understanding the underlying ideologies of Cantonese standardization and its political, social, and cultural meanings.

CANTONESE LANGUAGE AUTHORITIES

Between 1994 and 1996, a media campaign was launched to teach *correct Cantonese pronunciation* to the Hong Kong public. The campaign initiator was Man Wui Ho, at that time a professor of classical Chinese literature at the Chinese University of Hong Kong, a justice of the peace, and an occasional television broadcaster. Ho's campaign was the first (and probably last) of its kind, as it was the first time Cantonese pronunciation was systematically taught in the public media and was sponsored by a government-funded media institute.

In addition to Ho, during the years leading up to the handover, there were other language authorities which advocated ideas about Cantonese pronunciation in Hong Kong. Their language prescriptions and underlying ideologies can be explained by exploring the authorities' social and political positions and perspectives. In general, three sectors were involved as major sources for language prescription: pre-tertiary education administered by the Education Department, academia, and the mass media. I begin by analyzing the prescriptive discourse of the Education Department of the Hong Kong government, followed by those from the academic, quasi-official Committee for Standardizing Cantonese Pronunciation. Finally, I will turn to Ho's media campaign. Although these were not the only language authorities in Hong Kong at the time, they were certainly the most influential players prescribing Cantonese pronunciation and dominating public debate about its standardization process.

The Hong Kong Education Department

Language use in schools plays a significant role in codifying a language, maintaining a standard, and implementing official language policies. In this section, I discuss key

Education Department guidelines pertaining to Cantonese pronunciation and its status in education before and after the handover, and how those guidelines perpetuate the political and cultural ideologies at the time. In the preceding, I discussed the peculiar definition of *Chinese language* in Hong Kong: a perceived single language whose spoken form and written form in fact come from two different linguistic systems (spoken Cantonese and Mandarin/Putonghua as the basis of the written form). The Education Department guidelines reinforced this perception throughout the colonial period, and only changed after 1997, when Putonghua was introduced in the system as one of the three languages authorized for use in education.

During the colonial period, the Curriculum Development Committee of the Education Department of Hong Kong published three syllabi (Curriculum Development Committee, 1978, 1990, and 1995) for teaching the Chinese language in Hong Kong schools. The 1978 syllabus included instructions for teaching Cantonese pronunciation and "guid[ing] students to correct mistakes in pronunciation" (指導學生改正發音上的錯誤) (p. 68), and the same instructions were repeated in the 1990 syllabus. The committee listed four pairs of variations ([n] and [l], [ʔ] and zero, [kw] and [k], [khw] and [kh]), and suggested that schoolteachers follow dictionary prescription instead of the colloquial forms (Curriculum Development Committee, 1978, p. 92). The 1978 syllabus also addressed the issues of the medium of instruction and the national language of China: "Cantonese is commonly used in school teaching in Hong Kong (香港通用粵語教學), while the national language (國語) is the standard language of Chinese (而中文的標準語是國語)" (p. 67). This is the first time a government authority had specifically mentioned Cantonese, rather than the fuzzy term *Chinese* (Bruche-Schulz, 1997, p. 1), as the teaching medium for the Chinese language. This statement served to perpetuate the conception of the Chinese language in Hong Kong as consisting of spoken Cantonese and Standard Written Chinese. As the school system supported this conception, the mismatch of the written and spoken versions of a conceptually unified *Chinese language* was accepted by the schools as well as the Hong Kong public, ideologically erasing the difference between the two linguistic systems. The second statement about the "national language" as the "standard language of Chinese" probably refers only to the use of Standard Written Chinese for the written form, as the term 國語 ("national language") rather than Putonghua is used. The Education Department provided guidelines on variation in pronunciation, thus demonstrating the government's proscription against lazy pronunciation and its role in the standardization of Cantonese and the elevation of its status in Hong Kong.

This notion of the Chinese language, however, changed after the handover in 1997, when the Education Department enforced a new policy of "mother tongue education" in which three-quarters of the 400 public secondary schools in Hong Kong were required to use the "mother tongue" as the medium of instruction for all subjects, and only a selective quarter of schools could use English as the medium of instruction. The Department's justification for the policy was that using the mother tongue is pedagogically beneficial for student learning (Education Bureau, 1997). As Hutton (2012) argues in his discussion of what he calls "mother-tongue fascism," the notion of a *mother tongue* was highly controversial, used politically to further extreme nationalism during World War II. Therefore it is no surprise that the Hong Kong public and stakeholders in education were skeptical of the policy. At the beginning of policy implementation, questions were raised by the academic, educational, and public sectors about which version of the "Chinese mother-tongue" the government was referring to—Cantonese or Putonghua.

One concern was whether the mother-tongue policy was a stepping-stone toward using Putonghua as the medium of verbal instruction at schools. The Education Department clarified in its 1997 *Guidance for Secondary Schools* that one of the goals of Hong Kong education was to train students to be trilingual in spoken Cantonese, English, and Putonghua, and bi-literate in written English and Standard Written Chinese, and that Cantonese would continue to be the main medium of instruction at school, while Putonghua would be taught as a subject. The Department stated, "Our community is essentially Chinese. We speak, read and write Chinese in our daily life. The government has therefore been promoting the use of Chinese over the years" because the use of the "mother-tongue" in education benefits students' learning (Education Bureau, 1997, n.p.). In the two decades following the handover, however, the "stepping-stone" concern became real as the government began actively promoting Putonghua as the medium of instruction for Chinese language subjects, which caused much controversy and debates in the community (this issue has been discussed in detail by Lai & Byram, 2003; Li, 2009; Tsui, 2004; and Zhang & Yang, 2004).

Thus the guidelines and policy of the Education Department during the colonial period followed and reinforced popular language ideologies and contributed to the conception of the Chinese language in Hong Kong in which Cantonese was given a more elevated status than in China. During the time of political change after 1997, the Department took a more active role in modifying and aligning Hong Kong's language-in-education policy with China's national language policy, by officially including Putonghua as a compulsory subject and by introducing the mother-tongue education policy that eventually became a way to implement Putonghua as the medium of verbal instruction for Chinese language subjects.

In the next section, I turn to an overtly political institution, the scholarly Committee for Standardizing Cantonese Pronunciation, which attempted to direct Cantonese standardization toward the national language, Putonghua.

The Committee for Standardizing Cantonese Pronunciation

The two decades before the handover in 1997 saw a massive increase in publications and media attention on every aspect of Hong Kong. With reference to Cantonese

language studies, it was also a time of peak interest in scholarly work, with conferences on Cantonese held in mainland China and Hong Kong, numerous publications
of Cantonese dictionaries and syllabaries, books on etymologies of Cantonese words
and related cultural history, Cantonese textbooks for teaching Mandarin speakers,
and linguistic works in a Western linguistic tradition (e.g., see Pan, 1982; Wong, 1996;
Yu, 1989; Zhan, 1997). In 1990, seven years before the handover, a mainland scholar,
Bohui Zhan, initiated the organization of a language academy, the Committee for
Standardizing Cantonese Pronunciation (廣州話審音委員會), with the aim of
producing *A Standard Cantonese Pronouncing Dictionary* [廣州話正音字典]
(Zhan, 2002). Members of the committee included twenty-four scholars from
China, Hong Kong, and Macau, as well as two government officials from China—
the assistant head of the Guangdong Television Department and the assistant
head of the Guangdong Education Department. The goal of the committee was
to decide on a *correct* pronunciation and to set up a standard for Cantonese
(為廣州話審訂出正確的音讀, 樹立標準) (Zhan, 1990, p. 9).

The committee laid out nine principles of standardization that it used to prescribe pronunciation of over 30,000 Chinese characters (see Chang, 1993, for all
nine principles, and Chen, 1998, pp. 102–103, for English translation). The fifth principle raised controversy among committee members as well as outside scholars because of its underlying political implications: "The principle of leading [Cantonese]
towards the common language (向共同語靠攏) should be followed when there are
cases of variation." Zhan (1990), the chair of the committee, commented that "[t]he
relationship of Putonghua and regional dialects is that of the master and followers
(普通話是「主」, 各地方言是「從」)" (p. 8). Another member of the committee,
Huang (1989), made a similar comment: "The Cantonese pronunciation should be
led (引導) towards the direction of the common language [referring to Putonghua]
(向共同語靠攏), so that it will facilitate the unification of the Han Chinese language
(有利於漢語的統一發展)" (p. 18).

These principles established by the committee and implemented in their codification work were politically charged. The analogy of "master" and "follower," and
the concept of "the unification of the Han Chinese language" were underpinned by
the political ideology of Chinese nationalism. From the perspective of the mainland
scholars and officials, Cantonese, which had flourished in Hong Kong with the status
of a language rather than a dialect, needed to be put in its rightful place as a dialect
now that Hong Kong was to be a part of China. By extension, this was arguably also
an attempt to put the people of Hong Kong in their rightful place, as a part of China
and not an independent political unit with an elevated local dialect that could pose a
threat to "the unification of the Han Chinese language" and perhaps also to the unification of the people of China.

The Committee was the first Cantonese language academy to draw upon scholars
from China, Hong Kong, and Macau, and might have been expected to generate
much interest among scholars who actively debated Cantonese pronunciation in

education, academia, and public media. In reality, however, very few Hong Kong scholars participated in the committee's work. Man Wui Ho, for example, one of the most prominent scholars in the debates in Hong Kong over Cantonese pronunciation, did not participate; his advocacy on cultural and literary grounds against Cantonese following Putonghua pronunciation would not have been welcomed by the committee.

In the next section, I turn to Ho's prescriptive discourses and Cantonese ideologies, which are grounded in the cultural and literary tradition of Lingnan culture that can be traced to Middle Chinese.

Ho's Media Campaign and Cantonese ideologies

The focus of this section is on a media campaign that aimed to promote correct Cantonese and on the language ideologies underpinning this campaign. The figure responsible for the media campaign is Man Wui Ho, a professor of classical Chinese literature at the Chinese University of Hong Kong. The main thrust of his advocacy was that correct Cantonese pronunciation preserves the essence of traditional Chinese culture, literature, and language that can be traced to the Sui, Tang, and Sung dynasties (around 600 to 1000 C.E.). Speaking with lazy pronunciation, therefore, is morally reprehensible not only because the speakers are lazy and not working hard enough, but also because they are "destroying Chinese culture" (在催毀中國文化) (Ho & Bou, 1989, p. 6). The ideas and ideologies he advocated were not new, as similar discourses circulated among pre-1949 southern Chinese and Cantonese intellectuals, as well as in the schools and in the public media–complaint tradition in Hong Kong. But Ho was the most influential voice, and it was Ho who made the most significant impact in education, academia, and the media.

Between 1994 and 1996, with the support of Radio Television Hong Kong (RTHK), a government-owned broadcasting corporation, Ho launched the largest ever media campaign on television and radio to promote correct Cantonese pronunciation (see Ho, 1994–1996). This media campaign consisted of two television series broadcast at prime time on weekdays with an average Nielsen-scale viewer score of 9.4 to 11.2 points (each point representing 1% of the Hong Kong population at the time, i.e., about 500,000 to 600,000 viewers) (Ho, 1995, p. 125). Here we focus on the prescriptive discourses and their underpinning ideologies in Ho's media campaign and publications (for details of the content of the media campaign, see Chen, 1998).

Ho's most important claim was that Cantonese is an older form of Chinese that preserves the essence of Chinese culture. Other discourses stemming from this central claim were ideologically driven rationalizations to justify the prescriptivists' cause, such as the essentialization of the moral character of speakers of lazy pronunciation as "lazy" and "childlike"; condemnation of lazy speakers' inability to manage "complicated sounds"; and the fear that lazy pronunciation destroys the aesthetic qualities of Cantonese (Ho, 1990, pp. 33–51). In what follows, I examine the origin of this ideology and how it is connected with other discourses.

The idea that Cantonese is an older form of Chinese and preserves the essence of Chinese culture can be seen in Ho's discussion about what model to follow in Cantonese pronunciation. Ho considered *Guangyun* (廣韻), a rhyme book published in 1008 C.E. in the Sung dynasty, as the "correct" model of pronunciation. Ho described *Guangyun* as an "ancient standard" (圭臬) that represented the "real and orthodox convention recognised officially" (是真真正正的約定俗成, 而且得到官方承認) (Ho & Bou, 1989, p. 3), while "Cantonese pronunciation is the descendant of the *Guangyun* system" (粵音是《廣韻》系統的遺裔) (Ho & Bou, 1989, p. 4). He therefore argued that "Cantonese pronunciation should be in accordance with the pronunciation of *Guangyun*" (粵音仍要以《廣韻》切音為依歸) (Ho & Bou, 1989, p. 4) and that "Cantonese has an important mission of preserving the Chinese traditional culture and appreciating Chinese classical literature" (在保存中國傳統文化和欣賞中國古典文學方面, 粵音承擔了重要的使命) (Ho, 1995, p. 151). Therefore, by using pronunciation that deviates from the ancient standard, speakers of lazy pronunciation are "destroying Chinese culture" (在催毀中國文化) (Ho & Bou, 1989, p. 6). Ho's use of words such as "real," "official," and "standard" to describe *Guangyun*, and his claim that Cantonese is the descendant of this tradition, elevates the status of Cantonese among other Chinese languages. By implication, the official and national language of China, Putonghua, is of a subordinate cultural and linguistic status. Therefore, Ho argued strongly against having standard Cantonese pronunciation "follow" Putonghua. Indeed, given the principles of the Committee for Standardizing Cantonese Pronunciation, it is no surprise that Ho, the most well-known scholar on Cantonese pronunciation, was not involved in the work of the Committee.

If we examine Ho's discourse more closely, two problems arise with his claim that Guangyun is the model of modern Cantonese pronunciation. First, Guangyun is a schematic representation of a standardized speech of 1008 C.E. compiled by the imperial officials; there is no indication that it was an accurate record of speech sounds of the general public at that time. Second, Guangyun uses *fanqie* (反切), a linguistic system developed as early as the Tung Han dynasty (25–220 C.E.), for indicating the pronunciation of one character by means of another two characters. Through time, the characters used for indicating pronunciation also underwent sound changes. Thus, when they are used to indicate the pronunciation of another character in modern Cantonese, the result may not be the actual representation of how the character was pronounced in the past.

Nevertheless, there is some linguistic basis for Ho's argument that Cantonese, as the descendant of *Guangyun*, is a more suitable language than Putonghua for reciting classical poetry. Ho claimed that the phonological changes from Middle

Chinese (the time period when *Guangyun* was compiled) to modern Cantonese were smaller than changes from Middle Chinese to modern Mandarin (or Putonghua). Historical linguistic reconstruction of Middle Chinese compared with modern Cantonese and Putonghua phonology supports this claim. For example, modern Mandarin lost all [p], [t], [k] syllable finals, and it maintains just four tones, while Cantonese kept the final voiceless stops and six to seven tones (depending on the variety of Cantonese) from Middle Chinese. As a result, many poems written in the Tang dynasty (618–907 C.E.) and Sung dynasty (960–1279 C.E.), particularly 近體詩/今體詩 modern-style poetry (that is, modern within the Tang dynasty in comparison to older classics before the Tang dynasty), which has specific meter and rhyme schemes, still maintain their rhymes and rhythm when recited in Cantonese, but not in Putonghua.

From this main idea that Cantonese is an older form of Chinese that preserves the essence of Chinese culture, other discourses followed as rationalizations and justifications for prescriptive rules. Most important, speakers who do not follow prescribed pronunciation, which is important to their cultural heritage and identity, must be morally flawed ("lazy," "indecent," and "childlike"). Ho (1995) explained that incorrect pronunciation "is mainly caused by people choosing the easy rather than the difficult, therefore it is called the 'lazy pronunciation'" (起音唔準確, 主要就係取易不取難, 所以叫做懶音) (p. 5). He also ridiculed lazy pronunciation speakers as childlike: "a lot of adults in their thirties and forties, when they were children their pronunciation was indecent, therefore as adults they still pronounce [keoi] (3rd person pronoun he/she/it) as [heoi], they sound like babies who just begin to learn the language, and it is extremely uncomfortable to listen to" (很多三、四十歲的成年人, 因為小時候發音不檢點, 現在仍然把「佢」說成 *heoi*, 像牙牙學語一般, 聽起來令人非常不舒服) (Ho 1990, p. 51). Such moral sanctioning implied that the speakers themselves, like the language they use, are morally flawed; the flawed qualities (of the speech) become the flawed essence of the speakers. This powerful ideology became naturalized in the collective minds of the community to the extent that most Hong Kong people know about it and many feel guilty for using lazy pronunciation. Some members of the community, however, disregard such a prescriptive ideology and instead consider lazy pronunciation to be natural colloquial speech (see Chen, 1998, for interview accounts of Hong Kong speakers' attitudes toward lazy pronunciation).

Thus the discourses and ideologies of three major language authorities of Cantonese—the Education Department, the Committee for Standardizing Cantonese pronunciation, and Ho's media campaign and publications—responded to the shifting social, cultural, and political situation of the territory. In the final section, I summarize the social meaning of Cantonese standardization for Hong Kong people and the relevance of the Hong Kong case to the larger scholarly analysis of standardization, language ideologies, and politics.

CONCLUSION: THE POLITICS OF LANGUAGE STANDARDIZATION

This chapter has introduced the so-called Cantonese lazy pronunciation, which descriptive linguists consider as common phonological variations and sound change phenomena, while prescriptivists evoke ideological sanctioning of the features as well as their speakers. The adjective *lazy* (懶) in Chinese implies the same moral judgment as in English—that the *non-lazy, correct* pronunciation is a moral imperative. Those who use lazy forms are regarded as not trying hard enough, and their usage thus provides an indication of the moral character of the speakers. This is an example of how a language form becomes indexical to its speakers. This kind of moral judgment about language is not uncommon. For example, Andersson and Trudgill (1990) comment on *h*-dropping in non-standard British English, noting that many prescriptivists claim that dropping the initial *h* sound is "slovenly," "careless," "lazy," and "wrong" (p. 129). Aitchison (1996) quotes a letter of complaint about her series of Reith lectures broadcast by the BBC in Britain: "The speech patterns you endorse are the direct result of downright bone idleness in the speech of the cockneys." In response, Aitchison uses basic phonetics to point out that "the most noticeable cockney speech feature, the glottal stop, requires considerable muscular tension, and could not be due to laziness" (1996, p. 19). Yet evoking phonetics to counter the prescriptivist complaint may be beside the point: what is significant about complaints about Cockney speech, Cantonese lazy pronunciation, and other non-standard forms is that they serve to perpetuate the moral imperative of the standard, along with its associated social class and political hierarchy, at the expense of non-standard forms and their speakers. In addition, complaints about language are more than simply effective ways to shame and therefore to mobilize speakers to adhere to the standard: they are also called into service for causes that are broader than individuals' moral character—in this case, in support of a Hong Kong identity that is claimed to be more authentically Chinese than that in mainland China.

Indeed, the language ideology that underpins language standardization processes in Hong Kong is one of authenticity (cf. Bucholtz, 2003; Eckert, 2003; Woolard, 2016), in which the value of the language is rooted in its relationship with a place and signals the speaker's identity. As Young (1996) notes, Chinese intellectuals in Hong Kong consider Cantonese to be "the real Chinese language" and "pure[r]" than other varieties (p. 9), an ideology that has its root in the southern Chinese Lingnan culture (for further readings on Lingnan culture, see Wu, 1999 and Szeto, 2001). Thus Cantonese, with its associated southern culture grounded in a specific locality—southern China, including Hong Kong—signals not only one's identity as a southerner, but one's authenticity as "real" and "pure" Chinese compared to speakers of other (northern) Chinese varieties, including the national language, Putonghua.

Although Ho takes this ideology as a cultural one and does not explicitly connect it with the politics of language and national identity, the discourse is unavoidably political when it claims that Cantonese is the true representation of Chinese culture, and thus by implication other languages, including Putonghua, are historically and culturally subordinate.

In the years leading up to the handover, the Education Department encouraged the teaching of Putonghua in primary and secondary schools. Soon after the handover in September 1997, the Education Department issued a trilingual (English, Cantonese, Putonghua) and bi-literate (English and Standard Written Chinese) language policy for the Hong Kong school system, officially making Putonghua a compulsory subject for all schools. In addition, schools were encouraged to use Putonghua as a medium of instruction for teaching Chinese language subjects and were given funding for implementation. This language policy eventually became a topic of heated debates in Hong Kong. In the two decades since the handover, the discourse surrounding Cantonese has become increasingly politicized, as the rise of localism and the cultural, social, and political conflict between China and Hong Kong has intensified (e.g., in the Occupy Central movement of 2014 in Hong Kong). There have also been frequent public debates about whether Putonghua is pedagogically a better medium of instruction for Chinese language subjects, and whether the increased use of Putonghua in education and the community threatens the Cantonese language, and with it the distinctive local identity.

Thus the Hong Kong case suggests that language standardization and the ideologies underpinning its practice and discourse are never purely linguistic, but political and cultural in nature, as decades of research on standardization and language ideologies have shown. What is interesting about the Hong Kong case is that the changes in Hong Kong's political sovereignty, from its position as a Chinese Qing dynasty–ruled rural island, to a British crown colony, and then to a Special Administrative Region of the People's Republic of China, make a unique and interesting study for language standardization processes and shifts in language ideologies. The development of the Cantonese language tells its political and cultural history: Cantonese was a heritage from local southern Chinese culture with a standardization process that dates back hundreds of years; it flourished as a *language* in Hong Kong during the colonial period (vs. its status as a *dialect* in China), while in the background there were political, cultural, and ideological tensions among the British rulers, the Hong Kong colonial subjects, and China's leaders, especially after 1949; and it became a central issue in the return of Hong Kong's sovereignty to China with the renegotiation of the language and identity of Hong Kong's people. The ideological tugs-of-war among these multiple elements in different periods of time are key to understanding the larger issues of language, identity, and power, and ultimately the system of human relationships, in Hong Kong and mainland China.

ACKNOWLEDGMENTS

The author is especially grateful to the editors, James Tollefson and Miguel Pérez-Milans, who read through drafts of this chapter and gave detailed and insightful suggestions for improvement. All errors remain mine. Some material in this chapter first appeared in an unpublished thesis, Chen (1998). Research on Cantonese and Hong Kong identity has benefited from the Hong Kong Research Grants Council General Research Fund (GRF, HKU 742311H).

NOTES

1. Because of space limitation, another type of pronunciation variation, called *incorrect reading pronunciation* (錯讀), which is often mentioned together with *lazy pronunciation*, is not included. For further reading on this type of variation, see Chen (1998) and Yueng (1984).
2. Describing spoken Putonghua and Standard Written Chinese as coming from the same linguistic system is an ideological construct in itself, since language boundaries and definitions are fluid and changeable. Certainly there are distinctions between the two, given the different modality as well as regional differences, among other factors. But for our discussion, this description serves the purpose of establishing the different conceptions of *Chinese language* in China and Hong Kong.

REFERENCES

Aitchison, J. (1996, March 15). Madam, how dare you distort, desecrate and defile the English language. *The Times Higher Education Supplement*, p. 19.

Andersson, L., & Trudgill, P. (1990). *Bad language*. Oxford: Blackwell.

Ball, D. J. (1883, 1924). *Cantonese made easy*. Hong Kong: Kelly and Walsh.

Bauer, R. S. (1982). *Cantonese sociolinguistic patterns: Correlating social characteristics of speakers with phonological variables in Hong Kong Cantonese*. PhD dissertation, University of California, Berkeley.

Bauer, R. S. (1988). Written Cantonese of Hong Kong. *Cahiers de Linguistique Asie Orientale* 17(2), 245–293.

Bauer, R. S., & Benedict, P. K. (1997). *Modern Cantonese phonology*, Vol. 102. Berlin: Walter de Gruyter.

Bourdieu, P., & Thompson, J. B. (1991). *Language and symbolic power*. Cambridge, MA: Harvard University Press.

Bourgerie, D. S. (1990). *A quantitative study of sociolinguistic variation in Cantonese*. PhD dissertation, University of California, Berkeley.

Bruche-Schulz, G. (1997). "Fuzzy" Chinese: The status of Cantonese in Hong Kong. *Journal of Pragmatics* 27(3), 295–314.

Bucholtz, M. (2003). Sociolinguistic nostalgia and the authentication of identity. *Journal of sociolinguistics* 7(3), 398–416.

Chang, S. H. (1993). The work of Cantonese standardisation *Newsletter of Chinese Language* 27, 8–12. Hong Kong: T.T. Ng Chinese Language Research Centre, Institute of Chinese Studies, The Chinese University of Hong Kong.

Chen, H. Y. (1998). *Norms of pronunciation and the sociolinguistics of Cantonese in Hong Kong.* Unpublished thesis, University of Hong Kong.

Curriculum Development Committee. (1978). *1978 Chinese syllabus for secondary schools.* Hong Kong: Education Department of Hong Kong.

Curriculum Development Committee. (1990). *1990 Chinese syllabus for secondary schools.* Hong Kong: Education Department of Hong Kong.

Curriculum Development Committee. (1995). *Chinese syllabus for secondary schools (Target oriented curriculum).* Hong Kong: Education Department of Hong Kong.

Eckert, P. (2003). Elephants in the room. *Journal of Sociolinguistics,* 7(3), 392–397.

Education Bureau. (1997). *Guidance for secondary schools: Why should we teach in the mother tongue?* Retrieved from http://www.edb.gov.hk/en/edu-system/primary-secondary/applicable-to-secondary/moi/key-events-moi-fine-tuning-bg/moi-guidance-for-sec-sch/sep-1997/mother-tongue/index.html

Ho, G. C. (Ed.) (1990). 常用字廣州話讀音表 *A list of commonly used Chinese characters with standardised pronunciation in Cantonese.* Hong Kong: Government Printer (for the Institute of Language in Education).

Ho, M. W. (1991). *Introduction to the even and oblique tones in Cantonese* (Vol. 1) and *The correct pronunciation of Cantonese: Demonstration* (Vol. 2). Hong Kong: Publications (Holdings).

Ho, M. W. (1994–1996). Television and radio programs: TV series 1—*Celebrities unite to promote correct pronunciation* (August 1994, March 1995); Radio series 1—*Correct Cantonese pronunciation* (August 1994); TV series 2—*Marvellous detective of correct reading pronunciation* (January 1996); Radio series 2—*The three tests of correct reading pronunciation* (January 1996).

Ho, M. W. (1995). *A record of the teaching of Cantonese pronunciation.* Hong Kong: Chinese University of Hong Kong.

Ho, M. W., & Bou, Y. M. (1989). *Daily incorrect reading pronunciation.* Hong Kong: Hong Kong Professional Teacher's Association.

Huang, J. J. (1989). We should recognise the importance of correct pronunciation in Cantonese. *Yu Cong* 3, 18.

Hutton, C. (2012). *Linguistics and the Third Reich: Mother-tongue fascism, race and the science of language.* New York: Routledge.

Lai, P. S., & Byram, M. (2003). The politics of bilingualism: A reproduction analysis of the policy of mother tongue education in Hong Kong after 1997. *Compare* 33(3), 315–334.

Li, X. K., & 李新魁. (1995). 廣州方言研究. *Research on the Guangzhou Topolect.* 廣州: 廣東人民出版社.

Li, D. (2009). Towards "biliteracy and trilingualism" in Hong Kong (SAR): Problems, dilemmas and stakeholders' views. *AILA Review* 22(1), 72–84.

Matthews, S., & Yip, V. (2013). *Cantonese: A comprehensive grammar.* New York: Routledge.

Milroy, J., & Milroy, L. (1985). *Authority in language: Investigating language prescription and standardisation.* London; New York: Routlege & Kegan Paul.

Pan, P. G. (1982). Hong Kong Cantonese: A sociolinguistic perspective. *Working Papers in Linguistics and Language Teaching* 6, 1–16.

Ramsey, S. R. (1987). *The languages of China.* Princeton, NJ: Princeton University Press.

Rao, B. C. (1980). The problem of standardising the character readings of the Yue dialects. *Yuwen Zazhi* 5, 42–45. Hong Kong: Chinese University of Hong Kong Press.

Szeto, S.G. (2001). 司徒尚紀 (2001). 嶺南歷史人文地理: 广府, 客家, 福佬民系比较研究. 中山大学出版社. *Lingnan history and human geography: Cantonese, Hakka, Hokkien comparative study.* Guangzhou: Zungshan University Press.

Tsui, A. B. M. (2004). Medium of instruction in Hong Kong: One country, two systems, whose language? In J. W. Tollefson & A. B. M. Tsui (Eds.), *Medium of instruction policies: Which agenda, whose agenda?* (pp. 97–116). New York: Routledge.

Turner, M., & Ngan, I. (1996). *Hong Kong sixties: Designing identity.* Hong Kong: Hong Kong Arts Centre.

Wong, C. L. (1996). 王齊樂 (1996). 香港中文教育發展史. 香港: 三聯書店(香港). 有限公司. *The history of Hong Kong Chinese language education.* Hong Kong: Joint Publishing (Hong Kong).

Wong, K. P. (1996). Language favours the youth. In *Language education translation* (pp. 2–17). Hong Kong: Publication Workshop, Translation Department, Lingnan College.

Woolard, K. A. (2016). *Singular and plural: Ideologies of linguistic authority in 21st century Catalonia.* New York: Oxford University Press.

Wu, H. L. (1999). 胡巧利. (1999). 廣東方志與嶺南文化. 廣東史志出版. *Guangdong regional history and Lingnan culture.* Guangzhou: Guangdong History Press.

Yeung, B. W. (1984). 楊碧湖 (1984). 中文的誤讀誤寫誤用 *Incorrect pronunciation, writing, and using in Chinese.* 香港: 高明出版社 Hong Kong: Gou Ming Publication.

Yeung, H. S. W. (1980). *Some aspects of phonological variations in the Cantonese spoken in Hong Kong.* Unpublished MA dissertation, Hong Kong University.

Young, J. (1996). *Changing identities in Hong Kong: From British colonialism to Chinese nationalism.* Paper presented at the Annual meeting of the American Historical Association, January 4–7, 1996.

Yu, Zhufu (1989). We should take the proper attitude to the so-called lazy accent of Cantonese. *Yu Cong* 2, 46–47.

Zhan, B. (1990). 詹伯慧 關於廣州話審音問題的思考 中國語文通訊 A consideration of the problems of standardising Cantonese pronunciation. *Newsletter of Chinese Language* 11 (November), 8–13. Hong Kong: T. T. Ng Chinese Language Research Centre, Institute of Chinese Studies, The Chinese University of Hong Kong.

Zhan, B. (Ed.). (1997). 詹伯慧主編 第五屆粵方言國際研討會論文集 暨南大學出版社 *A collection of theses from the Fifth International Conference on Cantonese and other Yue dialects.* Guangzhou: Jinan University Press.

Zhan, B. (Ed.). (2002). 詹伯慧主編 廣州話正音字典 廣東人民出版社 *A standard Cantonese pronouncing dictionary.* Guangzhou: Guangdong Renmin Press.

Zhang, B., & Yang, R. R. (2004). Putonghua education and language policy in postcolonial Hong Kong. In M. Zhou & H. Sun (Eds.), *Language policy in the People's Republic of China: Theory and practice since 1949* (pp. 143–161). Houten: Springer Netherlands.

CHAPTER 11

GLOBALIZATION, LANGUAGE POLICY, AND THE ROLE OF ENGLISH

THOMAS RICENTO

In this chapter, I explore some of the ways that apparently incompatible claims from the language policy and planning (LPP) literature can be disambiguated and resolved by reference to political economy. In particular, I focus on the competing views regarding the role of English in the world today as either (a) a form of linguistic imperialism, or (b) a vehicle for social and economic mobility. First, I consider the case for English as *the* global lingua franca, citing statistics from a variety of sources that demonstrate the reach of English in academic publishing, economic activity, and international communication networks; evidence is also provided that the economic effects of English are both overstated and uneven. Next, I consider the role of English in economic development in non-English-dominant countries, using data on trade and other indices of economic development.

The available research shows that it is difficult to tease out the independent effects of English on economic development; the connections from language skills to foreign trade, foreign trade to gross domestic product (GDP), and GDP to development and quality of life are complex. Putting it differently, the distribution of skills in a language shared with a trading partner does not directly generate higher GDP, let alone enhance societal welfare. I then critically examine the TINA doctrine ("There Is No Alternative" to economic neoliberalism), a concept widely accepted by pundits and (often implicitly) by LPP scholars.

In analyzing the nature and effects of economic neoliberalism, as expressed in its globalized economic and political forms, I show that particular levels of proficiency in English are necessary for mobility for some people, in some economic sectors, mainly the knowledge economy, but such proficiency is generally not connected to socioeconomic mobility for the vast majority of the global workforce. I conclude with a brief discussion of neoliberal globalization and the role of English by answering the following questions: (1) Where does power reside? (2) Who has agency? (3) Who decides which language has value? and (4) Who has rights?

The Concept of Globalization

What does the term *globalization* mean? One of the most fashionable buzzwords of contemporary political and academic debate, *globalization* in popular discourse often functions as a synonym for one or more of the following phenomena:

- The pursuit of classical liberal (or "free market") policies in the world economy ("economic liberalization")
- The growing dominance of Western (or even American) forms of political, economic, and culture life ("Westernization" or "Americanization")
- The proliferation of new information technologies (the "Internet Revolution").

On the matter of globalization, three books written over the past decade reflect the range of views on globalization. In his book *The Collapse of Globalism and the Reinvention of the World*, John Ralston Saul (2005) argues that the West remains stuck on outdated ideas of growth, wealth creation, and trade expansion and that the world is headed for disaster. On the other hand, Thomas Friedman, *New York Times* columnist, argues in his 2000 book *The Lexus and the Olive Tree* that the driving idea behind globalization is free-market capitalism, and the more that market forces rule and the economy is opened to free trade and competition, the more efficient the economy will be. For Friedman, globalization means the spread of free-market capitalism to virtually every country in the world through the deregulating and privatizing of national economies in order to make them more competitive and attractive to foreign investment. Perhaps in the middle is someone like Joseph E. Stiglitz, Nobel Prize–winning economist, who in his book *Making Globalization Work* (2007), roundly decries the excesses and inequalities that have resulted from neoliberal global economic policies, but believes that changes in a range of policies can help level the playing field, especially for poorer countries that have fared the worst over the past forty years.

Among scholars interested in globalization and language, there is a range of views on how globalization affects language, and how language influences globalization, just as there is a range of views on the economic and political effects of globalization.

Some argue, for example, that the global spread of English has had many harmful effects, often captured by the term *linguistic imperialism*, made popular by British applied linguist Robert Phillipson in his 1992 book *Linguistic Imperialism*, and in a number of subsequent publications (e.g., 2001, 2003). In this model, English is viewed as an accomplice in the aggressive push of neoliberal economic policies and the spread of Western culture, often crowding out space for other languages, including medium-sized European languages, such as Catalan (with 5.7 million speakers in Catalonia) and Finnish (about 5 million in Finland).

Others argue, often triumphantly, that English can no longer be considered an imperial language, that it is the best and only choice for the global lingua franca, and that everyone should accept that fact and get busy learning English so they can improve their life chances and gain upward socioeconomic mobility. This view is championed by linguist David Crystal in *English as a Global Language* (2003), and by political theorist Philip Van Parijs in *Linguistic Justice for Europe and for the World* (2011). Despite their strong belief in the benefits of a global language, both Crystal and Van Parijs express concern about the real and potential negative consequences for other languages; thus, Van Parijs also supports the territoriality principle, by which smaller languages have protections in the states where they are the dominant or majority language. Crystal (2003, p. 191) warns that if in 500 years, English is the only language left to be learned as a second/additional language, "... it will have been the greatest intellectual disaster that the planet has ever known."

I have argued in Ricento (2015) that while English in non-English-dominant countries is tied to global economic forces and can provide an economic advantage to persons with the right educational credentials and skills relevant to knowledge-economy jobs, the particular histories and circumstances of nation-states and the policies of their governments greatly influence, even determine, the role and status that English and other global languages will have in society, especially in the education sector. There is no doubt that the ascendance of English as the dominant international language, especially since World War II, has had a measurable impact on the status and utility of languages in a number of domains where other languages previously had greater power. De Swaan (2001) describes what he calls the current "global language system" in which all languages are connected by multilingual speakers in a strongly ordered, hierarchical pattern.

The higher languages are in this hierarchy, the greater the number of other languages to which they are connected through multilingual speakers. In De Swaan's model, English is the "hypercentral language" at the hub that holds the entire constellation together. Below English are the "super-central," the "central," and, finally, the "peripheral languages." The eleven super-central languages (in alphabetical order) are Arabic, Chinese, French, German, Hindi, Japanese, Malay, Portuguese, Russian, Spanish, and Swahili. All except Swahili have more than one hundred million speakers, and each serves to connect the speakers of a series of central languages. All languages are, in today's *globalized* world, connected indirectly via chains of multilingual speakers. English may be the only language connected to virtually all other languages directly, since every language community contains some multilinguals with English in their repertoire.

Although the number of native speakers is not, by itself, a valid criterion for the internationality or globality of a language, it is a rough indicator of such a status. The number of non-native speakers also strongly correlates with the popular intuition that, for example, English and French are world languages compared to Hindi and Urdu, or even Chinese, even though those languages have many more native speakers than do English or French. Ammon (2010, p. 105) provides estimates from various sources on the number of non-native learners of English; the estimates range from 750 million to more than 1 billion (although Crystal [2003] estimates 2 billion users of English worldwide). Trailing far behind is French, with an estimated 82.5 million learners, followed by Chinese with 30 million learners worldwide (although another source estimates the number to be as low as 3 million [Ammon 2010, p. 105, n. b]). German learners are fourth at 16.7 million.

If we look at the number of native plus second-language speakers of major languages worldwide, Ammon (2010, p. 109), using data from *Ethnologue* (2005 [1984]), reports that in 2005 Chinese ranked first, with 1.051 billion speakers, followed by Hindi + Urdu (588 million speakers), English (508 million speakers), Spanish (382 million speakers), and Russian (255 million speakers) in the top five places. Using 1964 as the base year for comparison purposes, Ammon (2010, p. 109) shows that the following languages have declined in rank in the number of native and native plus second-language speakers of major languages worldwide: English, Japanese, French, Italian, and especially German (from 6th place to 11th place), while the rest have maintained their rank.

Comparison of the economic strength of speakers of different languages, however, yields a different ranking. Relying on data from *Ethnologue* (2005 [1984]), Ammon (2010, p. 110), shows that if the GDP of native and second-language speakers is divided by the percentage of the language's native speakers in the country's population, in 2005, English ranked first at \$12.7 billion, nearly three times stronger than Japanese (\$4.6 billion), and five times stronger than Chinese (\$2.4 billion). German moves from #11 in the number of native plus second-language speakers (123 million speakers) to #3 in terms of its economic strength (\$4.35 billion).

Another indicator of the international power and reach of English can be found in the number of countries and continents in which English is named as an official language. English has official status, including co-status with other languages, in 67 countries on all six continents, followed by French with official status in 29 countries on five continents, Arabic with official status in 22 countries on two continents, Spanish with official status in 21 countries on three continents, and German with official status in 7 countries on one continent (Europe) (Ammon, 2010, p. 112; updated figures on English from Wikipedia, 2015).

English is an official or working language in virtually all of the major international organizations, including the United Nations, the Commonwealth, the Council of Europe, the European Union, NATO, the World Bank, and the International Monetary Fund, and it is the only official language of the Organization of Petroleum Exporting Countries (OPEC) and of the European Free Trade Association.

In scholarly publications in natural sciences, social sciences, and humanities, English is by a very wide margin the dominant language. Hamel (2007) documented the dominance of English in the international scientific periodical literature. He found that in 1996, nearly 91% of scientific publications were in English, followed by 2.1% in Russian, 1.7% in Japanese, 1.3% in French, and 1.2% in German. In some fields, English is even more dominant; nearly 95% of all publications in physics between 1992 and 1997 were in English. In the social sciences and humanities, between 1974 and 1995, publications in English increased from 66.6% to 82.5%, and the second most common language was French, which decreased from 6.8% to 5.9% during this period. If we consider shares of languages in publications in the social sciences between 1880 and 2006, which includes overall average percentage for anthropology, political science, economics, and sociology, we find that in 2006, 80.8% of the publications were in English, followed by 6.1% in German, 4.0% in French, 2.1% in Russian, 1.6% in Spanish, and 0.9% in Italian (Ammon 2010, p. 116).

English and Economic Development

For some scholars, there is a tendency to view the current world neoliberal economic order as justifying the promotion of global languages, especially English, as a means of affording access to jobs and social mobility in developing countries. Philippe Van Parijs is a political theorist who has written extensively about the benefits of a lingua franca, such as English, in playing a role in diminishing poverty in poor countries, mainly by reducing the out-migration of highly trained, English-speaking citizens (e.g., Van Parijs, 2000). In *Linguistic Justice for Europe and for the World* (2011), Van Parijs claims that a lingua franca is urgently needed in Europe and across the world because

> [i]ts adoption and spreading creates and expands a transnational demos, by facilitating direct communication, live or online, without the cumbersome and expensive mediation of interpretation and translation. It enables not only the rich and the powerful, but also the poor and the powerless to communicate, debate, network, cooperate, lobby, demonstrate effectively across borders. This common demos . . . is a precondition for the effective pursuit of justice, and this fact provides the second fundamental reason why people committed to egalitarian global justice should not only

welcome the spread of English as a lingua franca but see it as their duty to contribute to this spread in Europe and throughout the world. (p. 31)

Following a similar line of argument, Brutt-Griffler (2002, 2005) argues that "exclusion from high proficiency [in] English [is] a prime determinant of lack of access to wealth in the world they [poor South Africans] inhabit" (2005, p. 29). She criticizes those who support the teaching of mother tongues over English as being insensitive to the economic aspirations of oppressed and impoverished people as they seek to escape poverty with the aid of English.

In many postcolonial countries, English is a language for the elite, specifically those who attend English-medium private schools and are educated overseas or in elite national universities. In South Africa, for example, the use of African languages for learning/teaching is restricted to underprivileged schools, while privileged schools have English as the language of learning. In a recent study, Casale and Posel (2011, p. 18) found that "English language proficiency [in South Africa] acts as a signal to employers of the quality of education that the worker has received, and hence, the worker's suitability for employment." Yet English-medium instruction may intensify educational disadvantage. For example, Rassool (2013, p. 53) reports that in Pakistan, "the country's focus on English as the medium of education has contributed to high levels of illiteracy amongst the population as a whole—53% in 2005; 57% in 2009." English-medium schools are dominated by children from the upper-middle classes and predominate in urban areas, while the urban poor and rural communities tend to become literate in the regional languages. Thus English (with Urdu) is available for the social and political elites, who run their own English-medium schools (Rahman, 2002), while for the poor rural majority, the lack of qualified teachers of English and limited resources restrict access to tertiary education and employment in the formal economy, where English is valued.

In Rwanda, the anglophone Rwandan Patriotic Front (RPF) took control of the country from the francophone Hutu-led government in 1994, and rapidly instituted a process of anglicization, in part for the same reasons that English has been adopted in many other countries: "Rwandans perceived that the future of globalization is written in English, and they wanted to be able to participate in that new world" (Samuelson, 2013, p. 219). Rwanda gained membership in the Commonwealth in 2009, despite the fact that estimates of the total number of English speakers in Rwanda range from only 1.9% to 5% of the population. Even though 99% of the population can speak Kinyarwanda, the emphasis on English in education through official government policies has blocked the use of mother-tongue education that would allow students to develop literacy in Kinyarwanda while also learning English (or French) as a subject in the early grades (p. 225).

In Rwanda, as in India, South Africa, Pakistan, Zambia, Tanzania, Malawi, Zimbabwe, and many other countries in Africa and elsewhere, decision-making about language policies in education tends to reflect the agendas of the most powerful groups, who seek foreign investment and loans to bolster their ability to maintain power, rather than to pursue broadly based economic development policies. Thus Williams (2014) summarizes the effects of the "Straight-for-English" policy in African countries in this way:

> To date . . . the evidence suggests that the dominant role of English in primary schools has, for the majority, proved to be a barrier to education, rather than a bridge. Students fail to acquire language capital, so human capital is not accumulated, and no economic capital accrues. It is no surprise, then, that whether one looks at development in terms of economic progress or of human needs, poor countries such as Malawi, Zambia and Rwanda that use ex-colonial languages in education have not hitherto made great strides. . . . (p. 137)

Despite such cases, the economic power of English is often assumed and often overstated. Although studies have shown that English can have an important influence on trade and wages, if other factors are taken into account, we find that English is just one factor in determining wages and level of trade. The following studies show that conclusions about the effects of English in trade and employment vary widely from one context to another:

1. Ku and Zussman (2010) found that in a survey over a thirty-year period of 100 countries in which English is not a first language, the acquisition of English-language skills could be seen as enabling the promotion of foreign trade. They base their conclusion largely on mean national test scores on the Test of English as a Foreign Language (TOEFL) over a period of thirty years; controlling for other factors that might influence trade, they found that English proficiency has a strong and statistically significant effect on trade flows. Their study included both industrialized and developing countries in all regions of the globe.

2. Using average TOEFL scores from fifty-four countries and GDP as the measure of development, Arcand and Grin (2013) found that widespread proficiency in English in countries in postcolonial Sub-Saharan Africa and Asia does not appear to be associated with higher levels of economic development, while widespread use of local languages positively correlates with economic development. They also found that English can covary with other variables, including income itself, and that English does not have unique effects on economic development or growth.

3. In studies that looked at market returns associated with English, there is some evidence that for individuals, English proficiency in South Africa has a direct positive effect on labor returns. For example, Casale and Posel (2011), controlling for an individual's amount of education, found that there is a significant wage premium for black South Africans with fluency in English literacy. On the other hand, Levinsohn (2007) found that English proficiency was more of an advantage for white South Africans compared to black South Africans.

4. In India, Azam and Prakish (2010) found that fluency in English (compared to no ability in English) increased hourly wages of men by 34%, and even a little proficiency in English increased male hourly wages by 13%; however, returns to English were lower for women, and were also significantly lower for members of India's Scheduled Castes. They conclude that upward mobility does not come automatically with English skills in India; some obstacles, including long-rooted discrimination against low castes, impede low-caste group members even when they have a skill that is valued by the modern labor market.

5. In a study on the relations between language diversity and foreign trade, Melitz (2008) found that despite the dominant position of English as a world language, English is no more effective in promoting trade than other major European languages. On the other hand, the major European languages as a group (including English) are more efficient than other languages in promoting trade.

Scholarly Acceptance of the TINA Doctrine

The policies and values associated with global economic neoliberalism tend to work against the very communal values that could benefit the sustainability of local economic development and, along with it, the sustainability of local languages, which are prerequisites for even minimal conceptualizations of justice within a global demos. In my view, the argument that "There Is No Alternative" (TINA) to global neoliberalism has been implicitly accepted by scholars such as Van Parijs and Brutt-Griffler, even though they may oppose the corrosive effects of neoliberalism, especially in the most impoverished countries in Africa, Asia, and Latin America. I concur with the sentiment expressed by Edwards (2003, p. 43), who says, ". . . we should cultivate a clearer and broader awareness of the real forces in the real world that bear upon language matters."

However, as with Van Parijs and Brutt-Griffler, Edwards does not question the impact of neoliberal economic policies on the fate of minority languages and cultures. In fact, Edwards (2010, p. 16) takes to task those scholars ". . . who are philosophically unwilling to find anything of moral value in modern, Western, capitalist society . . ." (p. 16) and who lament the loss of "authenticity" in a globalized economic system. He finds that a critique of neoliberalism ". . . naturally extends to the scientific culture per se, indeed to the generalities and 'universals' which many would see as the pivots of progress" (p. 17). To back up his claim, Edwards cites the British intellectual C. P. Snow, who concluded that "industrialization is the only hope of the poor"

(1959, p. 27), and Ernest Gellner (1968, p. 405), who argued for the superiority of the "scientific-industrial" way of life and claimed that modern society offered the best chances for individual freedom and "material liberation" (cited on p. 17). (For a critique of this view, see Saul [1992].)

Edwards's (2010) position makes explicit a view that is widely held by scholars who, even if espousing goals of social justice, tend to accept implicitly the TINA principle, that is, there is no alternative to modern orthodox political liberalism or its current global neoliberal economic instantiation. Yet the core elements that characterize contemporary neoliberal orthodoxy, which tend to reflect the interests of concentrated economic capital, are generally served by language policies that align with those same economic interests, including the promotion of linguae francae such as English. The problem with the position of Van Parijs is that he downplays the contradictions between the values and goals of economic neoliberalism and the values and goals necessary to promote a meaningful "democratic world order" in which economic justice can only be feasible if the debilitating values and manifest negative effects of the current neoliberal global regime—especially the lack of democratic participation in decision-making—are reversed, or at least severely modified. In other words, a global lingua franca is, or would be, an epiphenomenon of the very system that is antithetical to the values of a global, participatory demos.

The shortcomings of political liberalism, as practiced within Western(ized) political economies, have been apparent for a very long time (see Macpherson, 2012 [1973]), but these shortcomings have become greatly amplified over the past forty years. During this period, the decline of the distributive function of governments—largely though policies that have transferred public wealth to private corporations through favorable tax breaks, significant reduction of subsidies for social welfare programs, protective tariffs, and the financialization of natural resources and other goods and services, including intellectual property—has strengthened the role and power of corporate interests while reducing resources available to benefit the world's subordinate classes and shrinking the middle class in the industrialized nations. As Sandel (1982) puts it, liberals exaggerate the capacity for, and the value of, individual choice in the contemporary world. In the domain of language, as Holborow (2007, p. 55) observes, "[n]o one could fail to recognize the fact that real language choice hardly exists anywhere in the unequal world of today."

Proficiency in English (and in particular varieties of English), whether as a first, second, or third language, may provide an advantage for careers and employment in certain sectors of the global economy, but the number of available jobs and the number of jobs being created that require English is very small compared to the numbers of workers seeking jobs worldwide. The policies of the rich countries, especially the United States and the United Kingdom, supported and abetted by major international institutions, such as the International Monetary Fund, the World Bank, and the World Trade Organization, seek to exploit countries with relatively lower wages, limited workers' rights and environmental protections, relatively stable governments, and taxation and repatriation policies that provide a safe haven for foreign investors.

The jobs in these exploited countries are disproportionately very low-wage jobs for which only minimal competence, if any, in English is required. In cases in which a high degree of English is required, as with call centers in India and elsewhere, relatively small numbers of educated workers who also happen to speak, or can master, a variety of English acceptable to American consumers (Blommaert, 2009) have an advantage over those who don't speak this variety of English. But given the limited beneficiaries of English-promotion policies, English cannot be claimed to be a sufficient means to social mobility, let alone global justice for most individuals. Indeed, it is instead essential to address the underlying dynamics of transnational capitalism, particularly its effects on employment and migration patterns that often work against the development of local economies, especially in developing and poor countries.

NEOLIBERALISM, EMPLOYMENT IN THE FORMAL ECONOMY, AND THE ROLE OF ENGLISH

Castells (2006, p. 58) estimates that only about 200 million of the world workforce of 3 billion workers (about 7%) find work through the 53,000 or so multinational corporations and their related networks, yet this workforce is responsible for 40% of global GDP and two-thirds of world trade (Williams, 2010, p. 50). Linguae francae are used in these companies, regardless of their location, and English is by far the most common. Ammon (1995) reports that the German Chambers of Commerce recommend the use of English as the sole language of communication for transactions with 64 countries; German is recommended as a co-language for 25 countries, and Spanish for 17. These data suggest that English is a global lingua franca for players in the knowledge economy, and English, French, German, and Spanish are European linguae francae. Given that trade involving Japan, the United States, and Europe accounted for 50% of world GDP in 2000, the special status of these languages appears to be justified from a purely macro economic perspective.

The processes of neoliberalism and their globalized effects account for the movement of skilled labor to countries whose state or national language is English, or to companies who use English as the primary language of their activities. European mergers and acquisitions exceeded $1 trillion during 2005. The United States alone accounted for another $1.16 trillion in the value of mergers and acquisitions in 2005, followed by the United Kingdom ($305 billion). Many of these mergers involved technology companies. Because these new mega-companies have no obligation to retain their headquarters in the "home" countries, they increasingly move to countries with the most favorable corporate taxation regimes. In 2005, the most competitive countries with regard to taxation were Finland, the United States, Sweden, Denmark, Taiwan, Singapore, Iceland, Switzerland, Norway, and Australia (Williams, 2010, p. 30).

Only the countries that invest massively in education and research can appropriate the foreign technologies necessary to catch up with the rich countries. The United Nations Conference on Trade and Development (UNCTAD) claims that the poorer countries are the origin of only 8.4% of the spending on research and development (R&D) in the world, with 97% of this being in Asia (cited in Williams, 2010, p. 33). Therefore, foreign companies are not likely to locate in these countries, but rather will locate their head offices with high-paying jobs in the rich industrialized countries. Clearly, English is the dominant language in technology, and these countries have English either as the national language or a language spoken by high percentages of the relevant workforce. The trifecta of favorable corporate tax policies, a highly educated workforce, and one that speaks English helps perpetuate and increase disparities between poor and rich countries by attracting corporations beholden to shareholders' interests.

With outsourcing and offshoring, multinational corporations target certain regions of the world to create production facilities in order to market and sell products where they are produced. US facilities abroad produce $2.2 trillion a year for sales abroad and include factories and production facilities in many developing countries in Asia and Latin America. However, the outsourcing of New Economy activities requires a highly skilled and educated labor market, and with wages lower than those in the "home" country. Thus, India's technology industry employs 800,000, of which 300,000 (38%) work in Indian call centers. Indeed, a study by Deloitte in 2003 predicted that by 2010 as many as 25% of workers in the technology sector of the wealthiest countries would be de-localized into the emerging markets, with the zone of de-localization to include India, South Africa, Malaysia, Australia, and China, with India remaining the central point.

National governments in poor countries have had to choose between supporting fair wages, worker rights, environmental protection, and appropriate taxation policies on foreign investment, or the demands of the multinational corporations and banks (often referred to as conditionality), which oppose all of the preceding in order to ensure the greatest possible returns on investment. Citizens in these countries typically have no voice or vote in industrial policy (nor, in fact, do most citizens in more developed countries). Also, many of the jobs created in developing countries are temporary and without benefits, while fluctuations in global consumer consumption and currency exchange rates mean that local economic stability and growth is uncertain, as profits are repatriated to the rich countries.

CONCLUSION: LANGUAGE RIGHTS AND LANGUAGE POLICY

Brutt-Griffler accurately notes (2005, p. 31) that "*languages* do not have either power or rights, their speakers do. Languages can serve or hinder the purposes of their speakers, but on their own they are not social agents." In the neoliberal version of globalization, then, where does power reside? Who has agency? Who decides which language has value? Who has rights? The widely held tenets of contemporary neoliberalism offer answers to these questions:

- Corporations have more "rights" and protections, and certainly more power than individual human beings;
- Corporations have the "right" to hire any workers they please, anywhere in the world, at any wage, with few benefits and no job security;
- Individuals are on their own, each a disposable worker in a monetized, commodified system in which the only true right that remains, one that is virtually never questioned or opposed by the corporate media or economists, is the right to private property and the right to protect it at any cost;
- The right of private property and private ownership of national resources is claimed by the leaders of capitalist governments to be a necessary condition for "democracy" throughout the world.

As Harvey (2005, p. 176) puts it, "Neoliberal concern for the individual trumps any social democratic concern for equality, democracy, and social solidarities." A relatively few "world" languages serve the economic interests of large transnational corporations and banks, even though the percentage of the world's workforce that benefits is disproportionately skewed toward the most highly educated people from the richest countries, and especially multinational corporations themselves. Even in Europe, only about 4.5 million European citizens (about 1.4% of the total population) with tertiary-level qualifications are mobile across state boundaries within Europe (Williams, 2010, p. 50). The massive inequalities in global wealth occur not because of insufficient learning of English or other colonial languages, but rather because many of the poorest countries play a particular and narrow role in the global system, which is to provide cheap labor and natural resources to richer countries to be used in the manufacture of finished goods, with rich countries placing protectionist barriers on the exports by poorer countries of locally manufactured products, such as textiles and agricultural products.

This system has the effect of retarding local economic development that would require the use of local resources, including local/regional languages (Romaine, 2015). The belief that expanding access to English will help poor people escape poverty does not reflect reality on the ground. Even in poor countries, small numbers of socially and economically advantaged citizens benefit from neoliberal policies, because they have access to high-quality education (for example, in India and South Africa, as discussed in Ricento, 2010) and political power. "Free market" capitalism for the poor countries and corporate socialism for the rich countries means that language policies based on regimes of language rights will not succeed in reducing economic and social inequality. Groups who already speak dominant languages and have privileged access to education and cultural capital do not need more rights, and those who speak marginalized languages and lack access to high-quality education and cultural capital will not benefit by the granting of such rights.

I have suggested that the preference for English as a global lingua franca, especially over the past half-century, is conditioned by processes of economic globalization and expansion of the digitalized knowledge economy that disproportionately benefit some workers in some economic sectors and geographical regions, but mostly benefit the corporations that employ those workers. At this point in history, knowledge of certain varieties of English, coupled with particular skill sets obtainable only through high levels of education that are not universally accessible, is likely to enhance the social mobility of some individuals. States that provide affordable access to appropriate and high-quality English-language education, and which have highly educated workers with skills in demand in the knowledge economy, are in the game; states lacking in both will continue to lag far behind. But English is merely the language of the moment, not the inherent "hegemon," not the de facto oppressor, and most certainly *not* the ticket to social or economic mobility that it is claimed to be, either overtly or implicitly, by supporters and apologists for the current world neoliberal economic order.

ACKNOWLEDGMENT

Versions of some portions of the material presented in this chapter were previously published in Ricento, Thomas (2012), Political Economy and English as a "Global" Language, *Critical Multilingualism Studies* 1, 30–52; and in Ricento, Thomas (Ed.) (2015), *Language Policy and Political Economy: English in a Global Context*, Oxford: Oxford University Press.

REFERENCES

Ammon, U. (1995). To what extent is German an international language? In P. Stevenson (Ed.), *The German language and the real world* (pp. 25–54). Oxford: Clarendon.

Ammon, U. (2010). World languages: Trends and futures. In N. Coupland (Ed.), *The handbook of language and globalization* (pp. 101–122). West Sussex, UK: Wiley-Blackwell.

Arcand, J., & Grin, F. (2013). Language in economic development: Is English special and is linguistic fragmentation bad? In E. Erling & P. Seargeant (Eds.), *English and development: Policy, pedagogy and globalization* (pp. 243–266). Bristol, UK: Multilingual Matters.

Azam, M., & Prakish, N. (2010). The returns to English-language skills in India. Bonn: Institute for the Study of Labor. Discussion Paper No. 4802. Retrieved from http://ideas.repec.org/p/iza/izadps/dp4802.html

Blommaert, J. (2009). A market of accents. *Language Policy* 8, 243–259.

Brutt-Griffler, J. (2002). *World English: A study of its development.* Clevedon, UK: Multilingual Matters.

Brutt-Griffler, J. (2005). "Who do you think you are, where do you think you are?": Language policy and the political economy of English in South Africa. In C. Gnutzmann & F. Intemann (Eds.), *The globalization of English and the English language classroom* (pp. 27–39). Tübingen: Gunter Narr Verlag.

Casale, D., & Posel, D. (2011). English language proficiency and earnings in a developing country: The case of South Africa. *The Journal of Socio-Economics* 40, 385–393.

Castells, M. (2006). Globalisation and identity: A comparative perspective. *Journal of Contemporary Culture* 1, 56–66.

Crystal, D. (2003). *English as a global language.* Cambridge: Cambridge University Press.

De Swaan, A. (2001). *Words of the world: The global language system.* Cambridge: Polity.

Deloitte Research. (2003). *The cusp of a revolution: How offshore trading will transform the financial services industry.* London: Deloitte Research.

Edwards, J. (2003). Language and the future: Choices and constraints. In T. Tonkin & T. Reagan (Eds.), *Language and the twenty-first century* (pp. 35–45). Amsterdam: John Benjamins.

Edwards, J. (2010). *Minority languages and group identity: Cases and categories.* Amsterdam: John Benjamins.

Ethnologue: Languages of the world. (2005 [1984]). Dallas, TX: SIL International. .

Friedman, T. L. (2000). *The Lexus and the olive tree: Understanding globalization.* New York: Picador/Farrar, Straus and Giroux.

Gellner, E. (1968). The new idealism: Cause and meaning in the social sciences. In I. Lakatos & A. Musgrave (Eds.), *Problems in the philosophy of science* (pp. 377–432). Amsterdam: North-Holland.

Hamel, R. E. (2007). The dominance of English in the international scientific periodical literature and the future of language use in science. *AILA Review* 20, 53–71.

Harvey, D. (2005). *A brief history of neoliberalism.* Oxford: Oxford University Press.

Holborow, M. (2007). Language, ideology and neoliberalism. *Journal of Language and Politics* 6(1), 51–73.

Ku, H., & Zussman, A. (2010). Lingua franca: The role of English in international trade. *Journal of Economic Behavior and Organization* 75, 250–260.

Levinsohn, J. (2007). Globalization and the returns to speaking English in South Africa. In A. Harrison (Ed.), *Globalization and poverty* (pp. 629–646). Chicago: University of Chicago Press.

Macpherson, C. B. (2012 [1973]). *Democratic theory: Essays in retrieval.* Oxford: Oxford University Press.

Melitz, J. (2008). Language and foreign trade. *European Economic Review* 52, 667–699.

Phillipson, R. (1992). *Linguistic imperialism.* New York: Oxford University Press.

Phillipson, R. (2001). English for globalization or for the world's people? *International Review of Education* 47(3–4), 185–200.

Phillipson, R. (2003). *English-only Europe? Challenging language policy.* London: Routledge.

Rahman, T. (2002). *Language teaching and power in Pakistan*. Paper presented at the World Congress on Language Policies, Barcelona, Spain.

Rassool, N. (2013). The political economy of English language and development: English vs. national and local languages in developing countries. In E. Erling & P. Seargeant (Eds.), *English and development: Policy, pedagogy and globalization*, (pp. 45–67). Bristol, UK: Multilingual Matters.

Ricento, T. (2010). Language policy and globalization. In N. Coupland (Ed.), *The handbook of language and globalization* (pp. 123–141). Malden, MA: Wiley-Blackwell.

Ricento, T. (2012). Political economy and English as a "global" language. *Critical Multilingualism Studies* 1, 30–52.

Ricento, T. (2015). Political economy and English as a "global" language. In T. Ricento (Ed.), *Language policy and political economy: English in a global context* (pp. 27–47). New York: Oxford University Press.

Romaine, S. (2015). Linguistic diversity and global English: The pushmi-pullyu of language policy and political economy. In T. Ricento (Ed.), *Language policy and political economy: English in a global context* (pp. 252–275). New York: Oxford University Press.

Samuelson, B. L. (2013). Rwanda switches to English: Conflict, identity, and language- in-education policy. In J. W. Tollefson (Ed.), *Language policies in education: Critical issues* (pp. 211–232). New York: Routledge.

Sandel, M. (1982). *Liberalism and the limits of justice*. Cambridge: Cambridge University Press.

Saul, J. R. (1992). *Voltaire's bastards*. New York: Free Press.

Saul, J. R. (2005). *The collapse of globalism and the reinvention of the world*. Toronto: Penguin.

Snow, C. P. (1959). *The two cultures and the scientific revolution*. Cambridge: Cambridge University Press.

Stiglitz, J. E. (2007). *Making globalization work*. New York: W. W. Norton.

Van Parijs, P. (2000). The ground floor of the world: On the socio-economic consequences of linguistic globalization. *International Political Science Review* 21(2), 217–233.

Van Parijs, P. (2011). *Linguistic justice for Europe and for the world*. Oxford: Oxford University Press.

Wikipedia. (2015). Retrieved from https://en.wikipedia.org/wiki/List_of_territorial_entities_where_English_is_an_official_languageretrieved 04/25/2016

Williams, E. (2014). English in African politics of education: Capital or capital illusion? *International Journal of the Sociology of Language* 225, 131–145.

William, G. (2010). *The knowledge economy, language, and culture*. Clevedon, UK: Multilingual Matters.

CHAPTER 12

....

LANGUAGE RIGHTS AND LANGUAGE REPRESSION

....

STEPHEN MAY

THERE is a widespread belief that the recognition of language rights for linguistic minority groups and any associated endorsement of public bi/multilingualism is, by its very nature, a grave threat to social and political stability. Let me illustrate this with the following vignette. In the early 1980s, then US Senator from California, Samuel Hayakawa, proposed an English Language Amendment (ELA) to the Constitution of the United States that would make English, for the first time, an official rather than a de facto national language.[1] In his initiating speech, the senator gave the following reasons for his ELA (see Marshall, 1986, p. 23; emphasis added):

- a common language can unify; *separate languages can fracture and fragment a society*
- learning English is the major task of each immigrant
- only by learning English can an immigrant fully "participate in our democracy."

Hayakawa's proposal failed, but it spawned what has since come to be known as the *English Only* movement, at least in its contemporary form (similar attempts to make English the official language of the United States have been made for well over a century; for useful overviews, see May, 2014; Wiley, 2014). As Hayakawa's ELA proposal highlights, a key trope of the English Only movement is that political fragmentation necessarily ensues when separate languages are recognized and/or promoted in the public realm (via, e.g., bilingual education or voting provision). Such concerns become even more apocalyptic when they are linked specifically to wider ethnic conflict, separatism, and/or civil strife across the globe. Hayakawa makes exactly these associations in the following example:

> For the first time in our history, [the United States] is faced with the possibility of the kind of linguistic division that has torn apart Canada in recent years; that has been a major feature of the unhappy history of Belgium, split into speakers of French and Flemish; that is at this very moment a bloody division between the Sinhalese and Tamil populations of Sri Lanka. (cited in Nunberg, 1992, p. 492)

Likewise, Gary Imhoff, another early and vociferous advocate of the US English Only movement, asserts unequivocally, "language diversity has been a major cause of [international] conflict.... Any honest student of the sociology of language should admit that multilingual societies have been less united and internally peaceful than single-language societies" (1987, p. 40).

This is but one example of the by now almost de rigueur dismissal of minority language recognition and public bi/multilingualism as politically destabilizing. How have such perceptions become so deeply entrenched? In this chapter, I argue that there are three main sources: the negative ascription of ethnicity in both political and academic discourse; the construction of the ideal nation-state as ethnically and linguistically homogeneous, itself the product of the nationalism of the last few centuries; and the reinforcement of both via notions of common (undifferentiated) national citizenship.

I will first chart the trajectories of these three interlinked positions, outlining how they have contributed directly to language repression of minorities. As a consequence, minorities have been consistently excluded from, or at least relatively disadvantaged within, the public realm of modern nation-states. Ironically, this has led to ongoing and increasing political unrest, rather than its amelioration. I will thus conclude that a more pluralistic recognition of language rights is, in fact, the best means of achieving social and political stability, along with wider civic (and linguistic) participation, in modern nation-states.

COMMON IDENTITIES, UNIVERSAL RIGHTS, AND THE QUEST FOR POLITICAL STABILITY

In this section, I examine, first, the deep distrust of ethnicity and ethnic identity; second, the preoccupation with the linguistically homogeneous nation-state model; and, third, the promotion of individual citizenship. I argue that this triumvirate underpins the widespread disavowal of language rights for minorities in the modern era.

Denouncing Ethnicity

A key reason why language rights for linguistic minorities are viewed so skeptically is because of their often direct association with ethnicity. In this view, the recognition of minority languages is an inevitable prelude to ethnic conflict and separatism, a condition to be avoided at all costs. After all, fueled by lurid media reports of the immolation attending yet another "ethnic conflict," the wider public locate in ethnicity the principal cause of many of today's social and political problems. Places such as Rwanda, Sri Lanka, Northern Ireland, and the former Yugoslavia—to name just a few examples—suggest starkly the destructive and unproductive nature of ethnicity and ethnic mobilization. Indeed, since the end of the Cold War, the most common sources of political violence in the world have been ascribed to these so-called ethnic conflicts (Gurr, 1993, 2000).

Such developments are closely related, in turn, to the proliferation of a variety of ethnonational movements—movements based on ethnic affiliation, which aim to establish a national state of their own and which often, but do not always, resort to violence to achieve their ends (Fenton & May, 2002). The separatist ETA movement (Euzkadi 'ta Askatasuna) in the Basque Country, the IRA Republican movement in Northern Ireland, and the Tamil Tigers in Sri Lanka (see later discussion) can all be cited as examples here. In addition, there are minority groups who, while not necessarily wanting to establish a state of their own, want greater recognition, representation, and autonomy within existing nation-states. Most notable here, perhaps, are indigenous groups such as the Māori of Aotearoa/New Zealand, the Aboriginal peoples of Australia, Sámi (Lapps), Inuit (Eskimos), and Native Americans.

While these various developments present us with qualitatively different examples of ethnic minority affiliation and mobilization, and are often simply misrepresented reductively as ethnic conflicts,[2] they are nonetheless categorically held to be negative phenomena. And, given that language is often a key rallying cry in these political disputes, any related language rights' claims are also impugned as unnecessarily conflictual. This is so even when such groups may be seen to have legitimate and supportable claims.

The widespread dismissal of the legitimacy and value of ethnicity as a form of social and political identification lies in its historical juxtaposition with national identity and the modern nation-state from which the latter springs. I will deal with the question of national identity, along with its origins in the politics of nationalism, more fully in the next section. Suffice it to say at this point that, in this view, the nation-state is something to which we can legitimately give our allegiance, but ethnic groups are not. Nation-states are embracing and cohesive, whereas ethnic groups are exclusive and divisive. Nation-states represent modernity, while ethnic groups represent a harping, misinformed, and misguided nostalgia. Or so the story goes. But it is a story long told and with an impressive academic pedigree.

In the nineteenth century, for example, the British liberal John Stuart Mill argued in *Representative Government*: "Free institutions are next to impossible in a country made up of different nationalities. Among a people without fellow-feeling, *especially if they read and speak different languages*, the united public opinion, necessary to the working of representative government, cannot exist" (1972 [1861], p. 361; emphasis added). Mill proceeds to elaborate on why he deems alternative ethnic affiliations (and their languages) to be so counterproductive to the political organization of the nation-state. In so doing, he invokes a clear cultural hierarchy between different groups, arguing that "smaller nationalities"—the equivalent of "ethnic minorities" in modern political parlance—should be assimilated into the nation-state *via* its "national" culture and language, that is, the culture and language of the dominant (national) group:

> Experience proves it is possible for one nationality to merge and be absorbed in another: and when it was originally an inferior and more backward portion of the human race the absorption is greatly to its advantage. Nobody can suppose that it is not beneficial to a Breton, or a Basque of French Navarre, to be brought into the current of the ideas and feelings of a highly civilised and cultivated people—to be a member of the French nationality, admitted on equal terms to all the privileges of French citizenship . . . *than to sulk on his own rocks, the half-savage relic of past times*, revolving in his own mental orbit, without participation or interest in the general movement of the world. (1972, p. 395; emphasis added)

Likewise, the French nationalist and historian Michelet—a near contemporary of Mill—was to conclude of the French Revolution, often credited as the harbinger of nationalism (see later discussion): "this sacrifice of the diverse interior nationalities to the great nationality which comprises them undoubtedly strengthened the latter.... It was at the moment when France *suppressed* within herself the divergent French countries that she proclaimed her high and original revelations" (1946 [1846], p. 286; emphasis added). In this view then, a homogeneous national identity—reflected in the culture and language of the dominant "national" group—should supersede and subsume alternative ethnic and/or national identities and their associated cultures and languages.

It was not only liberal commentators who endorsed this position—so, too, and perhaps surprisingly, did the likes of the communist luminaries Marx and Engels. While championing the rights of "the working men" who "have no country," for example, Marx and Engels also endorsed the nationalist causes of "historic" nations where these were seen to facilitate and expedite the proletarian revolution (Marx & Engels, 1976a). However, any claims from "non-historic" nations or "historyless peoples" (*geschichtslosen Völker*)—minority ethnic groups, in effect—were simply ignored. In discussing the position of ethnic minorities, Engels [1849] could observe:

> There is no country in Europe which does not have in some corner or other one or several *fragments* of peoples, the *remnants* of a former population that was suppressed

and held in bondage by the [nation-state], which later became the main vehicle for historical development. These *relics* of nations [ethnic groups], mercilessly trampled down by the passage of history, as Hegel expressed it, *this ethnic trash* always become fanatical standard bearers of counter-revolution and remain so until their complete extirpation or loss of their national character, just as their whole existence in general is itself a protest against a great historical revolution. Such in Scotland are the Gaels. . . . Such in France are the Bretons. . . . Such in Spain are the Basques. . . . (Marx & Engels, 1976b, pp. 234–235; emphasis added)

As with their liberal contemporaries, "Marx and Engels were, to put it mildly, impatient with and intolerant of ethnic minorities" (Nimni, 1995, p. 68; see also Guibernau, 1996). What we see here, in effect, is the construction of ethnic minority cultures and practices, including the speaking of a minority language, as regressive and pre-modern. In contrast, *national* cultures and languages are associated specifically with modernity, and with the related presumptions of social and political inclusion (Bauman & Briggs, 2003). And yet, what gets consistently overlooked in this process of ethnic/national dichotomization is that these so-called national cultures and languages are invariably those of the dominant ethnic group in any given society. In other words, so-called national cultures and languages, which are themselves the specific product of the nationalism of the last few centuries, are simply elided with those of the dominant ethnic group (May, 2012), as the next section makes clear.

Nationalism, Nation-State Congruence, and the Politics of Homogeneity

The widespread negative ascription of minority ethnicities and their associated languages can only be fully explained when we also examine the central role of nationalism, and the nation-state system to which it gave rise. The era of nationalism is a recent one, emerging from the specific historical and social developments of modernization and its concomitants—industrialization, political democracy, and universal literacy—in eighteenth- and nineteenth-century Europe.[3] While there is ongoing debate about its specific origins, many commentators regard the French Revolution of 1789 as a key catalyst of this new political nationalism (see, e.g. Alter, 1989; Hobsbawm, 1990; Kedourie, 1960). Following from this, France is also widely regarded as the archetypal modern nation-state.

I am not able to rehearse here at any length how the modern French state emerged (see May, 2012, 2016, for further discussion), except to say that the establishment of post-revolutionary France by the Jacobin Revolutionaries was predicated on the relentless pursuit of an ethnically exclusive and culturally and linguistically homogeneous nation-state—a realm from which minority languages and cultures were effectively banished. The two key state institutions that effected this were the armed forces and, particularly from the nineteenth century onward, education.

The result was the transformation of the area we now know as France from a resolutely multilingual one to an almost exclusively monolingual one in its key public language domains. At the time of the French Revolution, for example, at least eight major languages were spoken, and even as late as the mid-nineteenth century only 25% of the population spoke French, including 50% of children (Weber, 1976). Now, French predominates as the national language in all language domains and less than 2% of the population now speaks languages other than French (Extra & Gorter, 2001, 2008).

The central principle underpinning this preoccupation with establishing national—and, by extension, linguistic—homogeneity, as illustrated by France, is *nation-state congruence*. Nation-state congruence holds that the boundaries of political and national identity should coincide. The view here is that people who are citizens of a particular state should also, ideally, be members of the same national collectivity. And if they are to be the same nationality, they should also, by extension, speak the same "national" language. The end result of modern nationalism, in this view, is the establishment of the ethnically exclusive and culturally homogeneous nation-state, represented ideally by one national language to which all must subscribe. As highlighted earlier, however, what is often overlooked in this process is that this "common" national language is almost invariably that of the dominant ethnic group. The effect of this is to banish minority ethnicities and their languages to the social and political margins. As the French sociologist and anthropologist Pierre Bourdieu observes of this process in relation to modern France, "measured de facto against the single standard of the 'common' language, they are found wanting and cast into the outer darkness of *regionalisms*" (1991, p. 54; emphasis in original). More broadly, Nancy Dorian highlights the deleterious consequences for all minorities: "it is the concept of the nation-state coupled with its official standard language . . . that has in modern times posed the keenest threat to both the identities and the languages of small [minority] communities" (1998, p. 18). Florian Coulmas observes, even more succinctly, that "the nation-state as it has evolved since the French Revolution is the natural enemy of minorities" (1998, p. 67).

The ongoing ascendancy of nation-state congruence is significant for issues of language rights and repression because, of course, the idea of a homogeneous nation-state is actually a social and political fiction. As Walker Connor (1993) highlights, for example, in 40% of all states there are at least five or more statistically and/or politically significant ethnic groups, while in nearly one-third of all states (31%) the largest national group is not even the majority. These groups comprise national and indigenous minorities in countries across the world. Examples include, among others, the Irish, Scots and Welsh in Britain; Hawaiians and Native Americans in the United States; Québécois and Aboriginal peoples/Native Canadians in Canada; Kurds in Turkey, Iran, Iraq, and Syria (see further discussion later in the chapter); Tibetans in China; Sámi in "Sápmi" (which includes areas of Russia, Finland, Norway, and Sweden); Ainu in Japan; and Māori in Aotearoa/New Zealand.

As a result of the increasing prominence of "superdiversity" (Vertovec, 2007), denoting the rapid expansion of migration and transmigration in this late modern age, these contexts also invariably include a wide variety of immigrant groups. The result is that most states are multinational (comprising a number of national minorities) and/or polyethnic (comprising a range of immigrant groups). Indeed, most countries in the world have been historically, and remain today, a combination of the two (Kymlicka, 1995, 2001, 2007). We can thus surely agree with Anthias and Yuval-Davis that "[t]oday there is virtually nowhere in the world in which . . . a pure nation-state exists, if it ever did, and therefore there are always settled residents (and usually citizens as well) who are not members of the dominant national collectivity in the society" (1992, p. 21). As they conclude, the fact that the notion of nation-state congruence remains so powerful is an "expression of the naturalising effect of the hegemony of one collectivity and its access to ideological apparatuses of both state and civil society. This constructs minorities into assumed deviants from the 'normal,' and excludes them from important power resources" (1992, pp. 21–22).

Liberal Political Theory, Individual Citizenship, and Human Rights

The third part of the triumvirate that leads to the claims of ethnic and linguistic minorities being viewed as so politically destabilizing is the dominance of liberal political theories of citizenship and their allied support in international law, particularly after World War II. Liberal conceptions of citizenship, exemplified most clearly in the work of John Rawls (1971), studiously avoid the recognition of ethnic, cultural, and/or linguistic differences as a basis for rights' claims. In other words, citizenship is defined by what we hold in common, not what differentiates us—much like the commonalities of national identity emphasized by nationalism. In the process, all citizens come to be treated as individuals dissociated from their ethnic, cultural, religious, and/or linguistic backgrounds. Citizenship rights are thus constructed as individual and universal rather than collective and particularistic, with the latter associated (negatively) with ethnic rights and/or the politics of multiculturalism (Barry, 2001; Schlesinger, 1992). As such, formal differentiation within the nation-state on the grounds of (ethnic) group association is rejected as inimical to the individualistic and meritocratic tenets of liberal democracy.

Where countenanced at all, alternative ethnic affiliations in this view should be restricted solely to the private domain, since the formal recognition of collective (ethnic) identity is viewed as undermining personal and political autonomy, and fostering social and political fragmentation. As the political philosopher Will Kymlicka observes, "the near-universal response by liberals has been one of active hostility to minority rights . . . schemes which single out minority cultures for special measures . . . appear irremediably unjust, a disguise for creating or maintaining ... ethnic privilege" (1989, p. 4). Any deviation from the strict principles of universal political citizenship and individual rights is seen as the first step down the road to apartheid.

Developments in international law, especially post–World War II, reinforce this skepticism toward any differentiated approach to citizenship rights. The cultural protection of minorities was actually a regular feature prior to World War II. In the nineteenth century, treaties were often employed for the protection of minority groups, initially on the basis of religion and later on the grounds of nationality (Duchêne, 2008; Oestreich, 1999; Thornberry, 1991a).[4] These practices culminated in the general organization of the League of Nations, established in the wake of World War I. The League endorsed a range of bilateral treaties that were overseen by the League's Permanent Court of International Justice (PCIJ) and which subsequently became known collectively as the Minority Protection scheme (MPS). The principal focus of the MPS was on the protection of so-called displaced minorities who had ended up on the wrong side of newly constituted borders as the result of the dissolution of the Russian, Ottoman, and Habsburg empires, and the reorganization of European state boundaries after World War I (Kymlicka, 2007; Packer, 1999).

This approach was to change significantly, however, with the advent of World War II and the associated excesses and abuses of the MPS by the Nazi regime, whereby Hitler used a supposed concern for the rights of German minorities elsewhere in Europe as a catalyst for the war. As a result, there was a postwar shift in emphasis to establishing generic human rights, irrespective of group membership. These developments were exemplified by the establishment of the United Nations, along with the implementation of its key legal instrument the (1948) Universal Declaration of Human Rights (UDHR). In the development of the UDHR, for example, it was assumed that no additional rights needed to be attributed to minorities. As Claude observed of this, "The doctrine of human rights has been put forward as a substitute for the concept of minority rights, with the strong implication that minorities whose members enjoy individual equality of treatment cannot legitimately demand facilities for the maintenance of their ethnic particularism" (1955, p. 211).

Consequently, all references to the rights of minorities were deleted from the final version of the UDHR.[5] Relatedly, a widespread conviction began to emerge among liberals that minority group rights were somehow incompatible with national and international peace and stability. Language rights were especially prone here to ongoing associations with the (unnecessary) promotion of ethnic particularism at the perceived expense of wider social and political cohesion. As the prominent sociolinguist Joshua Fishman ably summarizes it,

> Unlike "human rights" which strike Western and Westernized intellectuals as fostering wider participation in general societal benefits and interactions, "language rights" still are widely interpreted as "regressive" since they would, most probably, prolong the existence of ethnolinguistic differences. The value of such differences

and the right to value such differences have not yet generally been recognised by the modern Western sense of justice. . . . (1991, p. 72)

Some seventy years later, this view still holds wide sway (May, 2011, 2012). And yet, what is also increasingly apparent over this period is a clear pattern highlighting how this combination of political theory and international law has consistently disadvantaged minorities, who have been left subject to the majoritarian decision-making processes of nation-states. As Kymlicka observes, the result has been to render minorities "vulnerable to significant injustice at the hands of the majority, and to exacerbate ethnocultural conflict" (1995, p. 5), trends which the UN and other supranational bodies such as the European Union have only more recently begun to address (see also Kymlicka, 2007). Indeed, if this is true of Western liberal democracies, it is even more apparent in authoritarian contexts worldwide. In such contexts, issues of *securitization*, or the need to ensure the ongoing security of political regimes, often result in the active repression of minorities who are deemed to be a threat to the state (Kymlicka & Opalski, 2001; see also C. Charalambous, P. Charalambous, Khan, & Rampton, Chapter 31 in this volume).

I will provide a number of illustrative examples of these repressive policies toward minorities, and their languages, in the next section. Before doing so, however, let me foreground the key problem with this threefold combination of the denunciation of ethnicity, the valorization of nationalism and nation-state congruence, and notions of common citizenship and universal human rights. All emphasize individualism and universality as the basis for social and political inclusion and stability, and yet each actually promotes exclusion, division, and social and political disharmony, conflict, and instability. In combination, the deleterious effects are cumulative, as will be made clear in the next section.

RETHINKING LANGUAGE RIGHTS

In this section, I will illustrate how the active repression of minority languages often fosters ethnic conflict and entrenches political instability, rather than the reverse. I will then turn to examples where the recognition and use of language rights provide the basis for promoting, rather than undermining, social and political stability and ameliorating ethnic tension. In so doing, the reader may also want to revisit the veracity of the assertions by Hayakawa and Imhoff highlighted in the introduction to the chapter, since their apocalyptic statements are flatly contradicted by these examples.

Language Repression, Ethnic Conflict, and Political Instability

The political scientist David Laitin (2000) argues that questions of language repression and language rights are seldom a sufficient condition or cause for interethnic conflict. However, when these are coupled with the denial of political and/or economic rights, ethnic conflict can, and often does, ensue. Take Sri Lanka, for example. The conflict in Sri Lanka between the Sinhalese majority (comprising 75% of the population) and the Lankan Tamils (who comprise 12.5% of the remaining Tamil-speaking population) was most evident in the long-standing civil war waged by the Tamil separatist group, the Liberation Tigers of Tamil Eelam (LTTE), from 1976 until their defeat in 2009. The LTTE, based in the North and East of Sri Lanka, fought for a separate political state, but the conflict itself had its origins in the earlier denial of language and associated economic and political rights for Tamil Sri Lankans. In 1956, eight years after independence from the British colonial regime, Sinhala was made the sole official language, replacing English, in Sri Lanka. Up until that time, the Tamil minority had been favored over the Sinhalese as part of the British colonial regime's divide-and-rule policy. Tamils were until then disproportionately represented in the higher echelons of (English-medium) education and, subsequently, in the judiciary and civil service (de Silva, 1981). The 1956 Sinhala-Only language law quickly foreclosed these options for the Tamils and, when combined with their limited access to land, provided the basis for ongoing social and political discontent over the next fifty years, as they became increasingly marginalized in Sri Lankan society.[6]

The LTTE civil war can thus be traced back directly to issues of language, and wider political and economic, exclusion (Fishman & Solano, 1989; Little, 1994). Following the final defeat of the LTTE in 2009, the Sri Lankan government established the Lessons Learned and Reconciliation Commission in 2011. As a result of the Commission's recommendations, Sri Lanka is currently moving toward a formal trilingual state in Sinhala, Tamil, and English, with a particular focus on fostering greater bi/multilingualism in key public-language domains (Herath, 2015).

Another example of language repression fostering ongoing political unrest and armed conflict can be found in the long-standing repression of the Kurdish language within Turkey. Kurdish, an Indo-European language, is spoken predominantly in the territory of Kurdistan, an area with long historical associations for the Kurds that encompasses parts of present-day Turkey, Iran, Iraq, and Syria. There are approximately 35 million Kurdish speakers in total, and it is currently estimated that, of the 15 million Kurds within Turkey, approximately 4 million speak Kurdish as a first language (Skutnabb-Kangas, 2000).

The active repression and proscription of Kurdish by the Turkish state have been pursued for nearly a century and form part of a wider denial/rejection of Kurdish nationalist claims to be a distinct people, with attendant rights to secession, or at least greater autonomy within Turkey. This proscriptive language policy was first enshrined in Atatürk's Constitution of 1923 and was reiterated in the Turkish Constitution of 1982 (see Skutnabb-Kangas & Bucak, 1995). In the early 1990s there appeared to be a relaxation of these long-standing proscriptive laws, but by the late 1990s they had once again been reinforced. This move was presaged in March 1997 when secret Turkish interior ministry documents were made public which stated that "administrative and legal measures should be taken against those attempting to propagate the Kurdish language" (*The Guardian*, March 29, 1997). Criminal proceedings were subsequently implemented in 1998 against the Foundation for Kurdish Culture and Research—the first nongovernmental organization (NGO) in Turkey with an overtly Kurdish identity—for its promotion of Kurdish language courses. At the time, the Turkish National Security Council (NSC) summed up the key motivation behind this action. In its view, the ongoing use of the Kurdish language constituted a danger to "the existence and independence of the state, the unity and indivisibility of the nation, and the well-being and security of the community" (Skutnabb-Kangas, personal communication).

Over the last decade, there has been some movement toward a more open approach to Kurdish in Turkey, although these developments remain both limited and uneven. In the media, Turkey allowed private television channels to air programs in the Kurdish language for the first time from March 2006. However, clear limits were also imposed: broadcasting in Kurdish could only be for a maximum of 45 minutes a day or four hours a week and could not include any educational programs that taught the Kurdish language. These restrictions were only relaxed in 2009, with the advent of a new 24-hour Kurdish television station, as part of the state-run Turkish Radio and Television Corporation (TRT). Education for Kurds in Turkey, however, remains highly circumscribed. Kurdish-medium schools, for example, remain actively proscribed by the Turkish state, and Kurdish children do not even have the right to study Kurdish as a subject in school (Skutnabb-Kangas & Fernandes, 2008).

This ongoing marginalization of Kurdish by the Turkish state, along with a wider positioning of Kurds as a threat to the state, has resulted in long-standing political resistance and armed conflict within Turkey. This has been led most prominently by the PKK (Partiye Karkerên Kurdistanê—Kurdish Workers Party), which formed in 1978 and began an insurgent campaign in 1984. Despite a recent ceasefire between the PKK and the Turkish state that lasted three years (2012–2015), the armed conflict between Kurds and the Turkish state remains ongoing.

Language Rights as a Basis for Political Stability

If language repression fosters political unrest and ethnic conflict, the recognition of language rights for minorities, while not a panacea, can actively mitigate/ameliorate such tensions. There are two broad approaches that can be adopted here. The first is the *territorial language principle*, which grants language rights that are limited to a particular territory in order to ensure the maintenance of a particular language in that area (see Williams, 2008, for a useful overview). The most prominent examples of this principle can be found in, among others, Belgium, Québec, Switzerland, Wales, Catalonia, and the Basque Country.

In Belgium, for example, there had been linguistic conflict between its two principal language groups—the French in Wallonia to the south and the Flemish in Flanders to the north—since the inception of the Belgian state in 1830. However, much of this had to do with the de facto supremacy of French and the related marginalizing of Flemish (a dialect of Dutch) throughout its history, despite the fact that Flemish speakers (at 60%) were a numerical majority. This was, in turn, the result of the early industrialization of Wallonia in the nineteenth century, centered on the coal and steel industries, which meant that French speakers dominated economically and French became associated almost solely with social and economic mobility.

The ongoing conflict that these economic and linguistic disparities invoked led eventually to the adoption of linguistic legislation in 1962–1963, which ensured equal linguistic status for Flemish speakers. This legislation divided the country into three administrative regions: Flanders and Wallonia, which are both subject to strict monolingualism (Dutch and French, respectively), and the capital, Brussels, which is officially bilingual. However, even in Brussels the French/Flemish linguistic infrastructure is quite separate, extending to the workplace as well as to the more common domains of administration and education. This means that throughout the whole country there are only monolingual educational institutions, while administration is also monolingual, even in multilingual regions.

The result is that individual bi/multilingualism among Belgians, particularly French speakers, is significantly less than one might expect. That said, the recognition of both French and Flemish language rights has clearly contributed significantly to Belgium's sociopolitical and economic stability by ensuring the maintenance of group language rights (Blommaert, 1996; Nelde, 1997). This stability has been undermined somewhat in the last decade, with growing political support for greater devolution and autonomy for Flanders and the rise of the far-right Flemish nationalist party, the Vlaams Belang (Mnookin & Verbeke, 2009). Such developments highlight that the recognition of language rights does not, in itself, ensure ongoing political stability. Nonetheless, while Belgian federalism remains an increasingly contested option, its dissolution still seems unlikely. As Mnookin and Verbeke (2009) argue, a compromise that allows greater autonomy for Flanders within a still-federal Belgium is a far more likely scenario than secession. This is also broadly in line with recent developments across the European Union for greater linguistic and related territorial autonomy at regional level, as evidenced in Wales, Catalonia, and the Basque Country, for example (see May, 2012; Trenz, 2007).

The second broad approach to the granting of minority language rights is termed the *personality language principle*, which attaches language rights to individuals, irrespective of their geographical position. This provides greater flexibility than the territorial language principle in the apportionment of group-based language rights, although it also has its strictures. The most notable of these is the criterion *where numbers warrant—* that is, language rights may be granted only when there are deemed to be a sufficient number of particular language speakers to warrant active language protection and the related use of such languages in the public domain (May, 2011). Canada adopts the personality language principle, where numbers warrant, in relation to French speakers outside of Québec, via the (1982) Canadian Charter of Rights and Freedoms. A similar approach is adopted in Finland with respect to first-language Swedish speakers living there. Swedish speakers can use their language in the public domain in those local municipalities where there are a sufficient number of Swedish speakers (currently, at least 8%) for these municipalities to be deemed officially bilingual.

With over 200 language varieties spoken across thirty states and five Union territories, India provides perhaps the best example of this principle in operation. On the one hand, we have seen in India the long-standing promotion of English, and more recently Hindi, as the state's elite, pan-Indian, languages. On the other hand, there are eighteen languages recognized in India as *principal medium languages*, which, in addition to English and Hindi, include sixteen official state languages. The division of India's states along largely linguistic grounds means that, as a result, local linguistic communities have control over their public schools and other educational institutions. This, in turn, ensures that the primary language of the area is used as a medium of instruction in state schools (see Daswani, 2001; Pattanayak, 1990). Indeed, dominant regional language schools account for 88% of all elementary schools in India (Khubchandani, 2008). In addition, the Constitution of India (Article 350A) directs every state, and every local authority within that state, to provide adequate educational facilities for instruction in the first language of linguistic minorities, at least at the elementary school level. As a result, over eighty minority languages are employed as medium of instruction in elementary schools throughout India. More broadly, these language rights, and related educational provision, provide a key foundation for India's wider social and political stability, at least to date.

Conclusion: Language Rights and the Expansion of Democracy

To reiterate, the recognition of minority language rights on the basis of either the territorial or the personality language principle is not a political panacea and can also potentially be undone over time and in relation to evolving political circumstances. However, the recognition of language rights can and does support, rather than undermine, wider social and political stability in modern nation-states. In other words, nation-states can and should move beyond the historical preoccupation with linguistic homogeneity, arising from the politics of nationalism, in order to adopt a more plural and inclusive approach to minority groups. Continuing to ignore such demands, as we have seen, is only likely to escalate them, not least because minority groups are far less quiescent about the injustices attendant upon their long-standing cultural and linguistic marginalization as the price of civic inclusion in the (monolingual) nation-state model. Under these circumstances, as the academic jurist Fernand de Varennes, argues,

> any policy favouring a single language to the exclusion of all others can be extremely risky ... because it is then a factor promoting division rather than unification. Instead of integration, an ill-advised and inappropriate state language policy may have the opposite effect and cause a *levée de bouclier* [hue and cry]. (1996, p. 91)

More positively, if nation-states are reimagined in more plural and inclusive ways, there is potential for the recognition of not only greater political democracy but greater ethnocultural and ethnolinguistic democracy as well. Thus, far from undermining democratic principles—a common assumption among opponents of minority rights—the accommodation of cultural and linguistic group–based rights may well extend them. Indeed, my argument throughout this chapter has been that ethnic and national conflicts are most often precipitated when nation-states ignore demands for greater cultural and linguistic democracy, not—as is commonly assumed—when they accommodate them (see also Kymlicka, 2001, 2007; Parekh, 2000). The implications of this position are most evident in relation to the nation-state system. However, a more pluralistic approach to language rights is also consonant with the increasing salience of linguistic diversity in our globalized, late modern world. This requires us, in turn, to begin to rethink social and political organization in more overtly bi/multilingual terms at supranational and sub-state levels as well.

Notes

1. While often assumed to be, English has never been an official language of the United States. This can be traced back to the country's colonial foundations. Although both the Declaration of Independence and the Constitution were written in English, neither specified an official language for the United States. Underpinning this decision of the "Founding Fathers" was the centrality of the principle of individual choice. This was exemplified in the notion of free speech, and the related adoption of a laissez-faire language policy, deriving from the British model, which specifically eschewed the legislative formality of granting official status to English (see Marshall, 1986; Nunberg, 1992).
2. There are two points at issue here. Just because so-called ethnic groups are involved, does not mean that the conflict is driven by ethnicity (Fenton, 2003). Second, such conflicts are

not exclusive to ethnic groups or to postcolonial and/or "less stable" states with which they are usually associated. As Andreas Wimmer observes, "[what] we nowadays call ethnic cleansing or ethnocide . . . have in fact been constants of the European history of nation-building and state formation" (2004, p. 44; see the ensuing discussion of the nation-state system).

3. Blaut (1993) and Mignolo (2000, 2003) argue that the colonialism of the sixteenth and seventeenth centuries, particularly in the Americas, may also have been a key precursor to the rise of nationalism.

4. Indeed, examples of the protection of religious minorities can be traced as far back as the early Middle Ages, with a number of prominent treaties that included specific religious protection also evident in the seventeenth and eighteenth centuries (Oestreich, 1999). For a useful historical overview of minority protections, and the role and influence of the League of Nations (see later discussion), see Duchêne (2008, pp. 47–54).

5. Article 2 of the Declaration states, "Everyone is entitled to all the rights and freedoms set forth in this Declaration, without distinction of any kind, such as race [sic], colour, sex, religion, political or other opinion, national or social origin, property, birth or other status." Consequently, minorities, as such, do not enjoy rights in the Declaration. Various attempts at including a recognition of minorities in the text were strongly opposed at the draft stages, the consensus being that "the best solution of the problems of minorities was to encourage respect for human rights" (see Thornberry, 1991b, pp. 11–12).

6. While Tamil was subsequently recognized as a *regional language* in 1957 and was made an *official language* in 1987, the wider disparities between Sinhala and Tamil, and the related polarization of the two ethnic groups, remained largely unchanged. For example, by 2005, Tamils comprised only 8% of civil servants—the product of their wider social and economic exclusion over the last fifty years (Herath, 2015).

References

Alter, P. (1989). *Nationalism*. London: Edward Arnold.

Anthias, F., & Yuval-Davis, N. (1992). *Racialized boundaries: Race, nation, gender, colour and class and the anti-racist struggle*. London: Routledge.

Barry, B. (2001). *Culture and equality: An egalitarian critique of multiculturalism*. Cambridge, MA: Harvard University Press.

Bauman, R., & Briggs, C. (2003). *Voices of modernity: Language ideologies and the politics of inequality*. Cambridge: Cambridge University Press.

Blaut, J. (1993). *The colonizer's model of the world: Geographical diffusionism and Eurocentric history*. New York: Guildord Press.

Blommaert, J. (1996). Language and nationalism: Comparing Flanders and Tanzania. *Nations and Nationalism* 2, 235–256.

Bourdieu, P. (1991). *Language and symbolic power*. Cambridge: Polity Press.

Claude, I. (1955). *National minorities: An international problem*. Cambridge, MA: Harvard University Press.

Connor, W. (1993). Beyond reason: The nature of the ethnonational bond. *Ethnic and Racial Studies* 16, 374–389.

Coulmas, F. (1998). Language rights: Interests of states, language groups and the individual. *Language Sciences* 20, 63–72.

Daswani, C. (Ed.) (2001). *Language education in multilingual India.* New Delhi: UNESCO.

de Silva, K. (1981). *A history of Sri Lanka.* London: C. Hurst.

de Varennes, F. (1996). *Language, minorities and human rights.* The Hague: Kluwer Law International.

Dorian, N. (1998). Western language ideologies and small-language prospects. In L. Grenoble & L. Whaley (Eds.), *Endangered languages: Language loss and community response* (pp. 3–21). Cambridge: Cambridge University Press.

Duchêne, A. (2008). *Ideologies across nations: The construction of linguistic minorities at the United Nations.* Berlin: Mouton de Gruyter.

Extra, G., & Gorter, D. (Eds.) (2001). *The other languages of Europe: Demographic, sociolinguistic and educational perspectives.* Clevedon, UK: Multilingual Matters.

Extra, G., & Gorter, D. (Eds.) (2008). *Multilingual Europe: Facts and policies.* Berlin: Mouton de Gruyter.

Fenton, S. (2003). *Ethnicity.* Cambridge: Polity Press.

Fenton, S., & May, S. (Eds.) (2002). *Ethnonational identities.* Basingstoke, UK: Palgrave Macmillan.

Fishman, J. (1991). *Reversing language shift: Theoretical and empirical foundations of assistance to threatened languages.* Clevedon, UK: Multilingual Matters.

Fishman, J., & Solano, F. (1989). Cross polity perspective on the importance of linguistic heterogeneity as a "contributing factor" in civil strife. In J. Fishman (Ed.), *Language and ethnicity in minority sociolinguistic perspective* (pp. 605–626). Clevedon, UK: Multilingual Matters.

Guibernau, M. (1996). *Nationalisms: The nation-state and nationalism in the twentieth century.* Cambridge: Polity Press.

Gurr, T. (1993). *Minorities at risk: A global view of ethnopolitical conflicts.* Washington, DC: United States Institute of Peace Press.

Gurr, T. (2000). *People versus states: Minorities at risk in the new century.* Washington, DC: United States Institute of Peace.

Herath, S. (2015). Language policy, ethnic tensions and linguistic rights in post war Sri Lanka. *Language Policy* 14(3), 245–261.

Hobsbawm, E. (1990). *Nations and nationalism since 1780.* Cambridge: Cambridge University Press.

Imhoff, G. (1987). Partisans of language. *English Today* 3(3), 37–40.

Kedourie, E. (1960). *Nationalism.* London: Hutchinson.

Khubchandani, L. (2008). Language policy and education in the Indian subcontinent. In S. May & N. Hornberger (Eds.), *Encyclopedia of language and education*, 2nd edition, Vol. 1: *Language policy and political issues in education* (pp. 369–381). New York: Springer.

Kymlicka, W. (1989). *Liberalism, community and culture.* Oxford: Clarendon Press.

Kymlicka, W. (1995). *Multicultural citizenship: A liberal theory of minority rights.* Oxford: Clarendon Press.

Kymlicka, W. (2001). *Politics in the vernacular: Nationalism, multiculturalism, citizenship.* Oxford: Oxford University Press.

Kymlicka, W. (2007). *Multicultural odysseys: Navigating the new international politics of diversity.* Oxford: Oxford University Press.

Kymlicka, W., & Opalski, M. (Eds.). (2001). *Can liberalism be exported? Western political theory and ethnic relations in Eastern Europe.* Oxford: Oxford University Press.

Laitin, D. (2000). Language conflict and violence: The straw that strengthens the camel's back. *European Journal of Sociology* 4(1), 97–137.

Little, D. (1994). *Sri Lanka: The invention of enmity.* Washington, DC: United States Institute of Peace Press.

Marshall, D. (1986). The question of an official language: Language rights and the English Language Amendment. *International Journal of the Sociology of Language* 60, 7–75.

Marx, K., & Engels, F. (1976a). *Basic writings on politics and philosophy.* L. Feuer, Ed. Glasgow: Collins.

Marx, K., & Engels, F. (1976b). *Marx and Engels collected works.* London: Lawrence and Wishart.

May, S. (2011). Language rights: The "Cinderella" human right. *Journal of Human Rights* 10(3), 265–289.

May, S. (2012). *Language and minority rights: Ethnicity, nationalism and the politics of language.* 2nd edition. New York: Routledge.

May, S. (2014). Overcoming disciplinary boundaries: Connecting language, education and (anti)racism. In R. Race & V. Lander (Eds.), *Advancing race and ethnicity in education* (pp. 128–144). London: Palgrave Macmillan.

May, S. (2016). Language, imperialism and the modern nation-state system: Implications for language rights. In O. García, N. Flores, & M. Spotti (Eds.), *Oxford handbook of language and society* (pp. 35–53). New York: Oxford University Press.

Michelet, J. (1946). *The people.* C. Cooks, Trans. London: Longman (original, 1846).

Mignolo, W. (2000). *Coloniality, subaltern knowledges, and border thinking.* Princeton, NJ: Princeton University Press.

Mignolo W. (2003). *The darker side of the renaissance: Literacy, territoriality, and colonization.* 2nd edition. Ann Arbor: University of Michigan Press.

Mill, J. (1972 [1861]). *Considerations on representative government.* H. Acton, Ed. London: J. M. Dent.

Mnookin, R., & Verbeke, A. (2009). Persistent non-violent conflict with no reconciliation: The Flemish and Walloons in Belgium. *Law and Contemporary Problems* 72(2), 151–186.

Nelde, P. (1997). Language conflict. In F. Coulmas (Ed.), *The handbook of sociolinguistics* (pp. 285–300). London: Blackwell.

Nimni, E. (1995). Marx, Engels, and the national question. In W. Kymlicka (Ed.), *The rights of minority cultures* (pp. 57–75). Oxford: Oxford University Press.

Nunberg, G. (1992). Afterword—The official language movement: Reimagining America. In J. Crawford (Ed.), *Language loyalties: A source book on the Official English controversy* (pp. 479–494). Chicago: University of Chicago Press.

Oestreich, J. (1999). Liberal theory and minority group rights. *Human Rights Quarterly* 21(1), 108–132.

Packer, J. (1999). Problems in defining minorities. In D. Fottrell & B. Bowring (Eds.), *Minority and group rights in the new millennium* (pp. 223–273). The Hague: Kluwer Law International.

Parekh, B. (2000). *Rethinking multiculturalism: Cultural diversity and political theory.* London: Macmillan.

Pattanayak, D. (Ed.) (1990). *Multilingualism in India.* Clevedon, UK: Multilingual Matters.

Rawls, J. (1971). *A theory of justice.* Oxford: Oxford University Press.

Schlesinger, A. (1992). *The disuniting of America: Reflections on a multicultural society.* New York: W. W. Norton.

Skutnabb-Kangas, T. (2000). *Linguistic genocide in education—or worldwide diversity and human rights?* Mahwah, NJ: Lawrence Erlbaum.

Skutnabb-Kangas, T., & Bucak, S. (1995). Killing a mother tongue: How the Kurds are deprived of linguistic human rights. In T. Skutnabb-Kangas & R. Phillipson (Eds.), *Linguistic human rights: Overcoming linguistic discrimination* (pp. 347–370). Berlin: Mouton de Gruyter.

Skutnabb-Kangas, T., & Fernandes, D. (2008). Kurds in Turkey and in (Iraqi) Kurdistan: A comparison of Kurdish educational language policy in two situations of occupation. *Genocide Studies and Prevention* 3(1), 4–73.

Thornberry, P. (1991a). *International law and the rights of minorities.* Oxford: Clarendon Press.

Thornberry, P. (1991b). *Minorities and human rights law.* London: Minority Rights Group.

Trenz, H. (2007). Reconciling diversity and unity: Language minorities and European integration. *Ethnicities 7,* 157–185.

Vertovec, S. (2007). Super-diversity and its implications. *Ethnic and Racial Studies,* 30(6), 1024–1054.

Weber, E. (1976). *Peasants into Frenchmen: The modernization of rural France 1870–1914.* Stanford, CA: Stanford University Press.

Wiley, T. (2014). Diversity, super-diversity and monolingual language ideology in the United States. Tolerance or intolerance? *Review of Research in Education* 38(1), 1–32.

Williams, C. (2008). *Linguistic minorities in democratic context.* Basingstoke, UK: Palgrave Macmillan.

Wimmer, A. (2004). Dominant ethnicity and nationhood. In E. Kaufmann (Ed.), *Rethinking ethnicity: Majority groups and dominant minorities* (pp. 40–58). London: Routledge.

Language Policy and Planning in Institutions of the Modern Nation-State: Education, Citizenship, Media, and Public Signage

CHAPTER 13

MEDIUM OF INSTRUCTION POLICY

JAMES W. TOLLEFSON
AND AMY B. M. TSUI

BECAUSE medium of instruction (MOI) policies are ubiquitous worldwide, they have attracted a great deal of attention from scholars in language policy and planning (LPP). Beginning in the 1970s, research on MOI policies, particularly in North America, focused primarily on debates about the value of monolingual and bilingual approaches to instruction. Concerned with the relative effectiveness of competing instructional models (such as bilingual, pull-out, and immersion), this early research examined various measures of first- and second-language learning, as well as subject-matter content learning in a range of school subjects (Paulston, 1980). By the early 1990s, substantial evidence had been amassed that showed significant advantage for MOI policies that include use of learners' mother tongues, often in bilingual approaches, not only in primary schools, but also in secondary schools and adult education (Auerbach, 1993). Although the main aim of this research was to discover which model(s) should be adopted in schools, researchers began also to examine the links between MOI and the distribution of economic resources and political power in the wider society (Auerbach, 1995).

Among MOI researchers, the emergence of critical approaches to language in the 1990s, as well as the ongoing language rights movement, foregrounded such issues, shifting attention from the pedagogical goals of language and content learning to sociopolitical processes such as the formation of national and ethnolinguistic identities (Simpson, 2008), neocolonialism (Phillipson, 1992), globalization (Ricento, 2015), and the reproduction of various forms of social inequality in school settings (Skutnabb-Kangas, 2000; Tollefson, 1991, 1995). Despite growing understanding of the central role of MOI policies in such sociopolitical processes, however, policymakers in many contexts continued to emphasize pedagogical rationales for proposed MOI policies, while ignoring the political agendas that underlie those policies. Accordingly, the tension between pedagogical and political agendas has become an important focus of MOI policy research (Tollefson & Tsui, 2004).

Whereas the central pedagogical issues in MOI policy involve the consequences of various models of MOI for language learning, subject-content learning, and other forms of school performance, the central political issues involve the role of MOI policies in shaping relationships of power among different social groups. This latter issue concerns the impact of MOI on employment, income, language maintenance, and various measures of social justice. In New Zealand, for example, Māori-medium preschools (Te Kōhanga Reo) and immersion schools (Kura Kaupapa Māori) not only aid the education of Māori children; they are also crucial to the survival of Māori culture and to broad efforts to promote social justice in New Zealand (May, 2004). Elsewhere, MOI policies have been used to help resolve conflicts (e.g., South Africa), promote social inclusion (e.g., Nicaragua), and reduce economic inequality (e.g., Ecuador, Bolivia).

Yet MOI policies can also offer opportunities for powerful groups to further their own interests at the expense of others. For example, in the United States, English-only MOI is supported by anti-immigrant lobbying groups opposed to immigration and to political participation by the growing Latino population (see Yamagami, 2012). In the late 1980s and early 1990s, a period when state authority in Hungary, Czechoslovakia, and elsewhere in Eastern Europe was collapsing, some political leaders in Yugoslavia, in order to retain power, used MOI policy to promote conflict, leading eventually to a civil war (see Tollefson, 2002). Indeed, everywhere pedagogical debates may mask political agendas. For researchers, this means that MOI is best understood when classroom and school analysis is combined with historical and structural analysis within a single conceptual framework that links the everyday language practices in schools with related social, economic, and political forces.

This chapter[1] traces the main pedagogical and political agendas that are implicit in MOI policies. It begins with an important worldwide effort to promote mother-tongue MOI: the Education for All initiative. Although this initiative has gained wide support among education scholars, MOI policies that privilege former colonial languages remain dominant in many contexts. The next section focuses on such colonial and postcolonial contexts. In recent years, debates about MOI in postcolonial education have been superceded by a focus on the spread of English MOI under globalization. The following section examines globalization, specifically with the examples of Malaysia, Hong Kong, China, and European higher education. The next section examines a major counterforce to English MOI: the language rights movement. Finally, the chapter ends with a discussion of explicit efforts to use MOI to reduce inequality.

EDUCATION FOR ALL

The most important educational framework influencing MOI policies worldwide was established by the UNESCO World Conference on Education for All, held in Jomtien, Thailand, in 1990. The Education for All framework adopted at the meeting (UNESCO, 1990) declared a commitment to universal primary education, and in follow-up meetings, this commitment was extended to secondary and higher education, as well as adult education and lifelong learning.

Education for All stimulated worldwide debate about the importance of MOI policies in efforts to open access for all learners to quality education. Which MOI policies will offer *all* learners the chance for educational success? In response to this challenge, Bolivia, Ecuador, and Peru, for example, have increasingly supported the use of indigenous languages as MOI (Coronel-Molina, 2013), while Nicaragua has developed educational programs for indigenous languages in the Caribbean Coast region (Freeland, 2013). In Niger, Burkina Faso, and Mali, experimental bilingual programs have promoted the use of regional languages rather than French (Alidou, 2004), while Tanzania and Ethiopia have expanded the use of indigenous languages. In these and many other contexts, the expansion of mother-tongue education has achieved significantly better educational results than programs using a former colonial language (see the LOITASA project, Language of Instruction in Tanzania and South Africa; Brock-Utne, 2006; and Heugh et al., 2007).

Indeed, in the past three decades, substantial evidence supporting the use of children's mother tongues as MOI in primary and secondary education has been accumulated (Baker, 2011). In Hong Kong, for example, the change from English to Chinese MOI in secondary schools after the British handover to China in 1997 led to higher scores on secondary school examinations, better class participation, and improved access to higher education (Tsui, 2007). In Ethiopia, mother-tongue primary education has shown substantial pedagogical value, whereas English MOI not only limits students' achievement in all subjects, but also does not lead to better English-language learning. As Heugh et al. (2007) state, the use of mother tongue MOI is "fully supported by international literature on language learning and cognitive development, which show clearly that investment in learning through the mother tongue has short, medium and especially long term benefits for overall schooling performance and for the learning of additional languages" (p. 6).

Despite such evidence, in many educational systems (e.g., the United States), the value of mother-tongue MOI policies for educational achievement is not widely recognized (see Baron, 2011). Even international agreements that encourage the use of mother tongues in primary education (e.g., the European Charter for Regional and Minority Languages) are often equivocal, exempting state authorities from binding commitments to specific MOI policies (see Skutnabb-Kangas, 2008, and Skutnabb-Kangas & Phillipson, 1994, for analysis of such agreements). Instead, policymakers offer economic rationales (e.g., lack of textbooks and materials, the expense of training teachers) for maintaining policies that systematically privilege some groups over others (Tollefson, 2002). As a result, in many educational systems, a key question raised by follow-up work to the Jomtien conference remains relevant: "Can quality education for all be achieved when it is packaged in a language that some learners neither speak nor understand?" (UNESCO Bangkok, 2007, p. 1).

Nowhere is the ongoing debate over mother-tongue MOI more explicit and long-lasting than in colonial/postcolonial contexts, where policymakers weigh the relative advantages of mother-tongue MOI versus the use of colonial varieties.

MEDIUM OF INSTRUCTION IN COLONIAL AND POSTCOLONIAL SETTINGS

In colonial and postcolonial settings, MOI policies have been the focus of intense debate since the beginning of the colonial period, when the colonial language was often adopted as the preferred MOI, although indigenous languages were sometimes used when authorities believed they would be useful in preparing a loyal workforce. As Pennycook (2002) points out, regardless of the MOI, the goal of colonial education was the subjugation of colonized peoples. When indigenous languages were used in schools, they were intended to prepare an exclusive class of civil servants and other workers committed to colonial authority, or they were transitional languages in elementary education intended to provide students with a bridge to exclusive use of the colonial language (e.g., India). Even when used in schools, however, indigenous languages were usually treated as backward and primitive, and indigenous people were to be civilized only through the colonial variety (Pennycook, 2002). Such policies of linguistic assimilation led to the disappearance of many languages, such as Native American languages in the United States, or to their restricted use, as in the case of Māori in New Zealand in the nineteenth and twentieth centuries.

For postcolonial states facing MOI decisions, the legacy of colonialism has led to a variety of challenges. In many contexts, the colonial language was chosen as the main MOI, especially for secondary and higher education, and this choice was rationalized by the claim that it was politically and ethnically neutral, although access to the language was usually restricted to upper- and middle-class groups (Tollefson & Tsui, 2014). When colonial varieties have been used as MOI, indigenous languages also may be declared official, but such declarations often have limited practical impact on language use in schools. In India, for example, twelve regional languages (along with English and Hindi) are official languages of individual states, yet English is the only language taught in all states and is the most frequently chosen official MOI (Annamalai, 2013). In some postcolonial contexts, English and indigenous languages have been given co-official status, but English has retained a dominant position in MOI policies. This is the case in the Philippines and Hong Kong, where Filipino and Chinese, respectively, are co-official with English, but English is widely preferred as the MOI, even in early primary years. In most of Sub-Saharan Africa, French, English, Spanish, and Portuguese were adopted as MOIs, even though few people use them at home and most elementary students, with little ability in the colonial language, struggle to understand their teachers, textbooks, and materials (Alidou, 2004).

In some settings, indigenous languages had to be codified and standardized before they could be the basis for classroom materials, textbooks, and examinations. This is one reason why, in Sub-Saharan Africa, only Tanzania and Ethiopia adopted indigenous national languages throughout the school systems. Elsewhere, the lack of literacy materials made it difficult for schools adopting indigenous languages, as teachers and students had little to draw on for their work. In Niger, for example, efforts to adopt local varieties were constrained by what Alidou (2004) calls the lack of a "literate environment" (p. 207) in which learners can access a wide range of readings in local languages. In addition, many teachers in Niger never used their home language for schooling, and so teacher training must include language learning for literacy. Despite such challenges, however, some bilingual programs in Niger have been created, with regional languages serving as MOI in a limited number of experimental schools (see Alidou, 2004, for an account of the development of such programs).

In recent years, debates about whether to use the former colonial language or an indigenous variety have gradually been superseded by a new issue: the role of MOI in the processes of late capitalism (see Coupland, 2013). This new issue raises the question of the role of English in MOI policy, which is examined in the next section.

LATE CAPITALISM AND MEDIUM OF INSTRUCTION

The development of a transnational system of interlocking corporations that are not limited to one geographical area, largely unregulated international finance, and nation-states that have lost much of their control over their economies have contributed to important transformations in education, including MOI policies. These transformations include (1) a rapid decline in humanities and the arts and an increase in the study of science and technology, usually associated with a uniform curriculum (often termed a "global" curriculum; see Bloch et al., 2006); (2) the adoption of commercially prepared materials rather than those made by teachers in individual schools, which is part of the general "de-skilling" of teachers, who are losing control of classroom objectives, methods, materials, and assessment (Baumann, 1992); (3) the use of national and international standardized tests rather than teacher-made classroom assessments; (4) the subjugation of MOI policy to labor policy and national security (Spring, 2006); and (5) the use of English as MOI. These educational reforms are driven in many contexts (e.g., the United Kingdom and the United States) by neoliberal economic policies that entail significant reductions in state funding for education, which pushes the cost of education onto students' households, a change that is intensified by the expansion of private, for-profit institutions, resulting in significant student debt, especially in the United States (Union of Colleges and Universities, 2011). In addition, reductions in public funding have meant that many programs for migrants and speakers of minority languages have been eliminated, including newcomer programs and bilingual support in the United Kingdom and bilingual education in the United States (McGroarty, 2013). Although such changes have created major economic strains on middle-class and working-class households, they are rationalized by discourses that emphasize the opportunities of globalization and the instrumental value of *global languages* such as English (see, in this volume, Codó, Chapter 23; Pujolar, Chapter 24; and Martín-Rojo, Chapter 27).

Three important socioeconomic processes that have specific impacts on MOI policies are migration, urbanization, and the increasing demand for workers with advanced education and specific language and literacy skills. The migration of labor in recent years is no longer managed primarily by state programs to deal with labor shortages; rather, it is increasingly due to unregulated movements of workers internally and from poor regions of Latin America, Asia, and Africa to Europe and North America, to the oil-producing countries of the Middle East and North Africa, to city-states such as Singapore, to special economic zones (e.g., in China), and to regions with technology industries in the United States, India, and elsewhere. A second, related process is urbanization, not only in wealthy regions but also in South and Southeast Asia and Latin America. Third, employment in new categories of work in business and finance, service industries (e.g., call centers), government bureaucracy, and international nongovernmental organizations requires English or other so-called global varieties (e.g., French in North Africa), as well as literacy and technology skills usually learned in school.

These socioeconomic processes have several implications for MOI policies. First, migration and urbanization lead to reduced use of rural varieties and increased use of urban varieties—often former colonial languages (e.g., English in Pakistan)—spoken by the middle class; and urban migrants require school opportunities to learn these languages, thereby increasing demand for schooling. Second, new types of work require that workers learn English or other varieties used in business and government, which increases pressure for schools to adopt these varieties as MOI. Third, urbanization often leads to the formation of pidginized varieties, local varieties of the colonial language, regional lingua francas, and urban mixed varieties (Blackledge & Creese, 2014), yet most MOI policies do not take into account such complex linguistic ecologies. Fourth, the competition for places in school and for skilled jobs in the cities often lead dominant groups to favor repressive MOI policies in order to restrict access to good jobs by new urban migrants. Examples include English-proficiency requirements for immigration (e.g., the United States and Australia), English-only MOI laws (e.g., the United States), and reductions in the use of migrants' languages in schools (e.g., the United Kingdom). One major result of these important changes is that MOI policies favoring dominant languages (especially English) are overpowering family language policies and practices that support home varieties (see Macalister & Mirvahedi, 2017).

State education authorities have responded to these broad consequences of globalization in different ways. Some authorities, such as in Malaysia and Hong Kong, have tried to sustain indigenous official languages while also preparing students for globalized employment with English. Often the result is inconsistent MOI policies that shift between English MOI and local-language MOI. In other settings, such as China and the European Union, education authorities seek to transform many schools into English-medium institutions. In the rest of this section, we examine how these different responses to globalization are evident in the MOI policies in these four settings, beginning with Malaysia.

Malaysia

When Bahasa Malaysia was adopted as the *national* language after Malaysia gained its independence in 1957, the government adopted a mother-tongue policy that created Chinese-medium and Tamil-medium schools, in addition to the Malay-medium national school system (see Ministry of Education Malaysia, 1956). This policy particularly benefited the Chinese community (about one-quarter of the population), whose schools using Chinese as MOI came to be known for their high quality of education and successful graduates entering higher education and employment. From the 1960s through the early 1980s, as Malay was adopted as the MOI for all state-supported schools, the Chinese community undertook a significant fundraising effort to provide continuing support for the Chinese-medium schools. The result is a system of more than 1,200 primary and sixty secondary Chinese-medium schools (Centre for Public Policy Studies, 2012). Chinese parents' support for Chinese MOI does not mean, however, that they resist English for their children. Rather, because most Chinese in Malaysia are middle class, they have the resources to ensure that their children learn English, while also ensuring that they gain what many parents consider to be a superior education in the Chinese-medium or bilingual schools; and they are able to send their children to private, English-medium universities in Malaysia or to institutions overseas. Thus their support for Chinese is based on its pedagogical value and their confidence that their children will also be able to gain a highly prestigious English repertoire. In recent years, with the economic importance of China and growing interest in learning Mandarin Chinese (Putonghua) worldwide, many non-Chinese students (mostly Malay) attend schools that use both Putonghua and Malay as MOI.

In higher education, the policy of Malay MOI in state schools meant that publicly funded universities competed with privately funded English-medium institutions, whose graduates enjoyed a significant advantage in finding work in the private sector, where employers preferred workers with highly prestigious varieties of English. In contrast, graduates of the public institutions were limited mainly to lower-paid, Malay-medium government employment. Partly as a consequence, more than 90% of government jobs came to be filled by Malays (who comprise about 65% of the population). In response to this imbalance in employment and income (and to the perceived linguistic demands of late capitalism), the MOI policy was revised in 2003, so that science and math would be taught in English in public institutions (Gill, 2007). The new policy was met with resistance from many Malays and Chinese (who feared it would undermine the Chinese-medium schools), and so in 2009 the policy was revised once again, with Malay replacing English. Despite such resistance to English MOI, the most recent National Education Blueprint (Ministry of Education Malaysia, 2015) calls for continued expansion in the use of English (as well as Chinese and other languages), so that all graduates are multilingual by the year 2025.

Thus, Malaysian education authorities since independence have struggled to reach two divergent educational goals: ensuring that MOI policies support the link between language and identity in Malaysia, and helping students gain the skills in English, Chinese, and other languages required for employment. Changing official MOI policies over the years have reflected the changing relative priority of these two goals.

Hong Kong

After the British returned Hong Kong to China in 1997, the Hong Kong education authorities in 1998 implemented a *mother-tongue policy* of Chinese (i.e., Cantonese) MOI (CMI) in primary and secondary schools (with Putonghua as a compulsory subject). The government's rationale for the new policy was that CMI would help Hong Kong students achieve better academic results than English-medium instruction (EMI). Although Cantonese had long served as the MOI in primary schools, with this new policy, CMI was adopted too at the secondary level, with English and Putonghua taught as subjects. The policy goal came to be known as biliteracy (in Chinese and English) and trilingualism (in Cantonese, English, and Putonghua).

After the policy change, results of the secondary-level Hong Kong Certificate of Education Examination (HKCEE) suggested that CMI successfully raised students' academic performance compared to EMI classes (see Education and Manpower Bureau, 2005; Li & Majhanovich, 2010; Marsh, Hau, & Kong, 2000). Results of the pre-university Hong Kong Advanced Level Examination (HKALE), however, showed a decline in English language scores starting in 2005, while Chinese language scores showed a steady improvement (Li & Majhanovich, 2010). As a consequence of the HKALE tests, many parents—concerned above all with their children's English proficiency—began calling for the use of EMI in all secondary schools, a demand that persisted even though the CMI policy had provided better access to higher education for students in CMI schools.

As a result of parents' demands, as well as private-sector employers' resistance to CMI, in 2009 the government announced what it called a "fine-tuning" of the policy, which permitted secondary schools, with some restrictions, to use CMI or EMI for subjects other than languages beginning in the 2010 school year (Education Bureau, 2009). In its rationale for the policy change, the Education Bureau adopted a discourse of school choice: "Schools are in the best position to keep track of students' learning progress and teach according to diverse abilities. Accordingly, schools . . . should be allowed to determine their professional school-based MOI arrangements." As a result, different schools adopted varying MOI policies, including CMI only, EMI only, or a combination of CMI and EMI in different subjects.

Thus the CMI policy adopted in Hong Kong in 1998 had opened access to improved academic performance and to higher education for many students who previously could not compete in EMI secondary schools, but this policy was widely rejected by parents who believed that EMI schools offered better employment opportunities for their children, by businesses concerned about their ability to compete in a globalized economy that required English, and even by many CMI schools, which were widely perceived as inferior to EMI schools and thus were unable to compete for students. In addition, as political tension between Hong Kong and the Mainland has increased over the years, many Hong Kong residents fear that a CMI policy may be part of a long-term program to integrate Hong Kong with China by undermining the distinctive characteristics of Hong Kong society, particularly the important position of English.

By focusing solely on the question of EMI or CMI schooling, the MOI debate in Hong Kong has ignored the complex linguistic situation in the schools, where code mixing, hybrid Chinese-English varieties, and languages of South and Southeast Asian students are part of everyday interaction (Lin, 1996). The result is that policymakers have adopted simplistic MOI policies reflecting political pressures exerted by various stakeholders, rather than explicit pedagogical goals or an understanding of the linguistic repertoires of students and their families. In addition, the emerging issue of whether to use Putonghua as MOI in Putonghua classes has gradually received more public scrutiny, as growing numbers of students from Mainland China enter Hong Kong schools and as the tension intensifies between Hong Kong and the Mainland. With this additional complication, political agendas are likely to continue to dominate debates about MOI in Hong Kong schools in the years to come.

China

The most significant development in MOI policy in China in recent years has been the promotion of English MOI, commonly known as *bilingual education* (*shuangyu jiaoyu/jiaoxue*) (Feng, 2005; Hu, 2009). Programs that include content taught in English have been especially important in higher education, where many degree programs must include at least 10% of classes that are *bilingual* (i.e., use English at least half of the time) (Ministry of Education China, 2002). Because universities are evaluated, in part, according to the number of programs offering EMI, there has been a dramatic increase in the use of English, especially in elite universities.

In secondary education, the push for English presents significant institutional challenges, particularly finding teachers who can handle classes in English. In some schools, teachers are defined as *probationary* or *qualified* according to their English ability (e.g., in Shanghai; see Feng, 2005), and English-speaking instructors receive specialized training, higher salaries, and bonuses, paid in part by parents who want their children to attend EMI schools. As a result of these policies, schools in the wealthy coastal cities, with many middle-class parents able to pay the extra cost of EMI education, increasingly diverge in quality from schools in poorer regions in the interior of the country.

English-promotion policies have also had inequitable effects on the Han majority and the many ethnic minority groups in China. In most regions, linguistic minority children must learn Chinese and, in some schools, use it as the MOI, even if they are not fluent in it. Therefore English is delayed until after the period of compulsory schooling (the first nine years). In contrast, many Han children begin English study during the first three years of primary school. Not surprisingly, minority students are less competitive in university entrance exams that assess English ability. Indeed, the gap between university enrollment of Han and minority students has significantly widened in recent years, in part due to MOI policies that confront minority students with university programs in Chinese or English, both of which require high levels of proficiency that many students are unable to achieve (see Feng, 2009).

English-promotion policies also affect the study of minority languages by Han students in regions of China with large concentrations of minority-language speakers. In such regions, Han children previously studied minority languages, but now those languages are being replaced by English, as in Xinjiang, for example, where Uyghur is giving way to English in primary, secondary, and tertiary education (Tsung & Cruickshank, 2009). An important consequence is increasing tension between the Han majority and the ethnic minorities in some areas (Jia, Lee, & Zhang, 2012).

Thus English-promotion policies in China have increased the number of classes and programs using English MOI, which has led to a widening gap between the schools in wealthy and poor regions and between the Han and linguistic-minority populations. Perhaps for these reasons, government officials in 2016 considered (though eventually rejected) reducing the weighting of English in university testing (see Shao & Gao, 2017).

European Higher Education

The European Union, with twenty-four official languages and sixty regional and minority languages within its borders, has an explicit commitment to taking steps to ensure that citizens speak two languages in addition to their mother tongue. For example, a detailed plan adopted in 2003 was designed to extend language learning throughout education and to improve language teaching across the Union (European Commission, 2004; also see European Commission, 2008). Despite this commitment to broad programs of language teaching and learning, since the first decade of the 2000s English has increasingly become the medium of instruction in higher education in Europe at the expense of other languages.

The spread of English MOI has been encouraged by the Bologna Process, initiated in 1999 to create a European Higher Education Area to ease the transferability of university credits and degree qualifications across Europe (Phillipson, 2009). Following the adoption of the Bologna agreement, the growth in English MOI programs accelerated beginning in 2001–2002. In that year, less than a third of the 1,558 institutions of higher education in nineteen countries surveyed had at least one English MOI program (Maiworm & Wächter, 2002; also see Wächter, 2008), but by 2006–2007, the number had increased to more than 2,400 programs in twenty-seven countries (Wächter & Maiworm, 2008).

English MOI has been further encouraged by its identification with the internationalization of European higher education, which is evident in several ways. For example, because researchers who publish with scholars outside their home countries and who publish in English positively impact their university's position in the Times Higher Education University Ranking and similar ranking systems, hiring, promotion, and tenure policies favor scholars who work in English. Indeed, many universities have adopted incentives to encourage the use of English. In Norway, for example, a ranking system for publication is weighted to favor English over

Norwegian (Brock-Utne, 2007). In some universities, doctoral theses in specific departments must be written in English (Hilmarsson-Dunn, 2009), and financial incentives are offered to doctoral students writing in English (see Brock-Utne, 2007).

The widespread use of English MOI in European higher education means that English must be mastered for most young people wishing to attend universities in Europe. Indeed, the spread of English in higher education has increased pressure on secondary and primary schools to adopt English MOI as well. In addition, the European Commission's support for Content and Language Integrated Learning (CLIL) favors English, which is the most common MOI used in CLIL programs (European Commission, 2006; also see Relaño-Pastor, Chapter 25 in this volume). At the same time, however, languages other than English, including non-European languages such as Chinese, are becoming increasingly important in Europe, under an evolving language policy framework and neoliberal economic policies that have encouraged, for example, the spread of Chinese MOI in secondary schools (see Pérez-Milans, 2015b).

In sum, MOI policy in Malaysia, Hong Kong, China, and the European Union is characterized by ongoing debate about the appropriate roles for English and other languages. In Malaysia, government education authorities have fluctuated in their support for English vis-à-vis Malay, while most Chinese parents have strongly supported Chinese MOI. In Hong Kong, most parents support English MOI, despite evidence that many children benefit from Chinese MOI classes. This support is strong even among poor and working-class residents, who believe, despite contrary evidence, that English MOI schools offer the best opportunities for higher education and employment for their children. Similarly, in China public support for bilingual programs using English is fueled by the belief that such programs offer the best path to higher education and employment. Finally, in Europe, the long commitment to plurilingualism increasingly has come to mean *plurilingualism with English*, as English MOI spreads through universities and national education systems.

Yet the push for English worldwide is not unrestrained. One important factor contributing to policies that promote languages other than English is the movement for language rights (see May, Chapter 12 in this volume). In the next section we turn to this important counter-force to the spread of English MOI.

LANGUAGE RIGHTS IN MEDIUM OF INSTRUCTION POLICY

The central assumption of the language rights movement is that explicit statements of language rights can provide a framework within which ethnolinguistic minorities can achieve official recognition of their languages in the educational system, and that this recognition can help to reduce language-based inequalities. Such a system of rights is usually described as universal—that is, applicable equally to all people everywhere (Skutnabb-Kangas, 2000)—though this claim has been criticized as reflecting the limited perspective of European liberalism and as incompatible with sociolinguistic reality (Wee, 2011).

Assertions of a right to mother-tongue MOI are among the most commonly articulated of all language rights. Advocates for mother-tongue MOI offer three broad bases for those rights: territory, identity, and citizenship. A territorial basis protects MOI for identified ethnolinguistic groups that reside within particular geographical regions, usually those where minority groups constitute a significant portion of the population. In Slovenia, for example, language rights are constitutionally guaranteed within specific border districts where speakers of Italian and Hungarian are concentrated (Tollefson, 2004). In the United Kingdom, Welsh-medium schooling is provided in Wales, but it is not available to Welsh speakers in other areas of the country (Jones & Martin-Jones, 2004). In the United States, Navajo-medium education is available in areas of the Southwest, but not in urban areas where many Navajos live. Thus a right to MOI based on territory is not portable; it can be exercised only in designated geographical areas, usually those where speakers of minority languages reside. Because territory and language are rarely perfectly aligned, group members who reside across territorial boundaries may be excluded from MOI rights guarantees. In such circumstances, the potential for conflict can be significant, if political leaders exploit concern for individuals living outside their so-called home territory in order to create and sustain conflict. Examples include Germany/Poland in the 1930s, Serbs in Yugoslavia in the early 1990s (Tollefson, 2002), and Hungarians in Slovakia in the first decade of the 2000s (Longman, 2002).

A second basis for the assertion of a right to medium of instruction is ethnolinguistic identity. That is, members of recognized ethnolinguistic groups may be guaranteed specified MOI rights, without regard to territory (although in practice such rights often may be exercised only when enough speakers of the minority language are present). Many international documents, including UNESCO's Universal Declaration on Cultural Diversity, the European Charter for Regional or Minority Languages, the Council of Europe's Framework Convention for the Protection of National Minorities, and the United Nations' Declaration on the Rights of Persons Belonging to National or Ethnic, Religious and Linguistic Minorities, offer an identity basis for MOI rights. The latter document, for example, includes the following statement: "States should take appropriate measures so that, wherever possible, persons belonging to minorities have adequate opportunities to learn their mother tongue or to have instruction in their mother tongue" (paragraph 4.3). As this passage illustrates, such statements are often highly qualified, offering states broad leeway to implement MOI policies according to their own political and ideological agendas. Moreover, in most contexts, the number of ethnolinguistic groups with a right to MOI in their own language is limited, often to those with sufficient political power to assert those rights. Also, in many settings, migration may undermine notions of stable group membership that underlie such rights, particularly in this age of "superdiversity" (Vertovec, 2007) in which ethnic and linguistic group boundaries have become fluid and unstable.

A third basis for a right to mother-tongue MOI is citizenship. New Zealand, for example, has developed a complex concept of citizenship laid out in court rulings, treaties, and a vigorous discourse of equality and partnership within a multilingual citizenry (May, 2004). Accordingly, since the recognition of the Māori language as an official language of New Zealand in 1987, Māori communities have achieved significant gains in Māori-medium education. Similarly, in South Africa, constitutional statements about language, human rights, and equality are aimed at promoting tolerance and national unity, in part by specifying eleven official languages that may be used as MOI (although in practice, English is the MOI for approximately 80% of the population, even though less than 10% speak it at home) (Webb, 2004).

All three approaches to MOI rights tend to ignore the linguistic complexity of everyday life in schools. The heteroglossic nature of most environments and speakers' hybrid and fluid linguistic repertoires may not match well with policymakers' assumption that learners speak one or more distinct varieties having clear-cut linguistic boundaries, with code switching as the primary form of language mixing (see Blommaert, 2012). Indeed, MOI policies based on notions of a right to use a particular language may be inappropriate for some educational contexts (see Freeland, 2013, and McCarty, 2013). Alternatively, the concept of *translanguaging* offers a potentially fruitful framework for understanding "the language practices of bilinguals not as two autonomous language systems . . . but as one linguistic repertoire with features that have been socially constructed as belonging to two separate languages" (García & Wei, 2014, p. 4).

An example of the value and the limitations of a language rights basis for MOI policy can be found in the Andes region of South America, where more than ten million speakers of Quechua extend across areas of Peru, Ecuador, and Bolivia. Throughout the region, MOI policies have increasingly accommodated demands by activist movements for indigenous people's rights. In Peru, a national bilingual education policy adopted in the early 1970s was the first effort in the region to institute Spanish-Quechua bilingual MOI (Hornberger & King, 2001). In Ecuador in the 1980s and Bolivia in the 1990s, programs of bilingual intercultural education were adopted as a response to pressure from indigenous groups and international donors. Despite this long history of official state support for bilingual MOI, implementation has been difficult (King & Benson, 2004), due to limited resources such as trained teachers, the challenges of standardizing indigenous varieties, competing understandings of *bilingualism* and *bilingual education*, widespread heteroglossia and translingualism, political tension over centralized versus local control of education, and the long-standing prestige of Spanish as the language of economic and political power. Nevertheless, although bilingual intercultural education has had limited impact on underlying social and economic inequalities, the movement toward linguistic equality, marked by the increasing status of Quechua in the region, has been impressive, and provides hope that bilingual MOI may help to maintain indigenous languages (see Unamuno & Bonnin, Chapter 19 in this volume).

The challenge of implementing language rights in MOI has led some scholars to propose an alternative to the language rights discourse. Wee (2011), for example, proposes "deliberative democracy" (p. 164). Freeland (2013), based on her analysis of difficulties implementing language rights guarantees in Nicaragua's Caribbean Coast region, concludes, "if the language rights discourse is to provide any guarantee for minority languages, all its underlying concepts need deconstructing and reinventing in light of the local language ideologies of the target groups whose rights are to be vouchsafed" (p. 109). She suggests that alternatives such as "linguistic citizenship" (p. 109) may offer a firmer foundation for MOI policy decisions.

Although the language rights movement has had limited impact on entrenched economic, social, and political inequality, MOI policies in some settings have been explicitly aimed at mitigating inequality, with some important successes. The next section offers examples of such efforts.

Conclusion: Medium of Instruction to Reduce Inequality

Despite evidence around the world that MOI policies often serve the interests of dominant groups by providing them with privileged access to effective primary and secondary education, higher education, and employment opportunities, MOI policies in some contexts have been used to counter social and economic inequalities. Three such cases are Māori-medium schools in New Zealand, Kwara'ae-medium education in the Solomon Islands, and Navajo-medium schools in the US Southwest. Fortunately, a small number of LPP scholars have undertaken sustained and detailed research on such cases over many years (see May, 2004, on New Zealand; Watson-Gegeo & Gegeo, 1992, 2002, and Gegeo & Watson-Gegeo, 2002, 2013, on Solomon Islands; and McCarty, 2004, 2013, on the US Southwest). Based on this research, as well as research in many other contexts, four common features of successful programs to reduce inequalities can be identified.

First, effective programs that incorporate MOI policies in social justice efforts require an ideological and discursive foundation that links policy to important social values. In New Zealand, for example, Māori MOI is rationalized within the framework of a bilingual and bicultural Aotearoa/New Zealand citizenship that not only supports the maintenance of Māori culture but also appeals to the values of the dominant English-speaking population (May, 2004). In the United States, programs using Navajo as MOI are framed within a discourse of Native American self-determination, which helps to shield those programs from political conflicts over the use of Spanish in bilingual programs in the US Southwest (McCarty, 2002). In the Solomon Islands, Kwaraʻae-medium schools are embedded within an ideological framework that privileges indigenous knowledge and links MOI with local content and teaching methodologies (Gegeo & Watson-Gegeo, 2013). Elsewhere, such as in Europe, a discourse of multiculturalism and plurilingualism can provide support for the use of smaller languages in schools (though in Europe this discourse seems to be weakening).

Second, local community control over policymaking processes is a key to developing MOI policies that benefit linguistic minorities. For example, Māori-medium instruction in New Zealand was a direct outgrowth of community preschools (Kōhanga Reo) and primary schools (Kura Kaupapa Māori) created by Māori parents in the 1970s and 1980s outside of the state school system (May, 2004). Only later, at the initiative of parents, did the state incorporate the Māori schools within a framework proposed by the community. Thus the community provided the foundation for the spread of Māori MOI, which is perhaps the most important factor in its success. Similarly, the success of Navajo-medium schools in the United States is due largely to community control, even though state authorities exercise some administrative oversight (e.g., in testing). In war-torn Solomon Islands in the first decade of the 2000s, community leaders on the island of Malaita took the initiative in creating Kwaraʻae-medium schools for displaced Malaita youth. The decision to use Kwaraʻae reflected not only a belief in the pedagogical value of the mother tongue, but also a broader critique of state education in the country (see Watson-Gegeo et al., Chapter 20 in this volume). Elsewhere, too, such as in Hawaiian schools in the United States, Sámi-medium schools in Sweden, and Inuit schools in North America, community control of policymaking and the everyday practice of education is essential for program success.

Third, along with a discursive and ideological foundation, MOI policies for social justice require an appropriate legal framework that provides substantive legal protections for minority-language MOI and related programs that address inequality. For example, New Zealand's Treaty of Waitangi and the Māori Language Act of 1987 provide one of the most effective legal frameworks supporting community-led education. In the United States, Navajo MOI is supported by a less robust web of laws (such as the Indian Self-Determination and Education Assistance Act of 1975, the Native American Languages Act of 1990, and the Native American Housing and Self-Determination Act of 1996) that provide a legal framework for Navajo education but insecure funding and marginal support by federal or state agencies. Kwaraʻae-medium schools in the Solomon Islands, which were formed without state support and continue to function largely outside the state legal system, depend almost solely on community efforts.

Fourth, community support for educational programs depends on those programs meeting identifiable community needs, based on an understanding of the complex role of language in the life of individuals in the community. That is, MOI decisions must be based on an understanding of the full life trajectories of learners and their language repertoires in the linguistic ecology of the community, in school and beyond. In New Zealand, for example, because Māori preschools emerged directly from community efforts to create child care and early-childhood education programs, Māori MOI received strong community support that drove its spread to primary and secondary education. Similarly, Kwara'ae parents led the initiative to create new schools for Malaitan children who had been displaced by war and had no access to education, and so community schools were ensured strong support, in part because state education authorities had virtually no involvement. In the United States, Navajo schools often function as community centers for the geographically isolated communities that they serve.

Finally, efforts to use MOI to confront language-related inequalities have benefited from LPP research within the theoretical framework of what McCarty et al. (2011) call New Language Policy Studies, which argues that language policy is "a situated sociocultural process" (p. 335) in which ideologies and discourses are fundamental. When understood as ideological constructs, official policies can be linked to the interests of powerful groups that control state policymaking in education. The ideological foundation for MOI policy in India, for example, persuades even groups with no opportunity to use English for employment that English-medium education is the key to social mobility. Yet MOI policies also offer opportunity for marginal groups to pursue their interests. In the United States, Navajo-medium schools are part of a broad movement for indigenous "cultural continuance" (McCarty, 2013, p. 270), based on an ideology of self-determination that has gained force in recent decades. In New Zealand, the spread of Māori-medium schools is linked with the ideology of a multilingual and multicultural citizenry that has contributed to the long-term process of reinvigorating Māori social institutions. In Ecuador, Quechua-Spanish bilingual programs are under an independent administration charged with promoting the educational and economic interests of Quechua speakers. In these and many other contexts, MOI policy is an arena for action in influential movements for social change. As discursive constructs, MOI policies are embedded in complex and competing public discourses that often rationalize policies as a way to improve students' school performance. The educational discourses of opportunity through English in India and equality through English in the United States, for example, justify MOI policies that clearly disadvantage many learners. Thus MOI policies must be analyzed as discursive constructs that play an important role in broader social struggles.

Particularly fruitful is research using situated approaches (Pérez-Milans, 2015a) and trajectory-based analysis (Pérez-Milans & Soto, 2016), which means understanding local language practices in schools within local and global economic, political, and social conditions, in order to make explicit the links between MOI in classroom practices and the wider social life of communities. Situated approaches reflect new conceptualizations of language policy as a covert and implicit social process in which language serves to construct social hierarchies. MOI analysis, therefore, must explore the cultural logic of MOI within nation-states and global institutions, school systems, and individual households, to discover the links between individuals' everyday language practices and larger historical, ideological, social, and institutional systems.

NOTE

1. Parts of this chapter are adapted from Tollefson and Tsui (2014) and Tollefson (2013).

REFERENCES

Alidou, H. (2004). Medium of instruction in post-colonial Africa. In J. W. Tollefson & A. B. M. Tsui (Eds.), *Medium of instruction policies: Which agenda? Whose agenda?* (pp. 195–214). Mahwah, NJ: Lawrence Erlbaum.

Annamalai, E. (2013). India's economic restructuring with English: Benefits versus costs. In J. W. Tollefson (Ed.), *Language policies in education: Critical issues* (2nd edition; pp. 191–207). New York: Routledge.

Auerbach, E. R. (1993). Reexamining English only in the ESL classroom. *TESOL Quarterly* 27(1), 9–32.

Auerbach, E. R. (1995). The politics of the ESL classroom: Issues of power in pedagogical choices. In J. W. Tollefson (Ed.), *Power and inequality in language education* (pp. 9–33). Cambridge: Cambridge University Press.

Baker, C. (2011). *Foundations of bilingual education and bilingualism.* 5th edition. Bristol: Multilingual Matters.

Baron, D. (2011). Language and education: The more things change. In A. Curzan & M. Adams (Eds.), *Contours of English and English language studies* (pp. 278–297). Ann Arbor: University of Michigan Press.

Baumann, J. F. (1992). Basel reading programs and the deskilling of teachers: A critical examination of the argument. *Reading Research Quarterly* 27(4), 390–398.

Blackledge, A., & Creese, A. (Eds.) (2014). *Heteroglossia as practice and pedagogy.* Dordrecht: Springer.

Bloch, M. N., Kennedy, D., Lightfoot, T., & Weyenberg, D. (2006). *The child in the world/The world in the child: Education and the configuration of a universal, modern and globalized childhood.* New York: Palgrave.

Blommaert, J. (2012). Chronicles of complexity: Ethnography, superdiversity, and linguistic landscapes. *Tilburg Papers in Cultural Studies* 29. Tilburg, Netherlands: Tilburg University.

Brock-Utne, B. (2006). Language and democracy in Africa. In D. B. Holsinger & W. J. Jacob (Eds.), *Inequality in education: Comparative and international perspectives* (pp. 172–189). Hong Kong: Springer & the Comparative Education Research Centre of the University of Hong Kong.

Brock-Utne, B. (2007). Language of instruction and research in higher education in Europe: Highlights from the current debate in Norway and Sweden. *International Review of Education*, 57(4), 367–388.

Centre for Public Policy Studies. (2012). *Vernacular schools in Malaysia*. Kuala Lumpur: Centre for Public Policy Studies. Retrieved from http://www.cpps.org.my/upload/VERNACULAR%20SCHOOLS%20IN%20MALAYSIA%20REPORT%202012.pdf

Coronel-Molina, S. M. (2013). New functional domains of Quechua and Aymara. In J. W. Tollefson (Ed.), *Language policies in education: Critical issues* (2nd edition; pp. 278–300). New York: Routledge.

Coupland, N. (Ed.) (2013). *The handbook of language and globalization*. Malden, MA: Wiley-Blackwell.

Education Bureau (Hong Kong SAR). (2009). *Fine-tuning the medium of instruction for secondary schools*. Education Bureau Circular No. 6/2009, June 5. Retrieved from http://www.edb.gov.hk/attachment/en/edu-system/primary-secondary/applicable-to-secondary/moi/support-and-resources-for-moi-policy/lsplmfs-sch/d-sch/ow/sp/edbc09006e.pdf

Education and Manpower Bureau. (2005, August 10). *SEM pleased with HKCEE results* [Press release]. Retrieved from http://www.info.gov.hk/gia/general/200508/10/08100203.htm

European Commission. (2004). *Promoting language learning and linguistic diversity: An action plan 2004–06*. Luxemburg: Office for Official Publications of the European Communities.

European Commission. (2006). Eurydice Report. *Content and Language Integrated Learning (CLIL) at school in Europe*. Brussels: Eurydice European Unit.

European Commission. (2008). *Multilingualism: An asset for Europe and a shared commitment*. Communication from the Commission to the European Parliament, the Council, the European Economic and Social Committee and the Committee of the Regions. Retrieved from http://eur-lex.europa.eu/LexUriServ/LexUriServ.do?uri=CELEX:52008DC0566:EN:NOT

Feng, A. (2005). Bilingualism for the minor or the major? An evaluative analysis of parallel conceptions in China. *International Journal of Bilingual Education and Bilingualism* 8, 529–551.

Feng, A. (2009). English in China: Convergence and divergence in policy and practice. *AILA Review* 22(1), 85–102.

Freeland, J. (2013). Righting language wrongs in a plurilingual context: Language policy and practice in Nicaragua's Caribbean Coast region. In J. W. Tollefson (Ed.), *Language policies in education: Critical issues* (2nd edition; pp. 91–115). New York: Routledge.

García, O., & Wei, L. (2014). *Translanguaging: Language, bilingualism, and education*. Houndmills, UK: Palgrave Macmillan.

Gegeo, D. W., & Watson-Gegeo, K. A. (2002). The critical villager: Transforming language and education in Solomon Islands. In J. W. Tollefson (Ed.), *Language policies in education: Critical issues* (1st edition; pp. 309–325). Mahwah, NJ: Lawrence Erlbaum.

Gegeo, D. W., & Watson-Gegeo, K. A. (2013). The critical villager revisited: Continuing transformations of language and education in Solomon Islands. In J. W. Tollefson

(Ed.), *Language policies in education: Critical issues* (2nd edition; pp. 233–251). New York: Routledge.

Gill, S. K. (2007). Shift in language policy in Malaysia: Unravelling reasons for change, conflict and compromise in mother-tongue education. *AILA Review* 20(1), 106–122.

Heugh, K., Benson, C., Bogale, B., & Yohannes, M. A. G. (2007). *Final report: Study on medium of instruction in primary schools in Ethiopia.* Addis Ababa: Ministry of Education.

Hilmarsson-Dunn, A. M. (2009). The impact of English on language education policy in Iceland. *European Journal of Language Policy* 1(1), 39–59.

Hornberger, N. H., & King, K. A. (2001). Reversing Quechua language shift in South America. In J. A. Fishman (Ed.), *Can threatened languages be saved?* (pp. 166–194). Clevedon, UK: Multilingual Matters.

Hu, G. (2009). The craze for English-medium education in China: Driving forces and looming consequences. *English Today* 25(4), 47–54.

Jia, W., Lee, Y. T., & Zhang, H. (2012). Ethno-political conflicts in China: Towards building interethnic harmony. In D. Landis & R. D. Albert (Eds.), *Handbook of ethnic conflict: International perspectives* (pp. 177–196). New York: Springer.

Jones, D. V., & Martin-Jones, M. (2004). Bilingual education and language revitalization in Wales: Past achievements and current issues. In J. W. Tollefson & A. B. M. Tsui (Eds.), *Medium of instruction policies: Which agenda? Whose agenda?* (pp. 43–70). Mahwah, NJ: Lawrence Erlbaum.

King, K. A., & Benson, C. (2004). Indigenous language education in Bolivia and Ecuador: Contexts, changes, and challenges. In J. W. Tollefson & A. B. M. Tsui (Eds.), *Medium of instruction policies: Which agenda? Whose agenda?* (pp. 241–261). Mahwah, NJ: Lawrence Erlbaum.

Li, V., & Majhanovich, E. S. (2010). Marching on a long road: A review of the effectiveness of the mother-tongue education policy in post-colonial Hong Kong. *Gist Education and Learning Research Journal* 4(1), 10–29.

Lin, A. M. Y. (1996). Bilingualism or linguistic segregation? Symbolic domination, resistance and code-switching in Hong Kong schools. *Linguistics and Education* 8, 49–84.

Longman, J. (2002). Mother-tongue education versus bilingual education: Shifting ideologies and policies in the Republic of Slovakia. *International Journal of the Sociology of Language* 154, 47–64.

Macalister, J., & Mirvahedi, S. H. (Eds.) (2017). *Family language policies in a multilingual world.* New York: Routledge.

Maiworm, F., & Wächter, B. (2002). *English-language-taught degree programmes in European higher education: Trends and success factors.* Bonn: Lemmens.

Marsh, H. W., Hau, K. T., & Kong, C. K. (2000). Late immersion and language of instruction in Hong Kong high schools: Achievement growth in language and non-language subjects. *Harvard Educational Review* 70(3), 302–346.

May, S. (2004). Māori-medium education in Aotearoa/New Zealand. In J. W. Tollefson & A. B. M. Tsui (Eds.), *Medium of instruction policies: Which agenda? Whose agenda?* (pp. 21–42). Mahwah, NJ: Lawrence Erlbaum.

McCarty, T. L. (2002). *A place to be Navajo: Rough Rock and the struggle for self-determination in Indigenous schooling.* Mahwah, NJ: Lawrence Erlbaum

McCarty, T. L. (2004). Dangerous difference: A critical-historical analysis of language education policies in the United States. In J. W. Tollefson & A. B. M. Tsui (Eds.), *Medium of instruction policies: Which agenda? Whose agenda?* (pp. 71–93). Mahwah, NJ: Lawrence Erlbaum.

McCarty, T. L. (2013). Language planning and cultural continuance in Native America. In J. W. Tollefson (Ed.), *Language policies in education: Critical issues* (2nd edition; pp. 255–277). New York: Routledge.

McCarty, T. L, Collins, J., & Hopson, R. K. (2011). Dell Hymes and the New Language Policy Studies: Update from an underdeveloped country. *Anthropology and Education Quarterly* 42(4), 335–363.

McGroarty, M. (2013). Multiple actors and arenas in evolving language policies. In J. W. Tollefson (Ed.), *Language policies in education: Critical issues* (2nd edition; pp. 35–58). New York: Routledge.

Ministry of Education China. (2002). 普通高等学校本科教学工作水平评估方案 (试行) *Putong gaodeng xuexiao benke jiaoxue gongzuo shuiping pinggu fang'an (shixing)* [Assessment of quality of undergraduate teaching in higher education institutions (pilot)]. Retrieved from http://jw.zzu.edu.cn/glwj/new_page_2.htm

Ministry of Education Malaysia. (1956). *Report of the Education Committee 1956.* Kuala Lumpur: Ministry of Education. Retrieved from http://www.cpps.org.my/upload/Razak%20Report%201956.pdf

Ministry of Education Malaysia. (2015). *Malaysia education blueprint 2015–2025.* Kuala Lumpur: Ministry of Education.

Paulston, C. B. (1980). *Bilingual education: Theories and issues.* Rowley, MA: Newbury House.

Pennycook, A. (2002). Language policy and docile bodies: Hong Kong and governmentality. In J. W. Tollefson (Ed.), *Language policies in education: Critical issues* (1st edition; pp. 91–110). Mahwah, NJ: Lawrence Erlbaum.

Pérez-Milans, M. (Ed.) (2015a). Language education policy in late modernity: Insights from situated approaches. Thematic issue. *Language Policy* 14(2).

Pérez-Milans, M. (2015b). Mandarin Chinese in London education: Language aspirations in a working-class secondary school. *Language Policy* 14(2), 53–81.

Pérez-Milans, M., & Soto, C. (2016). Reflexive language and ethnic minority activism in Hong Kong: A trajectory-based analysis. *AILA Review* 29, 48–82.

Phillipson, R. (1992). *Linguistic imperialism.* Oxford: Oxford University Press.

Phillipson, R. (2009). English in higher education: Panacea or pandemic? *Angles on the English-Speaking World* 9, 369–378.

Ricento, T. (2015). *Language policy and political economy: English in a global context.* New York: Oxford University Press.

Shao, Q., & Gao, X. (2017). "Noisy guests shall not unseat the host": Framing high stakes English examinations in mainland China's state-controlled print media. *English Today* 33(3), 25–30.

Simpson, A. (Ed.) (2008). *Language and national identity in Africa.* Oxford: Oxford University Press.

Skutnabb-Kangas, T. (2000). *Linguistic genocide in education—Or worldwide diversity and human rights?* Mahwah, NJ: Lawrence Erlbaum.

Skutnabb-Kangas, T. (2008). Human rights and language policy in education. In S. May & N. H. Hornberger (Eds.), *Encyclopedia of language and education*, Vol. 1: *Language policy and political issues in education* (pp. 107–119). Berlin: Mouton.

Skutnabb-Kangas, T., & Phillipson, R. (Eds.) (1994). *Linguistic human rights: Overcoming linguistic discrimination.* Berlin: Mouton de Gruyter.

Spring, J. (2006). *Pedagogies of globalization: The rise of the educational security state.* New York: Routledge.

Tollefson, J. W. (1991). *Planning language, planning inequality: Language policy in the community.* London: Longman.

Tollefson, J. W. (Ed.). (1995). *Power and inequality in language education.* Cambridge: Cambridge University Press.

Tollefson, J. W. (2002). The language debates: Preparing for the war in Yugoslavia—1980–1991. *International Journal of the Sociology of Language* 154, 65–82.

Tollefson, J. W. (2004). Medium of instruction in Slovenia: European integration and ethnolinguistic nationalism. In J. W. Tollefson & A. B. M. Tsui (Eds.), *Medium of instruction policies: Which agenda? Whose agenda?* (pp. 263–281). Mahwah, NJ: Lawrence Erlbaum.

Tollefson, J. W. (2013). Language policy in a time of crisis and transformation. In J. W. Tollefson (Ed.), *Language policies in education: Critical issues* (2nd edition; pp. 3–10). New York: Routledge.

Tollefson, J. W., & Tsui, A. B. M. (2004). Contexts of medium of instruction policy. In J. W. Tollefson & A. B. M. Tsui (Eds.), *Medium of instruction policies: Which agenda? Whose agenda?* (pp. 283–294). Mahwah, NJ: Lawrence Erlbaum.

Tollefson, J. W., & Tsui, A. B. M. (2014). Language diversity and language policy in educational access and equity. *Review of Research in Education* 38, 189–214.

Tsui, A. B. M. (2007). Language policy and the social construction of identity: The case of Hong Kong. In A. B. M. Tsui & J. W. Tollefson (Eds.), *Language policy, culture and identity in Asian contexts* (pp. 121–141). Mahwah, NJ: Lawrence Erlbaum.

Tsung, L. T. H., & Cruickshank, K. (2009). Mother tongue and bilingual minority education in China. *International Journal of Bilingual Education and Bilingualism* 12(5), 549–563.

UNESCO. (1990). *World declaration on education for all and framework for action to meet basic learning needs* (adopted by the World Conference on Education for All Meeting Basic Learning Needs, Jomtien, Thailand, March 5–9, 1990). Paris: UNESCO.

UNESCO Bangkok. (2007). *Advocacy kit for promoting multilingual education: Including the excluded.* Bangkok: UNESCO, Asia and Pacific Regional Bureau for Education.

Union of Colleges and Universities. (2011). Draft resolution on higher education and research and the global financial crisis. *Congress Book 5: Draft Congress Resolutions, Education International 6th World Congress* (p. 43). Brussels: Education International.

Vertovec, S. (2007). Super-diversity and its implications. *Ethnic and Racial Studies* 30(6), 1024–1054.

Wächter, B. (2008). *Internationalisation and the European higher education area.* Report prepared for the Bologna Process Seminar Bologna 2020: Unlocking Europe's Potential—Contributing to a Better World, Ghent, May 19–20, 2008. Retrieved from http://www.ond.vlaanderen.be/hogeronderwijs/bologna/BolognaSeminars/documents/Ghent/Ghent_May08_Bernd_Waechter.pdf

Wächter, B., & Maiworm, F. (2008). *English-taught programmes in European higher education.* Bonn: Lemmens.

Watson-Gegeo, K. A., & Gegeo, D. W. (1992). Schooling, knowledge, and power: Social transformation in the Solomon Islands. *Anthropology and Education Quarterly* 23, 10–29.

Watson-Gegeo, K. A., & Gegeo, D. W. (2002). The critical villager: Transforming language and education in Solomon Islands. In J. W. Tollefson (Ed.), *Language policies in education: Critical issues* (1st edition; pp. 309–325). Mahwah, NJ: Lawrence Erlbaum

Webb, V. (2004). Language policy in post-Apartheid South Africa. In J. W. Tollefson & A. B. M. Tsui (Eds.), *Medium of instruction policies: Which agenda? Whose agenda?* (pp. 217–240). Mahwah, NJ: Lawrence Erlbaum.

Wee, L. (2011). *Language without rights*. Oxford: Oxford University Press.

Yamagami, M. (2012). The political discourse of the campaign against bilingual education: From Proposition 227 to Horne v. Flores. *International Multilingual Research Journal* 6(2), 143–159.

CHAPTER 14

LANGUAGE TESTS, LANGUAGE POLICY, AND CITIZENSHIP

KELLIE FROST AND TIM MCNAMARA

IN an era of mass global migration, language tests are now widely used by governments in various national contexts as screening or selection tools for controls, including restrictions, on immigration. The use of language tests in such policy contexts has led to efforts in the field of language testing to reconceptualise notions of test validity and fairness to include the social impact of test use, in order to account for the social and political roles that tests play, particularly when they operate within policy domains (McNamara & Roever, 2006; McNamara & Ryan, 2011). When language tests are viewed as embedded within sociopolitical spaces, the inevitable contestability of accounts of policy intentions will necessarily inform questions of test purpose and test consequences (Shohamy, 2001, 2006, 2009; Spolsky, 2004). Shohamy (2001, 2006, 2009) has repeatedly pointed out that tests are used for purposes far broader than simply measuring knowledge, and that the widespread acceptance of the legitimacy of tests means that potentially discriminatory and illiberal policy agendas remain hidden.

Much of the research has focused on identifying the underlying purposes of language-testing practices in the context of recent immigration policies in Europe, where many societies now have significant and increasing immigrant communities of recent origin (Extra & Van Avermaet, 2009; Hogan-Brun et al., 2009) and are experiencing varying degrees of social tension as a result of this demographic and cultural change. Less attention has been paid to problematising the existence of formal language test requirements within migrant selection processes in countries of immigration such as Australia, Canada, New Zealand, and the United States, which have typically encouraged immigration and have found it easier to embrace various forms of multiculturalism, despite some inevitable tensions. Nor has the impact of the language test requirements of immigration policies on the individuals who are subject to these requirements been explored, although since Foucault (1977) the effect of power on the examined subject has been a prominent theme.

To examine language tests in one country of immigration—Australia—we adopt a poststructuralist approach. Poststructuralism (McNamara, 2012b) as a lens through which to understand the social function of tests in general has been explored in the work of Ronell (2005); and poststructuralist analyses of language testing have begun to appear by those working within critical language testing (McNamara, 2012a; Shohamy, 2001, 2006). Fundamental sources for this re-evaluation of testing include Foucault's view of tests as instruments of surveillance in modernity and Derrida's notion of language as shibboleth (Derrida, 2005; cf. Derrida, 1998). Foucault, in his classic discussion of the role of surveillance in the operation of power in *Discipline and Punish*, discusses the way in which subjection to power creates the subject:

> Disciplinary power ... is exercised through its invisibility; at the same time it imposes on those whom it subjects a principle of compulsory visibility. In discipline, it is the subjects who have to be seen. Their visibility assures the hold of the power that is exercised over them.... The examination is the technique by which power ... holds [its subjects] in a mechanism of objectification. (Foucault, 1977 [1975], p. 187)

He adds:

> The examination as the fixing, at once ritual and "scientific," of individual differences, as the pinning down of each individual in his own particularity ... clearly indicates the appearance of a new modality of power in which each individual receives as his status his own individuality. (Foucault, 1977 [1975], p. 192)

The shibboleth appears first in a biblical story in which a test of pronunciation of a word is used to tell friend from foe. Derrida (2005) uses it as the basis for a discussion of the nature of language as a shared medium and as a site of power. The very means by which the individual exists as a social being, language, is also potentially the means by which the subject may be denied its rights, or even its existence. The fact that the shibboleth necessarily acts as a two-edged sword—inclusion always carries with it the potential for exclusion, and its potential for justice is simultaneously a potential for injustice—leads Derrida to speak of "the terrifying ambiguity of the shibboleth, sign of belonging and threat of discrimination" (2005, p. 27).

We adopt Foucault's notion of language tests as a form of surveillance and Derrida's conception of tests as shibboleth in order to examine the testing regime within which performance on language tests has become key to the chances of international students temporarily in Australia achieving permanent resident status there, and ultimately citizenship. We begin by summarising the changing role of language proficiency testing in Australia's skilled migration program, particularly emphasising its unpredictability and arbitrariness from the point of view of those subject to it. We then document the way in which the subjectivity of individuals subject to this regime is shaped by their experience of its demands as they make repeated attempts to pass the test. We conclude by considering the accounts of the test takers from a poststructuralist perspective and implications for further research in language policy and planning (LPP).

The Changing Role of Language Proficiency Testing in Australia's Skilled Migration Program

A formal migration program was created in Australia in 1945, with the establishment of the first federal immigration portfolio and specialised Immigration Department. In the early 1980s, the migration program was split from a single stream into the three categories that exist in the current policy: skilled, family, and humanitarian migration. Within the skilled migration category, a points-based model of selection, or points test, is used, and selection criteria are oriented towards selecting those with the potential to deliver benefits to the Australian economy, including an ability to communicate in English. As we will show, English ability has moved from an implicit to a central and explicit place within the policy.

English-language ability became a particularly salient issue in discussion of immigration policy during the 1980s as growing numbers of skilled migrants from diverse non-English-speaking backgrounds were entering Australia (Markus et al., 2009). Throughout this period, English-language ability was not mentioned explicitly in the list of points-weighted criteria, but it remained an important implicit criterion, as immigration officers were required to judge prospective migrants' settlement prospects on a five-point scale ranging from "settlement risk" to "outstanding" (Hawthorne, 1997, p. 12). Hawthorne (1997) points out that such judgements were based, at least in part, on an informal assessment of the migrants' English-language ability. In 1989, following a review of Australia's immigration policies, English-language competency was reinserted into the points system as an explicit criterion but was not listed as compulsory, and English-language points were not critical to selection for tertiary-qualified applicants of prime working age (Hawthorne, 1997).

By the early 1990s, however, as Australia, along with many other Organisation for Economic Co-operation and Development (OECD) economies, was in the midst of a worsening recession, skilled migrants from non-English-speaking backgrounds were increasingly identified as an economic burden. Perceptions that many were lacking the English skills needed for successful integration into the labour market fuelled calls for changes to migrant selection criteria (Brindley & Wigglesworth, 1997; Hawthorne, 1997). Consequently, in 1992 changes to the points test system were introduced, which made English competency a mandatory requirement for many occupations, listed as "Occupations requiring English." A new test, the Australian Assessment of Communicative English (*access:*), was commissioned and developed for skilled migration purposes by the National Centre for English Language Teaching and Research at Macquarie University (Brindley & Wigglesworth, 1997). The test was first administered in 1993, and in 1998 *access:* was replaced by the International English Language Testing System (IELTS), one of the tests currently recognised by the Australian government for skilled migration purposes.

In the late 1990s, the conservative Howard government (in office from 1996 to 2007) set about significantly increasing the skilled migrant intake and at the same time implementing reforms to the selection criteria in the points test. These reforms included an expansion of English-language criteria. By 1998, 85% of applicants were subjected to mandatory language requirements. In July 1999, mandatory language requirements were adopted as core migrant selection criteria (Birrell, Hawthorne, & Richardson, 2006; Chiswick et al., 2006). At the same time, the government also began prioritising temporary forms of migration, for work and study purposes (Koleth, 2010). While traditionally, skilled (and other) migration in Australia was conceptualised by governments and policymakers as necessarily involving the right to permanent residency (Markus et al., 2009), new forms of temporary visas were established, as a means of enhancing the flexibility of the migration program (Collins, 2013; Cully, 2011).

This shift towards temporary forms of skilled migration in the late 1990s coincided with government efforts to increase Australia's share of the international education export market. Intense global competition to attract and recruit highly skilled workers was a further driver of the promotion of Australia as a study destination, and attracting international students was viewed as a means of building an onshore supply of such workers. The introduction of the study-migration pathway in 1999, discussed in the following section, was a key policy measure in this context.

English Language Proficiency Testing within the Study-Migration Pathway

By the late 1990s, tertiary education was becoming an increasingly important and lucrative export industry in Australia, and international competition for both highly skilled migrants and international students was intense (Koleth, 2010). The purpose of the study-migration policy initiative was thus twofold: first, to provide an incentive (in the form of permanent residency) to attract international students to Australian institutions, thereby boosting the value of Australia's education export market; and second, and specifically in relation to skilled migration policy, to create an onshore supply of highly skilled and already acculturated migrant workers, as a means of efficiently augmenting the skill base and addressing skill shortages in the labour market (Gribble & Blackmore, 2012; Hawthorne, 2010; Koleth, 2010). According to Hawthorne (2010), international graduates were widely considered to be ideal migrants; they possessed locally recognised qualifications, and were thought likely to have already adapted and assimilated themselves to the local linguistic and cultural context. As a result, in 1999, existing skilled migration selection criteria were modified to grant additional points to applicants possessing qualifications from Australian institutions. This marked the beginning of the establishment of a link between study and permanent residency via the skilled migration program.

In 2001, the link was reinforced and expanded as international graduates of Australian institutions with qualifications in specified key skill areas, such as information and communication technologies, for example, became immediately eligible for permanent residency as skilled migrants upon completion of their studies. Applicants could now apply from within Australia (Koleth, 2010), and the basic work experience criteria, a compulsory requirement for offshore applicants wishing to gain an independent skilled visa, was waived for those who applied within Australia after having completed courses of at least one year in duration (Birrell, Hawthorne, & Richardson, 2006; Birrell & Healy, 2010).

International graduates of Australian institutions, even if their qualifications were not in key skill areas, were further advantaged compared to overseas applicants for permanent residency by other selection criteria in the points test. While applicants for skilled migration who had completed their qualifications overseas were required to demonstrate at least the minimum required level of English proficiency on a recognised language test, such as IELTS, those who had completed their studies onshore were, from 1999 until September 2007, assumed to possess adequate English skills and were thus exempt from any test requirement (Arkoudis et al., 2009).

The introduction of a study-migration pathway proved to be very effective in expanding Australia's education export market, with the number of international student enrolments rising from 133,384 in 1999 to 344,815 in 2005 (Australian Education International, n.d). Similarly, the pathway appeared to be effectively producing a supply of onshore skilled migrants in Australia, as intended. In 2003, almost half of the skilled visas granted were to former student visa holders (Koleth, 2010). As Koleth (2010) reports, a tightening of selection criteria ensued in July 2003 as the government sought to limit the likelihood of oversupply. The minimum period of study in Australia increased from one to two years before former students could access bonus points for Australian qualifications and have the basic work requirements waived. The points awarded to applicants with Australian higher degrees, such as master's degrees and PhDs, were also increased at this time.

By 2005, however, the efficacy of the study-migration pathway in addressing skill shortages in the labour market was beginning to be questioned. Concerns had emerged that international graduates transitioning to skilled visas were failing to gain employment in their fields, despite persistent skill shortages (Koleth, 2010).

Birrell, Hawthorne, and Richardson (2006) were commissioned by the immigration minister to examine how well skilled migration policy changes introduced since 1999 were achieving the general skilled migration program's broad aims, described as skill augmentation, addressing shortages in the Australian labour force, and sustaining Australia's labour force growth into the future. The investigation was primarily quantitative in nature, based on an examination of data from migrant surveys, including the Longitudinal Survey of Immigrants to Australia (LSIA). As part of their evaluation, migrant attributes, including English-language background and self-reported spoken English ability, were correlated with several economic measures of labour market integration. Their analyses revealed that skilled migrants from non-English-speaking backgrounds, including international graduates recruited onshore, were experiencing prolonged difficulties accessing the Australian labour market. Furthermore, the researchers found that when these migrants gained employment, they were often underemployed, unable to access job opportunities and pay rates commensurate with their qualifications. Not surprisingly, they also found that migrants' who reported speaking English very well generally achieved rapid integration into the labour market, and were more likely to attain jobs and pay rates consistent with their skill levels.

Although Birrell et al.'s (2006) evaluation provided broad support for the effectiveness of policy changes introduced since 1999 in terms of delivering improved labour market outcomes, they highlighted several problematic issues surrounding the study-migration pathway. For example, the researchers argued that bonus points attributed to applicants with in-demand qualifications, combined with bonus points for possessing Australian qualifications, created perverse incentives for overseas students. A Migration Occupations in Demand List (MODL) had been introduced in 1999 as part of a series of reforms to better align the skilled migrant intake with existing labour market shortages. All applicants for points-tested permanent skilled migration, not only former overseas students, benefited from bonus points for possessing qualifications in occupations listed on the MODL, as well as priority processing. The three researchers claimed that the double-benefit available to applicants with qualifications on the MODL and from an Australian institution was likely to encourage those with the primary goal of gaining permanent residency to enrol in relatively undemanding courses in areas that featured on the list, particularly if they possessed limited English-language proficiency. This, they suggest, was producing an over-concentration of graduates in a limited number of occupational areas, with no guarantee that they would possess good English communication skills.

As mentioned earlier, Birrell et al. (2006) supported their evaluation through an analysis of migrant survey data, whereby migrants were asked to provide a self-assessment of their own English proficiency by selecting the best option to describe how well they spoke English from the range: "very well," "well," "not well," and "not at all." Correlations with measures of labour market integration led to the conclusion that "in most dimensions of labour market success, the key is to have a level of English language competence that enables the respondent to report that they speak English at least 'very well'" (p. 92). Although Birrell, Hawthorne, and Richardson had already noted that there was "no way of aligning the answers of respondents to an objectively measured test of English proficiency such as IELTS" (p. 89), they nonetheless make the connection: "We equate this to about a 7 on IELTS, although it is a big stretch to do so" (p. 92).

Birrell et al.'s conclusions in relation to the study-migration pathway rest on an implicit premise that if positive self-assessments of English proficiency correlate with positive employment outcomes, then poor employment outcomes for graduates of Australian institutions from non-English-speaking backgrounds are likely attributable to their inadequate English skills. Such a view mirrors media discourses emerging from 2001 onwards in which the presence of international students was consistently associated with declining academic standards (Birrell, 2006; Devos, 2003). Birrell (2006), for example, drew on comparisons of IELTS scores achieved by the same test takers pre-entry to university and upon graduation to argue that there was little or no improvement in the English level of international students over the duration of their studies. This, he claimed, reflected declining academic standards as universities, reliant on income from international student fees, admitted international students despite their poor English-language skills and accommodated for this so-called deficit through lowering the standards of assessment. Such a claim served to further undermine the study-migration pathway, as international graduates were characterised in negative terms, as lacking the language skills for employment. As has been argued since, there is little empirical evidence to support this deficit perspective of the language skills of international students (see Benzie, 2010; Briguglio, 2011), and much evidence to suggest that barriers to their integration into the labour force are numerous and complex, and often are unrelated to language proficiency (Arkoudis et al., 2009; Gribble, 2014).

Nonetheless, this premise and the tenuous link these researchers established between speaking English "very well" and scores of IELTS 7 drove a series of reforms, from 2007 onwards, to the selection criteria for skilled migration. These reforms included an increase in the English-language requirements within the points test. In September 2007, the minimum language level for non-trade occupations was lifted from *vocational English*, defined then as IELTS 5, to the existing minimum level required—*competent English*, or IELTS 6. In addition, significant bonus points were attributed to above-minimum scores of IELTS 7—*proficient English*. Furthermore, international graduates of Australian institutions were no longer assumed to possess the required level of English, and have since been subjected to the same language test requirements as offshore applicants (Hawthorne, 2011). As Hawthorne (2011) points out, these reforms meant that IELTS scores became the key determinant of selection for permanent residency visas.

From December 2008, in the context of the global financial crisis and amidst persisting concerns that the skilled migration program was failing to adequately address skill shortages, the skilled migration program was again the subject of reforms in an attempt to ensure that those selected were readily employable and able to fill existing demand (Gribble & Blackmore, 2012). In January 2009, a new, more restrictive skills in-demand list was introduced. In March and again in May 2009, the government announced reductions in the skilled migrant intake. In July 2009, a further tightening of English-language test score requirements was implemented. Vocational English (IELTS 5) had remained sufficient for those in trade-related occupations until this point, when the requirement for these applicants was also increased to *competent English* (IELTS 6).

During this period, some of the issues that had been raised by Birrell, Hawthorne, and Richardson (2006) were being compounded by wider concerns over the integrity of Australia's export education industry and the student visa system, as well as the welfare of international students in Australia. These concerns stemmed from increasing evidence of unethical and exploitative practices by some English-language and international education providers, particularly in the context of rapidly increasing demand for courses that provided access to permanent residency, as well as the potential, due to inadequate regulation and quality assurance measures, for such providers to fraudulently align their courses with migration requirements (Hawthorne, 2011). Alarming reports of violent attacks against Indian international students in Australia further exacerbated welfare concerns. These factors, taken together, threatened to undermine Australia's reputation as a study destination for international students (Gribble & Blackmore, 2012). It had become increasingly apparent that the study-migration pathway was producing unforeseen and undesirable consequences; thus the government moved to assert a clear distinction between the purpose of the student visa program and the skilled migration program, which would effectively mean the removal of a direct link between study and permanent residency (Koleth, 2010).

The process of separating study and permanent migration included the announcement of significant reforms to the skilled migration selection criteria in 2010, and the implementation of a new points test in July 2011.

The Role of English-Language Proficiency in the New Points Test

This overhaul of selection processes reflected a marked preference for employer-sponsored migrants, with the bar significantly raised for other skilled applicants; from mid-2011 onwards, eligibility for skilled visas was restricted to those with high-level education qualifications, proven work experience, and advanced English ability (Gribble & Blackmore, 2012; Hawthorne & To, 2014).

The pass mark for the new points test is currently set at 60. The key changes between the points test in effect in 2010 and the new points test introduced in 2011 are summarised in Table 14.1. As shown, those gaining qualifications in Australia are no longer advantaged. Further, the pre-2011 minimum requirement of IELTS 6, *competent English*, remained in place in the new points test, but points were no longer awarded for meeting this requirement. Scores of IELTS 7 attracted 10 points, a slightly lower weighting than in the previous points test, but an extra discrete point item—*superior English*—defined as IELTS 8, was added for 20 points, accounting for a third of the overall requirement. Achieving points for English-language skills through scores of IELTS 7 or IELTS 8 became a necessity for many international

Table 14.1 Comparison of Key Criteria before and after Changes to the Points Test in Mid–2011

Points Test 2010: Pass Mark 120		New Points Test 2011: Current Pass Mark 60	
Criteria	Points	Criteria	Points
Occupational	60, 50, 40	N/A	
English language:		English language:	
IELTS 7	25	IELTS 8	20
IELTS 6*	15	IELTS 7	10
		IELTS 6*	0
Education:		Education:	
Australian doctorate	25	Doctorate (Australia or overseas)	20
Australian bachelor or above	15	Bachelor or above (Australia or overseas)	15
Australian trade qualification	5	Trade qualification (Australia or overseas)	10
Employment:		Employment#:	
60-point occupation + 3 years	10	1 year in Australia	5
Other SOL + 3 years	5	3 years in Australia	10
Closely related in Australia (1 year)	10	5 years in Australia	15
		8 years in Australia	20
Employment in Australia:		3 years overseas	5
One year relevant work experience	10	5 years overseas	10
		8 years overseas	15

* Minimum English test score required for eligibility

Employment in nominated occupation or closely related undertaken in past 10 years. Maximum points that can be awarded for any combination of Australian or overseas skilled employment is 20 points.

graduates wishing to obtain permanent residency in an increasingly competitive selection process, especially recent graduates who had yet to accumulate extensive work experience in their professions.

Since mid-2012, scores of IELTS 7 and 8 have become even more critical in the transition from temporary to permanent resident via the skilled migration program, regardless of work experience. At this time, occupational quotas were introduced into the selection process for permanent residency visas, such that the number of visas granted within any particular occupation is capped in line with labour market indicators on a bi-monthly basis. This has meant that in a given selection round (there are six per year), the number of applicants meeting the points test pass mark may exceed the number of visas available. In this case, applicants are ranked in point order, with priority given to those with the highest points score (DIAC, 2012). Those who are not granted a visa remain in the pool of applicants either until they are selected for permanent residency in a subsequent round or their temporary visas expire, in which case they are left with no option but to leave Australia.

Berg (2011) suggests that ever-increasing English-language test scores deliver an "implicit homogenising message that Australia wants migrants who sound like us and speak our language" (p. 110). She argues that the policy rationale of using English standards to promote inclusion and integration is, in this way, contradictory, as progressively raising English requirements potentially reinforces "an underlying nativism in Australia" (p. 110), supporting racist attitudes and behaviours, and further marginalising migrants who are linguistically unassimilated. This accords with concerns that the use of language tests in selection processes for immigration and citizenship promotes a predominately exclusionary political agenda (Blackledge, 2009; Horner, 2009; Shohamy, 2009; Van Avermaet, 2009).

But how is the policy experienced by those subject to an ever-changing, challenging, and allegedly exclusionary language-testing regime? In the rest of the chapter, we will consider the implications of these changing language requirements on two long-term temporary residents of Australia, both holding down professional jobs, and their experiences and changing attitudes as they make repeated attempts to achieve the levels of English proficiency on the IELTS test needed for them to be eligible for permanent residency in Australia. In Foucault's terms, how is their subjectivity constructed by their subjection to the requirements of immigration law as represented by the language test?

Two Individual Cases: Erfan and Ana

Erfan and Ana (both pseudonyms), aged in their thirties, were each residing in Australia on temporary visas and were in the process of seeking permanent residency via the skilled migration program, having completed their tertiary studies and having gained employment in Australia. Five in-depth, open-ended interviews were conducted by the first author with each of the two participants as they went through the process of repeated language test attempts in their efforts to gain permanent residency. The last interview with each participant was conducted after their fourth and final test attempt, in which both achieved the IELTS scores they needed for permanent residency. With Erfan, interviews were conducted between August 2012 and May 2013, and with Ana, between September 2012 and October 2013. The interviewer explained at the outset that the focus of the study was on participants' test experiences in the context of their migration journey, their perceptions of the language-test requirement, as well as how they felt about their language and their migration experiences generally. After this brief orientation, participants were invited to talk freely about their experiences. Biographical data was collected from each participant in the initial interviews. A brief profile of each of the two participants now follows.

Erfan

Erfan is from Iran and identifies Persian (Farsi) as his native language. He arrived in Australia in 2009, and had spent close to three and a half years in Melbourne by the time the interviews commenced. In Iran he had completed a bachelor-level degree in information technology (IT) and had worked as an IT professional there for three years. He came to Melbourne with the intention of studying for a doctorate, and had chosen Australia as a destination because of the option to apply for permanent residency upon completion. He began by applying for a master's degree in IT, and took the IELTS in Iran as part of the entry requirement. He was unable to achieve the score of IELTS 6.5 needed for direct entry into university, so he first undertook a ten-week preparation course in academic English as an alternative pathway. He graduated from his master's program in 2011 but did not achieve high enough grades to qualify for an international student scholarship to undertake a doctorate. In February 2011, he again took the IELTS and achieved the score needed to qualify for a three-year temporary graduate visa. In 2012, he commenced part-time work as a research assistant in his field at the university where he had completed his master's degree. He had been working there for just over three months when he participated in the first interview for this study. His plan was to apply for permanent residency so that he could apply to undertake a doctorate as a local student (local students currently pay no fees to undertake doctoral studies).

Ana

Ana is from Colombia and identifies Spanish as her native language. At the time the interviews commenced, she had been in Australia with her husband, also from

Colombia, for over three years, having arrived in 2009. Both Ana and her husband had completed bachelor-level degrees prior to coming to Australia, and both had been employed in skilled occupations in Colombia. Ana was an IT professional, and her husband worked in the finance industry. She began learning English when she arrived in Australia. After spending a year working as a cleaner and studying English, she enrolled in a master's degree program in networking systems. She successfully completed an academic English preparation course at a college affiliated with her university, which served as an alternative entry pathway to taking IELTS. She graduated from her master's program in March 2012. The first encounter she had with IELTS was in the middle of the last semester of her course, in September 2011, in order to meet the requirements for a temporary graduate visa, the first step in transitioning from international student to permanent resident status. She required an overall score of IELTS 6 to qualify for this visa and achieved IELTS 6.5. Since completing her master's degree she has been working as an administrative officer, in an area unrelated to her field of study.

Extracts from interviews with Erfan and Ana are presented in the following, as a means of shedding light on their perspectives on test purposes and their interpretations of the meanings of test scores. To begin with, details of their test encounters and their individual orientations to the test requirement are provided, including the stakes they each attach to the test and their attitudinal approach to achieving their score goals. This is followed by a discussion of their general perceptions of the use of an English-language test within migrant-selection procedures, and in particular, the weightings attributed to scores of IELTS 7 and 8 in the points test for skilled migration. Finally, we present participants' accounts of their perceptions of their test experiences, including the relevance of IELTS to their work contexts and their lives more broadly, and the meaning they attribute to particular score outcomes.

Test Encounters

For both Erfan and Ana, meeting the language test score requirement represented the final obstacle in their attempt to become permanent residents in Australia. Both had already satisfied all of the other criteria in the points test. They each needed scores of IELTS 7 across all four skills—speaking, writing, listening, and reading—to achieve the minimum points total required to become eligible to apply for permanent residency in Australia as skilled migrants, but they were each initially aiming for scores of IELTS 8. Achieving scores of IELTS 8 meant they would access 20 points instead of 10 for English language, which would push their points total above the minimum and increase the likelihood of selection if the number of applicants in their occupational areas exceeded the number of visas available. For each of them, achieving the minimum required scores of IELTS 7 involved four test encounters, with scores of IELTS 8 across all skills proving unattainable. Their test encounters and associated score outcomes are summarised in Tables 14.2 and 14.3.

Table 14.2 Test Encounters for Permanent Residency: Erfan

	October 2012	November 2012	February 2013	April 2013
Speaking	6.5	7	8	8
Writing	6	6	6.5	7
Listening	8	8.5	8	8.5
Reading	7.5	7	8	7

Table 14.3 Test Encounters for Permanent Residency: Ana

	October 2012	December 2012	May 2013	September 2013
Speaking	6.5	7	7	7
Writing	6.5	6	6	7
Listening	8	6	7.5	8
Reading	6.5	6	7.5	8

Perceptions of Test Stakes

As already mentioned, both Erfan and Ana needed scores of at least IELTS 7 to achieve the minimum points they required to become eligible for permanent residency. The stakes attached to gaining permanent residency, and thus test stakes for each of them, were very high, as shown in the following example.

> ERFAN: It's not very good, it's very difficult and you know the whole [of] my life depends on it.
> RESEARCHER: What will you do, I mean, if you didn't, if you weren't able to do that here would you move somewhere, or are you just not even thinking?
> ERFAN: I'm not even thinking. . . . Yeah because it's too devastating. I spent about $100,000 during these four years so it would be a complete waste of money and time.

Perceptions of Test Purpose

Erfan and Ana both supported the use of an English-language test in the process of migrant selection, even as they struggled to meet the requirements. They each saw learning English as an important responsibility on the part of migrants, necessary for social integration and for making a contribution to Australian society. They accepted the use of a test as an appropriate means of ensuring that migrants were capable of functioning in English.

Each participant hedged their support for test use, however, by drawing on their own personal experiences to reject the appropriateness of the heavy weighting of scores of IELTS 7 and 8, suggesting that such scores were unnecessary.

> ERFAN: So after working, after living for four years and two different universities, yeah, someone definitely has the ability to function in this country, but it might not be as high as 8 but it should be sufficient, at least, I think.
>
> ANA: But the, the thing is how they change the score so drastically from 6 to 7 or 8. . . . In that the way they, they, they jump from one score . . . I am functional. I work in an Australian company and if you ask them, I think, they have no problems with me and my communication.

They also suggested that privileging those with scores of IELTS 8, in particular, served to favour individuals from countries that are culturally and linguistically similar to Australia, and at worse to exclude those from non-European backgrounds. Each participant thus took a critical view of the current privileging of test scores of IELTS 8 in migrant selection. The points-weighting of such scores within selection criteria was seen to be unfair and in some ways racist. Particularly in Ana's case, these perceptions fed into a growing sense of injustice as she experienced difficulties achieving her own score goal: "Their English is not better than mine, they are not smart as, as smarter, smarter, smarter as I a- . . . anyway . . . and it seems that for them, everything is easy and, yes I have this feeling that everything is wrong with me."

Perceptions of Test Encounters and Score Outcomes

In addition to participants' perceptions of test purpose and the score requirements, their subjective experiences with IELTS as they encountered it informed their different understandings of the meanings of test scores they achieved. Erfan, for example, seemed to view the test purely as an arbitrary obstacle to overcome, with no real connection to how English is used in real life. He highlights the absurdity of having to perform tasks that are not only outside his professional domain, but that are also outside the realm of his experiences and capabilities even in his first language: "I can, I can write technical report very well but I can't write an essay about a social thing, so the unrelevant thing is this bit. . . . And the funny thing is I also, I, I even cannot write as in even in my first language the kind of quality that they expect me to write in English."

Similarly, he views the scores he achieves on the test as arbitrary and disconnected from his language abilities. He expressed a lack of confidence in his English ability in the first interview, before his first test attempt, despite his success in his studies in Australia and an ability to function effectively at work ("I still feel pressure and not comfortable in conversation"). In the fourth interview, despite achieving IELTS 8 on his speaking test, he felt that his English was inadequate for social interactions with native speakers of English ("I personally believe that it's not good enough to be engaged in social situations and friends, yeah").

By the fifth interview, he had achieved his target score in all skills, and thus qualified to apply for a permanent residency visa. As his explanation in the following suggests, however, he does not see his success on the test and his eligibility for permanent residency as evidence of his capacity to communicate sufficiently well in English. Instead, he continues to situate himself in a deficit position, inferior in skill to native English speakers and vulnerable to their judgment: "Ah, I just feel pressure when I'm talking to native people, native speaking people. I just feel I, I, I ah I don't want to make silly mistakes because it might give them a wrong impression of myself."

By contrast, Ana's perceptions of her English-language abilities shift on the basis of her test experiences. As shown earlier, she appears confident in her English-language abilities prior to her first test attempt for permanent residency. She asserts her ability to function effectively in English, evidenced by her social interactions and experiences at work, where she communicates with English native speakers on a daily basis without encountering any problems.

After her first test encounter, however, she loses confidence in her legitimacy as an English speaker and although her lack of success on the test is inconsistent with her successful non-test experiences using English, she starts to see her language use as problematic and feels that she has to try to modify how she speaks: "I think they follow a pattern, you know what I mean, a pattern? So if she thinks that, I think the rest will think the same, so I, what else can I do, you know?" After the poor scores she achieves in her second test encounter, the notion that her English skills are in need of improvement is reinforced and she re-situates herself as a language learner, linking test preparation and her broader life goals: "It's not just for the test, I want to get a better job. If I want to get a better job, I need to improve my language skills...."

After two further test attempts (four in total) over a period of one year, Ana achieves the scores she needs for permanent residency. At this point, she continues to situate herself as a work in progress in terms of her English usage, seeing her scores as indicative of only partial assimilation to the native speaker norms she is now aspiring towards: "I love Australia, I love English. Even it's, even if it's still broken, I love English.... English is my second language and I'm expecting to spend all my life in this country and I want to speak proper English. You have to honour your language, no?"

DISCUSSION AND CONCLUSION

The operation of tests, including language tests, in creating its subjects has been documented too little in studies of language tests. Bessette (2005) made a study of the experience of senior Anglophone civil servants in Canada who were forced to undergo rigorous assessment of high-level proficiency in spoken French as a condition of keeping their posts. The renewed enforcement of bilingual proficiency requirements via the test was a political response by Canadian federalists to the narrow defeat of the Québec separatist movement in a referendum in 1995. Bessette shows varying responses to the experience, which typically involved repeated attempts and repeated failure, and the necessity for long temporary absences from posts in order to undertake intensive language training, often requiring residence in French-speaking families in Québec. On the one hand, one informant discussed the experience in the following terms:

> There has to be a better way. . . . The process [is] set up for failure. . . . In a way, it's set up [so that] you go through, boom, [and] you pass or you fail and most people fail, . . . more than fifty percent fail; [. . . and] that's hard personally. Some incredibly brilliant people I know have taken eight times to actually pass.

This informant described the experience as a *ritual of humiliation*, echoing Foucault's characterisation of the examination. On the other hand, another informant embraced the construction of a new subjectivity through the experience: "On the whole, this participant 'surrendered himself'. . . . He felt that this experience has given him a fuller sense of himself as 'someone who represents the new Canada: visible minority person who speaks both official languages'" (Bessette, 2005, p. 55).

These findings resonate with the findings of our study, which show the complex ways in which the power of the language-proficiency requirement for residency shapes the subjectivity of our informants. Both informants acknowledge their subjection to the power of the test: "The whole [of] my life depends on it" (Erfan); "My husband depends on my results and we have built a life here and now my residency depends on that exam" (Ana). Neither showed any resistance to the existence of a testing regime in general, ventriloquising the discourse used to justify the existence of the regime in policy documents and public discussion: "There has to be some sort of test" (Erfan); "This is an English country, everyone speaks English and the government has to measure that in one or another way. . . . This is another culture, new rules, new people. I have to fix, I have to fit in that society. I can't swim against the flow" (Ana). Both felt an obligation to engage constructively with the power of the test: "I have to [feel positive about the test] . . . because you . . . everything what happens into your life, because you create it" (Ana); "It is a thing that I have to do and I have no way to escape so I don't want to mess my mind around with that . . . I don't want to blame anyone" (Erfan).

Despite their conformity in their attitudes and behaviour to the regime of the test, the irrationality of a policy which demanded levels of English higher than those actually and demonstrably required in their lives and work leads to suspicion of a discriminatory motivation for the test, as a mechanism for selecting out categories of immigrants culturally and linguistically similar to the majority. But that perception, a form of resistance to the policy, is not enough to shield them from its requirements and its effects on their self-perception. Through the process of interacting with the test on repeat occasions, Ana became increasingly conscious of a difference between her use of English and normalized forms of English usage, expressed through test scores and the feedback she received from English experts: "I have this feeling that everything is wrong with me" (Ana). Erfan, on the other hand, is protected from this self-deprecation by his awareness of the irrationality of the test as a measure: He feels it has no relationship to his own actual abilities, even when he does well on some section of it, or the abilities of others. Erfan's rejection of the authority of the test, however, does not mitigate his sense of vulnerability to judgement and potential exclusion from the more legitimate native English-speaker Australian community, despite his newly acquired eligibility for permanent residency status.

While disputing the practical relevance of the test as proof of a language proficiency clearly beyond the level required of their life and employment situations, both Ana and Erfan show an awareness of the complex ideological meanings of the testing regime: legitimate nation building on the one hand, covert discrimination on the other. Poststructuralist emphasis on the indeterminacy of signifiers (the disputed meaning of a test construct, for example) allows us to recognize the tension between the overt meaning of the construct, for example, *language proficiency*, and its covert meaning, in terms of the values or ideologies it represents. In other words, the interpretation of test scores as shibboleths can be made in reference to multiple constructs, open to various readings, and hence to dispute. In all this we see the power of the test in the lives of those who are subject to it: the test is the point of insertion of policy in the lives of individuals. We need more such studies, in many different contexts, to see how individuals experience this subjection, and in what ways and to what extent their subjectivity is constructed through it.

More generally, language policy and language planning practice are classic examples of modernist practices. Poststructuralist accounts can illuminate the complex impact of such practices on the subjectivity of individuals, as they locate themselves within the range of positions the language policy and planning regimes provide. While poststructuralism offers the potential for a critical engagement with such regimes, it also acknowledges the inevitability of power and its role in creating the very possibility of individual and social life. In this view, language policy is thus, like language itself, simultaneously creative and potentially destructive. We cannot escape this paradox of power; we must be continuously vigilant in recognising the complex and unpredictable effects of LPP practice, "the terrifying ambiguity of the shibboleth" (Derrida, 2005, p. 27).

References

Arkoudis, S., Hawthorne, L., Baik, C., Hawthorne, G., O'Loughlin, K., Leach, D., & Bexley, E. (2009). *The impact of English language proficiency and workplace readiness on the employment outcomes of tertiary international students.* Canberra: The Department of Employment, Education and Workplace Relations.

Australian Education International. (n.d.). *International student data 2005.* Retrieved from https://internationaleducation.gov.au/research/International-Student-Data/Pages/InternationalStudentData2005.aspx

Benzie, H. (2010). Graduating as a "native speaker": International students and English language proficiency in higher education. *Higher Education Research and Development* 29(4), 447–459.

Berg, L. (2011). "Mate speak English, you're in Australia now": English language requirements in skilled migration. *Alternative Law Journal* 36(2), 110–115.

Bessette, J. (2005). *Government French language training programs: Statutory civil servants' experiences.* Unpublished master's thesis, University of Ottawa, Canada.

Birrell, B. (2006). Implications of low English standards among overseas students at Australian universities. *People and Place* 14(4), 53–64.

Birrell, B., Hawthorne, L., & Richardson, S. (2006). *Evaluation of the general skilled migration categories.* Canberra: Commonwealth of Australia.

Birrell, B., & Healy, E. (2010). The February 2010 reforms and the international student industry. *People and Place* 18(1), 65–80.

Blackledge, A. (2009). Inventing English as convenient fiction: Language testing regimes in the United Kingdom. In G. Extra, M. Spotti, & P. Van Avermaet (Eds.), *Language testing, migration and citizenship* (pp. 66–86). London; New York: Continuum.

Briguglio, C. (2011). Quality and the English language question: Is there really an issue in Australian universities? *Quality in Higher Education* 17(3), 317–329.

Brindley, G., & Wigglesworth, G. (Eds). (1997). *access: Issues in language test design and delivery.* Sydney: Macquarie University.

Chiswick, B. Lee, Y., & Miller, P. (2006). Immigrants' language skills and visa category. *International Migration Review* 40(2), 419–450.

Collins, J. (2013). Rethinking Australian immigration and immigrant settlement policy, *Journal of Intercultural Studies* 34(2), 160–177.

Cully, M. (2011). Skilled migration selection policies: Recent Australian reforms. *Migration Policy Practice* 1(1), 4–7.

Department of Immigration and Citizenship (DIAC). (2012). *General skilled migration points test under SkillSelect.* Canberra: Commonwealth of Australia. Retrieved from http://www.acic.com.tw/files/7PDF/points-tested-migration-fact-sheet.pdf

Derrida, J. (1998). *Monolingualism of the Other; Or, the prosthesis of origin.* P. Mensah, Trans. Stanford, CA: Stanford University Press. (Translation of *Le monolinguisme de l'autre: ou la prothèse d'origin,* Paris: Éditions Galilée, 1996.)

Derrida, J. (2005). Shibboleth: For Paul Celan [Originally published as *Schibboleth: Pour Paul Celan.* Paris: Éditions Galilée, 1986]. In T. Dutoit & O. Pasanen (Eds.), *Sovereignties in question: The poetics of Paul Celan* (pp. 1–64). New York: Fordham University Press.

Devos, A. (2003). Academic standards, internationalisation and the discursive construction of "the international student." *Higher Education Research and Development* 22(2), 155–166.

Extra, G. Spotti, M., & Van Avermaet, P. (Eds.) (2009). *Language testing, migration and citizenship.* London; New York: Continuum International.

Foucault, M. (1977). *Discipline and punish: The birth of the prison.* A. Sheridan, Trans. London: Allen Lane [Originally published as *Surveiller et Punir: Naissance de la Prison,* Paris: Éditions Gallimard, 1975].

298 KELLIE FROST AND TIM MCNAMARA

Gribble, C. (2014). Employment, work placements and work integrated learning of international students in Australia. *International Education Association of Australia*, Research Digest 2.

Gribble, C., & Blackmore, J. (2012). Re-positioning Australia's international education in global knowledge economies: Implications of shifts in skilled migration policies for universities. *Journal of Higher Education Policy and Management* 34(4), 341–354.

Hawthorne, L. (1997). English language testing and immigration policy. In G. Brindley & G. Wigglesworth (Eds). *access: Issues in language test design and delivery* (pp. 9–29). Sydney: Macquarie University.

Hawthorne, L. (2010). How valuable is "two-step migration"? Labour market outcomes for international student migrants to Australia. *Asian and Pacific Migration Journal* 19(1), 5–36.

Hawthorne, L. (2011) *Competing for skills: Migration policies and trends in New Zealand and Australia.* Government of New Zealand, Wellington, and Government of Australia, Canberra. Retrieved from https://www.border.gov.au/ReportsandPublications/Documents/research/migration-policies-trends-fullreport.pdf

Hawthorne, L., & To, A. (2014). Australian employer response to the study-migration pathway: The quantitative evidence 2007–2011. *International Migration* 52(3), 99–115.

Hogan-Brun, G., Mar-Molinero, C., & Stevenson, P. (Eds.). (2009). *Discourses on language and integration.* Amsterdam; Philadelphia: John Benjamins.

Horner, K. (2009). Regimenting language, mobility and citizenship in Luxembourg. In G. Extra, M. Spotti, & P. Van Avermaet (Eds.), *Language testing, migration and citizenship* (pp. 148–166). London; New York: Continuum.

Koleth, E. (2010). *Overseas students: Immigration policy changes 1997–May 2010.* Parliamentary Library, Background note. Canberra: Commonwealth of Australia.

McNamara, T. (2012a). Language assessments as shibboleths: A poststructuralist perspective. *Applied Linguistics* 33(5), 564–581.

McNamara, T. (2012b). Poststructuralism and its challenges for applied linguistics. *Applied Linguistics* 33(5), 473–482.

McNamara, T., & Roever, C. (2006). *Language testing: The social dimension.* Malden, MA; Oxford: Blackwell.

McNamara, T., & Ryan, K. (2011). Fairness versus justice in language testing: The place of English literacy in the Australian citizenship test. *Language Assessment Quarterly* 8, 161–178.

Markus, A., Jupp, J., & McDonald, P. (2009). *Australia's immigration revolution.* Crows Nest: Allen & Unwin.

Ronell, A. (2005). *The test drive.* Chicago: University of Illinois Press.

Shohamy, E. (2001). *The power of tests: A critical perspective of the uses of language tests.* London: Longman.

Shohamy, E. (2006). *Language policy: Hidden agendas and new approaches.* London; New York: Routledge.

Shohamy, E. (2009). Language tests for immigrants: Why language? Why tests? Why citizenship? In G. Hogan-Brun, C. Mar-Molinero, & P. Stevenson (Eds.), *Discourses on language and integration* (pp. 45–60). Amsterdam; Philadelphia: John Benjamins.

Spolsky, B. (2004). *Language policy.* Cambridge: Cambridge University Press.

Van Avermaet, P. (2009). Fortress Europe? Language policy regimes for immigration and citizenship. In G. Hogan-Brun, C. Mar-Molinero, & P. Stevenson (Eds.), *Discourses on language and integration* (pp. 15–44). Amsterdam; Philadelphia: John Benjamins.

CHAPTER 15

....

LANGUAGE POLICY
AND MASS MEDIA

....

XUESONG (ANDY) GAO AND QING SHAO

RESEARCHERS who see language policy and planning (LPP) as a field of inquiry in the social sciences (e.g., Ricento, 2006) have called for "a constructive, interdisciplinary dialogue engaging in the different advantages of methods, concepts, and concerns" drawn from areas such as education, the sociology of education, and public policy (Peled, Ives, & Ricento, 2014, p. 296). In line with such a call, this chapter seeks to expand the links between LPP and media, based on an understanding of language policy as "processual, dynamic, and in motion" (McCarty, 2014, p. 2) and an acknowledgment of the important role that non-state actors such as the mass media (as well as other shapers of public opinion) play in the policymaking process (McGroarty, 2013; Wallace, 1993). Like other areas of public policy, language policies are proposed, interpreted, justified, negotiated, modified, implemented, resisted, and evaluated in an ongoing discursive process, with different parties "trying to tell a story that leads to [their] own most desired result" (Birkland, 2015, p. 243). In these discursive processes, research has begun to acknowledge the importance of media, which can "play a crucial role in information distribution and in the political market and public policy making" (Olper & Swinnen, 2013, p. 413).

Researchers have so far established that the mass media can play several important roles in language policymaking. First, social, political, and economic visions of society are defined and constructed by the media and communicated to the public, permitting different stakeholders to invoke these visions to strengthen their own arguments and weaken their opponents' positions in the relevant discursive processes (Yamagami, 2012). In addition, the media is an important site for "venue shopping" in which groups undertake great efforts "to gain a hearing for their ideas and grievances against existing policy" (Birkland, 2015, p. 185). Accordingly, the media is a platform for different policy stakeholders and the public to voice and (re) construct opinions. For example, Ron Unz, an opponent of bilingual education and a financial-software millionaire with no experience in bilingual education, emerged to be the most often quoted leading expert in the media coverage surrounding Proposition 227, which aimed to restrict the use of Spanish as a medium of instruc-tion (MOI) in the US state of California (Yamagami, 2012). In contrast to Unz, those who supported the use of Spanish as an MOI were discredited in media coverage as members of an entrenched bureaucracy motivated solely by economic self-interest. These media representations of opponents in the policy debate played a key role in the passage of Proposition 227.

This example shows that mass media does not just report on language-policy discussions, but also initiates and organizes these discussions to mobilize public opinion for or against particular policies. For instance, by making a query to the Norwegian Language Council, a Norwegian magazine started a heated debate in print and social media on what constitutes an *ethnic Norwegian* (Lane, 2009). In Arizona, Donahue (2002) found that the media persuaded voters, who were not nec-essarily informed about the relevant policy issues and had inaccurate understandings about the impacts of policy alternatives, to support an English-only educational ini-tiative that was eventually adopted.

Despite the media's significant role in the language policymaking process, Androutsopoulos (2009) has pointed out that "the media is not a key concept" in lan-guage policy research (p. 285). Most previous research on language policy and mass media has narrowly focused on "how the media plays a role in the management of language use" through policing of language forms (Lane, 2009, p. 210). For example, media outlets are involved in "language management" by setting out language-usage rules and restrictions on the use of obscene language (see Spolsky 2004, 2009). Studies have also explored language policy of particular media outlets (e.g., Kelly-Homes, Moriarty, & Pietikäinen, 2009), or the Internet as a channel for the commod-ification of language (e.g., Blommaert, 2009). Thus, the media has been understood primarily as one of the sources of relevant texts for language policymaking. Yet, con-sidering the media's "incentives to provide news to different groups in society" that "affects these groups' influence in policy making" (Olper & Swinnen, 2013, p. 413), it is necessary for researchers to expand their focus to the media as a meaning-making participant and an important player in the policymaking process.

To this end, this chapter reviews efforts to examine the construction and con-tent of media products, and the role of the mass media in the policymaking pro-cess, with a particular focus on framing in mass media coverage. In the following sections, we first elaborate what we mean by the term *framing*. Then we illustrate how the concept of framing can help researchers to explore the media's mediation of language policymaking in three specific debates: the *dialect crisis* in China; high-stakes English examinations in China; and MOI policy, with particular attention to the use of English, Cantonese, and Putonghua in Hong Kong and the use of English and Spanish in the US state of Arizona. We conclude with suggestions for expanding research on the role of mass media in language policymaking.

FRAMING LANGUAGE POLICY ISSUES IN THE MASS MEDIA

In social theory, *framing* refers to the schema on which individuals depend for interpretation of social phenomena (Goffman, 1974). With reference to the mass media, frames are the central "organizing principles" from which media contributors and users derive meaning, and thus frames become shorthand for representations of perceived reality (Reese, 2010, p. 17). Frames thus function in media "to promote a particular problem definition, causal interpretation, moral evaluation and/or treatment recommendation" (Entman, 1993, p. 52), and they impart coherence and meaning to a media text, often providing an implicit narrative and preferred policy solution for a given problem (Jefferies, 2009). For this reason, frames and their constituent elements (or themes) influence public understanding of phenomena such as language policies, and are the basis on which stakeholders make judgments about policy alternatives. As "an unavoidable reality of the public communication process," framing can result in challenges to the traditional norms of news reporting activities (e.g., objectivity, impartiality, and neutrality) (Nisbet, 2010, pp. 44–45).

Hence, analyzing media coverage of language policy discussions from a framing perspective reveals the media's agency as actors who seek to influence language politics and language policymaking. In such analyses, media coverage is conceptualized not as objective depictions of events, but rather as socially and culturally constructed phenomena that mediate language policymaking. This is important, "particularly given today's clichés about the media-driven nature of politics" (Phelan & Dahlberg, 2011, p. 6), in which mass media is an institution of power and authority often used by those with economic and political power to manage public perceptions about particular language policies (e.g., see Johnson & Milani, 2010).

Mass media participates in the language policymaking process through representation, legitimization, and delegitimization. *Representations* are "socially shared forms of knowledge about languages, ethnicities, nationalities, and other socially and culturally salient categories" (Tollefson, 2015, p. 137). Representations are important in media because actors in policymaking may "articulate representations as part of the policymaking process, drawing on their audience's shared knowledge of these representations in order to mobilize public support for specific policies, while also spreading these representations in order to shape public opinion" (Tollefson, 2015, p. 137; also see van Dijk, 1993). Policy actors use representations to *legitimize* or *delegitimize* individuals or groups. *Legitimization* refers to positive media representations that policy stakeholders use to strengthen their position against their opponents (Chilton, 2004). For instance, supporters of specific language policies may represent themselves as the true voice of those who may benefit from these policies, and they may legitimize their position by arguing that they are protecting the people's best interests. *Delegitimization* involves negative representations of others (such as opponents) through emphasis on differences (*othering*; see Palfreyman, 2005) and social boundaries. For example, opponents of bilingual education in 1998 in California accused bilingual education supporters of seeking personal financial gain (Yamagami, 2012). Thus, along with framing, the concepts of representation, legitimization, and delegitimization can help researchers investigate the role of media coverage of language issues in the policymaking process.

A limited number of studies have focused on the role of mass media in shaping education and language policy. Tsui and Tollefson (2007) note that an increasing number of MOI policy debates are taking place in the mass media with active participation of stakeholders and the wider public. As a major arena for language policy–related debates, the media is found to have shaped the policies adopted in multilingual contexts (Tollefson, 2015). For example, Crawford (1997) analyzed more than 600 newspaper articles on Proposition 227 published in a period that started from six months before the voting. He found that the media "define[d] the debate as Unz did" (1997, p. 5). More recent studies have analyzed the ways newspapers frame language policy incidents to construct and influence public opinion (e.g., Gao, 2015, 2017; Tollefson, 2015).

In the following sections, we explore in detail the role mass media play in language policymaking in mainland China, Hong Kong, and the United States (specifically, the state of Arizona). The three contexts are chosen to exemplify policymaking systems that can be characterized as top-down (mainland China), bottom-up (United States), and mixed (Hong Kong), and viewed on a continuum ranging from limited to extensive public participation in the policymaking process. In mainland China, ordinary citizens have limited participation in language policymaking, while in Arizona (United States) they can vote to decide relevant language policies, as was also the case in Proposition 227 in California. Hong Kong is often seen as a "semi-democratic but essentially liberal" city (Yung & Leung, 2014, p. 291).

First, we explore Gao's (2015) study of the coverage of the *dialect crisis* in China by state-owned print media, in which he finds that regional Chinese varieties (or *dialects*) were framed as identity markers, individuals' cultural heritage, and tools to resist cultural invasion from the outside. Second, we turn to framing in Chinese state-owned print media reports on English in high-stakes examinations, finding that newspapers in China "speak for the Chinese government's control of language policy formulation and implementation" (Shao & Gao, 2017, p. 29). Finally, we examine the role of media in MOI policy debates, particularly Tollefson's (2015) comparative analysis of MOI policy in Hong Kong and Arizona, and Shao's (2016) analysis of newspaper articles in Hong Kong, which reveals the active participation of the media in the policy process regarding the use of Putonghua as an MOI for teaching Chinese.

THE DIALECT CRISIS IN MAINLAND CHINA

The mass media coverage of the crisis of regional Chinese varieties (or *dialects*) reveals the Chinese government's use of the media to propagate its language policy (see Gao, 2015, 2017). Mainland China has a population of 1.3 billion people, which includes fifty-six ethnic groups. The dominant Han (汉) group comprises 91.5% of the total population and speaks at least "2,000 more or less distinct dialects or subdialects" (Li, 2006, p. 150; see also Coblin, 2000). The other fifty-five ethnic minority groups, including Mongolian, Tibetan, Uyghur, and Zhuang, speak over 290 languages (Lewis, 2009). Like many other governments, the mainland Chinese government has adopted an instrumental approach to language planning, propagating popular discourses that construct "majority languages as instruments of modernity and economic progress and minority languages as (merely) carriers of 'tradition' and 'cultural identity'" (Tan & Rubdy, 2008, p. 11).

Because a shared language has been historically seen as a crucial linguistic foundation for political unity, the government promotes Putonghua (literally, *a common speech*) as the national standard spoken Chinese (Chen, 1999). The nationwide promotion of Putonghua may reduce the vitality of regional varieties of Chinese and of minority languages, so that their survival in the future has become much less certain. This threat to regional varieties has become known as the *dialect crisis*.

Gao (2015) reports on a study that adopted content analysis (Hsieh & Shannon, 2005) to analyze the ideological framing of Chinese dialects or regional Chinese varieties in the mainland Chinese state print media coverage of the dialect crisis, and the associated efforts to sustain the use of these dialects, from 2002 to 2012. The study takes notice of the vulnerability of regional language varieties worldwide in relation to national standard varieties in light of many states' commitment to promoting a standard, usually as a crucial part of nation building (see Hara, 2005, on Europe; Tan, 2012, on Singapore; and Schilling-Estes & Wolfram, 1999, on the United States). Since regional language varieties are often assigned low standing in state promotion of national standard varieties, the struggles to preserve regional varieties often involve "a repudiation of the authority of state institutions" (Gal, 1993, p. 338). This raises the question of how the state print media would cover the issue of a dialect crisis in a context that is characterized by a centralized, top-down political system. In Gao's study (2015), a total of eighty related news reports from the Chinese state print media were analyzed to examine how dialects and dialect crisis were framed.

Analysis of these reports reveals a variety of frames of regional Chinese varieties advanced by individual citizens, corporations, and the state. More than half the reports argue that regional Chinese varieties should be preserved, either because they are closely associated with individuals' cultural heritage (36) or enable individuals to have different cultural experiences (7). Nine reports were also found to have related regional varieties to individuals' identities, and one report projected regional varieties as tools for individuals to protect their local ways of living against the erosion of culture from the influx of migrants from other regions. These reports also stress that learning these regional Chinese varieties is an important strategy for migrants to integrate themselves in the communities of their speakers. Many reports also justified the preservation of regional Chinese varieties because of commercial (14) and entertainment (14) values.

In addition, governments at various levels valued regional Chinese varieties as a better communication medium (9) to propagate state policies to the public, while business corporations believed they could use regional Chinese varieties to better promote their products among target consumers (9). Further analysis of the reports also found that individuals aspired to preserve regional Chinese varieties so that they could maintain their identification with particular social groups and regional cultures. It must be noted that individuals whose voices were featured in the coverage are those who were closely connected to the government and corporations, indicating the Chinese government's willingness to accommodate these diverse views and tolerate the relevant discussions (Zhang & Guo, 2012). This also suggests that individuals, business corporations, and state institutions might share similar beliefs about languages (Woolard, 1998, p. 17).

The coverage of individuals' voices with regard to the crisis of regional Chinese varieties also reflects a deepening process of what Yan (2010) terms *individualization* in Chinese society, a process that acknowledges the legitimacy of individuals' desires and pursuits. Individuals in economically developed regions (such as Shanghai and Guangzhou) were particularly vocal about demands associated with regional Chinese varieties, although the media coverage attempted to avoid creating any impression that individuals are in direct confrontation with state institutions. Although local and national Chinese governments are willing to legitimize individuals' demands about preserving regional Chinese varieties, this does not mean that the Chinese state will negate the official language policy promoting Puntonghua. Nevertheless, it has apparently adopted a highly pragmatic approach to relevant language policy issues, through which the state addresses individuals' concerns and insecurity about regional Chinese varieties while sustaining the state's unchallenged position as the sole language policymaker (Yan, 2010).

The Chinese state's pragmatic approach to resolving language-related disputes is also evident in the state print media coverage of the Protecting Cantonese Movement in Guangzhou (see Gao, 2017). In the light of dramatic social and economic changes, the Protecting Cantonese Movement is only one of hundreds of "mass incidents" that took place in China in 2010. Like many other such incidents, the Movement was underpinned by the ongoing tension between individual citizens and the Chinese government, though it was specifically about language issues (Qian, Qian, & Zhu, 2012; Zhang & Guo, 2012). Reportedly triggered by a proposal to reduce TV airtime in the medium of Cantonese, concerned local residents took to the streets to protest the proposed airtime cut and to demand that the government maintain the status of Cantonese as a regional lingua franca. In response to this open challenge to the government's authority in language policymaking, the state print media covered the Movement in a relatively conciliatory way, as the government used media coverage to justify its language policies.

Like the coverage of the dialect crisis, the extensive coverage by state media of the Protecting Cantonese Movement in Guangzhou suggests that the Chinese government is willing to engage with the public in the media about issues considered less threatening (Zhang & Guo, 2012). Although it may contribute to convincing readers of the sanctity of the national language policy, the Chinese government's use of the mass media also gives voice to "a wide range of actors, from the state to individuals, over civil society and corporate actors" (Blommaert et al., 2009, p. 203). Analysis of print media reveals that the majority of media texts (41 out of the 61 media texts) were rather sympathetic to the causes of the Movement. They acknowledged that the use of Cantonese as a regional lingua franca was critical to sustenance of regional culture. Nevertheless, they also denied that the decline of Cantonese as a regional lingua franca has anything to do with the national language policy that promotes Putonghua, drawing a clearly identifiable warning line against any open criticism of the central Chinese government and its language policy.

A total of twenty-three media texts were found to have framed the discussion on the status of Cantonese in terms of law and regulations that all readers need to abide by (Gao, 2017). These texts justify the national language policy to promote Putonghua with regard to its critical role in "[facilitating] communication between different ethnic groups and regions . . . [to achieve] national unity" in "a multi-ethnic, multilingual and multi-dialectal society" (Gao, 2017, p. 162). In light of an incontestable national language policy framework, regional governments were portrayed as active players in the preservation of regional cultures associated with regional Chinese varieties. For instance, governments in Guangdong were eager to clarify readers' potential misunderstandings about the national language policy.

Relevant media texts also listed a variety of efforts that the government has undertaken to sustain regional culture and refuted public criticism that government agencies have failed to do enough to protect Cantonese. The texts also praised individuals (especially young netizens) who actively participated in the Movement for their dedication to preserving cultural heritage in the region "even though those who were born in the 1990s may not be familiar with traditional cultures in Guangzhou" (Gao, 2017, p. 165). By focusing on the preservation of regional cultures, the media texts avoided presenting Cantonese as a means to "signal in-group membership" or exclude "members of an outgroup" (Giles et al., 1977, p. 307). In other words, the government and these netizens were all "committed to the preservation and development of Cantonese culture as a crucial strategy for the promotion of Lingnan culture" (Giles et al., 1977, p. 8). Such coverage of the movement represents the government and netizens as being on the same side, with the potential for social harmony between the two (e.g., Zhang & Guo, 2012).

As reflected in the media coverage, the government is aware that one of the most important causes for the decline of Cantonese as a regional lingua franca is the rising migration from other parts of the country to the region. However, government officials in Guangzhou stressed that "many of [migrants] have settled down [. . .] as 'new guest residents,' who 'are actively learning Cantonese'" (Gao, 2017, p. 166). Alternatively, the media texts present the city of Guangzhou as a city that accommodates people from different places and emphasize that "local residents could use Putonghua to socialize with the migrants" (Gao, 2017, p. 166). To argue against the decline of Cantonese as regional lingua franca, media texts cite "67 million Cantonese speakers, constituting a powerful economic community" as evidence (Gao, 2017, p. 163). These texts indirectly supported the view that the decline of regional Chinese varieties is a natural consequence of societal evolution underpinned by regional economic developments.

Analysis of the media coverage of the Protecting Cantonese Movement shows how the related media discussions took place within finely drawn boundaries in terms of legalistic, cultural, and socioeconomic development discourses, in which the national language policy is presented as inviolable because of the belief in the critical role that a shared language has in achieving national unity (Chen, 1999; Coblin, 2000). This means that efforts of regional governments to preserve regional cultures and regional Chinese varieties should not undermine this fundamental political objective of the central government's language policymaking. Indeed, at least three media texts accuse individuals who challenge the national language policy of undermining national unity by their parochialism. While these boundaries might have been meant to control language policy discussions, it is important to note that a discursive space, albeit constrained, has been opened up by these texts. Although they discourage the public from openly challenging the national language policy, as is evident in the media coverage, individuals are given some concessions so that they can undertake efforts to minimize the negative impact of national language policies on regional Chinese varieties and cultures.

The Chinese government's use of the state-owned print media to manage public response to top-down language policy decisions is also evident in the reform of the English-language examination in national matriculation (Gaokao), prescribed in the government's master plan for Chinese society (CCCPC, 2013). This will be the focus of the following section.

High-Stakes English Examinations in Mainland China

Researchers in educational language policy have noted that a frequently employed top-down practice is to "manipulate high-stakes examinations in the hope of motivating schools and teachers in terms of accountability or in achieving the desired washback effects in teaching and learning" (Gu, 2014, p. 287). High-stakes English examinations in China have served such purposes for decades. However, the way the state-controlled print media are mobilized to endorse reforms of language assessment policies remains underexplored.

To understand how mass media are used in language assessment policymaking, Shao and Gao (2017) examined newspaper coverage of policies affecting two major English examinations: Gaokao and the College English Test (CET). The first policy relates to a proposal in 2013 to reduce the weighting of the English section of Gaokao to 100 points from 150, while increasing the weighting of the Chinese section to 180. The second is about the policy practice related to the nationwide CET. It has been common for universities—but not the Ministry of Education—to prescribe satisfactory CET results as a precondition for degree conferment, but in recent years this practice has been increasingly challenged by the public. Shao and Gao (2017) inductively analyzed the relevant news texts to identify the framing strategies that state media outlets adopted to manipulate the public response to CET practice.

In the media coverage of English in Gaokao, first of all, frames such as *consensus*, *disagreement*, and *local practice* supported changes in the weighting of the sections of the test. The consensus frame presents the reduction of weighting of the English section as an agreement among the grassroots, especially the netizens (even though the decision was made in a top-down manner by the Beijing Municipal Commission of Education). Conversely, the disagreement frame highlights different opinions held by various stakeholders, suggesting that stakeholders had reached no consensus. Working as a counter-frame of the consensus frame, the disagreement frame represents a variety of opinions against the policy proposal and a lack of consistency among these opinions; that is, opposition to the proposal is framed as being characterized by lack of agreement. Finally, the local practice frame focuses on how the public responded to the policy initiative, by such actions as signing up for language training classes as usual, thereby implying that the proposed changes constituted only a mild policy move that was unlikely to undermine English-language learning in China.

In news reports about CET as a prerequisite for degree conferment, frames such as *victims, legitimacy*, and *utility and economic consequences* appear. Unfortunately, there have been reports of final-year university students committing suicide when unable to get a degree because of unsatisfactory CET results. In suicide-related reports, the victim frame is often used to interpret the tragedy as a direct consequence of the prerequisite, rather than a consequence of emotional challenges or psychological issues. These reports triggered debates over universities' autonomy to adopt such CET policies. The legitimacy frame typically adopts a top-down view of policymaking, as it often implies that only the Ministry of Education (MOE)—not universities—has the power to decide whether CET results can be set as a requirement for degrees. Reports using the legitimacy frame see CET results as an extra burden on students; because the MOE has never prescribed such a requirement, the legitimacy of the requirement is questioned. However, the MOE has not prohibited such a university-level policy decision, and that is where the controversy lies. In defense of universities, the utility and economic consequences frame frequently appears. A linguistic-instrumentalist view of the importance of English and CET in the news tends to emphasize the utility of English and the negative ramifications for their career prospects if students fail to reach a certain level of English proficiency. This frame highlights the importance of CET results, which many employers in China look at when recruiting new staff.

In the analysis of media coverage of the two high-stakes examinations, a clue emerges about how these frames work together to buttress the government's language policy initiatives and implementation. In reporting the proposed changes in the English section in Gaokao, the print media used consensus, disagreement, and local practice frames to secure the image of public opinion supporting the policy proposal in general. The proposal was thus legitimized. In the coverage of CET, those who are against the prerequisite practice invoked the authority of the Ministry of Education to support their claims. The implication is that only the central government is in the position to make educational language policies. Universities' own policy practices are thus delegitimized. This may reveal that media coverage of language policy in China constructs policymaking as a top-down process, despite the limited discursive space in the media for policy discussions. In addition, to advance their arguments, CET supporters emphasize the importance of English in the eyes of potential employers. There was, however, no discussion about whether a top-down educational language policy for the whole country could work equally well in different regional contexts, where regional factors, such as the status of economic development, differ greatly.

In the two previous sections, we reviewed how language policy issues have been covered by the state-controlled print media in mainland China. While the media in mainland China apparently colluded to support the government-led language policymaking and implementation, one may ask how corporate media in democratic or "semi-democratic" (Yung & Leung, 2014, p. 291) contexts cover language policies and discursively participate in the language policy process. For this reason, we turn to the media discussions of language policy issues in Arizona (United States) and Hong Kong.

MEDIUM OF INSTRUCTION DEBATES IN HONG KONG AND ARIZONA

In contrast to mainland China, mass media in Hong Kong and Arizona do not have an obvious media sponsor like the Chinese government. Instead, different stakeholders compete in an effort to actively use the media to influence public opinion. In this section, we review studies on the media coverage of MOI policies in these two contexts. We first present Tollefson (2015), in which he examines media coverage of MOI policies in both Hong Kong and Arizona. We then introduce Shao's (2016) study of Putonghua as an MOI in Hong Kong.

As Tollefson (2015) observes, MOI policies often have "political rather than educational agendas" in many contexts (p. 132). For example, MOI policies can have an impact on the composition of the labor force, or can help sustain the role of language as a gatekeeper in tertiary education and career development. In other words, MOI policies, apart from serving pedagogical purposes, are also "about economic and political agendas that shape the distribution of economic resources and political power" (Tollefson, 2015, p. 134). In light of such an understanding of MOI policies, Tollefson's comparative analysis of news articles in the print media on MOI debates in Hong Kong and Arizona uses a "conceptual framework of representation theory, legitimization theory and the framing of news" (2015, p. 136). Revealing discursive strategies adopted by the newspapers, he focuses on the debate over the fine-tuning of MOI policy in Hong Kong and the retrospective discussions ten years after adoption of Arizona's Proposition 203, which required schools in Arizona to use only English as MOI.

In Hong Kong, whether English or Chinese (i.e., Cantonese, the mother tongue of the majority of the local population) should play the role of MOI in secondary schools has been a controversial issue for many years. After the British handover of Hong Kong to China (1997), the Hong Kong government announced a mother-tongue education policy requiring a shift of MOI from English to Chinese in most secondary schools. Complaints were received from parents and school administrators because under such a policy, English became an MOI reserved for a privileged few, while schools adopting Chinese as the MOI were perceived as inferior to English-speaking institutions. Because the gatekeeping function of English in job seeking and university admission remains active in Hong Kong, the pressure for English is intense among parents and businesses. Thus in 2009, faced with opposition to the Chinese MOI policy, and more than a decade after the implementation of mother-tongue education, the Education Bureau fine-tuned the policy, granting schools greater autonomy to decide the MOI and adopt English.

Tollefson (2015) identifies six frames in media coverage of the MOI debate in Hong Kong: "globalization, identity, fairness, the purpose of education, stakeholders' rights and evidence" (p. 138). As a highly globalized metropolis, Hong Kong places great significance on English (globalization frame). However, some media texts also emphasize the importance of Cantonese for the identity of local residents (identity frame). Print media coverage also brought up the question of fairness, since only a limited number of schools could use English as the MOI. The debate over the purpose of education was linked with the rationale for mother tongue as MOI. The controversy also triggered discussions about stakeholders' rights in MOI-related decision-making: Who should decide MOI? Parents? Teachers? Government? The evidence frame, which emphasized the importance of research, generally supported Cantonese due to its pedagogical benefits as the mother tongue in classroom teaching. Thus the complexity of framing suggests that print media coverage of the Hong Kong MOI debate supported both English and Cantonese, both of which have supporters among the public.

In the United States, the most important MOI controversy has been whether bilingual education programs or an English-only MOI policy should be adopted (Tollefson, 2015, p. 134). In 2000, with the support of Arizona voters, Proposition 203 was passed by a margin of 63% to 37%. This Proposition required most schools to abandon Spanish and other languages as MOIs and to teach school subjects in English only.

Tollefson (2015) examined the media coverage of the Proposition around its tenth anniversary. Major frames adopted by newspapers at that time included a "fiscal frame, illegal immigration, science versus ideology, the failure of bilingual education, parental support, and choice" (p. 141). Framing Proposition 203 as a fiscal issue generally served to persuade readers that the public funds invested in bilingual education programs were a waste of taxpayers' money. Some newspaper articles juxtaposed bilingual education, "illegal" immigration, and Spanish speakers, implying that bilingual education somehow contributed to illegal immigration. Bilingual education programs were also portrayed as ideology-laden educational failures, while English-only MOI policy was said to be scientific, informed by research, and effective. Parents and students from immigrant families were depicted as English-only supporters whose freedom to choose English was violated by bilingual education programs using Spanish. Tollefson concludes that supporters of Proposition 203 were able to effectively "frame the issues in ways that offer[ed] advantages over their opponents" (p. 145).

Also from a framing perspective, Shao (2016) examines the local Chinese print-media coverage of the controversy over using Putonghua as a medium of instruction (PMI) for teaching Chinese in Hong Kong. His study of media over a twelve-month period beginning in February 2014 focused on the government's decision after the handover of sovereignty in 1997 to set the long-term goal of using PMI for teaching Chinese to the Cantonese-speaking student majority. (PMI has never become compulsory and is meant for teaching the Chinese subject only.) In 2014, the Education Bureau deleted two statements on its official website that had mentioned the lack of research evidence supporting PMI (Shao, 2016). This deletion triggered fear of the possible implementation of compulsory PMI. During this time, conflict between Hong Kong and the Mainland reached a climax, taking the form of the Umbrella Movement with its associated occupation of the main business district. In this context, the change in the Education Bureau website triggered street protests and significant media debates.

Shao (2016) inductively examined 138 articles from fifteen local Chinese print publications, identifying four issue-specific frames: the legal status of Cantonese, the culture and language crisis, politics, and pedagogy and linguistics. Each frame has a different "problem definition, causal interpretation, moral evaluation and treatment recommendation" about the policy at issue (Entman, 1993, p. 52). The legal status of Cantonese frame, appearing in six articles, identifies the problem as Cantonese having no legal protection. Although in the year 1974, the colonial government gave Chinese the status of a co-official language in Hong Kong, there was no mention of which variety of Chinese enjoys this status. In the news coverage, this was understood as a reason why Cantonese may be threatened by Putonghua. The treatment recommendation is that the relevant laws and ordinances should prescribe that Cantonese is a co-official language. Another problem definition was that while Putonghua is understood as a common language, Cantonese is relegated to the status of a regional variety—a dialect. This understanding was challenged by the local print media, because Cantonese, some articles argued, is a language recognized by the United Nations, and thus is not merely a dialect. Another eighteen articles used the culture and language crisis frame to define the problem as local culture and language currently under threat from Putonghua. To argue for this problem definition and to call for public response, the decline of Cantonese in Guangzhou and Shanghainese in Shanghai were used as supporting evidence. Only three articles maintained that there exists no such threat because PMI is only used for teaching Chinese, and other subjects would still be taught in English or Cantonese.

The local print media attempted to persuade readers that the threat from Putonghua must be resisted. As in Johnson's analysis (2005), a war metaphor was used to describe the current situation. In the most widely used frame—the politics frame—Daudet's short story *La Dernière Classe*, in which Prussian troops occupied French cities and banned the use of French, was cited. In total, fifty-eight articles used the politics frame. Half of them defined PMI as an embodiment of the Hong

Kong–Mainland conflict and a tool for the Communist Party to colonize Hong Kong. Moral evaluations were also conveyed by labeling Putonghua, its speakers, and PMI as *anti-democratic, anti-intellectual,* and *barbaric.* Fighting against PMI, and thus fighting against the Communist grip on Hong Kong, became the only morally and politically correct treatment.

In a similar vein, authors of another twenty-two articles tried to persuade readers that the current situation is not about language but about politics. Only ten of the fifty-eight articles refuted the anti-PMI campaign, representing it as fear-mongering. With a frame of pedagogy and linguistics, fifty-three articles recommended different treatments for various reasons. Ten recommended that Cantonese be the MOI for teaching Chinese because of the sheer beauty of the language. Thirteen supported Cantonese by questioning the efficiency of PMI. One argued for PMI from the perspective of linguistic instrumentalism. Twenty-nine articles advanced various arguments by taking real-life classroom scenarios into consideration, most of them supporting Cantonese.

Reflecting on these findings, Shao (2016) concluded that PMI was framed as "culturally invasive, politically wrong, pedagogically lame and linguistically inferior" (p. 778), revealing a highly negative stance against PMI. Thus the local print media coverage of the public debate over PMI delegitimized PMI, thereby contributing to the closing of the policy window for PMI.

CONCLUSION: MASS MEDIA IN LANGUAGE POLICY RESEARCH

The studies reviewed in this chapter focus on discursive strategies, such as framing, employed by the (print) mass media in coverage of language policy events and debates. These studies view the mass media both as a platform for public debate over language policies and as a participant in the language policy process. Reflecting on these studies, we contend that mass media's role in language policymaking deserves more attention.

With political and social life not only mediated, but also mediatized, the language policymaking process has become increasingly entangled with the mass media. As Strömbäck (2008) notes, "the important question no longer is related to the independence of the media from politics and society. The important question becomes the independence of politics and society from the media" (p. 228). Though media often claim that their coverage reflects public opinion, selective framing of language policy issues means that the definition of language problems and possible language policy responses are typically those that are endorsed by relevant media sponsors (see Molotch & Lester, 1975, on the competing sponsors approach to media analysis).

Of course the role of media in policymaking varies in different contexts. In mainland China, with a top-down political system, the government still plays the most important role in language policymaking, and all mass media outlets in China are ultimately state controlled. However, in many cases the media does not work directly as a propaganda organ to promote top-down language policies (e.g., Gao, 2012), but rather plays a more complex and nuanced role. Even in mainland China, the public demand explanations for policies and must be persuaded that the policies are legitimate. For this reason, frames are adopted in media coverage to create a sense that public opinion is considered in policymaking, even though what actually appears in the media texts is constrained by political considerations and is limited to official voices.

It must be noted that individuals whose voices were featured in the coverage are primarily those who are closely connected to the government and corporations (Gao, 2015). Nevertheless, the Chinese government's willingness to accommodate different views and to tolerate relevant discussions suggests an increasing concern about the legitimacy of policies and their public acceptance, especially when individuals may use Internet-based counter-media platforms, such as *Weibo*, to challenge top-down policies (although the Internet also is censored).

In contexts other than mainland China, such as Hong Kong and the United States, where the media cannot be labeled as state-owned or government-controlled, media framing means that some views—such as the alleged connection between bilingual education programs and illegal immigration, or the connection between Putonghua and the Communist regime—are dominant in shaping public understanding of language policy issues. In these contexts, public understandings may be critical to policy output. For instance, Proposition 227 in California and Proposition 203 in Arizona were initiatives subject to a public vote. In such contexts, the mass media's influence on public opinion must be considered by language policy scholars. By exposing discursive strategies used by the mass media in the coverage of language policy, empirical studies are in a position to understand the important role of the media in shaping dominant policy narratives and their alternatives. These studies can also lay bare the media's "practical goals, such as increasing readership and securing profit in the increasingly competitive media market" (Yang, 2017, p. 70).

To conclude, we reiterate the important role of the mass media in the language policymaking process. Yet in comparison with research in other fields of public policy, studies in language policy have devoted limited attention to the relation of mass media coverage to language policy. Therefore, more research is needed to reveal the hidden ideologies behind the coverage of language policy events and debates. The interplay between the mass media outlets and counter-media or counter-establishment platforms should be investigated as well. Comparisons between language policy debates in print media, on TV, and on YouTube channels, online forums, Facebook pages, and so forth, remain underexposed. Voices from journalists, editors, columnists, and other media practitioners also need to be heard.

The media's own interests (such as advertising revenue from language educators) should be examined, together with their reporting strategies. We do not claim that the media has a decisive influence on language policy output in all contexts. What we see in our studies and others is that "the media is not a key concept" in language policy research (Androutsopoulos, 2009, p. 285), yet it sometimes can be a key player in the language policymaking process, which deserves serious scholarly attention.

ACKNOWLEDGMENT

This chapter forms part of an ongoing research project entitled "Language Policy and the Mass Media in Hong Kong, Guangzhou and Arizona," which is funded by the Research Grants Council of the Hong Kong Special Administrative Region, China (RGC Ref No. HKU 17402414H).

REFERENCES

Androutsopoulos, J. (2009). Policing practices in heteroglossic mediascapes: A commentary on interfaces. *Language Policy* 8(3), 285–290.

Birkland, T. A. (2015). *An introduction to the policy process: Theories, concepts and models of public policy making*. 3rd edition. New York: Routledge.

Blommaert, J. (2009). A market of accents. *Language Policy* 8(3), 243–259.

Blommaert, J., Kelly-Holmes, H., Lane, P., Leppänen, S., Moriarty, M., Pietikäinen, S., & Piirainen-Marsh, A. (2009). Media, multilingualism and language policing: An introduction. *Language Policy* 8(3), 203–207.

CCCPC. (2013). 中共中央关于全面深化改革若干重大问题的决定 [Several major decisions to comprehensively deepen the reform made by the Central Committee of the Communist Party of China]. Beijing: People's Press.

Chen, P. (1999). *Modern Chinese: History and sociolinguistics*. Cambridge: Cambridge University Press.

Chilton, P. (2004). *Analysing political discourse: Theory and practice*. London: Routledge.

Coblin, W. S. (2000). A brief history of Mandarin. *Journal of the American Oriental Society* 120(4), 537–552.

Crawford, J. (1997). The campaign against Proposition 227: A post mortem. *Bilingual Research Journal* 21(1), 1–29.

Donahue, T. S. (2002). Language planning and the perils of ideological solipsism. In J. W. Tollefson (Ed.), *Language policies in education: Critical issues* (1st edition; pp. 137–164). New York: Routledge.

Entman, R. M. (1993). Framing: Toward clarification of a fractured paradigm. *Journal of Communication* 43(4), 51–58.

Gao, X. (2012). "Cantonese is not a dialect": Chinese netizens' defence of Cantonese as a regional lingua franca. *Journal of Multilingual and Multicultural Development* 33(5), 449–464.

Gao, X. (2015). The ideological framing of "dialect": An analysis of mainland China's state media coverage of "dialect crisis" (2002–2012). *Journal of Multilingual and Multicultural Development* 36(5), 468–482.

Gao, X. (2017). Linguistic instrumentalism and national language policy in mainland China's state print media coverage of the "Protecting Cantonese Movement." *Chinese Journal of Communication* 10(2), 157–175.

Gal, S. (1993). Diversity and contestation in linguistic ideologies: German speakers in Hungary. *Language in Society* 22(3), 337–359.

Giles, H., Bourhis, R. Y., & Taylor, D. M. (1977). Towards a theory of language in ethnic group relations. In H. Giles (Ed.), *Language, ethnicity and intergroup relations* (pp. 307–348). London: Academic Press.

Goffman, E. (1974). *Frame analysis: An essay on the organization of experience.* Cambridge, MA: Harvard University Press.

Gu, P. Y. (2014). The unbearable lightness of the curriculum: What drives the assessment practices of a teacher of English as a Foreign Language in a Chinese secondary school? *Assessment in Education: Principles, Policy and Practice* 21(3), 285–305.

Hara, K. (2005). Regional dialect and cultural development in Japan and Europe. *International Journal of the Sociology of Language* 2005(175–176), 193–211.

Hsieh, H., & Shannon, S. E. (2005). Three approaches to qualitative content analysis. *Qualitative Health Research* 15(9), 1277–1288.

Jefferies, J. (2009). Do undocumented students play by the rules? Meritocracy in the media. *Critical Inquiry in Language Studies* 6(1–2), 15–38.

Johnson, E. (2005). WAR in the media: Metaphors, ideology, and the formation of language policy. *Bilingual Research Journal* 29(3), 621–640.

Johnson, S., & Milani, T. M. (2010). Critical intersections: Language ideologies and media discourse. In S. Johnson & T. M. Milani (Eds.), *Language ideologies and media discourse: Texts, practices, politics* (pp. 3–14). London: Continuum.

Kelly-Holmes, H., Moriarty, M., & Pietikäinen, S. (2009). Convergence and divergence in Basque, Irish and Sámi media language policing. *Language Policy* 8(3), 227–242.

Lane, P. (2009). Mediating national language management: The discourse of citizenship categorization in Norwegian media. *Language Policy* 8(3), 209–225.

Lewis, M. P. (Ed.). (2009). *Ethnologue: Languages of the world.* 16th edition. Dallas, TX: SIL International. Retrieved from http://www.ethnologue.com/

Li, D. C. S. (2006). Chinese as a lingua franca in Greater China. *Annual Review of Applied Linguistics* 26, 149–176.

McCarty, T. L. (2014). Introducing ethnography and language policy. In T. L. McCarty (Ed.), *Ethnography and language policy* (pp. 1–28). New York: Routledge.

McGroarty, M. (2013). Multiple actors and arenas in evolving language policies. In J. W. Tollefson (Ed.), *Language policies in education: Critical issues* (2nd edition; pp. 35–57). New York: Routledge.

Molotch, H., & Lester, M. (1975). The Great Oil Spill as local occurrence and national event. *American Journal of Sociology* 81(2), 235–260.

Nisbet, M. C. (2010). Knowledge into action: Framing the debates over climate change and poverty. In P. D'Angelo & J. A. Kuypers (Eds.), *Doing news framing analysis: Empirical and theoretical perspectives* (pp. 43–83). Oxford: Routledge.

Olper, A., & Swinnen, J. (2013). Mass media and public policy: Global evidence from agricultural policies. *The World Bank Economic Review* 27(3), 413–436.

Palfreyman, D. (2005). Othering in an English language programme. *TESOL Quarterly* 39(2), 219–233.

Peled, Y., Ives, P., & Ricento, T. (2014). Introduction to the thematic issue: Language policy and political theory. *Language Policy* 13(4), 295–300.

Phelan, S., & Dahlberg, L. (2011). Discourse theory and critical media politics: An introduction. In L. Dahlberg, & S. Phelan (Eds.), *Discourse theory and critical media politics* (pp. 1–40). New York: Palgrave Macmillan.

Qian, J., Qian, L., & Zhu, H. (2012). Representing the imagined city: Place and the politics of difference during Guangzhou's 2010 language conflict. *Geoforum* 43(5), 905–915.

Reese, S. D. (2010). Finding frames in a web of culture. In P. D'Angelo & J. A. Kuypers (Eds.), *Doing news framing analysis: Empirical and theoretical perspectives* (pp. 17–42). Oxford: Routledge.

Ricento, T. (2006). Language policy: Theory and practice—An introduction. In T. Ricento (Ed.), *An introduction to language policy: Theory and method* (pp. 10–23). Malden, MA: Blackwell.

Schilling-Estes, N., & Wolfram, W. (1999). Alternative models of dialect death: Dissipation vs. concentration. *Language* 75(3), 486–521.

Shao, Q. (2016). Keeping the policy window closed: Framing Putonghua as a medium of instruction in Hong Kong. *The Asia-Pacific Education Researcher* 25(5–6), 771–779.

Shao, Q., & Gao, X. (2017). "Noisy guests shall not unseat the host": Framing high-stakes English examinations in mainland China's state-controlled print media. *English Today* 33(3), 25–30.

Spolsky, B. (2004). *Language policy*. Cambridge: Cambridge University Press.

Spolsky, B. (2009). *Language management*. Cambridge: Cambridge University Press.

Strömbäck, J. (2008). Four phases of mediatization: An analysis of the mediatization of politics. *The International Journal of Press/Politics* 13(3), 228–246.

Tan, S. (2012). Language ideology in discourses of resistance to dominant hierarchies of linguistic worth: Mandarin Chinese and Chinese "dialects" in Singapore. *The Australian Journal of Anthropology* 23, 340–356.

Tan, P., & Rubdy, R. (2008). Introduction. In R. Rubdy & P. Tan (Eds.), *Language as commodity: Global structures, local marketplaces* (pp. 1–15). London: Continuum.

Tollefson, J. W. (2015). Language policy-making in multilingual education: Mass media and the framing of medium of instruction. *Current Issues in Language Planning* 16(1–2), 132–148.

Tsui, A. B. M., & Tollefson, J. W. (Eds.). (2007). *Language policy, culture, and identity in Asian contexts*. New York: Routledge.

van Dijk, T. A. (1993). *Elite discourse and racism*. London: Sage.

Wallace, M. (1993). Discourse of derision: The role of the mass media within the education policy process. *Journal of Education Policy* 8(4), 321–337.

Woolard, K. A. (1998). Introduction: Language ideology as a field of inquiry. In B. Schieffelin, K. A. Woolard, & P. V. Kroskrity (Eds.), *Language ideologies: Practice and theory* (pp. 3–47). New York: Oxford University Press.

Yamagami, M. (2012). The political discourse of the campaign against bilingual education: From Proposition 227 to Horne v. Flores. *International Multilingual Research Journal* 6(2), 143–159.

Yan, Y. (2010). The Chinese path to individualization. *The British Journal of Sociology* 61(3), 489–512.

Yang, J. (2017). A historical analysis of language policy and language ideology in the early twentieth century Asia: A case of Joseon, 1910–1945. *Language Policy* 16(1), 59–78.

Yung, B., & Leung, L. Y. M. (2014). Facebook as change? Political engagement in semi-democratic Hong Kong in its transition to universal suffrage. *Journal of Asian Public Policy* 7(3), 291–305.

Zhang, X., & Guo, Z. (2012). Hegemony and counter-hegemony: The politics of dialects in TV programs in China. *Chinese Journal of Communication* 5(3), 300–315.

CHAPTER 16

MAINTAINING "GOOD GUYS" AND "BAD GUYS"

IMPLICIT LANGUAGE POLICIES IN MEDIA COVERAGE OF INTERNATIONAL CRISES

SANDRA SILBERSTEIN

UNDERSTANDINGS of language policy (LP) have broadened considerably in the past decade, with greater attention to the multiple ways that the practices of everyday social life constitute forms of LP. Thus, as evidenced in this volume, the field has recognized the utility of a range of tools and perspectives, from ethnography and critical discourse analysis to the conceptual frameworks of governmentality and linguistic landscapes. Reflecting this broadened understanding, Shohamy (2006, p. xv) points out that "language is used to create group membership ("us/them"; see also Silberstein, 2002), to demonstrate inclusion or exclusion, to determine loyalty or patriotism. . . . Language policy falls in the midst of these manipulations and battles, between language ideology and practice."

These new understandings have extended to new forms of analysis, such as attention to the discursive processes and techniques by which groups are formed, (re)created, (re)shaped, and resisted, and the life trajectories of individuals and groups whose social identities are forged within those processes. An important consequence of new and evolving understandings of LP is that researchers' attention extends well beyond traditional concerns with language forms—their complex systems, statutes, and changing roles in social life. New directions in LP are increasingly multidisciplinary, drawing from anthropology, sociology, political theory, and other disciplines in a multipronged effort to understand a broader range of ways in which language policy is immanent in social life.

A key issue in this attention to LP in everyday life is the question of who is allowed to speak—whose views count, whose stories matter? Often, this issue is explored narrowly, for example, in connection with the uses of different language varieties in interaction in different institutional contexts. But this can be explored also in other areas, as in mass media, in which verbal interaction is shaped by the demands of the ideological work in which it participates. As media analysis has shown, the ideological work of national and international media renders (inter) national crises intelligible, often without challenging systemic or institutional practices or the policy agendas of political elites (e.g., see Hodges, 2011; Silberstein, 2002). This ideological work shapes what becomes speakable and legible, through the telling and retelling of stories that often leave traditional victims and villains unchallenged. In reinscribing the sayable (Roy, 2014), the tales that are reproduced in mass media manifest implicit language policies: Who gets to speak and whose perspective is reported? Into whose identities are viewers interpellated? Whose aggressions are justified and whose mistakes understandable? Such questions draw researchers' attention to the intersection of media studies, discourse analysis, and language policy.

An important tool for analyzing mass media reporting is critical discourse analysis (CDA), which sees language use as a form of social practice (see, for example, Caldes-Coulthard & Coulthard, 1996: Fairclough, 2010, 2015; Gee, 2014; Lazar, 2007; Locke, 2004; van Dijk, 2001, 2008; Van Leeuwen, 2008; Wodak & Chilton, 2005; Wodak & Meyer, 2001, 2009). CDA focuses on how language is used to instantiate particular social relations, specifically relations of power. By analyzing a case of media reporting, this chapter shows how that instantiation is a form of language policy.

Fairclough and Wodak (1997, pp. 271–279) outline eight principles of CDA theory and method, all relevant here:

1. CDA addresses social problems.

2. Power relations are discursive.

3. Discourse constitutes society and culture.

4. Discourse does ideological work.

5. Discourse is historical.

6. The link between text and society is mediated.

7. Discourse analysis is interpretative and explanatory.

8. Discourse is a form of social action.

What makes subjects social (in the case under analysis here, media consumers) is their integration within a set of taken-for-granted understandings (i.e., their interpellation within particular ideologies). A central project of CDA and its foundational theories is understanding the material consequences of this process of integration, the consequences of language use itself. By examining a case of media coverage of two simultaneous international crises, this chapter provides a critical examination of how the implicit policies of the mass media shape and are shaped by public understandings.

In July 2014, US media consumers watched virtually simultaneous coverage of the downing of Malaysian Airlines Flight 17 (MH17) over Ukraine and the Israeli "Operation Protective Edge" into Gaza. In the days that followed these two events, CNN's audience jumped by 87% (Zara, 2014). For viewers in the United States and elsewhere, there were remarkable echoes in the CNN coverage of these two disasters. These allowed the intertexual construction of "good guys" and "bad guys," as prior texts (Becker, 1995) became almost instantaneously dialogic (Bakhtin, 1981): both locations were war zones with smaller geographies supported by major world players. There were disturbing reports of civilian casualties, particularly of children. In both cases, there were several unsuccessful attempts to arrange ceasefires, creating problems for reporters and aid workers and those trying to treat bodies with respect. In both instances there were contested rhetorics: Who was the aggressor, who a terrorist? Who was a victim? A CNN description of Ukraine could have been easily transposed to Gaza and Israel: "Regular men become radicalized.... They have seen their friends and family killed and the middle space for conversation and compromise is not there. . . . What looks to us as propaganda is truth to them." In part, what allows the viewer to make sense of these events is a process by which texts are rendered familiar, by tapping into Becker's (1995) "prior texts" or " 'lingual memory' [that] builds over a lifetime, giving resonance to things people say or hear" (p. 394). This prior knowledge allows potentially similar events to be starkly differentiated. But it falls to the ideological/policy work of the media to invoke lingual memory and to render texts familiar. What becomes speakable and legible in media products represents a form of language policy

In reporting these two events, the US media faced a rhetorical minefield as the two international crises had each left about 300 civilian fatalities (298 on MH Flight 17, on July 17; by July 19, 342 Palestinians were dead in Gaza; according to the United Nations, 70% of these were civilians, 72 children, "Death Toll," 2014). In one case, civilian fatalities were assumed to be the work of Russian-aligned "bad guys"; in the case of Gaza, most civilians were killed by a US ally. This chapter uses CDA, particularly Locke's (2004) "stories," to explore the implicit language policies that maintained "good guys" and "bad guys," victims and villains, in the context of ideological tensions and contradictions. In so doing, it makes the case for LP-inflected research into these implicit policies of public discourse and asks that we consider whose interests are served and what power hierarchies are sustained by them.

NEWS STORIES

Media coverage turns on storytelling. On CNN in the wake of 9/11, the attacks on the World Trade Center in New York City, the network advertised, "It's not just the story; everyone has great stories. You need to be a great storyteller." Why, one might wonder, did the media (in the case of newspapers, this happened quite early) embrace a term that announces its possible blurring of lines between the real and the imaginary in the service of entertainment? "Tell me a story" does not imply a request for a cogent, historically driven, critical account. For those interested in the workings of ideology, this definition from *dictionary.com*[1] is explanatory: Story: *a narrative*, either true or fictitious, in prose or verse, *designed to interest, amuse, or instruct the hearer or reader* (emphases added). Stories, with their ideological force, instruct us as they make sense of and reproduce a worldview. They invoke and become prior texts. The effects of this ideological work, this reproduction of dominant understandings, by news stories are material. For example, in the wake of the September 2001 World Trade Center attacks, the constant manufacturing of fear and the announcement that the United States was in a war on terror naturalized a coming war in Iraq, then Afghanistan (see Hodges, 2011, on what he calls the "War on Terror" narrative).

The analysis here focuses largely on a single day of consequential storytelling on the US edition of CNN (coverage that is often broadcast around the world). On July 17, 2014, CNN anchors found themselves with "breaking news on two fronts" (anchor Anderson Cooper), "two major international stories unfolding" (anchor Jake Tapper). The Israeli government had announced that they were entering into a ground offensive in Gaza, and a Malaysian Airlines passenger jet had been shot down over Ukraine. In examples of continuous intertexuality, the network shuttled back and forth between the stories and the reporters who were covering them.

Viewers and newscasters could have been forgiven if they had trouble distinguishing the two locales. This point is illustrated in the following with a modest sample of quotes that could have served to describe either context. Readers can test their ability to identify the referents, either MH17 or Gaza, unless otherwise indicated. Answers follow.

1. It certainly could be a major, major game changer.

2. The other breaking story today, of course, with far reaching implications. . . .

3. This is a tragic and horrific event and the human toll of this is going to be very difficult for people to bear. . . .

4. Regular men become radicalized. . . . They have seen their friends and family killed and the middle space for conversation and compromise is not there. . . . What looks to us as propaganda is truth to them.

5. These are not the terrorists I used to chase. They were pretty limited.

6. I want to bring in our experts, including Israeli retired Air Force General Asaf Agmon.

7. We wanted a situation where our civilians live in peace and quiet . . . and not be under the bombardment of rockets (Israeli speaking or Gazan?)

Answers: 1. MH17; 2. Gaza; 3. MH17; 4. MH17; 5. MH17; 6. MH17, then both; 7. Israeli

An inability to differentiate without aid of an accompanying gloss indexes the similarities between the events. The ability to accurately differentiate indexes sense-making stories at work. The events were, indeed, remarkably similar. And discussions of evidence and responsibility were ubiquitous, in the case of Gaza, with the killing of four boys playing soccer on a beach, and later as United Nations schools serving as civilian shelters were hit. But the two events would not be narrated as the same, arguably because in one case the majority of deaths arose from the actions of a US ally (Israel), whereas in the other, the deaths were presumed to result from the actions of a clear non-ally (Russian-allied separatists). How can two events that might be reported in similar ways be differentiated?

ANOTHER WAY TO THINK ABOUT STORIES

Terry Locke's (2004) *Critical Discourse Analysis* provides another way to think about stories. He theorizes ideology—commonsense, unexamined understandings that saturate society—in terms of stories. He begins with an advertising billboard displaying a large simulated note: "Kelly Browne's parents are away. PARTY at her place!!" The billboard is part of an insurance advertising campaign.

Drawing on Fairclough (e.g., 1992, 2010 [1995]), Foucault (1980, 1991), and Althusser (1971), Locke defines discourse as sense-making stories that circulate in society. Advertising, he notes, makes a virtue of being unoriginal, that is, telling viewers stories they tell themselves (invoking prior texts). I am arguing here that the same case can be made for mainstream media, which (re)teaches its audience the stories they tell themselves; the retelling of those stories is a form of instruction—an instruction, this chapter argues, that instantiates language policy and the sayable. This instantiation is understood within a poststructuralist model; in contrast to more positivist understandings, in which discourse is simply a reflection of society, the assumption here is of "a dialectical relationship between a particular discursive event and the situation(s), institution(s) and social structure(s) which frame it . . . the discursive event is shaped by [them], but it also shapes them" (Fairclough & Wodak, 1997, p. 26). The mutually constitutive nature of text and context, discursive and social structures, such that they are in fact indistinguishable, is a claim by post-structural theory in general that has been powerfully taken up by CDA.

For Locke, discursive events are built on familiar, sense-making stories. He observes that the Kelly Browne billboard ("Kelly Browne's parents are away. <u>PARTY</u> at her place!!") constructs young people, parties, and parents in particular ways:

- Young people prefer to socialize away from their parents.
- Parties are occasions for behaviour which parents may well disapprove of.
- Parents are party dampeners (2004, p. 6).

The billboard becomes interpretable through the recognition of stories that invoke and reproduce these constructions. In Althusser's (1971), or Judith Butler's (1997) terms, it becomes interpretable as the viewers are interpellated by this story into roles as younger or older people of a certain sort. Locke underscores that listing constructions as in the preceding highlights the constructedness of meaning. "It also makes it easier to engage in acts of dissent—to take issue with these constructions and to *resist* the *storied meanings* any text is positioning one . . . to subscribe to" (2004, p. 6; emphasis in original). This captures, in effect, the goal of much critical discourse analysis: to make visible the construction of what is the dominant construal of commonsense.

What then are the sense-making stories and constructions that made two news stories interpretable in particular ways in July 2014? And how were they invoked? As an initial example, Excerpt 1 comprises the first coverage of his day by CNN newscaster Anderson Cooper (Excerpts 1–4, Cooper, July 17, 2014). Recall that "it's not just the story, it's the storytelling." Emphases are added to highlight the structure of the coverage.

Excerpt 1

We begin with the downing of Malaysia Airlines Flight 17, and the search for who did it. **Who is responsible** for the loss of **nearly 300 lives** in a brief instant aboard an airliner over eastern Ukraine? The plane cruising at 33,000 feet one moment, pieces on the ground the next. That is the scene.

Wreckage of the Malaysia Airlines Boeing 777 bound for Kuala Lumpur from- from Amsterdam. And in that field of twisted metal, the remains of 298 men, women, children. Three of them we now know infants. In all, 283 passengers, 15 crew members, **298 souls** on board, 154 Dutch, 27 Australians, 23 Malaysian, 11 Indonesians, unclear how many if any of the rest were American. The list at this hour is incomplete.

So is our information about who ended their lives. We want to be very clear about that. **Who tracked the plane? Who aimed the missile? Who launched it and on whose behalf?**

The fact that it happened **in the heat of a civil war** that many believe was **fomented and fostered by Russia's Vladimir Putin** adding another dimension to **the tragedy**, potentially making it in the words of one analyst today **a game changer**.

The structure of the coverage tells a story of villainy. That story

- fronts and emphasizes: issues of responsibility;
- narrates: human details of "souls" lost (victims), which render this a tragedy;
- implies blame: the war was fomented by a non-ally;
- specifies significance: this is a game changer.

The issue of responsibility is taken up a few moments later. In Excerpt 2 (again, emphases added), the first sources cited by this US-based media outlet are those closer to America: the US government and Ukraine's Western-oriented (by then, NATO-supported) president.

Excerpt 2

COOPER: **A U.S. official** later confirming to CNN that the plane was brought down by a surface-to-air missile. And exactly who fired that missile is still unknown. **Ukraine's prime minister** quickly laid the blame squarely on separatists.

"We do not call it an incident or a catastrophe," he said, "but a **terrorist action.**"

From the point of view of Western-allied Ukrainians, the blame lay with Russian-allied separatists, who were responsible for the incident; what was a civil war was now a terrorist action. Similar to the Kelly Browne sense-making story, it is possible to see the positioning of actors that make this event interpretable to the CNN audience:

- Those who shoot down a passenger airliner committed a dastardly act, perpetrated on innocent victims.
- The victims are like any of us, souls from around the world.
- Vladimir Putin fomented the war that led to this.
- Those fomenting war are responsible for the consequences.
- People who take down passenger airplanes, killing innocent people, are terrorists.
- [Potentially implicit in this: Terrorists should be targeted by the worldwide war on terror.]

In Excerpt 3, Cooper's shift to Gaza coverage comes after a commercial break.

Excerpt 3

COOPER: Welcome back, the other breaking story today, of course, with far reaching implications: After 10 days of airstrikes, bombings and intense fighting, Israel has now launched a ground operation in Gaza. Israel's Prime Minister Benjamin Netanyahu and his defense minister ordered the ground offensive just a few hours ago.

Netanyahu's media adviser says **the point is to destroy tunnels from Gaza into Israeli territory, the kind of tunnels Hamas tried to use to infiltrate Israel just this morning** [emphasis added]. Hamas is condemning the ground action and says Israel will pay a heavy price for it.

There are similarities in the coverage of MH17 and Gaza that index who is the friend, and who the terrorist. Once again, the coverage places the viewer in the middle of hostilities. It indexes the ally by whose information is cited, and their reasoning is not questioned. There is no need to discuss provocations faced by non-allies (Russian-oriented Ukrainians or Hamas). Provocations, however, become important when the stronger party is an ally. In the instance of Gaza, the group with the massive military power, whom some might consider an aggressor responsible for the deaths of civilians and children, is an ally. In that context, the provocative actions and threats of those under bombardment, the non-allies, are fronted, that is, the building and use of tunnels (as well as the presence of rockets). In Excerpt 4, Cooper gives the floor to Wolf Blitzer, reporting from Jerusalem.

Excerpt 4

COOPER: Wolf, you've been talking to Israeli officials there in Jerusalem, what does Israel hope to accomplish with this?

WOLF BLITZER (CNN host, *The Situation Room*): They hope to destroy as much of Hamas infrastructure, **stockpiles of the rockets and missiles, but primarily the first objective is to go after these underground tunnels that they built. One was opened up this morning on the Israeli side, tunnel built from Gaza into Israel.**

The provocation is once again fronted in the next hour in the shift from Ukraine back to the Middle East (Blitzer, 2014a; emphases added), as shown in Excerpt 5.

Excerpt 5

WOLF BLITZER: It's a gruesome scene. Nearly 300 people are believed dead. We're getting in new pictures and new information this hour. [Not Gaza, although within days this will be equally true there.]

And here in the Middle East, Israel ground forces, they have now started moving into Gaza in big numbers. **It's promising to hit Hamas targets hard after militants refused to agree to a cease-fire.**

We want to welcome our viewers in the United States and around the world. I'm Wolf Blitzer in Jerusalem. You're in *The Situation Room*.

ANNOUNCER: This is CNN breaking news.

BLITZER: Let's get to the breaking news unfolding this hour in two very dangerous parts of the world. Stand by for a live report. **We will go inside Gaza on the Israeli ground operation** that is now under way. **Israel is blaming Hamas militants for the new bloodshed that's about to unfold here in the Middle East.** Much more on the story coming up this hour.

Beyond citing provocations, there is another rhetorical way in which the stronger party, the ally, remains a "good guy": reminding the viewer that both parties are at risk. Excerpts 6 and 7 emphasize losses that both sides are likely to suffer, even though the US ally announces that it tries to avoid inflicting losses when it can. First is an example from July 17, in which Wolf Blitzer stresses the dangers to both parties (Tapper & Blitzer, 2014; emphases added).

Excerpt 6

BLITZER: There aren't a whole lot of safe areas in the Gaza Strip right now. So there will be a lot of casualties. Presumably, Hamas insurgents will be killed, **but there will be a lot of civilian casualties, I suspect. There will be Israeli casualties as well.**

So far, **one Israeli has been killed** over the past 10 days of the missile and rocket strikes coming into Israel. **I suspect Israeli soldiers will be among those casualties,** because Hamas has been bracing for this. They have prepared for it. They have got some heavy weapons. So this could be pretty brutal.

Reporting from Gaza City, Ben Wedeman (Cooper, 2014; emphases added) also stresses the dangers to both sides. While he documents the devastation caused by Israeli assaults in 2009, he notes that "they avoided the really crowded areas."

Excerpt 7

WEDEMAN: Yes, of course. Keeping in mind that Gaza is a very crowded place and what we saw for instance in 2009 is even those **areas where the Israeli troops went in and avoided the really crowded areas,** but there are people living everywhere here. There were areas where we saw just one house after another completely destroyed. The roads ripped up and, of course, very high civilian casualties and that is of course the danger, as well.

Now for the Israelis, of course, they are entering into territory with the fighters, whether they are Hamas, the Popular Front for the Liberation. This is their turf. They know this area very well and Hamas has made it clear that they believe or they are confident that just as they have been able to increase the range of their rockets that their ground forces are better trained now, better trained now than ever before, so they are saying that they will be able to confront the Israeli troops, but we'll see if that's actually the case.

Here, then, is the constructed story of Gaza:

· The war in Israel/Palestine is ongoing.
· Now terrorists are trying to enter Israel through tunnels.
· The only way to destroy tunnels is through a ground offensive.
· In the past Israel has tried to avoid the heaviest populated areas.
· Even when one tries, it is not possible to avoid civilians.
· When fighting, there will always be military casualties as well.

To be clear, there are counter-narratives in the coverage, including descriptions of the misery of Gaza residents. Indeed, the issue of civilian casualties came to require more explanation as time went on. July 9 had seen the bombing of a cafe in Gaza, and July 16, the killing of four cousins (ages 9–11) playing on the beach in Gaza (the bombing of UN schools would come beyond the time frame covered by this chapter). Civilian casualties occasioned the opportunity for extensive explanation by an ally. On July 16, Wolf Blitzer (2014b) interviewed Mark Regev, identified as spokesman for Israeli Prime Minister Benjamin Netanyahu, and highly visible on CNN during this period. The rationale, illustrated in Excerpt 8, is a story that was repeated often enough on CNN to become a prior text.

Excerpt 8

BLITZER: We saw those horrible pictures, a horrible incident on a beach in Gaza City today. Israeli fire came and killed these four little boys. What happened?

REGEV: We don't know exactly. And we're checking it out, because we don't target civilians. We don't target children. And there's obviously been a mistake. And the army is investigating itself. It's appointed a full general to conduct the investigation. We want to find out what happened, what went—what went wrong.

BLITZER: Was this gunfire from a ship offshore? Is that what happened?

REGEV: It's not clear exactly. But our rules of engagement are very clear. And I cannot believe that if it was an Israeli army personnel who shot that missile, that they knew that they were targeting civilians. I cannot believe that. It must have been some sort of mistake.

And that's the ultimate difference between us, because Hamas randomly shoots into Israeli cities, trying to kill, indiscriminately, as many Israeli civilians as they can. We make a maximum effort—and you see that with the leaflets we've been putting out—to keep civilians out of combat zones, to make sure they're not caught in the crossfire between us and the terrorists.

BLITZER: But you see a lot of civilians, women, children, elderly, have been killed in these Israeli strikes.

REGEV: We don't want to see it. And we make a maximum effort to avoid that. And the truth is, the primary responsibility for the civilian toll on the Palestinian side is Hamas, that said no to the cease-fire.

BLITZER: So what do you say to the family of those four little boys who were killed today?

REGEV: We say we didn't want this conflict in the first place. I mean, we share with them their grief. We understand that, because we've had grief on our side, as well. But we didn't want this conflict. This conflict came because Hamas kept shooting rockets into Israel and we are forced to defend our people from those rockets.

These data from July 16 and 17, 2016, show the positioning of an ally:

- Allies get air time.

- Allies are us. Like/with us, they investigate and determine responsibility for their actions.
  - [Blitzer asks Regev, "What happened?"]
- When allies do bad things it is a dreadful necessity.
- Allies are forced to do bad things by bad people.
  - [It is Hamas who refuses a ceasefire, who shoots rockets into Israel; an unspoken prior text is the claim that they use human shields.]
- Viewers are interpellated into allies' worldview, sometimes literally.
  - [Note Jake Tapper's misspeak in that same broadcast: "Wolf, has the IDF or the Israeli government said at all whether or not US—I'm sorry—whether or not Israeli troops once they go in will be coming out?"]
  - [And the viewer physically becomes the IDF, in this coverage: "Coming up, we're live from Jerusalem. Split-second life and death decisions—we're about to get a look at an Israeli drone program that's used to try—to try to prevent civilian casualties."]

It is not that CNN never notices the parallels between MH17 and Gaza. But because of the underlying stories and positioning, because of the viewer's interpellation, the parallels can be ignored or explained away. An intertextual example from MH17 coverage (directly referencing the other crisis) comes from Jake Tapper (2014) on his CNN show *The Lead*, which can be seen in Excerpt 9.

Excerpt 9

This is a tragic and horrific event and the human toll of this is going to be very difficult for people to bear, especially people in the Netherlands, people in Malaysia, and who knows, maybe even in the United States. And the fact that it was intentional, that more people have now died in this plane crash than in this horror going on between Israel and Gaza, that somebody did it on purpose has serious ramifications beyond the human tragedy when it comes to world events.

In fact, it becomes clear early on that the downing of a passenger plane was unintentional. But non-allies don't get a free pass on mistakes. At best, they are unforgivably careless.

Conclusion

On July 17, 2014, two stories broke almost simultaneously, two stories that needed to be differentiated. The ideological work of national media rendered these international crises intelligible through the retelling of tales that left traditional victims and villains unchallenged. In reinscribing the sayable, these tales raise fundamental questions for LP scholars: Who gets to speak and whose perspective is reported? Into whose identities are viewers interpellated? Whose aggressions are justified and whose mistakes understandable? Whose lost lives are unqualified tragedies and whose unfortunate byproducts? These reinscriptions naturalize a status quo that rests on traditional good guys and bad guys, us and them.

This chapter makes the case for LP-inflected research into the implicit policies of public discourse. Three examples of the discursive positioning of Latino students and parents in the US context suggest how the kind of analysis offered here can be applied specifically to language issues in the mass media. First is Yamagami's (2012) analysis of media coverage of California's Proposition 227 campaign, which led to adoption of an initiative that banned most bilingual education in the state. Yamagami demonstrates that opponents of bilingualism won on the discursive playing field, "achiev[ing] a discursive victory" that "legitimized the anti-bilingual movement as the voice of children and families who do not speak English, [and] effectively blocked advocates of bilingual education from influencing language policy" (p. 144). Similarly, Crawford (2004) examined the media narratives of what became known as the Ninth Street Elementary School Boycott by Latino parents in southern California. According to the media, parents refused to permit their children to take bilingual classes, insisting instead on English-only instruction. The local incident, which was created and directed by a leader of the anti-bilingualism campaign, eventually became an iconic media story that inaccurately represented Latino parents as being opposed to bilingual education. A third example can be found in Jefferies's (2009) analysis of media representations of undocumented, mostly Spanish-speaking students as "not playing by the rules" in the "meritocracy" of the US educational system. Jefferies's analysis reveals the ideological positioning of migrant students as outsiders unwilling to submit themselves to the competitive US system. In all of these cases, dominant media narratives privilege the voices of actors who articulate monolingual ideologies that are normalized by media as the commonsense voice of the people. One wonders if a concurrent discourse analysis of these media portrayals might have allowed a more effective response.

Beyond mass media, public documents and rhetoric of all sorts embody the ideologies on which communal practices are based. This chapter invites LP scholars to become more attuned to these implicit policies and to the ways public discourse constrains the voices and perspectives that may be heard (see also Gao & Shao, Chapter 15 in this volume). Likewise, discourse analysts could become more aware of the language policy implications of their work. One example of a study with such implications is research on the media coverage of police sweeps of Seattle's homeless encampments (see Bawarshi et al., 2008, described in Silberstein, 2016). The multidisciplinary research traced discursive and ideological genealogies in legal, national policy, and public relations documents that underlay a media campaign designed to position the homeless as a threat to public safety. In effect, the research traced the genealogy of a language policy that favored the perspective of property owners and those who saw the homeless as a source of filth and contagion. Across discursive platforms, the voices of the homeless were silenced. As with all language policies, the task of the LP specialist studying mass media is to ask whose interests are served by the ideologies and policies analyzed, and what power hierarchies are sustained by them.

NOTE

1. Dictionary.com is the world's leading digital dictionary, with 5.5B word searches annually. Its proprietary source is the Random House Unabridged Dictionary, supplemented by American Heritage and Harper Collins.

REFERENCES

Althusser, L. (1971). *Lenin and philosophy and other essays*. B. Brewster, Trans. New York: Monthly Review Press.

Bakhtin, M. M. (1981). *The dialogic imagination: Four essays*. M. Holquist, Ed., C. Emerson & M. Holquist, Trans. Austin: University of Texas Press.

Bawarshi, A., Dillon, G., Kelly, M., Rai, C., Silberstein, S., Stygall, G., & Toft, A. (2008). *Media analysis of homeless encampment "sweeps."* Retrieved from http://faculty.washington.edu/stygall/homelessmediacoveragegroup/

Becker, A.L. (1995). *Beyond translation: Essays toward a modern philology*. Ann Arbor: University of Michigan Press.

Blitzer, W. (Presenter, Reporter). (2014a, July 17). Israel launches ground invasion of Gaza; Malaysia Airlines flight crashes in Ukraine. In *The Situation Room* [Transcript]. Retrieved from http://www.cnn.com/TRANSCRIPTS/1407/17/sitroom.02.html

Blitzer, W. (Presenter). (2014b, July 16). U.N. calls for limited cease-fire; first Hamas reaction to U.N. cease-fire plan; Israeli reaction to Hamas; Obama announces new policies on foreign affairs. In *The Situation Room* [Transcript]. Retrieved from http://www.cnn.com/TRANSCRIPTS/1407/16/sitroom.01.html

Butler, J. (1997). *Excitable speech: A politics of the performative*. New York: Routledge.

Caldes-Coulthard, C. R., & Coulthard, M. (Eds.). (1996). *Texts and practices: Readings in critical discourse analysis*. London: Routledge.

Cooper, A. (Presenter). (2014, July 17). Malaysia Airlines Flight 17 shot down. In *Anderson Cooper 360 Degrees* [Transcript]. Retrieved from http://www.cnn.com/TRANSCRIPTS/1407/17/acd.01.html

Crawford, J. (2004). *Educating English learners: Language diversity in the classroom*. 5th edition, Kindle edition. Portland, OR: Diversity Learning K12.

Death toll in Gaza rises past 300, more than 70% civilians: officials. (2014, July 19). CNN. Retrieved from http://pix11.com/2014/07/19/death-toll-in-gaza-rises-past-300-more-than-70-civilians-officials/

Fairclough, N. (1992). *Discourse and social change.* Cambridge, UK: Blackwell.

Fairclough, N. (2010 [1995]). *Critical discourse analysis: The critical study of language.* 2nd edition. London: Routledge.

Fairclough, N. (2015). *Language and power.* 3rd edition. London: Routledge.

Fairclough, N., & Wodak, R. (1997). Critical discourse analysis. In T. van Dijk (Ed.), *Discourse and interaction* (pp. 258–284). London: Sage.

Foucault, M. (1980). *Power/knowledge: Selected interviews and other writings 1972–1977.* New York: Pantheon.

Foucault, M. (1991). Politics and the study of discourse. In G. Burchell, C. Gordon, & P. Miller (Eds.), *The Foucault effect: Studies in governmentality* (pp. 53–72). London: Harvester Wheatsheaf.

Gee, J. P. (2014). *An introduction to discourse analysis: Theory and method.* 4th edition. London: Routledge.

Hodges, A. (2011). *The "War on Terror" narrative: Discourse and intertextuality in the construction and contestation of sociopolitical reality.* Oxford: Oxford University Press.

Jefferies, J. (2009). Do undocumented students play by the rules? Meritocracy in the media. *Critical Inquiry in Language Studies* 6 (1–2), 15–38.

Lazar, M. M. (Ed.). (2007). *Feminist critical discourse analysis: Studies in gender, power and ideology.* Hampshire, UK: Palgrave Macmillan.

Locke, T. (2004). *Critical discourse analysis.* London: Continuum.

Roy, A. G. (2014). What's Punjabi doing in an English film? In R. Rubdy & L. Alsagoff (Eds.), *The global-local interface and hybridity: Exploring language and identity* (pp. 153–169). Bristol, UK: Multilingual Matters.

Shohamy, E. (2006). *Language policy: Hidden agendas and new approaches.* London: Routledge.

Silberstein, S. (2002). *War of words: Language, politics, and 9/11.* London: Routledge.

Silberstein, S. (2016). Ethics in research and activist scholarship: Media/policy analyses of Seattle's homeless encampment 'sweeps.'" In P. DeCosta (Ed.), *Ethics in applied linguistics research: Language researcher narratives* (pp. 218–236). London: Routledge.

Tapper, J. (Presenter). (2014, July 17). Ukraine: Pro-Russia separatists shot down plane. In *The Lead with Jake Tapper* [Transcript]. Retrieved from http://edition.cnn.com/TRANSCRIPTS/1407/17/cg.02.html

Tapper, J. (Presenter), & Blitzer, W. (Reporter). (2014, July 17). Israel launches ground invasion of Gaza; Malaysia Airlines flight crashes in Ukraine. In *The Lead with Jake Tapper* [Transcript]. Retrieved from http://www.cnn.com/TRANSCRIPTS/1407/17/cg.01.html

van Dijk, T. A. (2001). Multidisciplinary CDA: A plea for diversity. In R. Wodak & M. Meyer (Eds.), *Methods of critical discourse analysis* (pp. 95–120). London: Sage.

van Dijk, T.A. (2008). *Discourse and power.* Hampshire, UK: Palgrave Macmillan.

Van Leeuven, T. (2008). *Discourse and practice: New tools for critical discourse analysis.* Oxford: Oxford University Press.

Wodak, R., & Chilton, P. (Ed.). (2005). *A new agenda in (critical) discourse analysis: Theory, methodology and interdisciplinarity.* Amsterdam: John Benjamins.

Wodak, R., & Meyer, M. (Eds.). (2001). *Methods of critical discourse analysis.* London: Sage.

Wodak, R., & Meyer, M. (Eds.). (2009). *Methods of critical discourse analysis.* 2nd edition. London: Sage.

Yamagami, M. (2012). The political discourse of the campaign against bilingual education: From Proposition 227 to *Horne v. Flores*. *International Multilingual Research Journal* 6, 143–159.

Zara, C. (2014). Cable news ratings: CNN, MSNBC sink despite July 2014 plane crashes, Israel-Gaza conflict. *International Business Times*. Retrieved from http://www.ibtimes.com/cable-news-ratings-cnn-msnbc-sink-despite-july-2014-plane-crashes-israel-gaza-conflict-1644120

....

CHAPTER 17

LANGUAGE POLICY AND PLANNING AND LINGUISTIC LANDSCAPES

....

FRANCIS M. HULT

WHILE the term *linguistic landscape* is sometimes used as a cover term to refer to the general linguistic circumstances of a polity, it is also the moniker for a rapidly expanding transdisciplinary field focused on investigating the use of language in public spaces (Gorter, 2013, p. 191). Its roots extend to work in the 1970s that examined public language use in bilingual cities, though the springboard that launched linguistic landscape (LL) analysis as it looks today was a landmark paper by Landry and Bourhis (1997) that labeled it as such and presented core principles that have continued to shape the field (Backhaus, 2007, p. 12; Gorter, 2013, p. 192). Following Landry and Bourhis, a growing field has emerged from an expanding number of studies and now includes a regular international meeting, along with *Linguistic Landscape* as a dedicated journal (Gorter, 2013, pp. 195–196).

Language policy and planning (LPP) was a foundational component of LL. As Landry and Bourhis explain, "it is in the language planning field that issues related to the notion of linguistic landscape first emerged," as officials in contexts like Belgium and Québec developed regulations for public signage in response to linguistic conflicts (1997, p. 24). LL, then, is a key consideration in LPP. The present chapter provides an overview of the relationship between LPP and LL, with illustrations from studies that have examined them together. I begin with a brief exposition of key LL principles and their relevance for LPP. I then turn to a discussion of direct connections between the two, when there is explicit LPP about LL, followed by various ways in which there are also indirect connections. Finally, I reflect on considerations for future research.

KEY PRINCIPLES

In their influential paper, Landry and Bourhis offer a definition of LL that remains widely used in current research: "The language of public road signs, advertising billboards, street names, place names, commercial shop signs, and public signs on government buildings combines to form the linguistic landscape of a given territory, region, or urban agglomeration" (1997, p. 25). Or, as Ben-Rafael et al. (2006) succinctly put it, LL is a "symbolic construction of the public space" (http://www.tandfonline.com/doi/abs/10.1080/14790710608668383). A basic premise is that LL is not randomly generated, but is the product of intersecting factors that mediate language choices, such as beliefs and ideologies about languages, language policies, and communicative needs (Ben-Rafael et al., 2010; Gorter, 2013; Shohamy & Gorter, 2009). Analyzing the ways in which language is used visually in public space, then, allows the researcher to read an LL as an expression of these factors, including possible sociopolitical tensions among them. For instance, as Shohamy notes, "the presence (or absence) of specific language items, displayed in specific languages, in a specific manner, sends direct and indirect messages with regard to the centrality versus the marginality of certain languages in society" (2006, p. 110).

As in LPP, a *top-down* versus *bottom-up* distinction is sometimes made. Signs created by an authority (e.g., government or corporation) are characterized as top-down or official because they are products of a centralized authority, while signs created by individuals are considered bottom-up or unofficial as they are ostensibly the product of personal choices (Backhaus, 2007, p. 27; Ben-Rafael et al., 2006, p. 10; Shohamy, 2006, p. 115). The distinction between the two is not always obvious. Is a laser-printed sign posted by a railroad stationmaster bottom-up because it was generated by one person, or is it top-down because it was created by an individual in his or her capacity as a railroad agent? At what point does a professionally commissioned commercial sign become top-down? When designed by an individual shopkeeper but manufactured by a sign company? When ordered by the senior member of a family-owned business? When decided upon by a local board of directors? When a franchise owner develops the content in relation to a company policy? When the content is generated and approved by a corporate body overseeing advertising or communication? The answer will depend on the circumstances and may vary from sign to sign.

Nonetheless, the top-down/bottom-up distinction points to ways in which LL relates to Spolsky's (2004, p. 5) tripartite characterization of language policy: language practices (habitual language choices and norms for interaction), language beliefs or ideology (situated values about languages), and language management (deliberate attempts to manipulate language practices or beliefs). LL research has focused variously and in different combinations on analyzing explicit management that targets visual language use, examining patterns of language choice in signage, and extrapolating language ideologies from visually projected linguistic relations (e.g., Shohamy, Ben-Rafael, & Barni, 2010; Shohamy & Gorter, 2009). LPP may relate directly and explicitly to LL when policies and planning specifically aim to manage public language use (Backhaus, 2009). The relationship may also be indirect, for example, when one can trace ideologies from general language policies to the configuration of language use on signage even when policy is not directly aimed at LL or when visual language use in LL becomes habituated to the point where norms become de facto policy (Shohamy, 2006, pp. 110–114; Spolsky, 2009, p. 252). It is to a closer consideration of these direct and indirect connections that I now turn.

LANGUAGE POLICY AND PLANNING ABOUT LINGUISTIC LANDSCAPES

The most obvious intersection of LPP and LL is when there is explicit policy and planning about visual language in public spaces. Studies of such contexts have documented compliance with or resistance to policy that aims to shape the LL (e.g., Hepford, 2017; Lamarre, 2014; Manan et al., 2015; Sloboda et al., 2010; Zabrodskaja, 2014), how individuals experience explicit policy and planning about LLs (e.g., Draper & Prasertsri, 2013; Sloboda et al., 2010), and using LLs to manage a sense of place (e.g., Akzhigitova & Zharkynbekova, 2014; Vigers, 2013).

Regulations for linguistic landscapes can be highly detailed and explicit. Manan et al. (2015, p. 35), for example, present the policy governing signage and advertising in the city of Kuala Lumpur, Malaysia:

> (1) The national language shall be used for all advertisements whether by itself or together with any other language; (2) If the national language is used with any other language in an advertisement, the words in the national language shall be—(a) 30% larger than the other language in measurement; (b) prominently displayed and (c) grammatically correct; (3) any person who fails to comply with paragraph (1) or

(2) shall be guilty of an offence and shall upon conviction be liable to a fine not exceeding 2000 ringgit (about 400 pounds) or to imprisonment not exceeding one year or both.

Hepford reports on the English-Spanish bilingual policy of the major US home improvement retailer Lowe's:

[S]igns should "group all English copy over Spanish copy, separated by a rule" and ever more specifically, "if the English font is 100 pt. or more, then the Spanish font should be 50% of the size of the English font and in a lighter font style." (Lowe's, 2011, A:2, as cited in Hepford, 2017, p. 655)

Such policies aim for consistency in the linguistic landscapes by attempting to regulate the linguistic behavior of those who generate and display signs, and there is often policing of the regulations (Backhaus, 2009). In Kuala Lumpur, for instance, authorities monitor compliance, and punitive measures resulting from infractions are frequently reported in news media (Manan et al., 2015, pp. 35–36). Lowe's has a centralized oversight process whereby signs created by individual store managers are first officially translated and then approved by a review board before they may be posted in a store (Hepford, 2017, p. 655). The Canadian province of Québec, and the city of Montréal in particular, has been well known since the 1970s for its detailed laws governing language use in public spaces (see Backhaus, 2009; Bourhis & Landry, 2002). Compliance with these laws is carefully monitored by *l'Office québécois de la langue française*,[1] which conducts periodic investigations and handles complaints from the public.

Despite explicit and detailed policies about signage and official attempts to enforce them, those who inhabit linguistic landscapes often find creative ways to subvert or resist the policies. Such resistance is common when official policies do not align with local sociolinguistic circumstances and communicative needs (Schiffman, 1996, p. 49; Spolsky, 2004, p. 222). It also suggests the important role of individual agency in the construction of LLs, which are ultimately aggregates of diverse values and experiences that are expressed visually (Ben-Rafael et al., 2006, p. 8: Jaworski & Yeung, 2010, p. 56). Lamarre (2014) documents resistance in the form of creative wordplay, what she terms "bilingual winks," in the signage of Montréal. A store name such as "T & biscuits" can be read as either French or English depending on the disposition of the viewer, and calling a footwear store *Chouchou* has a French appearance while cleverly invoking the English word *shoe* (Lamarre, 2014, p. 140). Such signage allows shop owners to playfully circumvent LL policies about the prominence of French in ways that are formally compliant and not aggressively political (Lamarre, 2014, p. 142).

Resistance can also come in the form of defying LL policies. Hepford (2017, p. 662) found that fully 51.5% of signs in one Lowe's store location were not in compliance with company LL policy, which she attributes to the agency of managers who subvert the policy when it does not align with the linguistic repertoire of the local community. More broadly, she notes that a greater proportion of signs were bilingual at a store situated in an ethnically diverse community than at one in a predominantly white neighborhood. Others have also documented local resistance to official LL policies. Zabrodskaja (2014) investigates the city of Tallinn in Estonia, where national language policy has focused on de-russification and the advancement of Estonian in all domains of society, including the linguistic landscape. Here, too, she finds that despite a Language Inspectorate that monitors compliance and levies fines for infractions, shop owners resist the monolingually oriented Estonian policy by using Russian and other languages to reach minority- and majority-language speakers (Zabrodskaja, 2014, p. 127).

Likewise, Manan et al. (2015), in their study of Kuala Lumpur, found that even with a highly detailed policy focused on advancing Bahasa Melayu, government monitoring, and media exposure of policy infractions, a range of languages are used to align with the local linguistic repertoire, including Arabic, English, Mandarin, and Myanmar/Burmese, in addition to Bahasa Melayu. This is not to suggest that LL policies do not have an effect. Indeed, developing explicit policy that includes the LL can be effective in managing linguistic behavior, as Gorter, Aiestaran, and Cenoz (2012) show in their study of Donostia–San Sebastián in the Basque Autonomous Community of Spain, where increased attention to LL in official policy appears to have resulted in the greater visibility of Basque. Similarly, as Marten (2010) demonstrates in his study of Rēzekne in post-Soviet Latvia, policy measures have contributed to promoting Latvian over Russian in LL and other domains, with regional and minority languages remaining peripheral.

How people experience LPP about LLs is another consideration. In her study of the LL of Tallinn, Zabrodskaja (2014) interviewed language students at Tallinn University about their attitudes toward multilingual signage, in addition to examining policy in relation to LL practice. She found that native-speaking Estonian students' attitudes aligned with the national policy favoring Estonian, as they generally had negative views of multilingual signs and of Russian or Russian-Estonian signs, in particular, while Russian-Estonian bilingual students had favorable views of multilingual signs, which they found creative and useful for reaching a wider audience (Zabrodskaja, 2014, p. 127). Sloboda et al. (2010) investigated LL policies in the Czech Republic, Hungary, and Wales in relation to how local residents experience their implementation. Working in two phases, they began by collecting data about the LLs themselves through photography and about their policy contexts via policy documents and reports, online sources, and media texts, and then conducted observations in three cities and interviews with residents, public officials, and visitors (Sloboda et al., 2010, p. 98). Triangulating these different data sources, Sloboda et al. offer a multidimensional perspective on a city in each context by mapping policy, how it is actually implemented, and how the implemented policy is experienced by different stakeholders. While the nature of policy, implementation, and stakeholder experiences differed in each context, a common finding was the role of individual agency in shaping the practical implementation of LL policy, thereby suggesting the value of not only formulating formal policy, but also managing the beliefs and emotions of stakeholders toward the languages being managed (Sloboda et al., 2010, pp. 110–111).

How people experience LLs is closely tied to the way in which visual language use contributes to the construction of a "sense of place" (Hult, 2014; Jaworski & Yeung, 2010). An LL is not passive scenery; it projects specific values that mediate inhabitants' interpretations of themselves and their relations to others in a space, thus forming a socially constructed "place" imbued with meaning (Curtin, 2009; Jaworski & Yeung, 2010, p. 155). Language planning about LLs is sometimes about deliberately managing the sense of place that people experience (Akzhigitova & Zharkynbekova, 2014; Dal Negro, 2009; Marten, 2010; Puzy, 2012; Sloboda, 2009). Draper and Prasertsri (2013), for example, describe a language maintenance and re-vitalization program for the Isan in Thailand, where attitudes toward the linguistic landscape were taken into account in planning efforts. The program, which involves pilot projects in certain municipalities that if successful could be expanded more widely, includes components related to traditional weaving, literacy education, cultural performance, and the development of multilingual signage in Thai, English, and the Isan language. The research-driven project involved surveying stakeholders about their attitudes toward multilingual signage. They found that there was gener-ally a positive view of multilingual signage, and the respondents saw the use of Isan on signage as facilitating identity development and the learning and maintenance of the language (Draper & Prasertsri, 2013, p. 628). Thus, there was alignment between the planning objectives to shape the sense of place through signage and people's beliefs about how the sense of place should be shaped. In contrast, Vigers (2013) shows tensions in Brittany between the projected sense of place through signage using Breton and the local experience, which is characterized by language shift to French. Signage in Breton serves to commodify the language as an index of heritage that offers the region a unique selling point for tourism, food, and industry, but not as an index of linguistic vitality, because "every Breton or bilingual sign becomes both a reconstructed *lieu de mémoire*, a memorialization of the language, and an ele-ment in the experience of Breton heritage" (Vigers, 2103, p. 175). In this case, LL pla-nning involves image planning (cf. Ager, 2005).

RELATING LINGUISTIC LANDSCAPES
TO LANGUAGE POLICY AND PLANNING

In addition to situations where there is explicit LPP about LL, there are circumstances when the connection is indirect as well. Research about such indirect relationships falls into three general areas. First, LL researchers tend to situate linguistic landscape analysis by interpreting visual language use in relation to sociopolitical context, which often includes general LPP that does not necessarily target signage directly but nonetheless provides insight into the ideological climate in which an LL is located (e.g., Hult, 2014; Isleem, 2015; Kasanga, 2012). Second, like language policy, LL has the potential both to reflect and to (re)produce language ideology, so the construction of LLs has itself also been noted as a kind of policymaking by practice, where the resulting semiotic aggregate is seen as a de facto language policy (e.g., Dal Negro, 2009; Shohamy, 2006, pp. 110–112; Sloboda, 2009). Third, because LL research brings to light ideological tensions about language that might be in need of management, analysts sometimes offer implications for LPP based on their LL findings (e.g., Coluzzi, 2009; Lazdiņa, 2013; Taylor-Leech, 2012). Each of these three areas is examined further in the following sections using empirical examples.

Situating Linguistic Landscapes in Policy Contexts

LL research is never decontextualized. A central purpose is to provide tangible evidence for the ideological climate that contributes to specific regimes of language in a particular polity (Blommaert, 2013, pp. 39–40; Shohamy, 2006, pp. 110–111; cf. Kroskrity, 2000). Both LL and de jure language policy are spaces in which values about language and linguistic relations are entextualized, or made into texts that legitimize certain ways of reading them (Blommaert, 2005, pp. 47, 185); thus, intertextual and interdiscursive analysis of policy and visual language use can highlight what specific values circulate widely in society as dominant discourses (Hult, 2015, pp. 224–225; Johnson, 2015). Policy, then, can be an ideological backdrop against which to view an LL, and an LL can be a place to see the resemiotization of policy discourses.

As an example of policy as LL context, Kasanga (2012) points to policy as one social factor among others (e.g., globalization, gentrification, and language attitudinal shifts) that contributes to the sociopolitical climate for the LL in Phnom Penh, Cambodia. The strong presence of Khmer relates to its status as the de jure official language, and language-in-education policy plays a role in enhancing attitudes toward and proficiency in English, which is outpacing French, a language with a long local colonial legacy, in visual space. Similarly, Isleem (2015) situates his LL study of two Druze communities in Israel in light of the policy history that has shaped the identity of this Arabic-speaking population in particular and the linguistic relations between Arabic and Hebrew in general. He finds that historically situated policy tensions are visible in the LL, where a power imbalance obtains between Arabic and Hebrew as the dominant language. Hult (2014) likewise situates the study of Spanish and English in the LL of San Antonio, Texas, within the context of national language ideologies and regional policies of linguistic assimilation that together provide a sociohistorical lens through which to view the contemporary dominance of English.

General language policies can be more than context; policy discourses about linguistic relations can be resemiotized, or transformed into other forms of expression, by being taken up by LL actors (Blommaert, 2013, p. 32; Hult, 2015, p. 224). As Lanza and Woldemariam (2009, p. 190) explain, "the impact of policies can be examined in light of language practices since language users may enforce or revolt against official national or regional policy in their public displays." They exemplify this relationship with their study of Ethiopia, which has a multilingual language policy of Amharic as the national language together with recognition of local languages within regional states, by investigating the LL in the city of Mekele, where the regional language of Tigrinya is an official working language. The national language policy and tensions related to it, Lanza and Woldemariam show, play out in Mekele's LL. Tigrinya is highly visible, especially in top-down signs, as is Amharic, which is equally balanced with Tigrinya on bottom-up signs, which they attribute to ongoing language ideological debate among local elites about the relative status of the regional language vis-à-vis the national language. Pearson's (2015) diachronic study of the LL of Butare, Ethiopia, in turn, shows that a shift over a six-year period from French to English as the dominant language in visual space coincides with a policy shift emphasizing English, suggesting that the general language policy has had an impact on how LL actors contribute to shaping the linguistic ecology. Cenoz and Gorter (2006), in a similar vein, compare the respective presence of Frisian in Friesland (Netherlands) and Basque in the Basque Country (Spain), noting that a more robust language policy for minority-language protection contributes to the slightly stronger presence of Basque in the city of Donostia–San Sebastián than Frisian in the city of Ljouwert-Leeuwarden.

In addition to general language policy, LLs can also be understood more broadly in relation to extralinguistic state ideologies that are sometimes also deliberately managed (Shohamy & Waksman, 2010; Sloboda, 2009). Sloboda (2009), for instance, comparatively analyzes the Czech Republic, Slovakia, and Belarus, which differ in that Belarus explicitly manages through education, politics, and media a particular overt ideology that celebrates the state and state actors (e.g., soldiers and police officers) whereas in the Czech Republic and in Slovakia state ideology implicitly advances political values around internationalization and citizen responsibilities (Sloboda, 2009, pp. 178–179). He finds that these ideological differences resonate in the respective LLs, where the minimal presence of international chain stores in Belarus aligns with the state ideology of a national market economy, while the presence of numerous chain stores in the Czech Republic and Slovakia speak to an ideology of participation in the transnational economy. In addition, the common presence of graffiti in the Czech Republic and Slovakia and its virtual absence in Belarus seem to relate to an ideology of order and the marginalization of sociopolitical opposition in the latter, in contrast to the former (Sloboda, 2009, pp. 180, 184–185).

Linguistic Landscapes and de Facto Language Policy and Planning

As Spolsky (2004, p. 222) avers, "the real language policy of a community is more likely to be found in its practices than in management." If policies can be thought of as institutionalized ideologies, and LLs are the ideological construction of places through visual language use, then one can read an LL as one expression of a community's de facto language policy (Dal Negro, 2009, p. 215; Lanza & Woldemariam, 2009, p. 189; Shohamy, 2006, p. 110).

This orientation falls into a growing perspective on LPP that highlights policy as emerging from daily practices that become codified in some way through habituation, which may occur with or without the existence of written policy texts (McCarty, 2011; Menken & García, 2010; Spolsky & Shohamy, 2000; cf. Hult, 2017). The focus, thus, shifts from centralized government policies and a linear path to their implementation to one of governmentality, whereby certain linguistic regulations emerge through iterative choices mediated by values about language that permeate multiple domains of society, including visual language use (Blommaert, 2013, p. 2; Pennycook, 2006). An important caveat is that the LL does not necessarily reflect regimes of language in non-visual modalities that might suggest alternative de facto language policies (Spolsky, 2009, p. 252; cf. Vigers, 2013). Nonetheless, LLs can be useful sites for observing the inscription of language ideologies, which can provide insight into de facto language policy, broadly speaking, and into the practiced language policies for LLs, in particular.

Dal Negro (2009) observes that LL is an "instrument through which a new course in language policy is made immediately apparent" (p. 206). The distribution of languages on signage can suggest the norms that govern visual language use and the latent ideologies that mediate those norms (Blommaert, 2013, p. 32). Hult (2009), for example, examines the LL of the Swedish city of Malmö in order to determine the "interaction order" (Goffman, 1983; Scollon & Scollon, 2004) that organizes visual language practices. Competing linguistic hierarchies were found in mainstream and minority contexts, with Swedish dominant in both, but English in second place in the former and minority language in second place in the latter. In both contexts, English tended to have metaphorical functions, suggesting that it is used more for indexing globalization than for instrumental communication, whereas Swedish was used prevalently for instrumental communication in both settings, and minority languages served a prominent instrumental function in the minority setting but rarely in the mainstream setting.

The de facto policy that emerges is that Swedish is the primary language that can be used widely for instrumental communication, that minority languages can be used for instrumental communication in minority contexts but not in mainstream contexts, and that English can be used to signal international cosmopolitanism, but it is not necessarily as relevant for day-to-day visual communication. Comparable values have been identified in official policies as well (e.g., Hult, 2012). In a similar way, Dal Negro (2009) found in her study of three rural Italian communities that the linguistic landscape suggested a de facto policy for German linguistic minority communities in a Walser village and in South Tyrol. While German was considerably less visible in the Walser village and substantially visible in South Tyrol, there was a notable difference in the variety of German. Standard German was used almost exclusively in South Tyrol, while a local variety of German was prominent in the Walser village, suggesting in the former a de facto policy of minority language standardization that aligns with the wider international German-language community, and in the latter a more limited de facto policy for tolerance of local minority-language use (Dal Negro, 2009, p. 213).

In another study that highlights the role of LL as de facto policy, Blackwood and Tufi (2012) compare French and Italian Mediterranean settings. They submit that while France is characterized by official policies that advance a concerted agenda for maintaining the prominence of French as the national language, Italy is characterized by language legislation that is vague nationally and uneven on regional scales such that the management of Italian in relation to other languages effectively amounts to "non-policy" (Blackwood and Tufi, 2012, pp. 114–115). Despite these legislative differences, they find that the national language dominates over regional languages in the LLs of both the French and the Italian communities. The prominence of French can be explained as the result of deliberate, official language management. In contrast, the prominence of Italian is the result of de facto policy that has emerged through the propagation of specific language ideologies through institutions like education, business, and administration that have legitimized Italian and delegitimized regional languages (Blackwood & Tufi, 2012, p. 124).

Ukraine has also been a context with tensions between de jure policy and de facto practice in LL (Bever, 2010; L'nyavskiy-Ekelund, 2016; Pavlenko, 2010). Language planning debates in Ukraine have focused on managing the relative positions of Ukrainian and Russian even before Ukraine gained independence in 1991 (L'nyavskiy-Ekelund, 2016, pp. 32–33). An existing constitutional provision provides for the national status of Ukrainian, and the 2012 *Law on State Language Policy* granted status to regional languages, making Russian a regional language in eastern and southeastern areas (Bever, 2015, pp. 255–256). A 2014 repeal of this policy sparked controversy and led to military aggression, as the repeal, which was later annulled, was framed in Russian media as an attempt to further marginalize Russian (L'nyavskiy-Ekelund, 2016, p. 8). LL research both before (Bever, 2010) and after (L'nyavskiy-Ekelund, 2016) the 2014 crisis show dynamic negotiation and coexistence of Ukrainian and Russian in metropolitan areas across the country, wherein top-down signage reflects the state's planning efforts to advance Ukrainian, and bottom-up signage reveals a de facto policy of multilingualism that aligns with the linguistic repertoires of local communities.

Even in settings where there are official policies about LL, there can be competing "covert" language policies that challenge or subvert de jure policies (Schiffman, 1996, p. 13). As Dal Negro remarks, "explicit and conscious interventions on language functions are typically reflected in LL, a privileged locus for language policy, both in top-down (institutional) and in bottom-up (counter-institutional) expressions" (2009, p. 216). While official policies reflect centralized or institutionalized attempts to intervene in LLs, covert policies emerge through the sedimentation of ideologically situated practices among those who live and work in LLs (Shohamy, 2006, pp. 110–111). Although LLs may appear at first blush to be singular structured places, in practice they are mosaics composed by multiple actors whose behaviors may be mediated by different sets of sometimes conflicting values (Ben-Rafael et al., 2006, p. 8; Hult, 2014; Jaworski & Yeung, 2010, p. 156). Accordingly, there may be multiple LLs within the same space, structured by a repertoire of de jure and de facto policies. In his study of the Dublin LL, for example, Kallen (2010) reveals multiple "frames" that regulate different sectors that each contribute to the LL: the civic frame that regulates state signage; the marketplace frame that regulates commercial signage; the portal frame that regulates signage related to virtual and physical migration and mobility; the less structured "wall" frame that encompasses posters, stickers, and other temporary signage; and the virtually unstructured detritus zone that includes discarded packing and other waste that may hold semiotic clues. These different dimensions of LL may intersect or operate in parallel.

Du Plessis (2010) offers an example of the interplay between covert and overt language policy in his investigation of the Mangaung Local Municipality in South Africa, where a constellation of national and municipal de jure policies target LL. The de jure municipal policy specifies Sesotho, Afrikaans, and English for municipal purposes, with the ostensible aim of advancing linguistic diversity and the African language of Sesotho in particular, following a 1994 government restructuring. National manuals for outdoor advertising and road signs are vague on specific language requirements and do not explicitly account for national legislation specifying that state institutions operate in at least two official languages. In practice, the LL shows English dominance with some degree of English/Afrikaans bilingual signage. The LL, thus, does not comply with the letter of the municipal policy nor fully with its spirit, as Sesotho remains underrepresented. This outcome, du Plessis (2010, pp. 90–91) suggests, follows from a covert policy to promote English as a language of liberation and modernization, whereas the status accorded to Sesotho was largely symbolic and not instrumental; indeed, some local officials seem to believe that the largely monolingual signage is actually in compliance with municipal policy, which points to the practical impact of de facto policy, especially in light of vague implementational guidelines. In a later study, du Plessis (2012) found a concomitantly powerful role for de facto LL policy in rural South African settings.

The juxtaposition of de jure and de facto policy in LL has been observed in a variety of other contexts as well. Muth (2014) considers the LL of Transnistria, a small autonomous region on the Moldovan border with Ukraine, that has a de jure language policy recognizing Russian, Romanian, and Ukrainian as official languages, corresponding with its ethnolinguistic demographics. In practice, the Russian language is central to Transnistria distinguishing itself culturally and politically from the Moldovan state, a position that is advanced through a de facto LL policy of the near monolingual dominance of Russian in a way that serves to visibly assert Transnistria as a distinct polity while also aligning it with the wider geopolitics of Russia (Muth, 2014, p. 44). Lado (2011), in turn, examines the Valencian community in Spain by comparing the management of LL in the cities of Gandía and Valencia. Both cities have de jure policies for the use of Valencian on signage, though the local political climates result in slightly different de facto policies reflected in LL practice, demonstrating variation within the civic frame. The left-wing-governed Gandía virtually eliminated official monolingual Spanish signs, whereas in right-wing-governed Valencia, Spanish continued to hold prominence as official monolingual signs remained in some areas even if Valencian was included on newer signage. Government policy had no obvious effect on the marketplace frame, as private sector actors consistently favored Spanish on commercial signs, providing evidence for the existence of parallel de facto policies.

Linguistic Landscape Analysis with Implications for Language Policy and Planning

Since LL offers a window into ideologies and power relations that mediate regimes of language, studies can bring to light possibilities for language management. The LL may suggest a de facto language policy, *vide supra*, that could be formally codified in de jure policy in order to align policy with sociolinguistic experiences in daily life (Schiffman, 1996, p. 49). Alternatively, the LL may draw attention to linguistic inequalities that could be redressed in de jure policy. Accordingly, LL researchers sometimes offer policy implications and recommendations based on their findings.

Lazdiņa's (2013) study of the ethnolinguistic vitality of Latgalian in Latvia illustrates how de facto developments in LL and other domains of society can prompt formal LPP. Although the use of Latgalian in LL is limited, its use in public space for both instrumental and symbolic purposes is part of a growing pattern of wider usage that suggests increased recognition of the variety's cultural and economic value, which, in turn, has led to more official interest in developing language revitalization efforts through education, including advancing it in schools through standardization and curriculum development. Lazdiņa (2013, p. 400) draws attention to issues that policymakers and language planners should consider, such as the need for training teachers of Latgalian and the creation of thorough and appealing teaching materials (cf. Kaplan & Baldauf, 1997, pp. 130–134). The Latgalian LL provided an ember to be stoked by LPP. Conversely, Gorter, Aiestaran, and Cenoz (2012) report that earlier LL research by Cenoz and Gorter (2006) seems to have influenced the municipal language planning in Donostia–San Sebastián based on what was missing from the LL, rather than on what was present. Successive revisions to the city's policy for the Basque language have included greater attention to the management of visual language use after the earlier research raised local officials' awareness about the dominance of Spanish in the LL (Gorter, Aiestaran, & Cenoz, 2012, pp. 154, 159).

In addition, LL research can bring to light linguistic inequalities and highlight related policy gaps. Coluzzi (2009) considers the regional languages of Milanese and Friulian in northern Italy and uses LL analysis to challenge what he argues are vastly overstated claims by dialectologists about the vitality of Italian regional languages. He argues that the lack of policy to promote Milanese and the limited policy supporting Friulian are inadequate, and he recommends the development of more comprehensive language policy to stimulate both public- and private-sector use of these languages. Taylor-Leech (2012) examines the LL of Dili, Timor-Leste, where Portuguese and Tetum-Praça are co-official, Indonesian and English are working languages, and sixteen Austronesian and Papuan languages are used. Although the official languages appear on official signage, they are less frequently used on non-official signs, where there is competition with English, Indonesian, Chinese, and other languages, leading her to "suggest that stronger measures from both official and non-official actors will be needed to ensure the visibility of the national languages and provide them with a secure, valued place in the linguistic landscape" (Taylor-Leech, 2012, p. 31). Du Plessis (2010), in light of his aforementioned study of the Mangaung Local Municipality LL in South Africa, concludes that LL actors are seemingly more influenced by covert policy than overt policy, and that more attention should be paid to covert language management.

Finally, it should be noted that the LL itself can be a site for engagement in meta-discursive debate about official policy. Moriarty (2012) provides the Dingle Wall in Ireland as a case in point. A government order that took effect in 2005 decreed that place names in the officially designated Irish-language region of Gaeltacht would become monolingual Irish rather than Irish-English bilingual. As a consequence, the town of Dingle would be renamed *An Daingean*, which sparked substantial local controversy. The Dingle Wall emerged as a physical space in the town that became a nexus point for residents, officials, and activists to post signs and images expressing their positions on the renaming. Accordingly, the Wall became a space in the LL for multimodal political debate about language (Moriarty, 2012, pp. 81–82).

Linguistic landscape analysis can also be useful in examining the semiotic production of public political debate beyond language issues. For instance, Chun (2014) examines how signs made by protesters and displayed in a Los Angeles park during the 2011 Occupy Movement in the United States contributed to the discursive framing of political debate about economic justice, and Aboelezz (2014) considers how protesters' signs in Tahrir Square during the Egyptian Revolution of 2011 served to construct the square as an index of revolutionary ideas and social change (see Martín Rojo, 2014, for additional examples of the wider political implications of linguistic landscapes).

FUTURE DIRECTIONS

While early LL research tended to focus on distributional description of the presence of languages on signage, recent developments highlight the importance of looking "behind the signs," as it were, to include historical foundations as well as lived experiences with visual space (Blommaert, 2013; Gorter, 2013, pp. 199–200). The study of LPP has moved in a similar direction from an early focus on the description of policies and their large-scale implementation to a situated perspective that takes into account how policies are experienced and negotiated by policy actors in daily life (Johnson, 2013, pp. 43–47; Menken & García, 2010).[2] Common to both of the latter-day situated perspectives is the application of ethnographic and discourse analytic approaches. Future LPP-oriented LL research, then, will benefit from developments in the ethnography of language policy, which emphasizes fieldwork in communities in order to gain insight into how de facto policies emerge, the situated impact of de jure policies, and the local transformation of language ideologies (McCarty, 2011). It will also benefit from the historical perspective that is part and parcel of an ethnographic approach, where history is not merely background, but rather is about situating individual life paths in a local context (Blommaert, 2013, p. 29).

LL research about LPP is already heading in this direction with studies that include local community histories (e.g., Lazdiņa, 2013; Shohamy & Waksman, 2010; Vigers, 2013) or that use observation and interviews to engage with individuals about their experience with signage (e.g., Marten, 2010; Zabrodskaja, 2014). In addition, LL research also has the potential to play a more substantial part in studies that seek a multidimensional understanding of LPP as a social system. As current research presented in this chapter demonstrates, LL is a major arena in which policy discourses play. Ethnographic and (critical) discourse analytic orientations, including approaches like nexus analysis or geosemiotics, can be used as spotlights to focus attention on the role of LL as a language policy mechanism in concert with other mechanisms like education (Dressler, 2012) and media (L'nyavskiy-Ekelund, 2016) within a larger policy system (Hult, 2015; Shohamy, 2006; cf. Scollon, 2008).

LPP was integral to the early development of LL work, and the two have had a symbiotic relationship ever since. LL research will continue to evolve in tandem with LPP because they complement one another in providing insight into how language is mediated by sociopolitical forces. LLs are not just the backdrop against which the politics of language is performed; they are tangible and visually salient manifestations of (language) ideologies. LLs are sites in which governments and other authorities attempt to influence linguistic behavior and beliefs by regulating language use, and they are also sites in which individual social actors can resist or reify ideologies through their own semiotic activities. LLs, then, offer potentially useful insight into the central concern of LPP as a field of inquiry—the dynamic interplay between language policy and practice.

NOTES

1. http://www.oqlf.gouv.qc.ca/accueil.aspx
2. A review of the history of LPP is beyond the scope of this chapter. It is worth noting, however, that while a situated orientation to LPP became more widely practiced in the first decade of the 2000s, there is, in fact, a history of ethnographic perspectives on LPP dating at least to the 1970s (Hult, 2017; Martin-Jones, 2011; cf. Heath, 1971; Hornberger, 1989).

REFERENCES

Aboelezz, M. (2014). The geosemiotics of Tahrir Square. *Journal of Language and Politics* 13(4), 599–622.

Ager, D. (2005) Prestige and image planning. In E. Hinkel (Ed.), *Handbook of research in second language teaching and learning* (pp. 1035–1054). Mahwah, NJ: Lawrence Erlbaum.

Akzhigitova, A., & Zharkynbekova, S. (2014). Language planning in Kazakhstan: The case of ergonyms as another scene of linguistic landscape of Astana. *Language Problems and Language Planning* 38(1), 42–57.

Backhaus, P. (2007). *Linguistic landscapes: A comparative study of urban multilingualism in Tokyo.* Clevedon, UK: Multilingual Matters.

Backhaus, P. (2009). Rules and regulations in linguistic landscaping: A comparative perspective. In E. Shohamy & D. Gorter (Eds.), *Linguistic landscape: Expanding the scenery* (pp. 157–172). New York: Routledge.

Ben-Rafael, E., Shohamy, E., Amara, M. H., & Trumper-Hecht, N. (2006). Linguistic landscape as a symbolic construction of the public space: The case of Israel. *International Journal of Multilingualism* 3(1), 7–30.

Ben-Rafael, E., Shohamy, E., & Barni, M. (2010). Introduction. In E. Shohamy, E. Ben-Rafael, & M. Barni (Eds.), *Linguistic landscape in the city* (pp. xi–xxviii). Bristol, UK: Multilingual Matters.

Bever, O. (2010). *Linguistic landscapes of post-Soviet Ukraine: Multilingualism and language policy in outdoor media and advertising.* Unpublished PhD dissertation, University of Arizona.

Bever, O. (2015). Linguistic landscape as multimodal and multilingual phenomena. In M. Laitinen & A. Zabrodskaja (Eds.), *Dimensions of sociolinguistic landscapes in Europe: Materials and methodological solutions* (pp. 233–262). Frankfurt: Peter Lang.

Blackwood, R., & Tufi, S. (2012). Policies vs non-policies: Analysing regional languages and the national standard in the linguistic landscape of French and Italian Mediterranean cities. In D. Gorter, H.F. Marten & L. Van Mensel (Eds.), *Minority languages in the linguistic landscape* (pp. 109–126). Basingstoke, UK: Palgrave Macmillan.

Blommaert, J. (2005). *Discourse: A critical introduction.* New York: Cambridge University Press.

Blommaert, J. (2013). *Ethnography, superdiversity and linguistic landscapes: Chronicles of complexity.* Bristol, UK: Multilingual Matters.

Bourhis, R. Y., & Landry, R. (2002). La loi 101 et l'aménagement du paysage linguistique au Québec [Law 101 and the management of the linguistic landscape of Quebec]. *Revue d'aménagement linguistique* [Review of Language Management]. Retrieved from http://www.oqlf.gouv.qc.ca/ressources/publications/publications_amenagement/sommaire_hs_ral.html

Cenoz, J., & Gorter, D. (2006). Linguistic landscape and minority languages. *International Journal of Multilingualism* 3(1), 67–80.

Chun, C. W. (2014). Mobilities of a linguistic landscape at Los Angeles City Hall Park. *Journal of Language and Politics* 13(4), 653–674.

Coluzzi, P. (2009). The Italian linguistic landscape: The cases of Milan and Udine. *International Journal of Multilingualism* 6(3), 298–312.

Curtin, M. L. (2009). Languages on display: Indexical signs, identities and the linguistic landscape of Taipei. In E. Shohamy & D. Gorter (Eds.), *Linguistic landscape: Expanding the scenery* (pp. 221–237). New York: Routledge.

Dal Negro, S. (2009). Local policy and modeling the linguistic landscape. In E. Shohamy & D. Gorter (Eds.), *Linguistic landscape: Expanding the scenery* (pp. 206–218). New York: Routledge.

Draper, J., & Prasertsri, P. (2013). The Isan culture maintenance and revitalization programme's multilingual signage attitude survey. *Journal of Multilingual and Multicultural Development* 34(7), 617–635.

Dressler, R. A. H. (2012). *Simultaneous and sequential bilinguals in a German bilingual program.* Unpublished PhD dissertation, University of Calgary.

Du Plessis, T. (2010). Bloemfontein/Mangaung, "city on the move": Language management and transformation of a non-representative linguistic landscape. In E. Shohamy, E. Ben-Rafael, & M. Barni (Eds.), *Linguistic landscape in the city* (pp. 74–95). Bristol, UK: Multilingual Matters.

Du Plessis, T. (2012). The role of language policy in linguistic landscape changes in a rural area of the Free State province of South Africa. *Language Matters* 43(2), 263–282.

Goffman, E. (1983). The interaction order. *American Sociological Review* 48, 1–17.

Gorter, D. (2013). Linguistic landscapes in a multilingual world. *Annual Review of Applied Linguistics* 33, 190–212.

Gorter, D., Aiestaran, J., & Cenoz, J. (2012). The revitalization of Basque and the linguistic landscape of Donostia-San Sebastián. In D. Gorter, H. F. Marten, & L. Van Mensel (Eds.),

Minority languages in the linguistic landscape (pp. 148–163). Basingstoke, UK: Palgrave Macmillan.

Heath, S. B. (1971). *Telling tongues: Language policy in Mexico, colony to nation.* New York: Teachers College Press.

Hepford, E. A. (2017). Language for profit: Spanish-English bilingualism in Lowe's Home Improvement. *International Journal of Bilingual Education and Bilingualism* 20(6), 652–666.

Hornberger, N. H. (1989). *Bilingual education and language maintenance.* Dordrecht, The Netherlands: Foris.

Hult, F. M. (2009). Language ecology and linguistic landscape analysis. In E. Shohamy & D. Gorter (Eds.), *Linguistic landscape: Expanding the scenery* (pp. 88–104). London: Routledge.

Hult, F. M. (2012). English as a transcultural language in Swedish policy and practice. *TESOL Quarterly* 46, 230–257.

Hult, F. M. (2014). Drive-thru linguistic landscaping: Constructing a linguistically dominant place in a bilingual space. *International Journal of Bilingualism* 18, 507–523.

Hult, F. M. (2015). Making policy connections across scales using nexus analysis. In F. M. Hult & D. C Johnson (Eds.), *Research methods in language policy and planning: A practical guide* (pp. 217–231). Malden, MA: John Wiley & Sons.

Hult, F. M. (2017). Discursive approaches to language policy. In S. E. F. Wortham & D. Kim (Eds.), *Discourse and education* (pp. 111–121). New York: Springer.

Isleem, M. (2015). Druze linguistic landscape in Israel: Indexicality of new ethnographic identity boundaries. *International Journal of Multilingualism* 12(1), 13–30.

Jaworski, A., & Yeung, S. (2010). Life in the Garden of Eden: The naming and imagery of residential Hong Kong. In E. Shohamy, E. Ben-Rafael, & M. Barni (Eds.), *Linguistic landscape in the city* (pp. 153–181). Bristol, UK: Multilingual Matters.

Johnson, D. C. (2013). *Language policy.* Basingstoke, UK: Palgrave Macmillan.

Johnson, D. C. (2015). Intertextuality and language policy. In F. M. Hult & D. C. Johnson (Eds.), *Research methods in language policy and planning: A practical guide* (pp. 166–180). Malden, MA: John Wiley & Sons.

Kallen, J. L. (2010). Changing landscapes: Language, space and policy in the Dublin linguistic landscape. In A. Jaworski & C. Thurlow (Eds.), *Semiotic landscapes: Language, image, space* (pp. 41–58). London: Continuum.

Kaplan, R. B., & Baldauf, R. B. (1997). *Language planning from practice to theory.* Clevedon, UK: Multilingual Matters.

Kasanga, L. A. (2012). Mapping the linguistic landscape of a commercial neighborhood in central Phnom Penh. *Journal of Multilingual and Multicultural Development* 33(6), 553–567.

Kroskrity, P. V. (Ed.). (2000). *Regimes of language: Ideologies, polities, and identities.* Santa Fe, NM: School of American Research.

L'nyavskiy-Ekelund, S. A. (2016). *Ukrainian language policy: The status of Russian in English language medium Ukrainian and Russian newspapers and in the linguistic landscape of four regions.* Master's thesis, Lund University. Retrieved from https://lup.lub.lu.se/student-papers/search/publication/8626476

Lado, B. (2011). Linguistic landscape as a reflection of linguistic ideological conflict in the Valencian community. *International Journal of Multilingualism* 8(2), 135–150.

Lamarre, P. (2014). Bilingual winks and bilingual wordplay in Montreal's linguistic landscape. *International Journal of the Sociology of Language* 228, 131–151.

Landry, R., & Bourhis, R. Y. (1997). Linguistic landscape and ethnolinguistic vitality: An empirical study. *Journal of Language and Social Psychology* 16(1), 23–49.

Lanza, E., & Woldemariam, H. (2009). Language ideology and linguistic landscape: Language policy and globalization in a regional capital of Ethiopia. In E. Shohamy & D. Gorter (Eds.), *Linguistic landscape: Expanding the scenery* (pp. 189–205). New York: Routledge.

Lazdiņa, S. (2013). A transition from spontaneity to planning? Economic values and educational policies in the process of revitalizing the regional language of Latgalian (Latvia). *Current Issues in Language Planning* 14(3–4), 382–402.

Manan, S. A., David, M. K., Dumanig, F. P., & Naqeebullah, K. (2015). Politics, economics and identity: Mapping the linguistic landscape of Kuala Lumpur, Malaysia. *International Journal of Multilingualism* 12(1), 31–50.

Marten, H. F. (2010). Linguistic landscape under strict state language policy: Reversing the Soviet legacy in a regional centre in Latvia. In E. Shohamy, E. Ben-Rafael, & M. Barni (Eds.), *Linguistic landscape in the city* (pp. 115–132). Bristol, UK: Multilingual Matters.

Martin-Jones, M. (2011). Language policies, multilingual classrooms: Resonances across continents. In F. M. Hult & K. A. King (Eds.), *Educational linguistics in practice: Applying the local globally and the global locally* (pp. 3–15). Bristol, UK: Multilingual Matters.

Martín Rojo, L. (Ed.). (2014). The spatial dynamics of discourse in global protest movements [special issue]. *Journal of Language and Politics* 13(4).

McCarty, T. L. (Ed.). (2011). *Ethnography and language policy*. New York: Routledge.

Menken, K., & García, O. (Eds.). (2010). *Negotiating language policies in schools: Educators as policymakers*. New York: Routledge.

Moriarty, M. (2012). Language ideological debates in the linguistic landscape of an Irish tourist town. In D. Gorter, H. F. Marten, & L. Van Mensel (Eds.), *Minority languages in the linguistic landscape* (pp. 74–88). Basingstoke, UK: Palgrave Macmillan.

Muth, S. (2014). Linguistic landscapes on the other side of the border: Signs, language and the construction of cultural identity in Transnistria. *International Journal of the Sociology of Language* 227, 25–46.

Pavlenko, A. (2010). Linguistic landscape of Kyiv, Ukraine: A diachronic study. In E. Shohamy, E. Ben-Rafael, & M. Barni (Eds.), *Linguistic landscape in the city* (pp. 133–150). Bristol, UK: Multilingual Matters.

Pearson, P. (2015, March 23). The utility of a diachronic comparative analysis in linguistic landscaping: Language shift across time. Presented at the American Association for Applied Linguistics Conference, Toronto.

Pennycook, A. (2006). Postmodernism in language policy. In T. Ricento (Ed.), *An introduction to language policy: Theory and method* (pp. 60–76). Malden, MA: Blackwell.

Puzy, G. (2012). Two-way traffic: How linguistic landscapes reflect and influence the politics of language. In D. Gorter, H. F. Marten, & L. Van Mensel (Eds.), *Minority languages in the linguistic landscape* (pp. 127–147). Basingstoke, UK: Palgrave Macmillan.

Schiffman, H. F. (1996). *Linguistic culture and language policy*. New York: Routledge.

Scollon, R. (2008). *Analyzing public discourse: Discourse analysis in the making of public policy*. New York: Routledge.

Scollon, R., & Scollon, S. W. (2004). *Nexus analysis*. New York: Routledge.

Shohamy, E. (2006). *Language policy: Hidden agendas and new perspectives*. New York: Routledge.

Shohamy, E., Ben-Rafael, E., & Barni, M. (Eds.). (2010). *Linguistic landscape in the city*. Bristol, UK: Multilingual Matters.

Shohamy, E., & Gorter, D. (Eds.). (2009). *Linguistic landscape: Expanding the scenery*. New York: Routledge.

Shohamy, E., & Waksman, S. (2010). Building the nation, writing the past: History and textuality at the Ha'apala memorial in Tel Aviv-Jaffa. In A. Jaworski & C. Thurlow (Eds.), *Semiotic landscapes: Language, image, space* (pp. 241–255). London: Continuum.

Sloboda, M. (2009). State ideology and linguistic landscape: A comparative analysis of (post) communist Belarus, Czech Republic and Slovakia. In E. Shohamy & D. Gorter (Eds.), *Linguistic landscape: Expanding the scenery* (pp. 173–188). New York: Routledge.

Sloboda, M., Szabó-Gilinger, Vigers, D., & Šimičić, L. (2010). Carrying out a language policy change: Advocacy coalitions and the management of linguistic landscape. *Current Issues in Language Planning* 11(2), 95–113.

Spolsky, B. (2004). *Language policy*. New York: Cambridge University Press.

Spolsky, B. (2009). *Language management*. New York: Cambridge University Press.

Spolsky, B., & Shohamy, E., (2000). Language practice, language ideology, and language policy. In R. D. Lambert & E. Shohamy (Eds.), *Language policy and pedagogy: Essays in honour of A. Ronald Walton* (pp. 1–41). Amsterdam: John Benjamins.

Taylor-Leech, K. J. (2012). Language choice as an index of identity: Linguistic landscape in Dili, Timor-Leste. *International Journal of Multilingualism* 9(1), 15–34.

Vigers, D. (2013). Sign of absence: Language and memory in the linguistic landscape of Brittany. *International Journal of the Sociology of Language* 223, 171–187.

Zabrodskaja, A. (2014). Tallinn: Monolingual from above and multilingual from below. *International Journal of the Sociology of Language* 228, 105–130.

II.C.

Language Policy and Planning in/through Communities

....

CHAPTER 18

REVITALIZING AND SUSTAINING ENDANGERED LANGUAGES

....

TERESA L. McCARTY

How and why do languages become endangered, and how can languages threatened with disuse be revitalized and sustained? Language endangerment is a global phenomenon, with expert predictions of the loss of as many as 50% to 90% of humankind's approximately 7,000 known spoken languages by the end of the twenty-first century (Grenoble, 2011). Of the "disappeared" languages, most will be Indigenous languages (McCarty, Skutnabb-Kangas, & Magga, 2008). At one level, the cause of endangerment seems straightforward: speakers stop speaking their mother tongue in favor of the language of wider communication (LWC). The process through which this occurs, called *language shift*, means that intergenerational language transmission is proceeding in a negative temporal and spatial direction, with fewer speakers, uses, and domains in which the language is primary in successive generations (Fishman, 1991).

Many endangered languages are relatively "small"—spoken by a few hundred people or less. But relatively "large" languages, such as Quechua, with millions of speakers in six South American countries, are endangered as well. How do we account for this significant variability in the relative "size" of endangered languages?

First, it is important to point out that "all languages change through time as a result of language-internal processes and as their speakers interact with other speech communities and cultural changes require new linguistic forms" (McCarty & Nicholas, 2014, p. 107). Linguistic change of this sort is different from community-wide shift, which occurs when the social structures supporting intergenerational language transmission break down, often as a result of violent dominant-subordinate encounters and the coerced abandonment of ancestral mother tongues. In these contexts, languages are not *re*placed but *dis*placed. Fishman (1991) describes language shift as an abstraction that is "concretely mirrored in the concomitant destruction of intimacy, family and community, via national and international ... intrusions, the destruction of local life [and] of the weak by the strong" (p. 4). When external forces interact with internal ones, they can produce feelings of linguistic ambivalence and shame, furthering the cycle of language loss.

Throughout the world, medium-of-instruction policies have been prime mechanisms of language shift (Tollefson & Tsui, 2004). By requiring education only in the dominant LWC, language-restrictive policies seek to "erase and replace" linguistically encoded knowledges and cultural identifications with those associated with dominant-class ideologies, values, and practices (Lomawaima & McCarty, 2006, p. xxii). Language-restrictive policies are associated with myriad educational, economic, and social disparities, including low rates of educational attainment and high rates of poverty, clinical depression, and teen suicide (Castagno & Brayboy, 2008). Hence, efforts to revitalize and sustain endangered and minoritized languages are not merely or even primarily about language per se, but are intimately tied to power asymmetries and minoritized communities' struggles for autochthonous lands, self-determination, and social justice.

This chapter proceeds on the assumption that linguistic and cultural diversity is an inherently enabling condition for individuals, families, and societies. To expand upon Ruiz's (1984) notion of language-as-resource, languages represent an irreplaceable reservoir of human intellectual, cultural, and scientific effort. For those who claim an endangered language, the loss is likely to be felt even more keenly as a break in communal heritage and identity. "We believe that First Nations, Inuit and Métis languages are sacred and are gifts from the Creator," the Task Force on Aboriginal Languages and Cultures affirms (2005, p. 3). Sustaining an endangered language represents a "larger effort by a community to claim its right to speak a language and to set associated goals in response to community needs and perspectives" (Leonard, 2011, p. 359).

In what follows, I explore the processes and prospects for endangered languages and their speakers, drawing on language planning and policy (LPP) research and practice from around the world. I intentionally frame these processes as *sustaining*, a conceptualization that foregrounds their dynamic and heteroglossic character. In comparison with notions of language maintenance and preservation, *sustaining* more accurately reflects what people actually *do* with their language practices, and the fact that linguistic forms, uses, and domains are ever in flux. I begin with some key definitions, followed by a discussion of language vitality and endangerment classificatory schemes. I then examine three language-in-education movements that illuminate the processes and contexts for sustaining languages that are severely minoritized and/or threatened with disuse. This is, by necessity, an attenuated view; my goal is to highlight key LPP issues related to revitalizing and sustaining endangered languages across a range of linguistic, cultural, and geographic/political contexts. I conclude by considering the kinds of sociolinguistic and sociopolitical changes needed to interrupt language endangerment, the relationship of local revitalization efforts to global movements, and the implications for linguistic human rights.

Defining the Endangerment-Revitalization Terrain

The terms we use to describe languages and sociolinguistic processes frame those languages and processes in ways that can reinforce or contest socially constructed linguistic inequalities (Skutnabb-Kangas & McCarty, 2008).[1] Throughout the chapter, I use the terms *heritage* and *ancestral* to refer to languages that are the object of revitalization efforts. As Wiley (2014) notes, while the terms *heritage language* (HL) and *heritage community language* (HCL) have wide usage, particularly in the United States, they carry a load of semantic freight, including backward-looking notions of an imagined pure linguistic form and equally problematic notions of native speakerhood and proficiency. Further, the term *heritage* may not be appropriate in some settings, such as Hawai'i, where *heritage* connotes immigrant languages, and Hawaiian, though minoritized, is a "Native American language official for a state" (Wilson, 2014, p. 219). Here, I use these terms to reference contextualized ethnolinguistic affiliations, recognizing that many HCL learners "might not be speakers of that language yet" (Wiley, 2014, p. 25). I also use the term *heritage mother tongue* (HMT), recognizing that even so-called sleeping languages for which there are no living first-language speakers are nonetheless languages of ancestry, identity, and connection to mother-place, and in this sense can and should be considered mother tongues (McCarty, 2008a, 2008b).

Language ideologies are beliefs and feelings held by users/claimers of a language about that language in relation to their own identities and the identities of others, and which influence everyday language choices and long-term linguistic trajectories (Kroskrity & Field, 2009). Language ideologies are both conscious and tacit, taken-for-granted assumptions about language statuses, forms, users, and uses that, by virtue of their "common-sense" naturalization, contribute to linguistic and social inequality (Tollefson, 2006, p. 47). For example, Dorian (1998) notes that a widespread Western European "ideology of contempt" has infused colonizing projects throughout the world, "to the serious detriment of indigenous languages" (p. 9). Like revitalizing and sustaining efforts themselves, language ideologies are not about language per se, but rather about identity, power, and "the very notion of the person and the social group" (Woolard, 1998, p. 3).

Language revitalization refers to activities designed to cultivate new speakers in situations in which intergenerational transmission has been so severely disrupted that children do not acquire their HMT in their childhood language socialization (Hinton, 2011). *Language regenesis, renewal,* and *reclamation* are often used synonymously with revitalization. However, recent sociolinguistic scholarship distinguishes *reclamation* as fundamentally political and decolonizing, aimed at dismantling the ideological forces that underpin social inequality and lead to language endangerment in the first place (Leonard & De Korne, 2017). Regenesis or regeneration, says Māori scholar Margie Kahukura Hohepa (2006), speak to "growth and regrowth," recognizing that nothing "regrows in exactly the same shape that it had previously, or in exactly the same direction" (p. 294). This reinforces the notion of sustaining (rather than maintaining or preserving) as a primary revitalization goal.

Languages that are the object of these efforts have been described as *moribund*—all speakers are beyond child-bearing age—or *dormant* or *sleeping*—the language is no longer spoken, but the potential for its awakening exists by virtue of documentary sources (e.g., written texts, audio recordings) and a heritage-language community that desires to learn it (Leonard, 2011). While these terms are useful, they require a word of caution, for they tend to separate languages from their users, and can make shift seem almost natural, obscuring the power relations that dispossess certain peoples of their languages while empowering certain classes of speakers of the LWC.

The question then arises, how do we evaluate what counts as endangered? As King et al. (2008, p. 1) ask, "Who makes such classifications, and what's at stake?"

Classificatory schemes devised to represent linguistic vitality use the following indicators: (1) the number, age, and relative proportion of speakers in a population; (2) the nature and extent of intergenerational language transmission; (3) extant domains for using the language; and (4) the potential for language revitalization (e.g., language documentation, official policies supporting or restricting language use, availability of teachers and teaching materials, etc.). Of these factors, Grenoble (2011) argues that the characteristics of the pool of speakers are most important—not only numbers of speakers, but also their distribution intergenerationally and proportions in the population as a whole (p. 38).

One frequently cited classification is Krauss's (1997, 1998) A–E scheme:

Class A: Languages spoken by all generations and "learned by practically all children";

Class A–: Languages learned by "nearly all or most children";

Class B: Languages spoken by the parent generation and older, "but learned by few or no children";

Class B–: Languages spoken by adults in their thirties "but not by younger parents, and probably no children";

Class C: Languages spoken by "middle-aged adults and older, forties and up";

Class C–: Languages spoken by adults in their fifties and older;

Class –D: Languages spoken by adults in their sixties and older;

Class D: Languages spoken by adults in their seventies and older;

Class D–: Language spoken by adults in their seventies and older, "fewer than ten"; and

Class E: Languages with no living speakers, described by Krauss as "extinct" (1997, pp. 25–26).

Grenoble and Whaley (2006) propose a six-way scheme that indexes speakers' ages and the extent of intergenerational transmission, from "safe" languages spoken by all generations in nearly all domains, to "at risk" languages having proportionately fewer speakers and use domains, to "disappearing" and "moribund" languages, to "nearly extinct" and "extinct" languages. The UNESCO Ad Hoc Expert Group on Endangered Languages (2003) uses a six-way framework of "safe," "vulnerable," "definitely endangered," "severely endangered," "critically endangered," and "extinct." Bauman (1980) has proposed a classification that ranks languages from "flourishing" to "enduring," to "declining," to "extinct."

Fishman (1991) developed a graded intergenerational disruption scale (GIDS), in which "the higher the GIDS rating the lower the intergenerational continuity and maintenance prospects of a language network or community" (1991, p. 87). Fishman's GIDS differs from other classification schemes in that he posits the stages as predictive (not simply descriptive) of language loss and recovery. In particular, he argues that stage 6, where the HMT remains the primary language of the home, constitutes "the heart and soul" of intergenerational language transmission: "*One cannot jump across or dispense with stage 6*" (1991, p. 95; emphasis in original).

Figure 18.1 compares these classification schemes. Here, another word of caution is in order. Although the schemes provide a sense of language trajectories, they also mask dynamic, power-laden processes of language use and shift. Further, the static nature of scaling and staging can discourage language revitalization efforts, especially for communities classified on the "critical" end of the scale. "No longer do we accept the 'e-word' (*extinct*) to describe *myaamia* [the Miami language]," Miami linguist Wesley Leonard (2011) asserts; "we instead use the term sleeping to refer to its status during its period of dormancy, noting that this term is not only more socially appropriate but also more accurate in that our language was never irretrievably lost" (pp. 141–142).

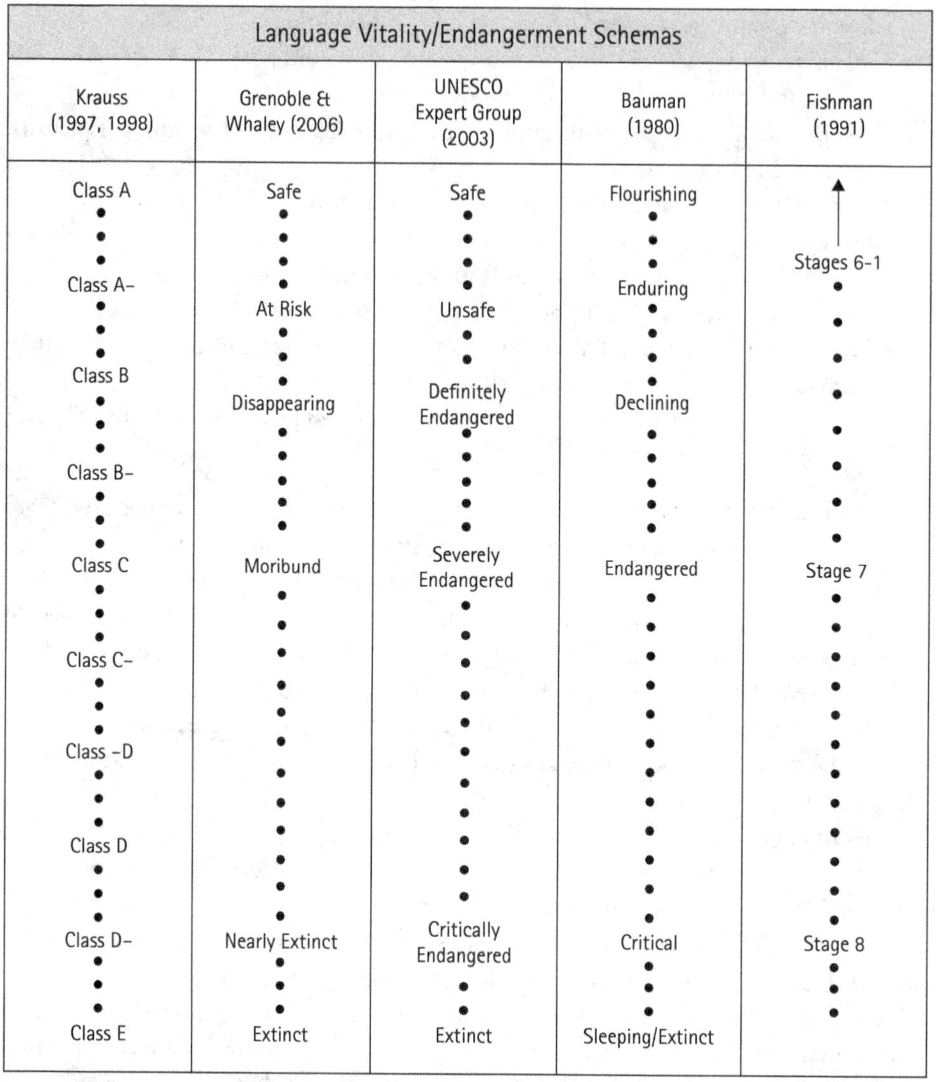

Language Vitality/Endangerment Schemas				
Krauss (1997, 1998)	Grenoble & Whaley (2006)	UNESCO Expert Group (2003)	Bauman (1980)	Fishman (1991)
Class A	Safe	Safe	Flourishing	↑
•	•	•	•	
•	•	•	•	Stages 6–1
•	•	•	•	
Class A–	•	•	Enduring	•
•	At Risk	Unsafe	•	
•	•	•	•	•
•	•	•	•	
Class B	•	Definitely	•	•
•	Disappearing	Endangered	Declining	
•	•	•	•	•
•	•	•	•	
Class B–	•	•	•	•
•	•	•	•	
•	•	•	•	•
Class C	Moribund	Severely	Endangered	Stage 7
•	•	Endangered	•	•
•	•	•	•	
•	•	•	•	•
Class C–	•	•	•	
•	•	•	•	•
•	•	•	•	
Class –D	•	•	•	•
•	•	•	•	
•	•	•	•	•
Class D	•	•	•	•
•	•	•	•	
•	•	•	•	•
Class D–	Nearly Extinct	Critically	Critical	Stage 8
•	•	Endangered	•	•
•	•	•	•	•
•	•	•	•	
Class E	Extinct	Extinct	Sleeping/Extinct	

FIGURE 18.1. Comparison of language vitality/endangerment schemas.

Source: McCarty (2013, p. 18); used with permission of Multilingual Matters.

In response to the problems of fixed and unitary language classifications, Leonard (2008) proposes a revised view of language vitality and endangerment that positions language varieties along a continuum of "less" and "more" endangered (Figure 18.2). As Fishman (1991) also stresses, language revitalization "must not be approached in absolute terms . . . but, rather, in functional, contextual, or situational terms [and] in terms of immediate vs. longer-range goals" (p. 12). As we will see, it is indeed possible, as Ó hIfearnáin (2015) maintains, "for a language to survive the loss of intergenerational transmission" (p. 60). We turn now to the cases illuminating those sociolinguistic processes.

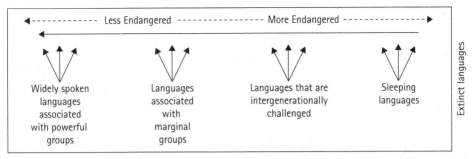

FIGURE 18.2. Leonard's (2008, p. 27) "revised view of the language endangerment continuum."

Source: McCarty (2013, p. 21); used with permission of Multilingual Matters.

THE NEW SPEAKER MOVEMENT: "CREATING A NEW PARADIGM"

By definition, language revitalization is about the cultivation of new speakers. In Europe and certain other national settings, a "new speaker" movement has emerged that gives a distinctive meaning to this process (see O'Rourke, Soler, & Darquennes, Chapter 30 in this volume). As described by O'Rourke, Pujolar, and Ramallo (2015), in the context of some European minoritized languages, *new speaker* refers to "individuals with little or no home or community exposure to a minority language but who instead acquire it through immersion or bilingual education programs, revitalization projects, or as adult language learners" (p. 1). The new speaker movement reflects what O'Rourke and her colleagues call a new sociolinguistic order based on "linguistic economies undergoing . . . profound transformation, in which the sources of linguistic authority are being displaced as we move towards a . . . post-national" modernity (O'Rourke et al., 2015, p. x).

Front and center in this new sociolinguistic order are the learners of endangered HMTs, whose language ideologies and practices force us to rethink static labels such as second-language (L2) learner and native speaker. These ideologies and practices also challenge us to reconsider how authority and authenticity are constructed in discourse, what counts as linguistic proficiency, and the ways in which individuals characterized as traditional (L1) speakers are often fossilized in time and space (O'Rourke & Walsh, 2015).

For example, in ethnographic research with new speakers of Breton in Brittany (*neo-bretonnants*) and Yiddish in Warsaw, Brussels, and London, Hornsby (2015) relates that "authentic" speakerhood lies "in the perceptions of the speakers themselves" (p. 110). Among both ethnolinguistic groups (all adults), so-called traditional language forms associated with older speakers and homelands were considered more authentic. Although teachers of Yiddish, some of whom were new speakers themselves, spoke the language "absolutely correctly," as one participant said, "it hasn't got the taste" of Polish Yiddish (p. 110). Similarly, "traditional" speakers of Breton distinguished between their language practices and the Breton "learned from books" (p. 110). Arguing that the needs of both sets of speakers must be recognized and valorized—and within those socially constructed categories, the needs of individual speakers—Hornsby calls for greater attention to new "hybrid forms of language use and of usership, . . . and of how [linguistic] repertoires reinforce or marginalize the power bases of different speakers" (p. 121).

In their research with Irish, O'Rourke and Walsh (2015, p. 64) make the point that, even as there has been a steady increase in the numbers of new speakers, public discourse and scholarship have "idealize[d] the notion of the traditional Gaeltacht speaker"—individuals who reside in core Irish-speaking districts located primarily in western, northwestern, southwestern, and southern Ireland. Drawing on in-depth interviews with fifty-four new speakers, O'Rourke and Walsh posit a continuum of language ideologies, from an essentialist notion of "real" speakerhood associated with a fixed linguistic form and place—"all Native speakers [in the Gaeltacht] should have historical Irish with no changing to English," said one participant (p. 69)—to a more nuanced, social constructivist view that confronts conflicting language ideologies and practices. The following statement by one participant, Sharon, who had been raised in English but attended an Irish-language *Gaelscoil*, illuminates these complex ideological and sociolinguistic positionings:

> [P]eople who weren't brought up with a language often . . . are more committed to it . . . because they understand the difficulties associated with language. . . . [T]he likes of me are probably creating a new paradigm. . . . I am proud of the fact that I have Irish . . . in case it might create a link between me and maybe somebody else. . . . (O'Rourke & Walsh, 2015, p. 77)

For new speakers like Sharon—increasingly the majority of HMT speakers in this sociolinguistic context—the socially and linguistically experienced break with the idealized native speaker is "creating a new paradigm" based on "a demand for ownership of Irish and recognition as speakers" (O'Rourke & Walsh, 2015, pp. 77, 79).

Manx Gaelic, one of Europe's smallest language communities, constitutes what Ó hIfearnáin calls a case of "extreme language shift" (ELS), in which the last "traditional" (L1) speaker has died. "When the last speaker of Manx died . . . ," write Nettle and Romaine (2000), "that was the end of the Manx language" (p. 48). Yet, Ó hIfearnáin maintains that Manx has "never ceased to be spoken and transmitted to new speakers without any break in that continuity" (p. 46). ELS languages, he adds, provide a rare window into the ways in which new speakers collectively construct the legitimacy of their language practices and forms.

In a sociolinguistic study of Manx on the Isle of Mann, Ó hIfearnáin (2015) documented fifty-five "completely fluent speakers of Manx," none of whom felt "bounded by the 'authentic speech' of the rural past," but who nonetheless distinguished between "competent speakers" and 'learners'" (p. 55). This research demonstrates two important points: first, that borders between individuals constructed as speakers and learners are porous and ever-shifting; and second, even in situations of ELS and absent traditional intergenerational transmission mechanisms, it is possible to sustain locally meaningful HMT communities of practice. As Ó hIfearnáin emphasizes, it is this community of practice—Manx speakers, learners, and non-speakers—who establish the right to claim their HTM and the shared values of what constitutes Manx authenticity (p. 61).

Research and practice on new speakerhood—which, in addition to the preceding examples, span sociolinguistic contexts as diverse as Basque, Catalan, Galician, and Cape Verdean in Spain (O'Rourke & Ramallo, 2015; Ortega et al., 2015; Pujolar & Pugdeval, 2015), Corsican (Jaffe, 2015), Welsh in Wales (Hornsby & Vigers, 2018), and Francoprovençal in France, Switzerland, Italy, and diasporic North American communities (Kasstan, 2018)—demonstrate that there is "no unitary or stable set of social uses of [HMTs] as a reference for 'authentic' use or even 'native' competence" (Jaffe, 2015, p. 41). Instead, there are very few speakers who have equivalent competencies "across all registers and linguistic domains" in both the HMT and the LWC (Jaffe, 2015, p. 41). These cases call upon researchers, practitioners, and policymakers to recognize the diversity and complexity of what it means to revitalize a language, the historical and ideological embeddedness of who and what counts as a speaker (and a language), and the ways in which these understandings can be used to support the individuals and communities who push against the grain to reclaim and sustain a minoritized heritage mother tongue.

INDIGENOUS REVITALIZATION IMMERSION: "PASSIONATE, POLITICAL, AND DEEPLY PERSONAL"

There are many parallels between the new speaker movement and recent research and practice in Indigenous LPP, which, by virtue of its revitalizing goals, is directly concerned with the creation of new speakers (Hinton & Hale, 2001). But there are important contrasts between Indigenous contexts and those of new speakers in Europe and European heritage communities. In this section I highlight one increasingly popular approach—Indigenous revitalization immersion—focusing on Native North America, the Pacific, and Scandinavia.

Immersion is a form of bilingual education in which at least 50% of subject-matter instruction takes place through the target (second or additional) language.

The goal, write Tedick, Christian, and Fortune (2011), is to promote bilingualism, biliteracy, and cultural pluralism by adding a new language to learners' communicative repertoires. This kind of additive immersion began in the 1960s with Canadian programs in which Anglophone students were immersed in French, the minoritized language, as a form of educational enrichment. Such programs are now found around the world.

Indigenous-language immersion draws on the principles of L2 acquisition used in French Canadian immersion, but is quite distinct. Unlike elite "one-way" immersion that serves children from dominant racial/ethnic/linguistic classes, or "two-way" immersion that brings together nondominant- and dominant-language students to be instructed in each other's language (Tedick et al., 2011), Indigenous-language immersion originates from a grassroots movement begun in the 1970s to reclaim and revitalize oppressed languages undergoing extreme language shift. These are contexts characterized by relatively small Indigenous populations in which learners represent nondominant, economically and socially marginalized communities for whom there is little out-of-school HMT support. They are also contexts characterized by profound and enduring education disparities. "What must be remembered in the case of Indigenous immersion programs," Wilson and Kamanā (2011) stress, is that their students come from underserved communities "where both ethnicity and socioeconomic status are associated with low achievement" (p. 46).

Given this sociolinguistic and educational context, immersion in these Indigenous settings has been described as "revitalization immersion" (RI) (McIvor & McCarty, 2016), "immersion revitalization" (García, 2009, pp. 128–129), and "education for language revitalization" (López & García, 2016, p. 123). RI approaches vary, and may be implemented inside and outside of school. In general, school-based programs share the goals of promoting students' cognitive, linguistic, and affective development equally with their cultural identity, thereby contributing simultaneously to learners' academic progress and the sustainability, empowerment, and well-being of their cultural communities.

Among the most promising school-based efforts are those by Hawaiians in the United States and Māori in Aotearoa/New Zealand. Hawaiian and Māori are closely related Eastern Polynesian languages, and their revitalization initiatives have followed intertwined paths. In both cases, Indigenous peoples experienced "political disenfranchisement, misappropriation of land, population and health decline, educational disadvantage and socioeconomic marginalization" associated with extreme language shift (May, 2005, p. 366). In 1978, as an outgrowth of Indigenous activism, Hawaiian became co-official with English in the state of Hawai'i, and in 1987, the Māori Language Act made Māori co-official with English (and subsequently with New Zealand Sign Language). By the early 1980s, full-immersion, parent-run Māori *Kōhanga Reo* and Hawaiian *Pūnana Leo* ("language nest") preschools set the stage for Indigenous-language tracks and whole-school immersion within the public school systems of New Zealand and Hawai'i, respectively. Immersion spread horizontally to other communities and vertically by grade. Today there are many Māori and Hawaiian full-immersion pre-K–12 schools, as well as tertiary education programs dedicated to promoting these languages in their respective national and state contexts.

As one example, Hill and May (2011) present an ethnographic case study of the Rakaumangamanga (Rakaumanga) Māori-medium school on New Zealand's North Island, one of the largest and oldest Māori-medium schools. Rakaumanga's philosophy embraces a *Kaupapa Māori* (Māori principles) framework, which emphasizes Māori control over Māori education (Smith, 2000). Entering students must have attended *Kōhanga Reo* for at least two years, laying the foundation for four years of full Māori immersion, after which English is introduced for three to four hours per week. The goal is full bilingualism and biliteracy. According to Hill and May (2011), by year eight, students reach or are approaching age-appropriate literacy in both languages. Moreover, these researchers say, this type of revitalization immersion is preparing Māori youth as "citizens of the world" (2011, pp. 173, 178).

Iokepa-Guerrero (2016) and Wilson and Kamanā (2011) report longitudinal data from Nāwahīokalaniōpuʻu (Nāwahī) Laboratory School in Keaau, Hawaiʻi, a pre-K–12, full-immersion school affiliated with the University of Hawaiʻi Hilo's College of Hawaiian Language and the nonprofit Pūnana Leo organization. Offering a college preparatory curriculum, the school teaches all subjects through the Hawaiian language and values, with the goal that students will achieve Hawaiian dominance alongside high levels of English fluency and literacy. Like Rakaumanga, Nāwahī has achieved impressive revitalization *and* academic achievement results, with students surpassing their non-immersion peers on state-required English-language tests and on high school completion and college attendance rates (Iokepa-Guerrero, 2016). On a broader scale, both the Māori and Hawaiian initiatives are widely recognized as RI "success stories" that have spearheaded re-vernacularization in their respective languages, offered viable alternatives to English-only schooling, and provided models for the exercise of Indigenous sovereignty (e.g., *Kaupapa Māori*).

Revitalization immersion is increasingly favored in Indigenous Canadian communities, where most Indigenous children no longer enter school speaking their HMT. The Canadian Census enumerates over 240,000 Aboriginal people who report fluency in their HMT. The fact that more Aboriginal people report Aboriginal language conversational proficiency than those who report an Aboriginal mother tongue suggests that "increasing numbers of Aboriginal language speakers in Canada are second language learners" (McIvor & McCarty, 2016, pp. 1–2). One recent study compared academic and linguistic outcomes, including postsecondary preparedness, for Mi'kmaq immersion and non-immersion students in New Brunswick. These researchers found that "students in the immersion program not only had stronger Mi'kmaq language skills compared to students in the [non-immersion] program, but students within both programs ultimately had the same level of English" (Usborne et al., 2011, p. 200). Similar findings have been reported for Mohawk, Cree, and Secwepemc RI in Canada, demonstrating that "success . . . is possible in immersion schooling, even within a small community with a relatively small number of speakers and students" (McIvor & McCarty, 2016, p. 7).

The Saami (also spelled Sámi) are the Indigenous people of present-day Norway, Sweden, Finland, and western Russia. Saami is a Finno-Ugric language with three major branches and eleven subgroups. According to Olthuis, Kivelä, and Skutnabb-Kangas (2013), the number of Saami speakers is about 22,000. In Finland, a unique approach is being used to revitalize Aanaar Saami, a linguistic variety with about 350 speakers, almost half of whom are elders (Olthuis et al., 2013). Full-immersion language nest preschools are key components. While the preschools have been highly successful, the focus on young children has left what Olthuis et al. (2013) call a "missing" generation: working adults between the ages of twenty and forty-nine, who straddle the child generation learning Aanaar Saami as a second language and elders for whom Aanaar Saami is a primary language.

The Aanaar Saami complementary education (CASLE) project supports this generation of working adults in recovering their HMT through formal classes, cultural field activities taught by local fisher-people, reindeer herders, and cooking specialists, and master-apprentice training in workplaces and elders' homes (Hinton et al., 2002). The latter approach involves informal immersion as language learner-apprentices spend time with master teacher-speakers, "talking and doing ordinary everyday things" (Olthuis et al., 2013, p. 80). The combination of preschool and adult RI has brought Aanaar Saami back into family homes. Thus, Olthuis et al. (2013) proclaim, it "is possible to revitalize a seriously endangered language!" (p. 1). (For more on Saami RI, see Huss, 2017.)

Indigenous RI faces the daunting challenges of dwindling numbers of speakers (hence, teachers are often second-language learners themselves); the need to create writing systems and teaching materials "from scratch"; and the lingering legacy of colonial ideologies that learning the Indigenous language "holds children back" (Wyman et al., 2010, p. 38). Additional challenges include the absence of supportive state-level policies—and in some cases, official policies that violate inherent Indigenous sovereignties and state-guaranteed language rights (McCarty, 2013)—and increasing urbanization, which separates learners from Indigenous community strongholds. The New Zealand Māori Council (2016) is addressing the latter challenge by calling on the government to establish Māori housing clusters near tribal cultural centers, with preference given "to those committed to speaking te reo [Māori language]" (para. 3). Other innovative strategies, such as Indigenous language houses "where people live together committed to using the language with each other," and language pods—"groups of speakers and advanced learners who get together on a regular basis to converse on various topics"—are addressing these challenges in Native American settings (Hinton, 2017, p. 266). Hinton's (2013) collection also features accounts of family-based RI endeavors for endangered languages around the world.

Like the new speaker movement, these revitalization efforts challenge hegemonic notions of speakerhood and bounded geographic territories of language acquisition and use. Instead, there is growing recognition of the heteroglossic, multi-sited, and hybrid character of Indigenous language practices and their enormous potential as resources for reclaiming and sustaining endangered Indigenous languages and ancestral knowledge systems. As Hermes, Bang, and Marin (2012) write, the Indigenous language revitalization movement is "passionate, political, and deeply personal, particularly for many Native people who are acutely aware that the [settler colonial state's] attempted genocide was the direct cause of Indigenous language loss" (p. 383).

Heritage Mother Tongue Bi/Multilingual Education: "Awakening the Sense of Injustice"

Like Indigenous revitalization immersion, forms of bi/multilingual education that systematically develop the HMT over the course of children's schooling can play a crucial role in the joint project of sustaining an oppressed language and decolonizing the power relations that structure that oppression. This section explores these efforts in the Indian subcontinent, Sub-Saharan Africa, and Latin America.

Within the Indian subcontinent, more than 750 languages are spoken—10% of all known spoken languages in the world. Nearly half are endangered. Mohanty and Panda (2017) relate this to a "double divide" between English and major regional/national languages, and between the latter languages and Indigenous languages. This multilayered linguistic hierarchy mirrors the unequal distribution of power and resources, "leading to disadvantage, marginalization, language shift and loss of linguistic diversity" (Mohanty & Panda, 2017, p. 2). In India, English is the language of power, while Hindi and other official languages (e.g., Bengali, Gujarati, Kannada, Marathi, Oriya, Punjabi, Tamil, Telugu, Urdu)—all with many millions of speakers—"are viewed as major 'Indian' languages" (Mohanty, 2010, p. 166). Similarly, Urdu and Bengali, respectively, are languages of Pakistani and Bangladesh national identity, but English is "the real language of power" (Mohanty, 2010, p. 166). In Nepal, say Hough, Magar, and Yonjan-Tamang (2009), "English is killing Hindi, which is killing Nepali, which is killing Nepal's major indigenous languages" (p. 163). At the same time, submersion education in dominant languages has led to widespread education failure for Indigenous students (Mohanty & Panda, 2017).

Under such conditions of profound educational and linguistic inequality, some experimental multilingual education programs show great promise. The Indian states of Andhra Pradesh and Orissa, for instance, are implementing mother tongue–based multilingual education in nearly 1,500 schools serving students from eighteen Indigenous-language groups. In these programs, the Indigenous language (Telugu in Andhra Pradesh and Oriya in Orissa) is the medium of instruction for all school subjects in grades 1 through 4, after which Telugu or Oriya is used alongside English, then Hindi. The Orissa program, called Multilingual Education Plus (MLE+), uses a culture-based pedagogy emphasizing community teaching and learning to "foster collaborative classroom learning and cultural identity" (Mohanty, 2010, p. 172).

In Nepal, where over 200 languages are spoken and half the nation's 23 million people are non-Nepali speakers, the Multilingual Education Project for All Non-Nepali Speaking Students of Primary Schools is a grass roots program in six Indigenous communities (Hough et al., 2009). In that project, education practitioners and community members work together to develop and implement a critical Indigenous pedagogy centered on local languages and knowledge systems, including herbal medicines and traditional healing practices, traditional practices relating to agriculture and food, tribal oral histories, cultural values such as collectivism and sharing, life cycle rituals, and a highly endangered Indigenous numerical system. While this "is still very much a work in progress," Hough et al. (2009) remark, data collected to date indicate the project is having a positive impact on curricular reforms within local schools and teacher training programs, and that it has become a bellwether for more systemic democratizing reforms (p. 175).

One such reform, examined in ethnographic research by Phyak (forthcoming) is the Indigenous Youth Critical Language Policy project in Kutipur, Nepal. The youth-led project, says Phyak, aims to interrogate and transform monolingualist policies based on ideologies of linguistic nationalism and neoliberalism, with the larger goal of "awakening the sense of injustice." Specifically, Limbu Indigenous youth are challenging *angreji moha*, the "English craze," through dialogic language policy workshops and organized protests, and by lobbying teachers, students, and policymakers "to ensure space for the Limbu language in education" (Phyak, forthcoming, p. 25). This represents an "engaged language policy" movement, Phyak maintains, "that keeps social justice at the center of analysis" (Phyak, forthcoming; see also Davis, 2014).

Postcolonial Africa presents an LPP context of similar linguistic divides in that there exists a proliferation of Indigenous languages (400 enumerated for Nigeria alone), which compete with a handful of colonial languages for status and a place in school curricula. Here the situation is complicated by artificial linguistic divides imposed by missionary/settler colonizers among mutually intelligible languages, as "misinvented" linguistic borders accompanied the deterritorialization of Indigenous peoples from their lands (Makoni, 2003). Despite the multilingualism throughout Sub-Saharan Africa, postcolonial "one nation–one language" ideologies serve to advance a single African language within nation-states (e.g., Amharic in Ethiopia, Setswana in Botswana), "invisibilizing" other languages and speakers (Heugh, 2009, pp. 109–111). Many former English colonies have adopted what Makalela (2015, 2017) calls a "straight-for-English," subtractive bilingualism approach.

Ethiopia is the second most populous country in Sub-Saharan Africa, home to eighty ethnolinguistic groups. Heugh (2009) reports on a government-commissioned Ethiopian study, undertaken following a new education policy in 1994 that extended the use of other Ethiopian languages (beyond Amharic) on a regional basis. The policy specifies eight years of mother tongue–medium schooling, plus Amharic as a subject for students who do not have this as a mother tongue, English as a subject to the end of year eight, and transition to English-medium instruction in year nine. In an exhaustive review of policy implementation across different regions of Ethiopia, Heugh and her colleagues found that students who experienced mother-tongue instruction for the full length of their primary schooling (eight years) performed as well as or better than their English medium-of-instruction peers on assessments of English, science, and mathematics. An earlier, six-year study of Yoruba-medium schooling in Nigeria reported identical findings (Kamwangamalu, 2016). As Makalela (2005) sums up 100 years of education research on the subcontinent, HMT bi/multilingual education "accelerates academic success, . . . provides psychological support necessary to nourish cognitive development [and] enhances an autonomous worldview" (p. 164). Meanwhile, of course, HMT bi/multilingual education sustains children's mother language(s), challenging the hegemony of colonial language policies.

Latin America encompasses twenty nation-states, nine dependencies, and a population of 568 million spread out across South, Central, and parts of North America (García et al., 2010). This vast region is home to 40 to 50 million Indigenous people—10% of the region's total population—who speak as many as 700 languages (López & Sichra, 2008). Maxwell (2016) notes that all minority language groups in Latin America are "losing young speakers to the hegemonic tongues" (p. 261).

Latin American republics were founded on an exogenous ideology of monolingual/monocultural national identity as a precursor to citizenship and equality for all. Yet there has been little equality, as this citizenship model has excluded women, the poor, and Indigenous peoples. Throughout the region, Indigenous language rights have come late and have confronted major gaps between official policies recognizing those rights and local conditions, including limited education resources, poverty, and racism. At the same time, there is general agreement that recent decades have witnessed important changes brought about by a growing "Indigenous conquest" of linguistic and education rights (Rockwell & Gomes, 2009). Today, the constitutions of most Latin American countries recognize the rights of Indigenous peoples to retain and sustain their distinctive languages and lifeways (Haboud et al., 2016).

At the heart of this conquest are programs of education for language revitalization (ELR) and bilingual/intercultural education (BIE) (López & García, 2016).

While BIE tends to be school-based, ELR, like Indigenous revitalization immersion, "goes beyond school activities" such that "homes, schools, and communities complement one another" (López & García, 2016, p. 121). One example of the strategic coupling of school- and community-based language planning is the long-standing Indigenous Bilingual Education Teacher Training Program of the Peruvian Amazon Basin (FORMABIAP). FORMABIAP prepares primary school teachers from fifteen Indigenous groups, some of whom, like RI teachers in North America, are learning their HMT as a second language. As multiple scholars and practitioners have pointed out, this is not simply linguistic or pedagogical work; it is also deeply political and emotional. López and García (2016) examine the "complex and conflicting experience" of Kukama-Kukamirias FORMABIAP participants, whose "external ascription as Indigenous was accompanied by the shame endured for not speaking Kukama" (p. 125; see also Lagunas, forthcoming, on Nahuatl). Elder-led language workshops, dialogue sessions, and community-based activities such as a Kukama literary competition helped the pre-service teachers recover their heritage language. Overall, say López and García (2016), "Kukamas are now convinced of the need to recuperate their language and culture" (p. 126).

Thousands of grassroots ELR and BIE efforts are under way throughout Latin America (see, e.g., examples in Coronel-Molina & McCarty, 2016). López and García (2016) report on a well-regarded Kaqchikel (Mayan)–medium school near Guatemala City that combines community-based cultural learning with bilingual Kaqchikel-Spanish instruction. "The school staff is determined to restore oral Kaqchikel in everyday life," these researchers state; the teachers' efforts have brought families and the community together in a language revitalization project called "'A dream come true'" (2016, p. 127). Maxwell (2016) and Messing and Nava Nava (2016) provide myriad examples of ELR and BIE for Nahuatl, Hñahñu, Isthmus Zapotec, and Chinatec in Mexico; Mayan in Guatemala; Quechua, Shuar, Aymara, and Guarani in the Andes; and Mapuche and Rapa Nui in Chile.

As demonstrated by the international literature discussed herein, the cognitive, academic, and affective benefits of these programs are well documented, and many have proven effective in promoting re-vernacularization. These successes notwithstanding, HMT bi/multilingual education continues to confront the "ideological paradox" of "constructing a national identity that is also multilingual and multicultural" (Hornberger, 2000, p. 173). In all these regional and national contexts, linguistic divides often force early exit from HMT bi/multilingual education where it exists, limiting children's acquisition of the HMT and the equality of its social standing (Mohanty & Panda, 2017). The root causes of these tensions are fundamental structural inequalities, ideologies of linguistic and cultural deficit, and the resultant remedial framing of bi/multilingual education as directed solely toward Indigenous and minoritized peoples rather than the population as a whole. López and Sichra (2008) sum up these issues for Latin America, but their point is equally relevant to other regional contexts: It is "urgent and mandatory to abandon once and for all the compensatory understanding of [bi/multilingual education] and to regard it as an approach for better educational quality in general" (p. 306).

FURTHERING LANGUAGE REVITALIZATION

At their core, the challenges facing those who seek to revitalize and sustain endangered and minoritized languages are challenges of *unequal power relations*. As Fishman (1991) wrote more than twenty-five years ago, sustaining a threatened language is difficult precisely because it entails rebuilding and defending linguistic and cultural community in the face of oppression. By necessity, language revitalization encompasses the political work of contesting unequal power relations and asserting "cultural autonomy" (Fishman, 1991, 2012; cf. Leonard & De Korne, 2017).

Mediating these fraught processes requires work at multiple levels, from the grassroots or bottom-up, to top-down official policy domains, and through the braided interstices of micro-, meso-, and macro-level language planning and policymaking. From a top-down perspective, multiple mechanisms are in place to support this work at the international level. Articles 13 and 14 of the hard-fought 2007 United Nations Declaration on the Rights of Indigenous Peoples states unequivocally that

> Indigenous peoples have the right to revitalize, use, develop and transmit to future generations their histories, languages, oral traditions, philosophies, writing systems and literatures . . . [and] to establish and control their educational systems and institutions providing education in their own languages. (United Nations General Assembly, 2007, Arts. 13 and 14)

The Organization for Security and Co-operation in Europe (OSCE) similarly links linguistic and human rights, affirming "the right to the maintenance and development of identity through [a minority] language" (OSCE High Commissioner on National Minorities, n.d., p. 6); and the action plan for UNESCO's (2001) Universal Declaration on Cultural Diversity specifically calls for "respecting the mother tongue . . . at all levels of education" (UNESCO, 2001, Annex II, No. 6). Many other international conventions and declarations provide an overarching framework for linguistic human rights (Skutnabb-Kangas & May, 2017). Yet these provisions are non-binding and include "exit clauses" that allow states to adopt a "minimalist approach" (Tollefson & Tsui, 2004, p. 6).

At the national level, many countries include linguistic rights and co-official status for endangered and minoritized languages through constitutional provisions and federal law, such as the Native American Languages Act (NALA) of 1990/1992 in the United States, and Mexico's 2003 General Law for the Linguistic Rights of Indigenous

Communities. In South Africa, nine Indigenous languages share co-official status with English and Afrikaans. Nonetheless, as we have seen, top-down policies and school-based programs, while important, are not sufficient in themselves to sustain endangered HMTs (Hornberger, 2008).

It is therefore in spaces of tension between possibility and constraint that the work of revitalizing and sustaining endangered languages takes place. At the national and regional levels, Kamwangamalu (2016) proposes "prestige planning" to raise the status of minoritized languages "so that members of the targeted speech community develop a positive attitude toward it" (p. 158). This can be achieved, he suggests, by requiring HMT ability for participation in desirable labor markets, providing dual-medium schooling in local languages and the LWC, and heightening "speakers' awareness about what [HMTs] can do for them in terms of upward social mobility" (pp. 163–169). Makalela (2015) proposes rethinking multilingual space to accommodate an "integrated plural vision" of sociolinguistic ecologies (p. 575). Based on the African notion of *ubuntu*—"I am because you are" (Makalela, 2015, p. 575)—this vision eschews a one nation–one language ideology and embraces instead translanguaging (García, 2009) as a pedagogic strategy in which "the use of one language is incomplete without the other" (Makalela, 2017, p. 527). Realizing such a vision is a long-term endeavor that will require coordinated action by all social sectors. Yet, as Kamwangamalu (2016) underscores, if linguistic, social, and educational inequities are to be transformed, it is just such complex multigenerational work that is needed (p. 220).

In the present moment, it is largely smaller-scale, bottom-up, grassroots endeavors that are propelling social-linguistic change. It should be remembered that it was a small group of Indigenous parents and elders who established the first *Kōhanga Reo* and *Pūnana Leo* in the early 1980s, at a time when Māori and Hawaiian were predicted to "die." Similarly, it was grassroots activism that led to passage of NALA in the United States, Mexico's General Law, numerous constitutional language rights provisions, and, after twenty-two years of political movement, the UN Declaration on the Rights of Indigenous Peoples. Among the Wampanoag of Massachusetts in the United States, a small group of tribal citizens has leveraged extensive linguistic documentation to resurrect Wôpanâak (Wampanoag), a language that had not been spoken in more than 150 years (little doe baird, 2013). Among the Miami of the southern Great Lakes region and the US state of Oklahoma, similar grassroots efforts have recovered *myaamia* (Miami), whose last "traditional" speaker died more than fifty years ago (Baldwin, 2003). As Miami language revitalizer Daryl Baldwin states (and not unlike the prestige planning proposed by Kamwangamalu for postcolonial Africa), the goal in these LPP efforts is "to change the language ideology of our own people and slowly raise the prestige of the language and culture . . .. [T]his is the real work of language revitalization" (cited in McCarty, 2013, p. 105).

Efforts like these are underway around the world, connecting the local with the global, bottom-up with top-down (Hornberger & McCarty, 2012). Such efforts refute—and refuse—grim prognostications of "failing" endangered languages (Meek, 2011), even as they illuminate the infinite plasticity of speakerhood and the generativity of people's language practices. It is to these efforts that LPP scholars and practitioners should look, as they direct us toward ever-new strategies for dismantling sociolinguistic hierarchies and the unequal power relations those hierarchies reflect and produce.

NOTE

1. Parts of this section are adapted from McCarty (2013, Chapter 1), and used with permission of Multilingual Matters.

REFERENCES

Baldwin, D. (2003). Miami language reclamation: From ground zero. Lecture presented by the Center for Writing and the Interdisciplinary Minor in Literacy and Rhetorical Studies, Speaker Series 24. Minneapolis: University of Minnesota. Retrieved from myaamiacenter.org/MCResources/baldwin_biblio/baldwin_ground_zero.pdf

Bauman, J. J. (1980). *Guide to issues in Indian language retention.* Washington, DC: Center for Applied Linguistics.

Castagno, A. E., & Brayboy, B. M. J. (2008). Culturally responsive schooling for Indigenous youth: A review of the literature. *Review of Educational Research* 78(4), 941–993.

Coronel-Molina, S. M., & McCarty, T.L. (Eds.) (2016). *Indigenous language revitalization in the Americas.* New York: Routledge.

Davis, K. (2014). Engaged language policy and practices. *Language Policy* 13(2), 83–100.

Dorian, N. C. (1998). Western language ideologies and small-language prospects. In L. A. Grenoble & L. J. Whaley (Eds.), *Endangered languages: Current issues and future prospects* (pp. 3–21). Cambridge: Cambridge University Press.

Fishman, J. A. (1991). *Reversing language shift: Theoretical and empirical foundations of assistance to threatened languages.* Clevedon, UK: Multilingual Matters.

Fishman, J. A. (2012). Cultural autonomy as an approach to sociolinguistic power-sharing: Some preliminary notions. *International Journal of the Sociology of Language* 213, 11–46.

García, O. (2009). *Bilingual education in the 21st century: A global perspective.* Malden, MA: Wiley-Blackwell.

García, O., López, D., & Makar, C. (2010). Latin America. In J. A. Fishman & O. García (Eds.), *Handbook of language and ethnic identity: Disciplinary and regional perspectives* (Vol. 1, pp. 353–373). Oxford: Oxford University Press.

Grenoble, L. A. (2011). Language ecology and endangerment. In P. K. Austin & J. Sallabank (Eds.), *The Cambridge handbook of language endangerment* (pp. 27–44). Cambridge: Cambridge University Press.

Grenoble, L. A., & Whaley, L. J. (2006). *Saving languages: An introduction to language revitalization.* Cambridge: Cambridge University Press.

Haboud, M., Howard, R., Cru, J., & Freeland, J. (2016). Linguistic human rights and language revitalization in Latin America and the Caribbean. In S. M. Coronel-Molina & T. L. McCarty (Eds.), *Indigenous language revitalization in the Americas* (pp. 201–223). New York: Routledge.

Hermes, M., Bang, M., & Marin, A. (2012). Designing Indigenous language revitalization. *Harvard Educational Review* 82(3), 381–402.

Heugh, K. (2009). Literacy and bi/multilingual education in Africa: Recovering collective memory and expertise. In T. Skutnabb-Kangas, R. Phillipson, A. K. Mohanty, & M. Panda (Eds.), *Social justice through multilingual education* (pp. 85–124). Bristol, UK: Multilingual Matters.

Hill, R., & May, S. (2011). Exploring biliteracy in Māori-medium education: An ethnographic perspective. In T. L. McCarty (Ed.), *Ethnography and language policy* (pp. 161–183). New York: Routledge.

Hinton, L. (2011). Revitalization of endangered languages. In P. K. Austin & J. Sallabank (Eds.), *The Cambridge handbook of endangered languages* (pp. 291–311). Cambridge: Cambridge University Press.

Hinton, L. (Ed.) (2013). *Bringing our languages home: Language revitalization for families.* Berkeley, CA: Heyday Books.

Hinton, L. (2017). Language endangerment and revitalization. In T. L. McCarty & S. May (Eds.), *Encyclopedia of language and education*, Vol. 1: *Language policy and political issues in education* (3rd edition, pp. 257–272). Cham, Switzerland: Springer International.

Hinton, L., & Hale, K. (Eds.) (2001). *The green book of language revitalization in practice.* San Diego, CA: Academic Press.

Hinton, L., Vera, M., Steele, N., & AICLS. (2002). *How to keep your language alive: A commonsense approach to one-on-one language learning.* Berkeley, CA: Heyday Books.

Hohepa, M. K. (2006). Biliterate practices in the home: Supporting Indigenous language regeneration. *Journal of Language, Identity, and Education* 5(4), 293–301.

Hornberger, N. H. (2000). Bilingual education policy and practice in the Andes: Ideological paradox and intercultural possibility. *Anthropology and Education Quarterly* 31(2), 173–201.

Hornberger, N. H. (Ed.). (2008). *Can schools save Indigenous languages? Policy and practice on four continents.* New York: Palgrave Macmillan.

Hornberger, N. H., & McCarty, T. L. (Eds.). (2012). *Globalization from the bottom up: Indigenous language planning and policy across time, space, and place.* Special issue, *International Multilingual Research Journal* 6(1), entire.

Hornsby, M. (2015). The "new" and "traditional" speaker dichotomy: Bridging the gap. *International Journal of the Sociology of Language* 231, 107–205.

Hornsby, M., & Vigers, R. (2018). New speakers in the heartlands: Struggles for speaker legitimacy in Wales. *Journal of Multilingual and Multicultural Development*, https://doi.org/10.1080/01434632.2018.1429452.

Hough, D. A., Magar, R. B. T., & Yonjan-Tamang, A. (2009). Privileging Indigenous knowledges: Empowering multilingual education in Nepal. In T. Skutnabb-Kangas, R. Phillipson, A. K. Mohanty, & M. Panda (Eds.), *Social justice through multilingual education* (pp. 159–176). Bristol, UK: Multilingual Matters.

Huss, L. (2017,). Language education policies and the Indigenous and minority languages of northernmost Scandinavia and Finland. In T. L. McCarty & S. May (Eds.), *Encyclopedia of language and education*, Vol. 1: *Language policy and political issues in education* (3rd edition, pp. 367–381). Cham, Switzerland: Springer International.

Iokepa-Guerrero, N. (2016). Revitalization programs and impacts in the USA and Canada. In S. M. Coronel-Molina & T. L. McCarty (Eds.), *Indigenous language revitalization in the Americas* (pp. 227–246). New York: Routledge.

Jaffe, A. (2015). Defining the new speaker: Theoretical perspectives and learner trajectories. *International Journal of the Sociology of Language* 231, 21–44.

Kamwangamalu, N. K. (2016). *Language policy and economics: The language question in Africa*. London: Palgrave Macmillan.

Kasstan, J. (2018). Exploring contested authenticity among speakers of a contested language: The case of Francoprovençal. *Journal of Multilingual and Multicultural Development*, https://doi.org/10.1080/01434632.2018.1429451.

King, K. A., Schilling-Estes, N., Fogle, L., Lou, J. J., & Soukup, B. (Eds.) (2008). *Sustaining linguistic diversity: Endangered and minority languages and language varieties*. Washington, DC: Georgetown University Press.

Krauss, M. (1997). The Indigenous languages of the North: A report on their present state. In H. Shoji & J. Janhunen (Eds.), *Northern minority languages: Problems of survival* (pp. 1–34). *Ethnological Studies* 44. Osaka: National Museum of Ethnology.

Krauss, M. (1998). The condition of Native North American languages: The need for realistic assessment and action. *International Journal of the Sociology of Language* 132, 9–21.

Kroskrity, P. V., & Field, M. C. (Eds.) (2009). *Native American language ideologies: Beliefs, practices, and struggles in Indian Country*. Tucson: University of Arizona Press.

Lagunas, R. (forthcoming). Language key holders for Mexicano: The case of an intergenerational community in Coatepec de los Costales, Mexico. In T. L. McCarty, S. E. Nicholas, & G. Wigglesworth (Eds.), *A world of Indigenous languages: Policies, pedagogies, and prospects for language reclamation*. Bristol, UK: Multilingual Matters.

Leonard, W. V. (2008). When is an "extinct" language not extinct? Miami, a formerly sleeping language. In K. A. King, N. Schilling-Estes, L. Fogle, J. J. Lou, & B. Soukup (Eds.), *Sustaining linguistic diversity: Endangered and minority languages and language varieties* (pp. 23–33). Washington, DC: Georgetown University Press.

Leonard, W. V. (2011). Challenging "extinction" through modern Miami language practices. *American Indian Culture and Research Journal* 35(2), 135–160.

Leonard, W. V., & De Korne, H. (Eds.) (2017). *Reclaiming languages: Contesting and decolonizing "language endangerment" from the ground up*. Special issue, *Language Documentation and Description* 14, entire.

little doe baird, J. (2013). Wampanoag: How did this happen to my language? In L. Hinton (Ed.), *Bringing our languages home: Language revitalization for families* (pp. 19–30). Berkeley, CA: Heyday Books.

Lomawaima, K. T., & McCarty, T. L. (2006). *"To remain an Indian": Lessons in democracy from a century of Native American education*. New York: Teachers College Press.

López, L. E., & García, F. (2016). The home-school-community interface in language revitalization in Latin America and the Caribbean. In S. Coronel-Molina & T. L. McCarty (Eds.), *Indigenous language revitalization in the Americas* (pp. 116–135). New York: Routledge.

López, L. E., & Sichra, I. (2008). Intercultural bilingual education among Indigenous peoples in Latin America. In J. Cummins & N. H. Hornberger (Eds.), *Encyclopedia of language and education*, Vol. 5: *Bilingual education* (2nd edition; pp. 295–309). New York: Springer.

Makalela, L. (2005)."We speak eleven tongues": Reconstructing multilingualism in South Africa. In B. Brock-Utne & R. K. Hopson (Eds.), *Languages of instruction for African emancipation: Focus on postcolonial contexts and considerations* (pp. 147–173). Capetown, SA; Dar es Salaam, Tanzania: Centre for Advanced Studies of African Society (CASAS) and Mkuki na Nyota Publishers.

Makalela, L. (2015). A panoramic view of bilingual education in Sub-Saharan Africa. In W. E. Wright, S. Boun, & O. García (Eds.), *The handbook of bilingual and multilingual education* (pp. 566–577). Malden, MA: Wiley Blackwell.

Makalela, L. (2017). Language policy in Southern Africa. In T. L. McCarty & S. May (Eds.), *Encyclopedia of language and education*, Vol. 1: *Language policy and political issues in education* (3rd edition, pp. 519–529). Cham, Switzerland: Springer International.

Makoni, S. (2003). From misinvention to disinvention of language: Multilingualism and the South African Constitution. In S. Makoni, G. Smitherman, A. Ball, & A. Spears (Eds.), *Black linguistics: Language, society and politics in Africa and the Americas* (pp. 132–149). New York: Routledge.

Maxwell, J. (2016). Revitalization programs and impacts in Latin America and the Caribbean. In S. M. Coronel-Molina & T. L. McCarty (Eds.), *Indigenous language revitalization in the Americas* (pp. 247–265). New York: Routledge.

May, S. (2005). Introduction. Bilingual/immersion education in Aotearoa/New Zealand: Setting the context. *International Journal of Bilingual Education and Bilingualism* 8(5), 365–376.

McCarty, T. L. (2008a). Native American languages as heritage mother tongues. *Language, Culture and Curriculum* 21(3), 201–225.

McCarty, T. L. (2008b). Schools as strategic tools for Indigenous language revitalization: Lessons from Native America. In N. H. Hornberger (Ed.), *Can schools save Indigenous languages? Policy and practice on four continents* (pp. 161–179). New York: Palgrave Macmillan.

McCarty, T. L. (2013). *Language planning and policy in Native America: History, theory, praxis.* Bristol, UK: Multilingual Matters.

McCarty, T. L., & Nicholas, S. E. (2014). Reclaiming Indigenous languages: A reconsideration of the roles and responsibilities of schools. *Review of Research in Education* 38, 106–136.

McCarty, T. L., Skutnabb-Kangas, T., & Magga, O.-H. (2008). Education for speakers of endangered languages. In B. Spolsky & F. M. Hult (Eds.), *The handbook of educational linguistics* (pp. 297–312). Malden, MA: Blackwell.

McIvor, O., & McCarty, T. L. (2016). Indigenous bilingual and revitalization-immersion education in Canada and the USA. In O. García, A. Lin, & S. May (Eds.), *Encyclopedia of language and education* (3rd edition). New York: Springer. doi: 10.1007/978-3-319-02324-3_34-1

Meek, B. (2011). Failing American Indian languages. *American Indian Culture and Research Journal* 35(2), 43–60.

Messing, J., & Nava Nava, R. (2016). Language acquisition, shift, and revitalization processes in Latin America and the Caribbean. In S. Coronel-Molina & T. L. McCarty (Eds.), *Indigenous language revitalization in the Americas* (pp. 76–96). New York: Routledge.

Mohanty, A. (2010). Languages, inequality and marginalization: Implications of the double divide in Indian multilingualism. *International Journal of the Sociology of Language* 205, 131–154.

Mohanty, A. K., & Panda, M. (2017). Language policy and language education in the Indian Subcontinent. In T. L. McCarty & S. May (Eds.), *Encyclopedia of language and education*, Vol. 1: *Language policy and political issues in education* (3rd edition, pp. 507–518). New York: Springer.

Nettle, D., & Romaine, S. (2000). *Vanishing voices: The extinction of the world's languages.* Oxford: Oxford University Press.

New Zealand Māori Council. (2016, July 18). Media statement on Māori language policy. Press Release. Retrieved from http://www.scoop.co.nz/stories/PO1607/S00199/maori-language-policy.htm

Ó hIfearnáin, T. (2015). Sociolinguistic vitality of Manx after extreme language shift: Authenticity without traditional native speakers. *International Journal of the Sociology of Language* 231, 45–62.

Olthuis, M.-L., Kivelä, S., & Skutnabb-Kangas, T. (2013). *Revitalizing Indigenous languages: How to recreate a lost generation.* Bristol, UK: Multilingual Matters.

O'Rourke, B., Pujolar, J., & Ramallo, F. (2015). New speakers of minority languages: The challenging opportunity—Foreword. *International Journal of the Sociology of Language* 231, 1–20.

O'Rourke, B., & Ramallo, F. (2015). *Neofalantes* as an active minority: Understanding language practices and motivations for change amongst new speakers of Galician. *International Journal of the Sociology of Language* 231, 147–165.

O'Rourke, B., & Walsh, J. (2015). New speakers of Irish: Shifting boundaries across time and space. *International Journal of the Sociology of Language* 231, 63–83.

Ortega, A., Urla, J., Amorrortu, E., Goirigolzarri, J., & Uranga, B. (2015). Linguistic identity among new speakers of Basque. *International Journal of the Sociology of Language* 231, 85–105.

OSCE High Commissioner on National Minorities. (n.d.). *Report on the linguistic rights of persons belonging to national minorities in the OSCE area.* The Hague, Netherlands: Author.

Phyak, P. (forthcoming). Transformation from the bottom-up: Ideological analysis with Indigenous youth and language policy justice in Nepal. In T. L. McCarty, S. E. Nicholas, & G. Wigglesworth (Eds.), *A world of Indigenous languages: Policies, pedagogies, and prospects for language reclamation.* Bristol, UK: Multilingual Matters.

Pujolar, J., & Puigdevall, M. (2015). Linguistic *mudes*: How to become a new speaker in Catalonia. *International Journal of the Sociology of Language* 231, 167–187.

Rockwell, E., & Gomes, A. M. R. (2009). Introduction to the special issue: Rethinking Indigenous education from a Latin American perspective. *Anthropology and Education Quarterly* 40(2), 97–109.

Ruiz, R. (1984). Orientations in language planning. *NABE Journal* 8(2), 15–34.

Skutnabb-Kangas, T., & May S. (2017). Human rights and language policy in education. In T. L. McCarty (Ed.), *Encyclopedia of language and education,* Vol. 1: *Language policy and political issues in education* (3rd edition, pp. 125–141). Cham, Switzerland: Springer.

Skutnabb-Kangas, T., & McCarty, T. L. (2008). Key concepts in bilingual education: Ideological, historical, epistemological, and empirical foundations. In J. Cummins & N. H. Hornberger (Eds.), *Encyclopedia of language and education,* Vol. 5: *Bilingual education* (2nd edition; pp. 3–17). New York: Springer.

Smith, G. (2000). Māori education: Revolution and transformative action. *Canadian Journal of Native Education* 24(1), 57–72.

Task Force on Aboriginal Languages and Cultures. (2005). *Towards a new beginning: A foundational report for a strategy to revitalize First Nation, Inuit and Métis languages and cultures.* Ottawa, ON: Aboriginal Languages Directorate, Department of Canadian Heritage.

Tedick, D., Christian, D., & Fortune, T. W. (2011). The future of immersion education: An invitation to "dwell in possibility." In D. J. Tedick, D. Christian, & T. W. Fortune (Eds.),

Immersion education: Practices, policies, possibilities (pp. 1–10). Bristol, UK: Multilingual Matters.

Tollefson, J. W. (2006). Critical theory in language policy. In T. Ricento (Ed.), *An introduction to language policy: Theory and method* (pp. 42–59). Malden, MA: Blackwell.

Tollefson, J. W., & Tsui, A. B. M. (Eds.) (2004). *Medium of instruction policies: Which agenda? Whose agenda?* Mahwah, NJ: Lawrence Erlbaum.

UNESCO. (2001). *Universal declaration on cultural diversity.* Retrieved from http://portal. unesco.org/en/ev.php-URL_ID=13179&URL_DO=DO_TOPIC&URL_SECTION=201. html

UNESCO Ad Hoc Expert Group on Endangered Languages. (2003). *Language vitality and endangerment.* Paris: UNESCO Intangible Cultural Heritage Unit.

United Nations General Assembly. (2007). *Declaration on the rights of Indigenous peoples.* Retrieved from http://www.un.org/esa/socdev/unpfii/documents/DRIPS_en.pdf

Usborne, E., Peck, J., Smith, D., & Taylor, D. M. (2011). Learning through an Aboriginal language: The impact on students' English and Aboriginal language skills. *Canadian Journal of Education* 34(4), 200–215.

Wiley, T. G. (2014). The problem of defining heritage and community languages and their speakers: On the utility and limitations of definitional constructs. In T. G. Wiley, J. K. Peyton, D. Christian, S. C. K. Moore, & N. Liu (Eds.), *Handbook of heritage, community, and Native American languages in the United States: Research, policy, and educational practice* (pp. 19–26). New York; Washington, DC: Routledge; Center for Applied Linguistics.

Wilson, W. H. (2014). Hawaiian: A Native American language official for a state. In T. G. Wiley, J. K. Peyton, D. Christian, S. C. K. Moore, & N. Liu (Eds.), *Handbook of heritage, community, and Native American languages in the United States* (pp. 219–228). New York; Washington, DC: Routledge; Center for Applied Linguistics.

Wilson, W. H., & Kamanā, K. (2011). Insights from Indigenous language immersion in Hawaiʻi. In D. J. Tedick, D. Christian, & T. W. Fortune (Eds.), *Immersion education: Practices, policies, possibilities* (pp. 36–57). Bristol, UK: Multilingual Matters.

Woolard, K. A. (1998). Introduction: Language ideology as a field of inquiry. In B. B. Schieffelin, K. A. Woolard, & P. V. Kroskrity (Eds.), *Language ideologies: Practice and theory* (pp. 3–47). New York: Oxford University Press.

Wyman, L., Marlow, P., Andrew, C. F., Miller, G., Nicholai, C. R., & Rearden, Y. N. (2010). Focusing on long-term language goals in challenging times: A Yup'ik example. *Journal of American Indian Education* 49(1–2), 28–39.

....

CHAPTER 19

"WE WORK AS BILINGUALS"

SOCIOECONOMIC CHANGES AND LANGUAGE POLICY FOR INDIGENOUS LANGUAGES IN EL IMPENETRABLE

....

VIRGINIA UNAMUNO AND
JUAN EDUARDO BONNIN

To be bilingual is not the same as being *a* bilingual. The former treats *bilingual* as an adjective: a descriptive term depicting some property of an entity. In contrast, the latter defines a category of beings: *a bilingual* is someone who is defined by his or her bilingualism. The definition of a speaker by her or his (multi)linguistic competences is not new; there is a globally valued order of languages that defines different "orders of indexicality" (Blommaert, 2010, p. 37), stratified axiological systems within which communicative competences are evaluated. Dominant languages in Western societies—English and Spanish in Latin-America—are a valuable linguistic capital that can be used by global speakers to achieve global goals, such as studying abroad or publishing academic papers. These speakers are bilingual, but they are not *the bilinguals*.

We observe this folk grammatical re-categorization that uses an adjective as a noun, in a rather specific phenomenon: the emergence of a new state-based job category that, unusually, requires Spanish–indigenous language bilingualism. Indeed, in

Chaco Province, Argentina, after several decades of invisibilization and social repression of indigenous languages, Moqoit-Spanish, Qom-Spanish, and Wichi-Spanish bilingualism are now required to access qualified jobs in the public educational and health-care system. Although it might be regarded as a successful outcome of many years of indigenous peoples' struggle, there is a more complex political process that situates bilinguals as an in-between class of social actors, whose Spanish–indigenous language bilingualism qualifies them for state positions in a particular way.

From this perspective, bilinguals in Chaco respond to a twofold problem that is characteristic of the formulation of national public policies within the context of regional integration processes. On one hand, the state interacts with international and multilateral organizations, thus "relinquishing some sovereignty and economic autonomy, in order to join a supranational regional group for prosperity and security purposes" (Wright, 2004, p. 182). On the other hand, the state also interacts with local actors—landowners and natives—to reduce social conflict: within a process of progressive reappropriation of the land as a means of subsistence for native populations, their social and economic demands are partially appeased with new government-provided jobs (Unamuno, 2014). The bilingual can be seen as a figure who works simultaneously at both levels. At the supranational level, this seems to respond to diplomatic commitments acquired in organizations such as the *Unión de las Naciones del Sur* (UNASUR) or the Pan-American Health Organization (PAHO) by somehow integrating so-called native people into educational and health institutions. At the local level, it helps to free roadblocks and decrease belligerence by indigenous organizations toward landowners in exchange for well-paid government-provided jobs (Unamuno, 2014).

As subjects *in-between*, the social and political meaning of the bilinguals is not homogeneous. On the contrary, different linguistic ideologies frame diverse conditions of understanding and encouraging the role of these new, emergent social actors. To the modern nation-state, the bilingual is a key actor in the *access* of minority populations to universally defined human rights. The ideology of access attributes to bilinguals the role of *translators* on the basis of two principles: (1) every minority should subordinate its particular identity to state-defined, Western universalistic policies (therefore adapting to dominant languages); and (2) language is a transparent code that objectively conveys information that can be completely translated from one code to another. To the communities, on the contrary, both principles are contested on the basis of an ideology of *identity*, which refuses to abandon their own worldview, based on a heteroglossic conception of language—not only bilingualism.

In what follows, we will present how we understand the role of the bilinguals in this contradictory position. First, we will explain the theoretical and methodological assumptions of our research. We understand language policies as a multidimensional political set of actions that, just like the bilinguals, exists between institutions and practices. Our approach to language policy and planning (LPP) therefore draws on ethnography, discourse analysis, and studies of interaction, combined in a comprehensive approach to data. Second, we will present a case study of indigenous teachers and health workers at El Impenetrable, Chaco, in the Argentinean context. This context will be observed first through the analysis of institutional discourses regarding language in health care and education, in order to better describe the *ideology of access* from the perspective of the Argentinean nation-state. Next, we will analyze ethnographic data to observe how this institutional ideology interacts with actual practices conducted at the local level by indigenous health workers and educators. The *ideology of identity*, materialized in daily practices and discourses, will (to a greater or lesser extent) silently confront the state view of language among indigenous actors in health care and education. The conflict between both ideologies is, up to a certain point, characteristic of the struggle between modern, state-oriented language policies and grassroots activism, including language as a part of a wider repertoire of political action. Following on this, we will conclude with an account of the further implications for LPP research.

Language Policies, Ethnography, and Discourse Analysis

Language planning and policies are usually related to practices, attitudes, and ideologies regarding the politics of language, or *glottopolitics*. As noted by Guespin and Marcellesi (1986, p. 14), "toute planification linguistique, dans une société de classes, est nécessairement la politique linguistique d'une classe sociale dominante" [language planning, at any given society of classes, is necessarily the linguistic policy of a dominant social class]. From this perspective, language policies are necessarily actions that (a) are meaningful and, as a result, can (and probably should) be discursively analyzed; and (b) are aimed at speakers rather than languages, affecting their social and economic realities. We therefore adopt a twofold perspective on language policies, which includes both discourse analysis of institutional texts and ethnographic analysis of language practices.

Language policies in Argentina have traditionally been studied through historical and discourse analysis of public texts, such as legal norms and political speeches (cf. Arnoux & Bein, 2010; Arnoux & Nothstein, 2014). Very little research seeks to explain language policies by taking into consideration political actions at different social levels or scales. However, the public field is a space of dispute in which historically confronted groups struggle to access, control, and transform goods and institutions. Land, education, health, and justice are political objects that different actors from different positions (and with different interests) seek to appropriate. In the context of these processes, languages play a key role. It is therefore hard to explain language policies without considering what is at stake in their symbolic and material dimensions.

Rather than considering language policies as the result of deliberate actions by state actors, undertaken to influence the use and/or transmission of language, we are interested in looking at the processes in which language is effectively intertwined with everyday political action (Tollefson, 1991, 2008). Our research seeks to understand complex multilateral processes in which language is a politically disputed capital, closely related to others such as educational degrees or professional qualifications. Instead of assuming that public agencies make decisions that other actors enforce, we are interested in the ways in which multiple decisions converge or diverge in the symbolic struggle to build and/or influence the public sphere regarding language-related issues.

These processes are complex research objects because, although contemporary, they require historical comprehension, and because, despite their strong interactional basis, their description requires simultaneous attention to different levels and degrees of context (Unamuno, 2015). Ethnographic sociolinguistics offers a series of meaningful tools for this kind of research (Heller, 2001, 2011; Hornberger, 1995; Codo, Patiño & Unamuno, 2012), especially regarding methods of multiple contextualizations in the process of reconstructing the meaning of the analyzed phenomena (Johnson & Ricento, 2013).

Ethnographic fieldwork and knowledge of a community help explain the actual effects of normative legal discourses. In Argentina, many public policies on languages, including their legal status (such as that of "official language"), do not lead to any political action over their use or transmission. Instead, they usually lead to innocuous symbolic recognition that does not necessarily have any transformative effect on the hegemony of Spanish.

The combination of discourse analysis and ethnography enables understanding of widespread institutional ideologies, as well as the actual agency of the mostly indigenous social actors who, through grassroots political activism and discourse struggle, can force emergent regulations or normative applications. We shall now turn to our research setting.

THE BILINGUALS IN CHACO: BETWEEN NATIONAL LEGISLATION AND LOCAL ROADBLOCKS

Chaco is a province in northeastern Argentina, inhabited by three indigenous nations—Qom, Moqoit, and Wichi—as well as descendants of eastern European immigrants. It was a pioneer province in the legal recognition of indigenous rights in general, and language rights in particular. The Law of the Chaco Aboriginal (Ley de las comunidades indígenas; Provincia de Chaco, 1987) is recognized, even today, as being very progressive on the subject of native people's rights. We gathered data for this chapter through our fieldwork, which has been ongoing since 2009. Our research focuses on the region of El Impenetrable, specifically on the communities that live by the Teuco River. We have accompanied these communities in different projects, especially regarding teacher training and the introduction of the Wichi language and culture in public schools.

It is worth noting two events in the recent linguistic history of these communities. One is the creation in 2007 of a branch of the Center for Research and Training for Indigenous Modality (Centro de Investigación y Formación para la Modalidad Aborigen), which provides teacher training and awards an official degree equivalent to that of any non-indigenous teacher. The other is the appointment in September 2009 of the first Wichi nurse in an executive position at the local hospital. Both events are meaningful milestones according to Wichi and non-Wichi local accounts, representing an about-face in interethnic relationships. In this new process, Wichi people have gradually gained access to previously unreachable state positions in the fields of education and health care. Thus, from 2009 to 2016, there has been an unusual increase in the number of Wichi teachers from only four to sixty-two, of whom 85% hold teaching positions in the public system. In a similar vein, from 2011 to 2016, 225 health-care workers joined the public health-care system, 63 of whom were Wichi.

Another series of events have taken place since the beginning of our research regarding language policy at different levels and dimensions. At the provincial level, in 2010, the Chaco Parliament enacted the law that makes Qom, Moqoit, and Wichi co-official languages. In 2013, after a long period of pressure from indigenous movements led by bilingual teachers, a Bill on Indigenous Intercultural Bilingual Community-Managed Public Education (Ley de Educación Pública de Gestión Comunitaria Bilingüe Intercultural Indígena) was proposed, and the law was enacted on August 13, 2014 (Provincia de Chaco, 2014). It enables indigenous communities to run schools, at which up to 50% of the appointed staff can be indigenous.

In the field of health care, it should be noted that in December 2007 a health emergency was declared in the Province of Chaco as a result of the death by malnutrition of more than twenty-two indigenous persons. Faced with this situation, various indigenous demonstrations took place in the province, with activists cutting off roads and occupying hospitals and health-care facilities. Chaco Aboriginal Institute, on behalf of indigenous communities, requested the intervention of the Ombudsman's Office, which filed a criminal complaint at the Supreme Court of Justice, causing the national and provincial governments to take immediate concrete action regarding indigenous health care. In this context of political pressure, the Aboriginal Health Council was created to advise the government of Chaco on health issues in indigenous contexts, creating new positions for bilingual nurses and new training programs for bilingual intercultural health workers.

As noted earlier, the bilinguals are subjects in-between. On the one hand, top-down, transnational indigenous movements project commitments, languages, and symbols from countries with more visible native activism (especially Bolivia, Peru, and Ecuador) onto others with more invisibilized native activism (like Argentina) through supranational organizations. On the other hand, bottom-up, daily struggles and protests result not only in community subsistence, but also in the revaluation of previously undervalued capital, such as native cultures and languages. These two different orders will be dealt with, in turn, in the following two sections.

Bilinguals as State Agents: The Ideology of Access

Health care and education are two basic human rights that are public, free, and universal in Argentina. Although the former is not explicitly included in the 1994 National Constitution, it is included in the Universal Declaration of Human Rights (1948) and the International Covenant on Economic, Social and Cultural Rights (1976), which Argentina ratified in 1986 (Giovanella et al., 2012, p. 26). In other words, health care appears as a human right through international instruments and commitments that the country has ratified. This helps explain the relevance of international organizations and their agendas in the formulation of health policies in Argentina.

On the other hand, the Argentinean Constitution explicitly recognizes the right to "intercultural bilingual education" (hereafter IBE; art. 75). The amendment, introduced in 1994, resulted from pressure by international multilateral agreements, specifically Argentina's ratification of the International Labour Organization's Indigenous and Tribal People's Convention of 1989 (ILO Convention 169), which explicitly includes IBE. Similarly, Argentina signed political commitments with UNESCO and UNICEF regarding the teaching of mother tongues and the protection of language-cultural diversity. However, formal recognition of IBE did not necessarily lead to actions regulating bilingual and intercultural teaching.

Although there is a long tradition of IBE and explicit reflection on language and education in Argentina (López & Küper, 1999; López & Sichra, 2008), no comparable importance is attributed to language in the field of health-care theory and practice. Something similar occurs with multilateral organizations such as the United Nations and the ILO, which tend to include indigenous languages explicitly when referring to education, but not when referring to health care. The United Nations Declaration on the Rights of Indigenous Peoples (2007) recognizes the right of indigenous people to "*their traditional medicines* and to maintain their health practices, including the conservation of their vital medicinal plants, animals and minerals" (art. 24; our emphasis). Knowledge of health and the body seems to be related to material objects and practices, and not to language, which is explicitly included when discussing education: "[i]ndigenous peoples have the right to establish and control *their educational systems and institutions* providing education in *their own languages*, in a manner appropriate to their cultural methods of teaching and learning" (art. 14; our emphasis).

The promotion of indigenous knowledge and practices in health care and education, despite differences regarding language, is complemented by universalistic discourse on *access* to state policies: "Indigenous individuals, particularly children, have the right to *all levels and forms of education* of the State without discrimination." (art. 14; our emphasis); "Indigenous individuals also have the right to *access*, without discrimination, *all social and health services*" (art. 24; our emphasis). The tension between indigenous medicine and education ("their") and universally defined policies proposed by the UN text ("all") poses a challenge to national states. The strategies used to face this challenge may often be understood as what we call the *ideology of access.*

The ideology of access, even when recognizing particular cultures and their values, has two principles, both based in the ideology of the modern nation-state, which links territory, identity, citizenship, and language (Blommaert, 2009). Its first feature is a *subordination of particular identities to state-defined, Western universalistic policies.* Under this principle, minorities are seen as excluded from policies because of their particularities; the state's duty is, therefore, to help them access universal rights, a corpus of Western knowledge and institutions that is fixed and static. Language may thus appear as a barrier to access: "[t]he main barrier [to health-care services] is the lack of geographic, cultural and economic accessibility [...]. Indigenous people receive substandard care at healthcare centers, due either to discrimination in the system or to communication difficulties because they speak different languages" (Ministerio de Salud de la Nación, 2012, p. 10; our translation).[1] Indigenous languages are not perceived as useful tools for health-care workers to access indigenous people, but rather as an obstacle faced by indigenous people, preventing them from accessing proper health care.

The main legal framework on IBE proposes language diversity as a basis for dialogue, rather than as an obstacle: "IBE promotes a mutually enriching dialogue of knowledge and values between indigenous peoples and populations that are ethnically, linguistically and culturally different, and encourages recognition and respect towards those differences" (Education Act 26.206, art. 52; our translation).[2] However, the normative ruling of the act replicates the conception of indigenous bi/monolingualism as a handicap. Thus, in the National Plan of Mandatory Education for years 2012–2016, language diversity is perceived as a feature of a population that has "special needs," almost as a disability: "as of 2016, all jurisdictions implement institutional formats for children with specific educational needs (rurality, deprivation of liberty of their mothers, interculturality and bilingualism, parents or students with disabilities, in hospital or in domiciliary care)" (Consejo Ferderal de Educación, 2012, p. 5; our translation).[3] As in the case of health care, bilingualism is perceived not as a competence of indigenous children that can be improved by the educational system but, on the contrary, as an obstacle that should be overcome in order for them to access Western, state-defined education.

The second feature of the ideology of access is a *monoglossic view on language as a transparent code* that allows information to be conveyed from one person to another. From this perspective, the issue of indigenous languages is regarded as a problem of indigenous bi/monolingual speakers who cannot access education or health offered by the Western, Spanish-monolingual state. This linguistic ideology sustains a reductive and conservative conception of interculturality: "communication between cultures or intercultural communication is basically understood as an exchange of information through language" (Ministerio de Salud, 2012, p. 50; our translation).[4] The definition of "intercultural communication" is based on a simplistic monoglossic view of language and culture whereby "exchange of information through language" assumes that *culture* equals *information* and that *communication* is, thus, an exchange of information that has language as a neutral medium, a code that can be perfectly translated into another. In the field of education, bilingualism and interculturality are not seen as the property of a specific educational policy or content, but rather as a contextual feature. IBE is thus intended to "extend and improve conditions and forms of access" at "kindergartens in intercultural and bilingual contexts," for "students in contexts of interculturality and bilingualism" (Consejo Federal de Educación, 2012, p. 17; our translation).[5]

To sum up, the ideology of access is a modern ideology that seeks universalistic inclusion of all citizens, helping them overcome their barriers or handicaps, such as language diversity, as a form of defending the equality of people born in different contextual conditions. This ideology is based on a monoglossic conception of language as a neutral code and thus leads to a strategy that aims to facilitate access to that code. Hence, the bilingual, from this point of view, is an interpreter capable of translating Western knowledge on education and health to the disadvantaged bi/monolingual indigenous population.

Nevertheless, at the local level of everyday language policymaking, the bilinguals' practices seem to be framed in the *ideology of identity*, in which ideas about language do not separate language and culture; at the same time, this ideology is based in a deeply heteroglossic view of language and communication. This is the hypothesis that we will explore next.

BILINGUALS AS LOCAL ACTORS: EDUCATION AND HEALTH CARE IN EL IMPENETRABLE

Many Wichi bilinguals have been hired for local state positions, despite social and ideological conflicts with the local white[6] population. Under these conditions, the revalorization of their linguistic capital played a key role in response to inclusive national laws regarding health and education. Indigenous bilingualism thus appears as a resource intended to ensure the access of the monolingual Wichi native population to general or common knowledge about the world. The ideology of access thus led to new institutional roles and dynamics that noticeably sought to appoint indigenous people to work as translators/interpreters. In what follows, we will observe, both at health-care and educational institutions, the tension between white authorities, who represent the state ideology of access, and indigenous bilinguals, who propose an alternative view of diversity and language.

The Wichi Health-Care Workers

The fieldwork vignette in Box 19.1 describes this process at the local hospital.

Box 19.1 "At the Hospital": Field Notes, September 2013

Dr. Nunez [pediatrician at the Hospital] explains that she has worked with bilingual health workers for a long time. "At the hospital there are now two people working with us. They translate when patients do not understand us. Women and children come here and sometimes they do not understand what they have to do. Flor and Marta explain to them in Wichi or ask them questions." I ask her for permission to observe consultations. She does not seem to like the idea very much, but agrees to it when Flor recognizes and greets me. Dr. Nuñez is sitting behind a desk next to Flor. On the left are a table and chair facing the desk. I stand there. A young Wichi woman in her twenties enters with a child in her arms. She hands the doctor a paper without saying a word. The doctor reads the paper and writes an order for powdered milk. Before returning the paper, she says she will weigh the child. Flor stands up and explains in Wichi what to do, asking the mother to put the baby on the scales. Flor announces the weight in Spanish to the doctor, who writes it down. She then hands the young mother the prescription for the milk and tells her to go to the hospital pharmacy. The woman leaves the room.

In the field notes, we can trace back to 2013 an initial intuition regarding the role of bilinguals as conceived by the state ideology of access—and its institutional agent, Dr. Nuñez. The role attributed to indigenous health workers—in this case, Flor— is that of interpreter or language assistant, subordinated to the white physician. Although Flor is not a physician, she has received formal training as a health-care worker. She belongs to the SASOI, the Service for Indigenous People's Orientation and Health Care (Servicio de Atención para la Salud y Orientación Indígena), a recently created office at public hospitals in Chaco that is entirely composed of bilinguals. We can observe in this vignette the two basic principles of the ideology of access. First, language appears as a handicap of indigenous people that prevents them from accessing Western health care. The physician therefore requires a translator in order to be understood by patients, not to understand them. Second, language appears as a transparent code that conveys information from one person to another. Flor herself—or her medical knowledge—does not appear to be relevant; the patient's mother remains silent throughout the whole process during which Dr. Nuñez gathers medical information without much actual interaction.

How do these bilinguals see their work? Do they share the ideology of access of Dr. Nuñez and official discourse? Box 19.2 provides some insights on these questions, as part of an interview granted by the local SASOI officer.

Box 19.2 Interview with Antonio, Local SASOI Officer (Participants: A: Antonio; R: Researcher)

A: Eso es una lucha constante de nosotros, porque vos verás que el que viene de arriba, le interesa mucho nuestro idioma porque quieren saber cómo eran nosotros, ¿no? Porque a través del idioma se entiende mucho lo que el . . . en la comunidad, lo que es el wichi, el aborigen, el originario como dicen (. . .) muchos de nuestros ancianos, de nuestros antepasados, no pudieron tener acceso a buena salud, a entender, a explicarle al doctor, al que viene de arriba lo que le pasaba. ¿Por qué? Por culpa de nuestro idioma, por muchas cosas que decimos en nuestro idioma. Lo traducimos en castellano y no es lo mismo, no. A veces yo digo, mirá, yo digo al doctor: "me duele . . . me duele . . . la panza." Claro que el doctor le va a dar cosas de la panza, y no era la panza, sino acá (se señala la zona de la panza). Y explicándole bien al doctor, bueno, puede ser estómago, porque nosotros decimos "la panza," toda la panza.

R: Ajá.

A: Y no era la panza, puede ser el hígado, la vesícula, o el estómago.

R: Ajá.

A: That is a constant struggle of ours, because you see that the people at the top are very interested in our language because they want to know what we were like, right? Because through the language you understand a lot that the . . . in the community, what is the Wichi, the aboriginal, the originary as they say [. . .] many of our old folks, of our ancestors, couldn't have access to good health, to understand, to explain to the doctor, to the one at the top what was wrong with them. Why? Because of our language, because of many things we say in our language. We translate into Spanish and it's not the same, no. Sometimes I say, look, I say to the doctor: "there's pain . . . there's pain . . . in my belly." Of course the doctor will give me things for the belly, and it wasn't the belly, but here (indicating the region of the belly). And, by explaining well, the doctor, well, it may be the stomach, because we say "the belly," the whole belly.

R: Mhm.

A: And it wasn't the belly, it could be the liver, the gall bladder, or the stomach.

R: Mhm.

In the interview excerpt, the health-care worker adopts an opposition between "us" (indigenous) and "them" (white people), introducing the issue of language as identity, rather than just a code: when explaining the interest of white people (mainly academics) in the Wichi language, he states that "through language you understand what the community, the Wichi, the aboriginal, the native people are." If language is not just a code that can be translated into another, but the very substance of "the community, the Wichi," it embodies a worldview that cannot be transposed from Wichi to Spanish: "we translate it into Spanish and it is not the same." This folk version of the Sapir-Whorf hypothesis is quite the opposite of the one adopted by the Ministry of Health, which defined "intercultural communication" as simply "exchanging information through language."

To Wichi health workers, language is not a monoglossic, transparent code homogeneously distributed among a given population. On the contrary, we can observe in their speech a reflection on both bilingual and monolingual medical practices, characterized as situations of intercultural communication.

In Box 19.3, this *cuento* (a story that might or might not have really happened) presents two characters: an inexperienced young physician, "newly graduated, from the city [. . .] with all his knowledge," and a *criollo* couple and their little child, who live in "a little village" (*un pueblito*). The opposition here is not between *criollos* or white people and Wichis (on this difference, see Unamuno, 2014), but between *criollos* from a small town and an inexperienced but competent white city physician. Both participants are defined by their wording of the pain suffered by the little boy who could not yet speak. In terms of Agha (2005, p. 39), Antonio's story introduces two distinct *social voices*, which can be defined as discursive figures that permit characterization in a metadiscourse of social types or personal attributes through characteristic lects or styles. In this case, the *criollos* are indexed by the "voice of the lifeworld" (Mishler, 1984): "problems in the stomach," "malaria," and "belly pain." The physician, on the other hand, rejects the parents' lay diagnosis ("he says no") and offers, instead, the "voice of medicine" (Mishler, 1984; see Bonnin, 2014, p. 159 ff.): "it's a gastroenteritis, it's nothing, it's gastroenteritis." The *criolla* woman does not understand ("what can it possibly be, she asks herself") or ask the physician for clarification. This is a typical sign of physician-patient asymmetry (due to their structurally different social roles), but does not necessarily refer to social distance between them (on this difference, see Bonnin, 2014, pp. 151–152). As the *criolla* woman cannot understand the technical term used by the physician, she arrives at a comic interpretation, mistaking "gastroenteritis" for "*gato enterito*" (whole cat).

This humoristic story provides a heteroglossic view of language that is not present at all in national or international institutional discourses: language barriers to health-care access are not just an inter-linguistic problem. Rather, in this example they are an inter-lect one, as the *criollo* couple cannot understand medical discourse. Thus, speakers of the same language may not understand each other because they embody different voices: the physician does not acknowledge the *criolla*'s account of her child's pain, and the *criolla* mishears the technical term used by the physician. This folk sociolinguistic hypothesis is opposed to the hypothesis of PAHO–Ministry of Health, which noted "difficulties in communication due to speaking different languages," addressing language contact as an obstacle to access.

Box 19.3   Interview with Antonio, Local SASOI Officer
(Participants: A: Antonio; R1: Researcher 1; R2: Researcher 2)

A: Aunque no lo creas, pero hay criollos también que, ¿no? criollos que no . . . tampoco no entienden su castilla. No sé si el castilla del blanco es . . .

R1: Es distinto. Mhm.

A: Tiene su interpretación, es distinto, no?

R1: Sí, es otra . . . otro dialecto digamos; aquí la gente criolla habla un dialecto del castellano muy cerrado y a veces muy diferente.

[. . .]

A: Sí, tengo un cuento de eso [. . .] resulta que había en un pueblito, era un doctor recién recibido, de la ciudad. Eh, está con todas las pilas, con todo su (choca las manos) su saber, (ríe) entonces viene al campo y viene una parejita de criollos, le llevaron a su hijito con problemas de estómago, de malaria, dicen ellos, de barriga, dolor de barriga. Entonces el doctor lo revisa bien, dice: "no, tu hijo tiene gastroenter- itis, no es nada; gastroenteritis tiene." La criolla lo mira, "qué será, gastroenter- itis," no sabe si entendió o escuchó mal. Entonces va al chico, lleva el chico y le preguntan "¿qué pasó?" "No," dice, "dice el doctor que no tiene nada el chico, dice que un gato enterito tiene en la panza."

A: Even though you may not believe it, there are *criollos* too who don't . . . *criollos* who either don't understand their Castilian [Spanish]. I don't know if the Castilian of whites is . . .

R1: It's different. Mhm.

A: It has its interpretation, it's different, right?

R1: Yes, it's another . . . another dialect, let's say; here *criollo* people speak a Castilian dialect that is very closed and sometimes very different.

[. . .]

A: Yes, I have a story about that [. . .] there was in a small village, it was a newly graduated doctor, from the city. Uh, he is full of energy, full of his (claps his hands) his knowledge, (laughs) then he comes to the countryside and a young *criollo* couple come, they brought their little son with problems in the stomach, with malaria, they say, with pain in the belly. Then the doctor checks him thoroughly, says: "no, your son has gastroenteritis, it's nothing; he has gastroenteritis." The *criolla* woman looks at him, "What can gastroenteritis possibly be?" She doesn't know if she un- derstood or heard wrong. Then she goes to the child, takes the child, and somebody asks "What happened?" "No," she says, "the doctor says the child has nothing, he says that he has a whole cat [*gato enterito* in Spanish] in his belly."

This theoretical view of language also extends to speakers: if medical interaction requires inter-lect communication, if languages are not neutral codes and there- fore cannot be perfectly translated into one another, then indigenous health workers are not simply interpreters who translate Wichi and Spanish in a single direction. Rather, they have a specific knowledge of health and the body that is relevant to the process of health-care communication.

The Wichi Educators

As in the field of health care, Wichi educators' ideas about language and knowledge differ from institutional ideas. The latter are embodied in the presence of bilingual assistants in classrooms who are intended to act as translators of non-indigenous teachers during their classes. These native teaching assistants, or NTAs (Auxiliares Docentes Aborígenes), have been appointed in Chaco Province since the 1990s and are the most common educational initiative in indigenous contexts.

In Box 19.4, the interview with a local school principal shows the institutional role attributed by white authorities to NTAs in the classroom.

Box 19.4 Interview with the Principal of 2256 School, September 2014 (Participants: SP: School Principal; R2: Researcher 2)

R2: ¿En qué grado están los auxiliares de los maestros?

SP: Están en primero y segundo.

R2: Los ADAs están en primero y segundo y los maestros también.

SP: También, pero están por una necesidad . . . que más se necesita de un maestro bilingüe o de un ADA es en primer grado o segundo grado porque son los chicos que recién ingresan a la escuela primera; ya tercero o cuarto ya hablan bien, para mí hablan bien

R2: In what grades do teaching assistants work?

SP: They're in first and second.

R2: The NTAs are in first and second and the teachers are as well.

SP: As well, but they're there in response to a need . . . that a bilingual teacher or an NTA are most needed in first or second grade because they are the children who are just starting school; by third or fourth they can speak well, in my opinion they speak well.

In this interview we observe, again, an institutional white authority who embodies the principles of the ideology of access. In first place, she describes the work of NTAs as "facilitators" who help monolingual Wichi children through their first years of schooling, until they are able to "speak [Spanish] well." As in the case of health-care workers, their role is not to adapt the school to indigenous students but, on the contrary, to allow indigenous people to overcome what appears to be their linguistic disability. Second, as in the case of indigenous health workers, NTAs have formal training as educators; their role should not be, therefore, to "assist" Wichi-speaking students but, rather, to teach classes to all students, both Wichi and white. Although they are supposed to work symmetrically in pairs with white teachers, forming a *pareja pedagógica* (pedagogical pair), they are often relegated to a secondary role as translators. We can observe this in Box 19.5.

In this example, Etelvina, an NTA, works together with Nora, the non-Wichi teacher. The roles, however, are not symmetrically distributed. Far from it: Nora

---

Box 19.5 Etelvina and Nora's Classroom, Kindergarten (Participants: E: Etelvina, NTA; N: Nora, Classroom Teacher; CH: Children, Pupils)

N: ¿Cómo se llamaba esto?

E: ¿HAP LEY?

CH: Tiza, tiza

N: ¿Y de color era esta tiza?

E: ¿EP HONTE T'OJH?

(a un niño) ¿YAJH WUYTSAMEJ
EP HONTE T'OJH?

CH: Rosada.

N: Rosada. Hoy vamos a trabajar ¿con?

CH: Tiza.

E: Con tiza; NAHONA TIZA.

N: Con una tiza mojada.

E: (a una niña que mira para otro lado)
¿Lucía?

N: En agua.

E: TISEÑHAT TOYHONA INOT,
TITSEWFNHU INOT

N: What was this called?

E: HAP LEY?

CH: Chalk, chalk.

N: And what color was this chalk?

E: EP HONTE T'OJH?

(to one child) YAJH WUYTSAMEJ
EP HONTE T'OJH?

CH: Pink.

N: Pink. Today we're going to work with?

CH: Chalk

E: With chalk; NAHONA TIZA.

N: With a wet chalk.

E: (to a girl who is looking the other way)
Lucía?

N: In water.

E: TISEÑHAT TOYHONA INOT (.)
TITSEWFNHU INOT

---

leads the class and proposes a painting task, and during the class, Etelvina provides linguistic assistance to Nora, monitoring the attention of Wichi children and offering supplementary explanations to ensure understanding and participation in the Spanish-driven activity. Again, the role of the NTA is not to bring white teachers closer to their students' language and culture but, instead, to enable indigenous pupils to participate in the class.

Over the past decade, however, the structure of the *pareja pedagógica* has been progressively displaced by another type of teaching organization, placing intercultural bilingual teachers solely in charge of the class. This new classroom organization is resisted by white institutions and their authorities. This resistance is visible at different levels. At schools, we have just seen that indigenous teachers are forced to accept an auxiliary role as interpreters or linguistic assistants of white teachers. In other spheres of public discussion, teaching unions do not recognize the professional competences of these new teachers in public education because indigenous teachers become competitors for jobs previously reserved to white workers (Unamuno, 2014). Nevertheless, the right to have their own classes is one of the strongest political vindications of indigenous movements in Chaco.

As we have documented in recent years, bilinguals have gradually gained positions in schools and have built up an effective pressure group at the provincial level to establish themselves as partners in the design and implementation of educational policies. Their view on the traditional roles attributed to Wichi teachers at schools is rather critical. As in the case of health care, they do not see themselves as linguistic assistants or interpreters. On the contrary, bilingual intercultural teachers demand a different relationship between education and languages regarding at least three aspects: (1) inclusion of the whole class (both Wichi and non-Wichi children) in the activities conducted in the Wichi language, in the understanding that bilingual education is an educational policy and not simply an aid to indigenous people; (2) inclusion of Wichi cultural contents that are not in the mandatory curriculum; and (3) teaching of Spanish as second language to many children who are monolingual, or almost monolingual, in indigenous languages.

The demands of Wichi teachers are new ways of bringing bilingualism into the classroom, including new contents they teach together with the Western curriculum. Outside the classrooms, these teachers have mobilized to oppose the limited traditional role attributed to them at schools. The vignette in Box 19.6, excerpted from fieldwork notes, illustrates this statement.

Box 19.6 "At a Teachers' Meeting": Field Notes, September 2014

Today we spent the whole morning at the Meeting of Wichi Teachers [. . .] After the speeches by Etelvina and Lucrecia, an interesting discussion arose: Lisandro supported an initiative of other teachers at his school who refused to translate the principal's speeches and patriotic songs. He also said that they could make a translated list of anniversaries to be used by all teachers. The rest agreed that they were also tired of translating. One of them, Joaquin, suggested preparing a collective document specifying the bilinguals' teaching duties and stating that translating is not one of them. "They should hire an interpreter" said Pablo, laughing.

CONCLUSIONS

In this chapter we have documented the emergence of bilinguals as an outcome of a recent phenomenon in Argentina: the valorization of Spanish-Wichi bilingualism as a professional qualification to apply for state positions in the field of public health care and education. This phenomenon responds simultaneously to different discourses. At the national and regional level, legislation (re)produces an ideology of access that seeks to guarantee the inclusion of native people in Western medicine and schooling. From this perspective, indigenous languages are a cultural barrier that prevents natives from accessing proper (Western) health care and education. The bilinguals are thus seen as interpreters whose main role is to facilitate this unidirectional access from particular deprived contexts to universal rights.

At the local level, however, bilinguals sustain a political discourse of identity, which rejects the monoglossic view of language as a neutral code and, instead, considers language and knowledge as two inseparable dimensions of their own identities. By casting off the ideology of access, indigenous health and education workers aim to transform the very same institutions that originally appointed them.

By doing so, the bilinguals address some core ideological meanings of the modern nation-state, as they reject both the identification of language and citizenship and a monoglossic conception of language. This active rejection is apparent in their explicit conceptions of language as an inseparable part of identity and also in their medical and educational practices, in which they dispute the subordinated role assigned to Wichi language and knowledge.

Analysis shows the actual production of language policies at different levels, which are contested and reinterpreted—practically and theoretically—from the margins, by the same indigenous people who are supposed to implement them passively. The use of ethnographically informed discourse analysis seems to be useful to reveal tensions between two ideologies: the institutional, which we call the ideology of access, and the indigenous, which we call the ideology of identity.

The case analysis presented herein discusses the role of local actors in the definition of language policies and their sense and performativity. Bilinguals' everyday actions and opinions, as they constitute the meaningful dimension of systematic actions regarding languages, are a veritable language policy that is designed, planned, and implemented by its own beneficiaries.

The actual scope of these alternative policies is not apparent. On the one hand, it could be argued that they will not have much effect on other native communities, as they are not encoded or materialized in laws and legal regulations. On the other hand, however, we observed that Wichis actually defy and confront laws and legal dispositions, engaging in grassroots activism by blocking roads or taking over state institutions, such as the local hospital. Through these political practices, Wichi people actually produce language policies on indigenous languages, sometimes regulating de facto ambiguous laws, sometimes creating new legal and juridical categories with (or without) special legal dispositions.

This process involves forceful action in the public space, and is not a top-down effect of international commitments. Moreover, it is framed by ideologies that provide symbolic support for policies, whether state- or indigenous-made, embodied in daily practices and discourses. Thus, it is at the crossroad of practices, discourses, and political action that language policies are actually made by the bilinguals in *El Chaco*. It is through daily interaction at hospitals and schools, and not through the legal discourse of the state, that we can best understand how politically powerful language policies might become.

In a wider sense, we think it is necessary to reconsider the central place that research gives to the role of the state as a LPP agent. We underline in this chapter the importance of including the study of the political actions of other actors regarding languages, in order to construct a deeper understanding of the complex relationships between agency and transformation of the sociolinguistic field. The consideration of the interplay between different actors and political actions allows us to denaturalize the repertoire of policy actions of the state, and place them in the frame of the ideological conditions in which they occur and of the interests to which they respond. In this sense, the ideology of access, described in public texts and in daily practices of state institutions, is linked to the state's role in the reproduction of the status quo. Its actions toward the recognition of cultural rights unlinked to economic rights are functional to this reproduction. Thus, grassroots activism—including language, but not limited to it—needs to be careful of its own success.

ACKNOWLEDGMENTS

This work is part of the project PICT-2013-2283 funded by the National Agency for Scientific and Technological Promotion. We want to thank Camilo Ballena and Lucía Romero for their collaboration with the transcripts. Also, we would like to thank the editors of this *Handbook*, who have helped us to improve this chapter in many ways. In particular, we would like to thank Wichi health workers and teachers for their interest in and support of our work. Thank you.

NOTES

1. "Accesibilidad a los servicios de salud [. . .] La principal barrera es la falta de accesibilidad geográfica, *cultural* y económica [. . .]. Las personas indígenas reciben deficiente atención en los centros de salud, ya sea por discriminación en el sistema o por las *dificultades para comunicarse por hablar lenguas distintas*" (Ministerio de Salud de la Nación, *Situación de salud, intervenciones y líneas de investigación para la toma de decisiones en salud con pueblos indígenas en Argentina*, p. 10).

2. "La Educación Intercultural Bilingüe promueve un diálogo mutuamente enriquecedor de conocimientos y valores entre los pueblos indígenas y poblaciones étnica, lingüística y culturalmente diferentes, y propicia el reconocimiento y el respeto hacia tales diferencias" (Ley 26.206, art. 52).

3. "Al 2016, todas las jurisdiccionales desarrollan formatos institucionales de atención a niños y niñas con necesidades educativas específicas (ruralidad, privación de la libertad de sus madres, interculturalidad y bilingüismo, alumnos/as-padres discapacidad, en atención hospitalaria y domiciliaria)" (*Plan Nacional de Educación Obligatoria y Formación Docente 2012–2016*; CFE No. 188/12).

4. "La comunicación entre culturas o comunicación intercultural, es entendida básicamente como intercambio de información a través del lenguaje" (Ministry of Health, *Interculturalidad y salud*, 50).

5. "Ampliar y mejorar las condiciones y formas de acceso," "jardines en contextos interculturales y bilingües," "estudiantes en contextos de interculturalidad y bilingüismo")" (*Plan Nacional de Educación Obligatoria y Formación Docente 2012-2016*; CFE No. 188/12).

6. The expression "white" is used by Wichi people to refer to non-indigenous people. In this chapter we take this native category in the sense in which they use it.

References

Agha, A. (2005). Voice, footing, enregisterment. *Journal of Linguistic Anthropology* 15(1), 38–59.

Arnoux, E., & Bein, R. (2010). *La regulación política de las prácticas lingüísticas* [The political regulation of language practices]. Buenos Aires: Eudeba.

Arnoux, E., & Nothstein, S. (Eds.). (2014). *Temas de glotopolítica: Integración regional sudamericana y panhispanismo* [Issues on glotopolitics: South American and Panhispanic regional integration]. Buenos Aires: Biblos.

Blommaert, J. (2009). Language, asylum, and the national order. *Current Anthropology* 50(4), 415–441.

Blommaert, J. (2010). *The sociolinguistics of globalization*. Cambridge: Cambridge University Press.

Bonnin, J. E. (2014). To speak with the other's voice: Reducing asymmetry and social distance in mental health care admission interviews. *Journal of Multicultural Discourses* 9(2), 149–171.

Codo, E., Patiño, A., & Unamuno, V. (2012). Hacer sociolingüística con perspectiva etnográfica: Retos y dilemas [Doing sociolinguistics with ethnographic perspective: Challenges and dilemmas]. *Spanish in Context* 9(2), 157–190.

Consejo Federal de Educación. (2012). *Resolución CFE No. 188/12: Plan nacional de educación obligatoria y formación docente 2012-2016* [Resolution CFE N° 188/12: National Plan of Mandatory Education and Teacher's Training]. Buenos Aires: Ministerio de Educación de la Nación.

Giovanella, L., Feo, O., & Faria, M. (2012). *Sistema de salud en Sudamérica: Desafíos para la universalidad, la integralidad y la equidad* [Health system in South America: Challenges or universality, integrality and equity]. Río de Janeiro: ISAGS.

Guespin, L., & Marcellesi, J. B. (1986). Pour la glottopolitique. *Langages* 21(83), 5–31.

Heller, M. (2001). Undoing the macro/micro dichotomy: Ideology and categorisation in a linguistic minority school. In N. Coupland, S. Sarangi, & C. N. Candlin (Eds.), *Sociolinguistics and social theory* (pp. 212–234). London: Longman.

Heller, M. (2011). Critical ethnographic sociolinguistics. In M. Heller (Ed.), *Paths to postnationalism: A critical ethnography of language and identity* (pp. 31–50). Oxford: Oxford University Press.

Hornberger, N. (1995). Ethnography in linguistic perspective: Understanding school processes. *Language and Education* 9(4), 233–248.

International Labour Organization. (1989). Convention No. 169. *Indigenous and Tribal Peoples Convention*. Retrieved from http://www.ilo.org/dyn/normlex/en/f?p=NORMLEX PUB:12100:0::NO::P12100_INSTRUMENT_ID:312314

Johnson, D. C., & Ricento, T. (2013). Conceptual and theoretical perspectives in language planning and policy: Situating the ethnography of language policy. *International Journal of the Sociology of Language* 219, 7–21.

López, L. E., & Küper, W. (1999). La educación intercultural bilingüe en América Latina: Balance y perspectivas [Bilingual intercultural education in Latin America: Balance and perspectives]. *Revista Iberoamericana de Educación* 20, 17–85.

López, L. E., & Sichra, I. (2008). Intercultural bilingual education among indigenous peoples in Latin America. In J. Cummins & N. Hornberger (Eds), *Bilingual education* (2nd edition; pp. 295–310). New York: Springer.

Ministerio de Salud de la Nación. (2012). *Interculturalidad y salud: Capacitación en servicio para trabajadores de la salud en el primer nivel de atención* [Interculturality and health care: Training at workplace for primary healthcare agents]. Buenos Aires: Ministerio de Salud.

Mishler, E. G. (1984). *The discourse of medicine: Dialectics of medical interviews*. Norwood: Alex Publishing.

Provincia de Chaco, Poder Legislativo. (1987). *Ley 3258 de las comunidad de indígenas* [Law 3258 of indigenous communities]. Retrieved from http://www2.legislaturachaco.gov. ar:8000/legisdev/ResumenDocumento.aspx?docId=L.3258&tipo=Ley.

Provincia de Chaco, Poder Legislativo. (2014). *Ley 7446 de educación pública de gestión comunitaria bilingüe intercultural indígena* [Bill on Indigenous Intercultural Bilingual Community-Managed Public Education]. Retrieved from http://www2.legislaturachaco. gov.ar:8000/legisdev/ResumenDocumento.aspx?docId=L.7446&tipo=Ley

República Argentina, Poder Legislativo. (2006). *Ley 26206 de educación nacional* [Act of National Education]. Retrieved from http://www.me.gov.ar/doc_pdf/ley_de_educ_nac. pdf

Tollefson, J. W. (1991). *Planning language, planning inequality: Language policy in the community*. London: Longman.

Tollefson, J. W. (2008). Language planning in education. In N. H. Hornberger (Ed.), *Encyclopedia of language and education* (pp. 3–14). New York: Springer.

Unamuno, V. (2014). Language dispute and social change in new multilingual institutions in Chaco, Argentina. *International Journal of Multilingualism* 11(4), 409–429.

Unamuno, V. (2015). Los hacedores de la EIB: Un acercamiento a las políticas lingüístico educativas desde las aulas bilingües del Chaco [The BIE makers: A close up to linguistic and educational policies at bilingual classrooms at Chaco]. *Archivos Analíticos de Políticas Educativas* 23(101), 1–35.

United Nations. (1948). *Universal declaration of human rights*. Retrieved from http://www. un.org/en/universal-declaration-human-rights/index.html

United Nations. (1976). *International covenant on economic, social and cultural rights*. Retrieved from https://treaties.un.org/Pages/ViewDetails.aspx?src=IND&mtdsg_no=IV-3&=4&clang=_en

United Nations. (2007). *United Nations declaration on the rights of indigenous peoples*. Retrieved from http://www.un.org/esa/socdev/unpfii/documents/DRIPS_en.pdf

Wright, S. (2004). *Language policy and language planning. From nationalism to globalisation*. New York: Palgrave Macmillan.

CHAPTER 20

CRITICAL COMMUNITY LANGUAGE POLICIES IN EDUCATION

SOLOMON ISLANDS CASE

KAREN ANN WATSON-GEGEO, DAVID W. GEGEO, AND BILLY FITO'O

The community has been the incubator of indigenous resistance . . .. But resistance is not an end, it is a means [to] achieve a people's own form of liberation.

—B. Maldonado Alvarado (2010, p. 369)

OUR community is not concerned with formal school curriculum and accreditation right now. We have hundreds of youth back on Malaita, we must do something before they return to Honiara in a deluge. The first thing is schools. Schools where nobody fails because learning is not measured by tests, but by lived experience, transformation, and empowerment—as in our indigenous ways of teaching. Where everybody learns literacy in their own language and English, and to critically analyze what is going on in the Solomons now, to prepare youth to build a life for themselves. The secondary school we're building in South Malaita is for basic education that these youth had no access to in the *Tenson* period.

—Robert Tetehano, former secondary principal
(interviewed by Gegeo, May 10, 2015)

WE live in an era of accelerating sociopolitical change, linguistic complexity, disappearing indigenous languages, and population pressures that both unite and divide people in their educational goals. Although national language policies dominate school systems in most countries, increasingly indigenous movements have sought to shape language policy and planning (LPP) at the local level. What are the effects of a shift in educational policymaking from the national (macro) level to the community (micro) level? How are macro- and micro-level concerns negotiated? Critical community language policy and planning in education (CCLPE) focuses on these and related questions, and is an interdisciplinary strand of research bringing together scholars in applied linguistics, anthropology, education, ethnic studies, and rural development theory.

The origins of CCLPE, as an area of study and a methodological approach, coincide with the turn to critical approaches and ethnography in the early 1980s. Critical approaches situate differential positioning of languages in a society as "a manifestation of asymmetrical power relations based on social structures and ideologies" (Ricento, 2006, p. 15), especially between national government institutions vis-à-vis communities and indigenous populations. Thus CCLPE researchers, working at the community level, necessarily need to understand specific situations in detail. By the mid-1980s, they adopted ethnographic research methods and critical discourse analysis (CDA) to study community language issues and analyze in-depth interviews with teachers and other educational stakeholders at the local level.

Several of the terms important to this chapter are illustrated in the opening quotations. Maldonado Alvarado, well-known Mexican anthropologist, has carried out critical ethnographic educational research for thirty years in rural Oaxaca. He addresses resistance, that is, local people resisting asymmetrical power relations with the national government that would obliterate their indigenous language. His work illustrates community autonomy grounded in place, culture, and language among indigenous people who have experienced loss of land to agribusiness and the undermining of their languages through nationally imposed Spanish-only schools. For these people, resistance is not just a refusal to comply with national policies; it is a group's assertion of their agency in shaping the language policy process, and therefore a form of liberation.

The second quotation, from educator Robert Tetehano, describes a secondary school that he and his community are building in South Malaita, Solomon Islands (SI). The curriculum of the school is rooted in indigenous epistemology. Indigenous epistemology and critical praxis are ancient constituents of what we term *deep culture* in SI societies (Watson-Gegeo & Gegeo, 2004). Indigenous epistemology refers to "a cultural group's ways of thinking and of creating, reformulating, and theorizing about knowledge via traditional discourses and media of communication, anchoring the truth of the discourse in culture" and experience (Gegeo & Watson-Gegeo, 2001, p. 58). Indigenous critical praxis refers to "people's own critical reflection" on culture, history, knowledge, politics, economics, language(s), and the "sociopolitical contexts in which they are living," and then acting on these critical reflections (p. 60).

Tetehano's goal parallels Freire's (1970, 1994) literacy for critical consciousness and empowerment, and is shared by many SI communities, especially now, in the aftermath of the ethnic conflict (see later discussion in this chapter). His use of the terms *experience, transformation*, and *empowerment* are direct English translations of words for these concepts in indigenous SI languages.

In the sections that follow, we first offer a brief overview of CCLPE, including engaged language policy (ELP), whereby many CCLPE researchers choose to work in communities as allies and learners, "engaging [community members] in critical dialogue as a life-changing process" (Davis, 2014a, p. 91). Then we turn to an example of CCLPE via our work in the Solomon Islands, focusing primarily on Malaita, in the wake of the *Tenson* (ethnic conflict) between Guadalcanal and Malaita (1998–2007). The political and social fallout from that period reverberates in multiple ways now that RAMSI (Regional Assistance Mission to SI), a United Nations–style military intervention led by Australia and New Zealand and sent to the Solomon Islands in 2003, substantially withdrew in 2013 (Fraenkel, Madraiwiwi, & Okole, 2014), and finally exited June 30, 2017 (Dobell, 2017, p. 1), leaving an uncertain future for the Solomons. We contextualize our analysis of the evolving educational situation of post-conflict Malaita by tracing the turning points for LPP in SI history. Our analysis is based on work by the first two authors on critical ELP with Kwara'ae people in Malaita since 1978, and Fito'o's (2016) completed doctoral research on current community educational initiatives in Malaita. Gegeo and Fito'o are both indigenous Kwara'ae.

Finally, we discuss implications of the SI case for community LPP and the future of education in the Solomons. While acknowledging the continuity between the institutional policies of the Solomon Islands as a modern nation-state, we focus on local processes of uncertainty and instability in times of sudden or rapid social change that have served to undermine community faith in the nation-state. We show through our case study that indigenous communities have learned over time that they can exert their agency to shape LPP from the bottom up, and that they recognize that the shaping must be grounded in indigenous language(s) and culture(s). This argument is not new, but it is consistent with the call for epistemological and ontological diversity that is increasingly being advanced in development theory, education, and related studies internationally (Dei, Hall, & Rosenberg, 2000; Gegeo & Watson-Gegeo, 2013b; Pallas, 2001).

PARADIGM SHIFTS IN LANGUAGE POLICY AND PLANNING

The scholarly study of LPP has been characterized over the past few decades by dramatic theoretical shifts, motivated by the rapid changes of globalization, neoliberalism, and hybridization in a world of superdiversity (the latter referring to the proliferation of language varieties and ethnic populations, especially through migration) (Blommaert & Rampton, 2011; Vertovec, 2007). These processes have affected most areas of the world, but often in differential ways. The shift away from conventional LPP models toward critical studies (Pennycook, 2001; Tollefson, 2006, 2013), ethnographic methods (Hornberger & Johnson, 2007), and ELP (Davis, 2014b) has challenged previous assumptions about agency in impoverished and politically disempowered communities. The degree to which linguistic minority populations can influence decision-making at the regional or national level, or can undertake local-level LPP, is affected by many processes, including sometimes unanticipated changes in national policy (Zhang, 2013).

In the earlier conventional paradigm formulated under modernization theory, *unplanned LPP* refers to local-level LPP. The assumption is that although community efforts may serendipitously produce favorable results, they often undermine official, national-level plans and policies (Baldauf, 1994). Modernization theory, which shaped development in decolonizing societies from the post–World War II era until recently, gave rise to national LPP, whereby the nation-state tasks its agencies with adopting a standard national language and/or promoting one or more international languages. These macro-level decisions are typically made with the help of expatriate professionals, but little community input. The research focus of this neoclassical model (Tollefson, 1991) is on learner variables, downplaying social, cultural, and political context. Individual learner variables are taken as the key measure for the success of LPP, the assimilation of linguistic minorities into a national or international language is assumed necessary, and little serious attention is paid to issues of minority identity.

In the 1980s and 1990s, critical scholars challenged the previously assumed political neutrality of LPP assumptions based on modernization theory. They argued that the conventional LPP framework was "detrimental to the development of equitable language policies in complex multilingual settings" (Ricento, 2006, p. 14). The resulting shift of perspective to power and inequality led researchers to examine the "impact of coercive policies on language learning and language behavior" (Tollefson, 2013, p. 26). If we ask why an individual chooses to speak a particular language, we prioritize "the social, political and economic factors [that] constrain or impel changes" in language structure and use (Tollefson, 1991, p. 7).

Modernization theory and the earlier conventional LPP model that emphasized macro-structural economic and linguistic planning seemed to point the way to success and prosperity for poor societies. But by the 1980s, the realization of the importance of micro-structural processes in education was driven by the failure of Eurocentric modernization theory to deliver on its promises for development. The dramatic historical changes brought by late capitalism, globalization, wars rooted in colonial history, and migration radically altered places where LPP professionals work. Tollefson (2013, p. 28) argues that the shift to a "relatively creative public sphere paradigm" emphasizes "the agency of all actors in the policy-making process," despite the "coercive and deterministic" circumstances in which they live. This shift is illustrated by the rise of ethnography, CCLPE, and ELP.

The rise of ethnography, also referred to as the *ethnographic turn*, includes the use of critical ethnographic theory and method, CDA, and a concern with linking micro and maco levels of analysis in order to produce *thick explanation*. The ethnographic turn, articulated in Hornberger and Johnson's (2007, 2011) proposal for an ethnography of language policy (2011, p. 273), emerged from work in the 1980s, maturing in the 1990s (Davis, 1994; Hornberger, 1988; Watson-Gegeo, 1988; Watson-Gegeo & Gegeo, 1992). Ethnography involves a "commitment to taking a long hard look at empirical processes that make no sense within established frameworks" (Blommaert & Rampton, 2011, p. 10). Critical ethnography (Carspecken, 1996; Madison, 2012), integrated with CDA (Fairclough, 2010; Van Dijk, 1993), is essential for relating micro-level interaction to macro-level social organization, and for moving beyond *thick description* to *thick explanation* (Watson-Gegeo, 1992).

As a result of this shift in LPP research, community LPP studies have multiplied since the first decade of the 2000s (see Canagarajah, 2004; Skutnabb-Kangas & Heugh, 2012). Kamwendo (2005) points out that many of these studies (including his in Northern Malawi) constitute *language planning from below* that emerges from grassroots activism rather than decisions by the state authorities. Moreover, local agents such as teachers are often the instigators of change, as in Nero's (2013) study of de facto language education policy in Jamaica, and Coelho and Henze's (2013) in rural Nicaragua (see Menken & Garcia, 2010).

Davis (2014a, p. 83) describes ELP as "grounded in critical theory and informed by political activism." She argues that "[m]oving towards the local suggests acknowledging not only traditions, but also innovation that realistically meets situated socioeconomic traditions" (pp. 83–84). Moreover, "[t]he practice of ELP, first and foremost, means focusing on the centrality of [researchers] engaging in critical dialogue as a life-changing process" with community members, teachers, and educational officials (pp. 91–92). Such a research program is exemplified especially by Davis and her co-researchers' work with teachers and youth in Nepal (Davis, Phyak, & Bui, 2012; Phyak & Bui, 2013).

We turn now to the specific case of community LPP in Malaita, Solomon Islands, where Watson-Gegeo and Gegeo have conducted CCLPE as engaged researchers undertaking critical dialogue with villagers and teachers since the late 1970s, and Fito'o (2016) recently. In the following section, we examine historical crises and turning points in LPP leading to and including the present, addressing how Malaitans have responded and continue to respond to current fluid social conditions at the national level, by building educational programs through critical community effort at the local level.

CRITICAL COMMUNITY LANGUAGE POLICY
AND PLANNING IN MALAITA

Located in the Western Pacific, the Solomon Islands consist of six major and hundreds of smaller islands and atolls, grouped into nine provinces with seventy indigenous languages, the official language of English, and the lingua franca SI Pijin (SIP), spoken in a total population of 550,000 (UNESCAP, 2013). Malaita Province is home to 27% of the nation's population, and ten to thirteen indigenous languages (see Solomon Islands Population and Housing Census, ca. 2010). Our focus is on the two main islands: Malaita and, at its southeastern tip, separated by a narrow ocean strait, South Malaita. Most of our data come from Kwara'ae, the indigenous language/culture with the largest number of speakers in the Solomons.

In the following sub-sections, we address historical crises and turning points for LPP on Malaita: missionization/colonialism, the Maasina Rule movement, modernization and the failure of rural development, the ethnic *Tenson* (conflict)/RAMSI period, and contemporary community initiatives in the post-*Tenson* present. Historical events and struggles over language are important background for understanding the contemporary situation of CCLPE because these events and struggles are still part of oral and written history passed across generations in villages. At the community level, current issues are always contextualized in past experience, thinking, and debates by participants in village meetings where decisions are made.

These meetings take place in high rhetoric, the formal discourse register of the Kwara'ae language. Even when speakers fail to command the intricacies of high rhetoric register, they attempt to follow the speaking style and structure of it. High rhetoric is semantically complex, involving a large, rich lexicon of abstract terms with subtle distinctions for discussing concepts and ideas. In critical discussion and debate, participants dialogically deconstruct and reconstruct history and planning, using a variety of named epistemological strategies that guide logical reasoning and the presentation of evidence (Gegeo & Watson-Gegeo, 2001, 2002, 2013b). It is through such traditional epistemological strategies that villagers draw lessons from the past and relate them to current circumstances and educational needs. In the case of CCLPE, the meetings and interviews we recorded cover five generations.

CCLPE DURING MISSIONIZATION AND
EARLY COLONIALISM

In the 1870s, several thousand islanders (primarily Malaitans) were taken, willingly on contract or forcibly by kidnapping (termed *blackbirding*), to work on plantations in colonial Australia (Akin, 2013; Bennett, 1987). There, Malaitans gained a reputation for hard work, stamina, and resistance to authority. The majority returned home when plantations began to be established on Guadalcanal (1880s–1890s). Returnees brought back an English-based pidgin created on plantations that by the 1970s had evolved into SIP, the lingua franca creole of today. Many also brought the South Sea Evangelical Mission (now Church, SSEC), formed by white missionaries on the plantations. During their years of plantation labor in Queensland, some islanders learned English, which they used to protest living conditions and contract terms (Watson-Gegeo, 1987). Back home on Malaita, in village meetings they shared their observations of white/European life, values, abuse of workers, racism, and protest. Villagers began to realize the potential power of acquiring English to push back against colonialism. However, because access to Western education and English was very limited at the time, traditional education continued in formal meetings and mentoring, using indigenous languages (Watson-Gegeo & Gegeo, 1990).

When the British Solomon Islands Protectorate (BSIP) was declared in 1893, missionization was already underway, having begun in 1848 with the establishment of the Melanesian Mission, Anglican (now Church of Melanesia, CM). A variety of other Christian denominations soon established missions throughout the Solomons. Although colonization was justified by the British as pacification, to end what was claimed to be constant warfare among tribes, it was instead aimed primarily at protecting missionaries and stopping German claims on the island chain (Bennett, 1987).

For many decades, the Anglican church exercised the primary influence on how schools developed in Malaita (Hilliard, 1978). From the beginning, the "vexing language question" (Whiteman, 1983, p. 180) was debated in the clergy and community: Which language (English or local indigenous languages) should be the medium of instruction in classrooms? Some supported English as the language of colonial administration, business, and "secular knowledge," arguing that such knowledge would be essential to islanders' future participation in the larger world (Hilliard, 1978, p. 204). Others supported indigenous languages, for children's depth and ease of understanding, and literacy development in their native language. Eventually, English became the official language for government, business, and schooling. Kwara'ae villagers used the term *sukulu* (from English *school*) to refer to Western education (including missionary church services), which they saw as different from traditional education (*fa'amanata'anga,* formal teaching in high rhetoric Kwara'ae that would create *ngwae ali'afu,* a "complete person").

However, for several decades before and after World War II, a division in attitudes toward Westernization grew between members of the SSEC (supportive) and CM (invested in traditional culture) (see Watson-Gegeo & Gegeo's [1991] discussion of language attitudes, discourse patterns, and linguistic differences by church affiliation in the late 1980s). The few village children who attended school, typically for one to three years, did learn some English. They transferred their literacy skills to Kwara'ae, and taught non-schooled children and adults to read and write Kwara'ae, using early orthographies developed by missionaries. Literacy skills in Kwara'ae meant that families could stay in touch with relatives working in plantations on Guadalcanal and elsewhere.

At the end of this historical period, villagers' critical community discussions acknowledged the overwhelming power of the colonial military police. When resistance to colonial policies (such as taxation of impoverished villagers) sporadically erupted at the local level, the British response was stern military retaliation, imprisonment, and executions (Fox, 1967; Keesing & Corris, 1980; Laracy, 1983). Treatment of workers on island plantations was also harsh. Villagers had aspirations for improving their situations, but the possibilities of doing so were very limited.

Village experience of English from the early colonial period was that English was the language of government, police, nurses/doctors, and missions. As communities realized that a measure of power and ability to enter more fully into the growing cash economy depended on going to school, villagers turned to making decisions about who should go to school. Missions did not provide free education, and tuitions were high, given village poverty. At the community level, critical discussion focused on keeping an oldest son and daughter at home, to be immersed in Kwara'ae language and traditional knowledge; the son would become head of the kin unit later in life. It was decided that at least one younger sibling would be sent to school. That decision was sometimes made on the basis of which younger child of a kin group seemed most apt to do well in school, and then group resources would be invested in that child. Children who went to school would learn English and Western knowledge, obtain a job in a colonial service, and then help support the larger family or kin group. *Support* involved helping to pay the government *head tax* on each adult male, and contributing to school tuitions for a sibling or relative. Critical praxis at this time aimed to share linguistic and monetary resources within communities, and balance the demands of a colonial world with traditional culture.

WORLD WAR II, THE MAASINA RULE MOVEMENT, AND NASCENT COMMUNITY LANGUAGE POLICY AND PLANNING

World War II brought many changes to the Solomons. As Bennett (1978, p. 19) aptly expresses it, World War II "shattered and totally destroyed the order of the white planters' world." Islanders' lives and perspectives were dramatically changed by the experiences of seeing the British retreat in front of the advancing Japanese. The American military invasion, beginning with the Battle of Guadalcanal in

1942, revealed the horror of artillery, bombs, and mass slaughter in modern war-fare. Malaitans (especially) were recruited by the British to join the Labour Corps, to serve in the war effort as soldiers, scouts, and carriers. Working side by side with Americans, islanders were impressed by the American soldiers' generosity and willingness to treat them as equals (unlike the British), as well as their support for Islanders' intentions to free themselves from British rule, as had the Americans be-fore them (White, Gegeo, Akin, & Watson-Gegeo, 1988). Moreover, as British co-lonial leaders fled Guadalcanal during the invasion, islanders felt that the British had abandoned them, in contrast to the Americans who came to rescue and fight beside them.

After the war, inspired by World War II experiences, in 1946 the Maasina Rule movement formed on Malaita and spread to Guadalcanal. Maasina Rule was both a cultural revitalization and a political independence movement (Worsley, 1968). Malaita had long been considered the "most politically fragmented island" (Laracy, 1983, p. 6) in the Solomons, because of its multiple languages and cultures. Now Malaitans came together with an island identity (even a "proto-nationalist polit-ical" identity; Worsley, 1968, p. 182), whether or not given individuals actually joined the movement (some pursued a separate path to self-rule from inside the colonial government).

English became the language of protest, generating "a mass of writing" in which islanders "spoke of and for themselves" (Laracy, 1983, pp. 6–7) for the first time. In lengthy community meetings using indigenous debate strategies, Maasina Rule members set up towns and a hierarchical administration, integrating a local view of colonial organization with traditional indigenous governance through chiefs, elders, and priests. The meetings used local Malaita or Guadalcanal languages where pos-sible, and a mix of SIP and English in cross-linguistic situations.

Although the British sought to discredit the movement by planting *cargo cult* ideas into some of its membership, ultimately in 1953 movement leaders succeeded in negotiating with a new resident commissioner the establishment of the first lo-cally governed Malaita Council (Bennett, 1987, p. 296). Delegates from various polit-ical factions on Malaita elected Salana Gaʻa (West Kwaraʻae, a Maasina Rule leader) as the Council's first president. Thus, Malaitans achieved a significant measure of self-rule through community action (Worsley, 1968). In the 1980s, Gegeo and Watson-Gegeo conducted extensive interviews of surviving Kwaraʻae activists, including Salana Gaʻa, Naphtali Rigamanu, Fr. David Ramotalau, and others on Maasaina Rule, and David Buamae on the Malaita Council movement. The success of the Malaita Council set the stage for self-governance of the Solomons in 1976, and full independence in 1978. Wanting to divest their expensive colonial possessions, the British were willing to turn the Solomons over to Australian/New Zealand he-gemony, and did little to prepare the islanders for nationhood.

Nevertheless, for many Malaitans, their resistance and successful struggle for in-dependence was an important experience in the power of community action and in communicating across language differences. As they reviewed their history going back to *blackbirding* days and forward to national independence, they felt optimistic about a future that would truly balance traditional culture and *ala'anga fanoa* (indigenous language) with English in nation building.

MODERNIZATION AND THE FAILURE OF RURAL DEVELOPMENT

The end of World War II was the beginning of the rural development era (1960s–1990s), guided by modernization theory. The Solomons were flooded with outside advisors and projects that devalued local cultures. The colonial (and national) government initiated several important development projects. One was the 1960s 'Asai Demonstration Farm in West Kwara'ae that dislocated and broke up kin groups that had originally formed a thriving and ecologically diverse community there (Gegeo, 1994). When 'Asai Farm failed miserably, the government abandoned it suddenly, leaving behind severe, permanent ecological damage, and great economic loss for local villagers. 'Asai farm's destruction injected into villagers' consciousness the capitalist notion of direct, individual land ownership, leading to many continuing land disputes. None of the development initiatives from government or outside consultants was based in indigenous knowledge or the local environment, and all left behind environmental destruction.

After independence, the national government took over control of schools from the missions, mandating English-only instruction. Expatriate teachers were replaced with SI teachers, often from other islands. Government teacher-training programs were set up, but a teacher shortage led to the government's posting individuals categorized as "partially trained" and "untrained" teachers to rural schools, often limiting "fully" trained teachers to more developed urban areas. In the 1970s–1990s, nearly 40% of Malaita's teachers were untrained and knew very little English, 40% of the children were not in school, 63% of the population had no schooled education, and in many years the national government sent no teaching materials to schools at all (Watson-Gegeo & Gegeo, 1994). Not surprisingly, Malaitans had the poorest record of all the Provinces for passing the national examination into secondary school.

Community responses to these conditions were variable. At times, delegations of village parents and teachers went to the Provincial headquarters in Auki to seek help in improving schools, arguing for the teaching of English through the use of indigenous languages, but the Province had neither the authority nor resources to help. In some villages, school leavers (with 3–6 years of schooling) set up impromptu lessons on Sunday afternoons to teach younger children who were unschooled or were faring poorly in school.

By the 1980s, the deep distrust Malaitans felt toward the colonial government had become redirected toward the new national government because of its failure to bring meaningful development to rural areas, its astounding level of corruption regarding logging contracts, bribes, and graft, and the growing gap in wealth between government officials in Honiara (the nation's capital on Guadalcanal) and rural villagers. The constant message from government agencies and outsiders that villagers were ignorant, inferior, and needed to give up their cultures and languages in order to "develop" (Watson-Gegeo & Gegeo, 1992, 1995) contributed to community disaffection with government-mandated English-only schooling. During the 1960s–1990s, village families made great sacrifices to pay for one or more of their children to attend school (tuitions skyrocketed after the government took over the schools). School was still about learning English well in order to get a job, yet jobs were few for graduates, and the great majority of students failed, returning in defeat and shame to live the lives of their parents in their home village. Partly for this reason, young adults with families (in a mid-1980s survey; Watson-Gegeo & Gegeo, 1991) argued that the most important language in which a Kwara'ae person needed to achieve fluency was high rhetoric Kwara'ae.

The 1980s also was the era of the *kastom* movement, a new cultural revitalization movement that valued indigenous cultures and languages in the wake of failed Western-style development. Teachers were actively engaged with communities, pushing for Kwara'ae as the language of instruction in lower grades. The need to develop teaching materials locally was discussed in community meetings. Under pressure by teachers and communities, the national government changed its policy to allow limited code-switching to children's indigenous languages for the sake of understanding. But some teachers in rural schools who had become aware of the international movement promoting bilingual education in the lower grades went further, alternating literacy lessons between English and the local language or Pijin.

Malaitans were called "stubborn and truculent" (Watson-Gegeo, 1987) by British colonial officials, because of the often resistant stance they took toward the colonial protectorate's institutions and practices. As shown here, we counter-argue that villagers are critical, a quality rooted in their indigenous epistemological processes of creating and examining knowledge to arrive at truth (*mamana'anga*). Their epistemological process led Kwara'ae and other Malaitans to expand their critique of large-scale development.

In 1978, the lead authors of this chapter arrived in West Kwara'ae for the first of nine research trips through the 1980s–1990s, initially to study Kwara'ae children's language socialization and schooling. On arrival we found villagers questioning why development projects and schools fail, and how to ensure the survival of Kwara'ae language and culture. They wanted to engage us on these issues because we were family, members of the tribe and sub-clan of David's home village, and they asked us to participate in village meetings and local gatherings where critical issues are debated. From the intense discussions that went on during and between our visits (many of them audio-recorded), we and the villagers together formed an epistemic community that co-constructed the idea of development based on indigenous episte-mology. The villagers had the knowledge that through colonialism their indigenous language had been suppressed and devalued. Our coming back to the community (in Gegeo's case) and focusing on indigenous language and knowledge helped villagers recognize the value of what they knew. Our work became ELP (Davis, 2014b).

In the early 1990s, villagers went on to create several development projects based on indigenous epistemology. Some of these focused on youth who, finding no em-ployment on Malaita, drifted to the national capital of Honiara (Guadalcanal), where after failing to find jobs, they often became involved in petty crime, contributing to the local reputation of Malaitans as "aggressive" (Gegeo & Watson-Gegeo, 2003). Other projects were cross-generational, multi-community efforts to critically debate and reconstruct traditional linguistic and cultural knowledge (Gegeo & Watson-Gegeo, 2001). Villagers also continued to press for community input to LPP in the schools, against the refusal of the Ministry of Education to listen.

ETHNIC *TENSON* AND THE RAMSI PERIOD

The ethnic conflict (*Tenson*) began in 1998, when Guadalcanal militants attacked Malaitan settlers and squatters (some legal and some not), burning down houses, beating and killing Malaitans, and driving out legal residents, as well. Resentment against Malaitans was fueled by decades of underdevelopment of rural Guadalcanal, cultural differences, and the perceived aggressiveness of Malaitans (Gegeo & Watson-Gegeo, 2013a; Moore, 2007), but was also manipulated by business factions for economic gain. During 1998–2000, Malaitan communities on Guadalcanal were under attack, national secondary schools were fired on and evacuated, and by June 2000, 20,000 Malaitans had fled to Malaita, even though many had never even vis-ited the island before. That month, a militia, armed and trained in secret on Malaita, invaded Honiara and overthrew the national government. They demanded the res-ignation of the prime minister and a new election. Once a new prime minister was installed, they vacated Guadalcanal.

Yet peace was hard to re-establish, and crime escalated on both islands. Eventually the national government asked Australia for help. RAMSI was posted to the Solomons initially from 2003 to 2013, tasked with restoring peace, educating the na-tional police force, and promoting nation building. While RAMSI did play a role in preventing new violence until everyone calmed down, a recent independent re-port on its impact (commissioned by the SI government) (Fraenkel, Madraiwiwi, & Okole, 2014) shows that it failed in its aims—especially nation building—and instead left behind a variety of serious social ills often promoted by RAMSI soldiers.

In the meantime on Malaita, the influx of 20,000 people created chaos, with shortages of food, medical supplies, and housing, as well as problems with land rights, crime, guns (which were suddenly numerous), and disruption of peaceful traditional villages. The death rate among village adults rose, due to illnesses, stress, and grief over relatives killed in Guadalcanal. Many returnees did not speak their heritage languages, but rather only SIP or English, and with their urban behaviors, considered themselves superior to rural villagers. In school, children who had grown up in town were ahead in English, spoke only SIP, and ridiculed village children for speaking indigenous languages. During the conflict part of the *Tenson*, most of the ongoing cultural projects came to a halt. Hundreds of village children who were either in secondary school on Guadalcanal (and evacuated to Malaita), or who were scheduled to go there, were suddenly closed out of continuing their education.

Malaita communities felt abandoned by the national government, and the Provincial government was unable to handle the crisis in Auki and other peri-urban areas. The churches stepped in to provide what aid they could, but as villagers told us in interviews, it was really up to the villagers themselves to survive the crisis.

The *Tenson* period led to a major paradigm shift, parallel to the rise of the Maasina Rule movement triggered by World War II. Communities, especially on Malaita, realized that the national government was deeply wounded and in crisis. They began holding day-long village meetings to plan what to do for youth and children with regard to schooling, and for the return of migrants whose problems included alcoholism, marijuana abuse, theft, and refusal to participate in cultural practices such as village conflict resolution and traditional formal teaching sessions. Existing primary schools added two grade levels to try to handle returning secondary students, although no appropriate teaching materials were available.

Some of the returnees to Malaita who spearheaded community development in this period were national government officials who had previously done development work for the government, and now wanted to do it for their own communities. A sense of shock began to be replaced by a sense of eagerness and transformation. After decades of struggling within the framework of national government control, villagers felt free to undertake the projects they had long wanted to pursue. An indication of the unity that this period brought was that virtually every development project taken up in village meetings in Kwara'ae was unanimously agreed upon. For example, communities organized to raise money and negotiate provincial government approval for establishing a technical school at Kilusakwalo in 2000. They contributed the building materials and labor themselves, and succeeded in securing assistance from AusAID, Taiwan, and Japan to hire teachers and obtain teaching materials (Gegeo & Watson-Gegeo, 2013a). Several such projects were started at this time, including community-built medical clinics, designed in community meetings and shaped by villagers.

In earlier decades, parents' disaffection with poor local schooling and their inability to have an effect on school curriculum had shown in their resistance to being involved in caring for school buildings. Now, however, villagers began to talk se-riously about "taking things into our own hands," given that they had waited and waited for the government to act, and "nothing came of it" (as many said to us in interviews). One of the major concerns was that with the back-migration of children who could not speak Kwara'ae, or any other Malaita language, communities were seriously faced for the first time with the potential loss of their indigenous languages.

New Community Initiatives in the Post-*Tenson* Period

The fallout from armed conflict and RAMSI occupation led to a new way of Malaitans, and Solomon Islanders generally, thinking about themselves, foreshadowed by the brief reconstruction of SI history described in the preceding. The shift in their thinking was away from the belief in a modern lifestyle emulating global culture and toward an appreciation of their own traditional way of life. They are integrating those aspects of global culture that they feel are positive and useful with those aspects of history and traditional culture that ground their sense of identity and provide the skills to live a rural life. Most of the new initiatives that have come about in the past decade are projects that focus on what has been lost or ignored by contemporary culture, with the belief that giving up what traditionally served villagers well threatens to create problems worse than the *Tenson* (Fito'o, 2016). Today on Malaita, the new generation of children and youth in urban and peri-urban areas speak primarily Pijin, their fluency in their indigenous language is poor or nonexistent, they prefer the knowledge produced in Western societies, and they believe that this will lead to the good life. Yet their parents, who also failed to learn much of their traditional culture mainly because they spent so many hours a day in English-medium classrooms that led to no employment, emphasize what has been lost. They and the elder generation (who were the young parents in our 1980s studies) realize that "chasing modernization" did not bring them the Kwara'ae ex-perience of the "good life" (*gwaumauri'anga*). These two generations together have started new initiatives in an almost desperate effort to revive their language, culture, and identity. We mention a few of these community initiatives here (see Fito'o, 2016).

Examples of language projects include the new Kwara'ae and Langalanga Bible translations replacing the old inaccurate missionary versions. The goal is to re-trieve indigenous languages that are dying and to revive important words in these languages that have been missing or incorrectly translated. Community members feel that these translation projects constitute the best immediate strategy for reviving indigenous languages because the Bible is now part of people's lives and creates a common bond among them.

New vocational secondary schools, including Malaita Technical School at Kilusakwalo (February 2012), are being built by the Central Malaita Farmers Association, a community organization. The Technical School replaces a temporary school built at the same location in 2000, providing an opportunity for secondary school dropouts at Form 3–6 to learn skills that will sustain them monetarily in rural areas, such as lapidary, cooking, indigenous medicine, and turning local resources into salable commodities. Another school for dropouts is the Asia Pacific Sustainable Development (APSA) institution at Gwaʻigeo school near Fiu village, started in 2001, which teaches traditional methods of raising pigs and aspects of gardening, including organic gardening. Its purpose is to help reverse the tendency of people to eat processed food, thereby improving local health. (Diabetes, cancer, heart disease, and other chronic diet-related diseases are on the rise.) These and other schools have found financial support from nongovernmental organizations (NGOs) and government.

In a continuation of the Kwaraʻae Genealogy Project (Gegeo & Watson-Gegeo, 2001) suspended during the *Tenson*, communities are organizing family, clan, and tribal meetings to teach and examine issues of land boundaries, genealogy, and traditional concepts. Such meetings involve the use of high rhetoric Kwaraʻae, indigenous epistemological strategies of argumentation, and critical praxis, discussed earlier. Related to these efforts are community power-sharing groups called *serving clubs*, including credit unions (to replace the failed outsider-introduced credit union movement of the 1980s), and communal mentorship programs of adults paired with youth to help guide them toward achieving their goals. Moreover, during 2003–2010, a group of Kuarafi tribe members from West Kwaraʻae moved back up into the mountains to their traditional/customary land that had been abandoned with missionization, rebuilding their original villages and strengthening their intra-community and tribal ties.

Women are taking a larger role in community decision-making, as well. In Kwaraʻae, the ʻAbero Women's club in Kilusakwalo, for instance, has been awarded funding for projects focusing on healthy living, sanitation, and gardening. One goal of such projects is to demonstrate that women can accomplish important development tasks and, unlike men, distribute work and rewards equally among themselves.

At the same time, a broader conversation that cuts across language lines is the political future of Malaita Province. Even as Malaitans waited two years before striking back in the ethnic conflict, keeping their plans secret while hoping that their Guadalcanal rivals would end their assaults, so today Malaitans are talking in community meetings about the future. Such conversations are being held all over the Solomons, of course. Malaitans are debating whether they want to secede from the SI nation, or push for a federal model to replace the current parliamentary model of government and expand their self-rule. A second preliminary draft of a constitution for a federal republic, changing provinces to states, is circulating as of this writing. Also, in 2015, Premier Peter Ramohia announced the appointment of a distinguished, educated task force to pursue Malaita Province's previously announced intention "to declare a sovereign nation of Malaita" (*Solomon Star*, September 20, 2015). A draft constitution for the Nation of Malaita was circulated and then withdrawn about a year later. The Solomon Islands has often been inaccurately termed a *failed state* (for a counter-argument, see Moore, 2007), when the real problem is that it is a highly corrupt state at the national level, and is in any case an artificial colonial construction. Malaitans' island identity was greatly strengthened by the conflict, but its national identity was, if anything, weakened.

After a decade of community and consultant pressure from several provinces that indigenous languages be used in primary schools, the Ministry of Education issued a policy statement mandating that primary grades should be taught in children's indigenous languages rather than English (Ministry of Education and Human Resources Development, 2010). The policy provided for a late exit–maintenance model of instruction and literacy primarily in children's first language through Grade 3, staged bridging to English in Grades 4–5, and maintenance of indigenous language arts classes through Grade 9. The road to implementing this change has been slow. In 2014, the Ministry of Education started a trial program in eight schools on South Malaita, in the Sa'a language, for seven years beginning with Grade 1 (SIL International, 2015). Sa'a was selected because basic linguistic studies had been done, including an established orthography; written materials were also developed, as well as curricula. Moreover, there was strong community support for the program (Luihenue, n.d.). A locally designed program is also underway, begun in 2015, on Santa Isabel. In 2012, the national government began a staged transition to free public education, starting at the first three primary grades, and now claims that all children are receiving free primary schooling.

CONCLUSION: IMPLICATIONS OF THE SOLOMONS CASE FOR LPP

If the federal form of government happens, or if Mala'ita has to go on its own, or even Kwara'ae is on its own, we can do it, we are ready. We feel we have what we need in this new cultural work to handle our own future.

—Augustine Maelefaka, rural villager (in a telephone call to Gegeo and Watson-Gegeo during a Malaita-wide cross-generational cultural celebration and organizational meeting in 2009) [Translated from Kwara'ae to English by Gegeo]

The "new cultural work" that Maelefaka refers to is development based on indigenous epistemology. In this chapter, we have presented a brief case study of the Solomon Islands since Western contact, highlighting crises and turning points that led Malaitans to turn to indigenous epistemology, bottom-up development, and schooling in both their indigenous language(s) and English (as Tetehano described earlier). We argued that the historical crises and turning points we have described shaped the current context for CCLPE on Malaita.

Education and LPP are essential activities in rural development. One implication of the Kwaraʻae case is that these activities are most successful when they are grounded in a local community's indigenous language(s) and epistemology(ies) through which villagers and communities can exercise their agency. This means that decision-making power relations between the central government and rural areas must at the least be shared and preferably initiated and planned at the local level. In other words, LPP for education and other strategies for development are not as successful and/or fail in many societies when they are designed top-down and imposed from the outside. We argue instead that development must "grow from within" (Gegeo & Watson-Gegeo, 2013b, p. 151). This point is not new in the theoretical literature; it began with the grassroots development movement decades ago (Escobar, 1992).

We believe that CCLPE offers the best approach to integrating local with national concerns, and that essential to community LPP in education is that researchers be engaged with communities in Davis's (2014a) sense; that is, they need to be willing to commit to long-term field research and collaboration with communities. Researchers need to be the learners and communities the teachers in knowledge construction, with learners immersing themselves in indigenous epistemology and forms of local critical praxis. Part of researchers' learning should focus on how the communities with which they work have been shaped by historical events and turning points—points of crisis and transformation—and how that history contributed to the local process of language and culture change (in Kwaraʻae, *falafala rokisiʻanga*). English or another international language does have an important role to play in development. We are not arguing for isolation of rural peoples from the global world, which would in any case be impossible. However, greater effort must be made to integrate English-language education with local cultural values, and to provide education in indigenous languages in meaningful ways.

Finally, the Solomon Islands today is a country of heightened fluidity, which in the postcolonial, globalized, contemporary world is the norm. Moreover, it has serious problems with government corruption, poverty, and disease. Yet we also see energy, innovation, and hope in the villages, which has not been seen for decades. Since the *Tenson* period, a new generation of youth has successfully completed higher education outside the Solomons and is now back home entering professional and governmental positions. Many Malaitans now hold graduate degrees (in law, political science, education, business, and sciences) and are determined to turn the country around.

Malaitans are also considering how to build on the institutions and values of their languages and cultures if it becomes necessary for Malaita to "go it alone," should efforts of national reform fail. The younger generation grew up in families where their grandparents and parents told stories of blackbirding, missionization, early co-lonialism, World War II, and Maasina Rule, and experienced the failure of rural de-velopment driven by modernization. They were exposed to the anti-Malaita rhetoric during the *Tenson* period, some lost family members and relatives, and their villages suffered. Even many who grew up in Honiara have a renewed sense of connection to their heritage communities in rural villages and to their home islands, which are struggling with the destruction and theft of local resources through the collusion of political corruption and multinational corporations. They are aware of the ur-gent need for sustainable local development, and they want to restore their indige-nous languages. In a few years they will replace the current generation of national leadership.

Locally on Malaita, the present situation is uncertain for villagers, but it also provides an opportunity to build a different society from the one that colonialism and neocolonialism left behind. The odds against being able to do this are great, given the power of international corporations, globalization, the invitation to greed for those in power, and dramatically changing ecological conditions, with global warming already altering the environment around which so much of indigenous knowledge is built.

It seems clear to us that CCLPE and critical community models of development built on indigenous epistemology will help shape the future, whatever path that future takes. Communities of parents and teachers working together in schools where children learn literacy in their first language during the initial years, and then continue first-language instruction as English is introduced, will be essential. Many of the returning PhD and MA graduates are seeking positions at SI National University's teacher-training college, and are pressuring for traditional cultural life practices, values, and ways of thinking and debating to figure prominently in the curriculum. They are bringing back with them knowledge of contemporary theories of education, especially critical perspectives, bilingual immersion, and indigenous knowledge/epistemology. Marion Luihenue (n.d., n.p.), the national pilot coordi-nator for the Sa'a bilingual project, argues that the project "is not exceptional and one day we'll be successfully up here in the world of [multilingual mother tongue education] for all," meaning the Solomon Islands as a whole.

That this has been a community-driven transformation from the beginning is an example of what Maldonado Alvarado (2010) meant by people's achieving their own form of liberation and Tetehano's (2015 interview) goal of schooling that prepares students for a life on their own. In this sense, the Solomon Islands is a case example of a "relatively creative public sphere paradigm" for LPP, emphasizing "the agency of all actors in the policy-making process" (Tollefson, 2013, p. 28).

REFERENCES

Akin, D. W. (2013). *Colonialism, Maasina Rule, and the origins of Malaitan* kastom. Honolulu: University of Hawai'i.

Baldauf, R. B. (1994). "Unplanned" language policy and planning. *Annual Review of Applied Linguistics* 14, 82–89.

Bennett, J. A. (1978). No "monstrous tongue." *Hemisphere* 22(4), 16–20.

Bennett, J. A. (1987). *Wealth of the Solomons: A history of a Pacific archipelago, 1800–1978.* Honolulu: University of Hawai'i.

Blommaert, J., & Rampton, B. (2011). Language and superdiversity. *Diversities* 13(2), 1–22.

Canagarajah, S. (Ed.). (2004). *Reclaiming the local in language policy and practice.* New York: Routledge.

Carspecken, P. F. (1996). *Critical ethnography in educational research: A theoretical and practical guide.* New York: Routledge.

Coelho, F. O., & Henze, R. (2013). English for what? Rural Nicaraguan teachers' local responses to national educational policy. *Language Policy* 13(2), 145–163.

Davis, K. A. (1994). *Language planning in multilingual contexts: Policies, communities, and schools in Luxembourg.* Philadelphia: John Benjamins.

Davis, K. A. (2014a). Engaged language policy and practices. *Language Policy* 13(2), 83–100.

Davis, K. A. (Ed.). (2014b). *Thematic issue: Engaged language policy and practices. Language Policy* 13(2), 83–242.

Davis, K. A., Phyak, P., & Bui, T. T. N. (2012). Multicultural education as community engagement: Policies and planning in a transnational era. *International Journal of Multicultural Education* 14(3), 1–25.

Dei, J. S., Hall, B. D., & Rosenberg, D. G. (Eds.). (2000). *Indigenous knowledges in global contexts: Multiple readings of our world.* Toronto: University of Toronto Press.

Dobell, G. (2017, April 10). Saving Solomon Islands from crocodiles: 14 years of RAMSI. *The Strategist: Australian Strategic Policy Institute Blog.* Retrieved from https://www.aspistrategist.org.au/saving-solomon-islands-crocodil...oSolomon%20Islands%20from%20crocodiles%2014%20years%20of%20RAMSI

Escobar, A. (1992). Reflections on development: Grassroots approaches and alternative politics in the third world. *Futures* 24(5), 411–436.

Fairclough, N. (2010). *Critical discourse analysis: The critical study of language.* 2nd edition. New York: Routledge.

Fito'o, B. (2016). *Citizenship education in a small island state: Exploring values for good citizenship in the Solomon Islands.* Unpublished dissertation, School of Education, University of the South Pacific, Suva, Fiji.

Fox, C. E. (1967). *The story of the Solomons.* Sydney: Pacific Publications.

Fraenkel, J., Madraiwiwi, J., & Okole, H. (2014, June 14). The RAMSI decade: A review of the Regional Assistance Mission to Solomon Islands, 2003–2013. Independent report commissioned by the Solomon Islands Government and the Pacific Islands Forum. Honiara: Solomon Islands Government.

Freire, P. (1970). *Pedagogy of the oppressed*. New York: Continuum.

Freire, P. (1994). *Pedagogy of hope: Reliving the pedagogy of the oppressed*. New York: Continuum.

Gegeo, D. W. (1994). *Kastom and Bisnis: Toward integrating cultural knowledge into rural development in the Solomon Islands*. Unpublished PhD dissertation, Department of Political Science, University of Hawai'i, Mānoa.

Gegeo, D. W., & Watson-Gegeo, K. A. (2001). "How we know": Kwara'ae rural villagers doing indigenous epistemology. *The Contemporary Pacific* 13, 55–88.

Gegeo, D. W., & Watson-Gegeo, K. A. (2002). The critical villager: Transforming language and education in Solomon Islands. In J. W. Tollefson (Ed.), *Language policies in education: Critical issues* (pp. 309–325). New York: Routledge.

Gegeo, D. W., & Watson-Gegeo, K. A. (2003). Whose knowledge? The collision of indigenous and introduced knowledge systems in Solomon Islands community development. *The Contemporary Pacific* 14(2), 377–409.

Gegeo, D. W., & Watson-Gegeo, K. A. (2013a). The critical villager revisited: Continuing transformations in language and education in Solomon Islands. In J. W. Tollefson (Ed.), *Language policies in education: Critical issues* (pp. 234–251). New York: Routledge.

Gegeo, D. W., & Watson-Gegeo, K. A. (2013b). (Re)conceptualizing language in development: Towards demystifying an epistemological paradox. *The Journal of Pacific Studies* 33(2), 137–155.

Hilliard, D. (1978). *God's gentlemen: A history of the Melanesian Mission 1849–1942*. St. Lucia: University of Queensland.

Hornberger, N. H. (1988). *Bilingual education and language maintenance: A southern Peruvian Quechua case*. Berlin: Mouton de Gruyter.

Hornberger, N., & Johnson, D. C. (2007). Slicing the onion ethnographically: Layers and spaces in multilingual language education policy and practice. *TESOL Quarterly* 41(3), 509–532.

Hornberger, N., & Johnson, D. C. (2011). The ethnography of language policy. In T. L. McCarty (Ed.), *Ethnography and language policy* (pp. 273–289). New York: Routledge.

Kamwendo, G. H. (2005). Language planning from below: An example from Northern Malawi. *Language Policy* 4, 143–165.

Keesing, R., & Corris, P. (1980). *Lightning meets the west wind: The Malaita massacre*. New York: Oxford University Press.

Laracy, H. (1983). Introduction. In H. Laracy (Ed.), *Pacific protest: The Maasina Rule movement, Solomon Islands, 1944–1952* (pp. 1–10). Suva: University of the South Pacific.

Luihenue, M. (n.d.). A 10 year journey towards MLE Pilot in the Solomon Islands. Retrieved from www.slideplayer.com/slide/3799522/

Madison, D. S. (2012). *Critical ethnography: Method, ethics, and performance*. 2nd edition. Los Angeles: Sage.

Maldonado Alvarado, B. (2010). *Comunalidad* and the education of indigenous peoples. In L. Meyer & B. Maldonado Alvarado (Eds.), *New world of indigenous resistance* (pp. 367–380). San Francisco: City Lights Books.

Menken, K., & García, O. (Eds.). (2010). *Negotiating language policies in schools: Educators as policymakers*. New York: Routledge.

Ministry of Education and Human Resources Development (MEHRD). (2010, November). Policy statement and guidelines for the use of vernacular languages and English in education in Solomon Islands. Honiara: Solomon Islands Government.

Moore, C. (2007). *Happy isles in crisis: The historical causes for a failing state in Solomon Islands, 1998–2004*. Canberra: Asia Pacific.

Nero, S. J. (2013). De facto language education policy through teachers' attitudes and practices: A critical ethnographic study in three Jamaican schools. *Language Policy* 13(2), 221–242.

Pallas, A. M. (2001). Preparing educational doctoral students for epistemological diversity. *Educational Researcher* 30(5), 6–11.

Pennycook, A. (2001). *Critical applied linguistics: A critical introduction*. New York: Routledge.

Phyak, P., & Bui, T. T. (2013). Youth engaging language policy and planning: Ideologies and transformations from within. *Language Policy* 13, 101–119.

Ricento, T. (2006). Language policy, theory and practice: An introduction. In T. Ricento (Ed.), *An introduction to language policy: Theory and method* (pp. 10–23). Malden, MA: Blackwell.

SIL International. (2015). MLE pilot project planned for Solomon Islands (pp. 1–2). Retrieved from http://www.sil.org/about/news/mle-pilot-project-planned-solomon-islands

Skutnabb-Kangas, T., & Heugh, K. (Eds.). (2012). *Multilingual education and sustainable diversity work: From periphery to center*. New York: Routledge.

Solomon Islands Population and Housing Census. (ca. 2010). *Provincial profile of the 2009 census: Malaita*. Honiara: Solomon Islands Government.

Solomon Star. (2015, September 20). Malaita pursues "sovereignty." Retrieved from http://www.solomonstarnews.com/news/national/8494-malaita-pursues-sovereignty

Tollefson, J. W. (1991). *Planning language, planning inequality: Language policy in the community*. London: Longman.

Tollefson, J. W. (2006). Critical theory in language policy. In T. Ricento (Ed.), *An introduction to language policy: Theory and method* (pp. 42–59). Malden, MA: Blackwell.

Tollefson, J. W. (2013). Language policy in a time of crisis and transformation. In J. W. Tollefson (Ed.), *Language policies in education: Critical issues* (2nd edition; pp. 10–34). New York: Routledge.

United Nations Economic and Social Commission for Asia and the Pacific (ESCAP). (2013). *Statistical yearbook for Asia and the Pacific*. Bangkok: United Nations.

Van Dijk, T. A. (1993). Principles of critical discourse analysis. *Discourse and Society* 4(2), 249–283.

Vertovec, S. (2007). Super-diversity and its implications. *Ethnic and Racial Studies* 30(6), 1024–1054.

Watson, K. A. (1987). English in the Solomon Islands. *World Englishes* 6(1), 21–32.

Watson-Gegeo, K. A. (1988). Ethnography in ESL: Defining the essentials. *TESOL Quarterly* 22(4), 575–592.

Watson-Gegeo, K. A. (1992). Thick explanation in the ethnographic study of child socialization and development: A longitudinal study of the problem of schooling for Kwara'ae (Solomon Islands) children. In W. A. Corsaro & P. J. Miller (Eds.), *Interpretive methodologies for the study of childhood socialization* (pp. 51–66). *New Directions in Child Development 58* (Winter). San Francisco: Jossey-Bass.

Watson-Gegeo, K. A., & Gegeo, D. W. (1990). Shaping the mind and straightening out conflicts: The discourse of Kwara'ae family counseling. In K. A. Watson-Gegeo & G. M. White (Eds.), *Disentangling: Conflict discourse in Pacific societies* (pp. 161–213). Stanford, CA: Stanford University Press.

Watson-Gegeo, K. A., & Gegeo, D. W. (1991). The impact of church affiliation on language use in Kwara'ae (Solomon Islands). *Language in Society* 20(4), 533–555.

Watson-Gegeo, K. A., & Gegeo, D. W. (1992). Schooling, knowledge and power: Social transformation in the Solomon Islands. *Anthropology and Education Quarterly* 12(1), 10–29.

Watson-Gegeo, K. A., & Gegeo, D. W. (1994). Keeping culture out of the classroom in rural Solomon Islands schools: A critical analysis. *Educational Foundations* 8(2), 27–55.

Watson-Gegeo, K. A., & Gegeo, D. W. (1995). Understanding language and power in the Solomon Islands: Methodological lessons for educational intervention. In J. W. Tollefson (Ed.), *Power and inequality in language education: Critical approaches* (pp. 59–72). New York: Cambridge University.

Watson-Gegeo, K. A., & Gegeo, D. W. (2004). Deep culture: Pushing the epistemological boundaries of multicultural education. In G. S. Goodman & K. Carey (Eds.), *Critical multicultural conversations* (pp. 235–256). Cresskill, NJ: Hampton.

White, G. M., Gegeo, D. W., & Watson-Gegeo, K. A. (Eds.). (1988). *The Big Death: Solomon Islanders remember World War II*. Suva: University of the South Pacific.

Whiteman, D. (1983). *Melanesians and missionaries: An ethnohistorical study of social and religious change in the southwest Pacific*. Pasadena, CA: William Carey.

Worsley, P. (1968). *The trumpet shall sound: A study of "cargo" cults in Melanesia*. New York: Schocken.

Zhang, Q. (2013). Language policy and ideology: Greater China. In R. Bayley, R. Cameron, & C. Lucas (Eds.), *The Oxford handbook of sociolinguistics* (pp. 563–586). New York: Oxford University Press.

CHAPTER 21

....

FAMILY LANGUAGE POLICY

....

XIAO LAN CURDT-CHRISTIANSEN

FAMILY language policy (FLP) is defined as explicit and overt as well as implicit and covert language planning by family members in relation to language choice and literacy practices within home domains and among family members (Curdt-Christiansen, 2009; King, Fogle, & Logan-Terry, 2008; Spolsky, 2012). Explicit and overt FLP refers to the deliberate and observable efforts made by adults and their conscious involvement and investment in providing linguistic conditions and context for language learning and literacy development. Implicit and covert FLP refers to the default language practices in a family as a consequence of ideological beliefs. Bridging the gaps between studies of child language acquisition and the field of language policy research, the study of FLP thus seeks to understand, inter alia: why (and how) members of some transnational families maintain their language while members of other families lose theirs; in what ways some children, growing up in a largely monolingual society, become bilingual while other children, growing up in a bilingual environment, become monolingual; what language planning and decisions caregivers make to support or discourage the use and practice of particular languages; and how these decisions and practices interact with broader language ideologies and educational policies (Curdt-Christiansen, 2013a; Fishman, 1991; Spolsky, 2012).

While focusing on close analysis of face-to-face interaction and social life within the family (Gafaranga, 2010; Lanza, 2004 [1997]; 2007; Li Wei, 1994), the study of FLP also takes into consideration external influences, such as public discourse as well as socioeconomic and political forces affecting families and contributing to the (dis)continuity of intergenerational transmission. As Curdt-Christiansen (2013a, p. 1) observes, "the study of FLP not only contributes to our understanding of the processes of language shift and change, it also sheds light on broader language policy issues at the societal levels. Most importantly, the study of FLP can make visible the relationships between private domains and public spheres."

This chapter starts with a brief introduction to the theoretical conceptualisation of FLP currently used by most researchers. It then provides a discussion of the major contributions to the field by focusing on three major themes: FLP and language-in-education policy; FLP and language ideology; and linguistic practices and the processes of language change. This is followed by an overview of recent developments in research methodology employed in the field. Finally, future directions in research resulting from increasing transnational migration and evolving political environments are outlined.

Conceptualising Family Language Policy

FLP is informed primarily by theories of language policy and language socialisation within the discipline of sociolinguistics. Much research in FLP draws on Spolsky's (2004, 2009) theoretical model, which consists of three interrelated components: language ideology—how family members perceive particular languages; language practices—de facto language use, what people actually do with language; and language management—what efforts they make to maintain language. Language socialisation theory is concerned with how children and other novices acquire sociocultural knowledge through language use and how they are socialised to use language through participation in social interactions (Duranti, Ochs & Schieffelin, 2011). The two theories combined can broadly provide theoretical understanding of the dynamic relationship between FLP and its wider sociolinguistic and sociocultural contexts. Figure 21.1 is a graphic representation of the interdisciplinary conceptual framework of FLP, illustrating how FLP is shaping and is being shaped by the external environments through language socialisation.

The inner circle represents the three core components of FLP. Within a family, there are rules and norms for speaking, viewing, acting, and believing. As such, FLP provides a cornerstone for language socialisation and language development (Duranti, Ochs, & Schieffelin, 2011; Lanza, 2007). Making decisions on what language(s) to practice and encourage or to discourage or abandon depends largely on the values that family members ascribe to certain languages. Curdt-Christiansen

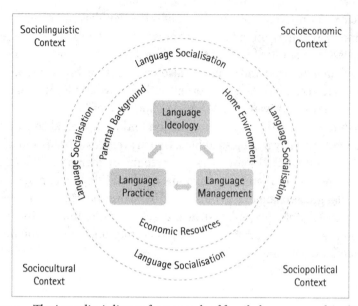

FIGURE 21.1. The interdisciplinary framework of family language policy (FLP).

Adapted from Curdt-Christiansen (2014).

(2009, 2012) contends that this decision-making process is also related to parental beliefs and goals for their children's multilingual development and educational success. Therefore, FLP decisions are influenced by the nature of intergenerational speech resources, parents' educational background, their own language learning experience, their migration experience, and the family's economic condition, in particular with regard to providing linguistic resources.

However tightly knit, families do not live in a vacuum, isolated from the larger sociocultural environment. On the contrary, they constantly interact with others in sociolinguistic, sociocultural, socioeconomic, and sociopolitical contexts (Spolsky, 2004, 2012). Such interaction takes place through the mediational means of language in the process of language socialisation. The dotted lines encircling the inner components of FLP and the outer settings of multiple social contexts act as walls, separating families from the outside world. They act, however, more like semi-permeable membranes, which allow external forces to penetrate, through language socialisation, into the family domain and, at the same time and to a certain degree, allow inner forces of FLP to pass in the opposite direction into the society.

In this regard, FLP is shaped by two types of forces: internal forces and external forces. The two types of forces, closely related and sometimes blurred together, form the ideological underpinnings of language choices, linguistic practices, and language investments at home (see Curdt-Christiansen, 2009, 2014). Because of the social nature of families, the study of FLP goes beyond parenting at home to encompass different domains related to family decisions, such as education, religion, and public linguistic space (Spolsky, 2009), as well as many different aspects of individual family members' everyday life, including emotions, identity, and cultural and political allegiances (Curdt-Christiansen, 2009, 2014, 2016; King, Fogle, & Logan-Terry, 2008; King & Logan-Terry, 2008; Pavlenko, 2004; Piller, 2002; Tannenbaum, 2012).

The development of FLP as a field of enquiry has undergone different phases, from viewing language acquisition as an uncontested state of private affairs in the early period to a broader view of language development as ideologically shaped social practices in recent years. This evolving development has advanced our understanding of FLP as a complex web, nested in a wide range of sociohistorical, political, cultural, and linguistic environments. But before moving on to the major recent contributions to the field, a review of the early developments will be presented in the following section.

Early Developments in Family Language Policy

Many of the early studies in FLP were centred on Western middle-class bilingual families. Those early works tended to focus on language input, parental discourse strategies, parents' language experiences, and their knowledge about bilingualism, with the purpose of achieving balanced bilinguals in intermarried families.

De Houwer (1990), for example, studied a bilingual Dutch-English child with regard to her morpho-syntactic development in the two languages. Using a naturalistic approach, she examined the effect of linguistic exposure from each parent on the child's language development in general. In this case study, the child was exposed to both languages from birth (bilingual first language learner) and the parents employed the One-Parent-One-Language (OPOL) approach. Analysing the child's utterances in Dutch and English, De Houwer found that the child's speech production resembled her monolingual peers in both languages. She concluded that the two separate linguistic input systems (OPOL) accounted for the child's language development in two separate languages.

Linguistic input thus motivated researchers to look at the different types of bilingual models/strategies that parents follow in raising bilingual children. Piller (2002), for instance, studied German and English élite bilingual couples to understand how and why parents undertook particular private language planning. Collecting her data from online newsletters and conversations between couples, she found that the majority of parents chose to raise their children by adopting the OPOL strategy (Ronjat, 1913), followed by the "home language versus community language" (hothouse strategy). Only a few couples acknowledged that they adopted a "mixed language and code-switching strategy" (see Romaine, 1995, for a full list of parental strategies).

While these communicative strategies provide essential means for parents to plan their FLP, two questions emerge as particularly relevant at this point: What types of linguistic input strategy have they actually adopted in their daily interactions with their children? Did these strategies lead to more efficient bilingual development? Drawing on language socialisation theory, Lanza (2004 [1997]) analysed parent-child interactions of bilingual English-Norwegian families. She identified five types of discourse strategy used by parents to socialise their children into a particular linguistic behavior: *minimal grasp, expressed guess, repetition, move on,* and *code-switching.* In *minimal grasp strategy,* adults pretend not to understand the children's language of choice in A (in a situation where the choice of the child's language is A and the parents' choice is B); the *expressed guess strategy* is used by adults posing yes/no questions in language B and accepting simple confirmation as answer; the *repetition strategy* means that adults repeat children's utterance in language B; the *move-on strategy* is employed by adults indicating comprehension and acceptance of children's language choice in A, so that a conversation continues without any disruptions; with *code-switching,* adults either switch over completely to language A or use intra-sentential change of language. These strategies demonstrate parental efforts in their conscious or unconscious private language planning, when children take an active role in making language choice decisions.

These early studies in FLP shed much light on language input and the linguistic conditions that parents provide in order to raise balanced bilingual children, yet making language choices and practising bilingual childrearing is not an easy journey. Okita's (2002) study of bilingual Japanese and English intermarried families in England illustrated that there were contextual demands and situational pressures that Japanese mothers had to face in their everyday lives when raising bilingual children. These pressures included parents' conflicting cultural values, mothers' conflicting feelings about using Japanese when children started school education in English, and language choice when other family members were involved. By interviewing twenty-eight families, Okita concluded that raising children bilingually was an emotionally demanding and "invisible" task, because mothers, largely by themselves, had to deal with matters that require "simultaneous accommodation of demands and goals, some of which may be diametrically opposed" (2002, p. 5).

Despite the difficulties parents encounter, some hold strong positive beliefs about raising additive bilingual children. This is evidenced from studies conducted by Caldas (2006), King and Fogle (2006), and Piller (2002), where parents strongly believed that bilingualism was an investment and asset. In his book entitled *Raising*

Bilingual and Biliterate Children in Monolingual Cultures, Caldas (2006) described how his three children grew up learning English and French in the United States. Caldas and his wife battled with peer influence and societal pressures to raise their three children not only orally, but also literately, in two languages. Also located in the United States, King and Fogle (2006) interviewed twenty-four middle-class families with regard to their beliefs about languages and parenting that framed their FLPs. Their findings revealed that parents' positive perception of additive bilingualism in Spanish and English was influenced by their own personal experiences in language learning. In addition to the asset perception of bilingualism, these parents also believed that raising bilingual children was related to notions of good parenting identity.

In sum, these important studies revealed how FLP was established and what linguistic mechanisms were used in Western middle-class bilingual families. As evidenced in this review, this line of work focused primarily on internal linguistic conditions involving two high-status European languages. Few early studies took into consideration the external social forces that shape FLP decisions in immigrant families and communities that speak a low-status or endangered language. The following section moves into more recent developments in the field, with a focus on understudied families in diasporic communities and in endangered language contexts.

Recent Research on Families in Transnational and Endangered Language Contexts

In recent years, studies into FLP have given greater attention to why different values are ascribed to different languages and how parents view bilingual development from sociopolitical and emotional perspectives. This has led to the expansion of FLP to include non-Western, non-middle-class, socioculturally and socioeconomically marginalised, and understudied transnational families, as well as those in indigenous and endangered language communities. Emphasising matters of language attitudes, language replacement, and language endangerment, the following discussion provides a review of FLP development in transnational immigrant families. This is followed by a critical discussion of language loss in intergenerational transmission in endangered language communities.

FAMILY LANGUAGE POLICY DEVELOPMENTS IN TRANSNATIONAL FAMILIES IN DIASPORIC COMMUNITIES

As researchers seek to understand why so many transnational families lose their home language within three generations while others are able to maintain their heritage language, the study of FLP has expanded its focus of attention to include migrant and transnational families across different geopolitical contexts (Curdt-Christiansen, 2009, 2014, 2016; Fogle, 2012; Gafaranga, 2010; He, 2016; Kang, 2015; King, 2013; Li Wei, 2011; Pérez Baés, 2013; Schwartz & Verschic, 2013; Sevinç, 2016; Tannenbaum, 2012; Tuominen, 1999; Wang, 2017; Zhu Hua & Li Wei, 2016).

Curdt-Christiansen (2009), for instance, studied a group of ten Chinese immigrant families in Quebec with regard to their children's language and literacy education in three languages, Chinese, English, and French. In this ethnographic study, Curdt-Christiansen focused on how multilingualism is perceived and valued, and how these three languages, seen from the parents' perspective, are linked to particular linguistic markets. Viewing FLP as "invisible" work, in contrast to "visible" language planning from governments or other authorities, she provided a detailed analysis of the ideological factors and the formation of ideologies underlying their FLPs. Looking into the influence of broader sociopolitical forces, she concluded that FLP in those immigrant families was established in relation to parents' educational background, their immigration experiences, the status of the minority and majority language, and their cultural disposition.

Exploring contextual factors involved in the processes of language shift and change, Seloni and Sarfati (2013) also studied Judeo-Spanish speakers in Turkey. They provided an account of how family members surrendered to external forces by ceasing the cultural and linguistic practices of the Sephardic Jewish community that settled during the fifteenth century around Ottoman Anatolia. Based on eighty-eight interviews found in historic archives, they documented the Turkish-Jewish community members' lived experiences in Turkey, and identified the factors that contributed to the decay of Judeo-Spanish.

Moving back to the contemporary context of intergenerational transmission, scholars have also engaged in studies focusing on families that travel back and forth between country of residence and home country. Pérez Baéz (2013), for example, studied a group of indigenous speakers of Zapotec (an Otomanguean language) from San Lucas in the state of Oaxaca, Mexico, who resided in Los Angeles, California. When looking at the processes of language shift in the families, she found that the shift in the diasporic community not only took place from Zapotec to Spanish and from Spanish to English; the shift was also "exported back" to the San Lucas home community as a consequence of intensified transnational movement of the family members back and forth between California and Oaxaca.

Transnational families can be complex in their composition, as many families live under the same roof together with grandparents, uncles, and aunts. In this regard, research into FLP has paid attention to such large families as well (Curdt-Christiansen, 2013b; He, 2016; Zhu & Li, 2016). Li Wei's (1994) study of *Three Generations, Two Languages, and One Family* in the United Kingdom illustrated how FLP was negotiated between family members (see also Li Wei, Chapter 29 in this volume). Also looking at three-generation families, Curdt-Christiansen (2016) located her study within the context of Singapore. By studying a trilingual Chinese family, a bilingual Malay family, and a bilingual Indian family, she showed how parents and other caregivers, including grandparents, perceived their languages differently, thus leading to conflicting language ideologies and contradictory language practices within the same family.

FAMILY LANGUAGE POLICY DEVELOPMENT IN ENDANGERED LANGUAGE COMMUNITIES

The analysis of FLP has also expanded to endangered language communities, where scholars have studied the processes of language change and FLP's function in language revitalisation (Ó hIfearnáin, 2013, 2015; Patrick, Budach, & Muckpaloo, 2013; Simpson, 2013; Smith-Christmas, 2016). Smith-Christmas's (2016) study was based on an eight-year-long ethnography during which she lived and observed the language practices of an extended family of three generations on the Isle of Skye in Scotland. The family consisted of grandmother (first generation), parents/uncles/aunts (second generation), and Maggie/Jacob (the third generation). Through analysing interactions between the children and adults, and interviews with different family members, she found that despite the adults' best efforts to use Gaelic with them, the children did not often speak Gaelic.

Similarly, Ó hIfearnáin (2013) studied an endangered language—Irish spoken by first-language Irish speakers in the southwest of Ireland, where "bilingualism is under great pressure from English monolingualism" (Ó hIfearnáin, 2013, p. 351). Unlike Smith-Christmas, Ó hIfearnáin used a quantitative survey and follow-up interviews to collect data on the attitudes and practices of first-language Irish speakers in Gaeltacht communities in relation to home language use and intergenerational transmission. He confirmed that, in order to persuade Irish-speaking parents to maintain their language, it is necessary to involve these speakers in government language policy decisions.

Patrick et al. (2013) studied FLP in an urban Inuit community in Ottawa, Canada. Through participant observation, participatory literacy activity, and interviews, the authors showed how literacy activities in the community centre can facilitate cultural and language learning at home. The study also showed that state-driven language policies can open up spaces for developing indigenous-defined language and literacy activities. Such activities, when brought back into the families, can provide opportunities for intergenerational sharing of Inuit experiences, cultural memory, and traditional storytelling.

As evidenced from this review of the different types of transnational families being researched across different parts of the world, studies of FLP continue to advance our understanding of language development, shift, loss, and change. While this review provides a glimpse of the historical trajectories of the cultural and linguistic development of non-middle-class families, the ways in which mobility and ongoing changes in sociocultural contexts as well as politico-economic accessibility impact FLP have also attracted the attention of many researchers. The following section will review major thematic contributions in the field.

Major Themes

As the field of FLP has steadily developed in recent years, contributions to the field have examined various aspects of FLP, including why different values are ascribed to different languages, how parents view bilingualism from sociocultural, emotional, and cognitive perspectives (Curdt-Christiansen, 2009; Fogle, 2012; King et al., 2008; Pavlenko, 2004; Tannenbaum, 2012), and what kinds of family literacy environment and what forms of parental capital are likely to promote bilingualism (Curdt-Christiansen, 2012; Li, 2007; Ren & Hu, 2013; Stavans, 2012). Importantly, these studies have expanded the inner working of the home domain into the domain of school to understand the conflicting demands of state-controlled education, on the one hand, and the intergenerational transmission of a heritage language, on the other (Curdt-Christiansen, 2012; Stavans, 2012; Spolsky, 2012; Wang, 2017). The following subsections bring into focus three major themes in the recent development of FLP: FLP, state language policy, and language in education policy; FLP, language ideology, and language hierarchies; and linguistic practices and the processes of language change.

Family Language Policy, State Language Policy, and Language in Education Policy

To understand how external influences underlie the formation of FLP, researchers are beginning to pay attention to how macro-level policies, such as government policy and school language policy, interfere with and support heritage language development or bilingual development (Curdt-Christiansen, 2014, 2015, 2016; Lane, 2010; Ren & Hu, 2013; Seloni & Sarfati, 2013).

Lane (2010) has studied a group of Kven (a Finnic language) speakers in northern Norway. The project, lasting eleven years, aimed to understand the macro-micro connections contributing to the massive language shift in this ethnic minority group. Using sociolinguistic interviews, participant observation, and feedback discussion with participants as the tools of enquiry, she collected data from forty-five participants from twenty to eighty-five years of age. Her study was situated within the context of the official Norwegianisation Policy of the 1970s; the long-lasting effect of the policy had coerced the Kven speakers to cease using Kven with their children, as the government had implemented a Norwegian-only language policy in all schools. The entire process of Norwegianisation had imparted a sense of inferiority and shame to the Kven speakers, who had little choice but to stop language transmission. In their words, "We did what we thought was best for our children" (Lane, 2010, p. 63). Similar findings have also been reported by Seloni and Sarfati (2013) in their study of Judeo-Spanish speakers in Turkey.

Shaming is not an unusual government strategy to convince people to change their language behaviour. Li Wei, Saravanan, and Ng (1997) have reported a visible language shift in the Chinese community in Singapore, where the government persuaded the speakers of so-called Chinese dialects to abandon their languages by openly stating that the dialects were underdeveloped varieties that had little value and could prevent their children from learning.

Also situated in Singapore, Curdt-Christiansen (2014, 2015, 2016) has demonstrated how state language policy and language-in-education policy affects FLP. Although the state language policy recognises four official languages—English, Mandarin, Malay, and Tamil (designated official mother tongues[1])—the language-in-education policy has promoted English as the language of instruction across all subjects in all schools at all levels. This political decision has resulted in much less curriculum time allocated to the teaching of mother tongue as a subject. In her study of bilingual Chinese families, Curdt-Christiansen found that there are competing ideologies with regard to developing Chinese and English simultaneously. Concerned about "losing out to English in a competitive society and a meritocratic educational system" that emphasises high proficiency in English, the parents had little choice other than to place Chinese and English in opposing positions (Curdt-Christiansen, 2014, p. 48). This has resulted in their lower expectations for their children's Chinese proficiency and less sufficient provision of Chinese literacy resources.

The preceding studies demonstrate clearly that decision-making is not a neutral private family matter. It is highly related to language status, language prestige, educational possibilities, and expectations of future socioeconomic gains. As Tollefson

(2002, 2013) noted, language policies in schools can create inequalities and provide access to resources, which may lead to rapid erosion of minority languages.

Family Language Policy, Language Ideology, and Language Hierarchies

Language ideology has been a recurring theme in many of the FLP studies, because it reflects "language users' evaluative perceptions and conceptions of language and language practices" (Curdt-Christiansen, 2016, p. 695). As language ideologies are socially constructed, they are typically associated with economic values, political power, historical roles, and social utilities (Blommaert, 2006; King, 2000; Kroskrity, 2010). In any given multilingual or monolingual society, languages are hierarchically ordered. An example of such ordering process is seen in the global spread of English as lingua franca and the associated hierarchies that come with it, as has been widely addressed in FLP research (Curdt-Christiansen, 2009, 2016; Garrett, 2011; Kirsch, 2012; Simpson, 2013; Wang, 2017).

Wang (2017) has examined Hakka Chinese families in Malaysia with regard to their FLP management. Because the Hakka community in Malaysia is situated within a complex sociolinguistic and political context, families must deal with daily discourses and ideologies that place English, Mandarin, Malay, Hokkien, and Hakka as tokens of global, regional, national, local, and home languages, respectively. These languages are thus hierarchically ordered, based on the family members' evaluation of their different values, including so-called communicative (Hokkien, Mandarin), instrumental (Hokkien, Malay, English) and sentimental (Hakka, Mandarin). In other words, although these languages play important roles in the family members' lives, they are ranked in terms of their importance in the socioeconomic and socio-linguistic market, as well as the scope of usage. In this regard, Wang concluded that despite the emotional role of Hakka in the private family domain, Hakka speakers are now slowly shifting to Mandarin. Likewise, although Hokkien is still a strong local variety of wider communication in the Penang area, it too has a tendency to give way to Mandarin because of the international prestige of the latter.

Similarly, in Curdt-Christiansen's (2016) study of three Singaporean families, there is a clear indication of language ordering in the families' management activities. The Indian family, for example, sent their son and daughter to a bilingual English-Chinese preschool to learn Mandarin and English, despite their Indian heritage and their heritage Tamil language. The Malay family adopted English-only practices in their daily communication, despite their pro-Malay ideology. The Chinese family is in the process of losing their heritage language, Hokkien, while adopting Mandarin as their family language because of its wider communicative and economic value in Asia. In their linguistic repertoire, English, Mandarin, and Hokkien are ranked differently because of different values ascribed to these languages by the family members.

These examples illustrate that in multilingual societies, language ranking and ideological conflicts can invoke complex systems of power relations that can inhibit intergenerational language transmission. Such hierarchical linguistic orders are particularly critical for minority language maintenance in societies with monolingual-dominant language settings, such as the United States and the United Kingdom. Kirsch's (2012) study of Luxembourgish families in Britain, for instance, shows the power relationship between English, the dominant societal and powerful global language, and Luxembourgish, the non-dominant European family language. Despite the prestige of its European origin, Luxembourgish has a difficult fight in the linguistic battleground of the United Kingdom. The case of Luxembourgish is not unique in that many migrant families, as reviewed earlier, have encountered the same issues when they struggled to fight against public discourse, school policy, and peer and political pressures in order to raise multilingual children in a largely monolingual society (Canagarajah, 2011).

Linguistic Practices and the Processes of Language Change

The third theme in the field of FLP concerns language practices at home, as scholars seek to understand the processes of language shift, language change, and language development. Gafaranga (2010) argues that research in language maintenance and shift should go beyond the analysis of language attitudes and ideology to actually describe everyday interactions between adults and children. The studies around this thematic category typically examine language exchanges among family members (Curdt-Christiansen, 2013b; Gafaranga, 2010), parental discourse models (Piller, 2002; Palvianinen & Boyd, 2013), and parental discourse strategies (Lanza, 2007; Meyer Pitton, 2013; Zhu Hua, 2008). Scholars look into how FLP is negotiated among family members, how parents and children translate their family language policies into everyday face-to-face interactions, what language input parents provide for their children, and how children comply with or reject parents' language choice.

Building on Lanza's (2007) discourse strategy framework, Gafaranga (2010) studied the language shift of Rwandan children in Belgium. He found that Kinyarwanda-French bilingual children constantly use *medium request* to ask for medium-switch from Kinyarwanda to French when speaking with adults. Describing the strategies that adults used to accommodate children's medium request, he showed how language policy was negotiated through face-to-face interactions, and how adults often accommodated to children's requests through medium negotiation. During the process of medium request, children's language production in Kinyarwanda began to decrease and French was used in almost all situations, thus leading to language shift.

Also studying language maintenance, Meyer Pitton (2013) reported a case study of Russian-French-speaking couples with young children living in Switzerland.

Observing interactions between parents and children, she focused specifically on their negotiating behaviour and language choice at the dinner table. Using language socialisation as her theoretical framework, she confirmed that language maintenance involving more than one language is often accompanied by language meshing and code-switching. In this regard, language maintenance through conversation in two or more languages during dinner table negotiation is not the primary concern of the families; rather, languages are used to socialise children into a particular behaviour.

Highlighting the role of linguistic practices in everyday interactions, Li Wei (2011) states that identity, attitudes, and relationships can be accepted and rejected, all in the process of interaction. Zhu Hua's (2008) work on bilingual intergenerational talk illustrated that conflictual sociocultural values and identities are intensely negotiated, mediated, and evaluated in bilingual interactions. Curdt-Christiansen (2013b), basing her work on discourse analysis of family talk in homework sessions, demonstrated that a range of FLPs are established and enacted in Singaporean Chinese bilingual families through parental discourse strategies, from highly organised and overt policies to unreflective, laissez-faire attitudes.

These interactional studies have also addressed an important topic—translanguaging (Garcia & Li Wei, 2014; see also Li Wei, Chapter 29 in this volume). They showed that in the process of language negotiation, language users rely on a linguistic theory of social relevance to index their beliefs. This is demonstrated by caregivers' intention to maintain heritage languages and children's agentive role to use new codes. In choosing a code, a bilingual speaker assesses the potential power of his or her choice, depending on the social situation in a given community. In Gafaranga's case, the Rwandan children used French as their choice to negotiate their rights and obligations in the processes of constructing FLP.

The previously mentioned studies, as well as others not included in this review, demonstrate that face-to-face interactional studies can enhance our understanding of how language practices are negotiated, in what ways cultural and linguistic values are transmitted, and why language and cultural practices are changed or abandoned. I will now turn to a more explicit account of methods used in FLP research.

METHODS IN FAMILY LANGUAGE POLICY RESEARCH

The interdisciplinary nature of FLP research has generated diverse methodological approaches to the study of language maintenance, multilingual development, and social cohesion. While these diversified research perspectives contribute a variety of new insights to the fields of bilingual education, multilingualism, and language policy, they can be generally grouped into three major approaches: quantitative, qualitative/interpretive, and sociolinguistic ethnographic. I address each of them in the following, in turn.

Quantitative Approach

De Houwer's (2007) study of 1,899 bilingual families in Flanders is one of most influential and representative quantitative studies of FLP. In this study, she examined the relationship between parental language input patterns and children's minority-language use. Using a one-page questionnaire, she collected data across Dutch-medium primary schools throughout Flanders. The questionnaire consisted of three questions: (1) Where is the family residence? (2) What are the languages spoken by the mother, the father, and each child? (3) What are the family members' ages and citizenships? All families spoke a variety of a minority language X and Dutch, but the language-use pattern involving the two types of language by family members varied. Using factor analysis, she was able to establish from this intergenerational transmission study that the OPOL strategy did not produce child language use in X language. The most successful parental input patterns that have an effect on children's use of language X were those where both parents used X, or one parent used only X and the other used X + Dutch. Her study showed that parents play an important role in their children's bilingual experiences.

In a more recent study, Kang (2015) investigated 480 Korean families in the United States about their FLPs. Using a web-based survey, she aimed to examine what types of FLP and demographic variables predict maintenance of the home language. The survey included five variables: (1) background information, including length of residence in the United States, mother's education, age of the parents and their children; (2) language practice, including eleven survey items on parents' language use during a twenty-four-hour period, covering Korean only, English only, or both Korean and English, as well as language-use patterns between family members; (3) language management, including five items concerning reading practice at home, TV watching, and attending heritage language school; (4) language ideology, including ten statements; (5) parents' assessment of children's skills in Korean. The results indicate that demographic variables, such as immigration status and the mother's education level, were not strong predictors of home language maintenance. Parental attitudes towards early bilingualism and parental management strategies strongly predicted the development of literacy skills in the home language. She concluded that simple exposure to authentic input at home may not be sufficient for developing literacy in the heritage language.

Similar quantitative studies using language surveys to explore parental language attitudes, language practices, and children's heritage language development have also been carried out in different parts of the world, such as Ó hIfearnáin (2013) in

Ireland, Sevinç's (2016) study of Turkish children in The Netherlands, Duursma et al.'s (2007) study of Spanish-English bilingual children in the United States, and Schwartz's (2008) study of second-generation Russian-Jewish children in Israel. These quantitative studies, however, tend to rely on parents' self-reports. What exactly happens at home needs to be examined through other measures and from children's perspective. For example, how do children perceive parental language input? In what ways do language practice patterns vary between family members? And how do language practice patterns index family members' ideologies and language beliefs?

Other types of quantitative studies are beginning to emerge, using longitudinal data collected across different periods in children's lives (Byers-Heinlein, 2013; De Houwer & Bornstein, 2016). This type of research still focuses on parental language input patterns and their effect on children's language production. These studies do not, however, consider the sociocultural environment factors that influence parental decisions about raising bi/multilingual children.

Qualitative and Interpretive Approach

Many FLP studies concerning language ideology are qualitative, in that researchers use interview and narrative inquiry to capture participants' lived experiences of raising multilingual children. Such approaches to studying FLP take into account the ways in which parents and children construct their intergenerational transmission experiences in relation to the broader sociocultural contexts.

One of the early studies in the field was conducted by Touminen (1999), who interviewed migrant parents in Seattle. The interviews were carried out either with the parents alone or in pairs, sometimes with their children present. Although she indicated that she also asked some children questions during the interview, the data and analysis of the conversations did not include the children's views on the matter of language transmission. Focusing on parents' deliberate actions of "creating language situations that allow and encourage the children to use that [minority] language" (Touminen, 1999, p. 60), she concluded that children were often the ones who decided what the family's language would be.

Interpretive enquiry through interviews and life history have contributed to our understanding of the role of FLP in minority/endangered language maintenance. Studies that I have reviewed earlier, such as Curdt-Christiansen (2009, 2014, 2015), Lane (2010) and Wang (2017), as well as those I have not reviewed here, such as Armstrong (2014), Chatzidaki and Maligkoudi (2013), and Simpson (2013), all employed these tools of enquiry to enhance our understanding of the interplay between language practice and language ideology.

Contributing to the ongoing investigation of the relationship between language and power, a special issue of *Language Policy*, dedicated to FLP and edited by

Curdt-Christiansen (2013a), has a particular focus on narrative and ethnographic data. Contributors to this thematic issue used life history (Seloni & Sarfati, 2013), interview and participant observation (Patrick et al., 2013; Pérez Baéz, 2013; Ren & Hu, 2013), and interview and ethno-theories (Fogle, 2013; Harkness & Super, 2006) to capture the multidimensional characteristics of FLP and the complex relationship between ideology and language practice. The articles in this special issue provide a different lens from that of quantitative methods to look at how parents make use of linguistic and cultural resources to facilitate, revitalise, and enrich minority-language practices at home (Patrick et al., 2013; Ren & Hu, 2013), and why and how family members surrender to external forces by ceasing the cultural and linguistic practices of their heritage language (Pérez Baéz, 2013; Seloni & Sarfati, 2013). These studies provide varied ways of conceptualising and analysing multilingual development and language shift phenomena, yet they still focus largely on parental experiences and perspectives.

Sociolinguistic Ethnography

The third major methodological approach to studying FLP includes audio- and videorecorded family interactional data, accompanied by texts and artifacts used in family activities. It is typically examined by interaction analysis and discourse analysis. The most representative works of this kind include Lanza's (2004 [1997], 2007) parental discourse strategies, Gafaranga's (2010) study of Kinyarwanda-French bilingual children in Belgium, and Li Wei's (1994) work on a three-generation Chinese family in the United Kingdom. These studies focused mainly on the processes of language shift and on the language experiences of multilingual families. As Li Wei (2011) states, this approach allows us to capture the moment-to-moment moves and the subtlety of translanguaging that contribute to language maintenance or language change among family members.

This approach to studying FLP has been emerging in recent years. In a special issue of the *Journal of Multilingual and Multicultural Development*, edited by Lanza and Li Wei (2016), contributors enriched the pool of data on FLP development. Drawing from this perspective, Curdt-Christiansen (2014, 2016) reported how Singaporean families' language practices are contradictory to their claimed beliefs, while Zhu Hua and Li Wei (2016) looked at how family members experience the gradual changes in languages in the United Kingdom. Also in this volume, Agnes He (2016) described how child and adult speakers construct meaning through repair and reformulation.

In sum, this review of methodological approaches to FLP illustrates the dynamic characteristics of FLP as an interdisciplinary enquiry. The data collected by using quantitative, qualitative, and interpretive as well as ethnolinguistic tools have extended our knowledge of the impact of parental language input on children's language output, have enriched our understanding of the powerful role of language socialisation in FLP, and have enhanced our awareness of the changing social and educational policies that influence family language decisions. Despite the vigorous approaches employed by researchers, the field can be further advanced by examining the essential interplay between macro-, meso- and micro-levels of linguistic practices and policy decisions. New ways of looking into FLP and new measures of examining FLP entail a critical understanding of family language planning as dynamic, fluid, and changeable in the life span of a given family.

It is particularly important to understand how families respond to constant social and political changes, make sense of educational policy initiatives, and reshape family language policies accordingly. These and other future research directions are discussed in the following section in more detail.

FUTURE DIRECTIONS

The study of FLP is focused on the role of language practice and language management in the family, both for intergenerational transmission and for developing multilingual speakers. Over the years, FLP research has moved beyond the notion that FLP is a private family matter to a broader sociopolitical concern that emphasises sociocultural values and power relationships among speakers of different language varieties. From this perspective, the study of FLP in recent years has given increased attention to language ideology and the sociopolitical contexts in which families are situated. Our understanding of the role of FLP in a given society can only be enhanced by interdisciplinary methods that examine the hybridity of language practices within the broader processes of language change and multilingual development.

Tollefson (2013) points out that intensified transnational migration and global flow of people entail "important social changes" (p. 22) during which "intense competition for places in schools and for the new jobs that require literacy and varying levels of fluency in English and other colonial and regional languages often leads to violence and the repression of minorities" (p. 23). Thus, interdisciplinary research into how family members continue or discontinue their family language practices in relation to the broader social and educational policy will continue to be welcome.

Ethnographic studies, for example, can reveal not only how individuals mobilise and react to different ideological perspectives in society, but also how they shape the language varieties used outside their home. In this respect, children's role in shaping FLP should be an important research focus, as Tuominen (1999) pointed out more than a decade ago in her study of "who decides the home language?." As children are agents of change, understanding ideologically shaped linguistic experiences from their perspective will shed important light on "how power is represented and reflected in and through languages" (Curdt-Christiansen, 2013a, p. 5). Home language observations across different communities and across different types of families will yield important insights into the social, cultural, and political complexities of family members' everyday experiences of migration and social changes.

Finally, constant changes in technology and their impact on children, parents, and extended family members require researchers to look beyond the confines of the home domain to include communications with family members living far away, sometimes across huge geographic distance. There is an urgent need for researchers to look into how these new technologies intervene in and facilitate intergenerational transmission and language development.

NOTE

1. The three official mother tongues are not necessarily the home languages for the three major ethnic groups. Singapore is a multi-ethnic and multilingual society in which each ethnic group speaks multiple varieties of their ethnic language. The Chinese community, for example, speaks eleven "dialects," including Hokkien, Teochew, and Cantonese; the Indians speak Punjabi, Malayalam, and several other languages; and the Malays' repertoire includes Bazaar Malay, Javanese, Buginese, and more. In order to manage this vast variety of language groups, the government decided that each ethnic group should have an official common mother tongue, which was also taught in schools.

REFERENCES

Armstrong, T.C. (2014). Naturalism and ideological work: How is family language policy renegotiated as both parents and children learn a threatened minority language? *International Journal of Bilingual Education and Bilingualism* 17(5), 570–585.

Blommaert, J. (2006). Language policy and national identity. In T. Ricento (Ed.), *An introduction to language policy: Theory and method* (pp. 238–254). Malden, MA: Blackwell.

Byers-Heinlein, K. (2013). Parental language mixing: Its measurement and the relation of mixed input to young bilingual children's vocabulary size. *Bilingualism: Language and Cognition* 16, 32–48.

Caldas, S. (2006). *Raising bilingual-biliterate children in monolingual cultures*. Clevedon, UK: Multilingual Matters.

Canagarajah, A. S. (2011). Diaspora communities, language maintenance, and policy dilemmas. In T. L. McCarty (Ed.), *Ethnography and language policy* (pp. 77–97). London; New York: Routledge.

Chatzidaki, A., & Maligkoudi. C. (2013) Family language policies among Albanian immigrants in Greece. *International Journal of Bilingual Education and Bilingualism* 16(6), 675–689.

Curdt-Christiansen, X. L. (2009). Visible and invisible language planning: Ideological factors in the family language policy of Chinese immigrant families in Quebec. *Language Policy* 8(4), 351–375.

Curdt-Christiansen, X. L. (2012). Private language management in Singapore: Which language to practice and how? In A. S. Yeung, C. F. K. Lee, & E. L. Brown (Eds.), *Communication and language* (pp. 55–77). Scottsdale, AZ: Information Age.

Curdt-Christiansen, X. L. (2013a). Editorial: Family language policy: Sociopolitical reality versus linguistic continuity. *Language Policy* 13(1), 1–7.

Curdt-Christiansen, X. L. (2013b). Negotiating family language policy: Doing homework. In M. Schwartz & A. Verschik, (Eds.), *Successful family language policy: Parents, children and educators in interaction* (pp. 277–295). Dordrecht: Springer.

Curdt-Christiansen, X. L. (2014). Family language policy: Is learning Chinese at odds with learning English in Singapore? In X. L. Curdt-Christiansen & A. Hancock (Eds.), *Learning Chinese in diasporic communities: Many pathways to being Chinese* (pp. 35–58). Amsterdam: John Benjamins.

Curdt-Christiansen, X. L. (2015). Family language policy in the Chinese community in Singapore: A question of balance? In Li Wei (Ed.), *Multilingualism in the Chinese diaspora worldwide* (pp. 255–275). London; New York: Routledge.

Curdt-Christiansen, X. L. (2016). Conflicting language ideologies and contradictory language practices in Singaporean bilingual families. *Journal of Multilingual and Multicultural Development* 37(7), 694–709.

De Houwer, A. (1990). *The acquisition of two languages: A case study*. Cambridge: Cambridge University Press.

De Houwer, A. (2007). Parental language input patterns and children's bilingual use. *Applied Psycholinguistics* 27, 411–424.

De Houwer, A., & Bornstein, M. (2016). Bilingual mothers' language choice in child-directed speech: Continuity and change. *Journal of Multilingual and Multicultural Development* 37(7), 694–709.

Duranti, A., Ochs, E., & Schieffelin, B. (Eds.). (2011). *The handbook of language socialization*. Oxford: Blackwell.

Duursma, E., Romero-Contreras, S., Azuber, A., Proctor, P., Snow, C., August, D., & Calderon, M. (2007). The role of home literacy and language environment in bilinguals' English and Spanish vocabulary development. *Applied Psycholinguistics* 28(1), 171–190.

Fishman, J. (1991). *Reversing language shift*. Clevedon, UK: Multilingual Matters.

Fogle, L. W. (2012). *Second language socialization and learner agency: Adoptive family talk*. Clevedon, UK: Multilingual Matters.

Fogle, L. W. (2013). Parental ethnotheories and family language policy in transnational adoptive families. *Language Policy* 12(1), 83–102.

Gafaranga, J. (2010). Medium request: Talking language shift into being. *Language in Society* 39(2), 241–270.

Garcia, O., & Li Wei. (2014). *Translanguaging: Language, bilingualism and education*. Basingstoke, UK: Palgrave MacMillan.

Garrett, P. B. (2011). Language socialisation and language shift. In A. Duranti, E. Ochs, & B. Schieffelin, (Eds.), *The handbook of language socialization* (pp. 515–535). Oxford: Blackwell.

Harkness, S., & Super, C. (2006). Themes and variations: Parental ethnotheories in Western cultures. In K. Rubin & O. B. Chung, (Eds.), *Parenting beliefs, behaviors, and parent-child relations: A cross cultural perspective* (pp. 61–80). New York: Psychology Press.

He, A. W. (2016). Discursive roles and responsibilities: A study of interactions in Chinese immigrant households. *Journal of Multilingual and Multicultural Development* 37(7), 655–666.

Kang, H. (2015). Korean families in America: Their family language policies and home language maintenance. *Bilingual Research Journal* 38, 275–291.

King, K. A. (2000). Language ideologies and heritage language education. *International Journal of Bilingual Education and Bilingualism* 3(3), 167–184.

King, K. A. (2013). A tale of three sisters: Language learning and linguistic identity in a transnational family. *International Multilingual Research Journal* 7, 49–65.

King, K. A., & Fogle, L. (2006). Bilingual parenting as good parenting: Parents' perspectives on family language policy for additive bilinguals. *International Journal of Bilingual Education and Bilingualism* 9(6), 695–712.

King, K. A., Fogle, L., & Logan-Terry, A. (2008). Family language policy. *Language and Linguistics Compass* 2(5), 907–922.

King, K. A., & Logan-Terry, A. (2008). Additive bilingualism through family language policy: Ideologies, strategies and interactional outcomes. *Calidoscópio* 6(1), 5–19.

Kirsch, C. (2012). Ideologies, struggles and contradictions: An account of mothers raising their children bilingually in Luxembourgish and English in Great Britain. *International Journal of Bilingual Education and Bilingualism* 15(1), 95–112.

Kroskrity, P. (2010). Language ideologies: Evolving perspectives. In J. Jaspers, J. Östaman, & J. Verschueren, (Eds.), *Society and language use* (pp. 192–211). Amsterdam: John Benjamins.

Lane, P. (2010). "We did what we thought was best for our children:" A nexus analysis of language shift in a Kvan community. *International Journal of the Sociology of Language* 202, 63–78.

Lanza, E. (2004 [1997]). *Language mixing in infant bilingualism: A sociolinguistic perspective.* Oxford: Oxford University Press.

Lanza, E. (2007). Multilingualism in the family. In P. Auer & Li Wei (Eds.), *Handbook of multilingualism and multilingual communication* (pp. 45–67). Berlin: Mouton de Gruyter.

Lanza, E., & Li Wei (2016). Multilingual encounters in transcultural families. *Journal of Multilingual and Multicultural Development* 37(7), 653–654.

Li, G. (2007). Home environment and second language acquisition: The importance of family capital. *British Journal of Sociology of Education* 28(3), 285–299.

Li Wei. (1994). *Three generations, two languages, one family: Language choice and language shift in a Chinese community in Britain.* Clevedon, UK: Multilingual Matters

Li Wei. (2011). Moment analysis and translanguaging space: Discursive construction of identities by multilingual Chinese youth in Britain. *Journal of Pragmatics* 43, 1222–1235.

Li Wei, Saravanan, V., & Ng, J. (1997). Language shift in the Teochew community in Singapore: A family domain analysis. *Journal of Multilingual and Multicultural Development* 18(5), 364–384.

Meyer Pitton, L. (2013). From language maintenance to bilingual parenting: Negotiating behaviour and language choice at the dinner table in binational-bilingual families. *Multilingua* 32(4), 507–526.

Ó hIfearnáin, T. (2013). Family language policy, first language Irish speaker attitudes and community-based response to language shift. *Journal of Multilingual and Multicultural Development* 34(4), 348–365.

Ó hIfearnáin, T. (2015). Sociolinguistic vitality of Manx after extreme language shift: Authenticity without traditional native speakers. *International Journal of the Sociology of Language* 231, 45–62.

Okita, T. (2002). *Invisible work: Bilingualism, language choice and childrearing in intermarried families.* Amsterdam: John Benjamins.

Palvianinen, Å., & Boyd, S. (2013). Unity in discourse, diversity in practice: The one person one language policy in bilingual families. In M. Schwartz & A. Verschik (Eds.), *Successful family language policy: Parents, children and educators in interaction* (pp. 223–248). Dordrecht: Springer.

Patrick, D., Budach, G., & Muckpaloo, I. (2013). Multiliteracies and family language policy in an urban Inuit community. *Language Policy* 12(1), 47–62.

Pavlenko, A. (2004). "Stop doing that, La Komu Skazala": Language choice and emotions in parent-child communication. *Journal of Multilingual and Multicultural Development* 25(2–3), 179–203.

Pérez Báez, G. (2013). Family language policy, transnationalism, and the diaspora community of San Lucas Quiaviní of Oaxaca, Mexico. *Language Policy* 12(1), 27–45.

Piller, I. (2002). *Bilingual couples talk: The discursive construction of hybridity.* Amsterdam: John Benjamins.

Ren, L., & Hu, G. (2013). Prolepsis, reciprocity and syncretism in early language and biliteracy practices: A case study of family language policy in Singapore. *Language Policy* 12(1), 63–82.

Romaine, S. (1995). *Bilingualism.* 2nd edition. Oxford: Basil Blackwell.

Ronjat, J. (1913). *Le development du langage osvervé chez un enfant bilingue.* Paris: Champion.

Schwartz, M. (2008). Exploring the relationship between family language policy and heritage: Language knowledge among second generation Russian-Jewish immigrants in Israel. *Journal of Multilingual and Multicultural Development* 29(5), 400–418.

Schwartz, M., & Verschik, A. (Eds.). (2013). *Successful family language policy: Parents, children and educators in interaction.* Dordrecht: Springer.

Seloni, L., & Sarfati, Y. (2013). (Trans)national language ideologies and family language practices: A life history inquiry of Judeo-Spanish in Turkey. *Language Policy* 12(1), 7–26.

Sevinç, Y. (2016). Language maintenance and shift under pressure: Three generations of the Turkish immigrant community in the Netherlands. *International Journal of the Sociology of Language* 242, 81–117.

Simpson, J. (2013). What's done and what's said: Language attitudes, public language activities and everyday talk in the Northern Territory of Australia. *Journal of Multilingual and Multicultural Development* 34(4), 364–384.

Smith-Christmas, C. (2016). *Family language policy: Maintaining an endangered language in the home.* London: Palgrave McMillian.

Spolsky, B. (2004). *Language policy.* Cambridge: Cambridge University Press.

Spolsky, B. (2009). *Language management.* Cambridge: Cambridge University Press.

Spolsky, B. (2012). Family language policy: The critical domain. *Journal of Multilingual and Multicultural Development* 33(1), 3–11.

Stavans, A. (2012). Language policy and literary practices in the family: The case of Ethiopian parental narrative input. *Journal of Multilingual and Multicultural Development* 33(1), 13–33.

Tollefson, J. W. (Ed.). (2002). *Language policies in education: Critical issues.* 1st edition. New York; London: Routledge.

Tollefson, J. W. (Ed.). (2013). *Language policies in education: Critical issues.* 2nd edition. New York; London: Routledge.

Tannenbaum, M. (2012). Family language policy as a form of coping or defence mechanism. *Journal of Multilingual and Multicultural Development* 33(1), 57–66.

Touminen, A. (1999). Who decides the home language? A look at multilingual families. *International Journal of the Sociology of Language* 140, 59–96.

Wang, X. (2017). Family language policy by Hakkas in Balik Pulau, Penang. *International Journal of the Sociology of Language* 244, 87–118.

Zhu, Hua. (2008). Duelling languages, duelling values: Codeswitching in bilingual intergenerational conflict talk in diasporic families. *Journal of Pragmatics* 40, 1799–1816.

Zhu, Hua, & Li Wei. (2016). Transnational experience, aspiration and family language policy. *Journal of Multilingual and Multicultural Development* 37(7), 655–666.

CHAPTER 22

....

LANGUAGE POLICIES AND SIGN LANGUAGES

....

RONICE MÜLLER DE QUADROS

THIS chapter argues for specific actions needed for language planning and language policies involving sign languages and Deaf communities, based on the understanding of what sign languages are, who the signers are, where they sign, and the sign language transmission and maintenance mechanisms of the Deaf community. The first section presents an overview of sign languages and their users, highlighting that sign languages are often used in contexts where most people use spoken languages. The acquisition of sign languages among children and adults is also discussed. The second section addresses the functions, roles, and status of sign languages in relation to spoken languages, as well as the relationship between Deaf communities and hearing society.[1] The medical view of deafness, which has a significant impact on language policies for Deaf people, is also critically considered. The third section offers examples of language policies, especially related to the use of sign languages in education, and an agenda for future work on sign language policy and planning.

SIGN LANGUAGES AND THEIR USERS

A discussion on sign languages requires first considering their social context, including their linguistic status and their acquisition. The range of people in Deaf communities needs to be described as well, such as Deaf people born to Deaf or hearing parents and who were exposed to sign language at different periods in their lives, and hearing people born into Deaf families. These familial circumstances impact conditions of transmission and maintenance of sign languages. All of these issues will be detailed in the subsections that follow.

The Linguistic Status of Sign Languages

Sign languages have specific grammatical features, are used across Deaf and hearing communities, and, as in the case of spoken languages, are shaped by patterns of geographical and social distribution. With regard to the grammar, and in contrast to speech articulation (using the mouth, tongue, etc.), sign languages are pronounced by the body, more specifically, arms, hands, and face, in a system in which words are combinations of visuospatial phonological units, including handshapes associated with locations and specific movements (Stokoe, 1978 [1960]). These articulators combine to produce multimorphemic meaning units, as words and sentences. From these morpheme combinations, phrases and sentences are built according to specific rules, following semantic and pragmatic specifications. Thus, sign languages are full languages from a linguistic point of view. This linguistic validation of sign languages has had a considerable impact on Deaf education. In particular, many Deaf community sign languages have been introduced into the Deaf education system within a bilingual educational framework (Hoffmeister & Caldwell-Harris, 2014; Marschark, Tang, & Knoors, 2014; Quadros, 1997).

Sign languages usually have grammars different from their surrounding spoken languages. For example, in Brazil, Brazilian Sign Language (Libras) and Brazilian Portuguese have different orders for adjectives and nouns, negation, and wh-structures (Quadros & Karnopp, 2004). American Sign Language (ASL) and English differ in similar ways (Aarons, 1994; Petronio, 1993; Stokoe, 1978 [1960]). Sign languages are also unrelated across country boundaries, even when a surrounding spoken language may be shared. British Sign Language (BSL) and ASL, Libras and Portuguese Sign Language (LGP), and Catalan Sign Language and Spanish Sign Language are all different sign languages. For example, in BSL and ASL, different sets of handshapes and movements make these languages completely unrelated. However, ASL, Libras, Mexican Sign Language (MSL), and French Sign Language (FSL) are related, because these sign languages were strongly influenced by FSL when Deaf teachers came from France to their respective countries to implement Deaf education in the nineteenth century (Diniz, 2011; Fenlon & Wilkinson, 2015; Quadros & Karnopp, 2004; Quer, 2012; Quinto-Pozos & Adam, 2015).

As a result of contact between signed and spoken languages, signed languages may use what is called *fingerspelling*, to create signs by using the handshapes representing the initial letters of words from the spoken language, or in some cases handshapes in a sequence that represents the complete word from the spoken language. Additionally, mouthing (i.e., mouth movements that follow the signs) can be used to include partial production of words from spoken languages (Quinto-Pozos & Adam, 2015; Sutton-Spence, 1994, 2007).

As for the relationship between Deaf and hearing communities, these communities share the same spaces in everyday life, though Deaf people create micro-universes in Deaf communities that use sign languages. Indeed, almost all Deaf children grow up within hearing families that use a spoken language. In some cases, members of these families learn sign language, but in most, the Deaf child will only have contact with sign language at school, where it may be used by their sign language interpreters or a sign language teacher, and in some cases with Deaf peers. As they grow up, most Deaf children will probably have contact with Deaf communities. In many countries, Deaf communities form associations that provide a space for Deaf people to meet, creating a comfort zone where they are able to interact with each other using their sign language. This was the case even when signed languages were forbidden in schools (for example, by the Milan Congress in 1880 [Fisher & Lane, 1993]).

Concerning the patterns of distribution, national sign languages usually exist in big cities, but there are also village sign languages and sign languages indigenous to local places (Aranoff et al., 2004; Nonaka, 2004).[2] For example, in Brazil, Brazilian Sign Language, a national sign language, is used throughout the country, whereas Urubu Kaapor Sign Language is used among the Urubu Kaapor indigenous community (Kakumasu, 1978) and Cena Sign Language is used in an isolated community in Piauí, Brazil (reported by Pereira, 2013). In these latter two communities, hearing and Deaf people use the local sign language and speak the local spoken languages. In these specific cases, the sign language occurs inside their communities within a wider community that speaks Brazilian Portuguese (BP). This situation creates a unique group of languages to discuss within a *heritage* language framework, defined by Benmamoun, Montrul, and Polinksy (2013) as minority languages in a specific context in which there is a different dominant language in the larger community.

In such contexts, use of the dominant language occurs in most public spaces, such as schools, media, and public institutions, usually as part of a policy-level *monolingual strategy* (Blommaert, 2010, p. 46) aiming to build monolingualism while simultaneously rejecting bilingualism. As a consequence, the impact on the heritage languages in these sociocultural environments tends to be incomplete acquisition, attrition, or even language death. I shall now turn to issues concerned with acquisition of sign languages in more detail.

Acquisition of Sign Languages

Understanding the process of sign languages acquisition requires a careful consideration of the family contexts in which these languages are used and learned, as well as of the issues and struggles among members of the Deaf community over who gets to own the language. Family contexts may vary depending on the linguistic profiles of the family members involved. Acquisition of sign languages will be explored with reference to how sign languages are passed on through generations, considering three different types of family configurations: (1) Deaf people from Deaf families; (2) Deaf children with hearing parents; and (3) hearing children of Deaf parents.

Compton and Compton (2014) consider Deaf people from Deaf families to be heritage signers, because they are in a Deaf family and in a Deaf community. Since access to spoken language is restricted by their hearing status, sign language is usually well established as the first language (L1) of such children. In this context, children commonly have much more contact with their sign language than with the spoken language of the wider hearing community, even when surrounded by speakers in the hearing community. Such Deaf children typically attend Deaf schools, where they will not experience the impact of an education in a spoken language, as do Deaf children who attend non-residential or mainstreaming programs (i.e., in hearing schools). Therefore, sign language is the language used most often for such Deaf people.

Deaf children with hearing parents may not have access to sign language until later years, because their parents, typically influenced by hearing professionals, often choose to teach them only the spoken language. In such situations, the attitude toward sign languages for young Deaf children is often that sign languages are related to special needs or are simply gestures based on spoken languages, rather than "real" languages. The myth of the superiority of monolingualism, based on an imagined monolingual and social uniformity (Blommaert, 2010), may also drive hearing parents' choices.

Many hearing people may not know about the existence of any sign language in their country. Because hearing parents are part of this wider community, they may believe (often encouraged by medical and speech professionals) that a single dominant spoken language should be used. Yet being born to hearing parents who do not know a sign language often results in limited sign language acquisition due to delayed input of either a sign language or a spoken language and the need for formal instruction over many years (Aranoff et al., 2004; Mayberry, 2010; Singleton & Newport, 2004). In some cases, Deaf children with hearing parents experience great difficulty acquiring the spoken language, and may create their own home sign system (Goldin-Meadow, 2003). As they mature and come in contact with the Deaf community, they may be exposed to a community signed language. This exposure at a later age may allow them to modify their home sign system and become conversant in a sign language, although there are negative consequences of late sign language acquisition (Davidson & Mayberry, 2015; Lieberman et al., 2014), such as the use of simple sentences, restricted L1 vocabulary, and difficulties in reading and writing the L2.

Variation in sign language input for Deaf children with hearing parents is dependent on family background and how early children have contact with the local adult sign language (Goldin-Meadow, 2003; Mayberry, 2010; Quadros, 1997;

Singleton & Newport, 2004). Indeed, the acquisition context of signers can be complex, so it is important to plan sign language acquisition for Deaf children carefully as part of sign language policies. Unless the social circumstances can ensure early access to a grammatically complete and lexically rich sign language, Deaf people will usually construct the lexicon of their natural language through an emerging language (Leite & Quadros, 2014). This situation makes sign languages vulnerable.

Two of the most common factors contributing to this form of endangerment include parents' decisions about the language policy at home and the attitudes about sign languages in their local communities. First, parents' choice can lead to restricted input, which in turn may critically impact the first years in which sign language acquisition takes place. This is particularly the case of the communication system used by hearing parents or hearing professionals, such as teachers or speech clinicians who do not have advanced sign language skills and are the primary communicative interactors with the Deaf child. Some parents may opt to interact with their Deaf child by using primarily a spoken language accompanied by gestures, while others may begin to learn sign language as a second language. If the former, the Deaf child is exposed to gestures that are not related to any dialect of a sign language. If the latter, the input will not initially be that of a fluent language since parents are learning the language along with the child; that is, the result may be a pidginized version of the sign language (a kind of interlanguage, according to Sánchez, 2015) used by second-language learners such as hearing teachers or hearing sign language interpreters who are not fluent signers (Leite & Quadros, 2014). Such input is common in non-residential and mainstream schools.

The second factor that makes sign languages vulnerable—attitudes toward sign languages and their users—is mainly concerned with stereotypes and inaccurate ideas about the nature of sign language and about the social status of Deaf people. Such ideas may be held by hearing teachers, sign language interpreters, and others in the community, thus creating a negative language learning experience (Bauman, 2010; Hill, 2013; Leite & Quadros, 2014).

Hearing children of Deaf parents may acquire and use the sign language of their parents at home, and acquire and use a spoken language with other hearing people who coexist in their environment, such as hearing family members, neighbors, and peers at school. In this kind of heritage language context, children often have ample access to the spoken language of their community as well as to their parents' and the Deaf community's sign language. Lillo-Martin et al. (2014) observed that there is also considerable variability in the balance of the languages acquired among hearing children of Deaf parents. Deaf parents vary in their ability to produce and interact in a spoken language: some are able to speak relatively clearly, and some are able to follow some speech (speechreading or lipreading), while others are only able to read and use print. When Deaf children become adults and have children, most of the children are hearing (estimates are the inverse of Deaf children born to hearing parents). The sign language backgrounds of Deaf parents vary considerably

(Mitchell & Karchmer, 2004; Singleton & Newport, 2004): some (10% or less) were exposed as children to signers from families with more than one generation of Deaf members, while others (up to 90%) learned to sign at later ages; in rare cases, some developed no sign language skills.

Hearing children who learn a sign language from a young age are called *bimodal bilinguals*, because they have two languages in two different modalities (sign and speech) (Lillo-Martin, et al., 2014). Emmorey et al. (2008) observed that sociolinguistic factors might influence the options in the language production of these children. They may use a bimodal mode, a blended mode in which signs and speech are produced simultaneously, or they may avoid one mode, depending on whom they are conversing with. Also, there may be a strong influence of the spoken language in their communication choices, since frequently the spoken language becomes their primary and dominant language; nevertheless, they still are able to distinguish between speech and sign contexts. When such hearing children grow up, we may see the effects of the dominant cultural and social attitudes toward sign and speech, for example when speech becomes their preferred primary language, or their first-language or sign-language ability experiences degradation or loss.

Chen Pichler et al. (2014) also stress variability in the language development of bimodal bilingual children. They found that Deaf families often contribute to the maintenance of sign languages, in that they encourage their hearing children not only to become fluent in sign language, but also to interact with a wide variety of Deaf people. This interaction provides insight as to how the wider community values sign language. The circumstances of school, peers, and hearing adults in the surrounding dominant language environment usually influence hearing children of Deaf parents to use spoken language much more than their heritage language. It is possible that the attitudes of different signers and speakers toward the language used by hearing children with Deaf parents may also play a role in their language choice, as is the case in other heritage language contexts in Brazil and in the United States (Kondo-Brown, 2006; Peyton, Ranard, & McGinnis, 2001). In many of these bimodal bilingual cases, significant variation in language interaction is reported; this variation is determined by multiple factors, among them, the status of the languages (Quadros, 2017).

The types of family environments outlined in the preceding provide a complex picture around issues of sign language acquisition. But how are sign languages transmitted down through the generations vis-à-vis community struggles over who gets to "own" the language? In general, Deaf adults and children in Deaf communities pass on their sign languages to other Deaf people (Dalcin, 2006), a type of peer transmission commonly experienced among the Deaf community (Lane, Hoffmeister, & Bahan, 1996). In this sense, Deaf-Deaf encounters are crucial for the establishment and transmission of sign languages around the world (Miranda, 2001; Wrigley, 1996). The idea of a Deaf-Deaf meeting is celebrated in the Deaf community, since it represents the perpetuation of the sign language heritage (Miranda, 2001), despite all the complexity involved in accessing this language. Children, hearing and Deaf, are part of the community, since they share their experiences, their culture, and their language. By extension, other Deaf people who are not from Deaf families are welcome in the Deaf community and are enabled to share in the sign language and culture of the Deaf community.

Through the recent increasing popularity of sign language in some countries (such as in the United States and Brazil), hearing people have increasing access to sign language, with many learning it as a second language. As a result, there is intensive discussion among members of the Deaf community about sign language ownership. Many Deaf people prefer to believe that it is *their* language (Facebook group *Sociedade em Libras*, 2015). However, hearing people who learn a sign language as a second language and become bilinguals may also consider themselves owners of this sign language. Similarly, Deaf people are becoming increasingly bilingual, learning the spoken and/or written language as a second language, and some feel that the spoken language is their language as well.

The following section examines the relationship between hearing and Deaf communities, including the medical view of Deaf people as physically deficient and the effects of this view on the functions, roles, and status of sign languages.

Tensions between Deaf and Hearing Communities

The relationship between speakers of sign languages and spoken languages is highly complex, often characterized by tension and uncertainty. One source of tension is that spoken languages are used in most communication and official settings, and are used as medium of instruction and taught as subjects in schools, whereas sign languages are often excluded from many institutional and social settings. The issue here is their difference in social status. A second issue for sign languages is the negative attitudes expressed in the medical perspective toward Deaf people and hearing loss (Balkany, 1993; Byrd et al., 2011; Hoffmeister, 1993; Lane, 1992; Miranda, 2001; Skliar, 1998; Wrigley, 1996). These two aspects have significant impact on language policies related to education and the approach of health-care professionals in their effort to solve what they consider to be the problem of deafness and hearing loss. Each of these will be explored in the following.

Social Status of Sign Languages

Tensions created by deaf communities' attempts to raise the social status of sign languages and resistance from certain areas of hearing society may be seen in various policy areas, of which some of the principal ones will be considered here. Specific issues that have had a direct effect on the language status of sign languages and policies affecting them include struggles over official recognition of linguistic diversity, appropriate provision of sign language in Deaf education, understanding of the structural relationships between spoken and signed languages, standardization, and language use in the media.

Efforts to raise the social status of sign language include intensive work by the World Federation of the Deaf (WFD, 2016) to help national Deaf organizations campaign for sign languages to be officially recognized as essential to local communities. In contrast to many hearing professionals, Deaf communities in several countries advocate a positive perspective about their national and local sign languages. In Europe, for example, the Catalan Deaf community recognizes Catalan Sign Language as a language of the community, and fights for its use as the language of instruction in education and for access to subject matter through Catalan Sign Language in specific programs, with written Catalan as a second language (Quer, 2012). In Brazil as well, the Deaf community fights for the right of Deaf children to have access to bilingual education in which Brazilian Sign Language is the language of instruction and Portuguese is taught as a second language (Quadros, 1997, 2012; Quadros et al., 2014).

However, language policies still tend to favor dominant spoken languages. For instance, in Spain, where the government recognized Catalan as one of the official languages of the country, sign languages are becoming recognized, but there remains a misunderstanding that Catalan Sign Language and Spanish Sign Language are variants of the same language, similar to dialect variation in spoken languages. In Brazil, despite the fact that Brazilian Sign Language (used by Brazilian Deaf communities across the country) is recognized as a *national* language through Law 10.436/2002, the educational system functions primarily in Brazilian Portuguese, the official language of the country. This vision of Portuguese as the sole language for education runs contrary to the Federal Government's National Institute of Historic and Artistic Heritage, which recognizes Brazilian Sign Language, as well as all the other languages used in Brazil, as national languages. In other words, despite Decree 7387/2010 (National Inventory of Linguistic Diversity), which should include all Brazilian languages, both signed and spoken, as part of the heritage of the country and recognizes them as part of the multiple identities of the country, the language policy has not been implemented effectively.

Brazilian Deaf organizations have used the law to claim their language rights, demanding a bilingual education for deaf children that uses Brazilian sign language and Portuguese. However, the government has prioritized the inclusion of sign language interpreters in schools, because it is still not widely understood that providing an interpreter is inadequate for bilingual education or education in sign language.

In the United States, unlike Brazil, there is no national language law recognizing American Sign Language (ASL), although the American Deaf community recognizes it as their language. Consequently, although some states do have a language policy to promote ASL, others do not, and there are efforts by medical, speech, and hearing professionals to suppress sign language in favor of the spoken language (Hill, 2013).

Further tensions in relation to the social status of sign languages arise from a lack of understanding of the structural relationship between sign languages and spoken languages. Indeed, in many countries there is a substantial difference between the way Deaf people see their languages and the hearing community's perspective toward sign languages. For instance, the influence of English on ASL may be viewed differently by Deaf and hearing communities. Kuntze et al. (2014; an article written by Deaf and hearing researchers) refer to fingerspelling as a part of sign languages, because it uses the body (hands) to express the letters; however, other people in Deaf communities may see fingerspelling as a tool forced upon their sign language by spoken language communities. Reagan (2010, p. 103), in support of this Deaf perspective, suggests that fingerspelling was one of the first efforts at corpus planning, as a way to fill lexical gaps that hearing people believed existed because of the lack of one-to-one correspondence with words from the spoken language. Such perceived gaps were the result of the lack of awareness among hearing second-language signers of the intricacies of sign language. Similar perceptions of a lexical gap occur among hearing second-language signers in Brazil.

As a result of the perceived threat to sign languages by the influence of spoken languages, some Deaf communities resist fingerspelling, even though some forms of fingerspelling may be naturally incorporated into sign languages. For example, in a series of videos of Deaf people discussing the use of fingerspelling in Brazilian Sign Language, the relationship between Brazilian Sign Language and Brazilian Portuguese was debated (*Sociedade em Libras* on Facebook, 2015). Through their comments regarding fingerspelling, some of the Deaf people expressed concern about the suppression of their sign language in favor of the spoken language. In particular, the generations of Deaf people who were physically punished for signing now resist the influence of spoken language in their sign language. However, further tensions arise even within the Deaf community, as younger generations of Deaf people are more open to diversity in communicating with multiple languages, including other sign languages, and to borrowing from signed and spoken languages.

Attitudes toward policies for the standardization of sign language are another significant source of tension, where Deaf and hearing communities differ in their approaches. Eichmann (2009) found that official efforts at standardization of German Sign Language (GSL) and British Sign Language (BSL) were not accepted by the Deaf communities in their respective countries, because the initiatives were spearheaded by hearing people. Eichmann concluded that standardization was related to the belief by the hearing community that sign languages were not good enough to express all concepts. Adam (2015), a Deaf author, however, has argued that standardization can play an important role in sign language planning, although it is critical to ensure that the Deaf community is involved in this process (cf. the question of language ownership, Eichmann, 2009).

Tensions produced by the power of users of spoken languages are also evident in mass media. As a result of policies behind equal access legislation, Deaf people in the United States can access information through English captions in almost all the programs available on TV. However, such a service is not available in American Sign Language. In some countries, the Deaf community asks for access, at least, to information such as a summary of the daily news in their own sign language, but this request is rarely implemented, even when the sign language is recognized as a language of the Deaf community, such as in Brazil. Among the few examples of such programs available in sign languages are BBC's (2016) *See Hear!* in the United Kingdom; *Hands on* (2016) in Ireland; and *TV Ines* (2016) in Brazil.

In countries where plurilingualism is a major aim of language planning and sign languages are included, the threat from the spoken language is reduced, and thus the tensions are reduced. Such is the case in Brazil, where language policies favor Brazilian Sign Language in several ways, and Deaf people are starting to access Brazilian Sign Language without restrictions (Quadros et al., 2014). The younger generation of Deaf people considers Brazilian Portuguese their language as well. As Brazilian Portuguese ceases to be a threat to their sign language, Deaf people begin to see it as another possibility for accessing information and communicating with the hearing community, using the written language. Also, they realize that they are able to use this language as a tool for empowerment in the hearing world.

Medical Perspective toward Sign Languages

A medical perspective toward sign languages has historically influenced attitudes and policies (Fischer & Lane, 1993; Hoffmeister, 1993). The medical view of Deaf people prioritizes a cure for deafness, to make Deaf people into hearing people. From this perspective, sign languages are equated with the lack of hearing and are merely tools to help Deaf people to become "normal" or "cured." Thus, this view conveys negative attitudes toward sign languages and their users, which can be grouped into four recurrent themes: (1) spoken languages are better languages than sign languages; (2) spoken languages capture concepts and ideas more precisely than sign languages; (3) spoken languages are more important than sign languages; and (4) sign languages are related to deafness which, from a medical perspective, is a problem that should be cured.

When held by hearing professionals, such negative ideas strongly influence attitudes related to sign languages and the planning and development of language policy. Some Deaf people may internalize negative attitudes, which especially tend to surface when Deaf people have hearing children. Deaf parents may be insecure and confused about how to manage the languages available to their hearing child, and may attempt to speak with their child instead of signing, thereby implying that it is better to speak than to sign. Many hearing children of Deaf parents mistakenly adopt this negative viewpoint, causing difficulty later in their lives (Quadros, 2017). The consequences of these negative attitudes are especially evident in education, as bilingual schools are closed in the name of inclusion, with bilingual schools for Deaf students often viewed as institutions for people with special needs compared to so-called regular schools. In this view, special needs students need to be together with hearing children, yet the impact of including Deaf students in hearing schools may be that Deaf children will not have Deaf peers. This isolation impacts both the Deaf child and their sign language, which may result in incomplete acquisition, language attrition, or language death. In addition, Deaf children in such schools often fall behind their hearing peers academically and socially, and over time feel excluded within the inclusive system (Lane, Hoffmeister, & Bahan, 1996; Quadros, 1997, 2012).

The dream of a cure for hearing loss, which positions Deaf people as disabled compared to hearing people (for an extended discussion of this view, see Lane, 1992; Lane, Hoffmeister, & Bahan, 1996,), was the basis for the decision at the Congress of Milan in 1880 to prohibit sign languages in schools throughout the world (Baynton, 1996; Fisher & Lane, 1993; Reagan, 2010). This conference, which brought together linguists, teachers of Deaf children, and policymakers, all of whom were hearing, decided that sign languages should be prohibited in the education of Deaf children, who, it was believed, should learn to speak the official spoken language of each country. This policy is widely considered by Deaf people to be an act of violence against Deaf communities worldwide, in which schools were used to forcibly control access to sign languages (Fischer & Lane, 1993; Laitin, 1993; Wrigley, 1996), by prohibiting the use of the language that is most accessible to Deaf children. Generations of Deaf children have been punished for using their hands and body to sign among themselves (Lane, 1992).

That historical event, remembered by Deaf communities in many countries as the worst period of their existence (Ladd, 2003; Lane, 1992), led to resistance by Deaf communities that preserved their sign languages behind the "curtains" or through the "windows," as Basso (2003) and Lane (1992) term it. Sign language was hidden from the hearing enforcers, in restrooms, at bedtime by candlelight, and when supervisors were not looking. This resistance is a matter of pride for Deaf communities all over the world, with stories about this time repeated at global and national conferences and in formal and informal Deaf meetings (Miranda, 2001; Sutton-Spence & Quadros, 2005). This event demonstrates the importance of awareness among Deaf people about the risks they face as a consequence of the medical perspective.

Despite such resistance, the medical perspective continues to be the basis for policies that restrict Deaf children's access to sign language, with most schools introducing speech only, forcing hearing technology into children's lives. In some schools and hospitals, families are not permitted to use sign language (Byrd et. al, 2011; Lane, 1992; Quadros, 1997). As a consequence, many Deaf children do not have access to sign language early in their lives and thus may fail to learn a spoken language or a sign language. Parents may be unaware that research indicates positive correlations between sign language skills and reading performance, as well as mathematical knowledge (Davidson & Mayberry, 2015; Hrastinski & Wilbur, 2016; Mayberry, 2010). For example, Hrastinsky and Wilbur (2016, p. 1) found that Deaf students highly proficient in ASL outperformed their less proficient peers in nationally standardized measures of reading comprehension, English language use, and mathematics. In fact, researchers have shown that sign language does not interfere with spoken language development, but instead provides a foundation for acquisition of a second language (Cruz et al., 2014; Davidson & Mayberry, 2015; Quadros et al., 2014). Thus policies that restrict the use of sign languages in early childhood have serious consequences for cognitive development and the ability to process and understand all forms of language (Davidson & Mayberry, 2015; Lane, Hoffmeister, & Bahan, 1996; Mayberry, 2010; Quadros & Cruz, 2011).

Yet the medical perspective continues to be empowered by current technology. In the first half of the twentieth century, hearing aids were considered a potential cure for deafness. Deaf children were equipped with hearing aids and were offered intensive speech classes, with the goal of learning to hear and to speak the dominant spoken language of the country (Lane, 1992). These methods did not achieve the desired results, as Deaf children continued to struggle with learning spoken language and continued to fall behind in school. Since then, this failed approach has been repeated many times in the history of Deaf education, as subsequent technological advances have led to similar failure to achieve adequate results (see, for example, Lane, Hoffmeister, & Bahan, 1996). Even with intensive speech therapy, hearing aids, and other technology, spoken language acquisition will not take place naturally (Quadros et al., 2014).

For Deaf people, access to a sign language as early as possible is crucial for maximizing language acquisition (for example, as proposed by the Laurent Clerc National Deaf Education Center at Gallaudet University, 2016). Bilingual language input that will allow a Deaf child the possibility of growing up with a sign language acquired naturally, along with spoken language, needs to be considered by policymakers (Mayberry 2010; Quadros, 1997; Quadros & Cruz, 2011; Quadros et al., 2015).

I now turn to an agenda for sign language policy and planning, with particular attention to education.

An Agenda for Sign Language Policy and Planning

Deaf communities and their representative organizations agree on the importance of sign language for their linguistic, cognitive, and personal development.

Whereas sign language is necessary for primary interactions and is part of the Deaf communities' heritage, Deaf people also recognize the importance of being bilingual and usually accept the dominant language as their second language, used for specific interactions among themselves and among the spoken community (e.g., Internet and texts in the written form). Nevertheless, not all countries recognize sign languages, and as a consequence impose policies that suppress sign languages.

Language policy and planning is an essential part of the agendas of Deaf organizations, which pressure decision-makers to adopt policies favoring sign languages. Although effective policies and plans usually require agreement and support from the community involved (Calvet, 2007), there may be conflicts about goals, often reflected in official documents that have ambivalent approaches to sign languages. For example, the Salamanca Statement and Framework for Action on Special Needs Education (1994) was a considerable advance in terms of Deaf education, since it recognized sign languages as languages of the Deaf community:

> Educational policies should take full account of individual differences and situations. The importance of sign language as the medium of communication among the deaf, for example, should be recognized and provision made to ensure that all deaf persons have access to education in their national sign language. (Salamanca Statement, 1994, p. 18, article 21)

However, other statements in this document emphasize the need for inclusion of Deaf children in general education, which conflicts with what most Deaf communities advocate, namely a full education in their own language. Despite such issues, planning for sign languages may yield many benefits. For example, the law that recognizes Brazilian Sign Language as a national language[3] has had a positive impact on the Brazilian Deaf community. Deaf people now have access to education in sign language, although a plan for bilingual education is still lacking. The law and its decree also created Brazilian Sign Language Programs to train teachers of Brazilian Sign Language and sign language translators and interpreters in four-year university education programs. As a result, sign language courses are required for all teacher training at the undergraduate level, which has had a positive impact on the status of this language in Brazil (Quadros et al., 2014).

Another law[4] established the National Inventory of Linguistic Diversity in Brazil, implemented by the Federal Culture Ministry, which established that sign languages are part of the heritage of Brazil to be preserved through documentation. The Ministry produced a documentation plan for all languages in Brazil, including Brazilian Sign Language. The documentation of Brazilian Sign Language includes data on its production across the country, including a demographic survey of users of the language and where it is signed (Leite & Quadros, 2014). This project will be extended to other sign languages in Brazil as well. This kind of documentation is currently under way in several countries with different sign languages, including Australia, the United Kingdom, Germany, and The Netherlands.[5]

In the view of Deaf communities, the major aims of sign language planning are related to sign language acquisition, sign language as a first language at school, sign languages as languages of instruction, acquisition of the spoken language as a second language, recognition of sign languages through language laws (not special needs laws or statements), and the establishment of sign language research, including language documentation (World Federation of the Deaf, 2015). Deaf organizations also argue that sign languages should be included in discussions of language rights (Universal Declaration of Linguistics Rights, 1998), which are highlighted in WFD guidelines for national Deaf organizations around the world (such as FESOCA, 2015, in Catalonia).

Based on the claims of Deaf organizations and Deaf communities, the following is an agenda for sign language policies as well as research in this area:

(a) Changes in policy and planning should move away from the medical perspective, particularly to revise laws that include sign languages as part of special needs rather than as an essential linguistic and cultural heritage.

(b) Deaf people should be authors and key actors in policy and planning. Historically, Deaf people have not participated in discussion about language policies and their implementation. Thus, empowerment of Deaf people in policymaking would help to ensure that policies reflect the needs and aspirations of Deaf communities.

(c) Sign languages need to be considered as the first language of Deaf children. Sign language is essential for Deaf children, since it is a visual language that they can acquire naturally. In this regard, policymakers must plan ways for children to access sign language as early as possible with their Deaf peers and Deaf adults. This goal requires involvement of health systems to identify deafness as early as possible.

(d) Status and education planning require a plan that considers sign language in a bilingual context, with the following provisions:

- Changes in attitudes toward sign language, associated with increased visibility of the language and affirmation of the Deaf community and its identity;
- Early sign language acquisition programs for Deaf children, with sign languages given the status of first languages;
- Second-language learning of the dominant language used in the society where Deaf children grow up;
- Bilingual education policies that include the guarantee of Deaf-Deaf meetings, sign language as the language of instruction, sign language as the first language for Deaf children, spoken language as the second language of Deaf children, and sign language as the second language of hearing children when they are in the same school with Deaf children;

- Diffusion of sign languages through the Internet and social networks, and publication of materials, movies, and other programs in sign languages;
- Systematization of teaching materials for sign languages as first and second language.

(e) Corpus planning needs to develop different areas with respect to sign languages, such as

- Corpora of sign languages;
- Descriptions of sign languages;
- Dictionaries of sign languages;
- Documentation of variation in sign languages.

CONCLUSION

This chapter has examined different aspects of language policies regarding sign languages: corpus, status, and acquisition planning, as well as language attitudes. Important variation exists among sign language users, including Deaf people from deaf families, Deaf people from hearing families, and hearing people from Deaf families. These different contexts impact sign-language acquisition in different ways. We have also seen that there is a tension among the attitudes, roles, and functions of signed and spoken languages and their users, often driven by the medical view of deafness. The status of sign languages varies according to language policies, popular beliefs about language, and attitudes toward languages. In addition, the linguistic status of sign languages has been recognized with developments in research, despite their continued repression in favor of spoken languages. Sign languages may have a strong value in some communities, but may not be recognized as a language at all by other communities. The consequences of these differences are especially evident in the education of Deaf children, as schools have an important role in sign-language acquisition and in shaping the status of and attitudes toward sign languages. The constant tension between a medical view and a linguistic view of Deaf people and their language has implications for language policies. To resolve this tension and to protect sign languages, Deaf people and researchers have to negotiate with policymakers in favor of sign languages as a linguistic right for Deaf children. Above all, Deaf communities must be included in the discussions and decisions about language policies that affect them.

ACKNOWLEDGMENTS

This research is supported in part by funding from CNPq (Brazilian National Council of Technological and Scientific Development) Grants # 303725/2013-3 and # 471355/

2013-5. I thank Rachel Sutton-Spence and Robert Hoffmeister for suggestions made to previous versions of this chapter, and James Tollefson and Miguel Pérez-Milans for relevant comments and suggestions during the review process.

Notes

1. The upper case *D* in Deaf people refers to people who use sign language as part of their culture in a Deaf community (for more details, see Ladd, 2003, p. 33).
2. Under the law in Brazil, a *national* language is one that is recognized as belonging to a community of speakers with status that is equal to other languages. Recognition of a sign language as a national language provides status and official equivalency to spoken languages having similar recognition.
3. Law 10.436/2002 in Brazil, with an implementation plan published through Decree 5.626/2005.
4. In Brazil, Law 7387/2010, National Inventory of Linguistic Diversity.
5. The following are websites with some access to the national sign languages corpora: Australia: http://www.auslan.org.au/about/corpus/; Germany: http://www.sign-lang.uni-hamburg.de/dgs-korpus/; England: http://www.bslcorpusproject.org/; Holland: http://www.ru.nl/corpusngtuk/; Turkey: www.cmpe.boun.edu.tr/pilab/BosphorusSign/home_en.html; Brazil: http://www.corpuslibras.ufsc.br/.

References

Aarons, D. (1994). *Aspects of the syntax of American Sign Language*. PhD dissertation, Boston University.

Adam, R. (2015). Standardization of sign languages. *Sign Language Studies* 15(4), 432–445.

Aranoff, M., Meir, I., Padden, C. & Sandler, W. (2004). Morphological universals and the sign language type. In G. Booij & J. van Marle (Eds.), *Yearbook of morphology* (pp. 19–39). Manchester: Kluwer Academic.

Balkany, T. (1993). A brief perspective on cochlear implants. *New England Journal of Medicine* 328(4), 281.

Basso, I. M. de S. (2003). *Educação de pessoas surdas: Novos olhares sobre velhas questões*. Dissertação (Mestrado em Educação), Universidade Federal de Santa Catarina, Brazil.

Bauman, D. (2010). What frames of reference have we used to see deafness in Deaf people? Retrieved from http://www.chs.ca/en/home/ministry.of.education-campaign/bauman-

Baynton, D. (1996). *Forbidden signs: American culture and the campaign against sign language*. Chicago: University of Chicago Press.

BBC. (2016). *See hear*. Retrieved from http://www.bbc.co.uk/programmes/b006m9cb

Benmamoun, E., Montrul, S., & Polinsky M. (2013). Heritage languages and their speakers: Opportunities and challenges for linguistics. *Theoretical Linguistics* 39, 129–181.

Blommaert, J. (2010). *The sociolinguistics of globalization*. Cambridge: Cambridge University Press.

Byrd, S., Shuman, A. G., Kileny, S., & Kileny, R. (2011). The right not to hear: The ethics of parental refusal of hearing rehabilitation. *Laryngoscope* 121(8), 1800–1804.

Calvet, L. (2007). *As políticas linguísticas*. I. de O. Duarte, J. Tenfen, & M. Bagno, Trans. São Paulo: Parábola Editorial; IPOL.

Chen Pichler, D., Lee, J., & Lillo-Martin, D. (2014). Language development in ASL-English bimodal bilinguals. In D. Quinto-Pozos (Ed.), *Multilingual aspects of signed language communication and disorder* (pp. 235–260). Bristol, UK: Multilingual Matters.

Compton, S. E., & Compton, S. (2014). American Sign Language as a heritage language. In T. G. Wiley, J. K. Peyton, D. Christian, S. C. K. Moore, & N. Liu (Eds.), *Handbook of heritage, community, and Native American languages in the United States* (pp. 272–283). New York: Routledge, Center for Applied Linguistics.

Cruz, C. R., Kozak, L. V., Pizzio, A. L., Quadros, R. M. de, & Chen Pichler, D. (2014). Phonological memory and phonological acquisition in bimodal bilingual children. In W. Orman & M.J. Valleau (Eds.), *BUCLD 38: Proceedings of the 38th Boston University Conference on Language Development* (pp. 103–115). Somerville, MA: Cascadilla Press.

Dalcin, G. (2006). Um estranho no ninho: Um estudo pscicanálitico sobre a constituição da subjetividade do sujeito surdo. In R. M. de Quadros (Ed.), *Estudos Surdos I* (pp. 186–215). Petrópolis, RJ: Arara Azul.

Davidson, K., & Mayberry, R. I. (2015). Do adults show an effect of delayed first language acquisition when calculating scalar implicatures? *Language Acquisition: A Journal of Developmental Linguistics* 22(4), 329–354.

Diniz, H. G. (2011). *História da língua de sinais dos surdos brasileiros*. Petrópolis: Editora Arara Azul.

Eichmann, H. (2009). Planning sign languages: Promoting hearing hegemony? Conceptualizing sign language standardization. *Current Issues in Language Planning* 10(3), 293–307.

Emmorey, K., Borinstein, H. B., Thompson, R., & Gollan, T. H. (2008). Bimodal bilingualism. *Bilingualism: Language and Cognition* 11, 43–61.

Fenlon, J., & Wilkinson, E. (2015). Sign languages in the world. In A. C. Schembri & C. Lucas (Eds.), *Sociolinguistics and Deaf communities* (pp. 5–28). Cambridge: Cambridge University Press.

FESOCA—Federació de Persones Sordes de Catalunya. (2015). Retrieved from http://www.fesoca.org/es/

Fischer, R., & Lane, H. (Eds.) (1993). *Looking back: A reader on the history of Deaf communities and their sign languages*. Hamburg: Signum.

Goldin-Meadow, S. (2003). *The resilience of language: What gesture creation in deaf children can tell us about how all children learn language*. New York: Psychology Press.

Hands on. (2016). *TV program in Ireland Sign Language*. Retrieved from http://www.rte.ie/tv/handson/index.html

Hill, J. (2013). Language ideologies, policies, and attitudes toward signed languages. In R. Bayley, R. Cameron, & C. Lucas (Eds.), *The Oxford handbook of sociolinguistics* (pp. 680–697). Oxford: Oxford University Press.

Hoffmeister, R. (1993). Response to the editorial, A brief perspective on cochlear implants, by T. Balkany, January 28, Vol. 328 (4). 1993. *New England Journal of Medicine*. Unpublished manuscript.

Hoffmeister, R., & Caldwell-Harris, C. (2014). Acquiring English as a second language via print: The task for deaf children. *Cognition* 132, 229–242.

Hrastinski, I., & Wilbur, R. B. (2016). Academic achievement of Deaf and hard of hearing students in an ASL/English Bilingual Program. *Journal of Deaf Studies and Deaf Education* 21(2), 56–70.

Kakumasu, J. (1978). Urubu Sign Language. In D. J. Umiker-Sebeok & T. Sebeok (Eds.), *Aboriginal sign languages of the Americas and Australia* (Vol. 2, pp. 247–253). New York: Plenum Press.

Kondo-Brown, K. (Ed.) (2006). *Heritage language development: Focus on East Asian immigrants*. Studies in Bilingualism 32. Amsterdam: John Benjamins.

Kuntze, M., Golos, D., & Enns, C. (2014). Rethinking literacy: Broadening opportunities for visual learners. *Sign Language Studies* 14(2), 203–224.

Ladd, P. (2003). *Understanding Deaf culture: In search of Deafhood*. Bristol, UK: Multilingual Matters.

Laitin, D. (1993). The game theory of language regimes. *International Political Science Review* 14(3), 227–239.

Lane, H. (1992.) *The mask of benevolence: Disabling the Deaf community*. New York: Alfred A. Knopf.

Lane, H., Hoffmeister, R., & Bahan, B. (1996). *A journey into the Deaf-world*. San Diego: DawnSignPress.

Laurent Clerc National Deaf Education Center. (2016). *ASL and spoken English: Maximizing language acquisition*. Retrieved from http://www.gallaudet.edu/clerc-center/learning-opportunities/webcasts/maximizing-language-acquisition-webcast.html

Leite, T. de A., & Quadros, R. M. de. (2014). Línguas de sinais do Brasil: Reflexões sobre o seu estatuto de risco e a importância da documentação. In M. R. Stumpf, R. M. de Quadros, & T. de A. Leite (Eds.), *Estudos da língua de sinais* (Vol. 2, pp. 15–28). Florianópolis: Editora Insular.

Lieberman, A. M., Borovsky, A., Hatrak, M., & Mayberry, R. I. (2014). Real-time processing of ASL signs: Effects of linguistic experience and proficiency. In W. Orman & M. J. Valleau (Eds.), *BUCLD 38: Proceedings of the 38th Boston University Conference on Language Development* (pp. 279–291). Somerville, MA: Cascadilla Press.

Lillo-Martin, D., Quadros, R. M. de, Chen Pichler, D., & Fieldsteel, Z. (2014). Language choice in bimodal bilingual development. *Frontiers in Psychology* 5 (article 1163), 1–15.

Marschark, M., Tang, G., & Knoors, H. (Eds.) (2014). *Bilingualism and bilingual Deaf education*. New York: Oxford University Press.

Mayberry, R. I. (2010). Early language acquisition and adult language ability: What Sign Language reveals about the critical period for language. In M. Marschark & P. Spencer (Eds.), *Oxford handbook of Deaf studies, language, and education* (Vol. 2, pp. 281–291). New York: Oxford University Press.

Miranda, W. (2001). *Comunidade dos Surdos: olhares sobre os contatos culturais*. Dissertação de Mestrado, Universidade Federal do Rio Grande do Sul, Brazil.

Mitchell, R. E., & Karchmer, M. A. (2004). When parents are Deaf versus hard of hearing: Patterns of sign use and school placement of Deaf and hard-of-hearing children. *Journal of Deaf Studies and Deaf Education* 9(2), 133–152.

Nonaka, A. (2004). The forgotten endangered languages: Lessons on the importance of remembering from Thailand's Ban Khor Sign Languages. *Language in Society* 33, 737–767.

Pereira, E. L. (2013). *Fazendo cena na cidade dos mudos: Surdez, práticas sociais e uso da língua em uma localidade no sertão do Piauí*. Tese de doutorado, Universidade Federal de Santa Catarina, Florianópolis, Brazil.

Petronio, K. (1993). *Clause structure in ASL*. PhD dissertation, University of Washington, Seattle.

Peyton, J. K., Ranard, D. A., & McGinnis, S. (Eds.). (2001). *Heritage languages in America: Preserving a national resource.* Washington, DC; McHenry, IL: Center for Applied Linguistics; Delta Systems.

Quadros, R. M. de. (1997). *Educação de surdos: A aquisição da linguagem.* Porto Alegre: ArtMed.

Quadros, R. M. de. (2012). Linguistic policies, linguistic planning, and Brazilian Sign Language in Brazil. *Sign Language Studies* 12, 543–564.

Quadros, R. M. de (2017). *Língua de Herança: Libras.* Porto Alegre: Editora Penso.

Quadros, R. M. de., & Cruz, C. R. (2011). *Língua de sinais: Instrumentos de avaliação.* Porto Alegre: ArtMed.

Quadros, R. M. de, & Karnopp, L. B. (2004). *Estudos linguísticos: Línguas de sinais.* Porto Alegre: ArtMed.

Quadros, R. M. de, Lillo-Martin, D., & Chen Pichler, D. (2015). Bimodal bilingualism: Sign language and spoken language. In M. Marschark & P. E. Spencer (Eds.), *The Oxford handbook of Deaf studies in language: Research, policy, and practice* (pp. 181–196). Oxford: Oxford University Press.

Quadros, R. M. de, Strobel, K., & Masutti, M. L. (2014). Deaf gains in Brazil: Linguistic policies and network establishment. In H. Dirksen, L. Bauman, & J. J. Murray (Eds.), *Deaf gain: Raising the stakes for human diversity* (pp. 341–355). Minneapolis: University of Minnesota Press.

Quer, J. (2012). Legal pathways to the recognition of sign languages: A comparison of the Catalan and Spanish sign language acts. *Sign Language Studies* 12(4), 565–582.

Quinto-Pozos, D., & Adam, R. (2015). Sign languages in contact. In A. C. Schembri & C. Lucas (Eds.), *Sociolinguistics and Deaf communities* (pp. 29–60). Cambridge: Cambridge University Press.

Reagan, T. G. (2010). *Language policy and planning for sign languages.* Washington, DC: Gallaudet University Press.

Salamanca Statement and Framework for Action on Special Needs Education (1994). Salamanca, Spain: UNESCO. Retrieved from www.unesdoc.unesco.org/images/0009/000984/098427eo.pdf

Sánchez, L. (2015). L2 activation and blending in third language acquisition: Evidence of crosslinguistic influence from the L2 in a longitudinal study on the acquisition of L3 English. *Bilingualism: Language and Cognition* 18, 252–269.

Singleton, J. L., & Newport, E. (2004). When learners surpass their models: The acquisition of American Sign Language from inconsistent input. *Cognitive Psychology* 49, 370–407.

Skliar, C. B. (1998). *A Surdez: Um olhar sobre as diferenças.* Porto Alegre: Editora Mediação.

Sociedade em Libras. (2015). *Facebook group.* Retrieved from https://www.facebook.com/groups/1627077764235022/

Stokoe, W. (1978 [1960]). *Sign language structure.* Silver Spring, MD: Linstok Press.

Sutton-Spence, R. L. (1994). The role of the manual alphabet and fingerspelling in British Sign Language. PhD dissertation, University of Bristol.

Sutton-Spence, R. L. (2007). Mouthings and simultaneity in British Sign Language. In M. Vermeerbergen, L. Leeson, & O. Crasborn (Eds.), *Simultaneity in signed languages* (pp. 147–162). Amsterdam: John Benjamins.

Sutton-Spence, R., & Quadros, R. M. de. (2005). Sign language poetry and Deaf identity. *Sign Language Linguistics* 8(1–2), 177–212.

TV Ines. (2016). *A primeira TV bilíngue do Brasil.* Retrieved from http://tvines.com.br/

Universal Declaration of Linguistic Rights. (1998). Follow up committee. Retrieved from http://www.culturalrights.net/descargas/drets_culturals389.pdf

World Federation of the Deaf. (2015). *Policies.* Retrieved from http://wfdeaf.org/databank/policies

World Federation of the Deaf. (2016). *Deaf rights.* Retrieved from https://wfdeaf.org/human-rights

Wrigley, O. (1996). *The politics of Deafness.* Washington, DC: Gallaudet University Press.

PART III

LANGUAGE POLICY AND PLANNING AND LATE MODERNITY

III.A.

Language Policy and Planning, Neoliberalism, and Governmentality: A Political Economy View of Language, Bilingualism, and Social Class

CHAPTER 23

LANGUAGE POLICY AND PLANNING, INSTITUTIONS, AND NEOLIBERALISATION

EVA CODÓ

As a form of sociopolitical action, language policy and planning (henceforth LPP) is intimately linked to the historically situated understanding of the interests, aspirations, and values of a polity. Traditionally, national states have been key players in the design and implementation of language policy measures. Today the role of the state in LPP is more nuanced than previously. On the one hand, new agenda-setting political actors have emerged, such as supranational agencies, like the Council of Europe (Sokolovska, 2016), and nonprofit international organisations (Muelhmann & Duchêne, 2007). On the other hand, as of the 1980s, the relationship between the state and the economic sector has been altered profoundly. The establishment of neoliberalism as a hegemonic political, economic, and moral orthodoxy worldwide, with its emphasis on efficiency, deregulation, and the lowering of public expenditure, has spurred the partial retreat of the state from key social fields, such as education, social services, and health care. As Harvey (2005) argues, (state) government has turned into (social) governance, where civil society organisations and private companies increasingly have taken on socially regulatory roles in lieu of or together with the state. This generates myriad tensions for partner organisations, tensions that materialise in (often contradictory) language policies, practices, and legitimising discourses (see Block, Chapter 28 in this volume).

Practices of institutional neoliberalisation cannot be delinked from globalisation processes; in fact, they are co-constitutive. Following Harvey (2005), I understand globalisation not only as the intensification of the circulation of capitals, people, and semiotic practices around the globe, but as a new mode of production predicated on the volatility of markets in rapidly evolving technological environments and on the flexibilisation of labour. Indeed, *flexibilisation* is the buzzword of neoliberal globalisation, and the condition and the outcome of neoliberal policy.

The institutional and economic transformations mentioned in the preceding are possible because neoliberalism is not only a mode of political-economic action or thought, but also an ethos, where the market is seen as the guiding principle for all human actions (Harvey, 2005). Individual subjectivities are corporatised, turned into Foucault's (2008) enterprising selves, where knowledge is reconceptualised as human capital (Holborow, 2012). Individuals are imagined as bundles of skills (which crucially include soft skills like language or communication), which are measurable and improvable (Urciuoli, 2008). These processes bring new dynamics to institutions, whether public, private or nongovernmental, to which issues of LPP are essential not only to their everyday functioning, but also to the accomplishment of their evolving social mission. Yet little attention has traditionally been paid in the field of LPP to issues of political economy (Ricento, 2015), thus often producing naïve accounts of the role of language in relation to the promotion of social justice.

As can be seen from the preceding, I understand LPP not as separate analytical levels, but as one complex whole (Spolsky, 2004). Policy is practiced (Bonacina-Pugh, 2012) and language practices enact de facto or declared policy. Policy and practice stand in a dialectical relationship to each other. My perspective also draws on Tollefson's (2006) defence of the political—in the sense of ideological and power-laden—nature of language policy in the reproduction of social inequality, and on Ricento's (2015 and Chapter 11 in this volume) need to comprehend language policy within broader processes of sociopolitical and cultural transformation. To investigate LLP in neoliberalising institutional spaces, it is thus necessary to understand its entanglement with emergent socioeconomic, political, and moral orders, as well as to investigate the conditions, constraints, and possibilities of language policy in specific institutional locales.

Institutions[1] are, by definition, sites of social struggle where actors have conflicting goals and distributed access to knowledge and power (Cicourel, 1980). They are structures of social selection based on linguistic performance. They process and sort individuals as a way of regulating access to scarce material and symbolic resources. Institutions are not neutral sites, but socio-institutional regimes which are deeply ideological in that they "'iron out' the contradictions, dilemmas and antagonisms of practices in ways which accord to the interests and projects of domination" (Chouliaraki & Fairclough, 1999, p. 26). Thus, as (interested) spaces of control and selection, institutions sustain and reproduce structures of power, though in ways that appear open, meritocratic, or simply commonsensical. In times of change, such as the present neoliberal epoch, institutions—if they are to survive—must cope with the tensions stemming from the need to redefine their social mission and values. Codó and Pérez-Milans (2014) have argued that this is, essentially, a discursive process, which affects LPP, language performance and assessment, and social and moral categorisation.

This chapter maps out the empirical research conducted on LPP in neoliberalising institutional spaces. The goal is not to be comprehensive, but to point readers towards key terrains, concepts, and authors. For organisational purposes, I have divided this chapter into three main types of institutional spaces that allow me to delve into the multilayered, interlocking transformations of LPP: individual subjectivities; institutional regimes; and political economy in contemporary institutions. The three fields presented are the workplace, education, and civil society organisations. In the first section, I will review studies that have investigated changing language policies and practices in relation to labour processes in the neoliberalised work environments of late modernity. In the second section, I will refer to the ways in which the neoliberalisation of education has impacted on and been achieved through language policies in that domain. In the third section, I will discuss research that has addressed the study of language policy in nongovernmental organisations (NGOs) providing services outsourced by the state. The chapter will conclude with a succinct discussion of possible avenues for further investigation on LPP, institutions, and neoliberalisation.

Language Policy in the Neoliberalising Workplace

LPP has not just become central to contemporary economic and labour processes, but constitutes a "privileged window into the workings of late capitalism, and a terrain on which we can see its tensions being worked out" (Heller & Duchêne, 2012, p. 14). Through the co-constitutive discursive tropes of "pride" and "profit," these authors show the multiple tensions emerging from the inscription of language, traditionally linked to national identity and the reproduction of the community, into the logics of the market, driven by considerations of flexibility, efficiency, and revenue.

One of the distinctive features of language in the new economy is that it has become a primary mode of production (Allan, 2013). In a number of contemporary workplaces, like call centres, translation agencies, or language teaching, language work constitutes the essence of the job. This entails and hinges on a "managerial conception of language" that "exploits all of a person's competencies" (Boutet, 2012, p. 223). As language is equated with productivity and outcomes, it is objectified, turned into a skill, regimented, regulated, and monitored (Cameron, 2000). Linguistic performances are conceptualised as "marketable commodities rather than as expressions of true selves or of relatively good or poor accomplishments of socially located personae" (Heller, 2010, p. 103; see also Pujolar, Chapter 24 in this volume).

The commodification of language, that is, the process by which "language comes to be valued and sought for the economic profit it can bring through exchange in the market" (Park & Wee, 2012, p. 125), is but one facet of the generalised commodification of the self in contemporary workplaces. Urciuoli describes how worker subjectivities are conceptualised as segmented selves that are then "recast as assemblages of productive elements" (2008, p. 224), subject to quantification and in need of constant improvement. Emphasis is placed on soft rather than on hard skills, that is, on relational and communicative abilities. Soft skill discourse promises professional success through self-transformation; this is because soft skills work as Foucauldian technologies of self. In other words, they claim to "empower" workers by shaping their personalities to modes of conduct and attributes needed for the workplace (Urciuoli & LaDousa, 2013; see also Del Percio, Chapter 26 in this volume).

In a case study of ELT programmes for migrants in Canada, Allan (2013) described how those programmes aimed to produce flexible workers for the Canadian knowledge-based economy. She showed how the institution had a clear neoliberalising agenda construed as "professional language training." Migrant underemployment was ideologically viewed not as a structural problem, but as stemming from migrants' lack of appropriate skills. Because the problem was individualised, the ELT programme became fertile ground for neoliberal governance. Not only was language teaching imagined as the teaching of soft skills, but migrants were advised to adopt an entrepreneurial stance, to self-marketise, and to self-imagine, as "tasks" in constant need of reflexive self-improvement, if they wanted to find a job. Allan observed how this "standardisation" of the self had to be reconciled with employers' search for individualised authenticity, predicated on the workers' identification with corporate values, which, significantly, were often conflated with general Canadian values.

Similar practices have been observed by Campbell and Roberts (2007) in job selection processes in the United Kingdom. The work interview has evolved significantly in recent decades in line with the neoliberal transformation of labour environments and shifts in the desired attributes of the workforce. In many industrialised societies, the competency- or skill-based interview is the current institutionalised regime for selecting new employees, even for unskilled posts. The contemporary job interview requires the blending in synthetic ways of various discursive modes: a formal and an informal register; personal and impersonal talk; and situated storytelling and abstract, analytical reasoning. The highly complex linguistic capitals that must be mobilised in order to perform successfully (i.e., display a credible individualised self which is aligned with corporate cultures) are not available to all candidates, in particular, those from migrant or ethnic minority backgrounds.

Despite the communicative arduousness of the situation, this type of interview is seen as a transparent way of evaluating candidate skills, and the interview itself is presented as a fair and equitable procedure. The key role of language is underestimated or simply overlooked. As a result, qualified foreign-born candidates underperform, even for low-skilled positions. As Robert states (2013, p. 92), "candidates may well be competent for the job but they are excluded from it because they are not competent for the interview." It seems clear, then, that implicit institutional language policies that require successful candidates to activate a complex bundle of linguistic and identity features in performing relatable neoliberal selves (Allan, 2013) work to reinforce preexisting socio-discursive inequalities.

As we have seen, contemporary labour is linguistic, and language *is* contemporary labour. One of the most visible language policy trends in neoliberalising workspaces is the Taylorisation of language work, typical of certain language industries such as call centres (Boutet, 2012). Scripted ways of performing (including register, tone of voice, vocal qualities, prosody contours, and the use of various strategies linked to the inscription of emotions in the process of creating closeness and trust in service interaction) are established beforehand independently of the worker, their language trajectories, emotional states, or the course of the exchange (Cameron, 2000). Standardisation requires regular monitoring and sanctioning, as well as the sanitisation of speech, especially (though not exclusively) in the case of bilingual or multilingual workers. These industries' language policies, with strong modernist ideologies of language, strive to erase all forms of linguistic variability, and impose stylised and formatted identities on workers. This has highly alienating effects, as they may be required to pass as native speakers of several languages in the same day or feign identities alien to them, as in the case of Indian call centre employees (Morgan & Ramanathan, 2009). Yet, as Urciuoli (2008) points out, not all employees are equally non-agentive linguistically, which questions the flat-hierarchy models saturating the neoliberal imagination of workplaces. In fact, agency is structured, as managerial staff is, on the one hand, less constrained to use language than frontline workers, and on the other, responsible themselves for the formulation of the language policies that those in the lower end of the work hierarchy will enact.

Another observable trend runs counter to the hygienising, standardising drive discussed in the preceding. In this case, linguistic diversity is not to be erased, but embraced. Multilingualism is tied to efficiency and productivity, with its adjoining consequences in terms of the reproduction of social inequalities. The diversification of languages, or multilingualisation of institutional spaces, becomes a strategy of localisation or market expansion (Duchêne, 2009; Heller, 2010). Rather than considering multilingual abilities as commodities per se with assumed value in the neoliberal market, these analysts enquire into the ways in which language policies are inscribed into business strategies, with what effects and for whom.

Duchêne (2009), for example, investigated the value of multilingualism in a Swiss tourist call centre. He concluded that the understanding of institutional language policies should be framed within organisational goals, on the one hand (i.e., the selling of Switzerland as a multilingual country), and within managerial interests on the other (i.e., enhancing productivity and efficiency). For example, it was observed that accentedness was accepted, contrary to habitual practices in the call centre industries. This acceptance was linked to the need to display "authenticity" by call centre operators as both knowledgeable interlocutors and local speakers, and it was only desirable because it was economically profitable for the institution.

A further study by the same author (Duchêne, 2011) revealed the structured value of multilingualism and the resulting socioeconomic inequalities in a Swiss airport. Again, he observed how this institution's language policy was inscribed into managerial considerations of flexibility and efficiency; but while multilingualism was a valuable means for the company to deliver effective services, the workers themselves, all low-qualified and occupying precarious job positions, never took advantage of their commodified multilingualism. The "neoliberalism of linguistic diversity," in Duchêne's words (2011, p. 82), compels us to investigate the intersecting economic and material constraints operating on the valorisation of multilingualism for individual workers.

All the case studies that have been reviewed in this section have pointed towards a profound transformation of the link between language, labour, and identity. Institutional language policies in the neoliberalising workplace are both instruments and outcomes of such transformations, which of course do not begin or end in the workplace. The inculcation of neoliberal values through a utilitarian ideology of knowledge pervades most educational systems in the world. These are the spaces to which I will now turn.

THE NEOLIBERALISATION OF EDUCATION AND LANGUAGE POLICY

The field of education, a key state instrument (together with the media), responsible for the ideological moulding of future generations, has been turned upside down through the implementation of neoliberal policies (Gray & Block, 2012). The neoliberalisation of education has affected the organisation of school systems worldwide, as well as the objectives and contents of education. Hirtt (2009) upholds that the goal of democratising access to education that was prevalent in Western democracies after World War II has been replaced by the goal of aligning the school system with the needs of the economic sector ("massification" to "marketisation"). The main objective of national educational systems is no longer the creation of national citizens, but of productive workers who can enhance the global competitiveness of the national economy.

Deregulation and decentralisation have been the driving forces behind most contemporary reforms in educational organisation, since decentralised systems are better able to adapt to the changing demands of the industrial and financial sectors. Interestingly, organisational decentralisation has run parallel to increased governmental regulation of outcomes and objectives, and the implementation of strict measures of institutional accountability—the "audit culture" that Urciuoli (2008) refers to. In a case study of two teacher-training programmes in the United Kingdom, Gray and Block (2012) showed how both teaching and teacher training have increasingly become product-oriented, subject to greater quality control and accountability requirements. Indeed, in the two courses examined, the emphasis was placed on "effective" curriculum delivery and "best" practice. This, they claim, has the effect of "sanitising" education (Hill & Kumar, 2009), providing fertile ground for the consolidation of neoliberal ideals. Teaching was constructed as the inculcation of instrumental skills and knowledge, stripped of opportunities for self-reflection and self-transformation.

The state's neoliberalising agenda and the growing influence of the business sector on defining the school curricula have had an impact on school contents. A utilitarian view of education has caused the dismissal of "general culture" in favour of a technicist and acritical curriculum (Hill & Kumar, 2009) that favours professional, social, and "transversal" skills (Hirrt, 2009) and lifelong learning. This technicist drive is most clearly reflected in the ascendance of certain school disciplines, like English and ICT (information and communication technology). Lo Bianco (2014) explains how English and ICT are disappearing as separate disciplines in the primary school curricula, and have instead entered the set of basic skills that all students should acquire. For Giroux (2009), the medium- and long-term effects of these transformations will be the widening of social inequalities (both among and within states), as the majority of pupils in schools will be trained for the service economy, which requires soft, relational skills, and only a (white) minority will acquire the knowledge necessary for highly skilled positions.

Another facet of the neoliberal marketisation of education is that it is increasingly seen as a profitable business; the attractiveness of private education is enhanced by the streamlining of budgets and the reduction of state expenditure on the public school system. The end result of this process, grounded on competition, selection, and exclusion, is the loss of equity (Hill & Kumar, 2009). Yet, what makes it particularly difficult to expose is that it is clad in the discourse of "choice" (of parents, students, and schools). For example, in a study in Cambodia, Clayton (2008) historicised English-language education policies and linked their evolution to the workings of international aid agencies and NGOs in the country. Despite the rhetoric of choice, the country's adoption of English as a main foreign language was, in fact, always highly constrained. It was shaped by hegemonic discourses linking the language to externally oriented modes of development, which in turn hinged on the constitution of an enabling state and the implementation of "open market" policies. On the individual level, Clayton showed how "choice" was unequally distributed and was actually employed to mask privileged social and class positions.

This case study takes me to one of the most influential lines of research in language policy in the educational field, namely that of the intensification of the demand for English worldwide. As the "ultimate commodified linguistic resource in the global market" (Park & Wee, 2012, p. 124), English is often constructed as both the arm of neoliberalism and the signal of its effects. Phillipson's linguistic imperialism (1992, 2009) is a classic in this field, but there is also research on less well-known aspects of the mutual implication of English and neoliberalism, such as the ways in which Anglo-American transnational corporations influence TESOL (Teaching English to Speakers of Other Languages) curricula and materials. As an example, Gray (2012) analysed the featuring of celebrities in English-language textbooks, and on the meanings and values that are transmitted by texts and activities, both in relation to the English language and with regard to desirable identity-types. In Gray's study, the ideal emergent subjectivity was that of the neoliberal enterprising self, self-marketed and self-branded, who presents him- or herself as an active shaper of his or her own fate through self-determination and a positive frame of mind.

The "craze" for English-language education is particularly visible in Expanding Circle countries, most notably in Europe and Asia (see Park, 2009, for an in-depth analysis of the South Korean case) and has translated into various forms of bilingual, multilingual, or simply English-medium education (EMI) (see Tollefson & Tsui, Chapter 13 in this volume).

From a language policy-making perspective, research on English language education worldwide has tended to focus on macro-level state policies, the factors contributing to their formulation, their social reception, and the problems envisaged in their implementation. Another approach has been to focus on the actual policy texts, their educational objectives, framing pedagogical principles, and grounding linguistic ideologies (e.g., Pan, 2011) with a view to critiquing their social effects in the (re)production of class, gender, and ethnicity-based inequalities (see Tollefson, 2006). Pennycook (2006) criticises the frequently expressed view that power is unidirectionally exerted by the state through language policy, and instead places the focus on the micro-level of classroom language use that, for him, is the true locus of governance. In that sense, Johnson (2009) defends the need for ethnographies of language policy as a way of establishing the connection between macro-level language policies and the interpretation and appropriation of those policies on the ground. In the case of English-language policies and practices in specific national, regional, and local contexts, such ethnographies are fairly rare.

One exception is the ethnographic study by Pérez-Milans (2013) of English-language education in three Chinese "experimental schools." The author investigated how a programme of neoliberally inspired reforms, linked to discursive tropes of academic excellence, meritocracy, and competition, was carried through in Chinese schools in order to modernise and improve the quality of the educational system. Organisational decentralisation and flexibilisation coexisted with state-defined goals and curricular contents, and frequent standardised controls in the form of school evaluations and student exams. In that context, the importance attached to English-language education became an emblem of the efforts made by the Chinese state to equip its citizens, and the national economy more generally, with the skills needed to compete in an internationalised global market.

English in Chinese schools was construed as a "technical" skill, stripped of any links to the values of (Western) liberal democracies, and was imbued with what were discursively represented as "Chinese characteristics." In the case of English pedagogies, this translated into a "specifically Chinese way of teaching English" (Pérez-Milans, 2013, p. 147), which combined the acquisition of English-specific skills and knowledge with the internalisation of the values of cooperation, motivation, and patriotism, featured as core Chinese values and discursively constructed as distinctive of the ongoing innovation reforms. Teaching practices on the ground, such as abundant stylised choral repetitions in the English-language classes, reflected and constructed institutional objectives and national policy agendas, and as the author claims, were "linked to sociocultural meanings that have a wider significance, beyond the classroom context" (p. 156).

In Europe, English-medium programmes are generally known as CLIL (Content and Language Integrated Learning), for many analysts a European development of CBL (content-based learning). The official CLIL rhetoric (European Commission, 2014) is yet fairly distinctive, and emphasises the fostering of key European values like social cohesion, democratic citizenship, and intercultural dialogue through CLIL.

Most CLIL research has been acritical, embracing the inherent goodness of this approach, and centring on assessing its effectiveness for raising students' proficiency levels (see Cenoz, Genessee, & Gorter, 2013, for an overview of existing studies and research gaps in the field). Few situated investigations have been conducted that explore the social inequalities engendered by CLIL programmes within and beyond the boundaries of schools. One exception is the research undertaken in a secondary school in Madrid (Martín Rojo, 2013; Pérez-Milans & Patiño-Santos, 2014). These studies showed that despite official emphasis on democratic values and social cohesion, the implementation of a Spanish-English bilingual programme created hierarchies among teachers, students, and the other existing language programme in the school, aimed to provide intensive Spanish training for migrant teenagers. The linguistic prerequisites to access the programme (a set level of English but also of Spanish, which excluded English-competent migrants) enforced a language-based student selection, which, coupled with broader social ideologies of English as linked to excellence and internationalisation, constructed the programme as elitist and the students as "academic/good."

Yet, in Relaño-Pastor (2015; also see Chapter 25 in this volume), based on data from the same school, we see how students resisted these ascribed identities, and foregrounded their working-class or middle-class affiliations. This study sheds light on the many contradictions that *practiced* language policy (Bonacina-Pugh, 2012) entails, among which are the discursive tensions between European policy texts and the views of socially situated stakeholders, who in that case held neoliberal ideas of English as commodity and added value. This investigation also questions globalist ideologies of English, and underlines the need to understand learning English as tied to local ways of "doing learning English" and their affective histories. In the case of the school investigated, this meant not only engaging in fluid Spanish/ English bilingualism, but also speaking English with a Spanish accent for social inclusion.

The association of English with the neoliberal agenda has spurred discourses that often fairly uncritically advocate for multilingualism to be put at the centre of a more democratic and inclusive language policy. However, Flores (2013) cautions against such naïve and celebratory views of multilingualism, and in particular of individual multilingualism, often referred to as plurilingualism. He claims that the idea of the plurilingual subject, as defined in many European policy documents (i.e., as somebody who can unproblematically employ several languages in the same conversation), aligns it with the dynamic and flexible neoliberal worker who is able to navigate cultural differences in heterogeneous work environments. Flores warns against the inequalities built into this policy ideal, which may actually work to benefit mobile plurilingual elites to the detriment of other (less mobile) social groups.

This section has outlined some of the effects of the neoliberalisation of education on language policy at primary and secondary school levels, but these effects are perhaps most visible at tertiary education, where a great deal of research on language policy and neoliberalisation has been conducted. This is the focus of the next section.

Markets of Higher Education, Internationalisation, and English

University education has become a major global industry (Lee & Lee, 2013), shaped by competition and neoliberally informed notions of educational quality, productivity, and efficiency. University credentials have become commodities with different values in the global and national markets. Students increasingly make educational choices that take into account the return value of their financial and personal investments in the labour market. The popularisation of often mass-mediated university rankings in the last two decades has corporatised and uniformised the higher education scene. Though often labelled "internationalisation," this process has been characterised as the wholesale acceptance of the US model of academic capitalism (Piller & Cho, 2013).

Universities increasingly adopt policies and practices that equip them to compete globally for top students, renowned scholars, and private and public funding to become "world-class research universities" (Piller & Cho, 2013). National governments have also been adept at enforcing implicit language policies through assessment procedures based on a set of ideologically defined criteria (see Hu, Li, & Lei, 2014, for the case of China). One such criterion is the number of courses taught through the medium of English. English-medium instruction (EMI) is an indicator of a university's degree of internationalisation, which is in turn a measurement of educational quality. Together, these three concepts (i.e., English, internationalisation, and excellence) form a pervasive indexical cluster (Lee & Lee, 2013). Universities have implemented EMI policies to enhance their own profile—through the indexical meanings associated with internationalisation—and that of their graduates, where English proficiency indexes greater social mobility and better career prospects, both at home and abroad. National economies benefit from an English-proficient workforce by becoming more competitive globally.

Hu, Li, and Lei (2014) discuss the exclusion mechanisms behind the ways in which such language policies have been implemented on the ground. In the Chinese context studied by the authors, EMI constituted an elite form of education, given student eligibility requirements (in terms of language proficiency and higher tuition fees). Inequalities also surfaced among faculty and staff both through the teaching eligibility criteria set and the system of material and symbolic incentives/rewards put in place. EMI language policy thus (re)produced social structures of inequality and strengthened the desirability of English. Piller and Cho (2013) argue that neoliberalism, through its rejection of any kind of regulation—including language policy—works as a covert language policy, imposing English while at the same time disguising its workings. EMI is the product of structures of competition, presenting the ascendance of English as cost-free and the result of the free market or individual determination.

Research is the other university domain where an English-only implicit language policy is being enforced. The use of English is linked not only to excellence in research output, but also to corporate notions of productivity and efficiency. These are increasingly being measured through the number of publications in internationally indexed journals (IIJ), which are almost exclusively in English and mostly are published in Anglophone countries (Piller & Cho, 2013). Research has focused on the role of institutional policies (e.g., for hiring, tenuring, promoting, and remunerating academic staff) in covertly extending the (almost exclusive) use of English as language of academic scholarship (Curry & Lillis, 2013; Piller & Cho, 2013). Lee and Lee (2013) investigated the neoliberal ideologies behind publishing policies in a Korean university. Producing English-language academic outputs was normalised as superior but equally accessible to everyone. Thus, publishing in IIJ was seen as a matter of individual talent or will, erasing structural and material constraints, as well as the pressure that this implicit language policy imposed on academics. The authors showed how ideologies of self-improvement as the path to self-satisfaction and international recognition underlie Korean professors' publishing choices.

So far, it has become evident that language policy in neoliberalised institutions cannot be detached from the establishment of subjectivity regimes grounded on individual self-governance and self-responsibilisation. The inculcation of desirable personality traits for inclusion and citizenship is no longer in the hands of states only, but actually is carried out by a variety of civil society institutions, to which I now turn.

LANGUAGE, THE STATE, AND CIVIL SOCIETY UNDER NEOLIBERALISM

The study of LPP in civil society organisations helps us to understand the transformation of the role of the state in the regulation of the social body at this historical juncture. As discussed previously, one of the effects of neoliberalisation has been the destabilisation (not disappearance) of the nation-state as *the* ideological frame of reference. This affects various levels of social governing, including the policing of legitimate languages, cultures, and identities. The state now interacts and in fact actually colludes with increasingly influential producers of discourses on language, such as international NGOs (Muelhmann & Duchêne, 2007). Indeed, these various organisations have become major actors in the production and circulation of discourses on language diversity. The concept of human rights has framed most discursive production in this field, clad in a universalising, egalitarian rhetoric, which, however, has never questioned the ideological framing of the nation-state (i.e. the idea of homogeneous social groups) or the dominant status of national languages. This research line points towards the importance of NGOs as new sites of linguistic regulation, where valuable resources, like certain languages, language varieties, or social identities, get (de)legitimised, visibilised, or ideologically erased.

A different line of LPP research in this social field analyses the role of civil society and nonprofit organisations in the neoliberal governance of populations and investigates the kinds of language policies that are legitimised in service provision practices. Some sociolinguists have applied the Foucauldian notion of *governmentality* (Foucault, 1991) to describe the ways in which nonprofit associations, often run by volunteers, actually partake in the regulation of peripheral social groups, like migrants, on behalf of the state (see also Martín Rojo, Chapter 27 in this volume). This is because in the post-social state, migrant-oriented welfare provision (including language education) has been largely downscaled to the nongovernmental sector, partly to reduce costs and partly to mask the state's (economic) investment in certain groups. Research in this area has shown that NGOs implement the state's ideological agenda. Codó and Garrido (2010), for example, compared the institutional policies and practices regarding language and multilingualism in two migrant services in Barcelona, more specifically a state immigration office and a free legal advice service run by an NGO. They concluded that both institutions had a covert language policy which de-problematised language issues, construed Spanish as the default, naturalised code of service provision, and imagined multilingualism as a threat to integration. This piece of research pointed at the reproduction by NGOs of the state's technologies of citizenship, among which is the national language.

A similar inculcation of the modernist linking of (national) language and citizenship was observed by Cleghorn (2000) in language education programmes for migrants in Canada, and by Garrido (2010) in similar spaces in Catalonia, Spain. The latter also documented the ways in which the language classes aimed to create "good citizens" through the re-socialisation of migrants into appropriate values and modes of conduct that went beyond language learning and concerned moral values, forms of knowledge, and various behavioural aspects. Along similar lines, Pujolar (2007) looked at the deployment of expertise discourses, presented as privatised and independent of the state, as a way of legitimising the regimentation of migrants in a volunteer-run language education scheme for African women in northern Catalonia. The notion of "integration" worked in this space and in society more generally as the ideological construct through which the management of migrants was achieved.

Another strand in this area has investigated the discursive tensions emerging in state subsidiary organisations as a result of their partnering with the state in the neoliberalisation of services for migrants. Codó (2013) investigated the evolution of the field of legal advice in Catalonia and exposed the many discursive, pragmatic, and role-identity contradictions that service providers had to face as intermediary, welcoming institutions, on the one hand, and veiled state bodies, on the other. Language policy (with Spanish as a prerequisite for access) emerged, quite significantly, as the locus where contradictions were neutralised and ideological continuity with the institutions of the nation-state was established.

After this unavoidably short presentation of LPP issues in three key institutional domains shaped by neoliberalising policies (i.e. workplace, education, and civil society organisations), I will now spell out what I consider are the major unaddressed topics in this area. I will conclude by suggesting some avenues for future investigation.

Avenues for Future Research
in Language Policy and Planning,
Institutions, and Neoliberalisation

This chapter has tried to map out the fairly unchartered territory of language policy as practiced in contemporary institutional spaces, traversed by processes of neoliberalisation, globalisation, and the tertiarisation and informatisation of the economy. One of the points I have made is that language policy and neoliberalism are co-constitutive. As Piller and Cho (2013) argue, neoliberalism *is* language policy insofar as the neoliberal free-market, free-choice ideology works to favour certain languages (especially English) to the detriment of others; in turn, language policy *is* neoliberalism because the service- and knowledge-based economy of late (neoliberal) modernity has communication as its central axis. I have claimed that, as legitimators of language and regulators of access to it, contemporary institutions are spaces defined by discursive tensions, where old and new policies, practices, and discourses coexist, compete, and interlock in unexpected ways.

Most of the studies I have reviewed here are ethnographic. My understanding of LPP as situated at the intersection of local institutional practice and trans-local socioeconomic processes foregrounds the need for a complexifying approach like that of institutional ethnography. Its integrative, holistic (Sarangi & Roberts, 1999) perspective allows researchers to move back and forth from institutional regimes to regional, national or continental agendas in order to comprehend the conditions of appropriation and redefinition of languages in processes of institutional neoliberalisation (Pérez-Milans, 2015).

More ethnographic studies are certainly needed in other kinds of spaces, both geographical and institutional. Geographically, we still know very little about how neoliberalisation is impacting institutional LPP in many parts of the world (e.g., the African continent). Yet I have exemplified here how fundamental a situated perspective is that understands the ways in which local sociocultural and economic imaginaries articulate with broader ideological processes. On the institutional front, more knowledge about neoliberally inspired LPP is needed in different institutional sectors than those currently investigated (e.g., social welfare, infant education, and health services).

In the institutional terrains discussed in this chapter, there are many aspects pending investigation. In the educational terrain, for example, there is a scarcity of studies on the transformation of the language curriculum to align language teaching with the linguistic needs of the contemporary workplace, the consequences of this transformation, and the ensuing tensions for LPP. In that sense, Block, Gray, and Holborow (2012) point out that (global) English pedagogies, which foster (neoliberal) ideas of interaction, participation, and problem-solving, may come into conflict with traditional ways of doing language education in local spaces. Data on these conflicts will shed important light on the ways in which institutional tension impacts LPP, that is, they will allow us to understand the various stages of language policy or the "language policy cycle" (Johnson, 2009, p. 142).

Another avenue for further exploration in language-in-education policy is the effect of the commodification of language on intercultural dialogue, one of the mandates of European CLIL education, as we discussed. In that sense, Kramsch finds that the current mystification of the global culture of communication compels students to "surf diversity" (2014, p. 302), rather than actually engage with difference.

All in all, research in this area of disciplinary intersection is, in many ways, just beginning to take off. New LLP data in different neoliberalising institutions will certainly provide more elements for a deeper understanding of the criss-crossing of global, national, and regional processes and specific institutional agendas.

Note

1. My thinking about institutions has been shaped by my participation in several research projects over the last fifteen years. I would like to acknowledge here the financial support of the Spanish Ministry of Science and Innovation for the latest (The Appropriation of English as a Global Language in Catalan Secondary Schools, ref. FFI2014-54179-C2-1-P), of which I am Principal Investigator. I would also like to thank the feedback received from the two editors of this volume. Any remaining shortcomings are, of course, my own.

References

Allan, K. (2013). Skilling the self: The communicability of immigrants as flexible labour. In A. Duchêne, M. Moyer, & C. Roberts (Eds.), *Language, migration and social inequalities: A critical perspective on institutions and work* (pp. 56–78). Bristol, UK: Multilingual Matters.

Block, D., Gray, J., & Holborow, M. (Eds.) (2012). *Neoliberalism and applied linguistics*. London: Routledge.

Bonacina-Pugh, F. (2012). Researching "practiced language policies": Insights from conversation analysis. *Language Policy* 11(3), 213–234.

Boutet, J. (2012). Language workers: Emblematic figures of late capitalism. In A. Duchêne & M. Heller (Eds.), *Language in late capitalism: Pride and profit* (pp. 207–229). London: Routledge.

Cameron, D. (2000). *Good to talk? Living and working in a communication culture*. London: Sage.

Campbell, S., & Roberts, C. (2007). Migration, ethnicity and competing discourses in the job interview: Synthesizing the institutional and personal. *Discourse & Society* 18(3), 243–271.

Cenoz, J., Genesee, F., & Gorter, D. (2013). Critical analysis of CLIL: Taking stock and looking forward. *Applied Linguistics* 13, 1–21.

Chouliaraki, L., & Fairclough, N. (1999). *Discourse and late modernity: Rethinking critical discourse analysis*. Edinburgh: Edinburgh University Press.

Cicourel, A. (1980). Three models of discourse analysis: The role of social structure. *Discourse Processes* 33, 101–132.

Clayton, S. (2008). The problem of "choice" and the construction of the demand for English in Cambodia. *Language Policy* 7, 143–164.

Cleghorn, L. (2000). *Valuing English: An ethnography of a federal language training program for adult immigrants.* Unpublished MA thesis, University of Toronto.

Codó, E. (2013). Trade unions and NGOs under neoliberalism: Between regimenting migrants and subverting the state. In A. Duchêne, M. Moyer, & C. Roberts (Eds.), *Language, migration and social inequalities: A critical perspective on institutions and work* (pp. 25–55). Bristol, UK: Multilingual Matters.

Codó, E., & Garrido, M. R. (2010). Ideologies and practices of multilingualism in bureaucratic and legal advice encounters. *Sociolinguistic Studies* 4(2), 297–332.

Codó, E., & Pérez-Milans, M. (2014). Multilingual discursive practices and processes of social change in globalising institutional spaces: A critical ethnographic perspective. *International Journal of Multilingualism* 11(4), 381–388.

Curry, M. J., & Lillis, T. (2013). Participating in academic publishing: Consequences of linguistic policies and practices. Special issue of *Language Policy* 12(3), 209–288.

Duchêne, A. (2009). Marketing, management and performance: Multilingualism as commodity in a tourism call centre. *Language Policy* 8, 27–50.

Duchêne, A. (2011). Néolibéralisme, inégalités sociales et plurilinguisme: L'exploitation des ressources langagières et des locuteurs. *Langage et Société* 136, 81–108.

European Commission. (2014). *Improving the effectiveness of language learning: CLIL and computer assisted language learning.* Retrieved from http://ec.europa.eu/languages/library/studies/clil-call_en.pdf

Flores, N. (2013). The unexamined relationship between neoliberalism and plurilingualism: A cautionary tale. *TESOL Quarterly* 47(3), 500–520.

Foucault, M. (1991). Governmentality. In G. Burchell, C. Gordon, & P. Miller (Eds.) *The Foucault effect: Studies in governmentality* (pp. 87–104). Chicago: University of Chicago Press.

Foucault, M. (2008). *The birth of biopolitics: Lectures at the Collège de France, 1978–1979.* New York: Picador.

Garrido, M. R. (2010). *"If you slept in Catalunya you know that here it's a paradise": Multilingual practices and ideologies in a residential project for migrants.* Unpublished MA thesis. Bellaterra: Universitat Autònoma de Barcelona.

Giroux, H. A. (2009). Neoliberalism, youth and the leasing of higher education. In D. Hill & R. Kumar (Eds.), *Global neoliberalism and education and its consequences* (pp. 30–53). New York: Routledge.

Gray, J. (2012). Neoliberalism, celebrity and "aspirational" content in English language teaching textbooks for the global market. In D. Block, J. Gray, & M. Holborow (Eds.), *Neoliberalism and applied linguistics* (pp. 86–113). London: Routledge.

Gray, J., & Block, D. (2012). The marketization of language teacher education and neoliberalism: Characteristics, consequences and future projects. In D. Block, J. Gray, & M. Holborow (Eds.), *Neoliberalism and applied linguistics* (pp. 114–161). London: Routledge.

Harvey, D. (2005). *A brief history of neoliberalism.* Oxford: Oxford University Press.

Heller, M. (2010). The commodification of language. *Annual Review of Anthropology* 39, 101–114.

Heller, M., & Duchêne, A. (2012). Pride and profit: Changing discourses of language, capital and nation-state. In A. Duchêne & M. Heller (Eds.), *Language in late capitalism: Pride and profit* (pp. 1–21). London: Routledge.

Hill, D., & Kumar, R. (2009). Neoliberalism and its impacts. In D. Hill & R. Kumar (Eds.), *Global neoliberalism and education and its consequences* (pp. 12–29). New York: Routledge.

Hirrt, N. (2009). Markets and education in the era of globalized capitalism. In D. Hill & R. Kumar (Eds.), *Global neoliberalism and education and its consequences* (pp. 208–226). London: Routledge.

Holborow, M. (2012). Neoliberal keywords and the contradictions of an ideology. In D. Block, J. Gray, & M. Holborow (Eds.), *Neoliberalism and applied linguistics* (pp. 33–55). London: Routledge.

Hu, G., Li, L., & Lei, J. (2014). English-medium instruction at a Chinese university: Rhetoric and reality. *Language Policy* 13, 21–40.

Johnson, D. C. (2009). Ethnography of language policy. *Language Policy* 8, 139–159.

Kramsch, C. (2014). Teaching foreign languages in an era of globalization: Introduction. *The Modern Language Journal* 98(1), 296–311.

Lee, H., & Lee, K. (2013). Publish (in international indexed journals) or perish: Neoliberal ideology in a Korean university. *Language Policy* 12, 215–230.

Lo Bianco, J. (2014). Domesticating the foreign: Globalization's effects on the place of languages. *Modern Language Journal* 98(1), 312–325.

Martín Rojo, L. (2013). (De)capitalising students through linguistic practices: A comparative analysis of new educational programmes in the global era. In A. Duchêne, M. Moyer, & C. Roberts (Eds.), *Language, migration and social inequalities: A critical perspective on institutions and work* (pp. 118–146). Bristol, UK: Multilingual Matters.

Morgan, B., & Ramanathan, V. (2009). Outsourcing, globalizing economics, and shifting language policies: Issues in managing Indian call centres. *Language Policy* 8, 69–80.

Muehlmann, S., & Duchêne, A. (2007). Beyond the nation-state: International agencies as new sites of discourses on bilingualism. In M. Heller (Ed.), *Bilingualism: A social approach* (pp. 96–110). London: Palgrave.

Pan, L. (2011). English language ideologies in the Chinese foreign language education policies: A world-system perspective. *Language Policy* 10, 245–263.

Park, J. S.-Y. (2009). *The local construction of a global language: Ideologies of English in South Korea.* Berlin: Mouton de Gruyter.

Park, J. S.-Y., & Wee, L. (2012). *Markets of English: Linguistic capital and language policy in a globalizing world.* London: Routledge.

Pennycook, A. (2006) Postmodernism and language policy. In T. Ricento (Ed.), *An introduction to language policy: Theory and method* (pp. 60–76). Oxford: Blackwell.

Pérez-Milans, M. (2013). *Urban schools and English language education in late modern China: A critical sociolinguistic ethnography.* London: Routledge.

Pérez-Milans, M. (2015). Language education policy in late modernity: (Socio)linguistic ethnographies in the European Union. *Language Policy* 14(2), 99–107.

Pérez-Milans, M., & Patiño-Santos, A. (2014). Language education and institutional change in a Madrid multilingual school. *International Journal of Multilingualism* 11(4), 449–470.

Phillipson, R. (1992). *Linguistic imperialism.* New York: Oxford University Press.

Phillipson, R. (2009). Linguistic imperialism continued. *TESOL Quarterly* 43, 335–339.

Piller, I., & Cho, J. (2013). Neoliberalism as language policy. *Language in Society* 42, 23–44.

Pujolar, J. (2007). African women in Catalan language courses: Struggles over class, gender and ethnicity in advanced liberalism. In B. McElhinny (Ed.), *Words, worlds and material girls* (pp. 305–347). Berlin: Mouton de Gruyter.

Relaño-Pastor, A. M. (2015). The commodification of English in "Madrid, comunidad bilingüe": Insights from the CLIL classroom. *Language Policy* 14(2), 131–152.

Ricento, T. (Ed.). (2015). *Language policy and political economy: English in a global context.* Oxford: Oxford University Press.

Roberts, C. (2013). The gatekeeping of Babel: Job interviews and the linguistic penalty. In A. Duchêne, M. Moyer, & C. Roberts (Eds.), *Language, migration and social inequalities: A critical perspective on institutions and work* (pp. 81–94). Bristol, UK: Multilingual Matters.

Sarangi, S., & Roberts, C. (1999). The dynamics of interactional and institutional orders in work-related settings. In S. Sarangi & C. Roberts (Eds.), *Talk, work and institutional order: Discourse in medical, mediation and management settings* (pp. 1–57). Berlin: Mouton de Gruyter.

Sokolovska, Z. (2016). *Les débats sur les langues dans une Europe en projet: Généalogie discursive, idéologies langagières et constructions (post)nationales au Conseil de l'Europe.* Unpublished PhD thesis. University of Strasbourg & University of Fribourg.

Spolsky, B. (2004) *Language policy.* Cambridge: Cambridge University Press.

Tollefson, J. W. (2006). Critical theory in language policy. In T. Ricento (Ed.), *An introduction to language policy: Theory and method* (pp. 42–59). Oxford: Blackwell.

Urciuoli, B. (2008). Skills and selves in the new workplace. *American Ethnologist* 35(2), 211–228.

Urciouli, B., & LaDousa, C. (2013). Language management/labour. *Annual Review of Anthropology* 42, 175–190.

....

CHAPTER 24

POST-NATIONALISM AND LANGUAGE COMMODIFICATION

....

JOAN PUJOLAR

In this chapter, I present the phenomenon of *linguistic commodification* as one prominent aspect of how contemporary societies intervene on language. As such, the chapter draws attention to the fact that language in late modern societies plays an increasingly central role in the economy, even as globalization undermines the strength of nation-states, which have been a major agent of language policies. The concept of commodification refers to the process whereby any object, tangible or intangible, is constructed as an element that can be brought into a process of economic exchange or accountability, be it through straightforward purchase (I pay, I get it), or through more complex forms of asset management. Thus, we are looking at *language as an economic asset*.

This chapter follows up ideas raised elsewhere in this volume, which include how tertiarization, neoliberalism, and globalization reconfigure the role of language in people's lives and the ways in which individuals and organizations treat languages (see, in this volume, Codó, Chapter 23; Del Percio, Chapter 26; and Martín Rojo, Chapter 27). Also included in these considerations are changing ideologies and practices of governance that point to a diminishing role of government in public life and in the economy. This has implications for language planning because it affects how public institutions may (or may not) intervene directly or indirectly in language, and conversely on the ways in which non-public institutions (such as businesses or

NGOs) also act, sometimes by determining public language uses and ideologies following their own interests. In relation to this, I will suggest that future research on language planning must expand its purview to the forms of linguistic governance determined by non-state actors. However, I argue that a more important point to learn from research on linguistic commodification is to appreciate that what we are witnessing is not so much a retreat of the state, but a transformation of its modes of intervention in public and economic life, and that language policy makes a particularly good lens to understand this transformation.

The concept of commodification is relatively recent in sociolinguistics (Heller, 2003), and it is still the subject of debate as to what it refers to, and whether it really designates a phenomenon that is new at all (McGill, 2013). Basically, it points to the complex imbrications of language and the economy, which the discipline largely associates with the work of Pierre Bourdieu. For Bourdieu, languages, utterances, and speakers are by definition subjected to a process of evaluation that is directly or indirectly connected to their standing in relation to symbolic and economic markets.

This central idea means that any utterance or any orientation from a speaker in relation to language follows a socioeconomic logic. From this perspective, the Roman elites who hired Greek tutors, the British upper and middle classes who took up French-speaking governesses in past centuries, and today's parents who send their children to English summer courses are not doing anything substantially different. Thus commodification does not refer to the general idea that economic calculation may be behind sociolinguistic phenomena, but rather to some recent specific developments that stick out as different from the way in which human beings were accustomed to use language and talk about language up until the late twentieth century.

The major received linguistic paradigm is the one in which most human groups have their own language, each possessing its own separate set of lexical, morphological, phonological, and grammatical resources. As industrial capitalism eventually led to the formation of liberal nation-states during the nineteenth century, languages were taken up as emblems of the communities and as justification of political sovereignty. Languages also became an object of state planning, studied and regulated by expert linguists, disseminated and controlled by teachers and publishers committed to the projects of nation building. From this viewpoint, there was a clear political economic logic behind the way in which languages were treated in this period; but the economics of language was masked behind forms of representation of language as a common group property, a vehicle of national culture, and a sign of the community's uniqueness.

Currently researchers on linguistic commodification argue that new ways of talking and using language are appearing in which the economic is made prominent; they propose that these alterations do not happen by chance, but are the product of important economic transformations in the last few years. Generally, we find that people and organizations now talk about language in ways that foreground their concerns about money, profits, or social mobility. And researchers believe that these new discourses emerge because the overall economic system is changing, that we have entered a phase called *post-industrial capitalism* or *late capitalism* in which linguistic performance is more central to processes of production than it used to be. Thus, this position can be counted among the lines of social science thinking in which the economy is seen as a major shaper of social practices, values, and institutions.

The terms *tertiarization, neoliberalism,* and *globalization* are commonly used to express this wide socioeconomic context of linguistic commodification. In the next section, I briefly define them. Then I examine three examples of commodification associated with language. In the final discussion section, I will bring together the implications of these phenomena for the ways in which we have traditionally restricted the scope of language planning (until recently) to aspects of the governmental intervention on language.

Tertiarization, Neoliberalism, Globalization—and Language Planning

Tertiarization, neoliberalism, and globalization can be said to affect language planning in different, albeit interconnected ways: tertiarization because it turns language into a particularly sensitive resource for economic actors; neoliberalism because it bears on the general idea of how governments should regulate social life; and globalization because it undermines the state's capacities to intervene in social and economic activities. *Tertiarization* refers to the dominance of so-called third- or tertiary-sector production in the economy. The primary sector covers agriculture, fishing, and extraction, and it was the predominant economic activity of humanity up to the twentieth century. The secondary sector includes any form of manufacture or building, activities that quickly became the largest producers of wealth and employment in industrial societies, as well as the source of unprecedented economic and demographic growth. The tertiary sector, also called the service economy, designates a heterogeneous set of activities that kept expanding in industrial societies until they overtook industry in overall size: finance, marketing, planning and government, design, hospitality and tourism, transport and distribution, wholesale and retail, education, policing, health care, social services, entertainment, communication, and professional services. The term *post-industrial society* often refers to contexts where this sector accounts for the largest share in gross domestic product (GDP) and employment, often after many manufacturing plants have been closed or moved to other countries where salaries and other production costs are cheaper.

Tertiarization is held to be associated with profound cultural changes that have been and are being examined by social scientists. Sociolinguists in particular have highlighted the fact that tertiarization affects and is affected by language in fundamental ways because most third-sector activities consist of producing linguistic goods or goods in which language is very important. The material shape of a novel, a theater play, an insurance contract, a marketing campaign, a training course, or a customer information service is basically linguistic. Social services, health care, and tourism may involve the exchange of material objects or resources, but they require social interaction, sometimes intense. What this means is that the contemporary twenty-first-century worker is no longer (predominantly) a manual worker but a language worker, no longer blue collar but white collar. As Duchêne (2009) puts it, the *main d'oeuvre* (*the workforce*) has become a *parole d'euvre* (*the wordforce*), which means that language is no longer important just as an emblem of national identity, but also as a component of individuals' professional selves and their socioeconomic standing. Predictably, this has consequences for the ways in which people talk about languages and what they mean to them; and it also has consequences for the organizations and corporations in which they work.

The term *neoliberalism* in its present usage generally refers to a specific ideology that posits that economic growth and stability is best achieved if governments abstain from intervening in how private companies and entrepreneurs operate. In this way, the capitalist economy would work like a jungle in which the fittest (e.g., the most efficient) arguably survive and improve the whole stock (Giroux, 2015). The idea is nowhere tested to an absolute limit, but conventionally it involves (a) selling public services like water or electricity to private companies, (b) passing new regulations that allegedly simplify or slim down former regulations, and (c) removing obstacles to trade, such as import tariffs or idiosyncratic authorization procedures. Neoliberalism is often considered to be the hegemonic political/economic ideology that drives globalization, which I discuss later.

Additionally, it is particularly relevant to language planning because it affects both the principles and the scope of language policies. First, it raises the question of whether the state should actively intervene in linguistic matters, particularly when these affect the economy and the conduct of private actors. Second, it effectively reduces the scope of what was traditionally considered as public affairs and hence of all the areas of society that were formerly run by state agencies and that used language following the logic of nation-state ideologies. This is also relevant to the idea of linguistic commodification in the sense that we are seeing parallel processes of the reconstitution of what were formerly presented as public goods (water, power, education, transport) in terms of products now subject to barter and competition.

Finally, *globalization* refers to the perception that economic, political, military, demographic, cultural, and environmental processes are intimately interconnected at a planetary scale to the point that most social issues cannot be understood by attending solely to their local circumstances. Although theorists of globalization place its start by the sixteenth century (Wallerstein, 1998), there is no question that recent improvements in transport and communication technologies have turned the world into a much smaller place. International trade and travel are consistently on the increase, while the Internet provides the means to multiply the networks of social activity that operate across large distances thanks to quasi-instantaneous flows of communications (which also boost the possibilities of the tertiary sector).

Globalization is relevant to language planning and to sociolinguistics in general on many counts, but particularly because it disturbs the ideas of social order fostered by industrial capitalism, in which the nation-state provided the fundamental means of sociopolitical organization, economic exchange, and the ideological constructs of what people thought they shared with their fellow citizens—namely language, culture, and a set of national values. Nation-states were not conceived for a world where people, goods, and capital move in and out of them all the time, or where workers and citizens operate and transact in multiple and changing languages. In short, globalization entails multilingualism as one more way in which the classical authority, legitimacy, and accountability of the nation-state is put in question. If languages and linguistic practices were until recently understood and evaluated in ways that followed the logic of how nation-states were organized, the question now is what happens in all those spaces and activities in which the state is not as relevant as it used to be.

I have so far highlighted how these three macro-trends seem to challenge or bypass state authority or its attendant linguistic ideologies. This is not intended to suggest that either nation-states or their ideologies have become irrelevant political structures or relics of the past. In fact, nation-states remain at present the only recognized source of political sovereignty, even in multinational setups such as the United Nations or the European Union. And even when they make a show of stripping down regulations (often by actually producing brand new regulatory frameworks), they still remain very active both nationally and internationally, furthering their national interests. Moreover, with regard to language, the classical view that they are bounded systems represented by their standard varieties that express the national character still dominates post-industrial societies, as debates on immigration clearly show. From this perspective, linguistic commodification does not appear as a new linguistic paradigm, but rather as an increasingly noisy dissonance within the dominant linguistic order. The examples I provide in the following section illustrate different manifestations of this dissonance.

BARTERING LANGUAGE: THREE EXAMPLES

I posit two main ways in which language can be presented as an economic asset: (a) as a component or property of a product; and (b) as an embodied capacity of individuals (i.e., as a skill). As one would expect, the two components rarely appear in specific contexts in completely separate fashions; they are not the poles of a continuum, nor do they exclude the presence of more classical nationalist constructions of language. Here I propose to examine three areas of activity that provide the means to discuss the forms of linguistic commodification and their social consequences that have so far been documented by sociolinguists: (1) the language learning abroad industry in Spain, (2) the policies of Francophone economic development in Canada, and (3) the multilingual call centers from the workers' perspective. The examples contain, respectively, an emphasis on (1) language as a product, (2) language as a property of a product, and (3) language as an embodied skill. They also exemplify slightly different modes of state involvement or non-involvement in the activities at hand.

Language Learning and Tourism

This first example illustrates how language can be mobilized as a product and hence inserted in new social activities and forms of representation that appear politically uncontroversial; but if we explore the backstage of the linguistic field we will find that traditional linguistic nationalism and colonialism is still a force to be reckoned with. Figure 24.1 displays the home website of a private language school in Barcelona that offers its courses to the segment of people who take up a language course in the country where the language is (allegedly) spoken, usually during their vacation time. I did not choose this particular school because it presented special features, but because it displayed explicitly most of the features associated with this kind of product. In it, language is offered as a product, although strictly speaking the product is rather the whole learning process, combined with tourist sociability. It is noticeable that the educational aspects are very briefly dealt with (class numbers, native-speaker teachers) in comparison with issues of accommodation, location, and amenities.

It appears that the authors are especially concerned with the *experience* quality of the product offered, so that the website presents features typically associated with travel preparations: accommodation close to the city center, vicinity to Barcelona's tourist attractions, and availability of "terrace" space for socialization and relaxation. The pictures also seem to suggest a youthful, informal environment with moderate racial diversity, and maybe the typically subdued promises of romance, which are much more explicit in other sites. Along with a varied array of conventional and intensive courses, customers can also take up "Spanish and Salsa" or "Spanish and Flamenco" courses. Through the conventional "customer comment" genre, there is an assurance of good management that explicitly responds to national stereotypes on Spanish informality: "very orderly, almost a little German. It is not what I expected of Spain."

One aspect of interest is the school's inscription into the wider networks of Spanish-language institutions, as signaled by the logos (top left) of FEDELE, the *Federación de Escuelas de Español como Lengua Extrangera* (Federation of Schools of Spanish as a Foreign Language) (located in Spain only), and of *Instituto Cervantes*, an

FIGURE 24.1. Learning Spanish in Barcelona.

Source: http://www.caminobarcelona.es/

agency equivalent to the British Council or the Goethe Institute, created by the government of Spain. FEDELE was created in 1999 as a conventional network of private businesses concerned with providing quality standards in the sector, and it became a member of the *Cervantes* board in 2014. FEDELE has another special partnership with *Turespaña*, the official agency of tourist promotion, which offers "learning Spanish" as one of the possibilities. Tourism is a space in which the language of marketing has long contributed to the articulation of discourses about the nation; but recently the Spanish government felt that it needed a more comprehensive approach, and so it created the *Alto Comisionado por la Marca España* (High Commission of the Spain Trademark), a governmental office charged with improving the image of Spain "at home and abroad" (http://marcaespana.es/que-es-marca-españa). *Marca España* takes also a special interest in language tourism; it reported that in 2012 Spain received €2 billion of income thanks to these language learners, although the datum itself is not very credible and the source seems to be equivocally handled (see España, 2013).

The growth of the language school industry is arguably consistent with the trend to tertiarization in its multiple dimensions, including the existence of a growing workforce with university qualifications, as well as a market in which individuals seek to acquire ever more skills to enhance their employability—again—in service industries. The expanding demand for education and training fuels competition and the development of new products. The term *edutainment* conventionally expresses new consumerist trends in education whereby educational products are encoded as components of specific lifestyles. These schools also build on new opportunities granted by the consistent growth of the tourist industry, which involves ever more people traveling, as well as its product diversification. Rather than offering *destinations* and *attractions*, the sector has in recent decades consistently moved toward a logic of *activities* and *experiences* in which products comprise complex combinations of learning, sightseeing, partying, and networking.

From a language planning perspective, we can look into how the state treats this specific area of activity. The sector follows the logic of private enterprise and is not the concern of the conventional educational system, in which state intervention is more encompassing and in which it has major organizational prerogatives. Institutional intervention here is thus primarily exerted through the control of accreditation procedures (the Cervantes' level certificates) and the articulation of *quality management* in partnership with a sector of the industry (FEDELE). Thus while the whole sector may be presented as an example of neoliberal deregulation in the sense that the state does not intervene in how or why someone sets up a language school, it nevertheless involves the deployment of specific forms of intervention by indirect means. Second, this industry is posited on the deployment of specific discourses about the value of Spanish for a constituency that is not the traditional national public, but the international market. Spain has a tradition of promoting or imposing the language among many of its own citizens through arguments that revolved around national identity, religious denomination, or ascription to modernity. However, a more recent example runs as such:

> *APRENDER ESPAÑOL: El idioma que hablan más de 470 millones de personas en el mundo. Aprender español en España es la mejor manera de acercarse al lenguaje universal de Cervantes. También es una forma de descubrir un país vitalista y moderno, con un inmenso legado cultural y artístico que te fascinará desde el primer momento.*

> TO LEARN SPANISH: The language spoken by over 470 million people world-wide. To learn Spanish in Spain is the best way to approach the universal language of Cervantes. It is also a way to discover a lively and modern country with an immense cultural and artistic legacy that will fascinate you from the start. (Turespaña, 2016)

With an implicit hint at the market value of Spanish internationally, the text lays its emphasis on Spanish as a vehicle of culture, which is consistent with traditional renderings of languages as vehicles for national cultures. There are no necessary contradictions between offering language as a commodity and reproducing its traditional image as an intangible good connected to national culture, particularly if the message need not be taken as an injunction for readers to stop speaking their own languages (as still happens in some contexts to Catalans or Mayas). The audience is not asked to become Spanish, or Catholic, or civilized, but to incorporate the language into its cultural baggage and—less explicitly—into its set of skills to bring into the labor market. An additional detail to note is that the target audience is no longer the traditional monolingual native speaker idealized by dialectology, mainstream linguistics, and nationalist primordialism, but the international consumer who seeks to accumulate (multilingual) linguistic and symbolic capital while on the move.

State interests and nationalism may not be explicit in the signs displayed, but they are still an important force behind the scenes of institutional and corporate strategy. As del Valle (2011) has documented, the Spanish-language teaching sector and its academic and state agencies are a part of a still wider picture of a program that brings together the political and economic interests of Spain and its most powerful banks and industries. This state-led program mobilizes hundreds of millions of euros to fund the Instituto Cervantes and specific projects of the Royal Spanish Academy to stage Spain's leadership in the Spanish-speaking world through language, even as banks and companies providing energy (gas, oil, electricity) or building infrastructures engage in a neocolonial comeback to Latin America. Old tensions between Spain and its former colonies, as well as with its own multilingual regions, were easier to find in a venue such as the *2008 Congreso Internacional del valor del Idioma Español: El español como recurso turístico, cultural y económico* (International conference on the value of the Spanish language: Spanish as a tourist, cultural and economic resource) in Salamanca:

> In this 3-day conference that included 44 papers or round-table sessions, as well as other events, presenters of about a third of the events began by criticizing the language policies deployed by the government of Catalonia (which is some 700 km. away). In this context, one member of the public went as far as proposing in a discussion that Barcelona's language schools should not be accredited because they were not located in a Spanish-speaking territory.

The event's agenda was meant to explore the rising international profile of the Spanish language and its impact on language teaching, research, trade, and foreign relations. However, this was done from an entirely *intra-national* perspective in which the participation of Latin American actors was minimal and the country's traditional obsession with its multilingual regions was palpable in the atmosphere. Although the spontaneous proposition in the preceding was met with silence and probably a certain embarrassment, and the response of the chair was short and non-committal, it was largely consistent with all the language-school websites, public and private, that in Castile and León claim to offer the best, the most original, or the purest variety of Spanish; or with the experience of a qualified Spanish teacher who recently was denied a post because of her Catalan origin. So while the public self-presentation of the Spanish-language teaching sector may draw on widely accepted idealizations of intercultural relations and multilingualism, a visit to the kitchen where these discourses are cooked provides a more sobering scenario in which traditional forms of linguistic nationalism and colonialism are still a force to be reckoned with.

Language in Heritage Tourism

Figure 24.2 features a poster publicizing areas (set in darker tones) inhabited by Canada's Easternmost Francophone Acadian communities as tourist destinations. The different colors display the fact that these areas fall under the administration of different Canadian provinces, with Nouveau/New Brunswick being the largest and the only officially bilingual one (in English and French). How such a representation came to happen, one that offers a linguistic minority as a tourist attraction, is what concerns us here, particularly in how these developments mobilize public and private actors. Monica Heller (2011a) and her colleagues have amply documented these processes, whose inception can be traced back to an address by the Canadian prime minister to attendees at the 1994 Acadian World Congress, where he vowed to mobilize the government for a plan of *développement communitaire* (community development) of minority-language communities.

In this example, we can see a subtly different way of inscribing language into tourist product development; but what is most interesting is the way in which state institutions changed gear in the way they understood their role in relation to the politics of Canada's two official languages. The concept of *développement communitaire* expresses a focus on economic policies addressed to largely francophone peripheral rural or fishing regions in crisis. The Employment Ministry (called *Ressources humaines et Développement des Compétences*) undertook a thorough task of evaluation of economic assets (including the professional skills of the workforce in the area) and investment strategies. Initiatives were channeled through an interministerial body called *Réseau de développement économique et employabilité* (Employment and Economic Development Network [RDEE]), which also included the participation of the Ministry of Culture (called *Patrimoine Canadien*) and the Canadian Tourist Commission.

FIGURE 24.2. acadievacances brochure.

Source: www.acadievacances.com

The initiative marked a momentous change of paradigm in communities that had previously cultivated francophone identity by way of education and cultural associations funded through government transfers. Gradually, access to funds was reconstituted as *investment* directed to projects aimed at the creation of innovative business ventures and infrastructures. Although the different regional committees have over the years identified different areas of economic opportunity (see http://rdee.ca/fr/reseau/), tourism has consistently featured as a key area of growth, in which the use and display of French language signage, local cultural celebrations, artistic performances, heritage sites, and cuisine have provided a narrative with the French language and Francophone identity presented as *valeur ajoutée* ("added value"). Numerous research projects have documented how different ventures have fared: the *Festival du Loup* in Lafontaine (http://festivalduloup.on.ca), the pageants *L'écho d'un people* in Casselman (http://echodunpeuple.ca/) and *La Fabouleuse Historie d'un Royaume* in Saguenay (http://www.diffusion.saguenay.ca/la-fabuleuse/la-fabuleuse-version-estivale/a-propos.html), the *Village acadien* in Caraquet (www.villagehistoriqueacadien.com/), *Le Pays de la Sagouine* (http://www.sagouine.com/) and *Les Trois Pignons* in Chéticamp (https://lestroispignons.com) (Heller & Pujolar, 2010; Heller, Pujolar, & Duchêne, 2014; Julien, 2012).

Generally speaking, these new tourist attractions constantly struggle to survive economically, and most have remained afloat with the help of government funding. However, in the process, Canadian authorities effectively provoked an overhaul in the institutional infrastructure of Francophone movements and forced a conceptual reconstitution of their position (and that of the languages) within Canadian society: in addition to a constitutive component of Canada's identity as a nation, French and Francophone communities were now an economic asset and were responsible for the exploitation of this asset.

Beyond the state's neoliberal approach, it is important to understand the economic context in which this process took place. Francophone communities devoted to agriculture, fishing, and forestry had traditionally been seen as historical and cultural emblems, the places *in the country* where Acadians were supposed to refer back to. During the 1980s, all these sectors started receding, as has happened in most industrial societies. Similarly, delocalization of industries threatened the employment base of the urban Francophone workforce. Thus, the state had to assist in the process whereby these populations moved into the tertiary sector, which was the essential charge of the RDEE.

As in the previous example, traditional linguistic nationalism has not really been replaced by an ostensibly business-oriented approach to language. Heller (2011b) has amply documented how the boards that run the new tourist venture typically agonized over the need to use English with tourist clients while maintaining the original commitment to public uses of French. In a way, Francophone cultural activists were confronted with the quandaries over linguistic rights and economic resources that they had formerly trusted that the state would resolve. In any case, as in the

Spanish example, new issues arose as to what constituted legitimate representations of Francophone language and identity. Given the focus on linguistic and cultural *authenticity* based on locality, a common occurrence in heritage sites was a greater visibility for local dialects that had traditionally been muted by educational authorities and the cultural elites.

Additionally, new forms of contemporary artistic production are emerging in which unconventional and hybrid linguistic practices (combining French and English) acquire a visibility that they had previously not enjoyed, and hence challenge the established practice of presenting French as a standard and unified language in the public domain (McLaughlin, 2010). Once authenticity is mobilized as a selling point for language and identity, old and new divisions emerge over the definition of what counts as authentic, and over who has the final say.

Multilingual Call Centers

Call centers provide a good setting to exemplify the post-national worksite in both their outward presentation and in their inner contradictions, as well as the complex ways in which workers may be subjected to specific forms of linguistic discipline. Call centers typically offer information services, so that the product is embodied in social interaction. Given that it consists basically of talk, workers can be hosted anywhere on the planet where the telecommunications infrastructure allows, which makes call centers potentially easy to outsource overseas (in theory). In the same way, given that they can potentially service many markets, call centers seem ideal for creating multilingual workplaces in which multilingual workers should thrive as they display and cash in multilingual skills that should arguably enable them to attend more flexibly to the diverse demands and needs of customers and employers. Call centers also make good sites to explore how language policies may be articulated following corporate logics, rather than those of social movements or governmental agencies.

There are three main aspects of interest in the management of communicative resources in call centers: the development of communication scripts; the establishment of the appropriate language variety; and the connections between workers' multilingualism and their compensation and status. Cameron (2000) described the trend in many service industries (not just call centers, but also fast food chains or other sales outlets associated with big transnational corporations with many branches and franchises) to systematize in a Taylorist style how workers should interact with customers:

> [...] call centre managers may set out to determine exactly what sequence of interactional moves is needed to accomplish a given transaction efficiently, and then institutionalize the preferred sequence in a model or script which all workers are required to reproduce in every transaction of the same type. (Cameron, 2000, p. 95)

Thus call center workers may be instructed in great detail on how to greet, identify themselves and callers, ask for information (probably withhold information, too), react to disagreement, describe the purview of the service, use specific tones of voice, and so on. Communication scripting also exemplifies ambivalences with respect to the exact character of the product being sold. A burger chain may be said to be selling burgers, although their marketing departments will realize that the entire premises and props (the space, tables, chairs, kids play areas, toys, etc.) are essential to what is being offered. Thus when deciding how workers must dress and be trained in how to negotiate orders with customers and pass them on to the kitchen, the burger chain in fact is inscribing social interaction into the process of product development. Linguistic commodification is especially caught up in this blurring of boundaries, in which even advertisements, with their injunctions and innuendos of gender and class-related lifestyles, may arguably be seen not just as vehicles of information about products, but as important components of the social worlds in which consumers are invited to participate.

Studies on multilingual call centers document the need to establish what linguistic varieties are used and how. First there is the choice of which languages, as conventionally understood, are made available for callers. As Duchêne (2009) explains, this is often done in terms of cost-benefit concerns. Given that each language requires an infrastructure and worker hours, the management must judge whether the customer base of the language is going to justify the investment. This can partly be presented as a political shift whereby decisions on public language uses formerly constructed in terms of rights now are decided following economic motivations. However, economic motivations are rarely negotiated in terms that are free from more traditional political concerns. Pujolar (2007), for instance, reports how the privatization of Spain's telephone services initially led to a decrease of customer service in Catalan. Strictly speaking, Catalan speakers have no trouble conducting business in Spanish, but popular protests and the pressure of Catalan public authorities constituted reasons enough to reverse the trend. Roy's (2003) studies of Canadian call centers provide a similar context, in which the economic reasons to cater to the country's French-speaking customers are partly coated by Canada's official linguistic duality.

It is the management of the varieties used by call center workers that provide a window into how these new forms of communication reconstitute how linguistic hierarchies were experienced and negotiated until recently. Roy (2003) documents how Canadian call centers treated local varieties of French as problematic, and selected workers able to conduct communication in the standard forms of French, or trained them to do so. In this case, the main problem was that local Francophones conventionally used many words or phrases from English and code-switched often between the two languages. In other situations, such as the Indian call centers researched by Shome (2006), it was the traces of accent and "non-American" turns of expression that the management sought to sanitize. These examples are sobering reminders that the kind of linguistic hygienism practiced by nation-state institutions might have been historically even more lenient than the class-based language hierarchies that were imposed in private life and in the economy.

This drive against hybridity and low-prestige varieties stands on important contradictions. First, these corporations establish their centers in areas known to be inhabited by a workforce ready to take up low-wage employment, such as India or, in the Canadian case, the Francophone areas that had recently suffered from deindustrialization. However, a low wage workforce is also one that by definition speaks low-value language varieties. A second contradiction is that the very customer base seeking those services may not necessarily have access to the standard or share the same expectations that the management takes for granted. Indeed, Duchêne (2009) found that, in a Swiss call center, callers often were in search not so much of standard languages, but of the local flavor and authenticity that natives were giving off (often inadvertently) in the form of regional or foreign accents. What these studies commonly show is that these *linguistic companies* generally ascribe to very conventional views of language as separate and bounded systems and as skills that can be ascribed to workers on a yes/no basis. In addition, because oral communication in real life is much more hybrid and complex, workers and customers often end up finding their own off-the-record solutions to overcome the contradiction that speaking in socalled "proper French" may actually make communication worse and more distant.

The final question in these contexts is how much multilingualism pays, and the answer is very little. As explained in the preceding, it is typical for call centers to include localization as part of its strategic planning. Thus, businesses do not really seek to attract a workforce with specific skills, but instead move to where this workforce is available and cheap and has no competitive value locally. Barcelona, for instance, has become a hub for European call services thanks to its constant floating population of young foreign students and tourists (Rodés, 2013). In the studies conducted by Roy and Duchêne, the multilingual workers were at the low pay levels, and a bilingual bonus had recently been introduced in the Canadian case, which did not so much underscore the difference between bilinguals and monolinguals, but the difference between those who could speak so-called proper French and those who spoke more vernacular forms. Duchêne (2009) argues that multilingualism was an asset for workers at the gatekeeping moment of obtaining the employment, but that their linguistic skills were banalized once in the job. It is thus telling that, in both places, multilingualism did not appear to have any bearing on workplace hierarchies, as the management could sometimes remain perfectly monolingual, which also shows how monolingual people in high-ranking managerial positions have to a degree contained the weight of linguistic skills in the corporate pecking order.

Call centers present contradictions that former political-economic structures had long exhibited. The professions that had traditionally required special oral and literacy skills (writers, journalists, publishers, teachers, lawyers, administrators) had been generally taken up by the educated elites who invested in standard languages. The contemporary service industry, however, has substantially relied on a new post-industrial proletariat characterized by low wages, job insecurity, and small prospects of social mobility, and hence the social segments least inclined to the linguistic discipline pursued by the state and the elites. The massive access of the population to electronic networks has further diversified the linguistic varieties accessible in the public domain.

Thus, the development of linguistic products for consumption, or the mobilization of language in specific forms of product development, as well as the increasing diversification of the linguistic professions, brings about representations and uses of language that are dissonant with inherited ideas about language and national identity and about linguistic propriety. These new contexts of production expose the sociolinguistic inequalities that former state institutions had done much to both suppress and legitimate through the school, the administration, and the public media. Private sector actors who had earlier tacitly participated in reproducing linguistic hierarchies (e.g., by providing certain jobs only to people with certain forms of education) now must explicitly inscribe linguistic ideologies into their production processes, following the logics of offer and demand. I will try to develop this line of thought in the final section.

FINAL CONSIDERATIONS: ON RESEARCH ON LANGUAGE POLICY AND PLANNING AND SOCIOLINGUISTICS

Linguistic commodification can therefore be understood as a term that addresses the sociolinguistic phenomena that emerge as language and language practices experience the pull of new socioeconomic practices and forms of cultural consumption. Zygmunt Bauman (Bauman, 2006 [2000]) is conventionally credited with expressing how contemporary subjectivities have reconstituted themselves in a sociopolitical world no longer structured around the logics of production, but according to the means and needs of consumption. While in pre-modern and modern times social identities were derived from each person's position within the structures of production (whether they were peasants, nobility, artisans, capitalists, or workers), in the past decades it is patterns of consumption that have increasingly featured as central to social belonging and the accumulation of symbolic capital. These shifts respond to the need of an economy in which the markets of manufactured goods become saturated and there is the need to ensure that people keep buying, be it by establishing the need for seasonal replacement (as in the fashion industry or tourism), through the constant renewal of entertainment products, by developing new specialized products that cater to ever smaller consumer bases (niche markets), or by commodifying new areas of activity such as utility supplies, education, or traditionally female family labor (child care, family care, cleaning). In this context, adherence to political structures and institutions such as trade unions, political parties, and even nation-states, according to Bauman, weakens as people invest more and more to inhabit the lifeworlds offered through advertising and the new physical and institutional spaces of socialization oriented to cost-effectiveness and consumption (such as shopping malls).

Thus, in a world in which work and consumption increasingly incorporate social interaction, it is not surprising that both languages and language practices become bound up with the development of new products and forms of work. The literature on linguistic commodification aims at understanding these processes as ever more diverse social actors develop interest in languages and language practices as properties of products and as skills of workers; which in turn leads them to analyze them, decompose them, and reconstitute them as elements of new products that can be marketed to accomplish specific tasks and/or bind the act of consuming with specific forms of social identity and affect. Fairclough (1992) posited the concept of "commodification of discourse" in a similar vein to refer to the ways in which commercial ventures, particularly the media, were reinscribing popular forms of interaction in their constant genre innovation; but also in the ways in which the semantics of corporate management was colonizing social activities formerly not experienced in commercial terms.

Indeed, now sociolinguists find that the informants that they interview increasingly express their relationships to language in terms of long-term economic strategies (Heller, 1999). Urla (2012) documents how Basque-language activists incorporate the language of quality management as they seek to engage with the private sector to promote the use of Basque in the workplace. Additionally, the increasing popularity of bilingual or immersion education in Europe and North America should also be examined in terms of the economic sense it makes for the new middle classes to invest in multilingual distinction, even when it applies to minority languages with very little weight in national and global markets.

Is this, however, a totally new sociolinguistic paradigm? Duchêne and Heller (2011) argue that this recontextualization of language within late modern forms of life brings about new forms of seeing language as an economic asset that often enters into conflict with the traditional approach to languages as emblems of national identity. It is not, however, that the old paradigm is being superseded by a new one in which people abandon their social or ethnocultural or nationalist attachments to languages. Rather, as we have seen in the three examples, the creation of new products and services is often done by recasting ideas and values attached to languages that derive from this nation-state paradigm. However, the tensions emerge when the linguistic constructs of the nation-state paradigm are brought to operate in social activities and in pursuit of agendas for which they were not made. The notion of a standard language made sense as a means of discipline that could be applied to pupils and schools and which was used, as Bourdieu has argued, in the process of reproduction of class hierarchies, which in turn was later legitimized by a capitalist economy where the educated occupied specific professional niches. As the middle and upper classes controlled the state apparatus, the industrial establishments in which language was instrumental at the managerial level, and the public circulation of print media supervised by language professionals, the match between language and the means of production and social differentiation could remain stable. However, these forms of control cannot be sustained in a world where populations and messages constantly cross borders, and particularly in an economy that chases every consumer and digs up any material or symbolic resource it can get hold of. The linguistic reproduction of class hierarchies is also complicated precisely in the context of a consumer economy that invests a lot in blurring the boundaries of social belonging, even as it must recruit the lower classes to accomplish the communicative work that helps to build the lifeworlds that it seeks to create and sell.

What are the implications of linguistic commodification for language planning? In my view, this is a question that should be handled with care. On the face of it, neoliberal approaches query what aspects of social life and resources must be managed by political institutions or should instead be left in the care of private persons or organizations. Thus, it raises the question of who should or who is actually doing language planning. However, in this chapter I have taken care to display my skepticism of the claims that neoliberalism effectively entails a *hands-off approach* to policy. In my view, as sociolinguists, we should not take these claims at face value, and should rather examine critically what transformations neoliberalism brings about in the ways in which different social actors intervene with language. This should include a very critical appraisal of how, after all, decisions are taken, who decides, and what the sociolinguistic consequences are.

In any case, given that nation-states have effectively let loose a good deal of what they (at least nominally) controlled half a century ago, and given that there are so many new kids in town who wish to tell us how languages can be accessed and evaluated, and given that there are now so many nongovernmental bodies (corporate or not) that play key roles in global governance, it seems necessary that researchers on language planning must increasingly step into these new spaces to understand the consequences of neoliberalism and what new forms of social and political control over language are thereby articulated.

However, it is important for language planning researchers to understand that this changes not just the object of study or the social settings in which research is conducted; it transforms in fundamental ways the position in which we as researchers are purported to speak and why; and this shift also affects the character of the conversation that the field has traditionally had with stakeholders outside academia. Whereas academia has traditionally adopted the position that it is pursuing general public interests, which justified that sociolinguists largely critiqued language planning institutions that also acted in the public interest, now we are increasingly dealing with actors who have a variety of organizational and corporate concerns intimately connected with economic accountability. Of course, the notion of *public interest* can in some contexts be easily translated into related concepts such as *corporate social responsibility*. But this does not take into account that the implications of neoliberalism are more profound and that they affect academia deeply. Thus, given the prospect of the increasing commodification of higher education, in which corporate research funding may render some research objects and orientations more profitable or viable than others, the ultimate challenge for language planning as an academic field will be to adopt an open reflexivity that acknowledges the ways in which its gaze is constituted by the specific historically bound social struggles over power in which language is a key resource.

ACKNOWLEDGMENTS

This text derives from the research Project "Language, Culture and Tourism: Identity Discourses and the Commoditization of Languages in Global Markets" funded by the Dirección General de Investigación of the Ministerio de Educación y Ciencia in Spain: Ref. HUM2006-13621-C04-04/FILO. It also benefited from collaboration with the project "Mobility, Identity and New Political Economies: A Multi-Sited Ethnography" funded by the Conseil de Reserche en Sciences Sociales et Humaines du Canada (Code 410-2008-0668).

REFERENCES

Bauman, Z. (2006 [2000]). *Liquid modernity*. Vol. 1. Cambridge: Polity Press.

Cameron, D. (2000). *Good to talk?: Living and working in a communication culture*. London: Sage.

del Valle, J. (2011). Política del lenguaje y geopolítica: España, la RAE y la población latina de Estados Unidos. In S. Senz & M. Alberte (Eds.), *El dardo en la academia: Esencia y vigencia de las academias de la lengua española* (pp. 551–590). Barcelona: Melusina.

Duchêne, A. (2009). Marketing, management and performance: Multilingualism as commodity in a tourism call centre. *Language Policy* 8(1), 27–50.

Duchêne, A., & Heller, M. (Ed.) (2011). *Language in late capitalism: Pride and profit*. New York: Routledge.

España, M. (2013, May 25). Turismo idiomático. Retrieved from http://marcaespana.es/ actualidad/cultura/turismo-idiom%C3%A1tico.

Fairclough, N. (1992). *Discourse and social change*. Cambridge: Polity Press.

Giroux, H. (2015). *Against the terror of neoliberalism: Politics beyond the age of greed*. New York: Routledge.

Heller, M. (1999). *Linguistic minorities and modernity: A sociolinguistic ethnography*. London: Longman.

Heller, M. (2003). Globalization, the new economy and the commodification of language and identity. *Journal of Sociolinguistics* 7(4), 473–492.

Heller, M. (2011a). Du Français comme "droit" au Français comme "valeur ajoutée" : De la Politique à l'économique au Canada. *Langage et société* 136, 13–30.

Heller, M. (2011b). *Paths to post-nationalism: A critical ethnography of language and identity.* New York: Oxford University Press.

Heller, M., & Pujolar, J. (2010). The political economy of texts: A case study in the structuration of tourism. *Sociolinguistic Studies* 3(2), 177–201.

Heller, M., Pujolar, J., & Duchêne, A. (2014). Linguistic commodification in tourism. *Journal of Sociolinguistics* 18(4), 539–566.

Julien, A. (2012). *Les festivals Francophones en Ontario: Vecteurs de la vitalité culturelle d' une communauté minoritaire—Une étude de cas multiples.* PhD dissertation, Université de Montréal.

McGill, K. (2013). Political economy and language. *Journal of Linguistic Anthropology* 23(2), 84–101.

McLaughlin, M. (2010). *L'Acadie postnationale: Producing Franco-Canadian identity in the globalized economy.* PhD dissertation, University of Toronto.

Pujolar, J. (2007). Bilingualism and the nation-state in the post-national era. In M. Heller (Ed.), *Bilingualism: A social approach* (pp. 71–95). Basingstoke, UK: Palgrave-McMillan.

Rodés, A. (2013). Apple respon als seus clients des de Barcelona. *Ara. Suplement: A Fons.* Retrieved from http://emprenem.ara.cat/Apple-respon-als-clients-Barcelona_0_859114091.html.

Roy, S. (2003). Bilingualism and standardization in a Canadian call center: Challenges for a linguistic minority community. In R. Bailey & S. R. Schecter (Eds.), *Language socialization in bilingual and multilingual societies* (pp. 269–285). Clevedon, UK: Multilingual Matters.

Shome, R. (2006). Thinking through the diaspora: Call centers, India and a new politics of hybridity. *International Journal of Cultural Studies* 9(1), 105–124.

Turespaña. (2016). Aprender español. Retrived from http://www.spain.info/es/que-quieres/aprender-espanol/.

Urla, J. (2012). "Total quality language revival." In A. Duchêne & M. Heller (Eds.), *Language in late capitalism: Pride and profit* (pp. 73–92). London; New York: Routledge.

Wallerstein, I. (1998). *Utopistics: Or, historical choices of the twenty-first century.* New York: New Press.

BILINGUAL EDUCATION POLICY AND NEOLIBERAL CONTENT AND LANGUAGE INTEGRATED LEARNING PRACTICES

ANA MARÍA RELAÑO-PASTOR

BILINGUAL education policy (BEP) as a type of language-in-education policy is defined in this chapter as involving education in two or more languages or linguistic varieties (Cenoz, 2012; García, 2009). In her comprehensive overview of the challenges posed by bilingual education in the twenty-first century, García claims that bilingual education is "good for all education, and therefore good for all children, as well as good for all adult learners" (p. 11). This beneficial perspective, however reasonable it sounds, is far from being undisputed, especially within critical approaches to language policy under the influence of neoliberalism. As Tollefson (2013) argues, language-in-education policies in the twenty-first century should be critically examined, particularly the elite's interests in promoting BEP at the local, regional, national, or global levels.

Critical analysis should focus on the resulting social inequality and marginalization of students, whose interactionally achieved acts of opposition toward controversial BEPs, such as the implementation of Content and Language Integrated Learning (CLIL) programs in Europe, is worth researching ethnographically (Relaño-Pastor, 2015). Similarly, Busch (2011) agrees that we should critically address the political context in which the implementation of innovative educational practices takes place. These practices are shaped by "sometimes complementary, sometimes contradictory discourses and policies" (p. 544), particularly in the European context, where most education systems are heavily influenced by "monolingual and monoglossic ideologies" (Busch, 2011, p. 545), which regard students' languages and language varieties as separate, bounded, and whole linguistic systems.

Language ideologies are deeply ingrained in language policies—more specifically, in language-in-education policies undertaken to deal with linguistic and cultural diversity—as well as in the teaching and learning of second and foreign languages. For Crawford (2004), language ideologies constitute the foundations of "folk linguistics" (p. 62) acquired from friends, relatives, media, community leaders, or schoolteachers, and popularized through reinforcement by society's dominant institutions. The field of language ideologies (LI) has consolidated over the last two decades (see the seminal work of Schieffelin, Woolard, & Kroskrity, 1998, for a comprehensive account of the field at that time). For example, Blommaert (2006) defines language ideologies as "socially and culturally embedded metalinguistic conceptualizations of language and its form" (p. 241). In addition, Kroskrity (2000, 2004) insists on the ubiquity of language ideologies in society, not necessarily coming from the ruling class, but including also, whether implicitly or explicitly, speakers' assessment of the role of language and communicative practices in society.

Kroskrity (2004) analyzes how language ideologies relate to language policies. In his view, investigating the relationship between ideology and policy requires attention to several issues, including the following: the perception of language and discourse among different cultural groups; the range of language ideologies according to different social divisions based on class, gender, elite status, or generation; opposition to and contestation of dominant language ideologies; individuals' awareness of local language ideologies; how language ideologies mediate between social structures and forms of talk; and the role of language ideologies in policymakers' decisions regarding which languages are used in the making of national identities and which are considered marginal in the nation-state (pp. 501–509).

In general, language policy decisions are usually less about language and more about underlying social and political conflicts. Whether at school, the workplace, home, or community spaces, language policies influence what languages or linguistic varieties we speak, judgments about linguistic appropriateness (*good/acceptable* or *bad/unacceptable*), and the values individuals attach to languages. Spolsky (2004) distinguishes three components of the language policy of a speech community: "its language practices; its language beliefs or ideology; and any specific efforts to modify or influence that practice by any kind of language intervention, planning or management" (p. 5). In addition, Shohamy (2006) believes that language policy serves as a "device to perpetuate and impose language behaviors in accordance with the national, political, social and economic agendas" (p. 3), so a critical view of language policy should analyze the mechanisms or "policy devices" embedded in language policy to understand the "battle between ideology and practice" (p. 45).

García (2009) offers one of the most comprehensive frameworks to understand BEP in relation to six characteristics: language ideologies (monoglossic or heteroglossic); linguistic goals (types of bilingualism, whether additive, subtractive, recursive, or dynamic); linguistic ecology (related to language shift, language maintenance, language revitalization, or plurilingualism); orientations toward bilingualism (bilingualism as a problem, a privilege, a right, or a resource); cultural ecology (how mono/biculturalisms are conceptualized); and the types of children involved (linguistic minorities and students situated at different points of the bilingual continuum) (pp. 120–122). Among the different types of BEP, García pays close attention to CLIL programs, which are characterized as "heteroglossic, fostering dynamic bilingualism, using languages as resources, providing students with a transcultural ecology, and serving children at different points of the bilingual continuum" (p. 134).

In Europe, CLIL-type bilingual education has been positively described and highly praised by the European Commission and the Council of Europe as an initiative that promotes "plurilingualism, linguistic diversity, mutual understanding, democratic citizenship and social cohesion" (Council of Europe, 2014) in order to meet the mother tongue plus two languages (MT + 2) mandate, according to which "every European citizen should master two other languages in addition to their mother tongue" (European Commission, 2012). Because of CLIL's importance in European bilingual education, this chapter will survey the latest research on CLIL in Europe as a type of bilingual education policy aimed at enhancing English-language education while successfully meeting the demands of the Council of Europe and the European Commission.

This survey of CLIL adopts a political economy perspective (Ricento, 2015) toward language policy, which relies on "a range of subject matters, including history, sociology, economics, politics, education, and linguistics in order to assess and explain real-world phenomena that do not fit neatly into boxes labeled 'economic,' 'social,' 'political' or 'cultural'" (Ricento, 2015, p. 2). Indeed, Ricento insists on the need to reinterpret, with a critical, political economic approach, the three main assessments of English as a global language, namely, "(1) a form of linguistic imperialism, (2) a vehicle for social and economic mobility, (3) a global lingua franca" (p. 3). The perspective of language policy as political economy goes hand in hand with critical interpretive approaches to language policy (Martin-Jones, 2007; Tollefson, 2006, 2013), which in the case of CLIL as a type of bilingual education means "to link insights from the close study of the interactional and textual fine grain of everyday life in educational settings with an account of specific institutional regimes, the wider political economy and the global processes of cultural transformation at work in contemporary society" (Martin-Jones, 2007, p. 163). This perspective contributes to what Busch (2011) calls "the second shift in research on language(s) in education in Europe," from the 1990s onward, which redefines linguistic diversity in relation to "transmigration, global mobility and the multidirectionality of communication flows" (p. 544). This shift in the conceptualization of language in European language policy research, far from considering language and linguistic varieties as "irregularities in a normally monolingual pattern," should instead account for their "heteroglossic disturbance," considered "an intrinsic and constitutive element of what is perceived as normality" (p. 545). Thus, following Pérez-Milans (2015), this chapter re-examines how CLIL, in promoting economic competitiveness, intercultural dialogue, social cohesion, and democratic citizenship, is deeply ingrained in neoliberalization and commodification processes.

The organization of this chapter is threefold. The following part surveys research on CLIL in Europe as the preferred model of bi/multilingual education by offering a summary of the major trends in policy and practice. The next section advocates for an ethnographic, political economy perspective to understand the complex relationships between bilingual language policy, stakeholders' circulating discourses about bilingualism, and CLIL bilingual classroom practices. This approach can help elucidate, among other things, neoliberalization and commodification processes involved in the global spread of English in Europe. The following section illustrates the case of bilingual programs in the south-central autonomous community of Castilla–La Mancha, Spain. The chapter ends with a discussion of some future directions for CLIL research in Europe.

CLIL RESEARCH IN EUROPE

Since the 1990s, the promotion of CLIL as a type of bilingual education policy has been strongly supported by both the Council of Europe and the European Commission in their effort to foster linguistic diversity, plurilingualism, plurilingual education, and English language education in the Union (see Baetens Beardsmore, 2009, for a review of the advocacy of CLIL by these European supra-national institutions). CLIL is defined in this chapter as an umbrella term that would include any type of language program in which a second language is used as the medium to teach a variety of content subjects, depending on policymakers' allocation of human and material resources across different educational sites (see Cenoz, Genesee, & Gorter, 2014; Lasagabaster & Ruiz de Zarobe, 2010; Ruiz de Zarobe, 2013, for discussions of CLIL programs in multilingual education research).

Although CLIL researchers admit that CLIL is a multifaceted phenomenon involving different stakeholders and different aspects of language and content learning, very few studies have emphasized the language policy dimension of CLIL, or adopted ethnographic perspectives that take into account the links between CLIL as a type of bilingual education policy, stakeholders' discourses, and classroom practices. Researchers such as Nikula et al. (2013, p. 72), following Dalton-Puffer and Smit (2007) and Dalton-Puffer et al. (2010), acknowledge "both holistic macro and particularized micro perspectives toward the phenomena studied in CLIL" and propose a visual diagram to explain the three dominant perspectives that, according to them, CLIL classroom discourse research is oriented toward: "(a) classroom discourse as an evidence-base for language learning, (b) language use and social-interactional aspects of CLIL classroom interaction, and (c) processes of knowledge construction in and through CLIL classroom discourse (Nikula et al., 2013, pp. 73–74). These authors conclude that CLIL classroom discourse research needs to be complemented with

> ethnographically oriented approaches that would help highlight both the participants' emic understandings of CLIL as well as reveal the whole ecology (van Lier, 2004) of CLIL extending beyond the confines of the classroom to institutional cultures, societal factors including policy-level considerations, and prevalent discourses around language and education that impact on classroom realities. (p. 92)

Similarly, the most recent overviews of CLIL research in Europe (Pérez-Cañado, 2012, 2016) and Spain (Dooley & Masats, 2015) identify the following as main foci of research in this area: " 'classroom discourse'; 'focus on content and/or language'; and 'teacher roles and teacher education' " (Dooley & Masats, 2015, p. 347), as well as "linguistic outcomes; longitudinal studies; assessment of language and content; CLIL methodology; CLIL teacher observation; and teacher training" (Pérez-Cañado, 2012, p. 331). Pérez-Cañado (2016) views CLIL research in Europe as shifting from what she calls "the CLIL craze" or "initial phase" that highlighted the benefits of CLIL and praised its implementation as a good model of bilingual education to "the CLIL conundrum," or "second phase," which "harbors a pessimistic outlook on its effects and feasibility" (p. 17). According to Pérez-Cañado (2016), researchers who question the positive outcomes of CLIL research base their criticism on the methodological shortcomings related to "variables," "research design," and "statistical methodology" (pp. 17–18). Despite the need for more qualitative CLIL research, described by Pérez-Cañado as including "extensive classroom observation," "videotaping," and "short face-to-face interviews with teachers" (pp. 18–19), ethnographic research on CLIL as policy and practice has been overlooked.

One of the exceptions that bridge the gap between policy and practice in CLIL research is Ruiz de Zarobe (2013), who points out that

> [t]he implementation of CLIL has been supported, on the one hand, by language policy-makers, stakeholders and European institutions and, on the other, by individual initiatives undertaken by school communities, teachers and parents, all of

them seeking to improve foreign language competence in a world where globalization and the knowledge society are encouraging foreign-language learning and communication. (p. 231)

Hüttner, Dalton-Puffer, and Smit (2013) also analyze stakeholders' beliefs about CLIL in Austria in relation to European language policy mandates to improve individuals' ability to communicate in more than one language (European Commission, 2012). Following Spolsky's (2004) tripartite model of language policy and planning that includes "language practices," "language beliefs," and "language intervention, planning or management" (p. 5), these authors conclude that participants in their study did not make reference to any CLIL policy in Austria or to CLIL as a European language-in-education policy, and instead they perceived CLIL as a pedagogic innovation that relied on their work. In Catalonia, Pladevall-Ballester (2015) analyzes CLIL teachers', students', and parents' perceptions about the implementation of CLIL in five primary schools using opinion questionnaires and interviews. She concludes that, overall, CLIL is perceived "as a positive practice that promotes motivation, learning and interest in the foreign language" although "more communication is needed among the groups of stakeholders to ensure a more realistic perception of CLIL implementation" (p. 57).

In sum, CLIL has been the most praised form of bilingual education policy in Europe, leading to the proliferation of CLIL-type bilingual programs that are widely seen as a "truly European approach for the integration of language and content in the curriculum as part of the international mosaic of multilingualism" (Ruiz de Zarobe, 2013, p. 233). However, with the exception of studies such as Labajos Miguel and Martín Rojo (2011), Martín Rojo (2013), Pérez-Milans and Patiño-Santos (2014), Relaño-Pastor (2015), and Codó and Patiño (2017), sociolinguistic ethnographies that address the complex relationship between policy and practice in CLIL-type bilingual programs and schools are still scarce (see Codó & Relaño-Pastor, forthcoming, for a discussion of ethnographic perspectives to multilingual education research).

The next section examines the successful implementation of CLIL in compulsory education across different EU states (Eurydice, 2006) by embracing a critical sociolinguistic ethnography perspective on CLIL as policy and practice to shed light on the neoliberalization and commodification processes at play in English-language education in Europe.

CLIL as Neoliberal Language Policy and Practice

Bilingual education policy and CLIL-type bilingual programs in Europe are shaped by "the economic dimension of English as a global language," which, according to

Ricento (2015), is "what determines its value and status in countries with aspirations to participate in the knowledge economy" (p. 37). Several scholars have argued for the political economy perspective in fields other than that of language policy (Ricento, 2015), including recent calls in applied linguistics (Block, 2017). In his state-of-the-art article, Block argues for a critical political economy approach to applied linguistics that addresses "the interrelatedness of political and economic processes and phenomena such as aggregate economic activity, resource allocation, capital accumulation, income inequality, globalisation and imperial power" (p. 35).

From this perspective, CLIL can be analyzed as a potential "mechanism for creating and sustaining systems of inequality that benefit the wealthy and powerful individuals, groups, institutions and nation-states, as well as for resisting systems of inequality" (Tollefson, 2013, p. 27). Yet at the same time, it is important to analyze "the agency of all actors in the policymaking process, particularly their ability to alter what seems to be the coercive and deterministic trajectories of class-based policymaking bodies and other institutional forms and structures" (p. 28). Thus research should, on the one hand, examine the conditions under which supranational policy bodies in Europe (e.g., Council of Europe, European Commission) favor CLIL as the preferred type of bilingual education and seek to impose their will on individuals and communities; and, on the other hand, interpret the conditions under which individuals and communities have the agentive power to change the material aspects of CLIL practice, for example the allocation of resources to teach content subjects through the medium of English. In this sense, the ethnographic agenda of language policy put forward, first by Ricento and Hornberger (1996) and later developed by Hornberger and Johnson (2007), provides one possible way of "examining the agents, contexts, and processes across multiple layers of what Ricento and Hornberger (1996) metaphorically referred to as the language policy onion" (Johnson & Ricento, 2013, p. 14).

As Hornberger and Johnson (2007) agree, "ethnographic language policy research offers a means for exploring how varying local interpretations, implementations, negotiations, and perhaps resistance can pry open implementational and ideological spaces for multilingual language education" (p. 511). Johnson and Ricento (2013) further argue that

> [c]ritical language policy theory continues to be influential and integral and is not at odds with other orientations (like the ethnography of language policy) that foreground agency and bottom-up language planning and policy. Indeed, a balance between structure and agency—between critical conceptualizations that focus on the power of language policy and ethnographic and other qualitative work that focuses on the power of language policy agents—is precisely what the field needs. (p. 13)

Ethnographic and critical approaches to language policy are also in line with critical sociolinguistic ethnography (Heller, 2011; Martín Rojo, 2010; Patiño-Santos, 2012; Pérez-Milans, 2013, 2015; Rampton, 2006), which addresses situated linguistic practices in relation "to institutional policies and wider socio-economic transformations" (see Pérez-Milans, 2015, for a comprehensive account of the inter-relationship between language-in-education policies, language ideologies, situated practices, and wider economic processes of late modernity such as neoliberalization and commodification). In the case of CLIL, neoliberalism, understood as "the voice of global capitalism" (Holborow, 2015, p. 1), plays a role in the commodification of English-language teaching and learning in CLIL-type bilingual education programs in Europe.

As a type of "economic ideology" (Piller & Cho, 2013), neoliberalism is embedded in language policy mechanisms that push for the global spread of English. In their study of "the cost of English" in South Korea at all educational levels, Piller and Cho (2013) analyze how English, particularly in higher education, is not merely the "result of the free linguistic market," but rather of a "systematic, organized, and orchestrated policy" (p. 38) that serves the interests of "neoliberal free-market fundamentalism" (p. 39), all of it under the naturalization of English as a "quantifiable index of glob-alization" (p. 39). Similarly, Park and Wee (2012), Gao and Park (2015), Martín Rojo et al. (2017), and Codó and Patiño (2017) emphasize the need to ground language policies and the resulting linguistic practices in the political and economic processes involved in the implementation of English-language programs such as CLIL: "We need to understand CLIL programmes as complex undertakings involving a multiplicity of social actors with various (and sometimes conflicting) interests, enmeshed in networks of shifting economic, political and material conditions, and as constructing or reinforcing unequal power relations" (Codó & Patiño, 2017, p. 4).

How should an ethnographic, political economy analysis of CLIL be undertaken? In the following section, I illustrate how neoliberal language policy agendas shape CLIL-type bilingual programs in the south-central autonomous region of Castilla–La Mancha, in Spain. I focus on the categorization processes involved in the labeling of schools and social actors in this region as *bilingual*, as they emerge in interviews with regional and local language planners as well as CLIL teachers participating in these bilingual programs. This data is part of an ongoing critical sociolinguistic eth-nography conducted in four bilingual schools in this region: two public, (i.e., state-run) primary and secondary schools, one religious semi-private (i.e., state-funded private) school, and one lay semi-private school.[1]

BILINGUAL CRAZE AND PRESSURE IN CASTILLA–LA MANCHA SCHOOLS

Castilla-La Mancha is one of the eleven autonomous regions where Spanish is the official language, alongside six other bilingual regions where, according to

Article 3 of the Spanish Constitution (1978), Catalan, Galician, and Basque are spoken and recognized as co-official languages (i.e., Catalonia, Galicia, the Basque Country, Navarre, Valencia, and the Balearic Islands). In the last two decades, bilingual programs in public and semi-private schools in Castilla–La Mancha have proliferated, transforming classroom practices as well as discourses and ideologies around what bilingual education entails and how bilingualism in Spanish and English is understood and embedded in the lives of different stakeholders (families, students, teachers, and language planners).

The first bilingual programs in Castilla–La Mancha started in 1996 as part of a signed agreement between the Spanish Ministry of Education (MECD) and the British Council to implement early bilingual Spanish/English education throughout the country. A total of forty-four Spanish primary bilingual schools were involved in the Bilingual School Project of this agreement, fourteen of which (seven primary and seven secondary) were distributed in the four provinces of Castilla–La Mancha. Since 2005, the institutionalization of bilingual programs under European language-in-education policy initiatives to promote "plurilingual and intercultural communication" (Council of Europe, 2014, p. 5; European Commission, 2012), as well as regional language planning efforts to democratize English-language learning for "all," has undergone different language planning phases and nomenclatures: European Sections (Secciones Europeas) (2005–2011); Bilingual Sections (Secciones Bilingües) (2011–2014); and Linguistic Programs (Programas Lingüísticos) (2014–present). In February 2017, the new plurilingualism decree, *Plan Integral de Enseñanza de Lenguas Extranjeras de la Comunidad Autónoma de Castilla–La Mancha* (Integral Plan for the Teaching of Foreign Languages in the Autonomous Community of Castilla–La Mancha), was drafted to be implemented in the academic year 2017–2018. Among the amendments proposed in this decree, the distinction between three levels of bilingual implementation (Initiation, Development, and Excellence) that had been used in CLM schools to the present was eliminated. That is, bilingual schools were no longer classified into one of these levels. Prior to 2017, the distinction among bilingual schools was made according to the number of DNL (Disciplinas No Lingüísticas) or content-subjects taught in English (one, two, or three or more), as well as the number of teachers who could certify at an accredited B2 level (i.e., independent user), in line with the Common European Framework of Reference for Language Learning (CEFR). In the case of the bilingual schools of excellence, in addition to being able to teach three DNL in English, they had to count on at least one accredited C1 teacher (i.e., proficient user).

In the academic year 2016–2017, a total of 588 bilingual programs operated throughout the five provinces of CLM. In the province of La Mancha (pseudonym), where the ethnographic research presented in this chapter was conducted, there are 151 bilingual schools, twenty-two of them located in La Mancha City (pseudonym; LMC, hereafter), with a population of 72,000 inhabitants. Among them, twelve public and eight semi-private schools use English as the medium of instruction in

DNL subjects; the two other schools (one primary and one secondary) are bilingual in French and Spanish.

Regarding the level of implementation, five of these schools are characterized as having implemented their Spanish-English bilingual programs at the *initiation* level, twelve at the *development* level, and only two of them (one primary and one secondary) at the *excellence* level. These two, together with two semi-private schools, whose Spanish-English bilingual programs are currently being implemented at the development level, are the focus of research in the ongoing sociolinguistic ethnography carried out in LMC bilingual schools (2015–present). Data include participant observation, field notes and audio recordings in DNL subjects taught in English as well as in English language classes, semi-structured and conversational interviews with stakeholders (language planners, education inspectors, heads of schools, bilingual program coordinators, bilingual teachers, students, and families), and language policy documents, classroom materials, and visual texts produced in these schools.

The aforementioned language policy initiatives are central to understanding the types of classroom practices and circulating discourses about bilingualism, bilingual programs, and bilingual teachers and students at LMC schools. Following Heller (2007), bilingualism is an ideological and social enterprise that needs to be understood as ideology and social practice, as well as revelatory of particular social processes in the neoliberal economic order of late modernity. As she puts it, "a critical social perspective on the concept of bilingualism, combining practice, ideology and political economy, allows us to examine the ways in which that idea figures in major forms of social organization and regulation" (p. 2).

As in other socially constructed monolingual Spanish autonomous regions such as Madrid, the commodification of this "bilingual boom" (Relaño-Pastor, 2015) has developed in line with what different stakeholders, families, and teachers refer to as "the bilingual pressures" that are intensifying in the Spanish educational system (see Relaño-Pastor, 2018b, for an analysis of the circulating narratives of bilingualism among families in LMC).

In what follows, I discuss how social categorization processes leading to academic hierarchies and social exclusion emerge in the ethnographic interviews conducted with regional and provincial language planners, the education inspector of the province of LMC, and CLIL teachers participating in these programs. For the analysis, I focus on participants' "moral stancetaking" (Jaffe, 2009; Ochs & Capps, 2001) in the narratives of bilingualism shared in these interviews. Following "social interactional approaches (SIA)" (De Fina & Georgakopoulou, 2012) and anthropological approaches to the study of conversational narrative (Ochs & Capps, 2001), narratives in this chapter are defined as situated, sense-making, mutually achieved social practices that individuals engage in at different points of time and space, and which are embedded in multiple discursive practices (for a discussion on the circularity and appropriation of narratives of bilingualism in ethnographic interviews, see Relaño-Pastor, 2018a). The analysis of moral stancetaking in these narratives sheds light on stakeholders' perspectives on how bilingualism and bilingual programs are being implemented in CLM schools and the moral meanings associated with them.

"Bilingualism Is On-Trend": Commodification and Social Hierarchization in Castilla–La Mancha Bilingual Schools

To serve the interests of the local and global English-language markets, English language education in Castilla–La Mancha has been resignified as bilingualism that is commodified, conveys added value to schools, and is sought as a source of "pride and profit" (Duchêne & Heller, 2012) among stakeholders. As Park and Wee (2012) point out, "English does not exist secluded in the economic market, but functions as a sign in all aspects of social life in which people either use or talk about English" (p. 124). In the case of LMC, stakeholders' shared narratives of bilingualism reveal how they take a stance toward English-language education in the region while engaging in social categorization processes involving types of schools, teachers, and students. The interpretation of these social categorization processes in LMC bilingual schools is tied to the understanding of "bilingualism as ideology, practice and political economy" (Heller, 2007) adopted by the critical sociolinguistic ethnography of CLIL policy and practice put forward in this chapter. The following extracts illustrate the hierarchization of schools, teachers, and students according to the levels of implementation of the bilingual programs, English proficiency, and academic performance, respectively.

Excerpt 1 is part of the interview conducted with Javier (J), the inspector of bilingual programs in the province of La Mancha City. Together with three researchers, Esther (E), May (M), and David (D), Javier discusses the differences between the implementation of bilingual programs in primary and secondary education. Whereas in primary schools all the students are expected to attend CLIL subjects, there is variation in secondary education: in semi-private schools, all the students are involved in bilingual programs from preschool to secondary education, in contrast to public schools, where they can choose whether to continue with the bilingual program at the secondary level (see transcription conventions used here in Appendix):

Excerpt 1. "Ghettos are created"

1. E: but don't you think that a small selection may exist↑=
2. J: =yes yes of course.
3. E: [implicit more in secondary than in primary=
4. J: =there is there is there is that's clear (.3) there's a selection of students (.2)
5. eh:: that's another thing:: that many:: that many parents and many teachers

6. eh:::n refer to to be against these programs=the fact that ghettos are created (.6)
7. that's the word that=I'm tired of hearing [that
8. M: [but is that something that:: is that what teachers or:::
9. J: both parents and >teachers=both<=for example in the admission applications
10. they tell you "I don't want this school because there=there are classrooms for
11. smart and dumb students"=literally (.) I saw it yesterday in one of the
12. applications (.) why ↑ because there is a bilingual section and in the bilingual
13. groups they say that's where the smart students are=
14. E: =but the law tries to avoid that
15. J: obviously ↑ only DNL students are grouped together
16. E: of course
17. J: >and only in the content subjects taught in the language but they are together in the
18. rest of the subjects <obviously you cannot have pure groups of
19. bilingual students but there exists the:: the:: generalized idea among parents
20. and teachers that ghettos are created and this is one of the things that leads to
21. the resistance among teachers =
22. D: =and when you talk about ghettos sorry ghettos would be:: eh: (.3) the ghetto=
23. J: =the elite and the non-elite ghetto
24. D: both things would be=
25. J: =obviously and many teachers (.) especially those who've been:: they've
26. been more years in the [bilingual program] they say that they are going to have
27. the bad:: group and the new teachers (.) the young ones with their level of
28. linguistic competence are going to teach the good students (1).

Stakeholders' talk about English-language education in our ethnography brought bilingualism as ideology and practice to the fore. In excerpt 1, Javier's moral assessment of the selection of students in bilingual programs echoes parents' and teachers' opinions about how bilingual programs result in "ghettos" of elite and non-elite students (lines 6, 23). One of the dominant conversational themes in our ethnography had to with the dominant social categorization process regarding bilingual and non-bilingual students. As Javier's narrative illustrates, the organization of bilingual programs at LMC schools involves the selection of students into bilingual and non-bilingual groups, who are morally evaluated according to their academic performance (i.e., "smart" versus "dumb" students, lines 10–13). This idea also circulated in line with the belief that teachers of bilingual students taught the "good" students (line 28). In this way, Javier's narrative incorporates parents' and teachers' voices of discontent regarding the hierarchization of students into "elite and non-elite ghettos" based on access to the linguistic capital of English. In the case of teachers, our ethnography shows that English becomes a mark of distinction having to do with improved teaching conditions (i.e., a lower ratio of students per class, best students in terms of academic and social behavior, and more academically involved families).

The same social categorization processes also emerge in the interview with Luis, the regional Head of the Division of Bilingual Sections and European Programs in Castilla–La Mancha, who assesses how the different levels of bilingual program implementation—in addition to creating hierarchies among bilingual and non-bilingual students and teachers—are a source of friction among secondary schools. At the time of the interview, in June 2016, Luis had been in his job for almost a year, and his main concerns involved potential changes that would take place from the new decree of plurilingualism he was responsible for planning and implementing in the 2017–2018 academic year. In the following excerpt, when researcher May (M) asks him about how different the new decree of plurilingualism was expected to be, Luis voices the intention of his team to eliminate the hierarchization of bilingual schools according to their levels of implementation.

Excerpt 2. "First-, second-, third-class schools"

1. L: = what I can tell you is that we have:: the idea of unifying a little bit (.)
2. unifying the structure of these programs
3. M: [uhm uh]
4. L: [I mean uh::] uh:: from my point of view hh u:::l (.) this distinction between programs
5. of initiation, development and excellence hh
6. M: Uhm uh =
7. L: = the only thing it has been generating is [eh:: (0.5) a disparity of levels among schools
8. M: [uhm uh] =
9. L: As you can imagine this already creates (.) [comparisons]
10. L: = among schools (.) [first class schools]
11. M: [uhm uh] =
12. L: = second class schools (.) third class uhm [so]
13. M: [uhm uh]
14. L: uhm so there you're already generating a problem
15. M: Uhm uh

Although the process of social distinction among bilingual schools regarding their material capacity to initiate, develop, or excel in the number of CLIL subjects and CLIL teachers with the required linguistic accreditation (B2, C1 levels) (lines 4–5) would be eliminated in the new decree of plurilingualism, Luis's moral assessment of schools according to levels of implementation (i.e., "first," "second," "third class") implies the continued unequal distribution of knowledge, resources, and spaces (Heller, 2007) in these schools (see lines 10–12). That is, schools at the initiation level would only implement one content-subject in English, would only need one accredited B1 CLIL teacher, and would only group bilingual students in one subject; whereas those schools having more resources in terms of teachers' linguistic capital and number of CLIL subjects would also be more exposed to tensions and dilemmas among teachers. For those participating in these bilingual programs, the emerging social categorization of bilingual and non-bilingual teachers brought to the fore differences in their English-language competence, professional development, and teaching conditions. Those teachers with the required linguistic accreditation were usually younger and less experienced, but could benefit from teaching the "best" students in smaller groups. In excerpts 3 and 4, Luis continues to evaluate the challenges that the implementation of bilingual programs has meant for LMC schools.

Excerpt 3. "Non-bilingual students"

1. L: But the biggest problem comes (.) with:: the twenty-eight or thirty students (.)
2. who are not bilingual=
3. M: = Uhm uh =
4. L: = which is generally the group where >the group< where you find the most [deprived]
5. M: [uhm uh] =
6. L: = socially (.) [uh:::]
7. M: [uhm uh] =
8. L: = academically (.) where on top of that you have [in those]
9. M: [uhm uh] =
10. L: = groups (.) students with [special needs::]
11. M: [uhm uh]
12. L: uh I mean (.) [the disruptive ones]
13. M: [uhm uh]
14. L: there [a time bomb] is created
15. M: [uhm uh] (.) uhm uh =

In this narrative, Luis categorizes non-bilingual students as being "the biggest problem" in schools (lines 1–2) and morally evaluates them not only in terms of academic performance, but also in terms of socioeconomic status and social behavior (lines 4, 6, 8, 10, 12). Another circulating theme in our ethnography had to do with significant disparity of class sizes, with the non-bilingual classes the most crowded. The dominant hierarchization of bilingual/non-bilingual students was in line with the hierarchization of bilingual/non-bilingual teachers based on English as linguistic capital. In the following excerpt, Luis explains the moral meanings associated with the knowledge of English.

Excerpt 4: "You are lucky to know English"

1. L: And that: (.) creates differences among students in terms of achievement uhm: (.)
2. the non-bilingual group lowers their academic performance uhhm and regarding the
3. teachers (.) what I was telling you earlier (.) [the:]
4. M: [uhm uh] =
5. L: = the suspicions (.) I mean (.) "you are lucky to:: uhm know English"↑
6. so then you are teaching the good twenty-five students group ↑ (.) and me who
7. doesn't know English =
8. M: = uhm uh =
9. L: = I have to teach the bad group hh with:: thirty-two (0.5) [that nobody]
10. M: [uhm uh] =
11. L: = would split (.) and on top of that I have been at this school for eleven years and
12. you just arrived ↑
13. M: Uhm uh
14. L: and so (.) that:: (.) [is what]

15. M: [uhm uh] =
16. L: = ends up [blowing out::]
17. M: [uhm uh] =
18. L: >sometimes [it doesn't happen all the time<]

In this narrative, Luis constructs English as an object with added value that polarizes teachers in bilingual schools into those who can enjoy better conditions, despite being less experienced (lines 6, 12), and those who have worse labor conditions, despite their greater professional experience (line 9). Once again, the social categorization process involving bilingual/non-bilingual teachers conveys moral meanings associated with bilingualism that can be measured (i.e., fewer students in class; better academic performance; more professional recognition) and results in tensions among teachers in some cases (line 16).

These last two excerpts illustrate how the desire for improving English-language education through CLIL-type bilingual programs brings about the academic *othering* of those students who do not participate in these programs. That is, both content and English teachers participating in these bilingual programs assessed their teaching experiences with bilingual and non-bilingual students very differently, from having very low expectations of non-bilingual students to full academic confidence in their bilingual students.

In excerpt 5, Ernesto, the CLIL physics teacher at San Marcos, the semi-private religious school of our research, takes a moral stance toward bilingualism as a trend in the Spanish educational system with consequences for the selection, distribution, and social hierarchization of students in bilingual and non-bilingual groups taught by bilingual and non-bilingual teachers. San Marcos, the oldest semi-private religious school in LMC, implemented the regional bilingual program at the development level in primary and secondary education in 2010. In addition, it also offers a trilingual program, starting in the third year of compulsory secondary education, where students are taught geography in French. The school is one of the Cambridge English examination centers in LMC, hires native English-language assistants, and belongs to the network of Catholic bilingual schools under the BEDA program (Bilingual English Development and Assessment).

Excerpt 5. "Bilingualism is on-trend"

1. E: Bilingualism is kind of a trend (1.0) it's almost inevitable uh uhm (.) it establishes two
2. learning speeds (1.0)
3. M: Uhm uh =
4. E: = Smart (.) dumb (.) it's almost inevitable (.) no single family (.5) whose children (.)
5. who have (.) normal children (2.0) uhm (1.0) would decide that their children are going
6. to study in Spanish [. . .]
7. E: and of course (1.0) bilingualism is creating two learning speeds among
8. students (2.0) and also (.5) among teachers

9. M: I see
10. E: Also among teachers (.5) because the bilingual teachers (1.0) I: have the
11. privilege of taking (.) the best students
12. M: [I see]
13. AL: [uhm uh] [I see]
14. E: [Who do I teach] [I teach the best students]
15. M: [I see] =
16. E: who do the non-bilingual teachers (.) [who]
17. M: [I see] =
18. E: = do the non-bilingual teachers teach↑ (.) the worst (1.0) and [of course]
19. M: [I see] =
20. E: = They are burned out
21. M: I see

Ernesto is the only teacher in this school accredited with a C1 level. In different in-formal talks and conversational interviews we conducted with him, he was always very critical of his school for requiring him to teach physics in English due to his C1 level, without professional development support in CLIL or English. In this ex-tract, Ernesto engages in a personal narrative of teaching experiences and positions himself as a privileged teacher who teaches the best students, compared to non-bilingual teachers who are "burned out" from having the "bad" students (lines 14, 20). He morally assesses the implementation of bilingualism at schools in LMC for establishing social hierarchies among teachers (bilingual/non-bilingual), students (the best and the worst), and levels of learning (fast and slow). Our ethnography shows that teachers who participated in the bilingual programs and taught both groups of students, bilingual and non-bilingual, shared similar pressures from the lack of support for improving their teaching methods, the scarcity of CLIL teacher training or professional development courses, as well as, in Ernesto's words, their "confidence about the level of English," which was particularly undermined in the case of those teachers accredited with a B2 level of English.

In sum, these excerpts illustrate how the institutional interest of the provincial and regional language policy administration to promote Spanish-English bilingual programs in Castilla–La Mancha is part of the neoliberal agenda to democratize English-language education for all. The examples show how this neoliberal agenda is creating social hierarchization processes along the lines of who counts as an ac-cepted bilingual teacher and student, and how schools are entitled to commodify English-language education to meet the demands of the local and global market of English. As the provincial head of the language planning section in La Mancha City put it: "in a world of tremendous competitiveness, where the job market is de-manding that you have to be an entrepreneur, whether you like or not, the knowl-edge of languages is basic, so having the opportunity to extend your education in these bilingual programs is very positive" (Interview with Miguel, Head of Division of Bilingual Sections and European Programs in the province of La Mancha City, June 3, 2016).

FUTURE DIRECTIONS

This chapter has offered an overview of the most recent CLIL research in Europe from a policy and practice perspective. However much CLIL has been investigated, there is still a scarcity of ethnographically oriented research. As a type of bilingual education policy, CLIL is still in need of being examined through an ethnographic lens to disentangle the messiness of everyday classroom practices against the backdrop of neoliberalization and commodification processes involved in the global spread of English. Thus this chapter has advocated for an ethnographic perspective toward CLIL policy and practice that recognizes the multidimensionality of social actors' circulating discourses and language ideologies about bilingualism.

Future research on CLIL policy and practice would benefit from the critical ethnography of language policy within a political economy perspective, together with critical sociolinguistic ethnography that emphasizes situated linguistic practices in relation to the wider sociopolitical, moral, and economic orders. A critical sociolinguistic ethnography of CLIL—and all forms of bilingual education—allows researchers to tell a comprehensive story of why social processes unfold the way they do and why social actors engage in the practices they do. Research on bilingual education should move forward by incorporating ethnographic approaches that reveal how social hierarchization processes like the ones discussed in this chapter can be followed in time and across different social spaces, and how these processes may be embraced or resisted by different social actors.

APPENDIX

TRANSCRIPTION CONVENTIONS

↑	rising intonation
↓	falling intonation
:::	elongated sounds
uhm uh	shows continuing listenership
(0.3)	time elapsed in tenths of seconds
(.)	micropause
[]	overlapping speech
[...]	extract deletion
=	no interval between adjacent utterances. (adapted from Sacks, Jefferson, & Schegloff, 1974)

Acknowledgments

Data presented in this chapter were collected as part of the research project APINGLO-CLM, "The Appropriation of English as a Global Language in Castilla–La Mancha Secondary Schools" (Ref.: FFI2014-54179-C2-2-P), funded by the Spanish Ministry of Economy and Competitiveness (MINECO), 2015–2017, of which I am Principal Investigator. I am particularly indebted to the four schools that opened their doors to this project and all the participants who kindly shared their conflictual, yet rewarding, stories with us. Special thanks to Ulpiano Losa Ballesteros for patiently transcribing interviews to move this project forward.

Note

1. All names of schools and individuals are pseudonyms.

References

Baetens Beardsmore, H. (2009). Language promotion by European supra-national institutions. In O. García (Ed.), *Bilingual education in the 21st century: A global perspective* (pp. 197–217). Malden, MA: Wiley-Blackwell.

Block, D. (2017). Political economy in applied linguistics research. *Language Teaching* 50(1), 32–64.

Blommaert, J. (2006). Language policy and national identity. In T. Ricento (Ed.), *An introduction to language policy: Theory and method* (pp. 238–255). Malden, MA: Blackwell.

Busch, B. (2011). Trends and innovative practices in multilingual education in Europe: An overview. *International Review of Education* 57(5–6), 541–549.

Cenoz, J. (2012). Bilingual and multilingual education: Overview. In C. Chapelle (Ed.), *The encyclopedia of applied linguistics* (pp. 1–8). Malden, MA: Blackwell.

Cenoz, J., Genesee, F., & Gorter, D. (2014). Critical analysis of CLIL: Taking stock and looking forward. *Applied Linguistics* 35(3), 243–262.

Codó, E., & Patiño, A. (2017). CLIL, unequal working conditions and neoliberal subjectivities in a state secondary school. *Language Policy*, doi:10.1007/s10993-017-9451-5.

Codó, E. & Relaño-Pastor, A. M. (forthcoming). Researching multilingual education: Ethnographic perspectives. In C. Siry & R. Fernández (Eds.), *Methodologies for research on teaching and learning*. Luxembourg: Sense Publishers (Bold Visions in Education Research Series).

Council of Europe. (2014). *Languages for democracy and social cohesion: Diversity, equity and quality. Sixty years of European co-operation.* Strasbourg: Council of Europe, Language Policy Division.

Crawford, J. (2004). *Educating English learners: Language diversity in the classroom.* Los Angeles: Bilingual Education Services.

Dalton-Puffer, C., & Smit, U. (Eds.). (2007). *Empirical perspectives on CLIL classroom discourse.* Frankfurt: Peter Lang.

Dalton-Puffer, C., Nikula, T., & Smit, U. (Eds.). (2010). *Language use and language learning in CLIL classrooms*. Amsterdam: John Benjamins.

De Fina, A., & Georgakopoulou, A. (2012). *Analyzing narrative: Discourse and sociolinguistics perspectives*. Cambridge: Cambridge University Press.

Dooly, M., & Masats, D. (2015). A critical appraisal of foreign language research in content and language integrated learning, young language learners, and technology-enhanced language learning published in Spain (2003–2012). *Language Teaching* 48(3), 343–372.

Duchêne, A., & Heller, M. (2012). *Language in late capitalism: Pride and profit*. New York: Routledge.

European Commission. (2012). *Key data on teaching languages at schools in Europe*. Retrieved from http://eacea.ec.europa.eu/education/eurydice/

Eurydice. (2006). *Content and Language Integrated Learning (CLIL) at school in Europe*. Brussels: European Commission.

Gao, S., & Park, J. S. Y. (2015). Space and language learning under the neoliberal economy. *L2 Journal* 7(3), 78–96.

García, O. (2009). *Bilingual education in the 21st century: A global perspective*. Malden, MA: Wiley-Blackwell.

Heller, M. (2007). *Bilingualism: A social approach*. Houndsmills, UK: Palgrave Macmillan.

Heller, M. (2011). *Paths to post-nationalism: A critical ethnography of language and identity*. Oxford: Oxford University Press.

Holborow, M. (2015). *Language and neoliberalism*. New York: Routledge.

Hornberger, N., & Johnson, D. C. (2007). Slicing the onion ethnographically: Layers and spaces in multilingual language education policy and practice. *TESOL Quarterly* 4(3), 509–532.

Hüttner, J., Dalton-Puffer, C., & Smit, U. (2013). The power of beliefs: Lay theories and their influence on the implementation of CLIL programmes. *International Journal of Bilingual Education and Bilingualism* 16(3), 267–284.

Jaffe, A. (2009). *Stance: Sociolinguistic perspectives*. Oxford: Oxford University Press.

Johnson, D. C., & Ricento, T. (2013). Conceptual and theoretical perspectives in language planning and policy: Situating the ethnography of language policy. *International Journal of the Sociology of Language* 219, 7–21.

Kroskrity, P. (Ed.). (2000). *Regimes of language: Ideologies, polities and identities*. Santa Fe, NM: School of American Research Press.

Kroskrity, P. (2004). Language ideologies. In A. Duranti (Ed.), *A companion to linguistic anthropology*, (pp. 496–518). Malden, MA: Blackwell.

Labajos Miquel, D., & Martín Rojo, L. (with M. López Muñoz). (2011). Content integration in bilingual education: Educational and interactional practices in the context of MEC-British Council partnership in Madrid region. In C. Escobar Urmeneta, N. Evnitskaya, E. Moore, & A. Patiño (Eds.), *AICLE-CLIL-EMILE: Educació plurilingüe. Experiencias, research & polítiques* (pp. 65–81). Bellaterra: Servei de Publicacions de la Universitat Autónoma de Barcelona.

Lasagabaster, D., & Ruiz de Zarobe, Y. (2010). *CLIL in Spain: Implementation, results and teacher training*. Newcastle, UK: Cambridge Scholars.

Martin-Jones, M. (2007). Bilingualism, education and the regulation of access to language resources. In M. Heller (Ed.), *Bilingualism: A social approach* (pp. 161–182). Houndsmills, UK: Palgrave Macmillan.

Martín Rojo, L. (2010). *Constructing inequality in multilingual classrooms*. Berlin: De Gruyter Mouton.

Martín Rojo, L. (2013). (De)capitalising students through linguistic practices: A comparative analysis of new educational programmes in the global era. In A. Duchêne, M. Moyer, & C. Roberts (Eds.), *Language, migration and social inequalities: A critical perspective on institutions and work* (pp. 118–146). Bristol, UK: Multilingual Matters.

Martín Rojo, L., Anthonissen, C., García-Sánchez, I., & Unamuno, V. (2017). Recasting diversity in language education in postcolonial, late-capitalist societies. In A. De Fina, D. Ikizoglu, & J. Wegner (Eds.), *Diversity and super-diversity: Sociocultural linguistic perspectives* (pp. 171–191). Washington, DC: Georgetown University Press.

Nikula, T., Dalton-Puffer, C., & Llinares, A. (2013). European research on CLIL classroom discourse. *International Journal of Immersion and Content Based Education* 1(1), 70–100.

Ochs, E., & Capps, L. (2001). *Living narrative: Creating lives in everyday storytelling.* Cambridge, MA: Harvard University Press.

Park, J., & Wee, L. (2012). *Markets of English: Linguistic capital and language policy in a globalizing world.* London; New York: Routledge.

Patiño-Santos, A. (2012). The discursive construction of school failure: A critical ethnographical sociolinguistics in a school in Madrid. *Spanish in Context* 8(2), 235–256.

Pérez-Cañado, M. L. (2012). CLIL research in Europe: Past, present, and future, *International Journal of Bilingual Education and Bilingualism* 15(3), 315–341.

Pérez-Cañado, M. L. (2016). From the CLIL craze to the CLIL conundrum: Addressing the current CLIL controversy. *Bellaterra Journal of Teaching & Learning Language & Literature* 9(1), 9–31.

Pérez-Milans, M. (2013). *Urban schools and English language education in late modern China: A critical sociolinguistic ethnography.* New York; London: Routledge.

Pérez-Milans, M. (2015). Language education policy in late modernity: (Socio) linguistic ethnographies in the European Union. *Language Policy* 14(2), 99–108.

Pérez-Milans, M., & Patiño-Santos, A. (2014). Language education and institutional change in a Madrid multilingual school. *International Journal of Multilingualism* 11(4), 449–470.

Piller, I., & Cho, J. (2013). Neoliberalism and language policy. *Language in Society* 42(1), 23–44.

Pladevall-Ballester, E. (2015). Exploring primary school CLIL perceptions in Catalonia: Students', teachers' and parents' opinions and expectations. *International Journal of Bilingual Education and Bilingualism* 18(1), 45–59.

Rampton, B. (2006). *Language in late modernity: Interaction in an urban school.* Cambridge: Cambridge University Press.

Relaño-Pastor, A. M. (2015). The commodification of English in "Madrid, comunidad bilingüe": Insights from the CLIL classroom. *Language Policy* 14(2), 131–152.

Relaño-Pastor, A. M. (March 2018a). Narrative circularity, disputed transformations, and bilingual appropriations at a public school "somewhere in La Mancha." In A. Patiño-Santos (Ed.), Storytelling in globalized spaces: A linguistic ethnographic perspective. *International Journal of the Sociology of Language*, 250 (March).

Relaño-Pastor, A. M. (2018b). Understanding bilingualism in Castilla-La Mancha: Emotional and moral stancetaking in parental narratives. *RESLA (Spanish Journal of Applied Linguistics).* Amsterdam: John Benjamins.

Ricento, T. (Ed.). (2015). *Language policy and political economy: English in a global context.* Oxford: Oxford University Press.

Ricento, T. K., & Hornberger, N. H. (1996). Unpeeling the onion: Language planning and policy and the ELT professional. *TESOL Quarterly* 30(3), 401–427.

Ruiz de Zarobe, Y. (2013). CLIL implementation: From policy-makers to individual initiatives. *International Journal of Bilingual Education and Bilingualism* 16(3), 231–243.

Sacks, H., Schegloff, E. A., & Jefferson, G. (1974). A simplest systematics for the organization of turn-taking for conversation. *Language* 50(4), 696–735.

Schieffelin, B. B., Woolard, K. A., & Kroskrity, P. V. (Eds.) (1998). *Language ideologies: Practice and theory*. Oxford: Oxford University Press.

Shohamy, E. G. (2006). *Language policy: Hidden agendas and new approaches*. New York: Routledge.

Spolsky, B. (2004). *Language policy*. Cambridge: Cambridge University Press.

Tollefson, J. W. (2006). Critical theory in language policy. In T. Ricento (Ed.), *An introduction to language policy: Theory and method* (pp. 42–59). Malden, MA: Blackwell.

Tollefson, J. W. (2013). *Language policies in education: Critical issues*. 2nd edition. New York: Routledge.

van Lier, L. (2004). *The ecology and semiotics of language learning: A sociocultural perspective*. Boston: Kluwer Academic.

CHAPTER 26

....

TURNING LANGUAGE AND COMMUNICATION INTO PRODUCTIVE RESOURCES

LANGUAGE POLICY AND PLANNING AND MULTINATIONAL CORPORATIONS

....

ALFONSO DEL PERCIO

SOCIOLINGUISTIC production has recently turned its attention to the analysis of language and communication in multinational corporations. These corporate organizations, which operate within and across national borders, contribute to the shaping of the globalizing economy through their practices and activities. While there is extensive literature looking at the ways in which language is used at work (see, e.g., Drew & Heritage, 1992), recent research has focused on the role of language and communication as an economic resource (Urciuoli & Ladousa, 2013). This research argues that language and communication have been resignified by managers, consultants, and marketing specialists as economic assets that contribute to the individualization or customization of products and services (Duchêne & Heller, 2012). This resignification of language occurs within an economic climate characterized by accelerated deregulation and the saturation of national economies, as well as a sense of increasing international competition and flexibilization of the production process (Appadurai, 1996; Fraser, 2003; Harvey, 2005).

Through their capacity to project specific qualities onto commercialized products, language and communication are said to contribute to the transformation of products and services into personalized symbols of identity and style (Kelly-Holmes, 2010; Piller, 2003). These semiotic resources also contribute to the shaping of desires, interests, and needs of highly knowledgeable and sophisticated niche markets (Duchêne, 2012; Jaworksi & Thurlow, 2010). Furthermore, the changing management styles that have been adopted in the context of global competition (Shore & Write, 2000) intensify awareness of language in corporate circles as something that needs to be strategically managed (Duchêne, 2011). Scholars note that managers' increasing interest in their workers' communication conduct as a domain of managerial regulation contributes to the enhancement of the production process (Boutet, 2012). They also document that language and communication emerge as crucial domains of investment for the production and circulation of supposedly better and more reliable information (Cameron, 2000a; Duchêne, 2009).

The aim of this chapter[1] is to discuss the techniques, tactics, and forms of expertise through which language and communication are governed and then turned into productive resources within multinational corporations. I hope to demonstrate that corporate actors' policing of language and communication is not merely linguistic policing. Rather, it is a means to discipline and express control over those actors producing language and communication. That is to say, such forms of policing are a method of enhancing multinationals' productivity and securing their competitiveness under changing market conditions.

In order to better understand how the governance of language and communication intersects with the management of productivity in multinational corporations, I will draw upon an analytical framework proposed by Duchêne (2009). He suggests that the management of language and communication in business should be viewed through the lens of the following four processes: (1) the selection of linguistic varieties and registers; (2) the standardization of language, communication, and the channels of communication at work; (3) the flexibilization of communicative processes, both in the business as a whole and of the actors and individuals producing language and communication; and (4) the exploitative activities of language and communication (i.e., the definition of who counts as a legitimate producer of the communicative resources and who can produce them at the lowest possible cost).

This chapter is structured as follows: I begin by focusing on the forms of expertise in language and communication that are produced by coaches, consultants, and communication specialists in the business sector. I particularly look at how these forms of expertise conceptualize language and communication in international business, and at how they problematize the ways in which communication shapes specific types of behavior and personae. In the next section, I attend to how multinationals invest in expertise on language and communication in international business, and I discuss how this form of investment contributes to the shaping of disciplinary practices governing languages and speakers within multinational organizations. This discussion will draw on ethnographic and historiographical research on language and branding that I conducted in Switzerland between 2008 and 2014.

EXPERTISE ON LANGUAGE AND COMMUNICATION

Before presenting an analysis of the techniques by which language and communication are managed within multinational corporations, I will discuss the forms of expertise informing this regulation. I will particularly examine what this expertise says about what language counts as desirable and productive.

Under current capitalist conditions, we can observe a multiplication of corporate actors including communication specialists, managers, and consultants who produce and sell expertise about language and communication in business to other corporate actors around the world (McElhinny, 2012). This is not to say that knowledge on how to behave appropriately and persuade others through speech has not always been circulated and consumed within business contexts and intellectual, upper-class circuits (see Cameron, 2000b, for a brief history on teaching talk). Clearly this knowledge is not specific to the current moment in capitalistic history. However, scholars have noted that businesses' increasing investment in language and communication for productive purposes has led to the emergence of a market where knowledge on language and communication is bought and sold. Crucially, this market allows corporate actors and academics to shape what counts as desirable and productive communication in business contexts.

One such actor is Communicationaid,[2] a worldwide multinational organization that assists other corporate actors in "mitigating the risks and maximising the opportunities of working in a complex and ever-changing international environment" (Communicationaid, n.d.[b]). According to the founder of Communicationaid,

> communication is no longer seen as a soft skill but is now a required skill for anyone wishing to work internationally [because] a lack of cultural sensitivity can lead to lost businesses, a failed assignment, poor client relationships, staff attritions and ultimately wasted time and investments. (Communicationaid, n.d.[a])

Accordingly, Communicationaid provides multinationals with training in "Business English" or "Financial English," involving modules such as "Key financial language and relevant terminology," "Drafting clear, accurate and concise written reports," "Skills for negotiating at a senior level," and a "Review of financial terms."

Similarly, Verizon, another multinational selling communication services around the world, states on its website that "Improving how your organization communicates leads to better business outcomes. The challenge is connecting all your employees, teams and locations with each other—and with your partners and costumers—for effective, productive conversations" (Verizon, n.d.). According to Verizon, customers "expect seamless, personalized and instant interactions"; they request "effective and efficient communication," as well as "unique, personalized experience during each interaction." To "improve productivity, reduce costs and increase revenue," Verizon offers services that help to prioritize business interactions, manage and standardize communication with customers, and improve technological devices that support and mediate communication, both within organizations and with stakeholders (Verizon, n.d.).

The knowledge sold by these two organizations theorizes language and the work process, and simultaneously gives practical advice on how to improve the productivity of business activity. Good communication is linked to qualities such as effectiveness, efficiency, and uniqueness, and it contributes to the competitiveness of any corporate actor. Furthermore, the value that customers assign to services and products is also imagined to be mediated by the quality of communication produced by the organization and its employees. Good communication seems to stand for professional expertise, and it is imagined that an organization within the world market can capitalize on it as a marker of distinction.

As mentioned previously, corporate consultants are not the sole actors in this market. In Switzerland, they compete with actors from the higher education industry in the production of expertise and the coaching of managers and communication specialists. The youngest Swiss university, for example, offers an executive master of science in communication management degree, which—for an annual fee of circa CHF50,000 (US$50,000)—trains decision-makers to

> understand the strategic and operational challenges of an organization and how they are linked to communication/develop communication strategies that address the complexity of a global environment/manage complex communications tasks— ranging from brand management and corporate culture to crisis communications and public affairs/develop and coordinate these tasks as integrated elements of corporate and marketing communications/[and] monitor the communications environment with reliable research methods. (EMScom Executive Master of Science in Communications Management, 2015, p. 13)

In a similar vein, the Institute for Competitiveness and Communication (the association between communication and competitiveness is already made clear in the name of this department), located in one of the leading Swiss universities of applied science, provides a master's degree of advanced studies in corporate communication management. For CHF33,000 (US$33,000), this MA program trains senior managers in public and corporate organizations on reputation and brand management, interpersonal communication, nonverbal communication, cross-cultural communication, online communication, crises communication, international communication, communication control, and communications ethics.

This language and communication knowledge, which is produced and sold to corporate actors and their (future) managers and employees, is aimed at providing strategies, standards, and instructions that improve communication processes. This knowledge is powerful, as it affects the way managers and officers think about language and communication in multinational corporations. It also influences how these individuals make sense of their own subjectivity and labor practice. Indeed, this expertise interpellates (Althusser, 1970) managers and officers as ideal communicators who regulate their own communication conduct, as well as the communication behavior of their colleagues and subordinates.

Not all multinational corporations buy services from corporations such as Communicationaid or Verizon or intentionally invest in the recruitment of managers and employees trained in business communication or intercultural communication. Sociolinguistic research on language policy and planning in corporate organizations shows that, while some do engage with these organizations, others have their own in-house communications specialists who coach and train managers and officers in ways that contribute to the planning of communication strategies. In other cases, managers and officers in multinational organizations seem to rely on tacit, internalized, and often implicit knowledge about language and communication in business in order to manage and plan customer relations, and to allocate resources and standardize processes (Cameron, 2000b; Gee, Hull, & Lankshear 1996).

I will now discuss the ways in which language and communication knowledge, which links good communication to professionalism, productivity, efficiency, and profit, is mobilized by actors operating in corporate settings. I will trace the multiple sources and trajectories of this regulatory knowledge and question how these individuals mobilize this expertise to allocate resources, organize and manage production, and regulate the conduct of their coworkers and partners. In order to do so, I will draw on ethnographic data that Alexandre Duchêne and I collected within Swisseco, a Swiss multinational organization based in the major economic center of German-speaking Switzerland.[3]

Making Language Safe for Branding

Swisseco, an organization with 200 employees, was mandated in 2008 by the Swiss federal state authorities and local, cantonal governments to promote the Swiss economy internationally. This mandate implies the attraction of potential international investors, capital, and entrepreneurs into Swiss territory. It also involves supporting, coaching, and consulting with Swiss companies regarding their export projects and activities. While Swisseco is mainly state sponsored, it is a typical multinational: it operates internationally and has, along with its three locations in Switzerland (Zurich, Lugano, and Lausanne), locations in the United States, Canada, Brazil, Spain, the United Kingdom, France, Germany, Italy, Austria, Poland, Russia, South Africa, India, China, Japan, South Korea, Hong Kong, Mexico, Turkey, Singapore, and the United Arab Emirates.

In order to examine and explain the ways in which language and communication are governed within and by Swisseco, I need to focus on the status of these specific resources within their production process. I argue that the management of language and communication must be understood in relation to the organization's need to shape and reproduce a specific image of Switzerland. In particular, this image must focus on the Swiss economy and its entrepreneurs, in a way that positions Switzerland as a solution to the challenges posed by the globalizing economy. Further, I claim that the regulation of these communicative resources needs to be understood as a part of Swisseco's attempts to stage expertise in the efficient management of a multilingual network of stakeholders located both within Switzerland (where Swisseco addresses linguistically diverse Swiss clients) and internationally (where the organization targets linguistically heterogeneous markets). The policing of language and communication also needs to be understood as interconnected with the organization's obligation to work with multilingual, international, and often geographically disconnected teams. Finally, the management of language and communication should be understood as resulting from the complex and often contradictory interests and agendas represented by those actors working with and for Swisseco. Swisseco complies with a multiplicity of stakeholders ranging from the Swiss federal state, local cantons and municipalities, and Swiss industries, as well as the interests of the markets, states, and economies that Swisseco addresses.

The following subsection focuses on the ways in which language and communication are regulated by different actors within Swisseco. Along with Duchêne's (2009) four analytical axes, I start my analysis by examining the tokens of language and communication that are considered to count as resources within Swisseco. With this first analytical step, I also reflect upon the logic whereby specific forms of language and communication are considered to be more productive than others.

Selecting the Resource

Swisseco attracts firms and entrepreneurs willing to invest in Switzerland as a location with three main objectives in mind: (1) to create new job opportunities; (2) to bring new technology and innovations to the country; and (3) to increase Swiss tax revenue. The Swiss federal government mandates Swisseco to attract entrepreneurs from a few select countries, namely the United States, Canada, Germany, France, Italy, and the United Kingdom, as well as Brazil, Russia, India, China, and Japan. The Swiss federal authorities believe that investors and entrepreneurs from these countries will fit the economic structure of Switzerland, and thus they are targeted through several strategies and activities.

The organization relies on two major promotional resources to attract investors. The first is what they call their *investor seminars*. As Swisseco needs to communicate the advantages of doing business in Switzerland, it organizes promotional events for potential investors in these selected countries. The second is the production of promotional brochures that present the unique selling potential represented by Switzerland's business location. Language and communication play a strategic role in both of these resources.

Indeed, the senior strategists at Swisseco, responsible for the location promotion section, decided that addressing every target market in what they consider its own language is a powerful feature of their strategy for attracting foreign investors. This is why the brochures, for example, are produced in English (with one version for the US and Canadian market, another for the Indian market, and a third for the UK market), German, French, Italian, Portuguese, Russian, Mandarin Chinese, and Japanese. According to the same principle, the investor seminars are held in the language of each target country.

The underlying rationalizations for this language choice are threefold. First, using the language of the target market facilitates efficient transmission of the promotional message and fosters mutual, cross-cultural understanding. This ensures that potential investors recognize the value of dislocating their activities to Switzerland and avoids miscommunication due to language. As one strategist explained, "While the firms and entrepreneurs in the targeted countries are used to operating internationally, they seldom speak English or German, so that using their own language is a means to make communication more transparent and efficient" (taken from field notes). Second, this choice of language changes the message of these resources. While not all brochures are adapted to the specific needs and desires of each target market (the investor seminars are), the strategic decision to invest in the language of the addressed market is part of a larger desire to package the promotional discourse in a way that is appealing to each specific country. Third, using the language of the markets being addressed also stages Switzerland's expertise and capacity for engaging in business in an international and increasingly multilingual global context. As Swisseco metonymically stands for the whole of Switzerland, this strategy is also coherent with Swisseco's promotional discourse that Switzerland's linguistic diversity and its workers' excellent multilingual skills are key advantages of doing international business from Switzerland.

Critically, the reproduction of the nationalist ideology of linguistically homogeneous nations is not unintentional. Indeed, as one of Swisseco's strategists explained, choosing, for example, German as a language to address a country that is ethnically and linguistically heterogeneous is an intentional way to select the entrepreneurs that Switzerland wants to attract. That is to say, not all entrepreneurs in Germany should be attracted—especially the many migrant businesses that are said not to fit the economic culture of Switzerland.

Language choice also affects the ways promotional discourses are put into text. Indeed, Swisseco's communications specialists (note the shifting source of authority and regulation) also decided that the style and register of the promotional text should change according to the textual genre that the promotional material represents. For example, informative texts, such as the *Handbook for Investors*, present basic information about Switzerland, its political, economic, legislative, and education systems, as well as knowledge about Swiss society, languages, and culture. Therefore, the communications specialists chose to use what they call a "descriptive, informative style." According to them, this communicative style is "factual, transparent and clear." However, for teaser brochures such as *Switzerland: Your No. 1 Location in Europe*, a "less descriptive, much more fancy and sexy language" must be used because they aim to foster public desire for Switzerland.

Different people are therefore seen as the experts in producing these two different genres. The *Handbook for Investors*, imagined to be a more descriptive text, is produced internally by Swisseco's location promotion team. This is legitimated by the fact that, here, the priority is the content of the brochure, so Swisseco employees are best placed to carry out this work. The writing of the brochure *Switzerland: Your No. 1 Location in Europe*, however, is outsourced to an external communication firm. The strategists of Swisseco exclusively provide the content of the brochure, while the external communication specialists are asked to transform this content into a powerful promotional text.

Swisseco's attempt to maintain control over the communicative registers that are used to promote Switzerland around the world are anchored within a larger attempt to standardize their branding. In what follows, I turn to the second analytical step, discussing how and why this multinational standardizes what is said about Switzerland.

Standardizing the Resource

While the promotional material and events are produced and circulated (or planned and conducted) by Swisseco and its staff, they are not allowed to make decisions on the messages (i.e., the content that is communicated to potential investors). The federal authorities have appointed a group of marketing experts that have developed a brand that embodies the specific qualities that Switzerland is imagined to stand for. These experts, positioned outside the structures of Swisseco, have been asked to define a set of stories about Switzerland (i.e., prefabricated bits and pieces of discourse about the strengths of Switzerland and its economy, culture, and society). These stories are then mobilized in the promotional marketing discourse. While Swisseco is a private and independent corporation, its government mandate obliges it to use these communication resources that standardize and prepackage the promotional discourse it produces and circulates (see Lorente, 2010, for how domestic workers in the Philippines are trained to embody such a prepackaged discourse).

Two main features characterize such prefabricated communicative resources. On the one hand, all promotional material and events must adhere to the qualities of "diversity," "humanitarian tradition," "close proximity to the citizen," "sense of quality," and "innovation"—these being defined by the marketing specialists as core qualities in the communicative representation of Switzerland both nationally and internationally. To specify the meaning of such qualities, the marketing experts added a list of features that those working with the qualities can use as instructions about how to interpret them. For the quality "diversity," for example, the specialists added "four languages, four cultures, high percentage of foreigners (coexistence), federalism, pluralism."

On the other hand, the promotional discourse also must be adjusted to a set of prefabricated stories about Switzerland; these are short texts to be integrated in the promotional discourse circulated about Switzerland. These stories are grouped in categories such as "Swiss culture," "Swiss population," "Swiss economy," and "Swiss science." The category of Swiss population, for example, is supposed to tell stories about the Swiss, including their strengths and values. The marketing specialists produced nine texts entitled, "Click and Vote," "Emancipation through Religion," "Tell's Apple," "The Desire to Help," "The Most Famous Girl in the World," "The Summit," "The Unlimited Freedom," "Unity in Diversity," and "The Loud Voice of Minority." "The Loud Voice of Minority" story is defined as follows:

> Conflicts between minorities and majorities about political, religious, and cultural issues often lead to war and violence. However, the founding of the newest canton in Switzerland proves that this does not always have to be the case and that conflicts can be resolved by peaceful means. In a popular vote, the Jurassian communes decided to break away from the Canton Bern. In 1978 the entire Swiss electorate voted in a referendum on the foundation of the new Canton Jura. The majority of voters respected the will of the French-speaking Jurassian minority to leave the German speaking Canton Bern and the Canton Jura became the 26th Swiss Canton.

This specific story is considered to be particularly important for demonstrating to countries that associate ethnic and linguistic diversity with political instability. Here they emphasize that Switzerland's linguistic and cultural diversity is not a risk for the economic climate or for the productivity of the country, but rather evidence of the solidity of the Swiss political system.

According to the government's marketing specialists, these prefabricated messages and stories, which are mobilized in handbooks, reports, and guidelines, are intended to exert control over communications about Switzerland. They also regulate the everyday work of those actors doing the promotional work, including those working for Swisseco, and beyond this to all other corporate actors mandated to market the nation's culture, tourism, and science. According to the marketing specialists, if global discourses of Switzerland and its qualities were too heterogeneous, this would confuse the markets and make Switzerland unrecognizable to a potentially interested public. This is why the prefabricated messages and content are assumed to assure coherence and recognizability of the promotional message, as well as a strict control of the ways Switzerland is described abroad. These standardizing practices are also said to empower individuals and organizations such as Swisseco, which circulate knowledge about the nation in their everyday routines.

However, this strict scripting of promotional practices is problematic for their strategists, as well as those officers doing the promotional work, because it contradicts Swisseco's strong focus on localized promotional messages. Certain prefabricated messages do not function in every national market. Certain markets, according to Swisseco's head strategist, are more complicated than others and need their own strategy. Thus, despite the prescribed promotional discourse, in certain cases Swisseco and its managers strategically decide to subvert the communicational strategy imposed by the federal authorities and produce an alternative discourse.

We observed this during an investor seminar in Paris, where Swisseco attempted to convince several French managers and investors about the advantages of opening a firm in Switzerland. In this specific case, Switzerland's linguistic and cultural diversity—a feature that is usually constructed as one of the nation's main qualities (in terms of multilingual work force, societal pluralism and cosmopolitanism, as well as political stability)—was completely erased from the promotional discourse. The officer of the targeting team finds that French investors often construct the German language as a source of unintelligibility and bureaucracy. They therefore view Switzerland's linguistic diversity, and more particularly the presence of the German language, as an obstacle to the successful implementation of their companies on Swiss territory. This is why, despite the governmental instruction to highlight national linguistic diversity as one of the nation's distinctive strengths, Swisseco systematically omitted this point during this seminar. Rather, they reframed the selling proposition of "diversity" as evidence of the linguistic proximity between France and French-speaking Switzerland.

Such strategic manipulation of the promotional practices codified and imposed by the government authorities is not an exception, say Swisseco's managers, but rather is part of a larger flexibilization strategy that contributes to the competitiveness of the organization within the Swiss market of consultancy firms. The next subsection speaks to this.

Flexibilizing the Resource

Swisseco's situation as a corporate actor is complicated. On the one hand, it is a private organization that competes on the free market with other Swiss and international consultancy firms for access to public and private services. On the other hand, through its recent mandate, the organization is entirely paid for by the state. This situation of privilege does not exempt Swisseco from the logics of efficiency, transparency, productivity, accountability, or flexibility that not only govern the everyday work of corporate actors, but are increasingly key principles in the neoliberal administration and auditing of public funding. This is why Swisseco's strategists are strongly committed to publicly showing the efficiency and flexibility of their services and practices. Within this framework, language and communication, and more specifically multilingualism, play a key role.

Indeed, historically, Swisseco invested in monolingual officers responsible for one specific market (for example, Italian-speaking officers for the Italian market). They requested these officers to master the language of the addressed market as well as English. However, the need for more flexibility, which came with the recent economic transformation, caused a redefinition of this managerial principle. Thus, officers are now increasingly requested to serve more markets simultaneously and, consequently, to be "trilingual" or even "quadrilingual." The multilingual officer is therefore invested in as a source of flexibility, able to compensate for the unpredictability of national and international markets.

This strategy of flexibilization of Swisseco's officers also came with the establishment of a so-called internal Academy, which is supposed to contribute to the training of the organization's personnel. The officers are asked to attend training activities to improve their productivity in domains such as export promotion, location promotion, and trade promotion. They are also expected to acquire competences that are mainly linguistic and communicational in nature. These are skills in business negotiation and intercultural communication, in addition to diplomatic and consulting techniques. The officers are also requested to work on their own flexibility and update their skills through online courses or self-assessments.

The flexibilization of the organizations' practices is also achieved through reorganization of the teams that address national markets. Teams are increasingly responsible for two or three markets that are considered to be related. The section of Swisseco responsible for the US market also now targets Canada. It is assumed that, given the geographical and linguistic proximity of the two markets, the team targeting US investors can also work on the Canadian market; the French-speaking investors in Canada were considered to be skilled enough in English to be addressed by officers with rather poor French competences. The same applied to the South and Central American regions, where the team assigned is asked to test whether the Spanish-speaking market would be profitable, both in terms of attracting potential investors to Switzerland and for export promotion. All Spanish-speaking countries, including Spain, were reconfigured into one single market. Using this same logic, Portugal was later integrated into a transnational Lusophone market along with Brazil.

In these cases, language was again seen as a tool for flexibilization. For all these Spanish-speaking countries (as for the Portuguese-speaking ones), Swisseco decided to produce only one brochure in Spanish or Portuguese, instead of one brochure for each country (as had been the case for India, the United States, and the United Kingdom, where brochures in different varieties of English were localized). The strategy was to expand the spectrum of addressed markets by investing in the language that the countries share while using existing brochures (for the Spanish-speaking market) or services (in the Canadian case) that had been developed for one specific country. This strategy enabled Swisseco to minimize risks and resources for emerging markets whose future development and profitability were not predictable.

It is important to note that while this strategy of flexibilization is imposed by Swisseco's steering board, it is mediated by a set of regulatory actors situated at different levels within the infrastructure of the organization. First, the human resources section now exclusively employs trilingual or quadrilingual personnel. They then ask existing officers and managers to work and improve their own linguistic and communication skills, given the necessity of flexible and multilingual employees. Second, the strategists in the location promotion section regroup the markets according to their linguistic affiliations and reallocate the human capital at their disposal to the different markets according to their current economic potentials. Finally, the officers and managers in the target markets who focus on their activities in new countries reallocate their (linguistic) resources accordingly. They then monitor the flexibility of these regulatory practices via training their own bodies to be more (linguistically) capable.

The need to continuously face demands for flexibility and expansion also involves processes of exploitation (of linguistic resources and human capital), which are discussed in the following.

Exploiting the Resource

In spite of (or probably because of) the situation of global economic stagnation that Swisseco has to face in its daily promotion of the Swiss economy, the organization is continuously expanding. More and more Swiss companies aim to benefit from Swisseco's service and to be supported by Swisseco's specialists and consultants. They seek their help in both their export activities and in the relocation of their productive infrastructure to so-called low-cost countries, where labor is cheaper and less regulated. The section of the organization that attracts investors to Switzerland is also experiencing more and more foreign investors who want to profit from the advantageous fiscal conditions and political stability that Switzerland can offer. In previous years, these two processes have led to an expansion of the organization's activity.

Swisseco manages and processes the work that this expansion entails, without needing to employ new human resources. The organization's steering board achieved this by reconceptualizing Swisseco as a platform that mobilizes different forms of expertise and resources (including linguistic resources) both within and outside the organization's structures. This platform is also supposed to efficiently connect different actors who have distinct economic interests and needs.

Swisseco has, for example, started to recruit multilingual personnel in the target countries that give the organization access to linguistic and communication expertise, as well as specific knowledge about the addressed market. In certain cases, as in emergent markets such as China, Japan, India, or Russia, this allows access to markets that would otherwise be difficult to access. These local multilingual officers are also imagined to provide Swisseco and its clients with local networks and business contacts, and to facilitate the implantation of Swiss firms in the target markets. The company has also started to build "pools of experts" in the target markets; these are Swiss entrepreneurs who have already been successful in export projects and who provide Swisseco with their knowledge about the local bureaucratic apparatus, as well as about economic issues. These actors, who often act as linguistic brokers between the Swiss entrepreneurs and the local authorities or economic partners, often offer their services and expertise for free. The involvement of the local expert is considered mutually beneficial by all parties: Swisseco is able to gain access to a precious resource (such as linguistic brokering services) for free, while Swiss companies see the possibility of accessing trustful partners and networks.

This is also a way for the local brokers to expand their business contacts and to become involved in export projects, which at a certain point have the potential to be exchanged with mandates. In addition, Swisseco has learned to involve and mobilize actors and communication resources from the local cantons and municipalities that are interested in accessing promotional spaces in which foreign entrepreneurs investing in their cities and regions can be approached. For the company, this human resource, which is employed and paid for by the local municipalities, is particularly useful, as it enables a sort of institutional and linguistic proximity—a level of support between entrepreneurs and local government authorities, which entrepreneurs often miss in their own countries. According to Swisseco's location-promotion experts, showing that future investors and municipal authorities (where investors will install and establish their firms) share a common language helps to establish trusting relations and is a competitive advantage that Swisseco wants to exploit.

Despite recruiting productive resources from outside the organizational architecture of Swisseco, the company does not lose control over the ways Switzerland is communicatively presented and marketed. Although the collaborators are employed in the target countries, they are trained in Switzerland and are allocated a partner from within the Swiss headquarters of Swisseco who supports them and provides them with instructions and guidance. These collaborators are coached in how to talk about Switzerland, the qualities they have to highlight, and how to present the promotional material. Sometimes they are even asked to learn a national language. Similarly, the personnel provided by the local, cantonal authorities are trained in producing the right discourse about Switzerland, including communicational techniques of presentation and negotiation.

It would be wrong, however, to assume that those recruited from outside of Swisseco are only executors of a communication practice designed and directed by a team of experts located from within. For example, we went to an investor seminar in Frankfurt, Germany, where a representative of a Swiss German municipality who had joined Swisseco's team for this specific event decided to deviate from the communication script imposed on him by the communication experts of Swisseco (see Del Percio, 2015, for an extensive account on this specific event). Normally, Swisseco would put forward the argument about the linguistic and cultural proximity of Germany and German-speaking regions in Switzerland when addressing German entrepreneurs. The common language is said to facilitate the implementation of German firms on Swiss territory, contribute to the avoidance of misunderstandings and inefficiencies in the management of new (as well as old) German-speaking networks of stakeholders, and give the investors access to a pool of laborers with whom they can communicate. "Switzerland is like Germany, just without the high taxation, the strong regulation of labour, and the inefficient bureaucratic apparatus." This is the script that the actors (both employees of Swisseco and externally recruited personnel) participating in investor seminars are asked to perform when addressing potential German investors.

In the context of this specific seminar, however, one of the representatives of a German-speaking municipality decided to mitigate this promotional argument. He noted in his speech that, for German entrepreneurs, the Swiss German dialect, though widely used in almost all oral, communicative situations, is not always intelligible to Germans. He also explained that sharing a language does not mean sharing an entrepreneurial culture. According to him, Germans often would be considered by their Swiss partners and stakeholders as arrogant, which then would lead to forms of conflict and intolerance.

The officer who subverted the promotional script imposed on him by Swisseco explained to me that he had decided to nuance the argument of Switzerland's linguistic proximity because otherwise German investors might come to Switzerland with false expectations. In certain cases, he argued, this leads to problems and delays in implementation processes and causes increased administrative work for officers like him who have to carry out these processes. His specification, he explained, was a way to make sure that entrepreneurs would be better prepared for the dislocation process, and would ensure that they are better informed about the cultural specificities of the Swiss market.

This deviation from the script created tensions among those who were selected for this specific investor seminar. The feedback suggested that German participants showed appreciation for this alternative evaluation of the linguistic and cultural similarity between Switzerland and Germany, and they considered this insight useful for a potential future relocation. However, Swisseco's management decided that such an alternative discourse could not be tolerated. As a consequence, in order to keep control over what was said about Switzerland and its linguistic character- istics to potential investors, Swisseco decided to remove this officer from its list of possible external speakers. They then sought a new representative who could better interpret the script dictated by Swisseco's management. In other words, if speakers produce alternative discourses about Switzerland and its qualities at these promo- tional events, it is seen to subvert the organization's standardizing and regulatory practice. As a result, these communicative deviances are sanctioned for the sake of order and homogeneity.

CONCLUSION

In this chapter, I have presented an analysis of the multiple techniques, logics, and forms of expertise enacted by a multinational organization turning language and communication into productive resources within a globalized, late capitalist economy. I have particularly pointed to the organizational processes that contribute to the regulation of language and speakers, as well as to the moments of subversion that challenge these regulatory forces.

In doing so, it was my intention to put forward an approach to language policy and planning that decenters language: that is, that understands the regulation of lan- guage and communicative practices as part of a larger regulation of the productive process of a given organization. Indeed, my account demonstrated that expertise in language and communication, as well as concrete policing practices of commu- nicative processes and language choices, does not target language per se. Rather, their ultimate targets are promotional campaigns, the production of documents and brochures, the use of middlemen and brokers, and the improvement of organ- izational processes and practices of accountability. In these terms, language and communication are always part of a package of activities that are subjected to disci- pline and regimentation. They cannot, therefore, be analyzed, nor understood and explained, in abstract (i.e., detached from the organizational practice in which they are anchored and which they serve).

Furthermore, my discussion of the policing practices regulating this multina- tional investment and of the use of language and communication aims to raise awareness within the field of LPP of the multiple sources of expertise that affect the use of language within a complex organization such as Swisseco. The regulation of language and communication in corporate organizations (as in every other domain of social life) is rarely orchestrated by a single, clearly identifiable logic or source of (linguistic) authority. The management of language and communication is rather the product of multiple, often coexisting, and sometimes contradictory sources of expertise and regulation, situated at different levels of an organization's architecture and following in certain cases divergent logics and agendas. As I have argued, even in highly regulated and controlled organizations such as Swisseco, the individuals who are asked to implement and embody these language policies have the ability to enact alternative modes of communicating and behaving linguistically. This, however, does not mean that their alternative practices are always successful, or that these remain unpunished. Sometimes they are successful and lead to organizational changes. In other cases, these alternative discourses lead to the stigmatization and exclusion of the people producing them.

Finally, this chapter aimed to highlight the value of (institutional) ethnography (Heller, 2009; Smith, 2005) as a powerful methodological tool, as it enables us to understand how the regimentation of language and communication is articulated with political economy (Del Percio, Flubacher, & Duchêne, 2016). The analysis provided here of the organizational activities documented within Swisseco has enabled me to demonstrate how ethnography provides access to specific logics, calculations, and forms of expertise that underpin organizations' choices of, and investment in, language and communication, and how organizations ascribe value to language and multilingualism. Finally, looking at language planning and policy through ethnography has helped me to research why language and communication matters to strategists and managers and to investigate the agendas and interests that this regulation of language and communication serves.

NOTES

1. These findings draw on research funded by the Swiss Research Foundation (SNF-FNS) entitled "Performing Swissness: Discourse, Institutions and Social Transformations" (SNF–100012 129885), directed by Alexandre Duchêne (University of Fribourg) and Vincent Kaufmann (University of St-Gallen).
2. The following cases of corporate and academic actors selling expertise on language and communication are emblematic for an industry of consultants and communication specialists selling communication services. These actors have been randomly identified through a Google search (I used the keyword "business communication consultant" and "business communication" as search options) and are presented here for illustrative purposes.
3. Swisseco is a pseudonym. Although the institution can be easily retrieved, we have maintained anonymity as agreed formally with the institution itself. The actors of the institution are perfectly aware of the impossibility of completely anonymizing our terrain and have agreed to that.

REFERENCES

Althusser, L. (1970). Idéologie et appareils idéologiques d'État. *La Pensée* 151, 3–38.

Appadurai, A. (1996). *Modernity at large: Cultural dimensions of globalization.* Minneapolis: University of Minnesota Press.

Boutet, J. (2012). Language workers: Emblematic figures of late capitalism. In A. Duchêne & M. Heller (Eds.), *Language in late capitalism: Pride and profit* (pp. 207–229). New York: Routledge.

Cameron, D. (2000a). Styling the worker. *Journal of Sociolinguistics* 4(3), 323–347.

Cameron, D. (2000b). *Good to talk: Living and working in a communication culture.* London: Sage.

Communicationaid (n.d.[a]). Cross-cultural training. Retrieved from https://www.communicaid.com/cross-cultural-training/

Communicationaid (n.d.[b]). The importance of "soft skills" in an interconnected world. Retrieved from https://www.communicaid.com/news/communicaid-news-the-importance-soft-skills-hr-review/

Del Percio, A., Flubacher, M., & Duchêne, A. (2016). Language and political economy. In O. Garcia, N. Flores, & M. Spotti (Eds.), *Oxford handbook of language in society* (pp. 55–75). New York: Oxford University Press.

Del Percio, A. (2015). Le plurilinguisme suisse à l'ère du capitalisme tardif: Investissement promotionnel sur un capital national. *Anthropologie et Société* 39(3), 69–89.

Duchêne, A. (2009). Marketing, management and performance: Multilingualism as commodity in a tourism call centre. *Language Policy* 8, 27–50.

Duchêne, A. (2011). Neoliberalism, social inequalities, and multilingualism: The exploitation of linguistic resources and speakers. *Langage et société* 136(2), 81–108.

Duchêne, A. (2012). Des marchés, des locuteurs et des langues. *Sociolinguistica* 26, 120–135.

Duchêne, A., & Heller, M. (Eds.). (2012). *Language in late capitalism: Pride and profit.* New York: Routledge.

Drew, P., & Heritage, J. (Eds.). (1992). *Talk at work: Interaction in institutional settings.* New York: Cambridge University Press.

EMScom Executive Master of Science in Communications Management. (2015). [Brochure]. Retrieved from http://www.emscom.usi.ch/sites/www.emscom.usi.ch/files/media/emscom_brochure-2015_web.pdf

Fraser, N. (2003). From Discipline to flexibilization? Rereading Foucault in the shadow of globalization. *Constellations* 10(2), 160–171.

Gee, J., Hull, G., & Lankshear, C. (1996). *The new work order.* Boulder, CO: Westview.

Harvey D. (2005). *A brief history of neoliberalism.* New York: Oxford University Press.

Heller, M. (2009). Doing ethnography. In Li Wei & M. Moyer (Eds.), *The Blackwell guide to research methods in bilingualism and multilingualism* (pp. 249–262). Malden: Blackwell.

Jaworski, A., & Thurlow, C. (2010). Language and the globalizing habitus of tourism: Toward a sociolinguistics of fleeting relationships. In N. Coupland (Ed.), *The handbook of language and globalization* (pp. 255–286). Oxford: Wiley-Blackwell.

Kelly-Holmes, H. (2010). Languages and global marketing. In N. Coupland (Ed.), *The handbook of language and globalization* (pp. 475–492). Oxford: Wiley-Blackwell.

Lorente, B. (2010). Packaging English-speaking products: Maid agencies in Singapore. In H. Kelly-Holmes & G. Mautner (Eds.), *Language and the market* (pp. 44–55). London: Palgrave-MacMillan.

McElhinny, B. (2012). Silicon Valley sociolinguistics? Analyzing language, gender, and communities of practice in the new knowledge economy. In A. Duchêne & M. Heller (Eds.), *Language in late capitalism: Pride and profit* (pp. 230–260). New York: Routledge.

Piller, I. (2003). Advertising as a site of language contact. *Annual Review of Applied Linguistics* 23, 170–183.

Shore, C., & Wright, S. (2000). Coercive accountability. In M. Strathern (Ed.), *Audit cultures* (pp. 57–89). Routledge: New York; London.

Smith, D. (2005). *Institutional ethnography: A sociology for people*. Oxford: AltaMira Press.

Urciuoli, B., & La Dousa, C. (2013). Language management/labor. *Annual Review of Anthropology* 42, 175–190.

Verizon (n.d.). Elevate your organization through effective, reliable communications. Retrieved from http://www.verizonenterprise.com/products/business-communications/

CHAPTER 27

NEOLIBERALISM AND LINGUISTIC GOVERNMENTALITY

LUISA MARTÍN ROJO

Economics are the method. The object is to change the soul.

—Margaret Thatcher

As a radical and laissez-faire capitalist set of economic policies, neoliberalism accomplishes extensive economic liberalisation by "eliminating price controls, deregulating capital markets, lowering trade barriers," and reducing state influence on the economy, especially through privatisation and austerity (Boas & Gans-Morse, 2009, pp. 137–161). In addition, what was initially an economic policy has become entrenched as a global ideology (Sklar, 1980), extending the logic of the market to all spheres of social life, education, language, urban space, and individuals' lives. This ideology imposes on different social fields—such as education, health care, and language—the need to be as profitable and competitive as markets, and the obligation to follow the same neoliberal principles. Thus, in recent decades, schools, families, and individuals have changed their language repertoires and have enhanced their language skills in order to become more competitive and more flexible for the labour market, and to enter into the global flow of capitals, people, and resources.

If a neoliberal logic rules, not only the economy, but society as a whole, as well as individuals, are compelled to behave according to the same principles, even at their most personal levels of existence. In this regard, neoliberalism goes well beyond an ideology and is also a form of governance. Thus it is urgent to understand the process by which a set of economic principles have become an ideology and a form of governance, at this moment in time when the crisis of neoliberalism as an economic and political order comes hand in hand with the rise of right- and left-leaning populism (and even neo-fascism) in different parts of the world. Accordingly, the object of research should be the knowledge, discourses, and practices that have made this mode of governance acceptable and through which it is exercised. This chapter, then, focuses on the interconnection of "what is said and what is done, rules imposed and reasons given, the planned and the taken-for-granted" (Foucault, 2008, p. 225).

In this context, two crucial questions arise: (1) What actually enables the processes that govern markets to colonise other spheres of our lives and of social organisation? (2) What role is played by language policies, ideologies, knowledge, and practices in the expansion and consolidation of a neoliberal order and the forms of governance that emerge from it? These issues are addressed in the present chapter. In the following section, I explore the current context of neoliberalism and explain how it can become a practice of governance of individuals and the population as a whole. I also introduce some crucial concepts, such as Foucault's governmentality, discuss to what extent a neoliberal governmentality can be traced, and consider its main features, including its linguistic components. The next two sections examine how a neoliberal understanding is transforming language policies, educational programmes, and practices through the discourses of personal enterprise and language as profit. Then, I study the impact of these discourses on speakers' experiences and trajectories, particularly in the processes of linguistic self-training and capitalisation. I then discuss how new forms of subjectivity emerge from these processes. In the final section, I turn to a discussion of how the effects of neoliberalism as a practice of governance provide a window to a better understanding of the changes and challenges of language policies.

NEOLIBERAL GOVERNMENTALITY

In order to understand what makes it possible for the processes that govern markets to colonise other spheres of human life and of social organisation, enabling neoliberalism to become an ideology and an extended mode of governance, we must first consider some of the main features of this prevalent economic model. Neoliberalism relies far more heavily than its predecessor, liberalism, on marketised ordering mechanisms. As Fraser observes,

> In the guise of neoliberalism, it vastly expands the scope of economic rationality, introducing competition into social services, transforming clients into consumers, and subjecting expert professionals to market discipline. In this regime of "de-statized governmentality," substantive welfare policy gives way to formal technologies

of economic accountability as auditors replace service professionals as the frontline disciplinarians. (Fraser, 2003, p. 168)

In this respect, Fraser notes, too, "vouchers replace public services and privatized 'risk management' replaces social insurance, individuals are made to assume new levels of 'responsibility' for their lives" (2003, p. 168). In Fraser's description of neoliberalism, market mechanisms have come to organise human activity, including its governing and self-governing capabilities. In this chapter, this feature is considered as the most significant characteristic of neoliberalism.

During the past two decades, the impact made by a neoliberal economic order on language management and policies has been examined, to some extent, by critical sociolinguistics and applied linguistics research. This research has revealed the effects of globalisation—increasing mobility, delocalisation, and the flexibilisation of markets—on the management of languages and linguistic resources, highlighting their potential as economic resources (Duchêne & Heller, 2012; Holborow, 2015; see also Pujolar, Chapter 24 in this volume, for an in-depth study). Researchers in the field of critical sociolinguistics have tried to describe the logic of resource distribution across social classes, genders, and ethnic groups, and the hierarchies of languages derived from the conditions of convertibility of languages into other sources of capital (Block, 2013; Duchêne, 2011; Martín Rojo, 2010, among others).

Research has also examined similar effects on language practices (for a general reflection on the impact of the study of practices such as translanguaging, polylanguaging, or metrolanguaging on sociolinguistic theory, see Jaspers & Madsen, 2016) and on language policies (Gal, 1989; Piller & Cho, 2013; Ricento, 2012), and these are not always framed or bounded within the nation-state. For example, Canagarajah (2013) proposed a new understanding of transnational social fields, allowing us to consider language as something that is shaped by liminal spaces between countries and communities. Thus, Pennycook (2007, p. 122) adapted the concept of *circles of flow* to refer to large networks in which highly diverse cultural and linguistic forms circulate and are exchanged, and can overlap and blend together in a global culture.

Without underestimating the effect of a neoliberal economy on language management, practices, and policies, and the correlative central role that language plays in the economy of late modern societies, what is significant in relation to the issue addressed by this chapter is that market mechanisms, as in other domains, have now come to some extent to organise speakers' trajectories and practices and to govern their conduct. Even decisions about children's language skills are entangled with market incentives and disincentives. Consider, for instance, how parents may attempt to raise a multilingual child, replacing the local language by an international and prestigious language, located at the top of the language rankings, with the expectation that this choice will increase the child's mobility (see Curdt-Christiansen, Chapter 21 in this volume). They establish this language as their normal language of exchange within the household, even if they themselves learned it at school or in late socialisation. In such circumstances, market rules, to a large extent, shape language practices, and can govern language conduct while also promoting self-regulation.

By studying the extension of neoliberal logic to language management and practices, we can understand the extent to which forms of power mutate, and identify some key changes that are currently taking place, in which languages and language policies are crucially involved (see Martín Rojo, 2016a; see also Heller, Chapter 2 in this volume). It is citizens' conduct that is governed or directed by the kind of power that in this chapter I call *governmentality*.[1] In 1971, Foucault introduced this term to refer to a technique in the exercise of power, which, in his view, is directly linked to liberalism in economy. He defined it as a kind of "power which has the population as its target, political economy as its major form of knowledge, and apparatuses of security as its essential technical instrument" (Foucault, 2009, pp. 107–108).

With this term, Foucault refers to the multiple forms of activity whereby human beings, who may or may not be part of government or of an institution, seek to control the conduct of other human beings—that is, to govern them. Thus, governmentality, like other power mechanisms, is not only exercised by state policies and institutional regimes, but from a multiplicity of nodal points and/or relations of power. In this regard, the parents in the previous example who allowed the rules of the market to shape their language choices in the socialisation of their children constitute one nodal point in the exercise of power, which amplifies and multiplies the extension of neoliberalism to other spheres of human life. Thus, *government* also encompasses self-control, guidance for the family and children, and management of the household.

Examples like linguistic socialisation in the family explain how "de-statized governmentality" (referred to by Fraser, earlier) is in fact part of a new global governmental rationality that has its roots in the generalisation of competition as a behavioural/conduct norm (Dardot & Laval, 2014). Indeed, as a general principle of this governmentality, *competitiveness* represents the extension of a neoliberal logic to all countries, to all sectors of public activity, and to all areas of social existence, including education, family, and interpersonal relations. This happens to such an extent that competitiveness shapes subjects, too, converting them into entrepreneurs capable of seizing opportunities for profit and ready to engage in the constant process of competition (see Fernández-González, 2016).

In contrast with the techniques of power considered by Foucault, such as discipline (see, particularly, *Discipline and Punishment*), governmentality targets the population as a whole, not particular sectors of our societies (students, the military, or "deviants" [Foucault, 1995]). However, as in the case of other techniques of power, through governmentality, power reaches individuals, their bodies, and their actions, attitudes, and conduct (Foucault, 1980, p. 39). Thus, this form of power ultimately aims to achieve self-government by the individual. For example, instead of imposing a language by force, the aim is to promote in speakers the desire to learn it, due to the social and economic benefits it brings.

Foucault offers a detailed study of the meaning of governmentality, explaining how it combined techniques of domination exercised over others with techniques of the self (2001, p. 1604). In this way, he incorporated the condition that in societies framed in liberalism, government requires liberty: To govern is not to govern against liberty, or despite it; it is to govern through liberty—that is, "to actively exploit the freedom allowed individuals so that they end up conforming to certain norms of their own accord" (see Dardot & Laval, 2014, pp. 10ff, for a full development of this approach). This action is believed to deliver a more democratic governance than traditional top-down exercise of power by the state; that is to say, the action vis-à-vis the subjects of governance often takes the form of self-mastery (i.e., individuals ultimately conform to certain norms of their own volition).

Authors like Bourdieu and Gramsci have also attempted to explain the reproduction of the social order and the acceptance of symbolic domination (Bourdieu, 1997) and hegemony (Gramsci, 2000) by the population. As in the case of Foucault, in order to explain this reproduction, they refer to the production of knowledge and/or ideologies, for example about the benefits of competition, the value of languages, and the unique competence of native speakers (Martín Rojo, 2016b). Following this logic, research should not capture the complexity of speakers' trajectories (Pujolar & O'Rourke, 2016) and their communicative life and sociolinguistic repertoires (Blommaert, 2010, p. 102ff) as a mere effect of increasing mobility in neoliberal economies. It must also be viewed as part of a new mode of governing linguistic conduct and as a response to newly coined models of speakerness that celebrate multilingualism.

Such a focus on governmentality has been initiated in the language disciplines through recent contributions in sociolinguistics and linguistic anthropology by authors such as Urla (2012), who focuses on language policies; Flores (2013), on education and language learning; Del Percio (2016), on the activities of nongovernmental organizations (NGOs); and Rampton (2014; see also Charalambous et al., Chapter 31 in this volume) on security and securitisation; and in discourse studies, by McIlvenny, Klausen, and Lindegaard (2016). The semantic linking of governing and mentalities, in Foucault's term *governmentality*, highlights the need to analyse the mentality underpinning current forms of governance. The previously mentioned practices of socialisation provide a useful example of how choices, desires, aspirations, needs, wants, and lifestyles have been mobilised and shaped by a neoliberal mentality of governance.

This mentality delineates a discursive field in which the exercise of power is "rationalized" (Lemke, 2001, p. 191). For this reason, in order to answer the two questions raised at the beginning of this chapter, I focus on the kind of knowledge that circulates in society in the form of discourses, and on how they contribute to extending the principles that determine how markets colonise other spheres of our lives and of social organization. Urciuoli (2008), Flores (2013), Boutet (2012), Block, Gray, & Holborow (2013), and Holborow (2015) have all analysed different aspects of what can be called the *neoliberal imaginary* or a *neoliberal epistemology*, which includes the representation of entrepreneurship and austerity, the concept of human capital, the commodification of language, and the personification of markets, among other key elements.

Some of these concepts form part of two discourses that share patterns of concerns, perspectives, concepts, or themes, and that seem to exert a significant impact on speakers' conduct. These discourses are that of *personal enterprise* and that of *language as profit*. Currently, both of these discourses are widespread, commonly reproduced by government agencies, institutions, and private companies. Moreover, as we shall see, they also seem to have been internalised by the population in our societies. In the next sections, I analyse these two discourses.

The Discourse of Personal Enterprise

One of the crucial extensions of neoliberalism to different domains of our lives takes place when processes that govern markets turn out to be a mode of social organisation and, moreover, correlate with a process of self-constitution. An illuminating example is the "flexibilization of markets and practices," whose hallmarks are fluidity, provisionality, and a short-term temporal horizon (Fraser, 2003, p. 169). Fraser explained that what networks are to space, flexibilisation is to time. This principle of flexibility is now ruling other domains of social life and is even informing the representation of the ideal worker. As Fraser states,

> so we have the "flexible individuals" (men and women) described by Richard Sennett, who frequently change jobs and even careers, relocating at the drop of a hat, whose collegial relations and friendships are trimmed to fit the horizon of no long term, and whose selfhood does not consist in a single meaningful, coherent overarching life-narrative. (Fraser, 2003, pp. 169–170)

A similar effect can be observed with the entrepreneurial order, which also correlates with a process of self-constitution, by means of which individuals are considered as enterprises that must ensure their own profitability. One of the paradigmatic examples of this colonisation of individuals' lives by market logic was provided by Aubrey (1994), an international consultant in California who has developed a method of professional training, adapting Foucault's concepts of self-care. In her prescriptive and performative proposals, every worker must seek out a customer, position herself in a market, set a price, manage her costs, undertake research and development, and train herself (Aubrey, 1994, pp. 85ff.). Aubrey's discourse of "personal enterprise" goes well beyond the proposition of a personal ethic in uncertain times: "Personal enterprise is finding a meaning, an engagement in the totality of one's life" (p. 297). And this happens very early on. Even the child must be an "entrepreneur of his/her knowledge" (p. 297), which underpins and highlights the significance of language education and language educational programmes.

In their study of Aubrey's concept of *self-mastery*, Dardot and Laval (2014, pp. 287ff.) point out that this means no longer leading one's life in a linear, rigid, and conformist way, but proving oneself capable of flexibility and entrepreneurship. The more choices that are available, the greater the obligation to enhance one's value in the market. Hence, an individual's value is no longer attached to rights acquired at birth, but, as Aubrey observes, is gained by "the enterprise one has, by one's wish not to make do with this world of rights in which everything is given, determined, inscribed, but to enter into a world that changes" (Aubrey 1994, p. 99). In this view, individuals, as enterprises, are ideally the site of all innovation, constantly changing and continually adapting to variations in market demand by constant self-work or self-improvement. Every individual should be her own expert, employer, inventor, and entrepreneur. Thus, neoliberal rationality encourages individuals to strengthen themselves in order to survive competition; all the activities must be compared to a form of production and viewed as an investment, subject to a cost calculation. The economy becomes a personal discipline that, as Flores (2013, p. 501) notes, meshes very well with the aim of creating flexible workers and lifelong learners to perform service-oriented and technological jobs. The equating of humans with capital is, for Holborow (2015, p. 16), at the centre of a competitive market world in which "human capital is owned and traded on a market" (Piketty, 2014, p. 46), as it is in slave-owning societies (as noted by Harvey, 2014, p. 185).

The lifelong-learning trajectories that the personal enterprise discourse demands constitute the process of "self-capitalisation" referred to by Rizvi and Lingard (2010), according to which individuals must accumulate symbolic capital in order to acquire profit for themselves and/or their organisation. From the moment we introduce the concepts of symbolic capital and of capitalisation/decapitalisation (developed by Martín Rojo, 2010, based on Bourdieu's notion of the convertibility of different forms of capital and social distribution [1986]), the question arises of access to valuable resources: How can participants intervene in the production and distribution of resources in everyday and in institutional practices? Capitalisation and decapitalisation refer to acts of conferring and withholding symbolic capital, such as access to language learning, which can be converted into economic capital, for instance, within the labour market or in the field of education.

The neoliberal discourse conceals the fact that access to the resources that capitalise individuals and make them profitable does not merely depend on the choices made by individuals, but instead on social class, gender, ethnicity, rural or urban origin, and age. Thus, as part of a neoliberal logic, not only are people pressured to compete, but this competition does not take place under conditions of equality (Block, 2013;

Duchêne & Heller, 2012; Martín Rojo, 2010, 2016b). Nevertheless, this competition is potentially productive for prospective employers (Urciuoli, 2010, p. 162), which leads us to the second discourse—that of language as profit.

THE DISCOURSE OF LANGUAGE AS PROFIT

Duchêne and Heller (2012) note the widespread emergence of discursive elements that treat language and culture primarily in economic terms, during the 1990s and into the twenty-first century. This discourse does not replace older ones that treat language as a political and cultural entity associated with the formation of the nation-state; rather, the two kinds of discourse become intertwined in complex ways (see Pujolar, Chapter 24 in this volume; also Heller, Chapter 2 in this volume). These authors present this discursive shift as part of a broader sociopolitical and economic change, by means of which the dominant discourse and ideology of language that are inextricably tied to identity and territory—and still central to the legitimisation of the nation-state as a particular historical mode of regulation of capital—is being challenged by the continual expansion and serial saturation of markets and the emergence of the tertiary sector as a defining element of the globalised new economy.

As a result of the commodification of languages, sociolinguistics researchers are increasingly bearing witness to the proliferation of discourses celebrating multilingualism. Linguistic skills are commodified, and constitute a key element in the process of *personal mastery* by which individuals make themselves competitive. As different authors have noted, these discourses of linguistic diversity oversimplify the societal position and role of languages. Indeed, bilingualism and multilingualism are still institutionally constructed as parallel/separate monolingualisms (see Creese & Blackledge, 2010; Heller, 2007; Pérez-Milans, 2015a; and many others). Furthermore, the values attributed to the different languages produce hierarchies that in many cases are rooted in former European colonial discourses (Errington, 2001; Fabian, 1986; Martín Rojo, Anthonissen, Sánchez, & Unamuno, 2017; Martín Rojo, Relaño-Pastor, & Rasskin, 2010).

Nevertheless, the discourse of multilingualism as a profit-producing mechanism impacts on language policies and speakers' linguistic trajectories and conducts. One example can be found in the educational policies implemented in the region of Madrid. In this region of Spain, as in many European countries, the valuation of language as capital seems to be restricted to English, to the point that it has been introduced, in parallel with Spanish, as a language of instruction in many schools. For the last two decades this region has been governed by conservative political forces that have advanced a strong neoliberal agenda. As a result, schools have been confronted with funding cuts, which in turn forces them to compete over students and resources. Thus public schools manage the withdrawal of state funding by competing with each other and with subsidised private schools (charter schools). Consequently, many schools have proclaimed the benefits of Spanish-English bilingual programmes in order to attract students, particularly those from relatively affluent middle-class families (see also Pérez-Milans, 2015b; Flubacher & Del Percio, 2017, for examples of how these developments are affecting the role of language and of language programmes in schools).

This is clearly illustrated in a flyer edited by the Madrid regional government, in which the region is defined as "Madrid, a bilingual community (Spanish & English)." The map in Figure 27.1 from the flyer shows how, starting from a situation of Spanish monolingualism in education for the larger part of the twentieth century, by 2013–2014, the region had 318 primary schools and 91 secondary schools distributed across the region, offering bilingual English/Spanish programmes.

The bilingual flyer also includes the following statement about the students' future:

> Example 1
> "Our students will be able to ..."
> · Travel to more than 120 countries
> · Communicate with more than 1 billion people
> · Study in the most prominent foreign universities
> · Work in all 5 continents

Thus, the bilingual programme is presented as a process of capitalisation that will prepare students to compete in a globalised world and to be the masters of their own destiny. The flyer claims that these acquired capabilities bestow social value on the students. In essence, the flyer hails multilingualism, presenting increased linguistic competences and skills as a requirement of our times. The last item ("Work on all 5 continents") carries a particularly powerful and pertinent message, given the high levels of unemployment among young people in Spain. What the students will gain is said to guarantee them entry into and mobility within the job market (Duchêne, 2011; Duchêne & Heller, 2012). This kind of publicity treats language (English) as a commodity that employers in the service industries use, and one by which those who possess it can benefit materially (see Holborow, 2015, p. 32, for a critical analysis of commodification in capitalist production and economies). If languages count as capital, only those that are socially valued can be competitive and thus render their speakers competitive.

The introduction of English as the language of instruction in schools in some regions of Spain, as well as elsewhere in Europe, represents a flexibilisation and deregulation of the national linguistic market compared to the traditional distribution of languages within Spain, in which the national language and other co-official languages had a favoured position in education and other areas of social life. Students must compete for access to these programmes, which are offered by state schools and in some private schools that are also subsidized by the state. Yet studies have

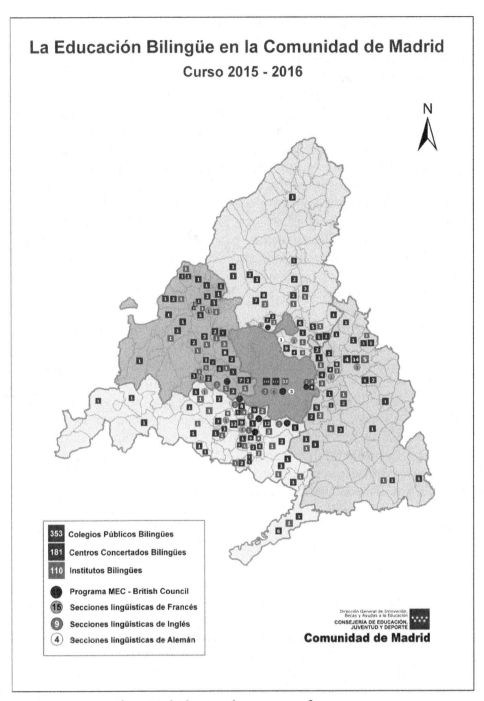

FIGURE 27.1. Map from Madrid regional government flyer.

Source: http://www.madrid.org/cs/Satellite?c=CM_Actuaciones_FA&cid=1354274775145&pagename=
PortalEducacion/CM_Actuaciones_FA/EDUC_Actuaciones

shown that access is not available to all on an equal basis, as students from migrant backgrounds or from disadvantaged social classes rarely have the same resources as those from middle-class families that can provide advantages in the competition for admission (Hidalgo, 2018).

By presenting the maximisation of linguistic competencies and skills as a contemporary requirement for entry into and mobility within the job market, schools are obliged to provide opportunities for such linguistic development. The deregulation of the national linguistic market thus provokes a deregulation of the schools, which have to be reorganised in accordance with the demands of these new programmes. Fast tracks are created for students with a high level of English, while those with lower English proficiency will be left behind. Similarly, a distinction is made between teachers in bilingual programmes and those who are not able to teach bilingually. Currently bilingual teachers enjoy certain privileges in the designated schools (bonuses or priority in choice of workplace; see Relaño-Pastor, 2015; also Relaño-Pastor, Chapter 25 in this volume). Thus, bilingual programmes in Madrid and beyond represent hierarchisation as yet another form of social organisation and control.

Urla (2012) has also examined forms of linguistic governmentality in the framework of national states being generalised through methods of evaluation that have the effect of classifying the population on the basis of linguistic competences and skills (for instance, in the Basque Country, distinguishing between *euskaldunes* [Basque speakers] and *non-euskaldunes* [non-Basque speakers], and among different levels of competences). In fact, as Duchêne & Humbert (2018) show there is a constant interrelation of state interests and the role of language statistics in governing speakers by numbers. Thus, in bilingual schools in Madrid, this particular assessment measure is applied in public education by large external assessment agencies, such as Cambridge *English Language Assessment*, which measures students' English proficiency. Teachers also have to pass a language proficiency test.

As a result of these developments, the school-going population is being organised, distributed, and compartmentalised into different language programmes. Possibly the most significant aspect of these outcomes is that the role of educational institutions has changed within this neoliberal order. Regarding the means of correct training, Foucault (1995) finds this to be discipline: "The chief function of the disciplinary power is to 'train,' rather than to select and to levy; or, no doubt, to train in order to levy and select all the more" (p. 170). In relation to language, schools are disciplinary institutions in which students are trained to speak in accordance with a model, such as the native speaker model, in which content, values, and ideologies are imparted. Thus they are encouraged to adopt the standard language and the associated norms of accepted language behaviour. Within a neoliberal logic, we are now seeing schools as institutions that orient pupils' conduct by broadly creating competition, rather than collaboration among them. As part of this competition, the compelling need is for students to become fully competent in at least one so-called international language as a mechanism of power in neoliberal economies. Such a context eventually not only produces the deregulation of the linguistic market but also reinforces marketisation and the privatisation of training.

The dynamics that turn market-governing processes into modes of social organisation and modes of self-constitution transfer the process of self-capitalisation to subjects who must enhance their own productivity by their own decisions. The analyses of the preceding discourses show how the behaviour of individuals, and that of the population in general, becomes regulated, particularly when one language is given prominence over others, by means of the development of training programmes, materials, and courses that transmit the need for students to master the language in question. Thus, self-capitalisation demands self-training, to which I will now turn.

LINGUISTIC SELF-TRAINING

Beyond the education received at school, individuals must master themselves and increase their own capital. Every item of knowledge (including crucially important linguistic knowledge) acquired in this process can be interpreted as a skill, an aspect of the self that is potentially productive for prospective employers (Urciuoli, 2010, p. 162). One of the difficulties individuals face in becoming productive is related to the demands of the market, which are never static, but change continuously in intensity and scope. Such fast-evolving demands are extremely difficult to meet, while, as Holborow notes, in other cases of commodification, language workers who do meet formerly acknowledged levels of proficiency are deprived of control over their skills and are often underpaid.

In spite of this, the number of languages in which speakers need to be proficient, the certificates required to endorse their competences, and the scopes of performance recommended to increase productivity are continuously expanding and increasing. Furthermore, the tensions individuals experience in order to fit these demands are evident in their discourses. As example 2 illustrates, they find themselves immersed in a global and flexible market, trying to design their language trajectories and conduct to fit such a context. The example provides an extract from the British Council in which the effects of high demands on speakers' trajectories and conduct are acknowledged:

Example 2
Every year the UK attracts over 500,000 international students. Around 9,000 Spanish students choose to study for an undergraduate or postgraduate qualification at UK institutions and over 40,000 Spanish students learn English at language

schools in the UK. More and more students are also choosing to spend a year in a British School or College. (https://www.britishcouncil.es/en/study-uk/fair)

The figures in example 2 give an impression of the mobility and effort invested by international students in language training, as well as the schools that offer language courses, organise examinations, award certificates, and provide diverse types of resources and symbolic capital that contribute to students' progress, achievement, and certification. As such figures show, Spanish students are singled out for their effort in learning one of the main languages in the global market, or increasing their levels of competence in order to be best prepared to compete. These "opportunities" are also offered to workers who take on extended stays abroad, especially during times such as the present when a flexible labour market has left many unemployed. Thus, the demand for language skills and their certification is also commodified.

In a context of capital and labour market deregulation in which jobs have become precarious, inequality has risen, and struggles for resources have increased (Fraser, 2003; Standing, 2011), people respond to this pressure by trying to meet market demands and by increasing their competencies in languages with high currency, even though not everyone has access to such stays abroad or the resources to fund them. The compelling need to become fully competent in at least one international language therefore constitutes a powerful regulatory mechanism in neoliberal economies, ultimately determining the behaviour of individuals and of the population at large (Martín Rojo, 2016b).

As a result, language (self-) training becomes an instrument for increasing competency and competitiveness, and fills the void resulting from long periods of unemployment in a precarious job market. Training in this context anticipates future situations in which it will be possible to "predict" and thus "prevent" or "prompt" events, as in controlling individuals' circulation, competitiveness, and employability. Language then becomes an "object of surveillance, analysis, intervention, modifications, and so on" (Foucault, 2000, p. 95).

Resorting to mobility as a means of complementing one's education reveals that the social and economic valuation of languages and of multilingualism does not represent a change in the canons of measurement or in the evaluation of skills and competences. In other words, the proliferation of multilingual speakers does not make this condition more highly valued, nor does it call for greater flexibility to enable such persons to make use of their multilingual abilities. On the contrary, (self-) language training still aims at targets based on particular models of speakerness. For example, it is important to *pass for a native* or to *sound local* in national and international languages. Figure 27.2 shows an advertisement circulated by one of the largest banks in Europe, Banco Bilbao-Vizcaya, which offers loans to young people for a single cause ("your goals have to be fulfilled"), namely, that of speaking English with "native-like" accent ("Learn English with an English accent"), probably meaning a British accent. This loan is available to those who can pay monthly instalments of

FIGURE 27.2. Advertisement for bank loans for English study.

150 euros. Thus, a so-called international language is required to fit a local (British) accent (see Márquez-Reiter & Martín Rojo, 2014, for a study of the same kind of contradiction in the case of Spanish).

This example illustrates two processes. First, it shows the dynamics that allow market governing processes to become modes of social organisation, and also modes of self-constitution. Second, it shows how the laws of supply and demand also apply to other spheres of human life. Speakers have to invest to be productive and to increase their opportunities; to achieve this goal, their linguistic skills are commodified. And, in the same way that discourses praising multilingualism often conceal the promotion of languages that are more highly valued for their role in the global economy, this commodification applauds only certain language variants. Yet there is no single market and no single convertibility rate for languages, accents, and so on. As observed by Blommaert (2016), the evaluations and the meanings of different language varieties and registers can vary according to the spatiotemporal configuration considered. For example, a Jamaican accent in English is negatively valued in the classroom, neutrally in the ethnically heterogeneous peer group, and positively in the after-school reggae club (Rampton, 1995). However, the prestige and the social significance of these linguistic varieties are not homogeneous either, and in those varieties that enable some social mobility, such as in education or the labour market, there continues to exist a model of speaker and speakerness that is linked to localness and even to birth.

This contradiction is highlighted by Woolard's (2008) distinction between, on the one hand, linguistic ideologies of authenticity, according to which the value of a language is located in its relation to a particular community, and on the other hand, linguistic ideologies of anonymity, which place the value of a language in its being socially neutral, universally available, and to some extent international. In this case, if the value of languages like English and/or Spanish lies in their universality, the demand that they be spoken with a local accent can be viewed as an "anonymity fake" (in Woolard's terms). Woolard (2008) and Moreno Cabrera (2015), among others, have shown that institutions (schools and language academies) position dominant languages as universally open and available to all. In so doing, they position languages in an ideology of hegemony (Gramsci, 2000) while also claiming that ethnic, class, and other differences have been erased. Then local and less widely distributed languages and language varieties are replaced by supra-ethnic and supra-social class and languages.

The experiences of the 500,000 international students in the United Kingdom, mentioned in Example 2, contradict this representation of the universality of so-called international languages. There is tension between anonymity and authenticity, so that the speakers' lived experiences face contradictory demands: They have to learn a language that is claimed to be international, and at the same time they have to speak it with a local, authentic-sounding, indeed "quasi-native," accent, in order to certify their competence. This means that they are required to acquire an accent that is socially, ethnically, and geopolitically marked, and not necessarily accessible to all.

Hence, those who seek to learn an international language must face normalising judgements. In fact, non-native speakers report a permanent and exhaustive surveillance of their language practices, which are still shaped by the native speaker model. In this regard, we recognise the same three instruments functioning in self-training as those upon which, according to Foucault (1995, p. 179), "the success of disciplinary power" depends: hierarchical observation, normalising judgment, and examination (1995, p. 170). Training is, in fact, the cornerstone of disciplinary power; however, it seems to be crucial in relation to governmentality as well. As soon as individuals start to transform themselves by means of training, competitiveness is extended to an individual dimension.

Summing up, at present the disciplinary effects of the native speaker model appear to be amplified within a neoliberal frame, in which individuals seek to advance themselves and/or their organisations. When training is done with a view to "self-capitalisation" (Rizvi & Lingard, 2010), so that subjects can "pass as a native" or "sound native," its impact on speakers' linguistic conduct and on their self-perception intensifies (see Martín Rojo, 2016b). It is precisely in this context that the concept of governmentality can be valuable, because it refers to a kind of "power which has the population as its target, political economy as its major form of knowledge" (Foucault, 2009, pp. 107–108). In this case, additionally, we see the maintenance of a disciplinary power that requires individuals to obtain training in accordance with a model of speakerness.

The following section examines the effects of this neoliberal rationality on individuals, and on how they understand themselves. As Margaret Thatcher (1981) clearly formulates in the quotation that opened this chapter, "Economics are the method. The object is to change the soul." Thus, the question is how subjects understand themselves within the frame of a neoliberal rationality that compels them to maximize their results by exposure to risks and taking full, personal responsibility for possible failures.

New Subjectivities

A first mode of objectification of the speaking subject can be detected in the discourses discussed in previous sections, one in which the competent speaker of profitable languages in a flexible market is equated to an entrepreneurial project in human resources and managerial literature, and in language industries. And as Dardot and Laval highlight, the major novelty of neoliberalism in relation to other economic orders consists "in triggering a *chain reaction* by producing *enterprising subjects* who in turn will reproduce, expand and reinforce competitive relations between themselves" (Dardot & Laval, 2014, p. 290). There is still much ground to cover in this new line of research if we are to understand what happens when humans are driven to examine themselves by evoking and internalising discourses like the ones studied in this chapter. If subjects have internalised legitimated and dominant discourses on language profit and self-capitalisation, they will use the categories of these discourses in understanding themselves (see Frost & McNamara, Chapter 14 in this volume). In fact, in defining themselves, people most frequently do so in terms of linguistic categories: bilingual, multilingual, native, competent, as well as by levels of achievement set by standardised tests, such as "I have a B2."

For example, in Madrid schools, students who follow the bilingual track are known as "the bilinguals," in contrast to others pupils, and as an element of distinction. This categorisation, rooted in the flexibilisation of linguistic and economic markets, has diminished Spanish-speaking pupils who do not follow an English track, as if they are less competent students and speakers, or "losers" who have not attained the basic goals required of them. Similarly, newcomers are located at an even lower level, as not even being fully competent in Spanish. Their multilingualism is judged differently from that of the bilinguals in that often it is not acknowledged or even recognised.

Thus we must inquire what happens when individuals internalise normalising discourses that construct them as incompetent and illegitimate speakers, or as "losers" who have not attained the required milestones. Do these speakers lower their social and educational expectations, or even exclude themselves completely from significant social areas of human activity? Could the internalisation of this ideology compel non-native speakers to train themselves indefinitely in order to adhere to the stipulated model of a native speaker? Or would this lead to self-censorship, or to placing their own linguistic practices in an evaluative and derogatory frame? How can the delusion be managed when even after mastering languages and acquiring the right accent, young people cannot find employment, or are not selected when they compete for a job, because of racial, ethnic, social, or gender inequality?

In a study conducted with María Cioé Peña and Emilee Moore at City College, part of the City University of New York system, located in Harlem (New York), we interviewed student-teachers in Bilingual Education or Teaching English to Speakers of Other Languages (TESOL) training programmes at the College, and examined the implications of traditional and new discourses about language for student-teachers' subjectivities (Cioé, Moore & Martín Rojo, 2016). All of the interviewees share diasporic trajectories, live transnational lives, and speak other languages in addition to English. Nevertheless, the *native and non-native dichotomy* emerges not only as salient in participants' self-perceptions of linguistic competence, but also in feelings of (un)preparedness for full participation in the teaching profession.

This example displays a "dividing practice" in which the competent/native/quasi-native who sounds local is pitted against a non-competent/non-native speaker who sounds foreign. The subject is either divided within herself or divided from others. Such a process will inevitably produce new understandings of speaking subjects. As with gender distinctions, binary thinking (monolingual vs. bilingual; native vs. non-native) is not only a fundamental obstacle to speakers' equity, but also a powerful mechanism in producing divided subjectivities—men/women, masculinity/femininity, or native/non-native, monolingual/bilingual. These distinctions also show that binaries involve a hierarchy, so that among language learners and teachers, nativeness is still placed at the dominant centre of rationality, while emerging bilinguals, non-profitable monolinguals, and non-profitable bilinguals are placed at the margins and positioned as the absent or wholly subordinate *other* (see Derrida, 1982, for a general reflection on the effects of binaries). However, and again similar to the case of gender, our research reveals a multiplicity of forms of being a speaker ("speakerness"), which challenges these language binaries and should provoke further research on the multiplicity and fluidity of speakerness.

We have proposed alternative categories, such as *legitimate speaker, resourceful speaker*, or *bi/plurilingual*, which may act in juxtaposition to that of *native*, or offer emancipatory ways forward. Following this argumentation, the proposal of the concept of *new speakers* calls for a disciplinary reorientation (see O'Rourke, Soler, & Darquennes, Chapter 30 in this volume). This is because *new speakerness* focuses on the experiences that an (ever)-increasing number of individuals go through as they traverse unique social and linguistic paths, joined by their common struggles for belonging. These experiences cannot be captured by traditional binarisms (native/non-native) (see also O'Rourke & Pujolar, 2015). To this end, an epistemological shift is needed that focuses on speakers and how they navigate across transnational contexts within superdiverse urban centres. The issue thus is that of unravelling the transforming, diverse, and complex nature of speakerness with a view to shedding new light on how individuals deploy their linguistic resources in relating to other people, while they operate in a highly complex, dynamic, and fluctuating social reality.

In claiming that social norms are internalized, we have not yet explained what internalization is, what it means for a norm to become internalized, or what happens to the norm in the process of internalization (Butler, 1997). Linguistic self-reflexivity, censorship, and shame (and pride) will be part of this process. There is still much research to be done in order to understand neoliberal or entrepreneurial subjectivities, and particularly, to understand why and how some individuals resist and do not internalise these discourses. In this line, Canagarajah's recent publication (2017) shows how African migrant professionals, by making use of the resources and networks of neoliberalism, enhance their skills and knowledge, and interact with each other to develop solidarity, and alternate social, ideological, and economic agendas.

IMPLICATIONS FOR LANGUAGE POLICIES

This chapter has shown how in recent decades, neoliberalism has turned out to be much more than an ideology, becoming a set of practices that affect not only the economy but society as a whole. One of the mechanisms that brought about this colonisation of other spheres of our lives is the dynamics that have turned market-governing processes into modes of social organisation and of self-constitution. The production of a neoliberal episteme that is built through such discourses as those of language as profit and self-training/capitalisation, is the cornerstone in the expansion of a neoliberal logic. This chapter has illustrated how these two discourses control entire communities and achieve securitisation within a global neoliberal order in two ways: on the one hand, individuals seek to obtain profit for themselves and/or their organisations by learning languages and by speaking them with a native accent; on the other, language training appears to be central to the process of governmentality. In this final section, I discuss the impact these processes are having on language policies, highlighting at least four major implications.

First, some deregulation and flexibilisation policies have been detected in the implementation of bilingual programmes in schools in some geopolitical areas. State language policies that establish and reinforce the national language have been removed or reduced, as a result of governments' commitment to neoliberal policies that directly interfere to construct a *free market* (Harvey, 2005, pp. 64–70). National languages are forced to compete with other languages in a globalised and flexible linguistic market. Thus, the laws of competence and of supply and demand seem to be replacing the policies of state language planning. Training takes place not only on a national scale, but also internationally, and not only on an institutional level, but also individually. Yet both private and public initiatives are ruled similarly by the emerging competitiveness among schools, languages, and language learners, as well as neoliberal or entrepreneurial speakers.

Second, introducing market forces of supply and demand into areas run by the state, in this case, language education in particular, and language policies in general, entails a process of marketization, by encouraging competition between schools and also among individuals. By celebrating multilingualism, language policies in a neoliberal context present the mere possession of selected languages and mastery of the right accent as a guarantee of individuals' success and ultimate satisfaction. Marketing is thus pervasive in language policy discourses: language education programmes, and the discourses of the language industries in general, are promoted by means of an incessant, ubiquitous incitement to enjoy. Emphasising fun and social advancement makes such marketing all the more effective. Thus, while a discourse celebrating multilingualism is put into circulation, it actually masks a simplification of current patterns of social mobility through language proficiency and training.

Third, the preceding analysis demonstrates that language policies are de facto reducing language diversity in the global economy. In particular, neoliberal discourses reduce multilingualism to the mastery of an international language, namely English, and to a lesser extent mastery of other, trade-related languages. In the same way, while such languages are presented as international, the most valued capital lies in being able to speak those languages with an accent that sounds local or even native. Languages are presented as commodities, thus also as capital that will improve individuals' competitiveness and productivity, but they do not necessarily offer a clear advantage to those who possess them, given that they are treated as a product of labour, whose benefits are primarily for employers (see Pujolar, Chapter 24 in this volume; also Holborow, 2015).

Finally, these language policies, which are shaped by the principles of flexibilisation and competence, are contributing to spreading neoliberal principles that seem to have been internalised by local populations. These discourses are produced at different levels, not just in government, and they are often reproduced by subjects who do not resist them. They represent the illusion that speaking certain languages assures success and personal satisfaction, while failing to achieve these linguistic goals means personal failure. As a result, the lack of access to these kinds of capital, which is suffered by many individuals, is concealed.

Language policies are in this regard playing a significant role within a neoliberal mode of governance. New entrepreneurial subjects are bi/multilingual. Nevertheless, they are restrained subjects who self-discipline in order to learn; they are divided by earlier, outdated linguistic categories that, far from disappearing, are now resignified and reinforced. In this context, the field of language policy needs to study the principles, nuances, and implications of the discourses that are shaping language policies at national and international levels, and to produce alternative discourses and policies, bearing in mind new forms of multilingualism and new speakers' subjectivities.

ACKNOWLEDGEMENTS

This chapter was made possible thanks to a visiting professors programme at the Advanced Research Center (CUNY), and has highly benefited from the discussion at the excellent seminar, Foucault 13/13, a year-long series hosted by the Columbia Center for Contemporary Critical Thought at Columbia Law School. I also thank Ofelia García, Emilee Moore, Joan Pujolar, Alfonso Del Percio, David Block, and Christine Anthonissen for their excellent comments and suggestions. I also thank the editors of this volume for their helpful and illuminating reviews.

Note

1. Foucault introduced this concept in his public lectures at the College de France, from 1971 until his death in 1984. See particularly Foucault (2000, 2008, 2009) and Foucault & Burchell (2011).

References

Aubrey, B. (1994). Le travail après la crise. *Ce que chacun doit savoir pour gagner sa vie au XXIe siècle.* Paris: InterÉditions.

Block, D. (2013). *Social class in applied linguistics.* New York: Routledge.

Block, D., Gray, J., & Holborow, M. (2013). *Neoliberalism and applied linguistics.* New York; London: Routledge.

Blommaert, J. (2010). *The sociolinguistics of globalization.* Cambridge: Cambridge University Press.

Blommaert, J. (2016). Superdiversity and the neoliberal conspiracy. *Ctrl+Alt+Dem.* Retrieved from https://alternative-democracy-research.org/2016/03/03/superdiversity-and-the-neoliberal-conspiracy/

Boas, Taylor C., & Gans-Morse, J. (2009). Neoliberalism: From new liberal philosophy to anti-liberal slogan. *Studies in Comparative International Development* 44(2), 137–161.

Bourdieu, P. (1997). *Méditations pascaliennes.* Paris: Le Seuil.

Bourdieu P. (1986). The forms of capital. In J. G. Richardson (Ed.), *Handbook of theory and research for the sociology of education* (pp. 241–258). New York: Greenwood.

Boutet, J. (2012). Language workers. In M. Dûchene, A. & M. Heller (Eds.), *Language in late capitalism: Pride and profit* (pp. 207–234). London; New York: Routledge.

Butler, J. (1997). *The psychic life of power: Theories in subjection.* Stanford, CA: Stanford University Press.

Canagarajah, S. (2013). Negotiating translingual literacy: An enactment. *Research in the Teaching of English* 2013, 40–67.

Canagarajah, S. (2017). *Translingual practices and neoliberal policies.* Berlin: Springer International.

Cioè Peña, M., Moore, E., & Martín Rojo, L. (2016). The burden of "nativeness": Four plurilingual student-teachers' stories. *Bellaterra Journal* of *Teaching* and *Learning Languages* and *Literature* 9(2), 32–52.

Creese, A., & Blackledge, A. (2010). Translanguaging in the bilingual classroom: A pedagogy for learning and teaching? *Modern Language Journal* 94, 103–115.

Dardot, P., & Laval, C. (2014). *The new way of the world: On neoliberal society.* London; Brooklyn: Verso Books.

Del Percio, A. (2016). The governmentality of migration: Intercultural communication and the politics of (dis)placement in Southern Europe. *Language and Communication* 51, 87–98.

Derrida, J. (1982). *Margins of philosophy.* A. Bass, Trans. Chicago: University of Chicago Press.

Duchêne, A. (2011). Néolibéralisme, inégalités sociales et plurilinguismes: L'exploitation des ressources langagières et des locuteurs. *Langage & Société* 136, 81–106.

Duchêne, A., & Heller, M. (Eds.) (2012). *Language in late capitalism: Pride and profit.* New York: Routledge.

Duchêne, A., & Humbert, Ph. N. (2018). Suvey-ing languages: The art of governing speakers by numbers. In A. Duchêne & Ph. N. Humbert (Eds.), *Survey-ing Speakers and the Politics of Census*. Special Issue in *International Journal of the Sociology of Language* 252.

Errington, J. (2001). Colonial linguistics. *Annual Review of Anthropology* 30, 19–39.

Fabian, J. (1986). *Language and colonial power. The appropriation of Swahili in the former Belgian Congo (1880–1938)*. Berkeley: University of California Press.

Fernández-González, N. (2016). Repensando las políticas de privatización en educación: el cercamiento de la escuela. *Archivos Analíticos de Políticas Educativas* 24(113). Retrieved from http://dx.doi.org/10.14507/epaa.24.2509

Flores, N. (2013). The unexamined relationship between neoliberalism and plurilingualism: A cautionary tale. *TESOL Quarterly* 47(3), 500–520.

Flubacher, M., & Del Percio, A. (Eds.) (2017). *Language, education and neoliberalism: Critical sociolinguistic studies*. Bristol, UK: Multilingual Matters.

Foucault, M. (1980). *Power/knowledge: Selected interviews and other writings, 1972--1977*. New York: Pantheon.

Foucault, M. (1995 [1977]). *Discipline and punish: The birth of the prison*. A. Sheridan, Trans. New York: Vintage Books.

Foucault, M. (2000). Governmentality. In J. D. Faubion (Ed.), *Essential works of Foucault*, Vol. 3: *Power* (pp. 201–222). New York: Norton.

Foucault, M. (2001). Les techniques de soi. In M. Foucault, *Dits et écrits II, 1976–1988*. Paris: Gallimard.

Foucault, M. (2008). *The birth of biopolitics: Lectures at the Collège de France, 1978–1979*. New York: Springer.

Foucault, M. (2009). *Security, territory, population: Lectures at the Collège de France 1977–1978*. New York: Picado.

Foucault, M., & Burchell, G. (2011). *The government of self and others: Lectures at the College de France, 1982–1983* (Vol. 7). New York: Macmillan.

Fraser, N. (2003). From discipline to flexibilisation? Rereading Foucault in the shadow of globalisation. *Constellations* 10(2), 160–171.

Gal, S. (1989). Language and political economy. *Annual Review of Anthropology* 18, 345–367.

Gramsci, A. (2000). *Cartas de la cárcel: 1926–1937*. México: Ediciones Era.

Harvey, D. (2005). *Neoliberalism: A brief history*. Oxford: Oxford University Press.

Harvey, D. (2014). *Seventeen contradictions and the end of capitalism*. Oxford: Oxford University Press.

Heller, M. (Ed.). (2007). *Bilingualism: A social approach*. Berlin: Springer.

Hidalgo, E. (2018). *The transition from primary to secondary bilingual education: Selection, access and hierarchisation of programmes*. Phd Dissertation, Universidad Autónoma de Madrid.

Holborow, M. (2015). *Language and neoliberalism*. London; New York: Routledge.

Jaspers, J., & Malai Madsen, L. (Eds.). (2016). Sociolinguistics in a languagised world. *Applied Linguistics Review* 7(3), 235–258

Lemke, T. (2001). The birth of bio-politics: Michael Foucault's lectures at the College de France on neo-liberal governmentality. *Economy and Society* 30(2), 190–207.

Márquez-Reiter, R., & Martín Rojo, L. (2014). *A sociolinguistics of diaspora: Latino practices, identities, and ideologies* (Vol. 6). New York/London: Routledge.

Martín Rojo, L. (2010). *Constructing inequality in multilingual classrooms*. Berlin: De Gruyter Mouton.

Martín Rojo, L. (Ed.). (2016a). *Occupy: The spatial dynamics of discourse in global protest movements*. Amsterdam: John Benjamins.

Martín Rojo, L. (2016b). Language and power. In O. Garcia, M. Spotti, & N. Flores (Eds.), *The Oxford handbook of language and society* (pp. 77–102). Oxford: Oxford University Press.

Martín Rojo, L., Anthonissen, C., García-Sánchez, I., & Unamuno, V. (2017). Recasting diversity in language education in postcolonial, late-capitalist societies. In A. De Fina, D. Ikizoglu, & J. Wegner (Eds.), *Diversity and super-diversity: Sociocultural linguistic perspectives* (pp. 171–190). Washington, DC: Georgetown University Press.

Martín Rojo, L., Relaño-Pastor, A. M. R., & Rasskin Gutman, I. (2010). Who is a "legitimate participant" in multilingual classrooms? Essentialising and naturalising culture. In L. Martín Rojo (Ed.), *Constructing inequality in multilingual classrooms* (pp. 261–304). Berlin: De Gruyter Mouton.

McIlvenny, P., Klausen, J. Z., & Lindegaard, L. B. (2016). New perspectives on discourse and governmentality. In P. McIlvenny, J. Z. Klausen, & L. B. Lindegaard (Eds.), *Studies of discourse and governmentality* (pp. 1–70). Amsterdam: John Benjamins.

Moreno Cabrera, J. C. (2015). *Los dominios del español: Guía del imperialismo lingüístico panhispánico*. Madrid: Síntesis.

O'Rourke, B., & Pujolar, J. (2015). New speakers and processes of new speakerness across time and space. *Applied Linguistics Review* 6, 145–150.

Pennycook, A. (2007). *Global Englishes and transcultural flows*. London; New York: Routledge.

Pérez-Milans, M. (2015a). Language education policy in late modernity: (Socio) linguistic ethnographies in the European Union. *Language Policy* 14(2), 99–107.

Pérez-Milans, M. (2015b). Mandarin Chinese in London education: Language aspirations in a working-class secondary school. *Language Policy* 14(2), 153–181.

Piketty, T. (2014). *Capital in the twenty-first century*. Cambridge, MA: Harvard University Press.

Piller, I., & Cho, J. (2013). Neoliberalism as language policy. *Language in Society* 42(1), 23–44.

Pujolar, J., & O'Rourke, B. (2016). New speakers, non-native speakers: Towards a post-national linguistics. Draft paper retrieved from https://www.academia.edu/30325038/Theorizing_the_speaker_and_speakerness_lessons_learned_from_research_on_new_speakers

Rampton, B. (1995). *Crossing: Language and ethnicity among adolescents*. London; New York: Longman.

Rampton, B. (2014). Gumperz and governmentality in the 21st century: Interaction, power and subjectivity. *Tilburg Papers in Culture Studies* 117.

Relaño-Pastor, A. M. (2015). The commodification of English in "Madrid, comunidad bilingüe": Insights from the CLIL classroom. *Journal of Language Policy* 14(2), 131–152.

Ricento, T. (2012). Political economy and English as a "global" language. *Critical Multilingualism Studies* 1(1), 31–56.

Rizvi, F., & Lingard, B. (2010). *Globalizing education policy*. London; New York: Routledge.

Sklar, H. (1980). Trilateralism: Managing dependence and democracy—An overview. In H. Sklar (Ed.), *Trilateralism: The Trilateral Commission and elite planning for world management* (pp. 1–55). Montréal: Black Rose Books.

Standing, G. (2011). *The precariat: The new dangerous class*. London: Bloomsbury.

Thatcher, M. (1981). Interview for Sunday Times. *Sunday Times* May 3, 1981. Retrieved from http://www.margaretthatcher.org/document/104475

Urciuoli, B. (2008). Skills and selves in the new workplace. *American Ethnologist* 35(2), 211–228.

Urciuoli, B. (2010). Neoliberal education: Preparing the student for the new workplace. In C. J. Greenhouse (Ed.), *Ethnographies of neoliberalism* (pp. 16–176). Philadelphia: University of Pennsylvania Press.

Urla, J. (2012). *Reclaiming Basque: Language, nation, and cultural activism.* Reno: University of Nevada Press.

Woolard, K. (2008). Language and identity choice in Catalonia: The interplay of contrasting ideologies of linguistic authority. In K. Süselbeck, U. Mühlschlegel, & P. Masson (Eds.), *Lengua, nación e identidad: La regulación del plurilingüismo en España y América Latina* (Vol. 122). Madrid; Frankfurt: Iberoamericana Editorial; Vervuert.

CHAPTER 28

....

INEQUALITY AND CLASS IN LANGUAGE POLICY AND PLANNING

....

DAVID BLOCK

As a field of enquiry, language policy and planning (LPP) has always drawn on research and scholarship in education as well as the social sciences in general (in particular sociology). Social theory has also figured as an important source of ideas and concepts, and critical LPP has arisen as a distinct strand of thought and research since the 1980s (Tollefson, 1991). More recently, critical LPP researchers have begun to turn to political economy as a source discipline, and neoliberalism has come to be a baseline concept for understanding LPP-related phenomena and practices in a range of contexts (Ricento, 2015a). Nevertheless, very often (though not always), the political economy angle in publications is not very well developed and neoliberalism, as a key construct, remains ill-defined and undertheorised. Most important, the rise of economic inequality and new forms of class struggle that have accompanied neoliberal policies and practices are effectively erased from analysis, or they are dealt with only in a cursory manner.

In this chapter, my aim is to elaborate on what political economy, neoliberalism, and in particular economic inequality and class might mean for LPP researchers. I begin with a brief exploration of my understanding of some of the key elements in LPP today, before discussing political economy, as a multidisciplinary field of enquiry; neoliberalism, as a key political economic construct for understanding the current form of capitalism dominant in the world today; and finally, economic inequality and class as key constructs for understanding the effects of neoliberalism on contemporary societies. This theoretical background is followed by a section in which I briefly examine how inequality and class have emerged as constructs in recent LPP research. I close with considerations about further research.

An Understanding of Language Policy and Planning

Einar Haugen's (1959) foundational work on the efforts of Norwegian language specialists to situate and establish Norwegian as a language independent of its neighbours, Danish and Swedish, is often cited as a possible beginning of LPP (Lo Bianco, 2010). In early discussions taking place once LPP had begun to be recognised as a field of enquiry, the two constituent terms, *language planning* and *language policy*, came to be distinguished. Language planning was said to occur when "changes in the systems of language code or speaking or both are planned by organizations that are established for such purposes or given a mandate to fulfil such purposes" (Rubin & Jernudd, 1971, p. xvi). Meanwhile, policy was seen as the implementation of planning by those in positions of power.

Such definitions have been carried forward, although they have been nuanced and embellished considerably as a less technical and more holistic, ecological perspective on LPP has taken hold. This line of thought can be seen clearly in general discussions of the field that have appeared in recent years, both in articles in journals such as *Language Policy* and *Current Issues in Language Planning*, as well as numerous edited volumes and monographs (e.g., Erling & Seargeant, 2013; Ferguson, 2006; Johnson, 2013; Ricento, 2006, 2015a; Shohamy, 2006; Spolsky, 2004, 2009, 2012a; Tollefson, 2013a; Wright, 2016). Indeed, these publications show that there is now a general consensus around the notion that LPP cannot be conceived of and analysed as if it existed in an asocial vacuum. LPP is a real-world phenomenon embedded deeply in societies, and attempts to understand it draw on a range of disciplines, including policy studies—specifically, education policy—as well as anthropology, political science, sociology, geography, and political economy, especially in the analysis of social class.

Spolsky (2012b) writes in a way consistent with this consensus, presenting his oft-cited three-component model, according to which LPP emerges at the confluence of language practices, language ideologies, and management practices. Many researchers sharing this perspective have focussed on a broad range of LPP phenomena, such as language description and codification; language standardisation, prescription, and proscription (what languages are to be used—and not used—and how they are to be used, by whom, where, and when); societal bi/multilingualism; language rights; and language pedagogy and learning (what languages are to be taught/learned, by whom, where, why, and when). Understood in this way, LPP has been researched extensively, often, as I noted earlier, from a politically engaged, critical perspective. In this sense, researchers working in this way "recognize the planning-policy-making process and the field of LPP itself as ideological and discursive, reflecting and (re)producing class, race, language and power" (McCarty, 2013, p. 40).

This critical approach can be traced back to the early work in the field by Tollefson (1991), who to some extent situated LPP in terms of class struggle, that is, as part of ongoing conflicts between the capitalist class/elites and the popular classes around control over the means of production, political power, and access to economic, social, and cultural resources. However, more recently, Tollefson (2013b) suggests that the critical approach has evolved and now examines how LPP is embedded not only in phenomena that are clearly political economic in nature (e.g., economic inequality, government policies impacting the interests and life chances of the working class and poor), but also in phenomena that might be seen as more broadly societal in nature. As Tollefson notes, these issues include the environment, ethno-national conflicts, global (in)security and violence, and the rise of religious fundamentalism and neo-fascism (which are inevitably accompanied by hostility to "outsiders").

In order to examine phenomena of this kind, we need to bring an explicit political economy orientation more firmly into LPP, which requires a more thorough understanding of the current state of capitalism (neoliberalism) as well as inequality and class. In the next three sections, I attempt to provide some clarification of what political economy, neoliberalism, inequality, and social class might mean in LPP research.

POLITICAL ECONOMY

Political economy may be understood as "the study of *the social relations, particularly the power relations, that mutually constitute the production, distribution, and consumption of resources*" (Mosco, 2009, p. 24; italics in the original). It is an area of enquiry with roots in scholarship focussing on the foundations of liberal economic theory (Mill, 2004 [1848]; Ricardo, 2004 [1817]; Smith, 2012 [1776])), as well as the critique of those foundations provided by Marx (1990 [1867]). Political economists analyse the relationship between the individual and society and between the market and the state, as they seek to understand how social institutions and social action intersect with capitalism (or indeed, any economic system). Any move to adopt political economy as a frame for research and discussion in LPP is consistent with the way in which LPP has always looked to the social sciences in general, and policy studies (as a subfield of sociology) in particular, as source disciplines.

As I argue elsewhere with regard to applied linguistics in general (Block, 2017a, 2018a), there is space for what we could call a "political economy turn" in LPP, which would mean applying themes arising in political economy literature to the study of Spolsky's language practices, language ideology, and language management. Such an approach means a substantial and sustained engagement with the foundational work of Smith, Ricardo, Mill, Marx, and others. It also means exploring recent work on issues such as the causes of the economic crisis (Harvey, 2010), austerity (Blyth, 2013), the rise of the neoliberal subject (Brown, 2005), increased inequality (Pikkety, 2014), and new forms of class division (Duménil & Levy, 2011; Harvey, 2014; Sayer, 2015). Finally, rather than merely mentioning in passing the term *political economy*, it means a more in-depth engagement with this dynamic field of enquiry.

The recent renewed interest in political economy in the social sciences and humanities has run parallel to the rise of neoliberalism as the globally dominant political economic ideology and the growing awareness of its effects, above all increasing inequality and the crisis that began in 2008 (Block, 2014). In effect, over the past decade we have seen in the media (television, newspapers, online publications) an endless succession of bad news about debt, bailouts, home repossessions, corrupt politicians and bankers, and the ubiquitous "markets." Thus, if in the 1990s a kind of celebratory globalisation predominated in many social, political, professional, and media circles (e.g., Ohmae, 1990), from the early part of this century onwards, more sobering realities have taken centre stage, particularly in those countries in the most economically developed parts of the planet. In the midst of such developments, there is a need to shift away from culture-dominant ways of understanding events to a more political economic view (Block, 2012). The execution of this shift requires, at a minimum, a clear and coherent understanding of key constructs such as neoliberalism.

NEOLIBERALISM

Neoliberalism may be understood as the generally accepted label for the latest incarnation of capitalism, in more intensively and extensively globalised and technologically advanced circumstances. In detailed discussions of the origins and rise to dominance of neoliberalism, scholars such as Mirowski (2013) and Stedman-Jones (2012) present it as a variety of economic liberalism that draws its inspiration from a distinctly interested reading of Adam Smith (2012 [1776]), along with the work of key figures such as Hayek (1944) and Friedman (1951). What Mirowski (2013) calls the "neoliberal thought collective" was forged as an international movement through an amalgam of schools of thought in Austria, France, Germany, Britain, and finally, the United States, where it came to be known as the "Chicago school." This recent American version famously came to the fore in the mid-1970s, when the Agosto Pinochet dictatorship in Chile became its first extensive testing ground. However, more famous examples of the ascendance of neoliberal policies and practices came in the 1980s after Margaret Thatcher and Ronald Reagan won elections in the United Kingdom and the United States in 1979 and 1980, respectively. During the 1980s, an increasing number of governments in countries around the world began to adopt neoliberalism as a working doctrine, if not dogma.[1]

In just two decades, the statement attributed to Milton Friedman in 1965—"we are all Keynesians now"—had become "there is no alternative [to neoliberalism]" (Reich, 2011, pp. 44–45; also see Ricento, Chapter 11 in this volume). Indeed, one could argue that a primary cause of the profound economic crisis in Europe at present (at the time of writing, far from over after nearly a decade of intervention by the European Central Bank and the International Monetary Fund) is the overly rapid shift away from the Keynesian/Social Democratic consensus, which dominated the continent for decades, to a full embrace of neoliberalism from the 1980s onward (Stedman-Jones, 2012).

In practice, neoliberalism entails a number of interrelated phenomena, activities, and behaviours, which have profoundly altered the lives of people around the world. First, neoliberalism means not less government, as is sometimes assumed, but more government, as the active involvement of state apparatuses (Althusser, 2008 [1971]) is necessary in the adoption and implementation of measures aimed at reducing, or even eliminating completely, government finance for most public services, such as education, medical care, transportation, and housing. It also means the partial or total privatisation of many of these public services: during the 1980s and 1990s, most European utility companies (water, gas, electricity), formerly state owned and operated, were either fully or partially privatised. Another practice associated with neoliberalism is the establishment and/or maintenance of regressive income tax reforms that disproportionately penalise working-class and middle-class incomes while allowing higher incomes a number of breaks and loopholes. Such tax policies are part and parcel of the abandonment of social democracy/Keynesianism and the notion that the state can and should act as an arbiter, redistributing wealth where necessary.

Neoliberalism is also associated with the partial and/or total deregulation of the financial markets, leading to capitalism without borders, in which financial institutions are under no legal or moral obligation to cater to the needs of societies; rather, it is only the market and profit that shape activity. This particular aspect of neoliberalism has become the main focus of government and media attention since the current economic crisis began in 2007–2008. Running parallel to this financial deregulation has been territorial deregulation, as a key element in twenty-first-century global production chains (Thun, 2014). Offshore outsourcing has become the most common means through which corporations reduce costs, by moving most or all of their production processes to parts of the world where labour costs are lower, there is less state protection of workers' rights, and environmental regulation is lax (if it exists at all in an effective and actionable form). The effect of such developments has been a global realignment of job markets both within and across nation-state borders. Thus, in the wealthier nations of the world today, the service sector has become dominant, while industrial production has, to a great extent, shifted to those countries where production costs are relatively lower.

In addition, neoliberalism has meant the adoption of the market metaphor as the dominant way to frame all manner of day-to-day activity. The notion of the market has been around for some time in political economy. Whereas for Smith, it was the generally self-regulating site where "by treaty, by barter, and by purchase . . . we obtain from one another the greater part of those mutual good offices which we stand in need of" (Smith, 2012 [1776], pp. 19–20), for Karl Marx (1990 [1867]), it was the site or social space (indeed, an uneven playing field) which compelled individuals (the proletariat) to enter into the processes of buying and selling commodities to satisfy their basic needs and wants. Those who support the market metaphor in discussions of the economy tend to adopt an oversimplification of Smith's version, along with the assumption that the markets are fair and open spaces of activity, in which participants are equal and free to act (and indeed to prosper).

One important effect of the adoption of the market metaphor in this way has been that domains of social activity that had previously been organised according to the need to build communities and institutions have come to be framed in terms of economic exchange. Moreover, in these processes, the individuals and collectives participating in the practices constituting social activity are positioned in terms of their roles as service providers and consumers. For example, the marketisation of education means the ways in which it is planned, delivered, and evaluated come to resemble (or, in effect, are the same as) those which apply in the private sector (see also Codó, Chapter 23 and Relaño-Pastor, Chapter 25 in this volume). Competition and the drive towards ever-greater efficiency replace the basic notions of functionality and public service provision for all (Lipton, 2011).

Finally, as a consequence of the previous phenomena, neoliberalism has had a profound impact on how individual and collective subjectivities are both publically constructed and privately lived. Important here is Becker's notion of human capital, which he developed over fifty years ago (see Becker, 1964). The basis of human capital is "the assumption that individuals decide on their education, training, medical care, and other additions to knowledge and health by weighing the benefits and costs. Benefits include cultural and other non-monetary gains along with improvement in earnings and occupations, while costs usually depend mainly on the foregone value of the time spent on these investments" (Becker, 1992, p. 43). This new way of framing human subjectivity was integral to a more general shift in the direction of what Foucault (2008) sees as neoliberal governance (see also Martín Rojo, Chapter 27 in this volume). As Foucault argued, the new idealised subject, the *homo economicus*, signalled broader changes in society. There was, as he notes, a shift in focus, from humans as social beings to humans as individuals, and the consequent shift from valuing collective activity to valuing individual activity.

All of this was part of the decidedly pessimistic view which persists to this day: that human beings only look after their own immediate and long-term self-interest, showing no concern for the collective good. The scholars who contributed to the construction of neoliberalism over decades believed that the collective good would take care of itself if human beings were allowed to pursue their individual interests untethered. Unfortunately, we now have ample proof that this optimistic assumption is misplaced, even if the ideology and its application persist.

INEQUALITY AND SOCIAL CLASS

As a direct result of the policies and practices of neoliberalism and the associated phenomena outlined in the preceding, inequality has increased dramatically in countries around the world, and the notion of class struggle has returned as a frame through which events unfolding before our eyes may be understood (Piketty, 2014). As both a reality and a construct, inequality has been around for centuries, going as far back as Plato's *Republic* in the fourth century BC, in which he wrote of the two states within every state, "the rich and the poor, at enmity with each other" (Plato, 2007 [380 BC], p. 124).

More recently, Göran Therborn (2006) outlines three general types of inequality. First, there is "vital inequality," which is about basic life-and-death chances and individuals' and collectives' relative exposure to life-threatening natural phenomena, such as disease, famine, flooding, and drought; self-inflicted human conditions, such as violence, alcoholism, and obesity; and larger human-made disasters, such as war, pollution, and the inability to reach and use vital natural resources. Second, there is "existential inequality," which is about systems of oppression that deny individuals and collectives what are understood today to be basic human rights. Social structures such as patriarchy, slavery, caste systems, racism, religious persecution, homophobia, and other forms of social ostracism, or attacks on ways of being, fall into this category. Third, there is "resource inequality," which refers to the variable access of individuals and collective to material and symbolic resources, from property to money to culture; contacts and social networks; and recognised legitimacy and respect (see Bourdieu, 1984, and his capital metaphors).

Since the mid-1970s, when the abandonment of the dominant Keynesian social democratic consensus in Western Europe, North America, and other parts of the world began (see the previous section), there has been a considerable increase in Therborn's *resource inequality*, especially material inequality. This turnaround has come about due to the adoption of economic policies and practices which have generated greater differences between the rich and the poor and the weakening and diminishing of the traditional middle class, not only in economic and material terms (around the ownership of assets, the relative stability of employment and income), but also in terms of the status and legitimacy which accompany it. In addition, inequality has increased even more rapidly in the years since the current economic crisis first began to emerge in 2007–2008 (Piketty, 2014). Among the populations of those countries most affected by the crisis, such as the southern-most states of the European Union, there is a growing realisation that the persistence and growth of resource inequality leads inevitability to a rise in Therborn's vital inequality, the collateral negative effects that come with society-wide impoverishment, such as ill-health (both physical and psychological) and a decrease in the quality of social services and publically available resources.

In the midst of this state of affairs, class remains a key construct in any discussion of capitalism, past or present, despite rumours of its demise. Drawing on scholarship ranging from Marx (1990 [1867]) to Bourdieu (1984), as well as more recent contributions by Atkinson (2015), Savage (2015) and Wright (2015), I understand class to be a multi-levelled phenomenon emergent in variable and ever-evolving constellations of dimensions, as summarised in Table 28.1.

All of these indicators of class, or what Wright (2015) has termed "individual attributes," as well as their intersections with well-established identity dimensions such as race, ethnicity, gender, and nationality, must be accounted for in any serious analysis of class in the lives of individuals and collectives (Block & Corona, 2014).

Central to an understanding of class is its relational nature: it is constituted in and emerges from the "systematic interactions of social actors situated in relation to each other" and is not necessarily best defined in terms of "quantitative names like upper, upper middle, middle, lower middle, and lower, but by qualitative names like capitalists and workers, debtors and creditors" (Wright, 2015, p. 33). In addition, these interactions involving social actors are further situated within larger market relations (in the realm of work) and beyond these market relations "within the relations of domination and exploitation in production" (Wright, 2015, p. 11). Emerging from these relations of domination and exploitation is the additional phenomenon of class struggle, which Wright (2005) defines as "conflicts between the practices of individuals and collectives in pursuit of opposing class interests . . . . [These conflicts/practices] range from the strategies of individual workers within the labour process to reduce their level of toil, to conflicts between highly organized collectives of workers and capitalists over the distribution of rights and powers within production" (pp. 20–21).

Table 28.1 Class as Constellation of Interrelated Dimensions

General Category	Dimensions
Material life conditions	Relations of individuals and collectives to the means of production: The circumstances of the provision of labour power to (and the exploitation of individuals and collectives by) those who own and control the means of production
Economic resources	Property: land and housing
	Property: other material possessions, such as electronic goods, clothing, books, art, etc.
	Income: salary and wages
	Accumulated wealth: savings and investments
Sociocultural resources	Occupation: manual labour, unskilled service jobs, low-level information-based jobs, professional labour, etc.
	Education: level of formal education attained and the corresponding cultural capital acquired
	Technological know-how: familiarity and ability to use evolving technologies
	Social contacts and networking: people regularly associated with as friends and acquaintances in class terms (the extent to which middle-class people tend to socialize with middle-class people, working-class people with working-class people, etc.)
	Societal and community status and prestige: embodied, achieved, and ascribed
Behaviour	Consumption patterns: choice of shops, buying brands or not, ecological/organic consumption, etc.
	Symbolic behaviour: how one moves one's body, the clothes one wears, the way one speaks, how one eats, etc.
	Pastimes: golf, skiing, cockfighting, participation in online fora
Sociopolitical life conditions	Political life: one's relative position in hierarchies of power in society
	Quality of life: in terms of physical and psychological comfort and health
	Type of neighbourhood: a working-class neighbourhood, a middle-class neighbourhood, an area in the process of gentrification, etc.
Spatial conditions	Mobility: physical movement, from highly local to global
	Proximity to other people during a range of day-to-day activities
	Dimensions and size of space occupied: layout of dwelling or place of work, size of bedroom; size of office, etc.
	Type of dwelling: trailer, house (detached/semidetached), flat (studio, small, large), etc.

However we understand class, there is little doubt, as suggested earlier, that it has had an up-and-down existence in the social sciences and humanities and that only recently does it seem to be experiencing something of comeback. In her work over the past two decades, Nancy Fraser (1995, 2008) has lamented what she sees as the marginalisation of class issues in public debate from the 1960s onward in parts of the world such as Western Europe and North America. In this period of time, laypeople and academics on the political left have, to varying degrees, abandoned a concern with issues around the distribution, understood as the structuring and allocation of material resources in an equitable fashion, in favour of a far greater focus on what Charles Taylor (1992) has called "recognition," understood as the acknowledgement of difference and respect for difference without condescension.

As a remedy to this imbalance, Fraser does not propose the abandonment of recognition claims, but she does argue for the need to explore how these recognition claims intersect with material inequalities arising from capitalism—both globally and locally—and vice versa. Dealt with separately or as intersecting claims, recognition and distribution can be treated in two different ways. On the one hand, they can be subjected to "affirmative" action, which provides "remedies aimed at inequitable outcomes of social arrangements without disturbing the underlying framework that generates them" (Fraser, 2008, p. 28). Recognition claims demand that diversity and difference are supported, promoted, and provided legal guarantees in diverse, multi-cultural societies. An example of an affirmative distributive action would be the application of social democratic principles whereby tax money is used to finance the provision of resources and services to citizens. In neither case is anything done to deal with underlying conditions that lead to the lack of acknowledgement of difference and to disrespect (what Taylor, 1992, calls "misrecognition") or the existence of gross economic inequality. Thus, for Fraser, affirmative policies and actions can never address the roots of injustice and inequality in society. For this to happen, "transformative" action, which provides "remedies aimed at correcting inequitable outcomes precisely by restructuring the underlying generative framework" (Fraser 2008, p. 28), is necessary. Transformative recognition means problematising and undermining group differentiations, such as gay versus straight, male versus female, or black versus white. Thus transformative distribution entails a deep restructuring of the political economy of a nation-state, that is, the arrival of socialism (or communism).

How, then, might political economy as a source discipline, neoliberalism as a construct meant to capture the current era, and inequality and class as key phenomena in this era, be applied to LPP? I provide some thoughts in response to this question in the final section of this chapter. First, however, I briefly consider a small sample of LPP research in which I see some attention to neoliberalism as a broad frame and inequality and class as emergent phenomena, even if this attention, in my view, is limited. My aim is not to be exhaustive; rather, I wish to highlight some research strands that I think move in the direction of situating economic inequality and class as central to LPP research.

NEOLIBERALISM, INEQUALITY, AND SOCIAL CLASS IN LANGUAGE POLICY AND PLANNING

There is a fairly abundant literature in LPP that situates neoliberalism as a key frame for enquiry, though most research deals with the topic only in a cursory manner at the theoretical level (the contributions to Ricento, 2015a, being exceptions). Some of this literature deals with the two key issues outlined earlier—namely, inequality and class, with the former being far more in evidence. For example, there is great deal of research in recent years focusing on the so-called "English divide" in East Asian and Southeast Asian contexts, which is carried out against the backdrop of the variegated versions of capitalism in these parts of the world.

The interest in East Asia and the Pacific Rim is no doubt driven by the rapid rise to prominence of the Chinese economy (now accounting for roughly 17% of the world economy). Yet it is worth considering how longer-term economic powerhouses such as Japan, South Korea, Taiwan, Hong Kong, and Singapore, as well as other centres of intense economic activity, such as the Phillipines, Malaysia, and Indonesia, have become key sites of research into how political economy and language practices, ideologies, and management interrelate. In particular, the South Korean context has proven to be fertile ground for explorations of how inequality emerges from neoliberal economic policies and practices, and how it is exacerbated by particular LPP practices. Thus, in research focussing on the role of English in the lives of Koreans living in South Korea and abroad in countries such as Canada, researchers (e.g., Park, 2009; Park & Lo, 2012; Park & Wee, 2012; Piller & Cho, 2013; Shin, 2012, 2014) have documented how the aspirational middle class and the upper classes are able to afford a range of behaviours, from paying for extra tuition in South Korea to moving to an English-speaking country, as they seek to ensure that their children will be highly proficient English speakers.

A central theme of this research is that in a job market which values English as a key skill and communicative resource, individuals must have what is considered a "good" command of English in order to be considered worthy of employment and, indeed, legitimised as successful citizens. From an LPP perspective, this is an example of language ideologies around ideal (neoliberal) citizenship, along with management actions taken in the educational sector and in private corporations (where hiring practices are embedded in and shaped by dominant ideologies) that intersect with language practices in a range of contexts (see Frost & McNamara, Chapter 14 in this volume). Similar trends can be found in other parts of East Asia and the Pacific Rim, as one sees in Kanno (2008) and Kubota (2011, 2015), focussing on Japan; Price (2014), focussing on Taiwan; Lin and Man (2010), focussing on Hong Kong; De Costa (2010) and Wee (2013), focussing on Singapore; Lorente (2012), focussing on the Philippines; and Butler (2013) and Gao (2014), focussing on China. Indeed, LPP based on the notion that the English language is the key to success is a worldwide phenomenon, as witnessed by the contributions to volumes such as Coleman (2011), Erling and Seargeant (2013), Ricento (2015a), Tan and Rubdy (2008), and Tupas (2015). In particular, the introduction of English-medium instruction into mainstream education engenders situations in which it is children and young adults from middle- and upper-class positions in society who have the most frequent and best-quality access to English (see Relaño-Pastor, Chapter 25 in this volume). This situation is also evident in bilingual English-Spanish schools in Madrid (Martín Rojo, 2010; Relaño-Pastor, 2015), bilingual English-Spanish schools in South America (de Mejía, 2005) and English-language instruction in mainstream schools in Mexico (López-Gopar & Sughrua, 2014).

In countries with a post-colonial relationship with English, issues around class and inequality, intermeshed with idealisations of the neoliberal citizen, are important factors in students' relative access to English. In postcolonial contexts, English mediates class divisions, and its introduction as a medium of instruction serves to deepen existing inequalities. Thus, with regard to India, scholars such as Annanmalai (2013), LaDousa (2015), and Ramanathan (2005) have noted how a lack of economic, political, social, and cultural resources leads to class division along linguistic lines, as access to English, and to a good command of English, has a direct impact on citizens' life chances. Moreover, those occupying the lower end of the class spectrum are those who benefit least from the push for English as the medium of instruction. A similar situation is evident in African contexts such as Lesotho, Swaziland, and Tanzania, where local governments pay lip service to the promotion of local languages (se-Sotho in Lesoto; siSwati in Swaziland; Kiswahili in Tanzania) while practices on the ground tell a different story. Thus, as Kamwangamalu (2013) explains with regard to these contexts, "government officials as well as most members of the ruling elite prefer to send their own children to schools where English is the sole medium of instruction" (p. 164), an example of *elite closure* (Myers-Scotton, 1993), whereby local elites "successfully employ official language policies and their own nonformalized language usage patterns to limit access of nonelite groups to political position and socioeconomic advancement" (p. 149).

A WAY FORWARD

Thus far in this chapter, I have discussed big concepts in political economy—neoliberalism, inequality, and class—followed by a brief survey of research that draws on these concepts to understand LPP in context. Most of the research cited, however, does not delve deeply into theories of inequality or class. Indeed, as is the case in applied linguistics in general, most LPP research that is situated as "political economy" includes a cursory and underdeveloped (or superficial) treatment of the field and constructs derived thereof. With regard to inequality, for example, there is tendency to deal with Therborn's (2006) existential inequality in the form of discrimination based on race, ethnicity, gender, language, nationality, and other dimensions of identity, while largely ignoring resource inequality and therefore a political economy perspective. Adopting such a position is to ignore, as Romaine (2015) reminds us, that "[t]he poor remain poor not because they do not speak English but due to deeply entrenched inequalities in the societies in which they live" (p. 253). In addition, this position does not clarify the extent to which researchers believe that the root causes of economic inequality and class struggle can be found in misrecognition and existential discrimination, rather than in the very logic of capitalism. This common position in LPP lets capitalism off the hook and constitutes a default acquiescence to neoliberalism.

In addition, in some LPP research, there is a tendency to use terms such as "middle class" and "working class" with little or no consideration of what they actually mean at a theoretical level. In such cases, the reader is left to wonder if the researcher is working according to a rudimentary model of class, based exclusively in family income or education level, which is a far cry from the multidimensional model outlined in Table 28.1. Similarly, class may be inserted into discussions as yet another identity dimension, alongside race, ethnicity, gender, and nationality. Yet class is primarily a material matter related to the distribution of resources in society and to various dimensions of class emerging from systems of distribution, and not merely a recognition issue that could be resolved if people respected one another.

Ricento (2015b) has recently suggested that "language policy scholars' lack of sophistication in political economy impacts their ability to critically address the effects of neoliberal economic policies on the status and utility of both global languages such as English, and non-global languages that could play an important role in local economic and social development in low-income countries" (p. 27). His edited volume *Language Policy and Political Economy* (Ricento, 2015a) is an attempt to frame and address LPP issues from a political economic perspective, focussing in particular on English as an international language against the backdrop of the relationship between the individual and society and between the market and the state in different contexts around the world. In this volume, contributors engage with a good range of publications emerging from political economy as they try to make sense of LPP issues.

Nevertheless, where inequality figures significantly there is still a tendency to focus far more on existential inequality over resource inequality, and class is only mentioned in passing when mentioned at all. For example, Bale (2015) provides an interesting discussion of global political economy, noting how various processes constituting neoliberalism impact on the regulation of languages in societies and ultimately the life chances of migrants. However, when the discussion might have situated migrants in existing class-based hierarchies and explored how class and resource inequality (and indeed, class struggle) intersect with phenomena such as racism, Bale remains in the realm of recognition, by focusing on language rights: "neoliberalism continues to reproduce nation-state structures that are used in part to regulate the linguistic lives of migrants and other minoritized communities" (2015, p. 93). Despite this limitation, Bale closes with a reminder similar to that found in Romaine (2015), noting how "learning English (or any particular language) is insufficient on its own to lead [to] greater prosperity" (p. 94). He also adds that "if inequitable access to English parallels the inequitable distribution of resources and jobs in society, then popular demands to establish the right to greater access to English have the potential to disrupt and otherwise challenge the system that breeds this sort of inequality" (p. 94). It would be instructive in this case to explore how class, as defined earlier, permeates the relative access to and competence in English in such a context—that is, the material life conditions, economic resources, sociocultural resources, behaviour, sociopolitical life conditions, and spatial conditions of those demanding greater access to English.

Elsewhere, Pérez-Milans (2015) focuses on the instruction of Mandarin in a "working class secondary school" in east London in the run-up to the 2012 Olympic Games. A broad frame for his study is EU policy, which ostensibly aims to promote diversity within Europe (multiculturalism, interculturalism, and multilingualism), and further to this, international cooperation beyond EU borders. From within this broad frame, Pérez-Milans takes EU language education policies to task because they "encompass a mélange of guiding principles, among which [are] economic competitiveness, intercultural dialogue, social cohesion and democratic citizenship" (Pérez-Milans, 2015, p. 154). One key problem here is that while it might be compatible with intercultural dialogue, economic competitiveness is very difficult to reconcile with social cohesion and democratic citizenship, given that it divides people between winners and losers and its promotion is part of the broader neoliberal agenda that has led to the rising vital, existential, and resource inequality discussed earlier.

The site of Pérez-Milans's research is the East London Secondary (ELS) School, founded in 2000 as a Specialist Language College offering French, Spanish, and Mandarin. Key stakeholders in the school are the British Council and the Hanban office (the Chinese equivalent of the British Council), the entities organising the Mandarin provision at the school. In addition, there are Mandarin teachers provided by the Hanban, as well as and local teachers and the students. With regard to the latter, Pérez-Milans writes that the overwhelming majority of students "were categorized as of low socio-economic background, and indeed 63% of them were entitled to free school meals" (p. 160). In this context, the LES School has been seen as a site of upward mobility for these students. In addition, Mandarin constitutes a mark of distinction (Bourdieu 1984), as the vast majority of British secondary school students study French.

Pérez-Milans's research is devoted primarily to the careful documentation of both discursive representations of Mandarin at the ELS school and as a sample of the actual practices taking place in classrooms. Among other things, he finds something of a disconnect between the underlying good intention of lifting students from poor backgrounds out of poverty through the learning of Mandarin and a range of events and practices that work against this ever actually happening. He sums up matters as follows:

> ... the story of ELS allows us to track the institutional tensions brought about by the socioeconomic conditions of late modernity. Institutional neoliberalization (i.e. selective deregulation and internationalization), shifts in the utility of language learning underlying the second language education policies (i.e. institutionalization of global languages with no regional or ethno-national roots in one territory), and the progressive destabilization of traditional relationships between students and teachers (i.e. teachers as powerful representatives of the state) seem to apply to the data analyzed in this article. (Pérez-Milans, 2015, p. 178)

While all of this is of great interest to LPP researchers interested in examining contexts from a multitude of angles on the way towards identifying the lack of alignment between planning and implementation, I would like to have seen the class angle explored in more detail. I say this especially because ELS, as the author notes, is identified as a school with a disproportionally high number of children from working-class and poor backgrounds. However, we do not know anything about the specific class profile of the children who are in the Mandarin programme, which means that we do not know if these children are the ones with the most economic and sociocultural resources, whose behaviour is most aligned with the dominant school culture. Also, it would be interesting to explore in more detail what the attempt to bring about upward mobility through the provision of Mandarin means in broader terms with regard to theories of social reproduction (Bourdieu, 1984). In this sense, the Mandarin programme may be seen as a rather weak attempt to stop and reverse the reproduction of lower-class conditions, via what is, in effect, a cultural palliative "aimed at inequitable outcomes of social arrangements without disturbing the underlying framework that generates them" (Fraser, 2008, p. 28).

Not all language policy contexts are about individuals who are, in effect, on the wrong side of the inequality divide. Van Mensel (2016) presents the interesting case of a couple living in Brussels, one Dutch speaking (Ann) and the other Spanish speaking (Ricardo), who must choose between Dutch-medium education and French-medium education for their young children, and beyond that, living their lives primarily in Dutch or primarily in French. Ann and Ricardo are described by Van Mensel as "highly educated middle-class parents... [who] have... law degree[s] and work as lawyers, for the European Commission and a private company, respectively" (p. 6). They are, therefore, empowered individuals with high levels of economic, social, and cultural capital (Bourdieu, 1984) and can be seen as *middling transmigrants* (Conradson & Latham, 2005), that is, "a type of migrants who are generally middle-class and well educated and who choose to change their place of residence and employment" (Van Mensel, 2016, p. 6). Van Mensel is explicit regarding this point, although the class issue soon disappears as he focuses primarily on how Ann and Ricardo talk about their lives lived among different languages and the ambivalence that they feel about living in Brussels: the city is both welcoming to transnational, cosmopolitan, middling transmigrants like themselves, and rigid and confining, as one must often choose between either Dutch or French as the possible mediators of social activities. As a way forward, Van Mensel suggests greater flexibility with regard to official language policies affecting language choice and use in institutions (e.g., education) and greater flexibility among the general population with regard to day-to-day language practices. Nevertheless, he also acknowledges that the educational system and the general public in Brussels are probably not ready for the kinds of changes that would benefit middling transmigrants like Ann and Ricardo. This, in turn, leads him to question their ability to effect changes in their lives with regard to language practices. Van Mensel then ends the paper with a reference to my work (Block, 2012), where I have called for a political economy turn and a return to social class as a way of understanding being in the world:

> Finally, I would like to argue that we should perhaps be more careful about attributing too much value to individual agency as a potential force vis-à-vis the structural forces. Block (2012) suggests that research in applied linguistics has gone too far in its fascination with notions like *fluidity* or *diversity* (in which the agency of social actors plays a primordial role), thus obscuring the role of historical or economic factors. When we look at the case of Ann and Ricardo, for instance, what provides them with the possibilities to still resist or counter the imposed language regime are precisely their economic resources, and the social and cultural capital that goes with it. Other families with fewer resources may not have the same possibilities and are thus left with even less room to maneuver. Therefore, I think . . . that in order to fully grasp the impact of language policies, a balance between structure and agency is needed in research, as the power of language policy agents is indeed contingent upon societal factors of a structural nature. (Van Mensel, 2016, p. 12)

I could not agree more with this assessment, and beyond the obvious importance of exploring how (social) structure and agency interact, there is a real need to examine the broader issue alluded to by Van Mensel, that is, how the lifestyles and class interests of middling transmigrants intersect with those of local middle-class and elite citizens, whilst standing in stark contrast to those of local working-class and poor citizens.

CONCLUSION

In series of recent publications, I have suggested that inequality and class should be key constructs in research focussing, for example, on language and identity (Block,

2016a), language and education (Block, 2017b), language and migration (Block, 2017c), and discourse in society (Block, 2018b). In this chapter, I have added LPP to this list. My main argument has been twofold: (1) first, that class-based inequality is endemic to capitalism, and that capitalism (and hence, neoliberalism) cannot be understood without an understanding of how class hierarchies and relations are constructed in capitalist societies; and (2) that research on LPP, as the sum of language planning and management practices taking place in societies, must have at its core a careful and in-depth consideration of these political economic phenomena. In this way, critical LPP research may be improved and made more relevant in neoliberal times, focussing not only on recognition issues (where it has traditionally been very strong), but also distribution issues (where it has not been as strong).

Acknowledgements

I would like to thank the editors of this volume, Jim Tollefson and Miguel Pérez-Milans, for their very helpful comments on an earlier version of this chapter.

Note

1. However, neoliberalism is above all a variegated phenomenon, playing itself out in different ways in different contexts, as local historical, political, social, cultural, and geographical characteristics come together to constitute local varieties of capitalism (Brenner, Peck, & Theodore, 2009). As Miguel Pérez-Milans (personal communication) reminds me, the case of China is especially interesting. In this sense, Harvey (2005) discusses "neoliberalism with Chinese characteristics," although it is worth noting Marx's (1990 [1867]) far earlier discussion of the "Asiatic mode of production" in *Capital 1*. More recently, Zhang and Peck (2016) have discussed the particularities of Chinese capitalism, and how "[t]he internal heterogeneity, cultural complexity and sheer size of the Chinese economy have . . . long confounded 'imported' theories, lending credence to what has been an equally long tradition of *sui generis* accounts of this ostensibly peerless model" (p. 54).

References

Althusser, L. (2008 [1971]). *On ideology*. London: Verso.

Annamalai, E. (2013). India's economic restructuring with English: Benefits versus costs. In J. W. Tollefson (Ed.), *Language policies in education: Critical issues* (pp. 191–208). London: Routledge.

Atkinson, W. (2015). *Class*. Cambridge: Polity.

Bale, J. (2015). Language policy and global political economy. In T. Ricento (Ed.), *Language policy and political economy: English in a global context* (pp. 72–96). Oxford: Oxford University Press.

Becker, G. (1964). *Human capital: A theoretical and empirical analysis, with special reference to education*. Chicago: Chicago University Press.

Becker, G. (1992). The economic way of looking at life. Nobel Lecture in Economics, Stockholm, Sweden, December 9, 1992. Retrieved from http://www.nobelprize.org/nobel_prizes/economic-sciences/laureates/1992/becker-lecture.pdf

Block, D. (2012). Economising globalization and identity in applied linguistics in neoliberal times. In D. Block, J. Gray, & M. Holborow (Eds.), *Neoliberalism and applied linguistics* (pp. 56–85). London: Routledge.

Block, D. (2014). *Social class in applied linguistics*. London: Routledge.

Block, D. (2016). Social class in language and identity research. In S. Preece (Ed.), *The Routledge handbook of language and identity* (pp. 241–254). London: Routledge.

Block, D. (2017a). Political economy in applied linguistics research. *Language Teaching* 50(1), 32–64.

Block, D. (2017b). Researching language and social class in education. In K. King & Y.-J. Lai (Eds.), *Encyclopedia of language and education*, Vol. 10: *Research methods* (3rd edition; pp. 159–169). New York: Springer.

Block, D. (2017c). Social class in migration, identity and language research. In S. Canagarajah (Ed.), *Routledge handbook of migration and language* (pp. 133–148). London: Routledge.

Block, D. (2018a). *Political economy and sociolinguistics: Neoliberalism, inequality and social class*. London: Bloomsbury.

Block, D. (2018b). Class and class warfare. In J. Flowerdew & J. Richardson (Eds.), *Routledge handbook of critical discourse analysis* (pp. 145–158). London: Routledge.

Block, D., & Corona, V. (2014). Exploring class-based intersectionality. *Language, Culture and Curriculum* 27(1), 27–42.

Blythe, M. (2013). *Austerity: The history of a dangerous idea*. Oxford: Oxford University Press.

Bourdieu, P. (1984). *Distinction*. London: Routledge.

Brenner, N., Peck, J., & Theodore, N. (2009). Variegated neoliberalization: Geographies, modalities, pathways. *Global Networks* 10(2), 182–222.

Brown, W. (2005). *Edgework: Critical essays on knowledge and politics*. Princeton, NJ: Princeton University Press.

Butler, Y. G. (2013). Parental factors and early English education as a foreign language: A case study in Mainland China. *Asia-Pacific Education, Language Minorities and Migration (ELMM), Network Working Paper Series, University of Pennsylvania* (pp. 5–8).

Coleman, H. (Ed.). (2011). *Dreams and realities: Developing countries and the English language*. London: British Council.

Conradson, D., & Latham, A. (2005). Transnational urbanism: Attending to everyday practices and mobilities. *Journal of Ethnic and Migration Studies* 31(2), 227–233.

De Costa, P. (2010). Language ideologies and standard English language policy in Singapore: Responses of a "designer immigrant" student. *Language Policy* 9, 217–239.

de Mejía, A.-M. (2005). *Bilingual education in South America*. Clevedon, UK: Multilingual Matters.

Duménil, G., & Lévy, D. (2011). *The crisis of neoliberalism*. Cambridge, MA: Harvard University Press.

Erling, E., & Seargeant, P. (Eds.) (2013). *English and development: Policy, Pedagogy and globalization*. Clevedon, UK: Multilingual Matters.

Ferguson, G. (2006). *Language planning in education*. Edinburgh: Edinburg University Press.

Foucault, M. (2008). *The birth of biopolitics: Lectures at the Collège de France 1979-1979*. London: Palgrave Macmillan.

Fraser, N. (1995). Redistribution to recognition? Dilemmas of justice in a "postsocialist" age. *New Left Review*, 212, 68–93.

Fraser, N. (2008). *Adding insult to injury: Nancy Fraser debates her critics?* K. Olsen, Ed. London: Verso.

Friedman, M. (1951). Neo-liberalism and its prospects. *Farmand*, February 17, 1951, 89–93.

Gao, A. (2014). Social-class identity and English learning: Studies of Chinese learners. *Journal of Language, Identity, and Education* 13(2), 92–98.

Harvey, D. (2005). *A brief history of neoliberalism*. Oxford: Oxford University Press.

Harvey, D. (2010). *The enigma of capital*. Oxford: Oxford University Press.

Harvey, D. (2014). *Seventeen contradictions and the end of capitalism*. London: Profile Books.

Haugen, E. (1959). Planning for a standard language in Norway. *Anthropological Linguistics* 1(3), 8–21.

Hayek, F. A. (1944). *The road to serfdom*. Chicago: University of Chicago Press.

Johnson, D. C. (2013). *Language policy*. London: Palgrave Macmillan.

Kamwangamalu, N. M. (2013). Language-in-education policy and planning in Africa's monolingual kingdoms of Lesotho and Swaziland. In J. W. Tollefson (Ed.) *Language policies in education: Critical issues* (2nd edition; pp. 156–171). London: Routledge.

Kanno, Y. (2008). *Language and education in Japan: Unequal access to bilingualism*. London: Palgrave Macmillan.

Kubota, R. (2011). Questioning linguistic instrumentalism: English, neoliberalism, and language tests in Japan. *Linguistics and Education* 22(3), 248–326.

Kubota, R. (2015). Neoliberal paradoxes of language learning: Xenophobia and international communication. *Journal of Multilingual and Multicultural Development* 37(5), 467–480.

LaDousa, C. (2015). *Hindi is our ground, English is our sky: Education, language, and social class in contemporary India*. New York: Berghahn Books.

Lin, A. M. Y., & Man, E. Y. F. (2010). *Bilingual education: Southeast Asian perspectives*. Hong Kong: Hong Kong University Press.

Lipton, P. (2011). *The new political economy of urban education: Neoliberalism, race, and the right to the city*. London: Routledge.

LoBianco, J. (2010). Language policy and planning. In N. Hornberger, & S. McKay (Eds.) *Sociolinguistics and language education* (pp. 143–174). Bristol, UK: Multilingual Matters.

López-Gopar, M., & Sughrua, W. (2014). Social class in English language education in Oaxaca, Mexico. *Journal of Language, Identity & Education* 13(2), 104–110.

Lorente, B. P. (2012). The making of workers of the world: Language and the labor brokerage state. In A. Duchene & M. Heller (Eds.), *Pride and profit: Language in late capitalism* (pp. 183–206). London: Routledge.

Martín Rojo, L. (2010). *Constructing inequality in multilingual classrooms*. Berlin: Mouton de Gruyter.

Marx, K. (1990 [1867]). *Capital 1*. Hardmondsworth, UK: Penguin.

McCarty, T. L. (2013). Language planning and cultural continuance in Native America. In J. W. Tollefson (Ed.), *Language policies in education: Critical issues* (2nd edition; pp. 255–277). London: Routledge.

Mill, J. S. (2004 [1848/1865]). *Principles of political economy*. London: Prometheus Books.

Mirowski, P. (2013). *Never let a serious crisis go to waste: How neoliberalism survived the economic meltdown*. London: Verso.

Mosco, V. (2009). *The political economy of communication*. London: Sage.

Myers-Scotton, C. (1993). Elite closure as a powerful language strategy: The African case. *International Journal of the Sociology of Language* 103, 149–163.

Ohmae, K. (1990). *The borderless world*. London: Collins.

Park, J. S.-Y. (2009). *The local construction of a global language: Ideologies of English in South Korea*. Berlin: Mouton de Gruyter.

Park, J. S.-Y., & Lo, A. (2012). Transnational South Korea as a site for a sociolinguistics of globalization: Markets, timescales, neoliberalism. *Journal of Sociolinguistics* 16(2), 147–164.

Park, J. S.-Y., & Wee, L. (2012). *Markets of English: Linguistic capital and language policy in a globalizing world*. New York: Routledge.

Pérez-Milans, M. (2015). Mandarin Chinese in London education: Language aspirations in a working-class secondary school. *Language Policy* 14(2), 153–181.

Piketty, T. (2014). *Capital in the twenty-first century*. Cambridge, MA: Harvard University Press.

Piller, I., & Cho, K. (2013). Neoliberalism as language policy. *Language in Society* 42(1), 23–44.

Plato (2007 [380 BC]). *The republic, Book IV*. Harmondsworth, UK: Penguin.

Price, G. (2014). English for all? Neoliberalism, globalization and language policy in Taiwan. *Language in Society* 43(5), 567–589.

Ramanathan, V. (2005). *The English-vernacular divide: Postcolonial language politics and practice*. Clevedon, UK: Multilingual Matters.

Reich, R. (2011). *Aftershock: The next economy and America's future*. New York: Vintage.

Relaño-Pastor, A. M. (2015). The commodification of English in "Madrid, comunidad bilingüe": Insights from the CLIL classroom. *Language Policy* 14(1), 131–152.

Ricardo, D. (2004 [1817]). *The principles of political economy and taxation*. Mineola, NY: Dover Publications.

Ricento, T. (Ed.). (2006). *Language policy: Theory and method*. Oxford: Blackwell.

Ricento, T. (Ed.). (2015a). *Language policy and political economy: English in a global context*. Oxford: Oxford University Press

Ricento, T. (2015b). Political economy and English as a global language. In T. Ricento (Ed.), *Language policy and political economy: English in a global context* (pp. 27–47). Oxford: Oxford University Press.

Romaine, S. (2015). Lingustic diversity and global English: The pushmi-pullyu of language policy and political economy. In T. Ricento (Ed.), *Language policy and political economy: English in a global context* (pp. 252–275). Oxford: Oxford University Press.

Rubin, J., & Jernudd, B. (1971). Introduction: Language planning as an element of modernization. In J. Rubin & B. Jernudd (Eds.), *Can language be planned? Sociolinguistic theory and practice for developing nations* (pp. xiii–xxiv). Honolulu: University of Hawaii Press.

Savage, M. (2015). *Social class*. Harmondsworth, UK: Pelican Books.

Sayer, A. (2015). *Why we can't afford the rich*. Bristol, UK: Policy Press.

Shin, H. (2012). From FOB to COOL: Transnational migrant students in Toronto and the styling of global linguistic capital. *Journal of Sociolinguistics* 16(2), 184–200.

Shin, H. (2014) Social class, habitus, and language learning: The case of Korean early study-abroad students. *Journal of Language, Identity & Education* 13(2), 99–103.

Shohamy, E. (2006). *Language policy: Hidden agendas and new approaches*. London: Routledge.

Smith, A. (2102 [1776]). *Wealth of nations*. Ware, UK: Wordsworth Editions.

Spolsky, B. (2004). *Language policy*. Cambridge: Cambridge University Press,

Spolsky, B. (2009). *Language management*. Cambridge: Cambridge University Press,

Spolsky, B. (Ed.). (2012a). *The Cambridge handbook of language policy*. Cambridge: Cambridge University Press.

Spolsky, B. (2012b). What is language policy? In B. Spolsky (Ed.), *The Cambridge handbook of language policy* (pp. 3–15). Cambridge: Cambridge University Press.

Stedman-Jones, D. (2012). *Masters of the universe*. Princeton, NJ: Princeton University Press.

Tan, P. K. W., & Rubdy, R. (Eds.) (2008). *Language as commodity: Global structures, local marketplaces*. London: Continuum.

Taylor, C. (1992). The politics of recognition. In A. Gutmann (Ed.), *Multiculturalism: Examining the politics of recognition* (pp. 25–73). Princeton, NJ: Princeton University Press.

Therborn, G. (2006). Meaning, mechanisms, patterns, and forces: An introduction. In G. Therborn (Ed.), *Inequalities of the world: New theoretical framework, multiple empirical approaches* (pp. 1–58). London: Verso.

Thun, E. (2014). The globlization of production. In J. Ravenhill (Ed.), *Global political economy* (4th edition; pp. 283–304). Oxford: Oxford University Press.

Tollefson, J. W. (1991). *Planning language, planning inequality: Language policy in the community*. London: Longman.

Tollefson, J. W. (Ed.). (2013a). *Language policies in education: Critical issues* (2nd edition). London: Routledge.

Tollefson, J. W. (2013b). Critical issues in language policy in education. In J. W. Tollefson (Ed.), *Language policies in education: Critical issues* (2nd edition; pp. 1–13). London: Routledge.

Tupas, R. (Ed.). (2015). *Unequal Englishes: The politics of Englishes today*. Basingstoke, UK: Palgrave Macmillan.

Van Mensel, L. (2016). Children and choices: The effect of macro language policy on the individual agency of transnational parents in Brussels. *Language Policy* 15(4), 547–560.

Wee, L. (2013). Governing English in Singapore: Some challenges for Singapore's language policy. In L. Wee, R. B. H. Goh, & L. Lim (Eds.), *The politics of English: South Asia, Southeast Asia and the Asia Pacific* (pp. 105–124). Amsterdam: John Benjamins.

Wright, E. O. (2005). *Understanding class*. London: Verso.

Wright, S. (2016). *Language policy and language planning: From nationalism to globalisation*. 2nd edition. London: Palgrave Macmillan.

Zhang, J., & Peck, P. (2016). Variegated capitalism, Chinese style: Regional models, multiscalar constructions. *Regional Studies* 50(1), 52–78.

III.B.

Mobility, Diversity, and New Social Media: Revisiting Key Constructs

CHAPTER 29

COMMUNITY LANGUAGES IN LATE MODERNITY

LI WEI

THIS chapter aims to reconceptualise the notions of *community* and *community languages* in late modernity and to recontextualise the discussion of language policy and planning (LPP) with reference to diaspora. Given the heterogeneity or superdiversity of the world today, the chapter raises questions about the meaning of *community* and its value in researching language. By extension, is the concept of *community language* still relevant? If it is not, can it be replaced by something else? In addition, scholars working with migrant groups are revisiting the notion of *diaspora*, emphasising its historical-cultural rootedness, global connections, and contemporary political, religious, and economic relevance. The chapter suggests how LPP in migrant communities and regarding migrant community languages could benefit from applying the new usages of *diaspora*. A particular focus will be on grassroots initiatives in LPP from within global diasporas.

The chapter consists of six sections (following this brief introduction). The first section presents a critique of the notion of *community* in late modernity. It argues that (1) community boundaries are fuzzy and multiple; (2) communities are mobile, intersecting, and connected; and (3) communities are locations and generators of grassroots responsibilities and power. The challenges that such features of the community in the twenty-first century present to the notion of *community language* will also be discussed. The second section looks at the renewed interest in the notion of *diaspora*. The third section examines the role of language and multilingualism. The fourth section discusses the possibilities and constraints of language policies and planning with regard to mobile and minority communities. The fifth section focuses on grassroots language planning actions, especially those that are carried out beyond institutionalised settings. The chapter concludes with a discussion of the new challenges facing community languages in late modernity, highlighting the dilemmas of post-multilingualism and suggesting translanguaging as a possible solution.

The Notion of *Community* in Late Modernity

Derived from the Latin *communitas*, the word *community* was originally used to refer to a settlement of people who interacted closely with each other. This sense of the term is still used in archaeology and other fields where physical proximity and material exchange are the defining criteria of a community. In his 1887 work, *Gemeinschaft und Gesellschaft* (translated as *Community and Society*), the German sociologist Ferdinand Tönnies emphasised communal networks and shared social understanding, or "unity of will," as he called it, as key to a community. McMillan and Chavis (1986) identified four elements of *sense of community*: (1) membership, (2) influence, (3) integration and fulfilment of needs, and (4) shared emotional connection. They further developed a Sense of Community Index (SCI), which has subsequently been adapted for use in schools, the workplace, and various types of communities. The shift of emphasis from physical closeness to unity of will is in part a recognition of the superdiversity of societies in the late-modern era.

As Vertovec (2007), who popularised the notion, recognises himself, superdiversity is by no means a new social phenomenon. But the emergence of the scale in recent decades and the multilayered experience of different groups within unequal power structures and social locations call for a reassessment of the traditional place- or ethnicity-based definitions of communities (Tollefson, 1991). More people move from more places to more places across the globe, rather than being tied to one location. Social formations become ever more complex, often marked by dynamic interplays of traditional variables such as ethnicity, language, country of origin, age, and gender, and by factors such as migration history, legal status, and access to social capital. In the meantime, a community can be virtual (Rheingold, 2000), with individuals interacting through specific social media crossing geographical and cultural boundaries, or imagined (Anderson, 1991), with members holding in their minds a mental image of their affinity without ever knowing, meeting, or hearing of each other.

As technological modernisation continues into the contemporary era, late modernity places the burden of responsibility on the individual, giving rise to the emergence of liquidity and reflexivity as key features of social life (Bauman, 2000). In turn, late modernity has given rise to a plethora of new terms with regard to community—online community, virtual community, LGBT (lesbian, gay, bisexual, transgender) community, learning community, knowledge community, brand community, community of practice, and so on—illustrating the fact that, under the cultural conditions of late modernity, individuals shift from one social position to another in a fluid manner. They change places, jobs, spouses, sexual orientations, political values, and more, as they take on the responsibilities for their own lives, as opposed to relying on traditional, localised support structures. There is a general trend to move from location-based communities or communities of places, for example neighbourhood, suburb, village, town or city, region, nation, or even the planet as a whole, to identity-based communities, ranging from the local clique, subculture, ethnic group, age, gender and sexuality, physical and mental capacity, religious, multicultural, or pluralistic civilisation, or the global community cultures of today (Castells, 2010).

In the meantime, organisationally based communities continue to exist, but expand from family- or network-based associations to more formal incorporated associations, political decision-making structures, economic enterprises, or professional associations on a national or international scale. Consequently, we can no longer talk about community as a geographical-physical entity. Instead, social scientists treat community as a sociological construct—a set of social interactions between people whose everyday behaviours have meanings and expectations (see discussions in Christensen & Levinson, 2003; Delanty, 2010). These meanings and expectations are understood and shared by members of the community, forming interests, beliefs, and values that are at the core of the construct. Paul James and his colleagues, for example, describe three kinds of relations that characterise different types of communities (James et al., 2012):

1. Grounded community relations, involving enduring attachment to particular places and particular people.

2. Life-style community relations, which give primacy to communities coming together around particular chosen ways of life, such as morally charged or interest-based relations, or just living or working in the same location.

3. Projected community relations, where a community is self-consciously treated as an entity to be projected and re-created. It can be projected through advertising slogans, for example "gated community," or it can take the form of ongoing associations of people who seek political integration, communities of practice based on professional projects, or associative communities that seek to enhance and support individual creativity, autonomy and mutuality. A nation is one of the largest forms of projected or "imagined" (Anderson, 1991) community.

Communities come in different shapes and sizes, with different interests and values, no two of which are alike. Here, I want to highlight three characteristics of the community in the twenty-first century that have important implications when we consider the relationship between language and community and with regard to language policy and planning in communities. These are concerned with their fuzzy boundaries, their mobile nature, and their grassroots responsibilities. I will detail each of them in the following.

Community Boundaries Are Fuzzy and Multiple

Unlike geography-bounded communities that are physically separated from other communities and where human interaction may consist primarily of relations between the residents living inside that location, communities in late modernity, whatever they may be, typically have interactions with other communities way beyond any geographical area. Individuals also typically have simultaneous memberships in several communities; for instance, a scientist in a knowledge community could be a member of a learning community and a virtual community when she uses an online platform to learn a new language, whilst simultaneously being a member of an LGBT community in Australia as well as a member of the Asian community there.

The same individual may have relatives and friends in different parts of the world. Memberships of the different communities are maintained through contacts that serve specific purposes and may be activated to different levels at different times. The increasingly easy accessibility of information and communication technologies and new media means that even the once traditional, place-bound communities can establish and maintain contacts and relationships far beyond their physical locations—that is to say, the boundaries of communities are not precise and singular.

Communities Are Mobile, Intersecting, and Connected

Mobility is not a new feature or product of late modernity. There have been communities of nomadic herders who walked long distances with their cattle, fishing groups who moved from time to time as the fish were available, and hunters who followed game. Large-scale migrations of people have resulted in diasporic communities of various kinds across the globe. This is continuing to be the case due to new developments of transportation, on the one hand, and humanitarian crises created by war, on the other.

At the same time, mobile technologies and new communication media have increased and enhanced the mobility and mobilisation of knowledge, ideas, resources, and values. People can be in contact with one another without physically moving places. In these terms, communities are both intersecting and connected: intersecting in the sense that there may be communities within larger communities in a cross-cutting matrix in relation to each other, and connected as they maintain multiple historical, spatial, and cultural contacts through various means. The latter is particularly important to diasporic communities, which I will discuss later.

Communities Are Locations/Generators of Grassroots Responsibilities and Power

Communities play a crucial role in shaping opinions, influencing behaviours, and ultimately changing social structures. This works in both directions: community can provide a normative mindset that impacts on individuals' everyday practices—if one wishes to remain a member of a community, he or she needs to behave in certain ways, like others in the community; in the meantime, individuals can determine whether or not change is needed and how it might happen through their everyday practices and ultimately the collective mindset and practices of the community. Communities are where power relations are built, cultivated, and mobilised. Anyone, either from inside or outside a community, who wishes to influence opinion and to introduce change will need to work through the relationships that already exist in the community, or what may be called *empowerment* of the community. Top-down decision-making would have limited effect without the buy-in of the communities concerned.

Individuals are expected to take responsibilities for their actions in the interest of the community; their reward would be that their opinions are heard and accepted by others, and social change could happen in a bottom-up way. The interconnectedness of communities that I talked about in the preceding also has important implications for social change itself: it means that change in any dimension of the intersections of a community has repercussions in the other dimensions and sections.

These three characteristics of the community in the twenty-first century present challenges to the notion of *community language*. Often believed to have been coined in Australia in the 1970s to denote languages other than English and Aboriginal languages (Clyne, 1991), the term has come to refer to languages used by members of minority groups or communities as their first languages within a majority language context. Some of these are languages that have been used for hundreds of years in the community concerned; others may be of more recent origin. The adoption of the term *community language* in preference to other terms, such as *minority, ethnic,* or *immigrant* languages, is in itself a reflection of the complexities and concerns of everyday life in late modernity. For example, the term *minority* languages suggests languages spoken by only a small number of people (manifestly not the case in relation to languages of world significance such as Arabic, Chinese, and Urdu) or languages that are somehow intrinsically of less value than *majority* languages. And terms such as *ethnic* or *immigrant* languages indicate that other characteristics, not necessarily relevant or easy to define, have to be taken into consideration. In comparison, *community language* would avoid many of the negative connotations that these other terms have attracted, and draws attention to the fact that languages are used in a range of shared social and cultural contexts. It also legitimises their continuing existence as part of a large society, and highlights the nested nature of contemporary communities: a *minority* language in one community could be a *majority* language in another community, and individuals can simultaneously have several different community languages as they belong to several different communities. It needs to be pointed out that those who use *community language* tend to emphasise the shared heritage and sociocultural practices amongst the language users, rather than any shared value that the term may imply, and acknowledge the issues arising from contested varieties and language standardisation.

A concept that is closely connected with that of *community* and that has been transformed significantly under conditions of late modernity is *diaspora*. I will turn to this in the following section.

Diaspora: Old Concept, New Potentialities

The concept of *diaspora* is a very old one, originally meaning the scattering of people between, through, and across different geographic locations. Its main reference was, for many centuries, the historical mass dispersions of the Jews, African slaves, and Chinese labourers. The emphasis on the involuntary nature of the displacement and dispersal in the historical references was easy to see. Studies of transnational human migration in the twentieth century tended to use terms such as *immigrants, guest workers, asylum seekers, ethnic minorities,* or *displaced populations* to refer to the different groups of migrants in contemporary society. As the world moved into the twenty-first century, though, there has been a renewed interest in the notion of *diaspora*.

Researchers increasingly find terms such as *immigrants* and *minorities* unsatisfactory. As Clifford (1997) suggests, "diasporic language seems to be replacing, or at least supplementing, minority discourse. Transnational connections break the binary relation of *minority* communities within *majority* societies" (p. 255). Scholars see a close link between the contemporary diasporic conditions and globalisation (Cohen & Vertovec, 1999). Diaspora in the twenty-first century is, to use a popular phrase, a *superdiverse* phenomenon (Vertovec, 2007). Individuals with different migration motivations and experiences, and different educational and socioeconomic backgrounds and statuses, come together; recent migrants are intermingled with long-term settlers; speakers of different languages, dialects, and accents are interacting with each other, often in a mixed mode. Yet they find sufficient common ground to identify themselves with each other as part of a diaspora, creating an imagined community (Anderson, 1991). This diasporic imagination often involves suppressing or neutralising past differences and establishing commonality and connectivity through which new identities can be negotiated (Sofos, 1996).

The rediscovered term of *diaspora* indicates a shift of interest from mobility to connectivity and of emphasis from the victimisation, uprooting, and displacement of the individuals and groups concerned, to their capacity for constructing new transnational spaces of experience that are complexly interfacing with the experiential frameworks that both places of settlement and purported places of origin represent (Morley, 2000). Tsagarousianou (2004), for example, talks about the *potentialities* of diasporas, that is, "the various creative possibilities opened by the activities of diasporas in both local and transnational contexts" (p. 58). She further argues that it is important to focus on "the ability of diasporas to construct and negotiate their identities, everyday life and transnational activities in ways that often overcome the ethnic identity versus assimilation dilemma" (p. 58), rather than the experiences of loss and displacement or the nostalgic fixation to a *homeland*. For Tsagarousianou, the diasporic communities' readiness and willingness to engage themselves with the building of a transnational imagination and connections differentiate them from *ethnic minorities*. In Brah's terms, "diasporas are . . . the sites of hope and new beginnings" (1996, p. 193); rather than looking back in a nostalgic effort of recovering or maintaining their identity, they discover or construct notions of who they are and what home is by essentially looking forward.

Such a shift in interest and emphasis in diaspora studies is echoed in applied linguistics research through the work of scholars such as David Block (2008), who challenges the appropriateness of the metaphor of *loss* in studying multilingual, transnational individuals and communities and calls for a move away from the excessively emotive and romanticised stances towards language maintenance and language shift. For many such individuals and communities, it is not what they have lost that occupies their minds in their everyday lives, but what they seek to develop and construct for themselves. The estrangement of an individual or a community in diaspora, to use Mandaville's words (2001, p. 172), "often leads to a particularly intense search for and negotiation of identity." It is therefore important to recognise the opportunity structures that the diasporic condition entails, which must include both the restrictive consequences of deterritorialisation and reterritorialisation and the creative potential of the multiplicity of connectivity. The multiplicity of connectivity creates an imagined, rather than given, community, continuously reinvented and reconstructed through the lengthy process of forging links amongst their members in both local and transnational contexts.

In an attempt to provide a theoretical framework for studying new communication media in diasporas, Tsagarousianou (2004) argues that migration movements in late modernity should not be framed in terms of isolation and solitude, but rather in terms of intense and constant interaction at a transnational level. Globalisation, in her view, means not simply rapid mobility over long distances, but also increased proximity and connectivity:

> Diasporas can be seen as situated at the centre of sets of intersecting transnational flows and linkages that bring together geographically remote locations. In turn, they contribute to the generation of transnational flows and, as a result, are considered to be in the vanguard of the forces that deepen and intensify globalization. (Tsagarousianou, 2004, pp. 60–61)

The renewed interest in the notion of diaspora brings forth the role of language in the construction of community. In fact, many traditional communities were defined along language lines, that is, individuals speaking the same language or language variety would be regarded as belonging to the same community, and individuals speaking different languages would be members of different communities. We now look at this issue further.

The Role of Language and Multilingualism

The previously mentioned norm-enforcement effect of the community means that members of the same community would share a set of norms and expectations regarding their use of language, too. This gave rise to the concept of *speech community* (e.g., Labov, 1972) as a group of people with shared community membership as well as shared linguistic communication:

> The speech community is not defined by any marked agreement in the use of language elements, so much as by participation in a set of shared norms: these norms may be observed in overt types of evaluative behavior, and by the uniformity of abstract patterns of variation which are invariant in respect to particular levels of usage. (Labov, 1972, pp. 120–121)

The notion of the speech community was designed to see linguistic varieties as associated with social strata within a single community, and for this reason it assumed a structural integrity of the linguistic system of each social group. Operationally, it assumed each social group within the speech community to form a neatly bounded unit, definable in terms of discrete and correlatable variables, such as ethnicity, race, class, gender, age, ideology, and specific formal variables of linguistic usage.

This conceptualisation worked well for Labov, who wanted to show that African American Vernacular English could not be seen as a structurally degenerate form of English, but rather as a well-defined linguistic code with its own particular structure. Yet, human relations and human behaviours are much more complex and fluid in the twenty-first century than ever before. Communities can no longer be identified on ethnic, race, or class terms alone, and, as interactional sociolinguistics research has demonstrated, there is much more intra-personal linguistic variation than was once understood. Choice of linguistic variant is often a situational choice made in relation to a specific speech context, rather than an expression of a permanent social identity, such as class, gender, or age. Furthermore, there is now much wider recognition that individuals of the same social group may not have exactly the same access to all linguistic forms, and the concept of the speech community as Labov defined it did not take account of power differentials within the community that sometimes work to restrict individual speakers' access to speech forms, or which impose certain linguistic varieties on certain groups and individuals.

It should be noted that Labov was by no means the only, or the first, linguist to develop an analytic concept of the linguistic community. Gumperz (1968), for example, described how social dialectologies had taken issue with the dominant approach in historical linguistics that saw linguistic communities as homogeneous and localised entities in a way that allowed for drawing neat tree diagrams based on the principle of *descent with modification* and shared innovations. Social dialectologists argued that dialect features spread through diffusion, and that social factors, often competing with each other, would determine how this happened in different communities. This insight prompted Gumperz (1968) to problematise the notion of the speech community as the community that carries a single speech variant, and instead to seek a definition that could encompass heterogeneity. He focused on the interactive aspect of language practice, because interaction is the path along which diffused linguistic features would travel. Gumperz defined the speech community as "any human aggregate characterised by regular and frequent interaction by means of a shared body of verbal signs and set off from similar aggregates by significant differences in language usage" (1968, p. 381). He further argued, "Regardless of the linguistic differences among them, the speech varieties employed within a speech community form a system because they are related to a shared set of social norms" (p. 382).

This definition does not aim to delineate either the community or the language system as discrete entities. In fact, Gumperz in his empirical work sought to compare the degree to which the linguistic systems of the community differed, so that speech communities could be multilingual, diglossic, multidialectal, or homogeneous, and the degree to which the use of different linguistic varieties were either set off from each other as discrete systems in interaction (e.g., diglossia where varieties correspond to specific social contexts) or habitually mixed in interaction (e.g., code-switching). Gumperz's work paved the way for later linguists to look at language from a practice theory (Bourdieu, 1977) perspective and speech community as a community of practice (Lave & Wenger, 1991). Hanks (1996), for example, studied the ways in which shared practices relate to the production of linguistic meaning and how linguistic practices are connected to a variety of inhabitable positions within the different social fields. Eckert (2000), in the meantime, examined how speaker groups employ linguistic practices to demarcate themselves from other such groups. For her, linguistic variations are *acts of identity* (Le Page & Tabouret-Keller, 1985) informed by ideologies. There are tensions between the goals and practices of subgroups coexisting within a macro-community, and these tensions interrelate and generate social change.

The replacement of the concept of *speech community* with more empirically anchored and differentiating vocabulary, such as *community of practice* or *network*, better captures "the often mobile and flexible sites and links in which representations of group emerge, move and circulate," as Blommaert and Rampton (2011, p. 4) suggest. But the more fundamental implication is for the conceptualisation of language in superdiversity. Since the 1990s, there has been a noticeable shift of attention from structural configurations of linguistic diversity and language contact to indexicality and the connotational significance of signs. The "interaction of meaningful sign forms, contextualised to situations of interested human use and mediated by the fact of cultural ideology" (Silverstein, 1985, p. 220) forms the total linguistic fact, which needs to be interpreted with reference to the specific activities and social relations in which it occurs, as well as the symbolic values it carries beyond the denotational and propositional meanings of words and sentences. There is much wider acceptance that multilingual practices are far more flexible than they were once thought and do not map neatly onto ethnic, cultural, or the so-called language groups. Even the local naming of the practices, such as code-switching, crossing, translanguaging, heteroglossia, polylingualism, metrolingualism, and translingualism, may itself be indeterminate and contested, among their users as well as among linguists (see further discussions in Garcia & Li, 2014; also Canagarajah, 2012; Jørgensen et al., 2001; Pennycook & Otsuji, 2015; Rampton, 2001).

The displacement and dispersal of people put speakers of different languages into direct contacts with each other. Multilingualism is a common, though not universal, outcome of such language contact. The need to build new connections with speakers of other languages in their newfound homes means that they need to learn and use new languages, whilst the need to maintain links with their former homelands and pass on their cultural heritage to their children means that they need to continue to use and teach the young their existing languages. Many diasporic communities are already multilingual before migration; migration only further enhances their multilingualism. Thus, multilingualism becomes an integral part of contemporary diasporas across the globe. Advancements in information and communication technologies provide new affordances for multilingual development: individuals and communities no longer have to migrate physically and geographically in order to come into direct contact with speakers of other languages. They also enable those who have migrated to maintain, even extend, their connections with others. Multilingualism adds an important dimension to the superdiversity of late modernity (Pérez-Milans, 2015).

Communities of whatever shape or form make decisions about their languages and language practices all the time, consciously and subconsciously. This will be explored in the following section.

POLICIES AND PLANNING: POSSIBILITIES AND CONSTRAINTS

A central question is to what extent a community should try to maintain its traditional languages and language use patterns or to adopt new languages (i.e., language maintenance and language shift). Different communities have different responses to the question, due to a variety of historical, sociopolitical, economic, ideological, and cultural reasons. On balance, most communities endeavour to preserve their traditional languages for some contexts and adopt new languages for others, often resulting in a dichotomy of we/in-group language and they/out-group language. Over time, the in-group and out-group languages may become primary languages of different generations, with the traditional community language being used primarily by older generations of speakers and the new languages by younger generations in the community. The former in-group language then becomes the heritage language, and the former out-group language becomes the *we* language of the younger generations.

The language experience of diasporic communities often goes through the processes of being resisted or marginalised, mainstreamed or assimilated, and memorialised (Li Wei, 2016a). Whilst individuals may be welcomed into the hostland communities, immigrant groups and their languages as a whole tend to be received negatively at the beginning. This may be largely due to ignorance and perceived threat to the cohesion of the local community. From the immigrants' point of view, if their number is small, they may feel isolated and their language use is restricted; and if the number is large, they might encounter segregation. Either way, they may experience marginalisation. The collective coping strategies for the immigrants often involve building the so-called "three pillars of the diaspora" (Li Wei, 2016a), namely, a community or townsfolk association, a school, and a communication network and media that usually begins with information newsletters and pamphlets, moving gradually to proper newspapers and magazines, and eventually to radio, television, and, increasingly, digital and online media. These three pillars of the diaspora play crucial roles in community language policy and planning.

Paradoxically, perhaps, the more successful an immigrant group is in building a community for themselves through establishing the three pillars of diaspora, the more pressure they may come under for mainstreaming and assimilation. Societies do not generally favour the idea of having too many different communities minding their own business and speaking their own languages. Under the discourse of community cohesion, immigrant communities, however successful and self-sufficient they may be, are pushed to assimilate with the so-called mainstream society. Of course, there are individuals and groups who do prefer to assimilate. And their efforts to do so often involve intermarriage, changing their names, and adopting a new language. Yet not everybody has the opportunity to assimilate, even if they wanted to. The vast majority of immigrant groups are ignored and become invisible over time, leaving the most and the least socioeconomically successful ones to stand out. In Britain, for example, different immigrant groups are perceived and treated very differently by the general public and the media. The majority of them rarely receive any notice or mention, but some are seen as forming problematic communities, such as the Bangladeshis in terms of their children's educational achievement and the Romanians in terms of their economic and labour market status. A few others, such as the Indian and the Chinese, are often held as examples of success, especially in educational and economic terms.

Many diasporic communities get memorialised over time, by both their own descendants and the mainstream society. Tsuda (2013), for example, talks about what he calls *double nostalgias*, the deflation of the romantic notions of both the homeland and the place of sojourn. Older immigrants are often invited to relive their own and their families' experiences during the earlier phases of migration and settlement and construct stories of prolonged struggle and eventual success. Younger generations are taught to learn lessons from such experiences, which are constructed to be relevant to the challenges of contemporary society. All over the world, we see the setting up of museums of history of migration. The "heritagisation" of community languages is another case in point. The processes of being resisted, mainstreamed, and memorialised may not be a simple linear one; they could happen simultaneously in some communities, where different generations or subgroups are being subjected to different pressures.

In addition to the three pillars of the diaspora, there are other community-based agencies for language reclamation, renewal, revitalisation, and revival, usually for communities that have already experienced language shift or loss. In the 1980s, Australia developed a language centre model, with the foundation of the Kimberley Language Resource Centre in the northwest of Western Australia. It is managed locally, and thus is more able to understand and meet the needs of local language communities. Some of the activities of the centre include coordinating local research projects, training staff in formal courses and through apprenticeship, hiring external linguists as necessary on short- and longer-term contracts, acting as regional repositories and archives for data, and as a resource production centre. Similar centres have been set up in other locations internationally, for example, the Yukon Native Language Center in Whitehorse, Yukon, and the Yinka Dené Language Institute in British Columbia, in Canada; the Centre for Endangered Languages Documentation (CELD) in Papua; the Academy for Kanak Languages, Agence de Développement de la Culture Kanak (ADCK), in New Caledonia; the Alaska Native Language Center, the Dena'ina Natuh, and the Sealaska Heritage Institute in Alaska; the Three Rivers Language Center in Indiana, and the Navaho Language Academy in Window Rock, Arizona, in the United States. (More information about such community language centres can be found at the website of the Resource Network for Linguistic Diversity: http://www.rnld.org/.)

There are, of course, constraints on what communities can do in terms of policy and planning regarding their own languages, and these constraints are not simply a matter of resources; rather, higher order social policies often have a crucial impact. More and more countries require new migrants to pass citizenship tests that also require the knowledge of the national language (Extra et al., 2009). Pupils from linguistic minority backgrounds in schools do not have equal rights to their *home* or *heritage* languages and can only receive education in the majority language. Indeed the idea of *home* or *heritage* language can be seen as a result of compartmentalisation and marginalisation of community languages. In public discourses, not speaking the national or majority language is often constructed as a cause of social problems affecting community cohesion and the sociocultural and economic welfare of the nation, even national security (Brecht & Rivers, 2000; Pérez-Milans, 2015).

The possibilities and constraints of language policy and planning facing mobile and minority communities highlight the need for grassroots actions beyond institutionalised contexts. We turn now to these.

GRASSROOTS AND THE EVERYDAY

The shift of sociological attention to the practice-based notion of community in late modernity points to the importance of grassroots actions and the everyday. For any policy and planning initiative to succeed, it needs buy-in from ordinary members of the community in their daily social practices. For that reason, initiatives and actions from the grassroots are more powerful and can influence not only individuals' everyday behaviour, but also their beliefs and values, which will have a long-term impact. The previously mentioned three pillars of the diaspora—townsfolk associations, heritage language schools, and community media—are agencies of grassroots actions from within the community. They play a crucial part in the everyday lives of transnationals and impact directly on their linguistic and other social practices.

Understanding the everyday practices of individuals provides insights into how society works overall. And there is no better place to understand everyday language policy and planning than in the family. In Spolsky's (2009) language management model, the family is an important domain for language policy and planning. It represents the everyday practices of individuals with shared heritage. Families are not given, but made. They are complex systems of relationships across time and space. They are the place where planning takes place on an everyday basis and where policies are developed, negotiated, accepted, or rejected. They are the location of grassroots actions. There is an increasing body of literature on family language policy (King, Fogle, & Logan-Terry, 2008; Curdt-Christiansen, Chapter 21 in this volume), and indeed effective management of family language policy is seen to be crucial in the maintenance and shift of community languages in particular.

Studies of multilingual diasporic families reveal a common recurrent pattern of first-generation migrants struggling to learn the languages of the new resident country, whilst their local-born children face the challenge of maintaining the home/heritage language (e.g., Lanza, 2007; Li Wei, 1994; Li Wei & Zhu Hua, 2011; Schecter & Bayley, 1997; Shin, 2005; Zhu Hua, 2008). If there are grandparents joining the family in their new setting, they often take up the responsibility of child care and interact primarily with other family and community members, and have relatively little opportunity for learning new languages. Members of diasporic families have to face these different challenges together as a unit: the presence of monolingual grandparents is as much an issue to them as children not wanting or being able to speak the home language in their everyday family life. Diasporic families also face the challenges of constructing new identities and fighting against prejudices and stereotypes, sometimes caused by their members not speaking the languages of the resident country.

Two issues have been highlighted by existing research on the changing sociolinguistic configurations in transnational families: necessity and opportunity. In most cases, it is necessary to have a good knowledge of the languages of the new resident country, as it would enable members of the transnational family to access services, education, and employment. Yet, opportunities for learning the languages are not always readily available. For instance, in the United Kingdom, funding for ESOL (English for Speakers of Other Languages) provision has been gradually removed, and the Ethnic Minority Achievement Grant, which was used to fund bilingual teaching assistants in schools for pupils whose English is an additional language, has been mainstreamed into the Direct Schools Grant, which covers everything from buildings to stationery (NALDIC, online; NASUWT, 2012).

Another example regarding home/heritage languages is that whilst transnational families often find it necessary to maintain them for domestic communication, especially where there are monolingual grandparents around, opportunities are not equally available across different home/heritage languages for the children to learn and maintain them. Again in the United Kingdom, some immigrant languages such as Bengali (150,000 speakers in the 2011 UK census) and Farsi (76,000 speakers) are taught in community schools and classes, while others such as Kashmiri (115,000 speakers) and Tagalog (70,000 speakers) are not. Within the same ethnic community, there are better opportunities to learn and use some languages than others. In the Chinese community, for example, varieties of Chinese such as Mandarin and Cantonese are taught in heritage language schools, but no school teaches Hakka (approximately 10,000 speakers in the UK) or Hokkien (approximately 4,000 in the UK), which also have significant numbers of speakers in the Chinese diaspora worldwide.

Families' and individuals' motivations for learning, maintaining, and using languages, however, often go beyond necessity and opportunity. They are tied to the families' and individuals' sense of belonging and imagination. As scholars in diaspora studies point out, transnationals construct and negotiate their identities, everyday life, and activities in ways that overcome the ethnic identity versus assimilation dilemma, suppressing or neutralising past differences and establishing commonality and connectivity in building a transnational imagination (e.g., Cohen, 1997). This imagination provides a site of hope and new beginnings (Brah, 1996, p. 193). Rather than looking back in a nostalgic effort of recovering or maintaining their identity, they discover or construct notions of who they are, and where and what home is, by essentially looking forward. The transnational imagination also motivates the families' decisions regarding their everyday language practices.

As well as the family, new, virtual communities are also important sources for aspiration and imagination and important sites for language policy and planning. The connectivities provided by the new media and information technologies also connect individuals, families, and communities across geographical and time boundaries. The Internet is now widely used as an effective tool for language maintenance and learning, as well as for everyday communication with relatives and friends in faraway places. Moreover, the netizens of the world exploit the affordances of the Internet and take control of the multilingual, multimodal, and multisemiotic resources available to them in creating communication spaces for the articulation of their experiences and subjectivities. These spaces present a challenge to language policy and planning by the state and public institutions. They are spaces for grassroots actions. Studies have shown that netizens use their multilingual creativity to escape censorship, to organise protests, and to promote activism (Li Wei, 2016b; Wozniak, 2015).

Thus far we have been discussing what mobile and minority communities and individuals have done and can do in response to the constraints of, as well as possibilities afforded by, the conditions of late modernity. The final section of this chapter will look at what new challenges such conditions pose to community languages and what the solutions may be.

New Challenges: Post-Multilingualism and Translanguaging

The connectivities and the flow of information and culture between individuals and communities across time and space that are characteristic of life in the twenty-first century present new challenges to multilingualism. Late modern societies are no longer content with simple recognition and acceptance of different languages, but are concerned with the process, as well as the consequence, of language contact. There seems to be a dilemma between the desire to protect the identity and integrity of individual languages whilst recognising and even promoting the fluidity of linguistic diversity and contact between languages. This is a particularly tough and sensitive question in the field of language endangerment, where tremendous efforts have been made to protect individual languages, whilst the sociolinguistic environment may be such that there is no monolingual speaker in the community who has ever had a monolingual experience. This is what I have called a *post-multilingualism challenge* (Li Wei, 2016b).

Another example of the post-multilingualism challenge is that language users increasingly find themselves having to deal with the question of how to express one's cultural values through a language, or languages, that is/are traditionally associated with the Other or Others. For many transnationals, their personal family history of migration often involves learning *foreign* languages that carry *foreign* values. They need to learn to use the language without necessarily accepting the cultural values and ideologies that the language typically carries; on the contrary, they need to learn to understand the values, ideologies, and practices through learning the language and to construct and articulate their own values, ideologies, and subjectivities through their newly acquired languages.

One response to the post-multilingualism challenges of the kind outlined here is translanguaging—the dynamic process whereby multilingual language users mediate complex social and cognitive activities through strategic and creative employment of multiple semiotic resources to act, to know, and to be (Garcia & Li Wei, 2014; Li Wei, 2011). Translanguaging represents a grassroots effort to push and break the boundaries between the old and the new, the conventional and the original, and the acceptable and the challenging. Studies in both educational and other settings have shown that multilingual language users, especially those in less privileged positions in the social hierarchies, have a natural tendency to question and problematise received wisdom and to fight against any imposed order and ideologies (Garcia & Li Wei, 2014; Li Wei & Wu, 2009). With regard to language, monolingual ideologies in the form of one language only, or one language at a time, still dominate many societies of today. Multilingual language users engage in translanguaging to challenge these ideologies. In doing so, they demonstrate their creativity and criticality.

As the contact and flow between people, cultures, and languages intensify in the twenty-first century, notions of the community, community language, and multilingualism change. The foci and challenges of language policy and planning also change. The liquidity and reflexivity that Bauman highlights of late modernity motivate hybridity and dynamic multilingualism, on the one hand, and protection and preservation of traditional, individual languages, on the other. Technological advances offer new affordances for communicating beyond the conventional linguistic boundaries, incorporating multimodal and multisensory semiotic resources. The translanguaging perspective aims to transcend not only the boundaries between languages, but also those between language and other cognitive and semiotic systems, as well as to transcend the divides between disciplines and research paradigms.

References

Anderson, B. (1991). *Imagined communities: Reflections on the origin and spread of nationalism.* Revised edition. London: Verso

Bauman, Z. (2000). *Liquid modernity.* Cambridge: Polity.

Block, D. (2008). On the appropriateness of the metaphor LOSS. In P. Tan & R. Rubdy (Eds.), *Language as commodity: Global structures, local marketplaces* (pp. 187–203). London: Continuum.

Blommaert, J., & Rampton, B. (2011). Language and superdiversity. *Diversities* 13(2), 1–22.

Bourdieu, P. (1977). *Outline of a theory of practice.* Cambridge: Cambridge University Press

Brah, A. (1996). *Cartographies of diaspora: Contesting identities.* London: Routledge

Brecht, R. D., & Rivers, W. P. (2000). *Language and national security in the 21st century: The role of Title VI/Fulbright-Hays in supporting national language capacity.* Dubuque, IA: Kendall/Hunt.

Canagarajah, S. (2012). *Translingual practice: Global Englishes and cosmopolitan relations.* New York: Routledge.

Castells, M. (2010). *The information age: Economy, society and culture,* Vol. 1: *The rise of the network society.* 2nd edition. Oxford: Wiley Blackwell.

Clifford, J. (1997). *Routes: Travel and translation in the late twentieth century.* Cambridge, MA: Harvard University Press.

Clyne, M. (1991). *Community languages: The Australian experience.* Cambridge: Cambridge University Press.

Christensen, K., & Levinson, D. (2003). *Encyclopedia of community: From the village to the virtual world.* Thousand Oaks, CA: Sage.

Cohen, R. (1997). *Global diasporas: An introduction.* London: UCL Press.

Cohen, R., & Vertovec, S. (Eds.) (1999). *Migration, diasporas and transnationalism.* Cheltenham, UK: Edward Elgar.

Delanty, G. (2010). *Community.* 2nd edition. New York: Routledge.

Eckert, P. (2000). *Linguistic variation as social practice.* Oxford: Blackwell.

Extra, G., Spotti, M., & Van Avermaet, P. (Eds.). (2009). *Language testing, migration and citizenship: Cross-national perspectives on integration regimes.* London: A&C Black.

García, O., & Li Wei. (2014). *Translanguaging: Language, bilingualism and education*. Houndsmill, Basingtoke, UK: Palgrave Macmillan.

Gumperz, J. (1968). The speech community. In D. Sills & R. K. Merton (Eds.), *International encyclopedia of the social sciences* (pp. 381–386). New York: Macmillan.

Hanks, W. (1996). *Language and communicative practices*. Boulder, CO: Westview Press.

James, P., Nadarajah, Y., Haive, K., & Stead, V. (2012). *Sustainable communities, sustainable development: Other paths for Papua New Guinea*. Honolulu: University of Hawaii Press.

Jørgensen, J. N., Karrebæk, M. S., Madsen, L. M., & Møller, J. S. (2011). Polylanguaging in superdiversity. *Diversities* 13, 23–37.

King, K. A., Fogle, L., & Logan-Terry, A. (2008). Family language policy. *Language and Linguistics Compass* 2(5), 907–922.

Labov, W. (1972). *Sociolinguistic patterns*. Philadelphia: University of Pennsylvania Press.

Lanza, E. (2007). Multilingualism and the family. In P. Auer & Li Wei (Eds.), *Handbook of multilingualism and multilingual communication* (pp. 45–67). Berlin: De Gruyter.

Lave, J., & Wenger, E. (1991). *Situated learning: Legitimate peripheral participation*. Cambridge: Cambridge University Press.

Le Page, R., & Tabouret-Keller, A. (1985). *Acts of identity: Creole-based approaches to language and ethnicity*. Cambridge: Cambridge University Press

Li Wei. (1994). *Three generations two languages one family*. Clevedon, UK: Multilingual Matters.

Li Wei. (2011). Moment analysis and translanguaging space: Discursive construction of identities by multilingual Chinese youth in Britain. *Journal of Pragmatics* 43, 1222–1235.

Li Wei. (2016a). Transnational connections and multilingual realities: The Chinese diasporic experience in a global context. In Li Wei (Ed.), *Multilingualism in the Chinese diaspora worldwide* (pp. 1–12). Oxford: Routledge

Li Wei. (2016b). New Chinglish and the post-multilingualism challenge: Translanguaging ELF in China. *Journal of English as a Lingua Franca* 5(1), 1–25.

Li Wei & Wu, C. J. (2009). Polite Chinese children revisited: Creativity and the use of codeswitching in the Chinese complementary school classroom. *International Journal of Bilingual Education and Bilingualism* 12(2), 193–211.

Li Wei & Zhu Hua. (2011). Voices from the diaspora: Changing hierarchies and dynamics of Chinese multilingualism. *International Journal of the Sociology of Language* 205, 155–171.

Mandaville, P. (2001). Reimagining Islam in diaspora: The politics of mediated community. *Gazette* 63(2–3), 169–186.

McMillan, D. W., & Chavis, D. M. (1986). Sense of community: A definition and theory. *Journal of Community Psychology* 14(1), 6–23.

Morley, D. (2000). *Home territories: Media, mobility, identity*. London: Routledge

NALDIC. (n.d.). Retrieved from http://www.naldic.org.uk/research-and-information/eal-funding

NASUWT. (2012). *Ethnic minority achievement*. Birmingham, UK: NASUWT.

Pennycook, A., & Otsuji, E. (2015). *Metrolingualism: Language in the city*. New York: Routledge.

Pérez-Milans, M. (2015). Language education policy in late modernity: (Socio)linguistic ethnographies in the European Union. *Language Policy* 14(2), 99–107.

Rampton, B. (2011). From "multi-ethnic adolescent heteroglossia" to "contemporary urban vernaculars." *Language & Communication* 31(4), 276–294.

Rheingold, H. (2000). *The virtual community: Homesteading on the electronic frontier.* Boston, MA: MIT Press.

Schecter, S. R., & R. Bayley. (1997). Language socialization practices and cultural identity: Case studies of Mexican-descent families in California and Texas. *TESOL Quarterly* 31, 513–541.

Silverstein, M. (1985). Language and the culture of gender. In E. Mertz & R. Parmentier (Eds.), *Semiotic mediation* (pp. 219–259). New York: Academic Press.

Shin, S. J. (2005). *Developing in two languages: Korean children in America.* Clevedon, UK: Multilingual Matters.

Sofos, S. (1996). Interethnic violence and gendered constructions of ethnicity in former Yugoslavia. *Social Identities* 2(1), 73–91.

Spolsky, B. (2009). *Language management.* Cambridge: Cambridge University Press.

Tollefson, J. W. (1991). *Planning language, planning inequality: Language policy in the community.* London: Addison-Wesley Longman.

Tönnies, F. (1887). *Gemeinschaft und gesellschaft.* Leipzig: Fues's Verlag. (Translated, 1957, by C. P. Loomis as *Community and society.* East Lansing: Michigan State University Press.)

Tsagarousianou, R. (2004). Rethinking the concept of diaspora: Mobility, connectivity and communication in a globalized world. *Westminster Papers in Communication and Culture* 1(1), 52–65.

Tsuda, T. (2013). When the diaspora returns home: Ambivalent encounters with the ethnic homeland. In A. Quayson & G. Daswani (Eds), *A companion to diaspora and transnationalism* (pp. 172–198). Oxford: Wiley-Blackwell.

Vertovec, S. (2007). Super-diversity and its implications. *Ethnic and Racial Studies* 30(6), 1024–1054.

Wozniak, A. M. (2015). River-crabbed shitizens and missing knives: A sociolinguistic analysis of trends in Chinese language use online as a result of censorship. *Applied Linguistics Review* 6(1), 97–120.

Zhu Hua. (2008). Duelling languages, duelling values: Codeswitching in bilingual intergenerational conflict talk in diasporic families. *Journal of Pragmatics* 40, 1799–1816.

CHAPTER 30

....

NEW SPEAKERS AND LANGUAGE POLICY

....

BERNADETTE O'ROURKE, JOSEP SOLER, AND JEROEN DARQUENNES

IN recent years, academic discussions around language policy and planning (LPP) have emphasized the multilayered and polycentric nature of language policymaking (Barakos & Unger, 2016; Blommaert et al., 2009; Halonen et al., 2014; Johnson, 2009, 2013). Instead of contrasting imposed or constructed divides between the *top-down* and *bottom-up* poles of opposition, there is now a growing body of scholarly work that attempts to analyze how discourses circulate across the language policy cycle (Canagarajah, 2006), and how actors position themselves vis-à-vis such discourses in order to open up or narrow down ideological spaces for the use of certain languages or linguistic varieties (Johnson, 2009). In this chapter we look at language policy through the *new speaker* lens and explore the many ways in which research on new speakers to date links to the discursive and ethnographic approaches that have recently come to the fore in language policy literature.

As O'Rourke and Pujolar (2013, p. 56) have observed, "notions such as 'new speakerness' and 'new speakers' have begun to be used to describe the ways of speaking and the social and linguistic practices of speakers which exist outside the traditional native-speaker communities." New speakers have emerged across a variety of contexts, including those in which attempts are made to revitalize autochthonous minority languages and urban settings characterized by different forms of migration and transnational, flexible workplaces. The capacity of the new speaker lens to cross-cut such a range of contexts and to draw out points of commonality in the varied sociolinguistic trajectories and repertoires of new speakers, as well as in the diverse challenges they face as speakers of another language, helps to bring the lived experience of becoming and being (recognized as) a new speaker into focus. Research on new speakers in the context of LPP thus reorients attention to the individuals who are in many ways impacted by policy and planning efforts: while LPP has in many cases fostered the contemporary emergence of new speakers, these individuals may draw on, negotiate, or resist official policy and planning measures over the course of their sociolinguistic trajectories. In all of these settings, the impact of language policy on the process of becoming and being a speaker of a given language has proven far-reaching for both authorities (i.e., language policymaking bodies and institutions) and individual speakers.

As most research on new speakers has to date addressed the context of language revitalization in European minority-language settings (e.g., O'Rourke et al., 2015), this chapter draws on this work as its point of departure. Starting with an overview of the context from which the concept has empirically and conceptually emerged, we then move to a brief overview of how indigenous minorities have historically been framed in language policy research. Following a brief discussion of how the new speaker concept itself facilitates a reconsideration of more traditional approaches to LPP in minority-language settings, this chapter will focus more specifically on LPP research in new speaker contexts. After setting out some of the challenges that research on new speakers in minority-language contexts has posed to traditional approaches to studying languages and their speakers, we discuss the theoretical and methodological underpinnings of new speaker research in connection to language policy. Noting that new speaker studies are not only situated in minority settings, at the end of the chapter we look at emerging areas of research beyond minority-language contexts.

New Profiles of Speakers in Minority-Language Contexts

In the early years of applied linguistics, particularly in the European context, language minorities were at the heart of LPP research. Working from a policy perspective, researchers examined how modern nation-states treated minority-language communities. Furthermore, they concentrated on and in some cases helped put in place top-down planning initiatives to halt or reverse the processes of language shift that many indigenous minority-language communities were undergoing.

Some studies such as Gal (1979) also paid attention to a broader profile of minority-language speakers. Later, the work of Dorian (1994) and others placed emphasis on the use and the role of less purist varieties of minority languages in language maintenance and revitalization strategies. Dorian also highlighted the need to focus on adult education in order to take account of the critical mass of minority-language speakers emerging outside the home domain. However, outside of these studies, there were "few if any attempts to explain the entire range of variation across 'new speaker' profiles through comparative theory building and research" (O'Rourke et al., 2015, p. 2).

This gap likely stems in part from the widespread recourse in research on language maintenance and shift to Fishman's influential work on language maintenance and language shift (1964) that culminated in his book on *Reversing Language Shift* (Fishman, 1991). This work focused on the idealized and prototypical representatives of indigenous language communities, that is, those speakers who had acquired and (still) used the minority language as their native language. Such speakers were seen to play a key role in the intergenerational transmission of the minority language in the home-family-neighborhood-community nexus, according to stage six of Fishman's Graded Intergenerational Disruption Scale (GIDS). Reflecting this importance placed on the intergenerational transmission of a language by its native speakers, indexes of language endangerment such as those proposed by Fishman (1991) and UNESCO's Red Book of Endangered Languages identified a break in home transmission as the single most important indicator of language decline, and in doing so established a direct link between the maintenance of a native-speaker community and language survival. As a result, language endangerment is often evaluated in relation to the strength of a native-speaker population and the level to which the language is transmitted from one generation to the next in the home.

This perspective on language revitalization has since been critiqued (cf. Darquennes, 2007). Models of language contact such as GIDS have tended, as Glynn Williams (1992, p. 121) argues, to draw on typologies and approaches that limit what can be said about the inherent conflict between language groups. Williams highlights the tendency in revitalization contexts to view the process of language shift from a functionalist perspective and therefore as one that is consensual, as opposed to conflictual. The playing down of potential conflict ignores power relations, and thus such approaches to language contact have been unable to account for apparent deviations from the sociolinguistic status quo such as is revealed in the behavior of new speakers. This restrictive approach, Williams argues, marginalizes minority languages and at the same time ignores the role of individual or collective agency in bringing about bottom-up change. Jernudd and Nekvapil (2012) are also critical of earlier models of language contact and call instead for models that take into account fluidity, permeability, and boundary-crossing.

The native-speaker-oriented approach to language revitalization that has come under critique within academia has also been challenged by dynamics on the ground, as the traditional communities of minority-language speakers enshrined in early language revival models are increasingly eroded as a result of increased urbanization, economic modernization, and globalization. To varying degrees, many of Europe's minority languages—including Scottish Gaelic, Welsh, Breton, Galician, Catalan, and Basque—follow this pattern. However, despite a decline in native-speaker populations, the number of second-language learners has increased in quite a number of minority-language settings as a result of LPP initiatives that have extended the uses of these languages beyond the home domain and into new social spaces, particularly through enhanced provision for minority languages in school curricula, the media, and other public domains.

Combined with community language development efforts and advocacy movements, these more supportive language policies have helped foster the emergence of new profiles of speakers of minority languages, distinguishable from the native speakers characteristic of the so-called traditional heartland areas, including those individuals who have (re)learned and have begun using the language that their families had stopped speaking in previous generations (Grinevald & Bert, 2011; Nelde, Strubell, & Williams, 1996; see also McCarty, Chapter 18 in this volume). In social and economic terms, this new profile of speakers is often characterized by a more urban middle-class educated status, and they tend to speak a more standardized variety of the language acquired through the formal education system (O'Rourke & Ramallo, 2011; Pusch & Kabatek, 2011).

The emergence of these new speakers, however, is not without complication: their growing prominence in minority-language contexts can in some cases have unintended consequences for revitalization agendas. Questions can emerge about language ownership, linguistic legitimacy, and the different values that language policies allocate (intentionally or not) to certain forms of language but not others. These tensions can sometimes lead to the alienation of certain speakers—sometimes new, sometimes not. In this context, Romaine (2006) has called for a reconsideration of what it means for a language to survive without home transmission and of the implications of this process for the development and evaluation of LPP initiatives in minority-language contexts. While such considerations have played a role in more holistic approaches to language maintenance and revitalization (Williams, 2000), they have only recently gained considerable momentum with the emergence of systematic research on new speakers. We shall now turn to this strand of research.

CONCEPTUALIZING THE NEW SPEAKER

While a variety of terms have traditionally been used to describe the new speaker phenomenon (i.e., *non-native, neo-speaker, L2, second-language speaker, learner*), the new speaker label itself is relatively new to English-language usage. Robert (2009),

for instance, used the term to refer to individuals who had gone through Welsh medium education and had acquired the language at school. In other language contexts,
however, the concept of the new speaker has a longer history of circulation. The term
euskaldunberri has long been used as a folk term to describe new speakers of Basque
(see Urla, 2012); similarly, in the context of one of Spain's other minority languages,
Galician, the term *neofalante* is often used to refer to Galician speakers who acquired
the language outside of the home (O'Rourke & Ramallo, 2011). *Neo-Breton* is used
to describe a similar type of profile among second-language speakers of Breton
(Hornsby, 2008; Timm, 2010), and nearly two decades ago Woolard (1989) was already using the term *New Catalans* to refer to second-language speakers of Catalan
who actively used the language and engaged in bilingual behavior. Other minority-
language contexts, while not making explicit use of the term, draw on other labels
to describe this general category of speakers. In the Irish context we find the term
gaeilgeoir. This term translates literally as *Irish speaker*, but is sometimes used to refer
more specifically to Irish-language enthusiasts in contrast to *cainteoirí dúchais*, the
term used for speakers brought up with the language in the home and within the traditionally Irish-speaking areas of Ireland.

Across all these contexts, the boundaries around who is or who is not a new
speaker are often fluid. They can be drawn by speakers who identify themselves as
new speakers of a language, or they can be traced by other speakers as a means of
categorizing a perceived level of competence and legitimacy. New speaker profiles
thus span a large spectrum and can range from second-language learners with very
limited linguistic competence in the language to what Piller (2002) refers to as "expert speakers" with high levels of proficiency and with an ability to pass as so-called
native speakers.

The explicit labeling of the new speaker phenomenon built on previous research
into these speaker profiles and began to be used by European-based researchers concerned with overlapping issues of legitimacy, linguistic authority, and language ownership in post-revitalization situations, specifically in the context of Catalan (Pujolar,
2007; Woolard, 2011) and comparative work on Galician and Irish (O'Rourke, 2011a).
The focus of these discussions was an attempt to understand the issues that arise in
situations in which these new profiles of speakers are emerging, as well as to explore
the tensions that often seem to be generated between traditional and new speakers
of minority languages in these situations. In this context, *new speakers* began to be
used as a generic term to refer to individuals who had acquired a minority language
outside of the home, often through the education system or as adult learners in the
context of language revitalization efforts.

In contrast to long-standing terms such as *L2* and *non-native*, the *new speaker* label
seeks to move away from the notion of deficit or deficiency and instead encapsulates
the possibilities available to the speaker to expand his or her linguistic repertoire
through active use of the target language. In this sense, it differs from *learner* in that
a learner may never actually use a language outside an educational setting, whereas

new speakers are active and regular users of their target languages or are attempting to achieve that goal (O'Rourke et al., 2015). The term thus also includes efforts by members of indigenous communities to learn their heritage language as a second or additional language (e.g., see the discussion in Wiley et al., 2014). Research on new speakers also emphasizes that a speech community can no longer be seen as something that is made up exclusively of those who have inherited the language through home transmission. As such, Pujolar and Puigdevall (2015, p. 171) stress the urgent need to "query how policies address and affect those who have 'adopted' the language" in other ways.

The challenging of native-speaker ideologies is not, of course, specific to minority-language contexts, but is one that has been going on in other academic fields. In sociolinguistics and related strands there has been a growing questioning of many of the underlying assumptions linked to the native-speaker ideology, and more fundamentally to the definition of a language. Within critical sociolinguistics there has indeed been a disinvention and reconstruction of the way we think about language and languages (Makoni & Pennycook, 2007). We have seen a critique of many of the basic concepts that defined our field and the emergence of a new metadiscursive approach that gives priority to communities of practice over bounded languages. This has prompted many scholars to look more closely at the in-between spaces that have often been absent from previous linguistic and sociolinguistic discussions (see Blommaert, 2010; Martin Jones, Blackledge, & Creese, 2012; Pennycook, 2007). A variety of terms have come into circulation to describe these spaces and have provided important analytical tools to capture non-standardized and mixed forms of language, including *translanguaging, translingualism, metrolingualism, lingolism*, and *superdiversity*. The concept of new speaker builds on such terminology in drawing attention to the in-between spaces occupied by minority-language speakers who acquired the language outside of the home. Such in-between spaces have often been lost in large-scale sociolinguistic surveys and census data, where languages are defined as discrete, bounded entities. As Urla (1993, 2012) has previously noted, in language revitalization contexts, census questions and surveys have been positioned as an important endeavor at regional, national, and international levels to count the number of speakers in the community and to measure levels of language decline or revival. As a result of such approaches, the in-between linguistic spaces and frequently more hybridized forms of language inherent in language contact situations have often been ignored in sociolinguistic discussion (Martin-Jones, Blackledge, & Creese, 2012).

In falling within these in-between spaces of linguistic practice, new speakers have tended to be overshadowed by native-speaker profiles, which were seen to represent users of real and authentic language, and as such were seen as more worthy of investigation. While in recent years this centrality has been challenged (see, for example, Bonfiglio, 2010; Cook, 1999; Davies, 2003; Doerr, 2009; Rampton, 1990), the ideal of the native speaker has remained remarkably consistent within linguistics, including the related fields of sociolinguistics and linguistic anthropology. In these latter domains, researchers working on minority-language groups have often tended to focus on those communicative practices believed to be the most traditional and authentic, thus designating them (albeit implicitly, perhaps) as the most (or only) legitimate representatives of a given community (Bucholtz, 2003, p. 400). In drawing attention to active speakers of minority language who fall outside the native category, the concept of new speaker helps redress the historical academic orientation toward a narrower, exclusive focus on certain speakers of these languages.

Moreover, the new speaker lens also seeks to shift the focus to the speakers themselves. While concepts such as *translanguaging* or *translingualism*, among others, focus more specifically on the processes involved in navigating multilingualism in contemporary societies, they arguably divert attention away from the speakers. Other concepts in circulation meanwhile focus more specifically on the multilingual speaker, such as Garcia and Kleifgen's (2010) notion of *emergent bilinguals* or Claire Kramsch's idea of the *multilingual subject* (2009). These concepts draw our focus more specifically to the individual speakers, to their experiences as multilingual social actors, and to the types of struggles they engage in as they move across different linguistic spaces and boundaries and, in so doing, negotiate and re-evaluate their own linguistic practices. By focusing on individuals and the opportunities and challenges they face in becoming, being, and being accepted as speakers of a language, the new speaker concept attempts to achieve a similar goal.

A review of this emerging tradition provides us with a good foundation with which to better grasp contemporary conceptualizations of the new speaker. We now shift our focus of attention to the theoretical and methodological contribution this concept can make to the development of innovative approaches to language policy research.

New Speakers and Language Policy: Theoretical and Methodological Underpinnings

As it challenges essentializing views of speakerhood—of what it means to be a speaker of a given language and to be able to claim legitimacy and authority in that language—the new speaker research has diverse contributions to make to language policy scholarship. Indeed, in line with Pennycook's (2006) call for a more postmodern approach to analyzing language policies, new speaker research can contribute to critical questioning of all preconceived notions of *language, policy,* and *mother tongue* (Pennycook, 2006, p. 62). In this section, we elaborate on the more specific theoretical and methodological strands of language policy to which new speaker studies can make a constructive contribution. We start with a brief overview of the centrality of work on language ideologies in the analysis of language policy, followed by a discussion of issues of language standardization and governmentality, two phenomena that have been identified as playing an important role in language policy and which are particularly relevant to new speaker settings. After that, we move on to methodological questions and situate new speaker research against the background of ethnographic and discursive approaches to the analysis of language policy.

Language Ideologies, Language Policy, and New Speakers

Language ideologies have been identified as playing a key role in informing both the development and implementation of language policy, and in the (at times challenging) processes of becoming and being a new speaker. According to Blommaert (2006, p. 244), language policy is invariably based on linguistic ideologies, that is, on images of societally desirable forms of language usage and of the ideal social and linguistic landscape; these images are themselves derived from larger sociopolitical ideologies. Ideological orientations in relation to assumptions about a specific language or language in general can thus be inferred from language policy decisions or statements. Similarly, as Spolsky (2004, p. 14) suggests, there may often be a consensual ideology that assigns values and prestige to certain varieties and not others because the members of a particular speech community share a general set of beliefs about appropriate language practices.

Language policies relating to indigenous minority languages, in particular, can often be traced to a common set of historically situated ideologies. Spurred on by the widespread legacy of language patriotism that emerged during the Age of Reason, European ethnocultural movements from the nineteenth century onward tended to draw on the image of the noble and uncontaminated peasant, who had kept the language pure and intact, as an important source of nationalist language planning (Fishman, 1972, p. 69). Such imagery articulates with anthropologically romantic notions surrounding the ideal of the native speaker linked to a bounded, homogenous speech community, to a particular territorial space, and to a particular historical past; that is to say, language itself, and the metadiscursive regimes that have come to be used when describing it, can be located in Western linguistic and cultural ideologies where the idea of language and territory are deeply engrained (Makoni & Pennycook, 2007). These ideologies were in turn frequently drawn upon in constructing revitalization agendas for minority languages, with the native speaker becoming part of this imaginary in the search for authenticity.

The ideological construct of authenticity, along with its opposite value, anonymity, often arise in discussions of the value of language in modern Western societies (Gal & Woolard, 1995). Authenticity situates the value of a language in its relationship to a specific community; according to Woolard (2008, p. 304), for a speech variety to be authentic it "must be very much 'from somewhere' in speakers' consciousness, and thus its meaning is profoundly local. If such social and territorial roots are not discernable, a linguistic variety lacks value in this system." In the context of minority language revival, authenticity and its link to identity can impede the acquisition and use of a minority language as a second language by a larger population (Woolard 2008, p. 315), the members of whom may perceive themselves as not sounding natural or real enough in comparison to native speakers. This may lead traditional native speakers to establish a social closure that functions as an identity control mechanism, effectively demarcating their privileged position as authentic speakers (O'Rourke & Ramallo, 2013). Such a situation can sometimes lead to frustration among newcomers to the language and may even discourage them from using it altogether (McEwan-Fujita, 2010; O'Rourke, 2011b).

In the face of the challenges posed to new speakerness by linguistic ideologies rooting the authenticity of minority languages in the speech of place-based communities of native speakers, the promotion of a standardized, anonymous form of the language through LPP efforts could be seen as offering a more equally accessible alternative. As the next section will explore, however, the standardization processes central to many minority-language revitalization policies do not necessarily resolve tensions around the valorization of certain forms of language.

New Speakers and Standardization

In the context of minority language revitalization, standardization can be seen as a broader process of corpus planning that often involves the modernization and codification of selected varieties that are meant to contribute (or to respond) to expanding domains of language use (cf. Darquennes & Vandenbussche, 2015). Standardization is often presented as an attempt to give a minority language the same value of anonymity as a public language, representing a "view from nowhere" (Woolard, 2008, p. 308) that is suitable for use across a range of domains and spaces—including those in which it previously had been deemed inappropriate and thus excluded. In moving the language toward a socially neutral, universally available form, standardization represents an attempt to demonstrate the equivalence of minority languages to the "world" languages more commonly associated with dominant public spheres (Urla, 1993, p. 246).

While standardization can be seen to have benefits for minority languages, however, the process can also lead to continued language loss (Grenoble & Whaley, 2006). Rather than strengthening speakers' dignity and self-worth (Cooper, 1989), it can lead to further stigmatization of certain varieties. Minority-language activists and planners often find themselves imposing standards that elevate literary forms and their users, thereby negatively sanctioning variability in order to demonstrate the reality, validity, and integrity of their languages (Woolard, 1998, p. 17). The purist ideologies shaping this process of standardization can disempower vernacular forms of the language spoken in everyday contexts. Standardizers often promote policies that reject loanwords, for example, in an effort to rid the minority language of influences from the dominant contact language, thus enforcing conservative and purist policies (Dorian, 1994). Such policies tend to suit—and are indeed frequently produced by—the educated urban elite, a situation that risks alienating speakers on the ground (Coulmas, 1989). Standardization can therefore have an adverse impact on minority-language revitalization, producing new forms of linguistic alienation and insecurity among the existing speakers of the language.

In pursuing these conservative purist standardization processes, the very movements that set out to save minority languages are often organized around "the same received notions of language that have led to their oppression and/or suppression" in the first place (Woolard 1998, p. 17). Standardization can often be presented as a neutral and necessary process in making a language more modern. However, as Fishman (2006) reminds us, the directional forces moving and guiding planning initiatives are more politically, ideologically, and value laden than they may first appear. As the preceding discussion argues, standardization goes far beyond the specificity of such overarching aims as modernization: this process inevitably has an impact on variation in that it creates new hierarchies of linguistic prestige.

In the contemporary European context, new speakers of minority languages are often the product of these revitalization agendas in which language policies have tended to be oriented toward standardization and the promotion of literacy, shaped by an underlying concern for purifying and defining the language (Urla, 1993, 2012). As Milroy (2001) highlights, an important effect of standardization has been the development of a consciousness among speakers of a so-called correct, or canonical, form of language. Through this process, the standard variety comes to represent a powerful filter for social mobility and effectively positions new speakers as legitimate speakers of the *langue autorisée* (Bourdieu, 1991). This process presents a challenge to the authority of traditional native speakers, whose language variety is effectively doubly stigmatized: first, by its historically subordinate position in relation to the socioeconomically and politically dominant contact language; and second, by its contemporary status alongside the newly developed standard for the minority language.

At the same time, however, new speakers often come to value these traditional vernacular varieties: in seeking out linguistic authenticity and the rooted language audibly "from somewhere," new speakers often look past the prestige of linguistic correctness and the value of anonymity associated with the standard (Woolard, 2008). Through such anonymity, as Gal and Woolard (1995) previously argued, publics potentially include everyone, but in doing so abstract from people's privately defined characteristics. As such, publics are seen to represent everyone because they are no one in particular. For new speakers, their more standardized varieties often seem inauthentic and artificial because they are seen as geographically and linguistically removed from the traditional dialectal varieties to which new speakers often aspire. In some cases, their self-perceived inability to emulate traditional forms can then prompt new speakers to construct more hybridized and anti-normative language practices in an attempt to shed themselves of the book-like formulations often associated with the standard and to authenticate new speakerness through more creative use of language.

This and the previous section have highlighted the role of language ideologies and standardization processes both as critical dimensions of the development of language policy and as powerful forces in shaping the lived experience of new speakerness. In the following section, we turn to how ideologically shaped language policies are actually implemented on the ground—and how new speakers make sense of, negotiate, and in some cases resist top-down efforts, thereby forcing LPP to develop more complex understandings of how power and agency circulate in language policy settings.

New Speakers and Governmentality

The focus recast by the new speaker lens on the speaker herself and her decisions in and experience of learning and speaking a new language effectively addresses an emerging critique of LPP research: while LPP literature has in the past focused on top-down policy agendas, this macro-level focus has come under criticism for its underestimation of the power of human agency. National language policy can sometimes be perceived on the ground as official legislation designed to control "people's linguistic lives" (Shohamy, 2009, p. 185). In such cases, social actors are often driven to resist and engage in what Pakir (1994) has referred to as "invisible language planning," or what Baldauf (1993) refers to as "unplanned language planning" through nongovernmental and spontaneous language planning of their own. While overlooked in earlier literature, such exercise of agency has long been manifested in language revitalization contexts through local social actors' efforts to resist official policies and introduce micro-level alternatives (McCarty, 2011; Ricento, 2000).

In taking human agency into greater account, LPP research has increasingly come to prioritize the understanding of how national policies are interpreted, implemented, and negotiated by social actors on the ground (Johnson, 2013). Critical language policy, which has been influenced by social theory (see Tollefson, 2006), has incorporated Foucault's notion of governmentality in an attempt to divert the focus away from official language policies and language ideologies and toward more local discourses and practices (Pennycook, 2006; see also Martín Rojo, Chapter 27 in this volume). Governmentality can be understood as a modality of power that seeks to govern every aspect of the life of an individual or of an entire population (Foucault, 1980), comprising rational efforts to influence or guide the conduct of people (Inda, 2005). At the macro-level, governmentality can be used to describe the ways in which governments produce citizens who fulfill their policies; more specifically, it addresses the ways in which governments draw on various organizational techniques and practices to mold individuals into the desired ideal for the citizens of a particular sociohistorical and geopolitical context. At the same time, governmentality refers to how power also operates at the micro-level of diverse practices and discourses, rather than in the macro-regulations of the state, drawing out how power circulates across a wide range of contexts. By bringing these macro and micro elements together, governmentality brings power differentials into focus, highlighting—and facilitating the questioning of—both the ways in which people are governed and the reflective processes that can prompt citizens to instigate change (Dean, 1999).

Through its emphasis on the diffuse nature of power, the Foucauldian concept of governmentality can provide a useful frame in which to understand the emergence of new speakers of minority languages. In many minority-language communities, macro-level governmentality has aimed to produce speaker-citizens who conform to language policy agendas that tend to generate passive support for the minority language but that do not always lead to any significant changes in its active use. While minority-language policies are usually overtly oriented toward encouraging (or even requiring) that people learn and develop a capacity to speak the language, language learners who become active new speakers sometimes fall outside the desired ideal citizen that language policies seek to produce. In other words, while they are in many cases a product of top-down language policies, new speakers can also be seen as reacting to language-focused governmentality through their active use of the language and their engagement in reflective sociolinguistic practices that challenge existing power structures. As Urla's (2012) analysis of the Basque contexts shows, an approach in terms of governmentality can also facilitate the study of resistance to such attempts at governing linguistic conduct. Drawing on Foucault's (1980) observations concerning resistance as a diagnostic of power, Urla (2012, p. 16) argues that "language-activist strategies can be seen as diagnostic of the ways in which the framework and assumptions of governmentality have in many ways set the terms of debate around language and shaped the way language practices and the speaking self are understood."

Through these brief discussions of the role of language ideologies, standardization, and governmentality in the development and implementation of language policies aiming to promote minority languages, we have tried to show how a focus on new speakers can enrich the theoretical underpinning of research on LPP by highlighting the questions of agency that characterize the new speaker experience. Building on this insight, we will now turn to the methodological dimensions of research that aims to bring such issues to the fore and to explore their sociohistorically situated realization.

New Speakers and the Ethnography of Language Policy

With respect to methodology, research on new speakers has generally drawn on ethnographic accounts. In this sense, new speaker research closely aligns with recent theoretical and methodological developments in LPP research that have more actively incorporated discursive and ethnographic perspectives (e.g., Barakos & Unger, 2016; Johnson, 2009, 2013; McCarty, 2011). Inspired by the ethnography of communication (Hymes, 1972) and critical discourse studies (Wodak & Meyer, 2016), discourse approaches to language policy seek to highlight the ideologically fraught nature of the language policy cycle. Ethnographic research, meanwhile, has emerged as central to research on LPP rooted in a range of disciplinary and epistemological traditions. Martin-Jones and da Costa Cabral's (Chapter 4 in this volume) critical ethnography draws on North American linguistic anthropology in focusing on language ideologies, for example, while Wodak and Savski's (Chapter 5 in this volume) critical discourse–ethnographic approach is shaped by the tenets of critical discourse analysis (CDA). Pérez-Milans (Chapter 6 in this volume) has also drawn on sociolinguistic and linguistic anthropology to develop an approach to language policy centered on the indexicality of language.

Of particular relevance to work exploring the complex relationship between language policy and new speakers (as outlined in the previous sections) is the ethnography of language policy (ELP), which aims to draw together the macro-level development and implementation of language policy and the situated realization and negotiation of, as well as resistance to, policy by social actors on the ground. The basic tenet of ELP is to examine "agents, contexts, and processes across the multiple layers of language policy creation, interpretation, and appropriation" (Johnson, 2013, p. 44). ELP's main objective is thus to move toward a resolution of the tension between critical theory's analyses of how power operates at a macro level and the agentive creativity of individual speakers. In short, the aim is to bridge the perennial gap in scholarship between the macro- and micro-level dimensions of social life (Hult, 2010). ELP, therefore, helps establish connections between the different (individual, institutional, national, supranational) layers of language policymaking (Hornberger & Johnson, 2007) and aims to unpack the social meanings of these interrelated processes. More specifically, "[f]or ethnographers of LPP this entails a view of policy as a situated sociocultural process: the practices, ideologies, attitudes, and mechanisms that influence people's language choices in pervasive everyday ways" (McCarty, 2015, p. 81).

In new speaker contexts, issues of agenda setting as well as the implementation and appropriation of, and resistance to, policy are central to understanding how ideological tensions develop and emerge between different social actors and are experienced by individuals. Jaffe (2015, p. 22), for example, used "the lens of the new speaker concept" in her efforts "to explore some of the complex identity and ideological issues that are raised about the legitimacy, authority, and authenticity of

Corsican language learners." In a context where the availability of the minority language is quite restricted (both in formal and informal situations), this question is of paramount importance given that "creating new speakers is a social project for Corsican society that is yet to be realised on a large scale" (Jaffe, 2015, p. 22). Along similar lines, Costa (2015) and Hornsby (2015) highlight the central role of questions of legitimacy and linguistic authority within minority-language communities and movements. The fact that more traditional profiles of speakers have lost (some of) their prominence in certain minority-language contexts raises questions as to who, then, can claim linguistic authority within the group, which can lead to the establishment of new forms of diglossic organization (Costa, 2015, p. 133).

As suggested by these recent works, a central dimension of much research on new speakers is the exploration of how different actors appropriate available discourses on language and speakerhood, and position themselves vis-à-vis these circulating discourses. Issues of identity and authority are fundamental in many minority-language contexts, from the smallest (Ó hIfearnáin, 2015) to the more well-established minorities (Ortega et al., 2015) in Europe, as well as in other language communities around the world (Mortimer, 2016). Metaphorically, if the aim of ELP is to slice the onion (the different layers of policy) ethnographically (Hornberger & Johnson, 2007), then new speaker research, with its grounded focus on different societal levels, is well situated to help expand and strengthen the scope of recent approaches to language policy analysis.

In sum, exploring how discourses circulate across multiple scales is central to both new speaker research and to ELP, with the shared goal of describing and critically assessing how ideological spaces fostering the use of (minority) languages are either opened up and enhanced, or narrowed down and hindered (Johnson, 2009). In addition to this common ground, and in view of Pérez-Milans's (Chapter 6 in this volume) critique of the ELP framework, new speaker research can contribute to answering the call to analyze language policy contexts beyond situated events, highlighting instead the performative nature of language, on the one hand, and the trajectories of agents and semiotic resources, on the other. ELP research has historically concentrated on educational contexts, in which it is relatively straightforward to apply the heuristic of the ELP framework. In such contexts, there usually exist official programs, curricula, and strategy plans devised by governing bodies (schools, municipalities, regional and national governments), and these materials and discourses can be analyzed to examine who creates such policy documents, what their ideological stances are, and what strategies they intend to use to apply those policies—in other words, to explore the creational dimension of language policy. Moreover, one can look at how such policies are received on the ground by teachers and students and what strategies are used to interpret and appropriate or resist the directives set out by the official policy documents, thereby illuminating the interpretation and appropriation layers of the metaphorical policy onion.

Indeed, the vast majority of the twenty-two studies with an ELP approach that Johnson (2013, p. 46) reviews have a focus on language in education. The ELP methodology would thus seem to have been primarily applied to contexts in which a certain official (language) policy exists, and the connections between its different layers can be traced. In order to build on this work but also expand the ELP approach beyond such settings, the ELP framework should be mobilized in the study of other contexts in which language policies are not formally and/or officially imposed (i.e., created) (see also Pérez-Milans, Chapter 6 in this volume). Johnson and Ricento (2013) indeed observe that recent work in LPP has ushered in a significant increase in the variety of settings that are being approached from an ethnographic perspective, including family and homes, religious organizations, call centers, and medical and health-care settings. It remains unclear, however, how the ELP framework primarily devised for studying language in educational contexts might be applied across such a range of settings. Based on the common ground outlined earlier, we believe that research on new speakers can fruitfully advance efforts to expand the scope of ELP research.

While studies of new speakers have thus far been primarily concerned with minority-language contexts such as those described here (see the collection of articles in O'Rourke et al., 2015; O'Rourke & Pujolar, 2015), attention has also been increasingly drawn to immigrant and transnational settings, in which the resonance of struggles over linguistic authority and legitimacy is also strongly felt. As the following section will discuss, recent research on new speakers and new speakerness across a wide range of contexts has pointed to the ways in which language policies—and the language ideologies they have historically reproduced—now align with contemporary social changes associated with such processes as globalization, migration (voluntary or otherwise), and the commodification of language. These insights position new speaker research as a fruitful terrain for exploring the evolution of language policy and efforts to manage multilingualism, as it will draw out speakers' experiences in negotiating questions of speakerhood, authenticity, legitimacy, and authority in the midst of accelerated social, cultural, political, and economic change.

New Speakers beyond Minority-Language Contexts

The formation of a research network in 2013 under the European Framework in Science and Technology provided a space within which to develop the connections between regional minority language and other perspectives on new speakerness, in particular in the context of migration and transnational movement. Through the international collaboration supported by this network, there has been a coming to-gether of researchers examining diverse dimensions of multilingualism to explore the new speaker phenomenon from a wider theoretical perspective, shedding new light on the processes of production and reproduction of sociolinguistic difference and ideologies of legitimacy. From this cross-cutting collaborative work has emerged a range of insights that will shape future research. The network's members have pointed in particular to the increasingly clear need for an intersectional approach to new speakers that pays close attention to dimensions of social class and gender and their link to the material conditions experienced by these speakers.

Caglitutuncigil (2015, p. 219), for example, shows how African female new speakers "need the language to become an active member of the labour market in Spain." Their ability to gain access to the legitimate form of language is crucial not only for their potential incorporation into the Spanish job market, but also for their capacity to resist and emancipate themselves from patriarchal forms of oppression. In a completely different setting but evoking a similar struggle for linguistic au-thority and legitimacy, Del Percio (2015) explores how language can be usefully em-ployed as a resource in order to maintain and reinforce sociolinguistic boundaries. In analyzing how a fan and a foreign coach of a Swiss football team draw on different varieties of German to access the local fan community's material and symbolic re-sources, Del Percio observes that "speakers are apportioned value in specific markets that are regimented by specific actors and institutions according to specific interests, logics, and agendas" (2015, p. 271).

As these studies suggest, even in contexts of highly celebrated hybridity, blending, and diversity, such as post-national football fandom and international migration, language is loaded with symbolic power and serves to (de)legitimize particular kinds of speakers, granting the control of given social spaces to some groups, while others, seeking access to those spaces, become subject to control. Other recent new speaker research has drawn out the enduring salience of the native/non-native dis-tinction, highlighting how the concept, which draws on the ideological framework of modern nationalism, takes on new meaning in contexts shaped by contemporary forms of globalization.

Focusing on refugees and asylum seekers in the United Kingdom, Sorgen (2015) illustrates how language plays a central role in shaping the chances of these individuals' integration into their new environments. Taking a critical stance on the native versus non-native divide, Sorgen (2015) highlights the importance of lan-guage acquisition not just from a proficiency perspective, but also in terms of finding the spaces and the support crucial to the efforts of the newly arrived to integrate more effectively. In The Netherlands, Thissen (2015) also focuses on the native versus non-native divide so as to challenge it: through her analysis of the construction of belonging in the everyday interactions in a Dutch supermarket, she brings to the fore how categories of nativeness and new speakerness are not given but instead emerge, shift, and are invested with fluctuating meaning through daily social life.

Within the new speaker research network, a specific strand of research activity has been oriented toward making connections between new speakers across a range of multilingual contexts and the role of language policy. In recent work, for example, Spotti et al. (2016) focus on the Chinese diaspora community in The Netherlands. Their work suggests that the younger members of the community may find it difficult at times to align themselves with the values and worldviews of older members, and they identify the Saturday school that some young members attend in order to learn Mandarin as an emergent site of identity work in which different ideological constructs and positionings are contrasted.

In their study of medical doctors who decide to move to Northern Europe (Sweden and Finland) after having completed university training in Hungary, Schleicher and Suni (2016) also highlight the heterogeneous nature of discourses around language and language learning, foregrounding the changing characteristics of speakers' repertoires as they enter new communicative spaces throughout their personal and professional trajectories.

Soler and Marten (2016) investigate the discourses of members of transnational communities in Estonia in relation to the country's official language policy, highlighting issues of resistance and adaptation to Estonian society by speakers of different backgrounds who have recently arrived in the country for professional and personal reasons. Navigating the tension between the need and desire to acquire the official language, Estonian, while finding opportunities to learn and practice it (enabled by the Estonian majority) is not straightforward for members of these transnational professional networks in a small country like Estonia; in this, the issues of linguistic authority and legitimacy these speakers face are not far from those encountered by new speakers of traditional minority languages.

Touching on questions of social inequality, (linguistic) legitimacy, migration, social integration, boundary drawing, and diasporic identity negotiation, the recent research surveyed here links new speakers and new speakerness to many of the most prominent processes and most critical challenges characteristic of the globalized era. As language policies are developed and implemented to respond to contemporary social, cultural, political, and economic shifts, new speaker research promises to offer crucial insight into individuals' lived experience of such efforts to manage multilingualism in the face of change at every interconnected scale, from the local to the global.

Concluding Remarks

In this chapter we have looked at language policy through the new speaker lens, highlighting the ways in which new speaker research thus far has drawn on ethnographic methods to illuminate the lived experience and active negotiation of language policy at the level of individual speakers. Soler and Darquennes (2016) highlight how research on new speakers can reveal the important role of individual agency in shaping (implicitly or explicitly) official and unofficial language policies. The detachment of individual agency from structure has long been problematized in the social sciences, with Giddens's (1982) work serving as a precursor to further developments in communication studies and LPP, which since the 1990s in particular have also drawn on insights from linguistic anthropology and ethnographic sociolinguistics. Much of this work, however, has focused almost exclusively on practice within institutions, leaving social actors backgrounded in holistic approaches to describing and analyzing institutional discursive arrangements (see Pérez-Milans, Chapter 6 in this volume). In light of this long-standing orientation of LPP research, the new speaker framework serves to bring to the fore the importance of addressing issues through the lens of individual speakers. Against the background of recent language policy literature that stresses the multi-sited nature of language policy, scholars working within the new speaker paradigm have attempted to shed light on the role of different types of actors (authorities, stakeholders), horizontally or vertically aligned, in language policy activities that involve new speakers across a range of geographical, social, and political spaces.

Such work has begun to bring together a heterogeneous group of scholars working across a different range of topics and areas, including historical and immigrant language-minority settings, migrant groups in diverse populations, language in the workplace, settings involving sign language users, and virtual-language environments. The aim of such work is to critically analyze and reflect on methodological and theoretical concepts that may illuminate the role and the interaction of actors in the cyclical process of language policy in specific language policy regimes involving new speakers.

ACKNOWLEDGEMENTS

The writing of this chapter has benefited from ongoing discussions on the new speaker theme as part of the EU COST Action IS1306 network entitled "New Speakers in a Multilingual Europe: Opportunities and Challenges." We would also like to acknowledge input from Sara Brennan and insightful comments and suggestions made by the editors of this volume.

REFERENCES

Baldauf, R. (1993). Unplanned language policy and planning. *Annual Review of Applied Linguistics* 14, 82–89.
Barakos, E., & Unger, J. (2016). *Discursive approaches to language policy.* Basingstoke, UK: Palgrave Macmillan.

Blommaert, J. (2006). Language policy and national identity. In T. Ricento (Ed.), *An introduction to language policy: Theory and method* (pp. 238–254). Oxford: Wiley Blackwell.

Blommaert, J. (2010). *The sociolinguistics of globalization.* Cambridge: Cambridge University Press.

Blommaert, J., Kelly-Holmes, H., Lane, P., Leppänen, S., Moriarty, M., Pietikäinen, S., & Piirainen-Marsh, A. (2009). Media, multilingualism, and language policing: An introduction. *Language Policy* 8(3), 203–207.

Bonfiglio, T. P. (2010). *Mother tongues and nations: The invention of native speaker.* Berlin; New York: Walter de Gruyter.

Bourdieu, P. (1991). *Language and symbolic power.* Cambridge: Polity Press.

Bucholtz, M. (2003). Sociolinguistic nostalgia and the authentication of identity. *Journal of Sociolinguistics* 7, 398–416.

Caglitutuncigil, T. (2015). Intersectionality in language trajectories: African women in Spain. *Applied Linguistics Review* 6(2), 217–239.

Canagarajah, S. (2006). Ethnographic methods in language policy. In T. Ricento (Ed.), *An introduction to language policy: Theory and method* (pp. 153–169). Oxford: Wiley Blackwell.

Cook, V. (1999). Going beyond the native speaker in language teaching. *TESOL Quarterly* 33(2), 185–209.

Cooper, R. (1989). *Language planning and social change.* Cambridge: Cambridge University Press.

Costa, J. (2015). New speakers, new language: On being a legitimate speaker of a minority language in Provence. *International Journal of the Sociology of Language* 231, 127–145.

Coulmas, F. (1989). Language adaptation. In F. Coulmas (Ed.), *Language adaptation* (pp. 1–25). Cambridge; New York: Cambridge University Press.

Darquennes, J. (2007). Paths to language revitalization. In J. Darquennes (Ed.), *Contact linguistics and language minorities* (Plurilingua XXX) (pp. 61–76). St. Augustin: Asgard.

Darquennes, J., & Vandenbussche, W. (2015). The standardization of minority languages: Introductory remarks. In J. Darquennes & W. Vandenbussche (Eds.), *The standardisation of minority languages* (Sociolinguistica 29) (pp. 1–15). Berlin: de Gruyter.

Davies, A. (2003). *The native speaker: Myth and reality.* Clevedon, UK: Multilingual Matters.

Dean, M. (1999). *Governmentality. Power and rule in modern society.* London: Sage.

Del Percio, A. (2015). New speakers on lost ground in the football stadium. *Applied Linguistics Review* 6(2), 261–280.

Doerr, N. M. (Ed.) (2009). *The native speaker concept: Ethnographic investigations of native speaker effects.* Berlin; New York: Mouton de Gruyter.

Dorian, N. (1994). Purism vs. compromise in language revitalisation and language revival. *Language in Society* 23(4), 479–494.

Fishman, J. (1964). Language maintenance and language shift as a field of inquiry: Revisited. *Linguistics* 9, 32–70.

Fishman, J. (1972). *Language in sociocultural change.* Stanford, CA: Stanford University Press.

Fishman, J. (1991). *Reversing language shift.* Clevedon, UK: Multilingual Matters.

Fishman, J. (2006). *DO NOT leave your language alone: The hidden status agendas within corpus planning in language policy.* Mahwah, NJ: Lawrence Erlbaum.

Foucault, M. (1980). *Power/knowledge: Selected interviews and other writings.* New York: Pantheon Books.

Gal, S. (1979). *Language shift: Social determinants of linguistic change in bilingual Austria.* New York: Academic Press

Gal, S., & Woolard, K. (1995). Constructing languages and publics: Authority and representation. *Pragmatics* 5(2), 129–138.

Garcia, O., & Kleifgen, J. A. (2010). *Educating emergent bilinguals: Policies, programs and practices for English language learners*. New York: Teachers College Press.

Giddens, A. (1982) *Sociology: A brief but critical introduction*. London: Macmillan.

Grenoble, L. A., & Whaley, L. J. (2006). *Saving languages: An introduction to language revitalisation*. New York: Cambridge University Press.

Grinevald, C., & Bert, M. (2011). Speakers and communities. In P. K. Austin & J. Sallabank (Eds.), *The Cambridge handbook of endangered languages* (pp. 45–65). New York: Cambridge University Press.

Halonen, M., Ihalainen, P., & Saarinen, T. (Eds.). (2014). *Language policies in Finland and Sweden: Interdisciplinary and multi-sited comparisons*. Bristol, UK: Multilingual Matters.

Hornberger, N., & Johnson, D. (2007). Slicing the onion ethnographically: Layers and spaces in multilingual language education policy and practice. *TESOL Quarterly* 41(3), 509–532.

Hornsby, M. (2008). The incongruence of the Breton linguistic landscape for young speakers of Breton. *Journal of Multilingual and Multicultural Development* 29(2), 127–138.

Hornsby, M. (2015). The "new" and "traditional" speaker dichotomy: Bridging the gap. *International Journal of the Sociology of Language* 231, 107–125.

Hult, F. (2010). Analysis of language policy discourses across the scales of space and time. *International Journal of the Sociology of Language* 202, 7–24.

Hymes, D. (1972). *Foundations in sociolinguistics: An ethnographic approach*. Philadelphia: University of Pennsylvania Press.

Inda, J. X. (Ed.). (2005). *Anthropologies of modernity: Foucault, governmentality, and life politics*. Oxford: Wiley Blackwell.

Jaffe, A. (2015). Defining the new speaker: Theoretical perspectives and learner trajectories. *International Journal of the Sociology of Language* 231, 21–44.

Jernudd, B., & Nekvapil, J. (2012). History of the field: A sketch. In B. Spolsky (Ed.), *The Cambridge handbook of language policy* (pp. 16–36). Cambridge: Cambridge University Press.

Johnson, D. (2009). Ethnography of language policy. *Language Policy* 8(2), 139–159.

Johnson, D. (2013). *Language policy*. Basingstoke, UK: Palgrave Macmillan.

Johnson, D., & Ricento, T. (2013). Conceptual and theoretical perspectives in language planning and policy: Situating the ethnography of language policy. *International Journal of the Sociology of Language* 219, 7–21.

Kramsch, C. (2009). *The multilingual subject*. Oxford: Oxford University Press.

Makoni, S., & Pennycook, A. (2007). Disinventing and reconstructing languages. In S. Makoni & A. Pennycook (Eds.), *Disinventing and reconstructing languages* (pp. 1–41). Clevedon, UK: Multilingual Matters.

Martin-Jones, M., Blackledge, A., & Creese, A. (2012). Introduction. In M. Martin-Jones, A. Blackledge, & A. Creese (Eds.), *The Routledge handbook of multilingualism* (1–26). Abingdon, UK: Routledge.

McCarty, T. (Ed.). (2011). *Ethnography and language policy*. New York; London: Routledge.

McCarty, T. (2015). Ethnography in language planning and policy research. In F. Hult & D. Johnson (Eds.), *Research methods in language policy and planning: A practical guide* (pp. 81–93). Oxford: Wiley Blackwell.

McEwan-Fujita, E. (2010). Ideology, affect, and socialization in language shift and revitalization: The experiences of adults learning Gaelic in the Western Isles of Scotland. *Language in Society* 39, 27–64.

Milroy, J. (2001). Language ideologies and the consequences of standardisation. *Journal of Sociolinguistics* 5(4), 530–555.

Mortimer, K. (2016). Producing change and stability: A scalar analysis of Paraguayan bilingual education policy implementation. *Linguistics and Education* 34, 58–69.

Nelde, P., Strubell, M., & Williams, G. (1996). *Euromosaic: The production and reproduction of the minority language groups in the European Union*. Luxembourg: Office for Official Publications of the European Communities.

Ó hIfearnáin, T. (2015). Sociolinguistic vitality of Manx after extreme language shift: Authenticity without traditional native speakers. *International Journal of the Sociology of Language* 231, 45–62.

Ortega, A., Urla, J., Amorrortu, E., Goirigolzarri, J., & Uranga, B. (2015). Linguistic identity among new speakers of Basque. *International Journal of the Sociology of Language* 231, 85–105.

O'Rourke, B. (2011a). *Galician and Irish in the European context: Attitudes towards weak and strong minority languages*. Basingstoke, UK: Palgrave Macmillan.

O'Rourke, B. (2011b). Whose language is it? Struggles for language ownership in an Irish language classroom. *Journal of Language, Identity and Education* 10(3), 327–345.

O'Rourke, B., & Pujolar, J. (2013). From native speakers to "new speakers": Problematizing nativeness in language revitalization contexts. *Histoire Épistemologie Langage* 35(2), 47–67.

O'Rourke, B., & Pujolar, J. (2015). New speakers and processes of new speakerness across time and space. *Applied Linguistics Review* 6(2), 145–150.

O'Rourke, B., & Ramallo, F. (2011). The native-non-native dichotomy in minority language contexts: Comparison between Irish and Galician. *Language Problems and Language Planning* 35(2), 139–159.

O'Rourke, B., & Ramallo, F. (2013). Competing ideologies of linguistic authority amongst *new speakers* in contemporary Galicia. *Language in Society*, 42(3), 1–19.

O'Rourke, B., Pujolar, J., & Ramallo, F. (2015). New speakers of minority languages: The challenging opportunity—Foreword. *International Journal of the Sociology of Language* 231, 1–20.

Pakir, A. (1994). Education and invisible language planning: The case of English in Singapore. In T. Kandiah & J. Kwan-Terry (Eds.), *English and language planning: A Southeast Asian contribution* (pp. 158–179). Singapore: Times Academic Press; Centre for Advanced Studies, National University of Singapore.

Pennycook, A. (2006). Postmodernism in language policy. In T. Ricento (Ed.), *An introduction to language policy: Theory and method* (pp. 60–76). Oxford: Wiley Blackwell.

Pennycook, A. (2007). *Global Englishes and transcultural flows*. Abingdon, UK: Routledge.

Piller, I. (2002). Passing for a native speaker: Identity and success in second language learning. *Journal of Sociolinguistics* 6(2), 179–208.

Pujolar, J. (2007). Bilingualism and the nation-state in the post-national era. In A. Duchêne & M. Heller (Eds.), *Bilingualism: A social approach* (pp. 71–95). Basingstoke, UK: Palgrave Macmillan.

Pujolar, J., & Puigdevall, M. (2015). Linguistic *mudes*: How to become a new speaker in Catalonia. *International Journal of the Sociology of Language* 231, 167–187.

Pusch, C., & Kabatek, J. (2011). Language contact in Southwestern Europe. In B. Kortmann & J. van der Auwera (Eds.), *The languages and linguistics of Europe: A comprehensive guide* (pp. 393–408). Berlin: Mouton de Gruyter.

Rampton, B. (1990). Displacing the "native speaker": Expertise, affiliation, and inheritance. *ELT Journal* 44(2), 97–101.

Ricento, T. (2000). Historical and theoretical perspectives in language policy and planning. *Journal of Sociolinguistics* 4(2), 196–213.

Robert, E. (2009). Accommodating new speakers? An attitudinal investigation of L2 speakers in south-east Wales. *International Journal of the Sociology of Language* 195, 93–116.

Romaine, S. (2006). Planning for the survival of linguistic diversity. *Language Policy* 5, 441–473.

Schleicher, N., & Suni, M. (2016). *To go or not to go? The role of language and language policies in the migration process of medical workers*. Presented at "New Speakers" Whole Action Conference, Hamburg University, Hamburg.

Shohamy, E. (2009). Language policy as experiences. *Language Problems and Language Planning* 33(2), 185–189.

Soler, J., & Darquennes, J. (2016). *"New speakers" in language policy research: Prospects and limitations*. Presented at British Association of Applied Linguistics, Anglia Ruskin University, Cambridge.

Soler, J., & Marten, H. (2016). *Resistance and adaptation to newspeakerness in educational contexts: Two tales from Estonia*. Presented at Sociolinguistics Symposium 21, Universidad de Murcia, Murcia.

Sorgen, A. (2015). Integration through participation: The effects of participating in an English conversation club on refugee and asylum seeker integration. *Applied Linguistics Review* 6(2), 241–260.

Spolsky, B. (2004). *Language policy*. Cambridge: Cambridge University Press.

Spotti, M., Li, J., & Kroon, S. (2016). *The new speaker 2.0 in a sociolinguistics of mobility perspective*. Presented at "New Speakers" Whole Action Conference, Hamburg University, Hamburg.

Thissen, L. (2015). "Because here we live in the Netherlands": Language cultural politics of belonging in a supermarket. *Applied Linguistics Review* 6(2), 195–216.

Timm, L. (2010). Language, culture and identity in Brittany: The sociolinguistics of Breton. In M. Ball & N. Müller (Eds.), *The Celtic languages* (2nd edition; pp. 712–752). Abingdon, UK: Routledge.

Tollefson, J. W. (2006). Critical theory in language policy. In T. Ricento (Ed.), *An introduction to language policy: Theory and method* (pp. 42–59). Malden, MA: Blackwell.

Urla, J. (1993). Cultural politics in an age of statistics: Numbers, nations, and the making of Basque identity. *American Ethnologist* 20(4), 818–843.

Urla, J. (2012). *Reclaiming Basque: Language, nation, and cultural activism*. Reno: University of Nevada Press.

Wiley, T., Peyton, J. K., Christian, D., Moore, S. C., & Liu, N. (Eds.). (2014). *Handbook of heritage, community, and Native American languages in the United States: Research, policy, and educational practice*. New York; London: Routledge.

Williams, C. H. (Ed.). (2000). *Language revitalization: Policy and planning in Wales*. Cardiff: University of Wales Press.

Williams, G. (1992). *Sociolinguistics: A sociological critique*. London: Routledge.

Wodak, R., & Meyer, M. (Eds.). (2016). *Methods of critical discourse studies*. 3rd edition. London: Sage.

Woolard, K. A. (1989). *Doubletalk: Bilingualism and the politics of ethnicity in Catalonia*. Stanford, CA: Stanford University Press.

Woolard, K. A. (1998). Introduction: Language ideology as a field of inquiry. In B. B. Schieffelin, K. A. Woolard, & P. V. Kroskrity (Eds.), *Language ideologies: Practice and theory* (pp. 3–47). Oxford: Oxford University Press.

Woolard, K. A. (2008). Language and identity choice in Catalonia: The interplay of contrasting ideologies of linguistic authority. In K. Süselbeck, U. Mühlschlegel, & P. Masson (Eds.), *Lengua, nación e identidad: La regulación del plurilingüismo en España y América Latina* (pp. 303–323). Frankfurt am Main; Madrid: Vervuert; Iberoamericana.

Woolard, K. A. (2011). Is there linguistic life after high school? Longitudinal changes in the bilingual repertoire in metropolitan Barcelona. *Language in Society* 40(5), 617–648.

CHAPTER 31

SECURITY AND LANGUAGE POLICY

CONSTADINA CHARALAMBOUS,
PANAYIOTA CHARALAMBOUS,
KAMRAN KHAN, AND BEN RAMPTON

SECURITY and war have often been significant influences in language policy, and in the 1940s, the term *applied linguistics* sprang from the marriage of Bloomfield's structuralism with language training in the US army (Howatt, 1984, pp. 265–269). But according to Liddicoat (2008, p. 129), "[l]anguage planning studies . . . have not dealt with security-related language planning in any systematic way. In fact, security is largely absent from most of the classic overviews of language planning." Liddicoat himself surveys the ways in which language planning features in how "states deal with those issues which impinge on questions of territorial integrity and national sovereignty" (p. 130), and he provides a fascinating account of the function and effectiveness of language policies addressing conflict management, conflict prevention, and state security needs. However, he also calls for "a more sophisticated understanding of the . . . conditions, approaches and contexts in [which] the language planning activity is carried out" (p. 148), and argues in conclusion that "[l]anguage planning theory focusing on security ha[s] . . . tended to focus only on the superficial features of communication without problematising how these superficial features in fact interact with both the context in which they operate and the ends to which they are to be used" (p. 150).

Liddicoat's call for security-related language planning to address context and ideology more fully points towards a wider shift in language policy research (Ricento, 2000). This finds expression in, for example, the ethnographic approach to language policy, which McCarty (2011, p. 2) describes as "processual, dynamic, and in motion. . . . [P]olicy never just 'is,' but rather 'does'. . . . We do not restrict our analysis to . . . official policy declarations and texts . . . but place these in context as part of a larger sociocultural system . . . inferred from people's language practices, ideologies and beliefs." There are also parallels with the *enactment* perspective on education policy developed by Stephen Ball et al. (2012, p. 3), who regard policy as "a process, as diversely and repeatedly contested and/or subject to different *interpretations* as it is enacted (rather than implemented) in original and creative ways within institutions and classrooms . . . but in ways that are limited by the possibilities of discourse." And most crucially for the present discussion, there are similarities to a relatively recent strand in security studies which criticises mainstream research on international relations for its idealisation of the sovereign nation-state, for its traditional dislike of "details, local events, or precise and complex life stories" and for its tendency to limit "the thickness of history and anthropology . . . to a varnish" (Bigo, 2014, pp. 190–191). In this perspective, security is not seen as the condition of being safe from external threat. Instead, security involves

> a practice of making "enemy" and "fear" the integrative, energetic principle of politics displacing the democratic principles of freedom and justice. . . . [S]ecurity can thus be understood as a political force. It is not simply a policy responding to threats and dangers. Neither is it a public good or value. It is a practice with a political content. It enacts our world as if it is a dangerous world, a world saturated by insecurities. It invests fear and enmity in relations between humans and polities rather than simply defending or protecting political units and people from enemies and fear. (Huysmans, 2014, p. 3)

In what follows, we will draw on this literature from critical security studies, a heterodox sub-branch of international relations, for two reasons: first, because it provides a great deal of highly informative description and commentary on the ways in which *security* is being reconfigured within the contemporary world, with developments in digital technology, large-scale population movements, and the privatisation of public services; second, because it is increasingly attentive to the ways in which geopolitics permeates the everyday. Within this literature, there is growing receptivity to ethnography (Goldstein, 2010; Maguire, Frois, & Zurawski, 2014), and as in much of sociolinguistics now (e.g., Coupland & Jaworski, 2009), practice theory broadly conceived (Ortner, 2006) is a major epistemological influence.

All this generates considerable scope for connection with studies of language in society (Bigo, 2016, p. 31), and in what follows, we offer two case studies of how *enemy* and *fear* have been active principles in language policy development. The first shows how security has become an increasingly influential theme in the United Kingdom

("Case Study 1" later in this chapter), and the second describes how legacies of large-scale violent conflict can generate rather unexpected ground-level enactments of language education policy, focusing on Cyprus ("Case Study 2"). But before that, the next section shows in a little more detail how the notion of security has been elaborated within critical security studies.

Securitisation, the State, Borders, and Surveillance: Critical Security Studies

Critical security studies has been strongly influenced by scholars like Foucault and Bourdieu, who have obviously been major influences in sociolinguistics as well. As already noted, security and insecurity are conceptualised as ways of seeing and acting in the world, experiencing relationships infused with fear and hostility, and a similar approach is taken to concepts like the *state*, *borders*, and *surveillance*. The congruence with sociolinguistics and situated discourse analysis can be seen very clearly in the notion of *securitisation*.

Securitisation refers to institutional processes that identify threats to the very existence of the state and other bodies, and that seek to suspend normal political rights and procedures (Emmers, 2013). With securitisation, a particular group or issue is said to present such a major risk—such an *existential threat*—that it needs to be moved out of the realm of ordinary politics into the realm of exceptional measures. According to Aradau (2004, p. 392), when accounts of securitisation speak of normal politics, they usually refer to the rules of liberal democracy, which can be said to involve (1) a certain degree of political equality and fairness instituted tangibly; (2) policies and actions as a product of popular power in some tangible sense; (3) basic procedures that are transparent, open to public scrutiny. By contrast, securitisation aims to

> institutionalize . . . speed against the slowness of [democratic] procedures and thus questions the viability of deliberation, contest of opinion and dissent. While the securitizing speech act has to be accepted by a relevant audience and remains within the framework of the democratic politics of contestation, the exceptionality of procedures is its opposite. The speed required by the exceptional suspends the possibilities of judicial review or other modalities of public influence upon bureaucratic or executive decisions. Securitisation re-inscribes issues in a different logic, a logic of urgency and exceptionalism . . . the politics of enmity, decision, and emergency. (Aradau 2004, p. 392)

Throughout the processes associated with securitisation, discourse plays a crucial part, both in declaring a particular group, phenomenon, or process to be an existential threat, and in persuading people that this warrants the introduction of special measures. In its earliest Copenhagen formulation (cf. Buzan & Waever, 2003), the theory of securitisation relied heavily on the speech act theory of Austin and Searle (see Aradau, 2004), but this limited model of communication has now been extensively criticised in security studies (e.g. Stritzel, 2007). In an edited collection that seeks to replace this earlier philosophical perspective with a more sociological and pragmatic account, there are references to Sapir, Goffman, Schegloff, Fairclough, Kress, Wetherell, Mey, Duranti, and Goodwin (Balzacq, 2011).

Traditionally in the study of politics and international relations, as well as in much common sense, the state has been seen as a sovereign entity that governs and protects a specified population within a given territory, and it exists alongside others in an international order made of similar sovereign states (Jabri 2007, pp. 41–42; cf. Liddicoat, 2008). But Foucault's account of the state has become increasingly influential in recent years (e.g., Huysmans, 2006), and instead of seeing the state as a monolithic power, this approach sees it as a plethora of different people, processes, types of knowledge, technologies, actions, and arguments:

> [t]he study of power should begin from below, in the heterogeneous and dispersed micro-physics of power[; it should] explore specific forms of [the exercise of power] in different institutional sites, and consider how, if at all, these were linked to produce broader and more persistent societal configurations. One should study power where it is exercised over individuals rather than legitimated at the centre; explore the actual practices of subjugation rather than the intentions that guide attempts at domination; and recognize that power circulates through networks . . . (Foucault, 1979, pp. 92–102; 2003, pp. 27–34). (Jessop, 2007, p. 36)

For Foucault, the state is a *polymorphous crystallisation* of these ground-level practices, one of the "broader and more persistent societal configurations" that emerge when these practices are coordinated, through mechanisms and organisations like policy, diplomacy, and the military (Jessop, 2007, pp. 36–37). But the whole assemblage is still rather precarious, and this bottom-up, practice-centred approach to the state complements the account of security sketched earlier (as well as the perspectives on policy cited in our introduction). It also extends to the crucial issue of borders.

In common sense, borders are viewed as relatively static geographical facts, lines around the perimeter of the territory governed by a particular state. But globalisation makes it increasingly difficult to operate with this definition, and the distinction between inside and outside loses a great deal of its fixity in the activities of the agencies set up to manage state borders. According to Bigo (2008, p. 14), "we can no longer distinguish between an internal order reigning, thanks to the police, by holding the monopoly on legitimate violence, and an anarchic international order which is maintained by an equilibrium of national powers vis-à-vis the armies and diplomatic alliances." Instead, there is a growing body of *security professionals* engaged in *border work*—police with military status, border guards, customs agents, immigration officers, intelligence officers, private security companies, specialist lawyers, academics, and others. Their interests and specialisms form a complicated, interconnected, but also relatively disorganised transnational field that often operates outside the auspices of the nation-state, but which nevertheless converges "towards the same figure of risk and unease management, the immigrant" (Bigo, 2002, p. 77).

In monitoring who belongs where, who is entitled to stay or visit, who presents what kinds of need, benefit, or threat, border work extends well beyond the moment when a person crosses from the territory of one state into another. Security professionals also make increasing use of digital technologies, building risk profiles of individuals and groups with computational algorithms that work on data sets assembled from the information traces left behind whenever people encounter bureaucracy or themselves use digital technologies (Bauman et al., 2014; Bigo, 2008; Huysmans, 2014). And of course it isn't only migrants who are affected by this surveillance. As matters of routine, most people in the West go online, visit websites, use swipe cards, carry cellphones, and so on. For much of the time, the data generated by these swift, convenient, and pervasive technologies are used commercially, as a resource for targeted marketing, promoting and monitoring consumption (Bauman & Lyon, 2013; Haggerty & Ericson, 2000; van Dijck, 2013). But these data can also be used to generate a risk profile for someone who wants health coverage, insurance, or a mortgage, and there is only a thin line between commercial and security surveillance (also Staples, 2014). Admittedly, there is no overall coordination between all the private, state, and transnational organisations involved in this surveillance, and there is also a good deal of political argument over privacy rights, so that in the view of scholars of security in the West, this doesn't all amount to *1984*'s Big Brother totalitarianism (Bigo, 2008, p. 11; Bauman et al., 2014). But as Edward Snowden's revelations show, the US National Security Agency and the United Kingdom's Government Communications Headquarters (GCHQ) collect phone calls, emails, text messages, Skype communications, and other data on a massive scale without public consent. Digital intelligence work starts with a particular suspect and then extends to friends of friends of friends. So "for a suspected person with 100 friends at the first hop, the person in charge of surveillance at the NSA or one of its private subcontractors can, without warrant, put under surveillance all 2,669,556 potential connections at the third hop" (Bauman et al., 2014. pp. 123–124).

In this section, then, we have reviewed some core concepts in the study of security. *Security* might sound like a clear-cut condition (safety from threat), just as the *state* might seem like a well-defined entity, but in the perspective discussed here, they are viewed as historically specific ensembles of practice and discourse—rationales, knowledges, technologies, and so on. Similarly, borders might seem like geographical facts remote from most people's everyday life at home, work, or recreation, but the proliferation of security professionals and technologies of surveillance means that almost everyone's routine conduct can have consequences for their mobility, status, and entitlements in ways that they don't immediately recognise.

SECURITISATION, LANGUAGE, AND LANGUAGE POLICY

The implications of all this for the study of language in contemporary social life are manifold. For example, in the burgeoning field of linguistic landscape research, analyses of multilingual signage risk a reductive account of the communicative dynamics of space, ethnicity, and migration if they neglect the placement, use, and effects of closed circuit television (CCTV) (cf. Staples, 2014; Vaughan-Williams, 2008). According to K. Ball, "the experience of surveillance has not yet been addressed in any detail. . . . The fact that individuals sometimes appear to do little to counter surveillance does not mean that surveillance means nothing to them" (2009, p. 640).

Similarly, research on language and superdiversity usually foregrounds (and sometimes celebrates) the challenge that the mobility associated with globalisation presents to established academic and bureaucratic demographic categorisation, but this risks overlooking the flexibility of digital surveillance (Arnaut, 2012; Rampton et al., 2015, pp. 8–10). So for example, "[o]n-line a category like gender is not determined by one's genitalia or even physical appearance. Nor is it entirely self-selected. Rather, categories of identity are being inferred upon individuals based on their web use. Code and algorithm are the engines behind such inference [constructing] identity and category online" (Cheney-Lippold, 2011, p. 165). As "a mode of governing that seeks to quickly adapt delivery of services, control and coercion to changing behaviours deriving and processing information directly from the everyday 'doings' of people" (Huysmans 2014, pp.166–167), the technologies of contemporary surveillance are attuned to the fluidity of identity and the (re)shaping that occurs in interactional practice, even though they are insensitive to the subtleties involved and their interpretations are skewed by their own driving preoccupations.

But what of language policy? In the two case studies that follow, *enemy*, *fear*, and *security* are central concerns in the contested and uneven unfolding of language policy, but the relationship between ordinary and securitised social relations can be seen as moving in opposite directions. Drawing attention to securitisation's growing influence in a liberal democracy, the first concentrates on the United Kingdom, where Muslims are increasingly treated as a security risk, where suspicion is articulated with growing force in public discourse, and there are contradictory effects on language policy. The second focuses on Cyprus, where there are now efforts to resolve the long-standing conflict between Greek- and Turkish-Cypriots, where opportunities to learn Turkish have been introduced for Greek-Cypriots, and where the aftermath of violent conflict generates rather distinctive and unanticipated ground-level enactments of language policy.

Case Study 1: The (In)securitisation of Language in Contemporary Britain

As already noted, the work of security professionals tends to converge on "the same figure of risk and unease management, the immigrant" (Bigo, 2002, p. 77). The negative portrayal of Muslims is long-standing in Britain, but over the last fifteen years, securitising discourses that abnormalise British Muslims and construct them as a *suspect community* have intensified. The term *suspect community* was originally used to refer to Irish communities in the United Kingdom, suspected of being sympathetic to the IRA (Hillyard, 1993). It refers to

> [a] sub-group of the population that is singled out for state attention as being "problematic" in terms of policing, and individuals may be targeted, not necessarily as a result of suspected wrong doing, but simply because of their presumed membership to that sub-group. Race, ethnicity, religion, class, gender, language, accent, dress, political ideology or any combination of these factors may serve to delineate the sub-group. (Pantazis & Pemberton, 2009, p. 649)

Since 2000, a number of events both in the United Kingdom and internationally have resulted in Muslims becoming the primary targets of suspicion. In the summer of 2001, there were riots in three northern English cities involving (mainly Muslim) British Asians, far-right extremists, and the police, and these led to calls for more emphasis on citizenship as a way of fusing together parallel communities (Cantle Commission, 2002). The 9/11 bombings occurred a few weeks later, and the view of Islamic communities as poorly integrated and a security risk became entrenched with the 7/7 London bombings in 2005, where three of the four bombers were born in the United Kingdom (Fortier, 2008). In 2007, Glasgow Airport was attacked by two Muslims driving a Jeep packed with petrol canisters into a terminal; in 2013, Fusilier Lee Rigby was murdered in Greenwich by Islamic militants; the Charlie Hebdo murders in Paris in 2015 once again focused attention on an Islamic *enemy within*; and more recently, the scale of ISIS's recruitment of young Muslims willing to leave a comfortable existence in the United Kingdom has intensified the portrayal of British-born Muslims as poorly integrated, potentially dangerous, and with questionable loyalty.

Over this period, the expression of hostility in public discourse has become much more explicit (see also Cooke & Simpson, 2012, pp. 124–125). *Political correctness* seems to be less of a concern, and the Overton Window—the range of ideas and policies that the public is willing to accept—has shifted to the right, as can be seen in, for example, Prime Minister Cameron's claim that too many Muslims "quietly condone" violent extremism (*Daily Mail*, 18 June 2015), or in the rise to prominence and acceptability of anti-immigration parties such as the UKIP (United Kingdom Independence Party). The public is now told that it is constantly under threat, and this can be seen in the British government's *Prevent* policy. In the post–9/11 era, the government has formulated a comprehensive anti-terrorism strategy consisting of four strands. The first, *Pursue*, aims to prevent terrorist attacks from happening; the second, *Prevent*, seeks to stop people becoming terrorists; the third, *Protect*, aims to safeguard areas both in the United Kingdom and abroad through, for example, stronger border control; and the fourth, *Prepare*, addresses the aftermath of a terrorist attack. *Prevent*, which is both ideological and material in nature, has been by far the most contentious of these strands, and its 2015 guidelines state three objectives:

> Respond to the ideological challenge of terrorism and the threat we face from those who promote it; prevent people from being drawn into terrorism and ensure that they are given appropriate advice and support; work with sectors and institutions where there are risks of radicalisation that we need to address. (HMG, 2015, p. 5)

The institutions identified "for partnership with *Prevent*" include local authorities, education from early child-care providers to higher education, health services, the prison service, and the police (HMG, 2015), and signs of this effort to alert the public to the threat of terrorism are now unavoidable in everyday life, whether these take the form of classroom surveillance, new measures in airports, or public signage about how to report suspicion. With the *Counter Terrorism and Security Bill (CTS) 2015*, educational institutions are obliged to report any children/individuals who might be being radicalised or *at risk*, with Muslim students—children—as potential terrorists and teachers as *de facto* security professionals, who can even receive training for this. Indeed, it was recently reported that

> [s]chools are being sold software to monitor pupils' internet activity for extremism-related language such as "jihadi bride" and "YODO," short for you only die once, ahead of the introduction of a legal requirement to consider issues of terrorism and extremism among children. . . . Several companies are producing "anti-radicalisation" software to monitor pupils' internet activity, including Impero, which has launched a pilot of its software in 16 locations in Britain as well as five in the US. . . . A spokeswoman for Impero said: . . . The system may help teachers confirm identification of vulnerable children, or act as an early warning system to help identify children that may be at risk in future. It also provides evidence for teachers and child protection officers to use in order to intervene in a timely and appropriate manner. (*The Guardian*, 10 June 2015)

These developments are contested: the 2015 conference of the National Union of Teachers considered the ways in which these developments shut discussion down in school classrooms, making Muslim students fearful that their teachers were undertaking surveillance; in higher education, over 280 academics signed a letter to *The Independent* arguing against *Prevent*'s "chilling effect on open debate, free speech and political dissent" (10 July 2015); and the trade union for Further Education and Higher Education stated, "the *Prevent* agenda will force our members to spy on learners, is discriminatory towards Muslims, and legitimises Islamophobia and xenophobia, encouraging racist views to be publicised and normalised in society" (UCU, 2015, p. 4). But the ground-level impact of this securitisation of British Muslims is likely to be considerable, and it has also affected language policy, repositioning of languages within policies on citizenship, anti-radicalisation, and recruitment for the military and intelligence services.

In the English education system, after extensive multicultural interest in the 1970s and 1980s, support for the multilingualism of minority ethnic students declined sharply in the 1990s, making way for a much more exclusive commitment to standard English (Rampton et al., 2001). But the events and discourses sketched in the preceding have led beyond this to an intensified emphasis on the need for adult migrants to learn English, and the teaching and learning of ESOL (English for Speakers of Other Languages) has been advocated as an essential ingredient in citizenship, an antidote to the ills of segregated communities and a vital instrument of social cohesion.

As Khan (2015) describes in detail, the 2001 riots were followed by a series of political speeches and policy documents calling for more attention to British citizenship, arguing that to be a citizen is to be a speaker of English (Blackledge, 2005; Cooke & Simpson, 2012, p. 125). In 2005, the *Life in the UK* test was introduced for migrants seeking British citizenship (and for those seeking Indefinite Leave to Remain in 2007), and over time, increasingly demanding English-proficiency requirements were tied into this, with, for example, a language requirement being introduced for the reunification of non-EU, non-English-speaking spouses in 2011. The spirit of these developments can be seen in the words of then Home Secretary Theresa May (2015):

> Government alone cannot defeat extremism so we need to do everything we can to build up the capacity of civil society to identify, confront and defeat extremism wherever we find it. We want to go further than ever before helping people from isolated communities to play a full and fruitful role in British life. We plan a step change in the way we help people learn English. There will be new incentives and penalties, a sharp reduction in translation services and a significant increase in the funding available for English. (Theresa May, Home Secretary, 23 March 2015, *A Stronger Britain, Built on Values*; https://www.gov.uk/government/speeches/a-stronger-britain-built-on-our-values)

Recourse to an interpreter is discouraged here, and arguments like these target other multilingual spaces as well, as evidenced in David Cameron's proposal that "as we develop our Counter-Extremism Strategy . . . we will also bring forward further measures to guard against the radicalisation of children in some so-called supplementary schools or tuition centres" (Cameron, 2015). Consistent with this, there has been a drop in funding for a number of modern- and heritage-language courses (Steer, 2014).

Of course, policy initiatives of this kind require the involvement of professionals from a range of sectors—immigration, education, city councils, and so on—and co-ordination of the ensemble of people, practices, knowledges, and mechanisms that constitute the state is often precarious. Some of the texture of the implementation of these policies is captured in Khan and Blackledge's (2015) account of citizenship in Britain. On the one hand, officials watch the mouths of participants to ensure that they utter the affirmation/oath to become British. At the same time, this gravity can be softened by the conduct of the officers in charge, as noted in Khan's field notes:

> All the citizens are standing together; they then make the pledge. As they go through the pledge, some are proud and speak clearly and loudly. Some people are a little more reserved and some look plain shy and embarrassed. B [the officiating dignitary] makes a joke: "we can't speak your language, so we need you to say it in English. Even if understanding English is difficult—do your best." He then makes the citizens aware that another hurdle remains. He even says: "I know you have jumped through a lot of hoops, but there is still a hurdle to go." He then says: "we'll be watching. Do your best. Try and do your best." (Khan & Blackledge 2015, p. 399)

The complexities of implementation emerged on a much larger scale in 2014, when Home Secretary Theresa May told the education sector "to put its house in order" and the English language tests for immigration run by the Educational Testing Service (ETS) were suspended, following allegations of widespread abuse ("fake sitters" and passes guaranteed for £500; *Times Higher Education*, 10 February 2014; *Daily Mail*, 10 February 2014). And when political calls for English-language proficiency as a prerequisite for citizenship coincide with extensive cuts to ESOL and adult educa-tion budgets (*Times Education Supplement*, 20 July 2015), the counter-extremist em-phasis on English for citizenship looks incoherent to the point of self-defeating.

In fact, for the British intelligence and security services, a dramatic fall in the number of students graduating with foreign-language degrees gives the multilin-gualism of the United Kingdom's ethnic minority population considerable stra-tegic significance. So in a 2013 response to potential cuts in heritage-language qualifications, GCHQ stated,

> We are concerned that there may be a move away from offering qualifications spoken by [minority ethnic] native speakers, as these qualifications not only allow speakers to develop their reading and writing skills and to learn about grammatical struc-ture of their language, but also demonstrate the value of having formally recognised native language skills. We would also support any initiative to increase the number of languages qualifications which cover native speaker or heritage languages. (British Academy, 2013, p. 30)

In its recruitment efforts, GCHQ has undertaken outreach work in schools, and in a similar vein, the British army has made a concerted effort to recruit more Muslims, not just because of its diversity targets, but also for their linguistic skills (British Academy, 2013; Carter, 2015). The difficulty is, of course, that just at the time when intelligence and the military want their linguistic abilities more than ever, Muslims are being portrayed as a *suspect community*, subjected to high levels of surveillance, scrutiny, and distrust (Khan, 2015).

So as an element in securitisation, language policy is no more coherent or unified than other aspects of this process. Even so, security concerns are far more prominent in the discourse and enactment of domestic language policy than they were at the end of the twentieth century, and we could not understand these developments if security is simply conceptualised as protection from a clearly identified external threat, as in traditional international relations research. Increasingly, cultural and linguistic difference has itself been constructed as a security risk, and in the everyday lives of many people with Muslim, migrant, diasporic, and/or multilingual backgrounds, this can be characterised as a process of *insecuritisation*, of being watched by a growing number of people pushed into the role of *security professional*, becoming increasingly vulnerable to *exceptional measures* (Bigo, 2008; 2014, pp. 198–202). And of course this isn't restricted to the United Kingdom. In the study of a town in Pennsylvania with a large community with links to Mexico, Gallo describes the enactment of "Secure Communities" from 2011 onwards:

> "Secure Communities" is a data sharing program in which local police officers submit a person's information to Immigration and Custom's Enforcement (ICE) when a person is stopped for any infraction, ranging from an arrest for an aggravated felony to a minor infraction such as a speeding ticket (Kohli, Markowitz, & Chavez, 2011). If this person does not have documentation for U.S. residency, he or she can be apprehended by ICE and undergo the deportation process. (2014, p. 477)

Ninety per cent of those deported are not released from detention prior to deportation, often not having the chance to say goodbye to their families (2014, p. 490), and Gallo describes in detail the traumatic effects on children and community (as well as the difficulties that schools hamstrung by test-oriented curricula have engaging with this) (de Genova, 2002; Gallo & Link, 2015).

Rather than highlighting political currents that are becoming more significant in liberal democracies, our second case points to a gap between the expectations of language policy in peace and stability, on the one hand, and on the other, the practices observed in environments where security has been a long-standing concern.[1]

Case Study 2: De-securitisation and Foreign Language Education in a Conflict-Affected Context

In the Council of Europe's *Common European Framework of Reference for Languages*, foreign-language education is generally assumed to contribute to peaceful coexistence. But what happens to dominant assumptions in a well-established field like this when teaching takes place in a conflict-ridden or post-conflict setting, where the language taught is associated with people who have been portrayed for many years as a threatening enemy?

Cyprus has a long history of interethnic conflict between the Greek-Cypriot and Turkish-Cypriot communities, going back to the beginning of the twentieth century. In an era of intense nation-building in both Greece and Turkey, the island's two main religious communities, Christians and Muslims, came to imagine themselves as incompatible *Greeks* and *Turks* under the influence of antagonistic nationalist discourses (Bryant, 2004). A bi-communal Republic of Cyprus was established in 1960, but in spite of this, interethnic violence broke out in 1963–1967, and in 1974 the political turmoil culminated in a military intervention by Turkey that left the island *de facto* divided into Turkish-speaking north and Greek-speaking, government-controlled south areas. Since then, a buffer zone patrolled by military personnel and UN peacekeeping forces has served as a physical border that separates the two communities and substantially inhibits communication between them.

Language played a crucial role in the historical development of these ethnic identities in Cyprus. It served as a tangible way of differentiating the population into two communities and was perceived as a pre-condition for their survival (Karoulla-Vrikki, 2004; Kizilyurek & Gautier-Kizilyurek, 2004). At earlier points in history, Turkish-Cypriots (the minority) used both Turkish and the local Cypriot variety of Greek, but during the conflict, nationalist discourses on both sides not only discouraged but also penalised bilingualism (Charalambous, 2012; Özerk, 2001). Speaking the language of the national *archenemy* (Papadakis, 2008) became undesirable and a sign of betrayal. So Turkish never featured in official Greek-Cypriot educational curricula, and learning the language was largely restricted to Greek-Cypriot police and intelligence services (Papadakis, 2005).

In 2003, however, after twenty-nine years of total isolation and *ethnic estrangement* (Bryant, 2004), in the midst of negotiations for Cyprus's entry to the European Union and the search for a political settlement of the Cyprus conflict, the Turkish-Cypriot authorities announced the partial lifting of the restrictions of movement across the buffer zone, and for the first time, people were allowed to cross the dividing line. Language was also drawn into a central role in this period of rapid political developments: just a week after the opening of the buffer-zone checkpoints, the (Greek-)Cypriot government announced the establishment of language classes for Greek-Cypriots wishing to learn Turkish as a foreign language, both in secondary schools and adult institutes, as well as classes for Turkish-speaking adults who wanted to learn Greek.[2] In educational documents, in interviews with senior ministry officials, and among many people who decided to attend the classes, these initiatives fitted into a rhetoric of reconciliation and were seen as an emblematic gesture of government goodwill (see Charalambous, 2012, 2013, 2014).

On the ground, though, things were more difficult, as the setting up of Turkish classes was not accompanied by an immediate change in educational and public discourse, which continued to construct Turks as the enemy posing an imminent threat to the Greek-Cypriot community (see Adamides, 2014). As a result, teaching and learning Turkish was often seen as threatening Greek-Cypriot education's Greek-centred—*Hellenocentric*—orientation. For Turkish-language teachers and learners, this generated a series of practical complications. In our 2006 study (see Charalambous, 2012), almost all interviewees reported being called a *traitor*, a *Turk*, or *Turkophile* by peers, friends, and occasionally by family members and other teachers, and as a result, they often hid their Turkish books, avoided mentioning the classes they taught or attended, and/or developed careful justifications in defence.

Formulated in terms from security studies, the lifting of border restrictions and the introduction of Turkish classes can be seen as *de*-securitising moves. Rather than seeking to shift a group from the sphere of ordinary politics into a zone of exceptional measures (securitisation), de-securitisation pushes in the opposite direction and seeks to normalise relations with what has hitherto been seen as an existential threat (cf. Aradau, 2004; Charalambous et al., 2017). But this involves discursive struggle and resistance, and analysis of the enactment of Turkish foreign-language policy in Cyprus points to practices and stances that challenge mainstream applied linguistic accounts of foreign-language education, thereby relativising them, while also suggesting unanticipated ways in which language education can contribute to processes of reconciliation.

In a great deal of the theory underpinning foreign-language policy, lessons are seen as occasions for practising communication, with a view to engaging with speakers of the foreign language outside class. Role-plays and materials with a degree of resemblance to the everyday world inhabited by the foreign-language speakers are often recommended (*authenticity*), and in recent years, there has been increased emphasis on students developing inter-cultural competence, the capacity to understand and manage cultural differences (Byram et al., 2001; Council of Europe, 2001). But in the de-securitisation process in Cyprus, Greek-Cypriot society was itself engaged in a still highly contested process of negotiating whether and how to move Turkish issues *into* the realm of ordinary civic life, *out of* the exceptional measures required for an existential threat. So for many Turkish language students, imagining oneself in the world of the target language was far from straightforward. A number of secondary students told us that they had no intention of ever talking to a Turkish-speaker, and as one teacher complained, "How am I going to practice dialogues in the classroom between sales-men and buyers, when students are not supposed to cross to the other side and buy things from the occupied territories?" (C. Charalambous field notes, 2006). Indeed, if a teacher made a positive comment about Turkish-speaking people even in passing in the classroom, this could spark intense reactions and at least momentarily jeopardise their authority, as C. Charalambous (2013) documents in detail.

So how did teachers cope? They developed several strategies, but the most common was to treat Turkish as just a lexico-grammatical code. Instead of emphasising the communicative and cultural aspects of the language, encouraging learners to "cope with the affective as well as cognitive demands of engagement with otherness" (Byram, 1995, p. 25), a lot of teachers tried to suppress the socio-indexical/socio-symbolic side of Turkish, and instead, they presented it in class as a neutral set of lexical items and syntactic structures. Of course, there is a strong philological tradition that supports pedagogy like this, but these teachers were quite explicit about the risks of attempting a communicative or intercultural approach (P. Charlambous et al., 2017). Their *de-culturalisation* of Turkish, in other words, was driven by acute cultural sensitivity.

And what of the young people? Why did they choose Turkish in the first place? "Because it's easy and gets you good marks" was one of the most common answers provided in interviews, and liking a particular teacher also played a part. But this oversimplifies the experience of learning the language of an enemy, and for a fuller understanding, it is important to look beyond the usual unit of analysis in the study of foreign-language learning motivation—the individual—and to situate learners in their families and family histories. In violent conflicts of the kind experienced in Cyprus, collective life is profoundly disrupted, with widespread loss of life and a great deal of forced relocation (Greek-Cypriot refugees moved south, and Turkish-Cypriots fled north). After the cessation of hostilities, the language of the enemy—in this case, Turkish—is likely to be bound up with lived, learned, and taught histories that are vividly remembered, indexing a set of experiences and relationships about which families still have very deep feelings. So to grasp how adolescents positioned themselves as learners of Turkish, we have to understand their intergenerational family relationships, and it was clear in interviews that family discussions could either constrain or enhance their scope for studying the language. Family losses, anger, and pain produced visible reservations among some learners, who worried about venturing too far with things Turkish, while for others, more positive family experiences in the pre-1974 period before the war—stories of friendship, collaboration, and exchange with Turkish-Cypriots—contributed to greater engagement, gradually reworking the negative associations of Turkish, often in continuing dialogue with older family members. In sum, secondary school students participated in these classes as the younger members of multi-generational families, balancing loyalty and responsibility to their kin with an awareness of geopolitical processes increasing the possibility of reconciliation. So here and more generally in post-conflict situations, an analysis that follows the usual route of focusing only on the motivation, aspirations, and choices of individuals is likely to be insufficient.

In the mainstream paradigm, foreign-language teachers prepare their students for visits abroad to the country where the language is widely spoken, but the situation was much more complex in Cyprus. While the political situation remained officially unsettled in the island, crossing to the other side was often treated as morally unacceptable. For some, the act of passing through a checkpoint gave recognition to an imposed dividing line that they regarded as illegitimate, bringing accusations of betrayal; some crossed occasionally but avoided economic transactions as a matter of principle; and others crossed more frequently and had ongoing relationships with people in the north. These differences were experienced among both adults and adolescents, and in the adult classes they were quite often acknowledged and discussed. When adults and adolescents did cross to the north, their perspective was also radically different from the *touristic* gaze most commonly assumed in foreign-language study (e.g., Sercu & Bandura, 2005). Instead, especially among adolescents, accounts of visits to the Turkish-speaking north often carried the aura of *pilgrimage*, and they were formulated as *narratives of return*, either to their parents' former home in the case of students from refugee families, or to places emblematic of Greek Orthodox identity. Indeed, even when talking about Istanbul in class, teachers tended to highlight its Greek roots, history, and character. In sum, locating the *target language* in time and space always bore the stamp of a troubled past, and it was far more difficult in these Turkish classes than is usually assumed in discussions of foreign-language education (Charalambous, 2013).

Admittedly, in defence of orthodox foreign-language education theory, one might argue that given the long history of Turkish in Cyprus, it is a mistake to call it a *foreign* language. But this was the categorisation used by the Greek-Cypriot education authorities, who placed it alongside Italian, French, Russian, and other languages in the secondary curriculum. Moreover, there is a case for saying that its very position as an everyday curriculum subject, as just one among a number of foreign languages, made a significant contribution to the reconciliation process. As we have said, it was very hard to normalise relations between Greek- and Turkish-Cypriots because it ran counter to the historic securitisation of Turks and Turkish-Cypriots. But for this, the very *ordinariness* of the foreign language class was itself a resource. Curricular foreign language learning is an unspectacular but long-term, widely established, institutionally organised activity that demands a significant investment of time and effort, and these Turkish language classes meant that Greek-Cypriots regularly shared a space where things and practices linked with Turkish had a low-key presence close at hand, travelling back and forth between school and home in homework bags, accessible for closer association if students wanted and were able.

According to Aradau (2004), effective de-securitisation in a liberal democracy needs to restore the "possibility of scrutiny as well as the expression of voice," practices that securitisation suppresses. To achieve this, it requires a "*slowness* in procedures that ensures the possibility of contestation" (p. 393; our emphasis), and "a different relation from the one of enmity . . . has to be *inscribed institutionally*" (p. 400; our emphasis). Slowness and institutionalisation were intrinsic to these Turkish classes. They brought people into the vicinity of otherness as a matter of routine (a teaching period twice a week for one or two years in the secondary curriculum), and they occupied their attention over periods of time that were long enough to host small and gradual shifts in outlook. Such shifts were, of course, far from guaranteed, but there was good evidence that Turkish lessons helped a number of students orient more constructively towards a peaceful future.

There is a risk, of course, of these classes being judged by the criteria most commonly applied in foreign-language education—the development of linguistic proficiency—even though the historical background of intense conflict meant that the working assumptions about communication, culture, and the person in time and space were very different from those operating in a Greek-Cypriot class of Spanish or Italian. An assessment of that kind would miss the significance of what was happening.

From research like Pavlenko's comparative account of foreign-language education in the war-oriented United States and Soviet Union (2003), Uhlmann's study of Arabic classes for Jewish school students in Israel (2010, 2012), and Karrebaek and Ghandchi's description of mother-tongue Farsi in the divided Iranian refugee community in Copenhagen (2015), it is clear that the Cyprus case isn't actually unique, and that when there are circumambient discourses of security and/or serious conflict in the background, the *target* culture may be excluded in culturally responsive language classrooms, along with anticipations of casual contact and tourist travel. To get proper recognition from policy actors, perhaps the vocabulary of language policy and pedagogy needs a new category capable of changing these expectations of success, such as *troubled* or *conflicted heritage language*. But of course policy enactment entails much more than just conception and design, and a formulation like *troubled/conflicted heritage* could undermine the low-key ordinariness of curricular Turkish-as-a-foreign-language that seemed to help students along the path from hostility to toleration (or beyond).

CONCLUSION

In this chapter, we have pointed to methodological compatibilities between ethnographic approaches to language policy, on the one hand, and critical security studies, on the other, both being grounded in a broadly based theory of practice. We began by describing the ways in which critical security studies is reconceptualising traditional concepts from international relations like the *state, security, borders*, and *surveillance*, and we suggested that in the process, linguistic ethnography becomes a potentially very valuable analytic resource. In addition, the interaction between sociolinguistics and critical security studies is warranted by the fact that over the last twenty years or so in parts of the West, issues of (in)security have gained much wider currency in both public and everyday discourse.

We illustrated this with a case study from the United Kingdom, showing how security policies are licensing and normalising new forms of racism, redefining the responsibilities of professionals, working through into new forms of monitoring, and respecifying the goals for language education. But at the same time—and in line with what policy ethnographies and critical security studies would both lead one to expect—we also saw that these processes were neither uncontested nor especially coherent.

Of course, in many places elsewhere, large-scale conflict can have a very prominent, wide-ranging, and long-standing impact on social life, and in the second case study, we turned to Cyprus, where teaching the language of the former enemy has featured in the (Greek)-Cypriot government's attempts to bring the Greek- and Turkish-Cypriot communities closer together. Here we focussed on the ground-level enactment of a *de-securitisation* policy, and we found language pedagogies that were hard to square with the orthodox theory and practice of intercultural communicative language teaching, even though they were very sensitively tuned to the possibilities at that particular time and place.

In fact, more generally, war, insecurity, and the legacies of violent conflict have featured in a number of different ways in studies of language and society (C. Charalambous et al., 2015). Close to front-line military conflict, there are accounts of language policy and communicative practice in, for example, intelligence gathering, translation and interpreting, language instruction, and allied personnel coordination (see Foottit & Kelly, 2012; Liddicoat, 2008). At one or more removes from the conflict itself, with enemies and experiences of violence looming in the background instead, there is significant work on language and discourse in asylum procedures and language pedagogy in settings receiving refugees (e.g., Karrabaek & Ghandchi, 2015; Maryns, 2006). There is also research on teaching and learning the *language of the enemy* (see the last paragraph in the preceding section), as well as language policy during and after conflict (Busch, 2010; Pavlenko, 2003). But for the most part, these studies lie outside the mainstream of applied and sociolinguistic research, and might be regarded as peripheral to discursive life in the polities in which they are conducted.

However, with a sense of geopolitical instability growing in many places, it is likely that *enemy* and *fear* will become increasingly powerful elements in politics, policy, and everyday institutional life, often "displacing the democratic principles of freedom and justice" (Huysmans, 2014, p. 3). As we have emphasised, the effects are unpredictable, and the changing configurations of security agent, threat, suspect, technology, policy, and communicative practice will need to be identified and described empirically. The terms *securitisation, insecuritisation*, and *desecuritisation* provide only a hint of the different ways in which *security* and language policy are likely to be related in the period ahead, but as a key resource for future investigations, there is an invaluable body of expert literature in critical security studies, which stands out for its compatibility with practice-centred language policy research.

Notes

1. The discussion draws on findings from two periods of linguistic ethnographic research focused on Turkish-language classes organized in Greek-Cypriot schools and adult institutes (2006–2009; 2012–2015). For a succinct overview, see Rampton et al. (2015).
2. For Turkish-Cypriots the language classes were only offered in afternoon governmental institutions, as schooling in both communities has been historically separate.

References

Adamides, C. (2014). Negative perceptions of foreign actors: An integral part of conflict perpetuating routines. In M. Kontos et al. (Eds.), *Great power politics in Cyprus: Foreign interventions and domestic perceptions* (pp. 197–222). Newcastle upon Tyne: Cambridge Scholars.

Aradau, C. (2004). Security and the democratic scene: Desecuritization and emancipation. *Journal of International Relations and Development* 7(4), 388–413.

Arnaut, K. (2012). Super-diversity: Elements of an emerging perspective. *Diversities* 14(2), 1–16.

Ball, K. (2009). Exposure: Exploring the subject of surveillance. *Information, Communication & Society* 12(5), 639–657.

Ball, S., Maguire, M., & Braun, A. (2012). *How schools do policy*. London: Routledge.

Balzacq, T. (Ed.) (2011). *Securitisation theory: How security problems emerge and dissolve*. London: Routledge.

Bauman, Z., & Lyon, D. (2013). *Liquid surveillance: A conversation*. New York: John Wiley & Sons.

Bauman, Z., Bigo, D., Esteves, P., Guild, E., Jabri, V., Lyon, D., & Walker, R. (2014). After Snowden: Rethinking the impact of surveillance. *International Political Sociology* 8, 121–144.

Bigo, D. (2002). Security and immigration: Toward a critique of the governmentality of unease. *Alternatives: Global, Local, Political* 27(1), 63–92.

Bigo, D. (2008). Globalized (in)security: The field and the ban-opticon. In D. Bigo & A. Tsoukala (Eds.), *Terror, insecurity and liberty: Illiberal practices of liberal regimes after 9/11* (pp. 10–49). London: Routledge.

Bigo, D. (2014). Afterword. In M. Maguire, C. Frois, & N. Zurawski (Eds.), *The anthropology of security* (pp. 189–205). London: Pluto Press.

Bigo, D. (2016). International political sociology: Rethinking the international through dynamics of power. In T. Basaran, D. Bigo, E.-P. Guittet, & R. Walkers (Eds.), *International political sociology* (pp. 24–48). London: Routledge.

Blackledge, A. (2005). *Discourse and power in a multilingual world*. Amsterdam: John Benjamins.

British Academy (2013). *Lost for words*. London: British Academy.

Bryant, R. (2004). *Imagining the modern: The cultures of nationalism in Cyprus*. London, New York: I. B. Tauris.

Busch, B. (2010). New national languages in Eastern Europe. In N. Coupland (Ed.), *Handbook of language and globalisation* (pp. 182–200). Oxford: Wiley-Blackwell.

Buzan, B., & Wæver, O. (2003). *Regions and powers: The structure of international security.* Cambridge: Cambridge University Press.

Byram, M. (1995). Intercultural competence and mobility in multinational context: A European view. In M. Tickoo (Ed.), *Language and culture in multilingual societies* (pp. 21–36). Singapore: SEAMEO Regional Language Centre.

Byram, M., Nichols, A., & Stevens, D. (Eds.). (2001). *Developing intercultural competence in practice.* Clevedon, UK: Multilingual Matters.

Cameron, D. (2015). Extremism. Retrieved from https://www.gov.uk/government/speeches/extremism-pm-speech

Cantle Commission. (2002). *Challenging local communities to change Oldham.* Coventry: The Institute of Community Cohesion.

Carter, N. (2015). *Transcript: The future of the British army: How the British army must change to serve Britain in a volatile world.* London: The Royal Institute of International Affairs.

Charalambous, C. (2012). "Republica De Kubros": Transgression and collusion in Greek-Cypriot adolescents' classroom "silly-talk." *Linguistics and Education* 23, 334–349.

Charalambous, C. (2013). The burden of emotions in language teaching: Renegotiating a troubled past in the language classroom. *Language and Intercultural Communication Journal* 13(3), 310–320.

Charalambous, C. (2014). "Whether you see them as friends or enemies you need to know their language": Turkish-language learning in a Greek Cypriot school. In V. Lytra (Ed.), *When Greeks and Turks meet: Interdisciplinary perspectives on the relationship since 1923* (pp. 141–162). London: Ashgate.

Charalambous, C., Charalambous, P., Khan, K., & Rampton, B. (2015). Sociolinguistics and security. *King's College Working Papers in Urban Language & Literacies* 177.

Charalambous, P., Charalambous, C., & Rampton, B. (2017). Desecuritizing Turkish: Teaching the language of a former enemy and intercultural language education. *Applied Linguistics* 38(6), 800–823.

Cheney-Lippold, J. (2011). A new algorithmic identity: Soft biopolitics and the modulation of control. *Theory, Culture & Society* 28(6), 164–181.

Cooke, M., & Simpson, J. (2012). Discourses about linguistic diversity. In M. Martin-Jones, A. Blackledge, & A. Creese (Eds.), *The Routledge handbook of multilingualism* (pp. 116–130). London: Routledge.

Council of Europe. (2007). *Guide for the development of language education policies in Europe: From linguistic diversity to plurilingual education.* Strasbourg: Council of Europe.

Council of Europe. (2001). *Common European framework of reference for languages: Learning, teaching, assessment.* Cambridge: Cambridge University Press.

Coupland, N., & Jaworski, A. (2009). Social worlds through language. In N. Coupland & A. Jaworski (Eds.), *The new sociolinguistics reader* (pp. 1–22). Basingstoke, UK: Palgrave Macmillan.

DeGenova, N. P. (2002). Migrant "illegality" and deportability in everyday life. *Annual Review of Anthropology* 31, 419–447.

Emmers, R. (2013). Securitization. In A. Collins (Ed.), *Contemporary security studies* (3rd edition; pp. 131–143). Oxford: Oxford University Press.

Footitt, H., & Kelly, M. (Eds.). (2012). *Languages at war: Policies and practices of language contacts in conflict.* Basingstoke, UK: Palgrave.

Fortier, A.-M. (2008). *Multicultural horizons: Diversity and the limits of a civil nation.* Abingdon, UK: Routledge.

Gallo, S. 2014. The effects of gendered immigration enforcement on middle childhood and schooling. *American Educational Research Journal* 51(3), 473–504.

Gallo, S., & Link, H. (2015). "Diles la verdad": Deportation policies, politicised funds of knowledge, and schooling in middle childhood. *Harvard Educational Review* 85(3), 357–382.

Goldstein, D. M. (2010). Toward a critical anthropology of security. *Current Anthropology* 51(4), 487–517.

Haggerty, K. D., & Ericson, R. V. (2000). The surveillant assemblage. *The British Journal of Sociology* 51(4), 605–622.

Hillyard, P. (1993). *Suspect community: People's experience of the prevention of terrorism acts in Britain.* London: Pluto Press.

HMG. (2015). *Prevent strategy duty guidance.* London: HM Government.

Howatt, A. (1984). *A History of English language teaching.* Oxford: Oxford University Press.

Huysmans, J. (2006). *The politics of insecurity.* Abingdon, UK: Routledge.

Huysmans, J. (2014). *Security unbound: Enacting democratic limits.* New York: Routledge.

Jabri, V. (2007). *War and the transformation of global politics.* Houndmills, Basingstoke, UK; New York: Palgrave Macmillan.

Jessop, B. (2007). From micro-powers to governmentality: Foucault's work on statehood, state formation, statecraft and state power. *Political Geography* 26(1), 34–40.

Karoulla-Vrikki, D. (2004). Language and ethnicity in Cyprus under the British: A linkage of heightened salience. *International Journal of the Sociology of Language* 168, 19–36.

Karrebæk, M., & Ghandchi, N. (2015). "Pure" Farsi and political sensitivities: Language and ideologies in Farsi complementary language classrooms in Denmark. *Journal of Sociolinguistics* 19(1), 62–90.

Khan, K. (2015). *"Suspect Communities" and multilingual solutions for intelligence and armed conflict.* Manuscript, University of Leicester.

Khan, K., & Blackledge. A. (2015). "They look into our lips": Negotiation of the citizenship ceremony as authoritative discourse. *Journal of Language and Politics* 14(3), 382–405.

Kizilyürek, N., & Gautier-Kizilyürek, S. (2004). The politics of identity in the Turkish Cypriot community and the language question. *International Journal of the Sociology of Language* 168, 37–54.

Liddicoat, A. (2008). Language planning and questions of national security: An overview of planning approaches. *Current Issues in Language Planning* 9(2), 129–153.

Maguire, M., Frois C., & Zurawski N. (Eds.) (2014). *The anthropology of security.* London: Pluto Press.

Maryns, K. (2006). *The asylum speaker: Language in the Belgian asylum procedure.* Manchester, UK: St. Jerome Press.

McCarty, T. (2011). Introducing ethnography and language policy. In T. McCarty (Ed.), *Ethnography and language policy* (pp. 1–28). London: Routledge.

Ortner, S. (2006). *Anthropology and social theory: Culture, power, and the acting subject.* Durham, NC: Duke University Press.

Özerk, K. (2001). Reciprocal bilingualism as a challenge and opportunity: The case of Cyprus. *International Review of Education* 47(3–4), 253–265.

Pantazis, C., & Pemberton, S. (2009). From the "old" to the "new" suspect community: Examining the impacts of recent UK counter-terrorist legislation. *British Journal of Criminology* 49(5), 646–666.

Papadakis, Y. (2005). *Echoes from the dead zone: Across the Cyprus divide.* London: I. B. Tauris.

Papadakis, Y. (2008). Narrative, memory and history education in divided Cyprus: A comparison of schoolbooks on the "history of Cyprus." *History & Memory* 20(2), 128–148.

Pavlenko, A. (2003). "Language of the enemy": Foreign language education and national identity. *International Journal of Bilingual Education and Bilingualism* 6(5), 313–331.

Rampton, B., Charalambous, C., & Charalambous, P. (2015). End-of-project report: Crossing languages & borders—Intercultural language education in a conflict-troubled context. *King's College Working Papers in Urban Language & Literacies* 178.

Rampton, B., Harris, R., & Leung, C. (2001). Education in England and speakers of languages other than English. *King's College Working Papers in Urban Language & Literacies* 18.

Ricento, T. (2000). Historical and theoretical perspectives in language policy and planning. *Journal of Sociolinguistics* 4(2), 196–213.

Sercu, L., & Bandura, E. (2005). *Foreign language teachers and intercultural competence: An international investigation* (Vol. 10). London: Multilingual Matters.

Staples, W. (2014). *Everyday surveillance: Vigilance and visibility in postmodern life.* 2nd edition. Lanham, MD: Rowman & Littleford.

Steer, P. (2014). We can't go on like this—Language qualifications in the UK. Retrieved from http://www.cambridgeassessment.org.uk/insights/why-we-cant-go-on-like-this-language-qualifications-in-the-uk/

Stritzel, H. (2007). Towards a theory of securitization: Copenhagen and beyond. *European Journal of International Relations* 13(3), 357–383.

UCU. (2015). *The Prevent duty: A guide for branches and managers.* London: UCU.

Uhlmann, A. (2010). Arabic instruction in Jewish schools and in universities in Israel: Contradictions, subversion and the politics of pedagogy. *International Journal of Middle East Studies* 42, 291–309.

Uhlmann, A. (2012). Arabs and Arabic grammar instruction in Israeli universities: Alterity, alienation and dislocation. *Middle East Critique* 21(1), 101–116

Van Dijck, J. (2013). "You have one identity": Performing the self on Facebook and LinkedIn. *Media, Culture & Society* 35(2), 199–215.

Vaughan-Williams, N. (2008). Borderwork beyond inside/outside? Frontex, the citizen-detective and the war on terror. *Space and Polity* 12(1), 63–79.

CHAPTER 32

··

LANGUAGE POLICY
AND NEW MEDIA
AN AGE OF CONVERGENCE
CULTURE

··

AOIFE LENIHAN

GLOBALISATION is undoubtedly a major force dominating the sociolinguistic reality, both online and off (cf. Ricento, 2010; Spolsky, 2004). Globalisation entails
recent changes in social, economic, media, technological, and political processes,
which have shifted from being primarily national concerns to global ones,
transcending boundaries and broadening their impact. Globalisation is a complex,
contested, and paradoxical notion, bringing commodification, commercialism, and
homogenisation, but also enabling localisation, glocalisation, and the empowerment
of individuals and communities. In the media context, technological globalisation
has brought fragmentation of audiences, a decentring of the media, and new spaces
for language use (Kelly-Holmes et al., 2009). In this new media context, audiences
and individuals expect to be able to find and interact with media that address their
particular perspective, appeal to their interests, and speak their language. New media,
such as Facebook, are primarily businesses, which are not traditional domains of enquiry in language policy research, though recent research points to the increasing
role of businesses in de facto language policy (cf. Shohamy & Gorter, 2009). As
O'Rourke (2011, p. 58) acknowledges, in the absence of explicit formal language
policies, decisions about language may be embedded in the agendas of commercial
interests, as in this study, the agenda of the Facebook website. Indeed, new media

organisations are translocal businesses involved in language policy formation, overt and covert, whether this is their intention or not (Shohamy, 2006; Spolsky, 2004).

Until recently, media were seen as a domain through which language planners could channel their endeavours (Jones & Singh, 2005). Spolsky (2004, 2009) notes, however, that a number of participants are involved in language management online, and that service providers are setting out language rules, for example, in relation to obscene language online. Indeed, language policy today is "rapidly expanding across the world in response to growing real-world communication problems in the wake of economic globalisation, mass migration and communication technologies" (Lo Bianco, 2010, p. 154). Yet, as Ricento (2006) points out, the language situation on-line might seem largely unregulated, with little of what is traditionally termed "top-down" (Kaplan & Baldauf, 1997) language policy on the Internet. In this context, understanding language policy in the new media environment requires close examination of the grass-roots, "bottom-up" (Hornberger, 1996) language policies that are made in new media contexts. Moreover, in line with Pennycook's argument (2006, p. 62), we must explore how new media impact "the very concepts of language [and] policy" and conceptualisations of language policy itself. Indeed, as will be discussed further, this research on new media problematises the traditional dichotomy of *top-down/bottom-up* language policy.

This chapter considers the implications of new media for language policy theory and research. To do so, I examine Facebook and its Translations application (app) over a three-year period using virtual ethnographic methods (Lenihan, 2013). In my analysis, the commercial entity Facebook and individuals participating in the Irish language Translations application are the primary language policy actors that develop the de facto language policy of this domain, also with wider impact affecting the multilingual World Wide Web (WWW). The discussion is organised as follows. First, I summarise a definition of language policy that emerges from recent work on the ethnography of language policy. I rely especially on Jenkins' (2006) concept of *convergence*, which is used to analyse language policy in new media through the methodology of virtual ethnography. Second, Facebook and its crowd-sourced Translations app, including the Irish Translations app community, are analysed with particular attention to the impact of individuals, commercial entities, and their technology on conceptualisations of language policy. Finally, I consider the future of languages and language policy online, asking if they will be located primarily in the practices of individuals and the business decisions and technological developments of commercial entities.

LANGUAGE POLICY IN NEW MEDIA

This chapter rests upon two contemporary shifts in language policy studies, one concerned with the notion of language policy itself, and the other with the understanding of language policy in new media. With regard to language policy, this notion is approached here as highly complex, explicit and implicit, and influenced by the ideologies, beliefs, and practices of its stakeholders. In McCarty's words, language policy is "overt and covert, top-down and bottom-up, de jure and de facto" (McCarty, 2011a, p. 2; see McCarty, 2011b). Schiffman (1996, 2006) grounds language policy in "linguistic culture," the beliefs and myths or mythologies of a speech community about language(s) and language policy. Language policy is thus a social construct dependent on the beliefs and behaviours of a language community (Spolsky, 2009), and immanent in the everyday decisions and actions of individuals and societal groups—"the dynamic, daily practice of language policy that resides in concrete activities" (Lo Bianco, 2010, p. 154).

Rephrasing Heath, Street, and Mill's (2008, p. 7) discussion of "culture as verb," McCarty (2011a, p. 2) concludes that "policy too is best understood as a verb; policy never just 'is' but rather 'does.'" Indeed, in much of the recent research on language policy, the starting point is "the notion of language policy as processual, dynamic, and in motion" (McCarty, 2011a, p. 2). This understanding of language policy draws attention to individuals as policy actors. Although Kaplan and Baldauf (1997, p. 12) include individuals in their analysis of language planning, they do so as "an accidental outcome," thereby highlighting the traditional focus of language policy research on institutions of the state. However, more recently, Shohamy (2009) emphasises the role of the individual in language policy, placing importance on personal experience and viewing language policy itself as experience. In Shohamy's view, a focus on language policy as experience draws attention to language policies originating in everyday language practices, distinct from authoritative top-down policies. In her view, the field of language policy has neglected the human, personal dimension, and she calls for the refocusing of language policy research from a "bureaucratic field into a human one" (2009, p. 186). An example of research that considers the role of individuals in language policymaking is work by Cameron (1996), who identifies "language mavens," or individual language enthusiasts who engage in language-related activities, such as collecting unusual linguistic expressions and advocating language-improvement schemes, in the absence of official or governmental language authorities. However, Cameron did not explore the role of such individuals in relation to language policy theory.

Following this line of thought, Shouhui and Baldauf (2012) explicitly consider individual agency in language planning, asking "who are the actors" and "what are their roles?" The focus of their study is the role of individuals in official prestige planning efforts. In particular, they point out that new media offer a new domain for individuals to be involved in language policymaking, with new techniques for communication on a global scale. In this regard, Lo Bianco's (2010) extension of the notion of the social in language policy is particularly relevant, since he allows room for the exploration of public texts, public discourses, and performative action as three sources of language policy activity—all of which are found in the new media context, such as the Facebook website and the Irish Translations app community.

In Lo Bianco's view, *performative action* is defined as "instances of language used both to convey messages in regular communication and at the same time to represent models for emulation of language forms" (2010, p. 161). Everyday, mundane language use reflects the taken-for-granted standards, norms, and rules of a speech community, and thus it is ideological. In this sense, everyday language operates as discursive language policy, "heavily laden with performativity and profoundly constitutive of its message; that is its use helps form and influence patterns of language, social relationships and meanings" (Lo Bianco, 2010, p. 162). In Pennycook's words (2006, p. 65), "in order to understand how the regulation of domains of life may be effected, we need to look not so much at laws, regulations, policing or dominant ideologies as at the operation of discourses, educational practices, and language use."

To understand language policy in new media, this chapter draws on Jenkins' concept of *convergence culture* (2006), which refers to the technological, industrial, and societal changes in contemporary culture where "old and new media collide, where grassroots and corporate media intersect, where the power of the media producer and the power of the media consumer interact in unpredictable ways" (pp. 1–2). To consider convergence culture, Jenkins proposes the concepts of *media convergence, participatory culture*, and *collective intelligence*. Media convergence "involves both a change in the way media is produced and a change in the way media is consumed" (Jenkins, 2006, p. 16), so that the roles of media producers and consumers converge, with both interacting as participants. Although not all participants are equal, with some able to participate more fully than others, the active participation of consumers is at the heart of Jenkins' concept of convergence culture; it signifies a cultural shift from passive media spectatorship to a participatory culture in which "consumers are encouraged to seek out new information and make connections among dispersed media content" (Jenkins, 2006, p. 3).

Participatory culture leads to what Bruns (2008) terms *produsers*, which refers to active media users and producers together acting as "producers of the shared knowledge base, regardless of whether they are aware of this role" (Jenkins, 2006, p. 2). Jenkins also notes the collective nature of convergence, drawing on Lévy's notion of *collective intelligence*, which describes how an individual cannot know everything, but individuals can bring together what they know, combining their knowledge for individual and collective action (Jenkins, 2006, p. 4). In Jenkins' view, this collective intelligence is "an alternative source of media power" that will lead to changes in how religion, politics, or advertising work (p. 4). Thus convergence, in Jenkins' dichotomous conceptualisation, is both "a top-down corporate-driven process and a bottom-up consumer-driven process" (p. 18). In other words, in this process, media companies are expanding the flow of media to gain viewers, markets, and opportunities, and to keep existing audiences engaged, while media consumers are gaining more control over these media and are interacting with other consumers. As Jenkins notes, "the promises of this new media environment raise expectations of a freer flow of ideas and content," with consumers "fighting for the right to participate more fully in their culture" (Jenkins, 2006, p. 18).

Convergence culture does not mean homogenisation, though. Media companies and media consumers can be at loggerheads, or they can work together toward a common goal, creating closer relationships between producer and consumer. In this case, Facebook and the Irish Translations community are working together to develop an Irish-language version of the website, thus diversifying (in language terms) both the Facebook website and the wider WWW. The Facebook website, the Irish Translations community, and the language policy processes they are involved in, as will be discussed later, are an example of convergence culture, with both the media producer and consumer participating in a flow of media and interaction, in this case in relation to language(s). The next section introduces the context of this research, the Facebook website and its method of translation—the Translations application.

FACEBOOK AND THE TRANSLATIONS APPLICATION

Facebook, a social network site (SNS) (boyd & Ellison, 2008) founded in 2004 by Mark Zuckerberg, is a phenomenon that grew from a computer network based in a Harvard dorm room and available only in English in 2004, to an international website in 2016 with user figures past the billion mark and growing. According to figures from June 2016 (Facebook, 2016), it is currently the largest social network site (Chaffey, 2016), with 1.13 billion active daily users on average, and the third most visited website globally, after Google.com and YouTube (Alexa, 2016). Searching for *Facebook* via Google returns "about 16,960,000,000 results [in] (0.42 seconds)" (Google, 2016). Thus Facebook is an appropriate case for examining new media due to its widespread popularity, rapid growth, and assimilation to and important role in popular culture.

Facebook's Translations app is one of many apps that users can add to their personal profile on the site to personalise it further. Apps vary widely in their type and purpose, and can be created by external developers or by Facebook. The Translations app was introduced by Facebook in 2008, first in Spanish, then French, followed by German, and in April 2008 an additional twenty-one languages. As a result of the Translations app, Facebook is now available in more than 100 languages, with Fula, Maltese, and Corsican the latest additions to the Translations app at the time of writing (Zuckerberg, 2016).

When Facebook users add the Translations app to their profiles, they become *translators* in Facebook's discourse and join the Translations community for the language they choose. The Translations app interface is available only in English, with users submitting translations via the interface; the wider language community then votes on translations and/or submits additional or different translations. The translations used on Facebook are the *winning* translations from this voting process. Facebook does not reveal how a translation *wins* in the voting, but from my virtual ethnographic research it seems that a *clear distance* is needed between competing translations for one to be deemed to have won and to be used on Facebook. (For more on the Translations app, the translation process, and its design and development, see Lenihan, 2013.) At its peak in 2012, the Irish Translations app comprised more than 500 individual translators. The exact date the Irish Translations app came into being is not known; however, the first post on its discussion board is from June 22, 2008. The app is composed of a number of elements, including voting, translating, and reporting sections, along with supporting areas such as a leaderboard of translators, discussion board and style guide, which is editable by the top twenty translators from the leaderboard.

The impact of the Translations app on Facebook was immediate: after the localisation of Facebook into French, German, and Spanish alone, Facebook's visitor numbers increased from 52 million to 124 million (Britton & McGonegal, 2007; Eskelsen et al., 2008). Facebook also expanded the availability and impact of the Translations app via Facebook Connect on the Facebook Platform. Facebook Connect "allows users to bring their Facebook account information, friends and privacy to any third party website, desktop app or device" running on it (Facebook, 2008). Any website or app that uses the Facebook Platform also has access to the Facebook Translations app and its language communities in order to translate its own website or app. This feature enables users to bring their language setting on Facebook (i.e., the language they have chosen to access Facebook) to any domain on the WWW that is on the Facebook Platform. In other words, the content is automatically presented in different languages, based on the user's Facebook language setting, negating the need for a language-selection process or language-gateway site (typically presented as a pop-up where a WWW user must select the language he or she wants to use on a website before accessing that site).

In my research, Facebook and its Translations app were examined over a three-year period using virtual ethnographic methods. Before proceeding further, it is worth detailing briefly what virtual ethnography entails.

VIRTUAL ETHNOGRAPHY

Virtual ethnography involves looking at computer mediated communication (CMC) in online networks and communities, analysing the language content, and observing the online interactions at the level of the users. In so doing, it "transfers the ethnographic tradition of the researcher as an embodied research instrument to the social spaces of the Internet" (Hine, 2008, p. 257). Like traditional ethnography, virtual ethnography is aimed at "thick description" (Geertz, 1983) from the participants' perspectives (Slater, 2002; Ward, 1999; Wouters, 2005). The key idea of ethnography is the immersion of the ethnographer in the context being investigated and the use of this experience to "try to learn how life is lived there, rather than coming in with a particular pre-formed research question or assumptions about the issues that will be of interest" (Hine, 2009, p. 6). Ethnography has moved on from its earlier field sites, which were distant and bounded cultures, and is now concerned with ethnography "at home" or in multiple locations (O'Reilly, 2009). The potential for online ethnography is bolstered by the development of multi-sited ethnography, connective ethnography, the ethnography of organisations, the use of discourse and network analysis, and narrative in ethnographic research (Davies, 2008). This research follows Hine's (2000) conceptualisation of virtual ethnography as a mixed methods approach, involving a number of qualitative and quantitative methods (for more on the virtual ethnographic approach of this research, see Lenihan & Kelly-Holmes, 2016, 2017).

A virtual ethnography of Facebook and the Irish language Translations app requires multiple data sources. In the following analysis, data sources include the Translations apps of a number of languages including Irish, the terms and conditions associated with the app, Facebook publications related to the app (press releases, blog posts, videos, regulatory documents, and academic presentations), as well as external sources such as websites and news media discussion and analysis of Facebook and the Translations app. Data was also gathered from a longitudinal study of the Irish language translations app and its community of translators.

Next, I summarise the findings of this research, exploring how Facebook, the Irish Translations app community, and its Translators are the primary language policy actors of this domain.

Language Policy Actors on Facebook

Facebook's language policy is not just the language policy of a commercial entity, but of a global communication domain/medium with over a billion users and a dominant position as the third most visited website on the WWW. Thus Facebook's language policy will have significant effects on the multilingual WWW. When discussing the Translations app, Facebook itself acknowledges that "everything here has such a huge impact for so many millions of people" (Facebook, 2009a). In the following I consider the role of Facebook and of the Irish Translations app community as language policy actors in the new media context, and their wider impact on the multilingual Web. I draw from Kelly-Holmes (2012), with the aim of accounting for the role of these two as agents of language ideology, status policy, corpus policy, and language diffusion and language learning. From this standpoint, media are examined as a major site of multilingualism.

Media play a primary role in both maintaining and challenging the language attitudes, ideologies, and regimes of a particular context. In language policy terms, the media can "be seen to carry out all of the key functions of language policy and planning for the regulation of linguistic variation and multilingualism in speech communities" (Kelly-Holmes, 2012, p. 337). Media can be agents of corpus planning, for example by using official terminology and/or disseminating (and creating) new terminology. This capacity can be considered a "strong feature" of minority language media in particular. Media can also act as agents of status planning by "allocating space, prominence, etc., to particular language(s) and variety(ies)" (p. 337). Furthermore, media can be agents of standardisation, using and therefore spreading a standard language and its accompanying attitudes/ideologies about norms. The media can be agents of language diffusion, that is to say, they can encourage people to learn a language by their decision to dub/subtitle programming, and agents of language learning by making available language-learning programmes. Finally, the media can be agents of language ideology, as they explicitly and implicitly constitute their speech community as mono-, bi- or multilingual; and, through their discourse about language(s), they can affect the views about language held by members of the speech community.

Next, this model (Kelly-Holmes, 2012) will be extended to the new media domain and applied to the practices of both Facebook and the individual translators of the Irish Translations app community.

Facebook

In internationalising its website to increase its market share, Facebook's language policy impacted, probably unwittingly, the de facto language policy and multilingual nature of the Web. In particular, Facebook acts simultaneously as an agent of language ideology, status policy, corpus policy, and language diffusion and language learning. First, its status as an agent of language ideology is related to its approach to internationalisation, multilingualism, and minority languages, which influences other commercial entities, individual users, and the wider WWW. It specifically influences the language diversity of new media, providing a space of use for minority-language communities and perhaps influencing other social and new media entities to do so as well. It has also impacted the mobile Web, as the Translations app and the language versions it develops are available to users who access the site through mobile devices. In August 2009, Facebook announced that the two Facebook mobile sites, a mobile browser and touch screen version, had been translated from the original English into other languages (Moissinac, 2009).

Second, Facebook's function as an agent of status policy on the Web derives from developing the Translations app, which may help minority and other less powerful languages gain a new domain of use and a space for their speakers and communities. When a language has completed the translation process, it is *launched* as part of the main Facebook site, giving it a place amongst the other languages available, a sort of online status and commercial value. This new domain of use gives minority languages status as viable, modern, and everyday languages, useful to their language community, non-speakers, and the wider online community, resulting in "a transformation of the ideological valuations of the language" (Eisenlohr, 2004, p. 24). The inclusion of minority languages in the Translations app also has the effect of commodifying minority languages (Heller, 2010), as they are valued as a commercial unit, market, and audience, as will be discussed further later.

Third, the capacity of Facebook and Facebook developers to act as agents of corpus policy is played out in the use of official or standard varieties on the site and in the dissemination of terminology and translations. Thus the status of Facebook can lead to the adoption and use of official or standard languages by other new media entities and their users online. According to the "Terms Applicable to Translate Facebook," in using the app, translators assign Facebook all rights to the translations and other submissions (comments, emails, etc.) they make via the app (Facebook, 2009b). Furthermore, they allow Facebook the "unrestricted use and dissemination" of their "submissions for any purpose, commercial or otherwise," and Facebook can "sublicense, to use, reproduce, display, perform, create derivative works of, distribute and otherwise exploit the Submissions in any manner" (Facebook, 2009b); that is to say, Facebook has access to, owns, and has the right to sell and distribute all of the translations submitted via the over 100 Translations apps.

An example is Facebook's testing of inline statistical machine translation (SMT) of Facebook users' content on the site. This SMT will include features from the Translations corpus created from the translations submitted via all the Translation apps (Ellis, 2009b, p. 2). Also, developers who use the Facebook Translations apps via the Facebook Platform have full use, control, and storage of the translations and other related data they receive from the app and its translators (Facebook, 2010). Ellis (2009a) reports that Facebook has a parallel corpus of over 4 million phrases in more than 90 languages that was "growing daily." These examples demonstrate the possible further life span and impact of translations from the app beyond the context of the Facebook website. Thus the Translations app could affect how multilingualism develops online both in terms of the presence of specific languages and also the specific terms in use online, as Facebook terms/translations may be adopted by other new media entities. Furthermore, the fact that Facebook can sell the translations submitted via the app is further evidence of Facebook's commercialisation of language.

Fourth and finally, Facebook operates as an agent of language diffusion and agent of language learning through playing a role in language learning and revitalisation. New media and the technologies they bring can aid language maintenance and revitalisation, as they offer reasonable and simple ways of documenting languages, creating and distributing teaching materials, and aiding the teaching of endangered languages, without tying these processes to a particular place or location (Eisenlohr, 2004). Although some of the Irish translators actively discourage language learners from using the app to improve or practice their Irish, Facebook participates in language teaching/learning, as bilingual Irish/English flashcards, tests, and games available online use some of the translations from the Irish app (Lindsey, 2009). This leads me to a discussion of the other primary language policy actors of this domain—the Irish Translations app community and its individual translators.

The Irish Translations Community and Its Translators

In line with Blackledge and Creese's (2010) finding in their micro-ethnographic research in other contexts, the Irish Translations community constructs its own language norms, rules, and language policy. The debates about language within the Irish Translations community (Lenihan, 2011, 2013) reveal the language attitudes and beliefs that influence the formation of the community's language policy. Also, the explicit efforts of translators to influence the language practices of their peers can be considered language management under Spolsky's (2004) tripartite model. In addition, translators' implicit or normative language and translation practices impact the language policy of the Irish Translations community. In other words, both as individuals and a collective group, the Irish translators and the Irish Translations app community are also simultaneously agents of acquisition policy, status policy, corpus policy, and language diffusion.

First, whether some translators mean to or not, the Irish Translations community acts as agents of acquisition policy by creating a new space of use for Irish in which learners can experience and interact in Irish via the site. Second, the Irish and other language communities involved in the Facebook Translations app act as agents of status policy in their campaigns to gain inclusion in the app, signalling each respective language as a modern language, usable in the new media domain. As a result, these language communities, including minority-language communities, gain prestige for their languages by their inclusion in the third largest website worldwide, normalising the use of their language in new media domains (cf. Honeycutt & Cunliffe, 2010).

Third, minority languages involved in the app are given new functions, as previously untranslated words and phrases are translated, discussed, and decided upon by the language community—a form of new media corpus planning (cf. Ó hIfearnáin, 2000). The new Facebook genre has led to the development of some new lexical items in Irish. For example, the Facebook activity of *poke[ing]* someone on the SNS has been translated as *tabhair sonc.*

Fourth, the Irish Translations community also decides which terminology/ translations to use over others. In doing so, community members disseminate existing terms, acting as agents of language diffusion. The language and translation activities of the Irish community thus lead to the development of a de facto language standard for this domain and (given the status of the Facebook SNS online) they contribute toward a (new) standard of Irish for new media/online use.

Finally, by providing (via the Translations app) new terminology relating to the online world, the Irish community may aid the uptake of minority languages by other new media entities and users, further evidence of the community acting as agents of language diffusion. This could consequently "re-index" the ideological perception of minority languages, making them more visible and providing new space for their communities and new opportunities to use the languages in other new media domains (Eisenlohr, 2004 p. 33). The translation of Facebook into languages other than English also guards against Honeycutt and Cunliffe's (2010) fear that the non-availability of the interface of websites in other languages could lead to the adoption of English/majority language terms into minority languages.

Now that we have examined how Facebook and the translators of the Irish Translations app community act as agents of language policy, the next section will consider how technological globalisation, new media, and convergence culture (Jenkins, 2006) provide a space for commercial entities and language speakers to create their own translation and language policy, as well as the implications for language policy theory and new media.

The Convergence of Language Policy

As the preceding analysis of Facebook and the Translation app suggests, new media and technological globalisation cause us to rethink the primary language policy actors of the new media context, as well as conceptualisations of language policy. The language policy of the Facebook SNS is the summation of the language ideologies and practices of a commercial entity, its technology in use, and individual language users. These are not just new agents of, actors in, or "folk" participants (Niedzielski & Preston, 2000) in language policy in this domain; and new media producers and consumers do not occupy separate roles in the language policy of this domain. Rather, in today's period of media convergence, participatory culture, and collective intelligence, both Facebook and its users/translators are participants in the creation of language policy, actively using language(s) online and creating language policy, whether intentionally or not. The implications of these changes are evident in four areas: the impact of new media technological developments on language policy; the commercialisation of minority languages; new forms of involvement in language policymaking; and new conceptualisations of language policy. Each is considered in the following.

The Impact of Facebook's Technological Developments

Technological developments by Facebook are one of the main influences on language policy online generally. Facebook has applied for a number of patents to the US Patent and Trademark Office for the method of translation developed via the Translations app (Wong, 2007; Wong et al., 2008), and similar translation efforts are popular elsewhere online, with both Google and Twitter crowdsourcing the localised versions of their sites. Given its status and influence, Facebook's approach to localisation/translation and the extension of the Translations app via Facebook Connect on the Facebook Platform will impact how other new media entities engage in localisation. In other words, Facebook's approach to and technologies of localisation are likely to shape the future of language policy in the new media context.

The extension of the Translations app to Facebook Connect demonstrates the major implications of technological developments by commercial entities for "the multilingual Internet" (Danet & Herring, 2007). As Inside Facebook (Smith, 2009) acknowledges, this development will aid non-English web users in particular and will increase the presence of languages online. This extension of a user's language settings will have wide resonance online. In 2012, 9 million apps and websites were integrated with the Facebook platform (Darwell, 2012). This method of localisation and the opening of the Translations app to Facebook Connect also will have implications at the micro level of new media users/consumers; as Facebook's vice president of growth (at the time) Chamath Palihapitiya wrote, "users will have access to even more great applications than ever before built by the world's best developers" (Facebook, 2008). In other words, web users will have access to more new media domains available in more languages other than English, as the Translations app and Facebook Connect change the multilingual nature of the WWW and the representation of language communities, speakers, and cultures online. Furthermore, it will give users more opportunities to use and engage with media in their languages.

The Commercialisation of Minority Languages

A number of researchers (Friedman, 2006; Giddens, 2002) point to the impact of globalisation in the inclusion and re-evaluation of local cultures and languages. An example is the concept of *long tail languages*, which entities such as Facebook,

Google, and Twitter term "minority" or "smaller" languages. Anderson (2004, p. 3) defines the *long tail market* as a market that includes all commodities, no matter how small or niche the audience (e.g., back catalogues, older albums, live tracks, B-sides, remixes). The key idea is that if a commercial entity has a number of niche/long tail markets, the result may be a market as large as a traditional mass market. In Facebook's case, the availability of the Facebook Translations app in a number of minority languages, including Irish, demonstrates the market value of such languages.

The notion of *long tail languages* is further evidence of the commercialisation of minority languages (cf. Heller, 2010) by new media entities as they identify languages directly with markets and with increasing user numbers. As discussed earlier, the impact of the Translations app on Facebook's user numbers was immediate, with visitor numbers effectively doubling. It can be argued that Facebook is dividing "the market into speakers of different languages and create[ing] glocalized marketing and advertising materials for these language groups" (Kelly-Holmes, 2012, p. 336). As Robertson (1994) notes, diversity sells, and given Facebook's potential impact on other new media entities, localisation and the Translations app may be viewed by some as another marketing technique. As Coupland (2010) notes, this re-evaluation of minority languages by commercial entities comes with the risk that these languages may be seen simply as shortcuts to authenticity, goodwill, and commercial gain, and will not be valued as important aspects of people's culture. As growth in online use of languages other than English continues, a key area for research will be the impact on the social value of different languages.

New Forms of Individual Involvement in Language Policymaking

Facebook and the translators of the Irish Translations app act in both *top-down* and *bottom-up* manners, depending on the context of the situation (Lenihan, 2014), leading to the need to reconsider the dichotomy of *top-down/bottom-up* in language policy theory. Thus one of the key contributions of new media is the possibility for language policy to be created and produced by these participants, interacting together in a convergent manner. In language revitalisation, for example, the involvement of language speakers in media production efforts, Eisenlohr (2004, p. 35) notes, promotes the " 'ownership' of revitalisation efforts by the speakers themselves." This notion of ownership can be extended to the development of language policy through the work of "produsers" (Bruns, 2008), in this case both corporate and individual. Thus new media create potential for new forms of ownership of language policy and new forms of involvement in policymaking by individuals previously cut out of the process.

Facebook and other new media entities create new social space(s) where any person can write a blog that may potentially be read by millions, can position him- or herself as a citizen journalist, start a website in a minority language, become a member of a virtual language community, or become a Facebook translator, implementing his or her own individual language policy with wide resonance. As Wright (2006) notes, much publishing, writing, translating, and responsibility for minority-language content lies with individual web users, with little or no input from professional translators or site authorities such as Facebook. Individual translators play a central role in translations developed across the Translation apps of many languages. For example, in the discussion board of the Irish Translations app community, one translator was responsible for 13% of the topics and 15.5% of the total posts analysed (Lenihan, 2013). Similarly, DePalma and Kelly (2011, p. 287) note that in the Spanish Translations community, "One volunteer, Fernando Pérez Chercoles, dominated the leader board for the first six months of the Spanish for Spain project with his translation of 36,824 winning words. This means that Señor Pérez provided approximately one word in eight of the total community-translated output during that period."

Thus Facebook positions individual language speakers at the heart of the Translations app, with technological globalisation (cf. Friedman, 2006) and today's convergence culture redefining the role and impact of the individual in language matters. Facebook, via the design and workings of the Translations app, creates a sub-community of "senior translators" within the Irish Translations app community (Lenihan, 2014). Those who are in the top twenty leaderboard of the Irish community have more translation functionality than other individual translators. Furthermore, in the discussions of the Irish community via the discussion board feature on the app, a number of translators, who feature in the top twenty leaderboard, position themselves as more authoritative "senior" (Lenihan, 2014) translators, explicitly telling the other translators how to translate and what to do, according to their opinions and attitudes. There is some resistance by the wider Irish community in these instances, but ultimately the "senior" translators' instructions are followed.

The impact and role of individual translators as "produsers" is also demonstrated by the expansion of the Translations app to developers via Facebook Platform. When developers use the Translations app to translate their content into a certain language, the glossary, style guide, and leaderboards from that language's app are transferred over. Thus the influence of the translators involved in the initial glossary stage of the translation process, the translators who have access to the style guide, and the "senior translators" of the community can extend beyond the Facebook site to other apps/websites and content on the WWW. Also, as previously outlined, the impact of individual translators must be acknowledged if Facebook reuses or sells the translations submitted via the app to other entities in the offline context. Accordingly, the influence of individual speakers and communities on the development of their language and its presence online can be extensive, in contrast to most official language policy efforts, in which only specific agents may exercise power in language policy matters. In other words, in new media contexts, policymaking authority is transferred from official agents to commercial, individual and community agents. In Shouhui and Baldauf's words, (2012, p. 18), "internet use provides public empowerment in domains that were previously monopolized by official bodies."

Although technological globalisation and convergence have led to the development of SNSs and their worldwide user bases, they have not led to a unified, homogenous community, but rather to new ideological and implementational space for languages and their speakers. In the case of Facebook and the Translation app, speakers and users of many languages are transformed into active consumers (Jenkins, 2006), media "produsers" (Bruns, 2008), translators, policymakers, and implementers. In the context of this cultural shift, the individual is no longer a passive spectator of media (Jenkins, 2006), but rather an active language policy "produser" utilising the collective intelligence of the language community (also see Appadurai, 1996).

Conceptualisations of Language Policy

New media and its non-traditional language policy actors also impact conceptualisations of language policy, making it global and convergent. As languages go global on the Web, expanding across the virtual world, so too does the concept of language policy. Facebook presents its site as a global entity, moving across state and country borders and even language barriers—a home for all language speakers and language communities, no matter how small. In this regard, Facebook's worldwide user base can be understood as a transnational community, a diverse linguistic community where language policy processes are ongoing as users interact and use the SNS. Language policy is enacted on the global SNS Facebook, affecting and influencing over one billion users and the numerous language communities they identify with. Of course, language policy here also occurs on the local level, affecting and influencing the language practices of individual Facebook users. In this media context, the nation-state is not the primary source of language policy efforts (cf. Blommaert et al., 2009); rather, the new source is the convergence culture of global media, their technologies, and local language users and communities.

Technological globalisation, convergence culture, and new media such as Web 2.0 contexts challenge traditional concepts such as *boundaries, location, language communities*, and, as problematised in this chapter, *top-down* and *bottom-up* language policy. The case of the Facebook SNS illustrates the complexity of the notion of language policy, with multiple actors interacting within one site of language negotiation. Facebook and the translators are both participants in this fluid, convergence context, where language policy is situated in hetereoglossic, late modernity conditions under which the traditional language policy aims of uniformity, stability, and homogeneity do not fit well (Blommaert et al., 2009). Thus language policy must be reconceptualised in this new media context.

New technologies and the new communicative contexts they bring illustrate the need to rethink the role of individuals and communities in language policy (Johnson & Ensslin, 2007). What this means for the future of language policy will be considered in the final section.

CONCLUSION: THE FUTURE OF LANGUAGE POLICY

Although a number of Irish translators are involved in language activism, mainte-nance, revitalisation, and community translation efforts both online and offline, it is not clear if the online Irish language community wants to play a role in official language policy efforts. Only one translator over the course of this virtual ethnog-raphy explicitly expressed a desire on the discussion board for the language commu-nity to play an active role in the creation of new terminology for Irish. Nevertheless, there is potential convergence of online and offline language policy efforts, with official, commercial, and individual language speakers participating in language policymaking, generally unregulated by agents controlling official, or traditional *top-down*, language policy.

One Irish language group, *Gaelport*, explicitly considers what this means for official translation efforts, asking, "Do projects such as this restore a voice to Irish speakers and Irish readers which is often lost in official translation?" (Gaelport, 2009). Efforts like the Translations app, involving participatory culture and collective intelligence, place individual Irish speakers at the heart of language policy, which was previously not the case. With individuals taking on the role of language mavens, folk linguists (Niedzielski & Preston, 2000), and language policy "produsers," we see the conver-gence of academic/professional and non-academic/non-professional participants (Niedzielski & Preston, 2000, p. 1), with commercial entities, language professionals, academics, localisation experts, and so-called ordinary language users working side by side to translate Facebook into over 100 languages.[1] Indeed, *Gaelport* (2009) takes the implications of the Facebook crowd-sourced translation effort further, acknowledging the potential effects of this method of translation beyond the new media domain to of-ficial language policy efforts, which it notes has already been considered on a number of Irish-language blogs (cf. iGaeilge, 2009, Kensei, 2009). As written in their *Cogar* publication (Gaelport, 2009), *Gaelport* states, "the main question being—is there a need for translators and spending money on the translation of official documents when the Irish speaking public is happy to do the work in projects such as this."

Thus the impact of the Facebook Translations app and similar convergence efforts could have wide implications for minority languages and language policy. Will the convergence nature of language policy online lead to commercial- and "produser"-driven efforts in offline, previously official language policy contexts? This question is particularly applicable in the current economic context, with funding for the Irish language and other minority languages being reduced and even eliminated (cf. McDonnell, 2012). In other words, given the success of crowdsourcing and localisation driven by commercial concerns and technology, will the future of languages and language policy be determined primarily by the online practices of individuals and the business decisions and technological developments of commercial entities?

ACKNOWLEDGEMENTS

I wish to acknowledge the support of the Irish Social Sciences Platform (ISSP), funded under the Programme for Research in Third Level Institutions, administered by the Higher Education Authority (HEA) and cofunded under the European Regional Development Fund (ERDF), which provided a doctoral scholarship for my research. I also wish to thank Prof Helen Kelly-Holmes, who supervised my doctoral research discussed here.

NOTE

1. It must be acknowledged, however, that the use of the Internet by language mavens and language communities is also a source of unequal power relations and potential exclusion.

REFERENCES

Alexa. (2016). Top sites. Retrieved from http://www.alexa.com/topsites

Anderson, C. (2004, 1 October). The long tail. *Wired*. Retrieved from http://www.wired.com/wired/archive/12.10/tail.html?pg=2&topic=tail&topic_set=

Appadurai, A. (1996). *Modernity at large: Cultural dimensions of globalization.* Minneapolis: University of Minnesota Press.

Blackledge, A., & Creese, A. (2010). *Multilingualism: A critical perspective.* London: Continuum.

Blommaert, J., Kelly-Holmes, H., Lane, P., Leppänen, S., Moriarty, M., Pietikäinen, S., & Piirainen-Marsh, A. (2009). Media, multilingualism and language policing: An introduction. *Language Policy* 8(3), 203–207.

boyd, D. M., & Ellison, N. B. (2008). Social network sites: Definition, history, and scholarship. *Journal of Computer Mediated Communication* 13(1), 210–230.

Britton, D. B., & McGonegal, S. (2007). *The digital economy fact book.* Washington, DC: The Progress and Freedom Foundation.

Bruns, A. (2008). *Blogs, Wikipedia, Second Life, and beyond: From production to produsage*. New York: Peter Lang.

Cameron, D. (1996). *Verbal hygiene*. London: Routledge.

Chaffey, D. (2016, 8 August). Global social media research summary 2016. *Smart Insights*. Retrieved from http://www.smartinsights.com/social-media-marketing/social-media-strategy/new-global-social-media-research/

Coupland, N. (2010). Introduction: Sociolinguistics in the global era. In N. Coupland (Ed.). *The handbook of language and globalization* (pp. 1–27). Chichester, UK: Wiley-Blackwell.

Danet, B., & Herring, S. C. (Eds.). (2007). *The multilingual internet*. New York: Oxford University Press.

Darwell, B. (2012, 27 April). Facebook platform supports more than 42 million pages and 9 million apps. *SocialTimes*. Retrieved from http://www.adweek.com/socialtimes/facebook-platform-supports-more-than-42-million-pages-and-9-million-apps/278492

Davies, C. A. (2008). *Reflexive ethnography: A guide to researching selves and others*. Oxon: Routledge.

DePalma, D. A., & Kelly, N. (2011). Project management for crowdsourced translation: How user-translated content projects work in real life. In K. J. Dunne & E. S. Dunne (Eds.), *Translation and localization project management* (pp. 379–408). Amsterdam: John Benjamins.

Eisenlohr, P. (2004). Language revitalization and new technologies: Cultures of electronic mediation and the refiguring of communities. *Annual Review of Anthropology* 33, 21–45.

Ellis, D. (2009a). Names in translation and social language modelling. *Facebook Note*. Retrieved from https://www.facebook.com/note.php?note_id=128753848919

Ellis, D. (2009b). Social (distributed) language modeling, clustering and dialectometry. In *Proceedings of the 2009 Workshop on Graph-based Methods for Natural Language Processing* (pp. 1–4). Singapore: Suntec.

Eskelsen, G., Marcus, A., & Ferree, W. K. (2008). *The digital economy fact book*. Washington, DC: The Progress and Freedom Foundation.

Facebook. (2008, 23 July). Facebook expands power of platform across the web and around the world. *Facebook Newsroom*. Retrieved from http://newsroom.fb.com/News/208/Facebook-Expands-Power-of-Platform-Across-the-Web-and-Around-the-World

Facebook. (2009a). Connecting the world: How we translated Facebook. *Facebook video*. Retrieved from http://www.youtube.com/watch?v=XZXBMSb7_eE&feature=plcp

Facebook. (2009b). Terms applicable to translate Facebook. Retrieved from http://www.littlewhitedog.com/modules.php?name=News&file=article&sid=5048

Facebook. (2010). Internationalization/Prepare. Retrieved from http://wiki.developers.facebook.com/index.php/Internationalization/Prepare

Facebook. (2016). Company info. *Facebook Newsroom*. Retrieved from http://newsroom.fb.com/company-info/

Friedman, T. L. (2006). *The world is flat*. London: Penguin Books.

Gaelport. (2009, 20 January). Déan cairdeas le . . . feidhmchlár (Facebook as Gaeilge!)/Make friends with . . . feidhmchláir (Facebook as Gaeilge!). *Cogar*. Retrieved from http://www.gaelport.com/uploads/documents/edition21.html

Geertz, C. (1983). *Local knowledge: Further essays in interpretive anthropology*. New York: Basic Books.

Giddens, A. (2002). *Runaway world*. London: Profile.

Google. (2016, 11 November). Facebook. *Google*. Retrieved from https://www.google.ie/?gws_rd=cr&ei=ktT8V5DyMsaOgAbTsI60AQ#q=facebook

Heath, S. B., Street, B., & Mill, M. (2008). *On ethnography: Approaches to language and literacy research*. New York: Teachers College Press.

Heller, M. (2010). The commodification of language. *Annual Review of Anthropology* 39, 101–114.

Hine, C. (2000). *Virtual ethnography*. London: Sage.

Hine, C. (2008). Virtual ethnography: Modes, varieties, affordances. In N. G. Fielding, R. M. Lee, & G. Blank (Eds.), *The SAGE handbook of online research methods* (pp. 257–270). London: Sage.

Hine, C. (2009). Question 1: How can qualitative internet researchers define the boundaries of their projects? In A. N. Markham & N. K. Baym (Eds.), *Internet inquiry: Conversations about method* (pp. 1–20). Los Angeles: Sage.

Honeycutt, C., & Cunliffe, D. (2010). The use of the Welsh language on Facebook. *Information, Communication and Society* 12(2), 226–248.

Hornberger, N. H. (1996). Language planning from the bottom up. In N. H. Hornberger (Ed.), *Indigenous literacies in the Americas: Language planning from the bottom up* (pp. 357–366). Berlin; New York: Mouton de Gruyter.

iGaeilge (2009, 12 January). Aistriúcháin in Aisce ar Facebook. *iGaeilge*. Retrieved from http://igaeilge.ie/2009/01/12/aistriuchain-in-aisce-ar-facebook/

Jenkins, H. (2006). *Convergence culture: Where old and new media collide*. New York: New York University Press.

Johnson, S., & Ensslin, A. (2007). Language in the media: Theory and practice. In S. Johnson & A. Ensslin (Eds.), *Language in the media: Representations, identities, ideologies* (pp. 3–22). London: Continuum.

Jones, M. C., & Singh, I. (2005). *Exploring language change*. London: Routledge.

Kaplan, R. B., & Baldauf, R. B. (Eds.). (1997). *Language planning: From practice to theory*. Clevedon, UK: Multilingual Matters.

Kelly-Holmes, H. (2012). Multilingualism and the media. In M. Martin-Jones, A. Blackledge, & A. Creese (Eds.), *The Routledge handbook of multilingualism* (pp. 333–346). Oxon: Routledge.

Kelly-Holmes, H., Moriarty, M., & Pietikäinen, S. (2009). Convergence and divergence in Basque, Irish and Sámi media language policing. *Language Policy* 8, 227–242.

Kensei. (2009, 12 January). Could translation of government documents to Irish be crowdsourced?. Retrieved from http://sluggerotoole.com/2009/01/12/could-translation-of-government-documents-to-irish-be-crowdsourced/.

Lenihan, A. (2011). "Join our community of translators": Language ideologies and/in Facebook. In C. Thurlow & K. Mroczek (Eds.), *Digital discourse: Language in the new media* (pp. 48–64). Oxford: Oxford University Press.

Lenihan, A. (2013). *The interaction of language policy, minority languages and new media: A study of the Facebook Translations Application*. Unpublished PhD dissertation, University of Limerick.

Lenihan, A. (2014). Investigating language policy in social media: Translation practices on Facebook. In P. Seargeant, & C. Tagg (Eds.), *The language of social media: Community and identity on the Internet* (pp. 208–227). London: Palgrave Macmillan.

Lenihan, A., & Kelly-Holmes, H. (2016). Virtual ethnography. In Zhu Hua (Ed.), *Research methods in intercultural communication: A practical guide* (pp. 255–267). London: Wiley-Blackwell

Lenihan, A., & Kelly-Holmes, H. (2017). Virtual ethnographic approaches to researching multilingualism online. In M. Martin-Jones & D. Martin (Eds.), *Researching multilingualism: Critical and ethnographic perspectives* (pp. 172–186). London: Routledge.

Lindsey, R. (2009). Facebook as Gaeilge. *Quizlet.* Retrieved from http://quizlet.com/674980/facebook-as-gaeilge-flash-cards/

Lo Bianco, J. (2010). Language policy and planning. In N. H. Hornberger & S. L. McKay (Eds.), *Sociolinguistics and language education* (pp. 143–174). Bristol, UK: Multilingual Matters.

McCarty, T. L. (2011a). Introducing ethnography and language policy. In T. L. McCarty (Ed.), *Ethnography and language policy* (pp. 1–28). New York: Routledge.

McCarty, T. L. (Ed). (2011b). *Ethnography and language policy.* New York: Routledge.

McDonnell, F. (2012, 6 March). Irish language endangered by austerity measures. *Gaelport.* Retrieved from http://www.gaelport.com/default.aspx?treeid=37&NewsItemID=7717

Moissinac, H. (2009, 3 August). Facebook Mobile: Now connecting 65 million people. Retrieved from https://blog.facebook.com/blog.php?post=129875017130

Niedzielski, N. A., & Preston, D. R. (2000). *Folk linguistics, trends in linguistics: Studies and monographs.* Berlin; New York: Mouton de Gruyter.

Ó hIfearnáin, T. (2000). Irish language broadcast media: The interaction of state language policy, broadcasters and their audiences. *Current Issues in Language and Society* 7(2), 92–116.

O'Reilly, K. (2009). *Key concepts in ethnography.* London: Sage.

O'Rourke, B. (2011). *Galician and Irish in the European context: Attitudes towards weak and strong minority languages.* Hampshire, UK: Palgrave Macmillan.

Pennycook, A. (2006). Postmodernism in language policy. In T. Ricento (Ed.), *An introduction to language policy: Theory and method* (pp. 60–76). Oxford: Blackwell.

Ricento, T. (2006). Language policy: Theory and practice—An introduction. In T. Ricento (Ed.), *An introduction to language policy: Theory and method* (pp. 10–23). Oxford: Blackwell.

Ricento, T. (2010). Language policy and globalization. In N. Coupland (Ed.), *The handbook of language and globalization* (pp. 12–141). West Sussex, UK: Wiley-Blackwell.

Robertson, R. (1994). Globalisation or glocalisation? *The Journal of International Communication* 1(1), 33–52.

Schiffman, H. F. (1996). *Linguistic culture and language policy.* New York: Routledge.

Schiffman, H. F. (2006). Language policy and linguistic culture. In T. Ricento (Ed.), *An introduction to language policy: Theory and method* (pp. 111–126). Oxford: Blackwell Publishing.

Shohamy, E. (2006). *Language policy: Hidden agendas and new approaches.* London: Routledge.

Shohamy, E. (2009). Language policy as experiences. *Language Problems and Language Planning* 33(2), 185–189.

Shohamy, E., & Gorter, D. (Eds.). (2009). *Linguistic landscape: Expanding the scenery.* New York; London: Routledge.

Shouhui, Z., & Baldauf, R. B. (2012). Individual agency in language planning. *Language Problems and Language Planning* 36(1), 1–24.

Slater, D. (2002). Making things real: Ethics and order on the Internet. *Theory Culture and Society* 19(5–6), 227–245.

Smith, J. (2009, 4 October). Can Facebook help translate the web? *Inside Facebook*. Retrieved from http://www.insidefacebook.com/2009/10/4/can-facebook-help-translate-the-web/

Spolsky, B. (2004). *Language policy*. Cambridge: Cambridge University Press.

Spolsky, B. (2009). *Language management*. Cambridge: Cambridge University Press.

Ward, K. J. (1999). Cyber-ethnography and the emergence of the virtually new community. *Journal of Information Technology* 14, 95–105.

Wong, Y. (2007). *Systems and methods for community translations on a Web-based social network*. Washington, DC: US Patent and Trademark Office.

Wong, Y., Grimm, S. M., Vera, N., Laverdet, M., Kwan, T. Y., Putnam, C. W., Olivan-Lopez, J., Losse, K. P., Cox, R., & Little, C. (2008). Community translation on a social network. Retrieved from http://appft.uspto.gov/netacgi/nph-Parser?Sect1=PTO2&Sect2 =HITOFF&p=1&u=/netahtml/PTO/search-bool.html&r=1&f=G&l=50&co1=AND &d=PG01&s1=facebook.AS.&s2=translation.AB.&OS=AN/facebook+AND+ABST/ translation&RS=AN/facebook+AND+ABST/translation

Wouters, P. (2005). The virtual knowledge studio for the humanities and social sciences. Presented at *First International Conference on e-Social Science*. Manchester, 22–24 June.

Wright, S. (2006). Regional or minority languages on the World Wide Web. *Journal of Language and Politics* 5(2), 189–216.

Zuckerberg, M. (2016, 30 September). Status update. Retrieved from https://www.facebook. com/zuck/videos/10103141435699471/

III.C.

Language, Ideology, and Critique:
Rethinking Forms of Engagement

CHAPTER 33

LANGUAGE IDEOLOGIES IN THE TEXT-BASED ART OF XU BING

IMPLICATIONS FOR LANGUAGE POLICY AND PLANNING

ADAM JAWORSKI

CONTEMPORARY art has been a site of intense linguistic production for several decades. Visual artists have been experimenting with new ways of displaying or enframing language, employing transformative processes and forms of symbolic manipulation that frequently contest or subvert dominant language ideologies. In this way, artists produce new *regimes of language* (or "regimes of discourse"; Pennycook, 2002, p. 92) that regulate or unsettle "moral and political visions that shape attitudes and behaviour" (Tollefson, 2011, p. 370).

When artists use language as a medium in their practice, their works enter a broader sociolinguistic field, whereby linguistic forms carry social values of distinctiveness and possibility as defined by participants' (artists' own, audiences', and critics') assumptions, perceptions, and interpretations, or—in other words—their language ideologies (Irvine, 2001). Irvine refers to language ideologies as "ideational schemes, whether about language or other things [that] have some relationship with point of view [. . .] and the viewer's baggage of history and partiality" (Irvine, 2001,

p. 24). But displays, or performances, of language in the form of art installations, especially on a vast scale, as is the case of some examples to be considered in this chapter, are not merely manifestations of the artist's ideologies of language. They are instances of historically consequential (Silverstein, 2001) language ideological debates that "develop against a wider sociopolitical and historical horizon of relationships of power, forms of discrimination, social engineering, nation-building, and so forth" (Blommaert, 1999, p. 2).

All the linguistic choices we make and the publics (Gal & Woolard, 2001) we *project* them onto result from some planning efforts, more or less conscious, individual or institutional. Woolard and Schieffelin (1994) suggest that all language policy and planning decisions are underpinned by specific language ideologies. Bolander goes as far as to consider "language policy *as* ideology" (2017, p. 262; original emphasis), in contrast to the view of "language policy as discourse" (Barakos, 2012, p. 169; see also Tollefson, 1991). Likewise, Lo Bianco (2004, p. 750) argues that "[i]n the absence of overt or explicit detailed planning [. . .] ideology operates as 'default' policy."

Naturally, debates about language ideologies take the form of discourses and metadiscourses, and they also presuppose, shape, and reshape language ideologies according to social actors' dominant regimes of representation (Blommaert, 1999). This is again echoed by Bolander (2017, pp. 261–262), who, building on Pennycook (2014, p. 2), argues, "that it is not so much language as language ideology that is the object of language policy." Furthermore, any public display of language, or so-called *linguistic landscape*, can be considered as a tool of and an arena for the implementation of specific language policies (Shohamy, 2006; also see Hult, Chapter 17 in this volume). Executing text-based works requires visual artists to make choices akin to the linguistic planning and policy decisions to be found in other areas of linguistic landscapes with regard to the selection of linguistic codes, genres, visual styling, emplacement, and so on.

Thus, language policy and planning cannot be separated from social actors' language ideologies, situated within the chains of broader language ideological debates. In the context of the present discussion, I focus on the field of artistic production as a site of sociolinguistic activity to underscore the role of individual agency in language policy, planning, and the execution or shaping of linguistic texts. In this sense, I follow Ricento's (2000) critical and postmodern perspective on language policy and planning, in which the notion of agency is understood as individual and group processes of language use, attitudes, and any overt policy decisions. Specifically, Ricento (2000, p. 208) poses the following question: "Why do individuals opt to use (or cease to use) particular language varieties for specific functions in different domains, and how do those choices influence—and how are they influenced by—institutional language policy-making (local to national and supranational)?" In response to Ricento's enquiry, Lane (2015), for example, demonstrates how efforts to standardize a minority language (in this case, Kven, a Finnic minority language in northern Norway) can lead to different reactions from its speakers, from embracing the idea of standardization by *fixing* its written version to resisting such standardization of Kven by considering it a *broken* language. In a radically different context, Roth-Gordon (2009) demonstrates how in Rio de Janeiro, Brazil, *gíria*, a *favela* (shantytown) slang, has come to be enregistered (Agha, 2003) in the 1990s alongside the Portuguese national standard. Confronted with violence from both the military police and drug gangs, the option of using, or disavowing, one register or the other allows individual speakers to navigate Brazil's regime of "differentiated citizenship" by strategically indexing different personas, places, and allegiances, and constructing newly vulnerable and newly marginalized city residents. Finally, Moriarty and Pietikäinen (2011) discuss two examples of individual, ad hoc language planning initiatives in the context of language revitalization and normalization: an American-born, long-term Irish resident performing stand-up comedy in his newly acquired Irish, and a Finnish-Sámi bilingual rapper performing his rap lyrics in Inari Sámi. The authors cite evidence of both artists receiving much exposure in their national communities through mainstream and online media and contributing to fresh perceptions of the two endangered, minority languages as *modern* (or *cool*) and appealing to young people.

Woolard and Schieffelin (1994) observe that the locus of language ideologies has been identified in language use as well as in metalinguistic discourse. Both these sites of linguistic ideology, which are also the *tools* of any language policy, are explored here through the examination of several works of text-based art by the artist Xu Bing (*language use*),[1] as well as the artist's own and various commentators' interpretations of his works (*metalinguistic discourse*). Collectively, they demonstrate how the field of artistic production and criticism contributes to language ideological debates about Chinese—in particular, about Chinese writing—and the nature of language more broadly.

In the following section I discuss briefly some aspects of Xu Bing's biography and artistic practice, specifically related to his use of language. Next, I discuss the diverse language ideological positions underpinning four of his major works. I conclude by offering some reflections on what students of language policy and planning might learn from extending the scope of their interest to text-based art.

Xu Bing and the Origins of His Language Art Practice

My key point of reference in this chapter is the contemporary conceptual artist Xu Bing. Xu Bing was born in 1955 in Chongqing (Sichuan Province, China) and was brought up in Beijing, where his father was a professor of history and his mother a staff member in the Department of Library Science, both at Beijing University. This environment provided Xu Bing with access to and interest in books. Although as a child he was unable to read them, he enjoyed their appearance on the rows of shelving, their texture, and the smell of paper and ink. His father encouraged and provided instruction in Xu Bing's study of calligraphy. As early as 1969 and 1970, during his time in middle school, Xu Bing developed a keen interest in typography, layout, and the visuality of writing more generally. He collected newspaper fonts and planned at some point to compile a "handbook of artistic lettering" (Erickson, 2001, p. 34).

Before Xu Bing graduated with a master's degree in printmaking from the Central Academy of Fine Arts in Beijing in 1987, his perspective on language was influenced greatly by his experience of the Cultural Revolution (1966–1976). For Xu, the most significant shift in the Cultural Revolution was the use of language as an instrument of propaganda, which had a direct impact on his family: "At the time there was a saying: 'Use your pen as a weapon and shoot down reactionary gangs.' My father was a reactionary" (Xu Bing, 2001, p. 16). In one interview, Xu Bing recounts an early memory of a particularly dramatic encounter with large-character posters, when he saw the name of his father, Xu Huamin, written in huge letters on a poster that proclaimed "Down with Xu Huamin" (Erickson, 2001, p. 34).

In 1974, as a well-educated young man, Xu Bing was sent for three years of "re-education" to the tiny village of Shouliang Gou in Yanqing county, some 80 kilometers northwest of Beijing. During these years, despite the tedium of peasant work and poor living conditions, Xu Bing drew and painted portraits and landscapes, designed notices for Chinese New Year celebrations, weddings, and funerals, and pursued the study of typography in his work for the mimeographed revolutionary periodical *Brilliant Mountain Flowers*. During this period, Xu Bing honed his skills as a draughtsman, calligrapher, and typographer, and, on his rare visits home, he benefitted from attending art exhibitions and occasional instruction from the husband of one of his mother's colleagues, the oil painter Li Zongjin (1916–1977). Aspects of his artistic practice were influenced by some of the literacy (and illiteracy) practices in the countryside. For example, he observed how some of the elders who struggled with writing and reading would locate characters from ritual texts in scraps of print and copy the characters onto white cloth, and he "marvelled at the writing he saw painted on furniture, where auspicious phrases of four characters were arranged overlaying each other as a single character" (Vainker, 2013, p. 14). Ultimately, although he considered the Cultural Revolution "an historically unprecedented experiment" that "resulted in disaster" (Xu Bing, 2011, p. 51), his experience of living among the peasants of Shouliang Gou turned him into an artist "with a socialist background" (p. 52) following Mao Ze Dong's (1893–1976) admonition to create "art for the people."

Xu Bing's early life was marked by a growing "mistrust of language" (Erickson, 2001). When he was very young, he was unable to read the books in his mother's library; when he was old enough to read them, he was not allowed to do so. Soon after he learnt to write and mastered traditional calligraphy, the government introduced the policy of simplifying Chinese characters in order to foster widespread literacy.[2] Once the grip of the Cultural Revolution began to loosen, Xu Bing started voraciously reading the books he had been forbidden to access in previous years and joined in countless intellectual debates. He felt overloaded by this new barrage of words, which he likened to a state of chaos: "I felt the discomfort of a person suffering from starvation who had just gorged himself. It was at this point that I considered creating a book of my own that might mirror my feelings" (*Book from the Sky*, see later discussion in this chapter) (Xu Bing, 2001, p. 14). Finally, at the age of thirty-five, he emigrated to the United States, where he was confronted with a new linguistic environment that required him to learn yet another way of speaking and writing. The resulting conflict between his actual level of knowledge and his ability to express that knowledge found expression in his later work (*Square Word Calligraphy*, see later discussion) (Xu Bing, 2001, p. 14).

Yet, the sources of Xu Bing's thematization of language, writing, and calligraphy in his work must be put into a broader perspective, reaching beyond his personal experience of early calligraphy education, training in printmaking, or typographic services for a revolutionary journal. Chinese communism, which Xu experienced since his early life, was as much a social as a national ideology, aiming at the restoration of the splendour of a great empire and civilization, in combination with Western-like modernization (Hobsbawm, 1994). As in other nation-building projects, the establishment and promotion of a national language, including a writing reform, was considered a necessary condition for the unity and modernization of China from the beginning of the proletarian revolution in the first half of the twentieth century (Chen, 1999), a sentiment shared earlier by nineteenth-century Protestant missionaries in China (Hutton, 2008b). In this respect, Chinese communist leaders adhered to the Herderian Romantic ideology of "the complex anchoring of language in national character, history, and society" (Bauman & Briggs, 2003, p. 170). Even if the enregisterment of Putonghua (Dong, 2010) as a national standard did not invoke Herderian references to national literature and literary language as capable of capturing the "national characteristics" of its people (Hutton, 2006, p. 85), the discourse of a shared language has always gone hand in hand with the discourse of Chinese nationalism, something that Xu has always been keenly aware of:

> Mao's transformation of culture was meant to "touch people to their very souls." Most deeply rooted was his transformation of language, because *the Chinese language directly influences the methods of thinking and understanding of all Chinese people*. To strike at the written word is to strike at the very essence of the culture. Any doctoring of the written word becomes in itself a transformation of the most inherent portion of a person's thinking. My experience with the written word has allowed me to understand this. (Xu Bing, 2001, pp. 13–14; emphasis added)

In this quote, Xu Bing echoes Herder's (and Mao's) position that for a nation (*Volk*) the "wealth of views on tradition, history, religion, and principles of life reside[s] in language, all of the people's heart and soul" (Herder, 1793; cited in Votruba, n.d.).

The next section explores how Xu Bing variably orients to the national language ideology in four different works/projects. Specifically, I will argue that the national language ideology is upheld and reinscribed in his video animation *The Character of Characters*, is subverted in the installation *Book from the Sky*, is inverted in the project *Square Word Calligraphy*, and is transcended in the project *Book from the Ground*.

THE WORKS

The four examples of Xu Bing's work to be considered in this section are derived from the following projects: *The Character of Characters* (2012), an animated video themed around the history of Chinese writing and China (Figures 33.1–33.5); *Book from the Sky* (*Tianshu*) (1987–1991), an installation featuring books and scrolls printed with "false" Chinese characters (Figures 33.6–33.7); *Square Word Calligraphy* (1994–), an ongoing project of writing (predominantly) English texts in a stylized Chinese script (Figures 33.8–33.10); and *Book from the Ground* (*Dishu*) (2003–), a multimedia project and novel "written" with visual symbols and icons drawn from "everyday" visual culture (Figure 33.11).

The Character of Characters (2012): Reinscribing National Language Ideology

In his video *The Character of Characters* (2012), Xu Bing tells the story of China through the story of the Chinese language, specifically its writing system and the art of calligraphy. The seventeen-minute animation, presented on a large, eleven-metre-wide screen, resembles an unfolding of a traditional Chinese scroll. It is premised on the idea that calligraphy has given rise to "the essential difference between Eastern and Western ways of thinking, which allows viewers to understand the Chinese national character, today's China, and the possibility of China's future through the Chinese writing system" (Xu Bing, 2012a, p. 60). A close link between the national language and the character of the nation is also invoked in the following quote, which explains the main "thesis" of the video:

> My intention in this animated film is to set forth my views on the origins of the Chinese people and their distinctive qualities—respect for tradition and ceremony, ability to bear hardship without complaint, firmness cloaked in gentleness, and ability to change with the circumstances—by means of analyzing, examining, and reimaging a handscroll by Zhao Mengfu now in the Guanyuan shanzhuang collection [. . .] *After watching the entire film, one will in fact come to understand the content of a "thesis" on*

calligraphy and the distinctive qualities of the Chinese people. (Xu Bing, 2012a, p. 27; emphasis added)

Xu Bing's story begins with the primordial first line, first brushstroke, embodied in the Chinese numeral one (一) (Figure 33.1). Its multiplications, permutations, and combinations give rise to a rich and complex writing system consisting of thousands of characters (Figure 33.2–33.3). Xu Bing locates the essence of Chinese writing, and implicitly of the entire Chinese culture, in the power of a single brushstroke.

Just as legitimizing claims to nationhood and to nation-states' bounded territories are typically located in the distant, indeed timeless, mystery-shrouded past (Anderson, 1983; Hobsbawm, 1990), the beginning of Xu Bing's history of Chinese writing is grounded in the legend of the mythical, four-eyed figure Cang Jie, whose extraordinary seeing powers allowed him to invent writing by observing patterns in nature. Cang Jie's written characters come to life as transformed patterns on turtle shells, bird feathers, mountain slopes, rivers, palms, and fingers. The characters come to signify objects (e.g., trees) and animals (e.g., birds) that may be long gone from view: "Through Cang Jie's mythic vision, humankind gained the ability to see and create meaning (and history) as our eyes connected to a brain that learns to make meaning in the factory of the mind" (Hammers, 2014, p. 112).

Xu Bing models his landscape in the early part of the animation on the painting *Autumn Colors on the Qiao and Hua Mountains* by the great artist of the Yuan dynasty (1271–1368), Zhao Mengfu (1254–1322). Zhao's landscape is brought to life, representing a world where the first sounds emerge from nature. A myna bird flies in and starts making sounds. A human figure then appears, and a battle of sounds between the bird and the human figure ensues. (Figure 33.4). The display of characters in the opening sequence (Figures 33.2–33.3) alludes to another famous work by Zhao,

FIGURE 33.1. Still image from Xu Bing, *The Character of Characters* (2012; sound and color; 16'45"); "一" approx. 00'57".

© Xu Bing Studio.

FIGURE 33.2. Still image from Xu Bing, *The Character of Characters* (2012; sound and color; 16'45"); all characters; approx. 01'02".

© Xu Bing Studio.

FIGURE 33.3. Detail of the leftmost part of Figure 33.2. Xu Bing, *The Character of Characters* (2012; sound and color; 16'45").

© Xu Bing Studio.

FIGURE 33.4. Still image from Xu Bing, *The Character of Characters* (2012; sound and color; 16'45"); landscape with myna bird and human figure, approx. 02'21".

© Xu Bing Studio.

his seven-scroll calligraphy of the *Sutra on the Lotus of the Sublime Dharma*, known for its grace and balance, and copied by many subsequent artists. By recontextualizing the scroll genre and a widely admired landscape painting by a past master, Xu Bing minimizes the "intertextual gap" between his work and the tradition of Chinese art, constructing for his viewers a sense of history, authenticity, and community (Briggs & Bauman, 1992; Gal & Woolard, 2001, p. 8; see also later discussion in this chapter).

In the following scenes, Xu Bing narrates how writing came to be central in all areas of Chinese social life: the slow process of literacy education, philosophy, divination, and ritual. For Xu Bing, Chinese characters are highly revered; they represent a supreme, artful expression of one's sophistication and demeanour, and an insight into one's personality. But writing is also a tool of political power, with emperors and rulers of China throughout Chinese history, down to Mao Ze Dong, introducing orthographic reforms and inventing new characters and fonts to make their mark and assert their authority over the people, who had to follow *their* way of writing and thinking (Kraus, 1991). In Figure 33.5, the first three images from left to right are captioned: "Calligraphy by Emperor Huzong of Song," "Calligraphy by Emperor Xuanzong of Tang," and "Calligraphy by Yongle Emperor." The fourth image is a stylized representation of the Communist Party Congress with a huge portrait and signature of Mao Ze Dong (going left to right) in his own, simplified calligraphy. Finally, both the tradition of copying Chinese characters and their ideographic nature are brought to the present and linked to mass-produced goods in Chinese factories, unauthorized copies of trademarked goods made in China, and Chinese people's apparent obsession with luxury brands and their logos (e.g., LV, CC, CK) (Erickson, 2012, p. 19). This is represented in the right-most image in Figure 33.5, by a hand holding a pen with a stylus, marking a shopping bag with a generic, red "X" symbol.

FIGURE 33.5. Still image from Xu Bing, *The Character of Characters* (2012; sound and color; 16'45"); history of character reforms, approx. 11'57".

In his aim to show "the relationship between the Chinese language and the unique origin of the Chinese national character" (Xu Bing, 2012a, p. 34), the artist *iconizes* (Irvine & Gal, 2000) Chinese script as distinct from the "Western" tradition (see earlier discussion) and as responsible for the artistry, perseverance, and spirituality of the Chinese people. A similar language ideology can be found among many post-Enlightenment scholars, who, according to Irvine and Gal (2000), believed that languages coincided with nations' cultural and spiritual dispositions, although pre-dating the political activity of constructing nationhood. This naturalness and distinctiveness of languages provided nineteenth-century linguists with a reliable basis for legitimating nation-states, or, in the case of the European colonial project, polities that were suitable for colonial administration. Implicit in this language ideology is the moral superiority of a nation united by a common and unified written script, indicative of the *erasure* (Irvine & Gal, 2000) of any linguistic diversity of the Chinese Empire, and subsequently, the Chinese nation-state. No matter how much Xu Bing aligns or misaligns with some of the narrated episodes (e.g., politically motivated orthographic reforms, or consumer-driven obsession with luxury brand logos), he tells the story of Chinese characters as an intertwined story of the Chinese national language and Chinese national identity, both of which arise in tandem through a dialectic process of mutual co-construction (Joseph, 2006; Silverstein, 2000).

Book from the Sky (*Tianshu*) (1987–1991): Subverting National Language Ideology

Dated 1987–1991, *Book from the Sky* was first exhibited in Beijing in 1988. Subsequent exhibitions of the enlarged, full-scale work, or its smaller versions, took place in numerous locations in Asia, North America, Australia, and Europe. The complete installation includes four stitch-bound volumes with indigo covers, referencing traditional Chinese binding style and scholarly content, presented with hand-carved walnut storage boxes, with additional copies opened and arranged as a massive rectilinear "carpet" on a low pedestal on the floor (Figure 33.6). Large, undulating scrolls hang from the ceiling over the open books, with additional panels hanging on the surrounding walls. The books and scrolls are all printed with approximately four

FIGURE 33.6. Xu Bing, *Book from the Sky* (1987–1991). Mixed media installation: hand-printed books, ceiling, and wall scrolls printed from wood blocks inscribed with "false Chinese characters"; dimensions variable. Installation view at "Crossings," National Gallery of Canada, Ottawa, 1998.

thousand "false" Chinese characters invented by the artist and carved onto pear-wood printing blocks.

When exhibited for the first time in Beijing's National Gallery in 1988, *Book from the Sky* attracted harsh criticism from the central government and created much anxiety, even anger, among the visitors who, upon entering the gallery space, inevitably assumed that they would be able to read the text, but on close inspection realized that it was not possible. Although it is commonly acknowledged that in much cursive calligraphy "the beauty of the brushstrokes and the structure of the characters" are deemed to be more important than the meaning of the words (Harrist, 2006, p. 33), Xu Bing's radical separation of calligraphy from literacy confused most of his audiences and angered many. Harrist explains that these reactions were compounded by two factors: first, Xu Bing's invented characters, at least at first glance, appear familiar, hence accessible, as they adhere to the conventions of symmetry and internal structure of real characters and are composed with "perfectly orthodox vertical and horizontal strokes, diagonals, dots and hooks" (Harrist, 2006, p. 40); and second, the typeface used by Xu Bing is based closely on the form of the characters known as the *Song style* (*Song ti*), widely used during the Ming dynasty (1368–1644), known as a golden age of printing in China (Harrist, 2006, p. 37) (Figure 33.7). Besides having no fixed meaning, Xu Bing's characters have no fixed sounds. Although some Chinese characters do carry some information of how they should be pronounced, they cannot be "sounded out" in the same way as unfamiliar words can in alphabetic scripts (Harrist, 2006, p. 39). Following Gal and Woolard (2001), by creating and displaying *Book from the Sky*, Xu Bing imagines a public of illiterates, in particular targeting the educated and typically literate speakers of Chinese. According to Silbergeld (2006, p. 20), the work creates a democratizing effect "in a kind of egalitarianism of induced illiteracy."

Most commentators on *Book from the Sky* emphasize the *meaninglessness* of its words, yet the "significance" of the piece and its various interpretations have been widely debated. In the absence of discernible propositional content, or perhaps because of this absence, the emphasis of the debate has often tended toward the questions of Chinese writing as a repository and manifestation of *Chineseness*, implicitly, and inevitably shifting the weight of the debate toward the idea of national language ideology—the idea that the installation subverts by questioning the standardization of Chinese characters.

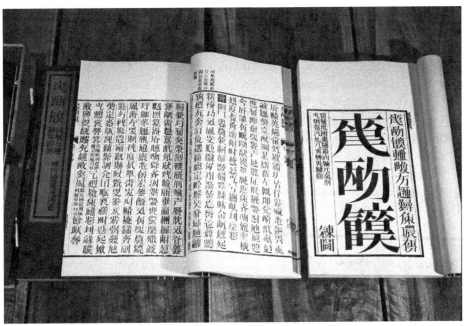

FIGURE 33.7. Xu Bing, *Book from the Sky* (1987–1991); detail.

From a sociolinguistic point of view, in addition to the apparent structural plausibility of the characters and the readability of their font, there is a third possible reason for the confusion and discontent felt by many gallery-goers, particularly those who can read Chinese—the work's genre. The volumes making up the installation are closely modelled on recognizable, historical Chinese formats of philosophical, medical, reference, and literary books. In their page layout, paper quality, folding, string binding, and the colour of the covers (indigo), the books follow meticulously the principles of traditional Chinese book-making. The walnut presentation boxes carefully assembled by hand, with wooden pegs and dovetailed joints, amplify the *authenticity* of the books' appearance and their gravitas. The only generic innovation, which points to the influence of Western art on Xu Bing in creating *Book from the Sky*, is that it is an art installation (Erickson, 2001, pp. 44–45).

Following Bakhtin (1986), Briggs and Bauman (1992) discuss genre as a structural property of texts—not as immanent, fixed, and unitary, but, despite being conventionalized, as open-ended, emergent, and ambiguous. Genre is also indexical, that is co-occurring with other entities such as the context or subject matter (Briggs & Bauman, 1992, p. 141). Briggs and Bauman consider genre to be "quintessentially intertextual," that is, linked "to generalized or abstracted models of discourse production and reception" (p. 147), rather than to single utterances, as, for example, is the case with reported speech. Thus, by invoking a genre, producers of discourse create associations between their utterances or texts with specific places, times, persons, or acts, and in doing so, they claim the authority to decontextualize and recontextualize these temporal, spatial, and social connections for their audiences.

The process of genre recontextualization can have different effects, depending on the degree of fit between a particular text and its generic model. When the "intertextual gap" (Briggs & Bauman, 1992, p. 149) is minimized, the text is maximally interpretable due to its closeness to its generic precedent, and the producer takes the authoritative stance by sustaining the conservative and traditionalizing textual formats. When the gap is maximized, a degree of disorder, chaos, and fragmentation is introduced to the text, possibly impeding its interpretability, while the producer claims authority by introducing individualizing and creative aspects into his or her discourse.

Through its title, *Book from the Sky* is metapragmatically framed as a *book*.[3] Its formal properties commented on earlier (printing technique, binding, page layout, typography, materiality, etc.), demonstrate great care in the artist's reproduction of recognizable traditional Chinese book formats. Its key *unreal* quality is its unreadable orthography. As has been mentioned, upon realizing that they could not read the text of *Book from the Sky*, Chinese speakers felt a degree of unease, confusion, or even anger. For them, probably, unreadable characters could be justified in some hard-to-read cursive calligraphy inscriptions or rubbings, but not in a printed *book*, especially with perfectly legible typography. What they may have failed to appreciate in that moment was that *Book from the Sky* creatively exploits an intertextual gap being presented in the *secondary* or *complex* genre (Bakhtin, 1986; Briggs

& Bauman, 1992, p. 154) of an art installation indexing the vast literary tradition of Chinese writing, libraries, and large-character posters of the Cultural Revolution era. Unwittingly, the visitors' reaction co-constructed and replicated the effect of overload and chaos in Xu Bing's "loss of meaning" that motivated him to make the work in the first place (Erickson, 2001, pp. 38–39).

Although beyond his control, some of these reactions may have been intended by the artist, precisely by exploiting and celebrating the intertextual gap of *Book from the Sky*. Characterized by its regular and orderly strokes, the *song-ti* typeface has come to be associated with (or *enregistered*; Agha, 2003) with a degree of formality, conveying factuality and accessibility; as Xu Bing explains, "over time it has become like the newsprint style of today [. . .] I didn't want to express my own personality. I wanted there to be a tension between the seriousness of the execution and the presentation and the underlying absurdity that animates the project" (Leung et al., 1999, p. 89). The piece is, then, a recontextualization of a tradition, or the *idea* of tradition in book writing, printing, and binding, but it is also an act of de-individualizing the author, a paradoxical move to create a *loss* of meaning or knowledge and a sense of disorientation in the "readers" who, upon realizing that the characters they are trying to decipher are deliberately wrong, are repositioned as an *Other*—marginalized outsiders and onlookers.[4] The invented script, a secret code that is opaque even to its inventor, establishes the stance of an outsider for the "author" and for the "reader" alike. But, in a throwback to Xu Bing's experience of the Cultural Revolution, it is also an act of defiance against language as propaganda in the hands of an oppressive regime.

Finally, the reportedly unsettling effect of *Book from the Sky* on the Chinese-reading public may have come from their orientation to *denotational ideology of language* (Silverstein, 1979), which considers the production of denotational (i.e., referential) meaning to be the sole rationale for the existence of language, and the *standard language*, especially in its written form, to be the ideal embodiment of this function. Thus, the deceptively traditional appearance of the books and scrolls in the installation led some visitors to insist on finding at least traces of denotational meaning in *Book from the Sky* (Abe, 1998).

Square Word Calligraphy (1994–): Dialogic Language Ideology

The sense of linguistic disorientation that Xu Bing achieved in *Book from the Sky* for his Chinese-reading audience has been replicated in his *Square Word Calligraphy* (1994–) for their English-reading counterpart, albeit with different resources and with different effects. Having moved to the United States in 1990, Xu Bing experienced a sense of linguistic limitation in functioning in the predominantly English-speaking environment (Xu Bing, 2001). As a way of reconciling his *cultural accentedness* (Blommaert & Varis, 2015), he created a script for writing English that resembles Chinese characters, which may be considered his linguistic self-portrait. He then developed the project as a means of engaging the broader public with contemporary art in the spirit of his socialist stance of *art for the people*.

Given Xu Bing's intended bilingual "strategic ambiguity" (Heller, 1988), for English-speakers, the text written in *Square Word Calligraphy* is, at first sight, unreadable, as it appears to be written in Chinese. On inspection, and not without some difficulty, readers of English can make out the words. The convincing, initial effect of the texts appearing to be Chinese calligraphy is achieved by strict reliance of rendering the letters of the Latin alphabet according to the elements of Chinese orthography. For example, *w* is rendered as the *shan* radical 山, and *o* as the *kou* 口 radical (Lee, 2015, p. 451). This systematicity makes it possible for Latin-script users to learn how to write in square word calligraphy. Some of the installations of *Square Word Calligraphy* include interactive "classrooms" with desks, exercise books, brushes, ink, blackboards, and video instruction manuals (Figure 33.8).

FIGURE 33.8. Xu Bing, *Square Calligraphy Classroom* (1994–1996). Mixed media installation: desk, chair sets, copy and tracing books, brushes, ink, video; dimensions variable. Exhibition and audience participation view at "Third Asia-Pacific Triennial of Contemporary Art," Queensland Art Gallery, Brisbane, Australia, 1999.

Subsequently, a computer programme has been developed to allow members of the public to type in their surnames in alphabetic writing and then display their surnames on a large panel in *New English Typography*.[5] Other works include banners and scrolls with Xu Bing's own handwritten or printed calligraphy, which, most famously, include Chairman Mao's slogan *Art for the People* on the banner displayed on the building of the Museum of Modern Art in New York as the motto for the 1999 exhibition *Project 70: Shirin Neshat, Simon Patterson, Xu Bing in the Museum of Modern Art in New York* (Figure 33.9). Other texts include Chinese poetry in English translation (Figure 33.10), poems by English-language poets, nursery rhymes, and so forth.

Erickson characterizes *Square Word Calligraphy* as Xu Bing's effort "to demystify Chinese culture and to share the pleasure of calligraphy" (Erickson, 2001, p. 55). This egalitarian stance, it appears, is underpinned by what might be referred to as Xu Bing's *dialogic language ideology*. In his aim to create a *dialogue* between *cultures*, he develops a linguistic tool premised on Bakhtinian *dialogism*, which Woolard, alongside Lüdi's (1987) notion of *translingualism*, takes as her starting point for the

FIGURE 33.9. Xu Bing, *Art for the People* (1999). Silk banner, 36 feet x 9 feet. Installation view at the entrance of Museum of Modern Art, New York, 1999.

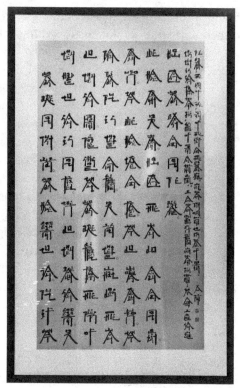

FIGURE 33.10. Xu Bing, *Square Word Calligraphy*, excerpts from *Zhuangzi's Discussion of Making All Things Equal* (2014). Exhibition view at "It Begins with Metamorphosis," Asia Society, Hong Kong Center, 2014.

© Xu Bing Studio.

discussion of linguistic simultaneity in bilingual communication. She considers three linguistic forms of simultaneity: *bivalency*, "the use by a bilingual of words or segments that could 'belong' equally, descriptively and even prescriptively, to both codes" (Woolard, 1998, p. 7); *interference*, by which she means "what Haugen calls 'interference in the strict sense' [. . .] a linguistic overlap arising from language contact, in which 'two systems are simultaneously applied to a linguistic item' (1956, p. 50)" (Woolard, 1998, p. 14); and *code-switching*, where the apparent use of two discrete languages cannot be easily teased apart on objective or ideological grounds (Gardner-Chloros, 1995).

The bivalent character of *Square Word Calligraphy* is most apparent with regard to interference. The execution of English (or other alphabetic) texts in this typeface by hand requires at least some basic familiarity with the technique of Chinese calligraphy, and its application results in the production of orthographically "accented" writing. These are decidedly linguistic forms, where elements from two distinctive linguistic traditions can be discerned. In fact, the entire raison d'être of the project is to bring them together into a dialogic tension, which, according to Holquist, can be seen as the purposeful enactment of three elements—*hybridity, heteroglossia*, and *polyglossia*:

> Within the overall concern that Holquist [1990] dubs dialogism, Bakhtinian simultaneities in language include: hybridity, "the mixing, within a single concrete utterance, of two or more different linguistic consciousnesses" (1981, p. 429); heteroglossia, "that locus where centripetal and centrifugal forces collide, [. . .] that which systematic linguistics must always suppress" (1981, p. 428); and polyglossia, "the simultaneous presence of two or more national languages interacting within a single cultural system." ([Bakhtin] 1981, p. 431) (cited in Woolard, 1998, p. 4)

Square Word Calligraphy exemplifies all the three elements. Lee (2015) considers the project as an instance of *translanguaging* (e.g., García & Li Wei, 2014) embodying a transcultural sensibility (hybridity). The novices learning and practicing square word calligraphy engage in acts of aesthetically driven, unidirectional double-voicing of code-crossing (Rampton, 1998), appropriating, imitating, and distorting Chinese orthography rather than *using* it (heteroglossia) (Jaworski, 2014b). Finally, and most evidently, *Square Word Calligraphy* introduces formal elements of Chinese writing into the texts and spaces typically functioning in other linguistic systems (polyglossia).

Although Xu Bing's *Square Word Calligraphy* is arguably one of the most sophisticated instances of the use of two distinct scripts in one text, it is certainly not a unique example of contemporary *heterography* (Blommaert, 2008) or *digraphia* (e.g., Angermeyer, 2012), and it is not limited to art. Contemporary commercial signage abounds in examples of similar mixing of scripts—for example, in the use of stylized, exoticizing features of different Asian scripts (Chinese, Hindi, or Arabic) in, say, English-language restaurant signs in the United Kingdom and other parts of the world (Jaworski, 2014a). In these instances, the texts become "accented" according to the simulated scripts in which they are written. *Square Word Calligraphy* has a similar *moiré* language effect (Jaworski, 2017a) found in the *metrolingual* (Pennycook & Otsuji, 2015) practices of individuals self-styling as cosmopolitans or transnationals, and in commercial signage creating symbolic added value of products and services positioned as translocal or global. Such displays of translingualism subvert the ideologies of homogeneous, bounded, and reified languages as formal systems. They bring home the idea that many people do not live in stable and uniform speech communities, instead moving across different geographical and social spaces, entering ever fluctuating and fleeting communities of contact (Pratt, 1987; Rampton, 2009).

Book from the Ground (*Dishu*) (2003–): Universal Language Ideology

The final example from Xu Bing's practice to be discussed briefly here is his project *Book from the Ground* (2003–), an "ongoing project that explores visual communication through archival material, an animation film, a pop-up concept store, original artworks, and a computer program that translates Chinese and English into the intermediate language of pictograms" (Borysevicz, 2012, p. 23). Inspired by the pictorial signage of international airports, airplane laminated safety manuals, and wrapper instructions for the disposal of chewing gum, Xu Bing has amassed and catalogued a wealth of visual symbols, icons, logos, emoticons, and punctuation marks from print and electronic sources. The culminating point of the project so far has been the publication of a novel, a twenty-four-chapter story of a man's life—Mr. Black—over the course of one day, *Point to Point, Book from the Ground*, or to give it its proper title, "• → ♟ → •" (Xu Bing, 2012b) (Figure 33.11).

Xu Bing's motivation for creating a universal pictographic language is no different from that of the inventors of innumerable verbal, "universal" languages over the past centuries (Okrent, 2009). Xu Bing explains:

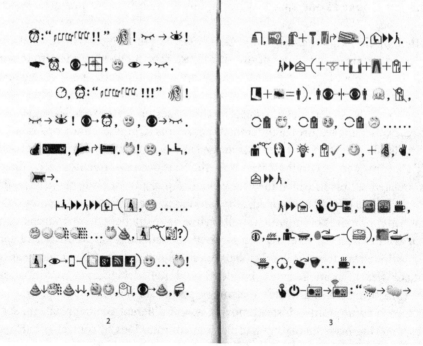

FIGURE 33.11. Xu Bing, *Book from the Ground* (2003–ongoing). Mixed media. Pages 2 and 3 from Xu Bing, *Book from the Ground*, Taipei: Cheng Pin Gallery, 2012.

> Our existing languages are based on geography, ethnicity, and culture (including all-powerful English), and all fall short. Written languages now face an entirely unprecedented challenge. Today, the age-old human desire for a "single script" has become a tangible need. This predicament requires a new form of communication better adapted to the circumstances of globalization. Only today can the implications of the Tower of Babel truly be revived. (Xu Bing, 2007, p. 71)

The ideology of a universal language driving this project is shared with all the other attempts at constructing a means of unimpeded, international communication. Silverstein (2001) discusses one historical example of a related endeavour, Charles Ogden's (1889–1957) Basic English, which, with just 850 *lexical primes* or *word units*, was meant to ameliorate language of the emotive burden that had led to war, destruction, and social pathology. In other words, it promised a "denotational utopia, marked by clear, unambiguous, and easily communicated thoughts" (Silverstein, 2001, p. 71). Basic English was also meant to be learnt quickly (three months, exactly) and used with ease by speakers of all and any language. Yet, as Silverstein argues, the project of Basic was premised on the untenable assumption of "freeing" people from the inadequacies of their own language and the possibility of a time- and culture-neutral communication system (despite the inclusion of some "primes" that are dated, from today's perspective, e.g., words such as *ink* and *porter*).

In his commentary on Xu Bing's pictorial language, Hutton also draws parallels with Ogden's Basic as well as Otto Neurath's (1882–1945) International System of Typographic Picture Education System (ISOTYPE), which had similar ambitions of "promoting international cooperation and preventing war" (Hutton, 2014, p. 136). Hutton is sceptical about the intended universality of all these languages. With regard to Xu Bing's attempt, he comments that it is likely to be accessible only to "an already highly literate and technologically integrated member of urban globalized society" (Hutton, 2014, p. 136). Yet, even members of well-educated globals may encounter problems in interpreting Xu Bing's pictorial language unequivocally. For example, Lee (2015, p. 125) reports issues of ambiguity when "reading" some of the icons, for which, in order to be disambiguated by the reader, an intersemiotic, visual-verbal dictionary would be needed, practically undercutting the autonomy of the pictorial language.

However, the success of Xu Bing's pictorial language as a universal language is only of secondary importance here. Even by his own admission, "[p]erhaps the idea behind this project is too ambitious, but its significance rests in making the attempt" (Xu Bing, 2007, p. 75). As long as it remains a conceptual art project, its value may lie precisely in testing the boundaries of the affordances of a pictorial language. Besides, not unlike numerous other artists (Jaworski, 2017b), *Book from the Ground* demonstrates yet again Xu Bing's commitment to a democratizing stance of his "language policy" across a number of his projects, whether turning *everyone* into illiterates or super-literates capable of transcending linguistic boundaries.

In my final section, I return to the link between language policy and/as language ideology and discuss some implications of engaging with text-based art in language policy and planning.

Conclusion

At the start of this chapter I linked the idea of language policy and planning with social actors' language ideologies and with their individual agency. This idea is not entirely new. While there are various tensions between *macro-* and *micro-*level language policies, especially at the interface between policy and implementation (Baldauf, 2006), various authors have commented on the possibility, a need even, to recognize language planning initiatives operating at different scale levels. For example, Mac Giolla Chríost (2006) discusses how the government-level attempts at maintaining the Irish language in the Gaeltacht and reviving it in other parts of Ireland are aided by community-based language-planning initiatives that are both economically relevant and socially inclusive. Micro-level language planning can foster positive attitudes to the minoritized language and can normalize its use across a wider range of social and institutional domains.

The link between the agency of individual speakers in relation to broader efforts of language planners to standardize (Lane, 2015) or revitalise (Moriarty & Pietikäinen, 2011) minority languages is now well-documented. Moriarty and Pietikäinen (2011, p. 365) go as far as to suggest that such localized language planning initiatives "can be seen to be tailored to the specific needs of the community." Roth-Gordon's (2009) work demonstrates poignantly how individual language choices are, de facto, micro-level policy decisions ensuring personal security and signalling speakers' allegiances to different versions of citizenship within a nation-state. Busch (2009) shows how localized, thoughtful, and liberal language policies valuing linguistic diversity can transform public institutions (in this case, the central library in Vienna) into non-restrictive, heteroglossic spaces, free from the hegemony of national language ideology and market-driven language hierarchies.

With regard to the display of languages in public space, Ben-Rafael et al. (2006) make a distinction between *top-down* and *bottom-up* flows of decisions (i.e., from public bodies and from undifferentiated individuals, respectively). The latter manifestations of language planning lie beyond policy documents. They are located in individuals' decisions, for example, as to which languages should be publically displayed, or erased from public view (Shohamy, 2006), or what place-names are chosen to designate urban spaces (Mac Giolla Chríost, 2007). Commenting on bilingual language display in Wales, Coupland (2010) discusses the rigidity and prescriptivism of key governmental institutions such as Bwrdd Yr Iaith (The Welsh Language Board) insisting on absolute language parallelism. Coupland notes how the linguistic landscape of Wales shaped *from below* (Coupland's preferred term in place of *bottom up*) demonstrates much variation, creativity, and blending of the two languages, escaping the easy parallelism formula couched in the Welsh government's consumerist and neoliberal discourse of (language) *choice*. As argued by Coupland, the policy of parallelism is itself rooted in the standard language ideology, which typically disregards linguistic creativity and innovation. Coupland contrasts the aesthetically bland and regimented language parallelism with commodified texts displayed on T-shirts sold by a small Welsh company Cowbois. Cowbois designs texts on its T-shirts with irony and obliqueness, playing with non-equivalence between Welsh and English, and deploying dense metacultural resources in articulating the (Welsh) culture that generates them. According to Coupland (2010, p. 98), for social actors who operate "in the much less strongly institutionalized periphery [. . .] conformity can give way to creativity and indirect indexicality."

There is only a fine line dividing commercially driven language display (such as on T-shirts) and conceptual text-based art, itself a commercial activity, frequently disseminated in the form of affordable, consumer language objects (Jaworski, 2015). However, as I tried to demonstrate in this chapter, despite operating within the powerful institutional frameworks of galleries and museums, individual text-based artists, like Xu Bing, create their own private or personal domains of language planning and language engineering. In so doing they respond to and comment on language planning at the level of the nation-state, or they transcend the nationalist agenda by developing an internationalist dream or a democratizing stance of planning a universal language for all humanity. With current emphasis in the studies of language policy on political economy, diversity, social justice, and social inclusion (e.g., Ricento, 2015), turning to text-based art may offer sociolinguists a useful lens through which to explore how hegemonic, unorthodox, non-normative, challenging, inclusive, or merely playful language ideologies may exist side by side.

In this sense, and following Wee's (2016) outlook on interventionist language policy, artists can be seen as both theorists (or ideologues) of language policy and planning and as the agents implementing the very policies (or ideologies) that underpin their works. Commanding language in all its multidimensional complexity (Wee, 2016, p. 345), often on a spectacular scale, in an aesthetically arresting manner, attracting large, diverse, and international publics, Xu Bing's ability to reinscribe (*The Character of Characters*), subvert (*Book from the Sky*), invert (*Square Word Calligraphy*), and transcend (*Book from the Ground*) the modernist, national language ideology can raise our awareness of the potentialities and the limitations of language, its value, and its role in shaping social relations. And that is why, I believe, the field of language policy and planning, and sociolinguistics more broadly, may benefit from paying more attention to the creative, aesthetic, and ideological dimensions of text-based art.

ACKNOWLEDGEMENTS

I thank Chris Hutton, Brook Bolander, Joe Gualtieri, Yeewan Koon, and the editors of the *Handbook* for their extremely helpful comments on earlier drafts of this chapter. The research for this chapter was supported by an HKSAR Government Funded Research Project (GRF), 2016–2019, titled "Word as Image: The Sociolinguistics of Art" (RGC ref. no. 17600415). All caveats apply.

NOTES

1. This is not to say that language use is ever devoid of the meta-level signification (Coupland & Jaworski, 2004), especially in the case of linguistic performance, which is always a "reflexive activity" (Bell & Gibson, 2011, p. 562) involving "heightened awareness of the act of expression" (Bauman, 1975, p. 293).
2. In a personal note, Christopher Hutton comments that the policy itself dates from the early 1950s, but there was a major initiative in 1964.
3. Due to limitations of space, I do not discuss here the evolution of the work's title (see, for example, Abe, 1998; Erickson, 2001, for discussion).
4. This interpretation of *Book from the Sky* focuses on its reception by Chinese reading audiences. Other interpretations of the installation have dominated in the West, particularly in the United States (Abe, 1998). For example, the first exhibition of *A Book from the Sky* in the United States at the Elvejhem Museum of Art, University of Wisconsin–Madison, was interpreted largely in light of the 4 June 1989 Tiananmen Square massacre. In the context of largely non-Chinese reading audiences, the emphasis has gradually shifted towards the form and aesthetic merits of the work, placing the viewers outside of the initial conceit of the piece to frustrate their attempts to "find" meaning in the text. The 1995 installation of *A Book from the Sky* at the Massachusetts College of Art did so literally by the absence of vertical scrolls on the gallery walls surrounding the central piece and the viewers. Furthermore, Abe frames his discussion of the reception of *Book from the Sky* in the West in the Orientalist treatment of Chinese writing as emblematic of *Chineseness* (see Hutton, 2006, 2008a).
5. For information about the programme, see http://www.xubing.com/index.php/site/projects/year/1998/your_surname_please; accessed 20 July 2016). The same installation in different formats was subsequently staged in other locations.

REFERENCES

Abe, S. (1998). No questions, no answers: China and *A Book from the Sky*. *Boundary 2*, 25(3), 169–192.

Agha, A. (2003). The social life of a cultural value. *Language and Communication* 23, 231–273.

Anderson, B. (1983). *Imagined communities*. London: Verso.

Angermeyer, P. (2012). Bilingualism meets digraphia: Script alternation and script hybridity in Russian-American writing and beyond. In M. Sebba, S. Mahootian, & C. Jonsson (Eds.), *Language mixing and code-switching in writing: Approaches to mixed-language written discourse* (pp. 255–272) London: Routledge.

Bakhtin, M. (1981 [1935]). *The dialogic imagination: Four essays*. M. Holmquist, Ed.; C. Emerson & M. Holquist, Trans. Austin: University of Texas Press.

Bakhtin, M. (1986 [1953]). *Speech genres and other late essays*. C. Emerson & M. Holmquist, Ed.; V. W. McGee, Trans. Austin: University of Texas Press.

Baldauf, R. B., Jr. (2006). Rearticulating the case for micro language planning in a language ecology context. *Current Issues in Language Planning* 7(2–3), 147–170.

Barakos, E. (2012). Language policy and planning in urban professional settings: Bilingualism in Cardiff businesses. *Current Issues in Language Planning* 13(3), 167–186.

Bauman, R. (1975). Verbal art as performance. *American Anthropologist* 27(2), 290–311.

Bauman, R., & Briggs, C. (2003). *Voices of modernity: Language ideologies and the politics of inequality*. Cambridge: Cambridge University Press.

Bell, A., & Gibson, A. (2011). Staging language: An introduction to the sociolinguistics of performance. *Journal of Sociolinguistics* 15(5), 555–572.

Ben-Rafael, E., Shohamy, E., Amara, M. H., & Trumper-Hecht, N. (2006). Linguistic landscape as symbolic construction of the public space: The case of Israel. In D. Gorter (Ed.), *Linguistic landscape: A new approach to multilingualism* (pp. 7–30). Clevedon, UK: Multilingual Matters.

Blommaert, J. (1999). The debate is open. In J. Blommaert (Ed.), *Language ideological debates* (pp. 1–38). Berlin: Mouton de Gruyter.

Blommaert, J. (2008). *Grassroots literacy: Writing, identity and voice in central Africa*. London: Routledge.

Blommaert, J., & Varis, P. (2015). Culture as accent: The cultural logic of hijabistas. *Semiotica* 203, 153–177.

Bolander, B. (2017). English language policy as ideology in multilingual Khorog, Tajikistan. In E. Barakos & J. W. Unger (Eds.), *Discursive approaches to language policy* (pp. 253–274). Basingstoke, UK: Palgrave Macmillan.

Borysevicz, M. (2012). (What) are we reading? In M. Borysevicz (Ed.), *The book about Xu Bing's Book from the Ground* (pp. 22–31). North Adams, MA; Cambridge, MA: MASS MoCA; MIT Press.

Briggs, C., & Bauman, R. (1992). Genre, intertextuality and social power. *Journal of Linguistic Anthropology* 2(2), 131–172.

Busch, B. (2009). Local actors in promoting multilingalism. In G. Hogan-Brun, C. Mar-Molinero, & P. Stevenson (Eds.), *Discourses on language and integration* (pp. 129–151). Amsterdam: John Benjamins.

Chen, P. (1999). *Modern Chinese: History and sociolinguistics*. Cambridge: Cambridge University Press.

Coupland, N. (2010). Welsh linguistic landscapes "from above" and "from below." In A. Jaworski & C. Thurlow (Eds.), *Semiotic landscapes: Text—image—space* (pp. 77–101). London: Continuum.

Coupland, N., & Jaworski, A. (2004). Sociolinguistic perspectives on metalanguage: Reflexivity, evaluation and ideology. In A. Jaworski, N. Coupland, & D. Galasiński (Eds.), *Metalanguage: Social and ideological perspectives* (pp. 15–51). Berlin: Mouton de Gruyter.

Dong, J. (2010). The enregisterment of Putonghua in practice. *Language and Communication*, 30(4), 265–275.

Erickson, B. (2001). *The art of Xu Bing: Words without meaning, meaning without words*. Washington, DC; Seattle: Arthur M. Sackler Gallery, Smithsonian Institution; University of Washington Press.

Erickson, B. (2012). Xu Bing's journey through language. In Curators of the Asian Art Museum (Eds.), *The Character of Characters: An animation by Xu Bing* (pp. 13–22). San Francisco: Asian Art Museum.

Gal, S., & Woolard, K. (2001). Constructing languages and publics: Authority and representation. In S. Gal & K. Woolard (Eds.), *Languages and publics: The making of authority* (pp. 1–12). Manchester: St. Jerome Publishing.

García, O., & Li Wei. (2014). *Translanguaging: Language, bilingualism and education*. Basingstoke, UK: Palgrave Macmillan.

Gardner-Chloros, P. (1995). Code-switching in community, regional and national repertoires: The myth of the discreteness of linguistic systems. In L. Milroy & P. Muysken (Eds.), *One speaker, two languages: Cross-disciplinary perspectives on code-switching* (pp. 68–89). Cambridge: Cambridge University Press.

Hammers, R. (2014). *The character of characters*: Imagining Can Jie: A response to Xu Bing. In Y. Koon (Ed.), *It all begins with metamorphosis* (pp. 112–114). Exhibition catalogue published on the occasion of Xu Bing's exhibition at Asia Society Hong Kong, 8 May–31 August 2014. Hong Kong: Asia Society.

Harrist, R. E., Jr. (2006). Book from the sky at Princeton: Reflections on scale, sense, and sound. In J. Silbergeld & D. Ching (Eds.), *Persistence | transformation: Text as image in the art of Xu Bing* (pp. 24–45). Princeton, NJ: P. Y. and Kinmay W. Tang Center for East Asian Art, Department of Art and Archaeology, Princeton University, in association with Princeton University Press.

Haugen, E. (1956). *Bilingualism in the Americas*. Gainesville, FL: American Dialect Society.

Heller, M. (1988). Strategic ambiguity: Codeswitching in the management of conflict. In M. Heller (Ed.), *Codeswitching: Anthropological and sociolinguistic perspectives* (pp. 77–96). Berlin: Mouton de Gruyter.

Herder, J. G. (1793). *Briefe zur beförderung der humanität: Erste sammlung*. [*Letters for the advancement of humanity: First collection*.] Riga: Johan Friedrich Kartnoch.

Hobsbawm, E. (1990). *Nations and nationalism since 1760*. Cambridge: Cambridge University Press.

Hobsbawm, E. (1994). *The age of extremes: The short twentieth century, 1914–1991*. London: Abacus.

Holquist, M. (1990). *Dialogism: Bakhtin and his world*. London: Routledge.

Hutton, C. (2006). Writing and speech in Western views of the Chinese language. In Q. S. Tong & D. Kerr (Eds.), *Critical zone 2: A forum of Chinese and Western knowledge* (pp. 83–105). Hong Kong: University of Hong Kong Press.

Hutton, C. (2008a). Human diversity and the genealogy of languages: Noah as the founding ancestor of the Chinese. *Language Sciences* 30, 512–528.

Hutton, C. (2008b). Language as identity in language policy discourse: Reflections on a political ideology. In K Süselbeck, U. Mütihlschlegel, & P. Masson (Eds.), *Lengua, nación e identidad: La regulación del plurilingüismo en España y América Latina* (pp. 75–88). Madrid; Frankfurt am Main: Iberoamericana; Vervuert.

Hutton, C. (2014). A new writing system? Xu Bing's visual language. In Y. Koon (Ed.), *It all begins with metamorphosis* (pp. 135–137). Exhibition catalogue published on the occasion of Xu Bing's exhibition at Asia Society Hong Kong, 8 May–31 August 2014. Hong Kong: Asia Society.

Irvine, J. (2001). "Style" as distinctiveness: The culture and ideology of linguistic differentiation. In P. Eckert & J. Rickford (Eds.), *Style and sociolinguistic variation* (pp. 21–43). Cambridge: Cambridge University Press.

Irvine, J., & Gal, S. (2000). Language ideology and linguistic differentiation. In P. Kroskrity (Ed.), *Regimes of language: Ideologies, polities & identities* (pp. 35–82). Santa Fe, NM: School of American Research Press.

Jaworski, A. (2014a). Xu Bing's transformative art of language. In Y. Koon (Ed.), *It all begins with metamorphosis* (pp. 74–87). Exhibition catalogue published on the occasion of Xu Bing's exhibition at Asia Society Hong Kong, 8 May–31 August 2014. Hong Kong: Asia Society.

Jaworski, A. (2014b). Metrolingual art: Multilingualism and heteroglossia. *International Journal of Bilingualism* 18(2), 134–158.

Jaworski, A. (2015). Word cities and language objects: "Love" sculptures and signs as shifters. *Linguistic Landscape* 1(1–2), 75–94.

Jaworski, A. (2017a). Epilogue: The moiré effect and the art of assemblage. *Social Semiotics* 27(4), 532–543.

Jaworski, A. (2017b). Television as art: Art on television. In J. Mortensen, N. Coupland, & J. Thøgersen (Eds.), *Style, identity and mediation: Sociolinguistic perspectives on talking media* (pp. 165–195). New York: Oxford University Press.

Joseph, J. (2006). "The grammatical being called a nation": History and the construction of political and linguistic nationalism. In N. Love (Ed.), *Language and history: Integrationist perspectives* (120–141). Abingdon, UK: Routledge.

Kraus, R. C. (1991). *Brushes with power: Modern politics and the Chinese art of calligraphy.* Oakland, CA: California University Press.

Lane, P. (2015). Minority language standardisation and the role of users. *Language Policy* 14, 263–283.

Lee, T. K. (2015). Translanguaging and visuality: Translingual practices in literary art. *Applied Linguistics Review* 6(4), 441–465.

Leung, S., Kaplan, J. A., Wenda Gu, Xu Bing, & Hay, J. (1999). Pseudo-languages: A conversation with Wenda Gu, Xu Bing, and Jonathan Hay. *Art Journal* 58, 86–99.

Lo Bianco, J. (2004). Language planning and applied linguistics. In A. Davies & C. Elder (Eds.), *Handbook of applied linguistics* (pp. 738–762). Oxford: Blackwell.

Lüdi, G. (1987). Les marques transcodiques: Regards nouveaux sur le bilinguisme. In G. Lüdi (Ed.), *Devenir bilingue: Parler bilingue* (pp. 1–19). Tübingen: Niemeyer.

Mac Giolla Chríost, D. (2006). Micro-level language planning in Ireland. *Current Issues in Language Planning* 7(2–3), 230–250.

Mac Giolla Chríost, D. (2007). *Language and the city.* Basingstoke, UK: Palgrave Macmillan.

Moriarty, M., & Pietikäinen, S. (2011). Micro-level language-planning and grass-root initiatives: A case study of Irish language comedy and Inari Sámi rap. *Current Issues in Language Planning* 12(3), 363–379.

Okrent, A. (2009). *In the land of invented languages: A celebration of linguistic creativity, madness, and genius.* New York: Spiegel & Grau.

Pennycook, A. (2002). Language policy and docile bodies: Hong Kong and governmentality. In J. W. Tollefson (Ed.), *Language policies in education: Critical issues* (pp. 91–110). Mahwah, NJ: Lawrence Erlbaum.

Pennycook, A. (2014). Language policies, language ideologies and local language practices. In L. Wee, R. Goh, & L. Lim (Eds.), *The politics of English: South Asia, Southeast Asia and the Asia Pacific* (pp. 1–18). Amsterdam: John Benjamins.

Pennycook, A., & Otsuji, E. (2015). *Metrolingualism: Language in the city.* Abingdon, UK: Routledge.

Pratt, M. L. (1987). Linguistic utopias. In N. Fabb, D. Attridge, A. Durant, & C. MacCabe (Eds.), *The linguistics of writing* (pp. 48–66). Manchester: Manchester University Press.

Rampton, B. (1998). Language crossing and the redefinition of reality. In P. Auer (Ed.), *Code-switching in conversation: Language, interaction and identity* (pp. 290–317). London: Routledge.

Rampton, B. (2009). Speech community and beyond. In N. Coupland & A. Jaworski (Eds.), *The new sociolinguistics reader* (pp. 694–713). Basingstoke, UK: Palgrave Macmillan.

Ricento, T. (2000). Historical and theoretical perspectives in language policy and planning. *Journal of Sociolinguistics* 4(2), 196–213.

Ricento, T. (Ed.). (2015). *Language policy and political economy: English in a global context.* New York: Oxford University Press.

Roth-Gordon, J. (2009). The language that came down the hill: Slang, crime, and citizenship in Rio de Janeiro. *American Anthropologist* 111(1), 57–68.

Shohamy, E. (2006). *Language policy: Hidden agendas and new approaches.* London: Routledge.

Silbergeld, J. (2006). Introduction. In J. Silbergeld & D. Ching (Eds.), *Persistence transformation: Text as image in the art of Xu Bing* (pp. 18–22). Princeton, NJ: P. Y. and Kinmay W. Tang Center for East Asian Art, Department of Art and Archaeology, Princeton University, in association with Princeton University Press.

Silverstein, M. (1979). Language structure and linguistic ideology. In P. Clyne, W. Hanks, & C. Hofbauer (Eds.), *Papers from the fifteenth regional meeting, Chicago Linguistic Society, April 19–20, 1979* (pp. 193–247). Chicago: Chicago Linguistic Society.

Silverstein, M. (2000). Whorfianism and linguistic imagination. In P. Kroskrity (Ed.), *Regimes of language: Ideologies, polities & identities* (pp. 85–138). Santa Fe, NM: School of American Research Press.

Silverstein, M. (2001). From the meaning of meaning to the empires of the mind: Ogden's orthological English. In S. Gal & K. Woolard (Eds.), *Languages and publics: The making of authority* (pp. 69–82). Manchester: St. Jerome Publishing.

Tollefson, J. (1991). *Planning language, planning inequality.* New York: Longman.

Tollefson, J. (2011). Language planning and language policy. In R. Mesthrie (Ed.), *The Cambridge handbook of sociolinguistics* (pp. 357–376). Cambridge: Cambridge University Press.

Vainker, S. (2013). The path to landscript: Works 1974–1987. In S. Vainker (Ed.), *Landscape/ Landscript: Nature as language in the art of Xu Bing* (pp. 12–25). Oxford: The Ashmolean Museum.

Votruba, M. (n.d.). Herder on language and nation. Retrieved from http://www.pitt.edu/ ~votruba/sstopics/slovaklawsonlanguage/Herder_on_Language.pdf

Wee, L. (2016). Are there zombies in language policy? Theoretical interventions and the continued vitality of (apparently) defunct concepts. In N. Coupland (Ed.), *Sociolinguistics: Theoretical debates* (pp. 331–348). Cambridge: Cambridge University Press.

Woolard, K. (1998). Simultaneity and bivalency as strategies in bilingualism. *Journal of Linguistic Anthropology* 8, 3–29.

Woolard, K., & Schieffelin, B. (1994). Language ideology. *Annual Review of Anthropology* 23(1), 55–82.

Xu Bing. (2001). The living word. Translated by A. Huss. In B. Erickson (Ed.), *The art of Xu Bing: Words without meaning, meaning without words* (pp. 13–19). Washington,

DC; Seattle: Arthur M. Sackler Gallery, Smithsonian Institution; University of Washington Press.

Xu Bing. (2007). Regarding *Book from the ground.* Jesse Coffino-Greenberg, Trans. *Yishu: Journal of Contemporary Chinese Art* 6(2), 70–75.

Xu Bing. (2011). Ignorance as a kind of nourishment. J. Coffino & V. Xu, Trans. *Modern China Studies* 18(2), 25–53 [Originally published in Bei Dao & Li Tuo (Eds.). (2008). *Qishi Niandai.* Hong Kong: Oxford University Press].

Xu Bing. (2012a). *The character of characters: An animation.* In Curators of the Asian Art Museum (Eds.), *The character of characters: An animation by Xu Bing* (pp. 27–62). San Francisco: Asian Art Museum.

Xu Bing. (2012b). *Point to point: Book from the ground.* Taipei: Eslite.

....

CHAPTER 34

LANGUAGE EDUCATION POLICY AND SOCIOLINGUISTICS

TOWARD A NEW CRITICAL ENGAGEMENT

....

JÜRGEN JASPERS

"EQUAL opportunities lead to three clear priorities: language, language and language," Flemish Education Minister Frank Vandenbroucke announced in 2007 at a colloquium the name of which alone ("Standing tall in Babylon, Languages in Europe") did not augur well for advocates of multilingualism. In saying this, of course, the Flemish minister had only a few languages in mind. His policy brief insisted that all pupils ought to acquire Standard Dutch in view of their equal opportunities, before learning a restricted set of economically attractive languages like French, English, or German. Pupils' diverse home languages (Arabic, Berber, Turkish, and so on) were not entirely ignored, but were presented as impracticably numerous and as contrary to equal opportunities, because "the importance of Dutch as a means to engage in society and to find an appropriate job has gradually increased" (Vandenbroucke, 2007, p. 5). Vandenbroucke's successor (2009–2014), also a Social-Democrat, staunchly supported these views, opposing pupils' non-Dutch home languages to a "rich knowledge of Standard Dutch" which is "the precondition for those wishing to learn, live and work in Flanders" (Smet, 2011, p. 3). The current Christian-Democrat education minister declares in her policy brief (2014–2019) that she will "follow up on the recently introduced innovations regarding the knowledge of Dutch as instruction language" (Crevits, 2014, p. 28) and recently pointed out that "Dutch [. . .] is the key to integration. I am hardcore in this: you need to learn and know the language [. . .] We must not budge one inch from Dutch as instruction language."[1]

This makes Flemish language education policy one that pays lip service to linguistic diversity. It invests in an orderly, executive style multilingualism, and at the same time problematizes the complex heteroglossic realities in the inner cities. Yet as a policy, it responds very well to widespread anxieties in Flanders, the Dutch-speaking north of Belgium. To be sure, this region can today look back on a nationalist struggle for language rights that has been so successful that it has gradually eroded the pertinence of accentuating Standard Dutch as the unifying symbol of a threatened sub-nation. Since the 1950s, it has also witnessed an economic boom that has transformed the region from a sending into a receiving area of migration, complicating representations of a distinct nation defined by a communal language, and raising concerns over social fragmentation. Adding to the unease are steady reports showing that Flemish education, to a greater extent than its neighboring regions, produces school failure along ethnic and socioeconomic lines—not to mention that, ironically after its political and cultural triumphs, Flanders is facing a globalized economy and an *end of the nation-state* discourse that celebrates diversity, cosmopolitanism, and choice over territorially bounded homogeneity.

To understand how an education policy responds to these concerns, we have to appreciate the symbolic function of policy formulation. As Lefstein (2013, p. 645) argues, following Edelman (1985), public policy does not simply have real-world effects in that it allocates limited resources differently, to the advantage of some groups more than others; it also has "symbolic effects, serving to reassure the less organised majority of the public that government is acting to protect their interests." Well-timed public displays of tax law enforcement, for example, help dispel public concern over tax evasion, despite the issuing of lucrative rulings to multinationals.

It is no accident, then, that Flemish language-education policy marries Standard Dutch emphatically with equal opportunities, in spite of the fact that successful Flemings are regularly criticized for speaking non-Standard Dutch. It effectively allows this language to be presented as an obligatory passage point for all speakers with other primary languages, promising social mobility to the latter as much as responding to fears of fragmentation and national identity loss among others. The focus on multilingual skills, to be acquired after Standard Dutch, at the same time addresses concerns over Flanders's participation in the globalizing market, projecting a path of investment in the knowledge economy via multilingualism, albeit founded on a reassuring national language base (cf. Hélot, 2010).

Similar symbolic effects, Lefstein continues, are pursued in education policy by what he calls *accountability theater*, or the organization of symbolic performances of responsibility, such as inspections, with which government demonstrates that it takes equal opportunities extremely seriously. This type of drama is "less expensive and more feasible than the reduction of educational gaps and inequalities" and therefore "a far more expedient means of maintaining the legitimacy of the neo-liberal educational order than actually transforming teaching practices and the distribution of educational resources" (2013, p. 657).

The pursuit of such effects transpires in the projection of an ethos of hard work, discipline, and duty. It does not cost much, while it conveys the impression of determination and concern. "Setting the bar high for languages at each school" accordingly served as slogan for Vandenbroucke's policy. Its introduction is peppered with phrases like "setting the bar high requires discipline" or "relativism and a laissez-faire attitude generally are a bad advisor in education, certainly when it comes to language" (Vandenbroucke, 2007, pp. 6, 4). The minister informed the press that "it is wrong to place responsibility exclusively with 'the system' [. . .]. Also pupils need to set the bar high for themselves. We expect them and their parents to make an effort."[2] And he regularly stated that "[e]very teacher is a language teacher. Not just the teacher of Dutch. Also the kindergarten teacher. The physical education teacher. The geography, accounting and carpentry teacher, up to the professor of constitutional law. The point is that teachers use correct language."[3] Earlier we saw that Crevits similarly projects a "hardcore" stance on learning and teaching Dutch because it is "the key to integration."

Such policies thus neutralize left-wing concerns over social inequality and individual emancipation, as well as right-wing anxieties about the economy and national identity. They fire hope that inequality can be changed, indirectly through language, while leaving structural inequalities untouched. They suggest genuine action by government, but already pass the buck for expected failure to teachers' or pupils' lack of hard work. They are, in other words, the perfect "Third Way" education policy, and like their illustrious inspiration in the United Kingdom, they have had a profound impact on local school practices.

Many other language education policies have been investigated on both sides of the Atlantic and across the Indian and Pacific oceans (Duchêne & Heller, 2007; Evans & Hornberger, 2005; Liddicoat, 2013; May, 2011; Pérez-Milans, 2013; Piller & Cho, 2013; Tollefson, 2002). These studies have shown that language education policies are pivotal elements in nation-states' negotiation of a globalizing economy and a diversifying population. They reveal that such policies play an authoritative role in associating particular linguistic resources with imagined pasts, presents, and futures, with all the consequences this entails for those seen to produce the wrong kinds of resources. As Harris et al. (2001, p. 9) conclude, such policies can turn national languages into "potent, condensed and multivalent symbol[s]" that stand for concerns as different as national unity, effective communication, social mobility, and civic duty. Frequently, too, these languages are severed from their sociohistorical origins and are presented as a neutral *technology of the mind* (Collins & Blot, 2003) that all those willing to make the effort can acquire. Language education policies are therefore deserving of our close attention.

I will argue on the next pages, however, that while language education policies merit critical examination, the suggestions for change that many critics recommend often reproduce some of the main assumptions behind the policies that they denounce. Some of these suggestions also have problems of their own. I suggest that this necessitates a reconsideration of the received opposition between sociolinguistics (broadly understood) and language education policy, and requires calls for change to take a different tack.

CRITICISM OF LANGUAGE EDUCATION POLICIES

Sociolinguists criticize language education policies because of the assumptions about language they entail and the consequences they are seen to have for particular groups of pupils. Such policies are, after all, frequently based on a view of monolingual nations. This view is inspired by the idea that there exist national languages, and that these need to be protected for their historical authenticity, as well as purified in order to ensure that they can be used in the performance of modern, civilized behavior. As a result, it has become customary to posit the existence of separate, countable, and improvable codes that require a territory to flourish unharmed, and to invest in language separation as a way of distinguishing the national standard variety from less modern predecessors (dialects) or rival varieties (foreign languages) (Bauman & Briggs, 2003). This is also the case in organized language learning and teaching: learners are typically oriented to forms of parallel monolingualism or sequential bilingualism; these orientations may translate into *one language at a time* classroom procedures, or into glorifications of full immersion as the ultimate language-learning experience.

Such views have in the past decades drawn a lot of criticism. Scholars not only insist on the ideological character of the notion of separate languages, but also on its descriptive and theoretical limitations for the study of language. Thus, they have been deconstructing bounded languages as a *myth* (Harris, 1998), a *Western ambition* (de Certeau, 1984, in Canagarajah, 2013, p. 19), or a foundational fiction of modernity (Bauman & Briggs, 2003). Much attention has been paid, as well, to spaces of intense linguistic contact—urban metropolises, digital communication—to argue that these present types of linguistic complexity that confound the imagination of distinct linguistic communities (Blommaert & Rampton, 2011). Instead of imagining that people use languages, several other concepts—among others, *polylingualism, metrolingualism, codemeshing,* and *translanguaging*—have been proposed to describe, name, and explain contemporary speech practices. Various sociolinguists have demonstrated the possibilities and efficiency of language learning through language mixing (Canagarajah, 2013; Creese & Blackledge, 2010; García & Li Wei, 2014; Hornberger, 2004).

It is clear, though, that most language education policies today take us down a different path by abstracting away from actual, often mixed, language use. In this sense, such policies "bring into being language-related problems" (Liddicoat, 2013, p. 12) because they make all language use that deviates from the idea of separate, bounded languages available for earmarking as disfluent or transgressive. Implementing language education policy has consequently been argued to involve symbolic violence, erasure, or disqualification of pupils' linguistic resources. Blommaert et al. (2006) argue in relation to a primary school class for newcomers in Antwerp that "the [home] linguistic resources disqualified by teachers are perfectly valuable as resources per se; but they do not qualify symbolically as language" (p. 36). Flores and García (2013) study newcomer classes for Spanish immigrants in New York and suggest that "[w]ell-meaning educators [. . .] insist on teaching Standard American English. Unfortunately, most efforts at doing this come in the form of delegitimizing the students' home language practices" (p. 243). Investigating linguistic practices across different secondary schools in Madrid, Martín Rojo (2010, p. 43) likewise concludes that "what prevails in schools is a diversity of languages, behaviors and cultures formally unrecognized and even actively suppressed in instructional processes."

Language education policies are regularly viewed, therefore, as reproducing power differences, or as serving the interests of a minority whose register is upheld as exemplary for all. Such a view chimes in with identifications of a *hidden curriculum*. These hold that although the official curriculum promises equal opportunities and claims to be ideologically neutral, its hidden aim is to reproduce the relationships of inequality that its subject matter, modes of transmission, and instruction language represent (García & Li Wei, 2014, p. 47; Martin Rojo, 2010; Shohamy, 2006; cf. Moore, 2007). A closely related dimension of this institutional bias proposes that the monolingual ideology education policy is based on negatively influences teacher attitudes and expectations. In line with the Pygmalion effect study (Rosenthal & Jacobson, 1968; but see Wineburg, 1987), it is then assumed that these attitudes and expectations have a detrimental impact on pupils' learning outcomes and well-being (e.g., Agirdag et al., 2013; Codó & Patiño-Santos, 2014, p. 62). As summarized by García & Li Wei (2014, pp. 55–56),

> language-minoritized children using home language practices in schools have been, and continue to be, severely punished [. . .]. Today [in contrast to before], the punishment is not corporal, but relies on instruction and assessments that follow monolingual language standards, ensuring that bilingual students get lower grades, are made to feel inadequate, and fail in schools. [. . .] Clearly the educational consequences of the sociopolitical inability to authenticate a multilingual and heteroglossic reality

[are] responsible for educational failure of many language minorities around the world. (2014, pp. 55–56)

These and similar postulations are usually influenced by neo-Marxist analyses of social class reproduction, according to which schools prepare students for their appropriate, class-related, position in the occupational structure, in spite of these schools' rhetoric of fairness (Bourdieu & Passeron, 1977; Bowles & Gintis, 1976). They are also attuned to a long-standing critical reflex in sociolinguistics: when working-class and black pupils in the 1960s were assumed to fail at school because of their *monosyllabic, deprived, absent* or *restricted* language, sociolinguists worked to demonstrate the regularity, complexity, and fluency of these pupils' linguistic skills (Cazden et al., 1972; Labov, 1972). In so doing, they sought to shift the gaze, when it came to school failure, away from pupils' presumed deficiencies or deprivation, to the institutions that devalued, failed to see, or misinterpreted pupils' linguistic skills (Collins, 2009; Jaspers, 2016).

The so-called deficiency of schools and curricula continues to inspire calls that language education policies require a quick and comprehensive makeover. Indeed, such calls are almost a tradition. Equally traditional, though, is the fact that policymakers are poor listeners when it comes to this type of appeal. The opposition even looks fairly overwhelming considering the re-emergence of (pupil) deficit discourses in popular and government opinion (Avineri et al., 2015; Grainger & Jones, 2013), the fact that nation-states with a more open outlook on diversity "have refocused away from linguistic diversity towards a narrower monolingualism" (Liddicoat et al., 2014, p. 269), and the depressing regularity with which accounts of negative teacher attitudes toward pupils' home languages come out.

These facts and assumptions about schooling—not to mention that school failure among working-class and ethnic-minority pupils remains sky-high—have shaped specific concerns and priorities in sociolinguistics, such as an interest in unofficial alternatives, accommodation, or resistance, and in a radical, transformative pedagogy. It is to these issues that I will now turn.

Translanguaging in the Classroom: Resistance and Critical Pedagogy

Faced with stiff opposition to their calls for a linguistically more diverse education, sociolinguists have been concerned with exploring unofficial and small-scale alternatives to language education policy, and with the pedagogical advantages this can entail. Such explorations are stimulated by the insight that teachers never passively implement policy (Johnson & Freeman, 2010) and that all "policies pose problems to their subjects, problems that must be solved in context. Solutions [. . .] will be localised and should be expected to display 'ad hocery' and messiness" (Ball, 1997, p. 270). Scholars thus, often ethnographically, describe how teachers flexibly and *à l'improviste* reconcile the expectations of a monolingual curriculum with a linguistically diverse pupil population, for example by tolerating pupils' code-switches and code preferences in class, or deliberately interspersing classroom time with pupils' better-known codes.

Such accommodations are explained as instructional strategies oriented to efficient classroom procedure (giving explanations, checking up on behavior or understanding, maintaining pace) and to keeping pupils' attention; or, in the longer run, to help pupils transcend the contradictions between the curriculum and the extra-curricular world they inhabit, by "mak[ing] links [. . .] between the social, cultural, community, and linguistic domains of their lives" (Creese & Blackledge 2010, p. 112; also see Heller, 1995; Macaro, 2006). Some teachers develop translingual pedagogies that constantly shift between curricular and pupils' primary language skills as they introduce pupils to officially ratified literacies (Canagarajah, 2013; García & Leiva, 2014; Hornberger, 2004). Such pedagogies are often seen to create so-called third spaces, that is, "symbolic or metaphorical space[s] that merg[e] the 'first space' of children's home, community and peer networks with the 'second space' of more formalized settings like school" (Combs et al., 2011, p. 195) and that thus generate alternative forms of collaboration and learning (Flores & García, 2013; Gutiérrez et al., 1999). Hélot (2010) describes in this context how two trainee teachers in the region of Alsace (France), working with heterogeneous kindergarten groups, constructed multilingual spaces by developing informal multilingual materials and providing translation. This eventually invited non-French-dominant pupils to start learning French and made their classmates curious to learn other languages that circulated at school.

The preceding studies commonly refer to language pedagogical insights according to which pupils' primary linguistic skills facilitate access to complex curriculum content; allowing them to use these skills, moreover, would accelerate their acquisition of the school language. Cummins (2000) proposes in this regard that pupils who acquire academic proficiency in their primary language will easily transfer the skills, strategies, and metalinguistic insights that this involves into a second or third language. Denying pupils the use and development of their primary linguistic skills in this view boils down to depriving them of a crucial scaffold for performing well at school, and to wasting valuable school time (Baker, 2011; Thomas & Collier, 2000). In this context we also find the development of pedagogies that seek to transfer pupils' skills in artistic plurilingual expressions, such as in hip-hop or creative writing, into more formal teaching and training contexts (cf. Alim, 2010; Hill, 2009; Holmes,

2014; Pennycook, 2007), along with calls for a culturally responsive or sustaining pedagogy (Paris & Alim, 2014).

Closely in line with these accommodative strategies is research that demonstrates participants' resistance to monolingual school policies. While some studies focus on teachers' opposition (see chapters in McCarty, 2011, and Menken & García, 2010; Pease-Alvarez & Thompson, 2014), most attention in this regard has gone to pupils' strategies as they sabotage, avoid, delay, or otherwise work against official language policy. Such work has included attention to how pupils' mixed and home language use frustrates teachers' monolingual and *one language at a time* policies (Heller, 1995; Pérez-Milans, 2011), and to how their playful language use can throw dominant linguistic expectations into critical relief (Charalambous, 2011; Creese & Blackledge, 2011; Jaspers, 2005). It has demonstrated, too, that some pupils recruit language policies for distinguishing themselves, jocularly or in earnest, from other pupils (Jaspers, 2011; Karrebæk, 2013; Talmy, 2009). When it comes to policy imposition and resistance, then, victims and offenders can be found on both sides of the teacher-pupil divide.

A third research strand proposes that translanguaging in the classroom ought not to be limited to "ensur[ing] that students learn content and academic language," or to "just another strategy to deal with a problem" (García & Li Wei, 2014, p. 93), but that it must instantiate a radically progressive pedagogy that "decolonize[s] the dominant intellectual knowledge" (García & Leiva, 2014, p. 211; cf. Flores & García, 2013; Martín Rojo, 2010). On the whole, such proposals take their cue from the Freirean (1970) perspective that sets out to replace a *banking concept* of education, treating pupils as passive receptors of knowledge, with a *problem-posing* one. The latter type incites pupils to develop their intellectual autonomy and to draw into question common truths that in fact hide systems of oppression and control. Rather than merely facilitating (language) learning, translanguaging in this view is seen to give minorities and bilinguals back "the voice that had been taken away by ideologies of monoglot standards" (García & Li Wei, 2014, p. 105).

This voice is subsequently suggested to generate new, fluid, linguistic subjectivities rather than monolingual ones, and to produce critical representations of the sociopolitical status quo: "fixed identities and meanings are questioned, and new signification is made" (García, 2013, p. 162). Such a view chimes in with calls for a critical language awareness (Alim, 2010; Hill, 2009) that invites pupils to investigate their own translingual practices. Validation of these practices as a subject of analysis is argued to lead to greater insight in linguistic regimentation at a larger scale, as well as to legitimize formerly devalued practices in a sacrosanct institutional space.

All of the previously mentioned studies have been invaluable for our understanding of the pedagogic and symbolic potential of language at school. They demonstrate that education policies significantly constrain teachers' and pupils' possibilities, but that these never determine actual classroom practice, or preclude critical reflection that may generate resistance and change. These studies have, in other words, exposed the school as a site of struggle and negotiation, rather than a harmonized place where participants act out the roles that larger systems of inequality have in store for them, and they provide insight into possible ways out. Underlying much of this work is a call that schools should valorize pupils' primary languages, pluralize the instruction language, or allow linguistic mixing, in the conviction that this will be beneficial to pupils' well-being, achievement, and future social opportunities. Intervention, in this perspective, is urgent. Yet, as I shall argue, although such calls are pedagogically exciting and justified on principle, they often share with the authorities they criticize representations of the policy implementation process, as well as assumptions about the presumed impact of educational reform on social inequality. Some of the more radical suggestions, in addition, complicate the emancipatory project of the school by reducing language use at school to group interests. Many calls for change may thus underestimate the difficulties for implementation, exaggerate their own effects, and overstate their critical character. I will address each of these issues in the next section.

Two caveats are in place, though. The first is that the challenges described in the following do not apply to each and every study mentioned earlier. I will be pointing out tendencies rather than universals; some of the previously mentioned studies do not even make suggestions for change. The second is that I am using *sociolinguistics* as a broad category here, including (critical) applied and educational linguistics, language policy studies, as well as discourse-analytic work. The idea is thus not to take a jab at sociolinguists (I am one myself), but rather to talk about tendencies observable in work by scholars of different but related disciplinary stripes.

Challenges for Intervention

In what follows I will concentrate on three tendencies that characterize much sociolinguistic reflection on language education policy: (1) an inclination for pointing a finger at teachers' behavior, awareness, or attitudes; (2) a conviction that with the right linguistic knobs turned, higher learning outcomes are a sure thing; and (3) a radical reduction of current linguistic practices at school to serving social rather than intellectual interests.

Disciplining Teachers

Despite their criticism of policymakers, many sociolinguists subscribe to a comparable process of disciplining teachers. Flemish education policy, as we saw earlier, contributes to this by insisting that *every teacher is a language teacher* if he or she cares about pupils' opportunities. Much research similarly contends that teachers with the appropriate attitude are criterial for genuine innovation. Thus one commonly finds appeals that teachers need to change their behavior or attitudes, usually through arguing that they need to be more aware or that they have a choice. This is visible in statements to the effect that "[t]eachers, students, all of us, have a choice to either uphold or disrupt that [monolingual, culturally homogenizing] hegemony" (Alim & Paris, 2015, p. 81), and that teachers "can create a space where dominant ideologies are interrogated and, over time, dismantled with the goal of providing equal language rights for all" (Alim, 2010, p. 227).

Others indicate that teachers had better make that choice in suggesting that they "hold as much responsibility for policy making as do government officials" (Menken & García, 2010, pp. 3–4), or intimate their appreciation of those who have made the right choice: "we are heartened by our experiences observing and working with a teacher collective that is resisting and [. . .] renegotiating policies of standardization" (Pease-Alvarez & Thompson, 2014, p. 166). Some imply that teachers do not really have a choice, because they should consider "social change as part of the job" (Cochran-Smith, 1995, p. 494, in Godley et al., 2006, p. 33), or that any choice they could make is constrained by requirements that teachers "need to be prepared to be bilingual teachers," that they "need [. . .] to be aware of language diversity," "need to develop a critical sociopolitical consciousness about the linguistic diversity of the children," and that they "need to act on all this information" (García & Li Wei, 2014, p. 122). There is frequent disappointment, too, about teachers' lack of susceptibility to sociolinguistic knowledge, their widespread negative attitudes toward linguistic variation, or their meager sense of responsibility and initiative (Agirdag et al., 2013; Alim, 2010; Codó & Patiño-Santos, 2014; Shohamy, 2006).

The least one can say about this is that sociolinguists have high expectations of teachers. But the image implicit in these accounts is also puzzling. Presented as independent actors with a choice, teachers only seem to have one genuine option, the others being uninformed, disheartening, or worse. Teachers' capacity for appropriation and resistance thus seems to be valued where official policy is concerned, but deplored when scholarly expectations are at stake. There is no reason, however, why the latter would be spared the fact that all policies, regardless of whether they have received the stamp of scientific approbation, will be negotiated by actors in their local conditions.

Moreover, suggestions that choosing the reasonable option is self-evident or a matter of will may be more informed by policymakers' representations than is apparent at first sight. They suffer from what Ball (1997) calls *isolationism*, that is, the tendency to concentrate on one policy in particular, bracketing out all others that circulate at school. Such isolationism overlooks that "the enactment of one [policy] may inhibit or contradict or influence the possibility of the enactment of others" (Ball, 1997, p. 265); and it reproduces policymakers' view that rather than the policies themselves and their complicated relation to other expectations, teachers' lack of interest or willingness contravenes application. Apart from easily slipping into a blaming culture, this perspective limits the focus of analysis on (dis) heartening responses in relation to one particular (in our case: language) policy, and it obfuscates teachers' navigation of multiple, sometimes structurally irreconcilable, concerns (cf. Ball, 1997, p. 270). Pachler et al. (2008, p. 440) usefully suggest in this context that teachers "orientat[e]—often simultaneously—towards different ideological *centers*: themselves, their colleagues, their groups of learners, the head teacher, the school as an institution with a tradition, the education system, the curriculum, the government, society-at-large, and so on. Their discourses reveal traces of such multiplicity and layering."

Teachers' behavior, in this view, must be approached not as straightforwardly revealing of their ignorance or lack of willingness, but as systematically ambivalent, as it orients toward different concerns at different scales (Jaspers, 2015; Martínez et al., 2015). Consequently, reporting negative attitudes toward pupils' primary language resources in relation to society at large can coexist with the informal recruitment of these resources for fostering learning or promoting rapport in small-scale interactions. More ambivalence of this kind can be anticipated in light of the growing tension between governments' investment in monolingual curricula, sociolinguists' emphasis on the opposite, pedagogues' promotion of positive learning environments, and pressure from parents that their children learn *real* languages. Understanding teachers' complex management of the resulting dilemmas confounds any representation of a simple choice between reproducing *or* disrupting power relations, because in many cases teachers will have to do both at the same time, in addition to many other things (cf. Heller, 1995; Pérez-Milans, 2013).

Language, School Success, and Social Inequality

A second challenge is that many suggestions for change share with policymakers fundamental assumptions about the relation between language, education, and social equality—notably that changing language in education will generate school success among those now failing, and that this educational change will redress social inequality. Indeed, while many sociolinguists and policymakers clash over the *type* of language that needs to be introduced (a standard variety, or a more diverse set of linguistic resources), in principle they are agreed that the *right* type of language at school will generate success (or well-being, as a precondition to this).

It is clear, of course, that language can play an important role in success or failure, just like other factors. In this regard it is useful to propose linguistic changes that facilitate learning, avoid misdiagnosing, or improve a transfer of skills. Yet assuming automatic links between curricular language and educational outcomes fails to explain particular outcomes, unless through invoking ad hoc effects. That is, while the disqualification of non-standard- or minority-language skills can be accurately described (and deplored), its occurrence does not prevent at least some domestic and ethnic minority groups to succeed nevertheless, in spite of negative attitudes or linguistic stigmatization (D'Amato, 1987; Erickson, 1987; Gibson, 1987; Moore, 2007; Ogbu, 1978; cf. also Rampton, 2006, pp. 271–276). Understanding the relation between instructional language and educational outcomes as contingent, rather than automatic, is equally required for explaining why medium-term experiments with ratifying home-language use in class, and providing extra tuition in that language (Ramaut et al., 2013), did not result in the predicted skills transfer.

This also holds for the relation between school achievement and the economy. Huge educational reforms in Western democracies (the massification of schooling after World War II, scholarship programs, and so on) have been inspired by the consensus view that democratizing education would redefine social opportunities. Sociologists have been emphasizing, however, that these massive reforms have not been able to redress social inequality to any significant degree, with few signs of any imminent change (Freeman-Moir & Scott, 2003; Moore, 2007; Reay, 2010; also see Marsh, 2011). "The irony is," Reay (2010, p. 399) indicates, "that the rhetoric of social mobility and equal opportunities within education has increased in volume and intensity as both have become less possible in practice." This sobering realization does not invalidate educational reform per se, but it raises caution as to its hoped-for effects: "[e]ducation can be significantly reformed and educational inequalities even significantly reduced, without this having any appreciable impact upon social opportunities and inequalities" (Moore, 2007, p. 170).

The main reason for this, Moore has been arguing in his work, is that educational expansion raises attainment levels for all groups (more people with formerly no or low degrees are now getting some or higher degrees), and so generates credential inflation. Successive generations therefore need more (that is, more expensive, exclusive, longer) education to maintain their status, which is affordable only to those groups who, prior to educational expansion, needed less education to distinguish themselves from those with no or low degrees. Consequently, "attainment levels increase and returns decline *pro rata*" (Moore, 2007, p. 152).

Neo-Marxist sociologists have sought to explain this through reversing the direction of the relation: schools do not have much impact on society, because as institutions they work to reproduce the class inequalities that already exist in that society. Apart from introducing a more pessimistic view on education, this explanation has also (and paradoxically, Moore argues) invited a range of radical pedagogies proposing that "forms of education that were 'the opposite' of those that [are] enshrined within the dominant system would automatically be subversive of capitalist social relations" (Moore, 2007, p. 108). Yet all these approaches maintain that relations in one field (the economy) are more or less copied and pasted into another (the school), or vice versa, and they struggle to explain behavior that is out of type (such as working-class pupils who eventually take up elite jobs).

What is needed, therefore, is a framework that accounts for the regularities and the exceptions, and this is one that approaches education and the economy as interactive but relatively independent fields (D'Amato, 1987; Moore, 2007). D'Amato argues that pupils apply themselves in school partly on the basis of a situational rationale, that is, their perception of the value of school for building relationships with peers or teachers, and for experiencing success and learning. Next to this situational rationale, pupils' investment in school depends on a structural one: their understanding of school performance in relation to perceived social opportunities, and in relation to their family's or community's expectations and experiences with school. Meager situational or structural rewards will in this view entail low investment in school. Pupils may also find only one rationale persuasive, leading to their endurance of tedious classes or the marginalization of their backgrounds as the price to pay for a valued degree; alternatively, it may invite their pursuit of cherished peer relationships in defiance of family expectations (Willis, 1977). Situational rationales can evolve from one classroom and teacher to another, while structural ones are interactive with changing economic opportunities, and with pupils' understanding of their own prospects relative to other pupils' (e.g., at *better* schools) expected school degrees (Reay, 2010). Even in the most ideal of worlds, therefore, where curricula are linguistically pluralized, we can expect schools to produce winners and losers in relation to what this institution means to those having to go through it.

Factoring in these two rationales implies that the beneficial impact of specific curriculum changes (e.g., a pluralized instruction language) on pupils' well-being, attainment rates, and social opportunity is an empirical matter rather than a theoretical one. This does not, of course, legitimate monolingual policies or condone negative teacher attitudes. But it means that singling out such policies or attitudes as the primordial cause for particular pupils' school failure, or inversely, assuming that translanguaging guarantees success, "exaggerat[es] both what schools can do and what they can be held accountable for" (Moore, 2007, p. 14).

Language and Group Interests

A third problem is that calls for a radical (translanguaging) pedagogy risk reducing curricular language and policies to serving particular group interests. To be sure, monolingual and translingual language use regularly appear on each side, respectively, of dichotomies such as colonizing versus decolonizing, bourgeois versus subaltern, old versus new, or white versus black. Exceptionally, this reduction manifests itself in claims that any linguistic expectation is a type of colonization. Because "language is personal and unique and varies from one person to another," Shohamy (2006, p. 2) suggests, "dictating to people how to use language in terms of accent, grammar and lexicon, etc., can be seen as a form of personal intrusion and manipulation." Such a view would seem to question the very principle of (language) teaching. More frequently, it is *hidden curriculum* analyses that trace language use at school back to group interests: since the curriculum hides the interests of a dominant group, its present monolingual character is taken to benefit a usually white, bourgeois, monolingual group. Changing the curricular language or setting up a translingual pedagogy is then seen to disrupt hegemonic norms, or to "decolonize the dominant intellectual knowledge" (García & Leiva, 2014, p. 211).

Obviously, current curricula are mostly monolingual, and there are good reasons for denaturalizing this state of affairs, as I will emphasize in the following. There is strategic merit, too, in essentializing for political action. Yet the more current curricular language is reduced to serving the interests of a self-conscious collectivity, the more this risks compromising the linguistic practices suggested as a replacement: they will serve the interests of a different group. The more, too, this downplays the capacity of linguistic practices to transfer knowledge we consider enlightening, at the same time as inevitably reflecting speakers' position in a stratified system.

Linguistic anthropologists have indeed insisted that all language use is doubly informative (Agha, 2007; Silverstein, 2003). It is inevitably indexical of speakers' social history, current conditions or activities, and of the type of social relation they seek to construct with others in the here and now. But language is equally used to produce cumulative and denotational coherence across sentences or turns of speech, resulting in what is conventionally called *information*. Reducing language to the first of these functions leads to postulations that all language use is inherently biased (*colonizing, bourgeois*). Reducing language to the second is positivistic and ignores that language is always produced from a particular position; there is no voice from nowhere.

A more moderate take on this, however, would argue that while language in its various shapes is inevitably indexical of speakers' position, we do not have to abandon the idea that it can be used to denote phenomena and share insights in a more or less accurate way. *How* accurate is an empirical concern, and this includes examination of the extent to which speakers' social background impacts more than superficially on what they say (Hammersley, 1992). When that impact is substantial, we are probably dealing with statements that advance or naturalize speakers' position. In the other case, though, speakers' social position may only be a trivial aspect of their language use (Moore, 2007, p. 18).

Translanguaging at school is not immune to this concern; neither is the default use of English for academic purposes. Indeed, no single way of speaking and writing is impervious to being recruited for excluding others or advancing one's own interests. Emancipation may, in other words, not so much reside in replacing an essentially bad old bourgeois language with essentially good, new, and subaltern translingual practices (cf. Hall, 1992, pp. 254–255). Rather, it may consist of teaching pupils that all language use at school will be socially locatable—and potentially group interest serving, in which case it is objectionable—but that this does not disqualify it per se for formulating the types of knowledge we think are worthy of exchange at school, irrespective of their value for specific groups.

Naturally, in the unlikely case that all language use in schools today is only trivially related to speakers' social backgrounds, this does not make its current, mostly monolingual character acceptable from a democratic or representational point of view, as I will underline in concluding.

Discussion and Conclusion

Many governments recruit language to neutralize concerns with national homogeneity and school failure among working-class and ethnic-minority pupils, imbuing it with promises of social mobility and prosperity. The education policies conceived in this spirit have been rightly criticized for their unsubstantiated premises and troublesome repercussions. Yet in their alternative suggestions, many scholars tend to demonstrate a similar investment in *language, language, and language* as a crucial tool for redressing social inequality and promoting emancipation. Even if in the case of governments this investment may have to be seen as relatively symbolic (cf. Lefstein, 2013), both parties in this way maintain the view that education motors social change, and that to the degree that it does not, urgent (linguistic) intervention is required. In consequently insisting on teachers' responsibility, it looks as if several policy critiques share with governments a penchant for disciplining behavior.

While such a common framework may be surprising, this does not make demands that current curricula be linguistically pluralized any less justified. Yet these demands may have to be made as a matter of principle, out of a political choice that school curricula should reflect the linguistic resources of the citizens they are designed for (and paid by). Such demands may be less vulnerable to criticism that sociolinguists are making overstated claims about the effects of language on pupils' well-being, achievements, and opportunities, or about the intrinsically oppressive or liberating qualities of particular linguistic resources, because they are legitimate regardless of pedagogical benefits or resultant social mobility.

The specific texture of this pluralization will depend on local needs and means, and on sociolinguistic insights. There is an acute need for more research that explores which opportunities and limitations emerge when employing mixed or translingual practices in class, offering translation and other types of linguistic assistance to pupils and/or parents, and reconciling this with the linguistic styles that the exchange of knowledge has come to be based on. It will be expedient to examine, understand, and potentially alleviate anxieties among parents, teachers, and the wider public, just as teachers can learn much from sociolinguists to recognize competence where none is usually presumed, or to help pupils recruit and value their primary language skills for acquiring subject matter and the school register(s) it is usually formulated in (cf. Alim, 2010; Godley et al., 2006). Additionally, in light of authorities' hitherto unwavering dedication to monolingualism, it will be in sociolinguists' interest to understand the ways in which schools are facing up to the complications this engenders, and to find out "how linguistic diversity surfaces under conditions that are clearly disfavoring it, and why or why not this happens" (Karrebæk, 2013, p. 356).

A principled demand for recognizing linguistic diversity at school—without guarantees for social mobility or well-being—may also help avoid reducing our interest in social equality to an educational issue. "Where education cannot compensate for society," Moore argues in echo of Bernstein (1970), "educational reform should not serve as a political substitute for direct social reform" (2007, p. 178); it is a costly strategy with limited effects. This is not to downplay the necessity of educational reform when linguistic diversity intersects with (lost) pedagogical opportunities or serves as a pretext for social distinction. Rather, it is to bear in mind, as Varenne and McDermott (1999) caution, that if education were perfectly tuned and fair, it would render illegitimate all protest against the unequal outcomes that Western-style schools must create to identify their above-average students. Our criticism should not be confined to language education policy; we must be critical as well of views that education, once linguistically pluralized, will fairly determine where we belong in an unequal world.

ACKNOWLEDGMENTS

The author thanks Kevin Absillis, Ciska Hoet, Lian Malai Madsen, Sarah Van Hoof, as well as the editors of this volume, for valuable comments on an earlier version of this chapter. All remaining shortcomings are my own.

NOTES

1. *De Tijd*, August 31, 2016.
2. *De Morgen*, May 20, 2006.
3. Suggested in "Language is a Social Issue," speech at the Symposium "Standing tall in Babylon: Languages in Europe," September 14, 2007.

REFERENCES

Agha, A. (2007). *Language and social relations.* Cambridge: Cambridge University Press.
Agirdag, O., Van Avermaet, P., & Van Houtte, M. (2013). School segregation and math achievement. *Teachers College Record* 115, 1–50.

Alim, H. S. (2010). Critical language awareness. In N. Hornberger & S. McKay (Eds.), *Sociolinguistics and language education* (pp. 205–231). Clevedon, UK: Multilingual Matters.

Alim, H. S., & Paris, D. (2015). Whose language gap? *Journal of Linguistic Anthropology* 25(1), 79–81.

Avineri, N., Johnson, E., Brice-Heath, S., McCarty, T., Ochs, E., et al. (2015). Invited forum: Bridging the "language gap." *Journal of Linguistic Anthropology* 25(1), 66–86.

Baker, C. (2011). *Foundations of bilingual education and bilingualism*. Clevedon, UK: Multilingual Matters.

Ball, S. J. (1997). Policy, sociology and critical social research. *British Educational Research Journal* 23(3), 257–274.

Bauman, R., & Briggs, C. (2003). *Voices of modernity*. Cambridge: Cambridge University Press.

Bernstein, B. (1970). Education cannot compensate for society. *New Society* 26, 288–314.

Blommaert, J., & Rampton, B. (2011). Language and superdiversity. *Diversities* 13, 1–21.

Blommaert, J., Creve, L., & Willaert, E. (2006). On being declared illiterate. *Language and Communication* 26(1), 34–54.

Bourdieu, P., & Passeron, J. C. (1977). *Reproduction in education, society and culture*. Beverly Hills, CA: Sage.

Bowles, S., & Gintis, H. (1976). *Schooling in capitalist America*. New York: Basic Books.

Canagarajah, S. (2013). *Translingual practice*. London: Routledge.

Cazden, C., John, V., & Hymes, D. (Eds.). (1972). *Functions of language in the classroom*. New York: Teachers College Press.

Charalambous, C. (2012). "Republica de Kubros": Transgression and collusion in Greek-Cypriot adolescents' classroom silly-talk. *Linguistics and Education* 23(3), 334–349.

Cochran-Smith, M. (1995). Color blindness and basket making are not the answer. *American Educational Research Journal* 32, 493–522.

Codó, E., & Patiño-Santos, A. (2014). Beyond language: Class, social categorisation and academic achievement in a Catalan high school. *Linguistics and Education* 25(1), 51–63.

Collins, J. (2009). Social reproduction in classroom and schools. *Annual Review of Anthropology* 38, 33–48.

Collins, J., & Blot, R. (2003). *Literacy and literacies*. Cambridge: Cambridge University Press.

Combs, M. C., González, L., & Moll, L. C. (2011). US Latinos and the learning of English. In T. McCarty (Ed.), *Ethnography and language policy* (pp. 185–203). New York; London: Routledge.

Creese, A., & Blackledge, A. (2010). Translanguaging in the bilingual classroom. *The Modern Language Journal* 94, 103–115.

Creese, A., & Blackledge, A. (2011). Separate and flexible bilingualism in complementary schools. *Journal of Pragmatics* 43(5), 1196–1208.

Crevits, H. (2014). *Policy brief 2014–2019*. Brussels: Flemish Ministry of Education.

Cummins, J. (2000). *Language, power and pedagogy*. Clevedon, UK: Multilingual Matters.

D'Amato, J. (1987). The belly of the beast. *Anthropology and Education Quarterly* 18(4), 357–360.

De Certeau, M. (1984). *The practice of everyday life*. Berkeley: University of California Press.

Duchêne, A., & Heller, M. (Eds.) (2007). *Discourses of endangerment*. London: Continuum.

Edelman, M. J. (1985). *The symbolic uses of politics*. Urbana: University of Illinois Press.

Erickson, F. (1987). Transformation and school success. *Anthropology and Education Quarterly* 18(4), 335–356.

Evans, B. A., & Hornberger, N. (2005). No child left behind: Repealing and unpeeling federal language education policy in the United States. *Language Policy* 4(1), 87–106.

Flores, N., & García, O. (2013). Linguistic third spaces in education. In D. Little, C. Leung, & P. Van Avermaet (Eds.), *Managing diversity in education* (pp. 243–256). Bristol, UK: Multilingual Matters.

Freeman-Moir, J., & Scott, A. (2003). *Yesterday's dreams*. Christchurch, NZ: Canterbury University Press.

Freire, P. (1970). *Pedagogy of the oppressed*. New York: Continuum.

García, O. (2013). From diglossia to transglossia: Bilingual and multilingual classrooms in the 21st century. In C. Abello-Contesse, P. M. Chandler, M. D. López-Jiménez, & R. Chacón-Beltrán (Eds.), *Bilingual and multilingual education in the 21st century: Building on experience* (pp. 155–175). Clevedon, UK: Multilingual Matters.

García, O., & Leiva, C. (2014). Theorizing and enacting translanguaging for social justice. In A. Blackledge & A. Creese (Eds.), *Heteroglossia as practice and pedagogy* (pp. 199–216). Dordrecht: Springer.

García, O., & Li Wei. (2014). *Translanguaging*. Basingstoke, UK: Palgrave Macmillan.

Gibson, M. A. (1987). The school performance of immigrant minorities. *Anthropology and Education Quarterly* 18(4), 262–275.

Godley, A., Sweetland, J., Wheeler, R., Mincinni, A., & Carpenter, B. (2006). Preparing teachers for dialectally diverse classrooms. *Educational Researcher* 35(8), 30–37.

Grainger, K., & Jones, P. (2013). The "language deficit" argument and beyond. *Language and Education* 27(2), 95–98.

Gutiérrez, K. D., Baquedano-López, P., & Tejada, C. (1999). Rethinking diversity. *Mind, Culture and Activity*, 6(4), 286–303.

Hall, S. (1992). New ethnicities. In A. Rattansi & J. Donald (Eds.), *"Race," Culture and Difference* (pp. 252–260). London: Sage.

Hammersley, M. (1992). *What's wrong with ethnography?* London: Routledge.

Harris, R. (1998). *Introduction to integrational linguistics*. Oxford: Pergamon.

Harris, R., Leung, C., & Rampton, B. (2001). Globalization, diaspora and language education in England. *Working Papers in Urban Language and Literacies* 17.

Heller, M. (1995). Language choice, social institutions and symbolic domination. *Language in Society* 24(3), 373–405.

Hélot, C. (2010). Tu sais bien parler maitresse! Negotiating languages other than French in the primary classroom in France. In K. Menken & O. García (Eds.), *Negotiating language policies in schools* (pp. 52–71). London: Routledge.

Hill, M. L. (2009). *Beats, rhymes and classroom life*. New York: Teachers College Press.

Holmes, S. (2014). Monsters, myths and multilingual creativity. *Working Papers in Urban Language and Literacies* 161.

Hornberger, N. (2004). The continua of biliteracy and the bilingual educator. *Bilingual Education and Bilingualism* 7(2–3), 155–171.

Jaspers, J. (2005). Linguistic sabotage in a context of monolingualism and standardization. *Language and Communication* 25(3), 279–297.

Jaspers, J. (2011). Talking like a "zero-lingual": Ambiguous linguistic caricatures at an urban secondary school. *Journal of Pragmatics* 43(5), 1264–1278.

Jaspers, J. (2015). Modelling linguistic diversity at school. *Language Policy* 14(2), 109–129.

Jaspers, J. (2016). (Dis)fluency. *Annual Review of Anthropology* 45(1), 47–62.

Johnson, D. C., & Freeman, R. (2010). Appropriating language policy on the local level. In K. Menken & O. García (Eds.), *Negotiating language policies in schools* (pp. 13–31). London: Routledge.

Karrebæk, M. (2013). "Don't talk like that to her!" Linguistic minority children's socialization into an ideology of monolingualism. *Journal of Sociolinguistics* 17(3), 355–375.

Labov, W. (1972). *Language in the inner city.* Philadelphia: University of Pennsylvania Press.

Lefstein, A. (2013). The regulation of teaching as symbolic politics. *Discourse. Studies in the Cultural Politics of Education* 34(5), 643–659.

Liddicoat, A. (2013). *Language-in-education policies.* Bristol, UK: Multilingual Matters.

Liddicoat, A., Heugh, K., Curnow, T., & Scarino, A. (2014). Educational responses to multilingualism. *International Journal of Multilingualism* 11(3), 269–272.

Macaro, E. (2006). Strategies for language learning and for language use. *The Modern Language Journal* 90(3), 320–337.

Marsh, J. (2011). *Class dismissed.* New York: Monthly Review Press.

Martín Rojo, L. (2010). *Constructing inequality in multilingual classrooms.* Berlin; New York: Mouton de Gruyter.

Martínez, R. A., Hikida, M., & Durán, L. (2015). Unpacking ideologies of linguistic purism: How dual language teachers make sense of everyday translanguaging. *International Multilingual Research Journal* 9, 26–42.

May, S. (2011). *Language and minority rights.* London: Routledge.

McCarty, T. L. (Ed.) (2011). *Ethnography and language policy.* London: Routledge.

Menken, K., & García, O. (Eds.) (2010) *Negotiating language policies in schools.* London: Routledge.

Moore, R. (2007). *Sociology of knowledge and education.* London: Continuum.

Ogbu, J. (1978). *Minority education and caste.* New York: Academic Press.

Pachler, N., Makoe, P., Burns, M., & Blommaert, J. (2008). The things (we think) we (ought to) do. *Teaching and Teacher Education* 24, 437–450.

Paris, D., & Alim, H. S. (2014). What are we seeking to sustain through culturally sustaining pedagogy? *Harvard Educational Review* 84(1), 85–100.

Pease-Alvarez, L., & Thompson, A. (2014). Teachers working together to resist and remake educational policy in contexts of standardization. *Language Policy* 13, 165–181.

Pennycook, A. (2007). *Global Englishes and transcultural flows.* London: Routledge.

Pérez-Milans, M. (2011). Being a Chinese newcomer in Madrid compulsory education. *Journal of Pragmatics* 43, 1005–1022.

Pérez-Milans, M. (2013). *Urban schools and English language education in late modern China.* London: Routledge.

Piller, I., & Cho, J. (2013). Neoliberalism as language policy. *Language in Society* 42(1), 23–44.

Ramaut, G., Bultinck, K., Van Avermaet, P., Slembrouck, S., Van Gorp, K., & Verhelst, M. (2013) *Evaluatieonderzoek van het project "Thuistaal in onderwijs" (2009–2012): Eindrapport* [Research Project evaluating the "Home Language in Education" project (2009–2012): Final Report]. Ghent; Leuven: Ghent University; KU Leuven.

Rampton, B. (2006). *Language in late modernity.* Cambridge: Cambridge University Press.

Reay, D. (2010). Sociology, social class and education. In M. W. Apple, S. J. Ball, & L. A. Gandin (Eds.), *The Routledge international handbook of the sociology of education* (pp. 396–404). London: Routledge.

Rosenthal, R., & Jacobson, L. (1968). *Pygmalion in the classroom.* New York: Holt, Rinehart & Winston.

Shohamy, E. (2006) *Language policy.* London: Routledge.

Silverstein, M. (2003). *Talking politics.* Chicago: Prickly Paradigm Press.

Smet, P. (2011). *Samen taalgrenzen verleggen* [Moving linguistic frontiers together]. Brussels: Flemish Ministry of Education.

Talmy, S. (2009). Forever FOB? In A. Reyes & A. Lo (Eds.), *Beyond Yellow English* (pp. 347–365). Oxford: Oxford University Press.

Thomas, W. P., & Collier, V. P. (2000). Accelerated schooling for all students. In S. Shaw (Ed.), *Intercultural education in European classrooms* (pp. 15–35). Stoke on Trent: Trentham Books.

Tollefson, J. (Ed.). (2002). *Language policies in education: Critical issues.* New York: Routledge.

Vandenbroucke, F. (2007). *De lat hoog voor talen in iedere school* [The bar high for languages in each school]. Brussels: Flemish Ministry of Education.

Varenne, H., & McDermott, R. (1999). *Successful failure.* Boulder, CO: Westview Press.

Willis, P. (1977). *Learning to labour.* Farnborough: Saxon House.

Wineburg, S. (1987). The self-fulfillment of the self-fulfilling prophecy. *Educational Researcher* 16(9), 28–37.

PART IV

SUMMARY AND FUTURE DIRECTIONS

CHAPTER 35

....

LANGUAGE POLICY AND PLANNING

DIRECTIONS FOR FUTURE RESEARCH

....

MIGUEL PÉREZ-MILANS AND JAMES W. TOLLEFSON

THIS *Handbook* has explored the links between language policy and planning (LPP) and the socioeconomic, institutional, and discursive processes of change taking place under the conditions of late modernity. A key organizational principle of the *Handbook* has been the tensions between these processes of change and the still-powerful ideological framework of modern nationalism—with its related discourses and policies about language, culture, and identity.

We set out not to produce a retrospective survey of LPP, but rather to explore in detail the important processes of change currently taking place in LPP and the social sciences more broadly (see Chapter 1 by Tollefson & Pérez-Milans). These processes include the following: the growing importance of non-state actors within political and administrative systems that continue to sustain a central role for nation-states; economic neoliberalization, which extends the logic of the market to all spheres of social life, including language, education, and the family, affecting individuals, in Martín Rojo's words, "even at their most personal levels of existence" (Chapter 27 of this volume); the accompanying forms of resignification of language and communication that reconfigure the role of language in social life, with subsequent impact on the unequal access that different socioeconomic groups have to institutional spaces and symbolic/material resources; new patterns of intensified transnational migration and their shaping of long-standing discourses about language, security, speakers, communities, and language learning; and new media technologies, along with the unpredictable relationships of power that they sometimes introduce in policymaking.

The consequences for LPP of such profound social, economic, and political transformations must be a central focus for LPP research in the years ahead. Although the chapters in this *Handbook* reveal the diverging circumstances for LPP under different configurations of global and local forces, they also point to several recurring key issues that we believe will be important in the future of LPP research.

ISSUES FOR LANGUAGE POLICY AND PLANNING RESEARCH

These recurrent issues are concerned with both ontological and epistemological dimensions in LPP research. They can be grouped into seven major strands: (1) the continued importance of critical approaches; (2) the paradox of agency; (3) the need for ethnographic approaches to move from recognition of their value to further engagement with epistemological awareness; (4) the challenge of creating new links between LPP and alternative philosophical traditions, beyond European political theory; (5) the increasing role of media in LPP; (6) the need for expanding collaborations and revisiting long-standing assumptions about community-based research, language rights, and activism; and (7) the imperative of addressing ethical issues in contemporary LPP research through researchers' reflexivity. In the following, we address each of these issues.

The Continuing Importance of Critical Approaches

Once considered to be marginal to LPP scholarship, critical approaches have become central to some of the most productive research, as evident in many of the chapters in this *Handbook*. Since the 1990s, the range of critical approaches has broadened from the early focus on historical-structural analysis and language rights to approaches that shed light on everyday interactions in varying local contexts that are linked with national and global policies and discourses (see, in this volume, Kamusella, Chapter 8, and Chen, Chapter 10). During this time, critical approaches have evolved considerably. For example, the analysis of governmentality, which has been productive in critical scholarship since the first decade of the 2000s, has shifted decisively from discourse analysis (e.g., Pennycook, 2002) to ethnography, particularly with recent calls for closer attention to new forms of political economy related to late capitalism (see Codó, Chapter 23; Pujolar, Chapter 24; Relaño-Pastor, Chapter 25; Del Percio, Chapter 26; and Martín Rojo, Chapter 27). Contemporary research on the processes of securitization, insecuritization, and desecuritization (see Chapter 31 by Charalambous, Charalambous, Khan, & Rampton) has also evolved, drawing from ethnography and practice theory in order to bring context and ideology into the conceptualization of security for a better grasp of the ways in which security and language policy are likely to be related in the period ahead.

Although the value of its evolving tradition in LPP seems clear, critical research continues to be misinterpreted. Among the most persistent of these misinterpretations is that it offers a "conspiracy theory" of LPP (e.g., Kamwangamalu, 2013, p. 548; Spolsky, 2004, p. 78). This dismissive term misleadingly suggests that critical scholars explain LPP with reference to "semi-secret" policies (Kamwangamalu, 2013, p. 548) developed by behind-the-scenes LPP agents who seek to disguise their efforts so that the negative effects of policies they support cannot be linked to them. On the contrary, critical approaches investigate the (usually) open pursuit of policy goals that are in line with the responsibilities, roles, and authorities of powerful institutions, groups, and individuals who dominate policymaking processes. In fact, some misunderstood critical work (e.g., on the role of British state educational authorities [Pennycook, 1998] and the British Council [Phillipson, 1992]) reveals English-promotion efforts over many decades that were almost entirely open to public view, and not at all conspiratorial or secretive in any meaningful sense.

Apart from such misunderstandings, critical approaches are widely recognized as offering useful analyses of some of the most important processes in LPP today: neoliberalism (including the neoliberalization of education), English under globalization, language commodification, the role of multinational corporations, linguistic governmentality, and class and inequality. Several chapters in this volume (by Ricento, Chapter 11; Tollefson & Tsui, Chapter 13; Frost & McNamara, Chapter 14; Codó, Chapter 23; Pujolar, Chapter, 24; Relaño-Pastor, Chapter 25; Del Percio, Chapter 26; and Martín Rojo, Chapter 27) demonstrate how critical approaches can productively engage with such processes. These chapters also challenge our understanding of the ways in which critical research shapes the meaning of LPP. As LPP becomes a window for exploring how old forms of socioeconomic inequality get (re) produced and legitimated under changing institutional and cultural conditions, the field is positioned as a discursive domain. That is to say, the prevalent ideas about what counts (and what does not) as LPP, at a given time, cannot be detached from the processes of inequality that LPP scholarship investigates (see Chapter 2 by Heller).

Nevertheless, the many achievements of critical research do not prevent critical approaches from needing to continue to evolve. As Jaspers points out in Chapter 34, too often critical scholars' attention to social (in)equality is reduced to an educational issue, which thereby ignores economic class or other factors that may severely constrain the ability of educational institutions and individuals working in them to confront the deep roots of inequality. In this regard, Block's call in Chapter 28 for critical scholars to develop a more explicitly theorized notion of class may permit more productive engagement with these broader forces that extend far beyond the institutions of education.

The Paradox of Agency

As David Cassels Johnson notes in Chapter 3, beginning in the late 1990s, historical-structural approaches were criticized for specific limitations that tended to make them overly deterministic, thereby underestimating the role of human agency, particularly of teachers, and for not fully describing language-planning processes in which local actors may exert significant influence over policy and practice. Following this critique, an increasing focus on situated practices has opened a wider window into the full complexity of language policymaking. Indeed, much of the most productive recent work in LPP has involved shedding light on new examples of tensions and contradictions arising from the localized production, circulation, and appropriation of language policies across different institutional and geographical contexts. This greater interest in situated practice has also revealed how the institutional and social are (re)produced, enacted, and made sense of in the discourses of everyday life, thereby expanding the critical lens beyond the historical and structural approaches of the 1990s (see, e.g., Jaworski, Chapter 33).

Yet this epistemological shift in LPP is not free from dilemmas concerned with a recurring question in the social sciences: How do we conceptualize the relationship between the theorization of agency and the one who acts (i.e., the self)? In contrast to cognitive-based developments that shaped European and North American concepts of the self in the social sciences from the nineteenth century to the mid-twentieth,[1] alternative approaches began in the late twentieth century to emphasize the self as a function of social and political context. But these approaches have often given different prominence to agency or structure in the explanation of how the self and the social world interact, depending on whether they align more closely with research philosophies stemming from objectivism, in which attention to societal structures predominates over analysis of social actors' actions (e.g., scientific realism), or subjectivism, which prioritizes agency (e.g., social constructionism). Marxist approaches, for example, have leaned more toward structural forces and determinism, while postmodernism has drawn more heavily from constructionism.

These two broad trends in research philosophies have been influential in LPP, where the foregrounding of social actors' practices and forms of making sense coexists with approaches that give greater attention to historical and structural forces. We do not argue that this paradox must be resolved, though we believe there are existing developments in the social sciences that address this paradox and deserve further attention in LPP research. One such development is contemporary social theory, which, for some decades now, has made serious theoretical efforts to account for the intersections of agency and structure, thus counterbalancing the long-standing polarization of agency/structure that often appears in LPP studies in the form of the *micro/macro* dichotomy, still widely in use in the field (see explicit discussions of this issue in Johnson, Chapter 3; Martin-Jones & da Costa Cabral, Chapter 4; and Pérez-Milans, Chapter 6). Alternative sociological theories are available to LPP scholars, among which the two most influential are structuration (Giddens, 1982) and critical realism (Archer, 1998; Bhaskar, 1989; Elder-Vass, 2015; Hartwig, 2007); whereas the former argues for the mutually constitutive nature of human agency and structural properties of social systems, the latter maintains that they should be analyzed separately, because structure precedes agency in social structure reproduction and therefore in analytical importance.

Although more work needs to be done in the epistemological formalization of critical realism in the language/discourse disciplines, the underpinnings of structuration theory have explicitly permeated contemporary developments in areas such as micro-sociology (Cicourel, 1978, 1980, 1992, 1996; Goffman, 1971, 1974, 1981), sociolinguistics (Blommaert, 2010; Heller, 2002; Martín Rojo, 2010; Rampton, 2006), and linguistic anthropology (Agha, 2007; Silverstein, 2005). Such work has provided relevant analytical perspectives with which to capture the ways in which historical products of institutions and socioeconomic structures, such as moral orders and conventional models/systems of social relations, get produced, recontextualized, entextualized, legitimated, and shaped within daily intersubjective discursive practices ordered across space and time (see, for instance, the analyses offered in Pérez-Milans, Chapter 6; Unamuno & Bonnin, Chapter 19; Relaño-Pastor, Chapter 25; Del Percio, Chapter 26; and Jaworski, Chapter 33). Increased effort to incorporate such work in LPP promises important benefits for theoretically informed agency/structure analysis.

Despite important work revealing the problematic consequences of the agency-structure distinction, the tension between different approaches to agency in LPP is not likely to disappear any time soon. The challenge for future research is therefore to sort through and make explicit the underlying ontological, epistemological, and personal/social underpinnings for researchers' claims. This effort may involve engagement with approaches that no longer privilege discourse in the study of social change, but instead focus more explicitly on the material realities of people understood not merely as disembodied life forms embedded in discursive systems, but rather as concrete human beings with substantial and inescapable material needs (cf. critical realism).[2] We look forward to future research that grapples with these important issues.

Ethnographic Research: From Recognition to Further Epistemological Awareness

With the 1990s and beginning of the twenty-first century as the key turning points, ethnography has gained momentum relatively late in LPP research, particularly if compared to the social sciences more widely, in which the ethnographic turn was initiated in the 1960s. Yet, there is a well-established consensus today in our field on the contributions of ethnographic approaches to understanding the ways in which policies are interpreted and appropriated by social actors, and the consequences of these local processes for participants and institutions involved (see overviews in Johnson, Chapter 3; and Martin-Jones & da Costa Cabral, Chapter 4). The value of ethnographic approaches is well attested in this *Handbook* through numerous chapters that report ethnographically on case studies in different contexts, including online (e.g., Lenihan, Chapter 32) and offline environments (e.g., Wodak & Savski, Chapter 5; Unamuno & Bonnin, Chapter 19; Relaño-Pastor, Chapter 25; and Del Percio, Chapter 26) or a combination of both (e.g., Pérez-Milans, Chapter 6). There are also calls for integrating ethnographic orientations into the study of relatively new LPP areas such as that of linguistic landscapes (see Hult, Chapter 17). Together, these contributions remind us that there is no such a thing as one way of doing ethnography of LPP. Instead, different ethnographic traditions, each with its own disciplinary roots, coexist in language policy research.

While all of the ethnographic chapters in this volume look at the discursive organization of institutions with the main goal of describing the links between local practices, institutional orders, and wider socioeconomic processes of change, they draw from different bodies of literature, depending on whether they stress critical discourse studies (Wodak & Savski, Chapter 5), ethnography of communication (Johnson, Chapter 3), linguistic anthropology of language ideologies (Martin-Jones & da Costa Cabral, Chapter 4), linguistic anthropology/sociolinguistics of the indexicality of language (Pérez-Milans, Chapter 6), ethnographic sociolinguistics (Unamuno & Bonnin, Chapter 19) or institutional ethnography (Del Percio, Chapter 26). In some cases, the boundaries between these approaches are fuzzy, though overall they reveal slightly different analytical sensitivities with regard to the analysis of the interrelation of texts, contexts, and meanings (see Pérez-Milans, Chapter 6, for a discussion of this issue).

The implications of acknowledging this apparently minor variation are vast, in our view, since such different sensitivities reveal an aspect of ethnographic research sometimes ignored in the social sciences: that ethnographic research is not just a methodological tool, but rather an epistemological framework (Mason, 2002); that is to say, ethnographic research entails more complexity than just adding interviews or observations to a given research design. Instead, doing ethnography of LPP involves asking particular types of questions that are tied to specific assumptions about what counts as relevant knowledge and, accordingly, about what are the most appropriate ways of collecting and analyzing data (even if interview-based, as pointed out by Pérez-Milans in Chapter 6), and these in turn have ramifications for different subdisciplines and areas of inquiry in language and communication studies. Accordingly, we believe that LPP would benefit from more epistemologically informed discussions of ethnographic alternatives. This would help the field move beyond recognition of the ethnographic lens as appropriate, toward a more detailed exploration of existing ethnographic traditions and their corresponding intellectual foundations. These discussions would allow room for more explicit acknowledgment of the different analytical sensitivities that such traditions bring with them, which in turn may create better conditions for a fruitful dialogue among ethnographically oriented approaches in LPP research.

Creating New Links between Language Policy and Planning and Alternative Philosophical Traditions

Several chapters in this *Handbook* (Peled, Chapter 7; Kamusella, Chapter 8; Ives, Chapter 9; and Ricento, Chapter 11) argue that LPP scholarship should work to develop more nuanced understandings of the important philosophical traditions that underlie theorizing in the social sciences, and specifically to systematically explore the links between LPP and political theory. In particular, they make the case for explicit attention to the value of European political philosophy for critically examining fundamental concepts such as *language, speaker, nation*, and *community*. We concur with these calls for greater connections between LPP and political theory and for continuing analysis of the philosophical foundations of nationalism. Yet it is also important to acknowledge that the chapters in this volume reveal a major limitation in LPP: the almost exclusive attention to European philosophical traditions.

This limitation is particularly problematic when LPP scholarship examines contexts outside Europe. In mainland China, Southeast Asia, or Japan, for example, Herderian (or other European) concepts of *language, nation*, and *state* may be less useful than Confucian or Daoist understandings of these concepts. Ives points out in Chapter 9, for example, that Mozi, the fifth-century B.C.E. pre-Confucian Chinese philosopher, offered a theory of language in which the emperor played a central role in planning for language unification (Pocock, 1973, p. 42); in many forms, the issue of language planning was addressed repeatedly during the subsequent history of Confucian philosophy (see Hall & Ames, 1998). A second area in which the Confucian tradition may be relevant to critical review of LPP is language rights. As many analyses explain (e.g., Laitin & Reich, 2003), the European language rights discourse rests on a liberal democratic notion of autonomous individuality and prioritizes a universal set of individual political freedoms and privileges over communal and environmental responsibilities. In response, the 1993 ASEAN Bangkok Declaration adopted a discourse that prioritized economic and cultural rights and rejected human rights universalism (see de Bary, 1998). This alternative conception of rights, however, must be understood in conjunction with its declared philosophical tradition, as well as with the political economies that underpin it (see Pérez-Milans, 2013, for a critique of the re-contextualization of Asian alternatives in the official discourse of "socialism with Chinese characteristics").[3] In order for LPP to more fully explore its links with political philosophy, such a tradition deserves attention. Other contexts, such as India and Malaysia, offer equally relevant platforms for the exploration of links between LPP and political theory.

A closely related issue is that LPP scholars are emerging in greater numbers from educational systems outside Europe, North America, Australia, and New Zealand. For this reason, too, it is important for the field of LPP to examine through a broader lens the ontological and epistemological traditions that underlie LPP research, and to work toward systematically incorporating alternative traditions such as Confucianism or Daoism into LPP theory. A project to widen the lens of LPP may benefit from creating new links between, for example, LPP, national studies in China, and Sinology. Such an explicit effort to move scholarship from China and elsewhere in East, South, and Southeast Asia toward the center of LPP research may also have the advantage of helping to moderate the privileged position currently held by European and North American scholars.

The Role of Media in Language Policy and Planning

As Chapter 15 by Gao and Shao points out, although there is a vast scholarly literature in media studies focused on framing and media effects, very little research in LPP has examined the impact of mass media on language policymaking. How do mass media shape the policies that are adopted in different social and political contexts? How may mass media be a policy actor in policymaking processes? Such questions focus attention on language policy debates as a form of political communication (Chilton, 2004) in which multiple state and non-state actors articulate their competing social visions, comprising discursive representations of languages, speakers, competing actors in policymaking, and specific language policy alternatives (e.g., see the analysis of the role of Man Wui Ho in Chen's Chapter 10, about Hong Kong). These competing representations are usually grounded in social, economic, and political antagonisms, articulated by the state and by political actors aligned with the state, and by actors who resist or subvert dominant state discourses and the policies they promote. As Gao and Shao reveal in Chapter 15, mass media in some contexts may play a decisive role in articulating these competing representations and the language policies associated with them, and in determining which policies are legitimized in public debates.

One focus of LPP research on mass media, therefore, should be the political and discursive processes by which diverse actors may establish a "plurality of struggles" (Laclau, 2005) in which their separate efforts combine into broader language movements. In the United States, for example, middle-class English speakers who support bilingualism for ideological reasons and dual-language immersion for instrumental reasons have joined forces with poor and working-class Latinos who support Spanish-language maintenance, language rights, and bilingual education. Under what conditions do groups with such divergent social networks, economic statuses, and language repertoires form alliances to support specific language policies? Answering this question is central to understanding how particular policy alternatives are legitimized and adopted.

In addition, Silberstein argues in Chapter 16 that mass media often constrain the voices that may be heard in policy debates, legitimizing some actors and delegitimizing others. How are some groups blocked from effective participation in policymaking? This question, which requires applications of discourse analysis to the mass media context, raises fundamental issues about policy actors' access to policymaking processes and to the networks of power that determine policy alternatives.

Whereas social media raise similar questions about the role of media in policymaking, Lenihan demonstrates in Chapter 32 that access to social media differs from access to mass media. With opportunities for direct participation as media producers, individuals and groups on social media potentially have direct access to participation in policymaking that may not be available in the mass media context. Individuals on social media can serve as policy practitioners and as policy analysts, in some cases replacing official actors, as Lenihan shows in the case of Irish translation. In the still emerging research area of social media, LPP scholarship can focus attention on social media as a form of language policymaking with new affordances for policy actors.

Community-Based Research, Language Rights, and Activism: Expanding Collaborations, Revisiting Assumptions

Since its origins, LPP has always been closely connected with the struggles, concerns, and dilemmas faced by various types of communities, ranging from families (see Curdt-Christiansen, Chapter 21) to indigenous groups and linguistic minorities (May, Chapter 12; McCarty, Chapter 18; Unamuno & Bonnin, Chapter 19; and Watson-Gegeo, Gegeo, & Fitoʻo, Chapter 20), to Deaf communities (Quadros, Chapter 22). These chapters reveal the links between policies promoting language maintenance and revitalization, on the one hand, and democratic forms of political participation and decision making, on the other.

McCarty, for example, in Chapter 18, not only analyzes the forces contributing to language endangerment and the opportunities for language maintenance; in addition, she advocates forms of sociolinguistic and sociopolitical change that are necessary to sustain endangered languages. Her decades of commitment to language maintenance efforts among speakers of Navajo, as well as her work to extend what she has learned to other communities, exemplifies a complex mix of analysis and action, of research and activism, and of professional and personal commitments. Similarly, Watson-Gegeo, Gegeo, and Fito'o (Chapter 20) articulate their commitment to critical community language policy and planning in education in Malaita, Solomon Islands. Their decades of research in their home community (Gegeo and Fito'o are from Malaita) involve not only scholarly analysis of language in education, but also direct action within community organizations to develop alternatives to the failed state educational system.

Though research and activist agendas may not always overlap, we believe it is necessary that LPP researchers continue to foster collaborations with those who engage in political work to challenge dominant language ideologies that reinforce entrenched systems of linguistic inequality. Indeed, we agree with Piller (2016) when she reminds us that bringing social justice into our research agendas requires understanding linguistic disadvantage as a form of structural disadvantage.

But bringing a social justice focus is not free from dilemmas and contradictions. First, academic research is not always perceived by activists as the most suitable platform for addressing social inequality, particularly in the context of contemporary academic institutions, which increasingly play a role in the unequal distribution of wealth by adopting corporate forms of organization that primarily serve the interests of privileged groups (see, for instance, Holborow, 2015). Nevertheless, in our view, there is still room for action, and these very institutions that LPP scholars work for are also made publicly accountable based on their ability to reach out to non-academic stakeholders and other community organizations that tackle peoples' pressing life struggles. Second, pursuing a social justice agenda in LPP research is fraught with ontological and epistemological tensions, forcing LPP scholars to continuously revisit our own assumptions so that we do not end up reinforcing the entrenched systems of linguistic inequality that we are trying to confront.

With this self-revisiting spirit in mind, and in line with Li Wei's Chapter 29, we believe LPP researchers interested in community-based work should critically reconsider long-standing conceptions of *language*, *dialect*, and *identity* that may fail to capture the complicated linguistic ecology and patterns of mobility of multilingual groups. In fact, LPP scholarship will be well served by this process of continually revisiting important concepts in light of ongoing collaborations with community activists. This effort equally applies to language revitalization actions, which, in their attempt to empower linguistic minorities, have long privileged so-called native speakers, as argued by O'Rourke, Soler, and Darquennes in Chapter 30 when they encourage LPP researchers to foreground the lived experiences and challenges that individuals face as they become (and are recognized as) speakers of another language.

Reconsideration of conceptions of language, dialect, and identity also demands careful engagement with notions of language rights that are linked with ideas of European nationalism and that may not be relevant to actual language use in many multilingual communities. Thus, while acknowledging Stephen May's argument in Chapter 12 that policies promoting language rights offer potential for social and political stability and the protection of certain linguistic minorities, we also note Freeland's (2013) important finding that groups supporting language rights may fundamentally disagree about what that means. Accordingly, Freeland calls for LPP to deconstruct and reinvent the language rights discourse "in light of the local language ideologies of the target groups whose rights are to be vouchsafed" (p. 109).

Ethical Issues and Researchers' Reflexivity

Combining research and activism raises important ethical issues that are increasingly foregrounded in LPP scholarship. In their introductory textbook on research methods in LPP, Hult and Johnson (2015) encourage LPP researchers' "public engagement" (p. 233) by acknowledging their potential contribution to schools and communities, to public policy debates (including various forms of media involvement and public appearances), and to interactions with politicians and policymakers. Such engagement has a long history in LPP, perhaps most notably in Joshua Fishman's decades-long commitment to language policies supporting language maintenance and multilingualism. Despite the esteem with which Fishman's public commitments have been viewed by LPP practitioners and researchers, however, engaged scholars are sometimes criticized for their failure to maintain objectivity in their research; such criticisms emerge from the positivist tradition in the social sciences, which assumes that objective data and analysis must be the focus of research, and that researchers should remain disinterested and neutral about issues of power, inequality, and social justice (see Miller et al., 2012, for a discussion of relevant issues). In addition, qualitative research, which raises important issues about scholars' positionality (Lin, 2015), increasingly entails notions of reflexivity that must be incorporated into the research process.

A consideration of the researcher's positionality requires what Peled in Chapter 7 calls "ethical reflection" through systematic forms of moral reasoning about the researcher's role. This attention to ethical issues extends beyond a concern for analyzing power relations and structural systems; instead, its aim, according to Peled, is to "identify the moral wrongs that [systems] may exhibit, and develop alternative structures that are capable of righting them." Such ethical judgments require consideration of a full range of epistemological issues, such as how knowledge is represented in research, whose knowledge counts as relevant to research, and the ways that participants are involved in designing research questions and gathering and reporting data. Thus standards for LPP scholarship increasingly require consideration of how the researcher's subjectivity, including ideologies, experiences, and values, can shape the research process. In addition, researchers are expected to reflect carefully on how communities' voices can be integrated into research: what research may be important to them, how it should be conducted and reported, and what benefits may accrue to the community (see Canagarajah & Stanley, 2015).

Commitments by researchers to community needs have led some LPP scholars to reconceptualize the research process as collaborative and transformative social practice, involving deep engagement with communities and requiring of researchers a continuing personal and epistemological reflexivity (see Langemeyer & Schmachtel-Maxfield, 2013). Scholarship thus driven by the effort to find alternatives to all forms of structural inequality places the ethical concern for social justice and the researcher's reflexivity at the center of the research agenda. Doing so ultimately may require that researchers take on new roles as apprentices to community mentors in experiences that matter to the community (Bishop, 2005). Accordingly, the process of ethical reflection may demand profound changes in researchers' identities. Expressing the close connection between the processes of social change and personal transformation, Man-Chiu Amai Lin wrote after more than two years of activist research on a community-driven language revitalization initiative in a Truku village in eastern Taiwan: "The project can effect change only to the extent that I have been changed" (Lin & Yudaw, 2016, p. 761).

We began this *Handbook* by acknowledging that particular forms of LPP emerged from the historic juncture at the middle of the twentieth century—the end of the colonial period—characterized by what were considered at the time to be the emerging "language problems" of new developing nations, requiring national language policies for the specific stated goals of modernization, development, and political and sociocultural integration. Now, in the second decade of the twenty-first century, the world is at another historic juncture, characterized by globalization, the apparent triumph of neoliberalism, the rise of neo-fascist social movements and political parties, and a depth of economic inequality not seen since the 1920s. LPP must respond to this crisis—which is a crisis of both capitalism and democracy[4]— with new research directions, the forms of which are still emerging. We have tried in this volume to articulate the outlines of some of these new directions.

ACKNOWLEDGMENT

We are grateful to John O'Regan for reading an earlier draft of this chapter.

NOTES

1. Two cognitive approaches were particularly influential in this understanding of the self. One, traceable in the European philosophical tradition to Thomas Hobbes, may be termed the *materialist* discourse, evident in neurophysiology, sociobiology, and Freudian and behaviorist psychology, and exemplified in language studies by the work of B. F. Skinner as well as in recent advances in neurobiology. The second is the *mentalist or formalist* discourse, evident in Platonic idealism, Cartesian philosophy, and phenomenology, and exemplified in language studies by Chomsky's theory of mind.

2. One criticism of discursive approaches in the social sciences and humanities is their tendency to understate the importance of individuals' material reality. For example, the concern that the concrete life problems of real people may be ignored in speculative discussions in philosophy is succinctly captured by Hall and Ames (1998) as follows: "It is one thing ... to realize in some abstract and speculative manner a vision of the harmony of . . . value and ... self-expression ... and quite another thing to come to grips with the concreteness of temporal experience. At the level of lived experience there seems to be no way of overcoming the concrete conflicts between the knowledge-bearing institutions, the propertied interests, and those technological activities that order the instrumentalities of society" (p. 13).

3. The European model of human rights tends to be state-centered and founded on the tradition of natural law and essentialist concepts of individual agency. In contrast, the Confucian critique of universal human rights involves not only a greater emphasis on communal responsibility, social harmony, and economic/cultural rights over individual political rights; it also entails a different foundational moral philosophy, grounded not on transcendent concepts of the rationalism of autonomous individuals, but rather on a presumption of social identity in which the individual cannot be separated from the social, cultural, and historical context. Henry Rosemont Jr. (1988) captures the Confucian critique of rational individualism as follows: "Contemporary [European] moral philosophy, the Confucian texts suggest, is no longer grounded in the real hopes, fears, joys, sorrows, ideas and attitudes of flesh and blood human beings. Since the time of Descartes, Western philosophy—not alone moral philosophy—has increasingly abstracted a purely cognizing activity away from persons and determined that this use of logical reasoning in a disembodied 'mind' is the choosing, autonomous essence of individuals, which is philosophically more foundational than are actual persons; the latter being only contingently who they are, and therefore of no great philosophical significance" (p. 175). An analysis of language rights controversies, particularly those involving China, Japan, and Taiwan, requires attention to such underlying issues.

4. Richard Posner, a conservative economist and a judge in the US 7th Circuit Court of Appeals, terms the current period a crisis of "capitalist democracy" (2010), whereas Wolfgang Streek, in the *New Left Review*, refers to the crisis of "democratic capitalism" (2011). The difference in terminology may reflect their differing underlying social theories, particularly the relative importance of structural economic factors.

REFERENCES

Agha, A. (2007). *Language and social relations*. Cambridge: Cambridge University Press.

Archer, M. S. (1998). Realism in the social sciences. In M. Archer et al. (Eds.), *Critical realism: Essential readings* (pp. 189–205). London: Routledge.

Bhaskar, R. (1989). *Scientific realism and human emancipation*. London: Verso.

Bishop, R. (2005). Freeing ourselves from neocolonial domination in research: A Kaupapa Māori approach to creating knowledge. In N. K. Denzin & Y. S. Lincoln (Eds.), *The Sage handbook of qualitative research* (3rd edition; pp. 109–138). Thousand Oaks, CA: Sage.

Blommaert, J. (2010). *The sociolinguistics of globalization*. Cambridge: Cambridge University Press.

Canagarajah, S., & Stanley, P. (2015). Ethical considerations in language policy research. In F. M. Hult & D. C. Johnson (Eds.), *Research methods in language policy and planning: A practical guide* (pp. 33–44). Malden, MA: Wiley Blackwell.

Chilton, P. (2004). *Analysing political discourse: Theory and practice*. London: Routledge.

Cicourel, A. (1978). Language and society: Cultural, cognitive and linguistic aspects of language use. *Sozialwissenschaftliche Annalen* 2, 25–58.

Cicourel, A. (1980). Three models of discourse analysis: The role of social structure. *Discourse Processes* 33, 101–132.

Cicourel, A. (1992). The interpenetration of communicative contexts: Examples from medical encounters. In C. Goodwin and A. Duranti (Eds.), *Rethinking context: Language as an interactive phenomenon* (pp. 291–310). Cambridge: Cambridge University Press.

Cicourel, A. V. (1996). Ecological validity and white room effects: The interaction of cognitive and cultural models in the pragmatic analysis of elicited narrative from children. *Pragmatics and Cognition* 4(2), 221–264.

de Bary, W. T. (1998). *Asian values and human rights: A Confucian communitarian perspective*. Cambridge, MA: Harvard University Press.

Elder-Vass, D. (2015). Developing social theory using critical realism. *Journal of Critical Realism* 14(1), 80–92.

Freeland, J. (2013). Righting language wrongs in a plurilingual context: Language policy and practice in Nicaragua's Caribbean Coast region. In J. W. Tollefson (Ed.), *Language policies in education: Critical issues* (2nd edition; pp. 91–115). New York: Routledge.

Giddens, A. (1982). *The constitution of society*. Berkeley: University of California Press.

Goffman, E. (1971). *Relations in public: Micro studies of the public order*. New York: Basic Books.

Goffman, E. (1974). *Frame analysis: An essay in the organization of experience*. New York: Harper & Row.

Goffman, E. (1981). *Forms of talk*. Philadelphia: University of Pennsylvania Press.

Hall, D. L., & Ames, R. T. (1998). *Thinking from the Han: Self, truth, and transcendence in Chinese and Western culture*. Albany: State University of New York Press.

Hartwig, M. (2007). *Dictionary of critical realism*. New York; London: Routledge.

Heller, M. (2002). *Éléments d'une sociolinguistique critique*. Paris: Hatier.

Holborow, M. (2015). *Language and neoliberalism*. London: Routledge.

Hult, F. M., & Johnson, D. C. (Eds.). (2015). *Research methods in language policy and planning: A practical guide*. Malden, MA: Wiley Blackwell.

Kamwangamalu, N. M. (2013). English in language policies and ideologies in Africa: Challenges and prospects for vernacularization. In R. Bayley, R. Cameron, & C. Lucas (Eds.), *The Oxford handbook of sociolinguistics* (pp. 545–562). Oxford: Oxford University Press.

Laclau, E. (2005). *On populist reason*. London: Verso.

Laitin, D. D., & Reich, R. (2003). A liberal democratic approach to language justice. In W. Kymlicka & A. Patten (Eds.), *Language rights and political theory* (pp. 80–104). Oxford: Oxford University Press.

Langemeyer, I., & Schmachtel-Maxfield, S. (2013). Introduction to the special issue on transformative social practice and socio-critical knowledge. *Outlines: Critical Practice Studies* 14(2), 1–6.

Lin, A. M. Y. (2015). Researchers positionality. In F. M. Hult & D. C. Johnson (Eds.), *Research methods in language policy and planning: A practice guide* (pp. 21–32). Malden, MA: Wiley Blackwell.

Lin, M. C. A., & Yudaw, B. (2016). Practicing community-based Truku (indigenous) language policy: Reflection on dialogue and collaboration. *Asia Pacific Education Researcher* 25(5), 753–762.

Martín Rojo, L. (2010). *Constructing inequality in multilingual classrooms*. Berlin: Mouton.

Mason, J. (2002). *Qualitative researching*. London: Sage.

Miller, T., Birch, M., Mauthner, M., & Jessop, J. (2012). *Ethics in qualitative research*. London: Sage.

Pennycook, A. (1998). *English and the discourses of colonialism*. New York: Routledge.

Pennycook, A. (2002). Language policy and docile bodies: Hong Kong and governmentality. In J. W. Tollefson (Ed.), *Language policies in education: Critical issues* (1st edition; pp. 91–110). Mahwah, NJ: Lawrence Erlbaum.

Pérez-Milans, M. (2013). *Urban schools and English language education in late modern China: A critical sociolinguistic ethnography*. New York: Routledge.

Phillipson, R. (1992). *Linguistic imperialism*. Oxford: Oxford University Press.

Piller, I. (2016). *Linguistic diversity and social justice: An introduction to applied sociolinguistics*. Oxford: Oxford University Press.

Pocock, J. G. A. (1973). *Politics, language and time*. New York: Atheneum.

Posner, R. (2010). *The crisis of capitalist democracy*. Cambridge, MA: Harvard University Press.

Rampton, B. (2006). *Language in late modernity. Interaction in an urban school*. Cambridge: Cambridge University Press.

Rosemont, H., Jr. (1988). Why take rights seriously? A Confucian critique. In L. Rounder (Ed.), *Human rights and the world's religions* (pp. 167–182). Notre Dame, IN: University of Notre Dame Press.

Silverstein, M. (2005). Axes of evals: Token versus type interdiscursivity. *Journal of Linguistic Anthropology* 15(1), 6–22.

Spolsky, B. (2004). *Language policy*. Cambridge: Cambridge University Press.

Streek, W. (2011). The crises of democratic capitalism. *New Left Review* 71, 5–29.

Index